The **Rough Guide** to

New Zealand

written and researched by

**Laura Harper, Tony Mudd
and Paul Whitfield**

**ROUGH
GUIDES**

NEW YORK • LONDON • DELHI

www.roughguides.com

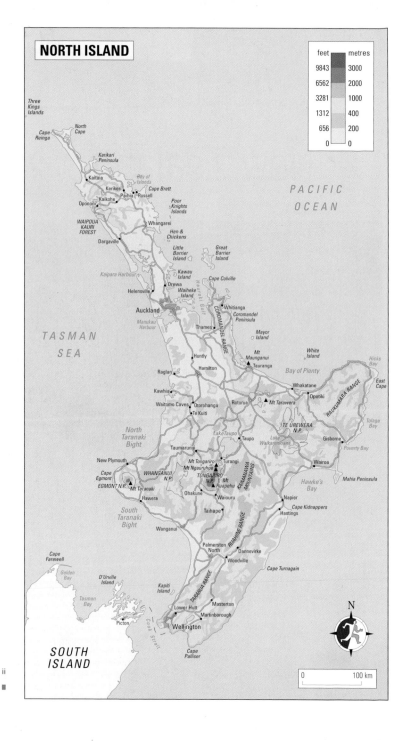

SOUTH ISLAND

feet	metres
9843	3000
6562	2000
3281	1000
1312	400
656	200
0	0

NORTH ISLAND

Kapiti Island

Wellington

Cape Palliser

Cook Strait

Cape Farewell
Farewell Spit
D'Urville Island
Marlborough Sounds

Golden Bay
ABEL TASMAN N.P.
Collingwood
Takaka
Tasman Bay
Picton

KAHURANGI N.P.
Nelson
Blenheim

Karamea Bight
Karamea

St Arnaud

KAIKOURA RANGES

Murchison

Westport
Cape Foulwind

NELSON LAKES N.P.
Kaikoura

PAPAROA N.P.
Reefton

Punakaiki
Lewis Pass
Hanmer Springs

TASMAN SEA

Greymouth
Lake Brunner

Hokitika
Arthur's Pass
ARTHUR'S PASS N.P.
Arthur's Pass Village
Ross

Christchurch
Banks Peninsula
Lyttelton

Whataroa
Methven
Akaroa

Franz Josef Glacier
Fox Glacier
WESTLAND N.P.
ADRAKI MOUNT COOK N.P.
Aoraki Mount Cook▲
Aoraki Mount Cook Village
Ashburton

Lake Tekapo

Haast
Twizel
Lake Pukaki
Timaru

Haast Pass

Jackson Bay
Lake Ohau

MOUNT ASPIRING N.P.
Mount Aspiring
Lake Hawea

Wanaka
Oamaru

Milford Sound
Milford Sound
Glenorchy
Arrowtown
Ranfurly

Mount Tutoko▲
Cromwell

George Sound
Queenstown
Alexandra
Palmerston

Lake Te Anau
Lake Wakatipu
Otago Peninsula

Secretary Island
FIORDLAND N.P.
Te Anau
Dunedin

Doubtful Sound
Manapouri
Lumsden

Ohai
Lake Manapouri
Balclutha

Resolution Island
Gore

Dusky Sound
Lake Hauroko
Invercargill
Tuatapere

Riverton
Bluff

Puyseger Point

Foveaux Strait
Oban (Halfmoon Bay)

RAKIURA N.P.

Stewart Island

PACIFIC OCEAN

Canterbury Bight

N

| 0 | 100 km |

iii

Abel Tasman National Park

Introduction to

New Zealand

New Zealand comes with a reputation as a unique land packed with magnificent, raw scenery: craggy coastlines, sweeping beaches, primeval forests, snow-capped mountains, bubbling volcanic pools, fast-flowing rivers, glacier-fed lakes, and unparalleled wildlife, all beneath a brilliant blue sky. Even Kiwis – named after the endearing, if decidedly odd, flightless bird that has become the national emblem – are filled with astonishment at the stupendous vistas and variety of what they call "Godzone" (God's own country).

All of this provides a canvas for boundless diversions, from moody strolls along windswept beaches and multi-day tramps over alpine passes to adrenalin-charged adventure activities like bungy jumping and whitewater rafting; in fact, some visitors take on the country as a kind of large-scale assault course, aiming to tackle as many challenges as possible in the time available. The one-time albatross of isolation – even Australia is fifteen hundred kilometres away – has become a boon, bolstering New Zealand's clean, **green** image (in truth, more an accident of geography than the result of past government policy) and helping to make it one of the world's safest destinations.

New Zealand lives up to these expectations, and despite its immense popularity remains unfettered by the crowds you'd find elsewhere. Almost

▽ Skytower, Auckland

Fact file

• Adrift in the south Pacific Ocean some 1500km east of Australia, New Zealand is one of the most isolated major land masses and was the last to be peopled, some 1000 years ago.

• At 268,000 square kilometres in area, New Zealand is a little larger than the UK and about two-thirds the size of California. With 4 million people, most parts of the country are thinly populated, though Auckland alone has over a million inhabitants.

• Physically, New Zealand is very varied with hairline fiords and glacier-weighted mountains in the south, rolling green hills fringed with golden beaches in the north, and abundant volcanic activity producing geysers and natural hot pools.

• For an instinctively conservative nation, New Zealand has often been socially progressive. It was the first country with votes for women and workers' pensions, and now pursues a bi-cultural approach to its race relations.

• NZ has almost 40 million sheep. That's ten for every inhabitant, down from twenty to one in the early 1980s.

• New Zealand's economy has traditionally been agricultural, and dairy products, meat and wool remain central to its continued prosperity, with forestry and fishing also playing a part. There is a growing "knowledge economy" and tourism is a big earner.

• New Zealand's flora and fauna developed independently giving rise to a menagerie of exotica: tall tree ferns, an alpine parrot (kea), a huge ground-dwelling parrot (kakapo), the odd-ball kiwi, and many more.

everything is easily accessible, packed into a land area little larger than Britain but with a population of only about 4 million, over half of it tucked away in the three largest **cities**: Auckland, the capital Wellington, and Christchurch on the South Island. Elsewhere, you can travel miles through verdant steep-hilled farmland rarely seeing a soul, and there are even remote spots that, it's reliably contended, no human has yet visited.

Geologically, New Zealand split off from the super-continent of Gondwanaland early, developing a unique **ecosystem** in which birds adapted to fill the role normally held by mammals, many becoming flightless through lack of predators. That all changed around 1000 years ago when the arrival of Polynesian navigators made this the last major land mass to be settled by humans. On sighting the new land from their canoes, Maori named it **Aotearoa** – "the land of the long white cloud" – and proceeded to radically alter the fragile ecosystem, dispatching forever the giant ostrich-sized moa, which formed a major part of their diet. A delicate ecological balance was achieved before the arrival of pakeha – white Europeans, predominantly of British origin – who swarmed off their square-rigged ships full of colonial zeal.

The subsequent uneasy coexistence between **Maori** and **European** societies informs both recorded history and the current wrangles over cultural identity, land and resource rights. The British didn't invade as such, and were to some degree reluctant to enter into the 1840 **Treaty of Waitangi**, New Zealand's founding document, which effectively ceded New Zealand to the British Crown while guaranteeing Maori hegemony over their land and traditional gathering and fishing rights. As time wore on and increasing numbers of settlers demanded to buy ever larger parcels of land from Maori, antipathy soon surfaced, eventually escalating to hostility. Once Maori were subdued, a policy of partial integration ensured the rapid dilution of their cultural heritage and all but destroyed **Maoritanga** – the Maori way of doing things. Maori, however, were left well outside the new European order, where difference was perceived as tantamount to a betrayal of the emergent sense of nationhood. Although elements of this still exist and Presbyterian and Anglican values have proved hard to shake off, the Kiwi psyche has become infused with Maori generosity and hospitality, coupled with a colonial mateyness and the unerring belief that whatever happens, "she'll be right". However, an underlying

Bungy jumping

Diving off tall towers with vines tied around the ankles has been a rite of passage for centuries in the South Pacific islands of Vanuatu, but modern bungy jumping was actually pioneered in Britain by members of the Oxford University Dangerous Sports Club, who jumped off the Clifton Suspension Bridge near Bristol in 1977, and were promptly arrested. Inspired by this, Kiwi speed skiers A.J. Hackett and Henry Van Asch began pushing the bungy boundaries, culminating in Hackett's jump from the Eiffel Tower in 1987. He too was arrested, but the publicity sparked worldwide interest that continues to draw bungy aspirants to New Zealand's half-dozen supremely scenic bungy operations, an adventure activity boom that shows no sign of slowing up.

The haka

Before every international rugby match, New Zealand's All Blacks put the wind up the opposition by performing an intimidating thigh-slapping, eye-bulging, tongue-poking chant. This is the Te Rauparaha **haka**, just one of many such Maori posture dances, designed to display fitness, agility and ferocity. The Te Rauparaha *haka* was reputedly composed early in the nineteenth century by the warrior Te Rauparaha, who was hiding from his enemies in the *kumara* pit of a friendly chief. Hearing noise above and then being blinded by light he thought his days were numbered, but as his eyes grew accustomed to the light he saw the hairy legs of his host – and was so relieved he performed the *haka* on the spot.

Touring teams have performed the *haka* at least since the 1905 All Black tour of Britain, and since the 1987 World Cup for home matches as well. The performance is typically led and spurred on by a player of Maori descent chanting:

Ringa pakia Slap the hands against the thighs
Uma tiraha Puff out the chest
Turi whatia Bend the knees
Hope whai ake Let the hip follow
Waewae takahia kia kino Stamp the feet as hard as you can

After a pause for effect the rest of the team join in with:

Ka Mate! Ka Mate! It is death! It is death!
Ka Ora! Ka Ora! It is life! It is life!
Tenei te ta ngata puhuru huru This is the hairy man
Nana nei i tiki mai Who caused the sun to shine
Whakawhiti te ra Keep abreast!
A upane ka upane! The rank! Hold fast!
A upane kaupane whiti te ra! Into the sun that shines!

inferiority complex seems to linger: you may well find yourself interrogated as to your opinions of the country almost before you leave the airport. Balancing this out is an extraordinary enthusiasm for **sports** and **culture**, which generate a swelling pride in New Zealanders when they witness plucky Kiwis taking on the world.

Only in the last couple of decades has New Zealand come of age and developed a true national self-confidence, something partly forced on it by Britain severing the colonial apron strings in the early 1970s, and partly by the resurgence of Maori identity. Maori demands have been nurtured by a willingness on the part of most *pakeha* to redress the wrongs perpetrated over the last century and a half, as long as it doesn't impinge on their high standard of living or overall feeling of control. More recently, integration has been replaced with a policy of promoting two cultures alongside each other, but with maximum interaction. The uncertainties of this future are further compounded by extensive recent **immigration**, partly from south Asia but the majority from China and Korea.

Where to go

New Zealand packs a lot into the limited space available and is small enough that you can visit the main sights in a couple of weeks, but for a reasonable look around at a less than frenetic pace, allow a month. However long you've got, look at spreading your time between the North and South islands: the diverse attractions of each region are discussed fully in the introduction to each chapter, but here's a quick top-to-toe summary. Obviously, the scenery is the big draw and most people only pop into the big cities on arrival and departure – something easily done with open-jaw air tickets allowing you to fly into Auckland and out of Christchurch.

Go-ahead **Auckland** is sprawled around sparkling Waitemata Harbour, an arm of the island-studded Hauraki Gulf. From here, most people head south, missing out on **Northland**, the cradle of both Maori and *pakeha* colonization, which is cloaked in wonderful sub-tropical forest harbouring New Zealand's largest kauri trees. East of Auckland the coast follows the isolated greenery and long, deserted, golden beaches of the **Coromandel Peninsula**, before running down to the **Bay of Plenty** resorts. The lands immediately south are assailed by the ever-present sulphurous whiff of **Rotorua**, with its spurting geysers and bubbling pools of mud, and the volcanic plateau centred on the trout-filled waters of **Lake Taupo** and three snow-capped volcanoes. Cave fans will want to head west of Taupo to the eerie limestone caverns of **Waitomo**. From Taupo it's just a short hop to the delights of canoeing on the **Whanganui River**, a broad, emerald green waterway banked by virtually impenetrable bush, or if you don't want to get your feet wet, head for the almost perfect cone of **Mount Taranaki**, whose summit

△ Sheep, Glenorchy

The Lord of the Rings

When Peter Jackson chose to locate his *Lord of the Rings* trilogy in New Zealand the country rejoiced; it even ap-pointed a special minister for the project. However, few could have anticipated how completely it would take over the country: Wellington's airport even has a sign reading "Welcome to Middle-earth".

For thousands of visitors, no visit to Aotearoa is complete without a tour of film locations. Despite efforts to minimise the impact on the land and remove all sets, enterprising individuals have set up tours to show where it all happened. While this is a good way to see some of the country's magnificent scenery, be prepared for some disappointment. Scenes rarely look as they did in the films. Mountains from one part of the country were often used as a backdrop for plains hundreds of kilo-metres away, and digital manipulation has rendered many landscapes unrecognisable.

For more information see books reviewed on p.980.

North Island

Matamata p.331 The gateway to Hobbiton.
Tongariro National Park p.347 Mount Doom and Mordor were mainly shot here.
Otaki Gorge p.297 Location for much of the Shire countryside around Hobbiton.
Putangirua Pinnacles p.480 Aragorn journeyed through on the Dimholt Road.
Wellington p.483 Helm's Deep was in the now-inaccessible Dry Creek Quarry; parts of the hobbits' flight from the Nazgûl were on Mount Victoria; the Embassy Theatre saw the world premiere of *The Return of the King*; and the city was temporary home for many of the actors during filming.

South Island

Nelson p.547 Jens Hansen jewellers made the "One Ring To Rule Them All".
Takaka Hill p.565 A beech forest here became Chetwood Forest.
Mount Owen p.574 Near Nelson, this was the location for Dimrill Dale.
Mount Sunday p.689 The foothills of the Alps became Edoras, capital of Rohan.
Twizel p.703 Barren fields west of town were the location for the Battle of Pelennor Fields, though Queenstown's Remarkables Range became the backdrop.
Wanaka p.864 The Black Riders chase sequence occurs near here.
Arrowtown p.826 The Ford of Bruinen was shot here and in Skippers Canyon.
Queenstown p.826 The Pillars of the Kings were shot on the Kawrau River near the bungy bridge; numerous scenes were shot at The Deer Park; and part of The Remarkables became Dimrill Dale.
Glenorchy p.857 Scenes of Isengard and Lothlórien were shot here and Saruman's tower, Orthanc, was digitally mapped onto the landscape.
Mavora Lakes p.864 The island of Nen Hithoel were shot here.

is accessible in a day. East of Taupo lie the ranges that form the North Island's backbone, and beyond them the **Hawke's Bay wine country**, centred on the Art Deco city of Napier, and the up-and-coming wine region of Martinborough. Only an hour or so away is the capital, **Wellington**, with its centre squeezed onto reclaimed harbourside land and the suburbs slung across steep hills overlooking glistening bays. Politicians and bureaucrats give it well-scrubbed and urbane sophistication, enlivened by a burgeoning café society and after-dark scene.

The **South Island** kicks off with the world-renowned wineries of **Marlborough** and appealing **Nelson**, a pretty and compact spot surrounded by lovely beaches and within easy reach of the hill country around **Nelson Lakes** and the fabulous sea kayaking of the **Abel Tasman National Park**. From the top of the South Island you've a choice of nipping around behind the 3000-metre summits of the Southern Alps and following the West Coast to the fabulous **glaciers** at Fox and Franz Josef, or sticking to the east, passing the whale-watching territory of **Kaikoura** en route to the South Island's largest centre, straight-laced Christchurch, a city with its roots firmly in the traditions of England. From Christchurch it's possible to head across country to the West Coast via Arthur's Pass on one of the country's most scenic train trips or shoot southwest across the patchwork Canterbury Plains to the foothills of the **Southern Alps** and **Aoraki Mount Cook** with its distinctive drooping-tent summit.

The flatlands of Canterbury run down, via the grand architecture of **Oamaru**, to the unmistakably Scottish-influenced city of **Dunedin**, a base for exploring the teeming wildlife of the **Otago Peninsula** with its albatross colony and opportunities for watching penguins. In the middle of the nineteenth century, prospectors arrived here and rushed inland to gold strikes throughout central Otago and around stunningly set **Queenstown**, now a highly commercialized activity centre where bungy jumping, rafting, jetboating and skiing hold sway. This is also the tramping heartland, with the **Routeburn Track** linking Queenstown to the rain-sodden

△ Rugby shirts hanging out to dry

Paua

Paua is New Zealand's endemic species of abalone, and is found in shallow waters, encrusted in a lime scale. With vigorous polishing this can be removed to reveal a wonderfully iridescent shell, all swirls of silver, blue, green and purple. Early Maori used slivers as lures to catch the eye of fish and inlaid shaped pieces into carvings, especially as the eyes of tiki figures. Its later use in tourist trinkets has produced some wonderfully kitsch items, but you're more likely to appreciate its use in Maori crafts; perhaps incorporated into a brooch or inlaid in a mirror frame.

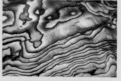

fiords, lakes and mountains of **Fiordland**, and the famous **Milford Track**. The further south you travel, the more you'll feel the bite of the Antarctic winds, which reach their peak on New Zealand's third land mass, the tiny and isolated **Stewart Island**, covered mostly by dense coastal rainforest that now forms part of New Zealand's newest national park. Here is your best chance of spotting a kiwi in the wild.

When to go

With over a thousand kilometres of ocean in every direction, it comes as no surprise that New Zealand has a maritime climate: warm through the southern summer months of December to March and never truly cold, even in winter.

Weather patterns are strongly affected by the prevailing westerlies, which suck up moisture from the Tasman Sea and dump it on the western side of both islands. The South Island gets the lion's share, with the West Coast and Fiordland ranking among the world's wettest places. The mountain ranges running the length of both islands cast long rain shadows over the eastern lands, making them considerably drier, though the south is a few degrees cooler than elsewhere, and sub-tropical Auckland and Northland are appreciably more humid. In the North Island, warm, damp summers fade almost imperceptibly into cool, wet winters, but the further south you go the more the year divides into four distinct seasons.

Such regional variation makes it viable to visit at any time of year, provided you pick your destinations. The **summer** months from December to February are the most popular and you'll find everything open, though often packed with holidaying Kiwis from Christmas to mid-January. Accommodation throughout summer is at a premium. In general, you're better off joining the bulk of foreign visitors during the **shoulder seasons** – October, November, March and April – when sights and attractions can be a shade quieter, and rooms easier to come by. **Winter** (May–Sept) is the wettest, coldest and consequently least popular time, though Northland can still be relatively balmy. The switch to prevailing

southerly winds tends to bring periods of crisp, dry and cloudless weather to the West Coast and heavy snowfalls to the Southern Alps and Central North Island allowing New Zealand to offer some of the most varied and least populated (and cheapest) **skiing and snowboarding** anywhere.

	Jan	Feb	Mar	Apr	May	Jun	Jul	Aug	Sep	Oct	Nov	Dec
Auckland												
av. max. temp. (°C)	23	23	22	19	17	14	13	14	16	17	19	21
av. min. temp. (°C)	16	16	15	13	11	9	8	8	9	11	12	14
av. rainfall (mm)	79	94	81	97	112	137	145	117	102	102	89	79
Napier												
av. max. temp. (°C)	24	23	22	19	17	14	13	14	17	19	21	23
av. min. temp. (°C)	14	14	13	10	8	5	5	6	7	9	11	13
av. rainfall (mm)	74	76	74	76	89	86	102	84	56	56	61	58
Wellington												
av. max. temp. (°C)	21	21	19	17	14	13	12	12	14	16	17	19
av. min. temp. (°C)	13	13	12	11	8	7	6	6	8	9	10	12
av. rainfall (mm)	81	81	81	97	117	117	137	117	97	102	89	89
Christchurch												
av. max. temp. (°C)	21	21	19	17	13	11	10	11	14	17	19	21
av. min. temp. (°C)	12	12	10	7	4	2	2	2	4	7	8	11
av. rainfall (mm)	56	43	48	48	66	66	69	48	46	43	48	56
Hokitika												
av. max. temp. (°C)	19	19	18	16	14	12	12	12	13	15	16	18
av. min. temp. (°C)	12	12	11	8	6	3	3	3	6	8	9	11
av. rainfall (mm)	262	191	239	236	244	231	218	239	226	292	267	262
Queenstown												
av. max. temp. (°C)	21	21	20	15	11	9	9	11	14	18	19	20
av. min. temp. (°C)	10	10	9	7	3	1	0	1	3	5	7	10
av. rainfall (mm)	79	72	74	72	64	58	59	63	66	77	64	62
Dunedin												
av. max. temp. (°C)	19	19	17	15	12	9	9	11	13	15	17	18
av. min. temp. (°C)	10	10	9	7	5	4	3	3	5	6	7	9
av. rainfall (mm)	86	71	76	71	81	81	79	76	69	76	81	89

things not to miss

It's not possible to see everything that New Zealand has to offer in one trip – and we don't suggest you try. What follows is a selective taste of the islands' highlights: outstanding buildings and natural wonders, adventure activities and exotic wildlife. They're arranged in five colour-coded categories, which you can browse through to find the very best things to see and experience. All highlights have a page reference to take you straight into the Guide, where you can find out more.

xiv

01 The Routeburn Track Page **860** • One of the country's finest walks, showcasing forested valleys, rich bird life, thundering waterfalls, river flats, lakes and wonderful mountain scenery.

02 **Whale watching** Page **593** • Whale watching off the Kaikoura Peninsula is justifiably highly popular, and you don't have to stick to a boat trip to do it, with plane- and helicopter rides on offer to up the adrenalin ante.

03 **Whanganui River Journey** Page **287** • This relaxing three-day canoe trip along a historic waterway takes you far away from roads through some of the North Island's loveliest scenery.

04 **Kauri Museum** Page **228** • The tiny settlement of Matakohe is home to one of the country's finest museums, totally dedicated to kauri wood, its extraction, and what you can do with it.

xv

05 **Hot Water Beach** Page **395** • Dig yourself a hole in the sand and luxuriate as the underground hot water wells up to mix with the incoming tide.

06 **Rugby** Page **62** • New Zealand's national game; if you get a chance to attend an international match, don't pass it up, not least for a chance to see the All Blacks perform the *haka*.

07 **Bungy jumping** Page **59** • New Zealand's trademark adventure sport can be tried at Kawerau Bridge, the original commercial jump site, or some of the super-high mega jumps nearby.

xvi

08 **Karori Sanctuary** Page **503** • On the edge of Wellington yet seemingly a million miles from anything urban, this beautiful fenced-in nature reserve is concentrating on restocking its 235 hectares with purely native flora and fauna.

09 Oparara Basin Page **784** • Gorgeous karst country, with disappearing rivers and wonderful limestone arches.

10 Hokianga Harbour Page **218** • As a low-key antidote to the commercialization of the Bay of Islands, the sand dunes, quiet retreats and crafts culture of the Hokianga Harbour are hard to beat.

11 Moeraki Boulders Page **660** • Don't pass through the Oamaru area without a visit to the Moeraki Boulders – large, perfectly round, naturally formed spheres with a honeycomb centre, just sitting in the surf.

12 Tongariro National Park Page **347** • Rafting, kayaking, tramping and skiing – there's an activity to suit most people in the popular area where three great volcanoes dominate the skyline.

13 White Island Page **420** • Take an appealing boat trip out to New Zealand's most active volcano, and stroll through the sulphurous lunar landscape to peer into the steaming crater.

14 **Tree ferns** Page **967** • New Zealand has a unique flora, its ubiquitous tree ferns sometimes reaching up to 10m in height and providing shade for more delicate specimens.

16 **Ninety Mile Beach** Page **211** • This seemingly endless wave-lashed golden strand is a designated highway, plied by tour buses that regularly stop to let passengers toboggan down the steep dunes.

15 **Hangi** Page **45** • Sample fall-off-the-bone pork and chicken along with sweet potatoes and pumpkin, disinterred after several hours' steaming in a Maori earth oven.

18 **East Coast** Page **425** • A varied coastline and the slow pace of life make the East Coast a place to linger and visit minor sights like the Anglican church at Ruakokore.

17 **Surfing at Raglan** Page **243** • A left-hand break that's one of the world's longest, coupled with reliable swells, makes Raglan a prime surfing destination.

19 Tongariro Crossing Page **356** • A superb one-day hike through the volcanic badlands of the Tongariro National Park passing the cinder cone of Mount Ngauruhoe, along the shores of turquoise lakes and with long views right across the North Island.

20 Wine Page **47** • New Zealand produces some world-beating wines, especially Sauvignon Blanc from the Marlborough region.

xx

21 Christchurch Arts Gallery Page **614** • The South Island's most extensive collection of New Zealand art is now housed in a striking modern building in the heart of Christchurch.

22 Art Deco, Napier Page **453** •
The world's most homogenous collection of small-scale Art Deco architecture owes its genesis to the devastating 1931 earthquake that flattened Napier.

24 Caving and cave rafting
Page **251** • Explore Waitomo's labyrinthine netherworld on adventure trips involving super-long abseils and floating underground streams on inner tubes while admiring the glowworms.

23 Wai-O-Tapu Page **330** •
The best of Rotorua's geothermal sites, Wai-O-Tapu offers beautiful, mineral-coloured lakes, plopping mud pools and a geyser that erupts on cue each morning.

25 Taieri Gorge Railway
Page **728** • Dating back to 1859, the Taieri Gorge Railway penetrates otherwise inaccessible mountain landscape and provides a dramatic journey at any time of the year.

26 **Penguin watching** Page **731** • Penguin Place, on the Otago Peninsula, offers the rare chance to see a protected penguin nesting area close up from a unique system of hides and tunnels.

27 **The Catlins Coast** Page **739** • Seals and dolphins and a slow pace of life make the Catlins a great place to unwind for a few days.

28 The glaciers Page **805** • The steep and dramatic Fox and Franz Josef glaciers can be explored by glacier hike, ice climbing and helicopter flights landing on the snow-fields above.

29 Jet boating Page **57** • This countrywide obsession finds its most iconic expression on Queentown's River Shotover, but there are numerous excellent jetboating opportunities all over the country.

30 Farewell Spit Page **571** • This slender 25km arc of sand dunes and beaches is a nature reserve protecting a host of bird species including black swans, wrybills, curlews and dotterels.

32 Abel Tasman National Park Page **554** • Kayaking the shoreline or hiking the Coast Track is a great way to see the Abel Tasman National Park.

31 Milford Sound Page **910** • Experience the grandeur and beauty of Fiordland on the area's most accessible fiord, an especially atmospheric place when the mist descends after heavy rainfall.

34 Carving Page **800** • In Hokitika's burgeoning arts scene Maori motifs are the basis for items made from wood, glass, bone and greenstone: you can even try your hand at bone-carving.

33 Kiwi spotting Page **762** • Stewart Island's Mason Bay provides one of the best opportunities to see these rare birds in the wild.

35 Museum of New Zealand (Te Papa) Page **496** • A celebration of the people, culture and art of New Zealand that's equally as appealing to kids as it is to adults, with an impressive use of state-of-the-art technology.

Contents

Using this Rough Guide

We've tried to make this Rough Guide a good read and easy to use. The book is divided into six main sections, and you should be able to find whatever you want in one of them.

Colour section

The front colour section offers a quick tour of the New Zealand. The **introduction** aims to give you a feel for the place, with suggestions on where to go. We also tell you what the weather is like and include a basic country fact file. Next, our authors round up their favourite aspects of New Zealand in the **things not to miss** section – whether it's a great food, amazing sights or a special hotel. Right after this comes a full **contents** list.

Basics

The Basics section covers all the **pre-departure** nitty-gritty to help you plan your trip. This is where to find out which airlines fly to your destination, what paperwork you'll need, what to do about money and insurance, about Internet access, food, security, public transport, car rental – in fact just about every piece of **general practical information** you might need.

Guide

This is the heart of the Rough Guide, divided into user-friendly chapters, each of which covers a specific region. Every chapter starts with a list of **highlights** and an **introduction** that helps you to decide where to go, depending on your time and budget. Likewise, introductions to the various towns and smaller regions within each chapter should help you plan your itinerary. We start most town accounts with information on arrival and accommodation, followed by a tour of the sights, and finally reviews of places to eat and drink, and details of nightlife. Longer accounts also have a directory of practical listings. Each chapter concludes with **public transport** details for that region.

Contexts

Read Contexts to get a deeper understanding of what makes New Zealand tick. We include a brief history, articles about wildlife and the environment, and a detailed further reading section that reviews dozens of **books** relating to the country.

Language

The **language** section gives useful guidance for Maori and Kiwi terms and phrases, and pulls together all the vocabulary you might need on your trip. Here you'll also find a glossary of words and terms peculiar to the country.

Index + small print

Apart from a **full index**, which includes maps as well as places, this section covers publishing information, credits and acknowledgements, and also has our contact details in case you want to send in updates and corrections to the book – or suggestions as to how we might improve it.

Chapter list and map

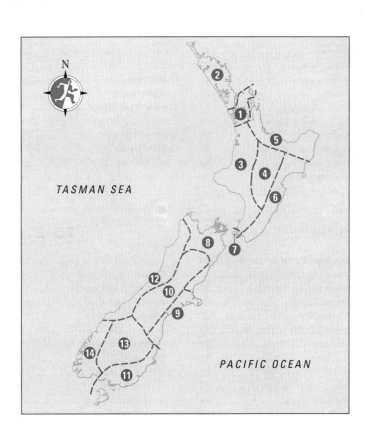

Contents

Colour section   i–xxiv

Basics   10–73

Guide   75–935

❼ Wellington and around

❽ Marlborough, Nelson and Kaikoura

❾ Christchurch and south To Otago

❿ Central South Island

Contexts   937–990

Language   991–998

Small print and Index   1011–1024

Basics

Basics

Getting there

The quickest and easiest way to get to New Zealand is to fly. It is possible to arrive by sea, but unless you own a boat, this means joining a cruise, paying for your passage on a cargo ship or joining a private yacht as crew – all of which are expensive and time consuming.

There are very few charter flights or all-in package deals to New Zealand, so flying there almost always involves **scheduled flights**. Airfares depend on the season, with the highest prices being asked during the New Zealand summer (Dec–Feb); fares drop during the shoulder seasons (Sept–Nov & March–May) and you'll get the cheapest prices during the low season (June–Aug). You can often cut costs by going through a specialist flight agent – either a consolidator, who buys up blocks of tickets from the airlines and sells them at a discount, or a discount agent, who in addition to dealing with discounted flights may also offer student and youth fares and a range of other travel-related services such as insurance, rail passes, car rentals, tours and the like.

A further possibility is to see if you can arrange a **courier flight**, although you'll need a flexible schedule, and preferably be travelling alone with very little luggage. In return for shepherding a parcel through customs, you can expect to get a deeply discounted ticket. You'll probably also be restricted in the duration of your stay. See ⓦ www.aircourier.co.uk for more UK-related information; ⓦ www.aircourier.org, ⓦ www.cheaptrips.com, ⓦ www.courier.org, or ⓦ www.nowvoyagertravel.com for US details.

If New Zealand is only one stop on a longer journey, you might want to consider buying a **Round-the-World** (RTW) ticket. Some travel agents can sell you an "off-the-shelf" RTW ticket that will have you touching down in about half a dozen cities (Auckland is on many itineraries); others will have to assemble one for you, which can be tailored to your needs, though this is liable to be more expensive.

Booking flights online

Many airlines and discount travel websites offer you the opportunity to book your tickets **online**, cutting out the costs of agents and middlemen. Good deals can often be found through discount or auction sites, as well as through the airlines' own websites.

Online booking agents and general travel sites

ⓦ **travel.yahoo.com** Incorporates a lot of Rough Guide material in its coverage of destination countries and cities across the world, with information about places to eat, sleep, etc.
ⓦ **www.cheapflights.co.uk** Bookings from the UK and Ireland only (for US,
ⓦ www.cheapflight.com; for Canada,
ⓦ www.cheapflights.ca; for Australia,
ⓦ www.cheapflights.com.au). Flight deals, travel agents, plus links to other travel sites.
ⓦ **www.cheaptickets.com** Discount flight specialists (US only).
ⓦ **www.etn.nl/discount.htm** A hub of consolidator and discount agent Web links, maintained by the nonprofit European Travel Network.
ⓦ **www.expedia.com** Discount airfares, all-airline search engine and daily deals (US only; for the UK ⓦ www.expedia.co.uk; for Canada ⓦ www.expedia.ca).
ⓦ **www.flyaow.com** Online air travel info and reservations site.
ⓦ **www.gaytravel.com** Gay online travel agent, offering accommodation, cruises, tours and more.
ⓦ **www.geocities.com/thavery2000/** Has an extensive list of airline toll-free numbers and websites.
ⓦ **www.hotwire.com** Bookings from the US only. Last-minute savings of up to forty percent on regular published fares. Travellers must be at least 18 and there are no refunds, transfers or changes allowed. Log-in required.

ⓦ**www.lastminute.com** Offers good last-minute holiday package and flight-only deals (UK only; for Australia, ⓦwww.lastminute.com.au).

ⓦ**www.opodo.co.uk** User-friendly, UK-only booking site – owned by major airlines such as BA and Air France – with good deals on flights and packages.

ⓦ**www.priceline.com** Name-your-own-price website that has deals at around forty percent off standard fares. You cannot specify flight times (although you do specify dates) and the tickets are non-refundable and non-transferable (US only; for the UK, ⓦwww.priceline.co.uk).

ⓦ**www.skyauction.com** Bookings from the US only. Auctions tickets and travel packages using a "second bid" scheme. The best strategy is to bid the maximum you're willing to pay, since if you win you'll pay just enough to beat the runner-up regardless of your maximum bid.

ⓦ**www.smilinjack.com/airlines.htm** Lists an up-to-date compilation of airline website addresses.

ⓦ**www.travelocity.com** Destination guides, hot web fares and best deals for car hire, accommodation and lodging as well as fares. Provides access to the travel agent system SABRE, the most comprehensive central reservations system in the US.

ⓦ**www.travelshop.com.au** Australian website offering discounted flights, packages, insurance, online bookings.

From Britain and Ireland

Over a dozen airlines compete to fly you from Britain to New Zealand for as little as £650, remarkably cheaply considering the distances involved but prices depend upon the time of year and rocket at Christmas to around £1600. However, going for the **cheapest flight** typically means sacrificing some comfort, which you may regret, given that your journey will last at least 24 hours, longer if your flight makes more than the obligatory refuelling stop. There are no direct flights to New Zealand from Ireland, and prices are proportionately higher, since the short hop to London (£70–90 return) has to be added on to the fare.

No matter how keen you are to arrive in New Zealand, it makes sense to break the journey, and most **scheduled flights** allow multiple **stopovers** either in North America and the Pacific, or Asia and Australia. The vast majority of direct scheduled flights to New Zealand depart from London's Heathrow, though Garuda Indonesia fly from London Gatwick (1 weekly), and Singapore Airlines use Manchester (around 4 weekly) as well as Heathrow. There are few overseas flights into Wellington or Dunedin, so the only real choice is between the main international airport at Auckland, in the north of the North Island, and the second airport at Christchurch, midway down the South Island. Christchurch receives fewer direct flights, but many scheduled airlines have a code-share shuttle from Auckland at no extra cost. The most desirable option, an open-jaw ticket (flying into one and out of the other), usually costs no more than an ordinary return and means not retracing your steps to get out of the country.

The best deals along fixed **Round-The-World** (RTW; usually valid for 12 months) routes include those such as the Aerolineas Argentinas/Thai combo that takes you from London through Buenos Aires, Auckland, Sydney, Perth and Bangkok for £1200–1800, or Alitalia/Air New Zealand's London-based circuit through Bangkok, Singapore, Bali, Auckland, Christchurch, Sydney/Cairns, Los Angeles or New York for £800–980; Trailfinders (see p.14) will usually knock a little off this using a slightly amended route. It is also possible to reduce your flight costs by incorporating an overland section into your round-the-world ticket: common land sectors include Delhi to Kathmandu, Brisbane or Sydney to Cairns, and Buenos Aires to São Paulo. Unusual routes combining the resources of two or more airlines in a RTW ticket are more expensive, and are almost infinitely variable.

If you are planning on doing a lot of travelling within New Zealand, especially between the North and South islands, it may be worth looking into **air passes** offered by Air New Zealand (see p.13). In addition, if you are combining Australia and New Zealand, there are handy air passes covering internal travel in each country and the joining flight. Air New Zealand do a **G'day Pass** that includes flights to Oz from New Zealand (though not including domestic travel in Oz) based on a zone system. Flying within a single zone is around £120, two zones £150 and over a second zone to a third £250. Qantas's **Boomerang Pass** is available to all international travellers (not just Qantas ticket holders), and comprises between two and ten coupons, each valid for a flight within Australasia: a one-zone coupon to fly within New Zealand or short hops in Oz costs around £120, a two-zone trans-Tasman coupon costs around £150.

Tourists and those on short-term working visas (see p.66) are generally required by New Zealand immigration to arrive with a ticket out of the country, so one-way tickets are really only viable for Australian and New Zealand residents. If you've purchased a return ticket and find you want to stay longer or head off on a totally different route, it's sometimes possible to cash in the return half of your ticket (though you'll make a loss on the deal) at the same travel agent where you bought it. Alternatively, you could try flogging it on the Internet but don't hold your breath.

Airlines

Aerolineas Argentinas UK ☎0845/601 1915, ⓦwww.aerolineas.com.ar. A couple of flights weekly from London Heathrow via Madrid and Buenos Aires to Auckland.

Air New Zealand UK ☎020/8741 2299, ⓦwww.airnewzealand.co.nz. Daily to Auckland, via Los Angeles and the popular South Pacific route with a choice of stopovers in Honolulu, Fiji, Western Samoa, the Cook Islands, Tahiti and Tonga. Easy connections to Christchurch.

British Airways UK ☎08750/850 9850, Republic of Ireland ☎1800/626 747, ⓦwww.britishairways.com. Daily flights from London Heathrow to Auckland and Christchurch, with stopovers in Australia or America, LA or Brisbane.

Air Canada UK ☎0870/5247 226, Republic of Ireland ☎01/679 3958, ⓦwww.aircanada.ca. Daily flights from London Heathrow to Auckland via Vancouver and Honolulu.

Cathay Pacific UK ☎020 8834 8800, ⓦwww.cathaypacific.com.

Garuda Indonesia UK ☎0807-1-GARUDA 427832, ⓦwww.garuda-indonesia.com. London Gatwick to Auckland via Bangkok and Bali.

Japanese Airlines UK ☎0845/7747700, ⓦwww.jal.co.jp. Three flights weekly from Heathrow to Auckland, via Tokyo.

Korean Air UK ☎0800/413 000, Republic of Ireland ☎501/799 7990, ⓦwww.koreanair.com. Flights per week vary at different times of the year, running from Heathrow to Auckland and Christchurch via Seoul.

Malaysia Airlines (MAS) UK ☎0161 835 3020, Republic of Ireland ☎01/676 1561 or 2131,

ⓦwww.mas.com.my. Two flights weekly from Heathrow to Auckland via Kuala Lumpur.

Qantas UK ☎020 8846 0466, ⓦwww.quantas.com.au. Daily scheduled flights from Heathrow to Auckland and Christchurch, via LA, Bangkok, Singapore, Sydney and Melbourne.

Singapore Airlines UK ☎01784 266122, Republic of Ireland ☎01/671 0722, ⓦwww.singaporeair.com. Flights from Heathrow (daily) and Manchester (daily) to Auckland and Christchurch via Singapore, long wait at Singapore on Manchester flights.

Thai Airways International UK ☎0870/606 0911, ⓦwww.international-thaiair.co.kr. Four flights weekly from Heathrow to Auckland, via Bangkok and Sydney.

Flight and travel agents

Austravel UK ☎08701 662 130, ⓦwww.austravel.net. Stopovers in Tokyo, Seoul, Singapore, LA or Fiji; also lays on "Focus Downunder" audio-visual presentations all over the UK to help you plan your trip.

Bridge the World UK ☎0870/4447474, ⓦwww.b-t-w.co.uk. Round-the-world ticket specialist, with good deals aimed at the backpacker market. Agents for Kiwi Experience.

Cresta World Travel UK ☎0161/927 7177, ⓦwww.mytravel.co.uk. Comprehensive range of flights and round-the-world tickets to New Zealand and Australia, with good backpacker deals.

Destination Group UK ☎020/7400 7000, ⓦwww.destination-group.co.uk. Good discount fares, especially on Garuda flights; Far East and USA inclusive packages.

Flightbookers UK ☎0870/010 7000, ⓦwww.ebookers.com. Low fares on an extensive selection of scheduled flights.

Joe Walsh Tours Dublin ☎01/872 2555 or 676 3053, Cork ☎021/427 7959, ⓦwww.joewalshtours.ie. General budget fares agent.

Jupiter Travel UK ☎020/8296 0309 or 8339 9929. Cheap and reliable agent with multi-stopover and round-the-world tickets to New Zealand.

London Flight Centre UK ☎020/8879 6789, ⓦwww.topdecktravel.co.uk. Long-established agent dealing in discount flights.

North South Travel UK ☎ & ☎01245/608 291, ⓦwww.northsouthtravel.co.uk. Friendly, competitive travel agency, offering discounted fares worldwide – profits are used to support projects in the developing world, especially the promotion of sustainable tourism.

Quest Worldwide ☎0870/442 3542, ⓦwww.questtravel.com. Specialists in round-the-world and Australasian discount fares.

STA Travel UK ☎08701/600 599,
ⓦwww.statravel.co.uk. Worldwide specialists in low-cost flights and tours for students and under-26s, though other customers are welcome. Experts on New Zealand travel with branches in major Kiwi cities.
Thomas Cook UK ☎508705/750 5711,
ⓦwww.thomascook.co.uk. Long established one-stop 24-hour travel agency for package holidays or scheduled flights, with bureau de change issuing Thomas Cook travellers' cheques, travel insurance and car rental.
Trailfinders UK ☎020/7292 1888,
ⓦwww.trailfinders.com, Republic of Ireland ☎01/677 7888, ⓦwww.trailfinders.ie. One of the best-informed and most efficient agents for independent travellers; produce a very useful quarterly magazine worth scrutinizing for round-the-world routes.
Travel Bag UK ☎0870/890 1456,
ⓦwww.travelbag.co.uk. Official Qantas agent. Discount flights to New Zealand, plus tours and adventure trips; agents for Kiwi Experience.
Travel Mood UK ☎0870/660 004
ⓦwww.travelmood.co.uk. Discount fares and round-the-world tickets; also car rental and bus tours, including Kiwi Experience.

Packages and tours

There are well over a dozen companies offering everything from flexible backpacker-oriented excursions through mainstream bus **tours** to no-expense-spared extravaganzas. If time is limited and you have a fairly clear idea of what it is you want to do, there are good deals going. Even if an all-in package doesn't appeal, there may be some mileage in pre-booking some accommodation, tours or a rental vehicle.

Full "see-it-all" packages can work out to be quite expensive but aren't bad value, considering what you'd be spending anyway. Basic bus tours range from 6 days around Northland for about £950 to 17- to 21-day nationwide tours staying in four-star hotels with all meals, and various cruises and sightseeing included, costing about £3750–4500. A number of companies, most notably Kiwi Experience and Magic Bus, operate flexible bus tours, which you can hop off whenever you like and rejoin a day or two later when the next bus comes through (see p.29 for details of these).

Pretty much all the major tour operators can also book you onto tramping trips, including some of the guided Great Walks

(see p.53); you'll still need to book way in advance, though. For skiing trips, the cheapest option is usually to contact ski clubs at the fields directly: check out the contacts at ⓦwww.snow.co.nz.
Australian Pacific Tours UK ☎020/8879 7444,
ⓦwww.aptouring.co.uk. Massive range of fully inclusive bus tours, a variety of 15-day national tours costing from around £2000.
Contiki ☎020/8290 6777, ⓦwww.contiki.com. Bus tours for 18–35s. Itineraries range from 3 days around the Bay of Islands (£150) to a 15-day grand tour (around £690 from Auckland), with accommodation and most meals included.
Explore Worldwide ☎01252/760 000,
ⓦwww.explore.co.uk. Small-group tours, staying in small hotels and including treks, canoeing and rafting (18 days on South or North islands £2200; 32 days for both £3400).
High Places ☎0114/275 7500,
ⓦwww.highplaces.co.uk. Trips to NZ specializing in high-country hiking and cycling.
Kuoni Worldwide ☎01306/741 111,
ⓦwww.kuoni.co.uk. A 15- to 17-night bus tour inclusive of flights from Britain and luxurious accommodation, plus some meals (around £2750–3000), as well as more flexible holidays ranging from 3 to 10 days.
Sunbeam Tours ☎1800/955 1818, ⓦwww.sunbeamtours.com. Offers bus tours, self-drive car and motorhome holidays, guided Great Walks and semi-independent tours at mid-range prices.

From the US and Canada

The only direct trans-Pacific flights to New Zealand are those from Los Angeles to Auckland, a flight of 12–13 hours. Air New Zealand and Qantas are the only companies flying planes, but assorted code-share partners – Air Canada, American Airlines, British Airways, etc – will sell tickets to New Zealand, usually offering several connections a day to the two other major airports, Wellington and Christchurch.

From the US an LA–Auckland round-trip Apex fare goes for around US$1000, rising to about US$1800 in peak season. Air New Zealand and others have special Internet fares as little as US$850 in low season. Expect to pay an extra US$50–100 for weekend travel. Flights from all other US cities are routed via Los Angeles. Off-peak you might expect to pay US$1300–1500 from New York or Chicago, but shopping around the discount agents or checking out the newspapers for special offers could save you more than a few bucks.

From Canada, United and Air Canada connect from most provincial capitals to LA. Depending on the season, sample Apex midweek fares are in the following ranges: from Vancouver CAN$2200–2500; from Toronto CAN$2500–2800; from Montréal CAN$2600–2800. Substantial savings can sometimes be made through discount travel companies and websites.

An alternative approach is to fly **via Asia**. It isn't as much of a detour as it sounds, especially if you're flying from Canada or the east coast of the US, and may work out cheaper. Korean Airlines have flights from Anchorage, Atlanta, Chicago, Dallas, Los Angeles, New York, San Francisco, Toronto and Vancouver all changing at Seoul (Incheon) before continuing on to Auckland. Singapore Airlines also have good deals from time to time, but again you have to fly via their home base.

RTW and Circle-Pacific routes

If New Zealand is only one stop on a longer journey, you might want to consider buying a **Round-the-World** (**RTW**) ticket. A sample itinerary of LA-Tahiti-Cook Islands-Fiji-Auckland-Sydney-Kuala Lumpur-Istanbul-London-LA would cost $2300 (low-season departure). An equally exotic option is a **Circle Pacific** ticket. Air New Zealand offer a "Pacific Escapade" ticket for $2700, valid for six months, originating from LA and with no limit to stopovers as long as you follow an onward circular route (no backtracking) and do not exceed 20,000 miles. However, a discount agent should be able to put together cheaper itineraries by combining sectors from different airlines, such as LA-Bangkok-Bali-Auckland-LA, starting from $1500.

Airlines in the US and Canada

Air Canada ☎1-888/247-2262, ⓦ www.aircanada.ca
Air New Zealand US ☎1-800/262-1234, Canada ☎1-800/663-5494, ⓦ www.airnz.com
American Airlines ☎1-800/433-7300, ⓦ www.aa.com

British Airways ☎1-800/247-9297, ⓦ www.british-airways.com
Korean Airlines ☎1-800/438-5000, ⓦ www.koreanair.com
Lufthansa US ☎1-800/645-3880, Canada ☎-800/563-5954, ⓦ www.lufthansa-usa.com
Mexicana ☎1-800/531-7921, ⓦ www.mexicana.com
Qantas Airways ☎1-800/227-4500, ⓦ www.qantas.com
Singapore Airlines ☎1-800/742-3333, ⓦ www.singaporeair.com
United Airlines ☎1-800/538-2929, ⓦ www.ual.com

Discount travel companies

Air Brokers International ☎1-800/883-3273, ⓦ www.airbrokers.com. Consolidator and specialist in round-the-world and Circle Pacific tickets.
Airtreks.com ☎1-877-AIRTREKS or 415/977 7100, ⓦ www.airtreks.com. Round-the-world and Circle Pacific tickets. The website features an interactive database that lets you build and price your own round-the-world itinerary.
Educational Travel Center ☎1-800/747-5551 or 608/256-5551, ⓦ www.edtrav.com. Student/youth discount agent.
SkyLink US ☎1-800/AIR-ONLY or 212/573-8980, Canada ☎1-800/SKY-LINK, ⓦ www.skylinkus.com. Consolidator.
STA Travel US ☎1-800/781-4040, Canada 1-888/427-5639, ⓦ www.sta-travel.com. Worldwide specialists in independent travel; also student IDs, travel insurance, car rental, rail passes, etc.
TFI Tours ☎1-800/745-8000 or 212/736-1140, ⓦ www.lowestairprice.com. Consolidator.
Travelers Advantage ☎1-877/259-2691, ⓦ www.travelersadvantage.com. Discount travel club; annual membership fee required (currently $1 for 2 months' trial).
Travel Avenue ☎1-800/333-3335, ⓦ www.travelavenue.com. Full-service travel agent that offers discounts in the form of rebates.
Travel Cuts Canada ☎1-800/667-2887, US ☎1-866/246-9762, ⓦ www.travelcuts.com. Canadian student-travel organization.
Worldtek Travel ☎1-800/243-1723, ⓦ www.worldtek.com. Discount travel agency for worldwide travel.

Specialist agents and tour operators

Abercrombie and Kent ☎1-800/323-7308, ⓦ www.abercrombiekent.com. Upmarket operator with customized tours and set packages. Their 8-day

Highlights of New Zealand sightseeing package is priced at US$2800 (land costs and internal flights only).

Adventure Center ☎1-800/228-8747 or 510/654-1879, ⊛www.adventurecenter.com. Hiking and "soft adventure" specialists with several NZ options.

Adventures Abroad ☎1-800/665-3998 or 360/775-9926, ⊛www.adventures-abroad.com. Adventure specialists often combining NZ with Australia and Fiji.

Australian Pacific Tours ☎1-800/290-8687, ⊛www.aptours.com. Various land-only packages from independent tours to fully escorted.

Collette Vacations US ☎1-800/340-5158, Canada ☎1-416/626-1661, ⊛www .collettevacations.com. Specialists in Australia and New Zealand travel. Their 19-day fully escorted tour of New Zealand, including trips to glaciers and rainforests, starts at US$2400 (land only).

Contiki Holidays ☎1-888/CONTIKI, ⊛www.contiki.com. Specialists in travel for 18–35s. Their several land packages range from a 3-day Bay of Islands tour (US$325) to a 12-day Grand Adventurer (US$1409).

Elderhostel ☎1-877/426-8056, ⊛www.elderhostel.org. Educational and activity programmes for senior travellers. In addition to joint Australia/New Zealand packages, there are specialist month-long tours like Land of Geysers and Greenstone (US$5151, land only).

Holidaze Ski Tours ☎1-800/526-2827 or 732/280-1120, ⊛www.holidaze.com. Short all-inclusive ski holidays to NZ.

Journeys International ☎1-800/255-8735 or 734/665-4407, ⊛www.journeys-intl.com. Offers several soft adventure tours such as the NZ Adventure (US$3400 for 15 days).

Newmans South Pacific Vacations ☎1-888/592-6224, ⊛www.newmansvacations.com. Specialists in New Zealand vacations, with around 25 package options in addition to fully independent tours. Their tours include a 12-day guided tour (from US$1825, land only).

REI Adventures ☎1-800/622-2236, ⊛www.rei.com/adventures. REI offer a 13-day hiking, cycling and kayaking tour of NZ for around US$2500.

Sunbeam Tours ☎1-800/955-1818, ⊛www.sunbeamtours.com. Customized tours, along with several set packages. Their 16-day sightseeing tour of the North and South Islands starts at US$1940 (land only).

Swain Tours ☎1-800/22-SWAIN, ⊛www.swainaustralia.com. South Pacific specialists offering customized individual and group

itineraries including a 12-day NZ highlights trip (US$3000 including domestic flights).

Wilderness Travel ☎1-800/368-2794 or 510/558-2488, ⊛www.wildernesstravel.com. Hiking and nature oriented trips around NZ including the 16-day Serious Fun (US$4100).

From Australia

Qantas, Air New Zealand, Freedom Air (a budget wing of Air New Zealand) and Pacific Blue all operate frequent flights between Australia and New Zealand, and the competition keeps **prices** reasonable. It may also be worth checking out the less frequent flights with Thai, Singapore, Emirates, Polynesian Airlines and Aerolinas Argentinas, especially if New Zealand is part of wider travels.

It's a relatively short hop across the Tasman: **flying time** from Sydney or Melbourne to Auckland or Christchurch is around three hours. There's an ever-changing range of special offers, and your best bet is to check the latest with a specialist travel agent (see p.17) or check the airlines' websites. Some of the **best deals** are with the budget-oriented Freedom Air who fly from Brisbane and the Gold Coast to New Zealand's main centres, and from Melbourne and Sydney to Hamilton, Palmerston North and Dunedin, all for around A$400 return in summer. Pacific Blue are equally competitive with direct flights from Brisbane to Christchurch, Sydney to Wellington and Christchurch, and Melbourne to Christchurch. Flights with Emirates start at around $450.

Qantas and Air New Zealand each fly several daily trans-Tasman flights, and prices vary enormously depending on demand: book well in advance in summer. By shopping around you should be able to land a return flight from most eastern cities to Auckland for A$500. There are fewer flights to Wellington and Christchurch and you might pay A$600–700, though A$500 tickets are possible. Flights from Perth start at around A$1000.

Open-jaw tickets – which let you fly into one city and out of another, making your own way between – can save a lot of backtracking, and add little (if anything) to the total fare. There are also various **air passes** for internal flights available (see "Getting Around", p.26, for details). If you're taking in New Zealand as part of your grand tour, it's worth considering a **Round-The-World** (RTW) ticket also taking in North or South America, Europe and Southeast Asia; the scope is enormous and rates start around A$2000.

Cruise ships do pass through the Pacific between November and January, but not on a regular basis; travel agents should be able to advise on which vessels are operating each season.

There's a huge variety of holidays and tours to New Zealand available in Australia. The holiday subsidiaries of airlines such as Air New Zealand and Qantas package short **city-breaks** (flight and accommodation) and **fly-drive** deals for little more than the cost of the regular airfare. In winter, there are accommodation **skiing** packages to New Zealand's skifields; all-inclusive four-day trips to Queenstown start from A$800, rising to A$1000 for a seven-day trip.

Airlines

Aerolineas Argentinas ☎ 02/9234 9000, ⓦ www.aerolineas.com.ar
Air New Zealand ☎ 13 2476, ⓦ www.airnz.com.au
Emirates Airline ☎ 1300/303 777, ⓦ www.emirates.com
Freedom Air ☎ 1800/122 000, ⓦ www.freedomair.co.nz
Pacific Blue ☎ 13 1645, ⓦ www.flypacificblue.com
Polynesian Airlines ☎ 1300/653 737, ⓦ www.polynesianairlines.com.au
Qantas ☎ 13 1313, ⓦ www.qantas.com.au
Singapore Airlines ☎ 13 1011, ⓦ www.singaporeair.com
Thai Airways ☎ 1300/651 960, ⓦ www.thaiair.com

Travel agents

Backpackers World Travel ☎ 02/8268 6001, ⓦ www.backpackersworld.com.au
Flight Centre Australia ☎ 13 3133, ⓦ www.flightcentre.com.au
STA Travel Australia ☎ 1300/733 035, ⓦ www.statravel.com.au.
Student Uni Travel Australia ☎ 02/9232 8444, ⓦ www.usitWorld.com
Trailfinders Australia ☎ 1300/780 212, ⓦ ww.trailfinders.com.au

Specialist agents and tour operators

Allways Dive Expeditions Australia ☎ 1800/338 239, ⓦ www.allwaysdive.com.au. All-inclusive dive packages, mostly around Northland.
Contiki Australia ☎ 02/9511 2200, ⓦ www.contiki.com. Frenetic tours for 18- to 35-year-old party animals.
Silke's Travel Australia ☎ 02/8347 2000, ⓦ www.silkes.com.au. Gay and lesbian specialist travel agent.
The Ski and Snowboard Travel Company ☎ 1300/766 938, ⓦ www.skiandsnowboard .com.au. Good deals on skiing trips to Queenstown, Wanaka and Mount Hutt. Rates vary with dates, standard of accommodation etc.
Talpacific holidays Australia ☎ 1300/137 727, ⓦ www.talpacific.com. Coach and independent travel around NZ.
travel.com.au and travel.co.nz Australia ☎ 1300/130 482 or 02/9249 5444, ⓦ www.travel.com.au. Comprehensive online travel company.
Value Tours ☎ 1300/ 361 322, ⓦ www.valuetours.com.au. Skiing and snowboarding holidays throughout New Zealand, plus airfares, car and campervan rental and accommodation passes.

BASICS | Getting there

Visas and red tape

All visitors to New Zealand need a passport which must be valid for at least three months beyond the time you intend to stay, although if your home country has an embassy or consulate in New Zealand that can renew your passport, you can get away with one month.

On arrival, British citizens are automatically issued with a permit to stay for up to six months, and a three-month permit is granted to citizens of most other European countries, Southeast Asian nations, Japan, the USA and Canada, and several other countries. Australian citizens and permanent residents can stay indefinitely.

Other nationalities need to obtain a Visitor's Visa in advance from a New Zealand embassy, which costs the local equivalent of around NZ$120 and is normally valid for three months. Visas are issued by the New Zealand Immigration Service (ⓦwww.immigration.govt.nz).

Embassies and consulates abroad

Websites and contact details for all New Zealand embassies and consulates abroad can be found at ⓦwww .nzembassy.com.

Australia

High Commission Commonwealth Avenue, Canberra, ACT 2600 ☎02/6270 4211, ⓔnzhccb@austrametro.com.au.
Consulates Level 10, 55 Hunter St, Sydney ☎02/8256 2000,
ⓔnzcgsydney@bigpond.com.au; Level 3, 350 Collins St, Melbourne ☎03/9642 1279, ⓔnzcgmelbourne@bigpond.com.

Canada

High Commission Suite 727, 99 Bank St, Ottawa, Ontario K1P 6G3 ☎613/238 5991, ⓔinfo@nzhcottawa.org.
Consulates Suite 2a West, 225 MacPherson Ave, Toronto M4V 1A1 ☎416/947 0000, ⓔandrina@attglobal.net; Suite 1200, 800 Dunsmuir St, Vancouver, British Columbia, V6C 3K4 ☎604/684 7388.

UK and Ireland

High Commission 80 Haymarket, London SW1Y 4TQ ☎020/7930 8422.
Consulate 37 Leeson Park, Dublin 6☎01/660 4233, ⓔnzconsul@indigo.ie; Ballance House, 118a Lisburn Rd, Glenavy, Co. Antrim BT29 4NY ☎0289/264 8098, ⓔballancenz@aol.com; 5 Rutland Square, Edinburgh EH1 2AS ☎0131/222 8109, ⓔiwscott@blueyonder.co.uk.

USA

Embassy 37 Observatory Circle NW, Washington, DC 20008 ☎202/328 4800, ⓔnz@nzemb.org.
Consulates Suite 1150, 12400 Wilshire Boulevard, Los Angeles, CA 90025 ☎310/207 1605; Suite 2510, 222 East 41st St, New York, NY 10017 ☎212/832 4038.

Customs regulations

In a country all too familiar with the damage that can be caused by introduced plants and animals, New Zealand's Ministry of Agriculture and Fisheries (MAF) takes a hard line on protecting the delicate environment of the country. Aircraft cabins are sometimes sprayed with insecticide before passengers are allowed to disembark, to kill off any stowaway insects or micro-organisms; the spray is apparently harmless to humans.

On arrival you'll be asked to **declare any food**, plants or parts of plants (dead or alive), animals (dead or alive), equipment used with animals, camping gear, golf clubs, used bicycles, biological specimens, and footwear (specifically walking boots). Fruit, vegetables and meat will be confiscated, but processed foods will usually be allowed through. Outdoor equipment and walking boots will be taken away, inspected and perhaps cleaned then returned a few minutes later. After a long flight it can all seem a bit of a pain, but such precautions are important and if you flout them you could be liable to fines ($200 on the spot for that orange you forgot you had), or at worst, they won't let you into the country. For more details visit Ⓦwww.maf.govt.nz/quarantine.

Visitors aged 17 and over are entitled to the following generous **duty-free allowance**: 200 cigarettes, or 250 grams of tobacco, or 50 cigars; 4.5 litres of wine or beer, plus one bottle of not more than 1125ml of spirits; and up to $700 worth of goods. Provided you have not already reached the $700 you may also bring in a couple of extra bottles of spirits.

There are **export restrictions** on wildlife, plantlife, antiquities and works of art. For more information on duty-free allowances and export restrictions visit Ⓦwww .customs.govt.nz.

Information, websites and maps

New Zealand promotes itself heavily and enthusiastically abroad through Tourism New Zealand (see below), where enquiries will trigger a deluge of glossy brochures. Much of this comprises inspirational, if rose-tinted, images of the country, of limited practical use. It is probably more fruitful to spend time surfing their extensive website Ⓦwww.purenz.com.

Many of the information centres listed below, as well as some cafés, bars and hostels, keep a supply of **free newspapers** and **magazines** oriented towards backpackers and usually filled with promotional copy, but informative nonetheless. Two of the best are the *New Zealand Backpackers News* (Ⓦwww.backpackernews.co.nz) and *TNT* (Ⓦwww.tntmagazine.com/au).

Visitor centres

Every town of any size has an **official visitor centre**, recognizable by its "i sites" logo. These are invariably well-stocked, staffed by helpful and knowledgeable personnel and sometimes offer some form of video or slide presentation on the area. Apart from dishing out local maps and leaflets, they offer a **free booking service** for accommodation, trips and activities, and onward travel. In the more popular tourist areas, you'll also come across all manner of places representing themselves as **independent information centres**, which usually follow a hidden agenda, typically promoting a number of allied adventure companies. While these can be useful, it's worth remembering that their advice won't be impartial.

Other useful resources are **Department of Conservation** (DOC; Ⓦwww.doc.govt .nz) offices and field centres, usually sited close to wilderness areas and popular tramping tracks, and often serving as the local visitor centre as well. These are highly informative and well-geared to trampers' needs, with local weather forecasts, intentions forms and maps as well as, in many cases, historic and/or environmental displays and audio visual exhibitions. Their website is a motherlode of stuff on the environment and the latest conservation issues plus details on national parks and Great Walks.

Tourism New Zealand offices

New Zealand PO Box 95, Wellington ☎04/ 917 5400, ℻915 3817.
Australia Level 8, 35 Pitt St, Sydney, NSW 2000 ☎02/9247 5222, ℻9241 1136.
Canada Information line only ☎1-866/639 9325.
United Kingdom New Zealand House, Haymarket, London, SW1Y 4TQ ☎020/7930 1662, ℻7839

8929, premium rated information line
℡ 09069/101010; also handles enquiries from
Ireland.

USA Suite 300, 501 Santa Monica Blvd, Santa
Monica, CA 90401 ℡ 310/395 7480 or 1-800/388
5494, ℉ 395 5453; Suite 1904, 780 3rd Ave, New
York, NY 10017-2024 ℡ 212/832 8482, ℉ 832
7602.

Websites

New Zealand has fully embraced the web
and throughout the guide we've supplied
websites for most businesses and any
accommodation places which have a web
presence. What follows is just a smattering
of useful travel planning sites and assorted
sites of general Kiwi interest.

Forest and Bird Society
ⓦ www.forestandbird.org.nz Mainstream
conservation site with info on biosecurity, at-risk
species and a handy bird finding guide.

Immigration ⓦ www.immigration.govt.nz Site
which deals with the ins and outs of staying in the
country longer term.

Kiwi Music ⓦ www.nzmusic.com Basic portal to
websites of most of the more popular and important
current Kiwi acts.

Maori Culture ⓦ www.culture.co.nz &
ⓦ www.aotearoa.maori.nz Labour-of-love sites
dedicated to all things Maori with everything from
personal profiles and Maori history to an online
cookbook. ⓦ www.maori.org.nz is another good
resource.

NZ Birds ⓦ www.nzbirds.com Comprehensive site
on everything feathery in New Zealand.

NZ Tourism Board ⓦ www.purenz.com Official
site and a good starting point for general travel
material.

Search NZ ⓦ www.searchnz.co.nz Leading NZ-
specific search engine.

Stuff ⓦ www.stuff.co.nz General portal from the
parent company of many of New Zealand's leading
magazines and newspapers, that also leads you into
ⓦ www.press.co.nz which includes the best daily
papers.

Tramping ⓦ www.tramper.co.nz Almost everything
you ever wanted to know about tramping in New
Zealand.

Women Travel ⓦ www.womentravel.co.nz
Essential information for the woman traveller in New
Zealand with links to retreats, women-oriented tour
operators and their newsletter.

Work ⓦ www.workingin-newzealand.com Site
which lists jobs throughout the country and gives a
few useful tips.

Maps

Specialist outlets (see below) should have a
reasonable stock of **maps** of New Zealand.
The best available is the two-sided
1:1,000,000 edition produced by International
Travel Maps (ⓦ www.itmb.com), with all the
important roads, and an attractive and instructive colour scheme giving a good sense of the
country's terrain. The 1:2,000,000 maps produced by GeoCentre and Bartholomew come
a distant joint second. **Road atlases** are
widely available in New Zealand bookshops
and service stations; the most detailed are
those produced by Kiwi Pathfinder, which indicate numerous points of interest and the type
of road surface – though some roads marked
as unsealed have since been tar-sealed. The
AA (see p.127) provide their members with
simple but effective strip maps of major touring routes free of charge. Finally, **Rough
Guides** have produced their own map of New
Zealand, water-proof, and tear-resistant it provides a birds-eye view of the country and is
invaluable in the planning of your trip.

With a road atlas and our city plans you
can't go far wrong on the roads, but more
detailed maps may be required for **tramping**. All the major walks are covered by the
Trackmap and Parkmap series, complete
with photos (around $14 from DOC offices
and bookshops in New Zealand), or go for
the larger scale Topo maps (around $14
also), which cover the whole country.

Map outlets

UK and Ireland

Stanfords 12–14 Long Acre, London WC2E 9LP
℡ 020/7836 1321, ⓦ www.stanfords.co.uk. Also at
39 Spring Gardens, Manchester ℡ 0161/831
0250, and 29 Corn St, Bristol ℡ 0117/929 9966.
Blackwell's Map and Travel Shop 50 Broad St,
Oxford OX1 3BQ ℡ 01865/793 550,
ⓦ maps.blackwell.co.uk. Branches in Bristol,
Cambridge, Cardiff, Leeds, Liverpool, Newcastle,
Reading and Sheffield.
Heffers Map and Travel 20 Trinity St, Cambridge
CB2 1TJ ℡ 01223/568 568, ⓦ www.heffers.co.uk.
Hodges Figgis Bookshop 56–58 Dawson St,
Dublin 2 ℡ 01/677 4754,
ⓦ www.bookshop.blackwell.co.uk.
John Smith & Son 100 Cathedral St, Glasgow G4
0RD ℡ 0141/552 3377, ⓦ www.johnsmith.co.uk.

James Thin Booksellers 53–59 South Bridge Edinburgh EH1 1YS ☎0131/622 8222, ⓦwww.jthin.co.uk.

The Map Shop 30a Belvoir St, Leicester LE1 6QH ☎0116/247 1400, ⓦwww.mapshopleicester.co.uk.

Newcastle Map Centre 55 Grey St, Newcastle upon Tyne, NE1 6EF ☎0191/261 5622.

The Travel Bookshop 13–15 Blenheim Crescent, W11 2EE ☎020/7229 5260, ⓦwww.thetravelbookshop.co.uk.

Traveller 55 Grey St, Newcastle-upon-Tyne NE1 6EF ☎0191/261 5622, ⓦwww.newtraveller.com.

In Australia and New Zealand

The Auckland Map Centre National Bank Centre, 205 Queen St ☎09/309 7725, ⓦwww.aucklandmapcentre.co.nz.

The Map Shop 6–10 Peel St, Adelaide, SA 5000 ☎08/8231 2033, ⓦwww.mapshop.net.au.

Map World 371 Pitt St, Sydney ☎02/9261 3601, ⓦwww.mapworld.net.au. Also at 900 Hay St, Perth ☎08/9322 5733, Jolimont Centre, Canberra ☎02/6230 4097 and 1981 Logan Road, Brisbane ☎07/3349 6633.

MapWorld 173 Gloucester St, Christchurch, New Zealand ☎0800/627 967 & 03/374 5399, ⓦwww.mapworld.co.nz.

Mapland 372 Little Bourke St, Melbourne, Victoria 3000 ☎03/9670 4383, ⓦwww.mapland.com.au.

In the USA

110 North Latitude US ☎336/369-4171, ⓦwww.110nlatitude.com.

Book Passage 51 Tamal Vista Blvd, Corte Madera, CA 94925 and in the historic San Francisco Ferry Building ☎1-800/999-7909 or 415/927-0960, ⓦwww.bookpassage.com.

Distant Lands 56 S Raymond Ave, Pasadena, CA 91105 ☎1-800/310-3220, ⓦwww.distantlands.com.

Globe Corner Bookstore 28 Church St, Cambridge, MA 02138 ☎1-800/358-6013, ⓦwww.globecorner.com.

Longitude Books 115 W 30th St #1206, New York, NY 10001 ☎1-800/342-2164, ⓦwww.longitudebooks.com.

Map Town 400 5 Ave SW #100, Calgary, AB, T2P 0L6 ☎1-877/921-6277 or ☎403/266-2241, ⓦwww.maptown.com.

Travel Bug Bookstore 3065 W Broadway, Vancouver, BC, V6K 2G9 ☎604/737-1122, ⓦwww.travelbugbooks.ca.

World of Maps 1235 Wellington St, Ottawa, ON, K1Y 3A3 ☎1-800/214-8524 or 613/724-6776, ⓦwww.worldofmaps.com.

Insurance

New Zealand's Accident Compensation Commission (ⓦwww.acc.co.nz) provides limited medical treatment for visitors injured while in New Zealand, but this is no substitute for having comprehensive travel insurance to cover against theft, loss and illness or injury.

Before paying for a new policy, however, it's worth checking whether you are already covered: some all-risks home insurance policies may cover your possessions when overseas, and many private medical schemes include cover when abroad. In Canada, provincial health plans usually provide partial cover for medical mishaps overseas, while holders of official student/teacher/youth cards in Canada and the US are entitled to meagre accident coverage and hospital in-patient benefits. Students will often find that their student health coverage extends during the vacations and for one term beyond the date of last enrolment.

After exhausting the possibilities above, you might want to contact a specialist travel insurance company, or consider the travel insurance deal we offer (see p.22). A typical travel insurance **policy** usually provides cover for the loss of baggage,

Rough Guides Travel Insurance

Rough Guides Ltd offers a low-cost travel insurance policy, especially customized for our statistically low-risk readers by a leading British broker, provided by the American International Group (AIG) and registered with the British regulatory body, GISC (the General Insurance Standards Council). There are five main Rough Guides insurance plans: No Frills for the bare minimum for secure travel; Essential, which provides decent all-round cover; Premier for comprehensive cover with a wide range of benefits; Extended Stay for cover lasting four months to a year; and Annual multi-trip, a cost-effective way of getting Premier cover if you travel more than once a year. Premier, Annual Multi-Trip and Extended Stay policies can be supplemented by a "Hazardous Pursuits Extension" if you plan to indulge in sports considered dangerous, such as scuba-diving or trekking. For a policy quote, call the Rough Guide Insurance Line: toll-free in the UK ℡0800/015 09 06 or ℡+44 1392 314 665 from elsewhere. Alternatively, get an online quote at ⓦwww.roughguides.com/insurance

tickets and – up to a certain limit – cash or cheques, as well as cancellation or curtailment of your journey. Most of them exclude so-called **dangerous activities** unless an extra premium is paid: in New Zealand this can mean scuba-diving, bungy jumping, whitewater rafting, windsurfing and even tramping under some policies.

Many policies can be chopped and changed to exclude coverage you don't need – for example, sickness and accident benefits can often be excluded or included at

will. If you do take medical coverage, ascertain whether benefits will be paid as treatment proceeds or only after return home, and whether there is a 24-hour medical emergency number. When securing **baggage cover**, make sure that the per-article limit – typically under £500 – will cover your most valuable possession. If you need to make a claim, you should keep receipts for medicines and medical treatment, and in the event you have anything stolen, you must obtain an official statement from the police.

Health

New Zealand is relatively free of serious health hazards and the most common pitfalls are not taking precautions or simply underestimating the power of nature. No vaccinations are required to enter the country, but you should make sure you have adequate health cover in your travel insurance, especially if you plan to take on the Great Outdoors (see p.56 for advice on tramping health and safety).

New Zealand has a fine health service, despite recent government cuts, and medical services are reasonably cheap by world standards. Although all visitors are covered by the accident compensation scheme, under which you can claim some medical and hospital expenses in the event of an

accident, without full accident cover in your travel insurance, you could still face a hefty bill. For more minor ailments, you can visit a doctor for a consultation (around $35) and, armed with a prescription, buy any required medication at a pharmacy at a reasonable price.

AIDS is as much of an issue in New Zealand as elsewhere but official attitudes are reasonably enlightened, and there are no restrictions on people with HIV or AIDS entering the country. Support organizations include the Auckland-based New Zealand AIDS Foundation (☎09/303 3124, ⓦwww.nzaf.org.nz), and the 24-hour HIV/AIDS National Hotline (☎0800/802 437).

Perhaps the most hazardous element of the whole New Zealand experience is getting there, in the light of a growing realization that long periods of time spent in cramped conditions on aeroplanes can contribute to deep vein thrombosis (DVT). All the airlines now have videos telling you to move about, perform stationary callisthenics and drink plenty of water. It also helps to limit the amount of booze you consume and, if you are unsure, contact your GP before travelling to find out if you are predisposed toward this problem and what you can do about it.

The sun and geological hazards

Visitors to New Zealand frequently get caught out by the intensity of the sun, its damaging ultra-violet rays easily penetrating the thin ozone layer and reducing burn times to as little as ten minutes in spring and summer. Stay out of the sun as much as possible between 11am and 3pm, and always slap on plenty of sunblock. Reapply every few hours as well as after swimming, and keep a check on any moles on your body: if you notice any changes, during or after your trip, see a doctor right away.

New Zealand is regularly shaken by **earthquakes**, but most are minor and it is not something to worry about. If the worst happens, the best advice is to stand in a doorway or crouch under a table. If caught in the open, try to get inside; failing that, keep your distance from trees and rocky outcrops to reduce the chances of being injured by falling branches or debris. New Zealand's **volcanoes** also have a habit of making their presence felt but vulcanologists are often able to predict periods of eruptive activity. If warnings are issued, get at least as far away as they suggest.

Wildlife hazards

New Zealand's wildlife is amazingly benign. There are no snakes, scorpions and other nasties, and there's only one poisonous creature: the little **katipo spider**. Mercifully rare, this six-millimetre-long critter (the biting female is black with a red patch) is found in coastal areas and only bites if disturbed. The bite can be fatal, but antivenin is available in most hospitals, is effective up to three days after a bite and no one has died from an encounter with the spider for many years. **Shark** attacks are also rare; you are more likely to be carried away by a strong tide (see p.131) than a great white, though it still pays to be sensible and obey any local warnings when swimming.

A far bigger problem are **mosquitoes** and **sandflies** which are a great irritant, but generally free of life-threatening diseases. The West Coast of the South Island in the summer is the worst place for these beasts, though they appear to a lesser degree in many other places across the country: a liberal application of repellent keeps them at bay.

At the microscopic level, **giardia** can be a problem. This parasite inhabits many rivers and lakes throughout the land and infection results from drinking contaminated water, with symptoms appearing several weeks later: a bloated stomach, cramps, explosive diarrhoea and wind. The Department of Conservation advises on the likely presence of giardia in national parks around the country. To minimize the risk of infection, purify drinking water by using iodine-based solutions or tablets (regular chlorine-based tablets aren't effective against giardia); by fast-boiling water for at least seven minutes; or by using a giardia-rated filter (obtainable from any outdoors or camping shop).

The relatively rare **amoebic meningitis** is another water-borne hazard, this time contracted from hot thermal pools. Commercial pools are almost always safe, but in natural pools surrounded by earth you should avoid contamination by keeping your head above water. The amoeba enters the body via the nose or ears, lodges in the brain, and weeks later causes severe headaches, stiffness of the neck, hypersensitivity to light, and eventually coma. If you experience any of these symptoms, seek medical attention immediately.

Costs, money and banks

New Zealand has a stable if not entirely burgeoning economy that has been much enhanced by the knock-on effect of a buoyant tourist trade. However, the value of the New Zealand dollar is still relatively weak by comparison with European currencies so most things will seem fairly cheap to Europeans, although less for North Americans. The quality of goods and standards of service you can expect are high and, on balance, the country offers very good value for money, though fluctuating exchange rates introduce some uncertainty.

The **currency** is the Kiwi dollar, or "buck", divided into 100 cents. There are $100, $50, $20, $10 and $5 notes made of a sturdy plastic material, and coins in denominations of $2 and $1, and 50¢, 20¢, 10¢ and 5¢; grocery prices are given to the nearest cent, but the final bill is rounded up or down to the nearest five cents. All the prices quoted in the Guide are in New Zealand dollars.

New Zealanders are a straightforward bunch and the price quoted is what you pay. In almost all cases, the 12.5 percent Goods and Service Tax (GST) is included in the listed price, and no tip is expected.

Basic costs

With the prevalence of good hostels, single travellers can live almost as cheaply as couples, though you'll pay around thirty percent more if you want a room to yourself. **Accommodation** costs from as little as a couple of dollars for a basic campsite, but a $12-per person pitch or a $18–25 dorm bed in a hostel is more common. Simple double rooms start from as little as $35, though you'll pay $70–90 for a motel unit, $70–120 for homestays and B&Bs, $150–300 for flash international-standard hotels, and anything up to $1000 a person for exclusive retreats. **Food** is good quality and great value; supermarkets are reasonably priced and you can usually find a filling plateful at a pub or café for under $16. A reasonable three-course meal will cost upwards of $35, though you can save on drinks by rooting out **BYO** (Bring Your Own) restaurants, where you can drink wine you've brought with you; though still quite common in smaller places, these are harder to find in the cities.

Given New Zealand's compact size, **transport** costs shouldn't be prohibitive, but if you find yourself moving on every couple of days it can soon add up. A good way of saving on travel is to check advance-booking prices, sometimes lower, or travel at unsociable times (early morning or late night). Though you are unlikely to return from New Zealand too laden with souvenirs, you can completely blow your budget on **adventure trips** – such as a bungy jump (around $150) or tandem parachuting ($200 and up). If you've got the money, by all means spend it; if not, think carefully about how best to get the maximum enjoyment from your visit.

Student **discounts** are few and far between, but you can make substantial savings on accommodation and travel by buying one of the backpacker or YHA cards (see p.40); **kids** and **seniors** enjoy reductions of around fifty percent on most trains, buses and entry to many sights.

Travellers' cheques, credit and debit cards

The safest way to carry your money is still as **travellers' cheques**, which can be exchanged efficiently at banks and bureaux de change all over New Zealand, can be replaced if they are lost or stolen, and usually offer a slightly better exchange rate than changing notes. Recognized brands – American Express, Thomas Cook, Mastercard and Visa – are accepted in all major currencies and, though travellers' cheques in New Zealand dollars relieve the uncertainty of fluctuating exchange rates, they aren't generally accepted as cash. You usually pay one to two percent commission when you buy travellers' cheques but there is seldom an additional charge when you cash them.

Visitors increasingly rely on **credit cards** – Visa, Mastercard, Bankcard and, to a lesser extent, American Express and Diners Club – which are widely accepted, though some supermarkets and many hostels, campsites and homestays will only accept cash. You'll also find credit cards useful for advance booking of accommodation and trips, and with the appropriate Personal Identification Number (PIN) you can obtain **cash advances** through 24-hour ATMs found almost everywhere. You should be aware that such withdrawals usually accrue interest immediately or are subject to a two percent premium – check with your bank before you go too wild. Most ATMs also have the facility for international **debit card** transactions using the Plus and Cirrus networks.

Banks and exchange

The best exchange rates are usually from **banks**. ASB, ANZ, BNZ, National Bank and Westpac have branches in towns of any size and are open from Monday to Friday 9.30am to 4.30pm except for public holidays. Outside banking hours, you'll have to rely on **bureaux de change** in the big cities and tourist centres, which are typically open from 8am to 8pm daily. If you get caught short, the larger hotels will often change travellers' cheques at any time, but rates tend to be poor.

Exchange rates tend to be fairly stable in relation to the Australian and US dollars, less so against European currencies. The New Zealand dollar currently trades at NZ$2.7 for £1, NZ$1.65 for US$1, NZ$1.8 for €1 and NZ$1.14 for A$1.

If you are spending some time in New Zealand – say a couple of months or more – you may want to open a **bank account**. The ease of doing so seems to depend largely on the whim of the bank clerk, so shop around: In Auckland, the Westpac branch at 79 Queen Street has been recommended by readers as being a particularly helpful starting point. Having a New Zealand address you can use for statements helps (though isn't always necessary), and you'll need a couple of pieces of ID. The big advantage of having an account is that you can get money from branches and ATMs using an **EFTPOS card**, which also enables you to pay for stuff at shops, service stations, restaurants, in fact just about anywhere, by swiping the card and punching in your PIN. Most shops will also give you cash, so you can go for weeks without ever visiting a bank.

Wiring money

The best way to get money sent out is to get in touch with your bank at home and have them **wire money** to the nearest bank. It may take a week but it is relatively cheap – you'll probably pay twice as much to have cash sent through Western Union (☎0800/270 000; ⊕www.westernunion.com) or through the nearest branch of Thomas Cook (⊕www.thomascook.com), who offer their own proprietary service and also use the faster Travelers Express MoneyGram (☎0800/262 263; ⊕www.moneygram.com). In all cases, the fees charged are independent of source or destination, and only depend on the amount being transferred: wiring NZ$1000, or equivalent, will cost NZ$70 for example. The funds should be available for collection at the company's local office within minutes of being sent, and by using this service the sender can dispatch cash by phone by using their credit card.

Getting around

New Zealand is a relatively small country and getting around is easy, with some form of public transport going to most destinations, though often you may be limited to one or two services per day.

Although it is possible to fly to many of the major destinations in New Zealand, you will appreciate the scenery better by travelling at ground level. You might take one or two flights, which can be quite reasonably priced if well booked in advance. The rail service is very limited and is also quite expensive, while competition on the ferries connecting the North and South islands keeps passenger fares good value, though transporting vehicles can be pricey. The cheapest and easiest, if most time-consuming, way to get around is by bus (sometimes known as coaches or shuttle buses).

For getting off the beaten track, you'll need your own wheels. If you shop around rental cars can be remarkably good value, especially for two or more people travelling together. If you are staying in the country for more than a couple of months, it's more economical to buy a car. New Zealand is renowned for its green countryside and cycling is an excellent way to see the country.

You'll still need to take to the air or the water (or go tramping) to reach the offshore islands and the remoter parts of the main islands that remain stubbornly impenetrable by road, though as each year passes some areas, such as Fiordland, become progressively easier to access by specialist tour or improved track, road and highway.

Regular long-distance bus, train and plane services are found under "Travel details" at the end of each chapter, with local buses and trains covered in the main text.

Domestic flights

Many visitors fly into Auckland at the beginning of their trip and out again from Christchurch at the end, so the Christchurch to Auckland leg is the only **domestic flight** they take. Those with a tight timetable want-ing to hit a few key sights in a short time might be tempted by some good value internal fares, the product of a reasonable amount of competition.

By far the biggest domestic operator is Air New Zealand which serves all the main centres and numerous minor ones (25 destinations in all). The main competition is from Origin Pacific, with frequent flights to around a dozen cities, and Qantas which just serves the half dozen main centres (including Rotorua and Queenstown).

Air New Zealand runs single-class planes with **fares** that come in three levels offering lower fares for decreased flexibility: there are fewer low-cost fares at popular times. For example, a one-way flight between Auckland and Christchurch might cost $80 as a Smart Saver, $150 as a Flexi Saver or $260 Fully Flexible.

Qantas and Origin Pacific both have a similar system often with slightly cheaper fares, though it always pays to check all three. **Children** (aged 2–11 inclusive) typically pay three-quarters of the adult fare, but don't expect backpacker or senior discounts: the best bet is to book early and be flexible enough to go for the budget fares.

Other flights you might take are scenic jaunts from Auckland to Great Barrier Island, the hop over Cook Strait and the short flight from Invercargill to Stewart Island.

Air companies

Air New Zealand ☎0800/737 000, ⓦwww.airnewzealand.co.nz. Extensive domestic and international flights.
Great Barrier Airlines & Air Coromandel ☎09/275 9120 & 0800/900 600, ⓦwww.greatbarrierairlines.co.nz. Flights between Auckland, Coromandel and Great Barrier Island.
Great Barrier Express & Mountain Air ☎0800/222 123, ⓦwww.mountainair.co.nz.

Flights between Auckland, Whangarei and Great Barrier Island.

Origin Pacific ☎ 03/547 2020 & 0800/302 302, ⓦ www.originpacific.co.nz. Low cost domestic flights.
Qantas ☎ 0800/808 767, ⓦ www.qantas.co.nz. Domestic and international flights.
Soundsair ☎ 0800/505 005, ⓦ www.soundsair .co.nz. Small planes across Cook Strait.
Stewart Island Flights ☎ 03/218 9129, ⓦ www.stewartislandflights.com. Scheduled services between Invercargill and Stewart Island.

Ferries

The **ferries** you're most likely to use are the vehicle-carrying services plying Cook Strait between Wellington on the North Island and Picton on the South Island. Two ferry companies vie for your business, one offering a fast-catamaran service: full details of these are given in the "Crossing Cook Strait" box on p.428.

There are also passenger ferries linking Bluff, in the south of the South Island, to Stewart Island, and both vehicle and passenger ferries connecting Auckland with the Hauraki Gulf islands, principally Waiheke, Rangitoto and Great Barrier. Information about these short trips is included in our accounts on Invercargill and Auckland.

Most visitors spend more boat time on cruises – whale watching, dolphin swimming or sightseeing – but you might also take **water taxis**. These principally operate around the Marlborough Sounds, some running a regular service to points along the Queen Charlotte Track, while others are hired as needed to reach lodges and hostels only accessible by water.

Ferries

Bluebridge ☎ 0800/844 844, ⓦ www.bluebridge.co.nz. Cook Strait ferries.
Foveaux Express ☎ 03/212 7660, ⓦ www.foveauxexpress.co.nz. Runs between Bluff and Stewart Island.
Fullers ☎ 09/367 9111, ⓦ www.fullers.co.nz. Hauraki Gulf ferries from Auckland.
The Interisland Line ☎ 04/498 3302 & 0800/802 802, ⓦ www.interislandline.co.nz. Cook Strait ferries.

Trains

There is very little left of New Zealand's passenger train service. There are **commuter train** services in Wellington (good) and Auckland (poor), and a few inter-city trains. The **long-distance services** that do exist are undoubtedly along scenic runs, but trains are so slow that they have ceased to be practical transport for most New Zealanders, and are primarily aimed at tourists. Minimal investment in infrastructure and rolling stock is beginning to have an effect on standards, but train travel remains a pleasant experience.

Trains have reclining seats, a buffet car with reasonable, good-value food, beer but no espresso, panoramic windows, and some services even have a glass-backed observation carriage so you can see where you've been. You also get a sporadic and not particularly diverting commentary about the places you pass through. A ticket guarantees a seat: passengers check in on the (usually fairly rundown) platform before boarding and bags are carried in a luggage van.

Long-distance trains are all run by **Tranz Scenic** (☎ 0800/872 467, ⓦ www .tranzscenic.co.nz), who operate just four passenger routes. The longest trip is **between Auckland and Wellington**, passing through some of the more rural areas of the North Island as well as the scenic Central Plateau with its volcanic peaks. Interesting stops along the way include Te Awamutu, Te Kuiti (where the daytime train is met by a shuttle bus to Waitomo Caves), and National Park (with access to Mount Ruapehu and the Tongariro Crossing). Two daily trains make the journey in each direction: the daytime *Overlander* leaves both Auckland and Wellington daily around 8.30am and reaches its destination around 7.30pm; and the nighttime *Northerner* departs Auckland 8.40pm and Wellington 7.50pm, and takes eleven hours. There are no sleeper cars on either train, just fairly comfortable reclining seats.

In the South Island, the *TranzCoastal* runs **between Christchurch and Picton**, a pretty run partly shadowing the coast. It leaves Christchurch at 7.30am for the run up through Kaikoura (10.30am) and Blenheim (12.20pm) to Picton (12.50pm). It then returns from Picton (1.40pm) through Blenheim (2.10pm), and Kaikoura (4.10pm) to Christchurch (7pm).

The finest rail journey in New Zealand, and one of the most scenic in the world is the *TranzAlpine* **between Christchurch and Greymouth** on the West Coast – all covered in detail on p.29.

Fares are slightly higher than the comparable bus fare but with discounts and the use of a travel pass (see p.29) travelling is reasonably good value. Unless you book at the last minute on a busy day you won't have to pay the standard fare. Most people get the **Saver fare** which gives a thirty percent discount in return for advance booking, limited availability and a maximum of fifty percent refund. Depending on demand you might even get a Super Saver or backpacker fare, with a further twenty percent off the Saver fare. Seniors (60 and over) and those carrying backpackers carrying YHA, BBH and VIP cards can get 20–30 percent discounts on standard fares, though you may find you can do better by going for a Saver or Super Saver.

Sample fares include: Auckland–Wellington (Saver $90–102, Super Saver & backpacker $64–73); Picton–Christchurch (Saver $57, backpacker $35); Christchurch–Arthur's Pass (Saver $50–60); and Christchurch–Greymouth ($84). Blind and other disabled travellers are entitled to a fifty-percent discount if they present authorization (from the DPA; see p.70). Train travel is also covered by some **travel passes**; see box, p.29.

Apart from a couple of short-run steam trains, the only other passenger trains are along the **Taieri Gorge Railway** (see p.728) between Dunedin and Middlemarch, again run almost entirely for the benefit of tourists and priced accordingly.

Long-distance buses

You can get most places on long-distance **buses** (sometimes called coaches) and the smaller **shuttle buses**, which essentially offer the same service but are more likely to drop you off and pick up at hotels, hostels and the like. Services are generally reliable, reasonably comfortable, and stiff competition keeps prices competitive. The larger buses are usually air-conditioned, and some have toilets, though all services stop every couple of hours, usually at wayside tearooms but also briefly at points of interest along the way.

Most of your fellow passengers are likely to be visitors to New Zealand so drivers will usually give some sort of commentary, the quality of which varies enormously.

InterCity and Newmans

Easily the biggest operator is **InterCity** (℡09/913 6100, ⊛www.intercitycoach.co.nz) who run high quality full-size buses all over the country. They operate closely with **Newmans** who pitch themselves as slightly more luxurious and concentrate more on sightseeing excursions. In practice, the two companies share a timetable and InterCity passes can often be used on Newmans buses: when we refer to InterCity we are generally referring to services run collectively by InterCity and Newmans.

Standard one-way **fares** are: Auckland –Rotorua ($40–50); Auckland–Wellington ($67–99); Picton–Christchurch ($46); Christchurch–Queenstown ($60); and Queenstown to Nelson (overnighting in Fox Glacier or Franz Josef Glacier: $198). Prices often plummet during off-peak periods and a range of discounted fares is available. Advance-purchase Saver fares offer 25-percent **discounts**, and there are a limited number of 50-percent discount Super Savers available: book early for the best prices. YHA and VIP (but not BBH) cardholders get 15 percent **discounts** off Standard fares but you'll often find you'll do better going for a Saver or Super Saver.

InterCity also offer numerous fixed-route **passes** such as: the Twin Coast Discovery Pass around Northland ($103); the North Island Value Pass between Auckland and Wellington ($153); the West Coast Passport from Picton to Queenstown ($149); and the Total NZ Experience loosely covering both islands ($680).

Kids aged 2–11 inclusive travel for two-thirds the adult fare.

Other buses

A host of **bus** and **shuttle bus** companies compete directly with InterCity / Newmans on the main routes and fill in the gaps around the country (especially in the South Island), often linking with the services of the major operators

B

Travel passes

If you're doing a lot of travelling by bus and train, there are savings to be made with travel passes. The most comprehensive is Tranz Scenic's **Best of New Zealand Pass** (☎0800/692 378, ⓦwww.bestpass.co.nz) which combines travel on Trans Scenic trains, the Taieri gorge Railway, *The Lynx* and *Interislander* ferries, and Great Sights and selected InterCity buses on a points system. You buy a number of points – 600 for $499, 800 for $649 or 1000 for $783 – and each journey that you take deducts so many points from your total. Although it involves a lot of pre-planning it is economic, particularly for those with a strict itinerary who book at least a couple of days in advance. The pass is valid for six months and you can expect to use up to 60 points for a coach trip from Auckland to Rotorua, 55–70 for a ferry across Cook Strait and 90 points for the TranzAlpine train journey. Stick to the main tourist routes and 600 points will see you around one island, and 1000 points will give you a full tour.

InterCity / Newmans offer their own **Flexi-Pass** (☎0508/353 947, ⓦwww.intercitycoach.co.nz) which lets you buy bus travel by the hour, and the more hours you buy the better the savings. You would typically need 45 hours ($340) to cover one of the main islands, more like 80 hours ($585) for a full tour, and if that's not enough you can top-up your pass with, say, 10 hours ($41). The Flexi-Pass is valid for 12 months and you get a free-call number to make onward bookings.

Travellers wanting to move around pretty quickly might be better off with one of the **New Zealand Travel Passes** (☎0800/339 966, ⓦwww.travelpass.co.nz). The *By-the-Month* variation gives unlimited travel on InterCity / Newmans for one month ($945), two months ($1080) or three months $1240). Add in ferry travel for a 2-in-One travelpass which is valid for a year and has various options from 5 days ($360) to 22 days ($898). Buses, ferries and trains are included in the 3-in-One Travelpass available from 5 days in a year ($446) to 22 days ($945).

Then there are the passes offered by the backpacker tours buses (see p.30), which offer lower prices in return for older buses and a more boisterous time.

---

to take you off the beaten track. They generally cost less (sometimes appreciably) and are often more obliging when it comes to drop-offs and pick-ups at your lodging, but seldom seem as comfortable over long distances. We've listed a number of the major operators below, but there are many more mentioned in the appropriate sections of the text.

Visitor centres carry **timetables** of companies operating in their area, so you can compare frequencies and prices. **Fare structures** are generally straightforward with fixed prices and no complicated Savers and discounts. Typical examples include: Auckland–Rotorua ($38); Picton–Christchurch ($25); Christchurch–Queenstown ($45); and Queenstown–Nelson ($120).

Buses

Atomic Shuttles ☎03/322 8883, ⓦwww.atomictravel.co.nz. Major long-distance bus operator in the South Island.

Guthreys Express ☎0800/759 999. Mostly covering the northern half of the North Island.
InterCity & Newmans Auckland ☎09/913 6100, Wellington ☎04/472 5111, Christchurch ☎03/379 9020, Dunedin ☎03/474 9600, ⓦwww.intercitycoach.co.nz & ⓦwww.newmanscoach.co.nz. Long-distance buses nationwide.
Northliner Express ☎09/307 5873, ⓔinfo@northliner.co.nz. Bus travel around Northland.
South Island Connections ☎03/366 6633, ⓦwww.southislandconnections.co.nz. Limited coverage of the South Island.
Southern Link Shuttles ☎03/358 8355. Nelson to Queenstown via Christchurch.
Wanaka Connexions ☎03/443 9122, ⓦwww.wanakaconnexions.co.nz. Linking Dunedin, Queenstown and Wanaka.

Backpacker buses

One of the cheapest ways to cover a lot of ground is on a **backpacker bus**, which combines some of the flexibility of independent travel with the convenience of a tour. You typically purchase a ticket for a fixed route (usually valid for twelve months), then take it at your own pace. Each of the major companies has several buses all following a number of fixed routes so that you can either stick with the one bus for the entire journey with nights spent at various towns along the route, or stop off longer in places and hop on a later bus. During peak times, it may not be that easy. Subsequent buses may already be full, so you may need to plan your onward travel several days in advance. Companies operate year-round, though services are much reduced in winter.

The emphasis is on experiencing the country rather than just travelling from one town to the next, so you'll be stopping off at places to bungy jump, hike trails or whatever. Being part of a group of forty rowdy backpackers arriving at some idyllic spot isn't everyone's idea of a good time, and by using assorted public transport it is often just as cheap to make your own way around New Zealand. But with almost everything organised for you, and a ready-made bunch of like-minded fellow travellers this sort of travel has undeniable appeal.

With all the companies listed below there are savings of 5–10 percent if you **book before you arrive** in New Zealand, and some deals are not available once you arrive. YHA, VIP, BBH, and ISIC cardholders get around five percent off most trips mentioned below. Tickets don't generally cover accommodation, activities (although these are often discounted), side-trips, food or travel between the North and South islands.

Easily the biggest and best known are the big green buses of **Kiwi Experience** (℡09/366 9830, ⒲www.kiwiexperience.com), which have a largely deserved reputation for attracting high-spirited revellers. They offer a huge array of passes from a loop from Taupo around the East Cape & Napier (minimum 4 days; $299) or a trip to Cape Reinga from Auckland (min 3 days; $173) to a basic countrywide trip (min 10 days; $679) or the Full Monty (min 29 days; $1542).

The pretender to the backpacker bus crown is **Magic Bus** (Auckland ℡09/358 5600, ⒲www.magicbus.co.nz) who offer a slightly less comprehensive selection of trips,

but guarantee you a seat if you book at least 24hr in advance. They work in with the YHA and target themselves at marginally older and more independently minded travellers. Their Freedom Passes cover the country in varying degrees of depth from a minimum of 11 days ($818) to a minimum of 23 days ($1322). YHA accommodation and inter-island ferry travel is included in their Highlights packages: either the South Island (min 9 days; $649), the North Island (min 8 days; $586), or the whole country (12–18 days; $950–1289). Shorter highlights trips (again with accommodation and some other extras) include the Coromandel Peninsula (min 3 days; $169), and Cape Reinga tour (min 3 days; $279).

Stray (NZ ℡07/824 3627, UK ℡020/7373 7737, Australia ℡1300/733 048; ⒲www.straytravel.com) is a relative newcomer to the field and are making a big effort to catch up to its major competitors. They aim to get further off the beaten track, are probably a little more personal, and guarantee beds each night. Trips are similar to the competition with better coverage of the south of the South Island but no East Cape of the North Island. Typical trips include: a South Island circuit (min 13 days; $614); a basic North Island circuit (min 7 days; $345); and the whole country (min 21 days; $884).

There's an altogether more free-spirited approach to the trips run by the eco-oriented **Flying Kiwi Wilderness Expeditions** (℡03/547 0171 & 0800/693 296, ⒲www.flyingkiwi.com), who get off the beaten track and eschew city hostels in favour of camping out. Converted buses are equipped with bikes, canoes, windsurfers, kitchen, awning, fridge, beds, tents and hot shower, and everyone mucks in with the cooking and dishes. Their trips operate all year and once on board you stick with the same group. Ten options range from the Northern Express from Wellington to Auckland via Taupo (2 days; $109) to a full NZ tour (27 days; $1275). On top of this you'll usually pay around $11 a night to camp and $16 a day for the food kitty.

Specialist tours

New Zealand really is a very easy place to travel independently, but for specialist insight, logistical help, or simply a little company along the way, you can't go past a multi-day guided tour.

Hiking, wilderness and wildlife

Active Earth ☎025/360 268 & 0800/201 040, Australia ☎1800/141 242, ⓦwww.activeearthnewzealand.com. Well organized guided wilderness tours suitable for anyone who is reasonably fit and wants to see things that few other tourists will. Good-humoured and informative guides take small groups tramping, climbing and wilderness camping in virtually untouched country throughout the North Island, with almost everything included – $595 for 5 nights to $990 for 9 nights – except a daily food and camp-fee kitty (around $10 a day) and any extra adventure activities.

Adventure South ☎03/941 1222, ⓦwww.advsouth.co.nz. This smallish, environmentally conscious company runs guided cycling and multi-activity tours around the South Island, with accommodation in characterful lodges, plus a two-week "Midlife Adventures" trip designed for "those too young to be called old, and too old to be called young". Consider trips such as 6 days cycling along the West Coast of the South Island ($2000), ten-days hiking, biking and sea kayaking in the northern half of the South Island ($4000), and 13 Midlife days throughout the country ($5100).

Kiwi Wildlife Tours ☎09/422 2115, ⓦwww.kiwi-wildlife.co.nz. Upscale small-group birding tours ranging from day excursions around the Auckland area ($150) or Arthur's Pass ($250) to a comprehensive 20-day all-inclusive NZ tour ($8400).

New Zealand Nature Safaris ☎025/360 268 & 0800/697 232, Australia ☎1800/141 242, ⓦwww.hikingnewzealand.com. Effectively the South Island arm of Active Earth (see above) with a similar range of trips including a Lord of the Rings-style tramp that covers some of the most beautiful country on the South Island.

Cycling

Pedaltours ☎09/302 0968 & 0800/302 0968, US freephone ☎1-888/222 9187, ⓦwww.pedaltours.co.nz. Guided road and mountain biking tours of both islands, from a week-long ride around the Nelson Lakes ($2300), to a full 22-day Grand Tour of the South Island (around $7400). High-standard accommodation and hearty meals are included, and bikes can be rented if needed (around $170 a week). Customized tours can be arranged for groups.

Cycle Touring Company ☎09/430 2030, ⓦwww.cycletours.co.nz. Tailored self-led tours of

Northland (or guided if you prefer), with several routes of two to twelve days, and the option to have your gear carried for you. Accommodation is in lodges and homestays (or a cheaper backpacker option) and prices are around $2000 for a week.

Pacific Cycle Tours ☎03/329 9913, ⓦwww.bike-nz.com. Lyttelton-based mountain bike and road bike tours around both islands with varying degrees of adventurousness ($2750 for 7 days to $3725 for 20 days), plus a self-guide four-day wine tour around Marlborough ($1650).

Motorcycling

Adventure New Zealand Motorcycle Tours & Rentals ☎03/548 5787 & 0800/848 6337, ⓦwww.gotournz.com. Nelson-based company who provide upmarket, small-group bike tours around the South Island; itineraries can often be tweaked to suit. Tours are accompanied by a luxury coach, and everything is done to the highest standard. Rates range from $9500 for a standard ten-day trip on a relatively modest bike to $23,000 for a full 21-day tour on a superbike.

New Zealand Motorcycle Rentals & Tours Auckland ☎09/377 2005, Christchurch ☎03/337 0663, UK freephone ☎0800/917 3941, US freephone ☎ 0800/917 3941; ⓦwww.nzbike.com. Specialist top-end company offering guided all-inclusive tours staying in quality accommodation (7-day $5300; 18-day $11,700); semi-guided tours (7-day $4000, 20-day $7500), and bike rental (see p.36).

Te Waipounamu Motorcycle Hire & Tours ☎03/372 3537, ⓦwww.motorcycle-hire.co.nz. These folk do upscale tours like the other companies but also offer a more budget oriented three-week Adventure Tour for $4800–5900.

Women's Tours

Wanderwomen ☎09/360 7330, ⓦwww.wanderwomen.co.nz. Auckland-based women-only outdoor adventure trips offering safe, enjoyable and enriching experiences for small groups. Try a few hours of kayaking, rock climbing or caving ($25–75), a weekend orienteering, alpine climbing or mountain biking ($250–400), or step up to multi-day adventure holidays (roughly $120 a day) including accommodation and food. They also do some **family excursions**.

South Sea Mermaid Tours ☎03/942 3264, ⓦwww.southseamermaids.co.nz. Christchurch-based company running women-only guided minibus tours of the South Island, either with all accommodation and meals included (10 days; $3335) or transport and guiding only (10 days; $950).

Driving

For maximum flexibility, it is hard to beat **driving** around New Zealand: you'll be able to get to places beyond the reach of public transport and to set your own timetable. With the freedom to camp or stay in cheaper places away from the centre of towns it may even work out cheaper overall for two or more people travelling together, though, this does come with an environmental cost.

In order to drive in New Zealand you need a valid **licence** from your home country or an International Driver's Licence (available from national motoring organizations in your home country). These are valid for up to a year in New Zealand and you must always carry your license when driving.

In New Zealand you **drive on the left** and will find **road rules** similar to those in the UK, Australia and the US. The one variation peculiar to New Zealand is that you must give way to all traffic crossing or coming from your right; this means that if you are turning left and another car coming from the opposite direction wants to turn right into the same side-road, you must let them go first. All occupants must wear **seatbelts**, and there is no provision for turning left on a red light, even if there is no traffic coming. Drivers must park in the same direction as that in which you are travelling; roadside **parking** facing oncoming traffic is illegal.

The **speed limit** for the open road is 100km/hr, reduced to 70 km/hr or 50km/hr in built-up areas. Speeding fines start at $80 and rapidly increase as the degree of transgression increases. Some drivers flash their headlights at oncoming cars to warn of lurking police patrols but the advent of hidden cameras makes this fairly pointless. **Drink driving** is a major problem in New Zealand: as part of a campaign to cut the death-toll, random breath tests have been introduced, and offenders are dealt with severely.

Road conditions are generally good and **traffic** is relatively light except around Auckland and at rush hour in Wellington. Most roads are sealed (paved), although a few have a metalled surface composed of an aggregate of loose chippings. Clearly marked on most maps, these are slower to drive along, are prone to wash-outs and landslides after heavy rain, and demand considerably more care and attention from the driver. Some rental companies prohibit the use of their cars on the worst metalled roads – typically those at Skippers Canyon and around the northern tip of Coromandel Peninsula. Always check conditions locally before setting off on these routes.

Other **hazards** include one-lane bridges: a sign before the bridge will indicate who has right of way, and on longer examples there'll be a passing place half way across. Even on relatively major roads you might also come across **flocks of sheep**, slow-moving farm equipment, and monstrous logging trucks, all made more of a nuisance by the paucity of passing lanes. Unleaded and super unleaded **petrol** and diesel are available in New Zealand and in larger towns petrol stations are open 24hr. In smaller town petrol stations may close after 8pm so be sure to fill up for long evening or night journeys. Prices currently hover around $1.04 a litre for unleaded, $1.10 for super unleaded, and 60¢ for diesel, with higher prices in more out-of-the-way places.

If you're driving your own vehicle, check if the **New Zealand Automobile Association** (ⓦ www.nzaa.co.nz) has reciprocal rights with motoring organizations from your country to see if you qualify for their cover; otherwise, you can join as an overseas visitor. Apart from free 24-hour **emergency breakdown service** (☎0800/224 357) – excluding vehicles bogged on beaches – membership entitles you to free maps, accommodation guides and legal assistance, discounts on some rental cars and accommodation, plus access to insurance and pre-purchase vehicle inspection services.

Vehicle rental

Visitors driving around New Zealand typically pick up a car in Auckland, tour the North Island to Wellington where they leave the first vehicle, cross Cook Strait, pick up a second car in Picton then drive around the South Island dropping off the car in Christchurch. The whole thing can be done in reverse, and may work out cheaper as there are savings in going against the flow.

New Zealand is awash with companies wanting to rent you a car and such competition has a wonderful effect on prices. You'll even see deals for under $20 a day, though this only applies to older small cars rented for over a month outside the summer season (Dec–March). Demand is high over the main summer season and prices rise accordingly.

Most of the **major international companies** – Avis, Budget, Hertz, National, Thrifty etc – are represented here and offer good deals for virtually new cars. **Nationwide firms** such as A2B, Ace, Apex, New Zealand Rent a Car, Omega and Pegasus can usually offer cheaper rates partly by minimising overheads but also by offering slightly older (but perfectly serviceable) vehicles. You may find even cheaper deals with cut-rate local companies which are fine for short stints, though for general touring the nationwide companies are probably the best bet. Their infrastructure helps when it comes to crossing between the North and South islands (see below).

In peak season it usually pays to have something **booked in advance**. At quieter times you can often pick something up cheaper once you arrive; and in winter (except in ski areas) you can almost name your price. Provided your rental period is four days or more the deal will be for **unlimited kilometres**. The rates quoted below are for summer season assuming a two-week rental period, but at any time, don't be afraid to haggle.

For two people a **small car** (1.3–1.8 litre) might cost $55–80 a day from the majors, $35–70 from national firms. Those requiring a little more comfort, or needing to fit in the kids, a **medium-sized car** (2–3 litre) would be more appropriate. This might cost $85–95 from the majors and closer to $80 from smaller companies. Unless you're here in winter and want to get up to the skifields without tyre chains you don't really need a **4WD**, which generally cost $100–150 a day; you'll do best to rent one for specific areas rather than long term.

If you are renting for several weeks from one company there is often no **drop-off fee** for leaving the vehicle somewhere other than where you picked it up. For shorter rental periods you may be charged $150–200, though if you're travelling south to north, you may be able to sweet-talk your way out of drop-off charges. At different times in the season Wellington, Picton, Christchurch and Queenstown often have a glut of cars that are needed somewhere else, and companies will offer great **relocation deals**. Look at hostel noticeboards, call the companies listed below or phone around companies listed under "Rental Cars" in the Yellow Pages. Some companies want quick delivery, while others will also allow you to spend a few more days en route for a much reduced rental rate.

Before you sign on the dotted line you must have a full, clean **driver's licence** and you must be over 21; drivers under 25 often have to pay more for insurance. In most cases insurance is included in the quoted cost but you are liable for any windscreen damage and the first $750 of any damage. This can usually be reduced to $250 or zero by paying an additional $8–12 a day Collision Damage Waiver. Before giving you a car, rental companies take a credit-card imprint or a cash bond from you for anything up to $1000. If you have an accident, the bond is used to pay for any damage: in some cases you pay anything up to the value of the bond; in others you pay the entire bond, no matter how slight the damage. Read the small print, look around the car for any visible **defects**, so you won't end up being charged for someone else's mistakes, and check whether there are any **restrictions** on driving along certain roads.

Car rental agencies in New Zealand

A2B Rentals ℡09/377 0825 & 0800/616 888, ⓦwww.a2brentals.co.nz
Ace Tourist Rentals ℡09/303 3112 & 0800/502 277, ⓦwww.tourist-rentals.co.nz
Apex ℡09/257 0292 & 0800/939 597, ⓦwww.apexrentals.co.nz
Avis ℡09/526 2847 & 0800/655 111, ⓦwww.avis.co.nz
Budget ℡09/256 8447 & 0800/652 227, ⓦwww.budget.co.nz
Hertz ℡09/256 8695 & 0800/654 321, ⓦwww.hertz.co.nz
National ℡09/275 0066 & 0800/800 115, ⓦwww.nationalcar.co.nz
New Zealand Rent a Car ℡09/275 2422 & 0800/112 345, ⓦwww.idealrentals.com
Omega ℡09/377 5573 & 0800/525 210, ⓦwww.omegarentals.com

Pegasus ☎09/358 5757 & 0800/354 510,
ⓦwww.rentalcars.co.nz
Thrifty ☎09/309 0111 & 0800/737 070,
ⓦwww.thrifty.co.nz

Car rental agencies abroad

Avis Australia ☎13 63 33, ⓦwww.avis.com.au;
Britain ☎0870/606 0100, ⓦwww.avis.co.uk;
Northern Ireland ☎028/9024 0404, Republic of
Ireland ☎01/605 7500, ⓦwww.avis.ie; US ☎1-
800/331-1084, Canada ☎1-800/272-5871,
ⓦwww.avis.com
Budget Australia ☎1300/362 848,
ⓦwww.budget.com.au; Britain ☎0870/153 9170,
ⓦwww.budget.co.uk; Republic of Ireland
☎0903/27711, ⓦwww.budget.ie; US ☎1-
800/527-0700, ⓦwww.budgetrentacar.com
Hertz Australia ☎13 30 39, ⓦwww.hertz.com;
Britain ☎0870/844 8844, ⓦwww.hertz.co.uk;
Republic of Ireland ☎01/676 7476,
ⓦwww.hertz.ie; US ☎1-800/654-3001, Canada
☎1-800/263-0600, ⓦwww.hertz.com
National Australia ☎13 10 45,
ⓦwww.nationalcar.com.au; Britain ☎0870/400
4581, ⓦwww.nationalcar.com; ☎1-800/227-
7368, ⓦwww.nationalcar.com
Thrifty Australia ☎1300/367 227,
ⓦwww.thrifty.com.au; Britain ☎01494/751 600,
ⓦwww.thrifty.co.uk; Republic of Ireland
☎1800/515 800, ⓦwww.thrifty.ie; ☎1-800/367-
2277, ⓦwww.thrifty.com

Campervan rental

Throughout the summer New Zealand roads
seem clogged with **campervans** (small
motorhomes) almost all being driven by
foreign visitors who rent them for a few weeks
and drive around the country staying in campgrounds and sneaking the odd free night in
wayside rest areas. This isn't strictly legal but
you're unlikely to be hassled in isolated areas.

A small campervan is generally suitable for
two adults and perhaps a couple of kids and
comes with a fold-down bed and compact
kitchen. Larger models sleep four or more
and often have a shower and toilet, but
don't expect to find American-style RVs the
size of a small house.

Campervan rentals (based on a 3–5
week rental) average about $160–250 a day
during the high season (Dec–Feb), dropping
a little for a couple of months either side and
plummeting to $50–90 in winter. The two

biggest rental firms are Maui and Brits (effectively the same company), but a few smaller
companies (listed below) offer cheaper rates,
saving 20–30 percent. The Backpackers
company offers particularly good rates down
to $85 a day in summer for a compact two-
berther. For that affordable and slightly off-
beat experience, go for a restored, classic
VW campervans (possibly with a pop-top)
from Picton-based Kool Kombi who charge
$85–120 a day in summer assuming a 3–5
week rental period.

There's usually a minimum rental period of
5–7 days, but you get unlimited kilometres,
a kitchen kit, and perhaps airport transfer.
Insurance is often included but you may be
liable for, say, the first $5000 and you'll need
to seriously consider paying extra fees to get
this liability reduced. Most companies have a
supply of tents, camping kits, outdoor chairs
and tables which can be rented for a few
dollars.

No special **licence** is required to drive a
campervan, but some caution is needed,
especially in high winds and when climbing
hills and going around tight corners. Finally,
have some consideration for other road
users and pull over to let others pass wherever possible.

Campervan rentals

Adventure NZ ☎09/256 0256, UK ☎0800/614
162, ⓦwww.nzmotorhomes.co.nz
Backpackers ☎09/833 5957 & 0800/226 769,
ⓦwww.backpackernz.co.nz
Britz ☎09/275 9090 & 0800/831 900,
ⓦwww.britz.com
Freedom Campers ☎03/259 4730 & 0800/325
939, ⓦwww.freedomcampers.co.nz
Kea Campers NZ ☎09/441 7833, Australia
☎02/8707 5500, ⓦwww.kea.co.nz
Kool Kombi ☎03/574 1295,
ⓦwww.koolkombi.co.nz
Maui NZ ☎09/275 3013 & 0800/651 080,
Australia ☎1300/363 80, ⓦwww.maui-rentals.com

Buying a used vehicle

Buying a used vehicle can be cost-
effective if you are staying in the country for
more than a couple of months and may
even be worthwhile for shorter periods.
Reselling can recoup enough of the price to
make it cheaper than using public transport

or renting. Of course, if you buy cheap there's also greater risk of breakdowns and expensive repairs. The majority of people buy cars in Auckland and then try to sell them in Christchurch, so there's something to be said for buying in Christchurch where you'll often have more choice and a better bargaining position.

Some of the best deals are found on backpacker **hostel noticeboards** where older cars and vans are typically offered for $500–4000. Realistically you can expect to pay upwards of $2000 for something half-decent. It may not look pretty and with a **private sale** there's no guarantee the vehicle will make yet another trip around the country, but you'll often have tables, chairs, cooking gear and assorted paraphernalia thrown in (or offered at a snip). Alternatively, trawl the local papers for likely candidates.

For a little more peace of mind, buy from a **car dealership**. There are plenty all over the country, especially in Auckland, Christchurch and Wellington. Prices begin at around $4500 and some also offer a **buy-back service**, usually paying about fifty percent of the purchase price. If you're confident of your ability to spot a lemon, you can try to pick up a cheap car at an **auction**; they're held weekly in Auckland and Christchurch (see listings p.127 & p.627), and are advertised in the local press. Be aware that you'll usually be liable for the **buyer's premium** of ten percent over your bid.

Before you commit yourself, consult the vehicle ownership section of the NZ Land Transport Safety Authority website (www.ltsa.govt.nz/vehicle-ownership) which has good advice on buying and the pitfalls. For general **technical pointers**, call the premium-rated AA Techline (Mon–Fri 8.30am–5pm; 0900/58324 from private lines only; $1 per min), who can fill you in on the good and bad points about a range of vehicles.

Unless you really know your big end from your steering column you'll want to arrange a mobile **vehicle inspection**, either from the AA (0800/500 333; $95) or from Car Inspection Services (0800/500 800 in Auckland and Wellington, www.carinspections.co.nz; $105). They'll come to you, and the cost may be offset by giving you ammunition to negotiate a price reduction. Finally, before you close

a private sale, call AA AutoReports (0800/500 333, www.autoreport.co.nz) which will fill you in on registration history, possible odometer tampering and any debts on the vehicle. It costs $25 for nonmembers.

Before they're allowed on the road, all vehicles must have a **Warrant of Fitness** (WOF), which is a test of its mechanical worthiness and safety, just like an MOT in the UK. WOFs are carried out and issued by specified garages and testing stations, and last for a year if the vehicle is less than six years old, or six months if older. Check the expiry date, as the test must have been carried out no more than one month before sale. The vehicle should also have current **vehicle license** which must be renewed before it expires (6 months, $112; 12 months, $217): post offices and AA offices are the most convenient for this.

You **transfer ownership** by filing a form (filled in by buyer and seller) at the post office: the license plates stay with the vehicle. Next you'll need **insurance**, either comprehensive (which covers your vehicle and any other damaged vehicles) or Third Party, Fire & Theft (which covers your own vehicle against fire and theft, but only pays out on damage to other vehicles in case of an accident). There are dozens of companies listed under "Insurance Companies" in the Yellow Pages: shop around as prices vary widely, but expect to pay a minimum of $250 for six months Third Party, Fire & Theft cover.

Motorbiking

Visitors from most countries can ride in New Zealand with just their normal license, though it (or your international licence) must specify motorbikes. Helmets are, of course, compulsory, and you'll need to be prepared for riding on gravel roads from time to time. Take it easy at first if you're not used to loose surfaces.

Few people bring their own bike but **bike rental** is available from the companies running guided bike tours (see p.31). It isn't cheap, so for a 650cc machine in summer you can expect to pay $155–175 a day. Bike Adventure New Zealand (027/498 8287 & 0800/498 600, www.banz.co.nz) offers 600cc enduro machines for $115 a day for short periods, dropping to $83 a day if you stay over two months.

Alternatively, try the same channels as for "Buying a used vehicle" above.

Cycle Touring

Cycle touring is an excellent and increasingly popular way of getting around New Zealand. Distances aren't enormous, the weather is generally benign, traffic is fairly light, and the countryside is gorgeous. Everywhere you go you'll find hostels and campgrounds well set up for campers but also equipped with rooms and cabins for when the weather really packs in.

But there are downsides: New Zealand's road network is skeletal so in many places you'll find yourselves riding on main roads; minor roads are often unsealed; even in summer it rains a fair bit; and much of the country is hilly making riding hard going.

Contrary to what you might think, cycling the South Island is an easier proposition than touring the North Island. The South Island's alpine backbone presents virtually the only geographical barrier, while the eastern two-thirds of the island comprise a flat plain. In the North Island you can barely go 10km without encountering significant hills – and you have to contend with a great deal more traffic, including overbearing logging trucks.

New Zealand law requires all cyclists to **wear a helmet**. Some **fitness** is important, but distances don't have to be great and you can take things at your own pace. If you'd rather go with a **guided group** see our recommendations on p.31.

For more **information** obtain the *Pedallers' Paradise* guides (ⓦ www.paradise-press .co.nz) to cycle touring the North and South islands or Bruce Ringer's *New Zealand by Bike* (for both see Contexts, p.987).

The bike

Since the vast majority of riding will be on sealed roads with only relatively short sections of gravel, it is perfectly reasonable (and more efficient) to get around New Zealand on a touring bike. But current fashion dictates most people use a **mountain bike** fitted with fat but relatively smooth tyres.

Most cycle tourists bring their **own bike**. If you're here for several weeks it is likely to be cheaper and you have the advantage of being able to set up everything perfectly before you leave home. On most international airlines bikes simply count as a piece of luggage and don't incur any extra cost as long as you don't exceed your baggage limit. You'll certainly be expected to remove pedals and handle bars and wrap the chain, but increasingly airlines demand you use a **bike bag** or box. Some airlines will sell you a cardboard bike box at the airport, though your friendly local bike dealer may give you one free. Soft bags are probably the most convenient (they're easy to carry on the bike once you arrive), but if you are flying out from the same city you arrive you can often store hardshell containers (free or for a small fee) at the backpacker hostel where you spend your first and last nights: call around.

Renting bikes for more than the odd day can be an expensive option, costing anything from $25–45 a day, depending whether you want a bike with little more than pedals and brakes, a tourer, or a state-of-the-art mountain bike. Specialist cycle shops do economical monthly rental for around $200 for a touring bike, $300 for a full-suspension superbike.

For long-distance cycle touring, it's generally cheaper to **buy a bike**. You'll be looking at a minimum of $500, and more likely $1000, to get fully kitted out with new equipment, but it is worth checking hostel noticeboards for **second-hand bikes** (under $300 is a reasonable deal), often accompanied by extras like wet-weather gear, lights, helmet and a pump. Some cycle shops offer **buy-back deals**, where you buy at full price and they guarantee to refund about fifty percent of the purchase price at the end of your trip. Contact Adventure Cycles, 36 Customs St East (☎ 09/309 5566 & 0800/335 566, ⓦ www.adventure-auckland.co.nz/advcy-chm.html) in Auckland. If you're bringing your own bike, the same folk will let you store the bike box you transported your machine in, help you organize an emergency package of spare parts and extra clothing to be forwarded at your request, and give your bike a final once-over before you set off, all for around $30. The best bet for similar treatment in Christchurch is Laurie Dawe Cycles, 838 Colombo Street (☎ 03/366 5639, ⓔ lauriedawecycles@kwik.net.nz)

Getting around

Lethargy, boredom, breakdowns or simply a need to transport your bike between islands mean at some point you'll need to use **public transport**. You can almost always hoick your bike onto a bus (generally $10) or train ($10 per journey) though space is often limited and you'll do well to book in advance. Crossing Cook Strait, the Lynx, Interislander and Blue Bridge ferries all charge $10.

Bikes usually travel free on buses, trains and ferries if packed in a bike bag and treated as ordinary luggage, though when flying, Air New Zealand and Qantas will still charge you $20 per flight.

Hitching and organised rides

Although many travellers enthuse about **hitching** in New Zealand – and it does enjoy a reputation of relative safety – the official advice is don't. Sadly, New Zealand has its share of unpleasant individuals and, with an extensive network of affordable transport and tours at your disposal, there's really little reason to take unnecessary risks. However if you are determined to work those thumbs then try to follow a few **rules**: hitch in pairs (no guarantee of avoiding trouble but safer than going solo); trust your instincts – there will always be another car; ask the driver where they are going, rather than telling them where you're headed; and keep your gear with you so you can make a quick getaway if necessary.

Finding the best hitching spots around the country is generally a matter of common sense, or common knowledge on the travellers' grapevine. Some town and city hostels drop their guests at hitching spots as a matter of course. Pick a spot where you can be clearly seen and drivers can stop safely.

It is generally safer to **organise a ride** before you set off, though it still demands some trust on both sides. Hostel noticeboards are the best bets, and if no one seems to be going where you want to go, stick up your own notice. Usually you'll be expected to share petrol costs

Accommodation

Accommodation will take up a fair chunk of your money while in New Zealand, though the expense is ameliorated by excellent standards. Almost every town has a motel or hostel of some description, so finding accommodation is seldom a problem – though it's advisable to book in advance from Christmas through to the end of January when Kiwis take their summer holidays, and a month or two either side when places fill with international visitors.

Many places are now accredited using the nationwide **Qualmark** system (@www.qualmark.co.nz), which grades different types of accommodation – exclusive, hotel, self-contained, guest & hosted, holiday parks, and backpackers – with a number of stars. Most fall between three stars (very good) and four plus (at the top end of excellent), but there is no way of knowing whether, for example, a 4-star backpacker is superior to rooms at a 5-star holiday park.

Kiwis travel widely at home, most choosing to self-cater at the country's huge number of well-equipped **campgrounds** (aka motor camps or holiday parks) and **motels**, shunning **hotels**, which cater mainly to package holidaymakers and the business community. An appealing alternative is the range of, **B&Bs**, **homestays**, **farmstays** and **lodges**

Accommodation price codes

Accommodation listed in this guide has been categorized into one of nine price bands, as set out below. The rates quoted represent the cheapest available double or twin room (single rooms generally cost only ten to twenty percent less) in high season – except for category ❶, which are per-person rates for a dorm bed. DOC hut and camping fees are also per person, unless otherwise stated. In the lower categories, most rooms will be without private bath, though there may well be a washbasin. From the ❺ band upwards, you'll more than likely have private facilities.

Prices normally include Goods and Services Tax (GST), as do our codes, though some more business-orientated places may give the GST-exclusive price.

❶	under $25 per person	❻	$121–150
❷	under $50 per room	❼	$151–200
❸	$51–70	❽	$201–250
❹	$71–90	❾	over $250
❺	$91–120		

which cover the whole spectrum from a room in someone's suburban home to pampered luxury in a country mansion.

Since the mid-1980s, New Zealand has pioneered the **backpacker hostel**, a less-regimented alternative to traditional YHAs, which have transformed themselves dramatically to compete. Found all over the country, hostels offer superb value to budget travellers.

Wherever you stay, you can expect unstinting hospitality and a truckload of valuable advice on local activities and onward travel. We've included a wide selection of New Zealand's best accommodation throughout the guide, and more detail can be gleaned from specialist accommodation guides.

Useful accommodation guides and websites

AA Accommodation Guide
Ⓦ www.aatravel.co.nz. Annually published advertising-based guide for the whole country; concentrates on motels and holiday parks but has some coverage of hotels and lodges. Nominally $15 if bought within NZ but available free from most motels.
Charming Bed & Breakfast Ⓦ www.bnbnz.com. Glossy B&B guide concentrating on mid-range places and with plenty of colour photos. Available through their website for the price of postage.
Friars' Guide Ⓦ www.friars.co.nz. An advertising-based annual guide with fairly comprehensive coverage of the country's more upscale B&Bs and boutique lodges. Available ($30) from NZ bookshops and vendors listed on their website.

The Bed & Breakfast Book Ⓦ www.bnb.co.nz ($20). Annually updated listing of member B&Bs, boutique lodges, homestays and farmstays, covering around 1200 places all over the country. Bear in mind that entries are submitted by the owners, so a little reading between the lines is advisable. Available from bookshops, visitor centres and many of the places listed in the book.
House rental Many Kiwis own a holiday home (aka *bach* or *crib*) which they rent out when they're not using them. Many are in superb locations next to beaches but you'll often have to agree to a minimum stay (perhaps four nights). Rates vary enormously peaking around Christmas (when availability is very low) and plummeting in winter. Sites to check out include Ⓦ www.bookabach.co.nz, Ⓦ www.holidayhouses.co.nz and Ⓦ www.beachhouses.co.nz

Hotels and motels

In New Zealand, **hotel** is a term frequently used to describe old-style pubs, which were once legally obliged to provide rooms for drinkers to recuperate from their excesses. Many no longer provide accommodation, but some have transformed themselves into backpacker hostels, while others are dedicated to preserving the tradition. At their best, hotels offer comfortable rooms in characterful, historic buildings, though just as often lodgings are rudimentary. Hotel bars are frequently at the centre of smalltown social life and, at weekends in particular, they can be pretty raucous; for the asking price of $50–60 a double, you may find a budget room at a hostel a better bet. In the cities and major resorts, you'll also come across hotels in the conventional sense, predominantly business- or tourbus-orientated places with all the usual trappings. Priced accordingly, they're seldom good value, usually costing $150–300 a room, though at quiet times and weekends there can be substantial discounts; it's always worth asking.

Most Kiwi families on the move prefer the astonishingly well-equipped **motels**, which congregate along the roads running into town, making them more convenient for drivers than for those using trains or buses. They come provided with bed linen, towels, Sky TV, bathroom, a full kitchen and tea and coffee, but are often fairly functional concrete-block places with little to distinguish one from another. Rooms range from all-in-one **studios** ($75–100 for two), with beds, kettle, toaster and a microwave; through **one-bedroom units** ($80–110 for two), usually with a full and separate kitchen; to two- and three-bedroom **suites**, sleeping six or eight. Suites generally go for the same basic price as a one-bedroom unit, with each additional adult paying $15–20, making them an economical choice for groups travelling together. Anything calling itself a **motor inn** or similar will be quite luxurious, with a bar, restaurant, swimming pool and sauna but no cooking facilities.

Guesthouses, B&Bs and lodges

While families might prefer the freedom and adaptability of a motel, couples are generally better served by a homestay or bed and breakfast (B&B). These terms are used almost interchangeably in New Zealand, though the cheaper places are more likely to call themselves **guesthouses**, offering simple rooms, usually with a bathroom down the hall and a modest continental breakfast included in the price.

A **B&B** may be exactly the same as a guesthouse, but the term also encompasses luxurious colonial homes with well-furnished ensuite rooms and sumptuous home-cooked breakfasts. Those at the top end are now fashioning themselves as **lodges**, **boutique hotels** and "exclusive retreats", where standards of service and comfort are raised to extraordinary levels, with prices to match.

Roughly speaking, **rates** for a double room are around $75–100 at guesthouses, $90–150 at B&Bs, $150–300 at boutique hotels and reach stratospheric levels when it comes to the exclusive retreats, where $800 per person per night is not unheard of (though that includes all meals and drinks). Rates drop in the low season, when these places can often be exceptionally good value. If you're travelling alone and don't fancy hostels, B&Bs can also be a viable alternative, usually charging **lone travellers** 60–80 percent of the double room rate, though some only ask fifty percent.

Homestays and farmstays

Homestays usually offer a guest room or two in an ordinary house where you muck in with the owners and join them for breakfast the following morning. Staying in such places can be an excellent way to meet ordinary New Zealanders; you'll be well looked after, sometimes to the point of being overwhelmed by your hosts' generosity. It is courteous to **call in advance**, and bear in mind you'll usually have to **pay in cash**. Rural versions often operate as **farmstays**, where you're encouraged to stay a couple of nights and are welcome to spend the intervening day trying your hand at farm tasks: rounding up sheep, milking cows, fencing, whatever might need doing. Both homestays and farmstays charge $80–120 for a double room, including breakfast; some cook dinner on request for $15–30 per person, and you may pay a small fee for lunch if you spend the day at the farm.

Hostels, backpackers and YHAs

New Zealand is awash with around four hundred budget and self-catering places, pretty much interchangeably known as **hostels** or **backpackers** and offering a bed or bunk for around $15–25. As often as not they're in superb locations – bang in the centre of town, beside the beach, close to a skifield or amid magnificent scenery in a national or forest park – and are invariably great places to meet others, hook-up to the travellers' grapevine and pick through the mass of local information, aided by genuinely helpful managers. Many of the best places have been specially built or converted, though some are substantially less appealing, wedged into former hotel rooms above pubs. Wherever you stay, you'll find a fully equipped kitchen, laundry, TV and games room, a travellers' noticeboard, and a stack of tourist information. **Internet access** (typically a coin-op booth) is now pretty standard, though a few rural places foster an away-from-it-all tenor by intentionally eschewing such mod cons. Depending on the area, there may be a pool, barbecue area, bike and/or canoe rental and information on local work opportunities. For **security**, many of the better places offer cupboards for your gear, though you'll need your own lock. If you **book ahead** – essential in January and February, and preferable in December and March – hostels may even pick you up from the nearest public transport. Almost all hostels in New Zealand are affiliated with local and international organizations that offer **accommodation discounts** to members, along with an array of other travel- and activity-related savings.

Many hostels allow you to pitch a tent in the grounds for $10–15 a person, but generally the most basic and cheapest accommodation is in a 6–12 bunk **dorm** ($15–19), with 4-bed rooms (known as **four-shares**) usually priced a couple of dollars higher. Most hostels also have **double**, **twin** and **family rooms** ($20–25 per adult), the more expensive ones with ensuite bathrooms. Many larger places also offer women-only dorms.

Around 60 places are classified as **YHA hostels** or affiliate YHA hostels, which have abandoned daily chores and arcane opening hours but maintain a predominance of single-sex dorms. Newer hostels have been purpose-built to reflect the YHA's environmental concerns, promoting recycling and energy conservation; older places are likely to be converted schools or large houses. Hostels are listed in the annual *YHA Hostel Guide* and the condensed *Quick Guide* version (both free to all and available from hostels and organization offices). Almost half of

the places listed are full YHA hostels open only to members: you should obtain a **Hostelling International Card** in your own country (see opposite for contact details), but you can stump up the $40 annual membership in NZ. Single night membership costs $4. The rest of the hostels are affiliated **associate hostels**, where no membership card is required, though there is often a discount of a dollar or so for members. At full YHAs all bedding is supplied, whereas associate hostels usually charge a small additional fee if you are not using your own sleeping bag or sheet. You can book ahead either from another hostel or through the YHA National Reservations Centre (see below) using a credit card or bank draft, and through Hostelling International offices in your home country.

YHAs are outnumbered six-to-one by other **backpacker hostels**, where the atmosphere is more variable; some are friendly and relaxed, others are more party-oriented. Most are aligned with the NZ-based **Budget Backpacker Hostels**, and are listed (along with current prices) in the BBH Accommodation guide (or simply "Blue Book") widely available from hostels and visitor centres. The entries are written by the hostels and don't pretend to be impartial but each hostel is given a percentage rating based on a survey of guests, an assessment that is usually a good indicator of quality, though city hostels seldom score as highly as the best rural places. Anyone can stay at BBH hostels, but savings can be made by buying a **BBH Club Card** ($40) which generally saves the holder $2–3 on each night's stay in either a bunk or a room. Cards are available from BBH and all participating hostels, and each card doubles as a rechargeable phone card already loaded with $20 worth of calling time.

Around eighty hostels are members of **VIP Backpacker Resorts**, an umbrella organization that offers a dollar off each night's stay to people who buy the annual VIP Discount Card ($39, valid in New Zealand, at 130 hostels in Australia and a few others dotted across Pacific islands).

For advice on backcountry camping and trampers' huts, see the "Outdoor Activities" section on p.52.

Hostel organizations

YHA offices

New Zealand PO Box 436, Christchurch
℡ 03/379 9970 & 0800/278 299, national
reservations centre ℡ 03/379 9808,
ⓦ www.yha.org.nz
Australia ℡ 02/9261 1111, ⓦ www.yha.com.au
Canada ℡ 1-800/663-5777, ⓦ www.hihostels.ca
England and Wales ℡ 0870/770 8868,
ⓦ www.yha.org.uk
Ireland ℡ 01/830 4555, ⓦ www.irelandyha.org
Northern Ireland ℡ 028/9031 5435,
ⓦ www.hini.org.uk
Scotland ℡ 01786/891 400, ⓦ www.syha.org.uk
USA ℡ 301/495-1240, ⓦ www.hiusa.org

Other backpacker organizations

BBH Club Card ⓦ www.bbh.co.nz
VIP Backpacker Resorts ℡ 09/816 8903,
ⓦ www.vip.co.nz

Motor camps, campsites and cabins

New Zealand has some of the world's best
camping facilities, so even if you've never
been camping before, you may well find
yourself using **motor camps** (also known as
holiday parks), which are geared up for
families on holiday, with space to pitch tents,
powered sites (or hook-ups) for campervans
and usually a broad range of dorms, cabins
and motel units. Elsewhere there is more
down-to-earth camping at wonderfully
located DOC sites.

Camping is largely a summer activity
(Nov–May), especially in the South Island
where winters can get cold. At worst, New
Zealand is very wet, windy and plagued by
voracious winged **insects**, so the first priority for tent campers is good-quality gear with
a fly sheet which will repel the worst that the
elements can dish out, and an inner tent
with enough bug-proof ventilation for those
hot mornings.

Busy times at motor camps fall into line
with the school holidays, making Easter and
the summer period from Christmas to the
end of January the most hectic. Make **reservations** as far in advance as possible at this
time and a day or two before you arrive anytime through February and March. DOC
sites are not generally bookable, and while

this is no problem through most of the year,
Christmas can be a mad free-for-all.

Free camping is not strictly legal, though
with huge areas of thinly populated land you
can often get away with a dusk-to-dawn
stay pretty much anywhere outside the
cities. Parking your **campervan** overnight in
roadside rest areas is also proscribed,
though many do and suffer no adverse consequences. In a few popular areas where
this relaxed approach has been abused
you'll see abundant "No Camping" signs:
respect these, use a little common sense,
and you'll have few problems.

Campgrounds and cabins

Campgrounds are typically located on the
outskirts of towns and are invariably well-
equipped, with a communal kitchen, TV
lounge, games area, laundry, and sometimes
a swimming pool; non-residents can often
get showers for $3–4. **Campers** usually get
the quietest and most sylvan corner of the
site and are charged $8–12 per person;
camping prices throughout the guide are per
person unless followed by "per site". There is
often no distinction between tent pitches
and **powered sites** set aside for campervans, which are usually charged an extra
dollar or so per person for the use of power
hook-ups and dump stations.

In addition, most campgrounds have some
form of on-site accommodation: the basic
dorm-style **lodge** ($12–18 per person);
standard cabins ($30–40 for two, plus $10
for each extra person), often little more than
a shed with bunks; larger **kitchen cabins** or
tourist cabins ($40–60, plus $12 each extra
person) have cooking facilities; and if you
step up to **tourist flats** ($45–70 for two, plus
$15 each extra person), you also get your
own bathroom. The flasher places also have
fully self-contained **motel units** ($60–90 for
two, plus $15–18 per extra person), usually
with a separate bedroom and a TV. Cabins
and units generally sleep two to four, but
motorcamps generally have at least one
place sleeping six or eight. In all but the
motel units, **sheets** and **towels** are not generally included, so bring a sleeping bag or be
prepared to pay $2–3 a night to rent bed
linen. Sometimes pans and plates can be

borrowed after handing over a small deposit, though for longer stays it is worth bringing your own.

Campgrounds are independently-run but some have now aligned themselves with nationwide organizations which set minimum standards. Ones to look out for are **Top 10** sites (ⓦ www.topparks.co.nz), which maintain a reliably high standard in return for slightly higher prices than the norm. By purchasing a $20 club card you save ten percent on each night's stay, and the card (valid two years) is transferable to Australia and the USA.

DOC campsites

Few holiday parks can match the idyllic locations of the two hundred and sixty **campsites** operated by the **Department of Conservation** (DOC) in national parks, reserves, maritime and forest parks, the majority beautifully set by sweeping beaches

or deep in the bush. This is back-to-nature camping, low-cost and with simple **facilities**, though sites almost always have running water and toilets of some sort. Listed in DOC's free *Conservation Campsites* leaflet (available from DOC offices throughout the land), the sites fall into one of three categories: **informal** (free), often accessible only on foot and with nothing but a water supply; the more common **standard** ($3–10 per person, typically $5), all with vehicular access and many with barbecues, fireplaces, picnic tables and refuse collection; and rare **serviced** ($8–12 per person), which are similar in scope to the regular motor camps described above. At any site children aged 5–15 are charged half price, and only the serviced sites can be booked in advance.

Other possibilities for using your tent include pitching in the grounds of many backpackers and along backcountry tramps.

Food and drink

Forget any preconceptions you may have about "slam in the lamb" Kiwi cuisine with a pavlova for dessert, New Zealand's food scene has forged ahead in recent years – both in terms of the quality of the food and the places where it's served.

New Zealand's **gastronomic roots** were nurtured in the British tradition of overcooked meat and two nuked vegetables, an unfortunate heritage that still informs the cooking patterns of older Kiwis and hasn't been completely displaced at some farmstays and guesthouses. Indeed, it is only in the last decade or so that New Zealand's chefs have really woken up to the possibilities presented by a fabulous larder of super-fresh, top-quality ingredients, formulating what might be termed **Modern Kiwi** cuisine. Taking its culinary cues from Californian and contemporary Australian cuisine, it combines traditional elements such as steak, salmon and crayfish with flavours drawn from the **Mediterranean**, **Asia** and the **Pacific Rim**: sun-dried

tomatoes, lemongrass, basil, ginger, coconut and many more. Restaurateurs feel duty-bound to fill their menu with as broad a spectrum as possible, lining up seafood linguini, couscous, sushi, Thai venison meatballs and a chicken korma alongside the rack of lamb and gourmet pizza. Sometimes this results in gastronomic overload, but more often the results are sensational.

Meat and fish

New Zealanders have a taste for **meat**. The quality of New Zealand lamb is matched by that of other meats such as beef, chicken and, more recently, farmed venison. Farmed ostrich has also gained fans for its leanness and superb taste, but the greasy charms of

cervena farmed venison

feijoa fleshy, tomato-sized fruit with melon-like flesh and a tangy, perfumed flavour

hogget the meat from a year-old sheep. Older and more tasty (though less succulent) than lamb, but not as tough as mutton

hot dog a battered sausage on a stick, dipped in tomato ketchup. What the rest of the world knows as a hot dog is known here as an American hot dog

kiwi fruit hairy, brown egg-sized fruit with a juicy green centre, which swept the world in the 1980s. Golden-fleshed kiwifruit are also available, and less acidic than their green counterparts. Note: kiwifruits are not called "kiwis" for short.

lamington sponge cake coated in chocolate or pink icing and rolled in desiccated coconut

muttonbird gull-sized sooty shearwater that was a major component of the pre-European Maori diet and tastes like oily and slightly fishy mutton – hence the name

paua the muscular foot of the abalone, often minced and served as a fritter

puha type of watercress traditionally gathered by Maori

silverside top-grade corned beef, cured in honey and often served with tangy mustard

stonefruit Collective term for any fruit with a stone eg peaches, nectarines, apricots etc.

swede rutabaga

tamarillo slightly bitter, deep-red fruit, often known as a tree tomato

Vegemite a dark, savoury yeast-extract spread that mystifies many but is much loved by antipodeans, who insist it is far superior to its British equivalent, Marmite

muttonbird remain a mystery to most. A traditional source of sustenance for Maori, each April and May these birds of the shearwater family are still plucked from their burrows on the Titi Islands, off the southwest tip of Stewart Island, and sold through fishmongers in areas with substantial Maori populations.

With the country's extensive coastline, it's no surprise that **fish** and seafood loom large on the culinary horizon. The white, flaky flesh of the snapper is the most common saltwater fish, but you'll also come across tuna, John Dory, groper (often known by its Maori name of *hapuku*), flounder, blue cod (a speciality from the Chatham Islands), the firm and delicately flavoured *terakihi* and the moist-textured orange roughy. You'll also see a lot of salmon – but not trout, which cannot be bought or sold (an archaic law originally intended to protect sport-fishing when trout were introduced to NZ for the pastime in the nineteenth century), though some hotel restaurants will cook your catch for you. One much-loved delicacy is whitebait, a tiny silvery fish mostly caught on the West Coast and eaten whole in fritters during the August to November season.

Shellfish are a real New Zealand speciality, and the king of them all is the *toheroa*, a type of clam dug from the sands of Ninety Mile Beach on the rare occasions when numbers reach harvestable levels. They are usually made into soups and are sometimes replaced by the inferior and sweeter *tuatua*, also dug from Northland beaches. On menus you're more likely to come across the fabulous Bluff oysters, scallops and sensational green-lipped mussels, which have a flavour and texture that's hard to beat and are grown in the cool clear waters of the Marlborough Sounds, especially around Havelock. Pricey crayfish is also delicious and, if you get a chance, try smoked eel and smoked marlin.

Fruit, vegetables and dairy produce

Fruit too is a winner, especially at harvest time when stalls line the roadsides selling apples, pears, citrus and stonefruits for next to nothing. Top-quality fruit and dairy products are the starting point for some delicious desserts, traditionally variations on the themes of ice cream, cheesecake and pavlova, though today supplemented by rich cakes and modern twists on British-style steamed puddings.

Vegetables are generally fresh and delicious. British favourites – potatoes, carrots, peas, cabbage – along with pumpkin and squash are common in Kiwi homes but on restaurant menus you're far more likely to encounter aubergines (eggplant), capsicums (bell peppers) and tomatoes. Pacific staples to look out for are *kumara* (sweet potato), which crops up in *hangi* and deep-fried as *kumara* chips, and the starchy **taro** and sweeter **yam**, both much more rarely seen.

New Zealanders eat a lot of **dairy produce** and all of it is first-rate. Small producers springing up all over the country – but especially around the Kapiti Coast (north of Wellington), Blenheim and Banks Peninsula (east of Christchurch) – are turning out some gorgeous individual cheeses, from the traditional hard cheddar-style to spicy pepper brie. Delicious ice cream of the firm, scooped variety is something of a New Zealand institution, and is available in a vast range of flavours, including intensely fruity ones and the indulgent hokey pokey – vanilla ice cream riddled with chunks of caramel.

Vegetarian food

An abundance of fresh vegetables and superb dairy food means that self-catering **vegetarians** will eat very well, though those who eat in restaurants are less well served. Outside the major centres you'll find few dedicated vegetarian restaurants, and will have to rely on the token meat-free dishes served at most regular restaurants and cafés. Pretty much everywhere you'll be able to get a salad, sandwich, or vegetarian pizza and pasta – but it can get a bit monotonous. **Vegans** can always ask for a simple stir-fry if all else fails. In terms of snacks, you may find yourself developing an unhealthy reliance on nachos or the ubiquitous vegeburger.

If you are taking a rafting expedition or 4WD tour on which food is provided, give them plenty of notice of your dietary needs – otherwise you might be left with bread and salad.

Eating out

The quality of **restaurants** in New Zealand is typically superb, the portions are respectable, and many are good value for money – especially at **BYO** establishments, where the cost is eased if you "bring your own" wine, sometimes for a small corkage fee (typically $5 or under). In most restaurants you can expect to pay upwards of $20 for a main course, perhaps $45 for three courses without wine. **Service** tends to be unpretentious and helpful without being forced, and there is no expectation of a tip, though a reward for exceptional service is always welcomed.

New Zealand's range of **ethnic restaurants** is improving all the time, with the major influx of east Asian immigrants enlivening the scene and lending a strong Thai, Chinese and Japanese flavour to the larger cities, alongside Indian and Mexican places. **Maori food** is barely represented in restaurants at all, but you shouldn't miss the opportunity to sample the contents of a *hangi* (see box opposite), an earth oven producing delectable, fall-off-the-bone meat and delicately steamed vegetables.

Often there is little ground between restaurants and the better **café/bars** that have sprung up all over the land and offer food that's just as good and a few dollars cheaper. Here, dining is less formal and you may well find yourself elbow to elbow with folk only there for the beer or coffee, but dining is very much part of the café/bar scene. Simpler **cafés** may only stretch to breakfasts, panini stuffed with Italian-inspired fillings, salads and cakes, but always produce good coffee and keep long hours.

Though common in the more cosmopolitan cities, cafés are less prevalent in the country towns – which are still ruled by traditional **tearooms –** daytime (most close around 5pm), self-service places that are low on atmosphere but high on value. Most are unlicensed, but offer machine coffee or tea, usually accompanied by a packaged sandwich, uninspiring savouries and either Devonshire (cream) Teas or home-style cakes. On main tourist routes, long-distance buses usually make their comfort stops at tearooms.

Some of the more civilized bars serve **pub meals**, often the best budget eating

The hangi

In New Zealand restaurants you'll find little or no representation of **Maori** or Polynesian cuisines, but you can sample traditional cooking methods at a *hangi* (pronounced nasally as "hungi"), where meat and vegetables are steamed for hours in an earth oven then served to the assembled masses. The ideal way to experience a *hangi* is as a guest at a private gathering of extended families, but most people have to settle for one of the commercial affairs in Rotorua or Christchurch. Though you'll be a paying customer rather than a guest, the *hangi* will be no less authentic.

First the men light a fire and place river stones in the embers. While these are heating, they dig a suitably large pit, place the hot stones in the bottom and cover them with wet sacking. Meanwhile the women prepare lamb, pork, chicken, fish, shellfish and vegetables (particularly *kumara*), wrapping the morsels in leaves then arranging them in baskets (originally of flax, but now most often of steel mesh). The baskets are lowered into the cooking pit and covered with earth so that the steam and the flavours are sealed in. A couple of hours later, the baskets are disinterred, revealing fabulously tender steam-smoked meat and vegetables with a faintly earth flavour. A suitably reverential silence, broken only by munching and appreciative murmurs, descends.

around with straightforward plates of steak and chips, lasagne or burritos, all served with salad for under \$15. One to look out for here is the nationwide chain Cobb & Co., formerly used as waystations by stagecoaches and now offering reliable meals and good breakfasts that will set you up for the whole day.

The country's burgeoning wine industry has spawned a number of **vineyard restaurants**, particularly in the main growing areas of Hawke's Bay and Marlborough. They're almost all geared around shifting their own product but are invariably good places to break your wine tasting. Most have outdoor seating close to or under the vines, and there may well be an area for a post-prandial game of petanque.

Breakfast, snacks and takeaways

New Zealanders generally take a fairly light "continental" **breakfast** of juice, cereals, toast and tea or coffee. Visitors staying at a homestay or B&B may well be offered an additional "cooked breakfast" probably along the lines of the traditional English breakfast of bacon and eggs; if you're staying in motels, hostels or campsites, you'll generally have to fend for yourself. In the bigger towns, you'll often find a **bakery** selling fresh croissants, bagels and focaccia, but increasingly New Zealanders are going out for breakfast or brunch, aided by the proliferation of cafés serving anything from a bowl of fruit and muesli to stupendous platefuls of Eggs Florentine and smoked salmon.

In the cities you'll also come across **food courts**, usually in shopping malls with a dozen or so stalls selling bargain plates of all manner of ethnic dishes. Traditional **burger bars** continue to serve constructions far removed from the limp international-franchise offerings: weighty buns with juicy patties, thick ketchup, a stack of lettuce and tomato and that all-important slice of beetroot. **Meat pies** are another stalwart of Kiwi snacking: sold in bakeries and from warming cabinets in pubs everywhere, the traditional steak and mince varieties are now supplemented by bacon and egg, venison, steak and cheese, steak and oyster and many others, though there is seldom a vegetarian version.

Fish and chips (or "greasies") are also rightly popular – the fish is often shark (euphemistically called lemon fish or flake), though tastier species may also be available, and the chips (fries) are invariably thick and crisp. Look out too for *paua* fritters, a battered slab of minced abalone that's something of an acquired taste.

Self-catering

If you're **self-catering** your best bet for supplies is the local supermarket: the warehouse-style Pak 'n' Save is cheap and found in most large towns and usually stays open until at least 8pm every day. The slightly more expensive but reliable New World is also found all over the country. Failing that, you'll notice a marked drop in scope and an appreciable hike in prices at the neighbourhood superette – IGA and Four Square are the biggies. Convenient corner shops (or dairies) stock the essentials, but, along with shops at campsites, also tend to have inflated prices, more so if located in isolated areas or anywhere with a captive market. Supermarkets sell **beer** and **wine**, but for anything stronger you'll need to visit a **bottle store**, which may well be attached to the local pub.

Drinking

New Zealand boasts many fine wines and beers, which can be sampled in cafés and restaurants all over the land. But for the lowest prices and a genuine Kiwi atmosphere you can't go past the **pub**. It's a place where folk stop off on their way home from work, the emphasis being on consumption and back-slapping camaraderie, with ambience and decor taking a back seat. In the cities, where competition from cafés is strong, pubs are sharpening up their act and comfortable, relaxing bars are more common, but in country areas little has changed. Rural pubs can initially be daunting for strangers, but once you get chatting, barriers soon drop. Some pubs are still divided into the **public bar**, a joyless Formica and linoleum place where overalls and work boots are the sartorial order of the day, and the **lounge bar**, where you are expected to dress up and are charged more for the privilege.

There is barely any limitation on the hours you can drink, most bars shutting up at around midnight on weeknights if it is quiet, more like 3am at weekends. The **drinking age** has been lowered to 18 (from 20) and anyone who looks under 25 can expect to be asked for identification.

Beer

Beer is drunk everywhere, and often. Nearly all beer is produced by two huge conglomerates – New Zealand Breweries and DB – who market countless variations on the lager and Pilsener theme, as well as insipid, deep-brown liquid dispensed from taps and in bottles as "draught" – a distant and altogether feebler relation of British-style bitter. Increasingly, Kiwi beer drinkers are turning to lager, especially their beloved Steinlager, which regularly bags international awards. There really isn't a lot to choose between them except for alcohol content, normally around four percent, though five percent is common for premium beers usually described as "export".

To find something truly different, seek out **boutique beers** such as those brewed near Nelson by Mac's. Try their dark and delicious stout-like Black Mac, or wait around for the Oktober Mac, a light and fresh concoction brewed in September and only available until it runs out. Small, regional brewers and in-house micro-breweries are increasingly establishing themselves on the scene – look out for the *Loaded Hog* and *One Red Dog* restaurant/bars. Most bottle shops stock a fair range of foreign brews and the flashier bars are always well stocked with the best of international bottled beers – at a price. On tap, you will only find New Zealand beer, except for the odd ersatz Irish bar pouring Guinness. A good source of information about all things beery in New Zealand is ⓦwww.brewing.co.nz.

Measures are standard throughout the country: traditionalists buy a one-litre **jug**, which is then decanted into the required number of glasses, usually a **seven** (originally seven fluid ounces, or 200ml), a **ten**, or even an elegantly fluted **twelve**. Despite 30 years under the metric system, handled **pints** (roughly half a litre) have now become widespread. Prices vary enormously, but you can expect to pay around $5 for a pint. It is much cheaper to buy in bulk from a bottle shop where beer is either sold in six-packs or cartons of a dozen ($15–20); serious drinkers go for refillable half-gallon **flagons** (2.25 litres) or their metric variant, the two-litre **rigger**; these can be bought for around a dollar and filled for $8–10 at taps in bottle shops.

Wines and spirits

Kiwis are justifiably loyal to New Zealand winemakers, who have made great strides in recent years and now produce **wines** that rank alongside some of the best in the world. New Zealand is rapidly encroaching on the Loire's standing as the world benchmark for Sauvignon Blanc, and there is an increasing band of fans for the bold fruitiness of its Chardonnay and the apricot and citrus palate of its Riesling. Certainly wine menus feature few non-Kiwi **whites**, but reds are often of the broad-shouldered Aussie variety. Nevertheless, New Zealand **reds** are rapidly improving and there are some very fine young-drinking varietals using Cabernet Sauvignon, Merlot and, the great red hope, Pinot Noir. A liking for **champagne** no longer implies "champagne tastes" in New Zealand: you can still buy the wildly overpriced French stuff, but good Kiwi Méthode Traditionelle (fermented in the bottle in the time-honoured way) starts at around $12 a bottle: Montana's Lindauer Brut is widely available, and justly popular. The latest drinking trend is **dessert wines** (or "stickies") typically made from grapes withered on the vine by the *botrytis* fungus, the so-called "noble rot".

Most bars and licensed restaurants have a tempting range of wines, many sold by the glass ($4–8, $8 and up for dessert wine), while in shops the racks are groaning with bottles starting from $8 ($12–15 for reasonable quality). Nowadays, the "chateau cardboard" wine bladders are considered passé, so do yourself (and your hosts) a favour and buy a decent bottle if invited to a barbecue or dinner.

If you want to try before you buy, visit a few **wineries**, where you are usually free to sample half a dozen different wines, though there is sometimes a small fee, especially to try the reserve wines. Among the established wine-growing areas, **Henderson** and the **Kumeu Valley**, 15km west of Auckland, is one of the more accessible though its urban nature makes it perhaps the least appealing to tour. On the east coast of the North Island, the area around **Gisborne** is good for a tasting afternoon, but wine connoisseurs are better

off in **Hawke's Bay**, where Napier and Hastings are surrounded by almost thirty vineyards open to the public. Further south, **Martinborough** has the most accessible cluster of vineyards, many within walking distance. The colder climate of the South Island effectively limits wine production to the northern part, though there is an increasing number of vineyards in **Central Otago** near Queenstown and Alexandra. The best are in **Marlborough**, close to Blenheim, which competes with Hawke's Bay for the title of New Zealand's top wine region. A good starting point for information on the Kiwi wine scene is ⓦwww.nzwine.com.

New Zealand also produces fruit **liqueurs**; some are delicious, though few visitors develop an enduring taste for the sickly sweet kiwifruit or feijoa varieties, which are mostly sold through souvenir shops. International spirits are widely available and their dominance is challenged only by one New Zealand-made **vodka** called 42 Below, and two single malt **whiskies**: Milford, made by the New Zealand Malt Whisky Co. (ⓦwww.milfordwhisky.co.nz); and Lammerlaw, made by Dunedin-based Wilson Distillers.

Soft drinks

New Zealand coolers are stocked with just about every international brand of carbonated soft drink, but one home-grown brand to look out for is L&P – originally **Lemon and Paeroa** after the Hauraki Plains town where it was first made – a genuinely lemon-flavoured pop. **Milkshakes, thickshakes** (usually with a dollop of ice cream) and **smoothies** made with blended fruit are popular thirst quenchers, and almost any café worth its salt serves glasses of **spirulina**, a thick, green goo made from powdered seaweed and often mixed with the likes of apple juice and avocado. Enthusiasts claim restorative properties when drunk the morning after a bender.

Tea and coffee

Tea is usually a down-to-earth Indian blend (sometimes jocularly known as "gumboot"), though you may also have a choice of a dozen or so flavoured, scented and herbal varieties. **Coffee** drinking has been elevated to an art form with a specialized terminology: an Italian-style espresso is known as a **short black** (sometimes served with a jug of hot water so you can dilute it to taste); a weaker and larger version is a **long black**, which, with the addition of milk becomes a **flat white**; **cappuccinos** come regular or chocolate-laced

as a mochaccino; while a milky café **latte** is usually sold in a glass but sometimes in a gargantuan bowl. Better places will serve all these decaffeinated, skinny or even made with soya milk. Flavoured syrups are occasionally available but are not common, and plunger and drip-style coffee is increasingly rare.

Communications and media

Communications services in New Zealand are generally first-rate, and excellent international networks make it pretty easy to keep in touch. The standard of media coverage sometimes leaves a little to be desired, but for the most part this is a well-informed country with relatively sophisticated tastes.

Email

For most people, the easiest way to keep in touch is by **email**, usually using one of the free **web-based email** addresses such as YahooMail or Hotmail – accessible through ⓦwww.yahoo.com and ⓦwww.hotmail.com. Once you've set up an account, you can use these sites to pick up and send mail from any Internet café, or accommodation with Internet access.

Almost everywhere you go in New Zealand you'll find someone offering **Internet access** and more are springing up all the time. Backpacker hostels almost always have access at reasonable rates, and increasingly motels, hotels and B&Bs will have a computer available. At more expensive places there'll be no charge, and for those carrying a laptop, a **dataport** may also be available. Failing any of these, there are abundant **Internet cafés** lining city streets – we've mentioned places in most town accounts, and visitor centres should be able to point you in the right direction. They typically charge $6–10 an hour, and often let you do a free email check on the assumption that you'll stay and reply, for which you'll be charged.

One useful website for details of how to plug your laptop in when abroad, phone country codes around the world, and information about electrical systems in different countries is ⓦwww.kropla.com.

Mail

Post boxes were traditionally white, black and red but, because they were so easy to miss, many have now been repainted red and silver. They are fairly common and usually give some indication of when and how often their contents are collected. Most New Zealand towns used to boast rather grand Victorian or Edwardian **post offices** in or near their centres but these days the majority have been sold off and postal services are now operated from much less picturesque, multi-purpose **post shops** (Mon–Fri 9am–5pm, plus Sat 9am–12.30pm) in large towns and cities.

The extremely efficient mail service operates two forms of **domestic delivery**: Standard (45¢, or 90¢ for larger envelopes), delivered to any destination within 2–3 days; and FastPost (90¢, or $1.35 for larger envelopes), delivered in 1 day from cities and 2 from rural areas. **International air mail** takes 3–6 days to reach Australia ($1.50), and 6–12 days to Europe, Asia and the United States ($2), depending on where it's posted; prices are higher for larger envelopes. **Aerogrammes** cost $1.50 to anywhere in the world, as do air-mail **postcards**. Make sure you send your missives by air mail, or the recipients could be in for a long wait. **Stamps** are sold at some newsagents, garages and general stores, as well as at post offices and post shops. For further information, contact NZ Post (☎0800/736 353, ⊛www.nzpost.com).

One post office in each major town operates a **Poste Restante** (or **General Delivery**) service where you can receive mail; we've listed the major ones in the "Listings" section of each town account, and you can get hold of a list of their addresses from the New Zealand Embassy or Tourism NZ in your home country or any Central Post Office in New Zealand. You need a passport or other ID to collect mail, which is returned to the sender after three months – though if you change your plans you can get it redirected (at a charge of around $10 within New Zealand, $10–25 internationally) by filling in a form at any post office. Most **hostels** and **hotels** will also keep mail for you, preferably marked with your expected date of arrival.

Phones and fax

There are only five **area codes** in New Zealand. The North Island is divided into four area codes, while the South Island makes do with just one; all numbers in the Guide are given with their area code. Even within the same area, you may have to dial the code if you're calling another town some distance away.

On a **private phone**, local calls are either free or cost just 20¢ for as long as you want, and long-distance and international calls cost between a third and a half the daytime rate when dialled outside **peak hours** (Mon–Fri 8am–6pm). Additionally, you can dial ☎013 before you make a national call (☎0160 for international) and the operator will call you back when you've finished to tell you the cost; however they will add $2.80 ($5–10 internationally) for the service.

Public telephones generally accept both major credit cards and slot-in phonecards ($5, $10, $20 and $50), which can be bought at post offices, newsagents, dairies, garages, visitor centres and supermarkets. You'll also see phones which accept these cards and coins (10¢, 20¢, 50¢, $1 and $2; no change given); and, rarely, phones which accept only coins. A **local call** on a public payphone costs 50¢ flat rate. Calls outside the local area go up from there, with calls to **mobile phones** (numbers prefixed ☎021, ☎025 ☎027, and ☎029) even more expensive. Off-peak calls are half price, though, and any ☎0800 and ☎0508 numbers are a **free call** nationwide, and require no coins or cards. Calls to **premium-rated** information lines (prefixed ☎0900) cannot be made from payphones. Prohibitive **international rates** virtually force you into using an account-based phonecard (see p.50).

Should you need to send a **fax**, you may well find your hotel, motel, or B&B happy to oblige for a fee of around $5 a page overseas and $1 a page within New Zealand: they'll usually receive for $1 a page. Most post offices offer a fax sending service, charging a basic transaction fee of $2.50 plus a per page fee of $1.50 within New Zealand, $1.60 to Australia, $3 to North America and $4 to Europe and Asia.

Useful phone numbers

National operator ☎010 (additional $2.80 for collect or price-required calls)
International operator ☎0170 (additional $5–9 for collect or price-required calls)
National directory assistance ☎018 ($0.50 for up to two numbers)
International directory assistance ☎0172 ($1.50 for up to two numbers)
Emergency services Police, ambulance and fire brigade ☎111 (no charge)

International dialling codes

To call **New Zealand** from overseas, dial the international access code (☎00 from the UK, ☎011 from the USA and Canada, ☎0011 from Australia), followed by ☎64, the area code minus its initial zero, and then the number.

To dial out of New Zealand, it's ☎00, followed by the country code (see p.50), then the area code (without the initial zero if there is one) and the number. Remember that there'll be a time difference between your country and New Zealand, which can be substantial (check out p.73 to avoid rude awakenings).

Country codes

Remember to dial ⊕ 00 first, then:
Australia: 61
Canada: 1
Ireland: 353
UK: 44
USA: 1

Phonecards and calling cards

For **long-distance and international calling** you are best off with pre-paid account-based **phonecards** (denominations from $5 to $50) that can be used on any phone. To make a call you dial the access number, the card number and your password (you choose it when you first use the card) followed by the number you are calling; the cost of the call is then deducted from your account which can be topped up using your credit card. There are numerous such cards around offering highly competitive rates, but be wary of the very cheap ones: they are often Internet-based and the voice quality can be poor and delayed. One reliable card is Telecom's Yabba (⊕ 0800/922 2248, ⓦ www.yabba.co.nz) which charges 30¢ a minute for calls within NZ, just 13¢ to Australia, Canada, Ireland, the UK and the USA, and 40¢ to South Africa and most of western Europe. Additionally they have a

maximum fee for calls up to two hours: $5 nationally, $10 to Australia and $15 to the UK, Ireland, the US and Canada.

There are also **discount phone centres** springing up in major cities and popular tourist destinations, though rates are little better than those offered by the phonecards.

Mobile phones

For sheer convenience you can't do better than a **mobile phone**, and it needn't cost the earth. Both analogue and digital networks exist in NZ so, if you're thinking of bringing your phone from home check with your service to see if your phone needs adapting for use in New Zealand or alternatively use your phone but buy a New Zealand SIM card. Telecom (ⓦ www.telecom.co.nz) and Vodafone (ⓦ www.vodafone.co.nz) run the two networks with the best coverage and have outlets in main streets of major towns. They'll both sell you a phone for under $100, and (depending on the special offers at the time) you may even get a pre-paid card thrown in. Shop around for other features like text messaging and voicemail, and if you are planning to spend time in remote areas you might appreciate the wider coverage of Telecom's analogue network.

Public holidays, festivals and opening hours

New Zealand's larger cities and tourist centres are increasingly open all hours, with cafés and bars open till very late, 24hr supermarkets abundant and shops open long hours every day. Once you get into rural areas, things change rapidly. Even quite large towns seem to shut up tight from Saturday lunchtime until Monday morning.

Holidays

In the southern hemisphere, **Christmas** falls in the middle of summer during the school **summer holidays**, which run from mid-December until the end of January. From

Boxing Day through to the middle of January Kiwis hit the beaches en masse so during this time you'll find a lot more people about, prices go up, and accommodation and travel can be difficult to book. To help you chart a path through the chaos, visitor centres are open for longer hours, as are some museums and many other tourist attractions. Other **school holidays** last for two weeks in mid- to late April, a fortnight in early to mid-July and the first two weeks of October, though these have a less pronounced effect. **Public holidays** (in bold below) are big news in New Zealand and it can feel like the entire country has taken to the roads, so it's worth considering staying put rather than trying to travel on these days. Each region also takes one day a year to celebrate its **Anniversary Day**, remembering the founding of the original provinces that made up New Zealand. We've listed official dates below, but days are usually observed on the nearest Monday (or occasionally Friday) to make a long weekend. Although this isn't a good time to actually arrive in town, if you're there already you can join in the shenanigans, usually consisting of an agricultural show, horse jumping, sheep shearing, cake baking and best-vegetable contests, plus a novelty event like **gumboot** throwing.

Public holidays and festivals

Many of the festivals listed below are covered in more detail in the relevant section of the Guide. National public holidays are in **bold**.

JANUARY

1	**New Year's Day; Whaleboat Racing Regatta, Kawhia; Highland Games, Waipu**
2	**Public Holiday**
Early to mid-Jan	Roots (reggae) Festival, Kaikoura
17	Anniversary Day (**Southland**)
22	Anniversary Day (**Wellington**)
29	Anniversary Day (**Auckland**, Northland, Waikato, Coromandel, Taupo and the Bay of Plenty). Massive regatta on Auckland's Waitemata Harbour

FEBRUARY

1	Anniversary Day (**Nelson**)
Second weekend	Flowers & Romance Festival, Christchurch ⓦ www.festivalof flowers .co.nz
6	**Waitangi Day**
Waitangi weekend	Harvest Hawke's Bay ⓦ www.harvesthawkesbay .co.nz; Rippon music festival, Wanaka

Second weekend	Wine Marlborough Festival, Blenheim; Coast to Coast multisport race
Third weekend	Art Deco Weekend, Napier Devonport Wine & Food Festival ⓦ www.devonportwine-festival.co.nz
mid-Feb to mid-March	Wellington Fringe Festival

MARCH

Late Feb to late March	NZ International Arts Festival, Wellington (even-numbered years only; Taranaki Festival of the Arts (odd-numbered years) ⓦ www.taranakifest .org.nz
First week	Golden Shears sheep-shearing competition in Masterton ⓦ www.goldenshears.co.nz
Early March	Maori Arts and Food Festival, Kaitaia
Mid-March	WOMAD festival, New Plymouth (odd-numbered years); Pasifika Festival, Auckland (ⓦ www.aucklandcity.govt.nz/ pasifika) a weekend of Pacific music, culture, food and crafts.
Second Saturday	Wildfoods Festival, Hokitika
Sun in mid-March	Round-the-Bays fun run, Auckland ⓦ www .roundthebays.co.nz
Closest Sat to March 17	Ngaruawahia Maori Regatta, near Hamilton
Late March	Te Houtaewa Challenge and Te Houtaewa Surf Challenge, Ahipara
23	Anniversary Day (**Otago**)
31	Anniversary Day (**Taranaki**)

APRIL

Late March to late April	**Good Friday and Easter Sunday**
Easter week	International Jazz n' Blues Festival, Auckland and Waiheke Island; ⓦ www.waihekejazz .co.nz; Highland Games, Hastings; Easter week Royal Easter Show, Auckland ⓦ www.royaleastershow.co.nz; Warbirds Over Wanaka International Airshow (even-numbered years
25	**ANZAC Day**
Last week	Arrowtown Autumn Festival

JUNE

| First Mon | **Queen's Birthday** |

Late June to early July	Two-week Queenstown Winter Festival ⓦwww .winterfestival.co.nz
JULY	
mid- to late July	Auckland International Film Festival ⓦwww.enzedff.co.nz; Wellington Film Festival ⓦwww.enzedff.co.nz
SEPTEMBER	
Second & third weekends	World of Wearable Art Awards Show, Nelson.
OCTOBER	
Fourth Monday	**Labour Day; Gumboot Day, Taihape**
31	Halloween. General Trick-or-Treating.
NOVEMBER	
1	Anniversary Day (**Hawke's Bay** and **Marlborough**)
5	Guy Fawkes' Night fireworks
Second week	Canterbury Show week
Third Sun	Toast Martinborough Wine, Food & Music Festival ⓦwww .toastmartinborough.co.nz
DECEMBER	
1	Anniversary Day (**Westland**)
16	Anniversary Day (**Canterbury**)

25	**Christmas Day**
26	**Boxing Day**

Opening hours

Banks open Monday to Friday, 9.30am to 4.30pm, with some city branches opening on Saturday mornings (until around 12.30pm). Core **shopping hours** (Mon–Fri 9am–5pm Sat 9am–noon) are often extended in bigger centres where tourist-orientated shops open daily until 8pm as a matter of course. In small towns the Kiwi tradition of **late-night shopping** (until 8 or 9pm on Thursday and Friday nights) still hangs on.

An ever-increasing number of **supermarkets** (at least one in or near each major city) now open seven days a week, 24 hours a day and small "**dairies**" (corner shops or convenience stores) also keep long hours and open on Sundays. **Museums** and **sights** usually open around 9am, although small-town museums often open only in the afternoons and/or only on specific days.

Outdoor activities

Life in New Zealand is very much tied to the Great Outdoors, and no visit to the country would be complete without spending a fair chunk of your time in intimate contact with nature.

Kiwis have long taken it for granted that within a few minutes' drive of their home they can find a deserted beach or piece of "bush" and wander freely through it, an attitude enshrined in the fabulous collection of national, forest and maritime parks. They are all administered by the Department of Conservation (DOC; ⓦwww.doc.govt.nz) which struggles to balance the maintenance of a fragile ecology with the demands of tourism. For the most part it manages remarkably well, providing a superb network of well-signposted paths studded with

trampers' huts; operating visitor centres that present highly informative material about the local history, flora and fauna; and publishing excellent leaflets for the major walking tracks.

The lofty peaks of the Southern Alps are perfect for challenging mountaineering and great skiing, and the lower slopes are ideal for multi-day tramps which cross low passes between valleys choked with sub-tropical and temperate rainforests. Along the coasts there are sheltered lagoons and calm harbours for gentle swimming and boating, but also sweeping strands battered by some top-class surf.

Hand in hand with this natural aptitude for outdoor life, the country also promotes itself as the adventure tourism capital of the world. All over the country you will find places to go bungy jumping, whitewater or cave rafting, jetboating, tandem skydiving, mountain biking, stunt flying, scuba diving, in fact you name it and someone somewhere organizes it. The New Zealand DIY ethic reigns supreme and it sometimes seems as though every Kiwi in possession of a minibus and a mobile phone runs an adventure-tourism business. While thousands of people participate in these activities every day without incident, standards of instructor training do vary. It seems to be a point of honour for all male (and they are almost all male) river guides, bungy operators and tandem parachute instructors to play the macho card and put the wind up you as much as possible. Such bravado shouldn't be interpreted as a genuine disregard for safety, but the fact remains that there have been quite a few well-publicized injuries and deaths in recent years – a tragic situation that's finally being addressed by industry-regulated codes of practice, independent system of accreditation and home-grown organizations that insist upon high levels of professionalism and safety instruction.

Before engaging in any adventure activities, check your insurance cover (see p.21).

Tramping

Tramping, trekking, bushwalking, hiking – call it what you will, it is one of the most compelling reasons to visit New Zealand, and for many the sole objective. Even if the concept sounds appalling, you should try it once; reluctant trampers are frequently bitten by the bug.

Tramps are typically multi-day walks, typically taking three to five days and following a well-worn trail through relatively untouched wilderness, more often than not in one of the country's national parks. Along the way you'll be either camping out or staying in idyllically located trampers' huts, and will consequently be lugging a pack over some pretty rugged terrain, so a moderate level of fitness is required. If this sounds daunting, you can

sign up with one of the guided tramping companies, which maintain more salubrious huts, provide meals and carry much of your gear, but at a price. Details of these are given throughout the Guide.

The main tramping season is in summer, from October to May. Some of the most popular tramps – the Milford, Routeburn and Kepler – are in the cooler southern half of the South Island, where the season is shorter by a few weeks at either end.

The tramps

Rugged terrain and a history of track-bashing by explorers and deer hunters has left New Zealand with a web of tramps following river valleys and linking up over passes, high above the bushline. As far as possible, we've indicated the degree of difficulty of all tramps covered in the Guide, broadly following DOC's classification system: a **path** is level, well-graded and often wheelchair-accessible; **walking tracks** and **tramping tracks** (usually marked with red and white or orange flashes on trees) are respectively more arduous affairs requiring some fitness and proper walking equipment; and a **route** requires considerable tramping experience to cope with an ill-defined trail, frequently above the bushline. DOC's estimated **walking times** can trip you up: along paths likely to be used by families, for example, you can easily find yourself finishing in under half the time specified, but on serious routes aimed at fit trampers you might struggle to keep pace. We've given estimates for moderately fit individuals and, where possible, included the distance and amount of climbing involved to further aid route planning.

Invaluable information on walking directions, details of access, huts and an adequate map are contained in the excellent DOC tramp **leaflets** (usually $1 apiece); as long as you stick to the designated route, there's really no need to fork out for specialized **maps** (see pp.20–21), unless you're keen to identify features along the way. In any case, most trampers' huts have a copy of the local area map pinned to the wall or laminated into the table. In describing tramps we have used "**true directions**" in relation to rivers and streams, whereby the left bank (referred to as the "true left") is the left-hand side of the river looking downstream.

Eight of New Zealand's finest, the most popular tramps and one river journey, have been classified by DOC as **Great Walks**; all are covered in detail in the text. On the North Island, the gentle **Lake Waikaremoana Circuit** (3–4 days) circumnavigates one of the country's most beautiful lakes; and the **Tongariro Northern Circuit** (3–4 days) takes in the magnificent volcanic and semi-desert scenery of the central part of the island. The popular **Abel Tasman Coastal Track** (2–4 days) skirts the pristine beaches and crystal-clear bays of the northern half of the South Island and avoids the difficult logistics of the **Heaphy Track** (4–5 days), which passes through the Kahurangi National Park, balancing sub-alpine tops and surf-pounded beaches. The tramping heartland is around Queenstown and Fiordland, where there are three magnificent alpine Great Walks: the world-famous **Milford Track** (4 days) passing through stunning glaciated scenery; the equally superb **Routeburn Track** (3 days), which spends much longer above the bushline; and the **Kepler Track** (4 days), intended to take the pressure off the other two, but no less appealing for that. Finally, there's the **Rakiura Track** (3 days) on Stewart Island, conveniently circular and partly along the coast.

Great Walks get the lion's share of DOC track spending, resulting in relatively smooth, broad walkways, with boardwalks over muddy sections and bridges over almost every stream. In short, they represent the slightly sanitized side of New Zealand tramping and are sometimes disparagingly referred to as hikers' highways. This is somewhat unfair since, even on the busiest tramps, by judiciously picking your departure time each morning, you can go all day hardly seeing anyone.

Access to tracks is seldom a problem in the most popular tramping regions, though it does require some planning. Most tramps finish some distance from their start, so taking your own vehicle is not much use; besides, cars parked at trailheads are an open invitation to thieves. Great Walks always have transport from the nearest town, but there are often equally stunning and barely used tramps close by which just require a little more patience and tenacity to get to – we've included some of the best of the rest in the Guide, all listed under "Tramps" in the index.

Backcountry accommodation: huts and camping

Going bush needn't involve too much discomfort as New Zealand's backcountry is strung with a network of almost nine hundred **trampers' huts**, sited less than a day's walk apart, frequently in beautiful surroundings. All are fairly simple, communal affairs that fall into five distinct categories as defined by DOC, which maintains the majority of them.

The simplest are the crude **Category 4** (free), mostly used by hunters and rarely encountered on the major tramps. Next up in luxury is **Category 3** ($5 per person per night), basic, weatherproof huts usually equipped with individual bunks or sleeping platforms accommodating a dozen or so, an external long-drop toilet and a water supply. There is seldom any heating and there are no cooking facilities. **Category 2** huts ($10) tend to be larger, sleeping twenty or more in bunks with mattresses; water is piped indoors to a sink – and flush toilets are occasionally encountered. Again, you'll need to bring your own stove and cooking gear, but heating is provided; if the fire is a wood-burning one, you should replace any firewood you use. More sophisticated still are **Category 1** huts – most of which have been converted to **Great Walk Huts** – found in the most popular walking areas and along the Great Walks. They tend to have separate bunkrooms, gas rings for cooking (but no utensils), gas stoves for heating, a drying room and occasionally solar-powered lighting. Most cost a modest $14 a night, though fees are substantially higher on the Kepler ($25), Milford ($105 for 3 nights) and Routeburn ($35) tracks, reflecting the extra costs involved in maintaining these fragile areas. In winter (May–Sept), these huts are often stripped of their heating and cooking facilities and revert to Category 3 status. Children of school age generally pay half the adult fee.

Hut fees are usually paid in advance at the local DOC office, visitor centre or other outlet close to the start of the track. For most tramps you buy a quantity of $5 tickets (valid for 15 months) and give the warden the appropriate number (one for a Category 3 hut, and two for a Category 2 hut) or post them in the hut's honesty box. You can sometimes buy tickets direct from wardens, but there is often a 25-percent premium on the price (60 percent on the Milford and Routeburn tracks). If you are planning a lot of tramping outside the Great Walks system, it may be worth buying an **Annual Hut Pass** ($65), which allows you to stay in all Category 2 and 3 huts. Throughout the summer Great Walks operate an **accommodation pass** system, guaranteeing trekkers a bed, although it's vital on the oversubscribed Milford, Routeburn, Lake Waikaremoana and Abel Tasman tracks, to make hut **reservations** as far in advance as possible. The easiest way to do this is direct through the relevant DOC office (see accounts in the Guide), or, by using a booking agent, stating which hut you intend to use each night. In winter (May–Sept) the huts on great walks are downgraded to Category 3 status, so if you have an annual hut pass you can use them, though possessing the pass or a ticket doesn't guarantee you a bunk. Beds go on a first come first serve basis, as they do on all tramps not designated Great Walks, so if the trail is busy you may find yourself in an undignified gallop to the next hut, in order to ensure you have somewhere soft to rest your weary bones.

Camping is allowed on all tracks except the Milford, and generally costs one hut ticket ($5–8) per night, though there are higher fees for camping on Great Walks: $15 on the Routeburn, $10 on the Lake Waikaremoana and Tongariro Northern circuits, and $6–9 on the others. Rules vary, but in most cases you're required to minimize environmental impact by camping close to the huts, whose facilities you're welcome to use (toilets, water and gas rings where available, but obviously not bunks).

Equipment

Tramping in New Zealand can be a dispiriting experience if you're not equipped for both hot, sunny days and wet, cold and windy weather. The best tramps pass through some of the world's wettest regions, with parts of the Milford Track receiving over six metres of rain a year. **Clothing** wise, it is essential to carry a good waterproof, preferably made from breathable fabric and fitted with a decent hood. Keeping your lower half dry is less crucial and most Kiwis tramp in shorts. Early starts often involve wading through long, sodden grass, so a pair of knee-length gaiters can come in handy. Comfortable boots with good ankle support are a must; take suitably broken-in leather boots or lightweight walking boots, and some comfortable footwear for day's end. You'll also need a warm jacket or jumper and a windproof shell, plus a good sleeping bag; even the heated huts are cold at night. All this, along with lighter clothing for sunny days, should be kept inside a robust backpack, preferably lined with a strong waterproof liner, such as those sold at DOC offices ($4).

Once on the tramp, you need to be totally self-sufficient. On Great Walks, you need to carry **cooking** gear; on other tramps you also need a cooking stove and fuel, both readily available in New Zealand. **Food** can be your heaviest burden; freeze-dried meals (available from all outdoors shops) are light and reasonably tasty, but they are expensive, and many cost-conscious trampers just carry quantities of pasta or rice, dried soups for sauces, a handful of fresh vegetables, muesli (granola), milk powder, and bread or crackers for lunch. Also consider taking biscuits, trail mix (known in New Zealand as "scroggin"), tea, coffee and powdered fruit drinks (the Raro brand is good), and jam, peanut butter or Vegemite. All huts have a drinkable **water** supply, but DOC advise treating water taken from lakes and rivers to protect yourself from giardia; see p.23 for more on this and suitable water-purification methods.

You should also carry basic supplies: a first aid kit, moleskin to prevent blisters, sunscreen, insect repellent; a torch (flashlight) with spare battery and bulb, candles, matches or a lighter; and a compass (though few bother on the better-marked tracks).

In the most popular tramping areas you can **rent equipment** (stoves, pans, sleeping bags and waterproofs). Most important of all, remember that you'll have to carry all this stuff for hours each day. Hotels and hostels in nearby towns will generally let you leave your surplus gear either free or for a small fee, perhaps $1 a day.

Safety

Most people spend days or weeks tramping in New Zealand with nothing worse than stiff legs and a few irritating sandfly bites, but **safety** is nonetheless a serious issue and every year there are cases of individuals failing to return from tramps. The culprit is usually New Zealand's fickle **weather**. It cannot be stressed too strongly that within an hour (even in high summer) a warm, cloudless day can turn bitterly cold, with high winds driving in thick banks of track-obscuring cloud. Heeding the weather forecast (posted in DOC offices) is some help, but there is no substitute for carrying warm, windproof and waterproof clothing.

Failed **river crossings** are one of the most common causes of tramping fatalities. If you are confronted with something that looks too dangerous to cross, then it is, and you should wait until the level falls (usually as quickly as it rose) or backtrack. If the worst happens and you get swept away while attempting a crossing, don't try to stand up in fast-flowing water; you may trap your leg between rocks and drown. Instead, face downstream on your back and float feet first until you reach a place where swimming to the bank seems feasible.

If you do get lost or injured, your chances of being found are better if you left word of your whereabouts either with a friend or with the nearest DOC office, which stock **intention forms** for you to declare your planned route and estimated finishing time. While on the tramp, fill in the hut logs as you go, so that your movements can be traced, and when you return, don't forget to check in with your contact or with DOC.

Animals are not a problem in the New Zealand bush. Kiwis never tire of reminding you there are no snakes, and there is only one poisonous spider, very rarely encountered. You might stumble upon the odd irate wild pig but the biggest irritants are likely to be kea, boisterous green parrots

that delight in sliding down hut roofs, pinching anything they can get their beaks into then tearing it apart. If you want to keep your boots, don't leave them outside when kea are around.

Swimming, surfing and windsurfing

Kiwi life is inextricably linked with the beach and from Christmas to the end of March (longer in the warmer northern climes) a weekend isn't complete without a dip or a waterside barbecue – though you should never underestimate the ferocity of the southern **sun** (see p.22 for precautions). Some of the best beaches (often stretching away into the salt-spray) are open to the pounding Tasman surf or Pacific rollers. **Swimming** here can be very hazardous, so only venture into the water at beaches patrolled by surf lifesaving clubs and always swim between the flags. Spotter planes patrol the most popular beaches and warn of any **sharks** in the area: if you notice everyone heading for the safety of the beach, get out of the water.

New Zealand's tempestuous coastline offers near-perfect conditions for **surfing** and windsurfing. At major beach resorts there is often a kiosk or shop renting out small dinghies, catamarans, canoes and windsurfers; in regions where there is reliably good surf you might also come across boogie boards and surfboards for rent, and seaside hostels often have a couple for guests' use.

Sailing

New Zealand's numerous harbours studded with small islands and ringed with deserted bays make **sailing** one of Kiwis' favourite pursuits. People sail year-round, but the summer months from December to March are busiest. Kids are often introduced to the tiny P-Class dinghies before they're riding bikes, and many grow up to own the yachts which choke the marinas for most of the year. Unless you manage to befriend one of these fortunate folk, you'll probably be limited to commercial yacht **charters** (expensive and usually with a skipper), more reasonably priced and often excellent **day-sailing trips**, or renting a small catamaran for some inshore antics along the bay. Most of what's available is in the northern half of the North Island with Auckland's Hauraki Gulf and the Bay of Islands being the main focal points, though there is some good sailing around Wellington, Christchurch, Dunedin and Bluff.

Scuba diving and snorkelling

The waters around New Zealand's coast offer some superb opportunities for scuba **diving** and **snorkelling**. What they lack in long-distance visibility, tropical warmth and colourful fish they make up for with the range of diving environments. Pretty much anywhere along the more sheltered eastern side of both islands you'll find somewhere with rewarding snorkelling, but much the best and most accessible spot is the **Goat Island Marine Reserve**, in Northland, where there's a superb range of habitats close to the shore. Northland also has world-class scuba diving at the **Poor Knights Islands Marine Reserve**, reached by boat from Tutukaka; wreck diving on the *Rainbow Warrior*, from Matauri Bay; other good spots lie close to Auckland in the **Hauraki Gulf Maritime Park** and off Great Barrier Island. In the South Island there are the crystal-clear **Pupu Springs**, some wrecks off **Picton** and

fabulous growths of **black and red corals** relatively close to the surface of the south-western fiords near Milford.

For the inexperienced, the easiest way to get a taste of what's under the surface is to take a **resort dive** with an instructor. If you want to dive independently, you need to be PADI qualified, which demands classroom instruction and a series of dives over a minimum period of a week. For more information, pick up the free, comprehensive, bi-monthly *Dive New Zealand* brochure from dive shops and the bigger visitor centres, or consult their website at Ⓦ www.divenewzealand.com.

Rafting

Whitewater rafting is undoubtedly one of the most thrilling of New Zealand's adventure activities, negotiating challenging rapids (see below for details of grading) amid gorgeous scenery. Visitor numbers and weather restrict the main **rafting season** to October to May, and most companies set the **lower age limit** at twelve or thirteen. In general you'll be supplied with a paddle and all the gear you need except for a swimming costume and an old pair of trainers. After safety instruction, you'll be placed in eight-seater rafts along with a guide and directed through narrow, rock-strewn riverbeds, spending an

Grading of rivers

Both rivers and rapids are graded according to the six-level **grading system** below, the river grade being dictated by the grade of the most demanding rapid. This lends itself to some creative marketing, and you need to take rafting company promotional material with a pinch of salt – a river hyped as Grade V might be almost entirely Grade III with one Grade V rapid. For maximum thrills and spills, the expression to look out for is "Continuous Grade ...".

I Very easy; a few small waves.

II A flicker of interest with choppier wave patterns. Dunking potential for inexperienced kayakers but no sweat in a raft.

III Bigger but still easily ridden waves make this bouncy and fun. Good proving ground for novice rafters.

IV Huge, less predictable waves churned up by rocks midstream make this excellent fun but dramatically increase the chance of a swim.

V Serious stuff with chaotic standing waves, churning narrow channels and huge holes ready to swallow you up. Best avoided by first-time rafters but thrilling nonetheless.

VI Dicing with death; commercially unraftable and only shot by the most experienced of paddlers.

average of a couple of hours on the water, before being ferried back for refreshments.

Thrilling though it undoubtedly is, rafting is also one of the most **dangerous** of the adventure activities, claiming a number of lives in recent years. Operators seem to be cleaning up their act with a self-imposed code of practice, but there are still cowboys out there. It might seem to be stating the obvious, but fatalities happen when people fall out of rafts: heed the guide's instructions about how best to stay on board and how to protect yourself if you do get a dunking.

Both the main islands have a major rafting centre – **Rotorua** on the North Island and **Queenstown** on the South Island – each with an enviable selection of river runs from mildly thrilling to heart-stopping. Less frequented but equally exciting rafting areas include Turangi on the North Island, and central Canterbury and the West Coast in the South Island.

In more remote areas, **helirafting** is common, with rafts and punters airlifted to otherwise inaccessible reaches by helicopter. This can involve a lot of expense and considerable hanging around, so make sure you know what you are letting yourself in for and be wary of extravagant claims – the water may be no more exciting than more accessible (and cheaper) rivers. That said, if it's a wilderness experience you are after then consider basing yourself in Hokitika, Greymouth or Karamea for the best West Coast rivers.

Rafts are exchanged for inner tubes to undertake **cave tubing**, which involves a generally placid drift through underground waterways, with the emphasis on exploration and viewing glowworms, though slightly more high-octane trips are also now available.

Canoeing and kayaking

New Zealand is a paddler's paradise, and pretty much anywhere with water nearby has somewhere you can rent either canoes or kayaks. Sometimes this is simply an opportunity to muck around in boats but often there is some kind of instruction or guided trips available, with the emphasis being on learning new skills and soaking up the scenery.

Grade II water is pretty much the limit for novices, making the scenic **Whanganui River** a perennial favourite. Despite its riverine nature, the **Whanganui Journey** (3–5 days) operates as a Great Walk and special arrangements apply to access and accommodation; several companies rent out all the necessary gear, often including the DOC hut passes as part of their all-inclusive price. Far shorter trips down similar water are run on the **Matukituki River** near Wanaka and the **Dart River** from Glenorchy.

Casual paddlers are much more likely to find themselves sea kayaking the near-land-locked harbours in Northland or the bays along the Abel Tasman Coastal Path; a perfect way to experience New Zealand's magnificent coastline and to encounter dolphins and seals.

Jetboating

The shallow, braided rivers of the high Canterbury sheep country posed access difficulties for run-owner Bill Hamilton, who got around the problem by inventing the **Hamilton Jetboat** in the early 1960s. His inspired invention could plane in as little as 100mm of water, reach prodigious speeds (up to 80km per hour) and negotiate rapids while maintaining astonishing turn-on-a-six-pence manoeuvrability.

Kayak or canoe?

In New Zealand, **canoe** seems to be the generic term for any small craft, whether it be fitted with a closed cockpit – elsewhere known as a kayak – or of the open variety paddled with a single-bladed paddle, sometimes differentiated by the term **Canadian canoe**.

To further confuse matters, some rafting companies run small **inflatable boats** akin to **mini-rafts** and paddled with a double-bladed paddle, which tend to be called **kayaks**.

The jetboat carried its first fare-paying passengers on a deep and glassy section of the Shotover River, which is still used by the pioneering Shotover Jet. Over half a dozen companies now run similar deep-water trips around Queenstown, while at nearby Glenorchy there's a wonderful wilderness trip along the shallow and twisting Dart River. Other key sites include the Wilkin River at Makarora and the Waikato River below Taupo's Huka Falls.

Thrills-and-spills **rides** ($65–85) tend to last for around thirty eye-streaming minutes, time enough for as much hot dogging and as many 360-degree spins as anyone really needs. **Wilderness trips** ($55–120) can last two hours or longer, pacing their antics.

Bungy jumping and bridge swinging

For maximum adrenalin, minimum risk and greatest expense, you can't go past bungy jumping. Not only is New Zealand the birthplace of commercial **bungy jumping**, it also has some of the world's finest jump sites – bridges over deep canyons and platforms cantilevered out over rivers. It is a complete head game; there's really nothing to fear but a massive rush of wind that lasts for ten seconds and a huge surge of adrenalin that can linger in the system for a day or so.

The craze was kicked off by Kiwi A.J. Hackett who, after a spectacular and highly-publicized jump from the Eiffel Tower in 1986, set up the first commercial operation just outside Queenstown on the **Kawerau Suspension Bridge** (43m). Its location beside the Queenstown–Cromwell highway, and the chance to be dunked in the river make this the most popular jump site, but there are now several other local sites and a handful of other sites around the country.

Wherever you jump, there'll be a boombox cranking out Limp Bizkit or suchlike while they strap the bungy cord to your legs. You'll be fed the jocular spiel about the bungy breaking (it won't) or not being attached properly (it will be) then you'll be chivvied into producing a cheesy (or wan) grin for a camera or three before shuffling out onto the precipice for the countdown. A swan dive is the traditional first jump, but there is often a substantial discount for second and subsequent jumps on the same day, giving jump veterans the opportunity to try The Elevator (just hopping off the platform, either forwards or backwards) or any number of variations. The pleasure is greatly enhanced by pre-jump banter and post-jump analysis, making the longer trips involving a drive into the site – the Skippers Canyon and Nevis sites in particular – all the more appealing. To show how brave you've been, this will all have been captured on video; there are also souvenir strips of used bungy cord to buy and a T-shirt, sometimes included in the jump package. **Prices** range from $99–170.

There have been a couple of injuries in the past but, on balance, bungy jumping is one of the safest adventure activities. The bungy cords are made from latex rubber (if it's good enough for condoms…) and only used 600 times, a quarter of their expected life. Some folk have been known to notch up over 1500 jumps without adverse effects, though bloodshot eyes aren't uncommon and there have been isolated reports of detached retinas, aggravated back injuries and people being thwacked in the face by the bungy rope.

A close relative of bungy jumping has hit the scene in recent years, and a couple of places are now offering **bridge swinging**, which involves a gut-wrenching fall and super-fast swing along a gorge while harnessed to a cable.

Canyoning and mountaineering

The easiest way to get your hands on New Zealand rock is to go canyoning, which involves following a steep and confined river gorge or streambed down chutes and over waterfalls for a few hours, sliding, jumping and abseiling all the way. This is currently only commercially available in a handful of places, the most accessible being in Auckland, Queenstown, and Wanaka, though there are bound to be more places in the near future.

In the main, New Zealand is better suited to mountaineering than rock climbing, though most of what is available is fairly serious stuff, suitable only for well-equipped parties with a good deal of experience. For most people the only way to get above the snow line is to tackle the easy summit of Mount Ruapehu, the North Island's highest point, or pay for a guided ascent of one of New Zealand's classic peaks. Prime candidates here are the country's highest mountain, Mount Cook (3754m), accessed from the climbers' heartland of Mount Cook Village, and New Zealand's single most beautiful peak, the pyramidal Mount Aspiring (3030m), approached from Wanaka. In both areas there is a comprehensive system of climbers' huts used as bases for what are typically twenty-hour attempts on the summit.

Flying, skydiving and paragliding

Almost every town in New Zealand seems to harbour an airstrip or a helipad, and there is inevitably someone happy to get you airborne for half an hour's **flightseeing**. The best of these cross the truly spectacular mountain scenery of the Southern Alps or the ice-sculpted terrain of Fiordland, either from Fox Glacier, Franz Josef Glacier, Mount Cook, Wanaka or Queenstown. Half an hour in a plane will set you back around $110; helicopters cost around fifty percent more and can't cover the same distances but score on manoeuvrability and the chance to land. If money is tight, you could always take a regular flight to somewhere you want to go anyway. First choice here would have to be the journey from either Wanaka or Queenstown to Milford Sound, which overflies some of the very best of Fiordland.

In **tandem skydiving**, a kind of double harness links you to an instructor, who has control of the parachute. After suitable instruction, the plane circles up to around 2500m and you leap out together, experiencing around thirty to 45 seconds of eerie freefall before the instructor pulls the ripcord. Again the Southern Alps and Fiordland are popular jumping grounds, but Taupo has established itself as the low-cost, reliable venue with the most choice, charging as little as $190 a shot; elsewhere $200–250.

A hill, a gentle breeze and substantial tourist presence and you've all the ingredients for **tandem paragliding**, where you and an instructor jointly launch off a hilltop, slung below a manoeuvrable parachute. For perhaps ten to twenty minutes of graceful gliding

and stomach-churning banked turns, you pay around $150; Queenstown, Wanaka and Nelson are prime spots. You might even come across variations on this theme such as **tandem hang gliding**, **parasailing**, where you are either winched out from the back of a boat then winched back in after a ten minute ride, or a variation on tandem paragliding where you and an instructor are winched way out from the back of a boat then released for a tandem flight back to the beach.

Skiing and snowboarding

New Zealand's **ski season** (roughly June to October or November) starts as snows on northern hemisphere slopes finally melt away. This, combined with the South Island's backbone of 3000-metre peaks and the North Island's equally lofty volcanoes, make New Zealand an increasingly popular international ski destination. Most fields, though, are geared to the domestic downhill market, and the eastern side of the Southern Alps is littered with **club fields** sporting a handful of rope tows, simple lifts and a motley collection of private ski lodges. They're open to all-comers, but some are only accessible by 4WD vehicles, others have a long walk in, and ski schools are almost unheard of. Conversely, lift tickets are only $35–55 a day, queues are short and there's usually a gear-rental shop not too far away. Throughout the country, there are also a dozen exceptions to this norm: **commercial resorts**, with high-speed quad chairs (lift tickets around $55–60), ski schools, gear rental and groomed wide-open slopes. What you won't find are massive on-site resorts of the scale found in North America and Europe; skiers commute daily to the slopes from nearby après-ski towns. **Gear rental**, either from shops in the nearest town or on the field, ranges from around $40 a day for a full set of decent equipment to around $50–70 for the fancy stuff or for snowboarding tackle.

The best up-to-date source of skiing information is the annual **Ski & Snowboard Guide** published by Brown Bear Publications, PO Box 31207 Ilam, Christchurch (☎03/358 0935, ⓦ www.brownbear.co.nz). It is freely downloadable from their website, and the printed guide can be picked up from visitor centres and ski area hotels for $2. For each field it gives a detailed rundown of facilities, expected season, lift ticket prices and an indication of suitability for beginners, intermediates and advanced skiers. Heliskiing is also dealt with and there's brief coverage of the main ski towns. Other **websites** for all things skiing in New Zealand are Ⓦwww.snow.co.nz and Ⓦwww.dailyshred.co.nz.

The main **North Island** fields include the country's two largest and most popular destinations, **Turoa** and **Whakapapa**, both on the volcanic Mount Ruapehu, which erupted during the 1995 and 1996 seasons but has remained quiet since. The Southern Alps give the **South Island** a great deal more scope, with the greatest concentration of commercial fields being around Queenstown – **Coronet Peak** and **The Remarkables** – and Wanaka – **Treble Cone**, **Cardrona** and the **Waiorau Nordic Ski Area**, New Zealand's only organized cross-country site. Further north, **Porter Heights** and Mount Hutt are within two hours' drive of Christchurch, and the Nelson region is home to New Zealand's newest commercial field, **Mount Lyford**. All these ski areas are covered in the relevant chapters of the Guide.

At weekends and school holidays the tow queues at the major fields can become unfeasibly long, and the ideal solution, if you have dollars to burn, is **heliskiing**. Guides conversant with the routes and skilled in reading avalanche danger take small parties onto virgin slopes high among the sparkling peaks of the Southern Alps. Provided you are an intermediate skier and are reasonably proficient at skiing powder you should be able to pass the ability questionnaire, but at $700–900 a day it isn't for everyone. If you can't resist, places to consider are the usual suspects of Fox Glacier, Wanaka and Queenstown; in Canterbury, you can ski the wonderful Tasman Glacier from Mount Cook Village or get a taster from the Mount Hutt skifield car park.

Fishing

Kiwis grow up fishing: virtually everyone seems to have fond memories of long days out on a small boat trailing a line for snapper, if only to stock the beachside barbecue. All around the New Zealand coast, but particularly in the north of the North Island, there are low-key canoe, yacht and launch trips on which there is always time for a little **casual fishing**, but you'll also find plenty of trips aimed at more dedicated anglers. Most sea trips aim to land something of modest size with good flavour: snapper, *kahawai*, *moki* and flounder being common catches. Bigger boats might hope for *hapuku*, then there's a step up to the **big-game fishing** boats. From December to May these scout the seas off the northern half of the North Island for marlin, shark and tuna. This is serious business and you're looking at around $250 per person per day to go out on a boat with three others, but on the smaller boats, a day out fishing might cost as little as $65, with all tackle supplied. Regulations and bag limits are covered on the Ministry of Fisheries website Ⓦwww.fish.govt.nz.

Inland, the **rivers** and **lakes** are choked with rainbow and brown trout, quinnat and Atlantic salmon, all introduced for sport at the end of the nineteenth century. Certain areas have gained enviable reputations: the waters of the Lake Taupo catchment are world-renowned for the abundance and fighting quality of the rainbow trout; South Island rivers, particularly around Gore, boast the finest brown trout in the land; and braided gravel-bed rivers draining the eastern slopes of the Southern Alps across the Canterbury Plains bear superb salmon. Archaic laws prohibit the sale of **trout**, so if you want to eat some you've got to go out and catch it.

A national **fishing licence** ($86 for the year from Oct 1 to Sept 30; $34 for 7 days; and $17 for 24 hours) covers all New Zealand's lakes and rivers except for those in the Taupo catchment area, where a local licensing arrangement applies. They're available from sports shops everywhere and directly from Fish and Game NZ (Ⓦwww.fishandgame.org.nz), the government's agency responsible for managing freshwater sportsfish fisheries. The website also lists bag limits and local regulations.

Wherever you fish, the **regulations** are taken very seriously and are rigidly enforced. If you're found with an undersize catch or an over-full bag, heavy fines may be imposed and equipment confiscated. Be sure to find out the local regulations before you set out.

Other fishy websites include ⓦwww.trout-newzealand.com, ⓦnewzealandfishing.com, and ⓦwww.fishing.net.nz.

Horse trekking

New Zealand's highly urbanized population leaves a huge amount of countryside available for **horse trekking**, occasionally along beaches, often through patches of native bush and tracts of farmland; there may even be an opportunity to swim the horses. There are schools everywhere and all levels of experience are catered for, but more experienced riders might prefer the greater scope of full-day or even week-long wilderness treks. We've highlighted some of the more noteworthy places and operators throughout the Guide, and there's a smattering of others listed at ⓦwww.truenz.co.nz/horsetrekking. As there are no nationwide safety standards, it's worth establishing your own and only using operators who offer riding helmets.

Mountain biking

If you prefer a smaller saddle, you'll find a stack of places renting out **mountain bikes**. For a quality machine, you might be paying over $45 a day, but for that you get a bike, a helmet and a headful of advice about local routes. The main trail-biking areas around Rotorua, Queenstown, Mount Cook and Hanmer Springs will often have a couple of companies willing to take you out on **guided rides** (the going rate is about $100 a half-day), usually dropping you at the top of the hill and picking you up at the bottom. For general information about the Kiwi **off-road biking** scene consult ⓦwww.mountainbike.co.nz.

Mountain bikes aren't allowed off-road in national parks and reserves, and elsewhere you must respect the enjoyment of others by letting walkers know of your presence, avoiding skid damage to tracks and keeping your speed down. For more information, consult the specific biking guides available in New Zealand.

Spectator sports

If God were a rugby coach almost every New Zealander would be a religious fundamentalist. The All Blacks are not a national passion, more the equivalent of a religion. The Kiwis are an active bunch on the whole, most preferring to fish, play some form of sport or tramp. Their Newspapers and TV news often give headline prominence to sport and entire radio stations are devoted to sports **talkback**, often dwelling on Kiwi underdogs overcoming better funded teams from more populous nations.

As elsewhere, most sport now is watched on TV, with all major games televised. Increasingly these are only on subscription channels such as Sky TV, which encourages a devoted following in pubs with large-screen TVs.

Anyone with a keen interest in sport or just a desire to see the less reserved side of the Kiwi character should attend a game. Local papers advertise important games along with ticket booking details. **Bookings** for many of the bigger events can be made through Ticketek (ⓦwww.ticketek.co.nz), which has a local number in each major centre; look under Ticketek in the white pages. Except for the over-subscribed international matches and season finals you can usually just buy a ticket at the gate.

Rugby

Opponents quake in their boots at the sight of fifteen strapping **All Blacks**, the national rugby team, performing their pre-match *haka*, and few spectators remain unmoved. Kiwi hearts swell at the sight, secure in the knowledge that their national team is always amongst the world's best, and anything less than a resounding victory is considered a case for mass mourning and much hand-wringing in the leader columns of the news-papers. Even a narrow win over northern hemisphere sides (until recently the weaker cousins of southern hemisphere rugby) was regarded as a disgrace. Sadly the All Blacks relative failure in the four-yearly **Rugby World Cup** – in 2003 they were defeated by the old enemy, Australia in the quarter finals – meant that the nation went into mourning and the media indulged in a modern-day witch hunt.

Rugby (or Rugby Union, though it is sel-dom called this in New Zealand) is played through the winter, the season kicking off with the **Super 12 series** (mid-Feb–May) in which regional southern hemisphere teams (five from NZ, four from South Africa and three from Australia, though controversially none from the Pacific Islands) play each other with the top four teams going on to contest the finals series. In the late 1990s the Auckland-based Blues (ⓦ www.blues-rugby.co.nz) were dominant while the Christchurch-based Crusaders, the most successful team, have won four out of eight championships (ⓦ www.crusadersrugby .com) and although good sides the Dunedin's Highlanders (ⓦ www.highlanders-rugby.com), Wellington-based Hurricanes (ⓦ www.hurricanes.co.nz) and Waikato Chiefs (ⓦ www.chiefs.co.nz) play the part of also-rans.

Super 12 players make up the All Black team which, through the middle of winter, hosts an international test series or two including the annual **tri-nations series** (mid-July to August) against South Africa and Australia. Games between the All Blacks and Australia also contest the **Bledisloe Cup,** which creates much desired bragging rights for one or other nation for a year.

The international season often runs over into the **National Provincial Championship** (NPC), played from the middle of August until the end of October. Each province has a team, the bigger provinces (Auckland,

Wellington, Canterbury, Otago and so on) competing in the first division with the minor provinces generally filling up the lower two divisions. Auckland currently, at the time of writing, hold the **Ranfurly Shield** (ⓦ www.ranfurlyshield.com), affectionately known as the "log of wood" (it's a wooden shield). Throughout the season the holders will accept challenges at their home ground, and the winner takes all. Occasionally minor teams will wrest the shield, and in the small-er provinces this is a huge source of pride, subsequent defences prompting a huge swelling of community spirit.

Tickets for Super 12 games cost $25–35, with international games costing a little more and NPC matches considerably less. For more information visit the NZ Rugby Union's official **website** ⓦ www.nzrugby.co.nz, or the more newsy ⓦ www.TheSilverFern.co.nz.

Rugby league (ⓦ www.rugbyleague.co.nz and ⓦ www.nzrl.co.nz) has always been regarded as rugby's poor cousin, though success at international level has raised its profile. Rugby League's World Cup was last held in 2000 with the NZ Kiwis only losing out in the final to their perennial nemesis, Australia. New Zealand's only significant provincial team is the Auckland-based **Warriors** who play in Australia's NRL during the March to early September season. The top eight teams in the league go through to the finals series in September, and though the Warriors haven't done especially well in recent years, they did make it into the final eight in 2001. Home games are usually played at Ericsson Stadium, where you can buy tickets at the gate.

Cricket

Attending a rugby match is something you shouldn't miss, but most visitors spend their time in New Zealand from October to March when the stadiums are turned over to New Zealand's traditional summer sport, **cricket** (ⓦ www.nzcricket.co.nz). The national team – the **Black Caps** – tend to hover around mid-table in international test and one-day rankings but periodic flashes of brilliance – and the odd unexpected victory over Australia – keep fans interested. Unless you are an aficionado, cricket is an arcane game and much of the pleasure of attending a game is sitting in the sun with a beer in your hand soaking up the ambience. This is particularly true of five-day international **test matches** that generally take place at Eden Park in Auckland, the Westpac Stadium and the Basin Reserve in Wellington, Jade Stadium in Christchurch, Carisbrook in Dunedin and a handful of provincial grounds. You can usually just turn up a buy a **ticket** (around $25), though games held around Christmas and New Year fill up fast. The same venues are used for **one day internationals** which are more popular, so it is best to book in advance.

International players are selected from **provincial teams** that contest the league-based championship during the November–March season; Auckland, Canterbury, Otago and Wellington are currently the strongest teams.

Other sports

Other team sports lag far behind rugby and cricket, though women's **netball** (@www.netballnz.co.nz) has an enthusiastic following and live TV coverage of international fixtures involving the current world champions – the Silver Ferns.

Soccer in New Zealand has always been thought of as slightly effete (especially in macho rugby-playing circles) though there are now more youngsters playing soccer than rugby. There was a brief surge of enthusiasm when the national team – the **All Whites** – reached the 1982 World Cup finals in Spain, but with their exit in the first round and subsequent lack of success the fires died out. National pride now rests with the **Football Kingz** (@www.footballkingz.co.nz), the nation's only representative in the Australian National Soccer League (NSL; @www.socceraustralia.com.au) and an almost permanent fixture close to the foot of the table. The season runs from October to early April and home games are played (usually on Friday evenings, sometimes Saturday) at Ericsson Stadium in Auckland; **tickets** ($15–25) can be bought at the gate or on the team's website.

Beyond these major team sports there is a reasonable following for women's **softball**, men's and women's **basketball**. In recent years there has been heightened interest in **yachting**: Auckland is a frequent midway point for round-the-world yacht races and has hosted the **America's Cup** (see box, p.94).

New Zealand's **Olympic** heritage is patchy with occasional clutches of medals from rowing and yachting and a long pedigree of **middle-distance runners**, particularly in the 1960s with Murray Halberg and Peter Snell, and in the 1970s with John Walker, Dick Quax and Rod Dixon but these days multi event championships and endurance events seem to dominate – like triathlons and the Iron Man race.

Crime and safety

Violent crime was once sufficiently novel in New Zealand that it was reported with front-page relish by the local media. These days it has lost its novelty value, and crime rates approach those in more developed and populated countries. But despite the statistics and the occasional grizzly story, New Zealand feels like a safe place to travel around, and as long as you use your common sense and don't drop your guard just because you're on holiday, you're unlikely to run into any trouble.

In the seedier quarters of the larger cities it is unwise for lone women to walk late at night, and obviously the more isolated a spot the less chance of getting help, but as long as you are reasonably careful you should be OK. Although this is by no means a rule, another area of difficulty for lone women involves taking up work in exchange for board and lodging not arranged through recognized organizations like WWOOF (see overleaf). If you want to taste the country life, stick with the WWOOF booklet when organizing your trip and remember that although it's very good, even so it's not a complete guarantee.

Car break-ins are a more widespread problem. When staying in cities it is easy enough (and a good idea) to move valuables into your lodging, but thieves also prey on visitors vehicles left at trailheads and while you go to take a picture of a waterfall. Campervans containing all your travelling possessions make obvious and easy pickings. When you leave your vehicle, take your valuables with you, and put packs and bags out of sight as much as possible. Beyond this, there isn't really a great deal you can do except get good insurance. When setting out on long walks use a secure car park if possible, where your car will be kept safe for a small sum. You may then have to get a shuttle bus to the start of the walk.

There is rarely any stealing in hostels apart from the odd case of mistaken identity when it comes to food in the fridge, although it doesn't do any harm to lock away stuff if you can.

Police and the law

As everywhere, there are cases of **police** corruption and brutality, but on the whole they're friendly and helpful. If you do get arrested, you will be allowed one phone call; a solicitor will be appointed if you cannot afford one and you may be able to claim legal aid. It is unlikely that your consulate will take more than a passing interest unless there is something strange or unusual about the case against you.

The laws regarding **alcohol consumption** in public are pretty lenient. Nobody's going to bother you if you fancy a beer on the beach or glass of wine at some wayside picnic area, and unless you are actively causing trouble, the police will give you a wide berth. The main exception is around New Year when some downtown areas and popular beaches impose a temporary (and rigidly enforced) alcohol ban.

The same does not apply to **drink driving** (see p.32), which is taken very seriously. **Marijuana**, has a reputation for being very potent and is pretty easily available. It is, however, illegal and although a certain amount of tolerance is sometimes shown towards personal use, the police and courts take a dim view of larger quantities and **hard drugs**, handing out long custodial sentences.

Prejudice

New Zealanders like to think of themselves as a tolerant and open minded people, and foreign visitors are generally welcomed with open arms. Racism is far from unknown, but you're unlikely to experience overt **discrimination** or be refused service because of your race, colour or gender, though on rare occasions (particularly in out-of-the-way rural pubs) women, foreigners, in fact anyone who doesn't live within a 10km radius, may feel like the cowboy stopping the music and conversation by walking through the door.

Despite constant efforts to maintain good relations between **Maori** and Pakeha (white New Zealanders), tensions do exist. Ever since colonisation, **Maori** have achieved lower educational standards, earned less and maintained disproportionately high rates of unemployment and imprisonment. Slowly Maori are getting some restitution for the wrongs perpetrated on their race, which of course plays into the hands of those who feel that such positive discrimination is unfair. "After all, we're all New Zealanders" is a refrain often heard.

Emergency phone calls

☎111 is the free emergency telephone number to summon the police, ambulance or fire service.

Recent high levels of immigration from East Asia – Hong Kong, China and Taiwan in particular – have rapidly changed the demographics in Auckland where most have settled. Central Auckland also has a large number of English-language schools which are mostly full of Asian students. The combined effect means that in parts of Auckland, especially downtown, white and brown New Zealanders are in the minority. It is a sensation that some Maori and Pakeha find faintly disturbing. There's little overt racism, but there are definitely calls from many quarters to reduce the rate of immigration.

Work

With the fairly low value of the Kiwi dollar, New Zealand isn't necessarily the best place to spend time working. But if you need extra income to fund multiple bungy jumps, skydiving lessons and the like you can find paid casual work, typically in tourism-linked service industries, or in fruit picking and related orchard work.

If you'd rather not tackle the red tape you can simply reduce your travelling costs without transgressing the terms of your visitor permit by working for your board.

Working for board and lodging

A popular way of getting around the country cheaply is to **work for your keep**, typically toiling for four hours a day in return for board and lodging. **FHiNZ** (Farm Helpers in New Zealand, 16 Aspen Way, Palmerston North; ☎ & ℱ06/355 0448, ⓦwww.fhinz.co.nz), organize stays on farms, orchards and horticultural holdings for singles, couples and families, and no experience is needed. Over 150 places are listed in their booklet ($25) and accommodation ranges from basic to quite luxurious. An organization run along the same lines is the international **WWOOF** (Willing Workers on Organic Farms, PO Box 1172, Nelson; ☎ & ℱ03/544 9890, ⓦwww.wwoof.co.nz), which coordinates some six hundred properties (membership and booklet $40), mostly farms but also orchards, market gardens and self-sufficiency orientated smallholdings, all using organic methods to a greater or lesser degree. They'll expect a stay of at least two nights, though much longer periods are common; armed with the booklet, you **book direct** (preferably a week or more in advance). Most hosts will work you three to four hours a day and vary the tasks to keep you interested, but there have been occasional reports of taskmasters; make sure you discuss what will be expected of you before you commit yourself. Property managers are vetted but **lone women** may feel happier seeking placements with couples or families. A similar organization is the online **Help Exchange** (ⓦwww.helpx.net), which supplies a regularly updated list of hosts on farms as well as at homestays, B&Bs, hostels and lodges, who need extra help for an average of four hours a day (sometimes less), in return for meals and accommodation; you register online for **free** and book direct.

Visas, permits and red tape

Anyone wanting any other kind of work in New Zealand (except for Australian citizens who are exempt) must first obtain a **Work Visa** (NZ$150 or equivalent), an endorsement in your passport which allows you to enter the country with the intention of working. You must then obtain a **Work Permit** ($90 or equivalent) which actually allows you to work (often with conditions limiting the type of work or even the employer's name). Typically you would apply for both before leaving for New Zealand, but it is possible to arrive on a visitor visa then apply for a Work Permit, though your chances of being granted one are lower and even if granted it will only last for the duration of your original visitor visa. Applications are made through the **New Zealand Immigration Service** (☎09/914 4100, ☜www.immigration.govt.nz), which has all the details and downloadable forms on its website.

You are only likely to be granted a visa or permit if you have an **offer of employment** for which you are qualified and for which there are no suitable New Zealanders available. With this limitation, some visitors are tempted to **work illegally**, something for which you could be fined or deported. In practice, the authorities sometimes turn a blind eye to infringements, especially during the fruit-picking season when there isn't enough local labour to fill demand.

The only significant exception to the Work Permit system is the **Working Holiday Scheme** for those aged 18 to 30, which gives you a temporary work permit valid for twelve months. Eight thousand Brits (plus 1000 Irish citizens, 800 Canadians, 500 Dutch and assorted French, Italians, Germans, Japanese, Koreans, Singaporeans and Malaysians) are eligible each year on a first-come-first-served basis starting on July 1; apply as far in advance as you can. You'll need a passport, NZ$120, evidence of a return ticket to New Zealand (or the funds to pay for it), and the equivalent of NZ$4200 or more to show you can support yourself (sponsorship from a New Zealand citizen is not accepted in place of this sum).

Anyone working in New Zealand (including, oddly, those working illegally without permits) needs to obtain a **tax number** from your local Inland Revenue office (☜www.ird.govt.nz), a process that can take from a day to a week. If you don't have a number then you may find your employer has trouble paying you, and that the authorities will be more likely to take an interest in you. The tax department rakes in twenty-four per cent of your earnings and you probably won't be able to reclaim any of this. Many companies will also only pay wages into a **bank account**, so you may need to open one, which is easy.

Casual work

One of the main sources of casual work is **picking fruit** or related **orchard work** such as packing or pruning and thinning. The main areas to consider are Kerikeri in the Bay of Islands for citrus and kiwifruit; Hastings in Hawke's Bay for apples, pears and peaches; Tauranga and Te Puke for kiwifruit; and Alexandra and Cromwell in Central Otago for stonefruit. Most work is available during the autumn **picking season**, which runs roughly from January to May, but this is also when most people are looking for work so you can often find something just as easily in the off-season. In popular working areas, some hostels cater to short-term workers and these are usually the best places to find out what's happening.

Picking can be hard and heavy work and **payment** is usually by the quantity gathered, rather than by the hour. When you're starting off, the poor returns can be frustrating but with persistence and application you can soon find yourself pulling in a decent wage. Don't expect to earn a fortune, but in an eight-hour day you should gross $70–100. Rates do vary considerably so it's worth asking around, factoring in any meals and accommodation, which are sometimes included. Indoor packing work tends to be paid hourly.

Finding other types of casual work is more ad hoc, with no recognized channels other than newspapers and hostel noticeboards; just keep your ear to the ground, particularly in popular tourist areas – Rotorua, Nelson, Queenstown – where people running **cafés**, **bars** and **hostels** often need extra staff during peak periods. If you have no luck, try your chances in more out-of-the-way locales, where there'll be fewer travellers clamouring for work. Bar and restaurant work usually pays around $9–12 an hour and tips are negligible. Generally you'll need to commit to at least three months. **Ski resorts** occasionally employ people during the June to November season, usually in catering roles. The traditional $9–12 an hour may be supplemented by a lift pass and subsidized food and drink, though finding affordable accommodation can be difficult and may offset a lot of what you gain. Hiring clinics for ski and snowboard instructors are usually held at the beginning of the season at a small cost, though if you are experienced it is better to apply directly to the resort beforehand.

Local hostels and backpackers are always good places to hear about likely work opportunities, and check out a number of handy **resources** and **websites**. Perhaps the best is NZ Job Search, ACB Backpackers, 229 Queen Street, Auckland (☎09/357 3996, ⓦwww.nzjobs.go.to), which details the legalities and helps place people in jobs. For fruit picking and the likes it is also worth checking out sites such as: ⓦwww.seasonalwork.co.nz, and ⓦwww.kiwijobs.co.nz.

Volunteering

A useful starting point is the online service from the UK-based **The Gapyear Company** (ⓦwww.gapyear.com) who offer free membership plus heaps of information on volunteering, travel, contacts and living abroad. The Department of Conservation's **Conservation Volunteer Programme** (click "Volunteers" on the ⓦwww.doc.govt.nz home page) provides an excellent way to spend time out in the New Zealand bush while putting something back into the environment. Often you will get into areas most visitors never see, and learn some skills while you're at it. Projects include bat surveys, kiwi monitoring and nest protection, as well as more rugged tasks like track maintenance, tree planting and hut repair – all detailed on the website. You can muck in for just a day or up to a couple of weeks, and sometimes there is a fee (perhaps $50–200) to cover food and transport. Programmes are often booked up well in advance so it pays to send in an application (forms available on the website) before you reach New Zealand.

Travellers with disabilities

New Zealand is disabled-traveller friendly, but that does not mean everything is rosy. Many public buildings, galleries and museums are accessible to disabled travellers, but as a rule restaurants and local public transport make few concessions.

Long-distance transport companies will generally offer disabled travellers help with boarding, but on-board access to toilets and other amenities can be difficult for wheelchair users. All accommodation in New Zealand should have at least one room or unit suitable for disabled travellers but the level of facilities and access varies considerably: try to go for newer places where possible. On the plus side, many tour operators are prepared to go to that extra bit of trouble to enable travellers with disabilities to participate in activities.

Planning a trip

There are organized **tours** and **holidays** specifically for people with disabilities – the contacts listed below will be able to put you in touch with any specialists for trips to New Zealand. If you want to be more independent, it's important to become an authority on where you must be self-reliant and where you may expect help, especially regarding transport and accommodation. It is also vital to be honest – with travel agencies, insurance companies and travel companions. Know your limitations and make sure others know them. If you do not use a wheelchair all the time but your walking capabilities are limited, remember that you are likely to need to cover greater distances while travelling (often over rougher terrain and in hotter temperatures) than you are used to. If you use a wheelchair, have it serviced before you go and carry a repair kit.

Read your travel **insurance** small print carefully to make sure that people with a pre-existing medical condition are not excluded. And use your travel agent to make your journey simpler: airline or bus companies can cope better if they are expecting you, with a wheelchair provided at airports and staff primed to help. A **medical certificate** of your fitness to travel, provided by your doctor, is also extremely useful; some airlines or insurance companies may insist on it. Make sure that you have extra supplies of drugs – carried with you if you fly – and a prescription including the generic name in case of emergency. Carry spares of any clothing or equipment that might be hard to find; if there's an association representing people with your disability, contact them early in the planning process. Once you're in New Zealand, several organizations provide information for travellers with disabilities and give practical advice on where to go and how to get there.

Accommodation

Current New Zealand law stipulates that any newly built hotel, hostel or motel must have at least one room designed or modified for disabled access and use. Many pre-existing accommodation establishments have also converted rooms to meet these requirements, including most YHA hostels, some motels, campsites and larger hotels. Older buildings, homestays and B&Bs are the least likely to lend themselves to such conversions.

For listings, go straight to Alexia Pickering's Accessible Options website (Ⓦ www.travelaxess.co.nz) which has a searchable database of lodging, and allows you to purchase the broad-ranging *Accessible New Zealand* book (NZ$17 in NZ, US$15 internationally, including postage).

Travelling

Few airlines, trains, ferries and buses allow complete independence. Air New Zealand provides a special wheelchair narrow enough to move around in the plane, and the rear toilet cubicles are wider than the others to facilitate access; for more details search for "Special Assistance" on their website. Other **domestic airlines** will provide help, if not always extra facilities. Cook Strait **ferries** have reasonable access for disabled travellers, including physical help while boarding, if needed, and adapted toilets. If given advance warning, trains will provide attendants to get passengers in wheelchairs or sight-impaired travellers on board, but moving around the train in a standard wheelchair is impossible and there are no specially adapted toilets; the problems with **long-distance buses** are much the same.

In cities there are some **taxis** specifically adapted for wheelchairs, but these must be pre-booked; otherwise taxi drivers obligingly deal with wheelchairs by throwing them into the boot and their occupant onto a seat. The **New Zealand Total Mobility Scheme** allows for anyone unable to use public transport to use taxis at half price; a list of participating areas and companies is available from the Disabled Persons Assembly (see "Contacts in New Zealand", below), who will also arrange for the necessary vouchers to be issued. There is also a **parking** concession for people with mobility problems, assuming they bring the relevant medical certificates with them; for more details email Ⓔ enabletour@xtra.co.nz. The staff on public buses will endeavour to lend a hand, but buses are difficult to board. Some small minibus conversions are available and shuttle buses will help you board and stow your chair, but it pays to let the operator know beforehand of your particular needs. Enable Tourism (see below) can provide lists of companies with **rental cars** adapted for disabled travellers, while some car rental operators will fit hand controls if they are given advance notice.

Contacts in New Zealand

Enable New Zealand ☎ 0800/171 981, Ⓦ www.enable.co.nz. Organisation assisting people with disabilities, though not specifically focused on travellers.

Disability Resource Centre 14 Erson Avenue, Royal Oak, Auckland ☎09/625 8069 & 0800/693 342, ⓦwww.disabilityresource.org.nz. General resource centre.

Disabled Persons Assembly 4/173–175 Victoria St, Wellington, New Zealand ☎04/801 9100 (also TTY), ⓦwww.dpa.org.nz. Resource centre with lists of travel agencies and tour operators for people with disabilities.

Enable Tourism 34 Whittaker Street, Shannon ☎06/362 7163, ⓦwww.enabletourism.co.nz. Provides a comprehensive service of contacts and advice.

Galaxy Motors ☎07/826 4020, ⓦwww.galaxyautos.co.nz. Auckland company with rental vehicle for those with special mobility needs, plus personalized tours with a guide, companion, carer or translator.

Physical Freedom and Manawatu Jet Tours Box 53, Ashhurst ☎06/329 4060, ⓔman-jet-tours@inspire.net.nz. Specialize in outdoor pursuits (bungy, whitewater rafting, kayaking, abseiling), have an accessible bus that accommodates five wheel chairs and offer personalized tours.

Ucan Tours 8 Campbell Street, Sumner, Christchurch ☎03/326 7881, ⓦwww.ucantours.com. Accessible group travel, customised independent tours and vehicle rental.

Contacts in Australia

ACROD (National Industry Association for Disability Services) PO Box 60, Curtin ACT 2605 ☎ 02/6282 4333, ⓦwww.acrod.org.au. Provides lists of travel agencies and tour operators for people with disabilities.

Contacts in the UK and Ireland

All Go Here ☎01923/840 463, ⓦwww.everybody.co.uk. Provides information on accommodation suitable for disabled travellers throughout the UK, including Northern Ireland.

Holiday Care 2nd floor, Imperial Building, Victoria Rd, Horley, Surrey RH6 7PZ ☎0845/124 9971,

Minicom ☎0845/124 9976, ⓦwww.holidaycare.org.uk. Provides free list of accessible accommodation in New Zealand.

Irish Wheelchair Association Blackheath Drive, Clontarf, Dublin 3 ☎01/818 6400, ⓦwww.iwa.ie. Useful information provided about travelling abroad with a wheelchair.

RADAR (Royal Association for Disability and Rehabilitation) 12 City Forum, 250 City Rd, London EC1V 8AF ☎020/7250 3222, Minicom ☎020/7250 4119, ⓦwww.radar.org.uk. Campaigning organisation and general resource for the disabled.

Tripscope Alexandra House, Albany Rd, Brentford, Middlesex TW8 0NE ☎0845/7585 641, ⓦwww.tripscope.org.uk. This registered charity provides a national telephone information service offering free advice on UK and international transport for those with a mobility problem.

Contacts in the USA

Access-Able ⓦwww.access-able.com. Online resource for travellers with disabilities.

Directions Unlimited 123 Green Lane, Bedford Hills, NY 10507 ☎1-800/533-5343 or 914/241-1700. Travel agency specializing in bookings for people with disabilities.

Mobility International USA 451 Broadway, Eugene, OR 97401 ☎541/343-1284, ⓦwww.miusa.org. Information and referral services, access guides, tours and exchange programmes. Annual membership $35 (includes quarterly newsletter).

Society for the Advancement of Travelers with Handicaps (SATH) 347 5th Ave, New York, NY 10016 ☎212/447-7284, ⓦwww.sath.org. Non-profit educational organization that has actively represented travellers with disabilities since 1976.

Wheels Up! ☎1-888/38-WHEELS, ⓦwww.wheelsup.com. Provides discounted airfare, tour and cruise prices for disabled travellers, also publishes a free monthly newsletter and has a comprehensive website.

Gay and lesbian New Zealand

New Zealand has in recent years become a broadly gay-friendly place, defying the odds in what has always been perceived as a fairly macho country. Certainly there remains an undercurrent of redneck intolerance, particularly in rural areas, but it generally stays well below the surface.

Homosexuality was decriminalized in 1986 and the **age of consent** was set at sixteen (the same as for heterosexuals). The human rights section of the **legislation** was passed in 1993, with none of the usual exceptions made for the military or the police. This also makes it illegal to discriminate against gays and people with HIV or AIDS, and makes no limitation on people with HIV or AIDS entering the country.

Such is the mainstream acceptance that the New Zealand Symphony Orchestra is quite upfront about one of its most prominent composers, Gareth Farr, doubling as a drag queen – though not mid-concert. This tolerant attitude has conspired to de-ghettoize the gay community; even in **Auckland** and **Wellington**, the only cities with genuinely vibrant gay scenes, there aren't any predominantly gay areas and most venues have a mixed clientele. Easy-going **clubbing** is generally the order of the day. Auckland's scene is generally the largest and most lively, but the intimate nature of Wellington makes it more accessible and welcoming. Christchurch has a few predominantly gay venues in the inner city, and Nelson has a moderately active gay community centred on Thursday nights at the Spectrum drop-in centre, 42 Franklyn Street (☏03/545 2284 & 2289). Elsewhere it's hard to find a gay network to plug into; even Queenstown is fairly quiet, though it has a gay information service at ⓦwww.gayqueenstown.com.

In 2005, Auckland's gay community will once again be celebrating its existence with its biennial two-week festival of film, theatre, dance and sport that culminates in an all-night dance party (ⓦwww.planetout.com). If you'd prefer a celebration out in the sticks, time your visit to coincide with the annual **Vinegar Hill Summer Camp**, held just outside the small town of Hunterville, in the middle of the North Island, from Boxing Day to just after New Year. It's a very laid-back affair with perhaps a couple of hundred gay men and women camping out, mixing and partying. There's no charge (except a couple of dollars for camping), no tickets and no hot water, but a large river runs through the grounds and everyone has a great time.

Publications

Express (fortnightly, $2.50; ⓦwww.gayexpress.co.nz), sold in almost any decent bookstore, graces the magazine racks of gay-friendly cafés and is often distributed free at gay venues; it is the best source of on-the-ground information and a good way to make contacts. Also keep your eyes peeled for the national bi-monthly **OUT!** ($6, ⓦwww.outnz.net.nz).

Travel information and websites

The non-profit **New Zealand Gay and Lesbian Tourism Association**, PO Box 24–558, Wellington 6015 (☏09/917 9184 & 0800/123 429, ⓦwww.nzglta.org.nz) provides travel information aimed at gay, lesbian and bisexual visitors, and vets businesses for standards of service and hospitality. The associated **Gay and Lesbian Visitor Information Network** (☏09/917 9182 & 0800/147 465, ⓦwww.gaynewzealand.com) offers a virtual tour of the country based on a gay and lesbian bent. Again closely linked, **Gaytravel Net** (ⓦwww.gaytravel.net.nz) offers a gay online accommodation and travel reservation service, and **Travellers to New Zealand** can also help with gay-friendly accommodation and the more way-out places to visit (contact Ron Harris, ☏03/465 1742, ✉ron .harris@xtra.co.nz). For the wild at heart there's ⓦwww.adventureout.co.nz, who organize adventure holidays all over New Zealand for gay men. They're based in Wellington (☎04/938 6539) and take small groups well off the beaten track. Another useful website is ⓦwww.gaynz.net.nz which gives direct access to all manner of gay, lesbian, bisexual and transgender information including the **New Zealand Pink Pages**, essentially a collection of linked pages including what's on in the gay community and a calendar of events all over the country. A worth-while website devoted to women's travel, accommodation and activities is ⓦwww.womenstravel.co.nz.

Directory

Airport tax The Airport departure tax of $25 is not included in airline ticket prices and must be paid (in NZ dollars; credit cards accepted) by each person aged 12 and over after check-in.

Children New Zealand is a child-friendly place: nearly every town of any size has Plunket Rooms, which can be used for changing nappies and sometimes host play groups; family rooms are commonly available in motels, and children are welcomed in most restaurants.

Cigarettes and smoking Smoking is outlawed on all public transport and in many public buildings. From December 2004 smoking will also be banned in the indoor areas of all restaurants, cafés and bars. Cigarettes are expensive and best bought duty-free on arrival.

Dates New Zealand follows Britain's lead with dates, and 1/4/2005 means April 1 not January 4.

Electricity New Zealand operates a 230/240volt, 50Hz AC power supply, and sockets take a three-prong, flat-pin type of plug. North American appliances require both a transformer and an adaptor, British and Irish equipment needs only an adaptor and Australian appliances need no alteration. Suitable adaptors are widely available in New Zealand and at most international airports.

Emergencies Dial ☎111.

Floors What would be called the first floor in the US is the ground floor in NZ, the one above is known as the first, and so on.

GST A Goods and Services Tax is charged at 12.5 percent on almost all items and services and is included in the price quoted,

Metric conversion table

1 metre (m) = 100cm	1 kilogram = 2.2lb
1 kilometre (km) = 1000m	1inch (in) = 2.54cm
1 hectare = 10,000 square metres	1 foot (ft) = 30.48cm
1 kilogram (kg) = 1000g	1 yard (yd) = 0.91m
1 centimetre (cm) = 0.394in	1 mile = 1.610km
1 metre = 39.37in	1 acre = 0.4 hectares
1 kilometre = 0.621 miles	1 UK gallon (gal) = 4.55 litres
1 hectare = 2.471 acres	1 US gallon (gal) = 3.85 litres
1 litre = 0.22 UK gallons	1 ounce (oz) = 28.57g
1 litre = 0.26 US gallons	1 pound (lb) = 454g
1 gram (g) = 0.035oz	

except for some business hotels where rates will be clearly marked GST-exclusive. GST exemption is available on more expensive items bought at shops bearing the "Duty-Free Shopping" sticker which are to be sent or taken out of the country.

Measurements New Zealand uses the metric system of measurements. Distances are in kilometres, petrol is bought in litres, and food is weighed in kilos (see opposite).

Photography Standard colour print film is widely available. Professional and slide film is harder to come by outside the main cities – Fujichrome Velvia seems to be particularly good at capturing New Zealand's intense blues and greens and costs around $30 for 36 exposures, plus $20 for processing. Camera shops everywhere will process your digital images onto CDs, and increasingly hostels have some way of allowing you to review your day's recordings.

Seasons Don't forget that in the southern hemisphere the seasons are reversed. Summer lasts from November to March, and winter from June to September, with a couple of transitional months that pass for spring and autumn.

Sunbathing Topless or nude sunbathing is not something you'll see much of in New Zealand except at naturist camps and recognized nudist beaches. New Zealand is by nature a conservative nation and as a matter of consideration to other beach users it's best to seek out one of the numerous secluded coves around the coastline.

Time New Zealand Standard Time (NZST) is 12 hours ahead of Greenwich Mean Time, so at noon in New Zealand, it's 10am in Sydney, midnight in London, 7pm the day before in New York, and 4pm the day before in Los Angeles. From the first Sunday in October to the third Sunday in March, Daylight Saving puts the clocks one hour further forward.

Tipping There is never an expectation of a tip, though reward for exceptional service is always welcomed.

Guide

Guide

Auckland and around

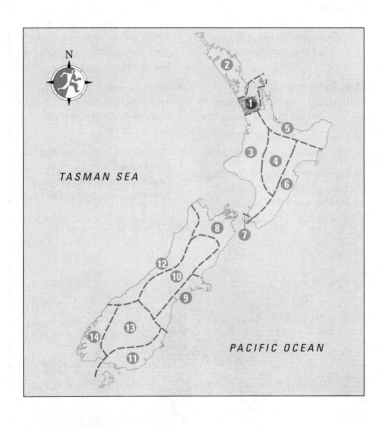

CHAPTER 1 # Highlights

* **Karangahape Road** Arguably New Zealand's funkiest street, with designer club-gear, Pacific Island grocers, and some of the city's best ethnic restaurants. See p.99

* **Auckland Museum** An exemplary Maori and Pacific Island collection is the highlight of this recently updated museum. See p.100

* **Kelly Tarlton's** It raised the bar for all modern aquariums and still cuts it. See p.104

* **Ponsonby Road** Auckland's premiere eat street. See p.106

* **Devonport** Refined waterside suburb that's home to a swag of sumptuous B&Bs. See p.109

* **Otara Market** Island print fabrics, veg stalls and a lot of life make this New Zealand's finest expression of Polynesian culture. See p.110

* **Rangitoto Island** Make a day-trip to this gnarled lava landscape draped in forest with great views back to the city. See p.139

* **Great Barrier Island** Enjoy island life, two hours but thirty years away from Auckland. See p.148

* **Tiritiri Matangi** The easiest place to see some of New Zealand's rarest birds in their natural habitat. See p.156

△ The waterfront, Auckland

Auckland and around

Auckland is New Zealand's largest city and, as the site of the major international airport, it is likely to be your introduction to the country. As planes bank high over the island-studded Hauraki Gulf, brightly spinnakered yachts tack through the glistening waters towards this "City of Sails". Indeed, Auckland looks its best from the water, the high-rise downtown dominated by the Skytower and backed by the low, grassy humps of some of the fifty-odd extinct volcanoes that ring the Waitemata Harbour. Beyond the central business district it is a low-slung suburban city, rarely rising above two stories and until recently characterized by prim wooden villas surrounded by substantial gardens, spreading off into the distance. As a consequence it is one of the least densely populated cities in the world, occupying twice the area of London and yet home to barely a million inhabitants. With its attractive harbour and warm climate, Auckland's fans rank it alongside Sydney, though on the whole it fails to live up to the claim, struggling to match Wellington, New Zealand's capital, for exciting culture and a vibrant night-life. Look beyond the glitzy shopfronts and Auckland has a modest small-town feel and measured pace, though this can seem frenetic enough in comparison with rural New Zealand.

Where Auckland stakes its claim to fame is as the **world's largest Polynesian city**. Around twelve percent of the city's population claim Maori descent while thirteen percent are families of migrants who arrived from Tonga, Samoa, the Cook Islands and other South Pacific islands during the 1960s and 1970s. Nevertheless, the Polynesian profile has traditionally been confined to small pockets, notably the nexus of **Karangahape Road** (universally abbreviated to K' Road), and it is only fairly recently, as the second generation reaches maturity, that Polynesia is making its presence felt in mainstream Auckland life, especially in the arts. Another and more obvious facet of the cities make-up, in the downtown area and retail outlets, is the large (ten percent), and still growing, Asian population that has made Auckland an intriguing, sometimes uneasy, tri-cultural melting pot.

Auckland is often regarded very much as a transit place, and many visitors only stay long enough for a quick zip around the smattering of key sights before moving on to far less metropolitan locales. You could be forgiven for doing the same, but don't miss the **Auckland Museum**, with its matchless collection of Maori and Pacific Island carving and artefacts. With more time, dip into the country's strongest collection of New Zealand fine art at the **Auckland Art Gallery**, and delve into the perspex shark tunnels of **Kelly Tarlton's Underwater World**. Auckland is even trying to catch up with the rest of the country by offering a clutch of new adventure activities like

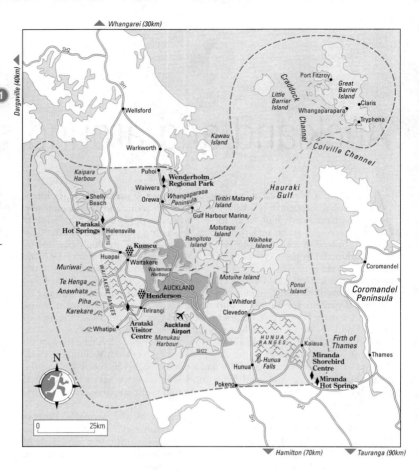

the harbour bridge walk and the **Sky Jump** from the Skytower. Beyond these, the pleasure is in ambling around the fashionable inner-city suburbs of Ponsonby, Parnell and Devonport, and using the city as a base for exploring what's **around Auckland** – the wild and desolate West Coast **surf beaches** less than an hour's drive from downtown, and the **wineries** nearby. Ferries based in the centre of the city open up the **Hauraki Gulf islands**: the botanically and geologically fascinating, the sophisticated city retreat of Waiheke Island and the time-warped and isolated Great Barrier Island.

Auckland's **climate** is often described as muggy; it's never scorching hot, and the heat is always tempered by a sea breeze. Winters are generally mild but rainy.

Auckland

AUCKLAND's urban sprawl completely smothers the North Island's wasp waist, a narrow isthmus where the island is all but severed by river estuaries probing inland from the city's two harbours. To the west, the shallow and silted **Manukau Harbour** opens out onto the Tasman Sea at a rare break in the long string of black-sand beaches continually pounded by heavy surf. Maori named the eastern anchorage the **Waitemata Harbour** for its "sparkling waters", which constitute Auckland's deep-water port and a focus for the heart of the city. Every summer weekend the harbour and adjoining Hauraki Gulf explode into a riot of brightly-coloured sails.

As the venue for the **America's Cup** in 1999 and 2002, Auckland's down-town was the focus for massive investment with new high-rises, more banks, hotels and some pleasing harbour development including stylish cafés and restaurants. The downside of all this is a marked loss of personality and despite Auckland's cosmopolitan bustle and harbourside setting, few fall in love with the city or stick around long enough to scratch below the surface. Those who persist might find some gems but rarely do people become as enthusiastic about the place as Aucklanders themselves.

Some history

The earth's crust between the Waitemata and Manukau harbours is so thin that every few thousand years, magma finds a fissure and bursts onto the surface, pro-ducing yet another volcano. The most recent eruption, some six hundred years ago, formed Rangitoto Island, to the horror of some of the region's earliest Maori inhabitants settled on adjacent Motutapu Island. Legend records their ancestors' arrival on the Tamaki Isthmus, the narrowest neck of land between the Waitemata and Manukau harbours. With plentiful catches from two harbours and rich volcanic soils on a wealth of highly defensible volcano-top sites, the land, which they came to know as Tamaki-makau-rau ("the spouse sought by a hun-dred lovers"), became the prize of numerous battles over the years. By the middle of the eighteenth century it had fallen to **Kiwi Tamaki**, who established a three-thousand-strong *pa* or fortified village on Maungakiekie ("One Tree Hill"), and a satellite *pa* on just about every volcano in the district, but was eventually over-whelmed by rival *hapu* (sub-tribes) from Kaipara Harbour to the north.

With the arrival of musket-trading **Europeans** in the Bay of Islands around the beginning of the nineteenth century, Northland Ngapuhi were able to launch successful raids on the Tamaki Maori which, combined with the pre-dations of smallpox epidemics, left the region almost uninhabited, a significant factor in its choice as the new capital after the signing of the Treaty of Waitangi in 1840. Scottish medic **John Logan Campbell** was one of few European residents when this fertile land, with easy access to major river and sea-borne trading routes, was purchased for £55 and some blankets. The capital was roughly laid out and Campbell took advantage of his early start, wheeling and dealing to achieve control of half the city, eventually becoming mayor and "the father of Auckland". After 1840, immigrants boosted the population to the extent that more land was needed, a demand which partly precipitated the **New Zealand Wars** of the 1860s (see p.945).

During the depression that followed, many sought their fortunes in the Otago goldfields and, as the balance of European population shifted south, so did the centre of government. Auckland lost its **capital status** to Wellington in 1865 and the city slumped further, only seeing the glimpse of a recovery when prospectors flooded through on their way to the gold mines around Thames in the late 1860s. Since then Auckland has never looked back, repeatedly ranking as New Zealand's fastest growing city and absorbing waves of migrants, initially from Britain then, in the 1960s and 1970s, from the Polynesian Islands of the South Pacific and, most recently, from Asian countries. Rising from the depression years of the early 1990s, and a brief slump after the Asian financial melt down, Auckland is a notable figurehead for New Zealand's renaissance as a modern nation.

Arrival and information

As New Zealand's major gateway city, Auckland receives the bulk of **international arrivals**, a few disembarking from stately cruise ships at the dock by the Ferry Building, but the vast majority arriving by air.

Auckland International Airport (T09/275 0789) is located 20km south of the city centre in the suburb of Mangere. The international terminal is connected to two domestic terminals - one operated by Air NZ, the other by Qantas - by a shuttle bus (every 20min) but if you've a light load it's only a ten-minute walk. Before leaving the international terminal you can grab a free shower (towels $6), though most travellers just head straight for the city. The well-stocked and helpful **visitor centre** (T09/275 6467) stays open for all international arrivals and will book you into a city hotel free of charge, or you can make use of the bank of courtesy phones nearby. There's also a branch of the BNZ **bank** that changes money at tolerable rates, and some **duty-free shops**, where inbound passengers can top up their quota.

A **taxi** into the city will set you back around $45, but there are plenty of **minibuses** vying for trade after each arrival, and most offer small discounts to backpackers in possession of a YHA or VIP card. The AirBus (every 20min 6am–10pm; $13 one-way, $22 return) follows a fixed route into the city (roughly 50min). Other buses operate a more or less door-to-door service. It's $20 for a single person with the price rising $5 per person and the total shared between all the passengers; for Devonport the rates start at around $32.

On arrival you just jump into the first one on the rank; for pick up on departure call Super Shuttle (T0800/SHUTTLE & 09/634 3960) or one of the various taxi companies (see p.128).

InterCity and Newmans operate most of the **long-distance bus services** that use the **Inter City Bus Terminal** under Auckland's Sky City casino complex on Hobson Street. Smaller operators – Northliner, Guthrey's, Go Kiwi and Supa Travel – stop outside the Northliner Travel Centre at 172 Quay Street, opposite the Ferry Building.

Trains pull in to the new Britomart, at the harbour end of Queen Street – although you're unlikely to use the poor commuter service much.

Information

Auckland has two main **visitor centres** –The Atrium, Sky City, corner of Victoria and Federal streets (Sun–Wed 8am–8pm, Thurs–Sat 8am–10pm; T09/979 2333, Wwww.aucklandnz.com), and on the wharf close to the Maritime Museum, Viaduct Harbour (daily 9am–5pm) – which share the same contact details. Both are efficient with the Sky City version being a crowded,

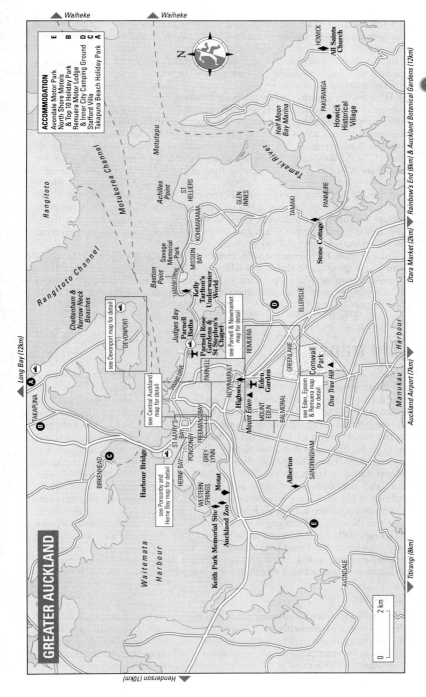

GREATER AUCKLAND

ACCOMMODATION	
Avondale Motor Park	E
North Shore Motels & Top 10 Holiday Park	B
Remuera Motor Lodge & Inner City Camping Ground	D
Stafford Villa	C
Takapuna Beach Holiday Park	A

N

Waiheke

Waiheke

Rangitoto

Rangitoto Channel

Motukorea Channel

Motutapu

HOWICK
All Saints Church

PAKURANGA
Howick Historical Village

Half Moon Bay Marina

Tamaki River

Cheltenham & Narrow Neck Beaches

DEVONPORT
see Devonport map for detail

Achilles Point
ST HELLIERS

Bastion Point
Savage Memorial Park

MISSION BAY
KOHIMARAMA

GLEN INNES

TAMAKI

PANMURE

Stone Cottage

TAKAPUNA

BIRKENHEAD

Harbour Bridge

see Central Auckland map for detail

TAMAKI DRIVE
Kelly Tarlton's Underwater World

Judges Bay
Parnell Baths
Parnell Rose Gardens & St Stephen's Chapel

PARNELL

see Parnell & Newmarket map for detail

REMUERA

ELLERSLIE

Manukau Harbour

see Ponsonby and Herne Bay map for detail

ST MARY'S BAY
FREEMANS BAY

PONSONBY
HERNE BAY

GREY LYNN

NEWMARKET

Highwic
Eden Garden

GREENLANE

Cornwall Park

see Eden, Epsom & Remuera map for detail

One Tree Hill

Keith Park Memorial Site
Auckland Zoo
Motat

WESTERN SPRINGS

MOUNT EDEN
Mount Eden

BALMORAL

SANDRINGHAM

Alberton

AVONDALE

Waitemata Harbour

Long Bay (12km)

Henderson (10km)

Titirangi (8km)

Auckland Airport (7km)

Otara Market (2km)

Rainbow's End (6km) & Auckland Botanical Gardens (12km)

0   2 km

83

1

fast-fix booking desk for pretty much everything in New Zealand while the latter is quieter, better set up and well stocked with leaflets from around the country.

Both visitor centres, as well as booking agents, hotels and hostels, stock a number of advertisement-heavy **free publications**, the best of which are the annual *Auckland A–Z Visitors Guide* and the bi-monthly *Auckland What's On*. Both have sketch **maps** that are adequate for most purposes, or you could splash out on the spiral-bound *Auckland* KiwiMap ($20). There are also several places specifically geared towards providing **backpacker information**, usually with low-cost Internet access, noticeboards for rides, vehicle sales and job opportunities and an extensive booking service for onward travel. The larger hostels (especially *Auckland Central Backpackers*) are useful, but the best place to go is the Travellers Contact Point, Dingwall Building, 87–93 Queen St (Mon–Fri 9am–6pm, Sat 10am–2pm; ☎09/300 7197, ⓦwww.travellersnz.com), which additionally organizes mobile phones, provides luggage storage (from $10 a week), almost always has people offering drudge work in return for accommodation, and offers a worthwhile mail forwarding service. Another good bet is Usit Beyond, 5–7 Victoria Street East (☎09/379 4224, ⓦwww.usitworld.co.nz; Mon–Fri 9am–5.30pm, Sat noon–3pm).

The compact **Department of Conservation (DOC) office**, in the Ferry Building at 99 Quay St (☎09/379 6476, ⓔaucklandvc@doc.govt.nz; Mon–Fri 10am–5.30pm, Sat 10am–3pm), stocks DOC material and does track bookings for the whole country but particularly specializes in the Auckland and Hauraki Gulf region.

City transport

Auckland's public transport is in a sorry state and periodic moves to improve it are hampered by the city's vast spread and low population density. That said, you'll find you can get to most places **on foot** (notably along the Coast-to-Coast Walkway, see p.113), by local **bus**, or with one of the city tour buses that shuttle between the major sights. Out on the harbour, **ferries** connect the city to the inner suburb of Devonport and numerous islands. **Taxis** are plentiful and can be flagged down, though they seldom cruise the streets and are best contacted by phone (see p.128). Few visitors will find much use for the Tranz Metro suburban **train** services (call Rideline on ☎0800/103080), which start from the new Britomart Centre and call at graffiti-covered and inhospitable stations in places that are low on most visitors' must-see lists; the two lines run south through Newmarket and Ellerslie, and west through Henderson then north to Waitakere. **Parking** isn't a major headache, but Auckland **drivers** aren't especially courteous and really you're better off renting a car once you're ready to leave the city. Hilly terrain and motorists' lack of bike-awareness render **cycling** a less than inviting option through city streets, but the situation is redeemed by a few dedicated routes.

Buses

The majority of **local buses** are run by Stagecoach Auckland, who also staff the Rideline **timetable** helpline (☎0800/103080 or 09/366 6400, ⓦwww.rideline.co.nz). The useful *Auckland Busabout Guide* leaflet is available free from visitor centres and newsagents including Victoria St Lotto & Newsagency, 67 Victoria St (Mon–Fri 7am–6.30pm, Sat 10am–7pm).

The single most useful **route** is the Link (Mon–Thurs 6am–11.45pm, Sat & Sun 7am–11.45pm; $1.20); these flashy silver and white buses ply a continuous loop through the city, Parnell, Newmarket, K' Road and Ponsonby every ten minutes during weekdays and every twenty minutes in the evening and at weekends. Of the remaining services, city-bound buses will be marked "Downtown" if terminating along lower Queen Street, or "Midtown" if ending their run at the corner of Victoria Street and Queen Street.

For buses other than the Link, **fares** are charged according to a zonal system: the inner city, Parnell, Mount Eden and Ponsonby are covered by one zone ($1.20 per journey), from the city to Newmarket is two zones ($2.40), Henderson is five zones ($5), and so on. You can save ten percent by buying a **Ten-trip Ticket** (price determined by the number of zones covered), which is also valid on the trains. For short-stay visitors, a better deal is the one-day **Auckland Pass** ($12 from bus drivers, ferry ticket offices and the train station; an $8-version doesn't include trains), which gives all-day relatively unlimited travel on the bus network (including the Link) and all ferries to the north shore (including Devonport). Late at night there's also a secure **NightRider** service designed to get you out of the city centre, from 1am–3am at weekends ($4 within zones A and B or $6 if travelling through both). During the day a limited view of the downtown city can be had for free on the bright red, eco-friendly **Circuit Bus** that begins on Queen Street, opposite the Britomart Centre, travels to the University and then crosses back over Queen Street to explore the west-side of downtown.

Tourist buses

To avoid dealing with complex timetables and numerous routes, you'll find it easier to get around the main sights on the hop-on-hop-off **Explorer Bus** (℡0800/439 756, ⓦwww.explorerbus.co.nz; $30, pay the driver), which runs every half-hour and comes with an en-route commentary. The circuit starts from the Ferry Building on Quay Street and goes along Tamaki Drive to Kelly Tarlton's Underwater World, up to Parnell and the Auckland Museum, and back via Victoria Park Market and Viaduct Harbour. During the summer months (Oct–April) there's a second loop taking in Mount Eden, the Auckland Zoo, MOTAT and the Auckland Art Gallery.

Ferries

The Waitemata Harbour was once a seething mass of ferries bringing commuters in from the suburbs. Services have been rationalized over the years, but the harbour **ferries** remain a fast, pleasurable and scenic way to get around. The main destinations are the Hauraki Gulf islands, but there are also services calling at Devonport, run by Fullers, the principal ferry company (℡09/367 9111, ⓦwww.fullers.co.nz). The **Devonport Ferry** (Mon–Thurs 6.15am–11pm, Fri & Sat 6.15am–1am, Sun 7.15am–10pm; every 30min; $8 return, bikes free) is the cheapest of the ferries, takes around fifteen minutes to cross the harbour, and is included in the Auckland Pass (see above). There are several other commuter services, the most useful being to Birkenhead (£8 return), which involves a passage under the harbour bridge.

Driving

With many of the Auckland region's sights conveniently accessible on foot or by public transport, there isn't a huge advantage in having a car while you're in the city, though you'll need one to explore gems like the Kumeu wineries and the surf beaches of the West Coast. As the main point of entry, Auckland is awash with places to **rent a car** (see p.127 for details of outfits in the city); and if you're planning on some serious touring, you may be interested in **buying a car** - see p.34 for some advice on the pros and cons, as well as the potential pitfalls.

Driving around Auckland isn't especially taxing, though it is worth trying to avoid the rush hours from 7–9am and 4–6.30pm. On first acquaintance, Auckland's urban freeways can be unnerving, with frequent junctions, poor signage and vehicles overtaking on all sides. Driving is on the left, though if you've just arrived after a long flight, you should consider waiting a day or so before driving at all. Inner-city streets are metered, which means that parking is best done in multi-storey **car parks** which are dotted all over the central city and reasonably well signposted; few are open 24 hours, so check the latest exit time – usually around midnight.

Cycling

Cycling around Auckland's hills can be a tiring and dispiriting exercise. However, a few areas lend themselves to pedal-powered exploration, most notably the harbourside Tamaki Drive east of the city centre, which forms part of a 50km **cycle route** around the city and isthmus – detailed in a free leaflet available from visitor centres. **Rental bikes** cost around $18–25 per day ($80–120 a week), depending on the sophistication of the model; see p.127 for details of outlets. In addition, there are several companies that offer monthly rental and **buy-back schemes** for long-stayers (see p.36).

Accommodation

Auckland has a broad range of accommodation, meeting the needs of most budgets, but that doesn't stop everywhere filling up through December, January and February, when you should definitely **book ahead**. At other times it is less critical and through the quiet winter months, from June to September, you'll be spoiled for choice with significant discounts on room rates, particularly if you're staying for a few days; it's always worth haggling.

More than anywhere else in New Zealand, Auckland is a place where you might choose to stay outside the **city centre**. Unless you have a mind to hit the clubs or have arrangements to make in the centre, you may have little cause to spend much time there. Most sightseeing can be done just as easily from the **suburbs**, such as **Ponsonby**, less than 2km west of the centre; **Mount Eden**, 2km south of the central city; peaceful and salubrious **Devonport**, a short ferry journey across the harbour; relaxed **Waiheke Island**, a forty-minute ferry ride away from the waterfront and, **Parnell**, 2km east of the centre. Besides which, all are well supplied with places to eat and drink, Ponsonby and Parnell's main streets ranking as the city's most vibrant, particularly at weekends.

The city centre remains the place to find international four- and five-star **hotels**, mostly geared towards business travellers and tour groups; walk-in rates are usually prohibitively high, though there are sometimes tempting weekend deals. Backpacker **hostels** congregate around the city centre and inner suburbs; **B&Bs** and **guesthouses** are strongest in Ponsonby, Devonport, Waiheke Island and the southern suburbs of Epsom and Remuera; and the widest selection of **motels** is just south of Newmarket in Epsom. Predictably, **campsites** are much further out and not really worth the hassle if you want to hang out in the city.

Hotels and motels

An increasing number of **hotels** pepper the city centre and inner suburbs, ranging from places little more salubrious than hostels up to swanky five-star affairs. High city rents force **motels** further out and you'll see them just about everywhere, but nowhere more so than the stretch of Great South Road in Epsom, immediately south of the Newmarket shops, where there are at least a dozen places within a kilometre. We've stuck to recommending places that are relatively convenient to the centre and the main sights.

City centre

See map on p.93.

Airdale Hotel 380 Queen St ☎09/374 1741, ⓦwww.scenic-circle.co.nz. Recently refurbished to its original 1950s Art Deco style, this impressive harbourside hotel has everything you could want: 101 rooms with fitted kitchens and summer deals that make it good value for money. ❺–❻

Aspen House 62 Emily Place ☎09/379 6633, ⓦwww.aspenhouse.co.nz. Compact hotel right in the heart of the city but surprisingly quiet and with a small garden and deck. Rooms aren't big and don't have private facilities but it's great value and a continental breakfast is included. ❹

Heritage 35 Hobson St ☎09/379 8553 & 0800/368 888, ⓦwww.heritagehotels.co.nz. Top class hotel fashioned from the original Farmers department store – once the city's grandest. Occasional bits of aged planking and wooden supports crop up in public areas, but it has had a major refit to a very high standard and many rooms have views across the harbour or into the glassed-in atrium. There are also tennis courts, a health club, and indoor and outside pools, the latter with views over the city rooftops. ❽

Hilton Princes Wharf, 147 Quay Street, Auckland ☎09/978 2000, ⓦwww.aucklandhilton.com. Newish international class hotel fabulously sited on

Airport accommodation

With a choice of several efficient door-to-door shuttle services into central Auckland there is little reason to stay near the airport except if you arrive at midnight or have a hideously early flight to catch. There is no accommodation actually at the airport site, but a dozen places line Kirkbride Road in Mangere, some 5km away at the end of the approach road and close to many of the car-rental pick-up points. All the places listed below provide their own free shuttle service to the airport (either on a fixed schedule or to order), and have a freephone at the airport: just give them a call and they'll pick you up. Alternatively, a taxi will cost $12-15. There isn't much of interest around the airport hotels, but the better hotels have bars and restaurants, and there are a couple of cheap restaurants and takeaways nearby.

Airport Bed & Breakfast 1 Westney Rd (at Kirkbride Rd) ☎ & ☎09/275 0533, ⓦwww.airportbnb.co.nz. Ten rooms (some en suite) in a converted suburban house that's well placed for the airport with breakfast thrown in and a very reasonable price. ❸

Jet Inn 63 Westney Rd ☎09/275 4100 or 0800/538 466, ⓦreservations @jetinn.co.nz. Business hotel with all the expected facilities – Sky TV, minibars, lovely outdoor pool – and decor attractively supplemented with traditional arts and crafts from the owners' native South Africa. Rates include a continental breakfast in the hotel restaurant. ❻

Pacific Inn 210 Kirkbride Rd ☎09/275 1129, ⓦpacific-inn.co.nz. Somewhat run-down but reasonably priced hotel with fairly spacious studio rooms, TV and tea- and coffee-making facilities, and a restaurant and bar downstairs. ❹

Skyway Lodge 30 Kirkbride Rd ☎09/275 4443, ⓦwww.skywaylodge.co.nz. Several grades of budget accommodation in friendly and relaxed surroundings with a refreshing pool, guests' kitchen and free luggage storage. Accommodation is in 4-bunk dorms, double and twin rooms and self-catering motel units. Dorms ❶, doubles ❷, en-suite doubles & units ❹

a wharf jutting into the harbour. Beautifully deco-rated rooms, all with terrace or balcony, are done in a fairly minimal style and start from around $260 but you'll pay at least $50 more for a good harbour view and fabulous waterside suites are around $1100. ❾

Kiwi International 411 Queen St ☎09/379 6487 & 0800/100 411, ✉kiwihotel@xtra.co.nz. Poor service, a rather characterless and ageing warren of rooms compensated for by off-street parking and low rates. The standard rooms are fairly comfortable, economy rooms come without a bathroom and there are bunks in dorms, though no self-catering facilities. Dorms ❶, economy rooms ❷, standard rooms ❹

Sky City cnr Victoria St & Federal St ☎09/363 6000 & 0800/759 249, ⓦwww.skycity.co.nz. Part of the casino complex, with all the facilities that entails: rooftop pool, gym, sauna, bars and restaurants. Rooms are standard, international-hotel style but nicely done, many with good harbour views. Rack rates start high and rise through the stratosphere, but walk-in rates (including breakfast and valet parking) are often lower, especially at weekends and in the winter. Specials ❽, otherwise ❾

Parnell

See map on p.103.

Kingsgate Parnell 92–102 Gladstone Rd ☎09/377 3619, ⓦwww.kingsgatehotels.co.nz. Well-managed extensive business and tourist hotel with city views, a brasserie, cocktail bar and comfortable rooms or villas (with full kitchens). Rooms ❻, villas ❾

Parnell Inn 320 Parnell Rd ☎0800/472 763 & 09/358 0642, ✉parnelin@ihug.co.nz. Compact and simple hotel attached to *The Other Side* café (which does room service) right in the heart of Parnell. Rooms are fairly small, some having cook-ing facilities, and off-street parking is available. Large rooms with view ❺, basic rooms ❹

Ponsonby, Herne Bay and Freeman's Bay

See map on p.107.

Abaco Spa 59 Jervois Rd ☎09/376 0119 & 0800/220 066, ⓦwww.abacospamotel.com. Recently refurbished mainstream motel close to Herne Bay and Ponsonby shops and restaurants, with budget kitchenless rooms and larger motel units, some with private spas and distant harbour views. ❺–❻

Unicorn 31 Shelley Beach Rd ☎0800/864 267 & 09/376 2067, ⓦwww.unicornmotel.co.nz. Top-quality, modern, air-conditioned motel with spa-cious fully equipped units; there's a private spa and a pool too. Famous for being the accommoda-tion used by the two French agents who blew up the Rainbow Warrior. ❻

Epsom

See map on p.111.

Greenpark 66 Great South Rd ☎09/520 3038, ✉green.park@xtra.co.nz. Renovated motel with standard and executive suites, all with separate bedrooms and full facilities. ❹–❺

Hansen's 96 Great South Rd ☎09/520 2804, ✉hansensmot@xtra.co.nz. One of the cheapest motels in town with small but perfectly formed self-contained studios and a nice swimming pool. ❹

Off Broadway Motel Newmarket 11 Alpers Ave ☎0800/427 623 & 09/529 3550, ⓦwww .offbroadway.co.nz. Business-orientated hotel with air-conditioned, soundproofed ensuite rooms. Plump for the much larger suites if your budget allows. Studios ❺, suites ❼

Siesta 70 Great South Rd ☎0800/743 782 & 09/520 2107, ✉reservations@siestamotel.co.nz. Good modern motel with kitchenless studios and self-catering units. ❹–❺

Tudor Court 108 Great South Rd ☎0800/826 878 & 09/523 1069, ✉stay@tudor.co.nz. Compact motel with small hotel-style rooms and slightly larger ones with kitchenettes. ❹

B&Bs and guesthouses

Auckland's stock of B&Bs and guesthouses is rapidly expanding. New places are continually opening, many pitching for the upper end of the market, with just a few rooms and an almost obsessive attention to the finest detail. Places are scattered widely around the **inner suburbs** on the south side of the har-bour, but in recent years the choice in the North Shore suburb of **Devonport** has mushroomed as a result of people trying to avoid the unattractive down-town area of Auckland but still wanting to be within easy travelling range of it. At last count there were over two dozen high-standard places, not all of them close to the ferry but all willing to pick up and drop off if you arrive that way.

Note that airport shuttle buses will drop you in Devonport for only a few dollars more than the central Auckland fare.

Parnell

See map on p.103.

Ascot Parnell St Stephens Ave ☎09/309 9012, ⓦwww.ascotparnell.com. Very swish and comfy accommodation with a large lounge opening on to a balcony overlooking the harbour, luxurious private bathrooms, Internet access and a filling breakfast. ❼

Chalet Chevron 14 Brighton Rd ☎09/309 0290, ⓦwww.chaletchevron.co.nz. Comfortable B&B with cheery and colourful en-suite rooms, some with distant sea views, and several well geared for singles. A full breakfast is served and there's free tea and coffee all day. ❺

St Georges Bay Lodge 43 St Georges Bay Rd ☎09/303 1050, ⓦwww.stgeorge.co.nz. Gorgeous and welcoming B&B in one of the four original St Georges Bay villas, tastefully renovated, fitted out in native timbers and hung with New Zealand artworks. Complimentary port and wine, and a full breakfast, are all part of the package. ❼

Ponsonby and Herne Bay

See map on p.107.

A1 Paddy's 25 John Street, Ponsonby ☎09/376 2180. Small, friendly and cheap homestay in a pioneer cottage with one single room and a garden studio double. ❺

Colonial Lodge 35 Clarence St, Ponsonby ☎09/360 2820. Great-value B&B in a turn of the century Kauri villa with two doubles and a single. Great breakfasts made from mostly organic grub plus alternative health therapies and massage. ❺

The Great Ponsonby B&B 30 Ponsonby Terrace, Ponsonby ☎09/376 5989, ⓦwww.greatpons.co.nz. Ultra-friendly boutique hotel in a restored 1898 villa three minutes' walk from Ponsonby Rd. Boldly decorated in ocean tones using native timbers and Pacific artworks, everyone has use of the sunny lounge and shaded garden and the breakfasts are a delight. All the luxurious rooms are en suite and come with Sky TV; there are also several self-catering studio units (❼). Rooms ❻

Herne Bay B&B 4 Shelly Beach Rd, Herne Bay ☎09/360 0309, ⓦwww.herne-bay.co.nz. Refurbished, low-key B&B in a large Edwardian house converted to accommodate three classes of room, and with a rooftop turret which is great for watching the sunset. Some rooms share facilities and have access to a small communal kitchen, some have their own kitchen, and the larger ones have a separate living area. Continental breakfast is served. ❹

Devonport and Birkenhead

See map on p.109.

Badgers 30 Summer St, Devonport ☎09/445 2099, ⓦwww.badger.co.nz. A sunny 1906 wooden villa where you will be pampered and spoiled, not only by the ultra-friendly hosts but by the surroundings. There are 5 doubles available, four of which are en suite and the range of breakfasts will set your head spinning. ❻

Cheltenham-by-the-Sea 2 Grove Rd, Devonport ☎09/445 9437, ⓦwww.cheltenhambythesea.co.nz. One of Devonport's cheapest B&Bs, right by Cheltenham Beach, twenty minutes' walk from the ferry. Rooms are spacious and simple, in a comfortable, modern home run by friendly folk. ❺

The Garden Room 23 Cheltenham Rd, Devonport ☎ & ℻09/445 2472, ⓔperrinehall@xtra.co.nz. Choose between the lovely private cottage in the leafy garden or the room inside the main house both of which are done to a very high standard; sumptuous breakfasts can be served under an arbour or in your room. ❼

Parituhu Beachstay 3 King Edward Parade, Devonport ☎ & ℻09/445 6559. Excellent budget B&B homestay in the heart of Devonport and overlooking the harbour. There's just the one room, with private bath and access to a secluded garden and self-service breakfast. ❺

Peace & Plenty Inn 6 Flagstaff Terrace, Devonport ☎09/445 2925, ⓦwww .peaceandplenty.co.nz. One of New Zealand's finest B&Bs. Elegantly restored kauri floorboards lead through to a lovely veranda, past exquisite rooms filled with fresh flowers and equipped with sherry and port. Venture outside the bounds of the inn, and you're right in the heart of Devonport. The communal breakfast is a major event, and the hosts will even take you sailing. ❽

Stafford Villa 2 Awanui St, Birkenhead ☎09/418 3022, ⓦwww.staffordvilla.co.nz. Located on a quiet street in one of the North Shore's more venerable waterside suburbs, where there are several good restaurants and the excellent Bridgeway Cinema, this top notch place offers just two period-furnished en-suite rooms in an elegant century-old villa. Guests have access to a drawing room and a comfy library (with complimentary port), and are treated to a sumptuous breakfast. ❽

Villa Cambria 71 Vauxhall Rd, Devonport ☎09/445 7899, ⓦwww.villacambria.co.nz. Beautifully decorated Victorian villa close to

Cheltenham beach and fifteen minutes' walk from Devonport with friendly and attentive hosts who provide lovely breakfasts and a relaxed atmosphere. All rooms en suite with complimentary port. Rooms ➎, large loft room ➑

Mount Eden, Epsom and Remuera

See map on p.111.

Aachen House 39 Market Rd, Remuera ✆09/520 2329 & 0800/222 436, ⓦwww.aachenhouse.co.nz. Elegant boutique B&B in an Edwardian house sumptuously decorated with antiques. Every comfort is catered for: rooms are spacious, beds

are huge, bathrooms are beautifully tiled and breakfasts are delicious. ➐

Bavaria 83 Valley Rd, Mount Eden ✆09/638 9641, ⓦwww.bavariabandbhotel.co.nz . Eleven-room B&B in a spacious, comfortable villa that boasts a pleasant deck and garden. It's popular with German speakers, has a buffet continental breakfast and can be reached on buses numbered in the 250s and 260s. ➏

Pentlands 22 Pentlands Ave, Mount Eden ✆ & ⓕ09/638 7031, ⓦwww.pentlands.co.nz. Peaceful, low-cost B&B ten minutes' walk from Mount Eden shops with plain bathless rooms but spacious lounges and a tennis court and barbecue area out back. Continental breakfast is served. ➍

Hostels

Auckland has stacks of **backpacker hostels**. The scene is highly competitive, and most are well set up for assisting new arrivals in planning their onward travel, even to the extent of having fully staffed on-site travel services – sometimes pushing favoured trips and activities, but generally offering fair and impartial advice.

There's a definite trade-off between proximity to the facilities offered by **downtown** hostels, and the relative quiet and comfort of places outside the centre. Those in the centre tend to cram in the beds and, with bars and clubs only a short stagger away, cater to party animals. The emphasis is firmly on having a wild time and the larger places have a reputation for being noisy at night; self-catering facilities seem like an afterthought and serve to encourage guests to eat out. Hostels in the **inner suburbs** – Parnell, Ponsonby and Mount Eden – tend to be less boisterous affairs often in old, converted houses, sometimes with gardens and always with parking.

As you'd expect, **prices** are a touch higher than at hostels in the rest of the country, though you can still get dorm bunks for around $20. Small dorms and four-shares hover around $22 and most doubles and twins are $50–65. If you're arriving during the peak summer season, try to book a couple of days in advance to be sure of getting a bed.

City centre

See map on p.117.

Albert Park 27–31 Victoria St East ✆09/309 0336, ⓔbakpak@albertpark.co.nz. Comfortable city centre backpackers; small, clean and fairly spacious with some large and several smaller dorms, reasonable doubles, adequate cooking facilities, bar and pool table. Dorms ➊, rooms ➌

Auckland Central 229 Queen St ✆09/358 4877, ⓦwww.acb.co.nz. Ever-expanding but very good hostel in a central, ten-storey converted office building with acres of parking. Despite the inevitable impersonality of housing so many, everything runs smoothly and it seldom feels too crowded. They've thought of everything including a downstairs bar, massive Internet centre, helpful travel office, large laundry, gear storage and even

electronic key access to rooms and public areas. Mixed dorms sleep up to eight but it is worth the extra $2 to stay in single-sex four-bed dorms supplied with sheets. Twins and doubles come either with or without en-suite bathroom. Dorms ➊, rooms ➌, en suites ➍

Auckland City YHA cnr City Rd & Liverpool St ✆09/309 2802, ⓔyhaauck@yha.org.nz. Large and central YHA with seven floors of mostly twin and double rooms – some with fine city views – plus well-equipped common areas and a large travel centre; even a bistro on site. Single sex dorms ➊, rooms ➋

Auckland International YHA 5 Turner St ✆09/302 8200, ⓔyhaakint@yha.org.nz. Just down the hill and even larger than its brother, this purpose-built YHA is thoroughly modern with excellent cooking facilities, spacious rooms, separate TV and smoking lounges, Internet access and a travel centre. Single sex dorms ❶, rooms ❸, en-suite rooms ❹

Central City 26 Lorne St ☎09/358 5685, ⓦwww.backpacker.net.nz. Large, busy and efficient hostel just off Queen Street with a lively atmosphere and stacks of local information plus a helpful travel agency and friendly bar downstairs. Four floors of ten-bunk dorms, four-shares and doubles are well equipped and fairly spacious. Dorms ❶, rooms ❸

Downtown 6 Constitution Hill ☎09/303 4768, ⓔbed@backpackers.co.nz. The smallest of Auckland's central backpackers, that's just changed hands, fills a couple of houses close to the city and mid-way to Parnell. It's homely in a ropey way with a small garden and fairly cramped four- and six-bunk dorms and double rooms. Dorms ❶, rooms ❷

The Fat Camel 38 Fort St ☎09/307 0181, ⓦwww.nomadsworld.com. With an emphasis on twins and doubles, though small dorms are also available, arranged in small flats with their own kitchens this is a solid hostel in the downtown region with its own bar and café. Dorms ❶, rooms ❷

Parnell

See map on p.103.

City Garden Lodge 25 St Georges Bay Rd ☎09/302 0880, ⓔcity-garden@computereb.co.nz. One of the city's friendliest backpackers in a spacious, well-organized villa surrounded by expansive lawns. For an extra dollar or two, the three- and five-person dorms have beds rather than bunks, and there are some lovely double and twin rooms. Dorms ❶, rooms ❷

International Backpackers 2 Churton St ☎ & ⓕ09/358 4584, ⓦwww.alansinternational.co.nz. Clean, peaceful hostel in a former YHA on a quiet street three minutes from Parnell with parking and a nice fenced garden. Dorms ❶, rooms ❷

Lantana Lodge 60 St Georges Bay Rd ☎09/373 4546. Small, spotlessly clean and friendly hostel with reasonable facilities and a homely feel. Dorms ❶, rooms ❷

Ponsonby

See map on p.107.

Brown Kiwi 7 Prosford St ☎09/378 0191, ⓦwww.brownkiwi.co.nz. Lovely little hostel in a restored Victorian villa right in the thick of the Ponsonby café zone but with a peaceful patio and tiny garden at the back. All the usual facilities and a relaxing atmosphere. Daytime parking is poor but it's easily accessible by the Link bus. Dorms ❶, rooms ❸

Uenuku (Rainbow) Lodge 217 Ponsonby Rd ☎09/378 8990, ⓦwww.uenuku.co.nz. Set back from the main road, this warren of an old boarding house is excellently located on the Link bus route and is gradually being converted into a comfortable, good-value hostel. Run by the same team as *Brown Kiwi*. Dorms ❶, rooms ❷–❸

Mount Eden

See map on p.111.

Bamber House 22 View Rd ☎ & ⓕ09/623 4267, ⓦwww.hostelbackpacker.com. Well-run, spacious and very clean hostel with all the facilities you could ask for, lawns right around the house and a great outdoor pool. The cheapest beds are in a cramped bunkhouse outside, but there are better dorms inside and well-priced doubles. Catch buses #255–258, #265 or #267 from Queen St just up from Victoria St. Dorms ❶, rooms ❷

Oaklands Lodge 5a Oaklands Rd ☎ & ⓕ09/638 6545, ⓦwww.oaklands.co.nz. Former YHA in a big old house right by Mount Eden shops. Beds come in large dorms, four-shares and doubles. Catch buses #274, #275 or #277 from Customs St East, downtown. Dorms ❶, rooms ❷

Campsites and motor parks

You'd have to travel a long way to find anywhere genuinely attractive to pitch a **tent**, but there are numerous well-equipped motor camps within the city limits which are fine for **campervans** and often have bargain **cabins**. However, without your own vehicle, you'll find yourself spending a lot of time and money on buses, the costs outweighing any saving you may make over staying in town.

Avondale Motor Park 46 Bollard Ave, Avondale ☎0800/100 542 & 09/828 7228, ⓦwww.aucklandmotorpark.co.nz. Restful and fairly central site 6km southwest of the city and accessible by buses #210–29 from Victoria St. Camping $10, on-site vans ❷, cabins & flats ❸

North Shore Motels & Top 10 Holiday Park 52 Northcote Rd, Takapuna ☎0508/909 090 &

09/418 2578, ⓦ www.nsmotels.co.nz. Well-appointed site on the North Shore, just off the northern motorway, with indoor swimming pool and extensive barbecue areas. Catch Stagecoach buses #921 and #922 from the corner of Victoria and Hobson streets. Camping $30 per site, cabins (❸) & motel units (❻).

Remuera Motor Lodge and Inner City Camping Ground 16 Minto Rd ☎ 09/524 5126 & 0508/244244, ✉ remlodge@ihug.co.nz. About the most central, convenient and appealing site, 6km east of the city in a quiet, sylvan residential area. There's even a swimming pool. Buses #625,

#645 and #655 from Customs St East will get you here. Camping $13, kitchen cabins & motel units ❹

Takapuna Beach Holiday Park 22 The Promenade, Takapuna ☎ & ⒻⒻ 09/489 7909, ⓦ takapunabeach.kiwiholidaypark.com. Beachside caravan park on the North Shore overlooking Rangitoto and within five minutes' walk of the Takapuna shops and restaurants. Stagecoach buses numbered in the 800s from the corner of Victoria and Hobson streets pass nearby. Camping $12, cabins & on-site vans ❷, en-suite cabins ❸, motel units ❺

The City Centre and the suburbs

Auckland's city centre clings to the southern shores of the **Waitemata Harbour**, with downbeat **Queen Street**, the main drag, striking south through a business district largely sustained by banks and insurance companies. In contrast, the city suburbs of Ponsonby, Parnell and Newmarket, now the subject of much redevelopment, have a relaxed, welcoming feel.

Queen Street meets the harbour at the Ferry Building, hub of ferry services to the North Shore, the maritime suburb of **Devonport** and to the islands of the Hauraki Gulf. Heading inland **Albert Park**, is wedged between the **University** and the **Auckland Art Gallery**, and halfway to **The Domain**, an extensive blanket of parkland that represents Auckland's premier green space, laid out around the city's most-visited attraction, the **Auckland Museum**. The Domain divides the city from the inner-eastern suburb of **Parnell**, ecclesiastical heart of the city with the **Cathedral**, one of Auckland's oldest churches and a couple of historical houses. To the east of Parnell, the harbourside **Tamaki Drive** runs past **Kelly Tarlton's Underwater World** to the city beaches of Mission Bay and St Heliers. West of the centre, the suburbs spread out beyond the reclaimed basin of Freeman's Bay to Auckland's most concentrated cluster of superb restaurants and cafés along **Ponsonby Road**, and out to Western Springs, home to the **Auckland Zoo** and the transport museum commonly referred to by its abbreviated name, **MOTAT**. To the south of the centre two of Auckland's highest points, **Mount Eden** and **One Tree Hill** with its encircling **Cornwall Park**, provide wonderful vantage points for views of the city.

Aucklanders with time on their hands and a penchant for thundering breakers leave the stresses of city behind and head to the surf **beaches** of the West Coast but there are local spots for a more impulsive dip, particularly compact and often-crowded coves along **Tamaki Drive** and the more expansive strands on the North Shore near **Takapuna**.

Downtown

Auckland's central city street names represent a roll call of prime movers in New Zealand's early European history. The city's backbone, Queen Street, along with attendant royal acolytes, Victoria and Albert streets, forms a central grid bedded with thoroughfares commemorating the country's first Governor-General, William Hobson; Willoughby Shortland, New Zealand's first colonial secretary; and William Symonds, who chivvied along isthmus Maori chiefs reluctant to sign the Treaty of Waitangi.

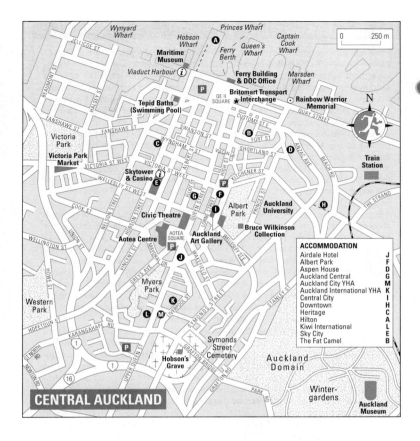

The central business district butts up against the **Waitemata Harbour**, formerly divorced from the city by docks, but now reconnected through the development of the **Maritime Museum** and the adjacent waterside rejuvenation of **Viaduct Harbour** and Princes Wharf, essentially flashy restaurants and residential accommodation around a marina.

There's little of abiding interest right in the city centre except for the **Auckland Art Gallery**, the country's foremost showcase for fine art. The highbrow theme continues to the east at the excellent **Auckland Museum**, packed with superb Maori and Pacific Island artefacts, which dominates **The Domain**, a vast swathe of trees and lawns sweeping down towards the harbour.

The waterfront

Auckland's waterfront is dominated by the Neoclassical 1912 **Ferry Building**, which is still the hub of the Waitemata Harbour ferry services, though the chaotic bustle of the days before the construction of the harbour bridge is now a distant memory. Nonetheless, there's a constant ebb and flow of commuters and sightseers boarding speedy catamarans to Devonport and Rangitoto, Waiheke and Great Barrier islands.

For a few glorious days in May 1995 **yacht-racing** eclipsed rugby as New Zealand's premier sport as **Peter Blake**, team captain of the *Black Magic* boat, wrested yacht-ing's most valuable prize, the America's Cup, from the Americans (for only the second time in the race's 144-year history). Blake was feted as a national hero and the crew were welcomed down Queen Street with a ticker-tape parade; the scenes repeated in March 2000 as New Zealand became the first nation (apart from the United States) to successfully defend the America's Cup.

The cup was first contested as the **One Hundred Guinea Cup**, with fifteen British boats and one American racing to circumnavigate the Isle of Wight, off the south coast of England, as part of imperial Britain's Great Exhibition in 1851. The schooner *America* romped away with the trophy and the New York Yacht Club held on to it through 23 defences, during which time the race became a battlefield for some of the world's most experienced crews and a proving ground for the latest boat designs, using space-age composite materials.

Finally, in 1983, the Perth Yacht Club's controversial winged-keel **Australia II** showed that the Americans didn't have an inalienable right to the silverware. The America's Cup became something of a holy grail for New Zealanders, and when everything finally came together in 1995, Kiwis went nuts. Peter Blake declared that the red socks he had been wearing were his lucky charm, and the entire nation – Prime Minister Jim Bolger and Governor-General Catherine Tizard included – donned red socks, the proceeds of sales going to fund the *Black Magic* crew, who went on to trounce the Americans five–nil in the final series. Peter Blake subse-quently retired from racing to pursue environmental concerns and, sadly, in late 2001, was killed by thieves in the Brazilian Amazon.

The victory in the seas off San Diego earned New Zealand the right to defend the trophy on home turf, in what was to be a five-month jibe-fest through the summer of 1999–2000. A scruffy fishing area known as **Viaduct Harbour** was given a com-plete makeover with the construction of new yacht berths, several apartment blocks going up, and dozens of flash restaurants opening. It didn't come without contro-versy and **Maori** groups with claims to the development sites struggled to get some remuneration from the event. For one disgruntled Maori, things came to a head in February 1997 when, driven by frustration, he smashed the cup – then on display in the Royal New Zealand Yacht Squadron's clubhouse – with a sledge hammer.

Nonetheless, by November 1999 half the world's multi-million-dollar super-yachts were filling the berths and the frenetic activity around the Viaduct Harbour had become the buzz of the nation. Meanwhile on the waters of the **Hauraki Gulf**, a dozen overseas challengers (five from the United States alone) competed to find who would win the **Louis Vuitton Cup**, and with it the right to challenge the Kiwi defender. The relatively inexperienced (but well-funded) Italian *Prada* team even-tually saw off such seasoned competition as Dennis Connor's *Stars and Stripes*. They did it with such grace and style that they gained a place in the hearts of Kiwis, who even hoisted the Italian flag next to the New Zealand ensign on the har-bour bridge. There was no love lost at sea, however, and when *Prada* took on the "black boat" of Russell Coutts' Team New Zealand they were trounced 5–0 in the best of nine series.

The Waitemata Harbour was once again host to the America's Cup in the summer of 2002–2003, developers and restaurant owners rubbed their hands with glee while even greater development went on around the harbour area, however things did not go according to plan. Internal politics and huge cash offers saw most of the original New Zealand team move to rival syndicates and one of those syndicates; the Swiss team, in *Alinghi*, drubbed the New Zealanders 5-0 and made off with the cup, which they will defend off the coast of Valencia, Spain. A run down on the history of the cup and its New Zealand connections can be found at ⓦ www.americascup.co.nz.

Since the 1999-2000 America's Cup challenge, the majority of the waterfront activity has shifted a couple of hundred metres west to Viaduct Harbour, where the re-paved wharves are strung with elegant lighting and lined by the outdoor seating of new restaurants. The area can seem a little too shiny and pleased with itself, but is fine for a stroll past the super-yachts moored alongside, maybe signing up for one of the harbour cruises, and idling away the afternoon over a cappuccino or chardonnay.

The only specific sight is the **National Maritime Museum**, Viaduct Harbour, on the corner of Quay Street and Hobson Street (daily: Nov–Easter 9am–6pm; Easter–Oct 9am–5pm; $12; Ⓦ www.nzmaritime.org), which pays homage to the maritime history of an island nation reliant on the sea for colonization, trade and sport. The short orientational, *Te Waka* video illustrates an imagined Maori migration voyage setting the scene for a display of outrigger and double-hulled canoes from all over the South Pacific. There's a huge variety of designs employed for fishing, lagoon sailing and ocean voyaging – the last represented by the huge 23m-long *Taratai*, which carried New Zealand photographer and writer James Siers and a crew of thirteen over 2400km from Kiribati to Fiji in 1976. Made entirely from traditional materials and propelled by an oceanic lateen sail, its intriguing method of operation is neatly demonstrated on a rig nearby. The creaking and rolling innards of a migrant ship and displays on New Zealand's coastal traders and whalers lead on to a collection of just about every class of yacht, culminating in the devotional exhibits on yacht racing – in particular, comprehensive coverage of the **America's Cup** (see opposite), its history and detailed scale replicas of key entrants. Other highlights include a very early example of the Hamilton Jetboat, which was designed for shallow, braided Canterbury rivers, a replica of a classic 1950s holiday *bach* and milk bar, with great archival film footage adding to the nostalgic flavour and the Edmiston Gallery, full of some excellent maritime art.

There are interesting guided tours (usually Mon–Fri 11am, Sat 11am or 2pm; free), and the possibility of a one hour **cruise** on the *Ted Ashby* (Tues, Thurs, Sat & Sun noon & 2pm; $15, $19 including museum entry), a 1990s replica of one of the traditional flat-bottomed, ketch-rigged scows that once worked the North Island tidal waterways.

If you want a focus to a waterfront stroll, follow the red fence from the Ferry Building along the redeveloped waterfront about 500m, past the Captain Cook and Marsden wharfs to the memorial plaque for the Rainbow Warrior, see p.201.

The city centre

The windswept **Queen Elizabeth II Square**, opposite the Ferry Building, makes an inauspicious introduction to the city centre, opposite the striking new Britomart transport interchange in the Neoclassical 1910 former post office. South, across Customs Street, lies the city's main axis, **Queen Street**, an inelegant canyon lined by shops, banks and offices threaded by arcades – notably Queen's Arcade and The Strand Arcade – running through to the parallel High, Lorne and Elliot streets. The foot of Queen Street once had a three-hundred-metre-long wharf extending out to deep water, but progressive reclamation has shifted the shoreline away from Fort Street (originally Fore Street), which, in keeping with its port-of-call past, is the downtown's red-light district. Jean Batten Place runs south off Fort Street, becoming **High Street**, which is energized by bookshops and trendy clothes shops, and is always the liveliest section of the central city. Most of the action happens around the junction with the former blacksmithing street of **Vulcan Lane**, now characterized by bars and swanky stores.

The city centre is dominated by the concrete **Skytower**, on the corner of Victoria Street and Federal Street (Sun–Thurs 8.30am–11pm, Fri & Sat 8.30am–midnight; $15 ($10 for YHA members), plus an extra $3 for upper viewing deck), built in the mid-1990s as a potent symbol for the city in the run-up to the new millennium. At 328m, it is New Zealand's tallest structure (just pipping the Eiffel Tower and Sydney's Centrepoint), and has the obligatory observation decks (192m and 220m) with a café and stupendous views right over the city and Hauraki Gulf. The tower has recently become the focus of a couple of **adventure activities** (see p.115) and you may see SkyJump practitioners hurtling through the air from the observation area.

The tower sprouts from **Sky City Casino**, a relative newcomer to the city that has managed to carve a niche for itself in a country where temperance is still revered. If you can demonstrate that you're over eighteen and eschew shorts, singlets and thongs (flip-flops), you can get on to a gaming floor awash in deep blue and green decor that's supposed to represent Polynesian demi-god Maui's underwater realm. All the usual distractions aimed at separating you from your money are here, along with cafés, bars, a high-roller room and *Alto Casino and Bar* for those who prefer the jacket-and-tie approach. Learner classes are held most mornings.

One of Queen Street's few buildings of any distinction is the Art Nouveau **Civic Theatre**, on the corner of Wellesley Street. The talk of the town when it opened in 1929, the management went as far as to import a small Indian boy from Fiji to complement the ornate Moghul-style decor. After renovation it reopened in its full splendour complete with a star-strewn artificial sky and an ornate proscenium arch with flanking lions, their eyes blazing red. It's well worth a look, but unless you happen to strike one of the infrequent open days, the only way to get inside is to see a performance (see p.126).

Bang next door, but architecturally miles away, is a chunky post-modern form (previously open as an Imax cinema). Adding little to the block's recent rejuvenation, it flanks **Aotea Square**, which is overlooked on its other sides by the recently refurbished Town Hall and the city's foremost concert hall, the **Aotea Centre**, which opened in a blaze of glory in 1990, with Kiri Te Kanawa honouring a longstanding promise to perform on the inaugural night. On Friday and Saturday, the arts, crafts, vintage clothing, jewellery and Pasifika stalls of the **Aotea Square Markets** bring the square to life and attempt to relieve visitors of a few tourist dollars.

The Art Gallery and Albert Park

Moving east of Queen Street, Wellesley Street runs up to the **Auckland Art Gallery** (Ⓦ www.aucklandartgallery.govt.nz) which comes in two parts – one predominantly traditional, the other resolutely contemporary – which jointly make up the world's most important collection of Kiwi art. The fee for any exhibition in the Heritage Gallery that contains mainly New Zealand works is waived on Monday, as is the entry fee to the New Gallery.

The Heritage Gallery

The elaborate mock-French **Heritage Gallery**, on the corner of Wellesley Street and Kitchener Street (daily 10am–5pm; $7, special exhibitions $5–12; free guided tours daily at 2pm; infoline Ⓣ09/307 7700), includes a small but respectable collection of quality works by internationally renowned artists – Brueghel, Corot, Maillol, Liechtenstein – but this is essentially a place to come to appreciate New Zealand art. Works change frequently, but you can expect to find original drawings by the artists on James Cook's expeditions setting the

△ Aotea Square

scene for overwrought and often crass oils depicting Maori migrations. These romantic and idealized images of Maori life seen through European eyes frequently show composite scenes that could never have happened, contributing to a mythical view that persisted for decades. Two works show contrasting but equally misleading views: Kennett Watkins' 1912 *The Legend of the Voyage to New Zealand*, with its plump, happy natives on a still lagoon; and Charles Goldie's 1898 *The Arrival of the Maoris in New Zealand*, modelled on Géricault's *Raft of the Medusa* and showing starving, frightened voyagers battling tempestuous seas.

Much of the rest of the early collection is devoted to works by two of the country's most loved artists – both highly respected by Maori as among the few to accurately portray their ancestors. Bohemian immigrant **Gottfried Lindauer** emigrated to New Zealand in 1873 and spent his later years painting lifelike, almost documentary, portraits of *rangatira* (chiefs) and high-born Maori men and women, in the mistaken belief that the Maori people were about to become extinct. In the early part of the twentieth century, **Charles F. Goldie** became New Zealand's resident "old master" and earned international recognition for his more emotional portraits of elderly Maori subjects regally showing off their traditional tattoos, or *moko*, though they were in fact often painted from photographs (sometimes after the subject's death). Contemporary landscape painters largely projected their European visions of beauty onto New Zealand landscapes, reducing vibrant visions of shimmering colour into subdued scenes reminiscent of English parkland, drab north European seas and Swiss Alps. It took half a century for more representative images to become the norm – an evolutionary process that continued into the 1960s and 1970s, when many works betray an almost cartoon-like quality, with heavily delineated spaces daubed in shocking colours. Look out for works by **Rita Angus**, renowned for her images of Central Otago in the 1940s, **Tony Fomison** (1939–90), painter of one of the gallery's most expensive works, *Study of Holbein's "Dead Christ"*. Completed in 1973, it's typical of his later, more obsessive period, combining the artist's passion for art history and his preoccupation with mortality. Also worth a look are the works of **Russell Clark** (1905–1966) who painted scenes from everyday working life.

The New Gallery and Albert Park

Across the street, the **New Gallery**, on the corner of Wellesley Street and Lorne Street (daily 10am–5pm; $7 for each section), has two light and spacious floors, signalling its more youthful and approachable nature. The exhibitions and site-specific installations by predominantly New Zealand, and particularly Maori, artists vary constantly. One name to look out for is **Colin McCahon**, who died in 1987, but whose fascination with the power and beauty of New Zealand landscape informs so much recent Kiwi art; indeed, there is a whole room set aside for his work. Others, such as **Gordon Walters**, draw their inspiration from Maori iconography, in Walters' case controversially employing vibrant, graphic representations of traditional Maori symbols – spirals, fernroot emblems and stylized human forms (for more on Maori design, see "Maoritanga" in Contexts).

The gallery's works spill outside, with George Rickey's stainless-steel 1984 *Double L Gyratory* and Neil Dawson's monumental semicircular *Throwback* sculpture creeping into **Albert Park**. These formal Victorian-style gardens spread uphill to the university, and are generally thronged with sunbathing students and office workers. Originally the site of a Maori *pa*, the land was successively conscripted into service as Albert Barracks in the 1840s and 1850s, and then as a labyrinthine network of air-raid shelters during World War II, before relaxing into its current incarnation as peaceful parkland. It comes filled with a century's worth of memorials, a floral clock, some beautiful oaks and Morton Bay Fig trees and the 1882 former gatekeeper's cottage containing the **Bruce Wilkinson Collection** (daily 10am–4pm; free), a small display of ornate clocks and figurines amassed by an Auckland businessman and donated to the city.

Karangahape Road

At its southern end, Queen Street climbs to the ridge-top **Karangahape Road**, universally known as K' Road, formerly an uptown residential area for prosperous nineteenth-century merchants, and long associated with Auckland's Polynesian community. For twenty years now, planners have hailed a mainstream shopping renaissance but K' Road remains determinedly niche, though development has headed up from the waterfront and is now taking over the Queen-Street-end of K' Road. Groovy cafés, music shops specializing in vinyl, and clothes shops selling budget designer garb and clubbing gear rub shoulders with colourful shops run by recently arrived East and South Asians. Pacific culture remains strong as witnesses by a couple of agents specializing in Pacific Island travel, the Niuean consulate, a Samoan Church and several shops selling island-print fabrics. There are no specific sights, but you can easily pass an afternoon browsing the shops and eating in budget ethnic restaurants.

K' Road is much loved by those who know it and much maligned, even feared, by those who don't – chiefly on account of the notoriety associated with its western end, a two-hundred-metre-long corridor of massage parlours, strip clubs and gay cruising clubs. It is certainly one of the seedier parts of town, but the raunchy places are interspersed with more mainstream nightclubs and there is always a vibrant feel that is seldom intimidating, though the usual precautions should be exercised at night.

Further east, K' Road crosses Symonds Street by the little-known and somewhat neglected **Symonds Street Cemetery**, one of Auckland's earliest burial grounds, with allocations for Jewish, Presbyterian, Wesleyan, Roman Catholic and Anglican faiths – the last two areas largely destroyed by the motorway cut through Grafton Gully in the 1960s. A patch of deciduous woodland shades the grave of New Zealand's first Governor, William Hobson (tucked away on the eastern side of Symonds Street almost under the vast concrete span of Grafton Bridge).

The Domain

Grafton Gully separates the city centre from **The Domain**, a vast swathe of semi-formal gardens draped over the low, irregular profile of an extinct volcano known to Maori as Pukekawa or "hill of bitter memories", a reference to the bloodshed of ancient inter-tribal fighting. In the 1840s, when Auckland was the national capital, Governor Grey set aside the core of The Domain as the city's first park, and it remains the finest, furnished with all the obligatory mid-nineteenth-century accoutrements: a band rotunda, phoenix palms, formal flower beds and spacious lawns. In summer, the scores of rugby pitches metamorphose into cricket ovals and softball diamonds, and every few weeks marquees and stages are erected in the crater's shallow amphitheatre for outdoor musical extravaganzas.

The Domain's volcanic spring was one of Auckland's original water sources. It was used to farm the country's first rainbow trout in 1884, and by the Auckland Acclimatization Society to grow European plants, thereby promoting the rapid

Europeanization of the New Zealand countryside. The spirit of this enterprise lingers on in the **Winter Gardens** (Nov–March Mon–Sat 9am–5.30pm, Sun 9am–7.30pm; April–Oct daily 9am–4.30pm; free), a shallow fishpond in a formal sunken courtyard flanked by two elaborate barrel-roofed glasshouses – one temperate, the other heated to mimic tropical climes – filled with neatly tended botanical specimens. Next door, a former scoria quarry has been transformed into the **Fernz Fernery** (same hours; free), a verdant dell with over a hundred types of fern in dry, intermediate and wet habitats.

Auckland Museum

The highest point on the domain is crowned by the imposing Greco-Roman-style **Auckland Museum** (Te Papa Whakahiku; daily 10am–5pm; $5 donation expected and valid for repeated entry on one day; @www.akmuseum.org.nz). Built as a World War I memorial in 1929, the names of World War II battles were duly added around the outer walls. The contents of Auckland's original city museum were moved here and the holdings expanded to form one of the world's finest collections of Maori and Pacific art. After a major revamp in the late 1990s the museum remains traditional in its approach, but now thoroughly contemporary in its execution, with each of the three floors taking on an individual identity – the people (ground), the place (middle), and New Zealand at War (top). Kids are catered for with the **Children's Discovery Centre** on the middle floor and if you're interested in buying Maori crafts while you're in New Zealand, check out the high-quality traditional and contemporary work in the museum **shop**. To round off the experience, head along to the 45-minute **Manaia cultural performance** (11am, noon & 1.30pm; $15) of song and dance, heralded by a conch-blast echoing through the building.

Auckland Museum is on the route of the Coast-to-Coast Walkway and city tour **buses**, and both the Link bus and regular buses #645 and #655 stop on Parnell Road, five minutes' walk away.

Ground Floor

Turn left as you enter the museum to reach the **Pacific Lifeways** room, dominated by a simple yet majestic, breadfruit-wood statue from the Caroline Islands depicting **Kave**, Polynesia's malevolent and highest-ranked female deity whose menace is barely hinted at in this serene form. In the main, this room concentrates on the daily life of Pacific peoples, characterized by an elegant vessel for holding kava (a mildly narcotic drink brewed from roots), polished with years of use; stunning tooth and shell necklaces; New Guinean and Solomon Island equipment for preparing betel nuts for chewing; and fine examples of patterned tapa cloth, made from the bark of the mulberry tree. If you're lucky they may even have folk sitting on rush mats and demonstrating the processes involved.

This leads on to **He Taonga Maori**, the extensive Maori collection that's the highlight of the ground floor collection. The transition from purely Polynesian motifs to an identifiably Maori style is exemplified in the **Kaitaia Carving**, a two-and-a-half-metre-wide totara carving thought to have been designed for a ceremonial gateway – guarded by the central goblin-like figure with sweeping arms that stretch out to become lizard forms at their extremities: Polynesian in style but Maori in concept. It was found around 1920 near Kaitaia and is estimated to date from the twelfth or thirteenth century, predating most Maori art so far discovered.

As traditional Maori villages started to disappear towards the end of the nineteenth century, some of the best examples of carved panels, meeting houses and food stores were rescued. Many are currently displayed here, though some of the exhibits are claimed by Maori groups throughout the country and may ultimately be returned to their traditional owners. The Taonga Maori is dominated by **Hotunui**, a large and wonderfully restored carved meeting house (*whare whakairo*), built near Thames in 1878, late enough to have a corrugated iron rather than rush roof, and re-erected here in 1929. Once again the craftsmanship is superb; the house's exterior is all grotesque faces, lolling tongues and glistening paua-shell eyes, while the interior is lined with wonderful geometric *tukutuku* panels. Outside is the intricately carved prow and stern-piece of **Te Toki a Tapiri**, a 25m-long war canoe (*waka taua*), the only surviving specimen from the pre-European era. Designed to seat a hundred warriors, it was hewn from a single totara log near Wairoa in Hawke's Bay and donated to the museum in 1885. Elsewhere is more magnificent work in the shape of storehouses and stand-alone statues, much of it by the renowned Te Arawa carvers from the Rotorua district. Several were emasculated by prudish Victorians.

Beyond the canoe you're into the main Pacific Island collection, known as **Pacific Masterpieces**, filled with exquisite Polynesian, Melanesian and Micronesian works. Look out for the shell-inlaid ceremonial food bowl from the Solomon Islands; ceremonial clubs; and a wonderfully resonant slit-gong from Vanuatu. The textiles are fabulous too with designs far more varied than you'd expect considering the limited raw materials: the Hawaiian red feather cloak is especially fine.

A couple of smaller but no less interesting galleries are tucked around the back: **Wild Child**, which explores the more entertaining aspects of growing up in the young colony; and **City**, covering how Auckland has grown from a tiny trading post to a million-strong city in the space of two long lifetimes.

Middle Floor

The middle floor of the museum comprises the **natural history galleries**, an unusual combination of modern thematic displays and stuffed birds in cases. It delineates the progress from the "Big Bang" through an exploration of plate tectonics and the break up of Gondwanaland, the geology and seismology of New Zealand and its flora and fauna. Dinosaur skeletons allude to their presence here until 65 million years ago, something scientists had discounted until fairly recently when fossils started turning up. Displays like the three-metre Giant Moa can't be missed, but there's a lot of stuff virtually hidden so be prepared to take your time. Armed with the knowledge of how New Zealand came to be, you proceed to a series of ecosystems such as a reconstruction of a cave in Waitomo complete with stuffed beasts and live animals in tanks and aquariums. Move on to a three-storey-high model of a kauri complete with lighting and sound that compresses a day of birdsong and animal chatter into a few minutes. The live animal theme follows through to the sealife section where you can walk across a tank full of crabs before learning more about how introduced species have affected New Zealand's unique environment.

Top Floor

A multi-levelled approach is used on the top floor in the **Scars on the Heart** exhibition, an emotional exploration of how New Zealanders' involvement in war has helped shape national identity. At any time you are able to divert from the main timeline and explore specific topics in more detail via interactive displays with personal accounts of the troops' experiences and the responses of those back home. Artefacts aren't completely ignored, but most of the uniforms, arms and memorabilia are neatly worked into the greater fabric of the exhibition, with the exception of the boldly displayed armoury. You enter through a slightly incongruous mock-up of an 1860s Auckland street that sets the scene for the New Zealand Wars, interpreted from both Maori and *pakeha* perspectives. World War I gets extensive coverage, particularly the Gallipoli campaign in Turkey, when botched leadership led to a massacre of ANZAC – Australian and New Zealand Army Corps – troops in the trenches. Powerful visuals and rousing martial music accompany newsreel footage of the Pacific campaigns of World War II, and finally New Zealand's foray into Vietnam is documented.

East of the city centre

The Auckland Domain separates the city from the fashionable inner suburbs of **Parnell** and **Newmarket**, the former an established, moneyed district of restaurants, boutiques and galleries with a modest line in churches and historical houses. To the east lies Auckland's prime waterfront, traced by **Tamaki Drive**, a twisting thoroughfare that skirts eight kilometres of some of Auckland's most popular city beaches – **Mission Bay**, Kohimarama and **St Heliers** – and some of the city's most expensive real estate. Throughout the summer it is the favoured hangout of roller-bladers and recreational cyclists, all jockeying for position. **Kelly Tarlton's Underwater World** is the only specific sight, but the harbour views out to Rangitoto and the Hauraki Gulf are excellent both from shore level and from a couple of headland viewpoints. The gentle hills behind are dotted with the secluded mansions of leafy **Remuera**, Auckland's old-money suburb. Further east you're well into the suburban heartland of Panmure, Pakuranga and the former "fencible" settlement of **Howick**.

Parnell

Forty years ago, few would have predicted the transformation of run-down **Parnell**, 2km east of Queen Street, into one of New Zealand's most sought-after addresses with restored kauri villas clamouring around the fashionable shops of the main thoroughfare, Parnell Road.

In fact, the district narrowly escaped the high-rise-concrete fate of many an inner-city suburb in the mid-1960s. Just as the bulldozers were closing in on the quaint but dilapidated shops and houses, eccentric dreamer **Les Harvey** managed to raise enough money to buy the properties, whisking them from under the developers' noses. In the guise of the now somewhat dated, ersatz-Victorian **Parnell Village**, the area blossomed, with rent from the shops and restaurants funding much-needed restoration. Meanwhile, Harvey successfully campaigned against New Zealand's strict trading laws, with the result that during the 1970s and much of the 1980s Parnell was the only place in Auckland where you could shop on a Saturday. Parnell Road soon established an enviable reputation for chic clothes shops, swanky restaurants and private art galleries.

Even if you're not buying, Parnell makes an appealing place to spend half a day browsing, sipping lattes at pavement cafés and exploring some of the marks left by the area's long history. At the southern end of Parnell Road stands one of the world's largest wooden churches, the **Cathedral Church of St Mary** (Mon–Sat 10am–4pm, Sun 1–5pm; free), built from native timbers in 1886. Inside, the most interesting feature is a series of photos taken on the dramatic day in 1984 when the church was rolled from its original site across Parnell Road to join its more modern (and more messy) kin, the **Auckland Cathedral of the Holy Trinity** (same hours; free). The original Gothic chancel was started in 1959 then left half-finished until the late 1980s, when an airy

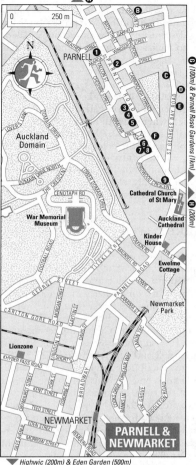

ACCOMMODATION		CAFÉS, RESTAURANTS & BARS	
Ascot	G	Antoine's	8
Chalet Chevron	H	Chocolate Boutique	7
City Garden Lodge	E	Di Mare	3
International Backpackers	B	Iguaçu	5
Kingsgate Parnell	A	Java Room	6
Lantana Lodge	C	Pandoro	9
Parnell Inn	F	Portofino	2
St Georges Bay Lodge	D	Strawberry Alarm Clock	1
		Zucchero	4

▼ Highwic (200m) & Eden Garden (500m)

nave with a Swiss chalet-style roof was grafted on, supposedly in imitation of the older church alongside. The result is shambolic. Nevertheless, it is worth admiring the new stained-glass windows; the bold and bright side panels symbolize Maori and Pakeha contributions to society. The Maori window has sea creatures frolicking in ribbed waves, while on the shore a basket of kumara is surrounded by shellfish, native birds and flowers. European influence is seen through Cook's arrival and the settlement that followed in his footsteps: the city skyline, sunbathing citizens on St Heliers Beach and cars careering along Tamaki Drive.

The Gothic flourishes of the nineteenth-century church show the influence of New Zealand's prominent missionary bishop, George Selwyn. With his favoured architect, Frederick Thatcher, Selwyn left behind a trail of trademark wooden **"Selwyn" churches**, distinguished by vertical timber battens - examples include St Stephen's Chapel, down the hill at Judges Bay (see p.104) and All Saints' at Howick (see p.105). In 1857, Selwyn commissioned Thatcher to build the nearby **Kinder House**, at 2 Ayr St (Tues–Sun 11am–3pm; $2), for the headmaster of the new grammar school – a post filled by John Kinder, an accomplished watercolourist and documentary photographer. Built of rough-hewn Rangitoto volcanic rock, the house contains some interesting photos and reproductions of Kinder's paintings of nineteenth-century New Zealand. Enthusiastic volunteers will flesh out the details both here and down the road at **Ewelme Cottage**, 14 Ayr St (Fri–Sun 10.30am–noon & 1–4.30pm; $3, $10 joint ticket with Highwic in Newmarket and Alberton; ☎09/379 0202), a pioneer kauri house built as a family home in 1864 for the wonderfully named Howick clergyman Vicesimus Lush, who wanted his sons to live close to the grammar school. The appeal of the place lies not so much in the house itself but in its contents: the furniture, fittings and possessions have been left just as they were when Lush's descendants finally moved out in 1968, the family heirlooms betraying a desire to replicate the home comforts of their native Oxfordshire.

Judges Bay and Newmarket

From the cathedral, you can continue south to Newmarket (see below) or north down Gladstone Road to Dove-Myer Robinson Park and the **Parnell Rose Gardens** (unrestricted entry; free), where five thousand bushes are at their glorious best from October to April. The park sweeps from the rose beds down to **Judges Bay**, named for three officers of the colony's Supreme Court who lived here from 1841, commuting to the courts on Symonds Street by rowboat. Bishop Selwyn used to stay with his friend, the Chief Justice William Martin, and had **St Stephen's Chapel** (usually closed) built nearby on a prominent knoll overlooking the harbour; the waterside Judges Bay Road leads to the open-air saltwater Parnell Baths.

The southern continuation of Parnell Road runs into Broadway, the main drag through fashion-conscious **NEWMARKET**, on the eastern flanks of Mount Eden which has several excellent restaurants and numerous motels. Specific sights are few, though you may be tempted by **Lionzone**, 380 Khyber Pass Road (tours daily 9.30am, 12.15pm & 3pm; bookings ☎09/358 8366, ⓦwww .lionzone.co.nz; $15), a highly self-promotional introduction to New Zealand's largest brewery involving a historical perspective on beer making, a look at the packing lines and a chance to sample the product. It's better than your average brewery tour, but at almost two hours it's a long-winded way to get a beer.

If you are staying over this way consider visiting the Gothic timber mansion of **Highwic**, 40 Gillies Ave (Wed–Sun 10.30am–noon & 1–4.30pm; $5, $10 joint ticket with Ewelme Cottage in Parnell and Alberton; ☎09/524 5729), built as a "city" property by a wealthy rural auctioneer and landowner in 1862. The estate, complete with its outbuildings and servants' quarters, gives a fair indication of the contrasting lives of the time. From here it's a short walk to **Eden Garden**, 24 Omana Ave (daily 9am–4.30pm; $5; ⓦwww .edengarden.co.nz), a verdant enclave created in a former quarry and tended by volunteers. There's year-round interest with a little of everything from water-gardens, cacti and proteas to Australasia's largest and most varied collection of camellias, in full bloom from April to October.

Along the Tamaki Drive waterfront

Quay Street runs east from the foot of Queen Street, soon becoming **Tamaki Drive**, which separates Waitemata Harbour from Judges Bay. Crossing the causeway to Okahu Bay brings you to one of the city's foremost attractions, **Kelly Tarlton's Underwater World and Antarctic Encounter**, 23 Tamaki Drive (ⓦwww.kellytarltons.co.nz; daily: Nov–Feb 9am–9pm; March–Oct 9am–6pm; $25). City tour **buses** and Stagecoach buses numbered #74 to 76 all stop outside.

Underwater World was the brainchild of Kiwi diver, treasure hunter and salvage expert, Kelly Tarlton, who wanted to share the undersea wonders off New Zealand's shores with the non-diving public. Having failed to secure a location in his home town of Paihia in the Bay of Islands, he settled on these huge tanks which, from 1910 until 1961, flushed the city's effluent into Waitemata Harbour on the outgoing tides. Opened in 1985, the aquarium pioneered walk-through acrylic tunnels, a novelty which lured 100,000 visitors in the seven weeks before Tarlton's untimely death from a heart attack at the age of 47. A moving walkway glides you through two tanks, both sculpted into the gnarled rock walls: the first is dominated by flowing kelp beds, colourful reef fish and twisting eels; the second with graceful rays and smallish sharks, all appearing alarmingly close in the crystal-clear water. You can step off the walkway for closer inspection at any time.

The remaining tanks have since been converted into the **Antarctic Encounter**, a synthesis of Antarctic history and penguin-atrium. An earnest video welcome from Sir Edmund Hillary introduces you to an accomplished replica of the prefabricated hut used by Robert Falcon Scott and his team on their ill-starred 1911–12 attempt to be the first to reach the South Pole and plant the British flag there; the original hut still stands at Scott Base, New Zealand's Antarctic foothold. Other Kiwi connections derive from the fact that Scott departed for the ice from Port Chalmers, near Dunedin, after first picking up a pianola donated by the people of Christchurch. Nor is a pianola the only unexpected thing you'll encounter in this capacious shelter: fittings include a fully-functional laboratory and a printing press – from which the *South Polar Times* rolled every few months throughout the three long years of the expedition. Contemporary footage and tales of their exploits add to the haunting atmosphere. Seamlessly moving from the sublime to the ridiculous, the **Snow Cat** is an inept attempt at a Disney-esque ride made bearable by the close-up views of King and Gentoo penguins shooting through the water and hopping around on fake icebergs.

A little further along Tamaki Drive, Hapimana Street leads up onto the grassy range of Bastion Point and the **M. J. Savage Memorial Park**, the nation's austere Art Deco homage to its first Labour prime minister, who ushered in the welfare state in the late 1930s. More recently, **Bastion Point** was the site of a seventeen-month stand-off between police and its traditional owners, the Ngati Whatua, over the subdivision of land for housing. The occupiers were finally removed in May 1977, but the stand helped to galvanize the land-rights movement, and paved the way for a significant change in government attitude. Within a decade, the Waitangi Tribunal recommended that the land be returned, along with a compensatory cash payment.

Bastion Point looks down on **Mission Bay**, the closest of the truly worthwhile city **beaches**, where a grassy waterside reserve is backed by an enticing row of cafés and restaurants. Swimming is best here close to high tide; at other times the water remains shallow a long way out. Similar conditions prevail at the sheltered beaches of **Kohimarama** and **St Heliers Bay**, both a short way further along Tamaki Drive, which finishes on a high note with excellent harbour views from **Achilles Point**.

Panmure and Howick

With your own transport it's easy enough to wind south from St Heliers through the low-rent suburbs of Glen Innes and Tamaki to **Panmure**, one of four **fencible settlements** – Panmure and Howick in the east, Onehunga and Otahuhu in the south – set up around the young capital as a defence against disgruntled Maori and ambitious French. So-called "fencibles" (pensioned British soldiers) were re-enlisted to defend these sites for seven years, in return for free passage and a block of land. Skirmishes were few, and the original shipments of men and their families formed the basis of small towns, all of which were subsequently engulfed by the Auckland conurbation. Panmure has relocated and restored **Stone Cottage**, at the corner of King's Road and Queen's Road (Fri & Sun 1–3pm; free), but the best place to get a sense of fencible life is at the

Howick Historica Village, Bells Road, Lloyd Elsmore Park (daily 10am–5pm, last admission 4pm; $9; ℡09/576 9506, Ⓦwww .fencible.org.nz), ten kilometres east of downtown through the numbing suburb of Pakuranga. Over thirty buildings dating from the 1840s and 1870s have been restored and re-sited from the four fencible settlements, and arranged in a believable village setting complete with a pond, a working blacksmith and market gardens. Volunteers role-play the diligently researched lives of real 1850s characters as they amble between the tents and makeshift Maori-style *raupo* huts used on arrival, the officers' cottages, hostelry, school hall and village shop.

The colonial village is one kilometre off Pakuranga Road, plied by all Howick & Eastern **buses**, which take about forty minutes to get out here from the Downtown Bus Terminal.

In the last fifteen years, droll Kiwis have dubbed the suburb of **Howick**, a further 5km east, "Chowick" – on account of its popularity with east Asians, who have constructed huge, florid mansions on former farmland to the south of town. For Aucklanders, these have become almost an attraction in their own right, mounting a challenge to Howick's more traditional sight, the distinctive, square-turreted **All Saints' Church**, the country's oldest active "Selwyn" church (see p.103), built in 1847.

West of the city centre

The suburbs of West Auckland developed later than their eastern counterparts, mainly because of their distance from the sea in the days when almost all travel was by ferry. The exceptions were the inner suburbs of Freeman's Bay, **Ponsonby** and Herne Bay, now enjoying renewed desirability for their proximity to the city and an unsurpassed array of the city's best restaurants, cafés and bars. Except for the flagging **Victoria Park Market**, sights are scarce until you get out to **Western Springs**, infant Auckland's major water source. The site of the springs is now part of **MOTAT**, a patchy transport and technology museum, and the small but go-ahead **Auckland Zoo**. To the south stands **Alberton**, once one of the city's grandest residences, but now just a brief distraction before you hit the wineries and West Coast beaches (see pp.130 & 131–134).

Freeman's Bay, Ponsonby and Herne Bay

Victoria Street climbs the ridge west of Queen Street and descends into **Freeman's Bay**, a flat basin long since reclaimed from the Waitemata Harbour to accommodate early saw-milling operations. The land is now given over to the popular rugby and cricket fields of Victoria Park, all overshadowed by the 38m-high chimney of Auckland's defunct incinerator, occupied since 1984 by **Victoria Park Market** (daily 9am–6pm; Ⓦwww.victoria-park-market.co.nz), a knot of stalls and restaurants. Despite having lost some of its more aspirational patrons to Ponsonby up the road, it's still an interesting enough place to mooch about for reasonably priced clothes and crafts, and a good place to break your walk out to Ponsonby. The **Link bus** passes on its way to Ponsonby, and city tour buses also stop here.

Early in Auckland's European history the areas around **Ponsonby** became fashionable neighbourhoods, only moving downmarket with the arrival of trams at the turn of the century. Inner-city living conditions deteriorated dramatically in the Depression of the 1930s, and the resulting low rents attracted large numbers of Pacific Islanders during the 1950s. Ponsonby took a bohemian turn in the Seventies and before long young professionals were moving in, restoring old houses and spending fistfuls of dollars in the cafés,

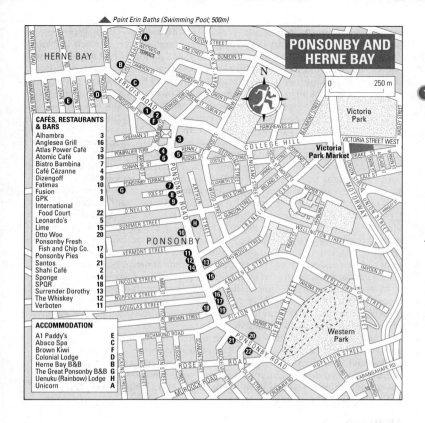

restaurants and boutiques along Ponsonby Road. The street itself may not be beautiful, but the people sure are: musicians, actors and media folk congregate to lunch, schmooze and be seen in the latest fashionable haunt. There's good reason to brave the poseurs, though, for some of New Zealand's classiest clothes shopping and eating.

Beyond St Mary's Bay and Ponsonby lies **Herne Bay**, which followed its neighbours' economic ebb and flow and now ranks as Auckland's most expensive suburb, the merchants' water-view villas fetching astronomical prices. There's little to see out this way, but you may find yourself staying here or indulging at one of the restaurants and cafés along Jervois Road.

Western Springs: MOTAT and the zoo

In the late nineteenth century the burgeoning city of Auckland, with its meagre supply of unreliable streams, was heavily reliant on the waters of **Western Springs**, 4km west of the city.

The area is now devoted to attractive parkland and two of Auckland's more significant sights. The **Museum of Transport, Technology and Social History** (MOTAT) on Great North Road (daily 10am–5pm; $10; infoline ℡09/846 7020) offers a trawl through New Zealand's vehicular and industrial past in a jumble of sheds and halls. It is worth visiting for two elements alone:

the restored Western Springs' pumphouse – where audio visual displays run through the 100-year history of the original engine – and the Pioneers of New Zealand – a massively improved exhibition concentrating on Richard Pearse (see p.648), the first man to achieve powered flight near Timaru, and Jean Batten, an internationally recognized air ace of the 1930s. These last two exhibitions contain a number of interesting bits and pieces but are fascinating primarily because of the extensive documentary audio-visual displays that focus not only on the pair's remarkable achievements but also on their personalities.

Admission includes entry to the **Sir Keith Park Memorial Site** (same hours), a kilometre away and linked to the main site by ancient rattling trams (every 10–20min; $2 return). This is one for aeroplane buffs, with a couple of dozen lovingly restored examples slotted into a hangar around the star attractions – one of the few surviving World War II Lancaster bombers, plus a double-decker flying boat, all decked out for dining in a more gracious age, which was used on Air New Zealand's South Pacific "Coral Route" until the mid-1960s.

The tram between the two sites also stops outside the **Auckland Zoo**, Motions Rd (daily 9.30am–5.30pm; $13), which has all but overturned the ancient regime of cages, replacing them with naturalistic habitats and captive breeding programmes. Although it's difficult to fathom why anyone would want to visit the zoo – it contains only ten percent of native New Zealand animals with the usual nocturnal kiwi house, a group of tuatara which form part of conservation work on offshore islands, and a large, walk-through aviary – it's a popular attraction, particularly for kids. The centrepiece is the trailblazing Pridelands development with lions, hippos, rhinos, giraffes, zebras and gazelles all roaming across mock savannah behind enclosing moats. Elsewhere, the "rainforest walk" threads its way among artificial islands inhabited by colonies of monkeys, you can walk through the wallaby enclosure unhindered, and the Sealion and Penguin Shores exhibit brings you face to face with these lovable animals, the former through underwater viewing windows.

Western Springs is reached by Stagecoach bus #045 from Custom Street East and is also on city tour **bus** routes.

Alberton

The only other diversion in the western suburbs proper is the imposing mid-Victorian mansion of **Alberton**, 100 Mount Albert Rd (Wed–Sun 10.30am–noon & 1–4.30pm; $5, $10 joint ticket with Highwic in Newmarket and Ewelme Cottage in Parnell), 3km south of the zoo, which began life as a farmstead built in 1863 by Allan Kerr-Taylor. This grand old house achieved its current form – replete with turrets and verandas – through a series of late-nineteenth-century additions befitting the centrepiece for an estate that once stretched over much of western Auckland. The last of Kerr-Taylor's daughters died in 1972 leaving a house little changed in decades: the family furniture and possessions remain surrounded by peeling century-old wallpaper.

The North Shore

Until the 1960s there was very little to the **North Shore**, just a handful of scattered communities linked to each other and the rest of Auckland by a web of ferries crisscrossing the harbour. The completion of the harbour bridge in 1959 provided the catalyst for development. By the early 1970s, the volume of traffic to the booming suburbs log-jammed the bridge – until a Japanese company attached a two-lane extension (affectionately dubbed "the Nippon Clip-ons") to each side. The bridge and its additional lanes can now be seen at close quarters on the Auckland Bridge Climb (see p.114).

The vast urban sprawl marches inexorably towards the Hibiscus Coast (see p.135), with most interest to be found in the maritime village of **Devonport**, and its quiet adjacent coves of **Cheltenham** and **Narrow Neck**, at the southern end of a long string of calm swimming **beaches** which stretch the length of this coast. Further north, try the more open and busier **Takapuna**, a short stroll from dozens of good cafés and reached by buses #80 and #90, and **Long Bay** (buses #83 & 85), with a grassy reserve and barbecue areas. All to some degree suffer from the Auckland curse of being shallow at low tide but beaches tend to be well attended throughout the summer days. Elsewhere, only harbourside **Birkenhead** has a smattering of appeal with its restored cinema and a few places to stay and eat.

Devonport

Devonport is one of Auckland's oldest suburbs, founded in 1840 and still linked to the city by a fifteen-minute ferry journey. The naval station was one of Devonport's earliest tenants, soon followed by wealthy merchants, who built fine kauri villas. Some of these are graced with little turrets ("widows' watches") that served as lookouts where the traders could watch for the arrival of their precious cargoes, and wives could watch hopefully for their returning husbands. Wandering along the peaceful streets and the tree-fringed waterfront past grand houses is the essence of Devonport's appeal, and there's no shortage of tempting bookshops, small galleries, cafés and restaurants along the main street to punctuate your amblings.

On Victoria Road, the main street, you can't fail to notice what was once Devonport's post office, now operating as **Jackson's Muzeum** (daily: summer 10am–9pm; winter 11am–4pm; $10), bedecked in old New Zealand and British telephone boxes. Longstanding wrangles with the local council over the museum's somewhat unorthodox use of a listed building have seen it closed in recent years but, now open again, it overflows with Bryan Jackson's lifetime collection of collections – a reflection of his philosophy that "more is more". This is an overwhelming hoard of just about everything imaginable: soda

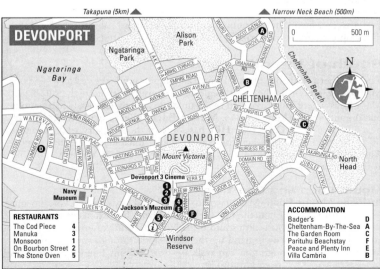

RESTAURANTS
The Cod Piece 4
Manuka 3
Monsoon 1
On Bourbon Street 2
The Stone Oven 5

ACCOMMODATION
Badger's D
Cheltenham-By-The-Sea A
The Garden Room C
Parituhu Beachstay F
Peace and Plenty Inn E
Villa Cambria B

siphons, hot-water bottles, gramophones, aquatint postcards, kauri gum, milk bottles and much, much more, ranging from the moderately special to the unbelievably ordinary. Access is through the *Venison Kitchen* restaurant.

Unless you have a soft spot for lifeless collections of uniforms and guns, you can blithely skip the **Navy Museum**, Spring St (daily 10am–4pm; donation advised), in favour of a stiff walk up one of the two ancient volcanoes that back Devonport. The closest, about fifteen minutes' walk, is **Mount Victoria** (Taka-a-ranga; unrestricted access for pedestrians; closed to vehicles from dusk on Thurs, Fri & Sat), from where you get fabulous city, harbour and gulf views. The hill was once the site of a Maori *pa* and fortified village, and the remains of terraces and kumara pits can still be detected on the northern and eastern slopes. A kilometre east, the grass- and flax-covered volcanic plug of **North Head** (Maungauika; daily 6am–10pm, vehicles 6am–8pm; free) guards the entrance to the inner harbour, a strategic site for Maori before it was co-opted to form part of the young nation's coastal defences. In the wake of the "Russian Scares" of 1884–86, which were precipitated by the opening of the port of Vladivostok, North Head became Fort Cautley, riddled with an extensive system of concrete tunnels linking gun emplacements. Most of the tunnels remain closed to the public, but you are free to poke around some of the peripheral remains and the gulf views are unbeatable.

Devonport is best reached on the **Devonport Ferry** (daily 6am–11pm, every 30min; $7 return, bikes free), which forms part of the Auckland Pass and Auckland Rover (see p.85). There's also a movie and ferry pass ($12) which gets you the ride over from the city and a screening at the Devonport 3 cinema (see p.126) for the same price you'd pay to visit a multiplex. Daytime ferries are met by Fullers' hour-long "Devonport Explorer Tour" (☎09/367 9111; daily 10am–3pm; $15), but really you're better off calling in to the **visitor centre**, 3 Victoria Rd (Mon–Fri 8am–5pm, Sat & Sun 8.30am–5pm; ☎09/446 0677, ⓦwww.tourismnorthshore.org.nz), picking up the free *Old Devonport Walk* leaflet, or a free map, and exploring at your own pace.

If you happen to be here around the middle of February, head for the **Devonport Food and Wine Festival** (ⓦwww.devonportwinefestival.co.nz) on the green opposite the ferry terminal, where for $20 you can buy the festival glass and spend the day sampling (for a small additional sum) the food and drink on offer from winemakers, market gardeners and restaurateurs.

South of the city centre

The southern tranche of Auckland, arching around the eastern end of Manukau Harbour, is the most neglected by visitors, though the airport at Mangere is where most arrive. In the main there are few unmissable attractions but the city's most lofty volcano, **Mount Eden**, offers superb views, and its near-identical twin, **One Tree Hill**, has some of the best surviving examples of the terracing undertaken by early Maori inhabitants. Further south, Auckland's Polynesian community plies its wares early each Saturday morning at the **Otara Market**.

Mount Eden and One Tree Hill

At 196m, **Mount Eden** (Maungawhau) is Auckland city's highest volcano and is named for George Eden, the first Earl of Auckland. The extensive views from the summit car park, just 2km south of the city, make it extraordinarily popular with tour buses which grind up the steep slope through the day and well into the evening, though you can walk up from Mount Eden Road or take buses #274 or #275 from Custom Street East.

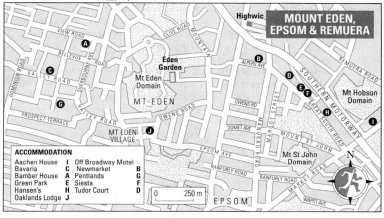

Highwic

MOUNT EDEN, EPSOM & REMUERA

Eden Garden

Mt Eden Domain

MT EDEN

Mt Hobson Domain

MT EDEN VILLAGE

Mt St John Domain

EPSOM

N

0   250 m

ACCOMMODATION

Aachen House	**I**	Off Broadway Motel	
Bavaria	**C**	Newmarket	**B**
Bamber House	**A**	Pentlands	**G**
Green Park	**E**	Siesta	**F**
Hansen's	**H**	Tudor Court	**D**
Oaklands Lodge	**J**		

More rewarding, though, is the area around **One Tree Hill** (Maungakiekie; 183m), 5km to the southeast. Although still one of the city's most distinctive landmarks, One Tree Hill is topped by a twenty-metre-tall granite obelisk, that was once accompanied by an ageing Monterey pine. For a century, until just before the arrival of Europeans, Maungakiekie ("mountain of the kiekie plant") was one of the largest *pa* sites in the country; an estimated 4000 people were drawn here by the proximity to abundant seafood from both harbours and the rich soils of the volcanic cone, which still bears the scars of extensive earthworks including the remains of dwellings and kumara pits. The site had already been abandoned when it was bought by the Scottish medic and "father of Auckland", Sir John Logan Campbell, who was one of only two European residents when the city was granted capital status in 1840. Through widespread land purchases and the founding of numerous shipping, banking and insurance companies, Campbell prospered, eventually becoming mayor in time for the visit of Britain's Duke and Duchess of Cornwall, in 1901. To commemorate the event, he donated his One Tree Hill estate to the people of New Zealand and named it **Cornwall Park** (daily 7am–dusk; free) in honour of his distinguished guests. The park puts on its best display around Christmas time, when avenues of pohutukawa trees erupt in a riot of red blossom. Campbell is buried at the summit, next to the obelisk, which bears inscriptions in Maori and English lauding Maori–Pakeha friendship. The summit is known in Maori as Te Totara-i-ahua, a reference to the single totara which originally gave One Tree Hill its name. Early settlers cut it down in 1852, and Campbell planted several pines as a windbreak, a single specimen surviving until the millennium. Already ailing from a 1994 chainsaw attack by a Maori activist avenging the loss of the totara, the pine's fate was sealed by a similar attack in 1999. The tree was removed in November 2000 and as yet plans for its replacement have come to nothing.

Free leaflets outlining a trail around the archeological and volcanic sites of the hill are available from the **visitor centre** (daily 10am–4pm), which is housed in **Huia Lodge**, originally built on the northern slopes by Campbell as a gatekeeper's house and now containing displays on the park and the man. Immediately opposite is **Acacia Cottage** (daily dawn–dusk; free), Campbell's original home and the city's oldest building, re-sited from central Auckland in the 1920s. Over the years, it has been heavily restored, but it's worth sticking your head in to see the simple construction and plain furnishings. Campbell devotees can round off their homage with a visit to the magisterial statue of him in mayoral garb at the northern end of the park by Manukau Road.

Fans of astronomy are better served on the southern side of One Tree Hill at the **Stardome Observatory**, on Manukau Road, where a frequently changing schedule of 45-minute multimedia programmes on the moon and the crystalline stars and distant galaxies of the southern skies is played out on the ceiling of the **planetarium** (Tues–Sat 8pm & 9pm; $12; infoline ℡09/625 6945, ⓦwww.stardome.org.nz). Weather and darkness permitting, the shows are followed by thirty minutes or so of telescope viewing; what you see obviously varies, but the moons of Jupiter, binary stars and Saturn's rings are all possibilities.

Most of Cornwall Park is closed after dark but the observatory and the summit are accessible from the southern entrance off Manukau Road, which can be reached on **buses** numbered #302, #305 and #312 from the corner of Queen and Victoria streets.

South Auckland

Head much beyond Cornwall Park and you are venturing into **South Auckland**, the city's poorest sector and the less-then-flatteringly-depicted gangland setting for Lee Tamahori's film *Once were Warriors*. There isn't a great deal to see down here, but neither is it a no-go zone and the **Otara Market** is certainly worth a look. Each Saturday morning, stalls sprawl across the car park of the Otara Town Centre, 18km south of central Auckland. Plausibly billed as the largest Maori and Polynesian market in the world, its authenticity has been somewhat diluted by an influx of market traders flogging cheap clothes and shoddy trinkets. The tat is alleviated by displays of island-style floral print fabrics, reasonably priced Maori carvings and truckloads of cheap fruit and veg, including many varieties peculiar to the islands like taro and yams. Your best bet for a bargain is the food: there are stalls where you can buy homemade cakes and Maori bread, and there's even a van ingeniously kitted out to produce an ersatz *hangi*. The market gets going around 5am and runs through to noon, though by 10am things are winding down, so get there early. Take the Otara exit off the southern motorway or catch buses #487 or #497 for the fifty-minute journey from the corner of Wellesley and Queen streets.

Parents with kids may well want to push on a few kilometres further south to **Rainbow's End**, Great South Rd, Manukau City (daily 10am–5pm; adults $37, kids $27; ℡09/262 2030 or 24hr infoline ℡09/262 2044, ⓦwww.rainbowsend .co.nz), New Zealand's largest theme park, where you get as many goes as you can handle on rides such as the corkscrew roller coaster, log flume, pirate ships, go-karts and flight simulators. Buses numbered #47 come out this way.

If you have your own transport, consider a jaunt to the **Auckland Botanic Gardens**, 102 Hill Rd (daily 8am–dusk; free), just by the Manurewa motorway turn-off, 27km south of the city centre. This extensive but relatively young collection of native and exotic plants opened in 1982, but came of age in 1998 when New Zealand's top horticultural show, the **Ellerslie Flower Show** (held annually in mid-Nov), was relocated here. The gardens come complete with interpretative visitor centre (Mon–Fri 9am–4pm, Sat & Sun 10am-4pm), a reference library, a café and a network of walks centred on two ornamental lakes.

Walks, cruises and adventure activities

Few visitors linger long in Auckland, most being content to make travel arrangement then head out to the "real" New Zealand, but if it's activities you're after, Auckland has plenty to offer. The relatively easy **Coast to Coast Walkway** is supplemented by more ambitious tramps in both the Waitakere (see p.131) and Hunua (see p.137) ranges. There are diverting ways to get out in the harbour, including **sailing** an America's Cup yacht and **swimming** with dolphins. And two of Auckland's largest structures provide the framework for the Auckland Bridge Climb and bungy jump and the Skyjump.

In addition, there are sightseeing tours to the city's west coast beaches and gannet colony (see p.134) and **wine tours** to the wineries of Kumeu and Huapai (see p.130).

Walks

The most ambitious walking normally attempted in Auckland is a stroll through The Domain or a more demanding hike up to one of the volcano-top viewpoints. The best of these have been threaded together as the well-marked **Coast to Coast Walkway**, a four-hour, 13-kilometre route straddling the isthmus from the Ferry Building on the Waitemata Harbour to Onehunga on the Manukau Harbour. By devoting a full day to the enterprise you can take in much of the best Auckland has to offer, including excellent harbour views from The Domain and the summits of Mount Eden and One Tree Hill, the Auckland Museum, Albert Park, and numerous sites pivotal to the development of the city. All is revealed in the free "Coast to Coast Walkway" leaflet available from the tourist offices, which includes an indication of where the walkway intersects with bus routes for walkers who want to tackle shorter sections.

More ambitious hikers can head to Rangitoto Island (see p.139) or out into the hills: west to the Waitakere Ranges (see p.131) or south to the Hunuas (see p.137).

Cruises, kayaking and dolphin swimming

Auckland is so water-focused that it would be a shame not to get out on the harbour at some point; and there is a welter of ways to do just that. The easiest and cheapest way is to hop on one of the **ferries** to Devonport (see p.110), or to one of the outlying islands (see "Islands of the Hauraki Gulf" from p.139), but for prolonged forays, consider one of the many **cruises** available; for a close-up perspective, a **dolphin swimming** or **sea-kayaking** trip offers a more intimate experience.

Cruises and sailing

As well as their ferry services Fullers offer a two-hour **Harbour Cruise** (daily 10.30am & 1.30pm; $30) which tours the inner harbour visiting the America's Cup team bases at Viaduct Harbour and coasting past Devonport and the Harbour Bridge. Similar ground is covered when you crew on Americas Cup **racing yachts** *NZL 40* or *NZL 41* (☎0800/724 569, ⓦwww .sailnewzealand.co.nz; $125 for a two-hour sail or $195 as part of a team in a race between the two boats), that give a real sense of power and speed. Built for New Zealand's 1995 cup challenge in San Diego they are now based quayside at the Viaduct Harbour and make several daily two-hour sailings. The same company also arrange cruises on Peter Blake's old Whitbread Cup round-the-world yacht, *Lion*, which runs from Auckland harbour to Whanagamunu or the Bay of Islands (2 days; $495).

Romantics might prefer a gentler trip **under sail** with *Pride of Auckland* (T 09/373 4557, W www.prideofauckland.com) who are based at the Maritime Museum and run a variety of cruises with coffee or a meal served on board: try the 45min basic cruise ($45), the Coffee Cruise (1hr 30min; $55), the Luncheon Cruise (1pm; 1hr 30min; $65) or the Dinner Cruise (7pm; 2hr 30min; $90). All cruises include entry to the Maritime Museum.

On most **summer weekends** you can help sail the *Søren Larsen* (T 0800/707 265 & 09/411 8755, W www.sorenlarsen.co.nz; mid-Nov to mid-Feb Sat 1–4pm, $57, & Sun 10am-3pm, $97 including lunch), a Danish Baltic trader built of oak in 1949 and later fitted with a nineteenth-century sailing rig. This majestic vessel starred in the 1970s TV series *The Onedin Line* and led the First Fleet re-enactment that formed a part of the Australian bicentennial celebrations in 1987. Passengers are free to participate – steering, hauling sheets and climbing the rigging – though maritime instruction tends to be a larger component of the mid-week trips to Hauraki Gulf and Coromandel (2–5 nights; $480–1100).

Dolphin swimming and kayaking

Though few Aucklanders are aware of it, the Hauraki Gulf is excellent territory for spotting marine mammals, best seen on five-hour dolphin and whale watching trips run by **Dolphin Explorer** (T & F 09/357 6032, W www .dolphinexplorer.com; $99) from beside the Ferry Building. Educational and entertaining trips head out daily (weather permitting) on a comfortable 20m catamaran, and dolphins are spotted ninety percent of the time (you get a second trip if there is no sighting). Over half the time passengers get to swim with common dolphins, and Bryde's whales are also frequently seen.

Several companies around Auckland will take you **kayaking**. One of the most popular trips is with Fergs Kayaks, 12 Tamaki Drive, Okahu Bay (T & F 09/529 2230, W www.fergskayaks.co.nz), kayaking the 7km across to Rangitoto Island (see p.139), watching sundown, hiking to the summit, then paddling back by torch- and moonlight (6–7hr; $75). They also do day-trips to Rangitoto and both day and evening trips 3km to Devonport, with a hike up North Head and a picnic supper (Oct–March daily 5.30pm; 4hr; $65).

If you'd rather go it alone, they offer **kayak rental** in either single sea kayaks ($12/hour, $25 a half-day) or doubles ($25/hour, $50 a half-day).

Adventure activities

Until very recently there were few diverting activities in Auckland, but a glut of recent openings has begun to put Auckland on the adventure sports map. Opportunities to walk to the top of the Harbour Bridge and jump off the Skytower are supplemented by canyoning trips in the Waitakere Ranges and further afield. As well as what's listed below, you could go **roller blading** along the waterfront east of the city where Tamaki Drive provides a smooth path (shared with bikes and pedestrians) and great harbour views; in-line skates can be rented from Fergs Kayaks (see above) for $10–15 per hour or $25–30 for a day.

Harbour Bridge Climb

Based on the Sydney Harbour bridge climb the **Auckland Bridge Climb**, 70 Nelson St ($110; T 09/625 0445, W www.ajhacket.com), gives you the opportunity to get decked out in natty overalls and sample the excellent city views from the highest point on the city's harbour crossing some 65 metres above the Waitemata Harbour. The two-and-a-half-hour trip is somewhat misnamed as there is no climbing involved, just strolling along steel walkways under the roadway then emerging onto the upper girders by means of ordinary stairs, all the while clipped by safety harness to a cable which runs the length of the walkway. Guides relate something of the history of the bridge, along with some of the region's Maori mythology and a good deal of detail on the bridge's fulcrums, pivots and cantilevers. Reservations are essential and anyone over ten can go. Cameras are not allowed, but there'll be someone on hand to take a snap and sell it to you later. On Saturdays, for an extra $10 you can undertake a **night climb**, starting around 8pm and wearing a head torch. Once the climb is over and if you crave an adrenalin rush, the new A J Hacket **Auckland Bridge Bungy** (contact details as above) should do the trick – it's apparently the only one of its kind, a 40m leap out over the water and will set you back $125.

Skyjump, Reverse Bungy and Vertigo

Auckland's 328-metre Skytower is the venue for two adventure activities, both exploiting its position as New Zealand's tallest building. On the **Skyjump** (Sun–Thurs 10.30am–7pm, Fri & Sat 10.30am–10pm; $195; booking recommended on ℡0800/759586, ⓦwww.skyjump.co.nz) – claimed as the world's highest tower-based jump – you plummet 192m towards the ground in a kind of arrested freefall at 75kph, with a cable attached to your back. Suitably kitted out in a jumpsuit and full body harness you climb to the tower's observation area before edging out along a gangplank and flinging yourself off. There's much the same stomach-in-your-mouth feeling as you get bungy jumping, but the cable maintains your descent at a steady pace, giving you a full 25-second ride until a giant rotating fan-brake slows you for a gentle landing. Keep your suit on and you can go again for $75.

If you'd prefer to go up rather than down, consider **Vertigo** (daily 9am–9pm; $145; ℡0800/483 784, ⓦwww.4vertigo.com), in which around half a dozen people are led up into the narrow confines of the slender pinnacle which tops the upper observation area. Climbing a vertical internal ladder surrounded by the high-tech cabling that feeds the mast-top broadcast and telecom equipment, you gain a further 50m and top out at the 270-metre level, where an open-air crow's nest gives a stupendous view over the city and Hauraki Gulf. Book in advance or simply front up at the desk inside the Sky City Casino building, where you'll be kitted out with overalls, body harness, helmet and earpiece then put through a simulator before being given the OK for the climb. Kids can go, provided they pass the simulation, and there are also dawn, sunset and after-dark climbs by arrangement; second-timers get a discount.

Last, and probably least, of these three money-grabbers is the **Sky Screamer**, a sort of cage for three people attached to bungy ropes that catapults you into the sky at about 200kph, with a 5G pull, where you bounce up and down for a while before being returned to the earth. Mostly it's people coming out of the pubs that take up this offer of speedy, if pointless, motion at $35, or $50 for two consecutive trips.

Canyoning

About the most fun you can have in a wetsuit around Auckland is to go **canyoning**, a combination of swimming, abseiling, jumping into deep pools and sliding down rock chutes. Two companies operate in the Waitakere Ranges, west of the city, both making pick-ups in Auckland and offering an excellentvalue day out. Canyonz (☏0800/422 696 & 09/357 0133, Ⓦwww.canyonz.co.nz) operates in Blue Canyon with a great variety of activities including an 8m-waterfall jump or abseil. The standard full-day trip ($145, 7hrs) can be condensed into a half-day ($125; 5hrs). Awol Adventures (☏09/630 7100, Ⓦwww.awoladventures.co.nz) runs similar trip near Piha, with more emphasis on abseiling. Join the day trip or go **night canyoning** (both $135) with just a headtorch and glowworms for illumination. Both companies' trips often end up with a visit to one of the West Coast surf beaches.

Canyonz also offers Auckland-based day-trips down the magnificent **Sleeping God** canyon near Thames (Oct–May only; $225). In this wonderfully scenic spot you descend 300 metres in a series of twelve drops using slides, and abseils as long as seventy metres (some actually through the waterfall), but also with the opportunity to leap 13m from a rock ledge into a deep pool. It's tough enough to require previous abseiling experience, best done by taking the Blue Canyon/Sleeping God combo ($345) over two days.

Eating

Aucklanders take their eating seriously and there is no shortage of wonderful **restaurants**, with ever more adventurous places opening all the time. They may only be following the trends of London, Australia or California but they're close behind and easily as good. If you're after a more casual eating experience, don't overlook the **pubs** (see "Pubs and bars" listings, starting on p.123), many offering a decent meal for under $15.

For several years, the best areas for grazing have been the inner-city suburbs, chiefly along **Ponsonby Road**, Auckland's culinary crucible; **Parnell Road**, the other main eating street; and **Devonport**, with a more modest but still tempting selection. In the wake of the 2000 America's Cup the **city waterfront** has been reinvented, with several dozen eating places now ringing the rejuvenated waterside and offering a full range of culinary styles.

Central Auckland and Viaduct Harbour

The centre of Auckland is undoubtedly the best place to grab something quick during the day with dozens of places geared up to cope with the **lunchtime** press of office workers and bank staff. Among the most popular are the **food halls**, seating plazas surrounded by numerous vendors, often tucked away in the basements of the shopping arcades that spur off Queen Street. Downtown's eating scene is spiced up with an increasing number of **Asian restaurants** that cater (sometimes almost exclusively) to the large numbers of recent immigrants who populate the central city apartment blocks. Chinese, Japanese, Korean, Lao, Thai and Indian places are liberally scattered.

The Asian influence continues along **K' Road** but is less influenced by the daytime business crowds; its selection of quirky places can be lively at any hour.

In the evening, parts of the city can feel pretty dead, but if you know where to look – **High Street** and **Lorne Street** are both good hunting grounds – there are plenty of places to eat. Nowhere are the restaurants so densely packed as around the **Viaduct Harbour** area where virtually all the waterside spots are occupied. The restaurants are out to impress just as much as the clientele, though this isn't reflected in the prices that are only a dollar or two above the city average.

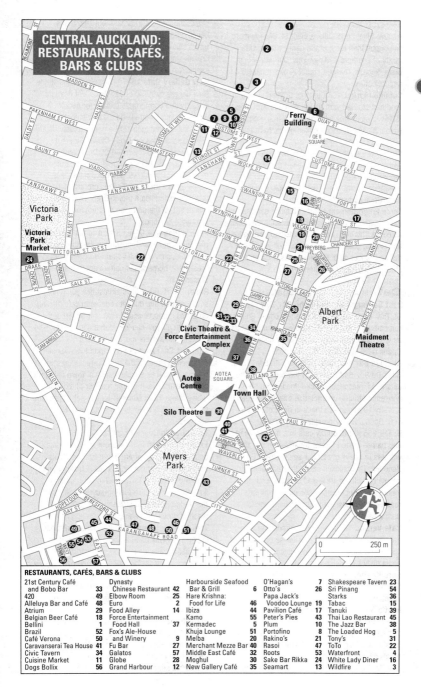

CENTRAL AUCKLAND: RESTAURANTS, CAFÉS, BARS & CLUBS

RESTAURANTS, CAFÉS, BARS & CLUBS

21st Century Café and Bobo Bar	33	Dynasty Chinese Restaurant	42	Harbourside Seafood Bar & Grill	6	O'Hagan's	7	Shakespeare Tavern	23
420	49	Elbow Room	25	Hare Krishna:		Otto's	26	Sri Pinang	54
Alleluya Bar and Café	48	Euro	14	Food for Life	46	Papa Jack's		Starks	36
Atrium	29	Food Alley	14	Ibiza	44	Voodoo Lounge	19	Tabac	15
Belgian Beer Café	18	Force Entertainment		Kamo	55	Pavilion Café	17	Tanuki	39
Bellini	1	Food Hall	37	Kermadec	5	Peter's Pies	43	Thai Lao Restaurant	45
Brazil	52	Fox's Ale-House		Khuja Lounge	51	Plum	10	The Jazz Bar	38
Café Verona	50	and Winery	9	Melba	20	Portofino	8	The Loaded Hog	5
Caravanserai Tea House	41	Galatos	57	Merchant Mezze Bar	40	Rakino's	21	Tony's	31
Civic Tavern	34	Globe	28	Middle East Café	32	Rasoi	47	ToTo	22
Cuisine Market	11	Grand Harbour	12	Moghul	30	Roots	53	Waterfront	4
Dogs Bollix	56			New Gallery Café	35	Sake Bar Rikka	24	White Lady Diner	16
						Seamart	13	Wildfire	3

Food halls

Atrium Elliot Food Gallery, Elliot St. Slightly more salubrious than most of the genre with a wide range of counters – Malay, Thai, burgers, Indian, pizza, kebabs, roasts, Chinese – plus a bakery and decent coffee.

Cuisine Market 106 Customs St West. A kind of food hall crossed with a high-end deli with a few tables to sip coffee while you tuck into delicate savouries and delicious baked goods from the surrounding stalls.

Food Alley 9 Albert St. Spartan two-level food hall with a strong Asian bias exhibited through counters selling Indian, Thai, Korean, Malaysian and Japanese cuisine along with a couple of noodle bars. Open daily until 10pm.

Force Entertainment Food Hall In the basement of the 12-screen multiplex cinema, Queen St overlooking Aotea Sq. This large food court caters to passing trade and cinema goers providing pizza, French, Chinese, deli and various other denominations of cheap and cheerful grub. Open daily from 10am.

Cafés and takeaways

21st Century Café and Bobo Bar 20 Wellesley St. Tiny, oddly named and insanely cheap Chinese-run café that offers great noodles and dumplings as well as English breakfasts, all for under $10. Opens daily at 7.30am, Not licensed.

Alleluya Bar and Café St Kevin's Arcade, 179 K' Rd ☎09/377 8482. Some of the best city views plus good, reasonably priced, food and a no-nonsense attitude characterize this spot hidden in a pretty 1920s arcade that's in need of a bit of TLC. Open daily for breakfast at 8.30am.

Brazil 256 K' Rd. Quirky café in a mosaic-lined and barrel-vaulted former theatre entrance that vibrates to heavy beats and jazz grooves. Eggs Benedict, Thai chicken salad, toasted bagels and veggie breakfasts are eased down by shakes or industrial-strength espressos made from beans roasted in the basement. Opens 8am weekdays, 9am weekends.

Café Verona 169 K' Rd. Longstanding muso hangout and general place-to-be-seen. Sup good coffee and tuck in to low-cost quiches, salads and pasta dishes in the comfy booths.

Hare Krishna: Food for Life 423 Queen St. Serene unlicensed restaurant serving wholesome vegetarian weekday lunches costing $3–8.

Melba 33 Vulcan Lane. Reliable – if expensive – café in the heart of the shopping and clubbing district that's justifiably popular for all-day bistro breakfasts, delicious muffins, coffee and light meals all day. Opens daily at 8am.

Middle East Café 23a Wellesley St. Tiny, simple, camel-themed eat-in or take-out café that's become an Auckland institution justly celebrated for its shawarma and falafel ($6–8), cloaked in creamy garlic, spicy tomato sauce or hot chilli sauce. Not licensed.

New Gallery Café 18–26 Wellesley St, inside the New Gallery ☎09/302 0226. Excellent daytime oasis, with a comfortable terrace for people watching and a coffee and cake or something more substantial (until 2.30pm) like a tasty risotto fish cakes or tandoori lamb. Closed Sun.

Pavilion Café 48 Shortland St. Deep leather chairs surrounded by artworks, sun streaming in through huge windows, and tasty coffee and cakes almost make up for the corporate tenor of this café, alongside a prohibitively expensive restaurant, in the pretentious atrium of an insurance building.

Peter's Pies 484 Queen St. Eat-in and takeaway pie shop – steak and mushroom, lasagne and vegetable, smoked fish – that also does bargain breakfasts, burgers and coffee; not licensed. Closed Sun.

Rasoi 211 K' Rd. It feels almost like you're in south India in this budget vegetarian café dishing up *dosas*, *uttappams* and *thalis* for $5–16 and there's an all-you-can-eat Maharajah *thali* for $14. Great Indian sweets too. Not licensed

Seamart Cnr Fanshawe & Market Place. Seafood deli serving some of the best sushi and sashimi around as well as a wide variety of fresh fish and accompaniments. A limited number of external tables make this a summer-lunch spot, unless you take your catch down to the waterfront. Not licensed.

Tanuki 319b Queen St ☎09/379 5353. Excellent yakitori and sake bar in a cave-like basement setting where you perch on stools and tuck into various delicacies – from grilled cloves of garlic to Teriyaki chicken (dinner $10–20), or if you're feeling adventurous one of the Badger's special dinners ($27–30) – all washed down with sake.

Thai Lao Restaurant 271 K' Rd. Authentic and super-fresh Thai and Lao cuisine served up at very low cost in basic unlicensed surroundings. At lunch the spicy seafood fried rice and pad krapow with Thai basil, bamboo shoots and baby corn (both $9) are excellent. The dinner menu is more extensive and dishes cost a few dollars more. Closed Sun.

Waterfront 161–173 Quay St, The Viaduct ☎09/359 9914. Stylish café that is unusually good-value. Serves generous portions of a wide range of cuisines and has a great waterfront seating.

White Lady Diner Cnr Queen St & Shortland St. Kerbside caravan in the club zone, open for refuelling throughout the night. Toasted sandwiches and burgers, notably the pack-in-the-works Aucklander, fit the bill – and the staff understand fluent drunk. Open 24hrs Sat & Sun.

Restaurants

Belgian Beer Café 8 Vulcan Lane. Former pub convincingly converted into a Belgian bar serving bargain pots of mussels dressed with lobster bisque and brandy, mustard and cream, or coconut cream and lemongrass. Every item on the menu comes with a suggested libation and the pouring of the beer is conducted with ritualistic zeal. The expected Hoegaarden, Stella and Leffe are supplemented by bottled fruit beers and a selection of Kiwi wines.

Caravanserai Tea House 430 Queen St. Relaxed Middle Eastern place decked out in Turkish rugs and cushions, some around knee-high tables. The extensive range of mezze, moussaka and kebabs go for around $13, or there are lighter snacks for half that.

Dynasty Chinese Restaurant 57–59 Wakefield St. Large restaurant that's always popular with Auckland's Chinese community especially for Sunday morning *yum cha*.

Euro Princes Wharf ℡09/309 9866. This popular, trendy place offers very high quality food and service. Their signature dish of rotisserie chicken on a bed of mashed potato and peanut slaw ($28) is superb, and the appetizers are all pretty tasty too.

Grand Harbour 18–28 Customs St West ℡09/357 6889. More opulent than most of the city's Chinese places, this bustling modern restaurant is always popular for business lunches and serves great yum cha daily.

Harbourside Seafood Bar & Grill 99 Quay St ℡09/307 0556. Classy but relaxed, award-winning Pacific Rim seafood restaurant upstairs in the Ferry Building. If it's warm, reserve a table on the harbour-view terrace, and feast on beautifully prepared and presented fish and crustaceans. Expect to part with at least $60 for a full meal, plus wine.

Kamo 382 K' Rd ℡09/377 2313. Stripped-down rowdy restaurant that is one of the very few serving Pacific-influenced dishes alongside Mediterranean favourites, all at reasonable prices. Try the *ika mata* (literally "fish prepared and eaten"), fresh fish marinated coconut cream and finely diced vegetables.

Kermadec 1st Floor (above *Loaded Hog*), Viaduct Harbour, cnr Lower Hobson St & Quay St (restaurant ℡09/309 0412, brasserie & bars ℡09/309 0413). Fashionable and imaginatively decorated seafood emporium, with a large bustling brasserie for classy versions of bistro favourites and the more formal, and expensive, Pacific Room for fine dining.

Merchant Mezze Bar 430 Queen St, cnr Mayoral Drive ℡09/307 0349. Buzzing café with a small deck outside, specializing in dishes from around the Mediterranean and the Middle East – anything from Spanish tortilla and grilled mushroom on polenta to Moroccan Meat Bake. Soups, salads, mezze ($8–14) and mains ($15–22) are served until 11pm, then drinks and coffee until midnight or later.

Moghul 2 Lorne St ℡09/366 0885. Good-value Indian curry restaurant that's great at any time but especially notable for lunches of five curry dishes plus rice and naan ($8.25). Another good bet is the $25 Moghul banquet (minimum two).

Ottos 40 Kitchener St, *Ascot Hotel* ℡09/300 9595. Among the most exalted of Auckland's fine dining restaurants, converted from a former magistrates' court and tastefully decked out in taupe and cream with huge potted palms. Try the wonderful chive linguini, roast venison, grilled crayfish or spinach ravioli but expect to pay $60–80 for three courses, plus drinks.

Portofino Viaduct Harbour ℡09/356 7080. The most fashionably sited of a small local chain of Italian places, with some seats out by the harbour. The food doesn't quite match the setting and service but is well priced for the location with most dishes served as both appetizer (around $16) and main ($25). Try the calamari Luciana with capers and garlic and the chicken risotto.

Sake Bar Rikka Victoria Park Market ℡09/377 8239. Excellent Japanese restaurant: settle down to their formidable platter of tempura, miso, sushi, chicken teriyaki and more for two people (under $40) and every kind of sake known to mankind including chilled versions. Closed Sun.

Sri Pinang 356 K' Rd ℡09/358 3886. Simple but ever popular Malaysian restaurant. Start with half a dozen satay chicken skewers ($6) and follow with perhaps sambal okra, beef rendang or clay pot chicken rice (all $11–20) scooped up with excellent roti. BYO only. Closed Mon & Sat lunch, and all day Sun.

Tony's 32 Lorne St & 27 Wellesley St ℡09/373 2138. Traditional, dark-wood, steak restaurant highly regarded for its juicy slabs of prime meat ($25–30); lunchtime menu cheaper. Always busy so worth booking ahead.

ToTo 53 Nelson St ℡09/302 2665. One of the city's finest modern Italian restaurants whose airy white room and terrace have become a lunchtime staple for TV execs from across the road and businessmen in the evenings. Main courses are around $20–25. Closed Sat & Sun lunch.

Wildfire Princes Wharf ⊕ 09/353 7595. Flashy Latin-influenced place with tables by the water or inside where a massive fiery grill flares up from time to time. Gourmet pizzas are overshadowed by the nightly rotisserie specials (quail, duck cervena; $26–28) and the Brazilian *churrascaria*, a vast selection of meats and seafood marinated in herbs and roasted over manuka coals. Served after tapas, the whole shebang costs $40.

Parnell

Parnell's eating places split into two camps; established restaurants with the accent on fine dining, and trendier, cheaper places catering to younger devotees, and backpackers from the nearby hostels. See map on p.103.

Antoine's 333 Parnell Rd ⊕ 09/307 8756. Enduring restaurant consistently rated among the best in Auckland and much favoured by Parnell and Remuera blue bloods. It's all very professionally, if somewhat conservatively, done, with a "nostalgia" menu full of game, offal and French classics alongside a modern counterpart. Mains start around $30.

Chocolate Boutique 323 Parnell Rd. Compact chocolate emporium selling hand-made choccies and a range of chocolate (and coffee) drinks. Tables inside and out, and it stays open late for that post-dinner dessert.

Di Mare Shop 9, 251 Parnell Rd ⊕ 09/303 1593. One of the best surf and turf restaurants in the city, serving excellent steaks and seafood to an appreciative crowd in this intimate restaurant in a back alley courtyard off the main road. Well-worth making the effort to find if only for the modern take on paella.

Iguaçu 269 Parnell Rd ⊕ 09/358 4804. Flashy conservatory-style brasserie frequented by a young corporate crowd, but worth a look in for a light meal or just a glass of wine. Sunday lunchtime jazz.

Java Room 317 Parnell Rd ⊕ 09/366 1606. Intimate restaurant serving loosely Indonesian-influenced dishes but stretching to dim sum, spicy fish cakes, Szechwan prawns and whole snapper in sambal.

Pandoro 427 Parnell Rd. Bakery specializing in Italian-style loaves, stuffed pizza bread – and chocolate brownies.

Portofino 156 Parnell Rd ⊕ 09/373 3740. Basic but reliable trattoria without the pretensions of much of this street, but with pasta and pizza favourites all exceptionally well done.

Strawberry Alarm Clock 119 Parnell Rd. Low-key café popular for breakfasts, a snack, or just hanging out over good coffee either inside or out in the rear courtyard.

Zucchero 259 Parnell Rd. From 7.30am this tiny café sells the best coffee in Parnell, along with bagels and panini, cooked breakfasts and a variety of cakes and light snacks, all accompanied by some dry urban wit and the local news rags.

Newmarket

Newmarket is rapidly heading the same way as Parnell, with interesting new places opening up all the time, though unless you are staying nearby it isn't worth making a special effort. See map on p.103.

Bodrum 2 Osborne St. Boisterous Turkish restaurant open nightly for feta- and potato-stuffed filo cigars, kebabs and regional favourites like falafel, moussaka, marinated lamb with jalapeno and spanakopita, all at moderate prices.

Mecca 61 Davis Crescent. Relaxed café with speedy service dishing up excellent blueberry pancakes with fresh fruit ($11) and a range of well-presented breakfast and lunch dishes including Thai chicken curry ($12) and an extensive selection of mezze ($9).

Vivo 10 Kingdon Place ⊕ 09/522 2311. Gourmet pizza place that serves excellent wood-fired pizzas including a glorious one with chorizo, capsicum, eggplant and lemon-fried capers and a chargrilled chicken one with veggies and banana – both under $25. Open daily till late

Zarbo 24 Morrow St. Auckland's finest deli/café with a fabulous range of products from around the world, put to good use in a superb range of breakfast and lunch dishes ($5–18). Lunch finishes at 3pm but they stay open until 5pm for salads, cakes and coffee.

Tamaki Drive: Okahu Bay and Mission Bay

If you find yourself peckish while visiting Kelly Tarlton's, roller blading along Tamaki Drive or just out for a swim at Mission Bay then head along to one of Mission Bay's cafés; *Hammerheads* is best saved for a more formal lunch or dinner.

Bar Comida 81 Tamaki Drive. Quality version of the typical Kiwi cover-all-the-bases café/restaurant/bar with woodfired gourmet pizza, great coffee and cakes, and a strong line in *pide*, Turkish flatbreads applied to anything from BLT to *lahmejan*, a lamb, parsley and lemon juice combo from Istanbul.

Bluefins cnr Tamaki Drive and Atkin Ave ☎09/528 4551. Classy terracotta-tiled seafood restaurant serving delicious seared scallops, tempura dishes and super-fresh daily specials. Mains around $25. Closed Sun & Mon.

Hammerheads 19 Tamaki Drive, Okahu Bay, by Kelly Tarlton's ☎09/521 4400. Popular waterfront seafood restaurant that sometimes suffers from slow service. The delectable food is worth the delay, though, and your wait is eased by dynamite cocktails and tremendous views.

Ponsonby and Herne Bay

At the cutting edge of Auckland's foodie scene is **Ponsonby Road**, a street where devotion to style is as important as culinary prowess. But don't be intimidated; the food is almost invariably excellent and though prices are generally a notch above those in more downbeat parts of the city, nowhere is prohibitively expensive, and there are several reasonably priced places hanging in there. Again, popular daytime cafés frequently ease into more rumbustious drinking later on, often until the wee hours. See map on p.107.

Cafés and takeaways

Atlas Power Café 285 Ponsonby Rd. Small modern café serving pricey but delectable sandwiches and salads for $11–15 and their own roast coffee.

Atomic Café 121 Ponsonby Rd. *Atomic*'s own-roast coffee has become a byword for quality espresso across town and here, in their home base, muffins reign supreme while macrobiotic and organic food dominates the blackboard. The sandpit in the grapevine-shaded courtyard make it a great place for parents.

Bistro Bambina 268 Ponsonby Rd. Café with a big central table stacked with magazines and newspapers. The food is reliably fresh and tasty from the all-day breakfast – try the ricotta hotcakes with fresh fruit ($12) – through to panini and open Turkish sandwiches. Great coffee too.

Café Cézanne 296 Ponsonby Rd. This casual, ramshackle place is great for reading the papers over hearty breakfasts, excellent quiches and huge wedges of cake.

Dizengoff 256 Ponsonby Rd ☎09/360 0108. Unlicensed breakfast and lunch café specializing in wonderful bagels, some Jewish deli favourites and luscious char-grilled vegetables, all at reasonable prices.

Fatimas 240 Ponsonby Rd ☎09/376 9303. If you fancy homemade, Middle-Eastern food then look no further than this friendly wee café-bar where nothing costs more than $10. Second branch in Takapuna, 20 Anzac St ☎09/489 6552.

Fusion 32 Jervois Rd. Enjoyable daytime café that's wonderfully relaxed inside and great out back under the parasols. A good range of breakfasts until 12.30pm, plus light lunches, great coffee and flavoursome fruit lassi drinks.

International Food Court 1st Floor, cnr Pollen and Ponsonby Rds. Small court where you can sample cheap but enjoyable grub including Indian, Japanese, Malaysian, Chinese, a burger grill and there's an attractive balcony bar for a drink.

Otto Woo 47 Ponsonby Rd. Excellent unlicensed noodle bar, primarily for take-outs but with a few stools at stark white tables. Choose from freshly prepared chicken bok choy, seafood laksa, satay vegetable noodles and a dozen other dishes (all $9–14) and finish off with some sweet rice balls and a fresh juice.

Ponsonby Fresh Fish and Chip Co 127 Ponsonby Rd ☎09/378 7885. One of the best basic fish, chips and burger takeaways around, frequently lauded in *Metro* magazine's annual readers' poll and always busy, so call ahead or trot across the road to the SPQR bar and wait. The vegetarian burgers are sensational. Unlicensed.

Ponsonby Pies 288 Ponsonby Rd. Basically a takeaway with a few chairs that's great for the most sumptuous pies in the land: apple and pork, silverbeet and cheese, pumpkin, bacon and smoked fish to name but a few. $8 for a full meal. Unlicensed.

Santos 114 Ponsonby Rd. Expensive, trendy little spot serving good cappuccinos and panini in a tired-looking Mexican hacienda.

Restaurants

Alhambra 1st Floor, Three Lamps Arcade, 283 Ponsonby Rd ☎09/376 2430. Excellent city views, tapas, good wine and beer help make this one of the coolest places in Ponsonby but the real crowning glory are the piano and live jazz nights most evenings.

Anglesea Grill C149 Ponsonby Rd ☎09/360 4551. Elegant surroundings and comfortable furniture are only half the story in this top seafood restaurant. Fresh fish is prepared in every conceivable way – chargrilled, steamed, fried, in

chowder and raw – with main courses from $20. Excellent wine list. Book ahead.

GPK 262 Ponsonby Rd ☎09/360 1113. Smart bar and restaurant wood-firing some of the tasty pizzas with avant-garde toppings such as Thai green curry or octopus. They're small, considering the $20 price tag, but well worth it.

Leonardo's 263 Ponsonby Rd ☎09/361 1556. About as authentic an Italian restaurant as you'll find in Auckland offering risotto but a great antipasta plate ($25 for two), pasta and gnocchi dishes (around $25), and *segundi piatti* ($25–30) such as fish in lemon caper parsley and white wine sauce, all served up with easy charm. Weekend lunches & dinner nightly except Mon.

Shahi Café 26 Jervois St ☎09/378 8896. Small and homely authentic north Indian restaurant serving reasonably cheap favourites include Dahl Maharani and that old standby Lamb Korma. Open daily for lunch & dinner.

Devonport

Devonport's range of places to eat has undergone a minor explosion and is rapidly catching up with Auckland's major foodie hangouts with plenty of worthwhile **lunch stops** and several quality restaurants for **evening dining**. See map on p.109

The Cod Piece 26 Victoria Rd. Sit-in and take-out fish and chip and gourmet burgers place, cheekily named by the gay owners. Open weekday evenings plus midday at weekends

Manuka 49 Victoria Rd ☎09/445 7732. Wood-fired pizza restaurant that's good at any time of the day for light snacks and salads or just for coffee and cake.

Monsoon 71 Victoria Rd ☎09/445 4263. There is seldom a bad word said about this excellent value-for-money Thai/Malaysian place with tasty dishes such as fish and Tiger prawns in a red curry sauce for around $18-20. Evenings only, from 5pm.

On Bourbon St 59 Victoria Rd ☎09/445 0085. Bar-restaurant that hums along with jazz, blues and excited conversation, particularly at weekends. The interior is softened by enveloping leather sofas and the atmosphere improved by the whiff of Louisiana gumbo, pork ribs and jambalaya, all for under $25.

The Stone Oven 3 Clarence St. Large, bustling bakery and café with a solid reputation for organic sourdough and cakes and pastries to take away or eat in; also popular for all day breakfasts (starting at 6.30am) and light lunches, quiches, pies and over-stuffed panini, accompanied by aromatic coffee.

Drinking, nightlife and entertainment

Auckland has some good nightlife and, with a million people to entertain, there's always something going on, even if it's just a night down at the local **boozer**. The best way to find out **what's on** is to pick up the *New Zealand Herald*. For gig information, buy the monthly *Real Groove* ($5), available from most record store and magazine shops, pick up the free weekly *Fix* leaflet from the same outlets or surf to the entertainment guide section of the bFM radio station website ⓦwww.95bfm.co.nz.

New Zealand produces plenty of **bands** and at any time you should be able to find some quality local acts bashing away in a club or dedicated venue; due to

Gay and lesbian Auckland

New Zealand has a fairly small but progressive and proactive **gay culture**, and Auckland and Wellington vie to be at its centre. Until recent times, the annual focus was the Hero Parade and the associated two-week Hero Festival, a smaller and considerably tamer cousin of Sydney's Gay Mardi Gras. Ongoing financial misman-agement and the far-from-liberal mayor, John Banks, may scupper plans to revive the festival.

The best way to find out what's happening and if the **Hero Parade** is taking place is to get hold of the fortnightly *Express* magazine ($2.50; ⓦwww.gayexpress.co.nz), which can be bought from branches of Maggazzino and the Out! bookshop (☏09/377 7770; 39 Anzac Ave), and is available for browsing in many cafés. It's also worth tuning in to **Round the Bend**, the Sunday evening gay and lesbian interest programme (8–9pm) on 95bFM (ⓦwww.95bfm.co.nz), preceded by an hour of *The Girls Own Show*. Look out too for **Queer Nation**, sporadically on TV2 late in the evenings.

The gay scene is fairly low-key, gently woven into the café/bar mainstream of Ponsonby, Parnell and Newmarket, and the western end of K' Road where strip clubs mingle freely with gay bars and cruise clubs. Among the **cafés** and **bars**, *Surrender Dorothy*, in Ponsonby is a good starting point. Along K' Road, *Staircase*, 340 K' Rd (☏09/374 4278), *Caluzzi*, 461 K' Rd (☏09/357 0778), and the leather-oriented *Urge*, 490 K' Rd, are the places to be. Recently there's been more going on around High Street and the parallel O'Connell Street, specifically at *Wunderbar*, 5 O'Connell St (☏09/377 9404), *G.A.Y*, 5 High St (☏09/336 1101) and *Flesh*, 16 O'Connell St, with both lounge and dance club sections.

Useful contacts

Auckland Pride Centre 281 K' Rd; postal address PO Box 5426, Wellesley St ☏09/302 0590, ⓦwwwpride.org.nz. The best place to tap into the scene, with a drop-in centre (generally Mon–Fri 10am–5pm, Sat 10am–3pm) and a good events noticeboard. Their website has an excellent links section.

Budget Travel 177 Parnell Rd; postal address PO Box 37–259, Parnell ☏09/302 0553, ☏358 1206. This branch of the nationwide chain of travel agencies special-izes in helping gay visitors plan their travels.

Gay and lesbian helpline ☏09/303 3584; Mon–Fri 10am–10pm, Sat & Sun 5–10pm.

Harvey World Travel 293 Ponsonby Rd ☏376 5011, ⓦwww.harveyworld.co.nz. Offers a similar service to Budget Travel.

New Zealand's remoteness, bands from North America or Europe are less fre-quent visitors. One of the best ways to see local bands is to attend one of the **free summer concerts** held in Aotea Square, Albert Park and The Domain under the *Free Summer* banner (☏09/379 2020, ⓦwww.akcity.govt.nz/freesummer/; mid-Dec to early Feb), mostly on Friday, Saturday and Sunday afternoons.

After a lull of a few years, Auckland's **arts scene** is picking up, and on any night of the week there should be a choice of a couple of plays, comedy and maybe some dance or opera.

Pubs and bars

In Auckland, as in much of the rest of the country, the distinction between eating and drinking places is frequently blurred, with cafés, restaurants and bars all just points along the same continuum. The factor uniting those listed over-leaf is their dedication to **drinking**: some are bars which may serve food but where drinking is the norm; others are old-time hotels in the Kiwi tradition, though even these have been dramatically smartened up and may do a sideline in inexpensive counter meals.

Drinking hours have relaxed markedly over the years, though Sundays still see some places close unconscionably early. The exceptions are Grey Lynn, which borders Ponsonby, and Mount Eden, which both relinquished their former "dry area" status in recent years but still have few pubs or licensed restaurants.

City centre

Bellini *Hilton Hotel*, Princes Wharf. Polish up your credit cards for this stylish cocktail bar with fabulous harbour views from the floor-to-ceiling glass. There's a wonderful range of champagne cocktails ($28), delicious martini variants ($20), a great selection of wines and tasty morsels to keep you going.

Civic Tavern cnr Queen St and Wellesley St. Two-in-one pub that's good for a quick drink before the movies up the road: choose between *Murphy's Irish Bar* downstairs and the *London Bar* upstairs where wood panelling, British beer and a menu of stodgy staples create the impression of a London pub. Live music and a lively feel on Friday and Saturday nights.

Dogs Bollix Cnr Karangahape and Newton Rds. Lively ersatz Irish bar with a soft spot for visitors, cheap bar food and live music every night (originals and cover bands).

Elbow Room 12 Durham Lane. Fashionable little bar often quiet midweek but with DJs at weekends and no cover.

Fox's Ale-House and Winery Viaduct Harbour. Pleasing corner bar where you can sip your drink and watch the trend-following locals trying to puzzle out which is the coolest place to be seen in.

420 373 K' Rd ☎021/597 876. Surprisingly stylish retro lounge with excellent inner city views – good for a quiet evening watching the sun go down.

Globe 299 Queen St, basement of the *ACB* (see Hostels). Long, thin, noisy backpackers-get-drunk bar that's full most nights of the week.

O Hagan's 101–103 Cutom's St West (☎09/363 2106). Irish style, predominantly wooden bar facing out on to part of the Market Square at the Viaduct Basin and endemic of its surroundings, with live bands at the weekends, DJ entertainment, food and within easy range of the other waterside diversions.

The Loaded Hog Viaduct Harbour. Vast, bustling, glass-walled bar with seating right on the quay, bar food, an impressive range of wines by the glass and four tantalizing micro-brewed beers; beware of the dress standards (no shorts, vests or thongs) enforced in the evenings.

Plum Market Sq, Viaduct Harbour. Sister bar to *Lime* (see below) trying to repeat the trick of making a success out of bar the size of a post box and succeeding.

Rakino's 1st floor, 35 High St. Good daytime café with tables shaped like Hauraki Gulf islands (including Rakino Island) which on Thursday, Friday and Saturday evenings transforms into a compact venue serving up anything from live jazz to DJs.

Shakespeare Tavern 61 Albert St. Not the liveliest or friendliest pub in the city but it does have an in-house micro-brewery producing a thirst-quenching low-alcohol ginger beer and a handful of commendable, stiffer brews – also sold in two-litre bottles to take away.

Starks Civic Theatre Bar, cnr Queen St & Wellesley St ☎09/377 0277. Open daily this deeply relaxing and stylish little cocktail bar offers the best gin and tonics in town, crossroads people watching, reasonable food and highly polished professional service.

Tabac 6 Mills Lane. Cosy establishment co-owned by former Crowded House singer/songwriter Neil Finn; good for a drink in the bar or take it through to the sofas of the intimate Velvet Room out back. Closed Sun & Mon.

The suburbs

The Carlton Club cnr Broadway & Khyber Pass Rd, Newmarket. Pub and brasserie offering good-value meals and presenting live music most weekends.

Galbraith's Alehouse 2 Mount Eden Rd. Microbrew pub with some of New Zealand's finest English-style ales plus hand-pulled Guinness, Orangeboom, Tuborg, Boddingtons and fifty-odd bottled varieties. Good back-to-basics bar meals include liver and onions and fish and chips along with hearty soups and desserts – all at very reasonable prices.

Lime 167 Ponsonby Rd. Longstanding locals' favourite with a reputation as a singles bar, primarily because its tiny and more than forty people means you end up with your hands in someone else's back pockets. Good cocktails, friendly staff and sing-along music, make this a fun late-night hang out (sister bar *Plum* on the Market Sq).

Mad Dogs and Englishmen 41 Albert St. Massive city sports bar, masquerading unconvincingly as an English pub, full of pool tables, big screen TV and booth seating, where you can pick up a pint of Irish stout, Newcastle Brown and John Smiths.

Sponge 198 Ponsonby Rd. A flashy oval bar adorns the centre of this modern cocktail bar-cum-smooth designer club, DJs spin house and hip hop, music and well-dressed, slightly older partygoers canoodle on the leather booth seating.

SPQR 150 Ponsonby Rd. Dimly lit and eternally groovy bar with an excellent range of wines (all sold by the glass) and beers, and fine Italian food (especially the pizzas); a good venue for spotting off-duty rock stars and actors.

Surrender Dorothy 175 Ponsonby Rd. An intimate and friendly bar with a strong gay following, that's great for a quiet drink anytime although it gets more lively on Friday and Saturday nights. Closed Sun & Mon.

Verboten 212 Posonby Rd. Next door to but not quite so louche as *The Whiskey*, this long thin bar takes the overspill from its neighbour but has a personality of its own and isn't a bad spot to stop for a couple of cocktails while sizing up the wildlife.

The Whiskey 210 Ponsonby Rd, Ponsonby. Stylish modern bar with something of the feel of a groovy gentleman's club, all chocolate leather sofas and white brick walls hung with superb photos of Little Richard, the New York Dolls, Jimi Hendrix and more.

Clubs and gigs

Auckland has a passable club scene and, by sheer weight of population, gets to see more bands than anywhere else in the country; indeed, the bigger international acts often make it no further. But if New York is the city that never sleeps Auckland is the city that dashes home for its slippers and dressing gown around midnight.

Though the area downtown around the junction of Vulcan Lane and High Street occasionally grasps the **clubbing** torch, the flame currently burns brightest along Karangahape Road, where you can join the nightly flow of bright (and not so) young things meandering between the bars and clubs. Unless someone special is on the decks or a band is playing, few clubs charge more than $5 admission (and many are free), encouraging sporadic and unpredictable evisits – just follow the crowds.

Many of the clubs have one area set up as a stage and on any night of the week you might find top Kiwi acts and even overseas **bands** blazing away in the corner; a few pubs may also put on a band from time to time. Bigger acts understandably opt for the larger venues; tickets can be booked through Ticketek (℡09/307 5000).

All venues listed are in the **city centre** unless otherwise specified; see map on p.93.

The Fu Bar 166 Queen St. A cool basement club with a good dance floor that kicks off about 10pm with DJ-inspired grooves and occasional alternative and progressive sounds. Big name platter spinners hit the spot regularly but are usually accompanied by prohibitive cover charges $20–40.

Galatos 17 Galatos St. ℡09/303 1928. Mellow lounge bar attached to a small venue offering a broad selection of DJ-led dance nights and off-beat live acts from around the globe. Closed Sun–Tues.

The Jazz Bar Cnr Queen and Rutland Sts ℡09/309 2512. Late-night, fun bar where live jazz acts bash out old favourites while people try to dance on the postage stamp dance-floor.

Ibiza 253 K'Road ℡09/302 3354. Level three of this lounge bar is a dance club playing house, R&B, retro and to a lesser extent progressive music; there's a bar and restaurant below.

Kings Arms 59 France St, Newton ℡09/373 3240. Popular pub and second-string venue hosting local and touring acts who can't quite fill the *Power Station*.

Khuja Lounge 536 Queen St ℡09/377 3711. Currently hot on the weekend circuit, this bar/club caters to a slightly-older, more musically inclined crowd, often mixing the styles – *khuja* means "melting pot" in Arabic. Closed Sun–Tues.

Papa Jack's Voodoo Lounge 9 Vulcan Lane ℡09/358 4847. Big bar with a party atmosphere that's heaving at weekends when it stays open to the small hours. Mixed dance and alternative rock DJs occasionally give way to top Kiwi touring bands when there'll be a small cover charge.

Roots 322 K' Rd ℡09/308 9667. Late-night club that's very much the place to go for DJs spinning reggae, Cuban and African beats.

Classical music, dance, theatre and comedy

Auckland's **theatre** scene is increasingly vibrant; though there is no professional company with a permanent venue, the Auckland Theatre Company (☏09/309 3395, ⊛www.auckland-theatre.co.nz) is now firmly established at both the Aotea Centre and the Maidment, with occasional performances elsewhere. The Aotea Centre doubles as the major venue for classical music, **opera** and **ballet**, but events are held only sporadically: the New Zealand Symphony Orchestra strikes up every month or so, the Wellington-based New Zealand Ballet calls in during its tours of the provinces from time to time, and the Auckland Opera puts on several shows a year. The **Auckland Philharmonia** (☏0508/266 237, ⊛www.aucklandphil.co.nz) also put on a number of shows at the Auckland Town Hall and Aotea Centre.

The **comedy** scene is equally lively, with a dedicated venue hosting regular stand-up comedy, while in late April and early May theatres and pubs around town are alive with local stand-up comics and top-flight international acts for the two-week **comedy festival**.

Aotea Centre Aotea Square, Queen St ☏09/307 5060. New Zealand's first purpose-built opera house, opened in 1990 and the home stage for New Zealand Symphony Orchestra and the New Zealand Ballet. The Auckland Theatre Company frequently performs in its Herald Theatre.

Civic Theatre cnr Queen St and Wellesley St ☏09/307 5058. Wondrously restored theatre (see p.96) worth visiting if there's anything at all on: could be dance, theatre or classic movies.

Classic 321 Queen St ☏09/373 4321, ⊛www.comedy.co.nz. Bar and comedy venue hosting all the best local names and the smaller

world-class acts when they're in town. Shows Wed–Sat (and sometimes other nights) but with the best line-ups at weekends when it is $15–20 for the main acts and $10 for the 11pm impro show.

Maidment Theatre cnr Princess St & Alfred St ☏09/308 2383, ⊛www.maidment.auckland .co.nz. Two university theatres, with mainstream works in the larger venue and more daring stuff in the studio.

Silo Theatre Lower Grays Ave ☏09/366 0339. Small venue specializing in less mainstream plays and events. Success varies, but there's usually something interesting on.

Cinema

Suburban multiplexes have virtually killed off smaller cinemas leaving central Auckland with just one twelve-screen monstrosity and one arthouse screen; **repertory** cinemas are more widely scattered, and are listed below. The annual **Auckland International Film Festival**, usually held in early July, presses many of these cinemas into service for arthouse and foreign screenings. **Admission** is around $15, though many cinemas drop their admission to $9 before 6pm on weekdays.

Academy 64 Lorne St ☏09/373 2761, ⊛www.academy-cinema.co.nz. Predominantly arthouse cinema with two screens tucked underneath the main library.

Bridgeway 122 Queen St, Birkenhead ☏418 3308. Recently renovated movie theatre on the North Shore that makes cinema-going even more of a pleasure with its intimate feel, good foyer food and coffee, luxurious seating and a wall-to-wall curved screen.

Devonport 3 48 Victoria Rd, Devonport ☏09/446 0999. First-run Hollywood movies. Accessible from the city with Fullers' Ferry & Movie Pass for much the same price you'd pay for just the movie on Queen Street.

Lido 427 Manukau Rd, Epsom ☏09/630 1500. Grab a beer or wine, sink into super-wide seats, and enjoy mainstream and classic movies with superb digital sound in this renovated suburban cinema.

Listings

Airlines Air New Zealand and Air New Zealand Link ☎0800/737 767; British Airways ☎09/357 8950; Cathay Pacific ☎09/977 2210; Canadian ☎09/309 0735; Garuda ☎09/366 1862; Freedom Air ☎0800/600 500; JAL ☎09/379 9906; Malaysian ☎09/379 3743; Qantas ☎09/357 8900; Singapore Airlines ☎09/379 3209; Thai ☎09/377 3886; United ☎09/379 3800.

Automobile Association 99 Albert St ☎09/377 4660, ⓦwww.nzaa.co.nz.

Bike rental Adventure Cycles, 36 Customs St East (☎09/309 5566, ⓦwww.adventure-auckland .co.nz), has city bikes for $18, mountain bikes from $25 and offers touring bikes at around $180 a month. Adventure Cycles also offers a service whereby you buy the equipment and they'll buy it back from you at the end of your trip for half the purchase price. Good deals can also be had at Cycles 4 Tour, 4 Hire, 4 Sale, Australia House, Custom Street East ☎09/309 5566.

Bookshops The biggest bookshops are downtown: Borders, at 291 Queen St (☎09/309 3377), and Whitcoulls, 210 Queen St (☎09/356 5400). In addition, try the more highbrow Unity Books, 19 High St (☎09/307 0731); and for a massive selection of secondhand books visit Hard to Find (But Worth The Effort) either at 238 K' Rd (☎09/303 0555), or over in Devonport at 81a Victoria St (☎09/446 0300). Out!, 39 Anzac Ave (☎09/377 7770), is the place for gay-interest books and magazines; and the Women's Bookshop, 105 Ponsonby Rd (☎09/376 4399), specializes in feminist literature and women's interest books.

Bus departures InterCity (☎09/913 6100, ⓦwww.intercitycoach.co.nz) runs the most comprehensive range of services to many destinations in conjunction with their partner, Newmans (☎09/913 6200, ⓦwww.newmanscoach.co.nz). Tickets for InterCity and Newmans can be bought at the office in the Sky City terminal on Hobson St. Guthreys (☎0800/759 999) runs to Hamilton, Rotorua, Taupo, Waitomo and Tauranga daily and offer very competitive prices.

Buying a car For general advice, consult Basics (see p.34), then peruse the noticeboards in hostels and at the main visitor centre or get along to one of the weekend car fairs, which are typically dominated by private sellers rather than dealers. The major venues are the Auckland Car Fair, Ellerslie Racecourse, Greenlane (☎09/529 2233, ⓦwww.carfair.co.nz), and the Manukau Car Fair, Manukau City Shopping Centre (☎09/358 5000). All take place in the morning from 9am to noon or

1pm (gates usually open around 8am) and are well organized, with qualified folk on hand to check roadworthiness. Alternatively, glance through the page of cars for sale in the weekly Auto Trader or Trade & Exchange magazines, or pick up Wednesday's or Saturday's New Zealand Herald newspaper.

Camping and outdoor equipment Bivouac, 109 Queen St (☎09/366 1966) and 300 Broadway, Newmarket (☎09/529 2298), have a good selection of quality gear for sale or rent; Kathmandu, 151 Queen St (☎09/309 4615), stocks all the major brands; and Doyles, 66 Hobson St (☎09/377 6998), have low-cost gear for sale. It's also worth checking the noticeboard in Auckland's main visitor centre and around the hostels for offers of camping and tramping gear for sale.

Car rental The international companies all have depots close to the airport and free shuttle buses to get you to them; smaller companies, frequently offering highly competitive rates in return for older cars and a poorer back-up network, are mostly based in the city or inner suburbs. Call around for the best deals. Ace Rentals 39–43 The Strand ☎09/303 3112, ⓦwww.acerentals.co.nz; A2B Rentals ☎09/377 0825 & 0800/616 888, ⓦwww.a2brentals.co.nz; Apex ☎09/257 0292 & 0800/737 009, ⓦwww.apexrentals.co.nz; Avis ☎09/379 2650 & 0800/655 111, ⓦwww.avis.com and airport ☎09/275 7239; Budget ☎09/265 2227 & 0800/283 438, ⓦwww.budget.co.nz and airport ☎09/256 8447; Hertz ☎09/367 6350, ⓦwww.hertz.com and airport ☎09/256 8695; National Car Rental ☎09/379 5080 & 0800/800 115 and airport ☎09/275 0066; NZ Rent a Car ☎09/308 9004 & 0800/809 005, ⓦwww.nzcars.co.nz; Rent-a-Dent ☎09/309 0066 and airport ☎09/275 2044; Thrifty Car Rental ☎0800/737 070, ⓦwww.thrifty.co.nz and airport ☎09/257 0562.

Consulates Australia ☎09/489 8249; Canada ☎09/309 8516; UK ☎09/303 2973; USA ☎09/303 2724.

Currency exchange Custom House Exchange, Level 2D, ABC Bank Centre, 135 Albert St ☎0800/660 037; Interforex 99 Quay St ☎09/302 3066; Tavelex 159 Queen St ☎09/379 3924 & 34 Queen St ☎09/377 2666; Money World 155 Queen St ☎09/366 3280.

Emergencies Police, fire and ambulance, ☎111; Auckland Central police station ☎09/302 6400.

Events Auckland Anniversary Weekend, sailing regatta on the Waitemata Harbour on the last weekend in Jan; Devonport Food and Wine Festival, third weekend in Feb; Pasifika Festival (ⓦ www.akcity/pasifika), a celebration of Polynesian and Pacific Island culture held at Western Springs Reserve, first or second Saturday in March; Round the Bays Run, when up to 70,000 jog 10km along Tamaki drive, last Sunday in March; Waiheke Jazz Festival, Easter week; Royal New Zealand Easter Show, Easter weekend, family entertainment Kiwi-style with equestrian events, wine tasting and arts and crafts, all held at the showgrounds along Greenlane; International Comedy Festival, late April and early May; Auckland International Film Festival, early July.

Internet access and discount phone centres There is Internet access in virtually all Auckland's accommodation as well as cyber cafes all over the central city mostly charging $3–7 an hour: try Cyber Max, behind the Queen St visitor centre; the 24hr Cyber Gates, 409 Queen St; the 24hr Hot Shotz, 13 Customs St East; Cyber City, 29 Victoria St, next to Albert Park Backpackers or Net, 2 308 Queen St.

Laundry Clean Green Laundromat, 18 Fort St ⓣ 09/358 4370; Mon–Sat 9am–8pm.

Left luggage Lockers at the Sky City Bus Terminal, Hobson St, and many hostels also have long-term storage for one-time guests at minimal or no charge.

Library Auckland Public Library, 44–46 Lorne St ⓣ 09/377 0209; Mon–Fri 9.30am–8pm, Sat 10am–4pm, Sun noon–4pm.

Maps Auckland Map Centre, 1a Wyndham St (ⓣ 09/309 7725), or Speciality Maps, 46 Albert St (ⓣ 09/307 2217).

Medical treatment Auckland Hospital, Park Rd, Grafton ⓣ 09/379 7440; Travelcare, 5th Floor, 125 Queen St ⓣ 09/373 4621, offers diving medicals, physiotherapy, X-rays and dental treatment and there's also the City Medical Centre, Cnr of Albert St and Mill Lane which has doctors and a pharmacy (Mon–Fri 8am–6pm, Sat 9.30am–1pm). Registered medical practitioners are listed separately at the beginning of the White Pages phone directory.

Newspapers and magazines Auckland's morning paper is the anodyne *New Zealand Herald* (ⓦ www.nzherald.co.nz), the closest New Zealand gets to a national daily. The best selection of international newspapers – mostly from Australia, UK and the US – is at Borders, 291 Queen St. This is also your best bet for specialist magazines, which are also sold at branches of Magazzino (123 Ponsonby Rd, Ponsonby; and 3 Mortimer Passage, Newmarket). These shops also sell *Metro*, Auckland's city monthly which, if nothing else, offers an insight into the aspirations of upwardly mobile Aucklanders.

Pharmacy The most convenient late-opening pharmacy is the Auckland City Urgent Pharmacy, 60 Broadway, Newmarket (Mon–Fri 6am–1am, Sat & Sun 9am–1am); emergency departments of hospitals (see "Medical treatment" above) have 24hr pharmacies.

Post office Auckland's main post office is just off Queen St in the Bledisloe Building, 24 Wellesley St ⓣ 09/379 6710 (Mon–Fri 8.30am–5pm), and has poste restante facilities.

Swimming Central pools include the indoor Edwardian-style Tepid Baths, 102 Customs St West (ⓣ 09/379 4745), the open-air saltwater Parnell Baths, Judges Bay Rd (ⓣ 09/373 3561), and the heated outdoor Point Erin Baths, cnr Shelley Beach Rd & Sarsfield St, Herne Bay (ⓣ 09/376 6863). Otherwise, simply head for one of the beaches (see "The North Shore", p.108).

Taxis Alert ⓣ 09/309 2000; Co-op ⓣ 09/300 3000; Corporate ⓣ 09/377 0773; Discount ⓣ 09/529 1000.

Travel agencies Budget Travel, 33 Lorne St (ⓣ 0800/808 040), and STA Travel, 10 High St (ⓣ 0508/782 872), are good for internal and international travel, or visit one of the specialist backpacker places (see p.90).

Women's centres Auckland Women's Centre, 4 Warnock St, Grey Lynn (Mon–Fri 9am–4pm; ⓣ 09/376 3227, ⓦ www.womenz.org.nz), offers counselling, health advice, massage and a library.

Around Auckland

For many, the best Auckland has to offer lies in the immediate vicinity, with its verdant hills, magnificent beaches and appealing seaside communities. Few would argue that the **Waitakere Ranges**, to the **west** of the city, rank among

Moving on from Auckland

Moving on from Auckland is a straightforward business, with frequent **buses** following the main routes north and south to most major destinations, and **trains** (Tranz Scenic ☎0800/802 802, ⓦwww.tranzscenic.co.nz) leaving daily for Hamilton, Palmerston North and Wellington. If you are **driving**, you have a couple of alternatives if you're heading north. You can take SH1 directly over the harbour bridge and make for Orewa, or go west around the head of the Waitemata Harbour past the wineries, West Coast Beaches and Waitakere Ranges to meet up with SH1 at Wellsford. **Cyclists** must use the Devonport Ferry rather than the harbour bridge if heading directly north but will do well to take the western route, possibly riding a suburban train to Waitakere (bikes carried free outside peak hours). Southbound cyclists are better off following the Seabird Coast, avoiding the Southern Motorway, the main route south out of the city for motorists.

The network of **ferries** and **flights** linking the islands in the Hauraki Gulf presents more interesting ways to get out of the city. By linking them together you can visit a few islands and continue on to Whitianga on the Coromandel Peninsula or Whangarei without returning to Auckland. The most useful combination is to take a ferry to Great Barrier Island (see p.149) and catch a flight from there, possibly adding Waiheke Island to your itinerary; contact Fullers (☎09/367 9111) and Great Barrier Airlines (☎09/256 6500 & 0800/900 600) for schedules and fares. Finally, if you're on your way out of New Zealand, remember to keep $25 aside for your **airport tax**, as this is payable on site, rather than being included in the price of your ticket.

New Zealand's most spectacular landscapes, but their proximity makes them a viable break from the urban bustle. The hills also serve to deflect the prevailing westerly winds, providing shelter for the **vineyards** of the Henderson Valley and Kumeu, home base for some of the country's top winemakers, most of which offer tastings.

Spectacular expanses of sand which can't be beaten for long moody strolls are found pretty much the full length of New Zealand's western seaboard, but it is only at Auckland's **West Coast beaches** that you will find surf-lifesaving patrols in reassuring numbers. Heading **north**, Auckland infringes on southern Northland, making the **Hibiscus Coast** a virtual suburb, enormously popular with day-trippers and holiday-home owners. South of Auckland, the **Hunua Ranges** offer a few modest walks and again provide a windbreak, this time for the **Seabird Coast**, where low shingle banks and extensive mudflats form an excellent breeding ground for dozens of migratory species.

West of Auckland

Auckland's suburban sprawl peters out some 20km west of the centre among the enveloping folds of the **Waitakere Ranges**. Despite being the most accessible expanse of greenery for over a million people, the hills remain largely unspoilt, with plenty of trails through native bush. On a hot summer day, thousands head up and over the hills to one of half a dozen thundering **surf beaches**, all largely undeveloped but for a few holiday homes (known to most Kiwis as *baches*) and the odd shop. The soils around the eastern fringes of the Waitakeres nurture long established **vineyards**, mainly clustered in the Henderson Valley but also stretching north to Kumeu, just short of the Kaipara Harbour town of **Helensville** and the **hot pools** at Parakai.

You'll need your own transport to do justice to the beaches and most of the ranges, unless you join one of the West Coast **tours**: Bush & Beach (T09/575 1458, W www.bushandbeach.co.nz) runs a half-day trip out west ($85) and a more satisfying full-day tour ($130) which takes in Piha Beach; and GeoTours (T09/525 3991, W www.geotours.co.nz) do a "Gannets & Volcanics of the West" trip (half-day; $80). You can also see something of the area on canyoning trips (see p.115) from Auckland.

As far as public transport goes, the Tranz Metro **trains** make it as far as Henderson and Waitakere – a boon for cyclists keen to get out of the city quickly – and Richies **buses** #054, #055, #064 & #066 run through Henderson to Kumeu.

The Henderson and Kumeu wineries

Much of New Zealand's enviable reputation as a producer of quality wine is the result of vintages emanating from West Auckland, the historical home of the country's viticulture. The bigger enterprises now grow most of their grapes in Marlborough, Gisborne and Hawke's Bay, but much of the production process is still centred 20km west of central Auckland around the suburban Henderson Valley, or 15km further north around the contiguous and equally characterless villages of **Kumeu** and **Huapai**.

As early as 1819 the Reverend Samuel Marsden planted grapes, ostensibly to produce sacramental wine, in Kerikeri in the Bay of Islands, but commercial winemaking didn't really get under way until Dalmatians turned their hand to growing grapes after the kauri gum they came to dig ceased to be profitable (see p.224 for the finer points of gum digging). Many of today's thriving businesses owe their existence to these immigrant families, a legacy evident in winery names such as Babich, Delegat, Nobilo and Selak. Today, the region is producing some quality wines and winning prestigious awards, usually with the key varietals of Cabernet Sauvignon, Merlot, Pinot Noir and Chardonnay. More than anywhere else in the country, this is where you can taste wines produced throughout New Zealand in one day.

The free *Winemakers of Auckland* leaflet available from Auckland visitor centres details the **wineries** that can be visited; most offer tastings. Give Henderson a miss and head out to the rural and broadly more appealing Kumeu where half a dozen places do tastings, notably Coopers Creek, SH16, Huapai (T09/412 8560, W www.cooperscreek.co.nz; Mon–Fri 9.30am–5.30pm, Sat 10.30am–5.30pm), Kumeu River, SH16 Kumeu (T09/412 8415, W www.kumeuriver.co.nz; Mon–Fri 9am–5.30pm, Sat 11am–5.30pm), Nobilo, Station Rd, Huapai (T09/412 9148, W www.nobilo.co.nz; Mon–Fri 9am–5pm, Sat 10am–5pm, Sun 11am–4pm), Harrier Rise, 748 Waitakere Rd (T09/412 7256; Sat & Sun noon–5.30pm) and Matua Valley, Waimauku Valley Rd, Waimauku (T09/411 8301, W www.matua.co.nz; Mon–Fri 9am–5pm, Sat 10am–5pm, Sun 11am–4.30pm). At the last, reserve a table to eat at the wonderful, if pricey, *Hunting Lodge* **restaurant** (T09/411 8259; lunch & dinner Wed–Sun; $25–35 for main dishes), which is beautifully set beside the vines. For more modest eating, visit *Carriages*, SH15 in Huapai, where excellent café-style food is served on a large deck or inside a couple of old railway carriages.

If you plan to do some serious tasting, designate a non-drinking driver or leave the car behind and join one of the West Coast tours (see above) which visit wineries as part of wider explorations. Better still, spend the day with Fine Wine Tours (T & F09/849 4519, W www.insidertouring.co.nz), which offers a selection of specialist small-group wine tours around west Auckland, some also visiting gannet colony. Their half-day tour ($119) visits three or four wineries, and allows time for a relaxed lunch, full-day tours ($149) often include extra wineries and food-tasting.

The Waitakere Ranges and the West Coast beaches

Auckland's western limit is defined by the bush-clad **Waitakere Ranges**, which rise up to five hundred metres. At less than an hour's drive from the city, the hills are a perennially popular weekend destination for Aucklanders intent on a picnic and a bit of a stroll. The western slopes roll down to the wild, black-sand **West Coast beaches**. Pounded by heavy surf and punctuated by preci-pitous headlands, these tempestuous shores are a perfect counterpoint to the calm, gently shelving beaches of the Hauraki Gulf.

The Kawarau a Maki people knew the region as Te Wao Nui a Tiriwa or "the Great Forest of Tiriwa", aptly describing the kauri groves that swathed the hills before the arrival of Europeans. By the turn of the century, diggers had pretty much cleaned out the kauri gum, but logging continued until the 1940s, by which time the land was economically spent. The Auckland Regional Council bought the land, built reservoirs and designated a vast tract as the Centennial Memorial Park, with two hundred kilometres of walking tracks leading to fine vistas and some of the numerous waterfalls which cascade off the escarpment.

The easiest access to the majority of the walks and beaches is the **Waitakere Scenic Drive** (Route 24), which winds through the ranges from the

Always swim between the flags

The New Zealand coast is frequently pounded by ferocious surf and even strong swimmers can find themselves in difficulty in what may seem relatively benign conditions. Most **drownings** happen when people swim outside areas patrolled by volunteer lifeguards. Every day throughout the peak holiday weeks (Christmas–Jan), and at weekends through the rest of the summer (Nov–Easter), the most popular surf beaches are monitored daily from around 10am to 5pm. Lifeguards stake out a section of beach between two red and yellow flags and continually monitor that area: always swim between the flags.

Before entering the water, watch other swimmers to see if they are being dragged along the beach by a strong along-shore **current** or **rip**. Often the rip will turn out to sea at some point leaving a "river" of disturbed but relatively calm water through the pattern of curling breakers. On entering the water, feel the strength of the waves and current before committing yourself too deeply, then keep glancing back to where you left your towel to judge your drift along the shore. Look out too for **sand bars**, a common feature of surf beaches at certain tides: wading out to sea, you may well be neck deep, then suddenly be only up to your knees. The corollary is that moments after being comfortably within your depth you'll be floundering around in a **hole**, reaching for the bottom. Note that **boogie boards**, while providing flotation, can make you vulnerable to rips, and riders should always wear fins (flippers).

If you do find yourself in **trouble**, try not to panic, raise one hand in the air and yell to attract the attention of other swimmers and surf rescue folk. Most of all, don't struggle against the current; either swim across the rip or let it drag you out. Around 100–200 metres offshore the current will often subside and you can swim away from the rip and bodysurf the breakers back to shore. If you have to be rescued (or are just feeling generous), a large donation is in order. Surf lifeguards are dedicated volunteers, always strapped for cash and in need of new rescue equipment.

dormitory suburb of **Titirangi**, in the foothills, to the informative **Arataki visitor centre** (Sept–May daily 9am–5pm; June–Aug Mon–Fri 10am–4pm Sat & Sun 9am–5pm). From here, walkways forge into the second-growth forest, where panels identify the multitude of species visible from a series of nature trails (20min–1hr) which loop around the centre, the longest visiting one of the few mature kauri stands to survive the loggers' onslaught. A felled kauri has been transformed by Kawarau a Maki carvers into a striking *pou*, or guardian post, the largest of several fine carvings around the centre. Arataki is also the place to pick up **camping** permits (call the Parksline in advance on ☎09/303 1530) for the twelve backpacker sites ($4 per person) scattered through the ranges and located on the *Waitakere Ranges Recreation and Track Guide* map ($8, available from the visitor centre).

Beyond the visitor centre, the scenic drive swings north along the range, passing side roads to the **beaches**, noted for their foot-scorching, golden-black sands and demanding swimming conditions. Before entering the water, read the box below, and heed all warning signs.

No **buses** run out this way, but Piha Surf Shuttle (☎025/227 4000; $20 each way; reserve at least 24hrs in advance) picks up in Auckland around 8.30am and leaves Piha for the city at 4pm.

Whatipu

Whatipu is the southernmost of the West Coast surf beaches, 45km from central Auckland and located by the sand-bar entrance to Manukau Harbour, the watery grave of many a ship. The wharf at Whatipu was briefly the terminus of the precarious coastal **Parahara Railway**, which hauled kauri from the mill at Karekare across the beach and headlands during the 1870s. The tracks were continually pounded by surf, but a second tramway from Piha covered the same treacherous expanse in the early twentieth century. Scant remains are visible, including an old tunnel which proved too tight a squeeze for a large steam engine whose boiler still litters the shore.

Over the last few decades, the sea has receded more than half a kilometre leaving a very broad beach backed by wetlands colonized by cabbage trees, tall *toe toe* grasses and waterfowl. It's a great place to explore, particularly along the base of the cliffs to the north where, in 30min, you can walk to the **Ballroom Cave**, fitted with a sprung dancefloor in the 1920s that apparently still survives, buried by five metres of sand that has drifted into the cave in the intervening years.

The only sign of civilization here now is *Whatipu Lodge* (☎09/811 8860, Ⓔwhatipulodge@xtra.co.nz; tent sites $12, rooms ❸). Occupying a 120-year-old former mill manager's house, the lodge only has electricity when the generator is fired up each evening, but has extensive communal cooking facilities, hot showers, a tennis court, a cosy library and a full-size billiard table.

Karekare, Piha and Te Henga

You can walk 5km north along the beach from Whatipu to **KAREKARE**, otherwise reached by a 17km road from Arataki visitor centre. Perhaps the most intimate and immediately appealing of the West Coast settlements, Karekare has regenerating manuka, pohutukawa and cabbage trees running down to a deep, smooth beach hemmed in by high promontories and only a smattering of houses more or less successfully integrated into the bush. In one hectic year, this dramatic spot was jolted out of its relative obscurity, providing the setting for beach scenes in Jane Campion's 1993 film *The Piano* and, at much the same time, the inspiration for Crowded House's *Together Alone* album. Spikes that once secured the Parahara railway tracks to the wave-cut platform around the headland to the south can still be seen from the **Gap Gallery Track** (15min each way), which winds around Korekau Point to the seemingly endless beach beyond – but beware, the track is submerged at high tide. The Karekare Surf Club patrols a safe swimming area on summer weekends, or there is the pool below **Karekare Falls**, a five-minute walk on a track just inland from the road. Despite the presence of the fine colonial Winchelsea House, there is nowhere to stay and no facilities at Karekare.

For decades **PIHA**, 20km west of the visitor centre at Arataki has been an icon for Aucklanders. It is the quintessential West Coast beach with its string of low-key weekend cottages and crashing surf that lures day-tripping families as well as a youthful partying set whose New Year's Eve antics hastened in a dusk-till-dawn alcohol ban on holiday weekends.

Piha feels on the brink of change; in the last few years some of the quaint old-time *baches* have been displaced by condo-style developments, and gentrification seems inevitable.

For the time being, though, a 3km-long sweep of gold-and-black sand is hemmed in by bush-clad hills and split by Piha's defining feature, the 101m **Lion Rock**. This former *pa* site, with some imagination, resembles a seated lion staring out to sea; the energetic climb to a shoulder two-thirds of the way up (20–30min return) is best done as the day cools and the sun casts a gentler light. The **Tasman Lookout Track** (30–40min return) leaves the south end of the beach, climbing up to a lookout over the tiny cove of The Gap where a spectacular blowhole performs in heavy surf.

Most **swimmers** flock to South Piha, the quarter of the beach south of Lion Rock where the more prestigious of the two surf-lifesaving clubs hogs the best **surf**. North Piha Road follows the beach north of Lion Rock for 2km to the second surf club. If battling raging surf isn't your thing, head for the cool **pool** below Kitekite Falls, a three-stage plunge reached on a loop track (1hr 30min) that starts 1km up Glen Esk Road, which runs inland opposite Piha's central Domain.

Most of Piha's visitors are day-trippers so facilities are limited to a general store, a fine traditional burger bar at South Piha (summer only), and a surf shop, Piha Surf (℡09/812 8723, ⓦwww.pihasurf.co.nz/), a couple of kilometres before the beach on the road in. There are a few **places to stay** including good-value, self-contained caravans at the Surf Shop (❶–❷), and the poorly shaded, year-round *Piha Domain Motor Camp* (℡09/812 8815; tent sites $10; on-site vans ❷), which is slightly set back from the beach and best booked well in advance. For something a little more upmarket try *Piha Lodge*, 117 Piha Rd, 3km before you reach the beach (℡09/812 8595, ⓦwww.pihalodge.co.nz; ❻), which has comfortable rooms and an outdoor pool.

The smaller and much less popular **TE HENGA** (also known as Bethell's Beach) lies at the end of a long road from Waitakere, 8km north along the coast. Less dramatic than Karekare, Piha or Muriwai, Te Henga is correspondingly less visited, making it good for escaping the crowds at the height of summer. There are no shops, but there is a surf club and **accommodation** (℡09/810 9581, ⓦwww.bethellsbeach.com) – at either the elegant pohutukawa-shaded *Te Koinga Cottage* (❽), which can house up to seven but comfortably sleeps two couples, or *Turehu Cottage* (❼), a smaller studio sleeping two; both have kitchens.

Muriwai

MURIWAI, the most populous of the West Coast beach settlements, lies 15km north of Piha, and 10km coastwards from Huapai. Again, there's wonderful surf and a long beach stretching 45km north to the heads of Kaipara Harbour. The main attraction here, though, is at the southern end of the beach where a **gannet colony** occupies Motutara Island and Otakamiro Point, the headland between the main beach and the surfers' cove of Maori Bay. The gannets breed here between September and March before migrating to sunnier Australian climes, a few staying behind with the fur seals which inhabit the rocks below. Gannets normally prefer the protection of islands and this is one of the few places where they nest on the mainland, in this case right below some excellent viewing platforms from where you can observe them gracefully wheeling on the up-draughts. Short paths lead up here from near the surf club and off the road to Maori Bay. The beach, dunes and exotic, planted forests to the north are best explored on **horse treks** run by the Muriwai Riding Centre, 290 Oaia Rd (℡09/411 8480; 2hr; $60).

The Waterfront **general store** serves light meals and booze but there's no indoor seating and keep in mind that the lease is up so there's no guarantee it'll be open. If you want to **stay** try either the *Muriwai Beach Lodge*, 380 Motutara Rd (℡09/411 8089; ●), a pleasing self-contained flat in a B&B near the beach or the shaded *Muriwai Beach Motor Camp*, (℡09/411 9262; tent sites $10). For those without transport, Bush & Beach Ltd (see p.130) run half-day and full day-trips out here.

The southern Kaipara: Helensville and Parakai

Venture beyond the vineyards of Kumeu and you'll soon find yourself in uninspiring **HELENSVILLE**, 45km from Auckland but more closely associated with Kaipara Harbour (see below). Like many Kaipara towns, Helensville was founded on timber which, following the completion of the rail link to Auckland in 1881, was floated here in huge rafts then loaded onto wagons. Dairying has replaced the kauri trade and, though the spread of the Auckland conurbation is threatening, Helensville still potters along. Photos of busier days are displayed at the **Helensville Pioneer Museum**, on Commercial Street as you enter the town (daily 10–4pm; $5 suggested donation) but you'll get a better idea of what the kauri logging days were like with Kaipara Action Tours (℡09/420 8466; Dec to mid-March, according to demand but mostly weekends), which ply the waters of Kaipara Harbour, visiting kauri mills and bush camps. The three-hour Historical and Nature Cruise costs around $25, while the full-day "Go North" Bus 'n' Boat Adventure ($95) links up with a 4WD sand bus to take you into Dargaville (see p.226) along Ripiro Beach, where chauffer-driven quad bikes take you up and down the dunes. Depending on the tide, boats leave either from the wharf at Springs Road in Parakai, just north of the Aquatic Park (see below), or from Shelly Beach wharf, 20km north of Helensville.

To get to Kaipara Harbour you have to drive through **PARAKAI**, 3km north of Helensville and chiefly noted for its Aquatic Park (℡09/420 8998; daily 10am–10pm; $12, private spa $5 extra per hour), where a series of pools are filled by natural hot springs; entry includes free use of a couple of buffeting water chutes.

Practicalities

Richies **buses** #066, #067 & #069 (℡0800/103080; Mon–Sat only) operate from the corner of Customs and Lower Albert streets in central Auckland to Parakai and Helensville, with one evening service continuing on to Orewa (see p.135). There's a **visitor centre**, 27 Commercial Rd (daily 9am–5pm; ℡09/420 8060, ⊛www.helensville.co.nz), right in the heart of town.

The best **place to stay** is the central *Malolo House*, 110 Commercial Rd (☎0800/286 060, ☎ & ☎09/420 7262, ☎malolo@xtra.co.nz), which operates as a high-standard backpackers with four-shares (❶) and doubles (❷) and a beautifully decorated B&B with en-suite rooms (❺). If this doesn't suit, try the *Mineral Park Motel*, 3 Parakai Ave (☎ & ☎09/420 8856; ❹), where each room has its own outdoor mineral pool, or the **campsite** adjacent to Parakai's Aquatic Park (☎09/420 8998; tent sites $15 including pool entry).

Helensville is basically **takeaway** land, with the notable exception of *Café Regent* (☎09/420 9148; licensed and BYO), at 14 Garfield Rd, the northern continuation of Commercial Road. Here, the foyer of an Art Deco former cinema offers filling snacks and coffee as well as an imaginative range of full meals at very reasonable prices; try the mussel fritters.

North of Auckland

The straggling suburbs of north Auckland virtually merge into **The Hibiscus Coast**, which starts 40km north of the city and is increasingly favoured by retirees and long-distance commuters. The region centres on the suburban Whangaparaoa Peninsula, the launching point for trips to Tiritiri Matangi Island (see p.156), and the anodine beachside community of **Orewa**, now mostly bypassed by an extension of the northern motorway. Immediately to the north, the hot springs at **Waiwera** herald the beach-and-barbecue scene of **Wenderholm** and the wonderful **Puhoi** pub. Travelling north, the account continues on p.163 with Warkworth.

Orewa

The most striking of the Hibiscus Coast beaches is the three-kilometre strand backed by **OREWA**, the region's main town, which garners just about all the accommodation and restaurants in the area. It is currently the centre of much development, primarily holiday and retirement homes and shopping malls. Swimming aside, there isn't a great deal to do here, though the visitor centre can point you towards pleasant bushwalks and minor diversions such as the town's stern-looking statue of Edmund Hillary.

South of Orewa, the **Whangaparaoa Peninsula** juts out 12km into the Hauraki Gulf, its central ridge traced by Whangaparaoa Road, which passes the small-time, narrow-gauge **Whangaparaoa Railway**, 400 Whangaparaoa Rd (Sat & Sun 10am–5pm, plus school holidays Mon–Fri 10am–4pm; $5) on the way to **Shakespear Regional Park** (8am–dusk; free), a pleasant enough place to swim and wander through regenerating bush spotting pukeko, red-crowned parakeets and tui. The peninsula's most enticing diversion, though, is a trip to the bird sanctuary of Tiritiri Matangi (see p.156), with boats leaving from the vast Gulf Harbour Marina just before Shakespear Park.

Practicalities

Auckland's Stagecoach **buses** (call Rideline ☎0800/103 080) run a complex timetable from downtown Auckland to the Hibiscus Coast, often requiring a transfer at Silverdale, just south of Orewa. These, and Northland-bound InterCity and Northliner buses, stop in central Orewa after passing the well-stocked **visitor centre**, 214a Hibiscus Coast Highway (Mon–Fri 9am–5pm, Sat & Sun 10am–4pm; ☎09/426 0076, ☻www.orewa-beach.co.nz). Bus routes

#898 and #899 run along Whangaparaoa Road to Shakespear Park several times a day, passing within 2km of the Tiritiri Matangi wharf.

The most convenient budget **accommodation** is *Pillows Travellers Lodge*, 412 Hibiscus Coast Hwy (☎09/426 6338, Ⓦwww.pillows.co.nz), which has modern dorms and four-shares (❶) and rooms, some en suite (❷–❸); while the very relaxing *Marco Polo Backpackers*, 2d Hammond Ave, 2km north at Hatfields Beach (☎09/426 8455, Ⓦwww.4success.co.nz), has some very nice dorms (❶) and rooms (❷) set around a lush garden. **Motels** that line Orewa's main drag, the Hibiscus Coast Highway, tend to be quite expensive during the summer months but try: the beachfront *Edgewater Motel*, at #387 (☎09/426 5260, Ⓕ426 3378; ❹); and the budget *Hibiscus Palms*, at #416 (☎ & Ⓕ09/426 4904, Ⓔhibiscuspalms@xtra.co.nz; ❸). Though it isn't beside the beach, the best **campground** is the peaceful *Puriri Park Holiday Complex*, Puriri Ave (☎0508/478 747 & 09/426 4648, Ⓕ426 2680; tent sites $10, cabins ❷, tourist flats ❸). If you fancy pampering yourself and don't mind staying out of town, try *The Ridge*, Greenhollows Rd (☎0508/843 743, Ⓦwww.theridge.co.nz; ❽), about 10km north of Orewa, though accessed via Puhoi (see p.137; call for directions). A luxurious eco-friendly lodge with panoramic views of the sea, farmland and bush, everything here is beautifully presented, with bush walks fanning out from the house and three-course dinners available ($45).

For straightforward **eating** try the gaudy *Creole Bar & Brasserie*, 310 Hibiscus Coast Hwy, which does decent Mexican, Thai and burgers at modest cost, and stays open late at weekends when there is usually some live entertainment. For something more fancy, visit the *Asahi Japanese Restaurant*, 6 Bakehouse Lane where the sushi is tasty and the teriyaki chicken ($18.50) is to die for (☎09/426 0065), or alternatively have a pie and a pint at the *Ship and Anchor* pub next door.

Waiwera and Wenderholm

The main highway north of Orewa (and bus #895) runs through the cluster of holiday and retirement homes that make up Hatfields Beach to **WAIWERA**, 6km north of Orewa, where Maori once dug holes in the sands to take advantage of the naturally hot springs. Bathing is now formalized in the **Waiwera Thermal Resort**, Waiwera Rd (Ⓦwww.waiwera.co.nz; daily 9am–10pm; $18), a vast complex of suicidal water slides and over twenty indoor and outdoor pools naturally heated to between 28 and 43°C. Private pools can be rented at $25 each per hour. If you're thirsty or peckish after a soak you could do worse than head for **Woody's Bar and Grill** opposite, where you wolf down a full breakfast for $12 or something a little healthier from $7–20.

Occupying a high headland between the estuaries of the Puhoi and Waiwera rivers, **Wenderholm Regional Park** was the first of Auckland's regional parks and is still one of the most celebrated. Its sweeping golden beach is backed by pohutukawa-shaded swathes of grass and is often packed with barbecuing families on summer weekends. Walking tracks ranging from twenty minutes to two hours wind up to a lovely headland viewpoint through nikau palm groves which have been turned into a "mainland island". By trapping and poisoning, the headland is kept free of introduced predators, allowing native birds to return, some reintroduced from Tiritiri Matangi (see p.156). You can also take a peek at **Coudrey House** (Jan daily 1–4pm, Feb-Dec Sat & Sun 1–4pm; $2 ☎09/528 3713), an 1860s colonial homestead.

The #895 bus terminates here on summer Sundays, and if you need to stay there's a nicely sited water-and-toilets **campground** ($5) with grassy plots and a barbecue beside the mangroves.

Puhoi

The village of **PUHOI**, 6km north of Waiwera, is now attracting attention from Auckland lifestylers, but for the moment remains a bucolic place which was settled by staunchly Catholic Bohemian migrants who arrived here in 1863 from Egerland, in the Austro-Hungarian Empire. Their descendants still form a small proportion of Puhoi's tiny population. As the land was found to be poor, the settlers were forced to eke out a living by cutting the bush for timber, and the horns of some of the more famed bullock teams are still ranged around the walls of the historic **Puhoi Tavern**, a colonial hotel containing a single-roomed bar festooned with pioneering paraphernalia and photos. Buy a beer, charm the bartender and you may be invited to see the dining room hung with an impressive collection of paintings of Maori chiefs and princesses. Come on the second or last Friday of each month to see ageing members of a local Bohemian band playing their accordions and supping jugs of beer or tucking into the generously-portioned pub grub.

Few visitors get much further than the pub, but there is an interesting **Puhoi Historical Society Museum** (Christmas–Easter daily 1–4pm; Easter–Christmas Sat, Sun & school holidays 1–4pm; $1 donation requested) in the former Convent School, as you enter the town, with a model of the village as it once was and a phalanx of volunteers brimming with tales of the old days.

For some gentle activity, you can **kayak** or paddle an open canoe along a tidal section of the river (kayak $30 per hour; canoe $25) or continue downstream to Wenderholm (2hr; kayak $60, canoe $60, including pick-up at the far end) with Puhoi River Canoe Hire (☎09/422 0891). For refreshments, hit the pub or drive 3km north to *The Art of Cheese* café with lawns running down to a small stream and a reasonable selection of snacks and light meals, several including some of the wonderful cheeses made on site.

Details on points north of here can be found in the Northland chapter, starting on p.159.

Southeast of Auckland

Most southbound travellers hurry along Auckland's southern motorway to Hamilton or turn off to Thames at Pokeno – either way missing out on the (admittedly modest) attractions of the **Hunua Ranges** and **The Seabird Coast** on its eastern shore. For **cyclists** in particular the coast road is an excellent way into and out of Auckland, avoiding the worst of the city's traffic, following Tamaki Drive from the city centre then winding through Panmure, Howick and Whitford to Clevedon and the coast.

Even for Auckland day-trippers the older and more rounded Hunuas definitely play second fiddle to the more ecologically rich Waitakeres, but there are a few decent walks – notably those around the **Hunua Falls**. There are greater rewards further south with excellent seabird viewing and hot pools at **Miranda**.

The Hunua Ranges

A considerable amount of rain is dumped on the 700m-high **Hunua Ranges**, 50km southeast of Auckland, and flows down into a series of four dams that jointly supply sixty percent of the city's water. The bush surrounding the reservoirs was once logged for kauri but has largely regenerated, providing a habitat for birds; bellbirds, long since extinct in the city, can sometimes be heard here.

Access to the region is easiest through the village of **CLEVEDON**, home to Auckland's polo club (games Dec–April; ℡09/292 8556), and with a couple of restaurants and a smattering of craft shops. Probably the best place to stop is Clevedon Coast Oysters, about 9km east of the town on SH25, where you can pick up a bargain bag full of delicious local oysters (Mon–Thurs 8am–4.30pm, Fri 8am–4pm, Sat 9am–2pm). Pressing on south to Hunua, you'll come across the **Hunua Ranges Park visitor centre** (daily 8am–4.30pm), that sells the *Hunua Recreation & Track Guide* ($9.50) – invaluable for extended walks in the ranges. The best of the walks are around the thirty-metre Hunua Falls, around 5km east, where the Wairoa River carves its way through the crater of an ancient volcano. A good half-day hike, passing some lovely swimming holes, crosses the River Wairoa at the falls and follows Massey Track to Cossey's Dam and back down the Cossey Creek Track to the falls.

The Seabird Coast and Miranda

The Hunua Ranges are bounded to the east by the Firth of Thames, a sheltered arm of the Hauraki Gulf which separates South Auckland from the Coromandel Peninsula. Its frequently windswept western littoral has become known as **the Seabird Coast**, in recognition of its international importance for migrating shorebirds; almost a quarter of all known species visit the region. During winter, the vast inter-tidal flats support huge 30,000-strong flocks of birds, with over fifty percent of the entire world population of the wrybill plover over-wintering here. During the southern summer (Sept–March), the arctic migrants are more significant – notably bar-tailed godwits and lesser knots, as well as turnstones, curlews, sandpipers and red-necked stints – who fly 15,000 kilometres from Alaska, Siberia and Mongolia.

The tidal flats butt up against the geologically significant "chenier plain" around Miranda, where the land has been built up from successive depositions of shell banks; much has been converted to farmland but newer shell banks in the making can be seen along the coast.

From Clevedon the coast road winds 35km past the small beach settlements of Kawakawa Bay and Orere Point, and the **Tapapakanga Regional Park** (primitive camping $5) to **KAIAUA**. Here you'll find the *Kaiaua Motor Camp* (℡09/232 2712; tent sites $9, cabins ❷) and a couple of places to eat in the form of the *Bay View Hotel*, which does a good grilled snapper, and the adjacent *Kaiaua Fisheries*, which has twice been voted the best **fish-and-chip** shop in the land (though not recently) and now operates a licensed seafood restaurant in the evening.

The coast's birdlife is thoroughly interpreted at the **Miranda Shorebird Centre**, 7km south of Kaiaua (daily 9am–5pm, and often later; ⓦwww.miranda-shorebird.org.nz); they'll fill you in on the current hot sightings and point you in the direction of the best viewing spots. With a sunny veranda for viewing, the centre also has good self-catering accommodation (℡09/232 2781 or see the warden in the cottage next door; dorms ❶, flat ❸). A further 7km south are the slightly alkaline **Miranda Hot Springs** (Mon–Sun 8am–9pm; $8, private spa $5 extra per half hour), with a large warm, open pool surrounded by grassy lawns and barbecue areas with private kauri spa tubs. Guests at the adjacent and upmarket *Miranda Holiday Park* (℡0800/833 144, ℡09/867 3205, ⓦmirandaholidaypark.co.nz; tent sites $15, dorms ❶, cabins ❺) have access to their own new and nicely landscaped mineral pool as well as a tennis court.

From here it's a twenty-minute drive to Thames (see p.379).

Islands of the Hauraki Gulf

One of Auckland's greatest assets is the island-studded **Hauraki Gulf**, a seventy-kilometre-square patch of ocean to the northeast of the city. In Maori, Hauraki means "wind from the north" – though the gulf is somewhat sheltered from the prevailing winds and ocean swells by the islands of Great Barrier and Little Barrier, creating benign conditions for Auckland's legions of yachties. Most are content just to sail but those who wish to strike land can choose from some of the 47 islands, administered by the Department of Conservation, and designated either for recreational use, with full access, or as sanctuaries for endangered wildlife, requiring permits.

Auckland's nearest island neighbour is uninhabited **Rangitoto**, a flat cone of gnarled and twisted lava which dominates the harbourscape. The most populous of the gulf islands is **Waiheke**, increasingly a commuter suburb of Auckland – but one with sandy beaches and a delightfully slow pace, enlivened by some quality wineries and an improving range of restaurants. Such sophistication is a far cry from the largest island hereabouts, **Great Barrier**, which until recently seemed trapped in a thirty-year time warp. However, the advent of fast ferries has put its sandy surf beaches, hilly tramping tracks and exceptional fishing within easy reach of holidaying Aucklanders and international visitors, many of whom continue on to the Coromandel (see p.369). The Department of Conservation's happy compromise of allowing access to wildlife sanctuaries is wonderfully demonstrated at **Tiritiri Matangi**, where a day-trip gives visitors an unsurpassed opportunity to see some of the world's rarest bird species. **Little Barrier Island** resists any such interference, and is pretty much off-limits except to researchers.

Frequent **ferries** run to the more popular islands from the wharves around Auckland's Ferry Building, at the foot of Queen Street; there's a DOC **information** centre conveniently located in the same complex. Around the corner is the Fullers Cruise Centre (Mon–Fri 7.30am–5.30pm, Sat & Sun 8am–5pm; bookings and enquiries ℡09/367 9111, timetable information ℡09/367 9102, Ⓦwww.fullers.co.nz,), which sells tickets for most island-bound boats. For more on cruising and kayaking the gulf, see "Adventure activities" starting on p.114.

Rangitoto and Motutapu islands

The distinctive, low, conical shape of **Rangitoto**, 10km northeast of the city centre, is a familiar sight to every Aucklander – yet few Aucklanders have actually set foot on the island. They miss out on a freakish land of fractured black lava, with the world's largest pohutukawa forest clinging precariously to the crevices. Alongside lies the much older and geologically quite distinct island of **Motutapu** or "sacred island", linked to Rangitoto by a narrow causeway.

A **day-trip** is enough to get a feel for Rangitoto, make the obligatory hike to the summit and tackle a few other trails, but **longer stays** are possible if you want to pitch your tent at the primitive campsite at Home Bay on Motutapu.

Rangitoto is Auckland's youngest and largest **volcano**. Molten magma probably pushed its way through the bed of the Hauraki Gulf around six hundred years ago - watched by Motutapu Maori, who apparently called the island

Rangitoto summit walk

The best way to appreciate Rangitoto Island is on foot; but bear in mind that, though not especially steep, the terrain is rough and it can get very hot out there on the black lava. Consequently the best walks are those that follow shady paths to the summit rather than the more open roads. A favourite is the clockwise **Summit/Coastal Path loop** (12km; 5–6hr; 260m ascent) around the southeast of the island. Turn left just past the toilets at Rangitoto Wharf and follow signs for the **Kowhai Grove**, a typical Rangitoto bush area with an abundance of the yellow-flowering kowhai that blossoms in September. Turn right onto the coastal road from Rangitoto Wharf then left into **Kidney Fern Grove**, which is packed with unusual miniature ferns that unfurl after rain. The well-worn **Summit Track** winds through patches of pohutukawa forest. Around three-quarters of the way to the summit, a side track leads to the **lava caves** (20min return), which probe deep into the side of the volcano. Further along the main track a former military observation post on the **summit** provides views down into the bush-shrouded sixty-metre-deep crater and out across Auckland city and the Hauraki Gulf.

Continue northwards to the east–west road across the island and follow it towards Islington Bay; from there, pick up the **coastal track** south, initially following the bay then cutting inland through some little-frequented forests back to Rangitoto Wharf.

"blood red sky" after the awesome spectacle that accompanied its creation. Others attribute the name to a contraction of Te Rangi i totongia a Tamatekapua ("the day the blood of Tamatekapua was shed"), recalling an incident when chiefs of the Arawa and Tainui clashed at Islington Bay.

Rangitoto's youth, lack of soil and the porous nature of the rock have created unusual conditions for **plant life**, though the meagre supply of insects attracts few birds, making things eerily quiet. Pohutukawa trees seeded first, given a head start by their roots, which are able to tap underground reservoirs of fresh water up to 20m below the surface, then smaller and fleshier plants established themselves under the protective canopy. Harsh conditions have led to some strange botanical anomalies: both epiphytes and mud-loving mangroves are found growing directly on the lava, an alpine moss is found at sea level, and the pohutukawa has hybridized with its close relative, the northern rata, to produce a spectrum of blossoms ranging from pink to crimson. Sadly, the succulent pohutukawa leaves were a big hit with **possums** and wallabies which were introduced in the 1880s and proceeded to ravage the forests. An eradication programme in the early 1990s has allowed the pohutukawa to rebound with vigour, and in fifty years' time Rangitoto will look completely different.

Europeans gave Rangitoto a wide berth until the Crown purchased the island for £15 in 1854, putting it to use as a military lookout point and a work-camp for prisoners. From the 1890s, areas were leased for camping and, in keeping with the defiantly anti-authoritarian streak that thrived in early New Zealand, unauthorized *baches* were cobbled together on the sites. By 1937, over 120 *baches* had sprouted, but subsequent legislation decreed that they could be neither sold nor handed down, and must be removed upon the expiry of the lease. Only 34 remain and, ironically, some of the finest examples are being preserved for posterity, their corrugated iron chimneys and cast-off veranda railings used as fenceposts capturing the make-do spirit of the times.

The moment you step across the **causeway** onto **Motutapu**, the landscape changes dramatically; suddenly, you are back in rural New Zealand with its characteristic grassy paddocks, ridge-top fencelines, corrugated iron barns and macrocarpa windbreaks. DOC's plan is to gradually restore its cultural and

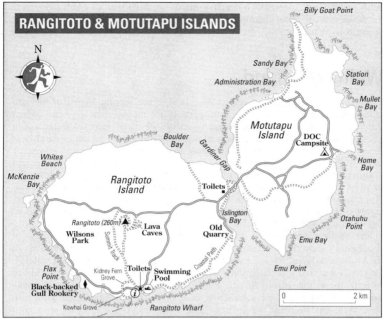

RANGITOTO & MOTUTAPU ISLANDS

N

Billy Goat Point

Sandy Bay

Administration Bay

Station Bay

Mullet Bay

Motutapu Island

DOC Campsite

Home Bay

Boulder Bay

Whites Beach

McKenzie Bay

Rangitoto Island

Gardiner Gap

Toilets

Islington Bay

Otahuhu Point

Rangitoto (260m)

Lava Caves

Old Quarry

Emu Bay

Wilsons Park

Summit Track

Emu Point

Flax Point

Kidney Fern Grove

Toilets

Swimming Pool

Coastal Path

Black-backed Gull Rookery

Kowhai Grove

Rangitoto Wharf

0   2 km

▼ Ferry to Auckland (15 km; 40 min) & Devonport (12 km; 30 min)

natural landscape, replanting the valleys with native trees – you can join their volunteer programme (see p.68) – restoring wetlands and interpreting the numerous Maori sites. Currently though Motutapu is drearier than Rangitoto: about the only thing to do is walk the Motutapu Walkway to the campsite and beach at Home Bay (6km; 1hr 30min one-way), then walk back again.

Practicalities

Fullers **ferries** (Christmas–April 3 daily; May–Christmas Mon–Fri 2 daily, Sat & Sun 3 daily; time of last returning ferry varies throughout the year; $20.40 return) take forty minutes to reach Rangitoto Wharf, where there is an **information kiosk**, which opens to coincide with summer ferry arrivals. Here you'll find a few bags of potato chips, a toilet block, the island's only **drinking water**, and a sun-warmed saltwater swimming pool (filled naturally by the high tide) that's great for kids. Apart from the Home Bay campsite and more toilet facilities at Islington Bay there's nothing else on the island, so bring everything you need – including strong shoes to protect you from the sharp rocks, sun hat, raincoat and, if you're planning a walk, carry plenty of water. Boats are met by the only transport on the island, a kind of tractor-drawn buggy which operates the two-hour **Volcanic Explorer Tour** ($49.40 including cost of ferry), a dusty summit trip with a full and informative commentary; the final 900m is on foot along a boardwalk.

The DOC has intentionally done all they can to ensure that the twin islands are the preserve of day-trippers. As a concession to the hardy and determined, there is a primitive but pleasant beachside DOC **campsite** ($6), with toilets and water, at Home Bay on the eastern side of Motutapu, over an hour's walk from Islington Bay and almost three hours' walk from Rangitoto Wharf.

Waiheke Island

Pastoral **WAIHEKE**, 20km east of Auckland, is the second-largest of the gulf islands and easily the most populous, particularly on summer weekends when Auckland day-trippers and weekenders quadruple the island's 8000 and rising resident population. The traffic isn't all one-way, though, and a fast and frequent ferry service makes it feasible for at least a tenth of the islanders to commute daily for work in the city – a trend that threatens to turn Waiheke into just another suburb. For the moment, with its chain of sandy beaches along the north coast and a climate that's slightly warmer and a lot less humid than Auckland, Waiheke retains its sybaritic character – and is increasingly being discovered by international visitors in search of a peaceful spot to recover from jet lag or to idle away their last few days before flying out.

The **earliest settlers** on Waiheke trace their lineage back to the crew of the Tainui canoe that landed at Onetangi and gave the island its first name of Te Motu-arai-Roa, "the long sheltering island". Waiheke, or "cascading waters", originally referred to a particular creek but was assumed by European settlers to refer to the whole island. Among the first **Europeans** to set foot on Waiheke was Samuel Marsden, who preached here in 1818 and established a mission near Matiatia. The island went through the familiar cycle of kauri logging, gum digging and clearance for farming. Gradually, the island's magnificent coastal scenery gained popularity as a setting for grand picnics, and hamper-encumbered Victorians, surreally attired in formal dress, arrived in boatloads.

Development was initially sluggish, but the availability of cheap land amid dramatic landscapes drew painters and **craftspeople** to the island's shores; others followed as access from Auckland became easier and faster. Since the mid-1980s, the city has been less than forty minutes away, and Waiheke has become increasingly **sophisticated**: dilapidated shacks have been replaced by swanky condos, cafés and restaurants are a match for many in Auckland and boutique **wineries** produce some of the finest Cabernet Sauvignon blends on the North Island.

Arrival, information and getting around

Fullers operate fast **ferries** (☎09/367 9111; 40min; $24 return, bikes free) every hour or two from the Ferry Building in Auckland to the Matiatia Wharf, where they are currently constructing a swish new ferry terminal, at the western end of Waiheke, just over a kilometre from the main settlement of Oneroa. If you're staying for a couple of days or longer, you may find it cost-effective to bring your vehicle over using the daily **car ferry**, a flat-deck barge run by Subritzky Line (☎0800/478 274 & 09/534 5663, ⓦwww.subritzky.co.nz; $110 return for a car only, plus $25 per passenger) from Half Moon Bay near Pakuranga in Auckland's eastern suburbs to Kennedy Point, between Huruhi and Putiki bays about 4km from Oneroa. With frequent fast ferries there is little advantage in **flying** here, though if you are planning to visit Great Barrier Island and don't need to return to Auckland you can fly there with Waiheke Air Services (☎09/372 5000; 2 daily; $80). The **airport** is 3km east of Ostend and is reached by taxi (see p.148) for around $10 from Oneroa.

WAIHEKE ISLAND

ACCOMMODATION
Blue Horizon	C
Castaway	H
Delamore Lodge	B
Island View B&B	E
Onetangi Beachfront Apartments	G
Palm Beach Backpackers	A
Palm Beach Lodge	D
Waiheke Island YHA	F

RESTAURANTS & CAFÉS
Mangrove Pizza	3
Sticki Fingers	1
Strand Café	2

▲ Auckland (20 km; 40 min)

▶ Half Moon Bay (15 km; 1 hr 20 min)

Information

Waiheke's main source of information is the efficient **visitor centre**, 2 Korora Rd, Oneroa (Mon–Sat 9am–5pm, Sun 9am–4pm; ☎09/372 1234, Ⓦwww.waihekenz.com), which can organize most things on the island, and stores bags for $2 apiece. **Shops**, a couple of **banks** and a post office are also clustered in Oneroa. The weekly *Gulf News* ($1.50) comes out on Thursday afternoons and has details of **what's on**, as well as a rundown of arts and crafts outlets. In the last week of January, a **Food and Wine Festival**, celebrates the produce of the island while the island goes mad at Easter for the four days of the **Waiheke Island Jazz Festival**.

Getting around

Ferry arrivals and departures connect with Fullers buses (☎09/366 6400) which run to Onetangi via Oneroa, Surfdale and Ostend, and to Rocky Bay via Oneroa, Little Oneroa and Palm Beach, which is the most useful. Tickets and a $10 day pass (which becomes worthwhile for return trips between Oneroa and Onetangi) are available on the bus. For more flexibility, head for from Waiheke Rental Cars (☎09/372 8635) at Matiatia Wharf and beside the tourist office, who **rent cars** ($50 a day plus 50¢/km) 4x4s ($65 plus 50¢/km) and **scooters** ($40), or try Waiheke Auto Rentals (☎09/372 8998), who do pretty much the same job, from the same location. **Bikes** cost around $25 per day, from Wharf Rats (☎09/372 7937) at the Matiatia wharf, and Blue Bikes, cnr Oceanview Rd and Korora Rd, Oneroa (☎09/372 3143); bear in mind that Waiheke is very undulating and you'll need to be pretty fit. For **taxis**, contact the companies (see p.148), which all run tours and drop-offs at accommodation around the island, with prices depending on numbers and destination.

Day-trippers will be well catered for by a number of **island tours**. Among those departing from Auckland, and including the return ferry trip, are Fullers Island Explorer (daily year-round departing Auckland 10am; $45), which includes an hour-and-a-half island tour, plus an all-day bus pass so you can explore further on your own, and their half-day Vineyard Explorer Tour (Dec–Feb daily, March–Nov Sat & Sun departing Auckland noon; $65) which spends three hours sightseeing and visiting the Mudbrick, Peninsula and Stonyridge **vineyards**: both tours allow a return to Auckland at a later date. On balance, this is the best way to tour the wineries, some of which are otherwise only open by appointment. Island-based operators include Ananda Tours (☎09/372 7530, Ⓦwww.waiheke.co.nz/anandatours.htm) who run personalized wine, eco, art and scenic tours around the island costing around $85 per person.

Accommodation

If your visit coincides with the Jazz Festival, the peak Christmas and January season, the Food Festival, or any weekend, be sure to **reserve** a room as far **in advance** as you can, though this tends to be less critical at the backpacker hostels dotted along the north coast beaches. At other times, accommodation is fairly plentiful, especially if you follow Aucklanders' lead and go for **B&Bs**; most are registered with the visitor centre and with the Fullers Cruise Centre at the Ferry Building in Auckland.

Camping is restricted to the grounds of the various hostels and a simple but attractive site at *Whakanewha Regional Park* ($5, reservations through the Parksline ☎09/366 2000) on the tidal Rocky Bay, with safe swimming, composting toilets, drinking water, cold showers and pleasant walks through the park. It is a couple of kilometres' walk from the nearest bus stop, though there are rumours of extending the bus route to the campsite.

Though there's a lot to be said for basing yourself at one of the quieter and more relaxing **beaches** like Palm Beach and Onetangi, many people prefer to stay close to Oneroa, for the convenience of being near the buses, restaurants, shops and other facilities.

Hotels, motels and B&Bs

Blue Horizon 41 Coromandel Rd, Sandy Bay ☎09/372 5632. Pleasing little, reasonably priced B&B with bright spacious rooms and a relaxed atmosphere. ❺

Delamore Lodge 83 Delamore Dr, Owhanake Bay ☎09/372 7372, ⓦwww.delamorelodge.com. A stunning building accompanied by extraordinary views over the bays, this is the luxury end of the market with bathrooms bigger than many people's houses. ❾

Giverny Inn 44 Queens Dr, Oneroa ☎09/3722200, ⓦwww.giverney.co.nz. Comfortable house rooms and a separate independent cottage with fantastic views over the bay make this very professional, modern, friendly outfit one of the best places on the island. ❾

Island View 9 Hauraki Rd, Palm Beach ☎09/372 9000, ⓦwww.gotowaiheke.com. A friendly, modern B&B with good sea views, but a fifteen-minute trek to the beach. ❺

Kiwi House 23 Kiwi St, Oneroa ☎09/372 9123, ⓔkiwihouse@clear.net.nz. A sociable place with several good rooms (with continental breakfast included); all have access to communal self-catering facilities, a TV lounge and barbecue. ❹

Onetangi Beachfront Apartments 27 The Strand, Onetangi ☎09/372 7051, ⓦwww .onetangi.co.nz. Upgraded waterfront motel units with kayaks, volleyball court, sauna and two spa pools all free to guests. Some units are quite old fashioned, some are brand new and well-equipped, some have beachfront access. ❺–❼

Palm Beach Lodge 23 Tiri View Rd, Palm Beach ☎ & ⓕ09/372 7763, ⓔpalmbch@orion.net.nz Luxurious salmon-pink guesthouse with lovely rooms, each with a balcony overlooking the sea. ❽

Punga Lodge 223 Ocean View Rd, Little Oneroa ☎ & ⓕ09/372 6675, ⓦwww.ki-wi.co.nz/punga .htm. Delightful B&B, well located in the bush close to Oneroa beach, with tea and muffins available all day from the helpful hosts. Accommodation consists of a range of comfortable and spacious en-suite doubles with verandas, and four self-catering apartments of different sizes. There's a spa pool, and good-value off-season deals. Free boat transfers. Rooms ❺, apartments ❻

Hostels

Castaway Orapiu, ☎09/372 6781. A relaxed feel-good hostel/lodge with kayaks, snorkel gear available – all just a 100m from the water's edge. Dorms ❶ Rooms ❷

Fossil Bay Lodge 58 Korora Rd, Oneroa ☎09/372 7569. A very relaxed, haphazard collection of huts, small dorms and self-catering units all located five minutes' walk from an all but private beach, a kilometre from town on an organic farm. Tent sites $10, dorms ❶, rooms ❷, units ❸

Hekerua Lodge 11 Hekerua Rd, Little Oneroa ☎ & ⓕ09/372 8990, ⓦwww.ki-wi.co.nz/hekerua.htm. Peaceful and friendly, pool-equipped backpackers' set in the bush ten minutes' walk from Little Oneroa Beach and Oneroa shops. With some private rooms and a self-contained unit. Tent sites $15, dorms ❶, rooms ❸, unit ❹

Waiheke Island YHA Seaview Rd, Onetangi ☎ & ⓕ09/372 8971, ⓔrobb.meg@bigfoot.com. A well-run associate YHA set high on the hill overlooking the beach, with a host of activities available to guests – mountain-biking, kayaking and snorkelling. Call Jaguar Tours (☎09/372 7312) before leaving Auckland for transport to the hostel. Dorms ❶, rooms ❷

Around the island

The bulk of Waiheke's population inhabits the western quarter of the island, chiefly around the main town of **Oneroa**, a kilometre east of the Matiatia Wharf. For many, Waiheke's finest beaches lie east of Oneroa: the almost circular Enclosure Bay for snorkelling, Palm Beach for swimming, and the more surfie-oriented Onetangi.

Waiheke has no shortage of diversions once you've tired of the beaches and surf. The lovely bays and headlands lend themselves to some short but often steep **walks** detailed in the free *Waiheke Island Walkways* leaflet, available from the visitor centre in Oneroa. One of the best and most accessible coastal tracks leads from Oneroa past Little Oneroa around to Enclosure Bay, while inland there's a shady stroll through the regenerating bush of the **Waiheke Forest and Bird Reserve**, up behind Onetangi. If you're still restless, take your pick from horse riding, kayaking, sailing and so on (see p.148).

Oneroa and around

The settlement of **ONEROA** is draped across a narrow isthmus between the sandy sweep of Oneroa Bay – one of the best and most accessible beaches on the island – and the shallow and silty Blackpool Beach. The ridge-top main street runs up to the island's visitor centre (see p.144), where you can pick up the free *Waiheke Winegrowers' Map* and the free *Waiheke Island Art Map*, a guide to the scattered **studios** of Waiheke's numerous artists and craftspeople. Artists' studio opening times tend to be erratic, so call ahead if you're set on visiting particular workshops. Local artists' work is also displayed in the adjoining Artworks gallery (daily 10am–4pm; free) and in the Waiheke Rocket Gallery daily 10am–4pm; free), just down the road. Adjacent to the visitor centre and in the same building as the local cinema and theatre is the slightly eccentric **Whittaker's Musical Experience** (daily except Tues 10am–4pm; $3; Ⓦwww.musical-museum.org), a room full of flageolets, piano accordions, player pianos, xylophones and more, some dating back two hundred years and all ably demonstrated during the "musical experience" performance (at 1pm; 1hr 30min; $10).

Two of Waiheke's **vineyards** are easily accessible from Oneroa: the Peninsula Estate, 52a Korora Rd, 1km northwest of town (Ⓣ09/372 7866; sales daily 1-4pm in summer; free tours and tastings by appointment only); and the more casual Mudbrick, 2km west on Church Bay Rd (Ⓣ09/372 9050, Ⓦwww.mudbrick.co.nz; tasting daily in summer), while a little further afield is the Onetangi Road Vineyard and Brewery (daily 11am–4pm) for those who have had too much wine and fancy tasting some excellent beer.

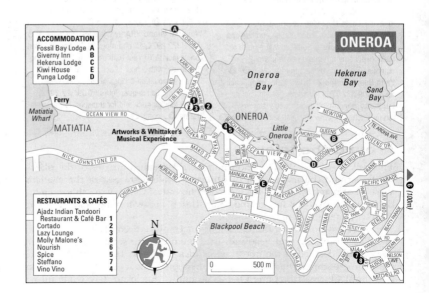

The rest of the island

What passes for a main road on Waiheke winds east from Oneroa through the contiguous settlements of Little Oneroa, Blackpool and Surfdale, and across the lagoon at Putaki Bay to **Ostend**. The island's light-industrial heart, far from any appealing beaches, Ostend is best ignored except on Saturday mornings (8am–1pm) when the Ostend Hall, corner of Ostend Road and Belgium Street, is given over to the **Ostend Market**, a very Waiheke affair with organic produce, arts and crafts, food stalls, massage, iridology readings and local entertainers.

A couple of Waiheke's most reputable **wineries** lie between here and Onetangi. At Goldwater Estate, 18 Causeway Rd (T09/372 7493, W www.goldwaterwine.com; sales & tastings daily 11am–4pm in summer), you can picnic in style, accompanied by one of their fine wines; you'll need to bring your own provisions, but there's no charge for glasses if you buy wine (typically $15 plus a bottle). The organic, hand-tended vineyards of Stonyridge, 80 Onetangi Rd (T09/372 8822, W www.stonyridge.co.nz), produce the world-class Larose, one of New Zealand's top Bordeaux-style reds. Each vintage is sold out before it's even bottled so there are often no cellar-door sales, but the **tour and tasting** (Sat & Sun 11.30am; $20) is entertaining and you can book ahead and stick around for an excellent, al fresco meal ($27–35) with views of the vines, olive trees and cork oaks.

Six kilometres east of Oneroa, **Palm Beach** takes a neat bite out of the north coast, with houses tumbling down to a small sandy beach separated by a handful of rocks from the nude bathing zone at the western end. Waiheke's longest and most exposed beach is **ONETANGI**, popular in summer with surfers, board riders and swimmers, and an occasional venue for beach horse races, usually Waitangi weekend at the beginning of February.

There are no shops or restaurants east of Onetangi, just tracts of open farm land riddled with fledgling vineyards and bordered by fine swimming beaches. One of the best of these is **Cactus Bay**, which is accessible down a short track from Man O' War Bay Road, 6km east of Oneroa. Jaguar Tours (T09/372 7312) runs trips out to the road end and to the start of the track from where you can walk just over 1km to the labyrinth of dank concrete tunnels which make up **Stony Batter**, abandoned World War II defences against the threat of Japanese attack – take a torch if you want to poke around.

Eating and entertainment

Oneroa is unchallenged on Waiheke for its **range** and **quality** of places to eat, with restaurants catering to the demands of city day-trippers. Elsewhere, the scene tends to be more ad hoc, with **beachside cafés** serving snacks and fast food.

Entertainment is more limited and sporadic, but there is sometimes **live music** at *Vino Vino*, in Oneroa, and occasional musical activity at *Molly Malones* in Surfdale.

Ajadz Indian and Tandoori Café Bar 2 Karora Rd. Surprisingly good Indian restaurant with authentic spicy food at bargain prices.

Cortado Espresso Bar 29 Waikare Rd, Oneroa. Wonderful cakes and coffee served up in this stylish little café with great views; really tasty fish and chips dished up daily from the building next door – but run by the same folk.

Lazy Lounge 139 Oceanview Rd. The place to hang out with an endless parade of the island's more interesting characters calling in for coffee, mushroom and pumpkin lasagne, pizza or a hearty slice of cake.

Molly Malones 6 Miami Ave, Surfdale T09/372 8011, W www.molly-malones.com. Irish restaurant and bar with dishes such as Irish beef stew ($14), a starter of mussels in white wine and garlic ($8), standard meat and fish dishes ($18–25) plus that all important Guinness and Kilkenny. Live music at weekends plus a garden seating.

Mangrove Pizza 30 Belgium St, Ostend ☎09/372 8789. The island's best chippy and burger bar, and they deliver.

Nourish 3 Belgium St ☎09/372 3557. Hearty breakfasts and excellent dinners from $14–25. Everything is made on the premises and comes with their own special relish: one of the few must-eat diners on the island.

Pizzeria and caffe da Stefano Miami Ave, Surfdale ☎09/372 5309. Coffee, panini and good pizza restaurant that will deliver for larger orders. BYO only. Closed Mon.

Spice 153 Oceanview Rd ☎09/372 7659. Licensed café next to *Vino Vino* where anything from breakfast to dinner goes down a treat. Try the creamy

coconut bread and butter pudding or the carrot and orange cake along with a strong cup of coffee.

Sticki Fingers Palm Beach ☎09/372 3608. Café-restaurant that's a new kid on the block offering an enticing combination of Indonesian, Thai and Mexican style foods in pleasant beachside surroundings from 7am–11pm.

Strand Café At the beach store, The Strand, Onetangi. Casual place, serving breakfasts, light meals and takeaways.

Vino Vino 153 Ocean View Rd, Oneroa ☎09/372 9888. Hard to beat for light meals, extending to bruschetta, warm salads and daily blackboard specials. Eat inside, or out on the deck with fabulous views across to the Coromandel.

Listings

Horse riding Waiheke Horse Trekking, Sunset Coral, Harbour Info Office, Pier One, Ferry Building, Quay St (☎09/372 6565). Guided treks of 1hr $55, 2hrs $75.

Internet access There's a cybercafé by the library on Oceanview Rd (daily 9am–5pm).

Kayaking Ross Adventures (☎09/372 5550, ⓦwww.kayakwaiheke.co.nz) runs from Matiatia and offers 4hr paddles ($65), moonlit evening trips (3hr; $65), full-day trips including a shuttle back to your starting point ($110) and round-the-island camping trips (2–4 days; $110 per day). They also rent sea kayaks from $30 a half-day. The Kayak Company (☎09/372 2112, ⓦwww.thekayakcompany.co.nz) offers an almost identical range of

tours at similar prices plus a full day out around Cactus Bay for $95, a moonlight tour and a half-day trip for $60.

Medical emergencies Waiheke Island Community Health Services, 5 Belgium St, Ostend (☎09/372 5005) and the Oneroa Accident and Medical Centre, Oceanview Rd (☎09/372 8756).

Sailing Flying Carpet, 104 Wharf Rd, Ostend (☎09/372 5621), offers trips on an ocean-going Cat (11am–4pm; $95, longer trips by arrangement).

Taxis Dial-a-Cab ☎09/372 3000; Waiheke Quality Taxi ☎09/372 7000; Waiheke Tuk Tuk ☎09/372 6127.

Great Barrier Island (Aotea)

Rugged and sparsely populated **Great Barrier Island** (Aotea) lies 90km northeast of Auckland on the outer fringes of the Hauraki Gulf and, though only 30km long and 15km wide, packs in a mountainous heart which drops away to deep indented harbours in the west and eases gently to golden surf beaches in the east. It's only a two-hour ferry or half-hour plane ride from the big city but seems a world apart, almost anachronistic in its lack of mains electricity or a reticulated water supply and it retains a sense of frontier lawlessness. There are no towns to speak of, no industry and no regular public transport, lending Great Barrier that sense of peace and detachment unique to island life, enhanced by **beaches**, **hot springs** and **tightly packed mountains** clad in bush and spared the ravages of deer and possums.

Ferries arrive in **Tryphena**, the southern harbour and major settlement, some continuing up the west coast to the minuscule hamlets of **Whangaparapara** and **Port Fitzroy**, both ideal jumping-off points for tramps in the Great Barrier Forest. **Claris**, in the east, is the site of the main airport and is convenient for the best beaches at **Medlands** and **Awana Bay**.

Some history

Great Barrier is formed from the same line of extinct **volcanoes** as the Coromandel Peninsula, and shares a common geological and human past. Aotea was one of the places first populated by **Maori**, and the Ngatiwai and Ngatimaru people were occupying numerous *pa* sites when Cook sailed by in 1769; recognizing the calming influence of Aotea and neighbouring Hauturu on the waters of the Hauraki Gulf, Cook renamed them Great Barrier Island and Little Barrier Island. The vast stands of kauri all over the island were soon seized upon for ships' timbers, the first load being taken in 1791. Kauri **logging** didn't really get under way until the late nineteenth century but continued until 1942, outliving some early copper mining at Miners Head and sporadic attempts to extract gold and silver from a large quartz intrusion in the centre of the island. Kauri logging and gum digging were replaced by a short-lived whale-oil extraction industry at Whangaparapara in the 1950s, but the Barrier soon fell back on tilling the poor clay soils and its peak population of over 5000 dropped back to little more than 1000.

The space and tranquillity of the island appealed to budding alternative lifestylers, many of whom trickled across from the mainland in the 1960s and 1970s. Much of the Seventies idealism has been supplanted by a more modern pragmatism, but **self-sufficiency** remains. Now more of a necessity in the face of isolation than a lifestyle choice, many people grow their own vegetables; everyone has their own water supply and the load on diesel generators is eased by wind-driven turbines and solar panels. However, **agriculture** is beginning to take a back seat to **tourism** and second-home-owners – a trend resisted to some degree by islanders, who fear that the Barrier will become just another commuter suburb for Auckland. For the time being, however, the fast ferry only operates a full service over the summer, the rest of year it's erratic.

Arrival, information and getting around

Points of entry are the **airport** at Claris on the east coast, the grass airstrip at Okiwi in the north, and the three main **harbours** of Port Fitzroy, Whangaparapara and Tryphena Harbour. Around the first two ports there's little more than a couple of lodges and a shop, leaving the bulk of the activity to the four main bays of Tryphena Harbour. Ferries arrive at Shoal Bay, from where shuttle buses, that must be pre-booked, run to Mulberry Grove, where there's a motel, or on to Stonewall Village, where there are several places to stay and eat, and a shop. Puriri Bay is a short walk along the coast from Stonewall Village. **Bad weather** occasionally causes ferries to be cancelled, but you can pre-empt the inconvenience this may cause by buying a boat/fly deal ($125), flying back or out and taking the ferry the other way.

The vast majority of visitors arrive from Auckland over the summer months aboard Fullers **ferries** (T 09/367 9111; Christmas to early Jan daily, Labour weekend (at the end of October), plus early Dec–Christmas & early Jan–Feb 3–4 weekly; 2hr), which runs to Tryphena for $118 ($109 if booked 3 days in advance; bikes free). Private shuttle buses will meet the ferry if pre-booked and charge around $10-15 to Stonewall Village, $15–20 to Medlands: ask around when you arrive.

With less urgency (or a desire to bring a car), travel with Sealink (T 09/373 4036 & 0800/732 546, W www.subritzky.co.nz), which runs two comfortable barges carrying passengers, cars and just about all the island's freight, leaving Wynyard Wharf in Auckland (Christmas-Jan daily, Feb-Christmas 5 weekly;

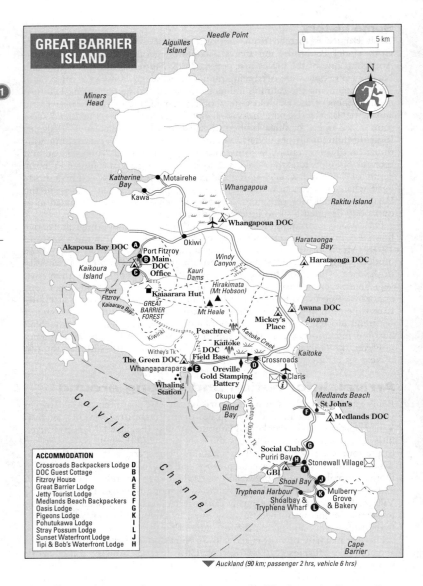

GREAT BARRIER
ISLAND

Needle Point
Aiguilles
Island

Miners
Head

Katherine
Bay ● Motairehe

Kawa

Whangapoua

Rakitu Island

Whangapoua DOC

Akapoua Bay DOC Ⓐ Port Fitzroy
Ⓑ Main
DOC
Office Ⓒ

Haurataonga
Bay

Harataonga DOC

Kaikoura
Island

Okiwi

Windy
Canyon

Kauri
Dams

Port
Fitzroy
Kaiaarara Bay

■ Kaiaarara Hut

GREAT
BARRIER
FOREST

Hirakimata
(Mt Hobson)

Mt Heale

Awana DOC

Awana

▲ Mickey's
Place

Peachtree

Kaitoke
DOC
Field Base

Kaitoke Creek

Kaitoke

Kiwiriki

Withey's Tk

The Green DOC
Whangaparapara Ⓔ

Crossroads Ⓓ

✉ Claris
ⓘ

Oreville
Gold Stamping
Battery

Whaling
Station

Okupu

Blind
Bay

Medlands Beach
St John's

Medlands DOC

Colville

Social Club
Puriri Bay

Stonewall Village ✉

GBI

Shoal Bay

Channel

Tryphena Harbour

Shoalbay &
Tryphena Wharf

Mulberry
Grove
& Bakery

Cape
Barrier

ACCOMMODATION
Crossroads Backpackers Lodge D
DOC Guest Cottage   B
Fitzroy House   A
Great Barrier Lodge   E
Jetty Tourist Lodge   C
Medlands Beach Backpackers F
Oasis Lodge   G
Pigeons Lodge   K
Pohutukawa Lodge   I
Stray Possum Lodge   L
Sunset Waterfront Lodge   J
Tipi & Bob's Waterfront Lodge H

▼ Auckland (90 km; passenger 2 hrs, vehicle 6 hrs)

4hr) for Tryphena, with one service a week (Tues) continuing to Port
Fitzroy. Fares are $85 return for foot passengers and return for a car ($500
in Dec & Jan).

By far the most reliable method of entry are the daily **flights**. The two main
players are Great Barrier Airlines (☎09/275 9120 & 0800/900 600,
Ⓔgba@gbair.co.nz; $189) and Great Barrier Xpress (☎0800/222 123 &
09/256 7025, Ⓦwww.mountainair.co.nz; $174 return), both of which operate

at least three scheduled flights a day from Auckland International Airport to Claris; services are met by shuttle buses, if they are pre-booked, which drop off in Medlands ($12 each way) and Tryphena ($15 each way). GBA also flies from the Barrier to Whangarei, Whitianga and Tauranga around three times a week.

Information

The island's **visitor centre** (daily 9am–4pm; ℡ & ℻09/429 0033, ⓌWww.greatbarrier.co.nz) is opposite Claris airfield. The main **DOC office** is the well-stocked and informative Port Fitzroy Field Base (Mon–Fri 8am–4.30pm; ℡09/429 0044, ℻429 0071), ten minutes' walk west of the Port Fitzroy wharf. There is now a **bank** on the island, West Force Credit Union (Wed & Thurs 10am–1pm; no outside ATM) and lots of places have EFTPOS facilities.

Getting around

Great Barrier has no scheduled public transport in the usual sense, though there is a **bus service** run by Aotea Transport (Nov–March daily April–Oct Mon–Fri only; ℡0800/426 832 & 09/429 0055) which travels from Tryphena to Port Fitzroy and back once a day; their Super Travel Pass ($45 for seven days unlimited travel) may be useful. Prices depend on numbers but expect from $12 from Tryphena to Medlands and $15 to continue on to the hot springs. Aotea also run tours of the island.

Many people **rent a car** for at least part of their stay, but rates are high, at around $75 for one day, dropping to $60 a day for longer rentals; note that all roads are gravel except for the run from Tryphena to Claris. **Mountain bikes** can be rented for around $30 a day, though the hills are steep and the roads dusty and hot in summer. See p.156 for details of car- and bike-rental outfits.

Accommodation

Accommodation on Great Barrier is broad ranging. Walkers and campers are well catered for with some pleasant but basic campsites, a trampers' **hut** and a cabin, which is well set up for groups. Most of these are towards the north of the island, close to the Great Barrier Forest: all six **DOC campsites** are marked on the map above, and tend to be empty most of the year except from Christmas to the end of January when you should definitely book in advance (℡09/429 0044); note that camping is not permitted outside designated campsites. There are several backpacker **hostels** scattered across the island, but most of the rest of the accommodation is concentrated around Tryphena Harbour and ranges from comfortable guesthouses to high-class **lodges**. Some of the best of the island's **self-catering cottages** are given below, but there are many more on lists held by the visitor centre; the owners often live close by and can arrange breakfast and sometimes dinner. In fact, given the dearth of places to eat, many lodges and **guesthouses** also have self-catering units.

Some places **pick up** from the harbours and airport, though those in Tryphena and Medlands will expect you to catch the transport which meets each boat or plane. The island's remoteness means that accommodation is generally more **expensive** than the mainland, particularly through the summer; some places further boost their rates from Christmas to the end of January when visitor numbers are at their peak – and you'll need to **book well ahead** to stand any chance of finding a place to stay. The price codes we've given overleaf are based on standard summer prices.

Lodges, guesthouses and cottages

DOC Guest Cottage Port Fitzroy ☎09/429 0044. Fully-equipped cottage sleeping up to ten, with gas cooking and wood supplied for barbecues. It is beautifully sited at Port Fitzroy adjacent to the DOC office and campsite and ten minutes' walk from the wharf. ❸

Fitzroy House Glenfern Rd, Port Fitzroy ☎09/429 0091, ⓦwww.fitzroyhouse.co.nz. One very comfortable self-contained cottage sleeping six, with views over the northern shore of the inner harbour. The emphasis here is on nature tourism with free use of canoes and a dinghy (sea kayaks are extra), a lovely walkway with a bridge to the top of a kauri, and combination walks where you get dropped off by Unimog (a kind of 4WD German military truck), do a hike, then get picked up by yacht. Bring your own food. ❻

Great Barrier Lodge Whangaparapara Harbour ☎09/429 0488, ⓦwww.greatbarrierlodge.com. This comfortable harbourside lodge is pretty much all there is at Whangaparapara, and also serves as the local shop. Accommodation is in cottages and studio units, and the main building houses a bar and restaurant serving home-style meals. Mountain bikes and kayaks are free for guests. Bunkroom $30pp, rooms & studios ❻

Jetty Tourist Lodge Kaiaarara Bay, Port Fitzroy ☎09/429 0050, ℻429 0908. Superbly sited place with bar and restaurant overlooking Kaiaarara Bay, around 2km from Port Fitzroy Wharf. B&B accommodation is in nicely decorated, self-contained chalets. ❻

Oasis Lodge Stonewall, Tryphena ☎09/429 0021, ⓦwww.barrieroasis.co.nz. One of the finest places on the island, with lovely en-suite rooms and great valley views and a couple of separate self-contained units. Rooms are let on a B&B basis, though you are encouraged to go full-board with delicious Asian-influenced meals. Unit ❼, rooms ❽

Pigeons Lodge Shoal Bay Rd, Tryphena ☎09/429 0437, ⓦwww.pigeonslodge.co.nz. Small, comfortable and classy B&B nestled in the bush near the sea, with en-suite accommodation, a self-catering chalet and a good licensed restaurant. ❺

Pohutukawa Lodge Stonewall, Tryphena ☎09/429 0211, ⓔplodge@xtra.co.nz. The pick of the places around Tryphena, homely, small and welcoming, with a great pub and restaurant spilling out onto the veranda and peaceful garden, all conveniently close to the shop; there are international newspapers on hand, and aromatherapy massage is available. Attractive rooms are let on a B&B basis, and there are compact three-bed backpacker dorms. Dorms ❶, B&B ❺

Sunset Waterfront Lodge Tryphena ☎09/429 0051, ⓦwww.sunsetlodge.co.nz. Motel-style accommodation with a generator which means there's power all the time and great views across the road to the sea. ❻

Tipi & Bob's Waterfront Lodge Puriri Bay Rd, Tryphena ☎ & ℻09/429 0550, ⓦwww.waterfrontlodge.co.nz. Good but pricey motel rooms, some with fine sea views, plus a self-contained cottage. ❻

Hostels

Crossroads Backpackers Lodge 1 Blind Bay Rd, Crossroads ☎09/429 0889, ⓦwww.aotealodge.com. Newish hostel with cabins let by the person, and double rooms, well sited in the middle of the island, close to the airport and facilities in Claris and within walking distance of the hot springs and island tramps. Beds ❶, rooms ❸

Medlands Beach Backpackers 9 Mason Rd ☎09/429 0320, ⓦwww.medlandsbeach.com. Basic, low-key backpackers' with two- and four-bed dorms, doubles and a secluded chalet on a small farm ten minutes' walk from Medlands Beach – making this place popular with surfers. There are boogie boards, mountain bikes and snorkelling gear for guests' use, but there are no meals and no shops nearby, so bring all your food with you. Dorms ❶, rooms ❸

Stray Possum Lodge Shoal Bay ☎0800/767 786 or ☎ & ℻09/429 0109, ⓦwww.straypossum.com. Very much part of the backpacker circuit, this activity-orientated hostel has a bar and on-site licensed pizza restaurant (which also serves breakfast) set in a spacious clearing in attractive bush. Beds are in four- to six-bed dorms or in well-appointed self-contained chalets ideal for groups of up to six. Daily trips visit the hot springs or drop-off for walks and horse rides, and there are mountain bikes, kayaks, snorkelling gear and surfboards for rent (see also p.156 for details of package deals from Auckland). Tent sites $12, dorms ❶, rooms ❸, chalets ❻

Campsites

Akapoua DOC Campsite Orama. Harbour-edge site right by the DOC office and an easy walk to the harbour and shop at Port Fitzroy. It comes equipped with coin-operated barbecues, cold showers and toilets. Tent sites $7.

Awana DOC Campsite Awana. Exposed site with separate tent and vehicle sites, all 400m from a good surf beach. Cold showers and toilets. Tent sites $7.

GBI Campground Puriri Bay, Tryphena ☎ 09/429 0184. A quiet sheltered campground nestled in bush by a fresh water stream near a safe swimming beach, 20min walk to shops. $8.50 per person.
The Green DOC Campsite Whangaparapara. Basic campsite with barbecues, water and toilets but without vehicular access. No showers but it's close to the sea and there's a stream to wash in. Tent sites $7.
Harataonga DOC Campsite Harataonga. Shady site 300m back from the beach, equipped with toilets and cold showers. Tent sites $7.
Medlands DOC Campsite Medlands Beach. Attractive beach-back site that gets very crowded in the peak season. Cold showers, stream water and toilets. Tent sites $7.
Mickey's Place Awana ☎ 09/429 0170. Hospitable commercial campsite 25km north of Tryphena that's less well located than the nearby DOC site but features hot showers, toilets and a cookhouse, all for $5.

Around the island

Sights are thin on the ground on Great Barrier and much of the pleasure here is in lazing on the beaches and striking out on foot into the **Great Barrier Forest**, a rugged chunk of bush and kauri-logging relics that takes up about a third of the island between Port Fitzroy and Whangaparapara. If you're looking for more structure to your day, there are a few small-time operators keen to keep you entertained by means of various activities and tours (see p.156). Tryphena has a particular dearth of things to do, though there is the appealing **Tryphena to Okupu Walking Track** (4hr) from Puriri Bay around coastal headlands to Okupu on Blind Bay.

Most people head straight for **Medlands Beach**, a long sweep of golden sands broken by a sheltering island and often endowed with some of the Barrier's best surf – though, be warned, there is no patrolled area. The pretty blue and white **St John's Church** looks suitably out of place for somewhere that was moved here from the mainland in 1986 by barge before being dragged over the dunes.

North of Medlands, the road leaves the coast for the airport at **Claris**, where the post office is planning to start up the gimmicky **Great Barrier Pigeon-Gram Service** again (summer only; $20 to send a pigeon-gram letter) in imitation of the original pigeon-mail service – said to be the world's first airmail service – set up in 1898 after it took a sobering three days to notify Auckland that the SS *Wairarapa* had been wrecked on the northwest coast. Birds took under two hours to cover the same distance, and were used until 1908 when a telephone was finally established. One or two letters are now attached to birds which fly to Auckland, where the letters are forwarded anywhere in the world.

Crossroads, 2km north of Claris, is just that – the junction of roads to Okupu, Port Fitzroy and the north of the island, and Whangaparapara. The Whangaparapara road runs past the scant roadside remains of the **Oreville gold stamping battery** (unrestricted entry) and the start of a path to **Kaitoke Hot Springs** (4km; 1hr 20min return; also on the Great Barrier Forest Tramp - see p.154), sulphurous dammed pools that aren't especially pretty but are perfect for an hour's wallowing. At Whangaparapara itself, a short stroll around the bay brings you to the foundations of a whaling station built here in the 1950s.

North from Crossroads, the Port Fitzroy road passes two excellent camping spots by the surf beach at Awana Bay, then the start of a short track to **Windy Canyon** (1km; 20–30min return), a narrow defile that gets its name from the eerie sounds produced by certain wind conditions. The narrow path winds through nikau palms and tree ferns to a viewpoint that gives a sense of the island's interior, as well as fabulous coastal views.

The island's highest point, Hirakimata, can be reached in three hours walking from Awana Bay or a similar time from **PORT FITZROY**, whose harbour remains remarkably calm under most wind conditions, a property not lost on

The Great Barrier forest tramp

The only decent walking map is the 1:50,000 Great Barrier Island Holidaymaker *($15); DOC also print a* Track Information *leaflet ($2 from DOC offices) which will just about do for most purposes but you are better off booking everything in Auckland.*

The **Great Barrier Forest**, New Zealand's largest stand of possum-free bush, offers a **unique** tramping **environment**. Because the area is so compact, in no time at all you can find yourself climbing in and out of little subtropical gullies luxuriant with nikau palms, tree ferns, regenerating rimu and kauri, up onto scrubby manuka ridges with stunning coastal and mountain views. Many of the tracks follow the routes of mining tramways past old kauri dams.

Access and huts

The tramp can be done equally well from Port Fitzroy or Whangaparapara, both having a reasonably well-stocked shop, a campsite and other accommodation. Port Fitzroy also has a 24-bunk **hut** nearby (Category 2; $10), and the main DOC office (☏09/429 0044; Mon–Fri 8am–4.30pm), which sells hut **tickets** and **maps**. In addition, Port Fitzroy's beautifully sited *Akapoua Bay* **campsite** ($7) is superior to Whangaparapara's simple site, *The Green* ($7).

If you have come specifically to tramp it is best to catch a ferry direct to Port Fitzroy, or call one of the shuttle operators in advance to organize transport from the airport or Tryhpena.

The tramp

From the wharf at **Port Fitzroy**, follow the coast road fifteen minutes south to the DOC office. From there the road climbs for half an hour over a headland with views over Kaiaarara and Rarohara bays, to a gate. The Kaiaarara Hut is roughly fifteen minutes on, along a 4WD track and across a couple of river fords. From **Kaiaarara Hut to Whangaparapara** (13km; 7–9hr; 800m ascent), the track soon leaves the 4WD track and crosses the Kaiaarara Stream several times as it climbs steeply to the first and most impressive **kauri dam** (see below), reached in under an hour. The well-defined path continues for another fifty minutes to one of the upper dams then begins a long and arduous series of boardwalks and wooden steps designed to

the dozens of yachties who flock here in summer. Apart from the shop and a few places to stay there's not a lot here, but Port Fitzroy makes the best base for **tramping** or shorter day-walks to some fine **kauri dams**. For three years from 1926, the Kauri Timber Company hacked trees out of the relatively inaccessible Kaiaarara Valley, shunning the tramways and trestle bridges employed in more manageable terrain in favour of six kauri dams – wooden structures up to twenty metres high and spanning the valley floor. Logs were cut and rolled into the reservoirs as the stream built up the water level behind the dams. The upper dams were then tripped, followed seconds later by the lower dams; the combined releases sent a torrent of water and logs sluicing down to Kaiaarara Bay, where they were lashed together in rafts and floated to Auckland.

Eating and drinking

The absence of stand-alone **restaurants** forces pretty much everywhere that provides a bed for the night to offer meals and drinks for both guests and non-residents; always book in advance. There's also a couple of shops where you can get snacks when you're on the move and pick up picnic provisions. **Drinking** tends to happen in bars attached to accommodation establishments or in the social clubs at Tryphena and Claris.

keep trampers on the path and prevent the disturbance of nesting black petrels. It'll take a good thirty to forty minutes to reach the summit of the 621-metre **Hirakimata** (Mount Hobson), where you'll be amply rewarded by panoramic views.

Less extensive boardwalks extend south around the dramatic spire of Mount Heale towards the junction of **two paths**. To the right a path follows the south branch of the Kaiaarara Stream **back to the Kaiaarara Hut** in around an hour and a half, making a four-to-five-hour circuit from the hut. The leftmost path follows an undulating but gradually descending route into Kaitoke Creek No.1 eventually reaching the edge of Kaitoke Swamp right by the hard-to-locate **Peach Tree Hot Spring** just beyond the northern-most tip of the swamp. Originally dug by kauri loggers, the pools here are hotter than the more widely used **Kaitoke Hot Springs** – the latter reached along a ten-minute track which spurs off south twenty minutes ahead; the more attractive hollows are to be found upstream. Back on the main track, you soon reach the 4WD forest road: follow it south for a hundred metres or so, then join the signposted track to the former site of Whangaparapara Hut, fifteen minutes on. From here it's ten minutes' walk to the DOC residence and half an hour to the Whangaparapara Wharf.

There are two main routes from **Whangaparapara to Kaiaarara Hut**, the direct and dull route following the Pack Track due north of the former site of Whangaparapara Hut and the 4WD forest road (11km; 5hr; 200m ascent), and the more appealing semi-coastal Kiwiriki Track (12km; 6hr; 300m ascent) which branches off the 4WD forest road just north of its junction with the Pack Track. The track cuts west from the forest road by the rocky knob of Maungapiko, leading to the picnic area at Kiwiriki Bay then climbing steeply over a ridge to Coffins Creek before a relatively gentle walk to a second picnic area at **Kaiaarara Bay**. From here it is half an hour to Kaiaarara Hut and another hour or so to the Port Fitzroy Wharf.

An alternative start to either route eschews the Pack Track and follows the far more interesting **Withey's Track**, which starts between the Whangaparapara DOC field base and the former hut site; it takes half an hour longer, but goes through some lovely bush with delightful streamside nikau groves.

Barrier Oasis Lodge Stonewall, Tryphena ☎09/429 0021, ⓦwww.barrieroasis.co.nz. Delicious meals using local and home-grown produce (including their own Cabernet Sauvignon and olive oil), frequently with Thai, Indian or seafood themes. The luncheon platter costs around $20, while evening meals are table d'hôte and will set you back $40.

Claris Texas Café Claris ☎09/429 0811. Easily the best café on the island with a sunny deck and a grassy patch for the kids. It's open daily 8am–5pm for light meals, panini, great desserts and excellent coffee; then for a la carte evening meals (summer nightly, winter Thurs–Sat) which might include chargrilled calamari or pan-fried sole with ginger and chive hollandaise.

Currach Irish Pub Stonewall, Tryphena. An Irish Pub that's about as traditional as you can get on a South Pacific island – a lot of the paraphernalia came from the owner's grandmother's pub, in County Kerry, which closed in 1950. What's more

they have Murphy's and Kilkenny on tap, and there's often live acoustic music, especially on Thursday when anyone is welcome to jam. Full breakfasts are served until 9.30am, and in the evening you might expect seafood chowder ($7.50), sirloin steak "pohutukawa" ($18.50) or fish 'n' chips ($11).

Great Barrier Island Sports & Social Club Whangaparapara Rd, at the foot of the road to Medlands Beach ☎09/429 0260. Cavernous public bar with pool tables and bar meals (Wed, Fr & Sat).

Jetty Tourist Lodge Kaiaarara Bay, Port Fitzroy ☎09/429 0050. Spacious restaurant with a large deck and a bar overlooking the bay. Hearty Kiwi meat and seafood dishes go for around $20, and breakfasts, lunches and Devonshire teas are also served.

Mulbarry Grove Store Mulberry Grove, Tryphena's new bar is well worth a visit as it makes the best coffee on the island. Also serves fish and chips alongside a range of other essentials.

Tipi & Bob's Waterfront Lodge Puriri Bay, Tryphena ☎09/429 0550. The rather soulless public bar and leafy garden bar are always popular

spots, as is the spartan seafood restaurant serving $20–25 mains and cheaper takeaways.

Whale Boat Bistro Whangaparapara Harbour. Bar and restaurant serving home-style meals indoors or on the spacious deck with harbour views.

Listings

Bike rental *Stray Possum Lodge* and *Great Barrier Lodge* both rent bikes to guests, or try Great Barrier Hire Centre in Claris (☎09/429 0417), which rents machines to all comers.
Car rental On the southern half of the island, try Tryphena's Better Bargain Rental (☎09/429 0092), GBI Rentals (☎09/429 0062) and in the north call Aotea Rentals (☎ & ℻09/429 0055).
Fishing To test Great Barrier's enviable reputation, head out for a day's fishing in the Colville Channel aboard any of the Tryphena-based boats who charge $450 a day for four people: try the *Vitamin C* (☎09/429 0949).
Golf Pioneer Park, Whangaparapara Rd, Claris (☎09/429 0420; green fee $10, club rental $5), is a nine-hole par-three course surrounded by bush and with pukeko strutting across the fairways;

every Thursday and Sunday the lively bar serves cheap drinks and decent meals.
Horse riding Great Barrier Island Adventure Horse Treks (☎09/429 0274) will take you out onto the beach and hinterland for $30 per hour.
Internet *Crossroads Backpackers Lodge* (see p.152) has Internet facilities open to all, as does the Stonewall Store, Tryphena.
Kayaking Tryphena-based Aotea Kayak (☎09/429 0664) run short paddling trips ($30), and joint 4–5hr kayak and snorkelling trips ($55) all year.
Tours Adventure Eco *Tours* (☎09/429 0699) offers 8-wheel drive trips ($49, 1hr), while Aotea Transport (☎09/429 0055 ⊛www.aoteatransport .co.nz) run round the island trips for $35, in addition to their scheduled service and a variety of other options, which include flights to Whitianga with Coromandel Air.

Tiritiri Matangi

No one with even the vaguest interest in New Zealand's wonderful birdlife should pass up the opportunity to visit **Tiritiri Matangi**, a low island 4km off the tip of the Whangaparaoa Peninsula and 30km north of Auckland. Tiritiri Matangi is run as an "open sanctuary", and visitors are free to roam through the predator-free bush where, within a couple of hours, it's quite possible to see takahe, saddlebacks, whiteheads, North Island robins, kokako, parakeets and brown teals. To stand a chance of seeing the little-spotted kiwi, you'll have to be here at night.

Judging by evidence from *pa* sites on the island, Tiritiri Matangi was first populated by the Kawerau **Maori** and later by the Ngati Paoa, both of whom are now recognized as the land's traditional owners. They partly **cleared the island** of bush, a process continued by Europeans who arrived in the mid-nineteenth century to graze sheep and cattle. Fortunately, **predators** such as possums, stoats, weasels, deer, cats, wallabies and the like failed to get a foothold on Tiritiri, so after farming became uneconomic in the early 1970s it was singled out as a prime site for helping to restore bird populations. The cacophony of birdsong in the Tiritiri bush is stark evidence of just how catastrophic the impact of these predators has been elsewhere.

When grazing stopped, a **reforestation** programme was implemented: a quarter of a million saplings raised from seeds found on the island have been planted out to form rapidly regenerating bush, though it is still far from mature. The **birds** seem to like it, however, and are mostly thriving – with nesting boxes standing in for decaying trees, and feeding stations equipped with video cameras and pressure-sensitive perches that weigh birds each time they alight.

Three of the species released here are among the rarest in the world, with total populations of around a couple of hundred. The most visible are the flightless **takahe**, lumbering blue-green turkey-sized birds long thought to be extinct (see p.971); birds moved here from Fiordland have bred well and are easily spotted as they seem unafraid of humans and are very inquisitive. **Saddlebacks** and **stitchbirds** (of which only seventy survive anywhere) both stick to the bush, but often pop out if you sit quietly for a few moments on some of the bush boardwalks. **Northern blue penguins** also frequent Tiritiri, and can be seen all year round – but are most in evidence in March, when they come ashore to moult, and from September to December, when they nest in specially constructed viewing boxes located along the seashore path just west of the main wharf.

Practicalities

Tiritiri Matangi is typically visited as a **day-trip**, giving almost five hours on the island; you'll need to take your own **lunch**, as there is no food available. The most reliable way to get here is with Fullers (☎09/367 9111), who depart from the Auckland Ferry Building (Oct–April Thurs–Sun 9am, May–Sept not Friday; $45 return) for the forty-minute run up to Gulf Harbour Marina on the Whangaparoa Peninsula, 30km north of Auckland (see p.135), from where it makes the twenty-minute crossing ($25 return) to Tiritiri. On other week-days (particularly Wednesday), the ferry is often chartered for school trips and you are usually welcome to tag along. Boats depart the island for Gulf Harbour and Auckland at 3.30pm.

Visitors arriving on scheduled ferries can join extremely worthwhile **guided walks** (1hr; $5), which leave from the wharf and are led by volunteers and DOC rangers steeped in bird-lore. Otherwise, you're free to wander the island at will or indulge in a little **swimming** from Hobbs Beach, a ten-minute walk west of the wharf (turn left as you step ashore), and the only sandy strand on Tiritiri.

It's also possible to **stay overnight** in a self-contained bunkhouse - bring a sleeping bag and food - near the lighthouse (call the rangers on ☎09/476 0010; ❶), but weekends are booked months ahead and even for week nights you'll need to book at least two weeks in advance; you can also get **general information** on this phone number.

Other gulf islands

There are dozens of other islands scattered around the Hauraki Gulf, several of them privately owned but more forming part of the Hauraki Gulf Maritime Park. The most easily accessible is the DOC-managed recreation reserve of **Motuihe Island**, just 3km south of Motutapu Island, a popular day-trip destination for Aucklanders keen to laze on the sheltered sandy beaches of the northwestern peninsula and spend three or four hours exploring the easy walking trails. The majority of the island is farmland, with small patches of bush around its fringes. The northwestern end of the island, where the boats dock, has had something of a chequered history. It was used as a smallpox and influenza quarantine station from 1873 until after World War I, doubling up as prisoner-of-war camp; during World War II, the same buildings served as a naval base associated with gun emplacements built in the northern tip of the island. Motuihe is most easily visited on Fullers Island Hopper service (early

Nov to Feb 4 daily; $20 return) giving up to six hours on the island and allowing you to combine your visit with a trip to Rangitoto. If you want **to stay** longer there are boats on Friday evening allowing you to stop over in a well-supplied farmhouse sleeping up to twelve ($12 per person, $60 minimum nightly charge), a bunkhouse (➊) and a campsite ($5). All are booked through the **kiosk** (☏09/534 8095), which is open daily in summer for groceries and takeaways.

No visitors make it out to **Little Barrier Island** these days (Hauturu), 80km north of Auckland, a nature reserve barred to those without the necessary DOC permit. Although around a third of its trees were felled for timber before the government acquired the island and set it aside as a wildlife sanctuary in 1884, mountainous Little Barrier remains largely unspoilt, its vast forests unaffected by introduced pests. The island is home to fascinating creatures – including giant earthworms up to a metre long, the prehistoric tuatara and a mouse-sized version of the grasshopper-like weta – and once cats were eradicated in 1975 Little Barrier also became a refuge for birds under threat on the mainland, such as the kakapo, kaka, stitchbird and the kokako.

Travel details

Trains

From Auckland to: Hamilton (2 daily; 2hr); National Park (2 daily; 5hr 30min); Ohakune (2 daily; 6hr); Otorohanga (2 daily; 3hr); Palmerston North (2 daily; 8–9hr); Wellington (2 daily; 11hr).

Buses

From Auckland to: Cambridge (4 daily; 3hr); Dargaville (2–3 daily; 3hr 15min); Gisborne (1 daily; 9hr); Hamilton (14–16 daily; 2hr); Hastings (3 daily; 7hr 30min); Helensville (Mon–Fri 8 daily; 1hr 10min); Kaitaia (1 daily; 7hr); Kerikeri (2 daily; 5hr); Kumeu (4–6 daily; 35min); Mangonui (1 daily; 6hr 30min); National Park (1 daily; 5hr 30min); Napier (3 daily; 7hr); New Plymouth (3 daily; 6–7hr); Ohakune (1 daily; 6hr); Opononi (3 weekly; 5hr 40min); Orewa (hourly; 45–60min); Paihia via Whangarei (3–6 daily; 4hr 20min); Paihia via Opononi (3 weekly; 8hr 30min); Palmerston North (4 daily; 9hr); Rotorua (8 daily; 4hr); Taupo (4 daily; 4–5hr); Taihape (3 daily; 6hr 30min); Tauranga (4–6 daily; 3hr 40min); Thames (5 daily; 2hr); Waipu (4–6 daily; 2hr 20min); Waitomo (3 daily; 3hr 15min); Warkworth (8 daily; 1hr); Wellington (4 daily; 11hr)Ω Whangarei (4–6 daily; 3hr);.
From Helensville to: Orewa (1 Mon–Fri; 40min).
From Orewa to: Auckland (hourly; 45–60min); Helensville (1 Mon–Fri; 40min); Waiwera (hourly; 15min); Wenderholm (summer Sundays 4 daily; 15min).

Ferries

From Auckland to: Devonport (every 30min; 10min); Great Barrier (2–5 weekly; 2–6hr); Motuihe (2–3 weekly; 50min); Rangitoto (2–4 daily; 40min); Tiritiri Matangi (4 weekly; 1hr 30min); Waiheke (7–10 daily; 40min).
From Gulf Harbour Marina to: Tiritiri Matangi Island (4 weekly; 20min).
From Half Moon Bay to: Waiheke (6–9 daily; 1hr).

Flights

From Auckland to: Bay of Islands (3–4 daily; 50min); Blenheim (2–3 daily; 1hr 20min); Christchurch (13 daily; 1hr 20min); Dunedin (3 daily; 2hr 30min); Gisborne (3–5 daily; 1hr); Great Barrier Island (5–10 daily; 30min), Hamilton (1–2 daily; 35min); Kaitaia (1 daily; 1hr), Napier (7–10 daily; 1hr); Nelson (2 daily; 1hr 30min); New Plymouth (5–8 daily; 50min); Palmerston North (5–8 daily; 1hr 10min); Queenstown (4 daily; 1hr 40min); Rotorua (4–5 daily; 45min); Taupo (2 daily; 50min); Tauranga (5–7 daily; 40min); Wanganui (2–3 daily; 1hr); Wellington (20–25 daily; 1hr); Whakatane (3–5 daily; 50min); Whangarei (5–7 daily; 40min).
From Great Barrier Island: to Whangarei (2 weekly; 30min); Whitianga (3 weekly; 20min).
From Waiheke Island to: Great Barrier Island (2 daily; 30min).

Northland

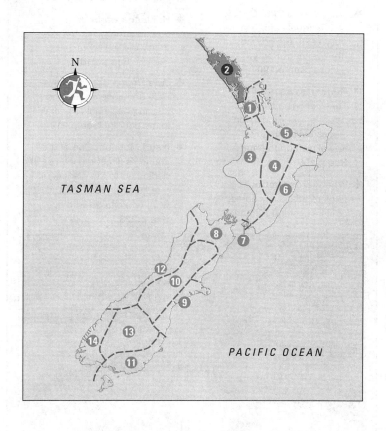

N

TASMAN SEA

PACIFIC OCEAN

CHAPTER 2 # Highlights

* **Poor Knights Islands** One of the world's ten best dive spots with caves, rock arches, abundant fish, and even a couple of wrecks. See p.176

* **Waikokopu Café** Classy yet informal café, beautifully set in the grounds of the Waitangi Treaty House. See p.190

* **Hundertwasser toilets** These imaginatively designed public conveniences have put tiny Kawakawa on the map. See p.190

* **Whangaroa Harbour** Explore this lovely corner of New Zealand from the decks of the yacht Snow Cloud. See p.202

* **Swamp Palace** Oddball rural cinema specializing in cult movies as well as the latest releases. See p.204

* **Hokianga Harbour** The quiet alternative to the frenzy of the Bay of Islands. See p.218

* **Tree House Backpackers** Hole up in one of the most relaxing backpacker hostels in the country. See p.219

* **Kauri Museum** One of the country's finest museums, dedicated to the giant kauri tree, its extraction, and what you can do with it. See p.223

△ Zoanthid polyps, Poor Knights Island

Northland

T he narrow and staunchly Maori province of **Northland** (Taitokerau; ⓦ www.northland.org.nz) thrusts 350km out from Auckland into the subtropical north, separating the Pacific Ocean from the Tasman Sea – two oceans that meet in the maelstrom off Cape Reinga, New Zealand's most northerly accessible road. The province is often described as the "Winterless North", and though the name only really holds true in the topmost part of the region, it rightly evokes the palms, citrus fruit and even bananas that thrive here and the warmer waters off its many gorgeous beaches.

Scenically, Northland splits down the middle. The **east coast** comprises a labyrinth of straggling peninsulas, with hidden coves between plunging headlands. The beaches tend to be calm and safe, their waters becoming choppy only during occasional Pacific storms, whose force is broken by clusters of protective barrier islands. There could hardly be a greater contrast than that with the **west coast**, one enormous dune-backed beach pounded by powerful Tasman breakers and broken by occasional harbours. Tidal rips and holes make swimming dangerous here, and there are no lifeguard patrols. Some beaches are even designated as roads, but are full of hazards for the unwary - and rental cars aren't insured for beach driving. Exploration of the undulating **interior** is both hampered and enlivened by the roads: the major routes are inland and often well away from the unspoiled and deserted beaches that are the main event in these parts, leading to long forays down twisting side roads.

North of Auckland's urban sprawl, the short **Kowhai Coast** begins to feel more genuinely rural and is popular with yachties sailing around Kawau Island, and snorkellers exploring the underwater world of the **Goat Island Marine Reserve**. The broad sweep of **Bream Bay** runs from the Scottish settlement of Waipu up to the dramatic crags of Whangarei Heads at the entrance to Northland's major port and the associated town of **Whangarei**. Off the coast here lie the **Poor Knights Islands**, New Zealand's premier dive spot. Tourists in a hurry tend to make straight for the **Bay of Islands**, a jagged bite out of the coastline dotted with islands perfect for cruising, diving and swimming with dolphins, and steeped in early New Zealand history. Everything north of here is loosely referred to as **The Far North**, a region characterized by the quiet remoteness of the **Whangaroa Harbour**, the popular resorts of **Doubtless Bay**, and the **Aupori Peninsula**, which backs **Ninety Mile Beach** all the way up to **Cape Reinga**.

The west coast feels very different from the east, marked by economic neglect over the last fifty years as kauri logging ended and dairying never successfully replaced it. First stop on the way back south from Ninety Mile Beach is the fragmented **Hokianga Harbour**, one of New Zealand's largest, with some fine sand dunes gracing the north head. South of here you're into

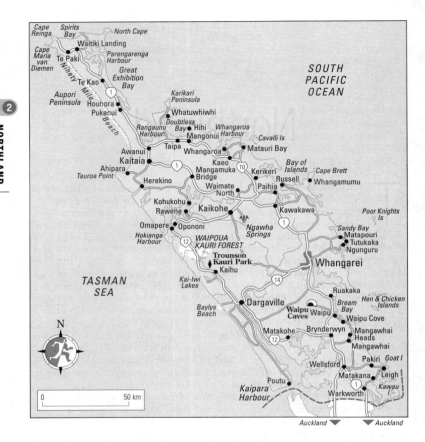

the **Waipoua Forest**, all that remains after the depredations of the kauri loggers, a story best told at the excellent **Matakohe Kauri Museum** on the shores of the Kaipara Harbour.

Northland has no passenger train services so **getting around** by public transport means travelling by **bus**. Kaitaia and the Bay of Islands airports have direct **flights** to Auckland and each other, Whangarei has flights to Auckland and Great Barrier Island, and Kerikeri has flights to Auckland and Kaitaia, but distances are relatively short and high prices act as a deterrent. Details of frequencies and journey times are given in "Travel details" at the end of the chapter (see p.229). If you're **driving** the choices are limited to a major road up each side of the peninsula. This forms a logical loop that has recently been formalized as the **Twin Coast Discovery route** (ⓦ www.twincoast.co.nz): there's no need to follow it slavishly, but the brown signs emblazoned with a dolphin and curling wave make a good starting framework.

Some history

Northland was the site of most of the early contact between **Maori** and **European settlers**, and the birthplace of New Zealand's most important document, the **Treaty of Waitangi**. Maori legend tells of the great Polynesian explorer Kupe discovering the Hokianga Harbour and, finding the climate and abundance of food to his liking, encouraging his people to return and settle there. It was their descendants in the Bay of Islands who had the dubious honour of making the first contact with Europeans, as whalers plundered the seas and missionaries sought converts. Maori society was ill-prepared for this onslaught, and its leaders petitioned Britain to step in. Without fully appreciating the implications or understanding the duplicity of the Pakeha, the northern chiefs signed away their **sovereignty** in return for assurances on land and traditional rights, which were seldom respected. There is still a perception among some Maori in the rest of the country that the five northern *iwi* gave Aotearoa away to the Pakeha.

As more fertile farmlands were found in newly settled regions further south, Northland fell into decline and the pattern became one of exploitation rather than development. Rapacious **kauri loggers** and **gum diggers** cleared the bush and later, as extractive industries died away, pioneers moved in, turning much of the land to **dairy country**. Local dairy factories closed as larger semi-industrial complexes centralized processing, leaving small towns all but destitute, though the planting of fast-growing exotic trees and sporadic pockets of horticulture keep local economies ticking over, aided by the cultivation of marijuana, a major cash crop in these parts.

The Kowhai Coast to Bream Bay

Auckland's influence begins to wane by the time you reach the **Kowhai Coast** around 50km north of central Auckland, a thirty-kilometre stretch of shallow harbours, beach-strung peninsulas and small islands. Freed from the shackles of the city, a more individual character becomes apparent, particularly once you pass sleepy **Warkworth** and head out either to **Kawau Island**, one-time home of Governor General George Grey, or up the coast to Leigh and the snorkelling and diving nirvana of **Goat Island Marine Reserve**.

There's little to detain you on SH1 between Warkworth and Waipu as it passes through dull Wellsford and the road junction at **Brynderwyn**, where SH12 loops off to Dargaville, the Waipoua Kauri Forest and the Hokianga Harbour. If you're heading north and want a scenic route, it's better to stay on the coast and follow **Bream Bay**, named by Cook when he visited in 1770 and his crew hauled in tarakihi, which they mistook for bream. The bay curves gently for 20km from the modest, rocky headland of Bream Tail in the south, past the entrance to Whangarei Harbour to the dramatic and craggy Bream Head. There are no sizeable towns here, only the small beach communities of **Mangawhai Heads** and **Waipu Cove**, looking out to the **Hen and Chicken Islands**, refuges for rare birds like the handsome wattled saddleback.

Warkworth and around

The economic focus of the Kowhai Coast is the easy-going small town of **WARKWORTH**, at the head of Mahurangi Harbour, and sheltered from the sea by its peninsula. For much of the year Warkworth is a peaceful and slow-paced rural town, only coming to life at the peak of the summer season, when thousands of yachties descend, mooring their boats in the numerous estuaries and coves nearby. From the late 1820s for about a century, the languid stretch of river behind the town seethed with boats shipping out kauri, initially as spars for the Royal Navy and later as sawn planks.

To learn more about the town's past, head 3km south to the **Warkworth and Districts Museum**, on Tudor Collins Drive, signposted off the main road (daily: 9am–4pm, June–Aug closes 3.30pm; $6), for a fairly dull exploration of the region's history through re-created rooms, and a five-metre-long, 130-link chain carved from a single piece of kauri. The two ancient kauri outside mark the start of two well-presented twenty-minute boardwalk nature trails through the **Parry Kauri Park** (9am–dusk; donation), an appealing stand of bush preserved as a public amenity. A free leaflet at the museum's entrance explains the trees in detail.

Following SH1 north of Warkworth, it's 4km to **Sheep World** (daily 9am–5pm; $7, or $13 to include show), where an entertaining, indoor sheep-shearing show (1hr, daily 11am, extra shows at weekends & holidays; ℡09/425 7444) allows you to try your hand at a little shearing. The complex also contains a minifarm and a short nature trail, as well as a campground and a backpackers (see below), plus a quality **Craft Co-op** (daily 9am–5pm), that's worth a quick peek. The **Dome Forest Walkway** begins 2km further north on SH1, leading through native forest to a lookout point (40min return), before climbing steeply to the summit (1hr 30min return) for superb views and descending gently to the twenty magnificent trees of the Waiwhiu Kauri Grove (3hr return).

Practicalities

Warkworth's **visitor centre**, 1 Baxter St (Christmas–Feb Mon–Fri 8.30am–5.30pm, Sat & Sun 9am–4pm; March–Christmas shorter hours; ℡09/425 9081, ⓦwww.warkworth-information.co.nz), is in the centre of town at the junction of Queen Street and Neville Street, where InterCity buses stop. Northliner buses pull up on SH1 near the ambulance station.

Bridge House Lodge 16 Elizabeth St ℡09/425 8351, ⓦwww.bridgehouse.co.nz. Twelve simple en-suite double rooms with TVs, and two en-suite backpacker rooms for $25 a bed; instead of a kitchen the lodge provides an attractive restaurant bar overlooking the river. ❹

Central Motel Neville St ℡09/425 8645, ⒺÌcentralmotel@xtra.co.nz. Reliable motel with twelve units and a spa and swimming pool. ❹

Rosemount Homestead 25 Rosemount Rd, 4km from Warkworth on the way to Matakana ℡09/422 2580, ⓦwww.rosemount.co.nz. A lovingly restored kauri homestead of 1900, blessed with wraparound verandas, extensive gardens and a pool; each of the three rooms is en suite. ❽

Saltings Guest House 1210 Sandspit Rd, Sandspit ℡09/425 9670, ⓦwww.saltings.co.nz. A gorgeous boutique B&B on a hill overlooking the estuary; all rooms are en-suite with their own patio and views of the estuary, and fine breakfasts. ❼

Sandspit Motor Camp 1334 Sandspit Rd ℡ & Ⓕ09/425 8610. Small campsite offering free use of canoes, dinghies and a small golf course. Camping $12, cabins ❷

Sheep World Caravan Park and Camping Ground 4km north of town, ℡09/425 9962, ⓦwww.sheepworldcaravanpark.co.nz. Attractive campground complex. Camping $12.50, dorms ❶, on-site caravans & cabins ❷, 4-bed chalets ❹ plus $12.50 per extra adult, 4-bed tourist flat ❷, plus $12 per extra adult.

Vintner's Haven 1210 Sandspit Rd, Sandspit ℡09/425 9670, ⓦwww.saltings.co.nz. Two stylish apartments and a double en-suite, which can all be rented separately (❻) or all together (from $450; sleeps 8; min 3 nights) run by the same owners as the *Saltings Guest House*. Both houses are within walking distance of the Kawau ferry wharf. ❾

Daytime **eating** is best done at the intimate *Unit A*, 7 Neville St, near the visitor centre, which focuses on seafood and Asian dishes; at the *Queen Street Corner Café & Bookshop*, on the corner of Queen and Neville Streets; or at the restaurant out at Heron's Flight winery (see p.166). In the evening make for the good-value *Millstream Bar & Grill* near the river bridge on Elizabeth St

(☎09/422 2292; closed Mon), which specializes in steaks for lunch and dinner and has a 32-seater movie theatre (free film before or after your meal), or the *Pizza Co.*, 18 Neville St (BYO & licensed), for fine pizza and great chowder. Alternatively drive 8km out to Snell's Beach, where *Pizza Construction* on Mahurangi East Rd (book in advance ☎09/425 5555) makes delicious pizzas (eat in or take away) and has a high-quality à la carte restaurant; or head 4km to Ascension Vineyard (see p.166; ☎09/422 9601).

Kawau Island

KAWAU ISLAND holds a special place in the hearts of the Hauraki Gulf yachting fraternity, as much for the safety of its straggling harbours as for the sandy coves wedged between modest cliffs. With a resident population of around a hundred, the island is chiefly given over to holiday homes. As a casual visitor, you can't do much without your own boat except visit the Mansion House at Mansion House Bay, and its exotic grounds.

Once farmed, the island is slowly reverting to kanuka scrub so it isn't an especially appealing place to walk around, and access is difficult to all but the DOC-managed southwestern tenth of the island. This area is where one of New Zealand's first export industries sprang up around a briefly profitable **copper trade** in the 1840s and 1850s. Mines in Dispute Cove yielded copper ore, which was processed at Smeltinghouse Bay on **Bon Accord Harbour**, the inlet that nearly cuts the island in two. The industry was defunct by 1862, when George Grey, then doing his second stint as New Zealand's governor, was looking for a private home and bought the mine manager's house and adjacent assay office, linking the two to form the **Mansion House** (daily 9.30am–3.30pm; $4). Grey was an austere man, so the house is simply decorated using kauri and totara panels. Apart from a collection of silverware, there's little in the house that belonged to Grey himself.

Grey's pursuit of the Victorian fashion for all things exotic resulted in grounds stocked with flora and fauna imported from all over the world. Although much of it was ill-tended after his departure, the dell is still a gracious place – Chilean wine palms, coral trees and a smattering of native species stud the formal lawns. He also brought in four species of **wallaby**, which have overtaken the island to the extent that they are now regularly culled. A path runs through the gardens to the tiny beach at **Lady's Bay** (5mins) and on to a network of short tracks that drop to the coves on Bon Accord Harbour and the ruins of the old copper mine, a walk of about forty minutes each way.

Practicalities

Boats to Kawau Island leave from the wharf at **Sandspit**, a small road-end community on the Matakana Estuary, 8km east of Warkworth. Throughout the year, Kawau Kat Cruises (☎0800/888 006 & 09/425 8006, ✉info@kawaukat.co.nz) operate the **Royal Mail Run** (daily 10.30am; 4hr; $59 return with barbecue lunch), delivering mail, papers and groceries to all the wharves on the island and giving you about two hours ashore at Mansion House Bay; their direct service (2pm; 26 Dec–April daily; rest of the year Fri–Sun only; $29 return or $16 one way) gives you more time at the bay. For a cheaper and more leisurely option, try the **Coffee Cruise** on the *MV Matata* (☎0800/225 292 & 025/960910; Christmas–Easter daily 10am & 2pm; rest of the year Tues–Sun 10am, with extra sailings at weekends & school holidays; $25 return, or $40 to include lunch and entry to Mansion House; buy your ticket on the boat), which follows a similar itinerary to the Royal Mail Run – though you'll need to go out on the early boat and come back on the later one if you want to linger on the island. Both companies run a range of other cruises in summer. Two **water taxi** services also operate daily year-round to various bays on the island – the 24-hour Reubens (℡09/422 8881 & 025 2746872; $15 per person or minimum call-out fee of $60 one way) and Kawau Water Taxi, operated by Kawau Kat Cruises (see p.165; 7am–7pm, $50 per person one way for up to 4 people or $12 per person for more than 4); book ahead or pop into their wharfside office (daily 8am–5pm). Bring whatever you need to Kawau as there are no stores or cafés. The only **payphone** at Sandspit is in the Kawau Kat office.

There are several **places to stay** on Kawau including *Pah Farm*, Moores Bay, Bon Accord Harbour (℡09/422 8765, ✉pah.farm@ihug.co.nz; tent sites $10, four-shares ❶, rooms ❷), equipped with a camp kitchen, restaurant and bar (both open daily), and kayaks for rent. Geared towards romantic weekends away is *The Beachhouse*, Vivian Bay (℡09/422 8850, ✉vivianbay@xtra.co.nz; ❾), charging from $320 with dinner and breakfast.

Matakana

MATAKANA, 8km northeast of Warkworth, is little more than a road junction at the heart of a fledgling wine-making region, though the surrounding area is dotted with the workshops of craftspeople. The catalyst for the region's development was the **Morris & James Pottery & Tileworks**, 2km from Matakana village at Tongue Farm Rd (Mon–Fri 8.30am–4.30pm, Sat & Sun 10am–5pm; free), which in the late 1970s exploited New Zealand's fortress economy by producing otherwise unobtainable handmade terracotta tiles and large garden pots made from local clay. You can catch a free 30min tour of the pottery (Mon–Fri 11.30am) before a visit to the pleasing café bar.

Despite received wisdom about high humidity and proximity to the sea being unsuitable for viticulture, half the valley seems to have been planted with **vineyards** during the last decade or so. The free and widely available *Matakana Coast Wine Country* leaflet currently details five wineries offering tastings, while two of the most interesting have restaurants. First stop should be *Heron's Flight*, 49 Sharp Rd (℡09/422 7915, ⊛www.heronsflight.co.nz; daily from 10am), styled along Tuscan lines and planting Sangiovese vines with considerable success. Mulberries, figs and olives are also grown here and sold in the deli, as well as appearing in dishes served up in the lovely **restaurant** overlooking the vines. For a small charge you can taste the Sangiovese and a range of New Zealand wines; for free you can stroll through the kitchen gardens and vineyards along short walks described in the winery's leaflet. Another good bet is *Ascension Vineyard & Café* (℡09/422 9601, ⊛www.ascensionvineyard.co.nz), on Matakana Rd, which also has a pleasant café-restaurant serving Mediterranean-style dishes (lunch daily, dinner Fri & Sat; bookings essential for weekend lunch or dinner all year and for dinner in summer), and offers a tasting of their complement of wines for $8. Matakana's original winery, *Hyperion Wines* (℡09/422 9375, ⊛www.hyperion-wines.co.nz; open daily Dec 27 to end of the first week in Feb, rest of the year by appointment), on Tongue Farm Rd 1km from Morris & James, also make a small charge for tastings of their diverse wines. For a high-quality **snack** try the tiny, award-winning *Pop-in Patisserie* in Matakana itself, on the corner of Matakana Valley Rd and Torea Rd (Mon–Fri 7am–2.30pm, weekends till 3pm).

Leigh and Goat Island

East of Matakana, the road runs 13km to the clifftop village of **LEIGH**, which boasts a picturesque harbour bobbing with wooden fishing boats, and the fine sandy bay of **Mathesons Beach**, 1km to the west. The boats attest to the abundance of fish where ocean currents meet the waters of the Hauraki Gulf. But overfishing has taken its toll, which underlines the importance of the **Goat Island Marine Reserve** (officially **Cape Rodney–Okakari Marine Reserve**, but usually known as Goat Island), located around some 4km northeast of Leigh. Established in 1975, this was New Zealand's first marine reserve, stretching 5km along the shoreline and 800m off the coast. It's named for its most prominent feature, a small, bush-clad island 300m offshore. Almost three angling- and shellfishing-free decades later, the undersea life is thriving, with large rock lobster and huge snapper. Feeding is discouraged – blue maomaos in particular developed a taste for frozen peas and used to mob swimmers and divers.

Easy beach access, wonderfully clear water, rock pools on wave-cut platforms, a variety of undersea terrains and relatively benign currents combine to make this an enormously popular year-round **diving** spot, as well as a favourite summer destination for families. **Snorkellers** enjoy a lush world of kelp forest with numerous multi-coloured fish; those who venture deeper find more exposed seascapes with an abundance of sponges. Snorkelling **gear** (from $13 for mask, snorkel and fins, plus wetsuits at $7 for a shortie or $12 full) can be rented from **Seafriends** (☏09/422 6212, ⓦwww.seafriends.org.nz) about a kilometre along Goat Island Road, where there's a restaurant and warm showers. The highly professional Goat Island Dive, 142a Pakiri Rd, next to the *Sawmill Café* at Leigh, (☏0800/348 369 & 09/422 6925, ⓦwww.goatislanddive.co.nz) rent gear for similar prices (plus full dive gear for $90) year round and also run trips to Goat Island Marine Reserve.

For an idea of what's under the water visit a series of small **aquariums** at Seafriends, which recreate different Goat Island ecosystems. Or, in fine weather (Sept–April only), join 45-minute boat tours around the island on the glass-bottomed *Aquador* (Sept–April; $18; ☏09/422 6334), which departs from the Goat Island Marine Reserve beach.

Practicalities

There's no public transport to Leigh or Goat Island, and the facilities are limited once you get here. You can **stay** at the welcoming *Goat Island Camping & Accommodation* (☏09/422 6185, ⓔgoatiscamp@xtra.co.nz; camping $12, dorms ❶, cabins & on-site caravans ❷), about 1km back from the reserve on the way to Goat Island, which has great bay views, plus snorkel gear rental at $10 for the day (mask, snorkel and fins; wetsuit is an extra $10). In Leigh, the *Leigh Sawmill Café*, 142 Pakiri Rd (☏09/422 6019, ⓦwww.sawmillcafe.co.nz), has five spacious en-suite doubles (❺), two bunkrooms (❶) and a communal kitchen; the *Leigh Motel*, 15 Hill St (☏ & ⓕ09/422 6179, ⓔleigh.motel@xtra.co.nz; ❹), has two-night deals from June to September.

There are several good **eating** options in the area. The slick *Leigh Sawmill Café* (see above), a vast sawmill sensitively converted into a smart café/bar (summer daily; winter Fri–Sun only), serves fine gourmet pizza and a range of well-presented dishes from brunch onwards; weekends typically draw touring bands. Good alternatives include Leigh's fish-and-chip takeaway (closed Mon & Tues except during school holidays), and the BYO and licensed restaurant at Seafriends (see above; daily: Oct–Apr 9am–8pm; May–Sept 10am–4pm), both serving excellent seafood, even if coming at it from very different angles.

Pakiri

Heading north up the coast, you can reach Mangawhai Heads (see below) from Leigh via a string of dirt roads through steep hills but it's not an especially striking journey, and you'll do better to return to SH1 in Warkworth – unless you want to visit the long, dune-backed white strand of **Pakiri**, with its few scattered houses, 10km north of Leigh. It's a gorgeous long beach with good surf, but the main attraction here is **horse-riding** with the highly professional Pakiri Beach Horse Riding, Rahuikiri Road, Pakiri Beach (Ⓣ09/422 6275, Ⓦwww.horseride-nz.co.nz), who operate year-round and run a pleasant café. Rides range from a brief jaunt along the beach and through a *pohutukawa* glade to full-blown safaris through stands of native bush and along the tops of sea-cliffs. Outings leave daily at 10am & 2pm, and there are three more departures in the peak summer season ($40 for an hour to $450 or more for overnight trips). If you'd like to stay over they have attractive **accommodation** in backpacker riverside cabins ($25), self-contained beachside cabins for two (Ⓢ), and a luxurious 4-bedroom beach house from $350 for two. **Campers** can stay nearby at the excellent *Pakiri Beach Holiday Park*, Pakiri River Rd (Ⓣ09/422 6199, Ⓦwww.pakiriholidaypark.co.nz; ❶–❽), where there's a broad range of accommodation, from bunkhouse cabins sleeping fifteen (❶) to a luxury beachfront lodge for four (❽ plus $50 per extra adult).

Mangawhai Heads and around

Back on SH1 and heading north, your next chance to turn off towards the coast is at the small roadside settlement of **TEHANA**, from where a winding country road runs 13km inland to tiny **Mangawhai**, little more than a crossroads until the arrival of the Smashed Pipi, 40 Moir St (Ⓣ09/431 4847; closed evenings Mon & Tues; book ahead), a gallery with an attached café and bar that draws the Auckland and Whangarei weekend set for brunch, lunch and dinner. Otherwise try the pasta and pizza dishes across the road at *Quatro Café* (Ⓣ09/431 5226). An organic fruit and veg market is held on Saturday mornings in the village hall on the corner of Moir Street and Insley Street.

The road continues 3km north to meet the coast at **Mangawhai Heads** at the mouth of the Mangawhai Harbour, marked by a cluster of holiday homes straggling over the hillsides behind a fine surf beach. Long a Kiwi summer-holiday favourite, Mangawhai Heads tends to be bypassed by outsiders due to its lack of specific attractions, but that's part of the charm, and a day or two lazing on the beach and body surfing can be enough. There's also the scenic **Mangawhai Cliffs Walkway** (2–3hr; closed in lambing season Aug to mid-Oct). Walk north along the beach for fifteen minutes then follow the orange markers up through bush-backed farmland along the top of the sea cliffs until the path winds back down to the beach. Provided the tide is below half, you can return along the beach through a small rock arch.

At Mangawhai Heads the town's shops are in the Wood Street shopping complex, in the centre and off Molesworth Drive. **Internet access** is available at The Nurv Computer Centre, in the Wood Street shops (Tues–Fri & Sun 9am–5pm, Sat 10am–6pm, closed Mon), who also repair computers.

Mangawhai Heads offers a backpackers and excels in more luxurious **accommodation**. The purpose-built *Bunk 'n' Brekkie Backpackers*, Mangawhai Heads Rd (Ⓣ & Ⓕ09/431 4939; tents $12, dorms ❶), offers dorms, and breakfast for an extra few dollars. It's 2.5km from the Wood Street shops and a 10-minute walk to the beach. Reserve as far in advance as you can to stay at *Milestone Cottages by the Sea*, 27 Moir Point Rd (Ⓣ & Ⓕ09/431 4018,

@ www.milestonecottages.co.nz; studio ❹, cottages ❻–❽ plus $35 for each extra person), a cluster of beautiful cottages amid sumptuous organic gardens and coastal bush within sight of the sea, and a short walk to a secluded estuary beach. All are self-catering and fully equipped, including a barbecue deck, TV and VCR; and there's free use of a lap pool and kayaks. If you want tremendous sea views and a more personal touch, opt for *Mangawhai Lodge*, 4 Heather St (☎09/431 5311, @ www.seaviewlodge.co.nz; ❻), high on a hill with tasteful rooms, three of them en-suite, all opening onto a wraparound veranda.

Mangawhai Heads offers a couple of good **places to eat** in addition to the restaurants in nearby Mangawhai. The licensed *Naja Garden Café*, 5 Molesworth Drive (☎09/431 4111) at a garden centre, makes a fine stop for a coffee and breakfast, or gourmet sandwiches; it's also open for dinner (summer nightly, winter Thurs–Mon), with a good range of well-priced mains. Alternatively, head for the airy *Sail Rock Café* on Wood St (☎09/431 4051) open for lunch and dinner, including gourmet pizzas. Or retreat to either of the two restaurants listed in Mangawhai (see above).

Lang's Beach and Waipu Cove

Lang's Beach, 12km north of Mangawhai Heads, is a delightful tree-backed strand where the *Lochalsh B&B* (☎ & ☏09/432 0053, @ www.lochalsh.co.nz; ❺), overlooks the beach from its perch above the main road and offers two double en-suite rooms. From here it's a further 4km to the top surf beach of **WAIPU COVE**, a cluster of houses by a sweeping stretch of Bream Bay. Accommodation is limited but right by the beach. There's camping at *Camp Waipu Cove*, 897 Cove Rd (☎09/432 0410, ℮info@campwaipucove.com; camping $10–17, modern cabins ❺), and stylish units at the *Waipu Cove Resort*, 891 Cove Rd (☎09/432 0348, @ www.waipucoveresort.co.nz; ❻). Or go for the modern cottages at the secluded *Waipu Cove Cottages and Camping*, Cove Rd (☎09/432 0851, ℮covecottages@xtra.co.nz; camping $10–12; single rooms $25, rooms ❷, 2-bedroom cottages ❹ plus $18 per extra adult, 1-bedroom unit ❸), just across a small estuary from the beach, with free use of dinghies.

Waipu and around

Driving through it, you wouldn't pick nondescript **WAIPU** as different from any other small Kiwi town but for an Aberdeen granite monument surmounted by a Scottish lion rampant in the middle of the main street. Erected in 1914 to commemorate the sixtieth anniversary of the town's founding, the monument recalls the Scottish home of the settlers who arrived here by way of Nova Scotia, following a charismatic preacher, the Reverend Norman McLeod. Like numerous other crofters dispossessed by the Highland clearances, McLeod left Scotland in 1817; he took with him as many as he could persuade to follow him and set down roots in St Ann's, Nova Scotia, where they stayed until famine and a series of harsh winters in the late 1850s drove them out. Some went to Australia, but most decamped to Waipu, forming a self-contained and deathly strict Calvinist community that eked a living from farming and forestry. The town is proud of its heritage, and sponsors someone every year to study pipes, drum or Scottish country dancing at the Gaelic College of Arts and Crafts in Nova Scotia. The biggest event of the year is Waipu's New Year's Day **Highland Games** (@ www.highlandgames.co.nz), in which competitors heft large stones, and toss cabers and sheaves in the Caledonian Park. The Scottish history and genealogy of the settlers is recounted in the **Waipu Heritage Centre** on the main street (daily 9.30am–4.30pm; $5; Ⓦwww.waipumusem.com), housing a well laid out exhibition of settlers' photos, their personal effects and an attractive display of carved and polished kauri gum.

Unless you happen to coincide with the Highland Games, there's nothing much to do in Waipu itself, though the **Waipu Caves** make a popular excursion to view one of the longest stalagmites in New Zealand in a 200-metre glowworm-filled passage, in the limestone country 16km to the northwest. Obtain a free map from the visitor centre in Waipu (see below), wear old clothes and good footwear, take a couple of good torches each – it's pitch-black and very disorientating inside the caves – and explore. The cave is signposted from Waipu Caves Road and is impenetrable when wet; you'll get muddy even in dry weather.

Horse trekking through local native bush and along river trails with one of New Zealand's best outfits begins only 10km to the northwest of Waipu, at North River Treks (Ⓣ0800/743 344 & 09/432 0565, Ⓔinfo@north-river.co.nz; reservations essential). Trips are geared to small groups of similar riding ability and last from 1hr ($35) to an overnight stay ($250). Favourites are the Trail Blazer (2hr, $65) for its coastal views, and The Caves (4–5 hr, $150), which stops for a BBQ lunch at Waipu Caves.

North from Waipu, the road runs parallel to Bream Bay, occasional turnings giving access to the long white **beach** that lies to the east. The best place to head to the sands is at **Uretiti**, 6km north of Waipu, where there's a primitive DOC camping area ($6), with water and cold showers, and an adjacent naturist beach.

Practicalities

InterCity and Northliner **buses** drop off and pick up on request outside the liquor store, on the main street, which also acts as a ticket agent (Ⓣ09/432 0225). A block away, the Waipu Heritage Centre (see above) contains the town's **visitor centre** (daily 9.30am–4.30pm; Ⓣ09/432 0746, Ⓦwww.waipumuseum.com). There are no banks or ATMs, but you can change travellers' cheques and currency (Mon, Wed & Fri 9.30am–3pm only) at the kiosk at Waipu Cyber Centre, next door to the liquor store on the main road, which also has **Internet access** (closed Sun).

Budget **accommodation** is found at *Waipu Wanderers*, 25 St Mary's Rd (Ⓣ09/432 0532, Ⓔwaipu.wanderers@xtra.co.nz; 4-bed dorms ❶, rooms ❷), which has nine beds in a separate house with its own kitchen and bathroom, within easy walking distance of the town centre. A full range of options is offered by the *Stone House*, on Cove Rd (Ⓣ09/432 0432, Ⓔstonehouse-waipu@xtra.co.nz; dorms ❶, cabin ❸, cottages sleeping 6 or 8 ❺ plus $20 each extra adult, B&B ❹). Set in extensive grounds near an ocean beach, some of the accommodation offers views across a lagoon and there's use of free dinghies.

For tasty **meals**, the best place is *The Pizza Barn*, 2 Cove Rd (Ⓣ09/432 1011), for a range of well-priced lunches and dinners in Waipu's former post office – either in the cosy log-cabin dining room/bar or in the garden.

Whangarei and around

On initial acquaintance, **WHANGAREI** is a bit of a disappointment. If you've come from the south, Bream Bay's sweeping coastline and the attractive Whangarei Harbour seem to promise more than Northland's provincial

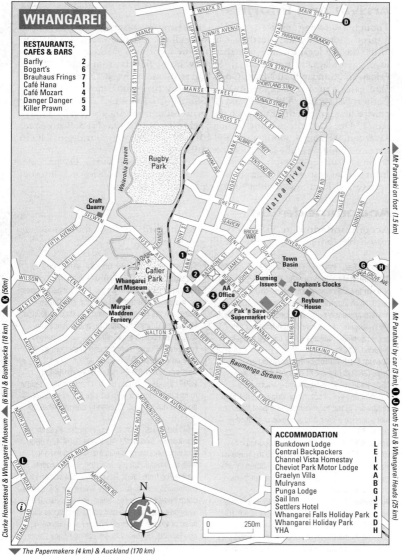

WHANGAREI

RESTAURANTS, CAFÉS & BARS

Barfly	2
Bogart's	6
Brauhaus Frings	7
Café Hana	1
Café Mozart	4
Danger Danger	5
Killer Prawn	3

ACCOMMODATION

Bunkdown Lodge	E
Central Backpackers	I
Channel Vista Homestay	K
Cheviot Park Motor Lodge	A
Graelyn Villa	B
Mulryans	G
Punga Lodge	J
Sail Inn	F
Settlers Hotel	C
Whangarei Falls Holiday Park	D
Whangarei Holiday Park	H
YHA	H

Map labels: **Ⓐ** (4 km), Whangarei Falls (4 km), **Ⓑ** (8 km) & Bay of Islands (70 km) · **Ⓒ** (3 km) · **Ⓓ** · Mair Street · Wrack St · Manse Street · Lupton Avenue · Dinnis Avenue · Wallace Street · Kamo Road · Mill Road · Parahaki · Rurumoki Street · Deveron Street · Western Hills Drive · Shortland Street · Manse Street · Donald Street · Neil · **Ⓔ** **Ⓕ** · Cross St · Wolfe St · Rugby Park · Bank St · Aubrey Street · Pentland Rd · Apirana Ave · Norfolk St · Hatea Drive · Hatea River · Aving Rd · Vale Rd · Dundas Rd · Waiarohia Stream · Grey St · Seaview · Bridge Way · Riverside · Craft Quarry · Selwyn · Fifth Avenue · Mont St · Dent St · Quay St · Town Basin · **Ⓖ** **Ⓗ** · Punga Grove Ave · Wilson Ave · Western Hills · Central Avenue · Rust Ave · Lovers Ave · Alexander · Cafler Park · Whangarei Art Museum · Bank St · James St · Robert St · John St · Burning Issues · Clapham's Clocks · Third Ave · Water St · Margie Maddren Fernery · Line St · Walton St · AA Office · Pak 'n Save Supermarket · Carruth · Dent St · Reyburn House · Reyburn St · Kaitika Road · Maunu Rd · Second Ave · First Ave · Rose St · Albert St · Clyde St · Siddom · Cameron St · Hannah St · Herekino St · Port Rd · Cooks St · Tarewa Road · Railway Rd · Raumanga Stream · Commerce Street · Bernard St · North Street · Anzac Road · Morningside Road · Kaka Street · Porowini Avenue · Otaika Road · Tarewa Road · Mountain Rd · Hilltop · The Papermakers (4 km) & Auckland (170 km) · Mt Parahaki on foot (1.5 km) · Mt Parahaki by car (3 km), **Ⓘ** & **Ⓙ** both 5 km & Whangarei Heads (25 km) · Clarke Homestead & Whangarei Museum (6 km) & Bushwacka (18 km) · **Ⓚ** (50m) · **Ⓛ** · N · 0 250m

capital is able to deliver. But it does have redeeming features, not least the riverside **Town Basin**, where sleek yachts are moored outside a renovated settlerstyle shopping and restaurant complex. Elsewhere there's a smattering of modest museums and sights and a few pleasant walks, but Whangarei is perhaps best used as a base either for a swimming and walking day-trip to Whangarei Heads, or for diving and snorkelling around the **Poor Knights Islands**.

NORTHLAND | Whangarei and around

2

Arrival and information

Though a rail line runs from Auckland to Whangarei, no passenger trains make it this far. InterCity and Northliner **buses** pull up on Bank Street, also the hub of the skeletal local town service that runs frequently on weekdays, slightly less so on Saturday, and not at all on Sunday. Daily **flights** from Auckland, and Friday and Sunday flights from Great Barrier Island arrive at Onerahi Airport, 5km east of town and linked to Whangarei by two shuttle taxi firms – Kiwi Carlton Cabs (℡09/438 4444) and A1 Shuttle (℡0800/483 3377). The **visitor centre** lies 2km south of town on the main route from Auckland at 92 Otaika Rd (27 Dec–Jan daily 8.30am–6.30pm; Feb–Christmas Mon–Fri 8.30am–5pm, Sat & Sun 9.30am–4.30pm; ℡09/438 1079, ⓦwww.whangareinz.org.nz). It's in the same building as the **DOC office** (℡09/430 2007; Mon–Fri 9am–5pm, Sat & Sun 10am–4pm, with extended hours in summer) and a decent café. **Internet access** is available at the visitor centre and at Klosenet Internet Services, 34 John St (Mon–Sat 10am–9pm, Sun 11am–6pm).

Accommodation

Accommodation in Whangarei is seldom hard to find and prices are reasonable, though there are few really special places.

Hotels, motels and B&Bs

Channel Vista 254 Beach Rd, Onerahi, 5km east of town towards Whangarei Heads ℡09/436 5529, ⓔchannelvista@igrin.co.nz. Luxurious modern homestay with two Queen suites overlooking Whangarei Harbour and 20m from a small beach; cooking facilities and a cooked breakfast included. ⑥

Cheviot Park Motor Lodge cnr Western Hills Drive (SH1) & Cheviot St ℡09/438 2341 & 0508/243846, ⓦwww.cheviot-park.co.nz. Cheerful and well-kept motor lodge about 1.5km southwest of the town centre, with pool, spa, room-service meals, and a choice of studios or suites. ⑤

Graelyn Villa 166 Kiripaka Rd, Tikipunga ℡09/437 7532, ⓔgraelyn@xtra.co.nz. Three en-suite rooms in a hundred-year-old suburban villa surrounded by lush gardens in a tranquil setting close to Whangarei Falls. ④

Mulryans Crane Rd ℡09/435 0945, ⓦwww.mulryans.co.nz. Elegant country B&B about 10km north of Whangarei, set amid large well-tended gardens with a tennis court, outdoor spa and pool. The two rooms are tastefully appointed and a generous farmhouse breakfast is served. Dinner is also available by prior arrangement for $45–55, including wine. ⑦

Punga Lodge 9 Punga Grove, off Riverside Drive ℡09/438 3879. One spacious en-suite B&B room beside the main house, overlooking the harbour and Town Basin from a central hillside location. ③

Sail Inn 148 Beach Rd, Onerahi, 8km from Whangarei ℡09/436 2356, ⓔsailinn@xtra.co.nz. An upmarket retreat in a light-filled modern house on the shore of a tranquil harbour. The Queen en-suite looks onto the water and has its own lounge, fridge and dressing room. The house is a 2min walk to the beach and 5mins to a good seafood restaurant. Picnic hampers and dinner are available on request. ⑦

Settlers Hotel 61–69 Hatea Drive ℡09/438 2699, ⓔsettlers@ihug.co.nz. Comfortable en-suite rooms in a complex with on-site bar, restaurant and swimming pool. Weekend rates available. ⑤

Hostels and campsites

Bunkdown Lodge 23 Otaika Rd ℡09/438 8886, ⓦwww.bunkdownlodge.co.nz. A spacious and well-run hostel in a pretty historic villa a couple of kilometres from town, but close to the visitor centre and with cheap bikes. There are 2 kitchens, dorm beds, four-shares, twins and doubles, and everyone gets free tea and coffee and access to a heap of videos. Guidance on Poor Knights diving, and tours of the beautiful limestone Abbey Caves (2hr; $25), plus lessons in portraiture. Dorms ①, rooms. ②

Central Backpackers 67 Hatea Drive ℡0800/437 6174, ⓔjulie@centralbackpackers.co.nz. Slightly cramped yet clean hostel in a converted suburban house containing dorms and a couple of compact units with kettle, fridge and stove. There's also a BBQ and they can help with choosing a diving trip. Dorms ①, rooms & units ③.

Whangarei Falls Holiday Park Ngunguru Rd at Tikipunga, 6km from town near Whangarei Falls ☎0800/227 222 & 09/437 0609, Ⓦwww.whangareifalls.co.nz. Less convenient than the other campsite, but the setting compensates – on the edge of the countryside, and with a pool and spa. It also has a pleasant bunkroom and spacious cabins, all 1km from a supermarket. Camping $10, dorms ❶, cabins. ❷

Whangarei Holiday Park 24 Mair St ☎09/437 6856, Ⓦwww.whangareiholiday.co.nz. Small and tranquil site in a pretty setting 2km from town with a range of accommodation to include well-equipped en-suite cabins and units. Camping $11, bunkroom ❶, cabins ❷, units ❸.

Whangarei Manaki Tanga YHA 52 Punga Grove Ave ☎09/438 8954, Ⓔyhawhang@yha.org.nz. Intimate hilltop hostel a steep fifteen-minute climb on foot from the centre of Whangarei, with good views over the town, and glowworms a ten-minute walk away into the bush. Accommodation is in twins, doubles and four- and six-bed dorms. Dorms ❶, rooms ❷.

The Town

The working port that originally brought Whangarei its prosperity is a few kilometres out of town, leaving the renovated **Town Basin** to restaurants and a smattering of tourist sights. Nearby, ranks of car-sales yards and print shops press in on the central grid of streets where the museum, fernery and craft quarry can occupy half a day. There's more interest just out of town at the cluster of museums around the **Clarke Homestead**, at **Whangarei Falls**, and in the smattering of local **walks**.

Central Whangarei

Whangarei's greatest concentration of sights is around the **Town Basin**, a prettified zone of upmarket galleries, shops and restaurants based around an 1880s villa. Call in at the kauri and fudge shops and maybe play with the giant chessboard pieces outside the **Burning Issues Gallery** (daily 10am–5pm; free), a glass and ceramics studio where you can watch glass-blowing most days. The main sight is **Clapham's Clocks** (daily 9am–5pm; $8), right by New Zealand's largest sundial, and packed with 1500 clocks. Nearby, Whangarei's oldest kauri villa, **Reyburn House** (Tues–Fri 10am–4pm, Sat & Sun 1–4pm; free), hosts the Northland Society of Arts' exhibition gallery, usually containing a few quality pieces. On the western side of the town centre, the small but well-kept **Cafler Park** is pleasant for a stroll – head for the Rose Gardens and the adjacent **Whangarei Art Museum** (daily 9am–5pm; donation), which houses a small permanent collection of New Zealand art and frequently changing exhibitions showcasing Kiwi artists. A footbridge crosses the stream running through Cafler Park to the restful and cool **Margie Maddren Fernery**, First Avenue (daily 10am–4pm; free), a collection of native ferns. These are flanked by two glasshouses, one containing New Zealand's more delicate fern species, the other stuffed with cacti. From here, it's ten minutes' walk to the **Craft Quarry** artists' co-operative, Selwyn Avenue (Mon–Fri 9am–5pm, Sat & Sun 10am–4pm; free), a focus for the local vibrant crafts community. You're free to wander among anarchic shacks built from adobe, timber and corrugated iron and watch the artisans at work (though few are here at weekends).

Suitably inspired, you may fancy having a go at making your own paper and cards at **The Paper Mill**, 4km south on SH1 at Otaika (Mon–Fri 9.30am–4pm; book ahead for tours on ☎09/438 2652; 40min tours daily 9.30am–2.30pm; $5 to make paper), where an interesting range of handcrafted paper is produced from natural and recycled materials in an eighteenth-century cottage – don't let the period costumes put you off.

Hikes and activities around Whangarei

Whangarei's most appealing feature is the number of small parks and easy **walks** within a few minutes of the town, the best of which are outlined in the free *Whangarei Walks* leaflet, from the visitor centre. Views over the harbour and town are the reward for climbing to the ugly sheet-metal war memorial atop the 240m **Mount Parahaki**, which can be approached by car along Memorial Drive (off Riverside Drive; 3km) or on foot along the steep Ross Track (40min ascent) from the end of Dundas Road.

Most visitors prefer the twenty-minute stroll around the broad curtain of the **Whangarei Falls**, where the Hatea River cascades over a 26-metre basalt ridge into a popular swimming hole. The falls are 5km northeast of the town centre (Kamo-bound buses pass close by) and can also easily be reached from an attractive remnant of kauri forest – the road out to the falls passes Whareora Road, which runs 1.5km to the **A. H. Reed Memorial Kauri Park**, where shady paths through native bush pass several mature kauri – look out for the ten-minute Alexander Walk, which links with a short, sinuous canopy boardwalk high across a creek before reaching some fine kauri. The Elizabeth track links with another track along the Hatea River to the Whangarei Falls (30min one way). For a longer walk to the falls you can begin in town, at the Parahaki Scenic Reserve on the opposite shore from the Town Basin (accessed from several points including Rurumoki Street off Hatea Drive), and follow the Hatea Walk (35min one way) to Whareora Road, continuing on to the A.H. Reed Memorial Kauri Park by following the signposts.

Three kilometres further along the same road, the fluted and weather-worn limestone formations of **Abbey Caves** (unrestricted access) invite comparison with Henry Moore sculptures. Though the caves are open to anyone, you need some caving experience to enter them on your own; or enrol on a 2hr **guided tour** from Whangarei (☏09/438 8886; $25).

Some 18km southwest of town on SH14, the **Bushwacka Experience** (reserve in advance on ☏09/434 7839 [no email]) offers fun packages of outdoor adventures amid interesting geology and thick bush hidden on a dairy farm. You can tailor your visit from a range of activities including 4WD safaris, exploring the "Squeeze" or one of the other deep volcanic rock crevices, abseiling into the "Black Hole", hiking to some giant kauri or just relaxing over a barbecue. The cost is $55 for two hours, $85 for half a day, including pick-up from Whangarei.

The Clarke Homestead and Whangarei Museum

There's another collection of museums ($5 each, or $8 combined ticket) at the **Whangarei Heritage Park**, 6km southwest of Whangarei on SH14 in Maunu, containing the **Clarke Homestead** (daily 10am–4pm), a rare example of an un-restored original homestead. Built in 1886 for a Scottish doctor, Alexander Clarke, the house was at its most vibrant in the 1930s, when Alexander's son hosted high-society parties here, and much of what you see dates from that era. The highlight is the unkempt, "*Boys Own*" bedroom of Alexander's grandson, Basil.

The **Whangarei Museum** (same hours; $5), in a modern building in the homestead grounds, has an intriguing selection of objects relating to local history, flora and fauna, plus a small yet interesting Maori collection. The prize exhibit is the *waka tupapuka*, a sixteenth-century wooden funerary chest decorated with bird-form carvings. The museum's **Kiwi House** (same hours; $5) is one of the best of its kind, well laid out and giving good visibility.

Eating and drinking

When it comes to **eating**, Whangarei has more choice than anywhere between Auckland and the Bay of Islands. A selection of popular **fast-food** franchises line Bank Street, while more imaginative **restaurants** cluster around the Town Basin and along Cameron Street. For **groceries**, Pak 'n' Save, on the corner of Robert Street and Carruth Street, has the best prices.

For details of **live music** gigs, check out Tuesday's "The Leader" newspaper.

Barfly 13 Rathbone St. Friendly all-day café/bar known for its excellent coffee, wood-fired pizzas, vegetarian dishes, à la carte dinner menu (except Sun & Mon nights) and lavish desserts.

Bogart's cnr Cameron St & Walton St. Easy-going, licensed dinner restaurant that's lively at weekends, serving crispy gourmet pizzas and a range of appealing mains for around $25.

Brauhaus Frings cnr Lower Dent St & Reyburn St (Ⓦwww.frings.co.nz) Welcoming microbrewery and small bar selling four beers that are brewed for sale on the premises only. German snacks and Kalte Platte are offered (food served Oct–May midday–8pm; rest of the year Wed–Sat evenings, lunch on Fri, & Sat afternoons from 2pm). The bar opens at 10am daily.

Café Hana 77 Bank St, next door to Town Hall Ⓣ09/430 8097. Excellent good-value Japanese restaurant in an unassuming venue for lunch and dinner (11.30am–2pm & 6pm onwards), as well as takeaway food; their set meals are a speciality.

Bookings are essential in summer for Thurs–Sat nights. Closed Sun & Mon, and for two weeks at Christmas.

Café Mozart 60 Cameron St Ⓣ09/438 1116. Swiss-run café and licensed restaurant for lunch and dinner in a former pharmacy, which still retains much of its original woodwork. An eclectic menu of international food, plus delicious fruit tarts and a good range of wines. Relax at the intimate bar before sitting down to eat. Closed Sun & Mon.

Danger Danger 37 Vine St. Kicking bar that boasts the biggest sports screen in Northland, which is switched to DJ use on dance nights. The bistro menu offers more than just basic bar food and there's a $6 Meal Steal (Tues–Sat for lunch & dinner).

Killer Prawn 28 Bank St. Conservatory-style bar and restaurant serving daytime and evening seafood; prawns are a speciality. Light snacks start at around $6; enormous mains at around $26. Closed Sun.

Around Whangarei

The best reason to spend some time in Whangarei is to explore the surrounding area, particularly to the east and north of the town where craggy, weathered remains of ancient volcanoes abut the sea. Southeast of the town **Whangarei Heads** is the district's volcanic heartland, where dramatic walks follow the coast to calm harbour beaches and windswept coastal strands. To the northeast, **Tutukaka** acts as the base for dive trips to the undersea wonderland around the **Poor Knights Islands**. Heading north from Whangarei or Tutukaka to the Bay of Islands, don't miss the **Hundertwasser toilets** in Kawakawa.

There's **public transport** to Tutukaka only (bus with MVS Limousines; book ahead Ⓣ09/438 9912), and the rugged terrain to any of these places can make cycling a challenge, but dive-trip operators run trips from Whangarei.

Whangarei Heads

The winding road around the northern side of Whangarei Harbour runs 35km southeast to **Whangarei Heads**, a catch-all name for a series of small beach communities scattered around jagged volcanic outcrops that terminate at Bream Head, the northern limit of Bream Bay. Numerous attractive bays provide safe swimming – **McLeod Bay** in particular – but there's really no reason to stop until the road leaves the harbour and climbs to a saddle at the start of an excellent, signposted **walk** (3km return; 2hr–2hr 30min; 200m ascent) up the 430m **Mount Manaia**, crowned with five deeply eroded pinnacles that are shrouded in legend. One story tells of a jealous dispute between two chiefs – Manaia, whose *pa* stood atop Mount Manaia, and the lesser chief, Hautatu, from across the water at Marsden Point, who was married to the beautiful Pito. Hautatu was sent away on a raid, leaving the coast clear for Manaia to steal Pito.

Hautatu returned and was chasing Manaia, his two children and Pito across the hilltop when all five were struck by lightning, leaving the figures petrified on the summit. These pinnacles remain *tapu*, but you can climb to their base through native bush, passing fine viewpoints. This walk and the three outlined below are described in DOC's *Whangarei District Walks* leaflet ($1), available from the Whangarei combined visitor centre/DOC office.

Beyond Mount Manaia, the road runs for 5km to **Urquharts Bay**, where a short walk (20min each way) leads to the white-sand **Smugglers Cove**. A longer trail (3hr return) continues to the small and pebbly beach of **Peach Cove**, which has a hut or you can camp, using the hut's water and toilet facilities (book through Whangarei DOC ✆09/430 2007, ✉ whangareivc@doc.govt.nz; $10 hut, $3 camping); very keen walkers could press on to **Ocean Beach** (5hr one way), a wild white-sand surf beach that's also accessible by road.

Tutukaka and the Poor Knights

The Tutukaka coast means one of two things to New Zealanders: big-game fishing or scuba diving – both based in tiny **TUTUKAKA**, set on a beautiful, deeply incised harbour 30km northeast of Whangarei. Boats leave from here for one of the world's premier dive locations, the **Poor Knights Islands Marine Reserve**, 25km offshore. Here the warm East Auckland current swirling around Cape Reinga and the lack of run-off from the land combine to create wonderfully clear water – visibility approaches 30m most of the year, though in spring (roughly Oct–Dec) plankton can reduce it to 15–20m. These waters are home to New Zealand's most diverse range of sea life, including a few subtropical species found nowhere else, as well as a striking underwater landscape of near-vertical **rock faces** that drop almost 100m through a labyrinth of caves, fissures and rock arches teeming with rainbow-coloured fish, crabs, soft corals, kelp forests and shellfish. The Poor Knights also lie along the migratory routes of a number of **whale** species, so blue, humpback, sei and minke whales, as well as dolphins, are not uncommon. As if that weren't enough, the waters north and south of the reserve are home to two navy **wrecks**, both deliberately scuttled. The survey ship HMNZS *Tui* was sunk in 1999 to form an artificial reef, and such was its popularity with divers and marine life that the obsolete frigate *Waikato* followed two years later.

Everything is protected within the Poor Knights reserve, but free-ranging species such as marlin, shark and tuna that stray outside the reserve are picked off by **big-game anglers** during the December to May season. Anglers wanting to rent a quarter-share of a charter game-fishing boat for the day should expect to pay $250 or more: for a list of operators contact the Whangarei Deep Sea Anglers Club (daily 8am–6pm during the season; ✆09/434 3818).

The reserve also contains myriad **islands**, though you're not allowed to land on any of them. They're a safe haven for geckos, skinks and thousands of tuatara, the sole survivors of a branch of prehistoric lizards, the rest of which became extinct sixty million years back. The islands are also rich in birdlife, the only place in the world where Buller's shearwaters breed, and they come in huge numbers.

Diving and snorkelling

You'll need prior diving experience to sample the best the **Poor Knights** have to offer, but there's plenty for novices and even snorkellers. Both Tutukaka and Whangarei can be used as **diving** bases, though **boats** all leave from Tutukaka. These offer broadly the same deal, with a full day out, two dives and all the equipment you need costing $170–190, including transport from Whangarei.

This reduces to $100–140 if you can provide some or all of your own gear; a day's **snorkelling** starts at around $65. First-time divers can try a **resort dive** ($210) with full gear and one-to-one instruction; a PADI open-water dive qualification will cost about $600 and take five days.

Half a dozen companies operate daily trips in the main season (Nov–April), and usually at least one of them goes out most days the rest of the year. The visitor centre in Whangarei (see p.172) has a full list of current **operators**, but two of the most professional in Tutukaka are Dive Tutukaka, Marina Rd, Tutukaka (℡0800/288 882 & 09/434 3867, Ⓦwww.diving.co.nz), who offer wreck dives and trips to the Poor Knights, putting you on a catamaran with similarly skilled divers, and even offering non-divers kayaking and snorkelling; and Pacific Hideaway, moored at Berth J1 at Tutukaka Marina, alongside the Whangarei Deep Sea Anglers Club (℡0800/693 483 & 09/437 3632, Ⓦwww.divenz.co.nz), who also take snorkellers and sightseers.

Cruising and sailing

You can otherwise appreciate these waters from the safety of a **cruise** on the *Wairangi*, a lovely wooden boat run by Greensea Ecocharters (℡09/434 3350, Ⓦwww.greensea.co.nz; around $80) – an ex-pilot boat skippered by a knowledgeable marine biologist. Day- and half-day trips leave from Tutukaka marina, stopping for snorkelling en route, and dolphin sightings are common. The *Wairangi* also operates overnight charters, comfortably accommodating twelve people. A **fast boat** trip – the Cave Rider – is run by Dive Tutukaka (see contact details above; 2hr30min, $65), zipping you out to spectacular sea arches and caves.

The most leisurely way to explore these waters is to **sail** on the 50ft yacht *Spirit of the Deep* on a 3-day trip with Paradise Eco-Ventures (℡09/434 4066, Ⓦwww.paradisecoast.co.nz; $175 per day including meals), snorkelling or diving at the Poor Knights on your way to Opua in the Bay of Islands, with kayaking opportunities on the second day.

Practicalities

The only amenities around the harbour at Tutukaka are **restaurants**, most notably the *Schnappa Rock Café*, Marina Rd (℡09/434 3774; summer daily; winter Wed–Sun from 4pm), a groovy bar-restaurant producing a tempting range of dishes, including vegetarian dishes, as well as bar snacks and a good range of evening mains (generally under $25); it's essential to book ahead for dinner in summer. *Moochas Bistro*, at the Whangarei Deep Sea Anglers Club building right beside the Tutukaka harbour, serves evening dishes for under $20 – as well as seafood you'll find Scotch fillet steaks and huge burgers.

Local **accommodation** is mostly on the headland just south of Tutukaka and accessed along Tutukaka Block Road, or 5km back towards Whangarei in **NGUNGURU**, which is strung along an attractive, sandy estuary that's fine for swimming if you dodge the jet-skis.

Ngunguru Holiday Park Papaka Rd ℡09/434 3851, Ⓔwater.edge@xtra.co.nz. Camping ($12.50) and cabins (❷) available at this pleasant waterside site, as well as chalets for backpackers (❷).
Malibu Mals Tutukaka Block Rd, Kowharewa Bay ℡09/434 3450 Ⓦwww.malibumals.co.nz. Diving groups are welcome at the two spacious and fully self-contained units (one sleeping 4, the other 6) in a secluded garden 5mins drive from Tutukaka marina. ❹ plus $15 each extra person.

Pacific Rendezvous Motel Rd, off the Tutukaka Block Rd ℡0800/999 800 & 09/434 3847, Ⓦwww.oceanresort.co.nz. Fabulously sited on the peninsula that forms the southern arm of Tutukaka's harbour, offering tranquil self-contained suites and apartments, as well as chalets with decks overlooking the ocean. ❺ plus $20 each extra person.
Poor Knights Lodge Tutukaka Block Rd, 2km from Tutukaka ℡09/434 4405,

ⓦ www.poorknightslodge.co.nz. Two luxurious self-contained suites in a spectacular setting; dinner is also available on request. ❽
Sands Motel Tutukaka Block Rd, 4km off the highway ☎ 09/434 3747, ⓦ www.nzmotels.co.nz/sands. Right beside the sands of Whangaumu Bay, this motel offers one and two-bedroom units. ❹ plus $15 each extra person.

Tutukaka Holiday Park Matapouri Rd, just around the corner from the harbour ☎ 09/434 3938, ⓦ www.tutukaka-holidaypark.co.nz. In a pretty valley 2mins walk from the harbour, this convenient site offers camping ($12), backpacker cabins sleeping twelve (❶) and a variety of cabins and flats sleeping up to 6 people (❸).

Beaches north of Tutukaka

Settlements north of Tutukaka are mostly nothing more than a few beachside holiday homes. Day-trippers flock from Whangarei for safe swimming in gorgeous bays tucked between headlands and dotted with numerous islets. Favourites include the village of **MATAPOURI**, 6km from Tutukaka, which backs a curving white-sand bay bounded by bushy headlands, and the pristine **Whale Bay**, 1km further north and reached by a twenty-minute bush walk. The only facilities along this stretch are *Dreamstay* (☎ 09/434 3059, ⓔ dreamstay@abel.net.nz; ❺), a stunningly located and immaculate B&B high above the gorgeous surf beach of **Sandy Bay**, and a shop and takeaway at Matapouri.

Heading inland from here the road is sealed all the way to **Hikurangi**, where it joins SH1. The coastal section between here and the Bay of Islands is most easily reached from Russell (see p.190).

The Bay of Islands

THE BAY OF ISLANDS, 240km north of Auckland, is one of the brightest stars in New Zealand's tourism firmament, luring thousands to its beautiful coastal scenery, scattered islands and clear blue waters. And although it's really no more stunning than several other spots along the Northland coast, such as Whangaroa and Hokianga harbours, what sets it apart is the ease with which you can get out among the islands, and the bay's rich history. This was the cradle of European settlement in New Zealand, a fact abundantly testified to by the bay's churches, mission stations and orchards. It's also a focal point for Maori because of the **Treaty of Waitangi** (see box on p.187) – still, despite its limitations, New Zealand's most important legal document.

Perhaps surprisingly, much of your time in the Bay of Islands will be spent on the mainland. There are no settlements on the islands, and there's only one on which you are allowed to stay overnight. Most visitors base themselves in beachside **Paihia**, which is well set up to deal with the hordes who come here eager to launch themselves on the various cruises and other excursions, as well as being the closest town to the Treaty House at **Waitangi**. The compact town of **Russell**, a couple of kilometres across the bay by passenger ferry, is prettier and more restrained, though almost equally convenient for cruises. To the northwest, away from the bay itself, **Kerikeri** is intimately entwined with the area's early missionary history, while **Waimate North**, inland to the west, was another important mission site and still has its Mission House, though the regional focus has now moved further south to **Kaikohe**.

As the main tourist centre in Northland, the Bay of Islands acts as a staging post for forays further north, in particular for day-long **bus tours** to Cape Reinga and Ninety Mile Beach (see box on p.212) – arduous affairs lasting eleven hours, most of them spent stuck inside the vehicle. You're better off making your way up to Mangonui, Kaitaia or Ahipara and taking a trip from

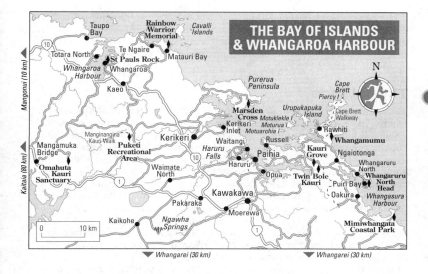

there, though if time is short you can take your pick from a wide range of Paihia-based excursions, including scenic flights over Northland.

Some history

A warm climate, abundant seafood and deep, sheltered harbours all contributed to dense pre-European **Maori settlement** in the Bay of Islands, with many a headland supporting a *pa*. The sheltered bay also appealed to **Captain Cook**, who anchored here in 1769 and prosaically noted in his journal, "I have named it the Bay of Islands on account of the great number which line its shores, and these help to form several safe and commodious harbours". Cook landed on Motuarohia Island at what became known as Cook's Cove, where he forged generally good relations with the inhabitants. Three years later the French sailor **Marion du Fresne**, en route from Mauritius to Tahiti, became the first European to have sustained contact with Maori, though he fared less well when a misunderstanding, probably over *tapu*, led to his death, along with 26 of his crew. The French retaliated, destroying a *pa* and killing hundreds of Maori.

Despite amicable relations between the local Ngapuhi Maori and Pakeha whalers in the early years of the nineteenth century, the situation gradually deteriorated to a point where historian Robert Hughes described the mid-nineteenth-century Bay of Islands as "a veritable rookery of absconders ... littered with grim little communities and patriarchal clans of convicts". With increased contact, firearms, grog and Old World diseases spread and the fabric of Maori life began to break down, a process accelerated by the arrival in 1814 of Samuel Marsden, the first of many **missionaries** intent on turning Maori into Christians. In 1833, James Busby was sent as the "British resident" to secure British interests and prevent the brutal treatment meted out to the Maori by whaling captains, but lacking armed back-up or judicial authority, he had little effect. The signing of the **Treaty of Waitangi** in 1840 brought effective policing yet heralded a decline in the importance of the Bay of Islands, as the capital moved from its original site of Kororareka (now Russell), first to Auckland and later to Wellington.

The Bay of Islands regained some degree of world recognition in 1927, when American writer **Zane Grey** came here to fish for striped and black marlin, making the area famous with his book *The Angler's El Dorado*. Every summer since, the bay has seen game-fishing tournaments and glistening catches strung up on the jetties.

The islands

The only island that accommodates overnight guests is **Urupukapuka Island**, where Zane Grey, author of best-selling westerns and avid hooker of marlin, set up a fishing resort at Otehei Bay. The resort largely burned down in 1973, but you can still stay in the **accommodation** units, which now operate as the *Zane Grey Lodge* (T 09/403 7009, W www.zanegrey.co.nz; dorm $20, rooms with spartan bunkrooms, and double rooms sharing a full kitchen plus the self-contained 4-berth *Zane Grey Cottage* in the grounds (❹). Adjacent to the lodge, the *Zane Grey* **restaurant** is a stopping point for Fullers cruises (see p.181), which provide regular access to the island. There are also basic DOC **campsites** ($6, booked through DOC at Russell, T 09/403 9005) in all except the western bays of the island and there are several Maori *pa* and terrace sites, which can be explored in a few hours by following signs on the island and the free *Urupukapuka Island Archeological Walk* leaflet.

Of the bay's other six large islands, by far the most popular is **Motuarohia**, more commonly known as **Roberton Island** after John Roberton, who moved here in 1839. The Department of Conservation manages the most dramatic central section, an isthmus almost severed by a pair of perfectly circular blue lagoons. Understandably, it's immensely popular with both private boaties and commercial cruises, and DOC have gone to the trouble of installing an undersea nature trail for snorkellers, waymarked by inscribed stainless-steel plaques. The wildlife sanctuary of **Moturua** lies adjacent, offering a network of walks through bush alive with spotted kiwi, saddlebacks and North Island robins.

Other sights that often feature on cruise itineraries include **the Black Rocks**, bare islets formed from columnar jointed basalt – these rise only 10m out of the water but plummet a sheer 30m beneath, allowing boats to inspect them at close quarters. At the outer limit of the bay is the craggy peninsula of **Cape Brett**, named by Cook in 1769 after the then Lord of the Admiralty, Lord Piercy Brett. Cruises also regularly pass through the **Hole in The Rock**, a natural tunnel through Piercy Island, an activity made more exciting when there's a swell running.

Exploring the bay

Unless you get out onto the water you're missing the essence of the Bay of Islands. Wherever you turn you'll find people keen to take you yachting, scuba-diving, dolphin-watching, kayaking or fishing. The vast majority of trips start in Paihia, but all the major **cruises** and bay **excursions** also pick up from Russell wharf around fifteen minutes later. Occasionally there are no pick-ups available, but the passenger **ferry** between Paihia and Russell only costs $5 each way. Prices can be quite high, especially during the summer months when demand outstrips supply and everything should be booked at least a couple of days in advance. Most hotels and motels book these trips for you and hostels can usually arrange some sort of "backpacker" discount of around ten percent, though better deals can sometimes be obtained by booking direct.

Almost all bookings can be made in or around the Maritime Building on Marsden Road with the main **tour operators**, King's, Fullers (plus their offshoot, Awesome Adventures) and Dolphin Discoveries.

Cruises

There are numerous different trips around the bay; all those mentioned below include a visit to the Hole in the Rock, by Cape Brett. Expect the boats to be full in peak season, and book in good time.

Fullers ☎ 0800/653 339 & 09/402 7421, ⓦ www.fullers-bay-of-islands.co.nz; adventure-oriented offshoot **Awesome Adventures** ☎ 09/402 6985, ⓦ www.awesomenz.com. Longstanding operator of large and stable craft. The leisurely Cream Trip is part of the Supercruise (Sept–May daily; June–Aug Mon, Wed, Thurs & Sat; 6hr 15min; $85) and delivers groceries and mail to wharves all around the bay. It includes a visit to the Hole in the Rock, ninety minutes at Otehei Bay, and cream tea. Their Hole in the Rock cruise (1–2 daily; 4hr; $65) speeds through the islands to Cape Brett and, when conditions permit, edges through the hole itself. By splitting your journey between the two daily summer trips, you can spend a few hours on Urupukapuka Island. To maximize your time on the island opt for an extended island stopover (Oct–Feb daily, for an extra $10), which gives up to five hours ashore.

King's ☎ 0800/222 979 & 09/402 8288, ⓦ www.dolphincruises.co.nz. Family-run firm, giving 10 percent discounts to AA members, backpacker cardholders and families. Their Hole in the Rock Scenic Cruise (2 daily; 3hr; $60) makes no island stops but includes dolphin and whale watching – and onboard Maori legend commentary. The Day in the Bay trip (Oct–May daily; 6hr; $85) is an approximation of Fullers Cream Trip, taking in the Hole in the Rock and giving an island stop of the captain's choice plus the chance to swim with dolphins.

Dolphin Discoveries ☎ 09/402 8234, ⓔ dolphin@igrin.co.nz. Relative newcomers who run similar trips in smaller boats. Their Discover the Bay trip on a fast cat (2 daily; 3hr 30min, $69 including a guaranteed dolphin sighting or you can go again for free) takes you to the Hole in the Rock and other sights on a flexible route, allowing for wildlife spotting throughout the year.

Fast boats

Mack Attack ☎ 0800/622528 & 09/402 8180, ⓦ www.mackattack.co.nz (Sept–July; 5 daily in summer, 2–3 daily in winter; 1hr 30min; $65). Open catamaran driven by 1320hp engines gives an adrenalin-pumping blast out to the Hole in the Rock and back; it's also the only boat that can take you right into Cathedral Cave.

The Excitor ☎ 09/402 7020, ⓦ www.excitor.co.nz (6 daily in summer, 2 daily in winter; 1hr 30min; $68). Another catamaran, that basically does the same thing. Seating 50, those at the front are kitted out with "horseback" seats for an even more extreme ride.

Sailing

Two companies run big sailing ships – a great way to experience the romance of the sea; for smaller yachts, see Snorkelling on p.182.

R. Tucker Thompson ☎ 0800/882537. A beautiful Northland-built schooner in the "tall ship" tradition, sails out on day-trips into the islands and anchors for a swim and barbecue lunch, taking up to 20 at a time. Late Oct to April daily; 6hr; $99 including morning tea with freshly baked scones and cream.

Ecocruz ☎ 0800/432 6278 & 025 592153, ⓦ www.ecocruz.co.nz. A three-day sail on

the twenty-two-metre twin-masted *Manawanui*, which takes up to twelve people around the Bay with the emphasis on exploration and appreciation of the natural environment. Excellent meals are included, along with on-board dorm-style and double-cabin accommodation, use of kayaks, snorkel gear, fishing tackle and a good deal of local knowledge and enthusiasm. $450.

Kayaking

Lack of previous experience is no impediment to kayaking in and around Paihia, with plenty of operators offering guided trips. If you want to go it alone, there are also various rental outfits to choose from.

Coastal Kayakers Waitangi Bridge ☎09/402 8105, ⊛www.coastalkayakers.co.nz. Open all year, running a variety of trips: half-day trips upstream to Haruru Falls ($50) and full-day trips ($70), which includes paddling around Motumaire Island; two- to three-day guided excursions operate from November to June, with camping options ($125–460 including all gear except sleeping bag). They also rent out kayaks for two or more people at a time ($10 per hour, $40 a day), and two-

person catamarans (Dec–March; $30 per hour). **Island Kayaks** Pipi Patch Lodge, 18 Kings Rd ☎0800/611 440, ⊛www.islandkayaking.co.nz. Operate all year, offering half-day ($59), full-day ($90) and twilight trips ($59) exploring the inner islands and bays.
Bay Beach Hire South end of Paihia Beach ☎09/402 7905. Rents double and single open and sea kayaks ($10 per hour, $40 a day), windsurfers ($25 per hour) and catamarans ($45 per hour).

Dolphin watching and swimming

Relatively warm water all year round and an abundance of marine mammals make the Bay of Islands one of the best places to go **dolphin watching**. You're likely to see bottlenose and common dolphins in pretty much any season, orca from May to August and Minke and Bryde's **whales** from August to January. If you don't see anything, most companies will take you out for a second chance, though lack of a swim doesn't usually earn a repeat cruise.

Though cruise boats and yachts will detour for a positive cetacean sighting, the best way to see dolphins and whales is on a cruise with one of the four companies licensed to actively search for and swim with dolphins. There's no swimming when dolphins are feeding or if they have juveniles with them (which can be any time of year), and only a dozen people are allowed in the water at a time. Since most trips carry around 40 people in the peak season, you can expect to be in the water about a third of the time that the dolphins are about.

Dolphin Discoveries Marsden Rd, opposite the visitor centre ☎09/402 8234, ⊛www.dolphinz.co.nz. The pioneers of dolphin swimming in this area and sensitive to the needs of the dolphins; 4hr, $99.
Dolphin Adventures ☎0800/653 339 & 09/402 7421, ⊛www.fullers-bay-of-islands.co.nz. Run by Fullers, this trip includes the option of a stopover on Urupukapuka Island for a few hours if you take the early boat at 8am; 4hr, $95.

King's ☎0800/222 979 & 09/402 8288, ⊛www.dolphincruises.co.nz. Dolphin watching is a feature of all their trips or you can swim with dolphins as part of their Day in the Bay cruise (see p.181).
Carino (see Snorkelling, below). A big catamaran that takes you on a day-trip around the islands, with a chance to swim with the dolphins if found in the right conditions.

Scuba-diving

Two main scuba-diving companies operate in the Bay, but their best trips are generally to the wreck of the **Rainbow Warrior** further north (see p.201).

Paihia Dive Williams Rd ☎09/402 7551, ℮divepaihia@xtra.co.nz. The main scuba-diving outfit will take you out in the Bay of Islands (from $185 with all gear) or on the wreck of the *Rainbow Warrior* ($185).

Dive North ☎09/402 7079, ⊛www .bay-of-islands.co.nz/diving/divenorth.html. A smaller company charging similar prices for comparable trips but most often to the *Rainbow Warrior*.

Snorkelling

A trip on a smaller yacht is the best way to get **snorkelling** and they usually take less than a dozen passengers: competition is tight and the standards high, with all bringing snorkelling and fishing gear and typically going out for six hours and including lunch. The pick of the boats are listed below.

Carino ☎ 09/402 8040, ⓦ www.sailinganddolphin.co.nz. A large red catamaran based in Paihia and skippered by a woman licensed to allow swimming with dolphins; $69, plus $5 for BBQ lunch.
Straycat ☎ 09/402 6130, ⓦ www.straycat.co.nz. A twelve-metre catamaran on which you can participate in the sailing. The focus is on swimming with fish and hand-feeding them, plus island walks; $79 including lunch.

Gungha II ☎ 0800/478 900, ⓦ www.bayofislandssailing.co.nz. A twenty-metre yacht on which you can also benefit from optional sailing tuition ($75 including lunch).
Tsunami ☎ 09/358 0259, ⓦ fullers-bay-of-islands.co.nz An exciting, high-speed 26-metre catamaran run by Fullers ($110 including BBQ lunch).

Fishing

There is a wider range and greater choice of **fishing trips** than any other activity: everything from a little line fishing for snapper to big game boats in search of marlin, shark, tuna and kingfish. Ask around and speak to the skippers to make sure you get a trip that suits; daily charter rates range around $60–80 for light tackle and $250 upwards for the big game boats.

Flights and parasailing

In addition to the water-based activities, you can see the bay in style from the air either parasailing or on scenic flights.

Salt Air Marsden Rd, near the Maritime Building, Paihai ☎ 0800/472 582 & 09/402 8338, ⓦ www.saltair.co.nz. See the bay in style from a small plane ($95 for 30min, $175 1hr (Hole in the Rock trip), or on a 20min helicopter flight (from $170, min 4 people).

Flying Kiwi Parasail based at Bay Beach Hire on Paihia waterfront ☎ 09/402 6078. Ten-minute tandem or solo flights from the back of a speedboat to around 200m ($60) or 300m ($75).

Horse riding and quad biking

On dry land there are a couple of activities to keep you entertained, that make reasonable wet-weather options too.

Big Rock Springs Trail Rides Near Okaihau, 35 km west of Paihia ☎ 09/401 9923 & 021/167 4878, ⓔ jennyking@xtra.co.nz. Full ($80) or half-day trips ($55) on scenic rides through bush in the hills inland near Okaihau, swimming the horses in the river and viewing glowworm caves; they pick up from Paihia.

Bush 'n' Bike Tirohanga Rd, near Kawakawa ☎ 09/404 1142, ⓦ www.bushnbike.co.nz. Professionally run horse rides in small groups (1hr 30min $45 or 2hr 30min, $70) and quadbiking tours (1hr 30min, $65) on powerful automatic 500cc bikes (90cc for kids) that climb rugged hill tracks to breathtaking views.

Paihia and Waitangi

PAIHIA is where it all happens. In its way, it is just as historically important as Russell, Waitangi and Kerikeri, but this two-kilometre-long string of waterside motels, restaurants and holiday homes has been overrun by the demands of tourism. Its location on three flat bays looking towards Russell and the Bay of Islands is pleasing enough and the encircling forested hills make an attractive backdrop, but the town itself could hardly be called pretty. Nevertheless, abundant well-priced accommodation, several good restaurants, a few boisterous bars and endless possibilities to get out on the water make this the goal of most visitors to the Bay of Islands.

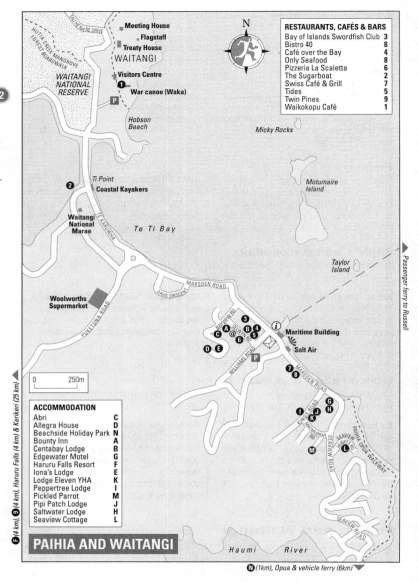

RESTAURANTS, CAFÉS & BARS

Bay of Islands Swordfish Club	3
Bistro 40	8
Café over the Bay	4
Only Seafood	8
Pizzeria La Scaletta	6
The Sugarboat	2
Swiss Café & Grill	7
Tides	5
Twin Pines	9
Waikokopu Café	1

ACCOMMODATION

Abri	C
Allegra House	D
Beachside Holiday Park	N
Bounty Inn	A
Centabay Lodge	B
Edgewater Motel	G
Haruru Falls Resort	F
Iona's Lodge	E
Lodge Eleven YHA	K
Peppertree Lodge	I
Pickled Parrot	M
Pipi Patch Lodge	J
Saltwater Lodge	H
Seaview Cottage	L

PAIHIA AND WAITANGI

Legend has it that the town was named in 1823 by the less than accomplished Maori scholar, the Reverend Henry Williams, when he was looking for a site to establish the Church Missionary Society's third mission. He apparently exclaimed, "*pai* [good] here!" – unlikely, but it makes a nice story. At the time, Maori were overwhelmed by the influx of Europeans and looked to the missionaries to intercede on their behalf. A plaque outside the current St Paul's

Anglican Church on Marsden Road marks the spot where, in 1831, the northern chiefs petitioned the British Crown for a representative to establish law and order. In 1833 King William IV belatedly addressed their concerns by sending the first British resident, James Busby. He built a house on a promontory 2km north across the Waitangi River in **WAITANGI** – the scene some seven years later of the signing of the **Treaty of Waitangi**, which ceded the nation's sovereignty to Britain in return for protection, even though Busby was ill-equipped to provide it.

Arrival, information and transport

MVS Limos (☎09/438 9912) run daily **buses** between Whangarei and Paihia (Oct–April; $22 one way), dropping off at accommodation. Northliner and InterCity buses arrive on the waterfront Marsden Road outside the Bay of Islands' main **visitor centre** (daily 8am–5pm, extended hours Oct–April; ☎09/402 7345, ⓔ visitorinfo@fndc.govt.nz). The adjacent **Maritime Building** contains booking desks for most of the major tour operators and often stays open until around 9pm in summer, and closes a little earlier in winter, according to business. Trips with smaller operators can be reserved through booking offices across the road on the corner of Marsden and Williams roads. The Bay of Islands **airport** is twenty-two kilometres away, near Kerikeri, receiving planes from Auckland, which are met by a shuttle bus (around $15). The passenger **ferry** from Russell ($5) lands at the wharf near the visitor centre, while the vehicle ferry ($8) lands 6 kilometres southeast at Opua.

Paihia isn't big, and everywhere is within walking distance. If you've got bags to carry, engage the services of the **Paihia Tuk Tuk Shuttle Service**, based outside the visitor centre (☎0274/866 071), who will pick up and drop off one to six people pretty much anywhere in town for $3 each and run up to Haruru Falls for $6 each. Alternatively, you can rent good-quality **mountain bikes** from Bay Beach Hire, at the south end of Paihia Beach (☎09/402 6078; $15 a half-day, $20 per day; Oct–April). **Parking** is difficult in high season; the best bet is the lot opposite the Four Square supermarket on Williams Road.

There's **Internet access** at the visitor centre; in the Maritime Building; and at Boots Off Travellers Centre on Selwyn Rd (☎09/402 6632).

Accommodation

Paihia abounds in good **accommodation** to suit all budgets although that's not to say it's cheap; for the couple of weeks after Christmas motel prices can be stratospheric. B&Bs and homestays tend to vary their prices less, and hostels maintain the same prices year round. Motels and B&Bs are scattered all over but there is a central cluster in the streets opposite the wharf; and Kings Road is a veritable backpackers' ghetto.

Hotels, motels and B&Bs

Abri 10 Bayview Rd ☎09/402 8003, ⓦwww .abri-accom.co.nz. Two high-standard separate modern studio apartments each sleeping two, in a pretty bush setting with great views over the town and bay from the sundecks. ❽

Allegra House 39 Bayview Rd ☎09/402 7932, ⓦwww.allegra.co.nz. A choice of luxury B&B or private apartment for two (both are air conditioned and have their own balconies) in a big, light and modern house at the top of a hill, with wide bay views; hot spa in native bush. ❼

Bounty Inn cnr Bayview Rd & Selwyn Rd ☎0800/ 117 897 & 09/402 7088, ⓦwww.bountyinn.co.nz. Pleasant, central yet quiet motel amid lush gardens, 100m from the beach. Each well-equipped unit is lined in timber and has a sundeck or balcony; other bonuses include a private spa, on-site restaurant and ample off-street parking. ❺

Edgewater Motel 10 Marsden Rd ☎09/402 7875, ⓔ edgewater_motel@xtra.co.nz. Small yet fully equipped quality motel right across from the beach with video, a spa pool, and a fenced playground for kids. ❻

Iona's Lodge 29 Bayview Rd ☏ & ⓕ 09/402 8072, ⓦ www.ionaslodge.com. Two central, self-contained units with a wonderful panoramic view of the bay, and reasonable rates that include a breakfast tray. ❺

Seaview Cottage 5 Sullivan's Rd ☏ 09/402 8516, ⓦ www.castlespas.co.nz. Charming two-bedroom cottage in a quiet bush setting with bay views and five minutes' walk to the beach. The double bedroom has a four-poster bed and there are TV/VCR, spa and BBQ. Book as far ahead as possible in summer. ❻

Hostels

Centabay Lodge 27 Selwyn Rd ☏ 09/402 7466, ⓦ www.centabay.co.nz. Central hostel near the beach and shops, with decent three- to six-bunk dorms, twins and doubles (some en-suite) and motel-style self-catering studios; free use of kayaks and bikes. Dorms ❶, rooms ❷, ensuite rooms ❸, studios ❹

Lodge Eleven YHA cnr Kings Rd & MacMurray Rd ☏ 09/402 7487, ⓔ lodgeeleven@hotmail.com. Good-value central hostel with four-share en-suite dorms and airy motel-style doubles and twins, all serviced daily. There are free bikes, a barbecue area and tennis courts next door. Dorms ❶, rooms ❸

Peppertree Lodge 15 Kings Rd ☏ 09/402 6122, ⓦ www.peppertree.co.nz. Deluxe, quiet and central hostel with spacious eight-bunk dorms, four-bunk dorms with own bathroom, great en-suite doubles and a self-contained flat. The TV room, lounge and kitchen are all in good condition and you can make use of a tennis court, free good-quality bikes, and kayaks. Be sure to book ahead October–May. Dorms ❶, rooms ❸, flat ❹

Pickled Parrot Grey's Lane, off MacMurray Rd ☏ 0508 727 768 & 09/402 6222, ⓔ theparrot@paradise.net.nz. One of Paihia's smaller hostels, tucked away in a central and peaceful spot with a courtyard. Secluded tent sites; 4- and 6-bed dorms as well as singles, doubles and twins, all with free breakfast thrown in, plus free pick-ups, bikes and tennis racquets. Tents $16, dorms ❶, single rooms $56, double & twin rooms ❸

Pipi Patch Lodge 18 Kings Rd ☏ 09/402 7111, ⓦ www.acb.co.nz/pipi.html. Central converted motel now operating as a well-kept hostel that's popular with Kiwi Experience, making it a party place. Accommodation is in en-suite dorms (sleeping up to eight) and fully self-contained twins or doubles (some with shared bathroom). Other benefits are Sky TV, a spa, plunge pool and bar. Dorms ❶, rooms ❸

Saltwater Lodge 14 Kings Rd ☏ 0800/002 266 & 09/402 7075, ⓦ www.saltwaterlodge.co.nz. Clean and efficiently laid out hostel, if a little lacking in character, with en-suite six- and four-share dorms, each equipped with a locker, and attractive en-suite motel-style rooms on the upper floor with great sea views. Facilities include a large lounge with video library, a barbecue area, small gym, tennis and kayaks. Dorms ❶, rooms ❺

Campsites

Beachside Holiday Park SH11, 2.5km south of Paihia ☏ 09/402 7678, ⓔ smithshc@xtra.co.nz. Small and peaceful waterside site with a range of cabins and units, as well as dinghies and kayaks for rent. Tent sites $13, cabins ❷ and units ❸

Haruru Falls Resort Panorama Puketona Rd ☏ 0800/757 525 & 09/402 7525, ⓦ www.haruru-falls.co.nz. Fabulous location by the river with commanding views of Haruru Falls, 4km north of Paihia, offering riverside tent sites and motel units around a pool. The resort has outdoor games such as pétanque and volleyball, a BBQ, and its own restaurant bar, plus kayaks and pedalboats for rent; plus a courtesy shuttle to Paihia. Tents $12.50–$14, motel units ❹

The Town

Paihia is primarily a base for exploring the bay, and there are no sights in town itself. If you'd like to study some fine bone and *pounamu* (NZ jade) carvings check out the Cabbage Tree counter in the Maritime Building (daily; summer 8am–8pm, winter 9am–6pm) or their shop on nearby Williams Street (daily; summer 9am–7pm, winter 9am–6pm). Around a kilometre north of the town centre, the Waitangi River separates Paihia from Waitangi and provides a mooring for the *Tui*, a three-masted barque, built as a sugar lighter in 1917, now home to *The Sugarboat* restaurant and bar (see p.190).

Waitangi Treaty Grounds

Crossing the bridge over the Waitangi River you enter the **Waitangi Treaty Grounds**, the single most symbolic place in New Zealand for Maori and Pakeha alike, and a focal point for the modern nation's struggle for identity. You can

The Treaty of Waitangi

The Treaty of Waitangi is the **founding document** of modern New Zealand, a touchstone for both Pakeha and Maori, and its implications permeate New Zealand society. Signed in 1840 between what were ostensibly two sovereign states – the United Kingdom and the United Tribes of New Zealand, plus other Maori leaders – the treaty remains central to New Zealand's **race relations**. The Maori rights guaranteed by it have seldom been upheld, however, and the constant struggle for recognition continues.

The treaty at Waitangi

Motivated by a desire to staunch French expansion in the Pacific, and a moral obligation on the Crown to protect Maori from rapacious land-grabbing by settlers, the British instructed naval captain William Hobson to negotiate the transfer of sovereignty with "the free and intelligent consent of the natives", and to deal fairly with the Maori. Within a few days of his arrival, Hobson, with the help of James Busby and others, drew up both the English Treaty and a Maori "translation". On the face of it, the treaty is a straightforward document, but the complications of having two versions (see Contexts, p.942) and the implications of striking a deal between two peoples with widely differing views on land and resource ownership and usage have reverberated down the years.

The treaty was unveiled in grand style on February 5, 1840, to a gathering of some 400 representatives of the five northern tribes in front of Busby's residence in Waitangi. Presented as a contract between the chiefs and Queen Victoria – someone whose role was comprehensible in chiefly terms – the benefits were amplified and the costs downplayed. As most chiefs didn't understand English, they signed the Maori version of the treaty, which still has *mana* (prestige) among Maori today.

The treaty after Waitangi

The pattern set at Waitangi was repeated up and down the country, as seven copies of the treaty were dispatched to garner signatures and extend Crown authority over parts of the North Island that had not yet been covered, and the South Island. On May 21, before signed treaty copies had been returned, Hobson claimed New Zealand for Britain: the North Island on the grounds of cession by Maori, and the South Island by right of Cook's "discovery", as it was considered to be *in terrorium nullis* ("without owners"), despite a significant Maori population.

Maori fears were alerted from the start, and as the settler population grew and demand for land increased, successive governments passed laws that gradually stripped Maori of control over their affairs – actions which led to the New Zealand Wars of the 1860s (see Contexts, p.944). Over the decades, small concessions were made, but nothing significant changed until 1973, when **Waitangi Day** (February 6) became an official national holiday. From 1971, Maori groups, supported by a small but articulate band of Pakeha, began a campaign of direct action, increasingly disrupting commemorations, thereby alienating many Pakeha and splitting Maori allegiances between angry young urban Maori and the *kaumatua* (elders), who saw the actions as disrespectful to the ancestors and an affront to tradition. Many strands of Maori society were unified by the *hikoi* (march) to Waitangi to protest against the celebrations in 1985, a watershed year in which Paul Reeves was appointed New Zealand's first Maori Governor General and the **Waitangi Tribunal** (see Contexts, p.956) was given some teeth.

Protests have continued since – including several infamous flag-trampling, egg-pelting and spitting incidents – as successive governments have vacillated over maintaining the commemorations at Waitangi or trying to defuse the situation by promoting a parallel event at the Governor General's residence in Wellington.

spend half a day here, taking in a thirty-minute cultural performance or a guided tour (see below), though most people give it around one and a half hours to take in the main sights. It was here in 1840 that Queen Victoria's representative William Hobson and nearly fifty Maori chiefs signed the Treaty of Waitangi (see box p.187), ceding Aotearoa's sovereignty to Britain, while ostensibly affording the Maori protection and guaranteeing them rights over land and resources. When the area was gifted to the people of New Zealand in 1932 by Governor-General Lord Bledisloe, the Treaty House was being used as a sheep shelter and the grounds were neglected, but a sudden desire to commemorate the 1940 centennial of the signing in fitting fashion provoked a flurry of restoration.

Paying to visit the **Waitangi Visitor Centre and Treaty House** (daily: Oct–March 9am–6pm; April–Sept 9am–5pm; $10), also gives you access to the grounds; in the visitor centre a twenty-minute audio-visual presentation sets the historical framework, bolstered by a small exhibition of Maori artefacts. Take your pick from a number of daily tours including Embrace Waitangi (1hr, Oct–Mar only; daily 10.30am, 12.30pm & 2.30pm; $20), filling you in on culture and history; and a well-presented cultural performance (30min; daily Oct–April, 11.30am, 1.30pm & 2.30pm; $10), based on song, dance, *poi* and *haka*. Highly recommended is the evening Sound and Light show (1hr 15min, Oct–March Mon, Wed, Thurs & Sat at 8pm; $45; book ahead on ☎09/402 5990, ⓦ www.culturenorth.co.nz) inside the meeting house – an engaging historical account of Maori life from the arrival of Kupe to the present-day, enacted with verve and mixing drama, song and dance with storytelling; pick-ups available from Paihia.

△ Wai kokopu café

The **Treaty House** was built in Georgian colonial style in 1833–34. Once described as "only a couple of rooms separated by a lobby", it's an unprepossessing structure, largely because James Busby's superiors in Sydney failed to supply the requisite materials. The original part is furnished as it would have been in Busby's time, while the wings added in the 1880s contain displays on Busby, Waitangi life and the treaty itself. The front windows look towards Russell over sweeping lawns, where marquees were erected on three significant occasions: in 1834, when Maori chiefs chose the Confederation of Tribes flag, which now flies on one yard arm of the central flagpole; the meeting a year later at which northern Maori leaders signed the Declaration of Independence of New Zealand; and, in 1840, the signing of the Treaty of Waitangi itself.

The northern side of the lawn is flanked by the *whare runanga*, or **Maori meeting house**, built between 1934 and 1940. Though proposed by Bledisloe and northern Maori chiefs, the construction of the house was a co-operative effort between all Maori. A short audio-visual presentation explains key elements on the richly carved panels. Housed in a specially built shelter in the Treaty House grounds is the world's largest **war canoe** (*waka*), the *Ngatoki Matawhaorua*, named after the vessel navigated by Kupe when he discovered Aotearoa. It's an impressive boat, built over two years from two huge kauri by members of the five northern tribes and measuring over 35m in length. It has traditionally been launched each year on Waitangi Day, propelled by eighty warriors. Near the visitor centre is the excellent *Waikokopu Café* in a relaxing setting (see p.190).

Westwards, the Waitangi Treaty Grounds extend beyond the Waitangi Golf Course to the scenic viewpoint atop **Mount Bledisloe**, reached by car 3km away. Two kilometres beyond that and accessed from the main road, are the **Haruru ("Big Noise") Falls**, formed where the Waitangi River drops over a basalt lava flow – though not that impressive by New Zealand standards, there's good swimming at their base. Haruru Falls are also reached from the Treaty House grounds via the very gentle **Hutia Creek Mangrove Forest Boardwalk** (2hr return) or on a guided **kayak** trip up the estuary and among the mangroves with Coastal Kayakers (see p.182).

Eating, drinking and entertainment

Paihia's range of **places to eat** is unmatched anywhere in the Bay of Islands and competition keeps prices tolerable. The restaurants are also good places to stick around for post-prandial drinking, and there are several more raucous **bars** along Kings Road: we list the best below. Across the water, near Russell, is the Omata Estate vineyard with its delightful café, restaurant and bar (see p.194).

If you fancy eating on the water, **Bay of Islands Mini Cruises** (2hr 30min, $65; ℡09/402 7848) depart from Paihia wharf and cruise along the Waitangi River to the Haruru Falls, where you tuck into pan-fried fish, T-bone steak or a veggie dish; but bring your own drinks. For **evening entertainment** with a contemporary approach to presenting Maori culture head for the **Sound and Light Show** at the Waitangi meeting house (see opposite). Paihia also hosts two **festivals – jazz and blues**, usually held during the second weekend in August (Ⓦ www.jazz-blues.co.nz), and **country rock** during the second weekend in May (Ⓦ www.country-rock.co.nz).

Bay of Islands Swordfish Club Marsden Rd. Private club, overlooking the bay and welcoming visitors outside the peak summer season for some of the cheapest drinks in town. Temporary membership (available at any time of year) costs $2.50. Simple but good-value food is served from 6pm. **Bistro 40** 40 Marsden Rd ℡09/402 7444. Sister restaurant to *Only Seafood* (see overleaf), located in the same atmospheric villa and open nightly for dinner. Sumptuous meals from an eclectic menu known for its high-quality beef and lamb dishes ($25–30), as well as seafood dishes.

Café Over the Bay Upstairs in the Paihia Mall, Marsden Rd. A good place for a daytime coffee on the veranda but also worth a visit for all-day breakfasts and reasonably priced lunches and dinners with an international slant. Licensed.

Only Seafood 40 Marsden Rd. As the name implies, it's seafood only at one of Paihia's finest restaurants, in a pretty villa with mains at $20–29, many of which can be enjoyed as cheaper entrées.

Pizzeria La Scaletta Selwyn Rd ☏ 09/402 7039. Gourmet pizza bar with beer on tap and outside dining, open for lunch and then for dinner, with nightly entertainment. Takeaway also available.

The Sugarboat On the *Tui*, beside the Waitangi Bridge ☏ 09/402 7018. The main draw is the cocktail bar on the deck of an atmospheric 1917 sugar lighter. The bar opens daily in summer at 5pm, with a chill-out hour from 5pm Tues–Fri offering discounted beer and wine. Down below is a dinner restaurant serving Mediterranean-style cuisine. Closed Mon & Tues in winter.

Swiss Café 48 Marsden Rd ☏ 09/402 6701. Intimate good-value dinner restaurant focusing on seafood and Swiss dishes accompanied by reasonably priced wines. Finish with Schumli Pflumli (a Swiss mountain coffee with Schnapps). Book ahead if you can Nov–end of March. Closed Mon in winter.

Tides Williams Rd ☏ 09/402 7557. Highly regarded, innovative and well-priced breakfasts, lunches and dinners, with the emphasis on fresh seafood and top-quality lamb.

Twin Pines Puketona Rd, Haruru Falls, 4km north of Paihia ☏ 09/402 7195. Fine old villa refitted as a restaurant and bar, open for dinner and for Sunday roast ($18 a head). It's cheaper than anywhere in town, the most expensive dish being steak at $22. There's also an attractive garden bar and a courtesy bus from Paihia during the peak summer season. Closed Tues in winter.

Waikokopu Café Treaty House Grounds, Waitangi ☏ 09/402 6275. Outstanding licensed café surrounded by lawns and a fish pond. Perfect for tucking into unusual and beautifully prepared breakfasts and lunches ($12–15), plus an excellent range of cakes and great coffee. They're also open for dinner in summer (Dec generally Sat only, Jan nightly; mains $20–25).

Around Paihia: Opua and Kawakawa

Drivers travelling between Paihia and Russell need to cross the narrow Veronica Channel at **OPUA**, 6km south of Paihia, where the small vehicle **ferry** leaves every ten to twenty minutes (daily 7am–10pm; car & driver $8 each way, pedestrians $1). Fans of mangroves and estuarine scenery can tackle the gentle **Paihia–Opua Coastal Walkway** (6km; 90min–2hr one-way) to get here.

As the Bay of Islands' only deepwater port, Opua was once an important freight entrepot, with rail connections south to Whangarei and beyond. The track now only extends 13km south to **KAWAKAWA**, a standard Kiwi small town with train tracks running down the middle of its only significant street. Regular passenger services last rumbled through town in the 1960s.

The only reason to stop is to visit Kawakawa's celebrated toilets on the main road and signposted from SH11, which were created in 1997 by the reclusive Austrian émigré **Friedrich Hundertwasser**, a painter, architect, ecologist and philosopher who made Kawakawa his home from 1975 until his death early in 2000, aged 71. The ceramic columns supporting the entrance hint at the complex use of broken tiles and found objects within. A steady trickle of visitors take a peek in both the Gents and the Ladies after suitable warning. The columns are echoed across the road at the Grass Hut, 35–37 Gillies Street, a gift shop selling Hundertwasser prints and cards.

Russell

New Zealand's most historic village, the small hillside settlement of **RUSSELL** is for much of the year a sleepy place favoured by city escapees, its isolation on a narrow peninsula with poor road but good sea access giving it an island ambience. But, during the summer, it's swamped with day-trippers piling off the passenger ferries from Paihia, a couple of kilometres across the water, and the

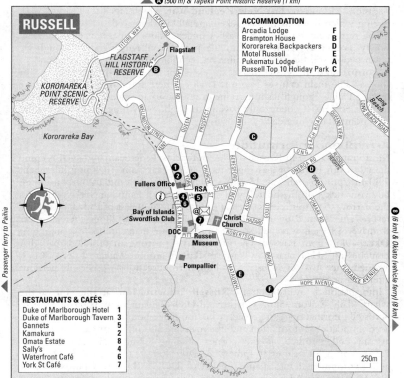

RUSSELL

ACCOMMODATION

Arcadia Lodge	F
Brampton House	B
Kororareka Backpackers	D
Motel Russell	E
Pukematu Lodge	A
Russell Top 10 Holiday Park	C

Passenger ferry to Paihia ▲

FLAGSTAFF HILL HISTORIC RESERVE Ⓑ

Flagstaff

KORORAREKA POINT SCENIC RESERVE

Kororareka Bay

N

Fullers Office

ⓘ

RSA

Bay of Islands Swordfish Club

DOC

Russell Museum

Christ Church

Pompallier

0   250m

RESTAURANTS & CAFÉS

Duke of Marlborough Hotel	1
Duke of Marlborough Tavern	3
Gannets	5
Kamakura	2
Omata Estate	8
Sally's	4
Waterfront Café	6
York St Café	7

vehicle ferries from nearby Opua. People come to explore the village's historic buildings and stroll along its appealing waterfront.

Evenings are more peaceful and romantic – the major exception being **New Year's Eve**, when half the nation's youth seem to descend and the revelry harks back to the 1830s when **Kororareka**, as Russell was then known, was a swashbuckling town full of whalers and sealers with a reputation as the "Hell Hole of the Pacific". Savage and drunken behaviour served as an open invitation to **missionaries**, who gradually won over a sizeable congregation and left behind Russell's two oldest buildings, the church and a printing works that produced religious tracts. By 1840, Kororareka was the largest settlement in the country, but after the signing of the Treaty of Waitangi, Governor William Hobson fell out with both Maori and local settlers and moved his capital progressively further south.

Meanwhile, initial Maori enthusiasm for the Treaty of Waitangi had faded: financial benefits had failed to materialize and the Confederation of Tribes flag that flew from Flagstaff Hill between 1834 and 1840 had been replaced by the Union Jack. This came to be seen as a symbol of British betrayal, and as resentment crystallized it found a leader in **Hone Heke Pokai**, Ngapuhi chief and son-in-law of Kerikeri's Hongi Hika. Between July 1844 and March 1845, Hongi and his followers cut down the flagstaff no less than four times, the last occasion sparking the first **New Zealand War**, which raged for nearly a year, during which Kororareka was sacked and all but destroyed.

The settlement rose from the ashes under a new name, Russell, and grew slowly around its beachfront into the peaceful village of today. Though far fewer people stay here than in Paihia on account of the limited range of budget **accommodation**, Russell makes an excellent base for exploring the rest of the bay. The main **cruises** (see p.181) all call here some fifteen minutes after leaving Paihia, though it's important to reserve in advance so that they know to pick you up. If you're only passing through, everything at Russell can be seen comfortably in a day.

Arrival and information

Most visitors arrive in Russell by way of **ferries**. Pedestrians and cyclists come directly from Paihia by passenger ferry (Oct–May 7am–10.30pm; June–Sept 7.30am–7pm; $5 each way; 15min), which runs every twenty to thirty minutes; buy your ticket on the boat. If you're **driving** from Paihia or SH1 you'll cross the narrow strait south of Russell at Opua, 6km southeast of Paihia, by vehicle ferry (7am–10pm; daily every 10min until 5.30pm, every 20min thereafter; car & driver $8 each way, pedestrians $1; buy your ticket onboard), landing at Okiato 9km from Russell. The **alternative route** – an unsealed road that branches off SH11 near Kawakawa to Russell around Waikare Inlet – is best avoided since it is very twisty with long narrow sections – especially perilous after rain or at night.

Information is available from **Russell Information**, at the end of the wharf (daily 8.30am–5pm, Christmas–March 7.30am–8pm; ☎09/403 8020, ✉russell.information@xtra.co.nz), who also make bookings for local trips and accommodation. Information and free maps are also offered, to a lesser degree, at the Fullers office, at the corner of The Strand and Cass St (daily 7.30am–5pm, Sun closes at 4pm; ☎ & ℱ09/403 7866). For specific walking and environmental information make for DOC's **Bay of Islands Visitor Centre**, The Strand (daily: Nov–May 9am–5pm; June–Oct 9am–4.30pm; ☎09/403 9005, ⊛www.doc.govt.nz), which is full of interesting displays and sells the useful *Russell Heritage Trail* leaflet ($1.20) and the *Bay of Islands Walks* leaflet ($1). Few places are more than half a kilometre away from the wharf, though if time is limited you may fancy the **Russell Mini Tour** (3 daily; 1hr; $17; ☎09/403 7866), which leaves from outside the Fullers office and visits the major sights. There's **Internet access** at Enterprise Russell on York St, next door to the *York Street Café* (daily 9am–5pm; ☎09/403 8843).

Accommodation

Accommodation in Russell is much more limited than across the water in Paihia and tends to be more upmarket. Apart from a handful of motels, hotels and backpacker lodges, most accommodation is in B&Bs and homestays; as well as those listed below, Russell Information or the visitor centre in Paihia can help you pick one out. Don't expect to find many vacancies in the three weeks after Christmas, when you'll have to book well ahead and pay inflated rates, which continue to the end of February.

Arcadia Lodge 10 Florance Ave ☎09/403 7756, ⊛www.arcadialodge.co.nz. One of Russell's gems: B&B in a historic, rambling wooden house encircled by decks on a quiet hill overlooking English cottage gardens and the bay. It's a five-minute stroll from the village and

some of the half-dozen wooden-floored suites and rooms (one en suite) enjoy sea views. Rooms ➐, suites for two ➑

Brampton House 79 Wellington St ☎09/403 7521, ✉brampton@xtra.co.nz. Two spotless and well-appointed suites (with separate entrances and terraces) in the highest house in Russell, surrounded by bush and commanding fabulous views all around. Deft touches such as complimentary wine and sumptuous breakfasts make this a treat. Closed for five months in winter. **⑦**

Kororareka Backpackers 22 Oneroa Rd ☎09/403 8494, ✉korobp@xtra.co.nz. Fairly simple yet adequate hostel five minutes' walk from town or to Long Beach, with three rooms (a double and two 4-bed bunkrooms) and good views from its wide decks. Dorms **①**, rooms **③**

Motel Russell Matauwhi Bay Rd ☎09/403 7854 & 0800/240 011, ⓦwww.motelrussell.co.nz. Despite the lack of sea views, this is the pick of Russell's motels, with pleasant self-contained units and studio units (some with kitchens), plus

an attractive pool and spa. Studios **⑤**, one-bedroom units **⑥**

Pukematu Lodge Flagstaff Hill ☎09/403 8500, ⓦwww.pukematu.co.nz. Beautifully sited boutique lodge with great 360-degree views and two spacious double suites ($295 all year) furnished in recycled native wood. A delicious breakfast is included, plus muffins and tea on arrival. **⑨**

Russell Top 10 Holiday Park Long Beach Rd ☎09/403 7826, ⓦwww.russelltop10.co.nz. Central, well-ordered and spotless campsite with tent and campervan sites, backpacker bunks (except in peak season) and an extensive range of high-standard cabins and motel units. Camping $13–15, dorms **①**, standard cabins **③**, kitchen cabins **④**, units **⑤**

The Town

Several historic buildings and Flagstaff Hill constitute the main sights in Russell, supplemented by a few diverting craft shops. Arriving on the passenger ferry, the single most striking building at the southern end of town is **Pompallier** (daily: Dec–April open access 10am–5pm, with interpreters taking you through the tannery and print room; May–Nov entry via 45-minute guided tours only at 10.15am, 11.15am, 1.15pm, 2.15pm & 3.15pm; $7.50), the last surviving building of Russell's Catholic mission, which was once the headquarters of Catholicism in the western Pacific. New Zealand's oldest industrial building, Pompallier was built in 1842 as a printing works for the French Roman Catholic bishop Jean Baptiste François Pompallier, who had arrived three years earlier to find the Catholic word of God under siege from Anglican and Wesleyan tracts, translated into Maori. The missionaries built an elegant rammed-earth structure in a style typical of Pompallier's native Lyons. The press and paper were imported, and a tannery installed to make leather book-bindings. During the next eight years over a dozen titles were printed, comprising more than thirty thousand volumes, which were some of the first books printed in Maori.

The printing operation only lasted until 1850 and the property became a private house, but restoration work has largely recreated its 1842 state. Artisans again produce handmade books – the production processes are explained in each room, and on the tour you can even get your hands dirty in what is New Zealand's only surviving colonial tannery. Outside, the grounds make a perfect place for a picnic.

Russell's only other building surviving from the same era is the prim, white, weatherboard **Christ Church**, Robertson Road, built in 1836 and New Zealand's oldest surviving church. Unlike most churches of similar vintage, it was not a mission church but built by local settlers: an appeal for public donations loosened the purse strings of Charles Darwin, who passed through the Bay of Islands at the time, long before he fell out with the church over his theory of evolution. In the mid-nineteenth century the church was besieged during skirmishes between Hone Heke's warriors and the British, leaving several still-visible bullet holes.

The small **Russell Museum** (Te Whare Taonga o Kororareka), close by on York Street (daily: late Dec to end Jan 10am–5pm; Feb to mid-Dec 10am–4pm; $5), shows a video telling the town's history and contains well laid out exhibits, including an impressive scale model of Cook's *Endeavour*, which called in here in 1769. From the museum, a stroll along The Strand passes the rooms of the prestigious Bay of Islands Swordfish Club, which was founded in 1924, and the *Duke of Marlborough Hotel* – the original building on this site held New Zealand's first liquor licence.

At the end of The Strand, a short track (30–40min return) climbs steeply to **Flagstaff Hill** (*Maiki*). The current flagpole was erected in 1857, some twelve years after the destruction of the fourth flagpole by Hone Heke (see Contexts, p.945), as a conciliatory gesture by a son of one of the chiefs who had ordered the original felling. The Confederation of Tribes flag, abandoned after the signing of the Treaty of Waitangi, is flown on twelve significant days of the year, including the anniversary of Hone Heke's death and the final day of the first New Zealand War. From Flagstaff Hill it's a further kilometre to the **Tapeka Point Historic Reserve**, a former *pa* site on a headland at the end of the peninsula – a wonderfully defensible position with great views and abundant evidence of terracing.

Another worthwhile stroll is to **Oneroa Bay** (Long Beach), 1km east of Russell on the far side of the peninsula, a gently shelving beach sheltered from the prevailing wind and safe for swimming.

Eating and drinking

The range of **restaurants** in Russell is not especially varied, they change hands quickly and prices are relatively high. **Drinking** options are no better, though there are a number of cheap private **clubs** – the RSA on Cass Street and the Bay of Islands Swordfish Club on The Strand, for example – which often welcome visitors.

The Duke of Marlborough Hotel The Strand ☏ 09/403 7829. Well-prepared traditional food is served in New Zealand's oldest licensed establishment, now a pricey hotel. The bar on the veranda is a good place to idle over a daytime coffee.

The Duke of Marlborough Tavern York St. Unreconstructed Kiwi pub with a lively atmosphere and mainstream bar meals all day, plus bands every Fri night, and on Sat in summer. À la carte evening menu is also served in the bistro.

Gannets cnr Chapel St & York St ☏ 09/403 7990. The decor may be rather uninspired, but the eclectic choice of food at this dinner venue is tasty and many of the dishes can be had as either a starter ($10–19) or main ($20–30). Closed Mon all year & Sun outside summer.

Kamakura The Strand ☏ 09/403 7771. Modern, licensed waterfront restaurant with an understated Japanese ambience and a varied menu of pricey but tasty and beautifully presented dishes. Closed Tues in summer; usually Tues & Wed in winter, and sometimes June & July.

Omata Estate Aucks Rd (the road to the vehicle ferry), 8km from Russell or 2km from the ferry wharf ☏ 09/403 8007, ⊛ www.omata.co.nz. Delightful café, restaurant and bar overlooking young vineyards with the inner bay as a backdrop. Lunch platters cost around $45–65 for two, dinner mains around $30, or just drop in for a coffee or a sundowner on the patio. The adjacent tasting room offers samples of several wines ($5) made from grapes grown on site. Advance booking essential for meals in summer.

Sally's 25 The Strand ☏ 09/403 7652. Relaxing and convivial restaurant, strong on modestly priced seafood and open for lunch and dinner, though it's worth booking ahead in peak season.

Waterfront Café The Strand. Simple café with great coffee, as well as snacks, all-day breakfasts and lunches. Closed Mon in winter.

York Street Café Traders Mall, York St. Relaxing and unpretentious café popular with locals for reliable fare ranging from full breakfasts to the best chowder in town and dinner dishes of Thai prawns, fish of the day or pizza. Closed Thurs in winter.

Around Russell: Whangaruru Harbour

To the south and east of Russell lies the mixed kauri forest of the **Ngaiotonga Scenic Reserve** and some wonderful coastline around the **Whangaruru Harbour**. The sealed Russell **coast road** twists through the region, closely tracing the shore from Orongo Bay, just south of Russell. Just beyond the Waikare Road turn-off for Kawakawa and Paihia, a signposted side road leads to some fine stands of kauri that can be visited on the **Ngaiotonga Kauri Grove Walk** (1km; 20min), the **Twin Bole Kauri Walk** (around 200m; 5min), and the **Ngaiotonga–Russell Forest Walkway** (21km; 9hr); the last is best tackled over two days with a tent (more information is available from DOC in Russell).

Continuing along the Russell coast road, you'll reach the turn-off to the scattered and predominantly Maori village of **Rawhiti**, the start of the challenging but rewarding **Cape Brett Tramping Track** (20km; 8hr each way; $30 track fee, payable in advance; hut bookings essential at the DOC Bay of Islands Visitor Centre in Russell). The walk, outlined in DOC's *Cape Brett* leaflet ($0.50) follows the hilly ridge along the centre of the peninsula with sea occasionally visible on both sides, and terminates at the end of the peninsula, where you either turn around and come back or take a water taxi to Rawhiti (Kiwi Eco Tours, ☎09/403 8823; $30 per person one way, minimum 4 people). Alternatively, take a water taxi from Rawhiti to the end of the track and walk back. If weather conditions won't allow the water taxi to make a landing at the cape, it drops you off at Deep Water Cove, from where it's a steep two-hour walk to the hut at the cape, a former lighthouse-keeper's house (23 beds, $12 in addition to track fee; annual hut pass not valid) with gas cooking stove and fuel, but no cooking utensils. The track crosses private land and you should check with DOC in Russell for the latest news about access to sections of the peninsula, where possum control is periodically undertaken.

The base of the Cape Brett peninsula is crossed by the **Whangamumu Walking Track** (4km; 1hr), which starts close to the Rawhiti Road junction, and runs through forest to a beach where the remains of a 1920s whaling operation can be seen.

At **Ngaiotonga**, 20km south of Rawhiti, a sealed road runs 8km through hilly farmland to the broad sweep of **Bland Bay**, with great beaches on both sides of the isthmus. You can **camp** at the simple *Bland Beach Motor Camp* (☎09/433 6759; camping $10), which has a basic shop, or press on a further 2km to **Whangaruru North Head Scenic Reserve**, with yet more lovely beaches, fine walks around the end of the peninsula and a DOC campsite ($6; closed Easter–Nov) with water and toilets.

The main settlement on the mainland side of the Whangaruru Harbour is **OAKURA**, 12km south of Ngaiotonga along Russell Road. Not a great deal happens here, but that is its appeal, and there's no shortage of places to swim and walk, as well as impressive sea and island views. There are a few **places to stay**, including the *Whangaruru Beachfront Camp*, Ohawiri Rd (☎09/433 6806; camping $10, cabins ➋, motel units ➍), and the *Oakura Bay Beach Holidays*, 24 Rapata Rd (☎ & ⓕ09/433 6066; ➌), which has a self-contained one-bedroom flat (➋), a family holiday cottage near the beach, with sea views ($165) plus evening meals ($25) and kayak rental ($5 per hour).

Kerikeri

KERIKERI, 25km northwest of Paihia, is both central to the history of and yet geographically removed from the Bay of Islands. On initial acquaintance it's an ordinary-looking service town, strung out along the main road and surrounded by the orchards that form Kerikeri's economic mainstay and offer abundant opportunities for casual work. Two kilometres to the east of town, the thin ribbon of the Kerikeri Inlet forces its way from the sea to its tidal limit

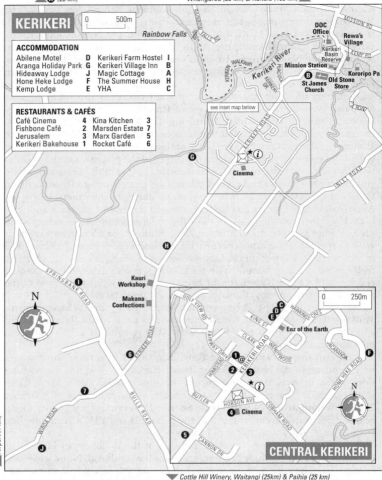

KERIKERI

0   500m

Rainbow Falls

Whangaroa (30 km) & Kaitaia (100 km)

A (20 km)

MISSION RD

RAINBOW FALLS RD

KERIKERI WALKWAY

Kerikeri River

KERIKERI RD

INLET ROAD

DOC Office

Rewa's Village

Kerikeri Basin Reserve

KEMP RD

Mission Station

Kororipo Pa

B   Old Stone Store

St James Church

IRI ROAD

ACCOMMODATION

Abilene Motel	**D**	Kerikeri Farm Hostel	**I**
Aranga Holiday Park	**G**	Kerikeri Village Inn	**B**
Hideaway Lodge	**J**	Magic Cottage	**A**
Hone Heke Lodge	**F**	The Summer House	**H**
Kemp Lodge	**E**	YHA	**C**

see inset map below

RESTAURANTS & CAFÉS

Café Cinema	**4**	Kina Kitchen	**3**
Fishbone Café	**2**	Marsden Estate	**7**
Jerusalem	**3**	Marx Garden	**5**
Kerikeri Bakehouse	**1**	Rocket Café	**6**

G

★ ⓘ

Cinema

H

Kauri Workshop

Makana Confections

SPRINGBANK ROAD

KERIKERI ROAD

BULL'S ROAD

WIROA ROAD

N

I

6

7

J

Airport (1 km)

CENTRAL KERIKERI

0   250m

HAWKING CRES

GOLF VIEW RD

KING ST

FAIRWAY DRIVE

CLARK RD

HOMESTEAD RD

KERIKERI ROAD

WENDYWOOD

JACARANDA

HONE HEKE ROAD

BUTLER

HOBSON AVE

COBHAM ROAD

CANNON DR

C
E

Enz of the Earth

1 @

2

3

★ ⓘ

4 Cinema

5

F

N

Cottle Hill Winery, Waitangi (25km) & Paihia (25 km)

at **Kerikeri Basin**, the site chosen by Samuel Marsden for the Church Missionary Society's second mission in New Zealand. John Butler, the first Anglican missionary, arrived here in 1819 but struggled to win the trust and assistance of the Ngapuhi, since he was unable to sell them the muskets they so wanted.

In the 1920s the area was planted with the subtropical crops that continue to thrive here – mainly citrus fruit, along with tamarillos, feijoas, melons, courgettes, peppers and kiwifruit. For most of the year it's possible to get **seasonal work** in the orchards, either weeding, thinning or picking. Work is most abundant from January to July, but this is also when competition for jobs is greatest, and you may find that your chances are just as good any month except August and September. The best contacts are the managers of the hostels and campgrounds (see especially *Aranga* and *Hideaway*), many of which also offer good weekly rates. In recent years Kerikeri has earned itself a reputation for its **craft shops**, dotted among the orchards.

Arrival and information

Air New Zealand **flights** from Auckland land 5km out of town towards Paihia at Bay of Islands Airport, from where Paihia Taxis operate an airport shuttle ($10 per person to Kerikeri, $15 to Paihia). Northliner and InterCity **buses** stop on Cobham Road, with several services to Paihia but just one bus heading north to Kaitaia daily: book through the Kerikeri Travel Shop on Fairway Drive (℡09/407 8013). At the time of writing there's no official visitor centre, but the leaflets in the unmanned foyer at the library on Cobham Road (Mon–Fri 10am–5pm, Sat 10am–noon; ℡09/407 9297) supply local **information**; and there's a **DOC office** at 34 Landing Rd (Mon–Fri 8am–4.30pm; ℡09/407 8474), which can advise on local walks and more ambitious treks into the Puketi and Omahuta forests (see p.200). For **Internet access** try Gadgit, a computer store at 98 Kerikeri Rd (Mon–Fri 9am–5pm, Sat 9.30am–noon; ℡09/407 5306).

Accommodation

Kerikeri is fairly well endowed with **accommodation** in all categories, but is particularly strong in budget places – a consequence of the area's popularity with long-stay casual workers. Seasonal price fluctuations are nowhere near as marked as in Paihia, though it's still difficult to find a place in January, when places are correspondingly expensive; prices quoted here are outside this post-Christmas period.

Motels, Cottages and B&Bs

Abilene Motel 136 Kerikeri Rd ℡09/407 9203, ℮abilene@kerikeri-nz.co.nz. Centrally located motel in a garden setting with pool, spa and Sky TV. ➎

Kemp Lodge 134 Kerikeri Rd ℡ & ℻09/407 8295. Three pleasant and modern self-contained chalets close to town, complete with TV and video, and pool. ➍

Kerikeri Village Inn 165 Kerikeri Rd ℡09/407 4666, ℠www.kerikerivillageinn.co.nz. Attractive modern home, with long views over rolling country and three comfy en-suite rooms, and a self-contained unit ideal for couples or families (available summer only; ➐ plus $30 per extra person). Complimentary port, chocolates and a tasty breakfast included. Rooms ➏, unit ➐

Magic Cottage Takou Bay Rd, Takou Bay, 20km northeast of Kerikeri ℡09/407 8065, ℠www.takouriver.com. A secluded and self-contained timber cottage for two, right beside the Takou River on a farm and near a pretty surf beach. $170 includes a gourmet organic breakfast.

The Summer House 424 Kerikeri Rd ℡09/407 4294, ℠www.thesummerhouse.co.nz. Classy environmentally aware boutique inn done out in French provincial style with three en-suite rooms. Sumptuous breakfasts are served in lovely gardens. Rooms ➐, self-contained ➑

Hostels and campsites

Aranga Holiday Park Kerikeri Rd ℡0800/272 642 or 09/407 9326, ℠www.aranga.co.nz. Large, beautiful streamside site on the edge of town with a spacious camping area, well-equipped standard cabins, comfortable self-contained units, and single rooms for long-stayers at a bargain $95 a week. Other attractions are two spas and a big barbecue on Friday nights. Tents $11–12, cabins ➋, units ➎

Hideaway Lodge Wiroa Rd (airport road), 4km west of Kerikeri ℡0800/562 746 & 09/407 9773, ℻407 9793. Large well-appointed hostel, some way out of town and catering almost exclusively to seasonal workers, who appreciate the reduced weekly rates, the large pool, games room and free trips into town. Camping $10, dorms ➊, rooms ➋, tourist flat ➌

Hone Heke Lodge 65 Hone Heke Rd ℡09/407 8170, ℮honeheke@xtra.co.nz. Pleasant hostel with six-bed dorms, each with a fridge and cooking gear, and doubles and twins, some en suite. There's also a games room and barbecue area. Dorms ➊, rooms ➋

The Town

The only way to get a sense of Kerikeri's past importance is to make for **Kerikeri Basin**, nearly 2km northeast of the current town. It was here, in 1821, that mission carpenters started work on what is now New Zealand's oldest European-style building, **Kerikeri Mission Station** (daily: Nov–April 10am–5pm; May–Oct 10am–4pm; $5, combined entry with Old Stone Store $7), a restrained, two-storey Georgian colonial affair. The first occupants, missionary John Butler and family, soon moved on, and by 1832 the house was in the hands of lay missionary and blacksmith James Kemp, who extended the design. Since the last of the Kemps moved out in the early 1970s it has been restored and furnished in mid-eighteenth-century style.

Next door is the only other extant building from the mission station and the country's oldest stone building, the **Old Stone Store** (same times as the Mission Station; $3.50), constructed mostly of local stone, with keystones and quoins of Sydney sandstone. Completed in 1835 as a central provision store for the Church Missionary Society, it successively served as a munitions store for troops garrisoned here to fight Hone Heke, then a kauri trading store and a shop, before being opened to the public in 1975. The ground-floor **store** sells goods almost identical to those on offer almost 170 years ago. The two **upper floors** house a museum stocked with old implements.

Opposite the Old Stone Store, a path along the river leads to the site of local chief Hongi Hika's **Kororipo Pa**, passing the place where, in the 1820s, he had a European-style house built. The *pa* commands a hill on a prominent bend in the river, a relatively secure base from which attacks were launched on other tribes using newly acquired firearms. Signs help interpret the dips and humps in the ground, but you'll get a better appreciation of pre-European Maori life from **Rewa's Village**, 1 Landing Rd (daily mid–Oct to April 9.30am–4.30pm; May to early Oct 10am–4pm; $3), a 1969 reconstruction of a fishing village across the river from the *pa* site. It comes complete with *marae*, weapons and *kumara* stores, as well as an authentic *hangi* site with an adjacent shell midden; the entrance kiosk screens a short video on the history of the area. Opposite is the **Kerikeri Basin Reserve** and the start of a track past the site of Kerikeri's first hydroelectric station (15min each way) and the swimming holes at Fairy Pools (35min each way) to the impressively undercut **Rainbow Falls** (1hr each way). The latter are also accessible off Waipapa Road, 3km north of the Basin.

Elsewhere, Kerikeri is dominated by orchards and the roads running between them (especially SH10 and Kerikeri Road), which are studded with **craft outlets**. The free and widely available *Kerikeri Art & Craft Trail* leaflet advertises the major ones; they're mostly open daily from 10am to 5pm, and you could easily spend a day trawling round them all. A few of the most highly regarded ones include The Enz of the Earth, right in town at 127 Kerikeri Rd (☎09/407 8367), which combines Indian and Indonesian handicrafts and clothing with an exotic garden; The Kauri Workshop, Kerikeri Rd (☎09/407 9196), which stocks anything you could make from kauri; and the nearby, Makana Confections, Kerikeri Rd (☎0800/625 262) produce handmade chocolates and you can watch the process.

Eating, drinking and entertainment

After years in the culinary wilderness, Kerikeri has an enviable selection of good **restaurants and cafés**. The town also boasts two **wineries**: *Cottle Hill Winery*, Cottle Hill Drive, about 4km south of town off SH10 (℡09/407 5203), which offers a big range of table wines, as well as port and dessert wines; and *Marsden Estate*, Wiroa Rd (the airport road; ℡09/407 9398), who make a broad variety of reds and whites sampled through free tastings, and run a restaurant (see below). **Entertainment** is thinner on the ground, though there's always the lovingly restored, sixty-year-old Cathay Cinema, on Hobson Avenue (℡09/407 4428), which shows mainstream first-run movies and has a good café attached (see below).

2

Café Cinema Hobson Ave ℡09/407 9121. Attractive café attached to the cinema, and usually offering a good movie-and-meal deal for $22. Mains include lamb sweetbreads, steaks and chicken and there's an extensive seafood menu. Open from 3pm; closed Sun.

Fishbone Café 88 Kerikeri Rd ℡09/407 6065. Great licensed café for breakfast and lunch, perennially popular for its high-quality Kiwi fusion food.

Jerusalem Village Mall ℡09/407 1001. Compact BYO and licensed Israeli café serving authentic, low-cost Middle Eastern dishes to eat in or take away. Summer Mon–Sat lunch and dinner, Sun dinner only; winter Mon–Fri lunch and dinner, Sat dinner only; closed all day Sun.

Kerikeri Bakehouse Fairway Drive. The best baked goods in town: sandwiches, pastries, superlative vegetarian pies and good coffee served in the small dining area. Closed Sun.

Kina Kitchen Village Mall, 132 Kerikeri Rd ℡09/407 7669. Convivial and bustling restaurant serving hearty portions of well-prepared dishes for $25 upwards, including a vegetarian dish of the evening. Some outside seating. Licensed & BYO.

Marsden Estate Winery & Restaurant Wiroa Rd ℡09/407 9398. Relaxed dining at moderate prices and with plenty of choice, either in the tasting room or outside in the lush gardens.

Marx Garden Kerikeri Rd ℡09/407 6606. One of Northland's best restaurants, on the outskirts of Kerikeri set by a tranquil garden. Lunch and dinner are served all year, plus breakfast in summer. Expect to pay at least $50 for three courses, excluding wine. Closed Mon or Tues in winter.

Rocket Café Kerikeri Rd, 3km west of town ℡09/407 3100. Excellent licensed café for breakfast and lunch in a pretty garden setting. Dishes include a fine range of quiches, pizzas and filo rolls stuffed with imaginative fillings, plus larger meals. Great coffee and cakes served outside or in the airy interior.

Around Kerikeri

Some 15km southwest from Kerikeri is **WAIMATE NORTH** and the colonial Regency-style **Te Waimate Mission House**, set in lush gardens (10am–5pm: Nov–24 Dec Mon–Wed, Sat & Sun; Jan–April daily; May to end Oct Sat & Sun or by appointment on ℡09/405 9734; $7.50), New Zealand's second-oldest European building. Now virtually in the middle of nowhere, in the 1830s this was the centre of a vigorous **Anglican mission**, the first to be established on an inland site, chosen for its fertile soils and large Maori population. Missionaries were keen to add European agricultural techniques to the literacy and religion they were teaching the Maori, and they made use of the grounds already cultivated by the missionaries' friend and Ngapuhi chief, Hongi Hika. By 1834 locally grown wheat was being milled at the river, orchards were flourishing and crops were sprouting – all impressing Charles Darwin, who visited the following year. For two years from 1842 this was the home of Bishop Selwyn and headquarters of the Anglican church in New Zealand but, ultimately, shifting trade patterns made this first European-style farm uneconomic, and the mission declined. The house itself was built by converts in 1831–32 and fashioned almost entirely of local kauri. Though slightly modified over the years, it has been restored as accurately as possible to its original design. Guided tours highlight prize possessions. The modest mission **Church of St John the Baptist** nearby is also open daily during daylight hours (free).

Ginns Ngapha Springs and the Puketi Forest

The nearest substantial town to Waimate North is **KAIKOHE**, almost equi-distant from both coasts. There's little reason to stop, though you might like to soak your bones at **Ginns Ngawha Springs** (daily 9am–9.30pm; $4 for 1–2hr), 5km southeast of Kaikohe, where eight individual pools are enclosed by native timber but otherwise untouched by tourist trappings.

The stands of the **Puketi and Omahuta native forests**, 20km north of Kaikohe, jointly comprise one of the largest continuous tracts of kauri forest in the north. The easiest and most rewarding access is to the east of the forest: head north off SH1 at Okaihau, or west off SH10 just north of Kerikeri along Pungaere Road. Both routes bring you to the **Puketi Recreation Area**, where there's a basic $6 campsite and a trampers' hut (from $7 in an 18-bunk main hut or two 3-bunk cabins; see Kerikeri DOC for keys) at the start of the twenty-kilometre **Waipapa River Track** - best done in one short (5hr) and one long (8hr) day, camping midway. This and several other worthwhile tracks are detailed in DOC's free *Puketi and Omahuta Forests* leaflet which, along with camping and hut details, can be obtained from the DOC office in Kerikeri.

North to Doubtless Bay

North of the Bay of Islands everything gets a lot quieter. There are few towns of any consequence along the coast and it is the peace and slow pace that attract visitors to an array of glorious beaches and the lovely Whangaroa Harbour. The first stop north of Kerikeri is tiny **Matauri Bay**, where a hill-top memorial commemorates the Greenpeace flagship, *Rainbow Warrior*, which was sunk in Auckland Harbour in 1985. The wreck now lies off the coast of Motutapere Island, a site that can be dived from here. A mostly sealed backroad continues north, offering fabulous sea views and passing gorgeous headlands and beaches including **Te Ngaire**, **Wainui Bay**, **Mahinepua Bay** and **Tauranga Bay**, before delivering you to **Whangaroa Harbour**, one of the most beautiful in Northland, and an excellent place to go sailing or kayaking.

Further north is the huge bite out of the coast called **Doubtless Bay**, which had two celebrated discoverers: Kupe, said to have first set foot on Aotearoa in Taipa; and Cook, who sailed past in 1769 and pronounced it "doubtless, a bay". The French explorer Jean François Marie de Surville was also close by and, a week later, became the first European to enter the bay, though he departed in an undignified hurry after a dispute with local Maori over a missing dinghy. Bounded on the west and north by the sheltering **Karikari Peninsula**, the bay offers safe boating and is popular with Kiwi vacationers. In January you can barely move here and you'll struggle to find accommodation, but the shoulder seasons can be surprisingly quiet, and outside December, January and February room prices drop to more affordable levels. Most of the bay's facilities cluster along the southern shore of the peninsula in a string of beachside settlements – **Coopers Beach**, **Cable Bay** and **Taipa Bay** – running west from pictur-esque Mangonui.

French nuclear testing in the Pacific

The French government has always claimed that nuclear testing is completely safe, and for decades persisted in conducting tests on the tiny Pacific atolls of **Mururoa** and **Fangataufa**, a comfortable 15,000km from Paris, but only 4000km northeast of New Zealand.

In 1966 France turned its back on the 1963 Partial Test Ban Treaty, which outlawed atmospheric testing, and relocated Pacific islanders away from their ancestral villages to make way for a barrage of tests over the next eight years. The French authorities claimed that "Not a single particle of radioactive fallout will ever reach an inhabited island" – and yet radiation was routinely detected as far away as Samoa, Fiji and even New Zealand. Increasingly antagonistic public opinion forced the French to conduct their tests underground in deep shafts, where another 200 detonations took place, threatening the geological stability of these fragile coral atolls. Surveys with very limited access to the test sites have since revealed severe fissuring; there is also evidence of radioactive isotopes in the Mururoa lagoon, as well as submarine slides and subsidence.

In 1985, Greenpeace co-ordinated a New Zealand-based protest flotilla, headed by its flagship, the **Rainbow Warrior**, but before the fleet could set sail from Auckland, the French secret service sabotaged the *Rainbow Warrior*, detonating two bombs below the waterline. As rescuers recovered the body of Greenpeace photographer Fernando Pereira, two French secret service agents posing as tourists were arrested. Flatly denying all knowledge at first, the French government was finally forced to admit to what David Lange (then Prime Minister of New Zealand) described as "a sordid act of international state-backed terrorism". The two captured agents were sentenced to ten years in jail, but France used all its international muscle to have them serve their sentences on a French Pacific island; they both served less than two years before being honoured and returning to France.

In 1995, to worldwide opprobrium, France announced a further series of tests. Greenpeace duly dispatched *Rainbow Warrior II*, which was impounded by the French navy on the tenth anniversary of the sinking of the original *Rainbow Warrior*. In early 1996 the French finally agreed to stop nuclear testing in the Pacific, paving the way for improved diplomatic relations between the French and New Zealand, and the following year the two foreign ministers met for the first time since the bombing of the *Rainbow Warrior*.

Matauri Bay

Some 20km north of Kerikeri, a high inland ridge provides a dramatic first glimpse of the long and sandy **MATAURI BAY** as it stretches north to a stand of Norfolk pines and the offshore **Cavalli Islands**. The northern limit of the main bay is defined by Matauri Bay Hill, topped by a distinctive stone and steel memorial to the *Rainbow Warrior* (see box above), now scuttled off Motutapere Island, one of the Cavalli Islands.

Missionary Samuel Marsden first set foot in Aotearoa in 1814 at Matauri Bay, where he mediated between the Ngati Kura people – who still own the bay – and some Bay of Islands Maori, a process commemorated by the quaint wooden **Samuel Marsden Memorial Church** on the road in, and a small memorial behind the beach. The strength of Maori culture in the bay is evident from the finely carved *Mataatua II waka* further north along the beach: constructed in the early 1990s, its name echoes the Ngati Kura's ancestral *waka*, which lies in waters nearby. The resonance of this legendary canoe partly led the Ngati Kura to offer a final resting place to the wreck of the *Rainbow Warrior*.

Sculptor Chris Booth's **Rainbow Warrior Memorial** comprises a stone arch (symbolizing a rainbow) and the vessel's salvaged bronze propeller. It's reached by a well-worn path from near the holiday park at the foot of the hill. Two-tank **dive trips** out to the wreck, ten minutes by boat, can be organized through Matauri Kat Charters (℗09/405 0525 or 021 244 1319), at the holiday park, who charge $95 for one dive, $165 for two – there are substantial discounts if you've got your own gear. Alternatively, try Seabed Safaris, based at Taipa, further north (℗09/408 5885) who charge $135 for two dives. The best visibility is typically in April; from September to November plankton sometimes obscure the view but it's still pretty good.

The only place for a bite to **eat** is the combined store and good-value café at the top of Matauri Bay Road, just before you descend to the bay, which is open all year, for general groceries, alcohol and a simple bistro menu. **Accommodation** in the bay is limited to the *Matauri Bay Holiday Park* (℗09/405 0525, Ⓦwww.matauribay.co.nz/camp; tent sites $12, powered sites $3 extra; on-site vans ❸), which has a small shop and, tucked around the corner from the camp, in a private bay, *Oceans on the Beach* (℗09/405 0417, Ⓦwww.matauribay.co.nz/oceans; ❺), a family and fishing resort with spacious units, lodges (with up to four bedrooms, from $200 for four adults to $410 for ten; less for children), a licensed **restaurant** (open daily in summer, weekends only in winter) and dinghies and kayaks for guests to rent.

Whangaroa Harbour

Inland from Matauri Bay on SH10 the small town of **KAEO** heralds the virtually landlocked and sheltered **Whangaroa Harbour**. Time spent around here is the perfect antidote to Bay of Islands commercialism. The scenery, albeit on a smaller scale, is easily a match for its southern cousin and, despite the limited facilities, you can still get out onto the water for a cruise or to join the big-game fishers. Narrow inlets forge between cliffs and steep hills, most notably the two bald volcanic plugs, **St Paul and St Peter**, which rise behind the harbour's two settlements, **WHANGAROA** and **TOTARA NORTH**.

The harbour wasn't always so quiet though, being among the first areas in New Zealand to be visited by European pioneers, most famously those aboard the *Boyd*, which called here in 1809 to load kauri spars for shipping to Britain. A couple of days after its arrival, all 66 crew were killed and the ship burned by local Maori in retribution for the crew's mistreatment of Tara, a high-born Maori sailor who had apparently transgressed the ship's rules. A British whaler avenged the incident by burning the entire Maori village, thereby sparking off a series of skirmishes that spread over the north for five years. Later the vast stands of kauri were hacked away; some were rafted to Auckland, while others were milled at Totara North, which claims the oldest mill in the country still operating (though only just).

Even if you're just passing through, it's worth driving the 4km along the northern shore of the harbour to Totara North, passing a boatyard or two and a sawmill, the last commercial remnants of this historic community.

Activities

The single best thing to do around Whangaroa is to spend a day on the eleven-metre *Snow Cloud* **yacht** (℗09/405 0523, Ⓦwww.kerikeri.net/snowcloud; 10–11hr; $80, including meals) – trips typically involve sailing out to the rugged uninhabited Cavalli Islands, stopping to let the small group of passengers snorkel, sunbathe and walk; it's great value for money. Alternatively, sail on a similar trip on the fifteen-metre steel cutter, *Sea Eagle* (℡09/405 1963, Ⓦwww.seaeaglecharters.com; full day $75 including meals), with pick-ups from Whangaroa or Totara North.

Summer **kayak** trips can be arranged with the knowledgeable Northland Sea Kayaking, on the northeastern flank of the harbour (℡09/405 0381, Ⓔnorthlandseakayaking@xtra.co.nz); half-day trips start at $50, a full day costs $70, overnight camping trips are available, and there's even self-catering accommodation (❶) for up to six people at the kayaking base. Two-tank **dive trips** to the *Rainbow Warrior* run from the *Whangaroa Harbour Holiday Park* (see below) and cost $85 for 4–5 hours, plus gear hire ($75).

Land-based activities primarily mean **walks**, two of the most rewarding being the 30-minute hike up St Paul from the top of Old Hospital Road in Whangaroa and DOC's Lane Cove Walk (1hr 30min–2hr each way) from Totara North, past freshwater pools, mangroves and viewpoints to the Lane Cove Cottage (❶) on the Pekapeka Bay, which sleeps sixteen people, but only opens for a minimum of four and is accessible by boat or on the walk. It has a solar-heated shower, water, toilets and plenty of sandflies, but you'll need your own cooking gear. Book well in advance in summer through Kerikeri DOC.

Practicalities

Though a combined InterCity and Northliner **bus** plies SH10 at the head of the harbour, public transport reaches neither the small community of Whangaroa, 6km off SH10 on the southern side of the harbour, nor tiny Totara North, 4km off the highway on the northern side.

Most of the harbour's limited **accommodation** clusters along the road to Whangaroa, first up being the tree-shaded *Whangaroa Harbour Holiday Park* (℡09/405 0306, Ⓔdyleewhangaroa@xtra.co.nz; tent sites $12.50, dorms ❶, cabins ❸), 3km south of the centre and boasting two small indoor pools, a BBQ and its own small grocery and shop selling takeaway food; three of the cabins are self-contained and all are equipped with a fridge. The *Sunseeker Lodge*, beyond the Gamefishing Club on Old Hospital Rd (℡09/405 0496, Ⓦwww.sunseekerlodge.co.nz; camping $13, spacious en-suite dorms ❶, rooms ❸, motel units ❹), perched on the hill overlooking the harbour, boasts a relaxing atmosphere, plus great sea views from the new spa, a kids' play area, and cheap sea kayak and fishing-gear rental. They also run a holiday house next door with spectacular views (❺). The hugely hospitable *Kahoe Farms Hostel* (℡09/405 1804, Ⓔkahoefarms@xtra.co.nz; tents $12, dorms ❶, rooms ❷), on SH10 1.5km north of the Totara North turn-off, is a beautifully restored homestead tucked into a corner of a working cattle farm, where people come to kickback for a few days. The attractive accommodation in a six-bed dorm and three spacious private rooms plus the separate, *The Villa* (Oct–April only; ❸), another large 19th-century homestead, with four double rooms sharing two bathrooms. All guests can enjoy excellent homemade dinners and generous breakfasts, plus kayak rental ($30 per day) and hiking trails to some superb swimming holes. Finally, all the units at the *Whangaroa Motel*, Church St (℡09/405 0022, Ⓔwhangaroamotel@xtra.co.nz; ❹) are self-contained and offer great bay views.

As for **eating**, there's decent seafood at Totara North's *Gumstore Bar and Grill*, 2km off SH10 (℡09/405 1703; daily from noon), which serves reasonable bar-style meals (around $20) and takeaways, and is enlivened by a collection of Kiwiana. Around 500m south of the Whangaroa turnoff on SH10 and 2km north of Kaeo, there's a touch of America at *Janit's Texas Diner* (8.30am–8.30pm or later: Jan daily; Nov, Dec, Feb–May Wed–Sun; ℡09/405 0569), which excels in big breakfasts, barbecue pork ribs and the like. Small **shops** in Whangaroa and Totara North provide for self-caterers.

Mangonui and around

There's an antiquated air to the friendly village of **MANGONUI**, attractively strung along a sheltered half-kilometre of harbour off Doubtless Bay. A handful of two-storey buildings with wooden verandas have been preserved and a couple of craft shops nestle between a clutch of cafés, but this is still very much a working village, with a lively fishing wharf and a traditional grocery perched on stilts over the water. It makes the most obvious stopping point on the way north, with excellent beaches nearby and a waterfront where you can catch your supper over an afternoon beer and have it cooked up at any of the local restaurants.

Mangonui means "big shark", a name recalling an incident when the legendary chief Moehuri's *waka* was supposedly led into the harbour by such a fish. But it was whales and the business of provisioning **whaling** ships that made the town. As whaling diminished, the kauri trade took its place, chiefly around Mill Bay, the cove five minutes' walk to the west of Mangonui.

While ships were being repaired and restocked at Mangonui, barrels were being fixed a couple of kilometres west beside a stream crossing the strand that became known as **COOPERS BEACH**. This glorious and well-shaded sweep of sand is now backed by a string of motels and blighted by a rash of construction sites for big new homes. The beach is popular in January and at weekends, but at other times you might still find you have it pretty much to yourself.

Another couple of kilometres west, the smaller settlement of **CABLE BAY** owes its existence to its short-lived role as the terminus of the 1902 trans-Pacific cable; in 1912, the telegraph station was moved to Auckland. Again, the water is the focus of the modern community, with an excellent swimming beach and good surf. The Taipa River separates Cable Bay from the beachside village of **TAIPA**, now the haunt of sunbathers and swimmers, but historically significant as the spot where Kupe, the discoverer of Aotearoa in Maori legend, first set foot on the land.

To get a feel for the layout of the bay, wander up to the views at **Rangikapiti Pa Historic Reserve**, off Rangikapiti Road (unrestricted entry), between Mangonui and Coopers Beach. For a deeper understanding, though, you'll need to drive 15km around the head of the harbour to Hihi and the waterside **Butler House and Whaling Museum** (open by appointment only on ℡09/406 0006; $10, grounds only $5). Butler House was originally built in 1847 by whaler, ship owner and local MP William Butler (and incorporates a still earlier house of 1843, which was floated across the bay from Mangonui), and is filled with early colonial and Victorian furniture. The adjacent whaling museum has a well-restored whaling boat complete with replica tryworks

---

The Swamp Palace

If you are staying anywhere around Doubtless Bay and have your own transport, don't pass up an evening at **The Swamp Palace** (℡09/408 7040 for screening info; $9, backpackers $7 closed Nov to first Thurs before Christmas), a quirky cinema in the Oruru Community Hall, 7km south of **Taipa** in the middle of nowhere. It caters to an eclectic mix of tastes – cult and classic movies, as well as the very latest releases – each introduced with an informed talk by the proprietor.

(where blubber was boiled down). Scrimshaw, in the form of carving and images etched into whalebone, hints at the boredom of ship life. All this is set in the lovely grounds of **Butler Point**, which occupies a former *pa* site studded with mature trees, including several enormous pohutukawas – one seven-hundred-year-old specimen has a trunk almost eleven metres in diameter, the broadest in the country.

In Mangonui, don't miss the reasonably priced selection of handmade **woven flax items** and other locally made crafts at Flax Bush, The Waterfront (daily 10am–5pm): the deals on woven baskets (*kete*) are among the best you'll find. Art of a different kind is found along the Waterfront in the old courthouse at **Exhibit A** (☏09/406 0455; 10am–5pm most days, and daily in summer), where Annie Tothill makes and sells vibrant wall-hangings, throws and clothes from natural fabrics, and exhibits work from a roster of Far North artists.

For something more active, you can **kayak** along the coast of the Karikari Peninsula to the northwest (see p.206) or in the Rangaunu Harbour (part of a world heritage centre for migrating birds) with A to Z Diving, based in Whatuwhiwhi (☏09/408 7077, ⓦwww.atozdiving.co.nz), who offer trips from one hour to a full day (from $20 an hour to $200 for a day), overnight guided trips, and accommodation. The same company also offer **diving** off the Karikari Peninsula (charging $135 for a half-day with full gear, $150 for a full day, with discounts if you bring your own gear), plus trips to the *Rainbow Warrior* wreck and day-trips to the Poor Knights Islands. Seabed Safaris (☏09/408 5885) also offer dives off the Karikari Peninsula such as to Brodies Pinnacle (boat dives start at $95), and for $135 you can dive the *Rainbow Warrior* – again, there are big discounts if you have your own gear. Mangonui also makes a good base for organized trips to **Cape Reinga and Ninety Mile Beach** (see box on p.212).

Practicalities

SH10 bypasses the Mangonui waterfront, which is reached on a two-kilometre loop road plied by the joint Northliner and InterCity **bus** service, which runs once a day in each direction between Paihia and Kaitaia. Buses stop outside the BP station on Waterfront Road (☏09/406 0024), which sells tickets for InterCity only; the adjacent Mangonui Stationery & Lotto (☏09/406 0233) sells Northliner tickets. The **visitor centre** just back around the corner (daily: Oct–April 10am–5pm, May–Sept 10am–2pm; ☏09/406 2046, ⓦwww.doubtlessbay.com) can point you to accommodation, both here and along the coast. There's fast **Internet access** at MCL, Waterfront Drive (Oct–April daily 9am–5pm or later, May–Sept closed Sun; ☏09/406 1716), next to the *Café Almarlin*.

Accommodation

Heath's B&B Homestay Hihi Rd, Hihi, 12km from Mangonui ☏09/406 0088, ⓔheathsbandb@xtra.co.nz. Pleasant homestay in a modern home with views across the water to Mangonui. Two en-suite rooms come with continental breakfast and freshly baked bread, and dinners are available on request. ❺

Mac 'n' Mo's 104 SH10, Coopers Beach ☏09/406 0538, ⓔMacNMo@xtra.co.nz. Extremely welcoming B&B with great views and four rooms, all of which have TV; breakfast is served on a deck overlooking the ocean. ❺

Macrocarpa Cottage 2 Bush Point Rd, Taipa ☏09/406 1245, ⓦwww.holidayhouses.co.nz/properties/1515.asp. An open-plan, self-catering cottage at the water's edge with one queen room, and two singles on a mezzanine, full kitchen and cable TV, plus fabulous views across the Taipa Estuary. Great for couples. ❺

Mangonui Hotel Waterfront Rd, Mangonui ☏09/406 0003, ⓔmangonuihotel@xtra.co.nz. Turn-of-the-century hotel, opposite the harbour and with an excellent upstairs veranda. Rooms (the doubles are en-suite) are fairly plain yet the best ones with harbour views go quickly, so book ahead or arrive early. ❹

Old Oak Inn Waterfront Rd, Mangonui ⓣ & ⓕ 09/406 0665. Hotel dating from 1861 with a few simple yet characterful rooms upstairs and two spacious dorms on the ground floor. Dorms ❶, rooms ❹

San Marino Motor Lodge San Marino Drive, off Kupe Rd, Coopers Beach ⓣ 09/406 0345,

ⓔ sanmarino@xtra.co.nz. Eight motel units, each with a small deck, and all sited with views and direct access straight onto the beach. Two minutes' drive to Mangonui waterfront. ❺

Time Out 6 Heretaunga Crescent, Cable Bay ⓣ 09/406 0101, ⓦ www.taketimeout.co.nz. An idyllic and spacious private studio for two with full self-catering facilities, stylish decor and direct beach access; Sky and cable TV. ❻

Eating and drinking

Doubtless Bay has the best range of **places to eat** north of Kerikeri, though admittedly it doesn't have much competition. Committed **drinking** mostly happens at the *Mangonui Hotel*, which often has bands at weekends.

Café Al Marlin Waterfront Rd, Mangonui. Good-value meals, mostly seafood with an Asian influence, open for breakfast and lunch (and dinner in summer, Tues–Sat).

Fresh & Tasty Waterfront Rd, Mangonui. Rival chippy to its more famous neighbour, and much frequented by locals happy to trade location for lower prices and equally good tucker.

Mangonui Fish Shop Waterfront Rd, Mangonui. A better-than-average fish-and-chip restaurant that is descended upon each summer afternoon

(usually 4.30–5.30pm) by several of the Cape Reinga tour buses. The bus groups take precedence. Guaranteed fresh, you can select your fillet from the catch of the day and retire to the great licensed deck over the water.

Waterfront Café Waterfront Rd, Mangonui ⓣ 09/406 0850. Reliable café and bar opening out to pavement seating just over the street from the harbour. Stop by for the best coffee in the district, breakfast, light lunches or a good range of dinner mains; or one of their fine pizzas.

The Karikari Peninsula

Doubtless Bay to the east and Rangaunu Harbour to the west are bounded by the crooked arm of the **Karikari Peninsula** as it strikes north, swathed in unspoiled golden- and white-sand beaches which, at least outside the peak Christmas to mid-February season, have barely a soul on them. There's no public transport, facilities are limited and, without diving or fishing gear, you'll have to resign yourself to lazing on the beaches and swimming from them – and there can be few better places to do just that.

The initial approach across a low and scrubby isthmus is less than inspiring, though it's worth stopping briefly at **Lake Ohia**, 1km off SH10, which has gradually drained to reveal the stumps of a 40,000-year-old kauri forest thought to have been destroyed by some prehistoric cataclysm. A kilometre on, the **Gum Hole Reserve** has a short trail past holes left by kauri gum diggers (see box on p.224 for more on their exploits). Eight kilometres later, a side road leads to the peninsula's west coast and the **Puheke Scenic Reserve**, a gorgeous, dune-backed beach that's usually deserted. There's another fine white strand nearby at the beachside hamlet of **RANGIPUTA**, with the *White Sands Motor Lodge*, right beside the beach (ⓣ09/408 7080, ⓕ408 7580; ❹) with attractive timber-lined units and, 1km back down the road, the attractive, spa-equipped *Reef Lodge*, Gillies Rd, off Rangiputa Rd (ⓣ09/408 7100, ⓔreeflodge@clear.net.nz; ❺), offering beachfront units, a couple of two-bedroom houses (❼ plus $15 each extra person) set among lawns, and safe swimming.

The peninsula's main road continues past the Rangiputa junction to the community of **TOKERAU BEACH**, a cluster of houses and a couple of shops at the northern end of the grand sweep of Doubtless Bay. The only accommodation nearby is the well-run *Whatuwhiwhi Holiday Park*, Whatuwhiwhi Rd (℡09/408 7202, ✉whatuwhiwhi@xtra.co.nz; camping $12–14, cabins ❷, units ❹, self-catering cabins ❸ and deluxe units ❻), set back from a gorgeous beach. One kilometre north of Tokerau Beach at the Carrington Club golf course and set high on a hill with good sea views, the **restaurant** (summer daily for breakfast, lunch & dinner; winter Thurs–Sat lunch & dinner, lunch on Sun; ℡09/408 7222) is, takeaways apart, the only place to eat on the peninsula. Guided **kayaking** trips off the peninsula are run by A to Z Diving (see p.205), who are based at Whatuwhiwhi Holiday Park and can also take you **diving** hereabouts, as can Seabed Safaris (see p.205).

The Karikari Peninsula saves its best until last: **Maitai Bay**, 20km north of SH10, is a matchless double arc of golden sand split by a rocky knoll, all encompassed by the *Maitai Bay Campground* ($6 per adult), the largest DOC campsite in Northland. Much of the site is *tapu* to local Maori, and you are encouraged to respect the sacred areas.

Kaitaia and around

KAITAIA, 40km west of Mangonui, is the Far North's largest commercial centre, situated near the junction of the two main routes north, but suffers from one of the highest unemployment rates in the country and is a place of limited charm or excitement. With your own transport you might want to whizz round the sights, refuel and push on, but it does make a convenient base if you're reliant on bus tours for some of the best trips to Cape Reinga and Ninety Mile Beach (see p.212), rather than doing longer trips from the Bay of Islands. Alternatively, with your own transport you might prefer to base yourself at the magnificent beach in **Ahipara** (see p.210), to sand toboggan the giant dunes or explore the old gumfields.

A Maori village already flourished here when the first missionary, Joseph Matthews, came looking for a mission site in 1832. The protection of the mission encouraged other European pastoralists to establish themselves here, but by the 1880s they found themselves swamped by the gum diggers who had come to plunder the underground deposits around Lake Ohia and Ahipara. Many early arrivals were young Dalmatians (mostly Croats) fleeing tough conditions in what was then part of the Austro-Hungarian Empire, though the only evidence of this is a Serbo-Croat welcome sign at the entrance to town, and a cultural society that holds a traditional dance each year.

The Town

The best place to gain a sense of the area is the **Far North Regional Museum**, 6 South Rd (Mon–Fri 10am–4pm & some weekends in summer; $4), with arresting displays on local life and history. The room of Far North Maori pieces is particularly striking; you enter under one of three copies of the twelfth- or thirteenth-century **Kaitaia Carving**, found around 1920 on the outskirts of Kaitaia, an example of the transitional period during which Polynesian art began to take on Maori elements; the original is held in the Auckland Museum. Pride of place in the main room goes to the earliest European artefact to be left in New Zealand: a huge one-and-a-half-tonne **anchor**, one of three abandoned by de Surville when he departed in haste in 1769 (see p.200).

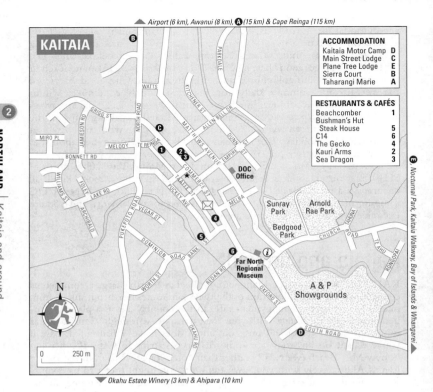

▲ Airport (6 km), Awanui (8 km), Ⓐ (15 km) & Cape Reinga (115 km)

KAITAIA

ACCOMMODATION

Kaitaia Motor Camp	D
Main Street Lodge	C
Plane Tree Lodge	E
Sierra Court	B
Taharangi Marie	A

RESTAURANTS & CAFÉS

Beachcomber	1
Bushman's Hut Steak House	5
C14	6
The Gecko	4
Kauri Arms	2
Sea Dragon	3

Ⓔ Nocturnal Park, Kaitaia Walkway, Bay of Islands & Whangarei

▼ Okahu Estate Winery (3 km) & Ahipara (10 km)

As elsewhere throughout the north, Maori people make up a large proportion of the population and strongly influence the **local culture**. One way to explore this is to join the excellent Tall Tale Travel 'n' Tours, 237a Commerce St, behind *KFC* and *Main Street Lodge*, on a Maori-led visit to the working Te Rarawa **marae**, just outside Kaitaia (℡ 09/408 0870, Ⓦ www.tall-tale.co.nz; $35). Tours last roughly two hours, though times and itineraries are flexible, and the emphasis is on fostering an understanding of Maori culture, in particular *marae* protocol, land issues and spiritual concepts of life, death and healing. They're run by the entertaining and informative Kitch, who also runs craft workshops, including bone carving ($25) and flax weaving ($55). In early March a **Maori arts and food festival** is held in Kaitaia – the arts housed in the *Whare Wananga* (Learning House) at *Main Street Lodge* and the food in the hostel's kitchen. This is two weeks before the annual **marathon** on Ninety Mile Beach, known as the Te Houtaewa Challenge, which is followed by the Te Houtaewa Surf Challenge, where six-man *waka* compete in sprints off Ninety Mile Beach (see p.215).

Another local attraction is a winery, **Okahu Estate**, 3.5km out on the road to Ahipara (℡ 09/408 2066, Ⓦ www.okahuestate.co.nz). Though experts have long claimed that the climate is too moist for successful wine making, the estate has produced small quantities of award-winning boutique wines – and offers free tastings.

Practicalities

The daily InterCity–Northliner joint **bus** service pulls up outside the Kaitaia Travel Bureau, Blencowe St (℡09/408 6120), which handles ticket sales for bus and airport (as does the visitor centre). The airport, 9km north of town near Awanui, is connected by direct **flights** to Auckland and the Bay of Islands with Air New Zealand (℡0800/737 000). A shuttle bus (℡09/408 0116 or 025 814962; $15) connects the airport to Kaitaia.

Kaitaia's **visitor centre**, South Rd (daily 8.30am–5pm; ℡09/408 0879, Ⓔkaitaiainfo@xtra.co.nz), stocks DOC leaflets such as *Kaitaia Area Walks* ($1) and *Cape Reinga and Te Paki Walks* ($1), and has **Internet access**, as does the hostel *Main Street Lodge*, 235 Commerce St (℡09/408 1275), offering good value. The **DOC office** is on Matthews Avenue (Mon–Fri 8am–5pm, ℡09/408 6014).

Accommodation

Accommodation can be tight in peak season, but prices are generally lower than at the coastal resorts to the east, and two attractive places are found outside the town, one at Ninety Mile Beach.

Kaitaia Motor Camp 69 South Rd ℡09/408 1212. Small and fairly ordinary campsite with tent sites ($9), powered sites ($11), communal kitchen and barbecue area.

Main Street Lodge 235 Commerce St ℡09/408 1275, Ⓦwww.tall-tale.co.nz/mainstreet. Welcoming and well-maintained YHA-associate hostel that promotes itself as New Zealand's first Maori backpackers and offers the opportunity to hand-carve bone pendants or weave items from flax; see opposite. They also provide free sand-toboggans to guests. Tent sites $12, dorms ❶, rooms ❷, en-suite rooms ❸

Plane Tree Lodge SH1, near Pamapuria, 10km south of Kaitaia ℡09/408 0995, Ⓦwww.plane-tree-lodge.net.nz. Choose between en-suite B&B in a pleasant timber home or a self-contained two-bedroom cottage attached to the house, all set in big, peaceful, English-style gardens. B&B ❻, cottage ❼

Sierra Court 65 North Rd ℡0800/666 022 & 09/408 1461, Ⓔsierracourt.kaitaia@xtra.co.nz. Attractive motor lodge with swimming and spa pools along with a selection of studios and larger units. ❹

Taharangi Marie Lodge 700 Sandhills Rd, Ninety Mile Beach, 15 km from Kaitaia ℡09/406 7462, Ⓦwww.90mile.co.nz. Luxury B&B or self-contained cottage sleeping four, in the grassy dunes right beside Ninety Mile Beach, with hosts well versed in Maori culture. The modern home has two en-suites (around $250 per room) and has Sky TV and a spa pool. Generous, excellent dinner is supplied on request ($50–65). B&B ❾, cottage ❼, plus $25 per extra person.

Eating and drinking

Beachcomber Restaurant 222 Commerce St ℡09/408 2010. Licensed restaurant strong on seafood but also with steaks ($25) and ostrich. The lunch menu also offers lighter fare including lamb koftas and pasta dishes for under $15, plus a range of veggie dishes. Closed Sat lunch and all day Sun.

Bushman's Hut Steak House 7 Bank St ℡09/408 4320. Licensed dinner restaurant decorated in rustic style serving a wide range of burgers, chicken dishes, fish and steaks at reasonable prices.

C14 14 Commerce St. Probably the pick of Kaitaia's cafés, open from breakfast until lunch (and dinner in summer), and serving up large portions of hearty Kiwi food at modest prices. Closed Sun in winter.

The Gecko 92 Commerce St. Kaitaia's best espresso is served at this daytime venue, open from around 7am – they also dish up muffins, sandwiches, nachos and the like. Closed Sun.

Kauri Arms Commerce St. Possibly the most popular of Kaitaia's workaday pubs, drumming up custom with local bands at weekends.

Sea Dragon 185 Commerce St ℡09/408 0555. Reasonably priced licensed and BYO Chinese restaurant and takeaway, for lunch Mon–Fri and dinner nightly.

Ahipara and the gumfields

At the southern curl of Ninety Mile Beach and on the west coast lies **AHIPARA**, a secluded scattered village 15km west of Kaitaia that grew up around the Ahipara gumfields. Bus tours along Ninety Mile Beach turn off long before reaching here but the long sandy crescent of Ahipara Bay attracts plenty of attention. **Quadbikers** are drawn to the expanse of beach and to impressive dunes nearby, which are great for sand tobogganing. But people also come for surfing, to walk in the gumfields, and to take a locally run bus tour to Cape Reinga. Ahipara is also the finishing point for the local annual marathon, the **Te Houtaewa Challenge** in mid-March (see p.215), run along Ninety Mile Beach and, a few days later, the annual six-man *waka* races of the **Te Houtaewa Surf Challenge** end here too.

To the north, a hundred kilometres of sand recede into sea spray, while to the south the high flatlands of the Ahipara Plateau tumble to the sea in a cascade of golden dunes. Beach and plateau meet at **Shipwreck Bay**, a surf and swimming beach immediately to the west of Ahipara Bay and named for the paddle-shaft of the *Favourite*, wrecked in 1870, which still sticks out of the waves. At low tide you can pick mussels off the volcanic rocks and follow the wave-cut platform around a series of bays for about 5km to the sand dunes – about an hour's walk – although most do it by quadbike or mountainbike. Continue exploring the numerous bays along the shore, and you head deeper and deeper into Maori land (access to the beaches is not restricted).

At their peak in the early twentieth century, the **gumfields,** on a remote sandy dune plateau to the south of town, supported three hotels and two thousand people. Unlike most fields, where experimental probing and digging was the norm, here the soil was methodically excavated, washed and sieved to extract the valuable kauri gum (see box on p.224). None of the machinery or dwellings remain on the plateau, but gum can still be found – particularly in the stream that washes down into Shipwreck Bay – and the gumfields make an eerie, desolately beautiful place to explore.

Activities

The best way to explore the dunes and gumfields is on **quadbike** guided tours with Tua Tua Tours (☎09/409 4875, ⒲www.ahipara.co.nz/tuatuatours) whose excursions range from the ninety-minute coastal Reef Rider ($80) to the excellent three-hour Gumfields Safari ($145), which includes some sand boarding. If you can manage without the local knowledge and riding instruction, head out on your own with quadbikes from the Ahipara Adventure Centre, Takahe Street, 100 metres past the store (☎09/409 2055, ⒲www.ahipara.co.nz/adventurecentre; $100 including a sand toboggan). They also rent out sand toboggans, surfboards, kayaks, mountain bikes ($10 per hour up to half-day rates; mountain bikes $25 half-day) and blo-karts (a micro land-yacht; $30 for first 30min and $25 per 30min thereafter), and run guided horse treks, mountain-bike or quadbike trips.

If you'd prefer to let someone else do the driving, take the 16-seater, **four-wheel-drive bus**, Unimog across the dunes and gumfields (book through the Adventure Centre, see above; Wildcat; 4hr, $45), which takes sand toboggans for the drop down the dunes to Tunatuna Beach.

Some accommodation places offer **boogie boards** for use on the dunes. Note that lying headfirst is not a good idea as it causes several injuries a year – try sitting instead or, better still, use a toboggan.

Very keen hikers might prefer to tackle the same area on a 6hr section of the tide-dependent **Gumfields Walk** (10km loop; free maps and tide times from the Ahipara Adventure Centre and *Main Street Lodge* in Kaitaia), which begins at the bridge at Shipwreck Bay and takes you into an eerie and desolate landscape of wind-sculpted dunes, then back along the beach. Let someone know where you're going and keep your eyes peeled for dull-looking lumps of kauri gum (if you're lucky you'll spot the tip of a big piece – digging with your hands might yield treasure), which can be polished up later. Take plenty of water and keep out of the way of the quadbikes.

Another shorter worthwhile **walk** takes you from the western end of the beach to a **lookout** (500m, 10min return), giving spectacular views all the way to Cape Reinga. The track begins at the end of Foreshore Road, which is unsealed for its last 3km.

Practicalities

Ahipara lies about eighteen kilometres southwest of Kaitaia, along a minor sealed road that's not served by public transport. Basing yourself here is a broadly more appealing proposition than staying in Kaitaia, even though there is no supermarket (a small store instead) or bank. The village is divided into two parts: on the main road, Takahe Street, are the store and the Adventure Centre (daily 9.30am–5pm; ℡09/409 2055, ⓦwww.ahipara.co.nz/adventure-centre), which acts as the focal point for **information**. Near the store you turn off for the beach along Foreshore Road.

When it comes to **eating** there's just a takeaway on Takahe St (summer breakfast–7pm, rest of the year from lunch) and one licensed dinner restaurant (and bar snacks in summer), the *Bayview Restaurant*, at *Ahipara Bay Motel*, 22 ReefView Rd (℡09/409 4888), which has poor service and food but benefits from sea views.

Accommodation

Virtually all the **accommodation** offers self-catering, and the village gets packed out for two weeks at Christmas.

Ahipara Bay Motel 22 Reef View Rd ℡09/409 4888, ⓦwww.ahipara.co.nz/adriaan. Opt for one of the six new units, which have tremendous sea views, although it's best to avoid the in-house restaurant/bar (see above). ⓺

Ahipara Motor Camp Takahe St ℡09/409 4864, ⓦwww.ahipara.co.nz. Basic campsite 5mins walk from the sea with camping ($10), basic cabins and self-contained cabins (⓷).

Beach Abode 11 Korora St ℡09/409 4070, ⓦwww.beachabode.co.nz. Two well-appointed beachfront units (one studio, the other 2-bedroom), each with a full kitchen, barbecue, deck and great views to the sea. Meals are available on request (breakfast $12; three-course dinner $35). Studio ⓹, 2-bedroom unit ⓹, plus $20 per extra person.

Endless Summer Lodge 245 Foreshore Rd ℡09/409 4181, ⓦwww.endlesssummer.co.nz. A relaxing and well-managed hostel in a fine 1880 homestead with kauri floors and fittings, which looks right onto the beach. It offers four comfortable doubles, two twins, and two 4-bed dorms, plus a herb garden and a BBQ; there are also free boogie boards and surf boards ($20) for guests. Dorms ⓵, rooms ⓶

Shipwreck Lodge 70 Foreshore Rd ℡09/409 4929, ⓦwww.shipwrecklodge.co.nz. Luxurious B&B right on the beachfront with stylishly furnished en-suite rooms, each opening onto a small private balcony with great sea views; Sky TV and stereo in the guest lounge. Full breakfast is included, and dinner ($65 plus) on request. ⓼

Ninety Mile Beach and Cape Reinga

Northland's final gesture is the **Aupori Peninsula**, a narrow, 100km-long finger of consolidated and grassed-over dunes ending in a lumpy knot of 60-million-year-old marine volcanoes. To Maori it's known as *Te Hika o te Ika*

The best way to experience the phenomenal length and wild beauty of Ninety Mile Beach is to take one of the **bus tours** based in Kaitaia, Ahipara, Mangonui, and Paihia in the Bay of Islands. Those from Paihia are the most numerous but are also the longest (11hr); tours starting further north give you less time in the bus and more for exploring. Paihia-based buses usually pick up along the way. The content varies but in essence the buses do the same trip, a loop up the Aupori Peninsula and back, travelling SH1 in one direction and Ninety Mile Beach in the other, the order being dictated by the tide. Highlights include **boogie boarding or tobogganing** down the huge sand dunes that flank Te Paki Stream; tobogganing is the best option since you sit upright and have more control; but if you're using a boogie board sit on it rather than lying down headfirst, which can lead to injury. Most of the companies give discounts to carriers of backpacker cards.

From Kaitaia there are currently three main bus companies (and a smaller independent), two of which run virtually identical trips to the cape: Harrison's Cape Runner, 123 North Rd (T09/408 1033 & 0800/227 373, Wwww.ahipara.co.nz/cape-runner; $40), and Sand Safaris, 221 Commerce St (T09/408 1778 & 0800/869 090, Wwww.sandsafaris.co.nz), who charge around $5 more and include a guided tour around the Gumdiggers Park. White Sand Adventures, based at Kaitaia and Ahipara (T07/863 5039; $55), also throw in a boat trip across Parengarenga Harbour to the remote white sands of Kokata Sandspit and offer pick-ups from Houhora and Pukenui for $10 less. All collect you from your accommodation around 9am and return around 5pm – they'll also drop you off and pick you up later if you want to do the three-day walk at Cape Reinga (see p.217). Alternatively, it's worth trying to get a group together (minimum 6) for the small-group trips run by Tall Tale Travel 'n' Tours, 237a Commerce St (T09/408 0870, Wwww.tall-tale.co.nz; $60 including picnic lunch, $90 including BBQ lunch), which emphasize the spiritual significance of the area for Maori through traditional stories, and usually includes shellfish gathering and a barbecue.

From Ahipara three companies operate: Wildcat (book through Ahipara Adventure Centre T09/409 2055; 8hr, $55 including picnic lunch); White Sand (see "From Kaitaia", above); and the more exclusive tour option, Outback Adventures (T09/408 0927, Wwww.farnorthtours.co.nz; 8hr, around $100, including morning tea and lunch), who take a maximum of five people off the beaten track in a four-wheel-drive rather than a bus, on tailor-made tours giving you the option to explore flora and fauna as well as archeological sites. They also have sole access among the tour groups to the white sands of Great Exhibition Bay.

From Mangonui, Paradise Connexion Tours (T0800/494 392 & 09/406 0460, Econnexion@xtra.co.nz) charge $55 for a bus tour including pick-up from your accommodation, and also have 4WDs for customized tours for up to four people ($450 day).

From Paihia, the two big cruise companies, King's and Fullers, dominate the Cape Reinga tour market. Most trips run daily, leaving at around 7.30am, returning about eleven hours later, and going via Kerikeri, Mangonui and Awanui in one direction and

("The tail of the fish"), recalling the legend of Maui hauling up the North Island ("the fish") from the sea while in his canoe (the South Island).

The most northerly accessible point on the peninsula is **Cape Reinga**, believed by Maori to be the "place of leaping", where the spirits of the dead depart. Beginning their journey by sliding down the roots of an 800-year-old pohutukawa into the ocean, they climb out again on Ohaua, the highest of the Three Kings Islands, to bid a final farewell before returning to their ancestors

passing Kaitaia and the kauri trees of the Puketi Forest in the other. King's (℡09/402 8288) run the all-in Cape Reinga Scenic ($90, plus $10 for picnic lunch). Fullers (℡09/402 7421) operate swanky, custom-designed buses on the sightseeing-oriented Cape Reinga Wanderer ($95, $110 with optional BBQ lunch), with sand tobogganing, swimming and shellfish digging. Both companies offer ten percent discounts if you sign up for both a cruise and a cape trip. Those young at heart or with a more adventurous spirit generally go with Awesome Adventures (℡09/402 6985; $95), who allow you to jump on or off and to stop at the top (helpful for the Te Paki walks); or Northern Exposure Tours (℡09/402 8644 & 0800/573 875; $85), who offer a fun, unstructured type of tour and also pick up from Kerikeri and all points en-route; or one of the smaller operators, who use more modest vehicles and take a less rigid approach, letting the group fine-tune the itinerary and not fussing overly if things run past the scheduled return time. Among the trips on offer from ④4 Dune-Rider (℡09/402 8681, ⑩www.dunerider.co.nz; $90, with a 10 percent discount for backpacker cards) are the personalised cape trips daily in a small and comfortable 4WD bus, so you can get right off the beaten track group and make several stops; they also pick up in **Kaeo**, **Mangonui**, **Taipa** and **Awanui**, and will drop you off and pick you up another day at no extra cost.

If you're intent on seeing Cape Reinga and not bothered about driving along Ninety Mile Beach, you can **drive to the Cape** via the main road and avoid the beach alto-gether. Alternatively you can **fly** there from Paihia with Salt Air (℡0800/475 582 & 09/402 8338; $345), who land at Waitiki Landing and cover the last section to Cape Reinga by 4WD, and take you to an east-coast beach and a west-coast beach; or from Kaitaia with Blue Sky Scenics (℡09/406 7320; 1hr 15min, $135).

Going it alone on Ninety Mile Beach
Rental cars and private vehicles are not insured to drive on Ninety Mile Beach – and for good reason. Vehicles frequently get bogged in the sand and abandoned by their occupants. If you get stuck there are no rescue facilities near enough to get you out before the tide comes in, and mobile phone coverage is almost nil: you could end up with a long walk.

If you are determined to take your own vehicle for a spin on the beach, seek local advice and prepare your long-suffering car by spraying some form of water repellent on the ignition system – CRC is a common brand. Schedule your trip to coincide with a receding tide, starting two hours after high water and preferably going in the same direction as the bus traffic that day; drive close to the water's edge, avoiding any soft sand, and slow down to cross streams running over the beach – they often have deceptively steep banks. If you do get stuck in soft sand, lowering the tyre pressure will improve traction. There are several access points along the beach, but the only ones realistically available to ordinary vehicles are the two used by the tour buses: the southern access point at **Waipapakauri Ramp**, 6km north of Awanui, and the more dangerous northern one along **Te Paki Stream**, which involves nego-tiating the quicksands of a river – start in low gear and don't stop, no matter how tempting it might be to ponder the dunes.

in Hawaiiki. The spirits reach Cape Reinga along **Ninety Mile Beach** (which is actually around 64 miles long), a wide band of sand running straight along the western side of the peninsula. Most visitors follow the spirits, though they do so in modern buses specifically designed for belting along the hard-packed sand at the edge of the surf – officially part of the state highway system – then negotiating the quicksands of Te Paki Stream to return to the road. The main road runs more-or-less down the centre of the peninsula, while the western ocean is kept tantalizingly out of sight by the thin pine ribbon of the **Aupori Forest**. The forests, and the cattle farms that cover most of the rest of the peninsula, were once the preserve of gum diggers, who worked the area intensively early this century. The last twenty kilometres of the drive to Cape Reinga on the main road are the hardest – on an unsealed and twisty road, shared with tour buses – so leave yourself plenty of time and remember not to park on a bend when you stop to take photos.

If you've made it this far north, you'll already be familiar with the paucity of facilities in rural Northland, so the Aupori Peninsula doesn't come as much of a surprise. There's sporadic **accommodation** along the way, ranging from some beautifully sited DOC campsites to motels, lodges and hostels. Most are reasonably priced, reflecting the fact that many visitors pass through without stopping; however, all are very busy immediately after Christmas. There are a few **places to eat**, though nothing stays open after around 8pm. Pukenui and Waitiki both have a shop and expensive **petrol**.

Awanui

AWANUI, 8km north of Kaitaia on SH1, is a dilapidated rural backwater notable chiefly for being the meeting point of the eastern and western roads north. The name is Maori for "Big River", though all you'll find is a bend in a narrow tidal creek that makes a great setting for the *Big River Café*, on SH10 and near the junction with SH1, which has some of the best eating hereabouts, until around 9pm in summer, 4.30pm in winter.

Almost all buses to Cape Reinga stop 1km north at the **Ancient Kauri Kingdom** (daily 8.30am–5pm; free), a defunct dairy factory now operating as a sawmill, cutting and shaping huge peat-preserved kauri logs hauled out of swamps where they have lain for between 30,000 and 50,000 years. You can wander around parts of the factory and watch slabs of wood being fashioned into all manner of things. Predictably, the emphasis is on the shop but be sure to climb up to the mezzanine on the spiral staircase hewn out of the centre of the largest piece of swamp kauri trunk ever unearthed, a monster three and a half metres in diameter.

Some 12km to the north of the Kauri Kingdom, 3km off SH1 and on Heath Road, the **Gumdiggers Park** (Tues–Sun 9am–5pm; $7) features an easy twenty-minute trail through manuka forest, leading past holes in the ground excavated by diggers early last century.

The main southern entrance to Ninety Mile Beach, the **Waipapakauri Ramp**, is just south of the Gumdiggers Park turn-off. You can **stay** near the ramp at *The Park*, (☎0800/367 719 & 09/406 7298, ⓦ www.ninetymilebeach .co.nz; camping $13, cabins ❸), a well-equipped Top 10 campsite five minutes' walk from the beach and with its own restaurant bar; or at Awanui at the modern *Norfolk Motel*, at the corner of SH10 and SH1 (☎0800/266 736 & 09/406 7515, ⓦ www.norfolkmotel.co.nz; ❺) in units with Sky TV and a heated pool and spa; they also have campervan sites ($10).

Houhora and Pukenui

Around 30km north of Awanui are the Aupori Peninsula's two largest settlements: scattered **HOUHORA**, and the working fishing village of **PUKENUI**, 2km to the north, where good catches are to be had off the wharf. At Houhora, a three-kilometre side road turns east to **Houhora Heads** and a campsite, a café with great harbour views and a couple of museums that are worth a look. It was here in 1860 that Polish pioneers – two brothers and their widowed

The legend of Te Houtaewa and the marathon

Each year competitors from around the world take part in a series of running, walking and *waka* events on Ninety Mile Beach in mid-March, originally inspired by the tale of a great Maori athlete.

According to legend, **Te Houtaewa**, the fastest runner of his day, enjoyed playing pranks on the enemies of his people. One day his mother asked him to collect some *kumara* from the gardens at Te Kao towards the northern end of the beach, but instead Te Houtaewa ran off south over the hard sands to annoy the **Te Rarawa** people living in Ahipara. Soon after, Te Houtaewa was spotted filling two large *kete* (baskets) from the Te Rarawa storehouse, and a line of people gathered to block his way back to the beach. Sprinting up a hill, Te Houtaewa drew his enemies in pursuit. After waiting for the Te Rarawa to draw close, Te Houtaewa (still clasping the baskets) ran back onto the beach, sending his pursuers sprawling. The Te Rarawa dispatched their best athletes in response, but despite his heavy load Te Houtaewa outran and outwitted them, arriving home to find the *hangi* hot, in readiness for his stolen *kumara*.

Today events range from the mammoth **Te Houtaewa Challenge**, a sixty-kilometre open marathon run by international competitors on a Saturday in mid-March and ending at Ahipara, to a six-kilometre **Walk for Life**. In the **Te Houtaewa Surf Challenge**, a few days after the marathon, a six-man *waka* race against each other, in 1000-, 3,000 and 5,000-metre sprints, finishing at Ahipara; again, anyone can enter. Contact Tall Tale Promotion (☎09/408 0870, ⓦwww.tall-tale.co.nz) for entry forms; fees are $50–70, depending on the event. The races are preceded by two weeks by a **Maori Arts and Food Festival**, held in and around *Main Street Lodge*, a hostel in Kaitaia (see p.209).

mother built the **Subritzky Homestead** (45min guided tours at 11.30am, 1.30pm & 3.30pm, $7.50; private tours outside these times $15; phone ahead on ☎09/409 8850). Although largely restored to its original state, some rooms still reflect the style of later inhabitants, particularly the last resident, Uncle Fred, who lived here until 1960. The best guide is Keith Wagener, one of the family's descendants, who brings the house and its family to life with his dry sense of humour and entertaining yarns. Back in the café building at the end of Houhora Heads Road is the **Wagener Historic Gallery** (daily: late Oct to early April 8.30am–5pm; rest of the year 10am–4pm; free), showing displays from archaeological digs at Mount Carmel, just across the harbour. The finds are believed to be among the oldest in New Zealand, shown alongside an excellent collection of kauri gum.

Practicalities

The area around Houhora and Pukenui has the greatest concentration of **places to stay** on the Aupori Peninsula. There are a couple of options close to the Subritzky Homestead including the spacious self-contained A-frame chalets of the *Houhora Chalets Motor Lodge*, cnr SH1 & Houhora Heads Rd (☎09/409 8860, ⓔchalets@xtra.co.nz; ➌), set in parklike grounds with a swimming pool. Alternatively, the beautifully sited *Houhora Heads Motor Camp*, Houhora Heads Rd (☎09/409 8564, ⓦwww.northlandholiday.co.nz; camping $10–12, on-site caravans ➋ plus $12 for power, backpacker dorms ➊, rooms ➋), right by the harbour heads – the backpacker rooms (4-bed rooms and 2-bunk rooms, plus a few doubles) are in the best spot and have their own kitchen. Guests can hire kayaks to ride to the local beach and mountain bikes for rides through forest to Ninety Mile Beach (both $15 a half-day), and there's

Internet access in the adjacent café. Two kilometres north of the Houhora Heads turnoff, back on SH1F, is the extremely hospitable *Houhora Lodge & Homestay* (☏09/409 7884, ⓦwww.topstay.co.nz; ❺), a stylish modern house offering en-suite rooms, a BBQ and great food making use of their organic veggie garden. **In Pukenui**, the YHA-affiliate *Pukenui Lodge,* cnr SH1 & Wharf Rd (☏09/409 8837, ⓔpukenui@igrin.co.nz; dorms ❶, rooms ❷, units ❸), offers plain, self-catering motel units, as well as doubles, and dorms in an old, basic house with its own kitchen, all occupying a lush, landscaped site with harbour views, a nice pool and barbecue area. Some 9km north, a side road winds 6km east to the excellent and secluded *North Wind Lodge Backpackers*, Otaipango Rd, Henderson Bay (☏09/409 8515, ⓦwww.northwind.co.nz; 5-bed dorms ❶, rooms ❷; no credit cards), a house with good facilities (including a small shop) 5 minutes' walk from a small pink-sand beach, 15 minutes to fine surfing at Henderson Beach (free boogie boards); pick-ups from Pukenui also available. Or you can B&B at the waterfront *Deepwater Lodge*, on the main road (☏09/409 8573, ⓔclubhouhora@paradise.net.nz; B&B ❺, cottage ❻), which has one en-suite king-sized double, and a double and a twin sharing a bathroom; next door there's a self-contained sunny cottage, also looking onto the harbour, with a double room and two single beds.

The only **place to eat** is the modern *Pukenui Pacific* on SH1 at Pukenui (☏09/409 8816), a good-value café bar and takeaway with harbour views (from 10am; the kitchen closes at 8pm); but you can always seek refuge at the waterside *Houhora Tavern*, 2km north of Pukenui, which is often claimed as New Zealand's northernmost pub.

The Parengarenga Harbour, Te Kao and Waitiki Landing

Beyond Houhora the road runs out of sight of the sea, though side roads give opportunities to reach the east coast, particularly at **Rarawa**, 10km north of Pukenui, where the fine sandy beach is as white as you'll find anywhere, and comes backed by a shady streamside DOC **campsite** ($6), 4km off SH1.

The white sands stretch over thirty kilometres north of Rarawa to the straggling **Parengarenga Harbour**, a place largely forgotten by most New Zealanders until 1985, when it was identified as the drop-off point for the limpet mines (delivered by yacht from New Caledonia) that were used to sabotage the *Rainbow Warrior*. Bends in the road occasionally reveal glimpses of the silica sands of the harbour's southern headland, which are pure white except in late February and early March, when hundreds of thousands of bar-tailed godwits turn the vista black as they gather for their 12,000km journey to Siberia.

This whole area is intensely Maori. The Ngati Kuri people own much of the land and comprise the bulk of the population, particularly in the settlement of **TE KAO**, just south of the harbour on SH1. The only reason to stop here, however, is for the twin-towered Ratana Temple, on the main road just before you reach the community – one of the few remaining houses of the Ratana religion, which combines Christian teachings with elements of Maori culture and spiritual belief.

The last place of any consequence before the land sinks into the ocean is **WAITIKI LANDING**, the end of the tarmacked road 21km from Cape Reinga and home to the last petrol station before the Cape, a shop and the *Waitiki Landing Complex* (☏09/409 7508, ⓔwaitiki.landing@xtra.co.nz; camping $7, backpacker rooms ❶, cabins ❸), with its campsite, timber-lined cabins, BBQ, smokehouse, and restaurant bar open till around 8pm for dinners (around $22) and takeaways; book as far ahead as you can for accommodation. The complex also rents boards for riding the dunes ($8 for 4hr) and can arrange transport for trampers wanting to be dropped off or picked up at the start or end of a walk. Alternatively you could join one of the very informative guided **hikes or kayak trips** run by Pack or Paddle Kayaking or Fishing (☏09/409 8445), based 2km south of Waitiki Landing beside SH1. Trips can be designed to suit, but expect to pay $125 a day, including backpacker-style accommodation.

From Waitiki Landing, a dirt road twists 15km to the gorgeous and usually deserted seven-kilometre sweep of **Spirits Bay** (Kapowairau), where you'll find a DOC **campsite** ($6) with pitches in manuka woods and cold showers. The main road continues towards Cape Reinga, passing a turn-off after 6km to the **Te Paki Stream entrance** to Ninety Mile Beach, where there's a small picnic area and parking, plus a twenty-minute **hike** to some huge sand dunes.

Cape Reinga

The last leg to **Cape Reinga** runs high through the hills before revealing the Tasman Sea and the huge dunes that foreshadow it. Magnificent seascapes unfold until you are deposited at the scruffy Cape Reinga car park, where you'll find toilets but little else. A well-trodden ten-minute path heads from here to the Cape Reinga **lighthouse**, dramatically perched on a headland 165m above Colombia Bank, where the waves of the Tasman Sea meet the swirling currents of the Pacific Ocean in a boiling cauldron of surf. On clear days the view from here is stunning: east to the Surville Cliffs of North Cape, west to Cape Maria van Diemen, and north to the rocky **Three Kings Islands**, 57km offshore, which were named by Abel Tasman, who first came upon them on the eve of Epiphany 1643.

Several dramatic **walks** radiate from the car park through scrub, sand and dunes giving great views: west to the long sweeping **Te Werahi Beach** (1.25km, 30min one way); or steeply east to great views and **Sandy Bay** (30min one way), continuing to the lovely **Tapotupotu Bay** (4.5km from the car park, a further 2hr one way) – the latter can also be reached by road and is a popular lunchtime picnic stop for tour buses. All these walks are described in the DOC leaflet *Cape Reinga and Te Paki Walks* ($1), containing a useful map of the area, available at Kaitaia and elsewhere. Beware of **rip tides** on all the beaches hereabouts and bear in mind the wild and unpredictable nature of the region's weather.

An increasingly popular option is the spectacular **Cape Reinga Coastal Walkway** (134km), which is walked from Kapowairua (Spirits Bay) along the east coast to Cape Reinga, then along the west coast to the impressive dunes of Te Paki Stream. Several Cape Reinga bus-tour operators (see box on p.212) will drop you off and pick you up. You need to be fit and self-sufficient and allow at least three days, bearing in mind that there are only two DOC campsites (both on the east coast), no other facilities, limited fresh water from streams, and mosquitoes at night, especially in summer. The walk also provides a starting point for the shorter strolls outlined above. The **dunes near Te Paki Stream** can also be reached from the end of a road branching off the Cape Reinga Road.

The only places to stay hereabouts are the beautifully located DOC **campsites** at Kapowairua (Spirits Bay) and Tapotupotu Bay (both $6), which come with toilets and cold showers.

Hokianga Harbour

South of Kaitaia, the narrow, mangrove-flanked fissures of **Hokianga Harbour** snake deep inland past tiny and almost moribund communities. For a few days' relaxation, the tranquillity and easy pace of this rural backwater are hard to beat. You will probably spend most of your time on the southern shores, from where the harbour's striking, deep-blue waters beautifully set off the mountainous sand dunes of North Head. The dunes are best seen from the rocky promontory of South Head, high above the treacherous Hokianga Bar, or reached by boat for a little sand tobogganing. The high forest ranges immediately to the south make excellent hiking and horse-trekking territory, and the giant kauri of the Waipoua Forest are within easy striking distance, but the focus is definitely the harbour.

It was from here that the great Polynesian explorer **Kupe** left Aoteaora to go back to his homeland in Hawaiiki during the tenth century, and the harbour thus became known as Hokianganui-a-Kupe, "the place of Kupe's great return". Cook saw the Hokianga Heads in 1770 but didn't realize what lay beyond, and it wasn't until a missionary crossed the hill from the Bay of Islands in 1819 that Europeans became aware of the harbour's existence. Catholics, Anglicans and Wesleyans soon followed, converting the local Ngapuhi, gaining their trust, intermarrying with them and establishing the well-integrated Maori and European communities that exist today. The Hokianga area soon rivalled the Bay of Islands in importance and notched up several firsts: European boat building was begun here in 1826; the first signal station opened two years later; and the first Catholic Mass was celebrated in the same year.

With the demise of kauri felling and milling (for more on which, see p.224), Hokianga became an economic backwater, with little industry, high unemployment and limited facilities. Over the last couple of decades, city dwellers, artists and craftspeople have snapped up bargain properties and moved up here in a small and fairly inconspicuous way, settling in **Kohukohu** on the north shore, **Rawene**, a short ferry ride away to the south, and the two larger but still small-time resorts of **Opononi** and **Omapere**, opposite the dunes near the harbour entrance.

You'll need to stock up with cash before exploring the harbour and kauri forests: there are **no banks** between Kaitaia and Dargaville, 170km away to the south, though all towns have EFTPOS facilities and the *Omapere Tourist Hotel and Motel* in the centre of Omapere will often change travellers' cheques, but at poor rates. The Hokianga region is served by a **visitor centre** in Omapere on SH12 (see p.221).

Kohukohu and the northern Hokianga

Heading south from Kaitaia, the hilly SH1 twists its way through the forested Mangamuka Ranges for 40km to reach **Mangamuka Bridge**, the western entrance to the Omahuta Forest (see p.200), from where a narrower and equally tortuous road heads towards the north shore of the Hokianga Harbour. An alternative route from Kaitaia winds 23km south from the Ahipara road to tiny **HEREKINO**, just a pub, a few houses and the *Tui Inn*, Puhata Rd (℡09/409 3883; beds $15), a fairly primitive backpackers with bargain tent sites ($7.50), where the main lure is the rural Kiwi tenor fostered by the owner, who offers superb horse trekking ($45) and fishing trips.

Both routes converge on **KOHUKOHU**, a blink-and-you-miss-it waterside village on the northernmost arm of Hokianga Harbour. Kohukohu was once the hub of Hokianga's kauri industry, but the subsequent years of decline have only partly been arrested by the recent influx of rat-race refugees, resulting in today's low-key settlement, which mostly consists of attractive, century-old wooden houses. Four kilometres further east at Narrows Landing is the northern terminus of the **Rawene Vehicle Ferry** (T09/405 2602; daily 7.30am–8pm; 15min; car & driver $14 one way, $19 return, pedestrians $2 each way), which runs across the harbour to Rawene, on the hour southbound and half-hour northbound.

The beauty of staying on the north side of the harbour is that there's almost nothing to do. You could try some **bone carving** to make your own *tiki* at Kohukohu Carving Studio, 2km up Rakautapu Rd (by appointment 10am–2pm, T09/405 5802; 3–5hr; $40 per person), while inspired by great hillside views of the harbour; or spend time **kayaking** around the mangroves and harbour with Misty Waters Kayaks (T09/405 5548; from $40).

Practicalities

The Kohukohu area makes a delightful place for a brief sojourn because of its excellent **places to stay**. Foremost among them is the *Tree House* (T09/405 5855, Wwww.treehouse.co.nz; tent sites $12–14, dorms ❶, house bus ❷, cabins ❸, cottage ❹), at Motukaraka, 2km west of the ferry, where people often stay far longer than they had planned, lulled into submission by the ultra-relaxing bush surroundings. Accommodation is scattered among the trees in two spacious dorms, plus double and twin cabins with sundecks, and a few tent sites; in summer there's also a well-equipped house bus in a macadamia orchard, and just down the road, near the water there's a self-contained two-bedroom cottage. Whichever option you go for you'll need to bring food, though essential supplies are sold at their small shop; and there's Internet access. The tasteful and aptly named *Harbour Views Guesthouse*, 32b Rakautapu Rd, Kohukohu (T & F09/405 5815; ❺), also makes a lovely spot for a peaceful night or two, with shady verandas and dinner for $20.

The Kohukohu **eating and drinking** scene, such as it is, has recently seen a resurgence, with the old pub and general store (the latter closing at 6pm) now supplemented by a quality takeaway, *The Palace Flophouse and Grill*, cnr Kohukohu Rd and Beach Rd (11am–7pm all year, closed Mon; T09/405 5858), which sells fabulous burgers (including lentil, chicken satay and veggie), great smoothies and espresso, and has a few tables inside. Right at the water's edge *The Waterline*, Kohukohu Rd, is a relaxing little licensed café serving great coffee, tasty breakfasts, snacks and lunches, as well as pizza (closed Mon & Tues in winter; also usually closed June & July).

Rawene

The Rawene Vehicle Ferry shuttles for fifteen minutes from Narrows Landing across to appealing **RAWENE**, a slightly livelier village than Kohukohu and occupying the tip of Herd's Point, a peninsula roughly halfway up the harbour. Though almost isolated by the mud flats at low tide, Rawene's strategic position made it an obvious choice for the location of a timber mill, which contributed material for the town's attractive wooden buildings, some perched on stilts out over the water.

On a sunny day Rawene is a pleasant place to saunter around, perhaps strolling along Clendon Esplanade to reach the **Mangrove Walkway**, a pleasant 15-minute return boardwalk through the coastal shallows. On Clendon Esplanade you pass the town's only significant distraction, **Clendon House**

(Nov–April Sat, Sun & Mon 10am–4pm; $4). This was the last residence of James Clendon, a pivotal figure in the early life of the colony. The house wasn't finished until 1868 and Clendon only lived in it for the four years prior to his death. The upper floor has been restored as a child's playroom and schoolroom, and one room beside the veranda has been retained as the post office it once was.

To go **kayaking** on the harbour in sit-on kayaks, contact Hokianga Blue, 49 Parnell St (T 021/263 1171, after hours 09/405 7675), who rent them out at $25 for a half-day; they also run guided tours around the harbour (from 2–3 hours at $35).

Practicalities

Rawene's proximity to the ferry (7.30am–7.30pm) makes it an ideal base for exploring both sides of the harbour. The main thoroughfare, Parnell St, passes the most convenient **accommodation**, the 1875 *Masonic Hotel* (T 09/405 7822, E masonic@igrin.co.nz; ❸), with small yet decent traditional hotel rooms. The hilltop *Rawene Motor Camp*, Marmon St, 1.5km from the ferry landing (T & F 09/405 7720; camping $9 & chalet cabins ❷), has harbour views, tent sites and self-catering cabins in bush enclaves, with a pool and BBQ. A short walk from the shops and cafés is a new self-contained studio, *Hokianga Blue*, 49 Parnell St (T 09/405 7675, W www.hokiangablue.co.nz; ❸ including breakfast), which has a queen-size bed, kitchenette and a private deck overlooking the harbour; dinner by arrangement.

For such a small place you can **eat** well. First stop should be the relaxing *Boatshed Café* (breakfast & lunch only; closed two weeks in Sept), on Clendon Esplanade and a stone's throw from the ferry, which is built out over the water and offers magazines to read on the sunny deck as you tuck into filo parcels or home-made cakes and the best espresso for miles around; they also stock plenty of good-quality local arts and crafts. The *Masonic Hotel* does good bar meals and reasonably priced à la carte dinners, has a peaceful deck overlooking the harbour on which to sup away the afternoon and hosts bands most summer weekends.

Opononi and Omapere

The two small-time resorts of **OPONONI** and **OMAPERE**, some 20km west of Rawene, run seamlessly for 4km along the southern shore of the Hokianga Harbour, with great views across to the massive sand dunes on the north side. Kiwis of a certain age can tell you all about Opononi and the eventful summer of 1955–56 when a wild bottlenose dolphin, dubbed "Opo", started playing with the kids in the shallows and performing tricks with beach balls. At the time dolphin-watching trips were decades away and signs had to be erected discouraging people from shooting the precocious dolphin. And yet Opo's antics captivated the nation: Christmas holidaymakers jammed the narrow dirt roads; film crews were dispatched; protective laws were drafted; and Auckland musicians Pat McMinn, Bill Langford and The Crombie Murdoch Trio cobbled together the novelty song, "Opo The Crazy Dolphin". Written and recorded in a day, the tape arrived at the radio station for its first airing just as news of Opo's untimely death broke – the song was still a hit.

Opononi has dined out on its fifteen minutes of fame ever since, though the only concrete reminders are a statue of Opo in the car park outside the *Opononi Resort Hotel* and her grave next door outside the War Memorial Hall. To get a better sense of the frenzied enthusiasm for Opo, head to Omapere –

just a roadside string of clapboard houses and a few places to stay and eat – where the local museum inside the visitor centre (see below) shows a short video in classic 1950s documentary style.

The only other attraction is **Labyrinth Woodworks**, Waiotemarama Gorge Rd, 6km southeast of Opononi (daily; they open the shop when you beep the horn; ☏09/405 4581), one of the region's better craft shops, whose wares include carved kauri pieces and excellent woodblock prints by noted local craftsman Allan Gale. There are also puzzles to play with and, from mid-December to April, a maize maze cut through a cornfield.

Activities and walks

Opononi and Omapere make good bases for exploring the surrounding area. The biggest of all the kauri trees, **Tane Mahuta**, is only 22km south of Omapere, and boats ply across the harbour to the sand dunes – though the vistas from the south side are so striking that it's enough just to visit the viewpoints. The most notable of these are immediately west of Omapere: **Arai te Uru Reserve**, along Signal Station Road, and the magical **Pakia Hill**, on SH12.

The **dunes** are most easily visited by boat from the Opononi wharf. Hokianga Express water taxi (☏09/405 8872 & 021 405872; $20) operate from 10am daily and will drop you off with sandboards and pick you up a couple of hours later. Hokianga Kayak Adventures (☏09/405 5844) run a number of guided kayak trips around the harbour, including the popular full-day Golden Gateway to sandboard on the dunes ($65), and a half-day jaunt in the remote mangrove forests of the upper harbour ($45); they also rent out kayaks from $20 for two hours. On land, Okopako Horse Trekking, at *Okopako Lodge* (see p.222), will take you **riding** ($20 per hour) into the bush and the hills, with views over the entire Hokianga Harbour.

The best and most popular of the short walks in the district is the **Waiotemarama Walk**, a two-kilometre loop through a lovely bush–clad valley full of ferns, nikau palms and kauri. From Labyrinth Woodworks, a ten-minute walk gets you to an attractive waterfall with a small swimming hole, and after another ten minutes you reach the first kauri. Another popular outing is the **Hokianga Track** (8km; 3–4hr), which heads from Hokianga South Head along Kaikai Beach and up the Waimamaku River back to SH12. More ambitious walkers could set two or three days aside for the **Waipoua Coast Walkway**, a fifty-kilometre coastal trek that continues south from the Hokianga Track to Maunganui Bluff and on to Kai Iwi Lakes (see p.225). Details are available in DOC's *Waipoua & Trounson Kauri Forests* leaflet ($1) and from visitor centres, though there are few facilities along the track.

Practicalities

Westcoaster run a limited **bus service** through the Hokianga on behalf of InterCity and Northliner (whose passes you can use on them), with a southbound service on Monday, Wednesday and Friday and northbound runs on Tuesday, Thursday and Saturday. They stop by the wharf in Opononi and on the main road in Omapere, outside the Hokianga **visitor centre** (daily 8.30am–5pm; ☏09/405 8869, ⓦwww.hokianga.co.nz), where you can book and buy bus tickets, and get information on the Waipoua Kauri Forest (see p.223), as well as on the more immediate area.

Accommodation

Top-end accommodation is hard to find around the Hokianga, but the twin towns are well served with **hostels** and a range of other options.

Globe Trekkers SH12, Omapere ☏ 09/405 8183, ⊛ www.globetrekkerslodge.com. Hillside hostel with harbour views; the dorms are five-bed and six-bed. Tent sites $10, dorms ❶, rooms ❷

Harbourside B&B SH12, at the western end of Omapere ☏ 09/405 8246. Lovely harbour views from two en-suite rooms with their own entrances and decking. ❹

House of Harmony, SH12, Opononi ☏ 09/405 8778, ⊛ www.geocities.com/harmonybak. Small and cosy hostel that has room for three to four tents; all dorms are four-bed and there's a BBQ. Camping $12–15, dorms ❶, rooms ❷

McKenzie's Accommodation 4 Pioneers Walk, Omapere ☏ 09/405 8068, ✉ dlmk@xtra.co.nz. Beachside options in either a spacious room rented as a double or a twin, with a separate bathroom and private entrance, or a self-contained two-bedroom cottage. B&B ❹, cottage ❹ plus $10 each extra person.

Okopako Lodge: The Wilderness Farm Mountain Rd, 5km east of Opononi ☏ & ℻ 09/405 8815. A peaceful combined B&B and YHA-associated hostel, with panoramic views from its hilltop position 1.5km up a twisting unsealed road. Organic farmhouse dinners are available for under $20 and breakfast at $10. They run daily horse treks through native bush to fabulous views. Tent sites $10, dorms ❶, rooms ❷

Omapere Tourist Hotel & Motel SH12, Omapere ☏ 09/405 8737, ⊛ www.omapare.co.nz. The best of the hotels, beautifully set opposite the dunes, with a solar-heated pool, bar and licensed restaurant. Tent sites $10, units ❺, beachfront units ❻, family apartments ❻ plus $15 each extra person.

Opononi Holiday Park SH12, Opononi ☏ 09/405 8791, ✉ harrybarlow@xtra.co.nz. Spacious if basic, harbourside campsite. Camping $11–12, cabins ❷, self-catering cabins ❷

Solitaire Historic Homestay SH12, 10km south of Omapere towards the kauri forests ☏ 09/405 4891, ✉ solitairehomestay@xtra.co.nz. Five comfortable rooms (two en suite) set in attractive gardens. ❺

Eating

Eating possibilities are severely limited. In Opononi there's just *Opo Takeaways* (daily 10am–7pm, later in summer) and the *Opononi Resort Hotel*, which offers the district's best eating, both bar food and daily à la carte. In Omapere the small *Harbourside Café* (by the BP garage) dishes up simple fare, while the *Omapere Tourist Hotel* serves good meals in its elegant yet reasonable à la carte restaurant and bar serving bistro meals, with a varied menu and great views over the lawns and harbour to the sand dunes.

The Kauri Forests and the northern Kaipara Harbour

Northland, Auckland and the Coromandel Peninsula were once covered in mixed forest dominated by the mighty kauri (see box on p.224), the world's second largest tree after the Californian sequoias. By the early years of the twentieth century, rapacious Europeans had felled nearly the lot, the only extensive pockets remaining in the **Waipoua and Trounson kauri forests** south of the Hokianga Harbour. Though small stands of kauri can be found all over Northland, three-quarters of all the surviving mature trees grow in these two small forests, which between them cover barely 100 square kilometres. Walks provide access to the more celebrated examples, which dwarf the surrounding tataire, kohekohe and towai trees.

This area is home to the Te Roroa people who, like their kin in the north, traditionally used the kauri sparingly. Simple tools made felling and working these huge trees a difficult task, and one reserved for major projects such as large war canoes. Once the Europeans arrived with metal tools, bullock trains, wheels and winches, clear felling became more manageable, and most of the trees had gone by the end of the nineteenth century. The efforts of several campaigning organizations eventually bore fruit in 1952, when much of the remaining forest was designated the Waipoua Sanctuary. It's now illegal to fell a kauri except in specified circumstances, such as culling a diseased or dying tree, or when constructing a new ceremonial canoe.

Driving through miles of farmland it's often hard to imagine the same landscape covered in dense forest. This is true of the lands to the south around the muddy shores of **Kaipara Harbour**, a labyrinth of mangrove-choked inlets, drowned valleys and small beaches that constitutes New Zealand's largest harbour. The harbour once unified this quarter of Northland, with sailboats plying its waters and linking the dairy farming and logging towns on its shores. Kauri was shipped out from the largest northern town, **Dargaville**, though the fragile boats all too often foundered on the unpredictable Kaipara Bar and were eventually washed up on **Ripiro Beach**, a fabulous salty strand which just pips Ninety Mile Beach to the title of New Zealand's longest, running for 108km (67 miles). Since the decline of harbour traffic, modern Dargaville itself survives on horticulture and a constant stream of tourists, bound for the kauri forests, who pause to explore the beach and the windswept Kaipara Heads. If you're pushed for time, skip the town in favour of a couple of hours at the **Matakohe Kauri Museum**, 45km south, which gives the best sense of what the kauri meant to the Northland economy and its spiritual significance for Maori.

Very infrequent **buses** run through the kauri forests from Omapere to Dargaville (northbound on Tues, Thurs & Sat; southbound on Mon, Wed & Fri), making a brief stop to glimpse the biggest tree; in addition, two or three buses a day run south from Dargaville, so judicious timing should enable you to see the Kauri Museum and get back again.

Waipoua and Trounson kauri forests

South of the Hokianga Harbour, SH12 twists and turns through nearly 20km of mature kauri in the **Waipoua Kauri Forest**, following the contours of the hills and skirting around the base of the big trees so as to cause minimal damage to their fragile and shallow root system. Just after you enter the forest you reach a small carpark, from where it's a three-minute walk to New Zealand's mightiest tree, the 1200-year-old **Tane Mahuta**, "God of the Forest". A vast wall of bark six metres wide rises nearly 18m to the lowest branches, covered in epiphytes. A kilometre or so further south on SH12, another car park marks the beginning of a ten-minute track to a clearing where three paths lead off to notable trees. The shortest (5min return) runs to the **Four Sisters**, relatively slender kauri all growing close together on the same mound of shed bark. A second path (30min return) twists among numerous big trees to the Big Daddy of them all, **Te Matua Ngahere**, the "Father of the Forest", ranked as the second largest tree in New Zealand on account of its shorter stature than Tane Mahuta but, if anything, more richly festooned in epiphytes than its brothers. The third, the **Yakas Track** (6km; 3hr), leads to the Waipoua Forest visitor centre in summer; even if you don't fancy the full track, walk the first thirty minutes to Cathedral Grove, a dense conglomeration of trees, the largest being the **Yakas Kauri**, named after veteran bushman Nicholas Yakas. This part of the track is open all year, the remaining section usually closes in winter.

In the heart of the Waipoua forest, a side road leads 1km to the **Waipoua Forest visitor centre** (Oct–April Mon–Fri 8.30am–5.30pm, Sat & Sun 9am–5pm; May–Sept Mon–Fri 8.30am–4.30pm, Sat & Sun 9am–4.30pm; ℡09/439 3011 ℮waipouavc@doc.govt.nz). The grounds contain a DOC **campsite** (tent sites $7, 1-bed cabins $8, 2-bed cabins $14 per person,

The **kauri** (*agathis australis*) isn't the tallest species of tree, nor does it boast the greatest girth, but as its gargantuan trunk barely tapers from roots to crown, it ranks alongside the sequoias, or redwoods, of California as one of the largest trees in existence. Unlike the redwoods, which are useless as furniture timber, kauri produce beautiful wood, a fact that hastened their demise and spawned the industries that dominated New Zealand's economy in the latter half of the nineteenth century.

The kauri is a type of pine which now grows only in New Zealand, though it once also grew in Australia and southeast Asia, where it still has close relations. Identifiable remains of kauri forests are found all over New Zealand, but by the time humans arrived on the scene its range had contracted to Northland, Auckland, the Coromandel Peninsula and northern Waikato. Individual trees can live up to 2000 years, reaching 50m in height and 20m in girth, finally toppling over as the rotting core becomes too weak to support its immense weight.

Kauri loggers

Maori have long used mature kauri for dugout canoes, but it was the young "rickers" (young trees) that first drew the attention of **European loggers** since they formed perfect spars for sailing ships. The bigger trees didn't escape attention for long, soon earning an unmatched reputation for their durable, easy-to-work and blemish-free wood, with its straight, fine grain. Loggers' ingenuity was taxed to the limit by the difficulty of getting such huge logs out of the bush. On easier terrain, bullock wagons with up to twelve teams were lashed together to haul the logs on primitive roads or tramways. Horse-turned winches were used on steeper ground and, where water could be deployed to transport the timber, dams were constructed from hewn logs. In narrow valleys and gullies all over Northland and the Coromandel, loggers constructed kauri dams up to 20m high and 60m across, with trap doors at the base. Trees along the sides of the valley were felled while the dam was filling, then the dam was opened to flush the floating trunks down the valley to inlets where the logs were rafted up and towed to the mills.

Gum diggers

Once an area had been logged, the **gum diggers** typically moved in. Like most pines, kauri exudes a thick resin to cover any scars inflicted on it, and huge accretions form on the sides of trunks and in globules around the base, further hardening off in time. In pre-European times, Maori chewed the gum, made torches from it to attract fish at night and burned the powdered resin to form a pigment used for *moko* (traditional tattoos). Once Pakeha got in on the act, it was exported as a raw material for furniture varnishes, linoleum, denture moulds and the "gilt" edging on books. When it could no longer be found on the ground, diggers – mostly Dalmatian, but also Maori, Chinese and Malaysian – thrust long poles into the earth and hooked out pieces with bent rods; elsewhere, the ground was dug up and sluiced to recover the gum. Almost all New Zealand gum was exported, but by the early twentieth century synthetic resins had captured the gum market. Kauri gum is still considered one of the finest varnishes for musical instruments, though prices don't justify collecting it; occasional accidental finds supply such specialist needs.

4-bed cabins $10 per person; bookings essential for cabins, through the visitor centre) with hot showers and a communal kitchen but no utensils; the 2- and 4-bed cabins have their own small kitchens and a stove, plus crockery, cutlery, pots and pans. South of here the highway runs through farmland 6km to the nearest formal **accommodation**, *Waipoua Lodge*, SH12 (℡09/439 0422, ⓦwww.waipoualodge.co.nz; ❼ including breakfast), with four luxurious new apartments in converted farm buildings in the tranquil grounds of a gracious and beautifully restored kauri villa – choose between the woolshed, stables, tack rooms and calf pen. Guests use the lodge for its dining room, lounge and sunroom library; fine evening meals are also available.

Immediately south of Waipoua Lodge, a side road leads to another small but superb stand of kauri, the **Trounson Kauri Park**, which since 1997 has been subject to intensive trapping and poisoning of native-bird predators – possums, stoats, weasels, feral cats, dogs and hedgehogs – to create a "mainland island" where North island brown kiwi can thrive. Numbers are up significantly, and you can join two-hour long guided night-time walks (every night, weather permitting, $15) to see kiwi, weta, glowworms and more from *Kauri Coast Holiday Park*, Trounson Park Rd (T0800/807 200 & 09/439 0621, Ⓔkauricoast.top10@xtra.co.nz; camping $13, dorms ❶, standard cabins ❷, self-catering cabins & motel units ❸). The forest can also be seen from a **short track** from the car park or from the simple but popular DOC campsite ($7), which is equipped with kitchen, toilets and hot showers.

A further 9km south of the Trounson turn-off, Aranga Coast Road branches west to the 460m **Maunganui Bluff**, the northern limit of Ripiro Beach (see p.226). Budget accommodation is available at the appealingly rural *Kaihu Farm Hostel*, on SH12 some 4km south of Aranga Coast Road (T09/439 4004, Ⓔkaihufarm@clear.net.nz; dorms ❶, single room $37, rooms ❷), with 3- and 5-bed dorms, glowworms in the bush and a seven-kilometre walk to the Trounson kauris.

Kai Iwi Lakes

The **Kai Iwi Lakes**, 11km west of SH12 and 20km south of Trounson, are a real change, with pine woods running down to fresh, crystal-blue waters fringed by silica-white sand. All three are dune lakes – relatively common along Northland's western seaboard – fed by rainwater and with no visible outlet. Though the largest, **Taharoa**, is less than a kilometre across, and **Waikere** and **Kai Iwi** are barely a hundred metres long, they constitute the deepest and some of the largest dune lakes in the country. Families flock here in the summer to swim, fish and waterski, but outside the first weeks in January you can usually find a quiet spot. There's no public transport to the lakes, but once here you'll find **accommodation** at the large and well-equipped *Kai Iwi Lakes Campground* (T09/439 8360; tent sites $8), which comprises the Pine Beach site on the gently shelving shores of Taharoa Lake, with water, toilets and cold showers; and the more intimate Promenade Point site with just long-drop toilets. The more substantial *Waterlea* at neighbouring Lake Taharoa (T & Ⓕ09/439 0749; studio unit ❺, house ❼), is just over the road from the lake and consists of a self-contained studio unit and a three-bedroom modern house with Sky TV; both have great views, and mountain bikes and kayaks for rent.

Walkers can follow the beach north from here to **Maunganui Bluff** (10km, 2hr one way) and walk back, or return along Aranga Coast Road inland (7km; 1hr 30min) to pick up a bus on SH12, which you wave down in the absence of a bus-stop (southbound Mon, Wed & Fri at about 12.15pm; northbound Tues, Thurs & Sat at about 12.30pm); or continue north along the **Waipoua Coast Walkway** to the Hokianga Harbour (about 50km, 3 days), walking at low tide only; detailed maps are available from the information centre at Dargaville.

Dargaville and around

Sleepy **DARGAVILLE**, 30km south of Kai Iwi Lakes, is trying to shake off its cow-town image by pitching itself as the capital of the so-called Kauri Coast, an amorphous region encompassing everywhere south from the Hokianga down and around the Kaipara. In fact it's more a service town for the region's farming community, traditionally dairy-based but burgeoning into the country's top kumara-growing district. The town was founded as a port in 1872, on the strongly tidal but navigable Northern Wairoa River, by an Australian, Joseph McMullen Dargaville. Ships came to load kauri logs and transport gum (see box on p.224) extracted by Dalmatian settlers who, by the early part of the twentieth century, formed a sizeable portion of the community. A building on Normanby Street still proclaims itself the Yugoslav Social Hall, and a statue on Hokianga Road of a jolly little gum digger commemorates their presence.

The town

The only specific sight is the **Dargaville Museum** (daily 9am–4pm; $5), in the hilltop Harding Park, 2km west of town and marked by two masts rescued from the *Rainbow Warrior* (see box on p.201). It contains extensive displays of artefacts recovered from the shifting dunes, which occasionally reveal old shipwrecks. The only pre-European artefact is the Ngati Whatua *waka*, which lay buried under the sands of the North Head of the Kaipara Harbour from 1809 until 1972, and is a rare example of a canoe hewn entirely with stone tools. A fine collection of kauri gum gives pride of place to an 84kg piece, reputedly the largest ever found.

Back at the western end of town, at the **Woodturners Kauri Gallery & Working Studio**, 4 Murdoch St/SH12 and near the junction with River Rd (T09/439 4975, E kauri4u@hotmail.com; daily 9am till dark), leading woodturner Rick Taylor demonstrates what can be done with the extraordinarily varied grains and colours of kauri, sells all manner of kauri products, and runs courses for those prepared to dedicate a day or more. There's a more industrial approach at **Zizania**, 90 River Rd, a working paper mill that puts the Manchurian wild rice grasses that grow hereabouts to good use in all manner of paper products, sold through the shop (Mon–Fri 9am–5pm; phone to check on public holidays). Tours (30–40min, $5; T09/439 0217) take place when numbers warrant or you can try just asking.

Baylys Beach and Ripiro Beach

West of Dargaville a minor road runs 14km to **Baylys Beach**, a conglomeration of mostly holiday homes on a central section of **Ripiro Beach**, the longest driveable beach in New Zealand (best done on a guided tour). The sands of Ripiro Beach are renowned for their mobility, with several metres of beach often being shifted by a single tide, and huge areas being reclaimed over the centuries; the anchors or prows of long-lost wrecks periodically reappear through the sand. As elsewhere on the West Coast, tidal rips and holes make swimming dangerous and there are no beach patrols. Beach driving is no less fraught with danger and shouldn't be undertaken without prior local consultation; vehicles frequently get stranded. Nevertheless, it's a fine place for long moody walks, digging up tua tua, the locally renowned shellfish (you find them with your feet by doing a sort of twist), and spotting seals and penguins in winter. When easterlies are blowing the coastline is adorned with kites, flown out from the shore and drawing fishing lines for anything up to a kilometre. They're left for twenty minutes or so then kite and line are hauled in, hopefully heavy with fish.

Several local operators run trips on Ripiro Beach and around the northern Kaipara Harbour, sometimes linking together to offer interesting combinations. If you fancy riding on **horseback** along the sands, try the excellent two-hour trips run by Baylys Beach Horse Treks (☏09/439 6630; $50).

Tours on wheels

Several operators run beach tours in specially designed vehicles, and some link with others to add quadbiking on dunes or cruising on the water. Call in advance as minimum numbers apply, and outside the peak summer season you may find little happening.

4x4 Sandcruiser Tours ☏09/439 8360. 4WD tour combined with a short harbour cruise on the *Kewpie To*; $45–60.
Kaipara Action Experience ☏09/439/1400, ⊛www.kaiparaaction.co.nz. Combined trips in a powerful catamaran from Dargaville to Pouto Point, where they connect with a sand vehicle to drive back along Ripiro Beach; $78–95 return.
Pete's Safari Tours ☏09/439 0515, ⒺInfo@petesafari.co.nz. Small personalized tours are taken along the beach in a Landrover, visiting the Kai Iwi Lakes and kauri forests (from

2hr, $45); an alternative excursion overnight to Pouto Point.
Pouto 4x4 Quad Tours ☏09/439 4298. Organized tours hook up with both Taylor Made Tours and 4x4 Sandcruiser Tours to take people quadbiking over the sand and dunes; $50 per hour.
Taylor Made Tours ☏09/439 1576 A specially designed six-wheeled truck operates along a wild and exposed section of Ripiro Beach to the disused Kaipara lighthouse, taking in shipwrecks on the way; full-day $55.

Practicalities

Two **bus** services stop on Kapia Street in Dargaville: InterCity (operated by Westcoast) runs between Paihia and Kaiwaka, where it connects with services to Auckland; and Mainline (☏09/278 8070) run direct from Dargaville to Auckland. Tickets for both are available from the **visitor centre**, 69 Normanby St (Mon–Fri 8.30am–5pm, Sat & Sun 10am–4pm, with extended hours in summer; ☏09/439 8360, Ⓔinfo@kauricoast.co.nz), which also has comprehensive accommodation listings for the region and **Internet access**.

Accommodation

Dargaville has a reasonable range, though you might prefer the sands of Baylys Beach or the solitude of Pouto Point.

Greenhouse Hoste 13 Portland St, Dargaville ☏09/439 6342, Ⓕ439 6327. A former 1920s schoolhouse in the town centre. Dorms ❶, single room $28, rooms ❷
Hunky Dory 29 Kelly St, Baylys Beach ☏09/439 0922, Ⓔaymditch@paradise.net.nz. Cheerful and intimate hostel near the beach. Dorms ❶, room ❷
Northern Wairoa Hotel crnr of Victoria St and Hokianga Rd, Dargaville ☏09/439 8923. Traditional pub beds (some en suite) in a 1922 hotel. ❸
Dargaville Motel 217 Victoria St, Dargaville ☏0800/466 835 & 09/439 7734. One of several reasonable motels, this one offering a view over the river and a lock-up garage for bikes. ❹
Kauri House Lodge Bowen St, Dargaville ☏09/439 8082, Ⓔkaurihouse@infomace.co.nz.

The town's grandest rooms in an engagingly low-key yet vast kauri villa with big en-suite rooms, a billiard room, library and swimming pool. ❼
Dargaville Holiday Park 10 Onslow St, Dargaville ☏0800/114 441 & 09/439 8296, Ⓔdargavilleholidaypark@xtra.co.nz. Well-managed site and hostel only 10 minutes' walk from town, providing a good range of cabins and units set in secluded park-like grounds. Camping $11, dorms ❶, cabins ❷, units ❹
Baylys Beach Holiday Park 24 Seaview Rd, Baylys Beach ☏09/439 6349, ⊛www.baylys-beach.co.nz. Well-run place, a short walk from the beach. Some of the cabins are en suite and the cottage sleeps seven; there are also quad bikes for rent at $60 for the first hour. Camping $10, caravans ❷, cabins ❷, units ❹, cottage ❺ plus $12 each extra person.

Lighthouse Lodge Pouto Point ☎0800/439 515, ⓦ www.lighthouse-lodge.co.nz. An hour's drive south and worth it for the isolation, fantastic harbour and sea views, comfortable en-suite rooms and three-course dinners from $30. **❼**

Eating

Eating in Dargaville is nothing special, though the *New Asian Restaurant*, 73 Victoria St (BYO & licensed), dishes up tolerable Chinese meals and take-aways, while the *Northern Wairoa Hotel* is locally renowned for its bargain pub meals and Sunday buffet served in an unusually elegant restaurant. A good alternative is to drive out to Baylys Beach to the *Funky Fish*, 34 Seaview Rd (reserve in advance for dinner in summer and for Sunday lunch all year ☎09/439 8883), a groovy modern café and bar where you'll find great fish and chips, a speciality beer-battered dory with chargrilled lemon and salad, plus a range of burgers, baguettes and a varied à la carte evening menu (summer daily from 11am; winter closed Mon lunch), and a great garden bar. Baylys Beach also has a store for basic groceries and takeaways.

Matakohe and the Kauri museum

South of Dargaville, SH12 runs 45km south to Matakohe, passing through countryside that is mostly flat except for the knobby **Tokatoka Peak**, 17km south of Dargaville. There are wonderfully panoramic views from the 180-metre summit of this extinct volcanic plug, reached in ten breathless minutes from a trailhead 1km off SH12 near the *Tokatoka* pub.

If there's one museum you must see in the north it's the **Kauri Museum**, Church Rd (daily: Nov–April 8.30am–5.30pm; April–Oct daily 9am–5pm; $12; ⓦ www.kauri-museum.com), on the outskirts of the village of **MATAKOHE**, 45km south of Dargaville. One of the best museums in the country, and deserving at least a couple of hours, it explains the way the second-largest tree in the world, the kauri, shaped the lives of pioneers in Northland through its superb timber and its highly sought-after resin, or gum. The displays focus on the makeshift settlements around logging camps, the gumfields, and the lives of merchants who were among the few who could afford to buy the fine kauri furniture or beautifully carved gum. Mock-ups of the various ways in which the huge logs are transported – kauri dams, wooden sleds, bullock trains and winches – lead on to a pit-saw operation and a turn-ing steam-driven sawmill. Downstairs, the museum has the most extensive and beautiful display of kauri gum anywhere.

Practicalities

By using two different **bus services**, it's possible to travel along SH12 with a stop of two to three hours at the museum. Alternatively, you can **stay** the night nearby, though none of the options are outstanding. Possibilities in Matakohe include *Matakohe House* (☎09/431 7091, ⓔmathouse@xtra.co.nz; **❻**), an invit-ing B&B right next to the museum with big, simply furnished en-suite rooms opening out onto a veranda, the complex also containing a golf driving range and licensed café (see opposite); and the nearby, hillside *Matakohe Top 10 Holiday Park*, Church Rd (☎ & ⓕ09/431 6431; camping $13; caravans & cabins **❷**; units **❹**), offering great harbour views. Slightly further afield, there's a broad choice of rooms at the atmospheric *Old Post Office Guest House*, SH12, 7km east in Paparoa (☎ & ⓕ09/431 6444; 3- or 4-bed dorms **❶**, rooms **❹**, B&B rooms **❹**), which has one drawback in the small kitchen but a BBQ and pretty garden help to compensate. There's more backpacker accommodation at the *Travellers Lodge*, on SH12 in Ruawai, 15km west of Matakohe (☎09/439 2283; camping $12, rooms ❷), where "dorms" are twin or single rooms costing $23–25 per person. There are a couple of reasonable licensed **cafés** right by the Kauri Museum, the best being *Matakohe House Café*, where food is served daily from breakfast to dinner and there's **Internet access**.

Travel details

Buses

Two major bus companies serve Northland. The most comprehensive operation is **InterCity** (☎09/913 6100, ⓦwww.intercitycoach.co.nz), who in combination with **West Coaster** run two routes, one up the eastern side from Auckland's Sky City depot through Warkworth, Brynderwyn, Whangarei, Paihia, Kerikeri and Mangonui to Kaitaia – the other spurring off at Kaiwaka and covering Dargaville, the Waipoua Forest, Omapere, Opononi and Kaikohe on the way to Paihia. Their Twin Coast Kauri Discovery pass ($103) is valid for three months and covers a loop from Auckland to Paihia and back through Opononi, the Waipoua Forest and Dargaville, or vice versa. **Northliner Express** (☎09/307 5873 in Auckland, ☎09/438 3206 in Whangarei; ⓦwww.northliner.co.nz) run almost identical services with a similar frequency from 172 Quay St, opposite Auckland's ferry building. North of Paihia InterCity and Northliner run a joint service. Northliner sell three useful passes, all valid for a month and all requiring some form of backpacker or student ID: the Bay of Islands Pass ($53) covers Auckland to Kerikeri via Paihia, the Loop Pass ($83) is identical to InterCity's Twin Coast Kauri Discovery, and the Northland Freedom Pass ($115), adds the leg up to Kaitaia. There is also one short-range operator from Auckland: **Mainline Coaches** (☎09/278 8070), who also serve Warkworth and continue on to Dargaville.
From Dargaville to: Auckland (2–3 daily; 3hr 15min); Opononi (3 weekly Tues, Thurs & Sat; 2hr 20min).
From Kaitaia to: Auckland (1 daily; 7hr).

From Kerikeri to: Auckland (2 daily; 5hr); Paihia (2 daily; 25min).
From Mangonui to: Auckland (1 daily; 6hr 30min).
From Opononi/Omapere to: Auckland (3 weekly Mon, Wed & Fri; 5hr 40min); Paihia (3 weekly Tues, Thurs & Sat ; 2hr), Dargaville (3 weekly Mon, Wed & Fri; 2hr 30min).
From Paihia to: Auckland via Whangarei (4–6 daily; 4hr 20min); Auckland via Opononi and Dargaville (3 weekly Mon, Wed & Fri; 8hr 30min); Kaitaia (2 daily; 2hr); Kerikeri (1 daily; 20min); Mangonui (1 daily; 1hr 20min).
From Waipu to: Auckland (4–6 daily; 2hr 20min); Whangarei (3–4 daily; 30min).
From Warkworth to: Auckland (7–8 daily; 1hr 15min).
From Whangarei to: Auckland (4–6 daily; 3hr); Paihia (4–6 daily; 1hr 15min); Warkworth (4–6 daily; 1hr 45min).

Ferries

From Kohukohu to: Rawene (hourly; 20min).
From Opua to: Okiato (every 10–20min; 15min).
From Paihia to: Russell by passenger ferry (every 20min; 20min).
From Rawene to: Kohukohu (hourly; 20min).

Flights

From Bay of Islands (Paihia/Kerikeri) to: Auckland (3–4 daily; 50min).
From Kaitaia to: Auckland (1 daily; 1hr).
From Whangarei to: Auckland (5–7 daily; 40min); Great Barrier Island (2 weekly; 30min).

Western North Island

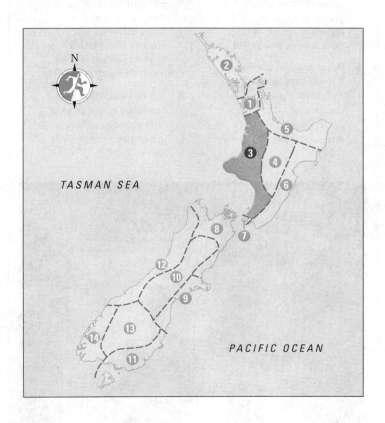

CHAPTER 3 # Highlights

✳ **Raglan** Pretty and sociable harbourside town within easy reach of some of New Zealand's finest surf. See p.243

✳ **Waitomo** A labyrinthine underworld illuminated by glowworms, all visited by abseiling, caving and cave tubing. See p.249

✳ **Whanganui River** Try a three-day canoe trip through the green canyons of New Zealand's longest navigable river. See p.261

✳ **Wind Wand** This iconic 45-metre carbon fibre sculpture swaying in the breeze was designed by Kiwi artist Len Lye. See p.271

✳ **Egmont National Park** Easy walks and steep hikes to the conical summit of the North Island's second highest peak. See p.275

✳ **Kapiti Island** This island sanctuary is one of your best chances of seeing endangered native birds. See p.299

△ Caving, Waitomo

Western North Island

M uch of the **Western North Island** is ignored by visitors, who make a beeline for the netherworld wonders of Waitomo and perhaps pay a visit to New Plymouth and the graceful Mount Taranaki then continue on to somewhere else. In fact, there's much more to the area and it is a place to absorb slowly, spending an afternoon in a timewarped fishing community or driving slowly along almost forgotten highways sampling their small-time charms and meeting the locals.

Much of the appeal is tied to its extraordinary **history** of pre-European settlement and post-European conflict. This region is deeply rooted in **Maori** legend and history for it was on the west coast at **Kawhia** that the Tainui people first landed in New Zealand. Kawhia was also the birthplace of **Te Rauparaha**, the great Maori chief who led his people from Kawhia to escape the better-armed tribes of the Waikato down the west coast to Kapiti Island and on to the South Island, pursuing his individual road to justice, fame and glory.

Approaching the region from the north you're into **the Waikato**, important farming country but with little of interest to the visitor. Much the same can be said of its provincial capital **Hamilton**, the fourth largest city in the land but only worth half a day of your time. It is far better to head to the west coast and **Raglan**, a wonderfully relaxing town with world-class surf and a great selection of places to stay and eat.

Backroads lead you south to harbourside **Kawhia**, a historic spot but a place where you can soak in hot springs at the edge of the surf. Inland, this rich dairying and agricultural region benefits from the fecund soil scattered by long-extinct volcanoes. Prim **Cambridge** exploits the rich grass by breeding thoroughbreds, while **Te Awamutu** is renowned for growing roses, and producing two of New Zealand's most celebrated musicians, the brothers Finn.

South of the Waikato is the **King Country**, which took its name from the King Movement (see p.247) and was the last significant area in New Zealand to succumb to the onrush of European colonization. Today it contains a number of stalwart communities coexisting with some extraordinary natural features – most famously the beautiful, creamy limestone **Waitomo Caves**, where unusual rock formations surmount a netherworld of glowworm-filled caverns. The farming towns of **Te Kuiti** and **Taumarunui** aren't much in themselves, but the former provides access to the tall-canopied **Pureora Forest Park**, while the latter is one of the main jumping-off points for spectacular canoe trips along the **Whanganui River** through the heart of the **Whanganui National Park** to the Bridge to Nowhere.

To the west, the giant thumb-print peninsula of **Taranaki** is dominated by the symmetrical cone of **Mount Taranaki** (2518m), the location of some

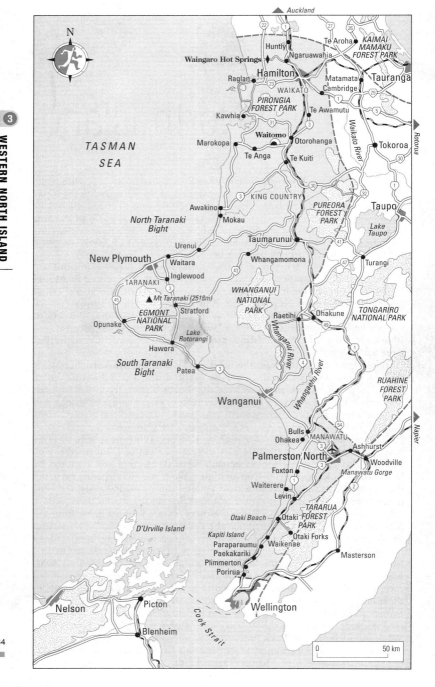

N

▲ Auckland

TASMAN
SEA

Huntly
Waingaro Hot Springs
Raglan
Hamilton
WAIKATO
PIRONGIA
FOREST PARK
Kawhia
Waitomo
Marokopa
Te Anga
Otorohanga
Te Kuiti

Ngaruawahia
Te Aroha
KAIMAI
MAMAKU
FOREST PARK
Matamata
Cambridge
Tauranga

Te Awamutu

▶ Rotorua
Tokoroa

KING COUNTRY

PUREORA
FOREST
PARK

Taupo

Awakino
Mokau
North Taranaki
Bight
Urenui
New Plymouth
Waitara
Inglewood
TARANAKI
▲ Mt Taranaki (2518m)
Stratford
EGMONT
NATIONAL
PARK
Opunake
Lake
Rotorangi
Hawera
South Taranaki
Bight
Patea

Taumarunui
Whangamomona

WHANGANUI
NATIONAL
PARK
Raetihi
Ohakune

Lake
Taupo
Turangi

TONGARIRO
NATIONAL
PARK

Whanganui River

Whangaehu River

RUAHINE
FOREST
PARK

▶ Napier

Wanganui

Bulls
Ohakea
MANAWATU
Palmerston North
Foxton
Waiterere
Levin
Otaki Beach
Otaki
Kapiti Island
Paraparaumu
Paekakariki
Plimmerton
Porirua

Ashhurst
Woodville
Manawatu Gorge

TARARUA
FOREST
PARK
Otaki Forks
Waikanae
Masterson

D'Urville Island

Nelson
Picton

Blenheim

Cook Strait

Wellington

0   50 km

superb hiking in the **Egmont National Park**. At its foot, **New Plymouth** warrants time spent at its excellent contemporary art gallery.

A multitude of surf beaches line the Taranaki coast, becoming wilder as they head south towards **Wanganui**, a small, ordered city where you can relive its river-port past on an elderly paddle steamer. The university city of **Palmerston North** is at the centre of the rich farming region of **Manawatu** and has some interesting architecture and a museum to show for its prosperity. A cluster of small communities line the highway to the south, the former flax-weaving town of **Foxton** providing the most interest until you reach the **Kapiti Coast**. Here, **Paraparaumu** is the launch point for boat trips to the wonderful bird sanctuary on **Kapiti Island**.

Paraparaumu is less than an hour from Wellington and by then you're firmly into commuter territory with only a couple of small towns warranting a brief stop, though **Waikanae**, **Plimmerton** and **Porirua** are all decent bases from which to visit the capital.

South from Auckland

Heading south from Auckland into the northern Waikato there's little reason to delay your progress into Hamilton. At **Huntly**, 95km south of Auckland along SH1, having gazed across the Waikato River at the twin 150m-high chimneys of New Zealand's largest power station, you may wish to pay a brief visit to the **Waikato Coalfields Museum**, 26 Harlock Place (daily 10am–4pm; $3), with its reconstructed mine tunnel, miner's cottage and displays on early life in the Waikato coalfield, which still provides fuel for the power station.

The most interesting and culturally significant spot in these parts is **NGARU-AWAHIA**, 14km further south on SH1, a farming centre at the junction of the Waikato and Waipa rivers. Both rivers were important Maori canoe routes, and the area has long held great significance for Maori: it is here that the **King Movement** (see p.247) has its roots, and the town is home to the current monarch, Te Arikinui Dame Te Atairangikaahu. It was also the scene of the signing of the Raupatu Land Settlement in 1995, whereby the New Zealand government agreed to compensate the Tainui for land confiscated in the 1860s.

The Maori heritage is most evident on **Regatta Day** (the closest Sat to March 17) when the waters of the two rivers host a parade of great war canoes before the Maori queen, and hurdle races and the like take place at the **Turangawaewae Marae** (generally closed except on Regatta Day; enquiries ☏07/824 5189) on River Road, off SH1 just north of the river bridge. For the rest of the year you'll have to content yourself with a view of the perimeter fence, made of the dead trunks of tree ferns interspersed with robustly sculpted red posts and a couple of finely carved entranceways. Through these you can glimpse the main features: the strikingly carved and decorated **Mahinarangi House**, which houses the Maori throne; **Turongo House**, the official residence of the present queen; and the Kimi-ora Cultural Complex, with its spectacular mural and a conspicuous octagonal roof.

On the opposite side of the river and road is **Turangawaewae House**, on Eyre Street, built in 1920 as the intended home of the Maori parliament. It isn't open to the public and is really just an ordinary Edwardian-style stucco building, except for the red-, black- and white-painted doors, carved barge boards and *pou* (guardian post).

Twenty-three kilometres west of Ngaruawahia, at the junction with SH22, are the popular though slightly run-down **Waingaro Hot Springs**, Waingaro Road (daily 9am–10pm; $6), a large pool complex based around a series of natural springs, which can get busy on summer weekends.

Hamilton

Most visitors pass through **HAMILTON**, 136km south of Auckland, but it is a pretty enough place, well sited on the banks of the languid green Waikato River and surrounded by parks. It is worth devoting a day to visiting the excellent **Museum of Art and History**, the tranquil **Hamilton Gardens**, and taking a **paddle-steamer cruise** on the river. And as befits New Zealand's fourth-largest city, there's a decent-sized student population, with a lively term-time nightlife. In mid-June the town hosts the annual four-day Fieldays **festival** (Ⓦ www.fieldays.co.nz), the largest agricultural field day in the southern hemisphere, at Mystery Creek Events Centre just outside the city.

Archeological evidence indicates that the **Tainui** settlement of **Kirikirioa** had existed on the current site of Hamilton for at least two hundred years before the **Europeans** arrived in the 1830s. The newcomers named their riverside settlement after **John Fane Charles Hamilton**, an officer of the Royal Navy who had died, either bravely or foolishly (depending whose interpretation you believe), at the battle of Gate Pa, near Tauranga, a few months earlier; a fictionalized account of the events leading up to his death appears in Maurice Shadbolt's excellent novel *The House of Strife*. The river remained the only supply route for the city until the railway came in 1878, effectively opening up the country to more European immigration, farming and commercial expansion.

Arrival, information and city transport

Hamilton **airport**, 15km south, is connected to the city by the door-to-door Super Shuttle (℡07/843 7778 & 0800/748 8853; $10), which meets all arrivals. The **train** station is on Fraser Street (℡07/846 8353) in the suburb of Frankton, a twenty-minute walk west of the city centre, or catch the #8 bus straight to the modern **Transport Centre**, right in the centre of town at the corner of Anglesea and Bryce streets, which is the hub for local and long-distance **buses**. Bus and train tickets are sold inside at the **visitor centre** (Mon–Fri 8.30am–5pm, Sat & Sun 10am–4pm; ℡07/839 3580, Ⓦ www.waikatonz.co.nz), where you'll also find **Internet access**, some **left luggage** lockers and a **taxi** rank. There's no **parking** outside the visitor centre, so head for the nearby car park at Centre Place Shopping Mall on Bryce St, or the one on Barton Street. The **DOC office** is three minutes' walk north at Level 4, 18 London St (Mon–Fri 8.30am–4.30pm; ℡07/838 3363).

Most of Hamilton's attractions are within walking distance of the centre; for those further afield pick up the free Busit timetable or call the information line on ℡0800/428 75463; fares are $2 a ride. Local **bus** companies also run scheduled services to the neighbouring communities of Paeroa, Raglan, Thames and Te Awamutu. Several services run between Auckland and Hamilton: Roadcat Transport (℡07/823 2559), Guthreys (℡0800/759 999), Go Kiwi (℡07/866 0336) and Silver Fern Shuttles (℡0800/021 130), the last-mentioned also running a daily shuttle service to Raglan.

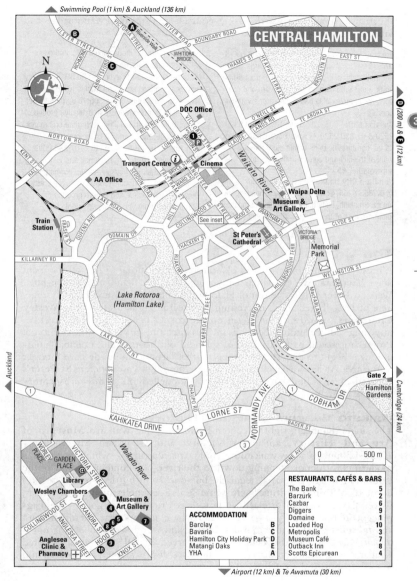

Swimming Pool (1 km) & Auckland (136 km)

CENTRAL HAMILTON

N

Riverside Walk

ULSTER STREET
RICHMOND ST
VICTORIA STREET
RIVER ROAD
BOUNDARY ROAD

B

C

WHITIORA BRIDGE
THAMES ST
HEAPHY TERRACE
EAST ST
BROOKLYN RD

MILL STREET
ABBOTSFORD ST
ROSTREVOR STREET
O'NEILL ST
LANDS RD
TE AROHA ST

NORTON ROAD
DOC Office
1
2

KENT ST
HALL ST
SEDDON ROAD
LONDON ST
CLAUDE ST
MEMORIAL DR

Transport Centre
Cinema

AA Office

LAKE ROAD
BRYCE ST
WARD ST
CHELSEA ST
ANGLESEA ST

Waikato River

Waipa Delta
Museum & Art Gallery

Train Station
QUEENS AVE
FRASER ST
DOMAIN DR
HILL ST
COLLINGWOOD ST
See inset
HOOD ST
GRANTHAM ST

St Peter's Cathedral

VICTORIA BRIDGE
CLYDE ST

KILLARNEY RD
THACKERAY ST
RUAKIWI RD
BRIDGE ST
HILLSBOROUGH TERR

Memorial Park
WELLINGTON ST
MacFARLANE ST
GREY ST

Lake Rotoroa
(Hamilton Lake)

PEMBROKE STREET
NAYLOR ST

LAKE CRESCENT

Auckland

ALISON ST
OHAUPO RD
COBHAM RD
NORMANDY AVE
JELLICOE DR

Gate 2
Hamilton Gardens

Cambridge (24 km)

1
KAHIKATEA DRIVE
1
LORNE ST
BADER ST
COBHAM DR

3
PINE AVE

D (200 m) & E (12 km)

0   500 m

RESTAURANTS, CAFÉS & BARS

The Bank	5
Barzurk	2
Cazbar	6
Diggers	9
Domaine	1
Loaded Hog	10
Metropolis	3
Museum Café	7
Outback Inn	8
Scotts Epicurean	4

WORLEY PLACE
GARDEN PLACE
VICTORIA STREET
Waikato River

@
2

Library

Wesley Chambers
3
Museum & Art Gallery
6 5
7
ALEXANDRA ST
ANGLESEA STREET
COLLINGWOOD ST
HOOD ST
KNOX ST

Anglesea Clinic & Pharmacy
10 9

ACCOMMODATION

Barclay	B
Bavaria	C
Hamilton City Holiday Park	D
Matangi Oaks	E
YHA	A

Airport (12 km) & Te Awamutu (30 km)

Accommodation

Hamilton's speciality is downtown business accommodation for farm company reps, and **motels,** which mostly line Ulster Street a little to the north. **B&Bs** are thin on the ground (the best option is outside the city) and even the selection of **hostels** is fairly limited. If you're only planning a short visit, it may be worth basing yourself in Raglan or Cambridge and visiting from there.

Barclay Motel 280 Ulster St ☎0800/808 090 & 07/838 2475, Ⓦwww.barclay.co.nz. Large, upmarket motel with self-contained, mostly ground-floor units, some with own private courtyard and spa pool; the complex also has a saltwater swimming pool. ⑤

Bavaria Motel 203–207 Ulster St ☎0800/839 2520 & 07/839 2520, Ⓦwww.bavariamotel.co.nz. Large, comfortable units within eight minutes' walk of the city and conveniently close to a supermarket. ④

Hamilton City Holiday Park Ruakura Rd ☎07/855 8255, Ⓦwww.hamiltoncityholidaypark .co.nz. Smallish, leafy and well-tended campsite a kilometre east of the centre with camping ($12),

basic and more luxurious cabins (❷), and some self-contained units. ❸

Matangi Oaks 634 Marychurch Rd/SH1B, midway between Hamilton and Cambridge ☎07/829 5765, Ⓦwww.matangioaks.co.nz. Superb upmarket B&B in an elegant modern house in extensive grounds, 12km from central Hamilton, with generous rooms (one en suite, two sharing a bathroom). ❻

YHA Hamilton 1190 Victoria St ☎07/838 0009, ⓔyha.hamilton@yha.org.nz. Small and welcoming hostel in a large, old house with airy dorms (max 5) plus single and double rooms. There's a pretty view from the terrace and superb grounds that lead down to the river. Dorms ❶, single $31, rooms ❷

The City

Almost everything of interest in Hamilton is either along or just off the main drag, **Victoria Street**, which runs along the west bank of the tree-lined Waikato River. While the rest of Hamilton exhibits a low, suburban cityscape, here at least there's some interesting architecture, notably the 1924 **Wesley Chambers** (now *Le Grand Hotel*) on the corner of Collingwood Street, an imposing edifice influenced by the architecture of boomtime Chicago. Progressing south past a handful of splendid old hotels and municipal buildings, you begin to discern the prosperity that farming and trade have brought to the area. At the corner of Bridge Street, the rough-cast concrete **St Peter's Cathedral** was built in 1915 but was modelled on a fifteenth-century Norfolk church.

Waikato Museum of Art and History

The single significant sight in central Hamilton is the **Waikato Museum of Art and History**, corner of Victoria and Grantham Streets (daily 10am–4.30pm; Ⓦwww.waikatomuseum.co.nz; donation), which occupies a modern construction stepping down to the river. The content of most of the exhibition spaces is rotated regularly, but one enduring feature is a section devoted to **Tainui culture**, with some superb examples of domestic items, woven flax, tools, ritual artefacts, and carvings. Pride of place goes to the magnificent *Te Winika* war canoe, surrounded by contemporary Tainui carvings, and *tukutuku* panels made from flax, leather and wood. Worth checking out is *Tainui, Ngati Koroki* the detailed wood-carved model of a *waka* by Fred Graham, periodically on display. You might see displays aimed at children and school groups; and a quality **café**.

Parks and gardens

Just across the river in **Memorial Park** you can step aboard the old paddle steamer *Waipa Delta* (Thurs–Sun & public holidays only; ☎0800/472 335, Ⓦwww.waipadelta.co.nz), which still **cruises** sedately along the Waikato River leaving the Memorial Park jetty at 12.30pm (1hr 30min, $39, incl lunch); 3pm (1hr, $20, incl afternoon tea); and 7pm (3hr, $55, incl smorgasbord).

From Memorial Park, another riverside path heads 2km south to the huge **Hamilton Gardens**, also reached by road or #10 bus from the Transport Centre. The gardens are on Cobham Drive/SH1 (two entrances: Gate 1 at the junction with Galloway Street, Gate 2 at the junction with Grey Street; always open; free; Ⓦwww.hamiltongardens.co.nz), with extensive displays of roses, tropical plants, rhododendrons, magnolias and cacti. Pick up a free map from the gardens' visitor centre (daily 10am–4pm; café attached), then duck next door to the inner sanctum of the **Paradise Gardens Collection** (daily 7.30am–dusk; free), six beautiful and inspiring enclosures each planted in a different style from around the world.

Eating, drinking and nightlife

The nucleus of Hamilton nightlife lies on Hood Street and around the corner, along the southern end of Victoria Street, where several places start as daytime **cafés** and progressively become **restaurants** and then **bars** as the day wears on.

The Village 7 multiplex **cinema** (℡0900/97 777), in the Centreplace Mall on Ward St, shows the usual mainstream releases. Check the daily *Waikato Times* for details of these and other happenings; comprehensive events and entertainment **listings** are in the Friday and Saturday editions.

The Bank Bar and Brasserie cnr Victoria St & Hood St. A former bank that has been transformed into a restaurant with a big-city bistro feel. There's always a crowd for the substantial snacks and good-value meals (lunch & dinner daily, brunch at weekends), or just for a drink, and at weekends DJ-led dancing from 10pm.

Barzurk Gourmet Pizza Bar 250 Victoria St. Excellent pizzas with a variety of toppings in a pleasant exposed-brick setting. Lunch Thurs–Sun, dinner daily.

Cazbar Brasserie The Marketplace, off Hood St. Stylish, dinner/night spot where snacks are served all day, and globally inspired dinner mains go for under $25. Live music Tues–Sat until 3am.

Diggers 17 Hood St. A drinkers' den, with a long kauri bar that provides welcome respite from the trendy city bars. It's the liveliest place at weekends with a great atmosphere and regular gigs on Sundays.

Domaine 575 Victoria St ℡07/839 2100. Vibrant modern restaurant open daily with streetside seating and booths in the back, both good for café dining throughout the day and a more formal yet reasonably priced evening menu including seafood laksa followed by venison steak.

Loaded Hog 27 Hood St. One of the most attractive bars in the city, this large double-gabled building is dotted with rural New Zealand memorabilia and has tables on the street out front. An array of excellent home-brewed ales is supplemented by a broad selection from around the country and full menu. DJ-cranked dancing on Wed–Sat nights.

Metropolis 211 Victoria St. A hip café that serves an eclectic range of tasty food for brunch, lunch and dinner, including veggie and vegan options and some good coffee and liqueurs; open daily till around midnight.

Museum Café 1 Grantham St ℡07/839 7209. Relaxing and stylish restaurant popular for its considered menu of beautifully prepared Modern Kiwi meals. Lunch dishes are around $15, dinner mains $20–25, and there's live jazz on Thursday evenings. Dinner reservations only; open for lunch daily, dinner Tues–Sat.

Outback Inn The Marketplace, off Hood St. The city's biggest bar, a loud and boisterous drinking hole with pool tables that's popular with students for the good selection of beers and a few snacks. There's dancing on Tues–Sat, with a DJ Wed–Sat, and occasional live bands.

Scotts Epicurean 181 Victoria St. An intimate, licensed modern café that makes a great spot for coffee, snacks, and excellent cakes, plus unusual dishes like Pytti Panna (Swedish bubble and squeak) or breakfast of buttermilk and poppyseed hotcakes. Open daily for breakfast, brunch and lunch.

Listings

Automobile Association 295 Barton St ℡07/839 1397.

American Express Calder and Lawson Travel Ltd, 455 Grey St ℡07/856 9009.

Bike rental R&R Sport, 943 Victoria St ☎07/839 3755 & 0800/777 767. About $30 a day for a mountain bike.

Bookshops Dimensions Women's Bookshop, 266 Victoria St; Browsers, 221 Victoria St; Crows Nest Books, Arcadia Building, Worley Place. The latter buys and sells secondhand books.

Car rental Budget ☎07/838 3585; Cambridge Car Rentals ☎07/823 0990; Hertz ☎07/839 4824; Rent-a-Dent ☎07/839 1049; Waikato Car Rentals ☎07/855 0094.

Library Central Hamilton library, Garden Place, off Victoria St (Mon–Fri 9am–8.30pm, Sat 9am–4pm, Sun noon–3.30pm), has Internet access.

Medical treatment Anglesea Clinic and Pharmacy, cnr Anglesea St & Thackeray St (daily 7.30am–11pm; ☎07/858 0800) offers consultations and fills prescriptions.

Post offices The main post office is in Bryce St near Victoria St.

Taxis Dial a Cab ☎0800/342 522; the Cab Company ☎0800 482 947.

Thomas Cook Garden Place ☎07/838 9391.

Travel agents Air New Zealand Travel Centre, 25 Ward St ☎07/839 9835; STA, 42 Ward St ☎07/839 1833.

Around Hamilton and the coast

Hamilton may not detain you for long, but there's plenty to soak up a couple of days' exploration in the immediate vicinity. South of the city, the genteel English charms of **Cambridge** contrast with the turbulent history of the former garrison township of **Te Awamutu**, but the region's real draws lie further west. Foremost among them is the sand-swathed coast, principally the surfie Mecca of **Raglan**, which has an enduring appeal. South of Raglan the surf-lashed coast borders the **Pirongia Forest Park**, a great spot for walks leading to the summit of wind-buffeted hills where you can appreciate the grisly, rough-hewn coastline to the south. It extends to **Kawhia**, a moribund little community on the site of the Tainui people's first landfall in Aotearoa – and still their spiritual home. The beaches south of Kawhia are typically black sand, steeped in isolation and lashed by wind and sea, though comfort can be taken in the thermal pools that bubble up at the shoreline close to Kawhia.

Cambridge

There's a peaceful understated air to the small town of **CAMBRIDGE**, 24km southeast of Hamilton. Founded as a militia settlement at the navigable limit of the Waikato River in 1864, Cambridge is today marooned in a broad agricultural belt renowned for stud farms. Attractive in a bucolic sort of a way, it has a big village green, tree-lined avenues and the elegant weatherboard **St Andrew's Anglican Church**, at the corner of Victoria Street and SH1, with its tall steeple, fine dark-wood interior and original stained-glass. Opposite the church lies the semi-formal **Te Koutu Park**, around a picturesque sunken lake and threaded by tracks through stands of tall chestnut and oak trees; pick up the free *Cambridge Welcomes You* brochure from the visitor centre to get the best from your amblings.

Practicalities

InterCity and Newmans **buses** between Hamilton and Taupo stop beside the Town Hall on Lake Street, while Cambridge Travel Lines (☎07/827 7363) run a local service from Hamilton (Mon–Fri only) that stops by St Andrew's church. Both stops are two minutes' walk from the **visitor centre**, at the corner of Queen Street and Victoria Street (Mon–Fri 9am–5pm, Sat & Sun 10am–4pm; ☎07/823 3456, ⓔcvc@wave.co.nz), who act as booking agents for the buses. There's **Internet access** at Corinthian Computers, 39E Victoria St (☎07/827 5824; Mon–Fri 8.30am–5.15pm, Sat 9am–12pm).

Just steps from the visitor centre *Park House*, 70 Queen St (☎07/827 6368, ⓦ www.parkhouse.co.nz; ❼), provides a good reason to **stay**, in an elegantly furnished, 1920s house where the rooms are in a separate wing and service is handled with easy grace. For cheaper B&B, try *Pamade*, 229 Shakespeare St (☎07/827 4916, ⓔ pamades@hotmail.com; ❺), two minutes' drive from central Cambridge; the well-appointed *Colonial Court Motel*, 37 Vogel St, off SH1 (☎0800/525 352, ⓦ www.nzmotels.co.nz/colonial.cambridge; ❺), or *Cambridge Motor Park*, 32 Scott St (☎07/827 5649, ⓔ cambridgemotorpark@paradise.net.nz; camping $11, cabins & kitchen cabins ❷, units ❸), ten minutes' walk west of town over the river.

Eating is best done at *The Deli*, corner Victoria Street and Empire Street, a small daytime venue open till around 4pm (2pm on Sun) that's great for coffee, snacks, light meals and Devonshire teas with mascarpone; or the daytime *Fran's Café*, 62 Victoria St (closed Sun; BYO), where you can grab simple snacks and light meals for under $10. For Italian food head for *Rosso's*, Alpha St (☎07/827 6699), serving snacks, lunch, dinner and weekend brunch (closed Mon). More value-for-money dinners can be had at the English pub-style *Prince Albert*, Victoria Plaza, off Victoria St.

Te Awamutu and around

The birthplace of fraternal Kiwi pop music icons Tim and Neil Finn, **TE AWAMUTU**, 30km south of Hamilton, is a placid place, surrounded by rolling hills, dairy pasture and overlooked by Mount Pirongia.

Local Maori trace their descent to the Tainui Canoe (see p.246), and by the nineteenth century there was a heavy Maori presence on the land, as evidenced by the many *pa* sites in the loops of rivers and on steep hilltops. During the 1863 **New Zealand Wars**, Te Awamutu was a garrison for government forces, and one of the most famous battles of the conflict was fought at the hastily constructed Orakau *pa*, where 2000 soldiers were held at bay for three days by just 300 Maori, an incident touchingly remembered in the local church.

The Town

Te Awamutu is locally renowned for its extensive **rose gardens**, at the corner of Gorst and Arawata streets, at their best between November and May. Immediately across the road is the visitor centre (see p.240), where fans of **Split Enz** and **Crowded House** might want to pick up the leaflet ($1) for the self-guided tour around frankly dull places of significance in the Finn brothers' formative years. The visitor centre also holds the key to **St John's Church**, just across Arawata Street, the very existence of which is a poignant reminder of the New Zealand Wars. Built as a garrison church in 1854, it was spared as other European buildings burned around it, because the Maori chieftain, Te Paea Potatau, had placed her *mana* upon it. Inside the church, a tribute from a British regiment, written in Maori, honours their Maori enemies, many of whom crawled, under fire, onto the battlefield to give water to their wounded British foes. The church also contains one of the oldest figurative, painted stained-glass windows in New Zealand.

Te Awamutu Museum, on Roche Street, about ten minutes' walk west of the visitor centre (Mon–Fri 10am–4pm, Sat 10am–1pm, Sun 1–4pm; free; ⓦ www.tamuseum.org.nz), contains an excellent collection of early Maori artefacts. The museum's pride and joy is *Uenuku*, a striking darkwood carving representing a traditional god as a rainbow. This sacred relic of the Tainui people is thought to have been carved around 1400AD. Along with displays about the European settlers and the New Zealand Wars there's the True Colours exhibit, a corner devoted to the Finn brothers, but concentrating on the life and times of Split Enz.

Practicalities

Trains on the main Auckland–Wellington line stop on Station Road, about 2km west of the visitor centre – a short walk, or call any of the cabs advertising at the station. InterCity **buses** (daily service between Auckland and Palmerston North) drop off at both Stuart Law's Garage, 90 Mahoe Street (which also acts as a ticket office) and at the visitor centre. Dalroys buses (daily service between Auckland and New Plymouth) stop at the **visitor centre**, at the corner of Gorst Avenue and Arawata Street (Mon–Fri 9am–5pm, Sat & Sun 10am–3.30pm, with extended hours in summer; ℡07/871 3259, ⓦwww.teawamutu.co.nz), from where just about everything in town is a short walk away. There's **Internet access** at *G.net café*, 59 Bank St (Mon–Fri 8am–5pm, Sat 10am–noon), which serves coffee, sandwiches and cakes.

Te Awamutu's **accommodation** and eating options are very limited. A safe bet just a few minutes' walk from the visitor centre is the *Road Runner Holiday Park*, 141 Bond Rd (℡07/871 7420, ℻07/871 6664), which has camping ($10) and cabins (❸). Modern comfort in luxury units is available at the *Albert Park Motor Lodge*, 299 Albert Park Drive (℡07/870 2995, ⓔalbert.park@xtra.co.nz; ❺). The **eating** situation is better with *Robert Harris*, 39 Arawata St, offering tasty breakfasts, snacks and coffee; the colourful licensed café *Zest*, where you can get coffee, lunch daily, good-value dinner mains (Wed–Fri) and all-day brunch at weekends; and the *Rose and Thorn*, 32 Arawata St, a café bar that's the best bet for generous **dinners**. The small French patisserie at *Salvador's*, 50 Alexandra St (Mon 10am–3pm, Tues–Fri 8am–4pm, Sat 8am–1.30pm; closed Sun), produces excellent pastries.

Yarndley's Bush and Pirongia

There is little to stop for along the straight highway north of town, except the atmospheric **Yarndley's Bush** (dawn–dusk; free), one of the largest remaining stands of the towering kahikatea on the North Island. To reach the reserve, turn off SH3 4km north of Te Awamutu, on to Ngaroto Road, and continue for 1500m to the signposted entrance. A **loop walk** (30min) winds through, past huge root buttresses, and midway along, a raised platform gives you a bird's-eye view of the constantly moving canopy. The drainage of marshland for farming and the use of odourless kahikatea wood to make boxes to transport butter overseas have hastened the demise of these magnificent native trees.

Dominating the landscape to the west of Te Awamutu is **Mount Pirongia**, scarred by redoubt trenches from the New Zealand Wars. The peak lies within the **Pirongia Forest Park**, an area traversed by a series of interesting nature **walks** described in the DOC *Pirongia and Karioi* leaflet ($1, from Te Awamutu visitor centre). The most popular is the Mangakara Nature Walk (3km, 1hr return), which meanders through ancient forest, descending from the Grey Road car park, 16km west of Te Awamutu, to a stream and circling back. Five longer **tramping routes** converge on the 959-metre summit, the most rewarding and one of the easiest being the Mahaukura Track (4km each way; 4–6hr up), from the Grey Road car park, which takes you via the Wharauroa Lookout (2–3 hours to the lookout; the last 30 metres are steep with chains in place to help). The summit ridge even has DOC's **Pahautea Hut** (8 bunks;

$5; book through Te Awamutu visitor centre or Hamilton DOC), which allows you to split your exploration over two days.

Raglan and around

Visitors often stay far longer than they intended at the small town of **RAGLAN** which hugs the south side of the large and picturesque Raglan Harbour some 48km west of Hamilton. Long a popular holiday and weekend destination from the provincial capital, it is seeing a renaissance, gaining permanent residents drawn by the town's bohemian arts-and-crafts tenor and the laid-back spirit engendered by the surf community. In fact, Raglan has an international reputation among **surfers** for the best left-handed break in the world, the lines of perfect breakers appearing like blue corduroy at Manu Bay and Whale Bay, both around 8km south of town.

Almost everything of note lines **Bow Street**, its central row of Phoenix palms shading banks, several good restaurants and a selection of crafts shops. At the street's western end it butts up against the sparkling harbour, where a slender footbridge over one arm provides access to the main campsite and a safe swimming **beach**.

To the south the horizon is dominated by **Mount Karioi** (site of an excellent hike; see p.245), which, according to Maori legend, was the goal of the great migratory canoe *Tainui*. They travelled towards it for a very long time, but when they reached the mouth of the harbour a bar blocked their way, so they named the harbour Whaingaroa ("long pursuit") and paddled south where they could finally land. The shortened epithet, Whangaroa, was the name used for the harbour until 1855, when it was renamed Raglan after the officer who led the Charge of the Light Brigade.

Arrival, information and accommodation

Hamilton City **buses** (2 daily; ☎0800 4287 5463) stop outside the library on Bow Street, just across from the **visitor centre** at 4 Wallis St (Mon–Fri 9am–3pm, Sat & Sun 10am–4pm, with extended hours in summer; ☎07/825 0556, ⓦwww.raglan.org.nz). Raglan Harbour Cruises run a **water taxi** service (☎07/825 0300; Nov to end April; rest of the year on demand) to various points around the bay, especially the northern shore, only accessible by boat. For explorations further afield contact Raglan Taxi (☎07/825 0506). Raglan Video, 6 Bow St, has **Internet** access (daily 10am–8.30pm), but it is expensive.

One of the reasons you may overdo your expected stay here is the abundance of excellent **accommodation** at all levels, some of the best located out by Whale Bay.

Accommodation

Belindsay's 28 Wallis St ☎ & ⓕ07/825 6592. Central accommodation in an upmarket yet good-value backpackers, set in a lovely 1930s house with polished wood floors, stained glass and a deep bath as well as shower. There are three-bed shares, a single ($35) and doubles, plus a sunny lounge and kitchen. Dorms ❶, rooms ❸

Harbour View Hotel 14 Bow St ☎07/825 8010, ⓔharbourviewhotel@xtra.co.nz. Pleasant rooms (including singles at $50) in the town's archetypal, two-storey hotel, some of them with a veranda overlooking the main street. ❹

Karioi Lodge Raglan Surfing School, 5 Whaanga Rd, Whale Bay ☎07/825 7873, ⓦwww.sleepinglady.co.nz. Pleasant hostel deep in coastal native bush 8km southwest of Raglan, with 4-bed dorms and doubles. There's a communal kitchen and evening meals supplied for $12 plus Internet access, mountain tracks, a flying fox and other amenities. Dorms ❶, doubles ❸

Raglan Backpackers & Waterfront Lodge 6 Nero St ☎07/825 0515, ⓔinfo @raglanbackpackers.co.nz. One of the finest backpackers around these parts – small but clean, comfortable and exceptionally friendly, and beautifully laid out around a courtyard that backs onto the estuary. It is also very centrally located and has free kayaks, rental surfboards ($10 per session) and surf lessons ($70 for two people). Dorms ❶, rooms ❷

Raglan Kopua Holiday Park Marine Parade ☎07/825 8283, ✉raglanholidaypark@xtra.co.nz. Central campsite that's 1km by road from town, but is quickly accessible by footbridge, and is well-sited next to Te Kopua, the harbour's safest swimming beach. Tents $10, single room $25, cabin dorms ❶, cabins ❷, kitchen cabins ❸

Rohi Manu Rose St ☎07/825 6831, ⓦwww.rohimanu.co.nz. Three upmarket and centrally located houses on Rose Street, above the wharf, all with gorgeous sea views and offering in-house holistic therapies such as medical herbalism and massage. Two-, three- and four-bedroomed houses costing $200–250 for a couple (price variation depends on the size of the house) and $35–50 per extra adult.

Sleeping Lady Lodgings Raglan Surfing School, 5 Whaanga Rd, Whale Bay ☎07/825 7873, ⓦwww.sleepinglady.co.nz. Six delightful self-contained holiday homes scattered through coastal bush 8km southwest of Raglan, sleeping from two to five ($120–210 a night for two; $275–300 for five). ❻

Solscape Wainui Rd, Manu Bay, about 5km south of Raglan ☎07/825 8268. Excellent idiosyncratic accommodation in the form of brightly painted, converted train carriages and cottages on top of a hill with panoramic views; other bonuses include free pick-ups from Raglan, surf lessons, plus surf-boards and boogie boards for rent. Sheltered camping $10–12, dorms ❶, twins and doubles ❷, self-contained studio unit ❺, self-contained carriage ❺, cottages ❻

The Town and its beaches

It's easy to pass a couple of hours just wandering along the foreshore, but there is little specific to see in town. The two-storey *Harbour View Hotel* looks suitably impressive overlooking the junction of Bow Street and Wainui Road, and you'll find several shops selling alternative art, tat and jewellery.

Housed in an old police station, the **Raglan Museum**, Wainui St (Sat & Sun 1–3.30pm; donation), has a modest local history collection, mostly European. For a more colourful version of local lore, you'd do better to see if there's a group you can join hopping aboard a **Raglan Harbour Cruise** (60min; $10–15 per person, depending on numbers; book ahead Dec–March on ☎07/825 0300), which leaves from the jetty at the bottom of Bow Street. The skipper keeps passengers amused with a string of amusing facts and fictions woven around the historic sites you pass.

Raglan has long been known as a prime **surfing** destination but is now making more of this asset and has its own Surfing School at Whale Bay, 8km southwest of town. Most of the action happens around **Whale Bay** and neighbouring **Manu Bay**, but the town itself also exudes a surf spirit, with board-topped old Holdens and Falcons parked outside the surf shop and a lot of baggy pants in the cafés. There are opportunities for novices to try their hand: guests at *Raglan Backpackers* can get low-cost lessons from the manager; or contact the excellent Raglan Surfing School (☎07/825 7873, ⓦwww.raglansurfingschool.co.nz) who charge $79 for a three-and-a-half-hour lesson on a specially made soft board including all gear and transport, and run their own hostel (see Karioi Lodge, p.243; surf packages available). They also operate a shack at **Ngarunui Beach**, 3km west of Raglan off Wainui Road, where you can rent boards ($15 per hour, $35 half-day), boogie boards ($5 per hour) and wetsuits ($5 per hour, $10 half-day).

Surf gear is also for rent in town from Gag, 9a Bow St (☎07/825 8702, ⓦwww.gagraglan.com; daily roughly 9am–5pm, 6pm in summer), in the centre of town set back from the main road, with boards ($30–45 a day) and **kayaks** ($30–40 a day) for rent. Kayaks are also available for rent at Raglan Backpackers (see p.243; $5 for 2 hours).

The safest **swimming** beach is Te Kopua, in the heart of town and reached via the footbridge from lower Bow Street or by car along Wainui Road and Marine Parade. Ocean Beach, just outside the town off Wainui Road and on the way to Whale Bay gives great views of the Raglan Bar and is a lovely picnic spot, but swimming is only safe in summer (when the beach is patrolled) between the flags because of strong undertows.

Eating and drinking

The explosion of surfers and travellers has spawned a minor **eating** revolution in Raglan with almost everywhere of note congregating around the intersection of Bow and Wainui streets; and good fish and chips at the takeaway on Bow Street.

Aqua Velvet cnr Bow St & Wainui Rd. A bright comfortable bar-café daily offering excellent organic coffee, good breakfasts, brunches and imaginative light lunches; also open in the evenings from Boxing Day to the end of Feb.

Department of Food 35 Bow St. An intimate deli-cum-espresso bar with great coffee, delicious cakes, muffins and snacks; and lunchboxes. Closed Mon & Tues.

Raglan Club 22 Bow St. The atmosphere's nothing to shout about but there's good basic pub fare in the evenings, around the $10 mark, plus a cheap Thurs night roast. Closed Mon & Tues.

Sushi Takeaways Aloha Market Place, cnr Bow St & Nero St. Small sushi bar, for eating in or taking away, with various hot rice and noodle dishes too (Thurs–Sun 11am–5pm, Sat 11am–7pm).

Tongue and Groove cnr Bow St & Wainui Rd. Another lively place with a good range of imaginative café fare and great coffee. Licensed & BYO.

Vinnie's World of Eats 7 Wainui Rd. The place that trailblazed the café scene hereabouts and remains excellent value, whether for weekend breakfast or lunch and dinner throughout the week. There's everything from snacks to seafood mains, and gourmet pizza (from $12) plus a great smoothies bar. BYO; closed Mon except in high summer.

Around Raglan

With a little time to spare it is well worth exploring the area south of Raglan around the **Karioi Range**, although the **Te Toto** track (8km return; 5–6hr) climbing steeply up to the 755-metre summit of **Mount Karioi** should not to be attempted in bad weather. Starting 12km south of Raglan along Whaanga Road, the track heads up a gorge and, after a strenuous and difficult climb within a cliff-lined cut to a lookout, reaches an easier final section to the summit and excellent views of the mouth of Raglan Harbour and up and down the storm-battered coast.

Twenty-three kilometres southeast of Raglan, a much easier walk (10min each way) leads to the **Bridal Veil Falls** hidden in dense native bush. Water plummets 55m down a sheer rock face into a green pool; some droplets evaporate before they hit the bottom, creating a shimmering veil, adorned with rainbows in sunny weather. From the Kawhia Road, a signpost indicates the track to the falls, which is about a ten-minute stroll beside a small stream. These sights can be combined on a winding gravel-road loop around the Karioi Range, to include **horse riding** with Magic Mountain Horse Treks, 334 Houchen Rd (☏07/825 6892, ⓦ www.magicmountain.co.nz), who charge $30 for an hour, $50 for two hours and $70 for a trek to Bridal Veil Falls. To get here, head 8km east of Raglan on SH23, then 6km up Te Mata Road, and 3km up Houchen Road; pick-ups can be arranged from the Bridal Veil Falls. They also have accommodation (❼).

Note that the minor road to Kawhia (55km or so) is mostly unsealed and twisty, with the added hazard of cattle trucks, so take your time or follow the inland highways.

Kawhia

Sleepy **KAWHIA**, 55km south of Raglan, perches prettily on the northern side of the large Kawhia Harbour. The town itself is little more than the harbourside Jervois Street, lined by a couple of petrol stations, a handful of combined shops and cafés, and the quaint little **Kawhia Museum** (Oct–March Mon & Tues 11am–4pm, Wed–Sun 10.30am–4.30pm and by appointment; donation; ℡07/871 0161), which reveals much about Maori culture (see p.957) and early European settlers, and includes an original kauri whaleboat built in the 1880s. In summer the resident population of 620 swells to 4000 or more when holidaying Kiwi families flock to **Ocean Beach** just outside town and its **Te Puia Hot Springs**, which bubble up from beneath the black sand between two hours either side of low tide (check times at the museum or in any of the local stores). You can reach the springs along the 4km unsealed Tainui/Kawhia Forest Road to the car park, from where a track leads over the dunes and straight down to the ocean. Look out for signs of sulphur or holes that others have dug to make springs near the sea: be warned that the black sand can scorch bare feet and this is not a safe swimming beach, with dangerous rips. Quadbike Sand Rover Trips ($8) also run along the beach from the Kawhia Camping Ground (see below).

Kawhia is the spiritual home of the **Tainui** people, whose legends tell of their 1350 arrival from the homelands of Hawaiki in the ancestral *waka* (canoe), or the **Tainui Canoe**. Kawhia Harbour was so bountiful that the Tainui lived on its shores for some three hundred years, until tribal battles over the rich fishing grounds forced them inland. In 1821, after constant attacks by the better-armed Waikato Maori, the great Tainui chief Te Rauparaha led his people to the relative safety of Kapiti Island. On arrival, the *waka* was tied to a pohutukawa tree, Tangi te Korowhiti, which still grows on the shore on Kaora Street, near the junction with Panera Street, 800m west of the museum – reached along an easy waterside footpath. The Tainui Canoe itself is buried on a grassy knoll above the beautifully carved and painted **meeting house** of the **Maketu Marae**, further along Kaora Street at Karewa Beach, with Hani and Puna stones marking its stern and prow.

With the arrival of **European** settlers and missionaries in the 1830s, Kawhia became a highly prosperous port, providing a gateway to the fertile King Country, although its fortunes declined in the early years of the twentieth century, owing to its unsuitability for deep-draught ships. These days the settlement is known throughout New Zealand for annual **whale-boat races** (Jan 1), when eleven-metre, five-crew whaling boats are rowed across the bay. To sample something of this maritime spirit, join a **cruise** around the harbour with Kawhia Harbour Cruises (℡07/871 0149; about $20), or Dove Charters (℡07/870 3493; $75 a day). Otherwise opt for harbour **kayaking** with Trak'n'Paddle (℡0800/872 567; 4hr, $60), who also run combined tramping and kayaking trips from Waitomo to Kawhia.

Practicalities

Kawhia Bus and Freight **bus** service from Te Awamutu (Mon–Sat; ℡07/871 0701) drops off in the centre at the general store. The museum (see above) acts as an unofficial **visitor centre**, dispensing free maps and details of local attractions.

Campers should stay at the well-kept *Kawhia Camping Ground*, 73 Moke St (℡07/871 0863, ⓦwww.kawhiacamping.co.nz; camping $8–10, cabins ❷), which rents out quadbikes for the beach at $35 for two hours; or the waterfront *Kawhia Beachside S-cape*, 225 Pouewe St/SH31 (℡07/871 0727, ⓔkawhiabeachsidescape@xtra.co.nz; camping $10–14, dorms ❶, cabins ❷, units ❹), which rents kayaks cheaply. For a basic but spacious holiday flat contact the local pub, *Blue Chook Inn*, Jervois St (℡07/871 0778, ⓔinfo@bluechook.co.nz; ❹);

and there's **B&B** at *Te Wharu Bay B&B* (☎07/871 0795; ❺), 3.5km east of Kawhia on SH31, in a self-contained studio overlooking the harbour.

The best place to get a **drink** is the *Blue Chook Inn*, a locals' haunt with a variety of beers, snacks and pizzas. Also on Jervois Street, the *Happy Flounder* serves burgers, good fish and chips, and other **snacks** during the day; and for coffee or something a bit more substantial in a pleasant setting visit the licensed *Annie's Café* (☎07/871 0198; closed Mon & Tues), adjacent to the *Blue Chook Inn* and open till 4pm, reopening for dinner on Fri and Sat. Last but not least are the excellent **fish and chips** at *Kawhia Seafoods*, on the quay opposite the museum (Wed–Sun, closes 6.30pm).

The King Country

The rural landscape inland from Kawhia and south of Hamilton is known as the **King Country**, an area that derives its name from more uncertain times when it became the refuge of **King Tawhiao** and members of the **King Movement** (see box below), as they were driven south in defeat during the New Zealand Wars.

The King Movement

Before Europeans arrived on the scene, Maori loyalty was solely to their immediate family and tribe, but wrangles with acquisitive European settlers led many tribes to discard age-old feuds in favour of a common crusade against the *pakeha*. Initially a response to poor communication and administration, **Maori nationalism** hardened in the face of blatantly unjust decisions and increasing pressure to "sell" their ancestral lands.

In 1856, the influential Otaki Maori sought a chief who might unite the disparate tribes against the Europeans, and in 1858 the Waikato, Taupo and some other tribes (largely originating from the *Tainui* Canoe; see p.243) chose **Te Wherowhero** as their leader. Taking the title of **Potatau I**, the newly elected king established himself at Ngaruawahia – to this day the heartland of the **King Movement**. The principal tenet of the movement was to resist the appropriation of Maori land and to provide a basis for a degree of self-government. Whether out of a genuine misunderstanding of these aims or for reasons of pure economic expediency, the settlers interpreted the formation of the movement as an act of rebellion – despite the fact that Queen Victoria was included in its prayers – and tension heightened. The situation escalated into armed conflict later in 1858 when the Waitara Block near New Plymouth was confiscated from its Maori owners. The fighting spread throughout the central North Island: the King Movement won a notable victory at Gate Pa, in the Bay of Plenty, but were eventually overwhelmed at Te Ranga. Seeing the wars as an opportunity to settle old scores, some Maori tribes sided with the British and, in a series of battles along the Waikato, forced the kingites further and further south, until a crushing blow was struck at Orakau in 1864. The king and his followers fled south of the Puniu River into an area that, by virtue of their presence, became known as the **King Country**.

They remained there, almost devoid of all European contact, until 1881, when **King Tawhiao**, who had succeeded to the throne in 1860, made peace. Gradually the followers of the King Movement drifted back to Ngaruawahia. Although by no means supported by all Maori, the loose coalition of the contemporary King Movement plays an important role in the current reassessment of Maori–*pakeha* relations, and the reigning Maori queen, **Te Arikinui Dame Te Atairangikaahu,** has been the recipient of many state and royal visits.

The area soon gained a reputation as an inhospitable Maori stronghold, renowned for difficult terrain and the type of welcome that meant few, if any, Europeans had the nerve to enter. However, the forest's respite was short-lived: when peace was declared in 1881, eager loggers descended in droves.

These days the most famous place in the King Country is **Waitomo**, a tiny village at the heart of a unique and dramatic landscape, honeycombed by limestone caves eerily illuminated by millions of glowworms, and overlaid by a geological wonderland of karst features. North of Waitomo is the small dairying town of **Otorohanga**, with the unexpected pleasure of a kiwi house and large aviary.

Workaday **Te Kuiti** remains devoted to sheep farming and bills itself as the shearing capital of the world. In the 1860s, the town provided sanctuary for Maori rebel Te Kooti, who reciprocated with a beautifully carved meeting house. Further south is the **Pureora Forest Park**, an enclave of rich lowland podocarp forest that was the site of a conservation battle in the late 1970s, and now provides access to some excellent walks and a home for the rare **kokako** bird, which prefers an ungainly walk to flight. The last community in the King Country, the rather jaded town of **Taumarunui** provides access to the Whanganui River, a historic drive to Stratford and the spectacular coastal road via **Mokau**, a tiny and intriguing coastal settlement, before heading through the Taranaki coastal plains to New Plymouth.

Otorohanga

Surrounded by sheep and cattle country some 30km south of Te Awamutu, **OTOROHANGA** is primarily of interest as a base for Waitomo (see p.249) and for the unusually visible birds at the **Kiwi House Native Bird Park**, Alex Telfer Drive, off Kakamutu Road (daily: Sept–May 9.30am–5pm; June–Aug 9am–4.30pm; $10; Ⓦwww.kiwihouse.org.nz), five minutes' walk from the town centre. The lifestyle of the kiwi is amply explained by attendants in the well laid out nocturnal house, which leads on to a section devoted to native lizards, geckos and the prehistoric lizard-like tuatara. Outdoor enclosures are given over to just about every species of New Zealand native bird, many in an extensive walk-through aviary: the kea and its cousin the kaka are always entertaining but there are also parakeets, tui, morepork, and myriad less sexy species.

Nearby on Kakamutu Road, the small **Otorohanga Museum** (Sun 2–4pm; other times by arrangement, ☏07/873 8849; donation) presents Maori flax weavings, dog-hair cloaks, and a splendid portrait of Wahanui Huatare, a one-time local elder. A separate room houses the 110-year-old wheelbarrow used in the inaugural ceremony for the railway, which finally opened up the King Country to Pakeha settlement.

In recent times, Otorohanga has decided to celebrate all things archetypally Kiwi through a series of light-hearted shop-window Kiwiana displays along the main **Maniopoto Street**. Take a few minutes to glance in Giltrap Gifts at #58 for the pavlova, and Otorohanga Sheepskins at #52 for Marmite. Perhaps more productively, check out the Karam and John Haddad Menswear Store, 65–71 Maniopoto St (☏07/873 8377), a stockist of Swanndri bushwear and Driza-Bone waxed coats, plus bucketloads of other great stuff, for men and women – vital gear for rural New Zealand, and considerably cheaper than elsewhere.

Practicalities

Auckland to Wellington **trains** pull in just off the main street behind the **visitor centre**, 21 Maniopoto St (Mon–Fri 9am–5.30pm, Sat & Sun 10am–4pm; ☏07/873 8951, Ⓦwww.otorohanga.co.nz), which is where

InterCity, Newmans and Dalroys **buses** stop. The visitor centre also has **Internet access**, or you can try the nearby library, just by the village green on Maniapoto St (Mon–Fri 9am–5pm, Sat 10am–noon). Otorohanga Taxis (℡0800/808 279 & 07/873 8279) run a shuttle to Waitomo, and the town has the **last amenities** of bank, supermarket and petrol before Waitomo, which has none.

If you want to **stay**, try the *Oto-Kiwi Backpackers*, 1 Sangro Crescent, off Domain Drive (℡07/873 6022, ✉oto-kiwi@xtra.co.nz; dorms ❶, rooms ❷), a small and comfortable hostel near the Kiwi House. Alternatively, the *Otorohanga Holiday Park*, 12 Huiputea Drive (℡07/873 7253, ⓦwww .kiwiholidaypark.co.nz; camping $11, cabin ❷, units ❸), is a well-equipped central campsite with its own gym. Moving upmarket there are the *Otorohanga & Waitomo Colonial Motels*, 59 Main North Road/SH3 (℡0800 828 289 & 07/873 7755, ✉oto@xtra.co.nz; ❹), and the luxurious, self-contained and peaceful *Kamahi Cottage* (℡07/873 0849, ⓦwww.kamahi.co.nz; ❽), 229 Barber Road, around 15km southeast of Otorohanga.

Eating in Otorohanga mostly revolves around a café-bar, the tearooms and takeaways along Maniapoto Street. The *Kiwiana Café*, at #13, is fine for coffee, snacks and lunches, but more fun is *The Thirsty Weta*, on the corner of Maniapoto Street and Wahanui Crescent, a small atmospheric evening bar serving good food.

Waitomo

WAITOMO, 8km west of SH3 some 16km south of Otorohanga, is a diminutive village with an outsize reputation for its wonderful **cave trips** and magnificent **karst limestone features** all around – dry valleys, streams that disappear down funnel-shaped sinkholes, craggy limestone outcrops, fluted rocks, and potholes and natural bridges caused by cave ceiling collapses. Below ground, seeping water has sculpted the rock into eerie and extraordinarily beautiful shapes visited on a number of tours from a gentle underground float through grottoes illuminated by **glowworms**, to full-on wetsuit-clad adventure caving trips involving hundred-metre abseils into the void and tight squeezes. Alternatively you can go glowworm searching independently for free on a nighttime walk through a **natural tunnel**.

Appropriately enough, Waitomo means "water entering shaft" and, for over a hundred years, visitors have flocked here to explore the surrounding caves. Passages were first discovered in 1887 by Maori chief **Tane Tinorau** and

---

Glowworms

Glowworms (*Arachnocampa Luminosa*) are found all over New Zealand, mostly in caves but also on overhanging banks in the bush where in dark and damp conditions you'll often see the tell-tale bluey-green glow. A glowworm isn't a worm at all, but the matchstick-sized larval stage of the fungus gnat (a relative of the mosquito), which attaches itself to the cave roof and produces around twenty or thirty mucus-and-silk threads or "fishing lines", which hang down a few centimetres. Drawn by the highly efficient chemical light, midges and flying insects get ensnared in the threads and the glowworm draws in the line to eat the insect.

The six- to nine-month larval stage is the only time in the glowworm **lifecycle** that it can eat, so it needs to store energy for the two-week pupal stage when it transforms into the adult gnat, which has no mouthparts. It only lives a couple of days, during which time the female has to frantically find a mate in the dark caves (the glow is a big help here) and lay her batch of a hundred or so eggs. After a two- to three-week incubation, these hatch into glowworms and the process begins anew.

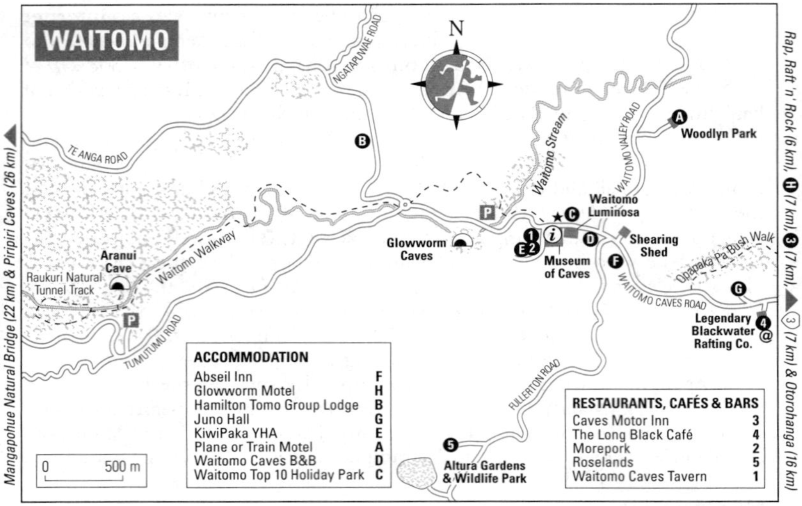
WAITOMO
N
NGATAPUWAE ROAD
TE ANGA ROAD
Waitomo Stream
WAITOMO VALLEY ROAD
Woodlyn Park
Waitomo Luminosa
Shearing Shed
Opapaka Pa Bush Walk
Glowworm Caves
Museum of Caves
WAITOMO CAVES ROAD
Legendary Blackwater Rafting Co.
Aranui Cave
Raukuri Natural Tunnel Track
Waitomo Walkway
TUMUTUMU ROAD
FULLERTON ROAD
Altura Gardens & Wildlife Park
0 500 m
ACCOMMODATION
Abseil Inn F
Glowworm Motel H
Hamilton Tomo Group Lodge B
Juno Hall G
KiwiPaka YHA E
Plane or Train Motel A
Waitomo Caves B&B D
Waitomo Top 10 Holiday Park C
RESTAURANTS, CAFÉS & BARS
Caves Motor Inn 3
The Long Black Café 4
Morepork 2
Roselands 5
Waitomo Caves Tavern 1
Mangapohue Natural Bridge (22 km) & Piripiri Caves (26 km)
Rap, Raft 'n' Rock (6 km), H (7 km), 3 (7 km), 3 (7 km) & Otorohanga (16 km)

English surveyor **Fred Mace**, who built a raft of flax stems and drifted along an underground stream, with candles as their only source of light. So impressed were they that further explorations ensued, and within a year the enterprising Tane was guiding tourists to see the spectacle. The government took over the operation in 1906 and it was not until 1989 that the caves were returned to their traditional Maori owners who now receive a percentage of all the revenue generated and participate in the site's management. Only a fraction of the forty-five kilometres of cave passages under Waitomo can be visited on **guided tours**, and the only caves you can safely explore **independently** are the Piripiri Caves west of the village (see p.254).

The ongoing process of **cave creation** involves the interaction of rainwater and carbon dioxide from the air, which together form a weak acid that flows down cracks in the rock; as more carbon dioxide is absorbed from the soil the acid grows stronger, dissolving the limestone and enlarging the cracks and joints and eventually forming the varied caves you see today. Each year a further seventy cubic metres of limestone (about the size of a double-decker bus) is dissolved.

Arrival and information

Trains and InterCity **buses** stop in Otorohanga, from where Waitomo Shuttle (☎0800/808 279; $8 each way) ferry people to Waitomo three times daily. Newmans buses run daily to Waitomo on their Auckland–Rotorua run, and there is also the Waitomo Wanderer (☎07/349 2509) which runs here once daily from Rotorua. Buses stop in the centre of the village outside the official **visitor centre** in the Museum of Caves building on the main road (daily: Jan & Feb 8am–8pm; Oct–Dec & March 8am–5.30pm; April–Sept 8.30am–5pm; ☎07/878 7640, Ⓦwww.waitomoinfo.co.nz). The centre is a booking agent for cave trips, trains and buses, as well as a post office. There's **Internet access** at the visitor centre, at the nearby *Cavelands Café*, beside the general store (daily around 7am–8pm) and at *The Long Black Café* (see p.254; daily 7.30am–4.30pm, later in the summer). Note that there is **no bank** or **petrol** at Waitomo and only a small store; the nearest towns with these amenities are Otorohanga and Te Kuiti.

Accommodation

Although backpackers are well provided for in Waitomo, other **accommodation** options are fairly limited. To make sure you get what you want, **book in advance**, particularly from November to January.

Abseil Inn 709 Waitomo Caves Rd, 400m east of the museum ☎07/878 7815, Ⓔabseilinn@xtra.co.nz. The pick of the B&Bs, relaxing, stylish and modern, on top of a hill with great views over rolling countryside. Each of the four en-suite rooms is decorated in its own style. ❻

Glowworm Motel cnr SH3 & Waitomo Caves Rd, 8km east ☎07/873 0882, Ⓦwww.glowwormmotel.co.nz. Simple motel with nine self-contained units, and a swimming pool. ❹

Hamilton Tomo Group Lodge 1.7km west of Waitomo ☎07/878 7442. Basic caving-club lodge that welcomes visitors and plies them with local knowledge. Large and clean, dorms are very cheap and have access to kitchen facilities and a wide sunny deck with BBQ. ❶

Juno Hall Waitomo Caves Rd, 1km east of Waitomo ☎07/878 7649, Ⓦwww.junowaitomo.co.nz. Comfy well-equipped hostel in a modern timber-lined building set on a low hill with a saltwater pool, barbecue deck and free transfers to and from Waitomo; other bonuses are volleyball, a tennis court, and free bikes. Camping $10, dorms ❶, rooms ❷, en suites ❸

KiwiPaka YHA Waitomo School Rd ☎07/878 3395, Ⓦwww.kiwipaka-yha.co.nz. Excellent, new

purpose-built complex right in the heart of Waitomo with beds in a lodge (four-share dorms, twins, doubles, en-suites), and chalets (double, twin, triple and quad) with their own bathrooms. There are also a café (see *Morepork*, p.254), travel-booking desk, and free pickup from the bus. ❶–❺

Plane or Train Motel Woodlyn Park, 700m up Waitomo Valley Rd, off Waitomo Caves Rd ☎07/878 6666, Ⓕ878 8866. Very popular accommodation in a well-preserved Bristol freighter imaginatively converted into two comfortable self-contained units; and a 1950s railway carriage containing a three-room unit – both on the site of Billy Black's Kiwi Culture Show. Best to book a month ahead for Dec–Feb. ❻

Waitomo Caves B&B Waitomo Caves Rd, 100m east of the museum ☎07/878 7641, Ⓔjancolbeeston@xtra.co.nz. Several comfortable, clean and spacious units built up a hillside in a peaceful garden; some are rather basic. ❹

Waitomo Top 10 Holiday Park, 12 Waitomo Caves Rd ☎0508/498 666 & 07/878 7639, Ⓦwaitomopark.co.nz. Spacious well-equipped campsite conveniently sited in the heart of town, with a swimming pool and spa. Camping $13, cabins ❷, self-contained units ❹

The Village

Above ground there's not much to **Waitomo Village** apart from the *Waitomo Caves Hotel*, which sits atop its hill, brooding like a rundown chateau. At its feet lie a campsite, a few places to stay, the visitor centre, a small general store, pub and a few offices for booking cave trips. Note that in very wet weather most **cave trips** are cancelled owing to perilous water levels, so phone ahead and allow extra time in case.

To enhance your cave experience, first stop should be the **Museum of Caves**, beside the visitor centre (daily 8am–5.30pm, late Dec to early March till 8pm; $5; Ⓦwww.waitomo-museum.co.nz), which has entertaining and informative displays on the geology and history of the caves. With interactive displays on the lifecycle of glowworms and cave wetas, it's a great place for kids. To test your aptitude for claustrophobic underground spaces before signing up for an adventure trip, try to wriggle through some of the tight crawl holes provided in the museum. A free 18-minute multimedia show is screened on request, telling you all you'll ever need to know about glowworms.

Visiting the Caves

Waitomo's original cave experience is **Waitomo Glowworm Caves**, 500m west of the visitor centre (daily 9am–5pm; $25), now very much geared to tour bus passengers who are herded through on forty-minute tours which begin every half hour. Paved walkways, and lighting that picks out the best of the stalactites and stalagmites, make for a gentle cave experience, finished off with a boat ride through the cave grotto, where glowworms shed pinpricks of ghostly pale-green light resembling constellations in the night sky of another planet. The best **tour** is the first of the day (9am), when there are fewer tourists, and it usually eases again after 3pm.

The glowworm caves office also sells tickets for the forty-five minute tours around the **Aranui Cave**, 3.5km west of the visitor centre (daily 10am, 11am, 1pm, 2pm & 3pm; $25), which is only 250m long, but is geologically more spectacular, with high-ceilinged chambers and magnificent stalactites and stalagmites. A two-cave combo costs $40, and a museum-and-cave special is $26.

If you want a gentle experience in a smaller group, seeing glowworms close up without getting wet and with almost an hour underground, consider **Spellbound** (book through the visitor centre or after hours on ℡0800/773 552; 3hr; $45, including entry to the Museum of Caves), which involves an underground hike through tunnels and caves followed by twenty minutes or so floating in a raft with a galaxy of glowworms just above your head.

Adventure caving

While the gentle cave trips are a good way to see glowworms and cave features, Waitomo really excels in **adventure caving trips**, which should be **booked in advance**, especially from November to January. The adrenalin factor varies considerably and the trick is to choose a trip that is exciting enough but won't scare you witless – most trips are not recommended for borderline claustrophobics. Operators are pretty adept at matching customers with the appropriate trip – most of which involve getting kitted out in your own swimwear plus wetsuit, caver's helmet with lamp and rubber boots – and combine two or more adventure elements as outlined below. In all cases, **heavy rain** can lead to cancellation as water levels rise too high, so it pays to have a day or two to spare. **Kids** under twelve are not usually allowed on adventure trips, and the wilder trips are for those of fifteen and over.

Cave tubing (also known as blackwater rafting) generally involves a gentle float through a pitch-black section of cave with your bum wedged into the inner tube of a truck tyre as you gaze at the glowworms overhead, unsure whether the cave roof is one or a hundred metres above your head. Access into some caves is by **abseiling** (rappelling) down a long rope, always with some safety system. Once underground you may do some genuine **caving**, working your way along passages, through fairly tight squeezes, clambering over rocks and perhaps jumping into deep pools.

Adventure caving operators

The Legendary Black Water Rafting Co. ℡07/878 6219 & 0800/228 464, @www.blackwaterrafting.co.nz. Roughly 1km east, Waitomo's original cave-tubing company, run two wetsuit-clad trips in Ruakuri Cave: Black Labyrinth (3hr, 1hr underground; $75) involves a short jump from an underground waterfall and an idyllic float through a glowworm cave; and the more adventurous Black Abyss (5hr, 2–3hr underground; $145), which adds abseiling and an eerie flying fox ride into the darkness. Museum of Caves entry is included in all their trips.

Rap, Raft 'n' Rock ℡0800/228 372, @www.caveraft.com; 4hr 30min, $95 including entry to the Museum of Caves, see p.250. Eight kilometres east of the Museum of Caves, at 95 Waitomo Caves Rd/SH37 or 1km from the junction with SH3. A small company that gives maximum value for money with small-group trips that start with a 27-metre abseil into a glowworm-filled cave explored partly on foot and partly floating on a tube, and finish with a rock-climb out to the starting point. There's also a high ropes course ($50 per half-day) among plantation pines close to the cave entrance, with all manner of confidence-testing escapades – trapeze, wobbly bridges and so on. A one-day cave and ropes combo costs $120.

Waitomo Adventures ☎07/878 7788 & 0800/924 866, ⊛www.waitomo.co.nz. The Waitomo Luminosa office in the centre of town is the base for a highly professional operation that offers a number of trips: Tumu Tumu Toobing (4hr; $85), a combination of walking, tubing and swimming through an especially spectacular cave; Haggas Honking Holes (4hr; $165), a madcap series of abseils, climbs and crawl-throughs; St Benedict's Caverns (3hr 30min; $100), a wetsuit-free "dry" trip into a very pretty cave, offering two short abseils and a flying fox, but no glowworms; Lost World Abseil (4hr; $225), another "dry" trip involving a gentle 100-metre rappel into the gaping fern-draped mouth of a spectacular pothole, followed by a short, dry cave walk before climbing out on a seemingly endless ladder – the first trip of the day is best. Cave junkies should go for the Lost World Epic (7hr; $355), with the abseil followed by several "wet" hours, working your way upstream through squeezes, behind a small waterfall and into a glittering glowworm grotto. **Waitomo Cave Club** ☎07/878 7442. Serious cavers with experience should contact this club, through the *Hamilton Tomo Group Lodge* (see p.251), who can usually arrange contacts or a trip.

Other activities

Other attractions include **Woodlyn Park**, 900m up Waitomo Valley Road from the village (☎07/878 6666, ⊛www.woodlynpark.co.nz), where a rustic barn hosts the hugely entertaining hour-long **Billy Black's Kiwi Culture Show** (daily 1.30pm, $15), which presents the history of logging and farming in an off-beat way, with loads of audience participation. Outside, you can pilot your own powerful single-seater jetboat around a specially designed racecourse ($47 for 8 laps). You can also tackle the rugged karst countryside around Waitomo on 4WD **quad bikes** with Waitomo Big Red (book through the visitor centre; 2hr, $75), and there's more sedate activity **horse riding** with Waitomo Caves Horse Treks (☎07/878 5065; 1hr, $40; 2hr, $50; 4hr, $90). Informative **scenic and cultural tours** are run by Waitomo Tiki Tours (☎0800 867 868; 5hr 30min; $80), who begin with a visit to the marae and take you to the west coast, viewing the Mangapohue Natural Bridge and the Marokopa Falls (see p.254) on the way, sharing Maori mythology and bush medicine; shorter tours are also possible.

Walks in and around Waitomo

Waitomo Village and the Aranui Cave are linked by the **Waitomo Walkway** (10km; 3hr return), which starts opposite the museum, disappears into the bush, then largely follows the Waitomo Stream to the Aranui Cave. The trail saves the best until last by linking with the **Raukuri Natural Tunnel** track (2km return; 45min), surely one of the most impressive short walks in the country. It starts from the car park for the Aranui Cave on Tumutumu Road, 3.5 kilometres west of the visitor centre, and follows the Waitomo Stream on boardwalks and mostly level walkways past cave entrances. Ducking and weaving through short tunnel sections, you eventually reach a huge cave where the stream temporarily threads underground. The Raukuri Natural Tunnel walk is especially magical at night when lit by glowworms in the bush on the banks. These walks are shown on the free Waitomo Caves **map** from the visitor centre.

Lastly, at the eastern end of the village, the **Opapaka Pa Bush Walk** (2km return; 45min) climbs past plants and trees traditionally used in Maori medicine to a *pa* site, which is thought to have been established in the 1700s.

Eating and drinking

Despite its position as one of New Zealand's tourist hot spots, Waitomo has a fairly limited range of **eating** options, particularly in winter, when opening times become very limited.

Caves Motor Inn 728 SH3, 100m south of Waitomo Caves Rd ☎07/873 8109. Some of the best and most reliable dinners in these parts are served upstairs at this out-of-town motel. The decor could be more inviting, but stick around for large portions of king prawns ($15), or their excellent chowder ($8.50) followed by tender steak ($20–25).

The Long Black Café 1km east of the museum. Cooked breakfasts, Waitomo's best coffee, simple snacks and light meals are served from 8am in summer (8.30am in winter) to around 4pm in this spacious room alive with people setting off on caving trips, playing pool, or hanging out on the sunny deck.

Morepork KiwiPaka YHA, School Rd. Pleasant, modern all-day café attached to the hostel and open from breakfast with a limited menu of sandwiches, pasta and salads, plus pizza in the evenings. BYO.

Roselands Restaurant 3km south along Fullerton Rd. Splendid buffet lunches (11am–2pm) of BBQ beefsteak and fish, with salads and vegetables served in a beautiful bush setting. They mainly cater to coach tours but independent travellers are welcome.

Waitomo Caves Tavern Immediately west of the museum. Almost everyone eventually ends up at this unreconstructed Kiwi pub, either for convivial boozing or good-value, large meals in the steak, seafood and burger tradition. There is occasional live music at weekends; the pub sometimes closes at 7pm or so, even in summer.

Around Waitomo: towards the coast

If you can't get enough of limestone scenery, or would prefer a less commercialized experience, drive the Te Anga Road for three free sights worth seeing in wet weather or fine. (Be sure not to leave your valuables in the car.) They kick off with the **Mangapohue Natural Bridge**, 24km west of Waitomo. An easy fifteen-minute loop trail winds through forest to a riverside boardwalk into a delightful, narrow limestone gorge topped by a remarkable natural double bridge formed by the remains of a collapsed cave roof. Dramatic at any time, it is especially picturesque at night when the underside of the bridges glimmer with myriad glowworms. In daylight don't miss the rest of the walk, which loops through farmland past fossilised examples of 35 million year old giant oysters.

Four kilometres further west, the **Piripiri Caves** are reached by a short path (5min each way) through a forested landscape full of weathered limestone outcrops. Inside the cavern you'll need a decent torch (and an emergency spare) to explore the Oyster Room which contains more giant fossil oysters, and you might spot a weta or two. A kilometre or so on, a track (5min each way) accesses the dramatic multi-tiered **Marokopa Falls** through a forest of tawa, pukatea and kohekohe trees.

The road continues west past tiny **TE ANGA**, with an archetypal country pub, the *Te Anga Tavern*, and the turnoff to a twisting loop road to Kawhia (see p.245), on towards the wind-lashed communities and long black-sand beaches of the coast. At **MAROKOPA**, stop at the Albatross Anchor, at the end of the road overlooking the beach, saved from the ship of the same name which foundered crossing the harbour bar, and take in the spot where the river meets the roaring white-capped waves – but be careful, the sea is dangerous and it's not unknown for fishermen to get dragged in.

Fun **guided tramps** in a small group through this spectacular region are led by Trak 'n' Paddle (☎0800/872 567, ✉info@traknpaddle.co.nz), who depart from Waitomo three times a week, offering one-day return trips ($100) or overnight stays ($150–350) that include kayaking in the Rakaunui Inlet and at Kawhia Harbour.

Te Kuiti and around

The hills narrow around the plain town of **TE KUITI**, 19km south of Waitomo, a regional farming centre that isn't much in itself but makes a reasonable base for Waitomo. On the main north–south rail line it sits near the junction of three routes: SH3, heading southwest to the coast and Taranaki; SH4, running south towards Taumarunui and the Tongariro National Park; and SH30, weaving south then east into the Pureora Forest Park.

Te Kuiti hosts the annual **New Zealand Shearing and Wool Handling Championships**, which are held in late March or early April, a celebration reinforced by the seven-metre-high statue of a man shearing a sheep at the southern end of Rora Street. More intriguingly, Te Kuiti also has a proud Maori history, for it was here that King Tawhiao and his followers fled after the battle of Rangiriri in 1864. Eight years later, Maori rebel Te Kooti (see p.449) also sought refuge here and lived under the Maori King's protection until he was pardoned. In return for sanctuary, Te Kooti left a magnificently carved **meeting house**, Te Tokanganui-a-noho, opposite the south end of Rora Street, on Awakino Road; you can look at it from the road and if anyone is there they might invite you onto the *marae*.

Practicalities

The **train station** is next to the visitor centre on Rora Street. InterCity and Newmans **buses** stop just down the road at the nearby *Tiffany's Restaurant*, which is their booking agent. Smaller services such as Dalroy's (℡06/755 0009; between Auckland and New Plymouth), Pioneer (℡07/895 8528), and Perry's Bus (which runs a regular **shuttle** to Waitomo and across to the coast; ℡025 6821084 & 07/876 7570) stop at the **visitor centre**, on Rora St (Oct–April daily 9am–5pm; May–Sept Mon–Fri 9am–5pm, Sat & Sun 10am–4pm; ℡07/878 8077, ✆tkinfo@xtra.co.nz. The **DOC office**, 78 Taupiri St (Mon–Fri 8am–4.30pm), has details of the Pureora Forest Park (see below). Travelling from the south, Te Kuiti is the **last stop** for a bank, petrol and a supermarket before you reach Waitomo, which has none.

Accommodation is available at the rural hillside *Casara Mesa Backpackers*, Mangarino Rd (℡07/878 6697, ✆casara@xtra.co.nz; dorms ❶, rooms ❷), 3km northeast but with free pick-ups from the visitor centre; the 4-bed dorms and some of the doubles are en suite. There are also units at the central *Motel Te Kuiti,* corner Carroll Street and King Street (℡07/878 3448, ✆moteltekuiti @xtra.co.nz; ❺). Alternatively, settle for the tranquil riverside *Te Kuiti Camping Ground*, 1 Hinerangi St (℡07/878 8966, ✆tewaka@hotmail.com; camping $7, 4-bed dorm ❶, caravans & cabins ❷), which also has a pool and a hostel in a pleasant house (dorm ❶, rooms ❷), plus Maori cultural and kayaking tours on the North Island (✇www.tewaka.com), for which you pay by donation.

The busiest place to **eat and drink** is *Tiffany's Restaurant*, at the corner of Rora and Lawrence streets, which has reasonable snacks, all-day meals and takeaways at low prices. There is better food and coffee a couple of kilometres north at the daytime *Bosco*, 57 Te Kumi Rd (℡07/878 3633; also open Sun eve), a promotional effort for New Zealand's plantation forest industry using renewable softwoods and glass in a modern structure. Political implications aside, it is a great place for breakfast, inventive sandwiches and mains, as well as desserts like sweet polenta and plum cake. Back in town, *Riverside Lodge*, beside the river off King Street (turn off by the bridge; closed Mon), runs a restaurant bar that does good pizza.

Pureora Forest Park

Straddling the Hauhungaroa Range some 50km southeast of Te Kuiti, the **Pureora Forest Park** only narrowly escaped clear-felling in 1978, when it became the site of a successful tree-top protest. Along with Little Barrier Island (see p.158) and a few pockets around Rotorua, this broad-leaf forest environment is now one of the few remaining habitats of the rare North Island **kokako**, a bluish-grey bird distinguished by the bright blue patches on either cheek. Poor fliers, they prefer to hop among the branches and nest close to the ground, making them vulnerable to introduced predators. On-going trapping and poisoning programmes attempt to redress the balance.

There is no public transport to the park, but SH30 provides access from the west, running 46km from Te Kuiti to the **DOC Pureora Field Centre** (Mon–Fri 7.30am–4pm; ☎07/878 1080), at the entrance to the forest. Here you can pick up leaflets describing various walks in the park ($1), and get details of the simple *Ngaherenga* DOC **campsite** ($7), 1km to the north. Half a kilometre north of the field centre, you can follow the wheelchair-accessible **Totara Walk** (800m loop; 15–30min), which winds through giant podocarps, past matai, rimu, tawa, kahikatea, ferns, vines and perching plants, with a screeching accompaniment from kaka high up in the canopy. Immediately south of the campsite, a signposted road runs 3km to the **Forest Tower**, which gives a twelve-metre-high protestor's-eye view of the surrounding area, close to the site of the landmark anti-logging protest. It's a fifteen-minute drive northeast of the field centre along SH30 to reach the **Pouakani Tree**, the largest totara ever recorded.

Link Road (also called Kakaho Road) runs east through the Pureora Forest to SH32, which provides access to the forest from the area around Lake Taupo. Along Link Road, coming from the field centre, there's challenging hiking and excellent views from the **Mount Pureora Summit Track** (4km return; 2–3hr; 300m ascent), which starts 10km east of the field centre; and the relatively easy but rewarding **Rimu Walk** (1.5km loop, 30min–1hr; 100m ascent), which goes through some lovely podocarp forest – predominantly rimu – and, after five minutes, past a cool swimming hole. The walk begins a further 16km east beside DOC's *Kakaho* **campground** ($7). From here it is 6km to SH32 which runs along the western side of Lake Taupo (see p.333).

The coast road to Taranaki

Heading southwest from Te Kuiti, **SH3** makes a beeline for the Tasman Sea, and the small but appealing coastal town of **Mokau**, then twists its way through tiny communities, sandwiched between the spectacular black beaches and steep inland ranges. Opportunities for exploration focus on walks near the **Tongaporutu** rivermouth, and there's refreshment a little further on at an excellent microbrewery. Eventually the scenery opens out onto the **Taranaki Plains** just north of New Plymouth; our coverage of New Plymouth and Taranaki starts on p.267.

Mokau

The first significant place to stop is the tiny community of **MOKAU**, 73km southwest of Te Kuiti, perched on a rise above the **Mokau Estuary** where the 90-year-old historic creamboat, MV *Cygnet* (☎06/752 9775; daily 11am & summer weekends 3pm; $30), runs **cruises** up river past a number of points of historic interest, old coal workings and abandoned farms. The river is noted for its run of whitebait, and in season (Aug 15–Nov 30) you'll find this delicacy available in Mokaus. The estuary also has good swimming though the two local black-sand surf **beaches** – Mokau and Rapanui – are dangerous and best left to surfers and those after the region's abundant **shellfish**. The wild scenery hereabouts provided the backdrop for several scenes from Jane Campion's 1993 film *The Piano*, particularly in the bush scenes and the fence line, seen in silhouette, along which the daughter dances.

In town, the local **Tainui Museum** (daily 10am–4pm; donation), charts the history of the small Maori settlements on either side of the Mokau rivermouth and of the 1840 European settlement beside the coal-rich river. Just over 2km north along SH3 the **Maniaroa Marae** and *pa* is the resting place of the Tainui Canoe's anchor stone from the alleged Great Migration, a historic *waka* and some excellent wood carvings; on entering the *marae* driveway, keep left to reach the cemetery where you must observe the anchor stone from outside the cemetery gates.

Buses between Auckland and New Plymouth stop outside the *Whitebait Inn* (⊕06/752 9713; camping $7–9, cabins ❷), where you can get **accommodation** and simple meals. From there it is 100m north to the cosy and well-kept *Palm House Backpackers* (⊕06/752 9081; dorms ❶, room ❷), and a similar distance to the museum, which acts as an unofficial **visitor centre**, and the *Mokau Roadhouse*, which has a limited supply of groceries, sells takeaways and serves basic bistro-style **meals**.

Tongaporutu and White Cliffs Brewery

Continuing south down the coast, after 18km you come to a fascinating **sea cave** just south of the **Tongaporutu rivermouth**. Signalled by two rock stacks on the beach opposite the entrance, the cave bears ancient footprints on its upper walls, about four metres up from the floor. For many years this coastal, tide-dependent route was the only access for Maori travelling between the Waikato and Taranaki districts, and this cave provided shelter. Local lore has it that the infamous chief Te Rauparaha, along with his most trusted female companion, rested in a sea cave to recover from a debilitating attack of boils. When the boils were lanced, the chief braced himself against the cave wall and, due to the combination of the sudden pain and his great strength, left impressions of his hands and feet in the rock. The chief was reputed to have six toes – as do eight of the foot imprints in the cave.

A little over 30km on and just north of Urenui keep your eyes skinned for a final worthwhile stop at **White Cliffs Brewery** (daily 10am–6pm; ⊕06/752 3676, ⓦwwwbrewing.co.nz/mikes.htm; free), a tiny organic microbrewery of international standing which produces just one super brew. The delicious Mike's Mild Ale will make you well disposed towards the entire region, and Mike may well be available for a quick tour of the facilities before selling you a few bottles.

Taumarunui and around

With its declining population and dwindling industries, five-thousand-strong **TAUMARUNUI**, 82km south of Te Kuiti, feels rather run-down. For most travellers the only reason to stop is to use the town as a base for canoe or jet-boat forays into the Whanganui National Park (see p.259) or to follow the **Lost World Highway** towards Stratford and Mount Taranaki.

Surrounded by national parks and forests at the confluence of the Ongarua and Whanganui rivers, Taumarunui was one of the last places to be settled by Europeans, who didn't arrive in large numbers until 1908, when the railway came to town. Finding a suitable route for the track on its steep descent towards Taumarunui from the area around the Tongariro National Park proved problematic, but surveyor R.W. Holmes proposed what's now known as the

Raurimu Spiral, a remarkable feat of engineering combining bridges and tunnels to loop the track over itself. The spiral can be seen from a signposted viewpoint 37km south of Taumarunui on SH4 (and actually closer to National Park; see p.359), and is still part of the Auckland–Wellington train line. Rail fans will want to view the model of the spiral in the Taumarunui visitor centre and make the one-hour **train trip** ($38 return, departs daily 2pm; book at the visitor centre) to National Park, returning by bus.

Practicalities

InterCity and Pioneer **buses** stop on Hakiaha Street (SH4) outside the **train station**, which contains the **visitor centre** (Mon–Fri 9am–4.30pm, Sat & Sun 10am–4pm; ✉ taumarunui.vic@xtra.co.nz). Staff here sell Whanganui National Park passes and hut tickets and offer general information. The **DOC office** (nominally Mon–Fri 8am–noon & 1–4.30pm, but often closed) is in Cherry Grove, off Taumarunui Street, about fifteen minutes' walk to the south. The library, opposite the ANZ Bank on Hakiaha St (Mon–Fri 10am–5pm, Sat 10am–1pm), has **Internet access**.

Motel **accommodation** is available at *Alexander Spa Motel*, 6 Marae St (☏07/895 8501, ✉ alexanderspa@xtra.co.nz; ❸–❹), which has comfortable units with continental breakfast included, and two budget units, plus two private spas; or there's camping and decent cabins at *Taumarunui Holiday Park*, 4km south on SH4 (☏07/895 9345, ✉ taumarunui-holiday-park@xtra.co.nz; camping $10–11, cabins ❷, units ❸), wedged between a patch of native bush and the Whanganui River, near the railway line.

Hakiaha Street has several **eating** places but only a couple stand out: *Rivers II Café*, corner of Hakiaha Street and Marae Street, Taumarunui's original version of a modern Kiwi café (daytime & Fri eve) with good coffee, breakfast, calzone, pies, steaks and various veggie options; and the pricier, European-style *The Flax*, corner Hakiaha Street and River Rd (☏07/895 6611; Wed–Sun breakfast to dinner, Tues till 3pm; closed Mon except in high summer).

Taumarunui–Stratford: The Lost World Highway

For a taste of genuinely rural New Zealand it's hard to beat the **Lost World Highway** between Taumarunui and Stratford (SH43), a rugged but mostly sealed 155-kilometre road that twists through the hills west of Taumarunui and is described in the leaflet of the same name (free from visitor centres). It skirts the northern reaches of the Whanganui National Park and is bordered by farmland, scenic reserves and about thirty points of historic and geographical interest. Some are very minor but others are worth a brief stop: we've outlined the best, and you should allow a minimum of three hours to travel the route, considerably longer if you want to spend time at any of the diversions along the way.

The first notable stop is **Maraekowhai Reserve**, signposted 18km down an unsealed road. A track from the road end follows a creek to a lookout over the **Ohura Falls** (10min). Just before the falls, another track branches off to the left over a small plank bridge, climbing to a former stronghold of the Hau Hau (see p.422) and site of some **nui poles**, which is also accessible from the Whanganui River (see p.261). Here in 1862 the Hau Hau erected a war pole, **Rongo–nui**, with four arms indicating the cardinal points of the compass, intended to call warriors to their cause from all over the country. At the end of hostilities, a peace pole, **Rerekore**, was erected close by.

Back on SH43, the road snakes through the sedimentary limestone of the Tangarakau Gorge, where a small sign directs you along a short trail to the picturesque site of **Joshua Morgan's grave**, the final resting place of an early surveyor. At the crest of a ridge you pass through the dark **Moki Tunnel** then descend to join a little used rail line which runs parallel to the road as far as the village of **WHANGAMOMONA**, around 90km from Taumarunui. It only has around thirty residents, but on October 28, 1989, it declared itself a republic after the government altered the provincial boundaries, taking it out of Taranaki. The declaration is celebrated every second year – the next in January 2005 and 2007 – with the swearing in of the president, whip-cracking, gumboot-throwing competitions, and a good deal of drinking and eating, all shared by hordes who come to witness and partake; special trains even run from Hamilton and Auckland.

Celebrations revolve around the only significant business, the 1911 *Whangamomona Hotel*, Ohura Rd (☏06/762 5823), where you can get your passport stamped or buy a Whangamomonian version ($3), while wetting your whistle. The **hotel** offers dinner, bed and breakfast for $60 a head, and serves **meals** and is open daily from 11am till the barman goes to bed. The hotel also runs the simple *Whangamomona Domain Camping Ground*, a kilometre down the road, and has **camping** ($10–5) and cabins (❶).

Climbing beside steep bluffs, SH43 passes a couple of saddles with views down the valley and across the **Taranaki Plains** before descending to flat dairy pasture, eventually rolling into **Stratford** (see p.280) as the permanently snow-capped Mount Taranaki looms into view.

Whanganui National Park

A vast swathe of barely inhabited and virtually trackless bush country immediately southeast of Taumarunui is taken up by the **Whanganui National Park**. Through it runs the emerald-green Whanganui River, which tumbles 329km from the northern slopes of Mount Tongariro to the Tasman Sea at Wanganui. The park itself sits on a bed of soft sandstone and mudstone (*papa*) that has been eroded to form deep gorges, sharp ridges, sheer cliffs and waterfalls. On this grows one of the largest remaining tracts of lowland forest in the North Island. Beneath the canopy of broad-leaved podocarps and mountain beech, an understorey of tree ferns and clinging plants extends down to the riverbanks, while abundant and vociferous **birdlife** includes the kereru (native pigeon), fantail, tui, robin, grey warbler, tomtit and brown kiwi.

Visiting the park is most commonly done on exhilarating multi-day canoe trips and on jetboat rides, which penetrate the interior and usually take in a visit to the intriguing Bridge to Nowhere. You can also hike through on two major well-kept tracks that are relatively easygoing despite the rugged country. Most who aren't taking a river trip are content to drive the roads that nibble at the fringes. SH43 provides limited access to the northwest, but only the slow and winding **Whanganui River Road** stays near the river for any length of time. This runs off SH4 near Ohakune, an easy 70km drive south of Taumarunui.

Information on the national park and the river is most readily available from the DOC office in Wanganui and visitor centres in Wanganui and Taumarunui, and directly from the widely available *In and Around the Whanganui National Park* booklet ($2.50). The two jetboats operators plying the river are also great sources of information (Bridge to Nowhere Jetboat and Wades Landing, both on p.261).

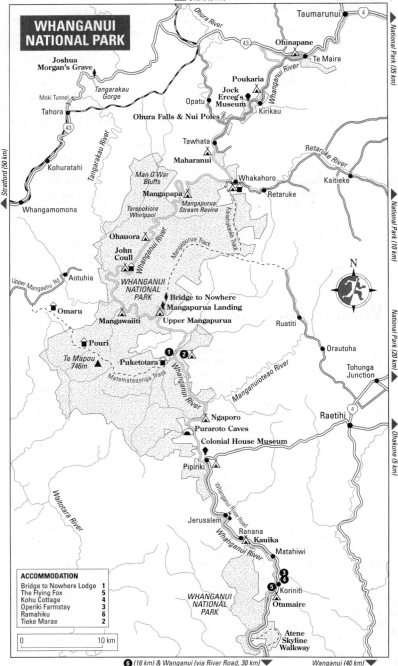

WHANGANUI NATIONAL PARK

Ohura (5 km)
Te Kuiti (80 km)

Taumarunui

Ohura River

Ohinapane
Te Maire

43

Whanganui River

Joshua
Morgan's Grave

Tangarakau
Gorge

Poukaria
Jock
Erceg's
Museum

Moki Tunnel

Opatu

Kirikau

Tahora

Ohura Falls & Nui Poles

43

Retaruke River

Tawhata

Kohuratahi

Maharanui

Tangarakau River

Whakahoro

Kaitieke

Whangamomona

Man O'War
Bluffs

Mangapapa

Retaruke

Tarepokiore
Whirlpool

Mangapurua
Stream Ravine

Kaiwhatakataka Track

Ohauora

Whanganui River

John
Coull

Mangapurua Track

Upper Mangaehu Rd

Aotuhia

WHANGANUI
NATIONAL
PARK

Omaru

Bridge to Nowhere
Mangapurua Landing

Mangawaiiti

Upper Mangapurua

Ruatiti

Pouri

Orautoha

Te Mapou
746m

Puketotara

1   2

Whanganui River

Manganuioteao River

Tohunga
Junction

Matemateaonga Track

4

Raetihi

N

Ngaporo

Puraroto Caves

Colonial House Museum

Pipiriki

Whanganui River

Waitotara River

Jerusalem

Whanganui River Road

Ranana
Kauika

Matahiwi

3
4

5   Koriniti

Otumaire

WHANGANUI
NATIONAL
PARK

Atene
Skyline
Walkway

ACCOMMODATION

Bridge to Nowhere Lodge	1
The Flying Fox	5
Kohu Cottage	4
Operiki Farmstay	3
Ramahiku	6
Tieke Marae	2

0   10 km

6 (16 km) & Wanganui (via River Road, 30 km)   Wanganui (40 km)

Some history

This is New Zealand's longest navigable river, and one much respected by **Maori**, who hold that each bend of the river had a *kaitiaki* (guardian), who controlled the *mauri* (life force). The *mana* of each settlement depended upon the way in which the food supplies and living areas were maintained: sheltered terraces on the riverbanks were cultivated and elaborate weirs were constructed to trap eels and lamprey. **European** missionaries started arriving in the 1840s, after which traders began to exploit this relatively easy route into the interior of the North Island, and from 1891 a regular boat service carried passengers and cargo to the settlers establishing towns at Pipiriki and higher up at Taumarunui. For the first two decades of the twentieth century, **tourists** came too, making the Whanganui New Zealand's equivalent of the Rhine with paddle steamers plying the waters to reach the occasional elegant hotel en route to Mount Ruapehu and central North Island.

European attempts to stamp their mark on this wild landscape have often been ill-fated. In 1917 the **Mangapurua Valley**, in the middle of the park, was opened up for settlement by servicemen returning from WWI, who little realized they were trading one battlefield for another. Plagued by economic hardship, remoteness and difficulty of access, many had abandoned their farms by the 1930s. A concrete bridge over the Mangapurua Valley was subsequently opened in 1936, but after a major flood in 1942 the bridge was cut off, the three remaining families ordered out, and the valley officially closed.

With the coming of the railway and better roads, the riverboat tourist-trade dwindled then ceased in the 1920s. Farms along the Whanganui continued to support a cargo and passenger service until the 1950s, but with the final loss of river traffic the region's isolation returned. This attracted recluses and visionaries fleeing the excesses of the civilized world, the most celebrated being poet **James K. Baxter** who set up a commune in the 1970s and was held in great affection by local Maori. Today, the only signs of habitation in the valley are the disappearing road, old fence lines, stands of exotic trees planted by the farmers, occasional brick chimneys and the poignant **Bridge to Nowhere**, a big concrete bridge over a deep gorge, which can be reached from the river or on the three-day Mangapurua Track.

Whanganui River trips

The best way to explore the Whanganui National Park is on a trip down the **Whanganui River**, which provides a safe and reliable route to the wilderness and is well furnished with riverside campsites as well as *marae* and farmstay accommodation. Canoes, kayaks and jetboats all work the river, allowing you to tailor trips to your needs; see p.263 for a list of operators. The flow of the rapids is rarely violent – mostly Grade I with the occasional Grade II, so this makes it an excellent canoeing river for those with little or no experience.

The navigable section of river starts at Cherry Grove in Taumarunui (see p.257) where there is a DOC office. From here it is about two days' paddle to **Whakahoro**, essentially just a DOC hut and a boat ramp at the end of a 45km mostly-gravel road running west from SH4. Between these two points the river runs partly through farmland with roads nearby, and throws up a few rapids appreciably larger than those downstream (but still only Grade II). The journey also takes you past several spectacular water cascades and the nui poles (see p.258), and **Jock Erceg's Museum** (open sporadically; free) with its collection of river memorabilia.

Downstream from Whakahoro you'll see the Mangapapa Stream Ravine, the **Man-o-war Bluff** (named for its supposed resemblance to an old iron-clad battleship) and the **Tarepokiore Whirlpool**, which once completely spun a river steamer. At Mangapurua Landing everyone stops for the easy forty-minute walk through the bush to the **Bridge to Nowhere** (and 35min to return), a trail that becomes the Mangapurua Track to Whakahoro. Further downstream you come to **Tieke Marae**, a former DOC hut built on the site of an ancient *pa* that has been re-occupied by local Maori; you can stay or camp here, and across the river at *Bridge to Nowhere Lodge*, an excellent base for all river activities. The last stretch runs past the **Puraroto Caves** and into Pipiriki.

River practicalities

The best source of practical **information** for river trips is the *Whanganui Journey* leaflet ($1) available from visitor centres and DOC offices in the region. All overnight river users must buy a **DOC Facility User Pass** ($25 in advance, $35 from rangers in the park), which covers the cost of staying up to six nights in DOC campsites and huts: these are scattered along the river and are marked on the map on p.260. All river users can buy passes from DOC offices and the Taumarunui visitor centre; those going on organized canoe trips will generally find that the pass is not included, but operators can often arrange one for you.

There are no shops along the river, so you need to take all your **supplies** with you – and don't drink the river water unless you have boiled it first.

Apart from the huts and campsites, you can find **accommodation** at the *Bridge to Nowhere Lodge* (☎0800/480 308 & 025/480 308, ⓦwww .bridgetonowhere-lodge.co.nz), which is only accessible from the river. It offers home-cooking and a bar, simple bunkrooms, doubles and a twin, all sharing bathrooms in a hillside lodge overlooking the river. You can self-cater (from $45 per person) or go for a dinner, bed and breakfast deal (from $115). There are also campsites ($5) and a cabin sleeping 6–8 ($10 per person). Non-canoeists pay extra for a 30min jetboat transfer from Pipiriki. Across the river is the relaxing *Tieke Marae*, where you can stay in big sleeping huts for a small donation, or camp on terraces by the river; if any of the residents are about you'll be treated to an informal cultural experience. You can just turn up, or book ahead through the Bridge to Nowhere Lodge (☎025/480 308). Booze is not allowed here. Alternative accommodation on the Whanganui River Road is listed opposite.

The quickest way to get about on the river is on **jetboat trips** (see p.263 for operators and details): Bridge to Nowhere Jet Boat Tours operate from Pipiriki and Wanganui, and River Spirit Jet operate from Pipiriki. They'll run you to the start of tramping tracks, drop you off for a few days' hiking and take you pretty much anywhere else you fancy going, but the main destination is the Bridge to Nowhere, which is appreciably closer to Pipiriki.

The real beauty, tranquillity and remoteness of the river is best appreciated on **canoe** and **kayak trips**. These range from one to six days, with most companies offering both **guided trips** and canoe or kayak **rentals** for independent paddlers. Companies supply pretty much everything you'll need (except possibly sleeping bags and tents for longer trips) and generally include transport to and from the river. Taumarunui, National Park and Ohakune are the most common bases.

Two-day canoe and kayak trips are normally on the upper section from Taumarunui to Whakahoro, but most people prefer the more scenic three- to four-day run between Whakahoro and Pipiriki. Five- and six-day marathons cover the whole stretch from Taumarunui to Pipiriki; few continue downstream from there. The river is accessible all year, but the paddling **season** is generally from November to April.

Tour and rental operators

Bridge to Nowhere Jet Boat Tours ☎0800 480 308 & 06/385 4128, ⓦwww.bridgetonowheretours .co.nz. Popular and regular jetboat tours for all ages from Pipiriki and Wanganui, plus transport to tramping tracks (from Pipiriki to Matemateaonga Track $50 per person; Mangapurua Track $70). Tours upstream from Pipiriki: to Bridge to Nowhere, which builds in the paddle itself (4hr, $75 return); an afternoon tour with *powhiri* at the Tieke *marae* (4–5hr, from $85; min 4 people); and a trip to the lodge for a lunchtime or evening BBQ ($65 return). They also work with Waka Tours to and from Tieke Marae, for 5–7 people. From Wanganui: any destination on the river, from $40 for 20min to a full-day to Taumarunui.

Bridge to Nowhere Canoe Hire ☎0800 480 308, ⓦwww.bridgetonowheretours.co.nz. Guided trips from Pipiriki, beginning by jetboat to the Bridge to Nowhere hike, to collect your canoe and paddle to the Bridge to Nowhere Lodge for the night. The next day you either paddle back to Pipiriki, or take the jetboat (2 days; from $125); also self-guided trips from $80, including jetboat from Pipiriki to the destination of your choice – optional overnight stay at the Lodge is extra.

Blazing Paddles 1033 SH4, 10km south of central Taumarunui ☎0800/252 946 & 07/895 5261, ⓦwww.blazingpaddles.co.nz. Self-guide gear rental with prices including drop-off, pick-up and looking after your vehicle (1 day for $50 per person to 5 days for $140); they can get you onto the water from Taumarunui, Whakahoro or Ohinepane and also organize guides (from $100 a day).

Canoe Safaris 6 Tay St, Ohakune ☎0800/272 335 & 06/385 9237, ⓦwww.canoesafaris.co.nz. Professional well-established outfit offering all-inclusive guided canoe trips from $300 for two days up to $785 for five days. They also do canoe and kayak rentals for self-guided trips charging

$125 per person for a 3-day trip, $140 for 4 and $150 for 5; rental prices include transport to and from the river from Ohakune.

River Spirit Jetboat Tours ☎06/342 1718, ⓦwww.riverspirit.co.nz. Jetboat day-trips from Pipiriki to the Bridge to Nowhere ($80); also one-hour tours of the river ($50 per person), and a shuttle service for trampers to Matemateaonga $50 per person, to Mangapurua $80).

Wades Landing Outdoors/Whanganui River Jet ☎07/895 5995, ⓦwww.whanganui.co.nz. Whakahoro-based operator running jetboat trips from the northern end of the river (Whakahoro to the Bridge to Nowhere and the Mangapurua track for $110); and self-guided canoe and kayak trips (2 days from Taumarunui to Pipiriki for $90 per person, 3 days for $125, and five days for $140). You can also kayak for a day downstream and catch a jetboat back ($85). Guided trips start at $495 for four days.

Waka Tours 17A Ballance St, Raetihi ☎06/385 4811, ⓦwww.wakatours.net.nz. Excellent 3-day guided tours ($420) from Whakahoro in 2- and 6-seater canoes on the scenic middle reaches, learning about the river environment from a Maori perspective, taking bush walks and staying in *marae*, where you're given a traditional welcome and hospitality. A true cultural exchange; longer trips available.

Whanganui National Park Rural Mail Tour ☎0800/377 311 & 06/344 2554, ⓦwww.rivercitytours.co.nz. This is a genuine mail delivery service which doubles as a Whanganui-based full-day tour (take a packed lunch) calling at sites of interest along the Whanganui River Road and offering the opportunity to spread your trip over several days taking jetboat rides into the heart of the park and canoeing back down. Trips depart Mon–Fri at 7.30am ($30).

Whanganui Park hikes

With the undoubted lure of canoe trips down the Whanganui River few people bother to tackle serious **hikes** in the area. In fact the country is so rugged that few tracks trace the deep valleys and bush–clad slopes, and those that do spend much of their time in the forest with only occasional lookouts. The prime hiking **season** is October to April, when track conditions are at their best. **Huts** along the way are managed by DOC and you'll need to buy hut tickets or an annual hut pass before setting out. Unless you fancy doing the walks in both directions, you'll also want to arrange for a **jetboat pick-up** either with the Bridge to Nowhere outfit from Pipiriki or Wades Landing Outdoors from Whakahoro. A popular option is to stay another night on the river at the Bridge to Nowhere Lodge (see p.263).

For general **advice** on tramping, see p.53; the best **map** is the 1:80,000 Whanganui National Park Parkmap ($13.50).

The Kaiwhakauka/Mangapurua Track

The park's most manageable and appealing multi-day tramp follows the **Kaiwhakauka and Mangapurua Track** (40km one way; 3 days; 660m ascent) from Whakahoro south past the Bridge to Nowhere to Mangapurua Landing where you can be picked up by jetboat. There is a hut near the start of the track at Whakahoro, but otherwise you stay overnight in clearly marked camping areas, with side streams providing water. Day one (8hr) follows old road routes and consists of easy riverside walking up the Kaiwhakauka Valley before dropping into the Mangapurua Valley, where you pitch camp. Day two (6hr) heads through bush and along sections hewn from sheer papa bluffs, but day three (6hr) is the highlight, taking in the Bridge to Nowhere and beyond to the Mangapurua Landing, where signs mark the **jetboat pick-up point**.

The Matemateaonga Track

The isolated **Matemateaonga Track** (42km one way; 4 days; 732m ascent), starts on the western side of the park just off the Upper Mangaehu Road at a turning off SH43, 48km from Stratford. Using old Maori trails, you are able to push deep into the dense forest before emerging at the river for a pre-arranged jetboat pick-up.

Day one (1hr 30min) heads up the Kohi Saddle overlooking the Matemateaonga Range and along to the **Omaru Hut** (12 bunks; $10). On day two (5hr), the track continues along the range through dense bush with occasional small clearings; after about three hours, you can take the side-track to Mount Humphries (90min return), for spectacular views across the park to mounts Taranaki and Tongariro, before continuing along the main track to the **Pouri Hut** (12 bunks; $10). Day three (7hr) is an easy gradient along a well-defined track, mostly along a ridge crest, before ascending to a clearing where the **Ngapurua Shelter** provides an ideal spot for lunch, before the final descent to the **Puketotara Hut** (12 bunks; $10). The last day (1hr) comprises a steep descent from the hut to the river, where a large sign marks the **jetboat pick-up point**.

The Whanganui River Road

Canoe and jetboat trips navigate the main body of the Whanganui National Park, but there are outlying sections to the south which can be accessed along the mainly unsealed **Whanganui River Road**. Accessed either from Raetihi, a small town near Ohakune, or Wanganui, the River Road hugs the river's left bank from the riverside hamlet of **Pipiriki** 78km downstream to Upokongaro, just outside **Wanganui**. It is a rough twisting road that is prone to floods and land slips, and even in the best conditions will take you a minimum of two hours.

Opened in 1934, the road is wedged between river, farmland and heavily forested outlying patches of the Whanganui National Park, and forms the supply route for the four hundred people or so who live along it. **Facilities** along the way are almost non-existent with no shops, pubs or petrol stations, and only a handful of places to stay.

If you don't fancy the drive, consider joining the **Whanganui National Park Rural Mail Tour** (see p.263), which leaves Wanganui each weekday for the four-hour run along the River Road up to Pipiriki, and back on the same day.

Pipiriki and around

The southern reaches of the Whanganui National Park are accessed from Raetihi along the winding 27km Pipiriki–Raetihi Road which meets the river at **Pipiriki** and is unsealed for the last third or so. While this is the most important community on the river road, and a major gateway and exit for the park, with most operators finishing canoe trips here, and a couple of jetboat companies running trips upstream, it comprises little more than a few houses. There's an unofficial **camping area** with toilets and water, and the **Colonial House Museum** (Oct–April daily 10am–4pm; $1), which is full of pictures, articles and information about the river. The other point of historical interest in the village is the 1904 **MV Ongarue**, the longest-serving riverboat on the middle reaches of the river, though these days the vessel sits high and dry on the riverbank and is in a sorry state. Nearby the signposted **Pukehinau Walk** (1km return; 30min) climbs above the settlement to the hilltop site of a former Hauhau stronghold.

Hiruharama

HIRUHARAMA (Maori for Jerusalem), 13km south of Pipiriki, was originally a Maori village and Catholic mission but is now best known as the site of the **James K. Baxter commune**, which briefly flourished here in the early 1970s. Baxter, one of New Zealand's most (in)famous poets, attracted upwards of two hundred of his followers to the area. A devout Roman Catholic convert, but also firm believer in free love in his search for a "New Jerusalem", he became father to a flock of his own, the *nga moki* (fatherless ones), who soon dispersed after his death in 1972. The main commune house is situated high on a hill to the northeast of the church, and Baxter is buried just below the house. To pay homage at his grave, ask for directions from the three remaining Sisters of Compassion, who still live beside the 1892 **church** (from the north head up the first driveway, with a mailbox marked "The Sisters"), which features a Maori-designed and carved altar; also in the church is a photo of Mother Mary Joseph Aubert (1835–1926), who established the first community of sisters in 1892, and a small portrait of Baxter, looking suitably messianic. The original wooden **convent** now offers basic yet clean self-catering **accommodation** (☎06/342 8190, ⓦwww.hoc.org.nz; $10, no linen) for up to twenty people in dorms with single beds separated by curtains.

From Moutoa Island to Koriniti

A couple of kilometres to the south lies **Moutoa Island**, scene of a vicious battle in 1864 when the lower-river Maori defeated the rebellious Hauhau warriors, both protecting the *mana* of the river and saving the lives of European settlers downstream at Wanganui. A cluster of houses 1km on marks **RANANA** (London) where there's a Roman Catholic mission church that's still in use today, and the *Kauika* **campsite** (☎06/342 8114; camping $5, powered sites $10 plus $5 per person), adjacent to the river, with toilets, showers, fresh water and a kitchen.

A further 4km downstream a hundred-metre track leads to the two-storey 1854 **Kawana Flour Mill**. One of a number of water-powered flour mills that once operated along the river, it's the only one that's been restored to its original condition (though it's not operational), along with the adjacent miller's cottage.

The only real settlement of note in these parts is **KORINITI** (Corinth), 9km from the flour mill and home to a lovely small church and a trio of traditional Maori buildings, the best being a 1920s **meeting house**, all down a side road. It is a fairly private community and you can enter the church, but the rest you view from the road.

The immediate environs of Koriniti offer three **accommodation** options, not least the welcoming *Operiki Farmstay*, 1km north of Koriniti (☎06/342 8159; ❺), surrounded by lush gardens, offering dinner, bed and breakfast for $55 per person. At Koriniti there's also the self-contained *Kohu Cottage*, set back from the main road (☎06342 8178, ✉kohu.cottage@xtra.co.nz; ❹), a restored one-bedroom colonial cottage in a rural setting. Five hundred metres south of Koriniti is the super-relaxing *Flying Fox*, (☎06/342 8160, ⓦwww.theflyingfox.co.nz), a romantic hideaway of unusual structures in organic gardens and bush, only accessed by boat or aerial cableway. You can camp ($10) or stay in a self-contained cabin modelled on a gypsy caravan (❷) or one of two self-catering rustic yet comfortable cottages (self-catering ❺; or dinner, bed & breakfast basis $80–100 per person), making use of the solar showers and wood-fired baths, and dining on excellent (mostly organic) food.

Around 2km south of Koriniti is the simple, well-kept and free Otumaire **campsite**.

From Atene to SH4

Almost 10km south of Koriniti, a few occupied houses mark what's left of the settlement of **ATENE** (Athens) and the start of the **Atene Skyline Track** (18km loop; 6–8hr), which makes a wide loop, ending with a two-kilometre walk along the road back to your vehicle. There are two entry points, upriver and downriver: begin from the upriver trailhead, marked by a discreet roadside sign and boardwalk, where the track climbs up to an old road that follows a gently ascending ridge line to a clearing, equipped with the hike's only potable water supply, toilets and space for **camping**. Shortly after this you reach the highest point, before skirting some impressive sandstone bluffs and descending steeply back to the river road.

A shorter **nature trail** (20min) shares the same starting point, taking you past examples of the flora and fauna of the region. A good base for the track is the **accommodation** at *Omaka*, on the main road 4km south (☎06/342 5595, ⓦwww.whanganuiriver.co.nz; camping $10, lodge rooms ❺), a riverside farm with tent sites and a modern, simple, self-catering lodge containing an en-suite double and two twins (plus breakfast basket on request). They also supply canoe rental and morning transport to Koriniti so you can canoe back along the prettiest stretch of the lower reaches (3hr; self-guided $40, guided $50).

Four kilometres further on, you pass the **Oyster Shell Cliffs**, roadside bluffs with oyster-shell deposits embedded in them, and **Hipango Park**, a scenic reserve on the riverbank that's only accessible from the river.

About six kilometres further (and 14km south of the Atene Skyline Track) is the last **accommodation** option, *Ramahiku* (☎06/342 5597, ✉ramahiku@xtra .co.nz), a picturesque farm on the other side of the river reached by aerial cableway, where you can camp ($10) or stay in one of two double rooms that share a bathroom ($60 per person, including all meals); they'll pick up from Wanganui.

Finally, just 3km from the point where the Whanganui River Road meets SH4, the road winds up to the summit lookout of **Aramoana**, giving a last look at the river snaking below. On a clear day you can enjoy views of the northeast horizon dominated by Mount Ruapehu. From the junction with SH4 it's 14 kilometres to Wanganui (see p.284).

Taranaki

The province of **Taranaki** juts out west from the rest of the North Island forming a blunt peninsula centred on **Maunga Taranaki** (aka **Mount Egmont**), an elegant conical volcano rising 2500m from the subtropical coast to its icy summit. Taranaki means "peak clear of vegetation", an appropriate description of the upper half of "the mountain", and a name adopted by one of the local Maori *iwi*, and the colonists when the province was formed.

As you tour the region the mountain remains a constant presence, though much of the time it will be obscured by cloud. Local wags are likely to tell you that if you can see the mountain, it's going to rain, and if you can't, it's raining already. You'll often see the summit in the early morning and just before sunset, though cloud frequently forms through the middle of the day – the bane of summit aspirants who put in all the hard work for no view.

Much of your time in Taranaki is likely to be spent in **New Plymouth**, the vibrant provincial capital with its collection of worthwhile sights and a decent selection of places to stay and eat. It makes a good base for a couple of days, perhaps for day trips into the **Egmont National Park** that surrounds the mountain or for short forays out to the surfing and windsurfing hotspot of **Oakura** or historic **Waitara**.

While New Plymouth and Egmont National Park are the undoubted highlights of the province, rural Taranaki has its share of minor attractions best sampled on a one- or two-day loop around the mountain. On the coastal SH45 **Surf Highway** west around the mountain, these are supplemented by ocean views from the multitude of surf beaches, and there's a hub of interest at **Hawera**, with a couple of entertaining museums and the opportunity to go **dam dropping**. The swift, virtually uninterrupted progress of the inland SH3 from New Plymouth to Hawera is dull by comparison to the Surf Highway, but compensates with good mountain access.

Some history

According to Maori, the mountain-demigod Taranaki fled here from the company of the other mountains in the central North Island. He was firmly in place when spotted by the first European in the area, **Cook**, who named it Egmont after the first Lord of the Admiralty. In the early nineteenth century few **Maori** were living in the area as annual raids by northern tribes had forced many to migrate with Te Rauparaha to Kapiti Island. This played into the hands of John Lowe and Richard Barrett who, in 1828, established a trading and whaling station on the Ngamotu Beach on the northern shores of the peninsula.

In 1841, the **Plymouth Company** dispatched six ships of English colonists to New Zealand settling at Lowe and Barrett's outpost. Mostly from the West Country, the new settlers named their community **New Plymouth**, which has grown into the region's largest city.

From the late 1840s many Maori returned to their homeland and disputes arose over land that had been sold to settlers, which from 1860 culminated in a ten-year armed conflict, the Taranaki Land Wars, part of the wider New Zealand Wars, slowing the development of the region and leaving a legacy of **Maori grievances**, some of which are still being addressed.

Once the hostilities were over, the rich farmlands that had caused so much strife were put to good use, primarily as grazing grounds for dairy cattle. For the next seventy years or so it seemed as though small **dairy companies** were springing up in every second field, but as economies

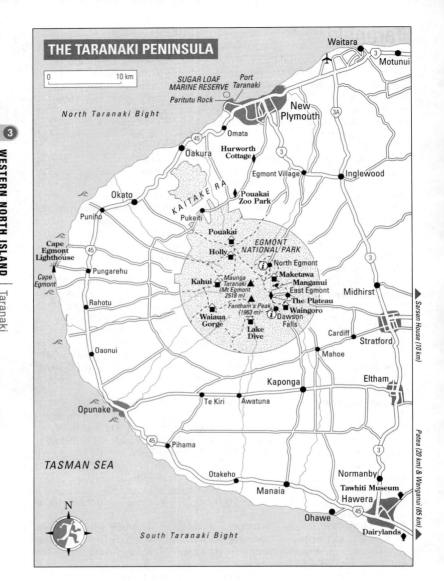

of scale became increasingly important, operations were consolidated and most plants closed down, finally leaving just one huge complex outside Hawera.

The discovery of large deposits of **natural gas** off the Taranaki coast in the early 1970s diverted attention from milk and cheese towards petrochemical industries. The government paid huge sums to American and Japanese firms for prefabricated modular factories, which were shipped over and assembled, mostly around Motonui, 20km east of New Plymouth, yet their long-term economic benefit remains debatable as gas supplies decline.

New Plymouth and around

The city of **NEW PLYMOUTH**, on the northern shore of the Taranaki peninsula, is the commercial heart of Taranaki, bustling with prosperity and bristling with a sense of its own importance. **Port Taranaki**, at the edge of the city, serves as New Zealand's western gateway and is the only deep-water international port on the west coast.

However, it's still a small city and one that's very approachable, with a tight grid of central streets flanked by an attractive **waterfront** enhanced by Len Lye's **Wind Wand**. A couple of streets back, the commercial centre contains the admirable **Govett–Brewster Art Gallery**, and a brand new regional museum and gallery complex known as **Puke Ariki**. The rest of the cityscape isn't especially appealing, but there's the fine public **Pukekura Park** as well as a lively restaurant and after-hours entertainment scene.

Just offshore is the **Sugar Loaf Islands Marine Reserve**, a haven for wildlife above and beneath the sea, and south of town is **Carrington Road**, a picturesque drive past a historic cottage and a small zoo to the colourful rhododendron gardens of **Pukeiti**.

Arrival, information and transport

From the **airport**, 12km northeast of town, Withers Coachlines shuttle into the city on request (℡06/751 1777; $14 for one, $18 for two). At the time of writing long-distance **buses** (InterCity/Newmans, Dalroy and White Star) were dropping off at a temporary site on St Aubyn Street, next to the **visitor centre** (Mon–Fri 9am–6pm, Wed till 9pm, Sat & Sun 9am–5pm; ℡06/759 6060, ⓦwww.newplymouthnz.com) on St Aubyn Street in the Puke Ariki complex. For specific information on Egmont National Park, visit the **DOC office**, 220 Devon St West (Mon–Fri 8am–4.30pm), which sells hut tickets, as does the visitor centre. There's **Internet access** at the library in the Puke Ariki complex (same hours as visitor centre).

Local bus services are run by Okato Bus Lines (℡07/758 2799) but there are few useful routes and services are infrequent; the mountain can be reached with Mountain Shuttle (see p.275).

Accommodation

New Plymouth has a reasonable range of **accommodation** with modest prices, but you might also like to consider staying outside of town, either at the surf beach of Oakura (see p.283), or up on the flanks of the mountain (see p.275).

Hotels, motels, farmstays and B&Bs

Airlie House 161 Powderham St ℡06/757 8866, ⓦwww.airliehouse.co.nz. Gracious and tastefully furnished B&B and self-contained flat in a large turn-of-the-century villa with crisp modern decor; one room is en suite, the other has a private bathroom with a claw-foot bath. ❻

Devon Hotel 390 Devon St East ℡0800/843 338 & 06/759 9099, ⓦwww.devonhotel.co.nz. A

smart, refurbished business hotel with a heated pool and spa, a dinner buffet restaurant and a range of rooms, as well as some suites for two. Rooms ❹, suites ❾

Henwood House 314 Henwood Rd, Bell Block, 5km east off SH3 ℡ & ℗06/755 1212, ⓔhenwood.house@xtra.co.nz. Grand late-Victorian homestead in a rural spot with mature trees and a big veranda; spacious en-suite rooms and twins share a bathroom. Dinner available at a day's notice ($40). ❼

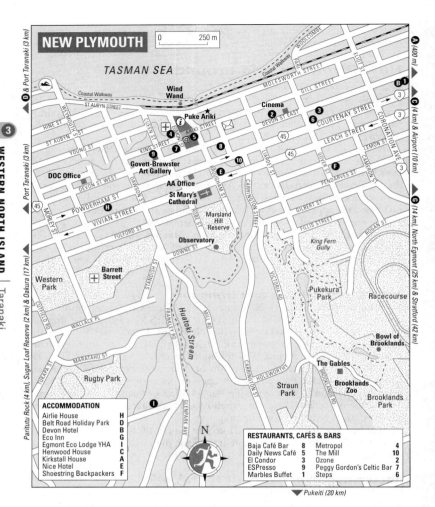

NEW PLYMOUTH

0   250 m

TASMAN SEA

ACCOMMODATION
Airlie House	H
Belt Road Holiday Park	D
Devon Hotel	B
Eco Inn	G
Egmont Eco Lodge YHA	I
Henwood House	C
Kirkstall House	A
Nice Hotel	E
Shoestring Backpackers	F

RESTAURANTS, CAFÉS & BARS
Baja Café Bar	8	Metropol	4
Daily News Café	5	The Mill	10
El Condor	3	Ozone	2
ESPresso	9	Peggy Gordon's Celtic Bar	7
Marbles Buffet	1	Steps	6

▼ *Pukeiti (20 km)*

Kirkstall House 8 Baring Terrace ☎ 06/758 3222, ✉ kirkstall@xtra.co.nz. An intimate and friendly B&B in an exquisitely furnished 1920s house with lovely views over a garden that slopes down to a river, fifteen minutes' walk from the city centre. Charming rooms, one of which is en suite. ④

Nice Hotel 71 Brougham St ☎ 06/758 6423, ⓦ www.nicehotel.co.nz. Intimate, restful and central boutique hotel with just 7 very stylish rooms, each unique, with a designer bathroom, contemporary artworks and luxurious fittings. There's also a good on-site dinner bistro. ⑦

Hostels and campsites

Belt Road Holiday Park 2 Belt Rd ☎ 0800 804 204 & 06/758 0228, ⓦ www.beltroad.co.nz. A scenic, seaside cliff-top site, twenty minutes' walk from the city centre, with camping and cabins (some en suite) in a tidy sheltered area. Camping $10, cabins ② & units ③

Eco Inn 671 Kent Rd, off SH3, between New Plymouth and Egmont Village ☎ 06/752 2765, ⓦ www.ecoinn.co.nz. A real alternative to the town hostels just 3km from the Egmont National Park boundary, an eco farm embracing a self-sufficient, low-impact ethos. Wind, water and solar energy supply the hostel's needs, and there are sleep-out

opportunities in a tree house, along with an organic garden, a wood-fired hot tub, and good hiking opportunities. Pick-ups available. Camping $12, singles $24, doubles and twins ❷
Egmont Eco Lodge YHA 12 Clawton St ☎06/753 5720, ⓦwww.taranaki-bakpak.co.nz. A friendly and comfortable associate YHA set in a peaceful garden, reached along a gentle streamside walking track (15min) from the city centre. Camping from $10, dorms ❶, rooms ❷

Shoestring Backpackers & Cottage Mews Motel 48 Lemon St ☎06/758 0404, ⓔshoestringb@xtra.co.nz. Only 5 minutes' walk from the visitor centre, with a sauna ($8), this self-catering joint, with a roomy kitchen and dining room, is one of the best places in town. Stay in the charming old house in four shares, doubles, twins or singles, or choose the quiet and pleasant bargain motel units next door. Dorms ❶, rooms ❷, units ❹

The waterfront

Arriving in the centre of New Plymouth you're immediately drawn towards the shore and the **Wind Wand**, a slender, bright-red, 45-metre carbon-fibre tube topped with a light globe that glows red in the dark and sways mesmerizingly in the wind. Designed by Len Lye (see below) in 1962, it wasn't erected until after his death in 2000 but fast established itself as a regional icon. Though a smaller version was constructed in Greenwich Village in 1962, and a slightly larger one at the Toronto International Sculpture Symposium in 1966, Lye's true vision was originally restricted by contemporary technology. However, more recent advances in polymer engineering enabled the construction of the

Len Lye

All of a sudden it hit me – if there was such a thing as composing music, there could be such a thing as composing motion. After all, there are melodic figures, why can't there be figures of motion?

Len Lye

Until recently, New Zealand-born sculptor, film-maker and conceptual artist **Len Lye** (1901–1980) was little known outside the art world, but his work is beginning to earn well-deserved recognition. Born in Christchurch, Lye developed a fascination with movement, which in his late teens expressed itself in early experiments in kinetic sculpture. His interest in Maori art encouraged him to travel more widely studying both Australian Aboriginal and Samoan dance. Adapting indigenous art to the precepts of the Futurist and Surrealist movements coming out of Europe, he experimented with sculpture, batik, painting, photography and animated "cameraless" films (he painstakingly stencilled, scratched and drew on the actual film). He spent time working on his films in London, but towards the end of World War II he joined the European artistic exodus and ended up in New York where he returned to sculpture, finding that he could exploit the flexibility of stainless-steel rods, loops and strips to create abstract "tangible motion sculptures" designed to "make movement real". The erratic movements of these motor-driven sculptures give them an air of anarchy, which is most evident in his best-known work, 1977's *Trilogy* – more commonly referred to as *Flip and Two Twisters* – three motorized metal sheets that wildly shake and contort until winding down to a final convulsion.

Lye envisaged his works as being monumental and set outdoors, but was always aware of the technical limitations of his era and considered his projects to be works of the twenty-first century. Just before his death in New York in 1980, friend, patron and New Plymouth resident, John Matthews, helped set up the Len Lye Foundation, which brought most of Lye's scattered work to New Plymouth's Govett-Brewster Art Gallery. The foundation has been instrumental in furthering Lye's work and the *Wind Wand* is the most visible and largest yet.

New Plymouth full-size model. That said, Lye's vision was greater still, but it seems unlikely that his forest of 125 wind wands swaying in the breeze together will be built in the near future.

Landscaping and pathways stretch a couple of hundred metres either side of the Wand making a waterfront park that's pleasant for an evening stroll. More ambitious walkers can follow the **Coastal Walkway** which stretches some 3km in each direction.

Downtown New Plymouth

The commercial heart of New Plymouth lies barely 200m from the waterfront, with shops and cafés lining Devon Street, which is divided into Devon Street West and Devon Street East. Near its junction with Queen Street lies the **Govett-Brewster Art Gallery**, corner of Queen Street and King Street (daily 10.30am–5pm; free; Ⓦ www.govettbrewster.org.nz), which is home to the **Len Lye Foundation**, the driving force behind the construction of the *Wind Wand*. The gallery owns a huge permanent collection of Lye's work, but only a small amount is on display at any one time. You can still watch some of Len Lye's films and a documentary on his life and work; if none are showing, just ask. The gallery has no other permanent exhibits but puts on a series of temporary exhibitions with a contemporary bias, which are usually challenging and always interesting. There is a good bookshop and excellent on-site café (see p.274).

The major new addition to the town centre is the **Puke Ariki**, St Aubyn Street (Ⓦ www.pukeariki.com), two minutes' walk east of the Govett-Brewster. This houses the visitor centre, town library and interactive city museum. Allow about two hours for the **museum**, which contains a large and permanent collection of local and national New Zealand paintings, and an extensive Maori section. Maori highlights on the top floor of the North Wing include the anchor from the *Tokomaru waka*, the canoe that brought Taranaki Maori to New Zealand and volcanic rock carvings and wood carvings of a style unique to Taranaki. But the free 12-minute multimedia show "Taranaki Experience" is deafening and not especially informative. The museum site also encompasses **Richmond Cottage** on Ariki Street, a stone cottage built in 1854 for local MP Christopher William Richmond, and moved to its current site in 1962.

Following Brougham Street south from Puke Ariki you reach Vivian Street and the Frederick Thatcher-designed **St Mary's Church**, the oldest stone church in New Zealand. It was built in 1845 along austere lines but is marred by a modern annexe that forms today's entrance. The church is worth visiting for its imposing gabled dark-wood interior and atmospheric graveyard with testaments to disease and war. Also inside the church is a striking Maori memorial with carvings by John Bevan Ford (see p.292) and *tukutuku* panels by Min Crawford; unveiled in 1972, the memorial invites forgiveness for past injustices by telling the story of Raumahora and Takarangi whose love for each other united two warring *iwi*.

Immediately behind the church, Marsland Hill Reserve contains **The Observatory**, Robe St (Tues: summer 8–10pm; winter 7.30–9.30pm; donation), where you are guided around the **night sky** by members of the Astronomical Society using their telescope.

Pukekura Park

Downtown New Plymouth is backed by the broad, hilly swathe of **Pukekura Park and Brooklands** (daily dawn–dusk; free), an oasis and one of New Zealand's finest city parks. Filming for *The Last Samurai* took place here, transforming the cricket pitch into a parade ground. The Pukekura section is mostly semi-formal with glasshouses and a boating lake. The more freely laid out Brooklands section occupies the grounds of a long-gone homestead and includes the **Bowl of Brooklands** outdoor amphitheatre, and numerous mature native and exotic trees including a 2000-year-old Puriri and a lovely big Ginkgo. Nearby a former colonial hospital from 1847 is now **The Gables** (Jan daily 1–4pm; Feb–Dec Sat & Sun 1–4pm; free), containing an art gallery and a small and mildly diverting medical museum. Here too is the **Brooklands Zoo** (daily 8.30am–5pm; free), that's firmly oriented towards children and tastefully presented. The whole area is a great place to wander at any time, but is best on summer evenings when the Pukekura section is given over to the annual **festival of lights** (mid-Dec to early Feb nightly dusk–10.30pm; free) when families and courting couples promenade along gorgeously lit pathways between illuminated trees, and take out rowboats festooned with lights; there's also live music most nights.

Paritutu Rock and the Sugar Loaf Marine Reserve

New Plymouth's port and ugly power station lie 4km west of the town centre at the foot of the 200-metre-high **Paritutu Rock**, a feature of great cultural significance to Maori and a near-perfect natural fortress that still marks the boundary between Taranaki and Te Atiawa territories. Despite its importance you are free to climb it from a car park on Centennial Drive, signposted off Vivian Street. It's a steep scramble (20–40min return) with a steel rope providing support, but the reward is a great view of the coast and sea, where a cluster of rocky islands comprise the DOC-administered **Sugar Loaf Marine Reserve**. These eroded remnants of ancient volcanoes were long occupied by Maori, but were given their current name by Captain Cook in 1770. The islands provide a sanctuary for rare plants, little blue penguins, petrels and sooty shearwaters; the surrounding waters harbour abundant marine life, including 67 species of fish and a wealth of multicoloured anemones, sponges and seaweeds in the undersea canyons. Humpback whales (Aug–Sept) and dolphins (Oct–Dec) migrate past the islands, and New Zealand's northernmost breeding colony of fur seals populate tidal rocks.

The **islands** themselves are off-limits, but Chaddy's Charters (3 times daily; 1hr, $25; ☏06/758 9133) run excellent if slightly eccentric **trips** around the islands in an old lifeboat launched from its shed at Ocean View Parade marina about 3km west of downtown.

Carrington Road

With your own wheels it makes a pleasant outing to follow Carrington Road south of the city towards the Taranaki foothills. First stop, 8km south, is the historic **Hurworth Cottage**, 906 Carrington Rd (open by appointment on ☏06/753 3593; $3.50). Built in 1856, and restored to its original appearance and furnished accordingly, it is the only survivor of a settlement called Hurworth, which was abandoned during the New Zealand Wars. The original occupier went by the name of Harry Atkinson, who later became New Zealand's Prime Minister four times – though two of these terms were only a year and one was just six days – and was one of the first politicians to advocate women's suffrage and welfare benefits.

Some 5km further south, the **Pouakai Zoo Park**, 1296 Carrington Rd (Tues–Sun 10am–4.30pm; $5), has an interesting walk-through bird enclosure, but the rest is pretty lacklustre. Around 20km from New Plymouth lies **Pukeiti**, 2290 Carrington Rd (daily: Sept–March 9am–5pm; April–Aug 10am–3pm; $8; ⓦwww.pukeiti.org.nz), a gorgeous rainforest garden of 360 hectares with New Zealand's largest collection of rhododendrons and azaleas. There's always something in bloom – though it is perhaps best in October and November when a **rhododendron festival** is held – and there's a café in the gardens serving light lunches, morning and afternoon teas. If you need transport, Cruise New Zealand Tours (☏06/758 3222; $35 return) will take you there.

Eating, drinking and entertainment

The majority of the cafés, **restaurants** and clubs are on what is known as the **Devon Mile**, on Devon Street between Dawson and Eliot streets. You'll seldom need to stray far from here for **drinking** either, though some exploration is needed to track down the excellent Mike's Mild Ale (see p.257). The Top Town Cinema 5, 119–125 Devon St East (☏06/759 9077), shows mainstream **movies**.

For those of a more cultural persuasion, the biennial **Taranaki Festival of the Arts** (ⓦ www.taranakifest.org.nz) takes place at venues all over town for about three weeks in late February and early March every odd-numbered year and is the biggest provincial arts festival in New Zealand. In mid-March every odd-numbered year the city hosts **WOMAD**, a three-day festival of World Music, Arts and Dance, (ⓦ www.womad.co.nz).

Baja Café 17–19 Devon St West. Popular all-day restaurant serving a good selection of mainly Mexican cuisine plus gourmet pizzas. The dance club out the back sparks off Thurs–Sat nights and settles into a sports bar/pool hall for the rest of the week.

Daily News Café Level 1, South Wing, Puke Ariki, St Aubyn St. Small and tranquil daytime café attached to the library, stocked with daily newspapers from around New Zealand, plus *The Guardian Weekly* from the UK, and serving excellent coffee and appetizing snacks.

El Condor 170 Devon St East. Small and simple Argentinian place with value-for-money pasta and gourmet pizza, mostly for under $20; they do takeaways too. Closed Sun & Mon.

ESPresso Govett-Brewster Art Gallery, cnr Queen St & King St. One of the most stylish daytime cafés in town for carnivores and vegetarians, with an imaginative variety of meals (under $15), a deli counter, good wine, luscious cakes and tasty coffee.

Marbles Buffet *Devon Hotel*, 390 Devon St East ☏06/759 9099. Worth a visit for its excellent evening $30 smorgasbord with cabaret entertainment at the weekends, when it gets crowded.

Metropol cnr King St and Egmont St ☏06/758 9788. A relaxed and airy restaurant with an imagi-

native menu with European influences for the $20–28 mark. They're well presented, tasty and accompanied by a select range of wines (many by the glass).

The Mill 2 Courtenay St. A massive converted flour mill with several bars for the late-night crowd, a wide range of beers and snacks, and live bands (or more likely a DJ playing Top 40 hits) at weekends.

Ozone 117 Devon St East. Specialist coffee roaster and groovy daytime café, with a small, well-made selection of panini, bagels, wraps. Closed Sun.

Peggy Gordon's Celtic Bar cnr Egmont St & Devon St. With pictures of Irish and Scottish folk heroes on the walls, an extensive range of single malt whiskies, twelve beers on tap, and live Irish music on Fri & Sat nights, it's no surprise that this is a popular haunt for both locals and travellers. The basement bar carries on after hours on Sat nights.

Steps 37 Gover St ☏06/758 3393. Widely regarded as New Plymouth's top restaurant, *Steps* is housed in a renovated villa with an attractive brick courtyard. Smart yet straightforward service brings Mediterranean-inspired dishes for lunch (and dinner Sat) and there's a short but well-chosen wine list. Closed Sun & Mon.

Listings

Automobile Association 49–55 Powderham St ☏06/757 5646.
Banks and exchange All the major banks have

branches along Devon St or within one block of the city centre; Thomas Cook 55–57 Devon St East ☏06/757 5459. Mon–Fri.

Bike rental Raceway Cycles, 207 Coronation Ave ☎06/759 0391; $20 a day. Cycle Inn, 133 Devon St East ☎06/758 7418; $30 a day.

Camping and outdoor equipment Kiwi Outdoors, 18 Ariki St ☎06/758 4152, rent and sell outdoor gear and camping equipment. They also have kayaks from $45 a day.

Car rental Avis ☎06/755 9600; Hertz ☎06/755 0700; Thrifty ☎06/757 4500.

Internet access At the public library

Library Puke Ariki, St Aubyn St (Mon–Fri 9am–6pm, Wed till 9pm, Sat & Sun 9am–5pm); with Internet access.

Medical treatment There's medical and dental care and a 24hr pharmacy at Medicross, Richmond Centre, 8 Egmont St ☎06/759 8915.

Post office The main post office, with a poste restante service, is at 21 Currie St (Mon–Fri 7.30am–5.30pm, Sat 9am–1pm).

Swimming The New Plymouth Aquatic Centre, Tisch Ave, Kawaroa Park (☎06/759 6060), is a massive complex with indoor and outdoor pools, wave machine, gym and fitness suite.

Egmont National Park

The province of Taranaki, and pretty much the whole western third of the North Island, is dominated by **Taranaki** (or Mount Egmont) a dormant strato-volcano that last erupted in 1755. From most angles its profile is a cone rising to a 2518-metre summit, a purity of form favourably compared to Japan's Mount Fuji. In winter, snow blankets almost the entire mountain, but as summer progresses this melts leaving only the crater filled with snow. The mountain is the focal point for **Egmont National Park**, the boundary of which forms an arc with a ten-kilometre radius around the mountain, interrupted only on its north side where it encompasses the **Kaitake Range**, an older and more weathered cousin of Taranaki.

Farmland lies all about, but within the national park the mountain's lower slopes are cloaked in native bush, which gradually changes to stunted flag-form trees, lopsidedly shaped by the constant buffeting of the wind higher up. Higher still, vegetation gives way to loose scoria slopes, hard work for those hiking to the summit.

Three sealed roads climb the sides of the mountain, all on the eastern side and all ending a little under half way up at car parks from where the park's 140km of walking tracks spread out in all directions. **North Egmont** is the most easily accessible from New Plymouth, but you can get higher up the mountain on the road through **East Egmont** to The Plateau; and there's particularly good walking (and the best alpine accommodation) around **Dawson Falls**. Both the DOC office and visitor centre in New Plymouth also have **information** on the park, and anyone interested in relatively easy hikes should obtain DOC's *Short Walks in Egmont National Park* brochure ($2.50). The main **visitor centre** is in North Egmont (see p.276).

With **accommodation** high on the mountain slopes close to all three major trailheads, it makes sense for avid hikers to base themselves inside the park. Day visitors can easily visit from New Plymouth, Stratford or Hawera, with all trailheads accessible in less than an hour by **car**. If you're relying on **buses**, your best bet is Mountain Shuttle (☎06/758 3222, ✉kirkstall@xtra.co.nz; $25 one way, $35 return) which departs New Plymouth daily at 7.30am for North Egmont. It leaves to return at 4.15pm giving just enough time for a summit attempt. Competitive alternatives include Seaspray Tours (☎06/758 9676).

If you'd rather go on **guided walks**, call either Mt Taranaki Guided Tours (☎025/417 042, after hours 06/751 3542, ✉alpineguidesmac@xtra.co.nz) or Top Guides (☎0800/448 433, ⓦwww.topguides.co.nz). Both offer bush walking, guided summit treks and a range of more technical stuff. Guides will normally take up to ten clients for summer hiking and summit attempts, but perhaps only two clients for winter expeditions, rock climbing or instruction. Guiding rates are around $250–300 for two or three people, plus $60 each per day if you need instruction.

If you're here in February, you can join one of the local **alpine clubs**' inexpensive day trips to the summit; enquire at the North Egmont or Dawson Falls visitor centres.

Egmont Village and North Egmont

The easiest access point to the park, and the closest to New Plymouth, is tiny **Egmont Village**, 13km southeast of New Plymouth on SH3. From here, the 16km sealed Egmont Road runs up the mountain to **North Egmont** (960m), by far the best base for summit ascents. Before heading up (or on any of the numerous easier tracks) be sure to call at the park's main information source, the **North Egmont visitor centre** (daily: Sept–May 8am–4.30pm; June–Aug 9am–4.30pm; ☎06/756 0990, ✉nevc@doc.govt.nz), which has interesting displays about the mountain, maps of all the tracks, good viewing windows, weather updates and a decent café.

Short walks around North Egmont are outlined in DOC's *Short Walks in Egmont National Park* leaflet ($2.50), and include the unusual and atmospheric **Ngatoro Loop Track** (1km loop; 45min–1hr; 100m ascent), which winds through the hidden valley of the Goblin Forest, with its kaikawaka trees, alpine plants and gnarled trunks hung with ferns and mosses. There's also the **Veronica Loop Track** (2.5km loop; 2hr; 200m ascent) which climbs to a ridge through mountain forest and scrub with fine views of the ancient lava flows known as Humphries Castle, and beyond to New Plymouth and the coast. Note that **water supplies** at North Egmont are limited and you should bring some with you.

With so much good hiking, you may want a **place to stay** around these parts, something easily found at *The Camphouse* (book through the North Egmont visitor centre; ❶), a large 1891 hut renovated for trampers, with four bunkrooms (each sleeping ❽; bring a sleeping bag), a communal lounge with electric heating, full kitchen and hot showers. Alternatively, stay at the foot of the mountain in Egmont Village at *The Missing Leg*, SH3 (☎06/752 2570, ✉jo.thompson@xtra.co.nz; camping $8, dorms ❶, rooms ❷), a fairly basic but hospitable and low-cost backpackers 300m south of the Egmont Road/SH3 junction.

East Egmont

The highest road on the mountain goes through **East Egmont**, simply a parking area and the site of the *Mountain House* (see p.278). From here, the **Curtis Falls Track** (3.5km return; 2–3hr; 120m ascent), which is part of the lower Around the Mountain Circuit, crosses several streams, via steps and ladders, to the Manganui River Gorge, where you can follow the riverbed (no track or signs) to the base of a waterfall. The **Enchanted Track** (3km one-way; 3hr return; 300m ascent), also begins at the car park heading through dense vegetation before climbing up to The Plateau (see below).

East Egmont is reached from Stratford (see p.280), from where Pembroke Road runs 14km west to East Egmont then a further 3.5km to **The Plateau**, a rugged and windswept spot 1172m up on Taranaki's flanks, which is on the upper route of the "Around the Mountain Circuit" (see p.279) and acts as the wintertime parking area for the small clubfield, **Manganui Skifield** (🌐www.snow.co.nz/manganui).

△ Egmont National Park

Accommodation is available at the *Mountain House*, Pembroke Rd (☎06/765 6100, ⓦ www.mountainhouse.co.nz), a beautifully sited but flagging **hotel**, 846m above sea level with en-suite rooms (❺), some with spa-bath (❻), and self-contained chalets (❺). They have a **restaurant** with a bias towards game and quality Swiss dishes (mains $20–25), and also manage *Anderson's Alpine Lodge* (same contact details; ❻), a lovely, modern chalet-style building offering three B&B rooms 5km downhill on the edge of the national park.

Dawson Falls

The most southerly access up Taranaki follows Manaia Road to **Dawson Falls**, roughly 23km west of Stratford and 900m above sea level. Here you'll find the **Dawson Falls visitor centre** (daily 8am–4.30pm; ☎0274/430 248), with a few displays including a mock-up of Syme Hut, a mountaineers' hut located high up on the mountain. Several tracks branch off from the visitor centre, or nearby, most notably to the seventeen-metre-high **Dawson Falls** (600m return; 40min; 30m ascent), which plummet over an ancient lava flow. This hike begins just

---

Taranaki summit hikes and cicuit hikes

The majestic conical shape rising direct from the surrounding sea makes Taranaki an obvious target for summit aspirants. Although it is an exhausting hike, it is quite possible in a day for anyone reasonably fit, but don't underestimate the mountain. The upper mountain is off limits to ordinary hikers in winter, but even during the summer **hiking season** (Jan to mid-April) bad weather, including occasional snow, sweeps in frighteningly quickly, and hikers starting off on a fine morning frequently find themselves groping through low cloud before the day is through. Deaths occur far too often: be sure to consult our **hiking advice** in Basics (see p.53); get further advice and an up-to-date **weather forecast** from one of the visitor centres or DOC offices on the mountain rather than in the cities; carry an **ice axe** and plenty of **warm clothing** at any time of year; climb with at least one other person or mountain guides (see p.275), and leave a **record of your intentions** before you set out. At the time of writing no DOC leaflets describing the summit routes were available, only a free information sheet supplied by the visitor centres.

There are two main **summit routes**, both requiring a full day, so you'll need to set off early, say around 7.30am. If you want to spend longer than a day on the mountain and are happy to forgo the goal-driven dash to the summit, the **Pouakai (or Northern) Circuit** might fit the bill or, for the most dedicated climbers only, the spectacular and testing **Around the Mountain Circuit**.

Summit routes

The **Northern Route** (10km return; 6–8hr; 1560m ascent) is the only recommended summit route for all but the keenest mountaineers and is the most frequented of all the tracks. It begins at North Egmont – there are good shuttle access from New Plymouth (Mountain Shuttle, see p.275), handy accommodation at the trailhead, and the path is reasonably well defined. It begins at the top car park at North Egmont and initially follows the gravel Translator Road to *Tahurangi Lodge*, a private hut run by the Taranaki Alpine Club. A wooden stairway leads to North Ridge and after that you're onto loose slopes of scoria (a kind of jagged volcanic gravel) up the Lizard Ridge leading to the crater. After crossing the crater ice and a short scoria slope, you reach the summit rocks. After (hopefully) taking in views that stretch over half the North Island, return by the same route.

The longer and poorly marked **Southern Route** to the summit (11km return;

down the road and can be extended along the **Kapuni Walk** (1km return; 1hr; 50m ascent). Another good walk leads to **Wilkies Pool** (1km loop; 1hr; 100m ascent), where the waters of the Kapuni Gorge rush through a staircase of rock pools, and there's a tougher hike to **Hasties Hill** (2km loop; 1hr 30min–2hr; 100m ascent) involving a passage across the flank of the mountain to a lookout and returning via **Kaupokoponui Falls**. Only very experienced climbers can also tackle the summit from here (see box on p.278).

At Dawson Falls there's budget **accommodation** at *Konini Lodge* (reservations through the visitor centre; ➊), an oversized hikers' hut with separate bunk rooms mostly sleeping eight (bring a sleeping bag), a communal lounge, hot showers and a kitchen equipped with stoves and fridges. You can also go more upmarket at the nearby *Dawson Falls Mountain Lodge* (☎06/765 5457, ⊛www.dawson-falls.co.nz), a homely Swiss-style lodge with a sauna and plunge pool. They offer a dinner, bed and breakfast deal in a single room ($150) or suites for two (➒) lined with pine, and have a **bar** and daytime **café**. Casual diners can also partake of three-course *table d'hôte* dinners in the **restaurant**.

8–10hr; 1620m ascent) is a more exacting proposition only suitable for those with extensive mountain experience; you'll need crampons and ice axes at any time of year. The route starts at the Dawson Falls car park and climbs through bush before making a rapid ascent up a staircase to the Lake Dive Track. From there on it is a steep and exhausting series of zig-zags up scoria slopes.

The Northern Circuit

The new **high-level Pouakai (aka Northern) Circuit** (25km; 2 days) makes an irregular loop around Taranaki varying in altitude from 700m to 1300m and starting at North Egmont. The views from the top of the Pouakai Range are great. At the time of writing the last and most dangerous 400-metre section was still to be completed (suitable only for the most experienced alpine trampers), but work was due to be completed in 2004. DOC had not yet printed useful maps either, so check with the visitor centres on the mountain before considering this one. The route has two **huts**, the 38-bed *Holly*, which can get very busy, and the 16-bed *Pouakai* ($10 each; buy hut passes from one of the DOC visitor centres). **Camping** is allowed outside the huts ($5) but nowhere else on the route.

The Around the Mountain Circuit

For dedicated climbers only, two circuits make their way around the mountain (at the time of writing DOC leaflets were not available for either, so get hold of a topographical map from DOC). The **low-level Around the Mountain Circuit** (44km; 3–5 days) makes another irregular loop around Taranaki varying in altitude from 500m to 1500m but is not maintained by DOC so check on its state before considering it. During midsummer (generally Dec–Feb) the snow melts enough for hikers to tackle the more strenuous **high-level route**, which is essentially the same but makes a few shortcuts by heading higher up the slopes. Thus you can shave a day or so off the lower circuit. There are six well-spaced **huts**, all costing $10 except for the tiny *Kahui Hut* (both $5) and *Syme Hut*; use your DOC annual hut passes or buy hut tickets from one of the DOC visitor centres. **Camping** is allowed anywhere on the circuit (free), but it's best to camp beside the huts so you can use their facilities.

The circuit is best walked clockwise from Dawson Falls and highlights include Lake Dive, the upper Beehive, Brames Falls and Ahukawakawa Swamp.

Along SH3 and SH3A: between New Plymouth and Wanganui

The quickest way to the upper slopes of the mountain, and the fastest road south to Wanganui, is **SH3** which runs 74km to Hawera where it meets the coastal SH45 Surf Highway (see p.283). Along the way it passes through minuscule **Egmont Village** where a good road accesses the mountainside trailhead at North Egmont (see p.276). At **Inglewood** SH3 is joined by **SH3A** from **Waitara**, a small coastal settlement worth a brief exploration. **Stratford** is the starting point for two more roads that head up walking trails in Egmont National Park. Stratford itself shouldn't detain you long from pressing on to **Hawera**, the most substantial and interesting town in rural Taranaki, or tiny **Patea** on the coast road to Wanganui.

Waitara and around

Leaving New Plymouth on the inland route south it's only a short detour to the small coastal settlement of **WAITARA**, 15km to the northeast. Once an important port, it is now quiet but marks the beginning of the **Waitara Campaign Trail**, a nineteen-kilometre drive marked by boards and plaques tracing the culture clash that sparked the first Taranaki Land War. For more details call at the Waitara **visitor centre**, 39 Queen St (Mon–Fri 9am–4pm; ☎06/754 4405, ✉waitarapr@xtra.co.nz).

Should you fancy sampling or buying fruit wines – especially kiwifruit and boysenberry – along with killer golden scrumpy and hair-raising gin, visit the **Sentry Hill Winery**, 152 Cross Rd (☎06/752 0778; Tues–Sun 10am–5pm; free tastings), signposted 4km off the SH3a some 8km south of Waitara.

Inglewood and Stratford

SH3 and SH3a meet at diminutive **INGLEWOOD**, a nondescript farming service town worth a brief stop to sample the excellent *MacFarlane's Café*, at the corner of Kelly and Matai streets in an 1878 building.

Just over halfway between New Plymouth and Hawera and 23km south of Inglewood is the small town of **STRATFORD**, which provides direct access to the slopes of Mount Taranaki, particularly East Egmont and the Manganui Skifield. Stratford isn't an especially attractive place, made less so by a truly grotesque mock-Elizabethan **clock tower** (built in 1996 to hide the 1920s version), from which lifesize figures of Romeo and Juliet emerge to mark the hour at 10am, 1pm and 3pm. If you're bound for the centre of the North Island, Stratford marks the start of the **Lost World Highway**, covered from p.258.

Intercity and White Star **buses**, as well as locally based Dalroy Express (☎0508/465 622), stop outside the central **visitor centre** on the corner of Prospero Place and Miranda St (Mon–Fri 8.30am–5pm, Sat & Sun 10am–3pm; ☎06/765 6708, ✉info@stratford.govt.nz).

There are a couple of **places to stay**, mostly patronized by the ski crowd. The well-cared-for *Stratford Top 10 Holiday Park*, 10 Page St (☎06/765 6440, ✉stratfordholpark@hotmail.com; camping $9, backpackers lodge ❶, cabins ❷, units ❹), is central and has bike rental for $25 a day, while *Taranaki Accommodation Lodge*, 7 Romeo St, Stratford (☎06/765 5444, ✉info@mttaranakilodge.co.nz; dorms ❶, rooms ❷) occupies a former nurses' home, with mostly twin rooms. For something much more rural, visit *Te Popo Gardens B&B*, 636 Stanley Rd (☎06/762 8775 🌐www.tepopo.co.nz; ❻), 15km northeast of Stratford but worth the journey for relaxing accommodation amid lovingly tended gardens. Rooms are en suite and well appointed and there's an apartment sleeping four ($170 for 2 & $20 for each extra adult). Self-cater or join the congenial hosts for dinner by arrangement ($60).

Stratford's **eating** scene is limited, but you can try the daytime *Urban Attitude* on Broadway (near the visitor centre), for breakfast, snacks and light meals.

Hawera

The eastern and western routes around Taranaki meet at **HAWERA**, a tidy town of eight thousand surrounded by gently undulating dairy country. Primarily a service and administration centre for the district's farmers, its survival is largely dependent on the fortunes of Kiwi Co-op Dairies, the world's largest **dairy factory** complex just south of town. Through the peak of the milk production season around the end of October the plant processes thirteen million litres a day. Year-round it handles twenty percent of the country's milk production, mostly gathered from the rich volcanic soils of Taranaki but also brought by rail from other parts of the North Island.

You can't visit the complex, but instead can call in at the **Dairyland** café and visitor centre. Elsewhere you can see how a former dairy factory has been transformed into the **Tawhiti Museum**, arrange to visit a fabulous **Elvis collection** and consider **dam dropping**.

The town and around

Hawera was the birthplace and home of one of New Zealand's most celebrated authors, **Ronald Hugh Morrieson** (see p.984) who loved jazz, wrote well-observed and amusing novels about small-town life and liked a drink or two. The only memorial to his existence here is *Morrieson's Café and Bar* near the junction of Victoria Street and High Street, which contains a few of his books, his old staircase, and tabletops made from timbers salvaged from his house demolished to make way for KFC. The café serves a good range of reasonably priced dishes from 11am, plus pizzas and takeaways.

The only other sight in Hawera is the irresistible **Elvis Presley Memorial Record Room**, 51 Argyle St (visits by appointment, ☎025 982 942 & 06/278 7624, ⓦwww.digitalus.co.nz/elvis; donation), a garage shrine to the King where the owner often dresses the part. It is about ten minutes' walk from the visitor centre, and contains thousands of rare recordings, photographs and memorabilia.

Elements of kitsch also poke through at **Dairyland**, SH3, 3km south of town (Mon–Fri 9am–5pm, Sat & Sun 9am–5pm & 6pm till late; $3), the public face of the local dairy industry. It is an interactive museum to all things lactic, where you're treated to an insightful series of displays to a soundtrack of lowing. Some of the content is fairly technical, and much is blatant industry promotion, but there are highlights including a couple of "moovies" and an engaging 10-minute simulator of a day-in-the-life-of-a-milk-tanker. Afterwards, retire to the café and gaze out at Mount Taranaki until the cows come home.

Economy of scale has put paid to many of the dozens of small dairy factories that once dotted the town's surroundings. Many of the buildings survive in other guises, the most interesting being the **Tawhiti Museum and Bush Railway**, 401 Ohangai Road (Sept–May Fri–Mon 10am–4pm; June–Aug Sun only; $8), just off Tawhiti Road, 4km east of Normanby, which in turn is 6km north of Hawera. The unique exhibits bring the past to life, using a multitude of lifesize figurines modelled on local people by owner and creator, Nigel Ogle. The social and technological heritage of both Maori and Pakeha is explored through the extensive use of photographs, models and dioramas, some of the most impressive being representations of *pa* sites. Other highlights include a diorama of 800 miniatures depicting the 1820s intertribal musket wars; an extraordinary account of the 1860s Land Wars, seen through the eyes of a deserter from the British Army who lived out his days with the local Ngati Ruanui tribe; and a small-scale **bush railway** (first Sun in the month, every Sun during school holidays & every public hol; $3) that trundles 1km through displays recounting Taranaki's logging history.

For something more active, try **dam dropping**, a variation on whitewater sledging conducted by Kaitiaki Adventures (☎021 461 110, Ⓦwww.kaitiaki.co.nz). You'll be equipped with a wetsuit, helmet, fins and buoyant plastic sledge, ready to slide six to nine metres down the face of a dam. This is more fun (and less scary) than it sounds, and you can do it as many times as you like before the gentle scenic float down the Wainongoro river with the guide, who imparts local Maori history and folklore. Choose to go dam dropping only ($50; 1hr), or take the full three-hour trip downstream ($80).

Practicalities

Long-distance **buses** travelling between New Plymouth and Wanganui stop at the **visitor centre**, 55 High St (Mon–Fri 8.30am–5pm, Sat & Sun 10am–3pm; ☎06/278 8599, Ⓔvisitorinfo@stdc.govt.nz), easily found at the base of the redundant water tower that dominates the townscape. There's no local transport other than Hawera Taxis (☎06/278 7171) and Southern Shuttles (☎06/278 4567) will run you out to the Tawhiti Museum and other local sights.

Hawera has a reasonable range of **accommodation**, most cheaply at either the small *King Edward Park Motorcamp*, 70 Waihi Rd (☎ & Ⓕ06/278 8544; camping $9, cabins ❷), right in town, or *Wheatly Downs*, 46 Ararata St, 4km past the Tawhiti Museum (☎06/278 6523, Ⓦwww.taranaki-bakpak.co.nz; tent sites $10, dorms ❶, rooms ❷, self-catering unit ❸), a friendly farmstay and backpackers with views of Mount Taranaki. Back in town are standard units at the *Furlong Motor Inn*, 256 Waihi Rd/SH3 (☎06/278 5136, Ⓔthefurlong@xtra.co.nz; ❹), and boutique B&B in a grand 1875 kauri mansion called *Tairoa Lodge*, at the corner of Puawai St and SH3 (☎06/278 8603, Ⓦwww.tairoa-lodge.co.nz; ❼), with a pool, mature grounds, en-suite rooms, and dinners on request (from $40); or in their two-bedroom cottage for $195 including breakfast.

When it comes to daytime **eating**, try *Morrieson's* (see p.281) for bar meals or time your explorations to dine at the cafés at Dairyland or the Tawhiti Museum. In the evening make straight for the *Fuse Factory*, 47 High St (closed Sun), a relaxing restaurant bar with a pool table.

Patea and around

Cutting through heavily cultivated farmland, SH3 splits **PATEA**, the only major community between Hawera and Wanganui. The township has a big model of the *Aotea* Canoe at the western end of the main street, commemorating the settlement of the area by Turi and his *hapu*, a good surfing beach at the mouth of the Patea River and a safe freshwater swimming hole, overlooked by the Manawapou Redoubt and *pa* site.

Some 47km south of Patea (and 24km north of Wanganui) is the turn-off for **Bushy Park Historic Homestead and Scenic Reserve**, 796 Rangitatau East Road (daily 10am–5pm; $4; free guided tours on request), well signposted 8km off SH3. The huge park contains a 1906 homestead and a big stand of thick native bush with several tracks including a 20-minute loop walk to the largest rata tree in New Zealand (12m in circumference and 43m tall). Notable features in the house include striking stained-glass windows at the entrance and a carved over-mantel and fireplace in the dining room; you can soak up the gracious atmosphere by **staying** (Ⓣ06/342 9879, Ⓦwww.bushypark-homestead.co.nz) on a B&B basis in the homestead (❺; shared bathrooms), self-catering in the chalet or bunkhouse (❶), or camping ($10–20). Dinner is available for guests ($18–40).

Along SH45: the Surf Highway

Despite its name, the **Surf Highway** (or SH45), running from New Plymouth to **Hawera**, mostly runs about 3km inland with myriad roads running down to tiny uninhabited bays. It's just over a hundred kilometres in length, but with its beachy charms it can consume half a day, longer if you want to sample the surf for which the coast is becoming increasingly known. Even among surfers it is still something of a backwater, but few who've sampled its glassy, even breaks doubt that this coast offers New Zealand's most consistent surfing. **Windsurfing** is good too, with near constant onshore winds that buffet the coastal trees.

Surf beaches are everywhere, but the only surf-oriented communities are **Oakura**, which is becoming increasingly populated by New Plymouth commuters, and **Opunake**, which retains its beach-resort feel. Between both lies Cape Egmont with its picturesque **lighthouse**.

Oakura

Heading west through New Plymouth's suburbs you're briefly among fields before arriving at **OAKURA**, 17km west of town. Rapidly becoming a dormitory community, it still retains a counter-culture tenor thanks to the boardriders here to surf the local breaks and experience the best windsurfing beach in Taranaki.

For **surfboard rental**, go to Vertigo, 605 Main St (Ⓣ06/752 7363, Ⓔvertigosurf@xtra.co.nz), who also have boards for windsurfing and run a **surf school** (Ⓣ06/752 8283; $60 for a 2hr lesson for 2 people). Standing up is virtually guaranteed with Tandem Surfing (Ⓣ06/752 7734, Ⓔgregpage @cookietime.co.nz), where $75 an hour gets you riding two-up on a specially elongated board.

While in Oakura, a visit to the **Koru pa** is well worth a brief detour: turn towards Mount Taranaki on the Wairau Road and left into Surrey Road, from which an easy walk (15min) brings you to the stronghold of the Nga Mahanga, its stone-faced ramparts now mostly strangled by native vegetation.

If you want a **place to stay**, try the beachside *Oakura Beach Camp*, 2 Jans Terrace (Ⓣ06/752 7861, Ⓔoakurabeachcamp@internet.co.nz; camping $10, cabins ❷, unit ❹), with an on-site café; or head 4km southwest along SH45 to *Wave Haven*, corner SH45 and Ahu Ahu Rd (Ⓣ06/752 7800, Ⓔwave.haven@xtra.co.nz; dorm ❶, rooms ❷), a rustic backpackers frequented by avid surfers. Ahu Ahu Road runs for 3km down to the coast and to *Ahu Ahu Beach Villas*, 321 Ahu Ahu Rd (Ⓣ06/752 7370, Ⓦwww.ahu.co.nz; ❻), several gorgeous self-contained villas sleeping four (❺; $200 for four), on a rise overlooking the ocean and built from an intriguing blend of salvaged materials and luxurious modern fittings. You can **eat** well in Oakura at *Green Ginger Café*, near the BP station on SH45 (daytime daily in summer and Thurs–Sun evenings; in winter closed Tues & Wed).

Cape Egmont and Opunake

At Pungarehu, about 25km further on, Cape Road cuts 5km west to the cast-iron tower of **Cape Egmont Lighthouse**, moved here in 1877 from

Mana island north of Wellington. Now automated, it perches on a rise on the westernmost point of the cape overlooking Taranaki's windswept coast; a great spot around sunset with the mountain glowing behind. As the wind and tidal conditions alter, surfers range along this coast but the real surfing hub in these parts is 20km on at **OPUNAKE**, a large village with a great golden beach and a relaxing atmosphere since there's little to do but swim, surf and cast a line.

If you fancy **staying**, try the beachside *Opunake Beach Camp*, Beach Rd (☎06/761 7525; camping $10, on-site caravans ❷, units ❸), or *Opunake Motel and Backpackers*, 36 Heaphy Rd (☎06/761 8330, ⓔopunakemotel@xtra.co.nz), which has a four-bed room (❶), doubles (❷), cottages (❸) and motel units (❹). **Eating** is best done at the upbeat and BYO *Sugar Juice Café*, 42–44 Tasman St (Tues–Sun daytime, plus dinner Wed–Sat; closed Mon), which also does takeaways.

Wanganui and around

There's an old-fashioned and charming feel to **WANGANUI**, with its slow pace and sense of civic pride evident in its museums and well-tended streetscape. Founded on the banks of the **Whanganui River** – the longest navigable watercourse in New Zealand – Wanganui is one of New Zealand's oldest cities and was the hub of early European commerce by virtue of its access to the interior and coastal links with the ports of Wellington and New Plymouth. The river traffic has long gone and the port is a shadow of what it was, but the city has given itself a facelift with an eye to the settlement's colonial past: the late Victorian and early Edwardian facades have been refurbished, and mock gaslamps installed along re-cobbled streets. With its riverbank charm, it's a pleasant little place to spend a day or two, perhaps taking a ride on a restored **river steamer**, visiting the excellent museum, and idling away an hour in the nationally renowned **art gallery**, or enjoying one of its biennial **festivals** (see p.51). Perhaps best of all you can join a **rural mail run** (see p.263) to see some of the tiny settlements further upstream beside the Whanganui River or drive yourself for a day-trip along the Whanganui River Road (see p.264). On the water, you can explore the river's lower reaches by canoe; or jetboat to the upper reaches and canoe back down (see p.262).

By the time **Europeans** arrived in the 1830s, the Maori population was well-established, and land rights quickly became a bone of contention. Transactions that Maori perceived as a ritual exchange of gifts, the New Zealand Company took as a successful negotiation for the purchase of Wanganui and a large amount of surrounding land. Settlement went ahead regardless of the misunderstanding, and it was not until the **Gilfillan Massacre** of 1847 that trouble erupted again – when a Maori was accidentally injured, his tribesmen took *utu* (retribution), massacring four members of the Gilfillan family. Further violent incidents culminated in a full-scale but inconclusive **battle** at St John's Hill. The next year the problems were apparently resolved by a payment of £1000 to the Maori; local tribes took no action during the wars in Taranaki, even helping European settlers by defeating Hauhau warriors at Moutoa Island in 1864. More recently, tensions came to a head in town at **Moutoa Gardens** (see p.287), today a peaceful patch of urban greenery.

Arrival, information and city transport

The **airport** receives flights from Auckland and is 5km southwest of the city centre, linked by Ash's Shuttles (☎06/347 7444; around \$12). **Buses** drop off at various places around town: InterCity and Newmans at The Wanganui Travel Centre, 156 Ridgway St (☎06/345 4433), and White Star at 161 Ingestre St (☎06/347 6677).

The **visitor centre**, 101 Guyton St (Mon–Fri 8.30am–5pm, Sat & Sun 10am–3pm; March–Oct Sat & Sun closes 2pm; ☎06/349 0508, ⓦwww .wanganuinz.com), takes bookings for InterCity and provides useful **maps** and

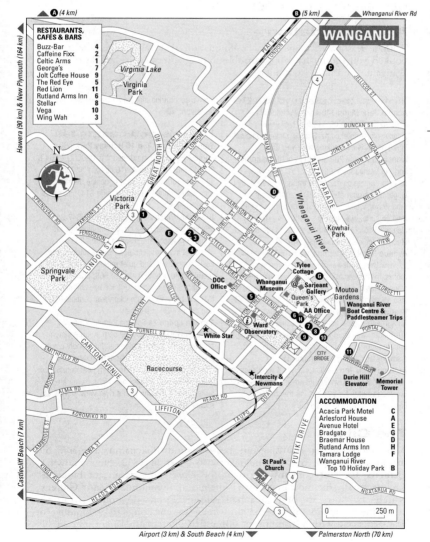

WANGANUI

RESTAURANTS, CAFÉS & BARS

Buzz-Bar	4
Caffeine Fixx	2
Celtic Arms	1
George's	7
Jolt Coffee House	9
The Red Eye	5
Red Lion	11
Rutland Arms Inn	6
Stellar	8
Vega	10
Wing Wah	3

ACCOMMODATION

Acacia Park Motel	C
Arlesford House	A
Avenue Hotel	E
Bradgate	G
Braemar House	D
Rutland Arms Inn	H
Tamara Lodge	F
Wanganui River Top 10 Holiday Park	B

(4 km) • (5 km) • Whanganui River Rd

Hawera (90 km) & New Plymouth (164 km)

Castlecliff Beach (7 km)

Airport (3 km) & South Beach (4 km) • Palmerston North (70 km)

0   250 m

leaflets, including timetables for the local Tranzit buses (☎06/345 5566), who run a limited Monday to Saturday **bus service** round the city and to the beaches at the rivermouth. If the buses don't suit then either walk (the city centre is easily manageable on foot) or try River City Cabs (☎06/345 3333). The **DOC office**, on the corner of Victoria Ave and Ingestre St (☎06/345 2402; Mon–Fri 8am–5pm), sells leaflets on the Whanganui National Park, plus hut and camping passes. There's **Internet access** at the visitor centre and the Davis Library in Queens Park (Mon–Fri 9am–8pm, Sat 9am–4.30pm). **Banks** are all on Victoria Ave or within one block of it, the **post office** has two branches, one on Victoria Avenue and the other at Trafalgar Square, and the **AA office** is at 78 Victoria Ave (☎06/348 9160).

Accommodation

With a reasonable range of accommodation that seldom gets completely booked you should have little trouble finding somewhere suitable to stay in Wanganui, and rates are modest.

Hotels, motels and B&Bs

Acacia Park Motel 140 Anzac Parade/SH4 ☎0800/800 225 & 06/343 9093, ⓦwww .acacia-park-motel.co.nz. Simple, clean rooms set in big grounds overlooking the river. ❹

Arlesford House 202 SH3 to New Plymouth, 7km north of Wanganui ☎06/347 7751, ⓦwww .arlesfordhouse.co.nz. Set in tranquil gardens, this elegant, Georgian-style 1930s country home has rimu floors, wood paneling and generous rooms (two en suite, two sharing a bathroom). There's also a 3-bedroom secluded cottage ($120 for two, plus $35 for each extra adult). B&B ❼

Avenue Hotel 379 Victoria Ave ☎06/349 0044, ⓦwww.theavenuewanganui.com. A range of rooms, from clean and budget ones to plush spacious suites in a fairly modern complex; there's also an on-site restaurant and swimming pool. ❺

Bradgate 7 Somme Parade ☎ & ⓕ06/345 3634. An agreeable 1907 house overlooking the river, a 10-minute walk from the city centre and offering three comfortable rooms with high ceilings (one is a single), all sharing a bathroom. ❹

Rutland Arms Inn cnr Victoria Ave & Ridgeway St ☎06/347 7677, ⓦwww.rutland-arms.co.nz. Luxurious suites for two in a central, historic, English-style building at the top end of all the town's accommodation, in a complex with bar and restaurant. ❻

Hostels and campsites

Wanganui River Top 10 Holiday Park 460 Somme Parade, 6km northeast ☎0800/272 664 & 06/343 8402, ⓦwww.top10.co.nz. Well-tended site 6km from the city centre, beside the river in the shade of giant trees. Camping $14, cabins ❷, motel units ❹

Braemar House 2 Plymouth St ☎06/347 2529, ⓦwww.braemarhouse.co.nz. Combined guest-house and associate YHA in a large 1895 home-stead set in lawns, equipped with a kitchen and cosy lounge. Airy and quiet rooms share a bath-room (single only $50, double $60; or B&B at $60 a single, $80 a double). Outside are tent sites ($10), cabins (❷) and backpacker doubles (❷) and dorms (❶) in cabins.

Tamara Lodge 24 Somme Parade ☎06/347 6300, ⓦwww.tamaralodge.com. A large historic building with pretty gardens and a friendly atmos-phere, five minutes' walk from the city centre. Offers free bikes, kayaks for rent, neat comfortable four-bed dorms, doubles and twins (some en-suite), plus a balcony with a river view. Dorms ❶, rooms ❷

The City

The cultural heart of Wanganui beats around Pukenamu, a grassy hill that marks the site of Wanganui's last tribal war in 1832. Now known as **Queens Park**, it contains a trio of the city's most significant buildings. Architecturally, the most impressive is the gleaming hilltop **Sarjeant Gallery**, which by car is best reached along Drews Avenue (Mon–Sat 10.30am–4.30pm & Sun 1–4.30pm; free), an engaging 1919 building of Oamaru stone with a magnificent dome that filters natural light. The highly regarded permanent collection concentrates on contemporary New Zealand art and photography and is augmented by various touring exhibitions. Immediately north of the gallery sits one of Wanganui's oldest buildings, the weatherboarded **Tylee Cottage**, at the corner of Cameron and Bell streets, built in 1853 and now providing accommodation for artists in residence at the Sarjeant Gallery.

Southwest of the gallery, the Veteran Steps lead towards the centre of the city past the **Whanganui Museum** (Mon–Sat 10am–4.30pm, Sun 1–4.30pm; $2), founded in 1892. It contains an outstanding collection of Maori artefacts and three impressive canoes, all displayed in the central court shaped like a traditional meeting house. In smaller galleries hang portraits of Maori in full ceremonial dress and *moko* (traditional tattoos) by Gottfried Lindauer. His portraits are sometimes criticized for the sitters' apparent passivity, but look long enough and the strongest impression is of great *mana* (dignity and pride).

Towards the river, on Somme Parade, lie the historic **Moutoa Gardens**, just a small patch of grass but a historic one. Traditionally Maori had lived at Moutoa during the fishing season until it was co-opted by *pakeha* settlers, who renamed the area Market Square. It was here that Maori signed the document agreeing to the "sale" of Wanganui, an issue revisited on Waitangi Day 1995 when simmering old grievances and one or two more recent ones reached boiling point. Maori occupied Moutoa Gardens, claiming it as Maori land, and began an 83-day occupation. This ended peacefully in the High Court, but created much bitterness on both sides, neither of which particularly distinguished themselves during the occupation. By 2001 a more creative atmosphere prevailed, and the government, city council and local *iwi* agreed to share management of the Gardens.

Following Ridgeway Street until it meets Victoria Avenue you reach the pretty **Watt Fountain**, which is surrounded by a number of ornate classical buildings, including the old Post Office and the striking Rutland Building. The Cinema 3 Complex provides a welcome counterpoint in the form of a stylish Art Deco (although actually built in the early 1950s) exterior, foyer and mezzanine lounge, not to mention luxurious ladies' powder rooms.

Continuing west you come to **Cook's Gardens**, known in New Zealand as the place where in 1962 local hero **Peter Snell** set a new world mile record of 3min 54.4sec, on grass. There's still a running track here along with a velodrome and the 1901 **Ward Observatory**, where every Friday night you can look through the 24-centimetre refractor, the largest unmodified version in use in New Zealand (from around 9pm in summer, 7pm in winter; otherwise by arrangement on ℡06/345 6954 or through the visitor centre; $2).

The evening is also the best time to take a stroll around **Virginia Park**, almost 3km north on SH3, to enjoy a colourful ornamental fountain in Virginia Lake, and illuminated pathside trees; there's even an imitation glowworm bank.

The river

Wanganui's history is inextricably tied with the Whanganui River, and though commercial river traffic has virtually stopped you can still ride the *Waimarie* **paddle steamer**, hopping aboard at Taupo Quay (Nov to end April daily 2pm; May–Oct, weekends, public & school holidays 1pm; $25; ℡0800/783 2637 & 06/347 1863, @www.wanganui.org.nz/riverboats; booking advisable), New Zealand's last surviving paddle steamer, which makes a two-hour run up a tidal stretch of the river. It's a relaxing trip – the huffing of the coal-fired steam engine and the slosh of the paddles a soothing background to an afternoon's sunning on deck or retiring to the wood-panelled saloon for cakes and tea.

The *Waimarie* was built by Yarrow and Company of London, in 1899, to a shallow-draught design with a tough hull making it suitable for river work. It was transported to New Zealand in kit form, then put to work on the Whanganui River, where it saw service during the pre-Great War boom in tourism, when thousands of people from all over the world came to travel up the Whanganui River and stay at the hotel at Pipiriki. In 1949 the *Waimarie* made her last voyage and three years later sank at her moorings. It wasn't until 1993 that the boat was salvaged and, thanks to skills passed on from half a century ago, the ship returned to the river in 1999.

The restoration took place at the admirable **Whanganui River Boat Centre & Museum** (Mon–Fri 9am–4pm, Sat & Sun 10am–4pm; donation), flanked by old warehouses and stores at Taupo Quay. Housed in an 1881 two-storey timber-framed building, the museum concentrates on the river and its history in relation to the town.

To explore further upstream consider a jetboat tour with Bridge to Nowhere Jet Boat Tours (see p.263) who'll take you to any destination on the river, including the eerie Bridge to Nowhere (see p.262) and also organise accommodation.

The left bank

Crossing City Bridge to the east bank of the river leads straight towards the **Durie Hill Elevator** (Mon–Fri 7.30am–6pm, Sat 9am–5pm, Sun 11am–5pm; $1 each way), where a Maori carved gateway marks the entrance to a 213-metre tunnel at the end of which a historic 1919 elevator carries passengers 66m up through the hill to the summit. At the top of the hill two excellent vantage points grant extensive views of the city, beaches and inland. The viewpoint atop the elevator's machinery room is the easy option, but the best views are 176 steps up at the top of the 34-metre **Memorial Tower** (daily 8am–dusk; free). Head back to town using the 191 steps to the river – it only takes about ten minutes, and provides more satisfying views.

It is about 2km south along Putiki Drive to **St Paul's Memorial Church**, Anaua Street (donation requested), which looks like any other small white-washed church but contains magnificent Maori carvings adorned with *paua*, a painted rib ceiling (as in Maori meeting houses), two beautifully etched-glass windows and two stained-glass, and *tukutuku* panels. The church is sometimes locked – you can get a key from the house on the same side of the road, on the corner with the main road, or from its mailbox.

The beaches and Bushy Park

Wanganui isn't noted for its great swimming beaches, but the strands either side of the mouth of the Wanganui River are great places for moody walks. Around 5km southwest of town, **South Beach** is a vast desolate tract of sand accessible from the old airport road, while north of the mouth **Castlecliff Beach** offers a broad sweep of black iron-sand and driftwood: it is around 8km west of town along Heads Road. For swimming head 15km north along SH3 for **Mowhanau Beach**, a spectacular beach surrounded by papa cliffs (sandstone and mudstone) and renowned for good windsurfing. Twenty-four kilometres north from Wanganui along SH3 is the turn-off to good walks at **Bushy Park Historic Homestead and Scenic Reserve** (see p.282).

Eating, drinking and entertainment

There are few culinary stars in Wanganui's firmament, but if you've just emerged after days in the Whanganui National Park the range is welcome. Either way, there's enough choice to keep you sated for a night or two.

For entertainment there's the Embassy 3 **cinema**, 34 Victoria Avenue (℡06/345 7958). If you happen to be here in late March and early April in an even-numbered year, check out the one-week **Wanganui Arts Festival** which has events all over town; October in odd-numbered years brings the **Blooming Artz Festival**, a celebration of gardens and art. For **listings** of any gigs or events check out the daily editions of the *Wanganui Chronicle*.

Cafés and restaurants

Caffeine Fixx 71 Liverpool St. Great little daytime café with sofas in which to relax over all-day breakfasts, panini, salads and aromatic coffee. Also has Internet access.

George's 40 Victoria Ave. A local institution, this old-fashioned fish-and-chip shop also sells good-value fresh fish: the best in town. Closed Sun.

Jolt Coffee House 19 Victoria Ave. Upbeat coffee house with an American diner feel, thanks to gleaming chrome and red plastic sofas (newspapers supplied). The great coffee is accompanied by a counter of rolls, cakes and sandwiches. Open Mon–Fri 7.30am–4.30pm, Sun 1–5pm.

The Red Eye 96 Guyton St ℡06/345 5646. Bohemian café, with eye-brightening coffee and tasty dishes for lunch or dinner, including Tandoori chicken, Indonesian stir-fry pizza slices. There is sometimes live music at weekends. Essential to book for Fri & Sat nights; closed Sun & Mon, also Tues dinner.

Stellar 2 Victoria Ave. Big all-day restaurant bar, also boasting lounge areas and a sports bar, with a comprehensive menu (mains around $25), light lunches and gourmet pizzas. Live bands some Fri nights.

Vega cnr Victoria Ave and Taupo Quay ℡06/345 1082. The best restaurant in town in an airy converted warehouse with two relaxing bars, one outdoors that backs onto the river; good-value café-style in the day, more romantic at night. Closed Mon.

Wing Wah 330 Victoria Ave ℡06/345 6096. Good-quality Chinese restaurant and takeaway offering reasonable prices, with generous banquet meals for two or more. Closed Mon & Tues lunch.

Bars

Buzz-Bar 321 Victoria Ave. Popular sports bar, café and student hangout with big-screen TV, all-day bar snacks, Wed "happening" nights, Fri happy hours (3.30–8pm) and an upstairs nightclub, with a DJ and dance music Thurs–Sat night.

Celtic Arms 437 Victoria Ave. Bargain pub food from breakfast onwards, plus live folk, jazz or rock on some Fri nights.

Red Lion 45 Anzac Parade. An atmospheric pub with a sports bar and a more comfortable café bar, a wide selection of beers and bar meals, plus live music every Sat night.

Rutland Arms Inn cnr Victoria Ave & Ridgway St. An old-style English pub, with 14 beers on tap and a full range of mainstream meals served in the restaurant or in a sunny courtyard.

South to Palmerston North

Southbound traffic along both SH1 and SH3 meets at **BULLS**, 44km north of Palmerston North, worth a brief pause to marvel at how the locals have let their sense of humour get the better of them with their signage. For example, the police station comes billed as Const-a-Bull, the medical centre as Medic-a-Bull, and the town hall as Soci-a-Bull.

At **OHAKEA**, 7km south, anyone with an aeronautical bent should stop off at the **Airforce Museum**, SH3 (daily 9.30am–4.30pm; $8), where you can spend half an hour or so browsing through the remnants of old planes, make pretend on flight simulators, pick up some history or just gaze from the café window at the RNZAF base next door.

Palmerston North and around

PALMERSTON NORTH is the thriving capital of the province of Manawatu, and with around 75,000 people it's one of New Zealand's largest landlocked cities. The term-time presence of students from **Massey University** makes the city a lively place with plenty of action around the

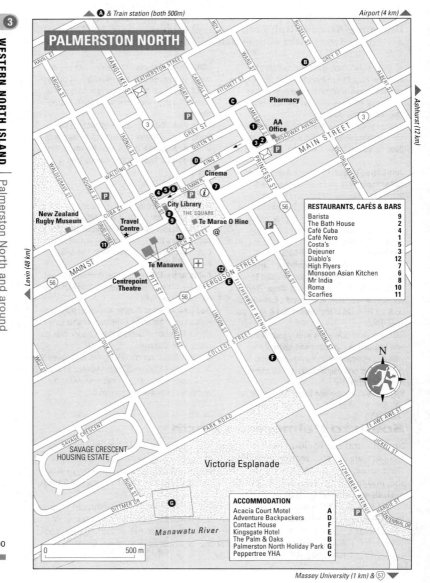

PALMERSTON NORTH

⬤ & Train station (both 500m) · *Airport (4 km)*

Ashhurst (12 km)

Levin (48 km)

Pharmacy

AA Office

Cinema

City Library
THE SQUARE
Te Marae O Hine

New Zealand Rugby Museum

Travel Centre

Te Manawa

Centrepoint Theatre

Victoria Esplanade

SAVAGE CRESCENT HOUSING ESTATE

Manawatu River

RESTAURANTS, CAFÉS & BARS	
Barista	9
The Bath House	2
Café Cuba	4
Café Nero	1
Costa's	5
Dejeuner	3
Diablo's	12
High Flyers	7
Monsoon Asian Kitchen	6
Mr India	8
Roma	10
Scarfies	11

ACCOMMODATION	
Acacia Court Motel	A
Adventure Backpackers	D
Contact House	F
Kingsgate Hotel	B
The Palm & Oaks	E
Palmerston North Holiday Park	G
Peppertree YHA	C

Massey University (1 km) & 57

restaurants and bars, but during the day there's no single must-see attraction, and the place is often ignored by tourists.

After the arrival of the rail line in 1886, Palmerston North grew from little more than a crossroads to a city of commerce based on its pivotal position at the junction of road and rail routes. Today its identity is reflected in some fine civic buildings, notably an excellent **museum** and **gallery** and a stunning **library**.

Arrival and information

Frequent Air New Zealand flights from Auckland, Wellington and Christchurch land at Palmerston North's **airport**, 3km northeast of the city, from where **taxis** run into town: try Palmerston North Taxis (℡0800/355 5333 & 06/355 5333; around $12). The **train station** is on Matthews Avenue, about 1.5km northwest of the city centre, and **long-distance buses** (InterCity/Newmans and White Star) stop at the Palmerston North Travel Centre, at the corner of Pitt and Main Streets. **Local bus** services run from Main Street, near the visitor centre, in a series of loops ($2 single) with reduced services outside term time. Timetables can be obtained from the **visitor centre**, The Square, opposite *High Flyers* bar on Main St (Mon–Fri 9am–5pm, Sat & Sun 10am–3pm; ℡06/350 1922, ⓦwww.manawatunz.co.nz), which also stocks an excellent weekly events sheet. **Internet access** is available at the library on The Square and for long hours at *iCafé* on the corner of The Square and Fitzherbert Avenue.

Accommodation

There's a decent range of **accommodation**, though the paucity of tourists means most places are geared towards university business and visiting parents.

Acacia Court Motel 374 Tremaine Ave ℡0800 685 586 & 06/358 3471, ⓦwww.acaciacourtmotel .co.nz. A friendly welcome and attractive place with fully self-contained, ground-floor units; Sky TV. ❹

Adventure Backpackers 95 King St ℡06/358 9595, ⓦwww.adventure-backpackers.com. Clean and spacious hostel close to the centre with all facilities, plus bike hire and transport to/from the airport. Dorms ❶, singles $30, rooms ❷

Contact House 186 Fitzherbert Ave ℡06/355 3653, ⓔcontact.us@mail.com. The pick of the bunch in terms of value for money and only ten minutes' walk from the square. Pay for a room only ($45 single, $55 double), in a modern block with shared bathrooms, or B&B for an extra $16. There's also a one-bedroom (❹).

Kingsgate Hotel 110 Fitzherbert Ave ℡0800/808 228 &06/356 8059, ⓦwww.kingsgatehotels.co.nz. A modern hotel complex containing 4 bars and a carvery restaurant only five minutes' walk from the square, offering a variety of rooms largely for corporate custom. Prices drop at weekends and during school holidays. Budget rooms from ❸

The Palm & Oaks 183 Grey St ℡06/359 0755, ⓦwww.thepalm-oaks.co.nz. Choice of B&B in a gracious 1926 house (rooms share a bathroom) or a luxurious, self-contained villa in a modern Italian-Deco-style (with breakfast provided) secluded in big gardens, with four double rooms. Enjoy top-quality fittings and an outdoor hot tub. B&B ❼, villa $200 per room

Palmerston North Holiday Park 133 Dittmer Drive ℡06/358 0349. Spacious campsite close to the Manawatu River with a wide range of accommodation and excellent facilities. Camping $10–11, cabins ❷, self-catering units ❸

Peppertree YHA 121 Grey St ℡06/355 4054, ⓔpeppertreehostel@clear.net.nz. A comfortable associate YHA hostel within easy walking distance of the central square. Run by friendly and helpful folk, this is a small place, so phone ahead. Dorms ❶, singles $40, rooms ❷

The City

Palmerston North centres on **The Square**, a simple grassy expanse marred by a central car park, and the ugly intrusion of the Civic Centre, along part of the western side. The Square is improved by **Te Marae o Hine**, or the Courtyard of the Daughter of Peace, an open area largely populated by skateboarders and graced by a couple of five-metre-high Maori figures carved by John Bevan Ford (see below). The Maori name is the one suggested for the settlement's central square by the chief of the Ngati Raukawa in 1878, in the hope that love and peace would become enduring features in the relationship between the Manawatu Maori and incoming *pakeha*.

Around The Square, the mish-mash of architectural styles – classical Victorian and Edwardian, Art Deco and so on – enhances the impact of the **City Library** (Mon, Tues & Thurs 10am–6pm, Wed & Fri 10am–8pm, Sat 10am–4pm & Sun 1–4pm), a Post-Modern conversion sensitively poking its nose from behind the classical facade of the 1927 C.M. Ross building on the southeast side. Designed by Ian Athfield (see box on p.493) and opened in May 1995, the facade fronts a challenging environment of colour and contrast, light and texture in which all the reading materials are arranged according to "subject living rooms" furnished with armchairs and sofas.

Immediately west of the square lies **Te Manawa** (daily 10am–5pm; access by car is from Main Street), the city's main cultural focus. It is divided into three parts centred on the **Life Galleries** (free), a museum devoted to the history and culture of the Manawatu region. Much of the space is given over to high-standard touring exhibitions, but one room is devoted to a large impressive Maori exhibit. In the same building, **Mind Galleries** ($6) offers top-quality hands-on science displays and experiments predominantly aimed at children. Adjacent stands the **Art Gallery** (free), which displays *pakeha* and Maori art from its permanent collection alongside touring exhibitions.

A short stroll northwest of the square, the **New Zealand Rugby Museum**, 87 Cuba St (Mon–Sat 10am–noon & 1.30–4pm, Sun 1.30–4pm; $4), is chiefly for die-hard rugger fans who can marvel at all manner of ephemera, plus a reference library of games on video and the bronzed boots of famous players.

South to the Manawatu River

The city's main southern axis is Fitzherbert Avenue, which runs 3km to the leafy campus and modern buildings of **Massey University**, on the southern side of the Manawatu River. The tree-filled parklands of **Victoria Esplanade** (daily dawn–dusk; free) stretch along the opposite bank, with manicured lawns and flowerbeds, bird aviaries, a miniature railway, beautiful rose gardens and many excellent spots for a picnic.

Around Palmerston North

The small town of **ASHHURST**, 13km to the northeast of Palmerston North along SH3, is the home of **John Bevan Ford** (ⓦ www.fordart.co.nz), one of New Zealand's leading contemporary artists whose works are held by some of the world's most prestigious museums. He produces finely wrought coloured-ink drawings on handmade watercolour paper and, more famously, large wooden carvings using traditional Maori and more contemporary techniques, as well as bright designs for Dilana rugs, again innovative yet retaining their native origins.

It is also worth popping 3km northwest of Ashhurst to the relaxing **Herb Farm and Café** (Wed–Sun 10am–4.30am; $4), to stroll around the garden of medicinal plants, herbs, grasses and trees. The café has excellent salads as well as pastries and hot herbal toddies, and the shop sells essential oils and remedies.

From Ashhurst take Oxford Street, which becomes Cloyton Road, then turn down North Grove Road.

Ashhurst sits at the entrance to the **Manawatu Gorge**, a narrow 10km-long defile through which a train line, SH3 and the Manawatu River all squeeze. Head through town and travel 3km down Gorge Road to reach **Go 4 Wheels** (☏06/376 7136, ✉go4wheels@amcom.co.nz), to experience one of the North Island's better quadbike excursions (2hr; $115 includes bike tuition). You climb modified cattle tracks to a summit to enjoy staggering views of the plains below and see **Tararua Wind Farm** up close, its 48 wind turbines, each 40m high, producing enough electricity to supply 15,000 homes. You can also drive to the wind farm by car – follow Gorge Road to the first right turn (Hall Block Road, a narrow, twisty gravel road; drive with caution) and follow it to the top.

Eating, drinking and entertainment

With its prosperous business community and large student population, Palmerston North supports a lively **restaurant** scene ranging from straight-forward cafés to fancy restaurants. Many places morph into vibrant **bars**, some of the best lining **George Street**, home of Palmerston North's café society.

For entertainment, there's the **Centrepoint Theatre**, cnr Church and Pitt streets (☏06/354 5740, ⓦwww.centrepoint.co.nz), an intimate performance space, with a pleasant pre-show and interval bar; and **movies** at the Downtown Cinema 8, on Broadway Avenue between Princess Street and The Square (☏06/355 5655). "The Pulse" pull-out section of Saturday's *Evening Standard* has entertainment **listings**.

Barista George St. Minimalist espresso bar where they grind their own and serve great cakes, snacky meals ($8–24), lunch mains around the $20 mark, dinner mains for $25–30, and a full range of breakfasts, including bagels.

The Bath House 161 Broadway Ave ☏06/952 5570. A restaurant and lounge bar in a former bathhouse decorated in "Fall of the Roman Empire" bacchanalia, with courtyard dining. The moderately priced food is suitably decadent: French- and Italian-influenced meals, finger food, brunches, lunch and dinner.

Café Cuba cnr George St and Cuba St. Funky all-day café, a bit of a local institution for breakfast, all-day brunch, lunch and dinner; a good place for food late night on Thurs–Sat when the kitchen closes at 11.30pm. Licensed & BYO.

Café Nero 36 Amesbury St ☏06/354 0312. Congenial café, restaurant and bar in a large gabled house. Excellent spot for relaxing over a coffee or glass of wine, or meal inside or out. Mains at around $24.

Costa's 282 Cuba St; book Fri & Sat ☏06/356 6383. Inexpensive evening restaurant with arched windows looking down on the street. The food is inexpensive (mains under $25) and includes light meals, pasta and Tex-Mex. Licensed & BYO.

Dejeuner 159 Broadway Ave ☏06/356 1449, ⓦwww.dejeuner.co.nz. The finest dinner restau-rant hereabouts and longstanding city favourite offering great service, style and French/Asian fusion cuisine with mains at around $30. Licensed & BYO; closed Sun.

Diablo's cnr Fitzherbert Ave and Ferguson St. Popular bar that serves food and is worth visiting late in the week when the lively party is DJ piloted. There's also outdoor seating where you can cool off after dancing up a sweat.

High Flyers cnr Main St and The Square. Central bar/club attracting a young crowd at night, especially to DJ dance nights Thurs–Sat. There's bar food on offer, and stone-grill pizzas.

Monsoon Asian Kitchen 200 The Square. Value-for-money Chinese, Malaysian and Singaporean cuisine. It isn't licensed but they will order drinks for you from the bar across the street.

Mr India 79e George St ☏06/354 5075. Superb, authentic and charismatic restaurant where you get too much to eat at good prices. Open for lunch Mon–Sat; dinner daily. Licensed & BYO.

Roma 51 The Square. Authentic Italian restaurant with a cosy atmosphere, easy-going service and many dishes available as a starter or a main. Dishes include an antipasto plate as well as thin-crust pizza to eat in or take away.

Scarfies cnr David St & Main St. A three-bar extravaganza aimed at students, with DJ enter-tainment Thurs & Sat.

Listings

AA (Automobile Association) office 185
Broadway Ave ☎06/357 7039.

Banks and exchange Most banks are within a
couple of blocks of The Square; there's also
Thomas Cook, cnr Broadway Ave & Princess St
☎06/359 1655.

Bookshop Best in the region is Bruce

McKenzie Booksellers, 51 George St ☎06/356
9922.

Medical treatment The Doctors, 27 Linton St
☎06/354 7737 (daily 8am–9pm). Full facilities
and a pharmacy on-site.

Post office The main post office is at 338
Church St.

South to the Kapiti Coast

To the south of Palmerston North and the Manawatu, the peaks of the rugged and inhospitable **Tararua Mountains** corral the **Horowhenua** region into a strip along the coast. Renowned for its gentle landscape, lakes, walkways, fruit and vegetable growing, rivers and beaches, the area has a few mildly diverting settlements, but lacks any substantial attractions. The northern towns are popular with retirees, but further south lies the commuter belt, just an hour or so from Wellington. This is the **Kapiti Coast** – named for the island 5km offshore – a narrow coastal plain between the mountains and sweeping beaches that's peppered with dormitory suburbs and golf courses.

Transport-wise, the coastal towns are served by the main north–south rail link between Auckland and Wellington and the main bus companies, but once you get outside your options are limited: it is a region best explored by car.

The best bet for a stop is tourist-orientated **Foxton**, with its plethora of museums and an extraordinary long flat beach facing its seaside offshoot community of **Foxton Beach**. Workaday **Levin** only warrants a stop if you're intent on exploring the **Tararua Forest Park** to the east, though this rugged bush country is more easily accessible from **Otaki Forks**, accessible from the small town of **Otaki**.

For waterfowl and a kiwi house visit the Nga Manu Sanctuary at **Waikanae**, but otherwise press on to burgeoning **Paraparaumu**, home to the comestible pleasures of the Lindale Centre, and launching point for trips to the wonderful bush-covered bird sanctuary and marine reserve of **Kapiti Island**, 5km offshore.

Paekakariki marks the southern end of the Kapiti Coast, before the relaxing charms of **Plimmerton** on the shores of Porirua Harbour, a good base to avoid staying in the capital city. **Porirua** only warrants a brief stop if you're into the history of law enforcement, then it is just 20km into Wellington.

Foxton

The most interesting little town around these parts is **FOXTON**, 38km southwest of Palmerston North, where you step back in time: the town has old-style shop facades, cobblestoned paving and several **museums**.

Archeological evidence suggests that there was a semi-nomadic **moa-hunter** culture in this area between 1400 and 1650 AD, pre-dating larger tribal settlements. **Europeans** came to the area in the early 1800s and settled at the mouth of the Manawatu River, but struck problems with land purchases and soon retreated to found Foxton. It quickly became the **flax-milling** capital of New Zealand, adopting and adapting the techniques perfected by local Maori who had long relied on handmade flax items for their everyday needs. Flax was exported from the small river port for use in woolpacks, as binder twine, fibrous plaster lashings, upholsterers' tow and carpet. In an effort to streamline the stripping and weaving processes, mills were constructed alongside swamps and on riverbanks in Manawatu and Horowhenua in the 1880s, and the history of this industry is recounted in the pick of the town's museums, the **Flax Stripper Museum**, Main Street, near the visitor centre (mid-Dec to first week in Feb daily 1–3pm; rest of the year every Sat 11am–1pm; $3). Just behind the museum, a hundred-metre-long strip of riverbanks contains a flaxwalk, a display of sixty-five types of flax, all growing in an unkempt manner and with no signs to tell you what's what, so you'll need the free explanatory leaflet available from the visitor centre or the museum.

You can't miss the **de Molen windmill**, beside the visitor centre on Main Street (daily 10am–4pm; 15min tour, $5) an exact replica of a 17th-century Dutch flourmill, which produces stoneground wholemeal flour. The short tour takes you upstairs to watch the operation.

At the north end of Main Street, in Coronation Hall, the **Museum of Audio Visual Arts and Sciences**, Avenue Rd (Sat & Sun 11am–3pm; $5), offers an insight into early broadcasting and home entertainment through its collection of over 14,000 records going back to the early 1890s, assorted gramophones, cameras and so on.

Foxton Beach is 5km away on the coast, where there's a long sandy beach with good surfing, safe swimming areas and abundant birdlife around the Manawatu River estuary. The small community is full of *baches* for vacationing New Zealanders, as well as a campsite and a few motels. The beach stretches 20km north of here making it a perfect spot for sand-yachting, a sport mostly conducted at the settlement of **Himatangi Beach**, 10km north.

Practicalities

InterCity/Newmans **buses** stop outside the **visitor centre**, 80–88 Main St (daily 8.30am–4.30pm; ☏06/363 8940, ℮thestation@xtra.co.nz), located in the old rail and tram station, also housing a good daytime **café**, and a horse-drawn tram that is hauled out every summer for tourist rides around town (15min; $2). When **food** cravings hit, make for the *Laughing Fox* (daytime daily & evenings Thurs–Sun), easily spotted on SH1 by its odd-looking turret, offering filling quiches, satay, salads, curries, pastries and lavish cakes.

Levin and around

The main southbound road routes converge 19km south of Foxton at **LEVIN**, the principal community in the Horowhenua region. The town makes a living from clothes manufacturing and horticulture – witness the abundance of **factory shops** flogging discount clothing – and the orchards where **fruit-picking** work can often be had (Nov–May). In January the three-day annual **Organic River Festival** takes place at the Kimberley Reserve (ⓦwww.ecofest.co.nz), just outside town, where you can camp during the festival.

Drivers on SH1 need only take a two-kilometre detour to reach the **Papaitonga Scenic Reserve**, 4km south of Levin, for a gentle boardwalk stroll to the Papaitonga Lookout (20min return) and great **views** of Lake Papaitonga and the surrounding wetlands, which provide a refuge for many **rare birds**, including the spotless crake, Australasian bittern, and New Zealand dabchick. It's a further ten-minute walk to the Otomuiri Lookout, though the views are no better.

It takes considerably more commitment to tackle the near impenetrable barrier of the Tararua Range immediately east of Levin, specifically the hikes within the rugged **Tararua Forest Park**. The tracks are narrow, poorly marked and subject to fog, high winds and snow funnelled from the Cook Strait, and the huts are basic, but if you're still keen, consider one of the shorter walks such as the **Mount Thompson Track** (2–4hr). This ascends one of the smaller peaks in the range, but offers good views of the coast and Kapiti Island. The walk begins around 100m past the Panatewaewae car park on North Manakau Road, a side road off SH1 some 10km south of Levin.

Practicalities

Auckland–Wellington **trains** stop at an unmanned station beside SH1, a ten-minute walk from the town centre; and **buses** pull into the Levin Mall car park in the town centre. The **visitor centre**, 93 Oxford St (Mon–Fri 9am–5.30pm, Sat & Sun 10am–3pm; ☏0508 467 6943, ✉visitorinfo@horowhenua.govt.nz), is five minutes' walk from both the station and the bus stop.

Fantails B&B, 40 MacArthur St (☏06/368 9011, ⓦwww.fantails.co.nz; ➎), provide excellent **rooms** in a peaceful country setting with organic breakfast, and great dinners on request ($45), plus two self-contained cottages (➏); or for something cheaper try *Mountain View Motel*, The Avenue/SH1 (☏06/368 5214, ⓕ368 4091; ➌), at the northern end of town, where most units have cooking facilities and there are two chalets.

For **something to eat** your best bet is to head for the all-day *Stephan's*, on SH1 at Manakau, thirteen kilometres south (☏06/362 6520; closed Mon & Tues), where excellent and good-value European food is served in a streamside setting with pretty gardens; or opt for the dinner restaurant at *Byron's Resort*, Otaki Beach (see p.297). Reasonable **places to eat** in Levin itself are limited to the daytime and old-fashioned *Ruffles*, 246 Oxford St (Sat closes 2pm; closed Sun), and *Cobb & Co.*, corner Oxford Street and Durham Street, open for simple lunches and dinners, and one of the best of this chain in New Zealand.

Otaki and around

OTAKI, 20km south of Levin, marks the northern gateway to the Kapiti Coast, and sits beside a broad, braided section of the Otaki River, in a market-garden area. For most of the year, this is a quiet place with a strong Maori heritage but, like other towns along this coast, it changes beyond recognition during the high-summer months of December to March, when its population of 4500 swells by a further 2000 or so, mainly Kiwi tourists.

The outskirts of Otaki line the highway with a smattering of services but the town itself is 2km towards the sea along Mill Road. In the town centre, Te Rauparaha Street leads 200m to the reconstructed **Rangiatea Church**, built on the site of an 1849 church devastated by fire in 1995, which was the finest Maori church in New Zealand. The new church opened in 2003 (key available from the vestry behind the church), its soothing, simple interior an exact replica of the original. Of note are the *tukutuku* panels on the walls, their pattern representing stars (and those who have gone before), and the rafters, painted in Maori design representing hammerhead sharks (symbols of power and privilege). The only item salvaged from the original church is the exquisite model of the *Tainui waka*, which was absent at the time of the fire. Outside, the grave of the Maori chief Te Rauparaha is found in a row of three under a mighty Norfolk pine and marked by a simple grey slate headstone on the far left, but he is thought to be buried on Kapiti Island.

A further 500m along Te Rauparaha Street is Pukekaraka, New Zealand's **first Catholic mission**, established in 1844. Today two churches stand beside one another, near a *marae*. The simple original church has a pretty interior decorated by stained-glass windows in contrast to the stark lines of its 1992 counterpart.

A further 2.5km along Mill Road brings you to the long gently curving, dune-backed **Otaki Beach**, rendered safe for swimming in summer by the presence of a surf patrol.

Otaki Gorge and Otaki Forks

A kilometre south of the town, the scenic and partly unsealed **Otaki Gorge Road** branches off SH1 and threads 19km into the hills along the picturesque gorge of the Otaki River to **Otaki Forks**, the main western entrance to the **Tararua Forest Park**.

Most of the forest park is accessible only to serious trampers, though there are a few shorter and less intimidating **walks** from a series of three parking areas, all close to each other at the end of Otaki Gorge Road. First up is the **Boielle Flat** picnic area, immediately followed by **Gibbons Flat**, where a resident ranger provides assistance and information, and keeps an intentions book. Nearby, crossing a swing bridge over the river and walking 200m brings you to Parawai Lodge, a **trampers' hut** where those with a sleeping bag and cooking equipment can stay ($5) or pitch a tent ($14). Half a kilometre up the road from Gibbons Flat there's a basic **campsite** ($4), and there's another 1.5km further on at the road end.

Armed with the *Otaki Forks* leaflet (20 cents, available from area visitor centres) you can explore the region and its remains of old boilers, stone walls, and remnants of abandoned logging and farming endeavours gradually being engulfed by regenerating bush. One good bet is the **Fenceline Walk** (3km; 2hr), offering excellent views of the river flowing down the valley to the coast.

Otaki practicalities

There's a **train station** in the centre of town, two minutes' walk away from the **visitor centre**, near the corner of SH1 and Mill Rd (Mon–Fri 8.30am–5pm, Sat & Sun 9am–3pm, with extended hours in summer; ℡06/364 7620, ⓦwww.kapititourist.co.nz), where **buses** stop. The visitor centre has free town maps and sells **hut passes** for tracks in the Tararua Forest.

It is just five minutes' walk across the rail tracks to pleasant backpacker **accommodation** at the rural *Otaki Oasis*, 33 Rahui St (℡06/364 6860, ⓦwww.otakioasis.co.nz; dorms ❶, rooms ❸) set on an orchard with free range eggs, horse riding, and a supermarket two minutes' walk away. Out at Otaki Beach, try the simple but well kept *Otaki Beach Motor Camp*, 40 Moana St (℡06/364 7107, ⓕ364 8123; camping $9.50, cabins & on-site caravans ❷), just one block back from the beach, or *Byron's Resort*, 20 Tasman Rd (℡0800/800 122 & 06/364 8121, ⓦwww.byronsresort.co.nz; camping $13–23 for two, tourist flat ❸, motel units ❹, one-bedroom beachside cottage ❹ plus $16 per extra adult), a multi-faceted complex with a popular restaurant bar (closed Mon & Tues except over Christmas & Jan), plus spa and swimming pool.

Daytime eating in Otaki is best done at *Brown Sugar*, on the corner of SH1 and Riverbank Rd at the southern outskirts of town, near the Otaki River bridge (daily 9am–4pm; get here early for lunch). Probably the best little **café** on the Kapiti Coast, it serves the likes of veg frittata, or sun-dried tomato and olive salad on focaccia, along with delicious cakes and great coffee, either inside or in a leafy garden. Otherwise try the **restaurant bar** at *Byron's Resort* (see above), which offers good-quality dinners at moderate prices, plus daytime snacks and light meals. But best of all is *Stephan's* in nearby Manakau (see p.296).

Waikanae

WAIKANAE, 10km south of Otaki, is divided between the highwayside settlement and a beach community, 4km away along Te Moana Road where the
broad, dune-backed **beach** has safe swimming.

The only reason to stop is the **Nga Manu Nature Reserve**, a large man-
made bird sanctuary (daily 10am–5pm, extended hours from Boxing Day to
end Jan; $7.50), with easy walking tracks and some picnic spots. A circular track
(1.5km) cuts through a variety of habitats, from ponds and scrubland to swamp
and coastal forest, which attract all manner of birds. There is also a nocturnal
house containing kiwi, morepork and tuatara, plus eels which are fed at 2pm
and 7pm daily. To get here, follow Te Moana Road off SH1 for just over a kilometre and turn right at Ngarara Road; the sanctuary is a further 3km.

About 3km south of Waikanae, the **Southward Car Museum**, Otaihanga
Road (daily 9am–4.30pm; $7), signposted off SH1 and 200 metres from the
highway, presents a stunning collection of veteran, vintage and classic cars, kept
in mint condition and displayed in a specially built showroom. Gems include
Marlene Dietrich's Rolls-Royce, a 1915 Stutz Racer, and a 1955 gull-winged
Mercedes Benz.

The **visitor centre** is in the library in Mahara Place shopping centre, next
to Woolworths car park, accessed from Marae Lane, off Te Moana Rd
(Mon–Fri 10am–3pm, Sat 9am–noon; ℡04/293 3278). The Kapiti Coast's
main **DOC office** is also here, at 10 Parata St, one street west of the main
highway, turn at the BP station (℡04/296 1112, ℻296 1115; Mon–Fri
8am–12.30pm & 1–4.30pm but sometimes unmanned).

Paraparaumu and around

PARAPARAUMU, 7km south of Waikanae, is the Kapiti Coast's largest settlement and the only jumping-off point to Kapiti Island. Though 45km short
of Wellington it is a burgeoning dormitory community, with commuters lured
here by the proximity of the long and sandy **Paraparaumu Beach**, 3km to
the west along Kapiti Road, which is safe for swimming and looks directly out
onto Kapiti Island.

There's precious little land-based interest here, though tour buses all flock to
the touristy **Lindale Centre**, 2km north on SH1 (daily 9am–5pm; free), where
you can sample the excellent cheese and ice-cream at **Kapiti Cheeses**, both
among New Zealand's finest. Its success has attracted a number of other food and
craft shops, a kind of petting zoo (farm walk $5) and a well-priced **café** (daily
7am–5pm), offering hearty snacks, light lunches and great cakes and coffee.

Those with a sweet tooth might prefer the **Nyco Chocolate Factory**, at the
corner of SH1 and Raumati Rd, 1km south of Paraparaumu (Mon–Sat
10am–4.30pm), which produces 90,000 chocolates daily and sells them
through a shop stuffed with goodies.

Practicalities

The **visitor centre**, SH1, in the Coastlands shopping centre car park
(Mon–Sat 9am–4pm, Sun 10am–3pm; ℡04/298 8195, ℮kapiti.info
@clear.net.nz), has local and DOC information. InterCity and Newmans'
buses drop off at the **train station** opposite, as do local services from
Wellington. There are few genuinely tempting **places to stay**, though the
revamped YHA *Barnacles Seaside Inn*, 3 Marine Parade, Paraparaumu Beach
(℡04/902 5856, ℮barnacles@paradise.net.nz; dorms ➊, singles $30, doubles
➋), in an attractive 1923 hotel is comfortable and overlooks the beach. There's

more luxury at *Wrights by the Sea*, 387 Kapiti Rd (T04/902 7600, Ewrights @paradise.net.nz; ❹), a motel two minutes' walk from the beach; while one of the newer motels in the main town is *Elliott's*, 33 Amohia St/SH1 (T04/902 6070, Wwww.elliottsmotorlodge.co.nz; ❺), within walking distance of the shops and transport. Just north of town, off SH1, is the *Lindale Motor Park* (T & F04/298 8046; camping $10–14, kitchen cabins ❷).

Apart from *The Farm Kitchen* at Kapiti Cheeses, **eating** is best done at Paraparaumu Beach where the intimate *Brier Patch*, 9 Maclean St (T04/902 5586; book ahead Thurs–Sat evenings; BYO & licensed), specializes in superb, moderately priced Creole and Cajun food for dinner and weekend brunch (10am–3pm); there's a separate bar for casual drinking, coffee and desserts; and new cafés regularly open up along the beachfront.

Kapiti Island

One of the few easily accessible island **nature reserves** in New Zealand, the 10km-long by 2km-wide **Kapiti Island** is a magical spot, its bush, once cleared for farmland, now home to birdlife that has become rare or extinct on the mainland. In 1822, infamous Maori chief **Te Rauparaha** captured the island from its first known Maori inhabitants and, with his people the Ngati Toa, used it as a base until his death in 1849: it's thought that he may be buried somewhere on the island, but the site of his grave is unknown. For this, and other reasons, the island is considered extremely spiritual to Maori, and was designated a reserve in 1897.

Late January and February are the best months to visit, when the **birdlife** is at its most active, but at any time of the year you're likely to see kaka (bush parrots that may alight on your head or shoulder), weka, kakariki (parakeets), whiteheads (bush canaries), tui, bellbirds, fantails, wood pigeons, robins and a handful of the 200 takahe that exist in the world. The island can be explored on three **walking tracks**, two of them linking up to lead to the island's highest point (521m), which gives spectacular views, though the best variety of birdlife is found along the lower parts of the tracks - take your time, keep quiet and stop frequently (allow about 3hr for the round-trip). Most visitors only have time to go to the top and back, most easily achieved by ascending **Trig Track** and returning along the steeper, and sometimes slippery, **Wilkinson Track**. The third option (2–3hr), **North Track**, follows the coast to the island's northern end, climbing quite steeply in places to about fifty metres above sea level and leading to a lagoon thronged with waterfowl such as royal spoonbills.

The exceptionally clear waters of the marine reserve make for great **snorkelling** around the rocks close to the shore and **scuba diving** (see overleaf for dive operators), particularly to the west and north of the island, where there are some interesting formations such as a rock archway known as the Hole-in-the-Wall. Three types of habitat – a boulder bottom, sheltered reef and sand bottom – are home to a rich variety of marine life, including orange and yellow sponges (some very rare), and luxuriant seaweed beds feeding kina and paua. Visiting ocean fish like moki and kingfish are common, and occasionally you'll see rare and subtropical fish.

Practicalities

DOC manage the island but allow limited numbers of visitors on **day-trips** (daily except Christmas Day & New Year's Day). Obligatory **landing permits** ($9 per person, valid for 6 months in case weather prevents a crossing) limit visitation to fifty a day: **book** a few days in advance but note that weekends from

December to March are filled three months ahead. Booking can be done through DOC in Wellington (☎04/472 7356; see p.488) or directly with the two **launch operators**: Kapiti Marine Charter (☎04/297 2585 & 027 4424850), or Kapiti Tours (☎0800 527484, ⓦwww.kapititours.co.nz); both trips depart from Paraparaumu Beach at 9am and return around 3.30pm, charging $30 return per person for the ten- to fifteen-minute trip. DOC are so sensitive about the reintroduction of pests that they insist your bags are checked for any stray mammals before leaving for the island. On arrival, you are greeted by the ranger, who informs you of the flora and fauna, so there's no real need to book the guided walks on offer (1hr; $10); a copy of the informative DOC booklet, *Kapiti Island Nature Reserve* (usually $2), is included in the price of the landing permit.

Qualified **divers** can arrange a full-day trip with Dive Spot, 9 Marina View, Mana, near Wellington (☎04/233 8238, ⓦwww.divespot.co.nz; $75) or New Zealand Sea Adventures, 65 Omapere St, Wellington (☎04/236 8787; $80), both of whom can supply gear and transport.

The island has a single toilet at the landing point, and if you take a picnic lunch be sure to bring back all the rubbish.

Paekakariki

There'd be no reason to stop in **Paekakariki**, a tiny village 10km south of Paraparaumu, were it not for a couple of good places to **stay** near a safe swimming beach, a couple of good cafés and easy transport into Wellington, saving you a small fortune in car parking fees. The intimate *Paekakariki Backpackers*, in the village at 11 Wellington Rd (☎04/902 5967, ⓔpaekakbackpack@paradise.net.nz; tents $11, dorms ❶, rooms ❷) is a lovely, peaceful spot with ocean views close to the train station for trips into the city. Tasteful decor sets the tone in the share-rooms and in the two en-suite rooms in the house, and there's a separate quiet cabin. Alternatively, try the well-appointed *Paekakariki Holiday Park*, 180 Wellington Rd (☎04/292 8292, ⓔpaekakariki.holiday.park@xtra.co.nz; camping $10, cabins ❷, units ❸), right by the beach. The village also contains a pub and small store.

Plimmerton and Porirua

South of Paekakariki the highway cuts inland for a few kilometres and rejoins the sea at **PLIMMERTON**, which hugs the shores at the mouth of the double-armed Porirua Harbour. Beautifully set and with a peaceful character it makes a relaxing base for the capital, with a good train service and even late-night buses at weekends. There's more bustle 7km south at the rapidly growing commuter city of **PORIRUA**, booming on account of its proximity to Wellington just over the hills to the southeast. For the passing visitor there are few reasons to stop.

In central Porirua the **Pataka Porirua Museum of Arts and Cultures** (Mon–Sat 10am–4.30pm, Sun 11am–4.30pm; free), at the corner of Norrie and Parumoana streets, shows local works, plus exhibitions by leading contemporary New Zealand artists, and hosts regular Maori and Pacific Island dance performances. You can watch them practise in the dance rehearsal rooms if you ask first.

More of a curiosity, the **New Zealand Police Museum** (Wed–Sun 10am–4pm; ☎04/238 3141, ⓔmuseum@police.govt.nz; $5), signposted from the Papakowhai exit off SH1, 1km north of Porirua, details New Zealand police history, with particular emphasis on the sinking of the *Rainbow Warrior* (see p.201) and the 1981 Springbok Tour (see p.952). See the *Rainbow Warrior's*

3

engine-room clock, stopped at the moment the blast ripped through the hull, and a mounted Springbok head given by the rugby team to the New Zealand Police to thank them for their efforts in policing the tour. Bus #30 leaves Porirua station on the half hour for the museum.

For a change of pace, tackle the moderately hard **Colonial Knob Walkway** (7.5km loop; 3–4hr), a track across forested hills to the west of Porirua reaching the 468-metre Colonial Knob, the highest point within the Wellington urban area, from where there are amazing **views** of Mana and Kapiti islands, Mount Taranaki to the north, and south as far as the Kaikoura Ranges. This and many other local walks are detailed in the free *Walking and Cycling Tracks in Porirua City* leaflet.

Practicalities

In Porirua, InterCity/Newmans **buses** stop on the main road, two minutes' walk from the visitor centre. TranzMetro trains and local buses between Wellington and the Kapiti Coast stop at the combined bus and train station, a few minutes' walk from the **visitor centre** at 8 Cobham Court (Mon–Sat 9am–5pm, Thurs to 6pm, Sat 9am–4pm, Sun 10am–2pm; ☎04/237 8088, ⓔ visinfo@pcc.govt.nz), which acts as an agent for buses, trains and ferries, and can help you find somewhere to stay near the capital but out of the hubbub.

For the budget-conscious, the best **accommodation** choice is the excellent *Moana Lodge*, corner Moana Rd and Cluny Rd, Plimmerton (☎04/233 2010, ⓦ www.moanalodge.co.nz; 3-share dorms ❶, rooms ❷), an Edwardian villa beautifully sited on the shore with sea views from some rooms, and extra rooms in a three-bedroom seafront cottage (❸). It's a cut above most and offers free kayak and mountain-bike usage, as well as stacks of local advice from the enthusiastic hosts.

Plimmerton has three **eating** places within a stone's throw of each other, though the best is *Café Vella*, 12 Steyne Ave, open daily during the day and for dinner Tuesday to Saturday.

Travel details

Trains

A single train line (with one daytime and one overnight service) runs south from Auckland to Wellington through Hamilton, Te Awamutu, Otorohanga, Te Kuiti, Taumarunui, National Park, Ohakune, Palmerston North, Levin and Paraparaumu. Frequent commuter services run from Wellington as far as Paraparaumu.

From Hamilton to: Auckland (2 daily; 2hr); Ohakune (2 daily; 3hr 40min); Otorohanga (2 daily; 40min); Palmerston North (2 daily; 6hr 40min); Te Awamutu (1 daily; 20min); Wellington (2 daily; 8hr 40min).

From Levin to: Paraparaumu (2 daily; 40min); Wellington (2 daily; 1hr 30min).

From Otorohanga to: National Park (2 daily; 1hr 40min); Palmerston North (2 daily 6hr).

From Palmerston North to: Auckland (2 daily; 8–9hr); Hamilton (2 daily; 6hr 40min); Wellington (2 daily; 2hr).

From Paraparaumu to: Paekakariki (half-hourly or more; 8min); Plimmerton (half-hourly or more; 25min); Porirua (half-hourly or more; 35min); Wellington (half-hourly or more; 50min–1hr).

From Taumarunui to: Hamilton (2 daily; 2hr 20min); Palmerston North (2 daily; 4hr 20min); Wellington (2 daily; 6hr 15min).

Buses

From Cambridge to: Auckland (4 daily; 3hr); Hamilton (7 daily; 20min).

From Hamilton to: Auckland (14–16 daily; 2hr); Cambridge (7 daily; 20min); Ngaruawahia (11 daily; 15min); New Plymouth (3 daily; 4hr 20min); Otorohanga (4 daily; 45min); Paeroa (1 daily; 1hr

30min); Raglan (4 daily; 45min); Te Aroha (1 daily; 1hr 10min); Te Awamutu (5 daily; 30min); Te Kuiti (5 daily; 1hr 20min); Rotorua (8 daily; 1hr 45min); Taupo (3 daily; 2hr 30min); Tauranga (1–2 daily; 2hr); Thames (3 daily; 1hr 50min); Wanganui (2 daily; 6–8hr), Wellington (4 daily; 9hr).

From Otorohanga to: Hamilton (4 daily; 45min); Te Kuiti (4 daily; 25min); Waitomo (6 daily; 30min).

From New Plymouth to: Auckland (3 daily; 6–7hr); Hamilton (3 daily 4hr 20min); Te Kuiti (3 daily; 2hr 40min); Wanganui (1 daily; 3hr); Wellington (3 daily; 6hr 45min).

From Palmerston North to: Auckland (4 daily; 9hr); Hastings (4 daily; 3hr); Levin (6 daily; 45min); Masterton (4 daily; 1hr 35min); Paraparaumu (6 daily; 1hr 15min); Rotorua (2 daily; 5hr 30min); Taupo (3 daily 3hr 30min); Wanganui (3 daily; 1hr 5min); Wellington (6 daily; 2hr).

From Taumarunui to: Te Kuiti (1 daily; 1hr); Wanganui (1 daily; 3hr).

From Te Awamutu to: Hamilton (5 daily; 30min); Kawhia (Mon–Sat 1; 1hr 30min); Otorohanga (5 daily; 25min).

From Te Kuiti to: New Plymouth (3 daily; 2hr 40min); Taumarunui (1 daily; 1hr).

From Wanganui to: Hamilton (2 daily; 6–8hr); New Plymouth (1 daily; 3hr); Palmerston North (3 daily; 1hr 5min); Taumarunui (1 daily; 3hr).

From Waitomo to: Auckland (3 daily; 3hr 15min); Rotorua (2 daily; 2hr–2hr 30min).

Flights

From Hamilton to: Auckland (3 daily; 30min); Nelson (1 daily; 1hr 15min); Palmerston North (1–2 daily; 1hr); Wellington (8 daily; 50min).

From New Plymouth to: Auckland (5–7 daily; 50min); Nelson (1 daily; 1hr); Wellington (5 daily; 55min).

From Palmerston North to: Auckland (5–8 daily; 1hr 10min); Christchurch (4–6 daily; 1hr 25min); Hamilton (1–2 daily; 1hr); Nelson (1 daily; 50min); Wellington (6 daily; 35min).

From Wanganui to: Auckland (2–3 daily; 1hr).

Central North Island

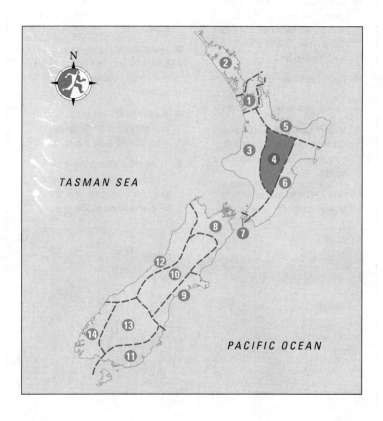

N

TASMAN SEA

PACIFIC OCEAN

CHAPTER 4

Highlights

* **Polynesian Spa** Bathe in outdoor mineral pools or opt for the landscaped luxury of the massage and spa section. See p.314

* **Agrodome** A cheesy but enjoyable look at sheep with nearby adventure activities to make your fleece stand on end. See p.317

* **Kaituna River** Raft this excellent short river and shoot its seven-metre fall. See p.318

* **Maori cultural performance** Chants, dance, songs, stories and a *hangi* feast. See p.321

* **Wai-O-Tapu** Iridescent pools, glooping mud and a performing geyser make this the best of Rotorua's thermal areas. See p.330

* **Lake Taupo** Cruise New Zealand's largest lake, haul trout out of it, or approach at speed while skydiving. See p.340

* **Huka Falls** For volume and power alone this is the country's finest waterfall. See p.343

* **Rapids Jet** The only commercial jetboat trip that tackles real rapids. See p.345

* **Tongariro Crossing** Quite simply the finest and most popular one-day hike in New Zealand. See p.356

△ Champagne Pool, Wai-o-Taipu

Central North Island

The **Central North Island** contains more than its fair share of New Zealand's star attractions, many of them a result of its explosive geological past. The area is dominated by three heavyweight features: **Lake Taupo**, the country's largest; **Tongariro National Park**, with its trio of active volcanoes; and the volcanic field that feeds colourful and fiercely active thermal areas, principally around **Rotorua**. If you are ticking off Kiwi icons, then time is well spent around Rotorua, where boiling mud pools plop next to spouting geysers fuelled by superheated water, which is drawn off to fill the hot pools found all over town. You'll also find the most accessible expression of Maori culture here, with highly regarded Arawa carvings and any number of groups ready to perform traditional dances and *haka*, and feed you with fall-off-the-bone meat and juicy vegetables cooked in a *hangi* steam oven.

The dramatic volcanic scenery is all the more striking for its contrast with the encroaching pines of the **Kaingaroa Forest**, one of the world's largest plantation forests, with serried ranks of fast-growing conifers marching to the horizon. When the country was being carved up for farming, this region was all but abandoned as cattle grazed here soon contracted "bush sickness" and died. In the 1930s, scientists discovered that the disease was caused by an easily rectified deficiency of the mineral cobalt, but by this stage the free-draining pumice soils had already been planted with millions of radiata (Monterrey) pine seedlings by gangs of convicts and Great Depression relief workers. Since then, sylviculture has continued to consolidate its position as the region's chief earner through pulp and paper mills at Kinleith, near Tokoroa, and Kawerau.

The rest of the region is loosely referred to as the **Volcanic Plateau**, a sometimes-bleak high country that is overlaid with a layer of rock and ash expelled two thousand years back when a huge volcano blew itself apart, the resultant crater being filled by **Lake Taupo**. This serene lake, and the streams and rivers feeding it, have since become a fishing mecca for anglers keen to snag brown and rainbow trout, but the area is no less appealing for the lure of its watersports and the thundering rapids of the Waikato River, which drains the lake. South of Lake Taupo rise the three majestic volcanoes of **Tongariro National Park**, created in 1887, since when it has become a winter playground for North Island skiers and a summer destination for trampers drawn to the spectacular walking trails.

If you're driving down from Auckland, you've got a choice of **routes**: the direct SH1 through Hamilton; or the faster, less congested and broadly more appealing journey along SH2, which branches east at Pokeno, 50km south of Auckland, then along SH27 as it cuts south across the fringes of the Hauraki Plains. The two routes converge on the small town of Tirau, where SH1 heads almost 100km south to Taupo and SH5 crosses the Mamaku Plateau to Rotorua, 52km away to the east.

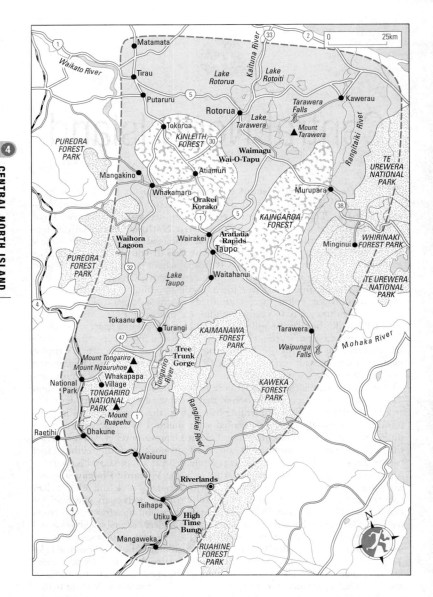

Climate wise, the altitude of the Volcanic Plateau lends Taupo, the Tongariro National Park and environs a refreshing crispness even in high summer, when it is a welcome retreat from the stickiness of Auckland and the north. Spring and autumn are tolerably warm and have the added advantage of freedom from the summer hordes, though the often freezing winter months from May to October are best left to winter-sports enthusiasts. The Rotorua area is more balmy on the whole, but can still be cool in winter, making the thermal areas steamier and the hot baths all the more appealing.

Rotorua and around

There is little doubt that **Rotorua** is the North-Island's tourist destination *par excellence*. It is one of the world's most concentrated and accessible geothermal areas, where twenty-metre geysers spout among kaleidoscopic mineral pools, steam wafts over cauldrons of boiling mud and terraces of encrusted silicates drip like stalactites. Everywhere you look there's evidence of vulcanism: birds on the lakeshore are relieved of the chore of nest-sitting by the warmth of the ground; in churchyards tombs often have to be built topside as digging graves is likely to unearth a hot spring; and hotels are equipped with geothermally fed hot tubs, perfect for easing your bones after a hard day's sightseeing. Throughout the region, sulphur and heat combine to form barren landscapes where only the hardiest of plants brave the trickling hot streams, sputtering vents and seething fumaroles. There's no shortage of colour, however, from iridescent mineral deposits lining the pools: bright oranges juxtaposed with emerald greens and rust reds. The underworld looms large in Rotorua's lexicon: there is no end of "The Devil's" this and "Hell's" that, a state of affairs that prompted George Bernard Shaw to ruminate on his colourful past while visiting the Hell's Gate thermal area and famously quip, "It reminds me too vividly of the fate theologians have promised me".

But constant hydrothermal activity is only part of Rotorua's appeal. The naturally hot water lured **Maori** to settle around Lake Rotorua and Lake Tarawera, using the hottest pools for cooking, bathing in cooler ones and building their *whare* (houses) on the hot ground to drive away the winter chill. Here they managed to hang on to their traditions and tribal integrity more than almost anywhere else in the country, forging a strong and vibrant culture that is part of the daily life of a third of the region's people. Despite the inevitably diluting effects of tourism, there is no better place to get an introduction to Maori values and traditions, dance and song than at one of the concert and *hangi* evenings held all over Rotorua and on nearby *marae*.

Maori-owned and operated tour companies often make the most insightful, not to say entertaining, ways of exploring Rotorua's surrounding area. To the south and east, the forests are punctuated by two dozen **lakes** tucked into bush-girt hollows and overlooked by the mountainous products of ancient volcanic activity and its more recent manifestation, the shattered five-kilometre-long chasm of **Mount Tarawera**. During one cataclysmic night of eruptions in 1886 this chain of volcanoes split in two, destroying the region's first tourist attraction the reputedly beautiful Pink and White Terraces, entombing the nearest settlement, the so-called **Buried Village** (see p.328), and creating the **Waimangu Volcanic Valley**. Waimangu is just one of four magnificent thermal areas open to the public; the others being the Pohutu Geyser at **Whakarewarewa**, on the outskirts of Rotorua, and the Lady Knox Geyser at **Wai-O-Tapu**, to the south of Waimangu.

Some history

The Rotorua region is home to the Arawa people, who trace their ancestry back to the **Arawa canoe**, believed to have journeyed from the Polynesian homelands of Hawaiki sometime in the fourteenth century, striking land at Maketu at the mouth of the Kaituna River on the Bay of Plenty. According to Maori oral history, one of the first parties to explore the interior was lead by the *tohunga* (priest), **Ngatoroirangi**, who made it as far as the freezing summit of Mount Tongariro (see p.349), where he feared he might die from cold. His prayers to the gods of Hawaiki were answered with fire, which journeyed underground, first surfacing at the volcanic White Island in the Bay of Plenty, then at several more points in a line between there and the three central North Island volcanoes. Ngatoroirangi was saved, and he and his followers established themselves around Lake Rotorua, where they lived contentedly until another Arawa sailor, the wily **Ihenga**, duped Ngatoroirangi out of his title to the land. The victor named the lakes as he reached them along the Kaituna River: Lake Rotoiti ("small lake") and Lake Rotorua ("second lake").

In revenge for an earlier raid on an island in nearby Green Lake, the Northland Ngapuhi chief, **Hongi Hika**, led a war party here in 1823. The Arawa got wind of the attack and retreated to the sanctuary of Mokoia Island, in the middle of Lake Rotorua; undaunted, Hongi Hika and his warriors carried their canoes overland between lakes (the track between Lake Rotoiti and Lake Rotoehu still bears the name Hongi's Track). The Ngapuhi, equipped with muskets traded with Europeans in the Bay of Islands, defeated the traditionally armed Arawa then withdrew, leaving the Arawa to regroup in time for the New Zealand Wars of the 1860s, in which the Arawa supported the government. This worked in their favour when, in 1870, **Te Kooti** (see box on p.449) attacked from the east coast, and the colonial troops helped turn them back.

By this time a few **Europeans** – notably a Danish trader Philip Hans Tapsell and the missionary Thomas Chapman – had already lived for some years in the Maori villages of Ohinemutu and Whakarewarewa, but it wasn't until Te Kooti had been driven off that Rotorua came into existence. **Tourists** began to arrive in the district to view the Pink and White Terraces using Ohinemutu, Whakarewarewa and Te Wairoa as staging posts. The Arawa, who up to this point had been relatively isolated from European influence, were quick to grasp the possibilities of tourism and helped turn Rotorua into what it is today.

Rotorua

You don't smell **Rotorua** long before you see it but it's hard to convince yourself otherwise after arrival. Hydrogen sulphide, drifting up from natural vents in the region's thin crust, means that the whiff of rotten eggs lingers in the air, but after a few hours you barely notice it. No amount of bad odour, however, will keep visitors away from this small, ordered city clinging to the southern shores of the near-circular **Lake Rotorua**. Rotorua's northern and southern limits are defined by the two ancient villages of the Arawa sub-tribe, Ngati Whakaue. The lakeshore **Ohinemutu** and the inland **Whakarewarewa** were the only settlements before the 1880s, when Rotorua became New Zealand's only city with its origins firmly rooted in tourism. Specifically, Rotorua was

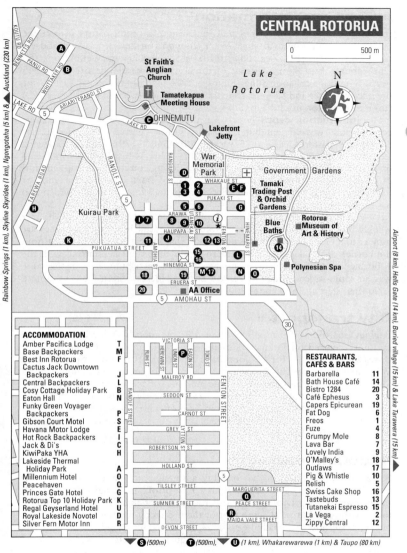

CENTRAL ROTORUA

0   500 m

N

Lake Rotorua

Auckland (230 km) ▲ & Ngongotaha (5 km) & Skyline Skyrides (1 km), Rainbow Springs (1 km),

Airport (8 km), Hells Gate (14 km), Buried village (15 km) & Lake Tarawera (15 km) ▶

Ⓐ
Ⓑ

St Faith's
Anglian
Church

Tamatekapua
Meeting House

Ⓒ OHINEMUTU

Lakefront
Jetty

War
Memorial
Park

Government Gardens

Tamaki
Trading Post
& Orchid
Gardens

Rotorua
Museum of
Art & History

Blue
Baths

Polynesian Spa

Kuirau Park

Ⓗ

Ⓚ

WHAKAUE ST
❶
❸
❷
ⒺⒻ
PUKAHU ST
❺ **❻**
ARAWA ST
Ⓘ❼
❽ **❾** **❿**
HAUPAPA ST
Ⓖ
ℹ️
HINEMARU ST
⓮
⓫
⓬ **⓭**
PUKUATUA STREET
⓯
⓰
HINEMOA ST
Ⓛ
⓲
⓳ **Ⓜ⓱**
ⓃⓄ
ERUERA ST
⓴
■ AA Office
AMOHAU ST

RANGIURI ST
RUAWAHIA ST
RANOLF ST
TAREWA ROAD
LAKE RD
ARIARITERANGI ST
WHITTAKER RD
GLENHOLME RD
PANUI RD
LAKE RD

FENTON ST
TUTANEKAI ST
AMOHIA ST

30

ACCOMMODATION

Amber Pacifica Lodge	T
Base Backpackers	M
Best Inn Rotorua	F
Cactus Jack Downtown Backpackers	J
Central Backpackers	L
Cosy Cottage Holiday Park	B
Eaton Hall	N
Funky Green Voyager Backpackers	P
Gibson Court Motel	S
Havana Motor Lodge	E
Hot Rock Backpackers	I
Jack & Di's	C
KiwiPaka YHA	H
Lakeside Thermal Holiday Park	A
Millennium Hotel	O
Peacehaven	Q
Princes Gate Hotel	G
Rotorua Top 10 Holiday Park	K
Regal Geyserland Hotel	U
Royal Lakeside Novotel	D
Silver Fern Motor Inn	R

VICTORIA ST
RUM ST
HERERUNI ST
LINDUS ST
EASTON ST
TIKO ST
Ⓟ
MALFROY RD
RANOLF STREET
SEDDON ST
CARNOT ST
FENTON STREET
GREY ST
LYTTON ST
ROBERTSON ST
HOLLAND ST
5
TILSLEY STREET
MARGUERITA STREET
SUMNER STREET
PEACE STREET
MAIDA VALE STREET
Ⓡ
DEVON STREET

**RESTAURANTS,
CAFÉS & BARS**

Barbarella	11
Bath House Café	14
Bistro 1284	20
Café Ephesus	3
Capers Epicurean	19
Fat Dog	6
Freos	1
Fuze	4
Grumpy Mole	8
Lava Bar	7
Lovely India	9
O'Malley's	18
Outlaws	17
Pig & Whistle	10
Relish	5
Swiss Cake Shop	16
Tastebuds	13
Tutanekai Espresso	15
La Vega	2
Zippy Central	12

Ⓢ (500m)   **Ⓣ** (500m),   **Ⓤ** (1 km), Whakarewarewa (1 km) & Taupo (80 km)

set up as a **spa town** on land leased from the Ngati Whakaue, under the auspices of the 1881 Thermal Springs Districts Act. By 1885, the fledgling Rotorua boasted the Government Sanatorium Complex, a spa designed to administer the rigorous treatments deemed beneficial to the "invalids" who came to take the waters. The original **Bath House** and recreational **Blue Baths**, both set amid the oh-so-English **Government Gardens**, are now part of the **Rotorua Museum** which successfully and entertainingly puts these early enterprises into context.

Arrival and information

InterCity and Newmans **buses** pull up outside the information centre (see below), as do Guthreys (℡0800/759 999), who run here from Auckland via Hamilton. Air New Zealand **flights** from Auckland, Wellington and Christchurch land 8km northeast of town at the lakeside airport (℡07/345 6175). The door-to-door Super Shuttle (℡07/349 3444) charges $10-15 for the first passenger and $2 for each extra to the same place, and **taxis** (see p.323) run into town for around $15-20.

The **information centre**, at 1167 Fenton St, contains a foreign-exchange counter and two efficient but often busy visitor centres (daily: Nov–Easter 8am–6pm, Easter–Oct 8am–5.30pm; ℡07/348 5179, ⓦwww.rotoruanz .co.nz): one dealing with local tourism, the other with New Zealand-wide travel and ticketing. For DOC track and hut tickets, countrywide maps and lots of local outdoorsy information visit The Map & Track Shop, 1225 Fenton St (daily 9am–6pm; ℡ & ℻07/349 1845 ⓔmap-track@clear.net.nz), which also has internet access.

For a general round up of what's happening around town, pick up the free weekly *Thermal Air Visitor's Guide*. Note that Central Rotorua **addresses** are subject to a block-based numbering system that increases south and west from the corner of Whakaue and Hinemaru streets near the lake, starting with the 1000 block. Confusingly, outlying areas haven't been numbered in the same way, so some streets – such as Fenton Street – increase from 1000 to around 1600 then start again at about 200.

City transport

Richies Coachlines (℡07/345 5694) provide the most basic level of urban **bus** transport, centred on Pukuatua Street between Tutanekai and Fenton streets. Buses leave daily for Ngongotaha, passing Rainbow Springs and Whakarewarewa (roughly every 90min), and costing around $2 each way or $7 for an all-day pass. There are a large number of bus **tours**, mostly geared towards the more distant sights (see p.325) but nearly all the points visited by the sightseeing/shuttle buses are within 7km of central Rotorua and there are no substantial hills, so **cycling** is a viable way to go; **car-rental** rates are also fairly competitive here (see p.323).

Accommodation

Rotorua's accommodation has one big advantage: no matter how low your budget, you can stay somewhere with a **hot pool**, and for a little more you might even get a private tub in your room. In fact there is barely a place in town without a hot pool – the best of them directly fed with mineral water, but most are now artificially heated.

The range is wide, including a clutch of quality **hostels**, all within walking distance of the city centre and all eager to advise on local activities. There's a huge range of **motels**, most of them lining the busy Fenton Street, which runs south towards Whakarewarewa; competition is fierce and at off-peak times you may well get rock bottom prices. There's also a good range of **B&Bs** and

A recent problem around Rotorua's centre has been theft from cars, with thieves targeting those parked near hostels. It makes sense to take any valuables into your room or ask to use a safe.

guesthouses, while **hotels** mostly cater to bus-tour groups and usually charge prohibitive prices if you just walk in off the street. We've mainly recommended **campsites** right in town, but there are dozens of others scattered around the region; most are listed with the visitor centre, who can advise on availability.

Between Christmas and March you would do well to make **reservations** a few days in advance.

Hotels and motels

Amber Pacifica Lodge 1296 Hinemaru St (off Fenton St) ☎0800/426 237 & 07/348 0595, ⓕ348 0795. Middle-of-the-road motel with only average rooms but well situated close to the town centre. ❹

Gibson Court Motel 10 Gibson St ☎07/346 2822, ⓕ348 9481. Small motel in a quiet location, simply decorated but with nice private mineral pools. ❹

Havana Motor Lodge 1078 Whakaue St ☎07/348 8134 & 0800/333 799, ⓕ348 8132. Quiet, well-sited motel close to the lakefront with spacious grounds, a heated pool and two small mineral pools. Many of the units have recently been renovated. ❹

Millennium Hotel cnr Eruera and Hinemaru sts ☎07/3471234 ⓦwww.millenniumhotels.com. Swanky, big tourist hotel within spitting distance of the lake and Polynesian Spa where everything is laid on. ❾

Princes Gate Hotel 1057 Arawa St ☎07/348 1179 & 0800/696 963, ⓦwww
.scenic-circle.co.nz. The sole survivor from the days when all of Hinemaru Street was lined with hotels catering to the ailing, who took the waters at the bathhouse across the road. This lovely old wooden hotel is now restored with en-suite rooms fronting onto lovely wide verandas, a tennis court and in-house video. Off-peak B&B specials are sometimes available. ❼

Regal Geyserland Hotel 424 Fenton St ☎07/348 2039 & 0800/881 882, ⓔgeyserland @silveroaks.co.nz. Book early to get a third- or fourth-floor room with unsurpassed views over the Whakarewarewa thermal area. The rooms and public areas have seen better days, but are quite adequate and there's an outdoor pool, small gym and restaurant/bar. Some viewless rooms are ❺, but that rather defeats the object of staying here. ❻

Royal Lakeside Novotel Lake end Tutanekai St ☎07/346 3888 & 0800/444 422, ⓦwww
.novotel.co.nz. Swankiest of the big hotels, with elegant modern rooms, some with lake views, and all the usual facilities, plus thermal pool and massage facilities. The normal rate comes out at ❾, though for most of the year there are specials at ❼–❽

Silver Fern Motor Inn 326 Fenton St ☎07/346 3849 & 0800/118 808, ⓦwww.silverfernmtorinn
.co.nz. Modern top-of-the-line motel with studios and one-bedroom units, all with spa baths, Sky TV, sunny balconies and oodles of space. ❻

B&Bs and guesthouses

Ariki Lodge 2 Manuariki Ave, Ngongotaha (see map p.324) ☎07/357 5532,
ⓦwww.arikilodge.co.nz. Excellent, welcoming B&B perched right beside the lake and serving sumptuous breakfasts. The rooms, one with excellent lake views, are both en suite, and there's an enormous suite with a spa bath. It's around 8km northwest of Rotorua and is reached from central Ngongotaha along Taui St. ❻

Best Inn Rotorua 1068 Whakaue St ☎ & ⓕ07/347 9769. Modern B&B right in the centre with attractively simple, clean rooms and Japanese-style onsen mineral baths. ❺

Eaton Hall 39 Hinemaru St, ☎07/347 0366. A comfy B&B with three en suites as well as seven rooms with shared facilities, right in the heart of town. Friendly and well-priced, with a full cooked-breakfast served. ❹

Jack & Di's 21 Lake Rd ☎07/346 8482, ⓔreservations@jackanddis.co.nz. Welcoming and attractively decorated B&B right by Ohinemutu with good lake views and three en-suite rooms. Continental breakfast is served and there's free tea, coffee, biscuits and fresh fruit all day. ❹

The Lake House 6 Cooper Ave (see map p.324) ☎07/345 3313 & 0800/002 863, ⓦwww
.thelakehouse.co.nz Spacious B&B in a 1930s house beautifully sited right on the lakeshore with views across lawns to Mokoia Island. As well as a comfortable lounge, guests have free use of kayaks and windsurfing equipment and can swim safely from the beach. Breakfast is substantial and there's a new spa to lounge in. Located just off Robinson Ave, itself off SH30 7km north of Rotorua. ❻

Lynmore Hilton Rd (see map p.324) ☎345 6303, ⓦwww.babs.co.nz/aroden. Comfortable B&B in the suburb of Lynmore, just off the Tarawera Rd 4km from central Rotorua, with very welcoming well-travelled hosts, nicely appointed rooms, lush gardens, a separate guest lounge, and tasty breakfasts. ❺

Peacehaven 10 Peace St ☎ & ⓕ07/348 3759, ⓔpeacehaven@clear.net.nz. Suburban homestay close to Whakarewarewa with friendly hosts,

comfortable rooms, a large thermally heated pool in the back yard and a lovely little mineral pool. ❹
Sandi's B&B 103 Fairy Springs Rd ☏07/347 0034, ℮sandi.mark@xtra.co.nz. Three comfortable, nicely decorated rooms close to the Rainbow Springs thermal park, with continental breakfast. ❸

Hostels

base Backpackers 1140 Hinemoa St ☏0800/843 392 & 07/350 2040, ⓦwww .basebackpackers.com. Central and well-appointed hostel with separate music, TV and games rooms and a 20m indoor climbing-wall, overlooked by an independently owned bar. City bikes rented for $30 a day. Dorms, four-shares, singles, doubles and en suites ❶–❸

Cactus Jack Downtown Backpackers 1210 Haupapa St ☏0800/122 228, ℮cactusjackbp@xtra.co.nz. A snazzy paint job and enthusiastic staff add character to this ageing warren of rooms and cabins, doors close at 8pm, with reasonably spacious dorms, twins and doubles. A large spa pool and pool table ensure it is always pretty lively. Dorms ❶ rooms ❸

Central Backpackers 10 Pukuatua St ☏ & ℻07/349 3285, ℮rotorua.central.bp@clear.net.nz. Small but spacious, homely and easygoing hostel in an immaculately kept large house, with beds rather than bunks in the four- and six-bed dorm rooms. There's low-cost bike rental and a spa pool too. ❶–❷

Crash Palace 1271 Hinemaru St ☏07/348 8842, ⓦwww.crashpalace.co.nz. Revamped former YHA with spacious and airy public areas, a spa pool and rooms, four-shares and doubles all made up with sheets. Dorms ❶, rooms ❸

Funky Green Voyager Backpackers 4 Union St ☏07/346 1754, ℻350 1100. Very relaxed hostel in a suburban house, ten minutes' walk from downtown with an easy-going communal atmosphere fostered by the idiosyncratic owner. Cooking facilities in particular are excellent and there's a hot tub and a cosy, TV-less lounge. Dorms, doubles and en suites. Dorms ❶, rooms ❷

Hot Rock Backpackers 1286 Arawa St ☏07/347 9469, ⓦwww.acb.co.nz/hot-rock. Large, lively and, at weekends, noisy hostel, a perennial favourite with patrons of the backpacker tour buses who are kept entertained in the two mineral pools, a heated outdoor swimming pool and the *Lava Bar* next door. Accommodation is mostly four-share dorms, each with private bathroom, there are backpacker

doubles, and en suites with kitchens as well. Dorms ❶, rooms ❸

KiwiPaka YHA 60 Tarewa Rd ☏07/347 0931, ⓦwww.kiwipaka-yha.co.nz. This huge, well-organized modern complex is only a five-minute walk from the town centre (on the far side of Kuirau Park) yet it's far enough away to avoid late-night party noise. Accommodation is great-value and split between the "lodge" area, with four- or five-bed rooms, and the en-suite chalets centred around the free thermal pool. There's an excellent low-cost café and a travel desk run by very helpful staff (their sister hostel is in Waitomo). Dorms ❶, rooms ❸

Campsites and motor parks

Blue Lake Top 10 Holiday Park Tarawera Rd, Blue Lake (see map p.324) ☏0800/808 292 & 07/362 8120, ⓦwww.topparks.co.nz. Large and well-organized site 9km from Rotorua on the way to the Buried Village and just across the road from Blue Lake. Extensive facilities include a games room and a spa pool. Camping $10, cabins & kitchen cabins ❷, s/c unit ❸, motels ❹

Cosy Cottage Holiday Park 67 Whittaker Rd ☏07/348 3793, ℮cosycottage@xtra.co.nz. Excellent holiday park a couple of kilometres from town with an extensive range of comfortable cabins and tourist flats, powered and tent sites, some of which are on geothermally-heated ground – great in winter but less appealing in summer. There's a swimming pool, a couple of pleasant mineral pools, naturally fed steam-boxes for *hangi*-style cooking, and bikes for rent ($16 a day). Camping $12, cabins ❷, flats ❸

Lakeside Thermal Holiday Park 54 Whittaker Rd ☏ & ℻07/348 1693, ℮relax@lakesidethermal .co.nz. Small and compact lakefront tent/campervan park 2km from the city, with kayaks for guests' use, a barbecue overlooking the lake, a genuine mineral-water pool and mineral-water baths where you can adjust the temperature to suit. Camping $10, cabins ❷, kitchen cabins ❸

Rotorua Top 10 Holiday Park 137 Pukuatua St ☏07/348 1886, ⓦwww.rotoruatop10.co.nz. Very well-appointed holiday park that's the closest to the city centre, with an outdoor pool and spa. A spacious camping area has tent and powered sites, basic but serviceable cabins, and more luxurious self-catering tourist flats as well as motel units. Camping $10, cabins ❷, flats ❸, units ❹

The Town, Lake Rotorua and Whakarewarewa

Rotorua's sights are scattered: even those around the centre of town require some form of transport, though half a day can be spent on foot visiting the fine collection of Maori artefacts and bath-house relics in the **Rotorua Museum**, located in the former bathhouse in the formal **Government Gardens**, then strolling around the shores of **Lake Rotorua** to Ohinemutu, the city's original Maori village with its neatly carved church. For a soak in a hot pool in the slightly surreal setting of a native bird sanctuary, catch a boat out to **Mokoia Island**, the romantic setting for the tale of two lovers, Hinemoa and Tutanekai.

The majority of sights require a little more effort, though sight seeing/shuttle buses (see p.325) do the rounds. Top of most sightseeing lists is **Whakarewarewa**, a large thermal reserve now divided into two sections: the **Thermal Village**, where folk still go about their daily lives amid the steam and boiling pools; and the **Maori Arts and Crafts Institute**, with its two large geysers and a fascinating carving and weaving school. Where Rotorua's northwestern suburbs peter out, Mount Ngongotaha rises up, providing the necessary slope for a number of gravity-driven activities at the **Skyline Skyrides**. In its shadow, **Rainbow Springs**, an aquatic farm, provides a window into the life cycle of trout, with some fine specimens swimming in pools richly draped in ferns, while Rainbow Farm offers a slightly different twist on the sort of sheep-centred farmshow pioneered by the **Agrodome**, nearby.

Government Gardens and around

In the early years of the twentieth century, Rotorua was already New Zealand's premier tourist town, a fact it celebrated in confident civic style by laying out the **Government Gardens** east of the town centre. With their juxtaposition of the staid and the exotic the gardens are like some bizarre vision of an antipodean little England. White-suited bowls players mill around sulphurous steaming vents, palm trees loom over rose gardens, and, commanding the centre, there's the neo-Tudor **bathhouse**, built in 1908. Heralded as the greatest spa in the South Seas, it was designed to treat patients suffering from just about any disorder – arthritis, alcoholism, nervousness – and offered ghoulish treatments involving electrical currents and colonic irrigation as well as the thermal baths. As the era of the grand spas came to a close, it's surprising that the bathhouse limped along until 1963, when it closed from a combination of low patronage and high maintenance costs. For a modern version of the spa experience head to the **Polynesian Spa** (see p.314), just up the road.

Other than the attractions within the gardens themselves, on their southwestern edge you'll find the **Tamaki Trading Post**, a meeting point on the corner of Hinemaru St and Pukuatua St for tours of Tamaki Maori Village (see p.323).

The Rotorua Museum and the Blue Baths

The old bathhouse is now home to the wonderful **Rotorua Museum of Art and History** (daily: Nov to mid-March 9am–6pm, mid-March to Oct 9am–5pm; $10). One of the principal attractions is the old baths themselves, complete with gloomy green and white tiling and exposed pipes. Several rooms have been preserved in a state of arrested decay and filled with photos, some surprisingly frank, of the glory days, while an entertaining film recreates some of the history of both the area and the baths. The rest of the building is devoted to three main exhibitions. The small but exquisite and internationally significant **Te Arawa** display showcases the long-respected talents of Arawa carvers who made this area a bastion of pre-European carving traditions. Many pieces have been returned from European collections, and the magnificent carved figures, dog-skin cloaks, *pounamu* (greenstone) weapons and intricate bargeboards are all powerfully presented. Prized pieces include the flute played by the legendary lover Tutanekai (see p.315), an unusually fine pumice goddess, and rare eighteenth-century carvings executed with stone tools. The photos around the walls depict faces tattooed with detailed *moko* (traditional tattoos), and a portrait of the Tarawera guide standing outside the Whakarewarewa meeting house. Much of the remainder of the museum covers the dramatic events surrounding the **Tarawera eruption**. The extensive displays include an informative relief map of the region, eye-witness accounts and reminiscences, an audio-visual presentation and photos of the ash-covered Temperance Hotel at Te Wairoa and of the similarly smothered Rotomahana Hotel, both now demolished. The small section on the exploits of the **Maori battalion** during World War II is mainly for war buffs, but the half-hour video is very moving and well worth a look.

While the main bathhouse promoted health, the adjacent **Blue Baths** (daily 10am–5pm; included with Rotorua Museum entry) promised only pleasure when it opened in 1933. Designed in the Californian Spanish Mission style so popular at the time, this was one of the first public swimming pools in the world to allow mixed bathing. Like its neighbour, the Blue Baths hit hard times and closed in 1982, not reopening until 1999. You can still swim in an ancillary outdoor pool ($7), though the bulk of the building is now a museum charting its decades at the centre of Rotorua's social whirl. People's recollections are posted on panels amid the old changing cubicles, and serve to reinforce the sense of loss you get strolling around the main pool, now filled in and grassed over.

The Polynesian Spa

Immediately to the south of the Blue Baths lies the **Polynesian Spa**, Hinemoa St (daily 6.30am–11pm; Polynesian Pools $12, Lake Spa $30; ℡07/348 1328, Ⓦwww.polynesianspa.co.nz), a mostly open-air complex landscaped for lake views and comprising three separate areas. The main Polynesian Pools section comprises thirty-odd hot mineral pools claimed to treat all manner of ailments, principally arthritis and rheumatism. The vast majority of visitors bathe in either the slightly alkaline main pool or the small and turbid Radium and Priest pools, where the acidic waters bubbling up through the bottom of the tub vary from 36°C to 43°C. Private pools (an additional $12 per person for 30min), where you can adjust the temperature yourself, are ranged around the Radium and Priest pools, but for real exclusivity, opt for the adjacent **Lake Spa** section, with four attractively landscaped shallow rock pools of differing temperatures along with private relaxation lounge and bar. Reserve in advance for the hedonistic pleasures of the enormous range of massages, body scrubs, mud wraps and general pampering, from thirty minutes ($65, includes Lake Spa entry) to varying full-day detox programmes ($550–650). Families are catered for in the new **Family Spa** ($28 for up to two adults and four kids), with one chlorinated 33°C pool, a couple of small mineral pools and a water slide.

Lake Rotorua and Mokoia Island

From the Government Gardens it is a short walk along the waterfront to the Lakefront Jetty, the starting point for trips onto **Lake Rotorua** and out to **Mokoia Island** (7km north of the jetty), New Zealand's only inland,

The love story of Hinemoa and Tutanekai

The Maori love story of **Hinemoa and Tutanekai** has been told around the shores of Lake Rotorua for centuries, and is widely believed to be more fact than fiction. It tells of the young chief Tutanekai of Mokoia Island, and his high-born paramour, Hinemoa, whose people lived along the western shores of the lake. Hinemoa's family forbade her from marrying the illegitimate Tutanekai and prevented her from meeting him by beaching their heavy *waka* (canoe), but the strains of Tutanekai's lamenting flute still wafted across the lake nightly and the smitten Hinemoa resolved to swim to him. One night, buoyed by gourds, she set off towards Mokoia, but by the time she got there Tutanekai had returned to his *whare* (house) to sleep. Hinemoa arrived at the island but, without clothes, was unable to enter the village, so she immersed herself in a hot pool. Presently Tutanekai's slave came by to collect water, and Hinemoa lured him over, smashed his gourd and sent him back to his master. An enraged Tutanekai came to investigate, only to fall into Hinemoa's embrace.

predator-free bird sanctuary (the scene of a successful and longstanding breeding programme for saddlebacks and North Island robins – often spotted at the feeder stations). The island is better known, however, for the story of **Hinemoa and Tutanekai** (see box, above), the greatest of all Maori love stories. The site of Tutanekai's *whare* and **Hinemoa's Pool** can still be seen, along with the grave of the first *pakeha* born in the Rotorua district.

There are various ways to get to Mokoia Island (a $25 landing fee applies to all visitors) but by far the cheapest, most frequent and reliable is with **Rotorua Lake Cruises**, (℡07/347 9852, $30, guided tour) on the Ngaroto (The Old lady of the Lake). Alternatively try the Scatcat tour (℡07/347 9852; 4 daily; $30), a speedy **catamaran** from which, if you catch one of the early boats, you can be put ashore on Mokoia Island and picked up by a later boat, leaving time for an extended soak in a hot pool or to wander the trails with an eagle eye out for native birdlife. Finally if you fancy a more high-octane approach, roar out to the island on a **Kawarau Jet Boat** (℡07/3437600, 1hr guided tour, 90mins total, $69).

If it is just a lake cruise you are after, consider the leisurely *Lakeland Queen* (℡0800/862 784, ⓦwwww.lakelandqueen.co.nz), a replica **paddle steamer** that runs a series of hour-long trips including a meal – the Morning Tea Cruise (10am; $28); Lunch Cruise (12.30pm; $30); and Afternoon Tea Cruise (2.30pm; $28). They also do occasional dinner cruises ($55).

Ohinemutu

Before Rotorua grew up around its government buildings, the principal Maori settlement in the area was at **Ohinemutu**, 500m north of the centre, on the lakeshore. Ohinemutu remains an overwhelmingly Maori village centred on its hot springs and the small wooden **St Faith's Anglican Church**, built in 1914 to replace its 1885 predecessor. The church's simple half-timbered neo-Tudor exterior gives no hint of the gloriously rich interior where there is barely a patch of wall that hasn't been carved or covered with *tukutuku* (ornamental latticework) panels. The main attraction, however, is the window featuring the figure of Christ, swathed in a Maori cloak and feathers, positioned so that he appears to be walking on the lake. Outside is the grave of Gilbert Mair, a captain in the colonial army who twice saved Ohinemutu from attacks by rival Maori and became the only *pakeha* to earn full Arawa chieftainship.

At the opposite end of the small square in front of the church stands the **Tamatekapua Meeting House**, again beautifully carved, though the best work, some dating back almost two hundred years, is inside, which, unfortunately, is currently inaccessible. Between the two buildings, a signed passage leads down to Ohinemutu Maori Handicrafts, Mataiamutu St (☎07/350 3378), a small gallery where Tony Kapua, a locally renowned carver, turns out fine Maori pieces.

Immediately south of Ohinemutu, on Ranolf Street, lies **Kuirau Park**, its northern end pockmarked by fairly modest steaming hot pools, while the southern end has some minor thrills for kids: crazy-golf, a miniature railway, play areas and the like.

Whakarewarewa thermal reserve and forest park

To New Zealanders, mention of Rotorua immediately conjures up images of the **Whakarewarewa Thermal Reserve** – or Whaka, as it is more commonly known – the closest thermal area to the city. Until 1998 this was a single entity, but a dispute over ownership has split it into two entirely separate complexes. Around two-thirds of the active thermal zone has been inherited by the **NZ Maori Arts & Crafts Institute**, Hemo Rd, 3km south of central Rotorua (daily: Nov–March 8am–6pm, April–Oct 8am–5pm; $19.95; ⊛ www.nzmaori .co.nz; free hour-long guided tours on the hour), which is the start of a series of walkways past glooping pools of boiling mud, sulphurous springs and agglomerations of silica stalactites. The main attractions are New Zealand's most spectacular geysers, the ten-metre **Prince of Wales' Feathers** and the granddaddy of them all, the twenty-metre **Pohutu** ("big splash"), which once performed several times a day until 2000, when it surprised everyone by spouting continuously for an unprecedented 329 days. It has since settled back to jetting water into the air for around eighty percent of the time.

The complex also contains a **nocturnal house** with kiwi, a replica of a traditional **Maori village**, and the **Arts and Crafts Institute** itself (same hours; included with entry) where skilled artisans produce flax skirts and carvings, which can be bought in the classy but expensive shop. The institute also hosts **Mia Ora** (6.15pm; $70; ☎0800/494 252) comprising a Maori welcome, concert and steam-cooked feast and, weather permitting, a floodlit tour of the geothermal valley.

The rest of the thermal area falls under the auspices of the **Whakarewarewa, The Thermal Village** Tryon St, 3km south of central Rotorua (daily 8.30am–5pm; $18; ⊛ www.whakarewarewa.com), a living village founded in pre-European times. Although you can't get really close to the geysers, there is considerable compensation in being able to wander around the houses and you might even see people using steam boxes for cooking. You can also attend the free **cultural performance** (11.15am & 2pm), and partake in a **hangi** (served at 12.30, $30; *hangi* taster $15).

The western fringe of the Whakarewarewa thermal area borders the **Whakarewarewa State Forest Park**, experimentally planted a century back to see which exotic species would grow well under New Zealand conditions. Redwoods were found to grow three times faster than in their native California, creating the impressive **Redwood Grove**, which is threaded by a number of short paths. The forest's **Visitor Centre**, Long Mile Rd (Oct–March Mon–Fri 8.30am–6pm, Sat & Sun 10am–4pm; April–Sept Mon–Fri 8.30am–5pm, Sat & Sun 10am–4pm; ☎07/346 2082), has details of these in its free *The Redwoods* recreation guide, and information on the excellent **mountain-biking trails**. The Forest is also the venue for **horse rides** with the Maori-run Peka Horse Trekking (☎07/346 1755), who run one-hour ($35) and longer treks.

West of the Lake: Around Ngongotaha

Aside from visits to the thermal areas, much of Rotorua's daytime activity takes place around the flanks of **Mount Ngongotaha**, between five and ten kilometres northwest of the centre, which is increasingly being surrounded by the city's suburbs. Closest to downtown, there's all manner of gravity-driven activities at the **Skyline Skyrides** site, and gentler pursuits at either **Rainbow Springs** or around the mountain at **Paradise Valley Springs**. Sheep take centre stage (literally) a little further out at the **Agrodome**, centrepiece of an adventure park that is trying to wrestle the adrenaline torch from the Skyline Skyrides.

Skyline Skyrides, Rainbow Springs and Paradise Valley Springs

First stop, around 4km from town, is the **Skyline Skyrides**, where a ski-lift style gondola (daily 9am–late; $17; ⓦwww.skylineskyrides.co.nz) whisks you 200m up to the station on the mountain for superb views across the lake and town, scenic dining in the restaurant (the gondola runs return trips until the restaurant closes, 10–11pm most nights) and café, and a bevy of adventure activities including a **luge** ($6 per ride; gondola plus 5 rides $33) and the adjacent **Skyswing** ride ($30).

At the foot of the hill lies **Rainbow Springs** (daily 8am–5pm; $21.50), an all-too-neat series of trout pools linked by nature trails where you can view some of the largest rainbow, brown and North American brook trout you will ever see. Across the road, linked by a pedestrian tunnel, is the **Rainbow Farm Show** (included in ticket price; shows at 10.30am, 11.45am, 1pm, 2.30pm & 4pm), with a huge fluffy shop and a covered area from where you can watch sheepdogs rounding up a flock, followed by a fake auction and a display of shearing prowess.

For even more trout, but in the company of lions rather than sheep, eschew Rainbow Springs in favour of **Paradise Valley Springs**, 13km west of Rotorua on Paradise Valley Road (daily 8am–5pm; $18; ⓦwww.paradisev.co.nz). It's an altogether more peaceful setting, with boardwalks guiding you past pools of trout, native birds and an attractive wetland area, though, the biggest draw is the breeding pride of lions, who are fed at 2.30pm. Trout superfans should continue along Paradise Valley Road to reach the **Ngongotaha Hatchery** (daily 9am-4pm; free) where a small hatchery and a succession of rearing ponds gives an insight into the activities of government-run Fish & Game New Zealand, the outfit that stocks most of the lakes around these parts. Paradise Valley Road continues to the Agrodome.

The Agrodome and Agrodome Adventure Park

Just about every bus touring the North Island stops 10km north of Rotorua at the **Agrodome**, Western Road, Ngongotaha (shows at 9.30am, 11am & 2.30pm; show $18, farm tour $20, combined price $35; ☎07/357 1050, ⓦwww.agrodome.co.nz), where the star attraction is a slick 45-minute **sheep show**. Though undoubtedly corny, this popular spectacle is always entertaining: rams representing the nineteen major breeds farmed in New Zealand are enticed onto the podium; a sheep is shorn; lambs are bottle-fed; and there's an impressive sheepdog display. Afterwards, the dogs are put through their paces outside – rounding up sheep into pens and so on – and you can watch a 1906 industrial carding machine turn fleece into usable wool. There's also a 45-minute farm tour complete with honey tasting, deer viewing and, between April and June, kiwifruit picking.

A totally different market is catered for at the adjacent **Agrodome Adventure Park** (daily 9am–5pm or later), where they've gone all out to lure adrenaline junkies. Attractions include a forty-three-metre **bungy jump** ($99), the **Swoop** swing ride ($45 for one, $40 each for two, $35 each for three), and the **Agrojet** ($35) where tiny racing jetboats hurtle around a short artificial course. Nearby at the **Zorb** (one go $40, two goes $60) you can dive into the centre of a huge clear plastic ball and roll down a two-hundred-metre hill. Even more fun is the **Freefall Extreme** ($65), which simulates freefall using a powerful propeller above which you hover five metres up. Add to this the possibility of helicopter rides with Heli Pro (see p.326) and you've got yourself quite a day out and an empty wallet.

Activities

As you might expect in a place that attracts visitors in such numbers, numerous companies have sprung up in Rotorua to offer all manner of adventure activities – rafting, kayaking, mountain biking or even fishing. The **adventure tourism** scene hasn't quite snowballed to the degree it has in Queenstown, but there is still loads to keep you occupied. In addition to the activities detailed below, brochures everywhere advertise water-skiing on Blue Lake, horse riding, quad biking, hot-air ballooning plus particularly scenic **skydiving** with Tandem Skydiving Rotorua (℡07/345 7520; around $245).

Rafting, kayaking and sledging

Rotorua has developed a considerable reputation for its nearby whitewater rivers which you can tackle by **rafting**, **kayaking** (usually in tandem kayaks with a guide) or the more in-your-face "**sledging**" where you float down the rapids wearing safety gear and hanging on to a buoyant plastic sledge (only recommended for good swimmers). Trips cost around $90–$120 and include transport and all equipment. Much of the hype is reserved for the Grade IV **Kaituna River**, or at least the two-kilometre section of it after it leaves Lake Rotoiti 20km north of Rotorua which includes the spectacular seven-metre **Tutea's Falls**. The one to go for though, if you can get the timing right, is the Grade IV-plus **Wairoa River**, 80km by road from Rotorua, on the outskirts of Tauranga, which relies on dam-releases for raftable quantities of white water (Dec–March every Sun; Sept–Nov & April–May every second Sun). This is one of the finest short trips in the world, negotiating a hazardous but immensely satisfying stretch of water. This is essentially a trip for those with some experience and a good appreciation of the hazards of white water.

If your tastes lean more towards appreciation of the natural surroundings with a bit of a bumpy ride thrown in, opt for the Grade III **Rangitaiki River**, which also shoots Jeff's Joy, a Grade IV drop that's the highlight of the trip. With more time, and money on your hands, it is well worth considering a **multi-day wilderness rafting trip** on Eastland's **Motu River** (see box, p.424). You can also **rent kayaks** or undertake **kayaking courses** and **guided trips** on several of the larger lakes in the region with the emphasis on scenic appreciation, soaking in hot pools and maybe a little fishing.

Adventure Kayaking ℡07/348 9451, ⓦwww.adventurekayaking.co.nz. Rent sea kayaks ($40 a day) and undertake guided kayaking trips including the Twilight Paddle ($65) on Lake Rotoiti, the Lake Tarawera Full Day Tour ($75), or the Kayak Camp Out ($120)

with a hot swim, barbecue dinner and cooked breakfast.
Kaitiaki Adventures ℡0800/338 736, ⓦwww.raft-it.com. Well-run operator offering rafting and sledging trips down the Kaitiaki. They also add a cultural dimension, explaining the

significance of the river to Maori and have modified rafts and sledges better suited to the conditions.

Kaituna Cascades ☎0800/524 886, @kaituna.cascades.co.nz. Rafting on all the rivers mentioned above as well as kayaking on Lake Rotoiti.

Kaituna Kayaks ☎0800/465 292, @www.kaitunakayaks.com. Offer tandem kayaking on the Kaituna River and including the 7m Tutea's Falls, steered down the river by an experienced paddler in the driving seat behind you. Also specialize in kayak courses.

Raftabout ☎07/345 4652 @www.raftabout.co.nz. Rafting trips on the Kaituna, the Rangitaiki and the Wairoa and a variety of package deals including other adventure activities.

River Rats ☎0800/333 900, @www.riverrats.co.nz. Long-established company offering rafting on all the above rivers and adventure packages including quad biking and caving.

Sun Spots Kayak Shop SH33, Okawa Bay 14km north of Rotorua ☎07/362 4222, @www.sunspots.co.nz. They rent recreational kayaks (around $25 per half-day), sea kayaks ($35 per day), and full whitewater set-ups ($30–40 per day) and run all manner of courses including the half-day introduction to kayaking ($100).

Wet'n'Wild ☎07/348 3191, @www.wetnwildrafting.co.nz. One-day trips on the Kaituna, Rangitaiki and Wairoa as well as overnight- to five-day rafting expeditions further afield.

Mountain biking

Some of the country's finest and most accessible **mountain biking** lies just fifteen minutes' ride from central Rotorua, with large areas of the Whakarewarewa Forest's redwoods, firs and pines threaded by single-track trails especially constructed with banked turns and jumps under a sub-canopy of tree ferns. Altogether there's over 40km of track, divided into a dozen circuits in five grades of difficulty and all explained and colourfully illustrated on the waterproof **trail map** ($2) available in town from the Map and Track Shop (see p.310), or out at the forest from the forest Visitor Centre. Don't get carried away with the idea it's just for experts though, any level of peddler can get a great deal of pleasure from half a day mucking about in this atmospheric forest. There is **no charge** to enter the forest or use the trails, which are most easily accessed from the obvious car park on Waipa Mill Road, 5km south of town off SH38. For bike rental try:

Edzown ☎07/346 1717, @edzownbike @paradise.co.nz, around $50 for half a day), offer self-guided trips with top quality bikes and all the gear (helmets, gloves, puncture repair kit, various spanners and replacement links), a water bottle and muesli bar. They also rent bikes at the Skyline, for those who only want to go down hill, and run a variety of guided trips (day and night for around $50–70 for two hrs) for those in need of moral support.

Planet Bike ☎07/348 9971, @www.planetbike.co.nz. Rent bikes and gear for guided and self-guided mountain biking through the forest, for all experience levels and similar prices; they even offer "women guides for women's rides".

Fishing

The Rotorua lakes boast a reputation for trout fishing only matched in the North Island by the rivers and streams flowing into Lake Taupo. With two dozen gorgeous lakes, the angling could hardly be more scenic and almost all are stocked with strong-fighting rainbow trout; a typical summer catch is around 1.5kg, though in winter this can creep up towards 3kg. The proximity of **Lake Rotorua** makes it a perennial favourite, reached by charter boats from the Lakefront Jetty (2hr minimum; $90–100 an hour, including tackle but not licences – see p.320).

If you are going it alone, obtain up-to-date information on lake and river conditions from either the Map and Track Shop (see p.310) or sports shops such as O'Keefe's, 1113 Eruera St (☎07/346 0178, @cotter@thenet.net.nz). Both also stock the free *Lake Rotorua & Tributaries* leaflet published by Fish &

Game NZ that explains the rules of the fishery (which in broad terms is open year round), and will provide contacts for fly-fishing guides which will generally set you back around $500 a day. **Licences** (24hr, around $20; 7 days, $35; year, $85), which are valid for the whole country except for the Taupo fishery region, can be bought with a credit card from the free licence helpline (☎0800/542 362).

Eating, drinking and entertainment

In recent years Rotorua has made great culinary strides and there are now quite a few quality **restaurants**, most congregated along a short strip at the lake end of Tutanekai Street – known as "The Streat". Nowhere is outrageously expensive, but the assiduously budget-conscious will fare better further from the main drag. Unlike the shops, which close up for much of the weekend, the restaurants and bars are generally open all week, most staying open as long as custom demands; unless you're part of a large group, there's little need to reserve a table.

Rotorua remains a small city and despite a plethora of restaurants nightlife is limited. There are a few lively **bars** to keep you entertained, but almost everyone spends one evening of their stay attending one of the **hangi** and **Maori concerts** in one of the tourist hotels or, preferably, at one of the outlying *marae*.

Restaurants and cafés

Bath House Café Blue Baths (see p.314). Gracious tea rooms re-created in the renovated Blue Baths complex serving cakes off an Art Deco trolley and with a couple of huge portraits of the Queen and Duke of Edinburgh. Pick a window seat and watch the bowls or croquette outside in Government Gardens while you indulge in tiffin ($16.50), Devonshire tea ($11.50), or lunches such as shepherds pie or calzone.

Bistro 1284 1284 Eruera St. White linen tablecloths belie the relatively relaxed atmosphere in what is one of Rotorua's better restaurants. Try the fresh goats cheese ravioli with smoked mushroom sauce ($15.50) or grilled venison with gingered kumara ($29.50), but leave space for the dark-chocolate and mint torte. Dinner only; closed Sun & Mon.

Café Ephesus 1107 Tutanekai St. Unassuming, cheap and friendly spot where generous portions of Turkish, Mediterranean and Middle Eastern fare is dished up with the minimum of fuss. Try the *menemen* (Turkish omelette with tomatoes, red onions and sweet peppers) or traditional dishes like *dolmades*, and *lahmacun* or, if you're feeling boring, a wood-fired pizza ($11.95).

Capers Epicurean 1181 Eruera St. A relatively recent addition, this large airy café cum deli serves up breakfast from 7.30am daily as well as colourful salads, over-stuffed panini, a great line in Jamaican pork curry, lasagne and toasted brioche, all at very reasonable prices for lunch and dinner, in a bustling, slightly cosmopolitan atmosphere.

Fat Dog 1161 Arawa St. Always lively café and bar, with a relaxed atmosphere engendered by mismatched furniture, eclectic wall hangings and music. Drop in for coffee, some of the best in town, and cake or a plate of wedges, or go for the wide-ranging selection of hearty mains ($12–27).

Freos 1103 Tutanekai St ☎07/346 0976. Quality modern Kiwi café dining at reasonable prices both inside and out. Good for burgers, focaccia sandwiches, pasta dishes and chargrilled meats.

The Landing Tarawera Rd, 18km southeast of Rotorua (see map p.324) ☎07/362 8595. Quality European-influenced Kiwi grub at moderate prices make this waterside café, restaurant and bar – with great views across to Lake Tarawera towards Mount Tarawera – an essential stop if you're out this way. During the day it is informal with brunch and lunch but from 6pm (generally Wed–Sat) à la carte dining means it's best to book.

Lovely India 1123 Tutanekai St ☎07/348 4088. Surprisingly authentic Indian restaurant with a wide range of good quality vegetarian dishes as well as the standard lamb kormas and Tandoori chickens ($5–20), take-away available.

Relish 1149 Tutanekai St. Modern café (with an unreachable bright-red sofa suspended from the ceiling) serving home-made toasted muesli from 8am (Dinners Thurs–Sat), Italian treats and some glorious cakes all day and a fusion main-course menu at reasonable prices.

Skyline Cableway Restaurant Skyline, Fairy Springs Rd ☎07/347 0027. Worth a visit if only for the beautiful view of an illuminated Rotorua, this

NZ buffet combines the best available seafood, steaks, lamb, venison and vegetable selection in a value-for-money package. Don't forget to book a taxi to get you home after the return cable trip.

Swiss Cake and Confectionery Shop 1230 Tutanekai St. Excellent pastries and handmade chocolates to take away. Closed Sun.

Tastebuds Mexican Cantina 1213 Fenton St. Tiny, ever-popular Mexican eat-in and takeaway, serving hefty helpings of Tex-Mex staples at lowish prices.

Tutanekai Espresso 1226 Tutanekai St. Daytime café with a good line in breakfasts, panini, and BLTs, plus fine coffee. Closed Sun.

La Vega 1158 Whakaue St. Bustling restaurant and bar concentrating on gourmet pizzas cooked in a wood-fired oven, pasta and steaks.

Zippy Central 1153 Pukuatua St. Rotorua's grooviest restaurant, with haphazard retro 1950s and 1960s pop decor. Serves great coffee and small selection of imaginative and well-prepared food, from bagels and smoothies to marinated lamb and tabouleh salad, pumpkin gnocchi, and seafood laksa ($11–22).

Bars and clubs

Barbarella 1263 Pukuatua St. Rotorua's "black sheep", with a supposed bad reputation though the stories of occasional violence are made too much of locally. Popular chiefly for underground, alternative and dance nights (hip-hop and house), visiting DJs and occasional bands. Usually Wed–Sat 10pm–3am.

Fuze 1122 Tutanekai St ☎07/349 6306. Upscale downtown bar with comfortable seating and DJs (Fri), occasional live acts and bands (Sat). Closed Mon.

Grumpy Mole 1246 Arawa St. Big and brash Wild West theme-bar (part of a countrywide chain); happy hours, live sport and table dancing rule the roost. $3 cover on Fri & Sat from 9.30pm plus vague dress code.

Lava Bar 1286 Arawa St. A refurbished and enlarged house converted into a bar that's found favour with backpackers, rafting guides and local youth. Basic meals are available and there's an early-evening happy hour, pinball machines and a pool table – if you can get to them, plus late night music. $2 cover charge at weekends.

O'Malley's 1287 Eruera St. Ersatz Irish bar with a strong line in draught Irish beers and bargain meals. Live Irish-style bands Thurs & Fri plus happy hour.

Outlaws 1140 Hinemoa St. Saloon-style bar in the same building as base Backpackers, with big windows overlooking the climbing wall. Good for a few beers and some pool – occasional live music.

Pig & Whistle cnr Haupapa St & Tutanekai St. Lively bar in a former police station with some locally brewed beers on tap, a garden bar, and rock and pop covers bands or DJs and dancing at weekends when tidy dress is required and a small cover charge applies. There are also large and reasonably priced bar meals.

Hangi and Maori concerts

Rotorua is probably the best place to sample food steamed to perfection in the Maori earth oven or **hangi** and watch a **Maori concert**, typically an hour-long performance of traditional dance, song and chants. Although not entirely satisfactory introductions to Maori culture, these are at least accessible and good value. Almost a dozen groups vie for your custom, with offerings that fall into two distinct camps: extravaganzas laid on at the major hotels (typically $50–70) and invariably disappointing; or packages operated and organized by **Maori groups** ($70–80). All trips run for three or four hours, most starting around 6 or 7pm, with buses picking up and dropping off at hotels and hostels around town; some of the hotels offer *hangi*-only or concert-only deals for about half the cost. The groups running **out-of-town packages** are distinctly more rewarding, though they all follow largely the same format, giving instruction on *marae* customs and protocol (see "Maoritanga" in Contexts, p.957) as you are driven out to a Maori village, followed by a formal welcome.

Mitai ☎07/343 9132, ⊛www.mitai.co.nz. Probably the best of the bunch, and the most recent addition, offering a more in-your-face trip – you'll probably end up with wood smoke in your eyes, ash in your hair and an amused grin at the rough-round-the-edges initial show. The food doesn't tend to be as stunning as at other *hangi* but the finale and enthusiasm are unmatched by any other Maori experience in New Zealand.

△ Tamaki village

NZ Maori Arts and Crafts Institute ℡07/348 90 47, ⓦwww.nzmaori.co.nz. Offer the "Mai Ora - Essence of Maori" evening performance at their extensive complex in the Whakarewarewa Thermal Reserve (p.307) which adds an extra layer to the generally professional show they put on during the day.

Rotoiti Tours ℡0800/476 864 & 07/348 8969, ⓔrotoititours@xtra2.co.nz. Lacks some of the panache of the others, but offers a more engaging (and in some ways more authentic) experience, with almost the whole *whanau* (extended family group) contributing to the proceedings – in the beautifully decorated meeting house on the

Rakeiao Marae at Tapuaekura Bay on the shores of Lake Rotoiti some 20km north of Rotorua.
Tamaki Maori Village ℡07/346 2823, ⓦwww.maoriculture.co.nz. You, and several busloads, are driven out to a specially built "Maori village" south of town for a spine-chilling welcome. Everything is so professionally done that it is hard to quibble, though parts can feel a bit "Hollywood". Its popularity has become its biggest downfall and sightlines can be restricted at the busier times of year, however, the *hangi* is probably the best on offer from any tour (£75). It's also possible to visit the site independently to see the central Tribal Market (daily 9am–4pm; $15).

Listings

Airlines Air New Zealand Travelcentre, cnr Hinemoa & Fenton sts: ℡0800/737 000.
Automobile Association 1191 Amohau St ℡07/348 3069.
Banks and exchange ANZ, cnr Hinemoa St & Amohia St ℡07/348 2169; BNZ, cnr Haupapa St & Tutanekai St ℡07/348 1099; National, cnr Fenton St & Hinemoa St ℡07/349 5300; Westpac, cnr Hinemoa St & Tutanekai St. See also American Express and Thomas Cook.
Bike rental Rotorua Cycle Centre, 1120 Hinemoa St ℡07/348 6588. See also "Mountain biking" p.319.
Bookshops Idle Hour Book Inn, 1186 Eruera St for secondhand books; Whitcoulls, 1238 Tutanekai St for new.
Car rental Link, 1234 Fenton St (℡07/349 1629 & 0800/652 565, ⓦwww.autohire.co.nz), offers a fully insured unlimited mileage runabout for $60 a day (3-day minimum). Budget, 1230 Fenton St (℡07/348 8127, ⓦwww.budget.co.nz), matches these rates most of the time, and U-Drive, 152 Lake Rd (℡0800/837 483) usually undercuts them both with four-day deals from $40–50 a day.
Cinema The local multiplex is Hoyts Movieland 5, 1263 Eruera St but there's also the more intimate Basement Cinema, 1140 Hinemoa St (under base Backpackers) an art-house movie theatre of 33 seats and great character (Tues, Thurs & Sat, $12), plus a licensed café.

Internet access Numerous places around town, especially along Fenton St, where there's fast access at the Map & Track Shop, #1225, and a larger number of machines at Contact Cyber Café, #1217, and Nomads Cyber Café, #1195 also try Cybershed, Tutaneka St.
Left luggage At Travelex, in the visitor centre see p.310 ($2 for 3hr, $4 per day).
Library The public library is on Haupapa St (℡07/348 4177).
Medical treatment For emergencies and urgent healthcare go to Lakes Primecare, cnr Arawa St & Tutanekai St ℡07/348 1000. Daily 8am–11pm.
Pharmacy Lakes Care Pharmacy, cnr Arawa St & Tutanekai St ℡07/48 4385. Daily 9am–9.30pm.
Police 64-98 Fenton St ℡07/348 0099.
Post office The main post office, with poste restante facilities, is at 79–85 Hinemoa St ℡07/349 2397.
Taxis Fast Taxis ℡07/348 2444; Rotorua Taxis ℡07/348 1111.
Travelex Tourism Building, Rotorua Visitors Centre, 1167 Fenton St, ℡07/348 0373, offers left luggage and foreign currency exchange.
Travel agents holiday Shoppe, 1235 Tutanekai St ℡507/347 6227; Flight Centre, 1228 Tutanekai St ℡07/348 6151; Galaxy United Travel, 1315 Tutanekai St ℡07/349 7444.

Around Rotorua

Much of the best Rotorua has to offer lies outside the city among the lakes to the north and east and around the most dramatic of the volcanic zones half an hour's drive south towards Taupo. Shuttles and tours run by numerous companies (see p.325) mean that just about any combination of sights can be packed into a full day-trip, while if travelling independently, minor sights along the eastern shore of Lake Rotorua can be quickly dispatched, leaving time for the seldom-crowded and recently renovated **Hell's Gate** thermal area and the opportunity to watch terrified rafters plunging over **Tutea's Falls**. Hiring a boat opens up the best of lakes Rotoiti, Rotoehu and Rotama, though they're pleasing enough just to drive past on the way to Whakatane and the East Cape. Rewards are more plentiful to the east and south especially around Mount Tarawera which, in 1886, showered tonnes of ash on the settlement of Te Wairoa, now known as **Buried Village**, where partly-interred Maori dwellings graphically illustrate the volcano's immense power. As the village and the Pink and White Terraces were being destroyed, the **Waimangu Volcanic Valley** was

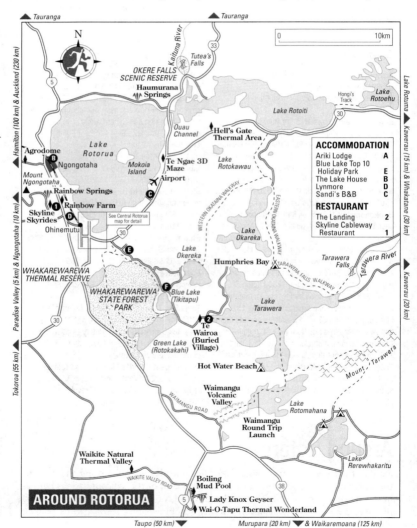

created and now ranks as one of the finest collections of geothermal features in the region alongside kaleidoscopic **Wai-O-Tapu**, with its daily-triggered **Lady Knox Geyser** and multicoloured pools.

Getting around

To get out to the sights around Rotorua without your own transport, you've got a choice of shuttles, which just do the running around, and a bewildering array of minibus tours, ranging from a couple of hours to a full day. The latter all include admission to sights, have a commentary of some description and the itineraries can be quite flexible, particularly when numbers are small. One destination that isn't accessible with your own vehicle is the shattered line of craters atop Mount Tarawera, which can be reached on foot (see box on p.326) or on tours with Mt Tarawera NZ.

Shuttle buses

Dave's Shuttles ☎07/348 7212. Picks up at hostels and hotels around Rotorua. A $20 all-day pass lets you get on and off as you please and includes an afternoon run out to the Buried Village. Probably one of the most comprehensive of the shuttle operators, Dave also runs to Wai-O-Tapu and Waimangu for $24, including entrance to the former.

Geyser Link ☎0800/004 321. Makes similar runs at similar prices to Dave's Shuttles including Wai-O-Tapu, Waimangu, Tamaki Maori Village and the Waikite hot pools.

Santa Fe Shuttle ☎07/345 7997. Will run you out to Wai-O-Tapu ($10 return), throw in Waimangu ($45 return), or just run you to Hell's Gate ($15 return).

Minibus tours

Carey's Tours 1108 Haupapa St ☎07/347 1197. Run a vast array of trips, including the Geothermal Wonderland (4hr; $85) out to Wai-O-Tapu and Waimangu; and the scenic Waimangu Round Trip (9hr; $190) which visits the Waimangu Volcanic

Valley, cruising across Lake Rotomahana, then bushwalking to a second cruise on Lake Tarawera, ambling around the Buried Village and finishing with a soak in the Polynesian Spa. Their back-packer-oriented trips – known as Carey's Capers – include lunch and a dip in natural hot pools in the bush but are otherwise almost identical.

Mt Tarawera NZ ☎07/349 3714, ⓦwww .mt-tarawera.co.nz. Have sole rights to the mountain. Either join their Rotorua-based half-day tour ($110) or their volcanic eco tour, taking in two thermal areas and Mt Tarawera for $195. If you've got some spare dosh you can get the best of both worlds by doing a fly-drive tour, a helicopter up to the mountain and drive back ($390).

Sonny's World ☎07/349 0290, ⓦwww .sonnysworld.co.nz. Offer a half-day tour ($55) including a *marae* visit.

TeKiri Trek ☎07/345 5016, ⓔtekiri@ihug.co.nz. Carry a maximum of five for a full day ($120) taking in Wai-O-Tapu and Waimangu, a 4WD safari through native forest, a big meal in the bush and a little hot-pool bathing.

Northeast of Lake Rotorua: Hell's Gate and the northern lakes

SH30 hugs the eastern shores of Lake Rotorua, bound for Whakatane and passing through the region's greatest concentration of lakes and plenty of twisting hill country. Scenery aside, there isn't a great deal to stop for along the way apart from the **Fairbank Maze**, opposite the airport, 7km northeast of Rotorua (daily 10am–5pm; $6), which ranks as the largest hedge maze in the country, and **Te Ngae 3D Maze**, 3km further on (daily 9am–5pm; $6), a wooden affair with bridges linking separate sections and complicating things immeasurably.

Immediately north of the maze, SH30 veers off right to Whakatane while SH33 continues north to Te Puke and Tauranga. A couple of kilometres along the latter, you'll cross the riverine Ohau Channel, which links lakes Rotorua and Rotoiti. Haumurana Road then spurs left around the shores of Lake Rotorua passing **Haumurana Springs**, 773 Haumurana Rd (daily 9am–5pm;

Scenic flights and walks around Rotorua

The scenery around Rotorua, like Mount Tarawera, is spectacular and can be breathtaking from the air. **Scenic flights** take in easily what you might find very difficult to access from the ground, like White Island and the volcanic spine that runs down through Rotorua. As a result there are various trips on offer, none cheap but many worthwhile if you are pushed for time.

Although Rotorua isn't especially well endowed with serious tramps, it does work well as a staging post for forays into the Whirinaki Forest (see p.330) and further afield to Waikaremoana (see p.330). If you're keen to stretch your legs around these parts, you are best off with there-and-back **day-walks**. Trying to link up multi-day hikes is all but impossible without a compliant driver to pick you up at the other end. The best **map** is the 1:60,000 Holidaymaker *Rotorua Lakes* map ($14).

Scenic flights

Some say the majesty of Mount Tarawera is best appreciated from the air; **plane flights** start from as little as $60 for a quick spin over the lake, $165 for Tarawera flights and something closer to $300 for an overflight of White Island out in the Bay of Plenty Volcanic Wunderflites (☏0800/777 359, ©wunderflites@xtra.co.nz), Volcanic Air Safaris (☏0800/800 848, ⓦwww.volcanicair.co.nz) and Lakeside Aviation (☏0800/535 363) all run competitive trips. For something a little different, consider biplane flights with either Red Cat (☏0800/733 228, ⓦwww.redcat.co.nz) or Adventure Aviation (☏07/345 6780) who both do scenic flights (15–20min for $130–160) and offer acrobatics for just a little more.

Helicopter flights will set you back a little more, with a short flight to Mt Tarawera and fifteen minutes on the ground going for $300 with Mt Tarawera NZ. HeliPro (☏07/357 2512, ⓦwww.helicopteradventures.com) and Wai-O-Tapu-based Heli-Kiwi (☏07/366 6611, ⓦwww.helikiwi.co.nz) both offer a range of flights, some overflying Mount Tarawera and combining with jet boat trips and the like.

Day-walks

Blue Lake (Tikitapu; 5.5km loop; 2hr; 500m ascent). A pleasant and none-too-arduous loop around the Blue Lake through regenerating bush then Douglas firs and past some sandy beaches perfect for a dip. The single major climb takes you away from the lake to a viewpoint over the Blue and Green lakes. Starts at the eastern end of the beach opposite the Blue Lake Holiday Park, 9km southeast of Rotorua.

Mount Tarawera (14km return; 4–5hr; 400m ascent). If you've got a car and don't want to pay for a 4WD ascent of Mount Tarawera, the alternative is to drive as far as you can then get out and walk; though it will cost you $25 per person to cross Ngati Rangitihi land. The reward is a fifteen-kilometre-long gash of craters that can be explored for as long as you wish, always keeping an eye out for cloud which can quickly disorientate in this trackless area. The hike starts on Bob Annett Road, off SH38 around 35km by road southeast of Rotorua. If road conditions are good and you have reasonable clearance on your rig, you should make it to the car park where you pay the fee, then continue on foot with 4WD vehicles and mountain bikes periodically clattering by.

Okere Falls Scenic Reserve (2.5km return; 40min–1hr). An easy stroll with river views and spectacular angles on rafters shooting Tutea's Falls (see opposite). Starts 18km north of Rotorua.

Tarawera Falls Walk (1–8km return; 30min–4hr; 100m ascent). Gorgeous bush walk to a great view of Tarawera Falls (see opposite), and on past swimming holes to the outlet of Lake Tarawera. Starts 80km by road from Rotorua, 24km south of Kawerau, and you can walk as far as you fancy before returning.

$6), which boast the largest natural spring in the North Island – though in a land where crystal clear waters are commonplace it seems strange to pay to see a spring.

Sticking with SH33, you soon come upon signs to the **Okere Falls Scenic Reserve**, which surrounds the rafting mecca of the Kaituna River – follow signs up Trout Pool Road, 4km north of the Haumurana Road junction. From the first car park, 400m along Trout Pool Road, a broad track follows the river to a second car park (2.5km return; 40min–1hr) passing glimpses of the churning river below, and a viewing platform that's perfect for observing rafters plummet over the seven-metre **Tutea's Falls**. From here, steps descend through short tunnels in the steep rock walls beside the waterfall to **Tutea's Caves**, thought to have been used as a safe haven by Maori women and children during attacks by rival groups.

Most of the traffic out this way sticks to SH30, the route to **Hell's Gate** (Tikitere; daily 9am–5pm; $16; ⓦ www.hellsgaterotorua.co.nz), 14km northeast of Rotorua. The least-visited and smallest of the major thermal areas, this is also one of the fiercest and most active, with an abundance of bubbling mud and seething gunmetal-grey waters. Its fury camouflages a lack of notable features, however, and the only real highlights are the bubbling mud of the Devil's Cauldron and the hot **Kakahi Falls**, whose soothing 38°C waters once made this a popular bathing spot (though now off-limits to bathers). By way of compensation you can soak in the hot waters and take a mud bath ($50, including hot swim) at the revamped spa.

Beyond Hell's Gate lies **Lake Rotoiti**, which translates as "little lake", though it is in fact the second-largest in the region and is linked to Lake Rotorua by the narrow Ohau Channel. This passage, along with the neighbouring **Lake Rotoehu** and **Lake Rotama**, traditionally formed a part of the canoe route from the coast. A section of this route, apparently used on a raid by the Ngapuhi warrior chief Hongi Hika, is traced by **Hongi's Track** (3km; 1hr return), a beautiful bushwalk which runs through to Lake Rotoehu passing the Wishing Tree, which is often surrounded by plant offerings.

Kawerau and Tarawera Falls

Around 6km beyond Lake Rotama, a good sideroad leads to the planned timber-mill town of **Kawerau**, which sits on a flood plain of the Tarawera River at the foot of the distinctive hump of Mount Edgecumbe (Putauaki). You are unlikely to want to stay longer than it takes to visit the **visitor centre**, Plunket St (Mon–Fri 8.30am–4.30pm, Sat & Sun 10am–3pm; ☏07/323 7550), for the compulsory **permit** ($2 here, or free from the forest's Visitor Centre in Rotorua) and directions to the region's main attraction, **Tarawera Falls**, 24km to the south. It is at its most impressive when the underground section of the Tarawera River appears to burst in a solid stream out of the cliff face. It is less impressive after a dry spell, but still worth the fifteen-minute walk (mostly flat) along the Tarawera Falls/Tarawera Outlet walkway to the falls viewpoint. You can see where the Tarawera River dives underground a further 10–20min walk upstream (and uphill), and by pressing on a further 5min you come across a wonderful safe swimming hole with natural diving spots and a rope swing. The track continues a further hour to DOC's popular lakeside Tarawera Outlet (Humphries Bay) **campsite** ($5; toilets and water only), also accessible by forest road. Note that **driving can be hazardous** on metalled forest roads – keep your headlights on at all times and keep clear of the billowing clouds of dust thrown up by huge logging trucks.

Southeast of Rotorua

Volcanic activity again provides the main theme for attractions southeast of Rotorua, most having some association with **Lake Tarawera** and the jagged line of volcanic peaks and craters along the southeastern shore, collectively known as **Mount Tarawera**, which erupted in 1886.

Before this, Tarawera was New Zealand's premier tourist destination, with thousands of visitors every year crossing lakes Tarawera and Rotomahana in whale boats and *waka*, frequently guided by the renowned Maori guide Sophia, to the **Pink and White Terraces**, two separate fans of silica that cascaded down the hillside to the edge of Lake Rotomahana. Boiling cauldrons bubbled away at the top of each formation, spilling mineral-rich water down the hillside where, over several centuries, it formed a series of staggered cup-shaped pools, the outflow of one filling the one below. The White Terraces (Te Tarata or "Tattooed Rock") were the larger, but most visitors favoured the Pink Terraces (Otukapuarangi or "Cloudy Atmosphere"), which were prettier and better suited to sitting and soaking. All this came to an abrupt end on the night of June 10, 1886, when the long-dormant Mount Tarawera erupted, creating 22 craters along a 17km rift, and covering over 15,000 square kilometres in mud and scoria. The Pink and White Terraces were shattered by the buckling of the earth, covered by ash and lava, then submerged deep under the waters of Lake Rotomahana which, dammed by earth upheavals, grew to twenty times its previous size.

The cataclysm had been foreshadowed eleven days earlier, when two separate canoe loads of *pakeha* tourists and their Maori guides saw an ancient *waka* glide silently out of the mist, with a dozen warriors paddling furiously, then vanish just as suddenly; this was interpreted by the ancient *tohunga* (priest) Tuhoto Ariki as a sign of imminent disaster. The fallout from the eruption buried five villages, including the staging post for the Pink and White Terrace trips, **Te Wairoa**, where the *tohunga* lived. In a classic case of blaming the messenger, the inhabitants refused to rescue the *tohunga* and it wasn't until four days later that they allowed a group of *pakeha* to dig him out. Miraculously, he was still alive, though he died a week later.

The chain of eruptions that racked the fault line during that fateful night in 1886 created an entirely new thermal valley, **Waimangu**, running southwest from the shores of the newly enlarged Lake Rotomahana. Still geothermally active, Waimangu struggles to outdo the supremely colourful thermal area of **Wai-O-Tapu**, a few kilometres further south.

Beyond the volcanic zone, the Kaingaroa Forest stretches away east to the little-visited tramping territory of the **Whirinaki Forest Park**, and the Kinleith Forest straggles west to **Tirau**, **Putaruru** and **Tokoroa**, minor way-stations on the route from Auckland to Taupo and the Tongariro National Park.

The Blue and Green lakes, the Buried Village and Lake Tarawera

To nineteenth-century tourists, Rotorua was merely a staging post before they continued their journey to the shores of **Lake Tarawera**, 15km southeast, where canoes would take them across to view the Pink and White Terraces. Latter-day sightseers still follow the same route, passing a ridge-top viewpoint that overlooks the iridescent waters of **Blue Lake** (Tikitapu) and **Green Lake** (Rotokakahi), which get their hues from subterranean mineral activity.

The road reaches the shores of Lake Tarawera just past the **Buried Village** (daily: Nov–March 8.30am–5.30pm; April–Oct 9am–4.30pm; $18;

Ⓣ 07/362 8287, Ⓦ www.buriedvillage.co.nz), the partly excavated and heavily reconstructed remains of a Maori settlement that, at the time of the Tarawera eruption, was larger than contemporary Rotorua. Numerous houses collapsed under the weight of the ash; others were saved by virtue of their inhabitants hefting the ash off the roof to lighten the load. Much of the village was excavated in the 1930s and 1940s, though work continues slowly today. Free **guided tours** take place on the hour (11am–3pm in the summer), or you can make your own way through the grounds where there is less of a sense of an archeological dig than of a manicured orchard: half-buried *whare* and the foundations for the Rotomahana Hotel sit primly on mown lawns among European fruit trees gone to seed, marauding hawthorn and a perfect row of full-grown poplars fostered by a line of fenceposts. Many of the *whare* contain small collections of implements and ash-encrusted household goods, contrasting with the stark simplicity of other dwellings such as **Tohunga's Whare**, where the ill-fated priest lay buried alive for four days before being released from his ashen tomb. Look out too for the extremely rare, carved-stone *pataka* (storehouse), and the bow section of a *waka* once used to ferry tourists on the lake and allegedly brought to the district by Hongi Hika when he invaded in 1823.

Beyond the formal grounds, a sequence of steep steps and slippery board-walks dives down the hill alongside **Te Wairoa Falls**, then climbs up through dripping, fern-draped bush on the far side. By the entrance to the Buried Village complex is a new **museum** which does a great job of capturing the spirit of the village in its heyday and the aftermath of its destruction, through numerous photos, some fine aquatints of the Pink and White Terraces and more ash-encrusted knick-knacks.

Cruises on Lake Tarawera go from the Tarawera Landing, 2km east of the Buried Village. Lake Tarawera Launch Services (Ⓣ07/362 8595) operate the *Reremoana* on a 45-minute scenic cruise on the lake (summer 1.30pm, 2.30pm & 3.30pm, winter 1.30pm; $17.50), and the Eruption Trail Cruise (11am; 2hr 30min; around $30) that takes you to the approximate site of the Pink and White Terraces and includes a short bush walk.

Waimangu

At the southern limit of the volcanic rift blown out by Mount Tarawera lies **Waimangu Volcanic Valley** (daily 8.30am–5pm; walking tour or boat cruise both $25; Ⓦ www.waimangu.co.nz), 19km south of Rotorua on Waimangu Road, via SH5, and 5km off the highway. Among the world's youngest thermal areas, this is also New Zealand's largest and most lushly vegetated.

A visitor centre by the entrance hints at the sights lining the streamside path, which cuts through a valley choked with scrub and native bush that has re-established itself since 1886. The regeneration process is periodically interrupted by smaller eruptions, including one in 1917 that created the 100m-diameter **Frying Pan Lake**, the world's largest hot spring. Impressive quantities of hot water welling up from the depths is the attraction of the **Inferno Crater**, an inverted cone where mesmerizing steam patterns partly obscure the powder-blue water. The water level rises and falls according to a rigid 38-day cycle – filling to the rim for 21 days, overflowing for 2 days then gradually falling to 8m below the rim over the next 15 days. More run-of-the-mill steaming pools and hissing vents line the stream, which also passes the muddy depression where, from 1900 to 1904, the **Waimangu Geyser** regu-larly spouted water to an astonishing height of 400m, carrying rocks and black mud with it.

The path through the valley ends at the wharf on the shores of Lake Rotomahana, where the rust-red sides of Mount Tarawera dominate the far horizon. From here, frequent free shuttle buses run back up the road to the visitor centre and gentle, commentated, 45-minute **cruises** (6 daily; $25) chug around the lake past steaming cliffs, fumaroles and over the site of the Pink and White Terraces.

Wai-O-Tapu

The tussle for Rotorua's geothermal crown is principally fought between Waimangu and the **Wai-O-Tapu Thermal Wonderland** (daily 8.30am–5pm; $18.50; ⓦwww.geyserland.co.nz), 10km south of Waimangu (and 30km from Rotorua), just off SH5. This combines a vast expanse of multi-hued rocks and pools, New Zealand's largest and most impressive lake of boiling mud and the **Lady Knox Geyser**, which is ignominiously induced to perform on schedule, at 10.15am daily. Buy your entrance ticket at the main entrance then double back 1km along the road to the geyser where, as the crowds fill the serried ranks of benches, a staff member pours a packet of soap flakes into the vent. Within a few minutes, the soap reduces the water's surface tension, and superheated steam and water are released in a jet which initially reaches around 10m and continues at half that height for anything up to an hour. Everyone then bundles into their vehicles and drives back to the main site for the crawl around the hour-long walking loop track as it wends its way through a series of small lakes which have taken on the tints of the minerals dissolved in them – yellow from sulphur, purple from manganese, green from arsenic and so on. The gurgling and growling black mud of the **Devil's Ink-Pots** and a series of hissing and rumbling craters pale beside the ever-changing rainbow colours of the **Artist's Palette** pools and the gorgeous, effervescent **Champagne Pool**, a circular bottle-green cauldron wreathed in swirling steam and fringed by a burnt-orange shelf. The waters of the Champagne Pool froth over **The Terraces**, a rippled accretion of lime silicate that glistens in the sunlight.

As you drive back to the main road, follow a short detour to a huge and active **boiling mud pool** which plops away merrily, forming lovely concentric patterns. On the opposite side of SH5, Waikite Valley Road runs 6km to **Waikite Valley Thermal Pools** (daily 10am–10pm; $5), a naturally fed geothermal pool that's a good deal more low-key than the pools in Rotorua, but hardly justifies a special journey; guests at the adjacent motor camp (tent sites $10) get in free.

Whirinaki Forest Park and the road to Lake Waikaremoana

Midway between Waimangu and Wai-O-Tapu, some 25km south of Rotorua, SH38 spurs southeast, running through the regimented pines of the Kaingaroa Forest towards the jagged peaks of Te Urewera National Park, a vast tract of untouched wilderness which separates the Rotorua lakes from Poverty Bay and the East Cape. The Kaingaroa Forest finally relents 40km on, as the road crosses the Rangitaiki River by the predominantly Maori timber town of **MURUPARA**. Apart from a couple of shops and takeaways, the only reason to pull over is the DOC's **Rangitaiki Area Visitor Centre**, 1km southeast of town on SH38 (Dec–March daily 8am–5pm; April–Nov Mon–Fri 8am–5pm; ☏07/366 1080, ⑤366 1082), with diverting displays and a stack of information on Te Urewera National Park and the Lake Waikaremoana region.

Particular emphasis is given to the easily accessible **Whirinaki Forest Park**, a wild and wonderful slice of country that harbours some of the densest and most impressive stands of bush on the North Island: podocarps on the river flats, and native beech on the steep volcanic uplands between them, support a wonderfully rich birdlife with tui, bellbirds, parakeets and even the rare brownish-red kaka. The forest is now protected from the loggers' chainsaw, after a close shave in the late 1970s and early 1980s, when it saw one of the country's fiercest and most celebrated **environmental battles**. In early 1978, protesters had succeeded in preventing logging by occupying trees in the Pureora State Forest to the west of Lake Taupo. Anticipating similar action at Whirinaki and fearing for their livelihood, the local Ngati Whare people blockaded the road into the forest; conflict was only avoided through intense negotiation. By 1987 logging of all native timber had ceased (except for totara cut for ceremonial-carving purposes), the mill had closed and the entire logging village of **MINGINUI**, 25km south of Murupara, was unemployed. It's now a moribund place with a community shop, only open sporadically.

River Road runs 8km south from Minginui to the Whirinaki car park, from where, in four hours or so, you can sample some of the best of the Whirinaki Forest Park – the Whirinaki Falls, where the Whirinaki River cascades over an old lava flow, and the churning Te Whaiti-nui-a-tio Canyon – on the first stretch of the **Whirinaki Track** (27km; 2 days). To penetrate deeper into the forest, you can follow the rest of this gentle track, though you'll need to carry your own cooking stove, food and sleeping bag. By linking several tracks and staying in some of the nine Category 3 **huts** ($5) that pepper the park, more robust walkers can tramp for four or five days. DOC's *Whirinaki Forest Park* leaflet ($1) covers the main routes, with expanded coverage on their *Whirinaki Short Walks and Tracks* leaflet ($1.50) and on the NZMS 260 series V18 *Whirinaki* map. It is also possible to explore the area with Rotorua-based Whirinaki Trax (☎07/366 4756), which offers a pick and drop-off service for the Whirinaki Track ($80, $60 per person for two), and uses Maori guides for its one-day **guided treks** ($112) that also visit a local vineyard.

The Hobbiton tour from Matamata

Diehard fans of the *Lord of the Rings* trilogy may fancy an excursion to **Hobbiton** village, near **Matamata**, eighteen kilometres north of Tirau on SH27. Tours to the site begin at the Matamata visitor centre, 45 Broadway (Mon–Fri 8.30am–5pm, Sat & Sun 9.30am–3.30pm; ☎ ✆07/888 7260, w✆www.hobbitontours.com; 2hr 15min; $50), who take all the bookings (InterCity/Newmans **buses** pull up outside). The main draw is the fact that this is the country's only LOTR film location still retaining remnants of a set, all others were dismantled soon after filming. No one knows how much longer the tours will be available, but there's no access to the site (a working sheep farm) other than on a guided tour. However, there's not that much left here – all you'll see are shabby plywood facades, attached to the "**hobbit holes**" in the hills, with nothing inside them (the interiors were created in Wellington). Nearby are a lake and the "Party Tree" (a big radiata pine), both of which were the main reason for this site to be picked for filming.

The tour begins with a 20-minute bus ride to the farm and lasts for about an hour and 30 minutes once there. From November to the end of April the number of tours varies according to demand but, at the time of writing, seven tours were running daily from 9.30am in the summer and fewer tours were planned for the winter. The visitor centre can also arrange **private tours** with a member of the Alexander family who own the farm ($250 minimum charge, $300 for 4 people, $350 for 5). If you want to **eat** in Matamata, try the offbeat *Workman's Café*, 52 Broadway (☎ ✆07/888 5498; closed Mon), the best licensed café in town and open from breakfast till 9pm or later.

Practicalities

For details of **transport** out this way contact the Rangitaiki Area Visitor Centre (see p.330) for advice, as it can be difficult to get to Whirinaki or through to Lake Waikaremoana without your own wheels. Even a car can be a liability as vehicles left at the Whirinaki car park aren't safe, so the best bet is to enlist the assistance of *Whirinaki Forest Holidays*, on Minginui Road, 1km south of its junction with SH38 (Ⓣ & Ⓕ07/366 3235). As well as running a pick-up service from Rotorua or Taupo ($30 each way), and a trampers' shuttle service for the Whirinaki Track (price dependent on numbers), the lodge also offers **accommodation** in comfortable dorms, cottages and motel units, or in the lodge with all meals included (dorms ❶, cottages ❷, units ❸, lodge ❺), and organizes horse treks ($25 per hour). *Jail House*, 2km south along Minginui Road (Ⓣ07/366 3234; ❹), also operates track transport from their self-contained jail-turned-chalet, which sleeps up to seven. Minginui itself has the informal riverside *Mangamate Waterfall campsite* ($6 per tent).

West of Rotorua: Tirau, Putaruru and Tokoroa

Fifty-odd kilometres northwest of Rotorua, SH5 and SH1 meet at the small farming settlement of **TIRAU**, a highwayside strip adorned with a wonderfully kitsch corrugated-iron sheep housing a wool shop. It has become something of a town icon and has spawned a sheet-metal biblical shepherd in the grounds of the church next door, and a similarly constructed sheepdog containing the **visitor centre** (Ⓣ & Ⓕ07/883 1202, Ⓦtirauinfo.co.nz; daily 9am–5pm). Here you can obtain the free *Tirau Visitors' Guide*, which highlights the town's recent reinvention of itself as something of an antique and crafts centre – several such shops now line SH1 and Hillcrest Street at the eastern end of town, some of which are quite interesting. There is a handful of **places to eat** along SH1, notably the *Alley Cats Espresso Café*, opposite the dog, which serves good quiches, pizza slices, spinach and feta wraps and cakes, and the *Loose Goose* (closed Tues) further east on SH1, which serves more substantial meals.

Beside the sheep, Okoroire Street runs 8km to the lovely **Okoroire Hot Springs**, a couple of private, concrete pools located (one open-air with a sandy bottom) in a glade by a cascading stream, each accommodating around twelve people. The pools cost $10 an hour, and can be booked at the adjacent *Okoroire Hot Springs Hotel* (Ⓣ & Ⓕ07/883 4876, Ⓦwww.okohotel.co.nz), which has budget rooms for $40 per person, recently renovated en-suite rooms (❸) and some chalets (❺) and allows camping ($10 per tent) among the mature poplars and conifers; the hotel also has a bar, serves meals, and lets you onto their nine-hole golf course for $10 a day.

South of Tirau the roads split again, with SH5 forging east, while SH1 turns southeast towards Taupo, passing through **PUTARURU**, 8km further on, and the **Putaruru Timber Museum** (Ⓣ07/883 7621; daily 9am–2.30pm; $5), a further 2km south, where the region's timber-milling heritage is pulled together in a well-laid-out collection of minor historic buildings relocated from around the district. If you do nothing else, climb the totara-built 1930s fire lookout to get an inkling of just how extensive the Kaingaroa Forest really is.

SH1 continues through rolling farmland to pungent **TOKOROA**, 25km southeast, a modern place downwind of the nearby Kinleith pulp mill, the principal reason for the town's existence. There's little to stop for, but it is almost 70km to Taupo, the next place of any consequence, so those needing a **place to stay** might choose the quiet, clean and friendly *Mayfair Court Motel*, 3 Logan St (☎ & 🖷 07/886 7399; ➍). Newmans and InterCity **buses** stop outside the visitor centre, on SH1 (Nov–March Mon–Fri 8.30am–5.30pm, Sat & Sun 9am–3pm; shorter weekend hours in winter; ☎ 07/886 8872, 🄴 tokoroa.info@xtra.co.nz). If the fast-food joints beside the highway aren't to your taste, try *Scoffers Café* (open daily; evening meals Thurs–Sat) on Rosebery Street, which runs parallel to the main highway.

The Western Bays Highway

Most likely you'll want to stick on SH1 to Taupo, but if the Tongariro National Park beckons, follow SH32 30km south from Tokoroa to Whakamaru and turn left (south) for the **Western Bays Highway** (still SH32) direct to Turangi. The road flanks the eastern side of the Pureora Forest, mostly accessed along Kakaho Road, 19km south of Whakamaru. Of additional interest 10km further south, a short side road leads to the **Waihora Lagoon Walk** (500m return; 15min), which ends at a gorgeous lake surrounded by rimu and kahikatea.

Taupo and around

The unobtrusive resort town of **Taupo**, 80km south of Rotorua and slap in the centre of the North Island, is slung around the northern shores of Lake Taupo, the country's largest lake. It attracts Kiwi and foreign tourists alike, the latter increasingly due to its attraction as the **skydiving capital** of New Zealand. From Taupo, views stretch 30km southwest towards the three snow-capped volcanoes of the Tongariro National Park, the reflected light from the lake's glassy surface combines with the 360m altitude to create an almost alpine radiance. Here, the impossibly deep-blue waters of the Waikato River ("flowing water" in Maori) begin their long journey to the Tasman Sea, and both lake and river frontages are lined with parks, lending Taupo a slow pace and an undeniably appealing tenor.

For decades, Kiwi families have been descending en masse for a couple of weeks' holiday, bathing in the crisp cool waters of the lake, fishing its depths and lounging around their holiday homes that fringe the lakeshore. Although you could easily follow their lead and spend a relaxing few days here, there is no shortage of stuff to see and do, most notably around the spectacular rapids and geothermal badlands of **Wairakei Park**, immediately north of town. Thousands more come specifically for the **fishing**: the Taupo area is perhaps the most fecund trout fishery in the world, extending south to Turangi and along the Tongariro River and with an enviable reputation for the quality and fighting-spirit of its fish. Year-round, you'll see boats drifting across the lake with lines trailing and, particularly in the evenings, rivermouths choked with fly casters in chest-high waders.

Lake Taupo (616 sq km, 185m deep) is itself a geological infant and, although no single eruption is responsible for its creation, a large part was played around 1800 years ago when the Taupo Volcano erupted, spewing out

24 cubic kilometres of rock, debris and ash – at least ten times more than was produced by the eruptions of Krakatoa and Mount St Helens combined – and covering much of the North Island in a thick layer of pumice. Ash was ejected so high into the atmosphere that it was carried around the world, enabling historians to pinpoint the date of the **eruption** as 186 AD – when the Chinese noted a blackening of the sky and Romans recorded that the heavens turned blood-red. As the underground magma chamber emptied, the roof slumped, leaving a huge steep-sided **crater**, since filled by, and forming part of, Lake Taupo. It is hard to reconcile this placid and beautiful lake with such colossal violence, though the evidence is all around: entire beaches are composed of feather-light pumice which, when caught by the wind, floats off across the lake. **Geologists** and **vulcanoligists** continue to study the Taupo Volcano (currently considered dormant) and treat the lake as a kind of giant spirit-level, in which any tilting could indicate a build-up of magma below the surface that might trigger an eruption.

The local Tuwharetoa people ascribe the lake's formation to their ancestor, **Ngatoroirangi**, who cast a tree from the summit of Mount Tauhara, on the edge of Taupo, and where it struck the ground water welled up and formed the lake. The lake's full name is **Taupo-Nui-A-Tia**, "the great shoulder mat of Tia" or "great sleep of Tia", which refers to an explorer from the Arawa canoe said to have slept by the lake.

Taupo

Nowhere in **TAUPO**'s compact low-rise core is more than five minutes' walk from the waters of the Waikato River or Lake Taupo, which jointly hem in three sides. The fourth side rises up through the gentle slopes of Taupo's suburbs. Most of the commercial activity happens on, or just off, SH1, which passes through the middle of town as the main Tongariro Street and the aptly named Lake Terrace. Room for expansion is limited to the southeastern quarter, where ever more motels and timeshares are springing up along the lakeshore and where many of the more bizarre architectural creations, in the form of holiday homes (bachs), blight this otherwise unpretentious little settlement.

Although Taupo bears little trace of the vigorous Tuwharetoa settlement that existed into the middle of the nineteenth century, there was scant European interest in the area until the New Zealand Wars of the 1860s, when the Armed Constabulary were trying to track down **Te Kooti** (see box on p.449). They set up camp one night in June 1869 at Opepe, 17km southeast of Taupo (beside what is now SH5), and were ambushed by Te Kooti's men, who killed nine soldiers. Garrisons were subsequently established at Opepe and Taupo, but it was Taupo that flourished, enjoying a more strategic situation and being blessed with hot springs for washing and bathing. By 1877, Te Kooti had been contained, but the Armed Constabulary wasn't finally disbanded until 1886, after which several soldiers and their families stayed on, forming the nexus of European settlement.

Taupo didn't really flourish as a domestic resort until the prosperous 1950s, when the North Island's roads had improved to the point where Kiwi families could easily drive here from Auckland, Wellington or Hawke's Bay. There are few attractions within the town itself but Taupo makes a great base for exploring the natural wonders of the surrounding area and ticking off skydiving from your "must do" list.

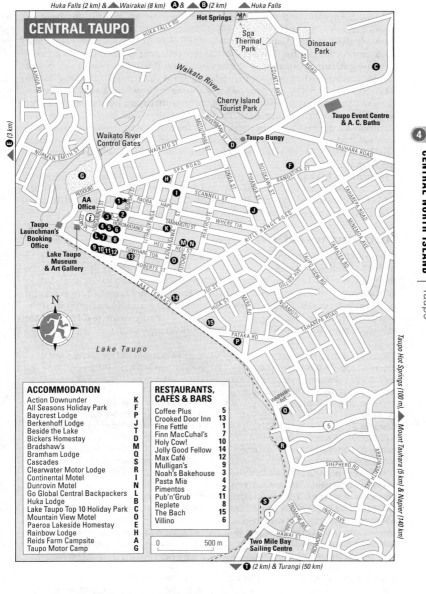

Taupo Hot Springs (100 ml) ▲ Mount Tauhara (5 km) & Napier (140 km)

CENTRAL TAUPO

Huka Falls (2 km) & ▲Wairakei (8 km) **A** & ▲ **B** (2 km) ▲Huka Falls

Hot Springs

Spa Thermal Park

Dinosaur Park

C

Waikato River

Cherry Island Tourist Park

Taupo Event Centre & A. C. Baths

Waikato River Control Gates

WAIKATO ST

SPA ROAD

D Taupo Bungy

TAUHARA ROAD

NORMAN SMITH ST

REDOUBT

SCANNELL ST

F

RANGATIRA ST

G

AA Office

PAORA

HAPE

WHERE TIA

J

Taupo Launchman's Booking Office

H

TITIRAUPENGA

HOROMATANGI

TAMAMUTU ST

RIFLE RANGE ROAD

K

Lake Taupo Museum & Art Gallery

KAIMANAWA

HEU ST

M **N**

TUWHARETOA

KETCHER

ROBERTS ST

13

LAKE TERRACE

TUI ST

14

GILLIES AVE

HUIA ST

MERE RD

15

PATAKA RD

P

NGAMOTU

TAHARAPA ROAD

Lake Taupo

N

NAIPAHIHI AVE

Q

SHEPHERD RD

R

5

INGLE AVE

HAWAI ST

Two Mile Bay Sailing Centre

T (2 km) & Turangi (50 km)

ACCOMMODATION

Action Downunder	K
All Seasons Holiday Park	F
Baycrest Lodge	P
Berkenhoff Lodge	J
Beside the Lake	T
Bickers Homestay	D
Bradshaw's	M
Bramham Lodge	Q
Cascades	S
Clearwater Motor Lodge	R
Continental Motel	I
Dunrovin Motel	N
Go Global Central Backpackers	L
Huka Lodge	B
Lake Taupo Top 10 Holiday Park	C
Mountain View Motel	O
Paeroa Lakeside Homestay	E
Rainbow Lodge	H
Reids Farm Campsite	A
Taupo Motor Camp	G

RESTAURANTS, CAFÉS & BARS

Coffee Plus	5
Crooked Door Inn	13
Fine Fettle	1
Finn MacCuhal's	7
Holy Cow!	10
Jolly Good Fellow	14
Max Café	12
Mulligan's	9
Noah's Bakehouse	3
Pasta Mia	4
Pimentos	2
Pub'n'Grub	11
Replete	8
The Bach	15
Villino	6

0 ——— 500 m

Arrival, information and transport

InterCity and Newmans **buses** (with direct connections from Rotorua, Tauranga, Hamilton, Auckland, Napier, Palmerston North and Wellington) stop at the Taupo Travel Centre bus station, 16 Gascoigne St (☎07/378 9032), around two hundred metres from Taupo's **visitor centre**, Tongariro Street (daily

8.30am–5pm; ☎07/376 0027, ⓦwww.laketauponz.com), right in the heart of town. Taupo's busy little **airport**, 10km south of the centre, is served by Air New Zealand flights; Airporter Shuttle (☎07/378 5713) meets all planes and costs around $17 for the first person, the fare reducing as more people get on.

As for **getting around**, almost everything you'll want to visit in the centre can be reached either on foot or with Top Cabs (☎07/378 9250) and Taupo Taxis (☎07/378 5100). To visit the surrounding sights without your own vehicle, use the Hot Bus (daily 10am–6pm), which makes an hour-long circuit of all the main sights (except Aratiatia Rapids) plus a few hostels, Taupo Hot Springs and the visitor centre. You pay $4 for a single journey, $7 return and $10 for a day pass. Alternatively join a **guided tour** with Paradise Tours (☎07/378 9955; 2hr 30min; $30) who visit most of the same places, including the Aratiatia Rapids.

Renting a bike gives greater freedom: the most sophisticated machines will set you back roughly $30 a half-day and $40 a day (see p.342 for rental outlets). For **car-rental**, try the Rental Car Centre, 7 Nukuhau St (☎06/378 2740), which undercuts the big guys.

Accommodation

Taupo manages to maintain a very high standard of accommodation for all budgets. Finding somewhere to stay is unlikely to be a problem except when the crush is on (Christmas to end-Feb), when you should **book** several days in advance, especially at weekends. As befits a Kiwi holiday resort, there is no end of places catering to families, with much of the lakefront taken up by **motels**, and grassy spots on the fringes of town given over to **campsites**. **Hostels** are abundant too and uniformly good, though differing in style.

Hotels and motels

Baycrest Lodge 79 Mere Rd ☎07/378 3838 & 0800/229 273, ⓦwww.baycrest.co.nz. Luxuriously appointed top-of-the-range motel with spacious multi-room units, a heated pool, poolside bar and Sky TV. ❼

Cascades SH1, Two Mile Bay ☎07//378 3774 & 0800/996 997, ⓦwww.cascades.co.nz. Classy motel with units either on the waterfront or with access to an attractive pool. Studio and family units are all spacious with deluxe fittings, a full kitchen, mezzanine sleeping area, a patio and a spa bath. ❻

Clearwater Motor Lodge 229 Lake Terrace ☎07/377 2071 & 0800/639 639. Beautiful lakeside accommodation with great views, in-room spas and some rooms with small balconies. ❻

Continental Motel 9 Scannell St ☎ & ☎07/378 5836. Comfortable, low-cost, central motel with small, well-maintained units. ❹

Dunrovin Motel 140 Heu Heu St ☎ & ⓕ07/378 7384 & ☎0800/386 768, ⓔinfo@dunrovintaupo.co.nz. Older, budget units that are well-kept and characterful, being built of wood rather than the ubiquitous concrete blocks. ❹

Huka Lodge Huka Falls Rd, 4km north of Taupo ☎07/378 5791, ⓦwww.hukalodge.co.nz. One of the first and still the best-known of New Zealand's exclusive lodges, located just upstream from Huka Falls. It costs a cool $1075 a night for a double, including cocktails, five-course dinner and breakfast. ❾

Mountain View Motel 12 Fletcher St ☎07/378 9366 & 0800/146 683, ⓔmt-view-motel@xtra.co.nz. Budget, central motel with spa pool, Sky TV, games room and kids' play area. The family units are huge, and the studios are at the bottom end of this price code. Studios ❹, family units ❻

B&Bs and guesthouses

Bickers Homestay 190 Spa Rd ☎07/377 0665, ⓔorbiii@reap.org.nz. Plain, simple and friendly non-smoking homestay made special by its sunny garden, on the cliffs high above the Waikato River and the views of Cherry Island and the Taupo Bungy. ❹

Beside the Lake 8 Chad St, 5km south of Taupo ☎ & ⓕ07/378 5847, ⓔfoote.tpo@xtra.co.nz. Two modern, tasteful and well-appointed luxury rooms (one with private bath, one en suite) beside a small park which fronts the lake. Rooms have lake views, a/c, and a terrace that catches the afternoon sun. A full breakfast is served. ❼

Bradshaw's 130 Heu Heu St ℡07/378 8288, ℻378 8282. Good-value guesthouse with pleasant floral decorated rooms with showers, let at very reasonable rates, with breakfast an optional extra. There are also new and good three-bedroom units that can be good value for groups. ❸

Bramham Lodge 7 Waipahihi Ave ℡07/378 0064, ⓦwww.bramham.co.nz. Spacious homestay with expansive lake and mountain views, a couple of comfortable rooms with private facilities, and delicious breakfasts. ❺

Paeroa Lakeside Homestay 21 Te Kopua St, Acacia Bay ℡07/378 8449, ⓦwww .taupohomestay.com. Luxurious homestay in a lush garden setting with great lake views five minutes' drive southwest of Taupo, with en-suite double all with balconies. ❼

Hostels

Action Downunder 56 Kaimanawa St ℡07/378 3311, ℻378 9612. Truly welcoming, modern associate YHA hostel close to town and with good lake and mountain views from the kitchen and barbecue balcony, and a spa pool. Dorms sleep three–five, there are doubles and twins, and bikes can be rented for $20 a day. Dorms ❶, rooms ❷

Berkenhoff Lodge 75 Scannell St ℡ & ℻07/378 4909, ⓔbhoff@reap.org.nz. Bustling and slightly cramped hostel fifteen minutes' walk from the centre. The games room and on-site bar are perennially popular and they run a barbecue every evening by the pool and spa. Each dorm has a bathroom, and doubles and twins come with linen. Dorms ❶, rooms ❷

Go Global Central Backpackers cnr Tongariro St & Tuwharetoa St ℡07/377 0044, ⓦwww.go-global.co.nz. Large, central hostel above a bar and popular with the backpacker

buses. The dorms and a multitude of rooms are all clean and comfortable and there's Internet access. Dorms ❶, rooms ❷

Rainbow Lodge 99 Titiraupenga St ℡07/378 5754, ⓔrainbowlodge@clear.net.nz. Spacious, relaxed and spotless purpose-built backpackers with a comfortable lounge, coin-op sauna, bike rental at $15–20 a day and fishing gear for $11 a day, a stack of local information and little touches that create a homely atmosphere. Dorms have six–nine beds and there are spacious triples and doubles, many of them en suite. Dorms ❶, rooms ❷

Campsites and motor parks

All Seasons Holiday Park 16 Rangatira St ℡07/378 4272 & 0800/777 272, ⓦwww.taupoallseasons.co.nz. Compact site just over 1km from town, with tent sites scattered among nice new cabins and a range of good tourist flats. Camping $13, cabins ❷, flats ❸–❹

Lake Taupo Top 10 Holiday Park 28 Centennial Drive ℡ & ℻07/378 6860, ⓦwww.taupotop10 .co.nz. Wonderfully spacious site 2km from town with good communal facilities and excellent range of clean kitchen cabins, tourist flats and fully self-contained flats, and easy access to the A.C. Baths. Camping $15, cabins, flats & cottages ❸–❺

Reids Farm Campsite 3km north of Taupo on Huka Falls Rd. Spacious free campsite right by the Waikato River just upstream of Huka Lodge left to the world by a previous owner who liked backpackers. The makeshift slalom course makes it a popular spot with kayakers.

Taupo Motor Camp 15 Redoubt Rd ℡ & ℻07/377 3080, ⓦwww.taupomotorcamp.co.nz. Very handy site on the banks of the Waikato River right in town. Camping $12, cabins ❷, on-site vans ❸

The Town

True to its family-resort status, Taupo specializes in entertainment for the kids and adventure activities for adults. However, one of its more intriguing spots is the much improved **Lake Taupo Museum and Art Gallery**, Tongariro Park (daily 10.30am–4.30pm; suggested donation $4), well worth a visit to see the beautiful *Reid Carvings*, gifted to the museum in 1960 and then inexplicably kept under the floor of the old War Memorial Hall until recently. Carved in 1927–28 by the famous master carver Tene Waitere, who produced 'treasures' for Marae throughout New Zealand, the pieces are exhibited in the form of a meeting house and are some of the finest Maori carving on display anywhere. Remarkably, Waitere was a survivor of the Buried Village of Te Wairoa, destroyed by the Tarawera eruption (see p.328) – reputedly he was responsible for much of the current Buried Village carving; the work on show here was intended as a gift for his niece, Mrs Lucy Reid. If this were not enough, the gallery section has regular exhibitions and contains a few Thomas Ryan water-colours of Ngati Tuwhareto chiefs which show the unmistakable influence of the artist's great friend Charles Goldie (see p.98); Ryan, born in England was also famous for his rugby, playing for the first representative New Zealand Rugby (All Blacks) team. The remainder of the museum is given over to exhibits covering pioneering days and fishing in some depth, and a curious collection of scale models of every plane which took part in World War II. From the museum, Tongariro Park sweeps down to the lakeshore and the Taupo Boat Harbour, the departure-point for cruises, fishing trips and a multitude of aquatic pursuits.

Away from the town centre, 3km southeast on SH5, is the family crowd-pleaser **Taupo Hot Springs**, (daily 7.30am–9.30pm; $8; ⓦ www.taupohotsprings .com), a couple of large outdoor pools filled with natural mineral water that's oddly slippery on the skin. For an extra dollar you can also soak in one of the private mineral pools, which come in a range of temperatures, while $5 gets you as many descents as you like on the hot-water hydroslide. Without your own vehicle, you'll find it more convenient to head for the **Taupo Events Centre**, A.C. Baths Avenue (Mon–Fri 6am–9pm, Sat & Sun 7am–9pm), a sparkling new sports hall and twelve-metre climbing wall (harness, shoes and chalk $7, plus $8 entry), alongside the long-standing **A.C. Baths**, a recently completely rejuvenated complex of swimming- and hot-pools. The private hot pools ($5 per person, 45mins) run off a thermal spring nearby while the swimming pool ($6.50, also gets you into the public hot pools) is divided into lanes for those who want some exercise between broiling sessions.

From the junction opposite the baths, Spa Road forges north to the site of the first hot spring used by the Armed Constabulary and now ignominiously overlooked by the thirty life-size ferro-concrete dinosaurs of the **Spa Dinosaur Valley** (daily 10am–4pm; $5). Jurassic Park it ain't, but the "realistic" dinosaur noises will probably still scare young kids witless. Just west, Spa Avenue runs down to the green swathe of **Spa Thermal Park**, where a path leads to the Waikato River past some naturally hot bathing pools (unrestricted entry) and, in an hour or so, downstream to Huka Falls (see p.343).

A few hundred metres upstream, the river swirls through the narrows of Hell's Gate, the 47m white cliffs providing the launch pad for **Taupo Bungy**, 202 Spa Rd (daily 9am–5pm, until 7pm in high season; $135 with t-shirt; ⓣ 0800/888 408, ⓦ www.taupobungy.co.nz), one of New Zealand's finest bungy sites cantilevered 20m out from the bank, and with optional (so they say) dunking.

Taupo activities

As you would expect of Taupo, there's plenty of activities to relieve you of your holiday money. These days the primary one is **skydiving**, Taupo is now one of the busiest drop zones anywhere in the world and it provides a spectacular setting toward which to plummet from a plane. Of the other activities some of the best are water-based, either **cruising** gently across Lake Taupo, **rafting** down the raging waters of the Tongariro or Rangitaiki rivers or **fly-fishing** the rivers and streams for trout.

Skydiving

Taupo has rapidly gained a reputation as one of the cheapest places to go **tandem skydiving** – and one of the best, with magnificent scenery all around, if you dare to look. At times it can feel like a production line, with three very professional companies processing dozens of people a day, each

Walking and horse riding

There are a few relatively easy **walks** near town. By far the most popular is the **Great Lake Walk**, which is more modest than it sounds: just follow the lakeshore east from town, covering as much of the 7km promenade as you like, passing hot springs right at the water's edge. On the northern edge of town, County Avenue leads to the **Spa Thermal Park**, where there's a pleasant thirty-minute bushwalk, which can be combined with a riverbank walk to **Huka Falls** (4km; 1hr one-way), and further extended to the Aratiatia Rapids (8km; 2hr one-way), though you've then got to get back – if you set off early, you could conceivably walk back via the Wairakei visitor centre and the Craters of the Moon (12km; 3hr). Finally, if you have your own transport and a taste for magnificent lake and town views, try the track to the summit of **Mount Tauhara** (6km; 2–3hr return), the hill behind Taupo, which is approached on Mountain Road, which turns off SH5 to Napier after 6km.

If you fancy **horse riding**, Taupo Horse Treks, Karapiti Rd ☎07/378 0356, do one-hour ($30) and two-hour ($50) treks through the pine forests around the Craters of the Moon (see p.344), and will do courtesy pick-ups for booked two-hour jaunts; Ge Ge Horse Treks ☎0274/912 872 offer farmland and forest horse treks ($30 per hr) and Moehiwa Horse Ventures ☎07/378 3727 run small groups on wilderness treks of about an hour or more at a similar rate.

offering an array of videos, photos and T-shirts which add to the basic jump price of around $200 for 12,000ft and $300 for 15,000ft. Despite the price, many people go for 15,000ft for the longer freefall time (45 seconds at 12,000ft, around a minute at 15,000ft). The difference between the various operators is primarily the pre- and after-jump package. If you can afford to stay longer, each company also offers reasonably priced **solo skydiving** courses.

Great Lake Skydive ☎0800/373 335 & 07/378 4662, ⓦwww.freefly.co.nz. Provides a friendly and professional service. A 12,000ft jump is $360, 15,000ft is $489, both with an individual freefall video and a roll of stills film.
Skydive Taupo ☎0800/586 766, ⓦwww .skydivetaupo.co.nz The smallest company, offering a more personal experience: picking you up in a stretch limo, providing an individual video – you choose the music – and presenting you with a

beer when you land. Currently only operating from 12,000ft it costs $330 for a jump, freefall video and roll of film, though they too will be working at 15,000ft by next season.
Taupo Tandem Skydiving ☎0800/275 934 & 07/377 0428, ⓦwww.tts.net.nz The biggest operation in terms of publicity but primarily competes with Great Lake in terms of service and numbers. 12,000ft is around $350, 15,000ft is $448, both with individual freefall videos and roll of film.

Scenic flights

If you'd prefer to stay in the plane, there are fixed-wing **scenic flights** over the lake and surrounds on a float plane from Taupo's Float Plane (10min; $60, 15mins $90, over the Rotorua lakes $225, and various other longer options; ☎07/378 7500 ⓦwww.tauposfloatplane.co.nz). Other operators include Skytrek Aviation (☎07/378 0172; 15min–2hr) and Taupo Air Services (☎07/378 5325) while the best helicopter trips are run by Helistar Helicopters (☎0800/435 478, ⓦwww.helistar.co.nz), on the Huka Falls Road, who offer a variety flights, including ones over the Huka Falls and Craters of the Moon (10min; $95), as well as a variety of combo deals with other adventure operators.

Mountain Boarding

As well as the bungy jump in town (see p.338), Taupo also offers a more affordable adrenaline rush in the form of **mountain boarding** at Gravity Hill, off

Rakaunui Road (ⓦ www.mountainboarding.co.nz), about 1km further on from the AC Baths. Mountain Boarding is an adventure activity combining the skills of skate boarding, snowboarding and surfing on large, almost 4WD, skate board and this is currently the best park in the world in which to practice. Five runs, all the gear and a lift back up the hill cost just $29. Be brave.

Lake Cruises

One of the most satisfying ways to relax in Taupo is to take one of the **lake cruises**, run from the Taupo Boat Harbour and setting course for some striking modern Maori rock carvings, which can only be seen from the water at Mine Bay, 8km southwest of town. The ten-metre-high carvings, date from the late 1970s and depict a stylized image of a man's face heavy with *moko*, together with tuatara (lizard-like reptiles) and female forms draped over nearby rocks. The most characterful of the sailing trips – as much for the sea-dog skipper as the boat – is aboard *The Barbary* (ⓣ 07/378 3444; 10am & 2pm; 2hr 30min; $30), a 1926 ketch once owned by Eroll Flynn (who, it is colourfully claimed, won it in a card game). If you're not too bothered about seeing the carvings, take the summertime-only sunset trip which is a little shorter and only costs $25.

For a touch of gin-palace style, opt for the *Cruise Cat* (ⓣ 07/378 0623 & 0800/252 628; 11.30am & 1pm; 1hr 30min; $28), which motors past the carvings while you sit back and watch the world go by. Different atmospherics are offered by the *Ernest Kemp* (ⓣ 07/378 3444; daily: Dec–Feb 10.30am, 2pm & 5pm; $28), a replica 1920s steamboat that chugs to the carvings and back in a couple of hours, though for sheer charm join up with the old sailors who restored and now run the *Alice*, a tiny vintage steam launch, built between 1861 and 79, that pootles round the lake's edge for an hour or so at weekends (Lakeside Bookings Office ⓣ 07/378 8659; $12).

Kayak tours and watersports

To get the most rewarding experience of the lake join Eco-Explorer (ⓣ 0800/529 255, ⓦ www.kayakingkiwi.com) for **kayak tours**, which either use a restored launch to get you to interesting sections of coastline, including the rock carvings (the boat acts as a base while you paddle around) or require you to paddle direct. Two- to three-hour trips to the carvings (Oct–April 8am, 1pm & 6.30pm; May–Oct 10am; $75) require no prior experience and take an educational, eco-sensitive approach. Longer charters, using the launch, can range from $495 and include excellent lunches and a wealth of information.

There are no whitewater rivers right on Taupo's doorstep, but the town makes a viable base for **rafting**. The main rivers run from Taupo are the Tongariro (covered under Turangi – see p.349), the Rangitaiki and the Wairoa, and a two-day trip on the relatively gentle upper section of the Mohaka, camping on the riverbank overnight. Rapid Sensations (ⓣ 07/378 7902 & 0800/227 238, ⓦ www.rapids.co.nz) run the Tongariro for $90, the Mohaka Gorge for $130 and various river kayaking trips, while Kiwi River Safaris (ⓣ 07/377 6597 & 0800/723 857, ⓦ www.krs.co.nz) organize rafting trips to the Wairoa ($90), the Rangitaiki ($90) and a one-day Mohaka trip $150, as well as longer excursions.

Bookings can be made either direct with operators, through the visitor centre or with the Taupo Charter Boats Booking Office, Redoubt Street (ⓣ 07/378 3444; 8am–5pm). The latter can point you in the direction of other lake-based watersports, such as **parasailing**, **waterskiing** and **jetbiking**. If you'd rather be self-propelled, head around the lake to Two Mile Bay, where 2 Mile Bay Sailing Centre (ⓣ 07/378 3299, ⓦ www.sailingcentre.co.nz; daily

9am–5pm in summer, otherwise sporadically) rents kayaks and canoes ($30 per hr), **catamarans** ($44 per hr), **windsurfers** ($30–50 per hr) and various sail boats (from $45, $250 overnight charter for cruisers).

Fishing

New Zealand's arcane fishing rules dictate that trout can't be sold, so if you've got a taste for their succulent flesh you'll have to catch it yourself and your chances are better here than at most places. Your best approach is to fish the lake on a boat chartered through the visitor centre or directly from the Taupo Charter Boat Booking Office. Smaller **boats** go out for a minimum of two hours, but more usually three or four, and cost $80 an hour, taking up to four people. **Book in advance** from mid-December to February – and at any other time of year if you want the booking offices to help reduce your costs by matching you up with other interested parties. Boat operators have all the tackle you need and will organize a Taupo District Fishing Licence ($12.50 per day, $27 per week, $37 per month and $58 for the full July-to-June year) for you.

The rivers flowing into Lake Taupo are the preserve of **fly-fishers**, particularly from March to September when mature rainbow trout enter the mouths of the streams and rivers and make their way upstream to shallow gravel hollows where they spawn. Brown trout are also in these waters, but they tend to be more wily. You can **rent tackle** from Taupo Rod & Tackle, 34 Tongariro St (℡07/378 5337), and the Fly & Gun Shop, Heu Heu St (℡07/378 4449), and pick your own spot, but average catches are much larger if you engage the services of a **fishing guide**, which will set you back close to $250 for half a day with gear and licence: the tourist office has a list of guides – two of the best are Chris Jolly and Will Kemp.

Eating, drinking and nightlife

Taupo's culinary stock has risen in recent years with new places opening all the time, many making use of settings with great views across the lake. A sprinkling of modern cafés supplement more traditional tearooms, and the better lakefront motor lodges all have pricey **restaurants**, some of them very good. For a small provincial town, there's a reasonable nightlife, with holidaymakers converging on several **pubs** and **clubs**.

Restaurants and cafés

The Bach 2 Pataka Rd ℡07/378 7856. Modern dining in an easy-going atmosphere. Choose from wood-fired crispy pizza, a select range of $30-plus mains and an extensive selection of cellared New Zealand wines by the bottle and glass.

Coffee Plus 11 Hiromatangi St. Relaxing coffee house, decorated predominantly yellow, with a juice bar on the street out front. The coffee is excellent, the energy giving juices are tasty and the food just about keeps apace, popular with locals.

Crooked Door Inn cnr Roberts and Titraupenga sts ℡07/376 8030. Legendary seafood in a mock Tudor building hidden just away from the main drag. Try the renowned main-course chowder in sourdough cob (à la San Francisco) $23, fresh seafood mains $20–30, including delicious blue

cod, and if you feel adventurous try the crocodile. Dinner from 6pm, daily.

Fine Fettle 39 Paora Hape St. Daytime organic wholefood café that's good for breakfasts, including Eggs Benedict ($14.50) and the all-encompassing "FF classic" ($13.50). Lunches include hearty soups ($8), an excellent mussel chowder ($9.50) panini and salads, many served with organic bread which is also available by the loaf.

Jolly Good Fellow 76–80 Lake Terrace. The nearest Taupo gets to a British pub, nothing like one in style but it has over a dozen English and Irish beers on tap, most of which seem to have travelled well. There are also pub meals in the English tradition with fish and chips ($17), toad-in-the-hole ($15) and breakfast served all day.

Max Café 38 Roberts St. Taupo's fast-food mainstay, serving a good standard of burgers, toasties and steak 'n' chips meals 24hr a day in an atmosphere-free zone with lake views.

Noah's Bakehouse 10 Heu Heu St. Open daily from 8am this little café provides low-cost simple food, including generous breakfasts for under $10, roast dinners and a range of other cheap Kiwi staples. Not licensed.

Pasta Mia 26 Horomatangi St, close to the cinema. Relaxed daytime café with a small but immaculate line in simple pasta dishes ($10–18), cakes and good coffee.

Pimentos 17 Tamamutu St ℡07/377 4549. Stylish restaurant specializing in fusion cookery with Thai and other Asian influences vying with jazzed-up European staples. Try the seared paprika Scotch fillet with roasted peppers and Yorkshire pud' ($21) or the rice stick noodles with mushrooms, bok choy, sliced ginger and chilli sauce ($19). Closed Tues.

Replete 45 Heu Heu St. Despite inconsistent service and surly staff this is a good deli and daytime café, serving quiches, pizza slices, cakes and coffee until 5pm Mon–Fri, 3pm Sat & Sun.

Villino 45 Horomatangi St ℡07/377 4478. Classy downtown restaurant and café open daily for lunch and dinner and serving a typically eclectic range of dishes which lean towards German and Italian, though they also do wonderful Pacific oysters for under $20. Mains ($26–35) might include duck confit, roast rack of spring lamb or fillet of beef.

Bars and clubs

Finn MacCuhal's cnr Tongariro St & Tuwharetoa St. Ersatz Irish bar very popular with the locals as well as the backpackers staying upstairs at *Go Global*. You come here for the Guinness, but they also do good-value steaks, pasta dishes and salads.

Holy Cow! 11 Tongariro St. Recently renovated, this is still the liveliest late-night bar in town, spinning an eclectic selection of rock and dance tunes and turning clubby late on. Very popular.

Jolly Good Fellow (see above). An excellent range of hand-pulled ales and a lively community pub feel with lots of dinners early on followed by revellers for the late shift.

Mulligan's 15 Tongariro St. Typical Irish-style bar with stout on tap, mischievous Kiwi bar staff, live music, quiz nights and massive plates of bar food. Popular with locals and tour buses alike.

Pub'n'Grub 4 Roberts St. Once known as *Red Barrel*, now a much-improved bar that serves very pleasant pub-style food but is primarily popular for its pool tables and lake views.

Villino 45 Horomatangi St. Swish cocktail bar where acoustic, jazz or operatic sounds drift late into the night. You pay for the atmosphere with slightly more expensive drinks.

Listings

Automobile Association 93 Tongariro St ℡07/378 6000.

Bike rental Most of the hostels have basic bikes for guests' use: *Rainbow Lodge* and YHA-associate hostel, *Action Downunder* also rent to non-guests.

Internet access Open longest are *Log On Internet Centre*, 71 Tongariro St, 8am–midnight. Nearly all the accommodation offer internet access and there are various other places springing up around town. The public library is another safe bet (9am–5.30pm).

Left-luggage Lockers are available at the Superloo, Tongariro St. Daily: Dec–Jan 7.30am–9pm; Feb–Nov 7.30am–5.30pm. $1 a day.

Medical treatment Taupo Health Centre, 115 Heu Heu St ℡07/378 7060 (8am–5pm).

Pharmacy Main Street Pharmacy, cnr Heu Heu St & Tongariro St (℡07/378 2636), is open daily until 8.30pm.

Police Story Place, by the museum and art gallery ℡07/378 6060.

Post office cnr Horomatangi St & Ruapehu St (℡07/378 9090), with poste restante facilities.

Travel Agents House of Travel, 37 Horomatangi St ℡07/377 2700; Flight Centre, 19 Horomatangi St ℡07/377 3554; United Travel, Taupo Travel Centre, 40 Heu Heu St ℡07/378 9709; James Travel Holiday Shoppe, 28 Horomatangi St ℡07/378 7065.

Around Taupo

Taupo's attractions are in many ways upstaged by those immediately to the **north**, a fabulously concentrated collection of natural wonders. Within a few minutes of each other you can find boiling mud, hissing steam harnessed by the

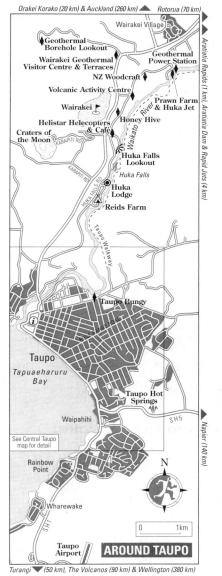

Wairakei Village

Geothermal Borehole Lookout

Wairakei Geothermal Visitor Centre & Terraces

Geothermal Power Station

NZ Woodcraft

Volcanic Activity Centre

Prawn Farm & Huka Jet

Wairakei

Honey Hive

Helistar Helecopters & Café

Craters of the Moon

Huka Falls Lookout

Huka Falls

Huka Lodge

Reids Farm

Aratiatia Rapids (1 km), Aratiatia Dam & Rapid Jets (4 km)

Taupo Walkway

Taupo Bungy

Taupo

Tapuaeharuru Bay

Taupo Hot Springs

Waipahihi

SH5

Napier (140 km)

See Central Taupo map for detail

Rainbow Point

N

Wharewake

0   1km

Taupo Airport

AROUND TAUPO

CENTRAL NORTH ISLAND | Around Taupo

4

Wairakei power station and the clear, blue Waikato River, which cuts a deep and swirling course northwards, occasionally turning wild as it squeezes through some of the country's most powerful rapids. The highlights – **Huka Falls**, **Aratiatia Rapids** and the **Craters of the Moon** geothermal area – are all within 10km of Taupo, but you'll have to venture further to reach a second thermal park, **Orakei Korako**, 40km north. To get out this way, you'll need your own vehicle, or the services of one of Taupo's tour companies (see p.336).

Moving **south** from Taupo, SH1 follows the lakeshore to Turangi, while heading east along SH5 towards Napier, there are a couple of things to detain you along the way.

Along Huka Falls Road

The bulk of the sights and activities flank the Waikato River as it wends its way north, and are lumped together under the collective title of **Wairakei Park**. The park is reached via Huka Falls Road, which loops off SH1 a couple of kilometres north of Taupo and passes the Reids Farm free campsite and the exclusive *Huka Lodge* (see p.336) en route to the first point-of-call, the impressive and justly popular **Huka Falls** (*hukanui*, or "great body of spray"). Here the full flow of the Waikato River, one of New Zealand's most voluminous rivers, funnels into a narrow chasm then plunges over a ten-metre shelf into a seething mael-strom of eddies and whirlpools; the sheer power of some four hundred tonnes of water per second make it a far more awesome sight than its relatively short drop would suggest. A footbridge spans the channel, providing a perfect vantage point for watching the occasional mad kayaker making the descent, usually on weekend evenings. The parking lot, toilets and snack stand are only open until around 6pm but you can park outside and walk in at any time.

343

Continuing along Huka Falls Road, a large Russian helicopter marks the launch pad for Helistar flights (see p.339) en route to the cutaway hives and educational video at the **Honey Hive** (daily 9am–5pm; free; ☎07/374 8553), 1km further north, which shouldn't divert you long, though they do have an excellent range of honey varieties, including the famous antibacterial *manuka* and a passable *manuka* beer. Press on to the **Volcanic Activity Centre** (Mon–Fri 9am–5pm & Sat–Sun 10am–4pm; $6), a highly instructional museum where the dense text is alleviated by striking photos and interactive computer displays on all things tectonic. Watch one of several films run continuously then check out the seismograph linked to sensors on Mount Ruapehu, an earthquake simulator and a large relief map of Taupo Volcanic Zone, which extends from Mount Ruapehu to White Island.

Moving swiftly past **NZ Woodcraft** (☎07/374 8555), essentially a shop selling turned native woods, you'll come to the Wairakei geothermal power station. Most of the excess heat generated by the station is discharged into the river, though a portion is channelled into large open ponds, where tropical (originally Malaysian) prawns are raised in a highly successful enterprise known as the **Prawn Farm** (daily: 9am–5pm, later in mid-summer, tours hourly, starting at 10am; $8; ⊛ www.prawnpark.co.nz). Even if the "Day in the life of a Prawn" tour doesn't stir your imagination, you can at least indulge in the scrumptious prawn platters dished up by the *Prawn River Restaurant* while seated by the deep-blue water of the Waikato. Also you might wonder why, if they love prawns so much, they've set up a golf tee overlooking the tanks, whereby you are encouraged to whack golf balls at targets which, when they miss, rain down on the prawns.

The peace is periodically shattered by the **Huka Jet** (30min; $75; ☎07/374 8572 & 0800/485 2538, ⊛ www.hukajet.co.nz) as it roars along the river between Huka Falls and the Aratiatia Dam. The boats leave from a jetty by the Prawn Park (courtesy bus from Taupo), and play all the usual tricks – close encounters with rock faces and 360-degree spins – but if you are looking for thrills opt for Rapids Jet (see opposite) or save your money for the jetboating heartland around Queenstown.

Craters of the Moon and the Wairakei Valley

The Huka Falls loop road rejoins SH1 opposite the **Wairakei International Golf Course** (☎07/374 8152), one of the country's finest. Just south of the intersection, Karapiti Road runs west to the **Craters of the Moon** (unrestricted entry but custodian on duty 8am–6pm; donation appreciated), an other-worldly geothermal area that sprang to life in the 1950s, after the construction of the Wairakei geothermal power station drastically altered the underground hydrodynamics. What it lacks in geysers and colourful lakes, it more than makes up for in hyperactivity: the belching steam is so vigorous that you should wear closed footwear to walk the 2km of trails that wind among roaring fumaroles and huge rumbling pits belching out pungent bad-egg smells. The culprit can only be visited via the self-promotional **Wairakei Geothermal Visitor Centre** (daily 9am–4.30pm; free), 3km north on SH1, with its relief map of the whole Tongariro and Waikato power schemes, an explanatory video shown on demand ($2), and plenty of stuff on the intricacies of harnessing the earth's bounty. Outside, shiny high-pressure-steam pipes twist and bend the 2km to the power station from the borefield, which can be viewed from the **Geothermal Borefield Lookout** just down the road.

The same forces that created the Craters of the Moon are on show at the revamped **Wairakei Natural Thermal Valley** (daily 9am–5pm; $18 for the walkway & thermal tour; ☎07/378 0913), Taupo's original thermal area where the self-guided tour takes you past carvings and pools much like others on view elsewhere. However, this park benefits from being visited in the evening as part of a **Maori cultural experience**, when suddenly it springs to life (pick ups from Taupo can be arranged). The small-scale evening tour (6pm; $75) begins with a challenge and welcome, followed by a guided tour of the site, during which Maori beliefs and history are interwoven with visits to the pools, a functioning life-size model village and carvings. Potentially more impressive are the beginnings of some man–made terraces in the mould of the original Pink and White Terraces (see p.328). To round the evening off there follows a *hangi* and concert. The whole thing takes about three hours and is conducted with a charm that indicates the devotion the organisers have to renewing the fortunes of what had become a rather run down thermal valley.

Aratiatia Rapids and around

Around 2km downstream from the Wairakei power station lies the first of the Waikato River's eight hydroelectric dams, the Aratiatia Dam, which holds back the Waikato immediately above the **Aratiatia Rapids**, a long series of cataracts that were one of Taupo's earliest attractions. In the 1950s, when plans to divert the waters around the rapids were revealed, public pressure succeeded in preserving the rapids; though it's something of a hollow victory, since the rapids are left empty most of the time and only seen in their full glory during three or four thirty-minute periods each day (Oct–March 10am, noon, 2pm & 4pm; April–Sept 10am, noon & 2pm). Stand on the dam itself or at one of two downstream viewpoints reached by an easy trail, and wait for the siren that heralds the bizarre spectacle of a parched watercourse being transformed into a foaming torrent of waterfalls and surging pressure waves, then easing back to a tame trickle.

The most exhilirating way to experience the rapids is with the great-value **Rapids Jet** (☎07/378 5828 & 0800/727 437, ⊛www.rapidsjet.com; $69), located on Rapids Road 3km beyond the Aratiatia Dam. This is no slick bus-them-in operation, but New Zealand's only true whitewater jetboating run, taking you down and up Fuljames rapid and throwing in a good deal of local lore and entertaining patter to boot. The entire boat gets airborne and the company makes no secret of having sunk three boats on the rapid, but no one has been injured: just listen closely to the safety spiel, hang on and prepare to get very wet.

If this is your kind of thing, you might also want to trip along to **Rock 'n' Ropes**, a maze of high ropes and wires on SH5 16km north of Taupo (daily 8.30am–4.30pm or later; ☎07/374 8111 & 0800/244 508, ⊛www.rocknropes.co.nz), where you can ride the Giant Swing ($15), a fifteen-metre swoop that's as heart-stopping as many a bungy and a whole lot cheaper. The swing is included in the Adrenaline Combo ($40), where you are attached to a climbing harness for a nerve-wracking walk along a horizontal pole suspended 15m above the ground, then goaded into leaping off and grabbing a trapeze.

The site is also home to the **Crazy Catz Adventure Park** (⊛www.crazycatz.co.nz; same hours) where the farm tour, mini golf and maze are no match for riding go-carts around a concrete track ($15 for 10min), or trying to steer around a track in a VW Beetle with its steering mechanism reversed ($10); if this doesn't appeal you can tear around on quad bikes.

Orakei Korako

There's yet more geothermal activity 40km north of Taupo at **The Hidden Valley of Orakei Korako** (daily: 8am–4.30pm in summer, 4pm in winter; $21; ☏07/378 3131, ⓦwww.orakeikorako.co.nz), which is reached by travelling 14km east off SH1 or 23km west off SH5. The site's main distinguishing feature is its means of access, via a short shuttle-boat journey across a dammed section of the Waikato River, which drops you at the foot of a large silica terrace tinged orange, pink and green by heat-loving algae. From here, an hour-long self-guided walking trail loops past bubbling mud pools, through an active geyser field, and down into the mouth of Ruatapu Cave, a sacred site once used by Maori women to prepare themselves for ceremonies – hence *Orakei Korako*, "a place of adorning".

You can **stay** on the opposite side of the river at *Orakei Korako Lodge* (dorms ❶, units ❻) in self-catering bunk-style budget accommodation and new motel units, with a big lounge, a pool table, hot tubs, and canoes for rent at $10 an hour.

The Taupo–Napier Road

Travelling beyond the immediate vicinity of Taupo, SH1 hugs the lake as it heads southwest to Turangi (see p.349), while SH5 veers southeast along the **Taupo–Napier Road**, a twisting ninety-minute run through some of the North Island's remotest country. Much of the early part of the journey crosses the Kaingaroa Plains, impoverished land cloaked in pumice and ash from the Taupo Volcanic eruption and of little use save for the pine plantations which stretch 100km to the north. The history of this route to Napier is traced by the **Taupo–Napier Heritage Trail**; pick up a free booklet from Taupo or Napier visitor centres. Many of the 35 stops are of limited interest, but be sure to call in at **Opepe Historic Reserve**, 17km from Taupo, where, on the north side of the road, a cemetery contains white wooden slabs marking the graves of nine soldiers of the Bay of Plenty cavalry, killed by followers of maverick Maori leader Te Kooti in 1869.

After another 11km, Clements Mill Road leads 30km south into the northern reaches of the **Kaimanawa Forest Park**, a remote rugged mountain wilderness, almost untouched, and little-visited by recreational trampers, but a perennial favourite with deer hunters and anglers. If you are experienced and determined, get hold of the detailed *Guide to Kaimanawa State Forest Park* map and set off on the remote **Te Iringa–Oamaru Circuit** (60km; 4–5 days), staying in a series of Category 3 huts ($5 per night). Some 25km southeast of the Clements Mill Road turn-off, the Waipunga River, a tributary of the Mohaka, plummets 30m over the **Waipunga Falls**, and continues beside SH5 through the lovely Waipunga Gorge, packed with tall native trees and dotted with picnic sites which double as overnight **campsites** with no facilities but river water. The highway descends to the Mohaka River and the accommodation at *Riverlands Outback Adventures*, 5km south of SH5 (☏06/834 9756, ⓔriverlnds @xtra.co.nz; camping $10, dorms ❶, rooms ❷, self-contained units ❸), a residential multi-activity centre where the prime attractions are **horse trekking** (2hr, $40; 4hr, $60) and **whitewater rafting** on Grade I–II stretches of the Mohaka (2hr, $70), or the more exciting and wonderfully scenic Grade III section (full day; $120), which runs through a narrow gorge that's just great for jumping off the cliffs either side. Beyond the Mohaka River, the highway climbs the Titiokura Saddle before the final descent through the grape country of the **Esk Valley** into Napier (see p.453).

Tongariro National Park and around

New Zealand's highly developed network of national parks owes much to Te Heu Heu Tukino IV, the Tuwharetoa chief who, in the *pakeha* land-grabbing climate of the late nineteenth century, recognized that the only chance his

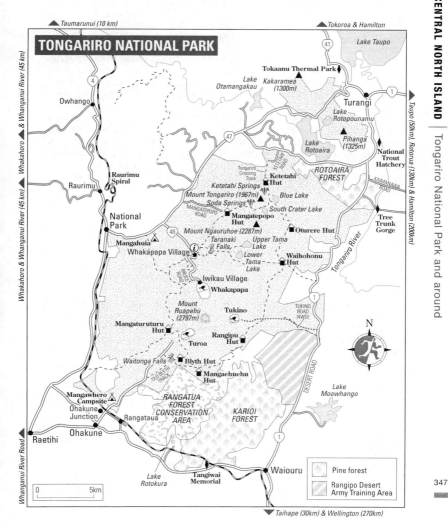

4

The Maori mountain legends

When Te Heu Heu Tukino donated Tongariro's central volcanoes to the Crown (see p.347), he was motivated by a deep spiritual need for their protection. According to Maori, the mountains at the heart of the park have distinct personalities and a genealogy and symbolize the links between the community and its environment. This significance was recognized in 1991 when the park became the first World Heritage Site included as a **cultural landscape**. The **Maori mountain legends** which follow explain some of the relationships between the peaks and their formation.

There are said to have been a lot more mountains in the past dominated by the chiefly **Ruapehu, Tongariro, Ngauruhoe** and **Taranaki**. Around them clustered smaller mountains including the beautiful **Pihanga** in the northern section of the park, whose favours were widely sought. Pihanga loved only Tongariro, the victor of numerous battles with her other suitors, including one that had brought him to his knees, striking off the top of his head, giving him him his present shape. Taranaki, meantime, defeated Ngauruhoe, but when he came to face Ruapehu, he was exhausted and badly wounded. He fled, carving out the Whanganui River as he made for the west coast of the North Island. Meanwhile the smaller **Putauaki** got as far north as Kawerau; but **Tauhara** was reluctant to leave and continually glanced back, so that by dawn, when the mountains could no longer move, he had only reached the northern shores of Lake Taupo, where he remains to this day, "the lonely mountain".

To the local Tuwharetoa people these mountains were so sacred that they averted their eyes while passing and wouldn't eat or build fires in the vicinity. The *tapu* stretches back to legendary times when their ancestor **Ngatoroirangi** came to claim the centre of the island. After declaring Tongariro *tapu* he set off up the mountain, but his followers broke their vow to fast while he was away and the angry gods sent a snow storm in which Ngatoroirangi almost perished before more benevolent gods in Hawaiki saved him by sending fire to revive his frozen limbs.

people had of keeping their sacred lands intact was to donate them to the nation – on condition that they could not be settled nor spoiled. His 1887 gift formed the core of the country's first major public reserve, **Tongariro National Park** which became a **World Heritage Site** in 1991 owing to its unique landscape and cultural significance (see box above). In the north a small, outlying section of the park centres on **Mount Pihanga** and the tiny **Lake Rotopounamu**, but most visitors head straight for the main body of the park, dominated by the three great volcanoes, which rise starkly from the desolate plateau: the broad-shouldered ski mountain, **Ruapehu** (2797m), its squatter sibling, **Tongariro** (1968m), and, wedged between them, the conical **Ngauruhoe** (2287m).

Within the boundaries of the park is some of the North Island's most striking scenery, the more forbidding volcanic areas were used as locations for Mordor and Mt Doom in the *Lord of the Rings* (see p.985), though, in reality, it's a beautiful mixture of semi-arid plains, steaming fumaroles, crystal-clear lakes and streams, virgin rainforest and an abundance of ice and snow. All of this forms the backdrop to two supremely rewarding tramps, the one-day **Tongariro Crossing** and the three-to-four-day **Tongariro Northern Circuit**, one of New Zealand's Great Walks. The undulating plateau to the west of the volcanoes is vegetated by bushland and golden tussock, while on the eastern side the rain shadow of the mountains produces the **Rangipo Desert**. Although this is not a true desert, it is still an impressively bleak and barren landscape, smothered by a thick layer of volcanic ash from the 186 AD

Taupo eruption. The park is part of the Taupo volcanic zone and captured world headlines in 1995 and again in 1996 when **Mount Ruapehu**, the highest and most massive of the three volcanoes, burst into life, blasting a plume of ash and dust 12km into the atmosphere and emptying the crater lake down the side of the mountain in great muddy deluges known as lahars. Although the **eruptions** drastically curtailed the ski season, they have had little lasting damage; what made them newsworthy was the dramatic contrast between the black plume of ash and the pristine snowy peak, all offset by a cloudless sky – images now endlessly recycled on the walls of local cafés and visitor centres.

The northern approach to the region is through **Turangi**, not much in itself but a reasonable base both for the Tongariro tramps and for rafting and fishing the Tongariro River. What it lacks is a sense of proximity to the mountains – something much more tangible in the service town of **National Park**, and more so again in **Whakapapa Village**, 1200m up on the flanks of Ruapehu. The southern gateway is **Ohakune**, a more appealing place than National Park but distinctly dead outside the ski season. Heading south, the Army Museum at Waiouru marks the southern limit of the Volcanic Plateau, which tails off into the pastoral southern half of the region set around the agricultural town of **Taihape** home to the North Island's highest bungy jump.

Pretty much everyone comes to the park either to **ski** or to **tramp**, staying in one of the small towns dotted around the base of the mountains. While a **car** makes life easier, there is a reasonable network of **minibuses** plying the more useful routes and providing trailhead transport for trampers (see box on p.355). Note that this whole region is over 600m above sea level, so even in the height of summer you'll need some **warm clothing**.

Turangi and around

Turangi, 50km south of Taupo, is a small, flat and characterless place, planned in the mid-1960s and built almost overnight for workers toiling away at the tunnels and concrete channels of the ambitious Tongariro Power Scheme (see box, p.352). It doesn't even make the best of its location – Lake Taupo is only 4km to the north and the town centre is separated by SH1 from its trump card, the fishing and rafting waters of the Tongariro River. Nonetheless, it is very popular with trout fishers, and works well enough as a base for a smattering of sights and activities in the immediate vicinity and for the Tongariro National Park (see p.347), just beyond the steep volcanic range to the south. It has also become a major jumping-off point for the Tongariro Crossing (see p.356) with a selection of hostels offering transport to and from the trailheads.

European settlement began early this century soon after trout were released into the Taupo fishery, but although the collection of fishing lodges warranted a shop and post office, no town existed until 1964 when well-paid work on the power scheme lured workers to the area, notably Italian tunnellers, many of whom subsequently settled here.

Arrival, information and accommodation

Alpine Scenic Tours and Tongariro Expeditions both run low cost daily **bus** services from Taupo dropping off pretty much where you want. InterCity and

Newmans drop off near the visitor centre, Ngawaka Place (daily 8.30am–5pm; ℡07/386 8999 & 0800/288 726, ⓦwww.laketauponz.com), which sells bus tickets and is packed with local **information**, including informative panels on trout fishing and a relief model of the Tongariro Power Scheme. They also sell Taupo fishing licences, topo maps, DOC tramping brochures and hut tickets, though if you have detailed tramping enquiries you can trot down the street to the small **DOC office**, Turanga Place (Mon–Fri 8.30am–5pm; ℡07/386 8607, ⓕ386 7086). A couple of the local adventure tour operators have turned the old bus station on Ohunga Rd into a booking centre offering packages of activities in the region as well as information and onward bookings. At the time of writing it was not open but may prove to be a useful place to coordinate transport or guides for the Tongariro Crossing.

Turangi's need to cater to anglers, skiers and trampers bound for the Tongariro National Park has left it with a decent range of **accommodation**; the budget places congregate in the town centre, while the plusher lodges and B&Bs line the Tongariro River to the east, though nowhere backs right onto the river.

Bellbird Lodge cnr Tautahanga Rd & Rangipoia Place ℡07/386 8281, ⓔbookings@bellbird.co.nz. A popular and homely backpackers, slightly rough at the edges, occupying several suburban houses, with home-made cakes each evening. Dorms ❶, rooms ❷

Club Habitat 25 Ohuanga Rd ℡07/386 7492. An activity-oriented associate YHA that comes with a spacious games bar and dining complex, a spa and sauna, and is a favourite with the backpacker tour buses. Camping $10, dorms ❶, cabins ❸, self-contained units ❹

Creel Lodge 183 Taupahi Rd ℡ & ⓕ07/386 8081. A simple, low-cost, fishing-oriented motel comprising a cluster of self-contained one- and two-bedroom units in grounds running down to the river edge with communal fish smoker and barbecue. ❹

Extreme Backpackers 26 Ngawaka Place ℡07/386 8949, ⓔebpcltd@xtra.co.nz. It's worth paying the extra dollar or so over the other hostels for the simply decorated rooms in this purpose-built backpackers set around a central courtyard. The amenable hosts sometimes run guests to the Tokaanu hot pools in the evening, there's also a good climbing wall and an amiable café. Camping $10, dorms ❶, rooms ❷, en suites ❸

Ika Lodge 155 Taupahi Rd ℡ & ⓕ07/386 5538, ⓦwww.ika.co.nz. This superior homestay-cum-fishing lodge by the Tongariro River has two en-suite rooms and a self-contained apartment, along with succulent game and fish dinners for $40. ❻–❽

Parklands cnr SH1 & Arahori St ℡0800/456 284 & 07/386 7515, ⓦwww.parklandsmotorlodge .co.nz. An extensive motor lodge with an outdoor pool, private hot tubs, games room and a small restaurant serving home-style dinners. Camping $10, studios ❹, units ❺

Founders Guest Lodge 253 Taupahi Rd, ℡07/386 8539, ⓦwww.founders.co.nz. Four extremely comfortable double rooms in a quiet and relaxing purpose-built homestay with cooked and continental breakfasts and friendly hosts. ❻

Activities

In order to get to the various activities around Turangi you'll either need your own transport or to arrange pick up by the operators or the Tongariro shuttles (see p.355). Four companies offer rafting year round on the lower reaches of the Tongariro River, which runs through one of the most scenic and accessible river gorges in the country. The river's natural flow patterns have been modulated by the Tongariro Power Scheme, limiting the possibilities of a really wild time on the Grade II and Grade III rapids, but what sets the Tongariro apart is the range of trips you can do on one piece of water – some involving a two-hour run in traditional river rafts, some employing sit-on kayaks and some combining fishing with the rafting.

All **operators** charge $90: handiest are Tokaanu-based Rock 'n' River Rafting (℡07/386 0352, ⓦwww.raftingnewzealand.com) and Turangi-based

Tongariro River Rafting, Atirau Road (℡07/386 6409 & 0800/101 024, 🅦www.tongariro-riverrafting.com). Taupo's Rapid Sensations (℡0800/227 238 & 07/378 7902, 🅦www.rapids.co.nz) and Kiwi River Safaris (℡07/377 6597, 🅦www.krs.co.nz) are also very competitive. All offer straightforward whitewater-rafting trips, though Tongariro River Rafting also allow you to paddle yourselves with a guide in hailing distance, and offer the Tongariro Duo ($120), which combines mountain-biking and rafting over the best part of a day. Big rafts can make the modest scale of the lower Tongariro seem a little tame, and more fun can be had on Tongariro River Rafting's **sit-on kayak** ($90 for 3hr) on a lower stretch of Grade II whitewater.

If you're keen to try hauling a trout from Lake Taupo or one of the local rivers, the visitor centre will help pair you with a **fishing** guide to match your experience and aspirations as well as a license ($12.50 a day); expect to pay around $100 for a couple of hours with gear and guiding. You can rent a boat and tackle at moderate prices from the Motuoapa Marina (℡07/386 7000, $30 per hr, minimum 3hrs), 8km north of Turangi on SH1. River fishing takes place pretty much year-round, but the spawning season is from April to October.

To combine the last two activities, Tongariro River Rafting will take you for a full day **raft fishing** (Dec–May only) which involves rafting the Grade III section of the Tongariro, stopping off at otherwise inaccessible pools along the way to cast a fly. Rates are $500 a day for two people – roughly the same as you'd pay for a fishing guide alone. They also rent out **mountain-bikes** at $20 for two hours ($40 per day) and can provide transport and guides for the 42 Traverse, an exhausting full-day ride along forest roads – a group of three or four will bring prices down to manageable levels.

Eating and drinking

Eating in Turangi is more limited than the range of accommodation would indicate, but you can eat tolerably well for a couple of nights with many of the best places attached to lodges.

Brew Haus Bar & Restaurant at *Club Habitat* on Ohuanga Rd ℡07/386 7492. Simple restaurant serving moderately priced hearty meals at breakfast (7–9.30am) and dinner (6–9pm). Its bar next door is probably the most hospitable in town and serves a range of beers brewed on site.
Grand Central Fry cnr Ohuanga Rd & Ngawaka Place ℡07/386 3344. Easily the best of the town's several takeaways doing great fish and chips and, of course, run by an Englishman.
Kaimanawa Bistro 258 Taupahi Rd ℡07/386 8709. Dinner-only restaurant outside the town centre towards the Tongariro River where you might expect char-grilled fillet steak, or fried salmon strips, venison hot pot and traditional desserts – three courses around $45. Closed Sun & Mon.

Mustard Seed Café 91 Ohuanga Rd. Casual, recently refurbished modern café with the usual range of breakfasts, panini, salads and cakes, plus decent espresso and internet access.
Turangi Smokehouse and Deli Shop 37, Town Centre Shopping Precinct. Eat-in or takeaway, serving locally caught trout and a range of lovely sausages. Daytime only, closed Sun.
Red Crater Café At *Extreme Backpackers*, see p.350. Excellent little café serving great coffee, good-value snacks, burgers and more substantial fare.
Valentino's Ohuanga Rd ℡07/386 8812. Mainstream and modestly priced restaurant serving reasonable, if not always consistent, Italian and Kiwi mains ($18–22) in 1970s trattoria surroundings. Closed Tues.

Around Turangi

The massive amount of trout fishing in this area, especially Lake Taupo, makes it essential that rivers are continually restocked with fingerlings raised at fish-breeding facilities such as the **Tongariro National Trout Hatchery**, on SH1,

The Tongariro Power Scheme

The **Tongariro Power Scheme** provides an object lesson in harnessing the power of water with minimal impact on the environment. Its two powerhouses produce around seven percent of the country's electricity, while the outflows that feed into Lake Taupo add flexibility to the much older chain of eight hydroelectric dams along the Waikato River. While some argue it is unacceptable to tamper with such a fine piece of wilderness, and while it has caused fluctuations in the levels of nutrients in the Tongariro River and erosion along some of the service tracks, the scheme has many admirers.

In fact, if it weren't for the scale models in visitor centres and the ugly bulk of the Tokaanu power station, only astute observers would be aware of the complex system of tunnels, aqueducts, canals and weirs unobtrusively going about their business of diverting the waters of the Tongariro River and myriad streams running off the mountain slopes, back and forth around the perimeter of the national park, using modified natural lakes for storage. Mount Ruapehu poses its own unique problems: the threat of **lahars** (see p.349) is ever-present and, after the 1995 eruption, **tephra** (a highly abrasive volcanic ash) found its way into the turbines of the Rangipo underground powerhouse, causing an unscheduled seven-month shutdown.

5km south of Turangi (daily 10am–3pm; free), recently revamped and set among native bush between the Tongariro River and one of its tributaries, the Waihukahuka Stream. There isn't a lot to see, it's more for kids, but you are free to wander through buildings where tanks hold the tiniest fish, among the rearing ponds outside and into an underground viewing chamber where you can view wild trout in the Waihukahuka Stream.

The pleasant **Tongariro River Loop Track** (4km; 1hr) is well worth the hour it takes to complete. The trail starts from the Major Jones footbridge at the end of Koura Street on the edge of town, it follows the right bank of the river north past a couple of viewpoints and over a bluff then crosses the river and returns along the opposite side. Ten kilometres south of Turangi, off SH47, the **Lake Rotopounamu Circuit** (5km; 90min) encircles a pristine lake surrounded by bush alive with native birds.

Tokaanu

Turangi's smaller neighbour, **Tokaanu**, 5km west, was the main settlement in the area in pre-European times. Maori were drawn by the geothermal benefits of what is now the **Tokaanu Thermal Park** (unrestricted entry; free), a compact patch of low scrub, beautifully clear hot pools and plopping mud threaded by a fifteen-minute trail. The adjacent **Tokaanu Thermal Pools**, Mangaroa Rd (daily 10am–10pm; $5), are great for soaking your bones after a day's tramping in the national park, with an open-air public pool and hotter, partly enclosed and chlorine-free private pools ($7 per hour, close at 9.30pm). Nearby you can spend a very pleasurable hour or two gently paddling along a narrow, lush, bush-fringed channel, past the hot tubs and back gardens of the locals in **kayaks** rented from Tokaanu Kayaks (daily 10am–5pm; ☏07/386 7558, ✉kayaks@reap.org.nz).They charge $25 for an hour, $45 for two and will even provide transport if you don't fancy paddling back upstream. To find them, take the Tokaanu road out of Turangi and look for the sign on the left, just over the bridge.

To **stay** in Tokaanu, try the *Oasis Motel and Tourist Park*, SH41 (☏07/386 8569, ✆386 0694; camping $10, cabins ❷, studios & units ❸), an extensive campsite with mineral hot pools, spa pools and simple but well priced on-site accommodation.

Whakapapa and around

Tiny **Whakapapa**, the only settlement set firmly within the boundaries of the Tongariro National Park, hugs the lower slopes of Mount Ruapehu some 45km south of Turangi on SH48, which spurs off SH47. Approaching from the north, an open expanse of tussock gives distant views of the imposing form of the *Grand Chateau* hotel which rises into view like an absurd mirage, framed by the snowy slopes of the volcano behind and overlooked by the arterial network of tows of the Whakapapa skifield.

From Whakapapa, SH48 continues as Bruce Road 6km to **Iwikau Village** (known locally as the "Top o' the Bruce"), an ugly jumble of ski-club chalets which, from late June through to mid-November, and in exceptional circumstances as late as Christmas, becomes a seething mass of wrap-around shades and baggy snowboarders' pants. Outside the ski season, the village dies, leaving only a couple of chair lifts (mid-Dec to mid-April; $17 return) to trundle up to the garish *Knoll Ridge Café*, New Zealand's highest at 2020m.

Practicalities

The only **bus services** to Whakapapa are the once-daily shuttle buses from Turangi and National Park (see box on p.355), which drop off close to DOC's helpful **visitor centre** (daily: Dec–Feb 8am–6pm; March–Nov 8am–5pm; ☎07/892 3729, ✉whakapapavc@doc.govt.nz). The centre is stocked with all the maps and leaflets you could need and is equipped with extensive displays on the park, including the tiny Ski History museum and a couple of videos that are shown on demand – *Volcanoes of the South Wind* (15min) is a fairly simplistic discussion of vulcanism in general and its manifestations here, including the '95 and '96 eruptions, while *The Sacred Gift of Tongariro* (25min) combines Maori legends surrounding Tongariro with impressive footage of the landscape through the seasons and the activities that take place in it. Each costs $3, or you can see both for $5.

Accommodation

There's not much to Whakapapa beside a few cafés, a pub and **places to stay**, all within a couple of minutes' walk of each other and all often booked up in advance. You'll do well to reserve as far ahead as possible through the ski season and over the Christmas and January school holidays. The most prominent hotel is the *Grand Chateau* (☎07/892 3809 & 0800/242 832, ⓦwww.chateau.co.nz; ⑥–⑨), a vast brick edifice built in 1929 with gracious public areas including a huge lounge with full-size snooker table and great mountain views; it's worth a visit for a cup of tea even if you're not a resident. Guests have use of the highest nine-hole golf course in New Zealand, tennis courts, gym and a small indoor pool, and stay in rooms modernized to international hotel standard; you'll need a premium room (⑨) if you're after plenty of space and good views, but you can save money in spring and autumn when there are often discounts of around thirty percent. The *Chateau* also has self-contained chalets (⑧), some sleeping up to six; and organizes the Tongariro trek (see p.356). The only other hotel is the *Skotel*,

about 50m up the hill beside the Grand Chateau (☎07/892 3719 &
0800/756 835, ⓦwww.skotel.co.nz; backpacker beds ❶, standard rooms ❺,
chalets ❻), a rambling "alpine retreat" with a sauna and a range of rooms
from self-catering hostel-style affairs (with very limited kitchen facilities) to
relatively luxurious rooms, some with views of Ngauruhoe and Tongariro.
Note that rates are hiked up considerably in the ski season (cheapest room
❹). The best budget option is the *Whakapapa Holiday Park,* entrance diagonally opposite the Visitor Centre (☎07/892 3897, ⓔwhakapapaholpark
@xtra.co.nz; camping $11, dorms ❶, cabins ❸, flat ❸), nicely set in a patch
of bushland with spacious tent and powered sites, simple cabins that are let
as backpacker dorms in summer, and a more luxurious en-suite tourist flat.
There is also DOC's toilets-and-water self-registration *Mangahuia campsite*
($4), on SH47 close to the foot of the Whakapapa access road.

   Iwikau Village has no public accommodation, only ski-club lodges and a
daytime café that's open throughout the year.

Eating and drinking

You can eat **lunches** and **snacks** cheaply at *Fergussons Café,* opposite the visitor centre, though you might prefer the better quality across the road at the
Chateau's *Pihanga Café and T Bar,* which serve more substantial fare ($15–20
from 11.30am to 9pm). Alternatives are the *Skotel,* which serves breakfast and
good-value bistro meals and has a bar. The cheapest booze and food, and some
might say the most atmospheric place to **drink**, is the *Tussock Pub* (open at
3pm with big screen TV) where the few locals tend to congregate. If you want
to reward yourself for the successful completion of a major tramp, the place
to do it is the Chateau's *Ruapehu Room,* with very good à la carte meals at à
la carte prices.

Around Whakapapa

Outside the skiing season (see box on p.358), Whakapapa is a lot less frenetic
but is still alive with trampers, since it makes a fine base for both short walks
and long tramps. The Tongariro Northern Circuit and the Round the
Mountain track (see p.357) can both be tackled from here, but there are also
easier strolls covered by DOC's *Whakapapa Walks* leaflet ($1). Three of the best
of these are the **Whakapapa Nature Walk** (1km; 20–30min), highlighting the
unique flora of the park; the **Taranaki Falls Walk** (6km; 2hr), which heads
through open tussock and bushland to where the Wairere Stream plunges 20m
over the end of an old lava flow; and the **Silica Rapids Walk** (7km; 2hr
30min), which follows a stream through beech forests to some creamy-
coloured geothermal terraces.

Tramping in Tongariro National Park

Tongariro National Park contains some of the North Island's finest walks. The
Tongariro Crossing alone is rated as the best one-day tramp in the country,
but there are many longer possibilities, notably the three- to four-day **Tongariro
Northern Circuit**; both pass through spectacular and varied volcanic terrain.
Mount Ruapehu has the arduous but rewarding **Crater Rim Walk** and a
circuit, the **Round the Mountain Track**, which offers a narrower variety of
terrain and sights than the Tongariro tramps, but is consequently less used.

The major bus companies don't run through the Tongariro National Park, leaving several smaller companies, many associated with backpacker hostels, to fill the void. Several of those servicing the Tongariro Crossing offer an Early Bird service getting you to the trailhead before the masses, though some only run at peak times and they all charge up to $5 extra for the privilege.

From Taupo: Alpine Scenic Tours (℡07/378 7412, ⓦwww.alpinescenictours.co.nz) pick up and drop off Tongariro Crossing-bound trampers ($30 return), will provide wet weather gear and walking poles, and since it is a scheduled service, will even go when the weather is poor. Tongariro Expeditions (℡0800/828 763 & 07/377 0435, ⓦwww.tongariroexpeditions.com; $30 return) compete directly, but only go when the crossing is viable.

From Turangi: Alpine Scenic Tours (℡07/386 8918, ⓦwww.alpinescenictours.co.nz) do a particularly useful run three times a day, calling at Whakapapa and the start and end of the Tongariro Crossing including one run (11am from Turangi) going right through to National Park. *Bellbird Lodge* (℡07/386 8281), *Club Habitat* (℡07/386 7492), and *Extreme Backpackers* (℡07/386 8949) each run similar services open to everyone, with most offering an early bus giving you a head start on the pack. Fares are very competitive – each charges $25 for the Tongariro Crossing drop-off and pick-up and $20–25 one-way to either Whakapapa or National Park. Alpine becomes a skifield shuttle in winter.

From Whakapapa: Tongariro Track Transport (℡07/892 3716) runs a daily shuttle leaving the visitor centre at 8am for the start of the Tongariro Crossing (around $20 return), and meeting you at Ketetahi at either 4.30pm or 6pm.

From National Park: Shuttle buses serve the trailheads in summer and skifields in winter. All the hostels will arrange transport, but the biggest operator is *Howard's Lodge* (℡07/892 2827) which runs its own all-comer buses, charging $20 for drop-off and pick-up at either end of the Tongariro Crossing. Tongariro Track Transport picks up in National Park at 7.45am then continues to Whakapapa and Mangatepopo.

From Ohakune: Tongariro National Park Shuttle Transport (℡0800/825 825) do door-to-door Tongariro Crossing shuttles ($30 return) and include a free DOC brochure. They're also helpful for linking Ohakune with National Park and Whakapapa.

Practicalities

The 1:80,000 *Tongariro Park* **map** ($15) is ideal for these tramps, but **DOC leaflets** ($1 each) covering the tramps separately are informative and perfectly adequate. The main **points of access** to the walks are Mangatepopo Road and Ketetahi Road for the Tongariro Crossing and Tongariro Northern Circuit; and Whakapapa for the Tongariro Northern Circuit, the Ruapehu Crater Rim and the Round the Mountain Track. Shuttle **buses** serve the trailheads from Turangi, National Park and Whakapapa, with the exception of the unmarked Crater Rim walk, the tracks are all well maintained and sporadically signposted, so you can judge your progress if you've a bus to catch.

Other than accommodation in Whakapapa Village, the only places to stay are the **trampers huts**, all of which have adjacent **campsites**. In summer (roughly late Oct–May), huts on the Tongariro Northern Circuit – Mangatepopo, Ketetahi, Waihohonu and Oturere – are classed as Great Walk huts ($14); in winter they lose their cooking facilities and revert to Category 2 ($10, camping $5). Hut tickets do not guarantee a bunk, so at busy times you could still find yourself on the floor. Campers (summer $10, winter $5) stay close to the huts and use the same facilities. Huts on the Round the Mountain Track – Whakapapaiti, Mangaturuturu, Blyth, Mangaehuehu and Rangipo – are Category 2 huts all year ($10, camping $5). Hut tickets can be bought in advance from DOC in Whakapapa and Ohakune, or DOC and the visitor centre in Turangi; if bought from a hut warden you pay an extra $4.

There are several **organized treks**, too: the *Grand Chateau* hotel in Whakapapa Village runs the Tongariro Trek (℡07/892 3809 & 0800/242 832, Ⓦwww.trek.co.nz; mid-Dec to mid-April; $1215, includes meals and accommodation), which, over four days, covers the Ruapehu Crater Rim walk and the Tongariro Crossing, returning each night to the hotel. The Whakapapa Skifield Guided Walk (℡07/892 3738; mid-Dec to mid-April daily 9.30am; $55, including chair-lift ride) ascends to the Ruapehu Crater Rim, providing interesting commentary on the geology and flora en route.

The **weather** in the mountains is extremely changeable, and the usual provisos apply. Even on apparently scorching summer days, the increased altitude and exposed windy ridges produce a wind-chill factor to be reckoned with, and storms roll in with frightening rapidity. Any time from the end of March through to late November there can be snow on the tracks, so if you are planning a tramp during this period, enquire locally about current conditions. Always take warm **clothing** and rain gear – and if you plan to scramble up and down the steep volcanic cone of Mount Ngauruhoe, take gloves and long trousers for protection from the sharp scoria rock.

Tongariro Crossing

The **Tongariro Crossing** (16km; 6–8hr; 750m ascent) is by far the most popular of the major tramps in the region and for good reason. Within a few hours you climb over lava flows, cross a crater floor, skirt active geothermal areas, pass beautiful and serene emerald and blue lakes and have the opportunity to ascend the cinder cone of Mount Ngauruhoe. Even without this wealth of highlights it would still be a fine tramp, traversing a mountain massif through scrub and tussock, before descending into virgin bush for the final half-hour. It can be a long day out if you're not particularly fit, but it's not excessively arduous. Note too that this isn't a wilderness experience – on weekends and through the height of summer well over a thousand people complete the Crossing, so it pays to aim for spring or autumn, or stick to weekdays. Another alternative is to turn the walk from a one-day into a two-day experience by doing it in reverse (see box below).

Car parks at both ends of the track have a reputation for break-ins and it is a good idea to leave your vehicle in Turangi, National Park or Whakapapa and make use instead of the many shuttle buses (see box p.355). The track can be walked in either direction but by going from west to east you save 400m of ascent, also all shuttle buses are scheduled around a west to east traverse, usually depositing their charges at Mangatepopo Road End car park, six gravel

Avoiding the crowds

To avoid the worst of the crush on the Tongariro Circuit, steal a march on other walkers by choosing a shuttle operator prepared to drop-off at Mangatepopo Road a little earlier; or dawdle behind the mob and plan to stay the night at Mangatepopo Hut; you could also try the trek in reverse by getting dropped off at Ketetahi Road late in the day and then sleeping at Ketetahi Hut ready for a crack-of-dawn start next day (though bear in mind this direction is much tougher).

kilometres east of SH47, at about 8.30am and picking up at Ketetahi Road around 4.30pm. Some shuttle operators do a 6pm pick-up allowing you to tack on an ascent of Ngauruhoe; ask when you book.

From Mangatepopo Road End the first hour is fairly gentle, following the Mangatepopo Stream through a barren landscape and passing the Mangatepopo Hut. The track gradually steepens as you scale the fractured black lava flows towards the **Mangatepopo Saddle**, passing a short side-track to the **Soda Springs**, a small wildflower oasis in this blasted landscape. The Saddle marks the start of the high ground between the bulky and ancient Mount Tongariro and its youthful acolyte, **Mount Ngauruhoe**, which fit walkers can climb (2km return; 2hr return; 600m ascent) from here and still make the shuttle bus at the end of the day. The two-steps-forward-one-step-back ascent of this thirty-five-degree cone of red and black scoria must be one of the most exhausting and dispiriting walks in the country, but it is always popular – both for the superb views from the toothy crater rim and for the thrilling headlong descent among a cascade of tumbling rocks and volcanic dust. If you're attempting it in **winter**, bear in mind that the ascent becomes a "sub-alpine" climb, when the use of mountaineering equipment, like ice axes, is advisable.

From the Mangatepopo Saddle, the main track crosses the flat pan of the South Crater and climbs to the rim of **Red Crater**, with fumaroles belching out steam, which obscures the banded crimson and black of the crater walls. Colours get more vibrant still as you begin the descent to the Emerald Lakes, opaque pools shading from jade to palest duck-egg, and beyond to the crystal-clear Blue Lake. Sidling around Tongariro's **North Crater**, you begin to descend steeply on golden tussock slopes to **Ketetahi Hut**, a major rest stop with views of Lake Rotoaira and Lake Taupo. From here you pass close to the steaming Ketetahi Springs, then begin the final descent through cool stream-side bush to the car park on Ketetahi road.

Tongariro Northern Circuit and the Round the Mountain track

If the Tongariro Crossing appeals, but you are looking for something a little more challenging, the answer is the **Tongariro Northern Circuit** (42km; 3–4 days at a gentle pace), one of New Zealand's Great Walks. The section from **Whakapapa to Mangatepopo Hut** (9km; 2–3hr; 50m ascent) is boggy after heavy rain but usually passable, though you could always get a shuttle to Mangatepopo. If you decide to walk you'll find the track undulating through tussock and crossing numerous streams before meeting the Tongariro Crossing track close to Mangatepopo Hut. From **Mangatepopo Hut to Emerald Lakes** (6km; 3–4hr; 660m ascent), you follow the Tongariro Crossing (described above), then have the choice of continuing on the Crossing to **Ketetahi Hut** (4km; 2–3hr; 400m descent) and returning to this point the next day, or branching right **to Oturere Hut** (5km; 1–2hr; 500m descent), descending steeply through fabulously contorted lava formations towards the Rangipo Desert. The initial section from **Otuere Hut to Waihohonu Hut** (8km; 2–3hr; 250m descent) crosses open, undulating country, then descends into the beech forests before a final climb over a ridge brings you to the hut, where you can drop your pack and press on for twenty minutes to the cool and clear Ohinepango Springs. The final day's walk, from **Waihohonu Hut to Whakapapa** (14km; 5–6hr; 200m ascent), cuts between Ngauruhoe and Ruapehu, passing the Old Waihohonu Hut (no accommodation) that was built

Mount Ruapehu skifields

Mount Ruapehu is home to the North Island's only substantial **skifields** which attract around two thirds of the nation's skiers. Every weekend from around **late June to early November**, cars pile out of Auckland and Wellington (and pretty much everywhere in between) for the four-hour drive to either Whakapapa, the more extensive skifield on the northwestern slopes of Mount Ruapehu, or Turoa, easily beaten into second place on the south side. Both fields have excellent reputations for pretty much all levels of skier and the orientation of volcanic ridges lends itself to an abundance of dreamy, natural half-pipes for snowboarding.

With over thirty groomed runs, a dozen major chair lifts and T-bars and the dedicated learners' area of Happy Valley, **Whakapapa** is New Zealand's largest and busiest ski area. It offers the longest North Island season (usually late June to early Nov and sometimes through to Christmas), 675 vertical metres of piste, plus snow-making equipment, ski schools, a huge gear-rental operation, crèche and a couple of cafés. **Access** is along the toll-free, sealed Bruce Road. Tyre chains are sometimes required, in which case a fitting service miraculously appears at a parking area beside the road. Car parking is free and there is a free courtesy bus from the lower car parks. Shuttle buses run from Whakapapa Village, National Park, Turangi and Taupo.

Turoa (typically mid- to late June through to late October) has developed in a much more controlled fashion than Whakapapa, and offers the country's greatest vertical range of piste (720m) and a skiable area almost as extensive as Whakapapa's with wide groomed trails particularly aimed at intermediate skiers; it also offers the region's best après ski at Ohakune. It is usually possible to drive straight up the sealed, toll-free, 17km access road from Ohakune without chains, and park for nothing. Again, the skifield operators will fit chains ($20) when needed, or you can rent from shops in Ohakune for a little less and fit them yourself. Several shuttle buses run up from Ohakune, charging around $20 return.

Practicalities

After rationalization brought on by short seasons, the two fields have now amalgamated under one company (☎07/892 3738, @www.mtruapehu.com). Lift passes at either fields cost around $63 a day, $262 for five days, and there is both a Discover Ski pack ($63) and a Discover Snowboard pack ($73) that includes gear rental, an hour-and-a-half lesson and a learners' area lift pass. On-site ski rental for one day and a pass costs $81, $102 for snowboard, pass and boots, and there are discounts for rentals of five or more days. Several places in National Park and Ohakune also offer competitive rates and a wide selection of equipment.

Neither field has public accommodation on site. Ski clubs maintain dozens of chalets at the foot of the main tows in Whakapapa's Iwikau Village, but casual visitors (unless they can get invited to a lodge as a guest) have to stay 6km downhill at Whakapapa Village or 22km away at National Park (see opposite). Almost everyone skiing Turoa stays in Ohakune (see p.361).

---

for stage coaches on the old road in 1901. The path then continues alongside Waihohonu Stream to the exposed **Tama Saddle** and, just over a kilometre beyond, a junction where side tracks lead to Lower Tama Lake (20min return) and Upper Tama Lake (1hr return), both water-filled explosion craters. It is only around two hours' walk from the saddle back to Whakapapa, so you should have time to explore the **Taranaki Falls** before ambling back through tussock to the village.

If you'd prefer to steer clear of the popular Northern Circuit but still circle around a mountain, try the **Round the Mountain Track** (71km; 4–5 days) which loops around Mount Ruapehu, most easily tackled from Whakapapa.

This track can also be combined with the Northern Circuit to make a mighty five- or six-day **circumnavigation** of all three mountains. For these two you need backcountry hut tickets or an annual hut pass. Huts are Cat 2 ($10) and camping is $5. A Great Walks pass is necessary for Waihohonu hut which is also part of the Northern Circuit Great Walk.

Ruapehu Crater Rim

The ascent to the **Ruapehu Crater Rim** takes around eight hours return from the Top o' the Bruce (15km), and a much more appealing five hours from the top of the **Waterfall Express chair lift** (9km), avoiding a long slog through a barren, rocky landscape. Even from the top of the chair lift, this is one of New Zealand's more gruelling short hikes, but the destination makes it all worthwhile. Volcanic instability makes it dangerous to go beyond the **Dome Shelter** (no accommodation), at 2672m the highest structure in the country and typically surrounded in snow. It perches on the rim of the crater, with great views across the upper reaches of a small glacier to the dramatic silhouettes of Cathedral Rocks, west to Mount Taranaki and down into the crater lake, currently in the process of refilling after thousands of tonnes of water were ejected during the 1995 and 1996 eruptions. The route is not waymarked, but from Christmas until the first snows arrive, the ascent can usually be made in ordinary walking boots without crampons or an ice axe. If you are in any doubt or would appreciate some commentary, join an organized trek (see p.356).

National Park

The evocative moniker attached to **National Park**, 15km west of Whakapapa Village, belies the overwhelming drabness of this tiny settlement – a dispiriting collection of A-frame chalets sprouting from a scrubby plain of pines, eucalyptuses and flax, with only the superb views of Ruapehu and Ngauruhoe to lend it any grace. The place owes its continued existence to skiers and trampers bound for the adjacent Tongariro National Park, and paddlers heading for **Whanganui River trips** (see p.261). With limited accommodation at Whakapapa Village, visitors are often forced to stay here, using shuttle buses (see box on p.355) to get to the Tongariro tramps.

Practicalities

National Park comprises a grid of half a dozen streets wedged between SH4 and the parallel rail line. **Trains** stop at the deserted platform on Station Road, while InterCity **buses** pull up outside what used to be the National Park Store, now just a telephone box 100m north on Carroll Street. Bus tickets can be bought a further 100m up the road at *Howard's Lodge* (see overleaf). There are no banks or cash machines in National Park so unless you have an EFTPOS card, bring plenty of cash.

Accommodation

Accommodation is in great demand during the **ski season** – when prices will be at least one price code higher than those given here – and can fill up from Christmas to the end of January, but otherwise it's plentiful. *Pukenui Lodge*, SH4 (☎0800/785 368, ⓦwww.tongariro.cc; camping $10, dorms ❶, rooms ❷, en suites ❸, units ❺), offers a spacious lounge and kitchen with great mountain views, a spa pool, plenty of assistance arranging activities, and a range of accommodation from plain and comfortable dorms and doubles, some en suite, to self-contained motel units. Similar standards are maintained at *Howard's Lodge*, 9 Carroll St (T & F07/892 2827, W www.howardslodge.co.nz; dorms ❶, rooms ❷, deluxe rooms ❸), which has its own track transport, a spa pool, and two accommodation sections – one catering to backpackers and the other offering plusher kitchen and lounge for the better-heeled guests. Rooms range from basic dorms (separate for men and women) and doubles to appreciably more modern and comfortable en-suite rooms; mountain bikes are available to rent ($20 for 2hr), as is tramping and climbing gear. Alternatives include the *Plateau Lodge*, Carroll St (T07/892 2993 & 0800/861 861, E plateaulodge @xtra.co.nz; dorms ❶, units ❷), offering marginally the cheapest dorms and some ageing but perfectly functional motel units; and National Park Backpackers, Finlay St (T & F07/892 2870, E nat.park.backpackers @xtra.co.nz; camping $12, dorms ❶, rooms ❷, made-up doubles ❸), with outdoor hot tub and generally good facilities, but chiefly notable for being built around an indoor climbing wall ($8, plus $2 for boots and harness). Guests only pay once for climbing during their visit.

Eating and drinking

All lodges serve breakfast for guests, but for main **meals** you're limited to steaks and bar-style meals at the usually rowdy *Schnapps Bar*, on SH4, next to Pukenui Lodge, or you can get fish 'n' chips and a jug of **beer** at the *National Park Hotel* on Carroll Street. *The Station* at the railway station is a relatively new café cum restaurant producing good quality food and coffee from 11am-10pm, though the bar stays open longer while the long-awaited *Elvin's* has re-opened at the corner of Carol St and SH4, it's open and airy with lots of large portions of kiwi favourites like steak and lamb as well as some Asian- and European- influenced soups and snacks, open from 4pm.

Ohakune and around

Ohakune, 35km south of National Park, welcomes you with a huge (artificial) carrot, celebrating its position at the heart of one of the nation's prime market-gardening regions. This is easily forgotten once you are in town among the chalet-style lodges and ski-rental shops geared to cope with the massive influx of winter-sports enthusiasts who descend from mid-June to early November for the **skiing** at Turoa (see box p.358), 20km north up Ohakune Mountain Road. During these months, the bars and restaurants swing into action, everyone makes their money for the year and then shuts up until next season. Consequently it is pretty quiet in summer, but once the snows have melted, the trails are open for tramping, mountain biking and horse trekking.

Practicalities

Ohakune is strung between two centres. The Auckland–Wellington rail line passes through **Ohakune Junction** where there's the **train station** and a cluster of hotels and restaurants mostly serving the skiing fraternity. **Central Ohakune**, the commercial heart of the town, lies 2km to the southwest, where InterCity **buses** on the Hamilton–Taumarunui–Wanganui run (daily except Sat) stop close to the **visitor centre**, 54 Clyde St (Mon–Fri 9am–5pm, Sat &

Sun 9am–3.30pm; ☎06/385 8427, ✉ruapehu.vic@xtra.co.nz), which has all the general information you'll need and sells both bus and train tickets. For more specific tramping information, the mountain weather forecast and a detailed low-down on local flora and fauna, make for the DOC **field centre** at the foot of Ohakune Mountain Road (Mon–Fri 9am–3pm; ☎06/385 0010, ✉ohakunevc@doc.govt.nz); weather and tramping information is available in the foyer which stays open 24hr. **Internet access** is available at The Video Shop, cnr of Goldfinch and Ayr sts.

There are no regular buses around Ohakune, so you might want to rent a **mountain bike** from either the Powderhorn Chateau, 194 Mangawhero Terrace ($25 per half-day, $35 full-day), or from The Big Red Ski Shed, 71 Clyde St (☎06/385 8887) where the machines range in quality and start from $15 for 1hr (tandems $25, or $65 for the day).

Accommodation

Ohakune has stacks of **places to stay**, though several of them close outside the ski season and are packed once the snows arrive – when prices get hiked up by around thirty percent more than those quoted here. Enough places are open in summer to satisfy almost all budgets, the most comprehensive and appealing being *Rimu Park Lodge*, 27 Rimu St, Ohakune Junction (☎06/385 9023, ⓦwww.rimupark.co.nz; dorms ❶, rooms & cabins ❷, units & carriages ❹, chalets ❹–❺), a 1914 villa containing spacious six-bunk dorms and comfortable doubles. The grounds are dotted with simple cabins, en-suite units with TV and fridge but no kitchen, fully self-contained chalets sleeping between four and ten, and several railway carriages fitted out as self-contained units with separate lounge and sleeping quarters. Also in Ohakune Junction you'll find the top-of-the-range *Powderhorn Chateau*, 194 Mangawhero Terrace, at the base of Ohakune Mountain Road (☎06/385 8888, ⓦwww .powderhorn.co.nz; ❻), an immense log-cabin style edifice with a lovely indoor swimming pool ($7 for nonguests), sun beds, and en-suite rooms, the best with balconies and forest views.

Folk arriving by bus will find it more convenient to stay in the main town, where there's budget accommodation at the vastly improved and welcoming *Matai Lodge*, 15–17 Clyde St (☎06/385 9169, ⓦwww.matailodge.co.nz; dorms ❶, rooms ❷); now combined with the *YHA* next door and offering various extras including transport and tours. Good budget beds can also be found at the *Alpine Motel Lodge*, 7 Miro St (☎ & ℱ06/385 8758, ⓦwww.alpinemotel .co.nz; dorms ❶, rooms ❷, units & chalets ❹), with basic four-share dorms and rooms, and some nicer studio units and fully self-contained chalets, all with access to Sky TV, a spa and drying room. For B&B try the basic but cosy *Penguins*, 56 Goldfield St (☎ & ℱ06/385 9411, ✉douglas.richard@xtra.co.nz; ❹), which has a shared bathroom and separate guest lounge; or the very tasteful and amiable *Whare Ora*, 14 Kaha St (☎ & ℱ06/385 9385, ✉whareora@xtra.co.nz; ❼–❽), 6km east in the village of Rangataua, with two rooms (one with spa bath and both with diverting modern art works), a lounge with unsurpassed mountain views, and delicious dinners available on request ($70 per person with wine, book in advance).

Campers have a choice of the *Ohakune Top 10 Holiday Park*, 5 Moore St (☎ & ℱ06/385 8561, ⓦ www.ohakune.net.nz; camping $12, cabins & kitchen cabins ❷, motel units ❸–❹), right on the edge of the bush but still central, and DOC's toilets-and-water *Mangawhero Campsite* ($4), 1.5km up Ohakune Mountain Road from the field centre.

Eating, drinking and nightlife

During the ski season, Ohakune Junction is very much the happening place to spend your evenings. In summer though, when hardly any of the half-dozen restaurants, bars and clubs bother to open, you're better off in **central Ohakune**, where the tastiest meals are served at the daytime *Utopia*, 47 Clyde St, an ideal spot for idling away an hour or two over great coffee and sumptuous all-day brunches; you might even catch them open in the evening, but don't bank on it. Other good bets are succulent gourmet kebabs from *Mountain Kebabs*, 29 Clyde St (winter only), where chicken, lamb, seafood and vegetarian fillings are doused with a stack of tasty sauces; and *O Bar and Restaurant*, 72 Clyde St, inside the Ohakune Country Hotel, a kind of upscale bar with pool table, roaring fire in winter and an extensive range of $15–25 dishes including pizza, steaks and Thai curry. Alternatively, try the *Mountain Rocks*, 53 Clyde St, a newish café-bar offering good beer and value-for-money grub.

At the **Ohakune Junction**, the *Powderhorn Chateau* harbours two restaurants: the excellent fine-dining *Matterhorn* (☎06/385 8888), serving large mains at $25–30, including salmon teriyaki, venison steaks and rosemary smothered lamb shanks; and the more modest *Powderkeg* brasserie/bar, which serves full bar meals in winter, when you'll need to fight for a prized place on the balcony (they don't take bookings). Next door, the *Fat Pigeon Garden Café*, Mangawhero Terrace, serves excellent café-style meals and coffee, in summer is often only open weekends, but suffers from an owner with a short fuse. In winter, *Margarita's*, 5 Rimu St, do warming and tasty enchiladas, tostadas and other Tex-Mex favourites, and the *Hot Lava* bar, kicks up a storm until the early hours.

Summer activities

Unlike at Whakapapa, the Turoa chairlifts rarely run outside the ski season, but the 17km Ohakune Mountain Road makes an impressive drive through stands of ancient rimu and provides access to a number of fine **walks**, including the Round the Mountain track (see p.357). The pick of the shorter trails are: the **Mangawhero Forest Walk** (3km return; 1hr), a short and well-marked loop track from opposite the DOC field centre; the **Waitonga Falls Walk** (4km return; 1hr 10min) to a spectacular waterfall, starting 11km up the Mountain Road; and the hike to **Lake Surprise** (12km return; 5hr), an undulating route along the Round the Mountain track to a shallow lake which starts from the 15km mark on Ohakune Mountain Road and passes evidence of volcanic debris which swept down the mountain during the 1975 and 1995 eruptions.

All the walking tracks, and any inside the bounds of the national park, are off-limits for **mountain biking**, but you can coast 17km down Ohakune Mountain Road on The Ohakune Mountain Ride, 16 Miro St (Nov–June; around $30; ☎06/385 8257), or rent a bike (see p.361) and head 12km east to the forest roads around Rangataua; consult DOC or the visitor centre for more details.

A less arduous approach is to let **horses** take the strain at *Ruapehu Homestead*, 4km east on SH49 (☎06/385 8799), which runs back-country trail rides through bush and rivers (2hr; $40), as well as easier trips for the less experienced.

The Desert Road and Waiouru

South of Turangi, and past the trout hatchery, SH1 sticks to the east of the Tongariro National Park running roughly parallel to the Tongariro River. This is the eerily scenic **Desert Road** (SH1), which climbs up over an exposed and barren plateau. This isn't a true desert (the rainfall is too high), but it's about as near as you'll get anywhere in New Zealand. Road cuttings reveal the cause as they slice through several metres of volcanic ash – a timeline of past eruptions – that's so free-draining that any vegetation struggles to take hold.

Initially you're deep in pine forest with side roads periodically ducking off to the east and the assortment of hydro-electric tunnels, intakes and tailraces of the Tongariro River. Some 9km south of Turangi, Kaimanawa Road runs 2km down to the river and beyond to a good free camping area by a stream (best found in daylight). After crossing the river, keep left on a tarmac road following signs to Waihaha Valley. The site is 500m back from the substation at the end of the road. A further 5km south along SH1, Tree Trunk Gorge Road leads again to the Tongariro River at a spot where it squeezes through a narrow fissure known as **Tree Trunk Gorge**.

Back on the highway you soon climb out of the forest for great views of the three volcanoes off to the west and the blasted territory ahead. It is a dramatic scene, somehow made even more elemental by the three lines of electricity pylons striding off across the bleak tussock towards Waiouru.

Waiouru and the Army Museum

The Desert Road and the roads flanking the western side of Ruapehu, Ngauruhoe and Tongariro meet at **WAIOURU**, an uninspiring row of service stations and tearooms perched 800m above sea level on the bleak tussock plain beside New Zealand's major **army base**. The serene view of the mountains from here can be fabulous but the peace is often disturbed by troop movements and even target practice.

The place to take cover is in the three concrete bunkers of the **QEII Army Memorial Museum** (daily 9am–4.30pm; $10), a showcase of national military heritage from the New Zealand Wars through the Anglo–Boer and two World Wars to New Zealand's involvement in Vietnam. Mannequins in regimental regalia set in lifeless dioramas do little to prepare you for the impact of the *Roimata Pounamu* ("Tears on Greenstone") **wall of remembrance**, where a veil of tears symbolizes mourning and cleansing as it streams down a curving bank of heavily veined greenstone tiles while the name, rank and place of death of each of the 33,000 New Zealanders who have died in the various wars is recited. A twenty-minute audio-visual presentation sets the scene for the rest of the chronologically arranged exhibits, which are brought to life by oral histories, including some heart-rending ones that recount the bungled Gallipoli campaign of World War I. The emphasis is small-scale and personal: one particularly affecting case contains artefacts made by soldiers in the trenches – cribbage boards, chess sets and a cigarette holder that completely encased the cigarette so it could be smoked at night without risk of the enemy seeing the telltale glow.

The *Rations* **café**, inside the Army Museum, is as good as any hereabouts. Should you need to **stay**, try the budget *Oasis Hotel and Motel*, SH1 (T & F 06/387 6779; ③–④), with mostly twin rooms and some motel units.

Taihape and around

Continuing south along SH1, you descend from the volcanic plateau into the **Rangitikei District**, with the Rangitikei River never far away, though seldom seen as its waters have carved through the soft young rock, to leave off-white cliffs as the only evidence of the river's course. This is prime farming country, where the pastoral nature of the region is reflected in the character of the region's largest town, **Taihape** (30km south of Waiouru) an agricultural service centre of only passing interest, though it works well enough as a base for some superb whitewater rafting, a bungy jump and some fine gardens. Taihape promotes itself "New Zealand's one and only Gumboot City", something it showcases each year on Labour Day in late October with **Gumboot Day**, a tongue-in-cheek celebration of this archetypal Kiwi footwear that culminates in a gumboot-throwing competition.

Most people hurry on by but if you fancy a bite to eat, Taihape has the best **eating** on SH1 between Taupo and Wellington. The main contenders here are: *The Venison Kitchen*, 65b Hautapu St, which claims to be the only farmed venison café in the country, and serves it in burgers, souvlaki and pies for under $10, closed Wednesday; the cottagey but expensive *Brown Sugar Café*, Huia St (℡06/388 1880), which serves excellent light meals, as well as dinner on Friday and Saturday evenings (booking advisable); and the more modern *Café Exchange,* Huia St (℡06/388 0599), which has a good deli selection. **Places to stay** include the rock-bottom rooms at the *Gretna Hotel*, corner of SH1 and Hautapu St (℡06/388 0638; dorms ❶, rooms ❷); units at the *Safari Motel*, SH1, 1km north (℡0800/200 046, ℻06/388 1116; ❹); and hilltop homestay at *Korirata*, 25 Pukeko St (℡ & ℻06/388 0315, ✉korirata @xtra.co.nz; ❹), which has great views over Taihape and Mount Ruapehu.

Activities

Driving through Taihape, there is little to suggest that the hilly country to the east hides one of New Zealand's most thrilling whitewater-rafting trips and the North Island's highest bungy jump.

The Grade V gorge section of the **Rangitikei River** is one of the toughest regularly used sections of **whitewater-rafting** river in the country. Ten major rapids are packed into the 2–3hr run. Operators will take first-timers, but novices can make it safer for everyone if they choose to raft elsewhere first. Trips on the Rangitikei are run from Mangaweka (see opposite), or more directly from *River Valley Venture*, Pukoekahu (℡06/388 1444, ⓦwww.river-valley.co.nz; ❶–❸), a mostly backpacker-oriented complex well-sited right by the Rangitikei at the pull-out point for the rafting trips some 30km east of Taihape. Morning, and occasionally afternoon, trips ($109) are run throughout the year, though when water levels are low, rafts are replaced by paddle-yourself one-person inflatable kayaks (also $109) launched in convoy with guides helping out the more tentative paddlers. *River Valley* also offer scenic rafting ($109; 5hr) down the quieter Grade II section immediately downstream of the lodge, **kayaking** ($109 same trip), **horse trekking** ($50 for 2hr), **mountain biking** ($35 per day), **abseiling** down a 40m cliff ($25) and 9-hole **pitch-and-putt** ($11).

Customers, many of them from the Kiwi Experience buses which call nightly, typically stay in sixteen-bunk or slightly pricier six-berth dorms (❶), pleasant double or twin rooms (❸), camping ($10), or ten-minutes up the road in shearers' quarters nicely converted into a self-contained house (❶). Straightforward low-cost meals are served and there's a bar on site.

If you are an adventure seeker get a detailed map and follow the backroads from *River Valley* to *Gravity Canyon*, or alternatively turn off SH1 at Uhutu, 7km south of Taihape, and follow the signs 15km east. Here you'll find an

80m **bungy jump** ($99; booking advisible; ☏06/388 910900, Ⓦwww
.gravitycanyon.co.nz) and the longest and fastest **Flying Fox** in New Zealand
(170m high, 1km long, $90, combo deals available) both of which have a
unique and rather pleasant water-powered lift to get you back to jumping-off
height. You jump from a bridge over Rangitikei River far below or you fly
from a specially built platform.

Mangaweka

The brightly-painted form of a DC3 airplane beside SH1, 24km south of
Taihape, is about the only indication that there might be a reason to stop in the
dilapidated hamlet of **MANGAWEKA**, scattered across a plain high above the
Rangitikei River. The *DC3 Café* is cheap, basic and an obvious lure, but there
is more of interest at the adjacent service station, from where the Manaweka
Adventure Company (☏ & Ⓕ06/382 5747, Ⓦwww.rra.co.nz) operate **whitewater rafting** down the Grade V Mokai Gorge ($134 or $120 for a full day
on the Rangitekei), along with more family-oriented fun rafting down a gentle
stretch of the river (1hr $30, half-day $55). From here it is 60km to Bulls (see
p.289), with little to see in between.

Travel details

Trains

From National Park to: Auckland (2 daily; 5hr
30min); Ohakune (2 daily; 30min); Palmerston
North (2 daily; 3hr 30min); Waiouru (2 daily; 1hr);
Wellington (2 daily; 5hr 30min).
From Ohakune to: Auckland (2 daily; 6hr);
Wellington (2 daily; 5hr).

Buses

From Kawerau to: Rotorua (2 daily; 45min);
Whakatane (2 daily; 45 min).
From National Park to: Auckland (1 daily; 5hr
30min); Ohakune (1 daily; 30min); Wellington (1
daily; 5hr 40min).
From Ohakune to: Auckland (1 daily; 6hr);
Wellington (1 daily; 5hr 15min).
From Rotorua to: Auckland (8 daily; 4hr);
Gisborne (1 daily; 4hr 30min); Hamilton (8 daily;
1hr 45min); Kawerau (2 daily; 45min); Opotiki (1
daily; 2hr 10min); Palmerston North (2 daily; 5hr
30min); Taupo (4 daily; 1hr); Tauranga (4 daily; 1hr
30min); Waitomo (2 daily; 2hr–2hr 30min);

Whakatane (2 daily; 1hr 30min).
From Taihape to: Auckland (3 daily; 6hr 30min);
Taupo (3 daily; 2hr); Turangi (3 daily; 1hr 10min);
Wellington (3 daily; 4hr).
From Taupo to: Auckland (4 daily; 4–5hr);
Hamilton (3 daily; 2hr 30min); Hastings (3 daily;
2hr 30min); Napier (3 daily; 2hr); Palmerston
North (3 daily; 3hr 30min); Rotorua (4 daily; 1hr);
Taihape (3 daily; 2hr); Tauranga (4 daily; 2hr
30min); Turangi (3 daily; 45min); Wellington (3
daily; 6hr).
From Tokoroa to: Hamilton (2 daily; 1hr 45min);
Taupo (2 daily; 45min).
From Turangi to: The Chateau (4 daily; 1hr).

Flights

From Rotorua to: Auckland (5 daily; 45min);
Christchurch (2 daily; 1hr 15min); Wellington (5
daily; 1hr 10min).
From Taupo to: Auckland (2 daily; 50min);
Wellington (3 daily; 1hr).

The Coromandel, Bay of Plenty and the East Coast

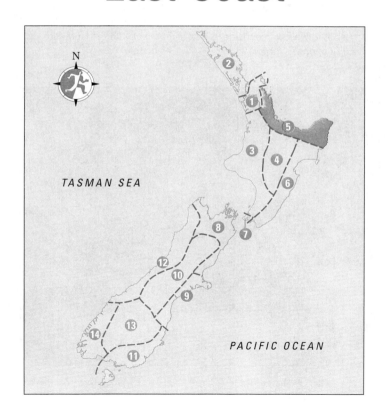

N

TASMAN SEA

PACIFIC OCEAN

CHAPTER 5

Highlights

5

* **Coromandel Peninsula** Untouched beaches, rich bush and a slow pace lull you into Peninsular time. See p.376

* **Driving Creek Railway** This modern narrow-gauge line climbs high through the bush for long coastal views. See p.386

* **Hot Water Beach** Grab a shovel and stake your spot to wallow in surfside hot springs. See p.395

* **Dolphin Swimming** There's always a high success rate in the waters off Whakatane. See p.419

* **White Island** Visit the otherworldly moonscape and sulphur deposits of New Zealand's most active volcano. See p.420

* **The East Coast** Rugged, isolated and solidly Maori, this is where you come to connect with the land and its people. See p.425

△ Coromandel Peninsula

The Coromandel, Bay of Plenty and the East Coast

The long coastal sweep to the east of Auckland is split into three distinct areas, among them two of the most popular summer-holiday destinations on the North Island; the other is one of the least-visited parts of the country, whatever the time of year. Heading east from Auckland by road you'll first cut across at least a portion of the **Hauraki Plains**, a wedge of dairy country at the foot of the Coromandel Peninsula with a few pleasant surprises for anyone willing to dawdle for a day or so. In the spa town of **Te Aroha** you can languish in a private soda bath, while at nearby **Paeroa** there are pleasant walks in the lush **Karangahake Gorge**, once the scene of intensive gold mining.

Directly across the Hauraki Gulf from Auckland, the long and jagged **Coromandel Peninsula** is blessed with some of the country's best sandy beaches and a gorgeous climate. But if this conjures up images of overcrowding and overdevelopment, think again. This is a place of great coastal scenery, solitude, walks to pristine beaches, and tramps in luxuriant mountainous rainforest. Its two coasts are markedly different, the east supplying the softer, more idyllic tourist beaches and short coastal walks; the west having a far more rugged and atmospheric coastline, plus easier access to the volcanic hills and ancient kauri trees of the **Coromandel Forest Park**. All this countryside is best explored from bases such as **Thames**, a small town rich in gold-mining history, or tiny **Coromandel**, set in rolling hills beside an attractive harbour. The principal towns in the east are **Whangamata** and **Whitianga**, both blessed with long, luxurious, sandy beaches. The latter is also handy for **Hot Water Beach**, where natural thermal springs bubble up through the sand lapped by the Pacific Ocean, and for **Cathedral Cove Marine Reserve**, ideal for dolphin spotting and snorkelling.

From the open-cast gold-mining town of **Waihi** at the base of the Coromandel Peninsula, the **Bay of Plenty** sweeps south and east to Opotiki, punctuated by an outstanding sequence of golden beaches and great surf, and traced along its length by the Pacific Coast Highway (SH2), which links

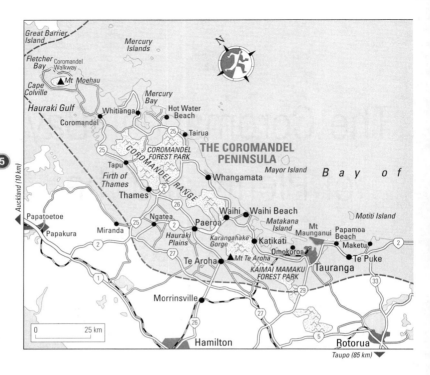

Auckland with Gisborne. The bay earned its name from **Captain Cook**, who sailed in on the *Endeavour* in 1769 and was struck by the number of thriving Maori settlements living off the abundant resources, as well as by the generous supplies they gave him. This era of peace and plenty was shattered by the **New Zealand Wars** of the 1860s, as fierce fighting led to the establishment of garrisons at both Tauranga and Whakatane, and the easternmost town of Opotiki gained notoriety as the scene of the death of a European missionary – allegedly murdered by a Maori prophet.

The Bay of Plenty has the best climate on the North Island, making it a fertile fruit-growing region (particularly citrus and kiwifruit) and another much-visited holiday area. The coast, though popular with Kiwi holidaymakers, has remained relatively unspoiled, offering great surf beaches and a good variety of offshore activities. On top of that, the region is home to one of the country's fastest-growing urban areas, centred on modern, vigorous **Tauranga** and the contiguous beach town of **Mount Maunganui**.

The eastern Bay of Plenty revolves around sunny **Whakatane**, primarily of interest for boat excursions to the fuming, volcanic **White Island**, opportunities to swim with dolphins, and as a base for wilderness rafting on the remote **Motu River**.

Contrasting with these two regions is the splendid, rugged and isolated **East Coast**, once a wealthy part of New Zealand but today run-down and sparsely populated. But with a dramatic coastline, and a rich and varied Maori history, this hospitable region provides a taste of a secluded way of life long gone in the rest of the country. At its easternmost point – the **East Cape** – is a lighthouse

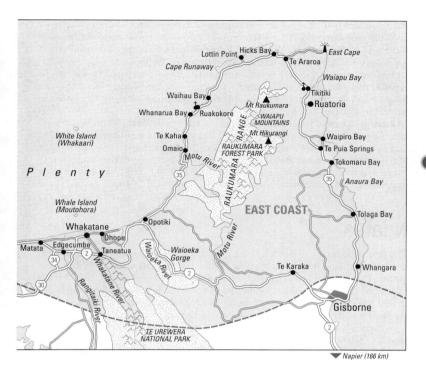

Napier (166 km)

that overlooks East Island, the first place in the country to see the sunrise. All of the region's small communities, each with its own distinctive personality, are dotted along the coastline – against the dramatic backdrop of the **Waiapu Mountains**.

The Hauraki Plains

Approach the Coromandel Peninsula from the west and you can't help but pass through at least a part of the fertile **Hauraki Plains**, a wedge of former swamp at the peninsula's southern end. It's bordered to the north by the Firth of Thames, final destination for a number of meandering rivers, which drain this sweep of rich pastoral farmland. Attractions are admittedly limited, and most people rush through on their way to the scenic splendour to the north and further east, missing out on at least a couple of sights worth a minor detour.

Journeying southeast from Auckland on SH2 you'll first strike the tiny settlement of **Ngatea**, worth a fleeting visit for the curiosity value of a warehouse crammed with rock crystals. The hub of the plains is **Paeroa**, not much in itself, but handy for the scenic **Karangahake Gorge**, which runs from Paeroa to Waihi (see opposite). This leafy landscape contains a few good walks along the banks of the rushing Ohinemuri River and past the skeletal remains of old gold workings, plus a short scenic train journey to Waihi.

However, the real jewel hereabouts is the Edwardian small town of **Te Aroha**, tucked away at the southern extremity of the plains, where you can hike Mount Te Aroha for breathtaking views, returning to soak your bones in natural hot springs of soda water.

Getting around the Plains by public transport isn't too difficult with InterCity running two or three services a day from Auckland through Paeroa and the Karangahake Gorge to Waihi and Tauranga. Supa Travel (☎07/571 0583) operate between Auckland and Paeroa once daily except Saturday. Te Aroha is out on a limb but Turley-Murphy (☎07/884 8208) run a service once daily between Hamilton and Thames via Te Aroha and Paeroa.

Ngatea

The first settlement you'll reach heading southeast on SH2 is tiny **NGATEA**, set amid green rolling hills 70km from Auckland. The only attraction is **Wilderness Gems**, 13 River Rd (daily 9am–5pm; free; ⓦ www.wildgems.co.nz), 200m off the main road and signposted just before the river bridge. It is essentially a warehouse stuffed with rock crystals from around New Zealand and all over the world. Petrified wood, agates and rose quartz compete for space with jewellery crafted from carved jade and bone, and geodes sliced to reveal the hollow crystalline interior. The best examples are just for display but some pretty snazzy specimens are available for as little as $3 – and as much as $3000. You can catch a glimpse of the cutting and polishing operation through a window, or press on to the small dark Fluorescent Room, where a five-minute programme illustrates how a range of minerals react to UV light, vibrantly glowing.

From here the highway continues to Paeroa, where you can branch off on SH26 northwards to the Coromandel Peninsula or southwards to Te Aroha.

Paeroa

Continuing 25km southeast from Ngatea on SH2 you reach the small and rather dreary **PAEROA**, which briefly became a significant port during the early gold-mining days when boats from Auckland could go no further up the Ohinemuri River.

To Kiwis, Paeroa is simply the birthplace of **Lemon and Paeroa** (L & P), a homegrown soft-drink that still holds its own against international competition, despite substituting the original natural mineral water – discovered here in the nineteenth century – with water from an Auckland bottling plant. Undaunted by this harsh reality, a giant brown L & P bottle stands at the junction of SH2 and SH26, greeting those arriving from the south, and Paeroa gets as much mileage as it can from the drink's promotional catchphrase "World Famous in New Zealand".

On Paeroa's main thoroughfare, Belmont Road, the limited **Paeroa Museum**, at no. 37 (Mon–Fri 10.30am–3pm; $2), neatly covers the town's history, early shipping and gold mining in the Karangahake Gorge. Of particular interest is a huge collection of Royal Albert bone china, while among the few

Maori artefacts is a stack of collection drawers containing tools and ornaments: stone adzes, cutting tools, bone fish-hooks and carved *tiki* (pendants).

Practicalities

Paeroa's **main street**, Belmont Road (SH2), runs south through town before becoming Normanby Road; the town centre is concentrated into a small area wedged between the Domain and the junction with SH26. Supa Travel **buses** stop at the *L & P Café* on the corner of Taylor Avenue and Seymour Street. InterCity, Guthreys and Turley-Murphy buses stop outside the **visitor centre**, 1 Belmont Rd (Oct–April Mon–Fri 9am–5pm, Sat & Sun 10am–3pm; May–Sept Mon–Fri 9am–5pm; ☏07/862 8636, ⓦwww.paeroa.org.nz), which takes bookings for all the buses, is well stocked with bumph on the Coromandel Peninsula and sells cans of L & P. **Internet access** is at the library on the corner of Belmont Road and William Street (Mon–Thurs 10.30am–4.30pm, Fri 10am–5.30pm, Sat 10am–noon).

There are a couple of reasonable **places to stay**, including the wooden, nineteenth-century *Criterion Hotel*, on the corner of Normanby Road and Te Aroha Road (☏ & ⓕ07/862 7983; single rooms \$25, ❷), where all double rooms are en suite. There's little to choose between the motels, but you could try the pleasant *Racecourse Motel*, 68 Thames Rd (☏07/862 7145, ⓕ862 7131; ❹), 1km north of town along SH26.

Café culture has come to Paeroa in the form of the *Lazy Fish*, 56 Belmont Rd, opposite Hughenden Street (summer daily; June–Oct Wed–Sun; licensed & BYO), so you can **eat** well on Mediterranean-inspired mains for lunch and dinner, or just grab a coffee and muffin. Otherwise, you're limited to fairly standard cafés such as the big *L & P Café*, on the corner of Taylor Avenue and Seymour Street, near the visitor centre, which is open from breakfast through to dinner, for the likes of pizzas and burgers.

The Karangahake Gorge

Paeroa visitors bound for the Coromandel Peninsula should still take time to explore the leafy tranquillity of the magnificent **Karangahake Gorge** immediately east of Paeroa. This was the scene of the Coromandel's first gold rush, in 1875, where independent miners, armed only with picks and sluice pans, were quickly superseded by large companies that could afford the powerful equipment needed to extract the metal. Today it's hard to envisage such frenetic activity in this scenic spot. The steep-sided gorge begins 8km east of Paeroa along the narrow, snaking continuation of SH2 as it traces the Ohinemuri River to Waihi. The **Karangahake Gorge Historic Walkway** (described in a \$1 leaflet available from the Paeroa visitor centre) covers 7km of a former rail line and is accessed from several points along the gorge, the best being the **Karangahake Reserve**, at the start of the gorge. Here a pedestrian suspension bridge crosses the river to join a **loop walk** (3km; 1hr), which heads upstream beside the Ohinemuri River past remnants of the gold workings and into the Karangahake Gorge, hugging the cliffs and winding through regenerating native bush. The loop is completed by crossing the river and walking right through a 1km-long tunnel (usually lit). This walk encircles the site of the Karangahake township, now reduced to the reliable *Talisman Café* on the main road, and the *Ohinemuri Estate Winery and Café*, Moresby St (☏07/862 8874, ⓔohinemuri.wines@paradise.net.nz), which has a delightful courtyard where you can sample the wines and tuck into well-prepared café fare (summer daily; winter Fri–Sun). On fine Sunday afternoons in summer there's a classical guitarist on duty, and you can **stay** in a smart, self-contained apartment for four built into the hayloft (❺ plus $10 per extra person).

At the eastern end of the gorge, the tiny village of **WAIKINO** comprises little more than a train station, the western terminus for the Goldfields Railway (see p.401), running three trains daily to Waihi and back. Inside are displays on local history and walks in the area, as well as the daytime *Waikino Station Café*, with outdoor seating on the platform.

Heading south from here, Waitawheta Camp Road runs for 8km along the rugged **Waitawheta Valley** to a trailhead for hikes into the scenic **Kaimai-Mamaku Forest Park**. Tracks follow old logging routes and rivers through a diverse mix of regenerating bush and podocarp forest, some of which are described in DOC's *Kaimai-Mamaku Forest Park Day Walks* leaflet ($1), and others in *Kaimai-Mamaku Forest Park Long Walks* leaflet ($1).

Te Aroha

On the fringes of the Hauraki Plains, 21km south of Paeroa on SH26, the town of **TE AROHA** is not really on the way to anywhere, despite its status as New Zealand's only intact **Edwardian spa**. It benefits from relative obscurity, and those prepared to make the journey for a peaceful day-trip are rewarded with a neat little town hunkered beneath the imposing bush-clad slopes of the **Kaimai-Mamaku Forest Park**. The 954-metre **Mount Te Aroha** rears up

Walks in and around Te Aroha

The most rewarding of Te Aroha's **walks** is undoubtedly the ascent of **Mount Te Aroha**, which tops out on the crest of the Kaimai Range to give sweeping views to the Bay of Plenty and, on exceptionally clear days, across to mounts Ruapehu and Taranaki. The **Te Aroha Mountain Track** (8km return; 4hr; 950m ascent), starts from just behind the Mokena Geyser in the Domain and climbs steeply through native bush, zigzagging up a well-defined path to a viewing platform at **Whakapipi** (or Bald Spur), before dipping to a small saddle. From here, the final climb (which can be muddy and slippery after rain) becomes increasingly arduous, and you'll need to use your hands to pull yourself up in places, but the stunning views make it all worthwhile. To return, follow the **Tui Mine Track**, which drops through a stark, heavily mined landscape to link with the Tui Road back to town in one direction, and with the **Tui–Domain Track** in the other, a pleasant bushwalk past a waterfall back to the Domain. If the thought of an uphill slog right to the top is too much, the **sector** as far as the **Whakapipi Lookout** (2km; 50min) gives good views over the town and its surroundings. These walks and others are listed in the *Te Aroha and Waiorongomai Walks* leaflet ($2) from the Te Aroha visitor centre.

Other walks of varied grades and duration lie south of Te Aroha in the **Waiorongomai Valley**, part of the **Kaimai-Mamaku Forest Park**. Formerly the scene of intense mining activity, several tracks following historic miners' trails are described in the leaflet *Guide to the Waiorongomai Valley* ($2.50), available from Te Aroha visitor centre (see p.376). Access is from a car park on the Waiorongomai Loop Road, which is signposted 4km south of town off the Te Aroha Gordon Road – but note that this is an extremely rugged area punctuated by old mines and shafts that are dangerous to enter. **Overnight hikes** should only be attempted by experienced, fit and well-equipped trampers; hut tickets ($5) can be bought from the visitor centre in Te Aroha.

immediately behind the town centre, providing a reasonably challenging goal for determined hikers, while gentler pursuits await in the hot **soda baths**.

The town itself was founded in 1880 at the furthest navigable extent of the Waihou River and the following year rich deposits of gold were found on Mount Te Aroha, sparking a full-scale **gold rush**, with the gold-bearing quartz producing handsome yields until 1921. Within a few months of settlement, the new townsfolk set out the attractive Hot Springs Domain around a cluster of soda springs which, by the 1890s, became New Zealand's most popular mineral spa complex, frequently compared with those of Vichy or Baden. People flocked to enjoy the therapeutic benefits of its waters and enclosures were erected for privacy, most rebuilt in grand style during the Edwardian years of the early twentieth century. The fine suite of original buildings has been beautifully restored and integrated with more modern pools fed by the hot soda springs. Perhaps the only drawback to time spent here is the strong and biting winds that assault the town from time to time.

The Town

Te Aroha's centrepiece is the **Hot Springs Domain** at the southern end of town on Whitaker Street, a 44-acre **thermal reserve** of formal gardens and rose beds. The baths are well signposted and a slightly smoky smell emanates from the modern **Spa Baths** complex (daily 10am–10pm; 30min: Mon–Fri, $10–12, Sat & Sun $15; book ahead at weekends ☏07/884 8717), which comprises five private, enclosed pools, each with hydro-therapeutic water jets. Choose a stainless steel one if you fancy adding aromatherapy oils; otherwise the wooden tubs are bigger and more comfy. A half-hour soak is plenty, said to extract polluting heavy metals from your system. Shower first to open up your pores and be sure to drink plenty of water during and after your soak, to help counteract the dehydrating effects of the mineral-rich water. The soda water keeps working on you afterwards so don't shower a second time. If you'd prefer more space, book the private 3-metre-long **No. 2 Bathhouse** (daily 11am–7pm; same prices as Spa Baths), opened in 1900 as one of the original communal bathhouses. It is contained in the nearby outdoor **Wyborn Leisure Pool** complex ($5 entry if you want to swim too). The bath house is usually heated to 40°C and can be booked by one person or a couple, even though it takes sixteen people.

You can indulge in more holistic **therapy** at Te Aroha Massage and Natural Therapies, on the corner of Whitaker Street and Burgess Street (Mon–Sat; ☏07/884 6620 & 025/265 0694), who charge $20–25 for 30min.

Just uphill from the baths is the erratic **Mokena Geyser**, which spurts to impressive heights on good days, going off roughly every half-hour. From here, a **trail** (see p.374) leads to the top of **Mount Te Aroha** which, legend has it, was named by a young Arawa chief, Kahumatamomoe, who climbed it after losing his way in the region's vast swamp while on his way home to Maketu in the Bay of Plenty. Delighted to see the familiar shoreline of his homeland, he called the mountain *Te Aroha*, meaning "love", in honour of his father and kinsmen.

An old sanatorium, just below the spa baths and in front of the croquet lawn, houses the town **museum** (Dec–March Sat, Sun & public holidays 11am–4pm; April–Nov Sat, Sun & public holidays 1–4pm; donation). It comprises three exhibit-packed rooms and two finely decorated Royal Doulton Victorian lavatories. Highlights are a collection of black-and-white photos of the town and its people, a chemical analysis of the local soda water, and memorabilia of an old silent movie called *Tilly of Te Aroha*, made when the film industry was in its infancy, and a racy picture for its time.

By the Boundary Street exit from the Domain you'll find the 1926 **St Mark's Anglican Church**, on the corner of Church Street and Kenrick Street, insignificant but for the incongruously sited 1712 organ, said to be the oldest in the southern hemisphere. Built in England by Renatus Harris, it is the sole survivor of ten made after Queen Anne petitioned Parliament to raise taxes in order that the finest pipe organs of the day might be installed in ten London churches. Brought to New Zealand in 1926, this particular organ was restored in 1985 by an Auckland firm who found that part of the finely carved, English heart-oak casework predates the organ and probably came from the famed Grinling Gibbons's workshop. If you can get a group of six or more together and are prepared to make a small donation, an organ recital can be arranged through the visitor centre.

Practicalities

The town's main street is Whitaker Street and everything of interest – banks, post office, library – is either along it or close by: the **visitor centre** (Oct–March Mon–Fri 9.30am–5pm, Sat & Sun 9.30am–4pm; April–Sept Mon–Fri 9.30am–4.30pm, Sat & Sun 10am–3pm; ☎07/884 8052, ⊛www .tearoha-info.co.nz) is at 102 Whitaker St by the entrance to the Domain, and has DOC information for the local area. There's **Internet access** at the library (Mon & Tues, Thurs & Fri 9am–5pm, Wed 10am–5pm, Sat 9am–1pm).

For a small place, Te Aroha has a reasonable choice of **accommodation**. The small *YHA* on Miro St, off Brick Street (☎07/884 8739, ⊜tearoha.yha@xtra.co.nz; dorms ❶, room ❷), is one of the simplest in New Zealand, about ten minutes' walk from the visitor centre in a wooden cottage on the lower slopes of Mount Te Aroha, with good views. Beside the Domain is the *Te Aroha Motel*, at 108 Whitaker St (☎07/884 9417; ⊜tearohamotel@xtra.co.nz; ❹), with functional, well-kept units. Campers should head 4km out on the road to Hamilton (SH26) to the *Te Aroha Holiday Park*, 217 Stanley Road South (☎07/884 9567, ⊛www.tearoha-info.co.nz/holidaypark; tent sites $10, on-site vans ❷, cabins & flats ❸), set among well-established oak trees.

Two cosmopolitan **cafés** vie for your business: the atmospheric *Café Banco*, 174 Whitaker St, occupies a former bank and serves breakfast, lunch and dinner (mains around $25) using plenty of organic produce (closed Mon & Tues plus Sun eve in winter); the café bar *Ironique*, corner Whitaker Street and Kenrick Street, does good coffee, snacks and evening meals in a place where black iron is used to imaginative effect. Simpler yet reliable food is on offer at the bistro in *The Grand Tavern*, on the corner of Whitaker Street and Rolleston Street. The low-key *Mokena Restaurant*, in a rambling old wooden hotel at 6 Church St (☎07/884 8038; licensed), is a big hit with locals, offering evening **smorgasbords** (Fri–Sun from 6pm; $28; best to book ahead) of fresh, home-cooked fare.

The Coromandel Peninsula

Auckland's Hauraki Gulf is separated from the Pacific Ocean by the long, broad thumb of the **Coromandel Peninsula**, a mountainous and bush-cloaked

PACIFIC OCEAN

Mercury Islands

Fletcher Bay

Cape Colville
Port Jackson
Poley Bay
Coromandel Walkway
Stony Bay
Port Charles

Fantail Bay
Mt Moehau 892m
Port Jackson Rd

Waikawau Bay
Little Bay

Colville

Colville Road

Kennedy Bay

New Chums Bay
Whangapoua
Matarangi
Kuaotunu

Driving Creek Railway
Te Rerenga

HAURAKI GULF

Coromandel

Castle Rock 521m

Waiau Waterworks

Mercury Bay

CATHEDRAL COVE MARINE RESERVE

Waiau Falls
Whitianga

Cathedral Cove

Kauri Grove

309 Road

Cooks Beach
Hahei

Hot Water Beach

Manaia

Kereta
25

Whenuakite

Coroglen
25

Tapu

COROMANDEL RANGE

Rapaura Water Gardens
Square Kauri

COROMANDEL FOREST PARK
The Pinnacles 759m

Tairua
Pauanui

Firth of Thames

Kauaeranga Valley
Broken Hills

Hikuai

Opoutere

Thames

Miranda

Kopu
25A

25
Pipiroa

Whangamata

Ngatea
2

Waihou River

Wentworth Falls
Wentworth Valley
25

COROMANDEL FOREST PARK

N

Hauraki Plains

27
26

Paeroa

Waihi
Waihi Beach

Karangahake Gorge
Waikino
2

KAIMAI-MAMAKU FOREST PARK

0   25 km

▼ Te Aroha (10 km)   ▼ Tauranga (57 km)

interior fringed with beautiful surf and swimming beaches, all basking in a balmy climate. Although the genuine sights are few, there's no denying the allure of a relaxing few days spent exploring or just lazing on a beach. Allow at least a couple of days here.

The peninsula's two coasts are starkly different. In the **west**, cliffs and steep hills drop sharply to the sea leaving only a narrow coastal strip shaded by **pohutukawa** trees, which erupt in a blaze of rich red from mid-November to December. The beaches are sheltered, safe and ripe for exploration, but most are only good for **swimming** when high tide obscures the mud flats. Except for the attraction of a couple of interesting small west-coast towns, most people prefer the **east coast**, a land of sweeping white-sand beaches pounded by impressive but often perilous **surf**. This is where Kiwis flock for long weekends and summer holidays, and the more fashionable beaches are lined with holiday homes. Increasingly people are finding ways to live here permanently, and one-time *baches* are being replaced by million-dollar beach-front properties.

Elsewhere on the peninsula low property prices in declining former gold towns, combined with the wonderful juxtaposition of bush, hills and beaches, have exerted a powerful effect on hippies, **artists** and New Agers. Keep your eyes peeled and you'll spot folk eking out a living from the land, running holistic healing centres and holding retreats. Less vigilance is required to find painters, potters and **craftspeople**, many of them very good, often hawking the fruits of their labours from their homes and studios. The free and widely available *Coromandel Craft Trail* leaflet details thirty or so mostly rural craft outlets all over the peninsula, ranging from silk flowers to bronze and concrete sculpture. As you might imagine, there's plenty of support hereabouts for the Green Party, illustrated by the fact that the Coromandel's Jeanette Fitzsimmons became New Zealand's first elected **Green MP** in 1999.

Maori spirituality is also important in the peninsula. The **Coromandel Range** that runs through the interior – sculpted millions of years ago by volcanic activity into a jagged and contorted skyline, since clothed in dense rainforest – is interpreted as a canoe, with **Mount Moehau** (at the peninsula's northern tip) as its prow, and Mount Te Aroha in the south (bordering the Hauraki Plains) as its sternpost. The **summit** area of Mount Moehau is sacred Maori-owned land, the legendary burial place of Tama Te Kapua, the commander of one of the Great Migration canoes, *Te Arawa*.

Notwithstanding the bohemian flavour and scenic splendour, there's not a great deal to do here, though a few towns warrant attention. At the base of the peninsula, the former gold town of **Thames** exhibits its heritage and makes a good base for exploring the forested **Kauaeranga Valley** with its walking tracks into the steep hills. Further north the lovely little town of **Coromandel** offers the opportunity to ride the narrow-gauge **Driving Creek Railway** and is close to the trans-peninsular **309 Road** where the **Waiau Waterworks** and an impressive stand of **kauri** are the main attractions. For really remote country head up to tiny **Colville** and the peninsula's northern tip, but the sealed highway continues east to **Mercury Bay**, centred on the appealing town of **Whitianga**. Nearby, digging a hole to wallow in surf-side hot springs lures hundreds to **Hot Water Beach**, while brilliant snorkelling and gorgeous bays draw others to the **Cathedral Cove Marine Reserve**. Yet more beaches string the coast further south, some of the best (and most populated) around **Whangamata** and at **Waihi Beach**, the coastal acolyte of **Waihi**, the peninsula's southernmost town, which still produces gold from its open-cast mine.

Peninsula practicalities

As one of the North Island's principal holiday spots, the Coromandel Peninsula becomes the scene of frenetic activity from **Christmas** until the end of January, when finding accommodation can become near impossible – book well ahead. Numbers are more manageable for the rest of the summer, and in **winter** much of the peninsula is deserted, even though the **climate** remains mild for most of the year.

It's easiest to negotiate the Peninsula by **car**. The main roads are mostly sealed, and though many of the more remote stretches are gravel, very few pose any real danger if you take it steadily – even the infamous roads beyond Colville to the northern tip are a lot better than they once were. **Bus** travel is a little more problematic and limiting, but still pretty good. Timetables all but dictate that you cover the peninsula in a clockwise direction, with InterCity providing a regular loop service from Thames, north to Coromandel, across to Whitianga and back south and across to Thames: the **Coromandel Trail** ticket costs $101 and incorporates the fare from Auckland to Rotorua. Go Kiwi (℡0800/446 549 & 07/866 0336) offers a competitive door-to-door service between Whitianga, Tairua, Thames and Auckland, running to Auckland in the morning and back in the afternoon. With limited time an **organized tour** with Kiwi Dundee Adventures (see p.399) is a great way to get a taste of the region.

You can **fly** to the peninsula with Great Barrier Airlines (℡0800/900 600; $99 one way, or $180–190 return), from Auckland to Whitianga via Great Barrier Island two to three times a week, with daily flights between Auckland and Great Barrier Island.

Thames and around

The small and rather dull former gold town of **THAMES** is packed into a coastal strip between the Firth of Thames and the Coromandel Range. It is the peninsula's main service town with a range of accommodation, a few reasonable places to eat, and transport connections for both the immediate surroundings and the rest of the peninsula.

The first big discovery of gold-bearing quartz was made in a Thames creek-bed in 1867, but mining activity tailed off during the 1880s, and little remained after 1913. Nonetheless, the legacy of the **mining** heyday forms the basis of the town's attractions, and you can easily spend half a day visiting them and wandering backstreets liberally dotted with the grand homes of erstwhile owners. Also within easy reach is the **Kauaeranga Valley**, a popular centre for hikers visiting the Coromandel Forest Park and often busy at weekends.

Arrival, information and transport

Combined InterCity/Turley-Murphy and Go Kiwi **buses** drop off all over town, including outside the **visitor centre**, 206 Pollen St (Mon–Fri 8.30am–5pm, Sat & Sun 9am–4pm; ℡07/868 7284, Ⓦwww.thames-info.co.nz), which has stacks of literature on the town and the Coromandel Peninsula (including Hot Water Beach tide times). Pollen Street, the main shopping thoroughfare, is home to what's left of Thames's gold-era hotels, and has a number of **banks**, and the **post office**. Nowhere is far from here,

THAMES

A (1.5 km), **B** (2.5 km), Butterfly & Orchid Garden (2.5 km), Coromandel (55 km) & Whitianga (100 km)

Goldmine Experience

WW1 Memorial & lookout

COROMANDEL FOREST PARK

Mineralogical Museum

Karaka Bird Hide

Pak 'n Save

Goldfields Mall

Firth of Thames

N

Thames Natural Soap Co.

DOC Field Centre & Kauaeranga Valley (13 km)

Kauaeranga River

ACCOMMODATION

Brunton House	F
Coastal Motor Lodge	A
Cotswold Cottage	G
Dickson Holiday Park	B
Far Horizons	E
Gateway Backpackers	D
Sunkist Lodge	C

RESTAURANTS, CAFÉS & BARS

Food for Thought & Second Thought	6
The Goldmine	5
Green Cheese Café	3
The Old Thames	4
Punters	1
Sola Café	2
Udder Bar	7

0   500 m

G (500 m), Auckland (115 km) & Tauranga (116 km)

but you can get around with **taxis** from Thames Gold Cabs (T07/868 6037), or **rental touring bikes** from Paki Paki Bike Shop, in the Goldfields Mall off Mary Street (T07/867 9026, Wwww.pakipakibikeshop.co.nz) or **mountain bikes** from Price & Richards, 430 Pollen St (T07/868 6157; $15 a day). There's also **car rental** from Michael Saunders Motors (T07/868 8398, F07/868 8168) and John Davy Rentals (T07/868 6868), both of whom allow their budget cars onto the peninsula's roughest roads. **Internet access** is at the visitor centre and World Wide Wash laundromat, 740 Pollen St (Mon–Fri 9am–9pm, Sat & Sun 10am–9pm; closes 8pm winter).

Accommodation

Accommodation in Thames is rather scattered, most of it lying outside the town centre, but it's generally of a good standard and there's plenty of choice.

Brunton House 210 Parawai Rd ℡ & ℉07/868 5160, Ⓦwww.bruntonhouse.co.nz. A fine, big Victorian villa within 15mins' walking of the centre. Three rooms share two bathrooms and guests can use the swimming pool and tennis court. Just ❺

Coastal Motor Lodge 608 Tararu Rd (SH25), 2.5km north of town ℡07/868 6843, Ⓦwww.nzmotels.co.nz/coastal. A complex of well-equipped "cottage" units and modern, spacious A-frame chalets (all self-contained and designed for two), overlooking the Firth. The best views are from the pricier chalets. Cottages ❺, chalets ❻

Cotswold Cottage 46 Maramarahi Rd, 3km south of town off SH25 ℡07/868 6306, Ⓦwww.cotswoldcottage.co.nz. Grand B&B in an old villa set in mature grounds on the outskirts of Thames, overlooking the adjacent river. Three richly furnished en-suite rooms have their own entrances. ❺

Dickson Holiday Park Victoria St, off SH25 ℡07/868 7308, Ⓦwww.dicksonpark.co.nz.

Large, well-run campsite in a pretty valley 3.5km north of the centre. Excellent facilities include a pool and bus pick-up from Thames. Tent sites $11, dorms ❶, cabins & onsite caravans ❷, flats ❸, unit ❹

Far Horizons 204 Hauraki Terrace ℡07/868 9711, ✉t1p1@xtra.co.nz. Budget B&B in a studio unit with good river views and continental breakfast. Transport by arrangement, but it is only a 15-min walk uphill from the visitor centre. ❹

Gateway Backpackers 209 Mackay St ℡07/868 6339. Intimate and welcoming hostel just a few paces from the visitor centre and InterCity bus stop; free bikes, luggage storage and transfer to Kauaeranga Valley. Dorms ❶, rooms ❷

Sunkist Lodge 506 Brown St ℡07/868 8808 & 0800/767 786, ✉sunkist@xtra.co.nz. An atmospheric hostel in a historic building. Services include baggage and bike storage, free pick-up at the visitor centre, and car insurance; the InterCity bus stops outside. Tent sites $14, dorms ❶, rooms ❷

The Town

The best introduction to the town's gold-mining past is at the **Goldmine Experience**, Tararu Road (daily 10am–4pm; $10; ℡ & ℉07/868 8514, Ⓦwww.goldmine-experience.co.nz), where you join an informative 45-minute tour through the old battery. The tour continues underground along a narrow horizontal shaft originally cut by hand by Cornish miners. Life down the mine is convincingly portrayed through sound effects, realistic-looking mannequins, anecdotes, and an extensive historical photo museum.

The **Mineralogical Museum**, on the corner of Brown and Cochrane streets (Wed–Sun 11am–3pm; $3.50), continues the mining theme with a vast collection of quartz, crystals, rocks and fossils displayed in cases – this is one for geology freaks only.

Fans of natural lotions and potions should pay a visit to the EcoPeople store, on the corner of Pollen and Grey streets (Mon–Fri 9am–5pm, Sat 9am–1pm), where you can join a one-hour tour of the **Thames Natural Soap Co.** factory (groups of 10 or more, Mon–Fri 11am, 1pm & 3pm; $10, ℡0800/326 777), complete with abundant essential oils to sniff.

Near the junction of Brown and Amy streets, a one-minute boardwalk across the mangroves leads to the **Karaka Bird Hide**: a couple of hours either side of high tide is the best time to spot migratory birds such as knots, godwits, shags and terns, especially between October and February. An information board details the species that frequent the mangroves. Winged creatures of a tropical variety can be seen at the magical **Butterfly and Orchid Garden**, 3.5km north of Thames, at the *Dickson Holiday Park*, Victoria Street, just off SH25 (daily: Nov–March 10am–4pm; April–Oct 10am–3pm; $9), where you can spend twenty minutes or more inside a hothouse delighting in the acrobatics of hundreds of butterflies (up to 25 species), and up to 50 orchids in bloom at any one time.

You can get a good view over the town and the Firth of Thames from the **lookout** at the war memorial; walk or drive up Waiotahi Road and Monument Road to a car park just below the monument, then climb a short flight of steps to the viewpoint.

Kauaeranga Valley

The steep-sided **Kauaeranga Valley**, to the east of town, stretches towards the spine of the Coromandel Peninsula, a jagged landscape of bluffs and gorges topped by **The Pinnacles** (759m), with stupendous views to both coasts across native forest studded with original giants such as rata, rimu and kauri.

Kauaeranga walks

The Kauaeranga Valley is blessed with a wonderful variety of easily accessible tramps ranging from a thirty-minute stroll to a satisfying two-day circuit with a night spent at the large and relatively plush **Pinnacles Hut** (80 bunks; $15; advance booking essential through Kauaeranga DOC ℡07/867 9080). There are also a couple of remote and very basic DOC **campsites**: one near the Pinnacles Hut and another at Moss Creek (both $7.50). The *Kauaeranga Kauri Trail* DOC leaflet ($1) covers the basics, though you might prefer the detail provided by the 1:50,000 Thames topo map ($12.50): both are available from the DOC office and the Thames visitor centre. You can **store luggage** or tents at the Kauaeranga DOC office at the roadend for $2 per person.

Nature Walk to Hoffman's Pool (1.5km loop; 30min). The valley's shortest walk, an easy loop beginning about 1km beyond the DOC office. Information panels make it a classic introduction to the valley's native forest. The track leads to a tranquil sand-edged pool in a river bend, an ideal picnic and swimming spot (toilets and changing sheds nearby). You return the same way or in a loop along the road.

Billygoat Landing (1.5km return; 20–30min). Begins 300 metres beyond the road-end, giving excellent views of the 180-metre Billygoat Falls.

Edwards Lookout (1km return; 40min–1hr). A fine viewpoint over manuka-towai forest from a rocky saddle reached by a track starting 5km beyond the DOC office.

Pinnacles Moss Creek Circuit (14km loop; 2 days). This is the way to really get to grips with the region, following the **Kauaeranga Kauri Trail** and overnighting in the *Pinnacles Hut* (see above) about a third of the way along. It is really just a day and a half, starting at the road end and spending the first 2–3hr following Webb Creek up to *Pinnacles Hut* and the well-restored Dancing Camp kauri dam. From the hut a steep 50min climb reaches The Pinnacles. The second day is longer (7–8hr) and can be muddy and difficult, involving a few unbridged stream crossings. It passes the sad remnants of a couple of kauri dams, an old logging camp and some more fine viewpoints, with Moss Creek campsite along the way. A there-and-back trip to the Pinnacles can be done in 6–7hr.

Webb Creek–Billygoat Circuit (9km loop; 4–5hr). Historically the most interesting of the walks, where info panels tell the story of the loggers and the various methods used to transport the logs from the hillsides. From the roadend the track crosses the river on a swingbridge and follows Webb Creek along an old packhorse route (steep in places) used by kauri bushmen in the 1920s. Linking with the Billygoat Track leads to a saddle with excellent views down the valley to the Hauraki Plains.

Wainora Track (6km return; 2–3hr). Moderate, well formed track to a couple of large kauri – pretty much the only accessible ones left standing hereabouts – that starts from the Wainora campsite, 6km beyond the DOC office, heading northeast.

All this is reached along a scenic and mostly sealed road snaking beside the river, providing access to some of the finest walks in the Coromandel Range, and the only backcountry DOC hut on the peninsula. *Sunkist Lodge* (see p.381) runs a shuttle bus along the road on request ($25–$35 return), picking up from accommodation; or you can **drive** by heading out of the southern end of Thames, along Parawai Road, which becomes Kauaeranga Road.

Thirteen kilometres along you reach the **DOC office** (daily 8am–4pm; ℡07/867 9080, Ⓕ867 9095), where you can stock up on maps, buy hut tickets and examine displays on early kauri logging in the valley. From here a loop track (500m; 10min) leads to a scale model of a kauri driving dam, the type once used extensively in this forest. Along the eight unsealed kilometres beyond the DOC office to the road-end, an assortment of tracks (see p.382) lead off into the bush containing scattered "pole stands" of young kauri that have grown since the area was logged a century ago: only a handful in each stand will reach maturity. Most of the hikes head into the bush near one of the half-dozen simple roadside **campsites** ($7; toilets and stream water) dotting the length of the stretch.

To really get off the beaten track consider **canyoning** down the Sleeping God canyon with Canyonz (see p.116), whose trips begin in Auckland but will pick up in Thames.

Eating and entertainment

Thames's old-style tearooms and traditional bars are being supplemented by a couple of more modern places, but evening entertainment still revolves mostly around the pub and the mainstream **cinema** in Goldfields Mall (℡07/867 9100). For **stocking up**, consider the small and friendly Organic Co-op, 736 Pollen Street (Mon–Fri 9am–5pm, Sat 9am–noon), and the Saturday morning **market** (9am–noon; food, clothing and more) held at the northern end of Pollen Street.

Food for Thought and Second Thought 574 Pollen St. Two small, central daytime cafés next door to one another, specializing in pastries, cakes and vegetarian dishes; plus great coffee too. Both closed Sun.

The Goldmine cnr of Pollen & Mary streets. Good-value restaurant and gaming bar, open from morning till late for mainstream meals in gargantuan portions, such as T-bone and chips or beer-battered fish and chips.

Green Cheese Café 701 Pollen St. Simple café for fresh juices, snacks and meals, specializing in organic food and locally made cheeses, with seating in a pretty garden. Open till 8pm in summer, 5pm in winter.

The Old Thames cnr of Pollen & Pahau streets. Popular family restaurant with a broad range of moderately priced dishes (including takeaway) and generous desserts. Licensed; lunch Thurs–Sun, dinner all week.

Punters 719 Pollen St ℡07/868 7033. Lively sports bar and betting shop with garden bar. Standard pub fare for reasonably priced lunch (Tues–Sun), dinner (Thurs–Sat), and all-day breakfast at weekends.

Sola Café 720b Pollen St. Modern vegetarian café and restaurant for excellent coffee and snacks during the day. Also open Wed–Sun evenings for good-value Italian-style mains; and a short vegan menu (plus some wheat-free). BYO.

Udder Bar cnr Pollen St and Sealey St. Sparsely furnished bar with a line in bar meals and a lively clientele who dutifully spill into the Krazy Cow club (in the same building) on Fri & Sat nights.

North to Coromandel

From Thames, SH25 snakes 58km north to Coromandel (the town after which the peninsula is named), tracing the grey rocky shoreline of the "**Pohutukawa**

Coast" past a series of tiny, sandy bays, most with little more than a few houses and maybe a campsite. Hills and sand-coloured cliffs rise dramatically from the roadside for the first 19km to **Tapu**, where the **Tapu–Coroglen Road** peels off to the Coromandel's east coast. It is a wonderfully scenic 28km run of narrow, unsealed yet manageable driving, leaving behind the marginal farmland on the coast and climbing over the peninsula's mountainous spine. Even if you aren't tackling the traverse, it is worth making a detour 6.5km along the road (and just beyond the end of the asphalt), to **Rapaura Water Gardens** (daily 9am–5pm; $10; ⓦ www.rapaurawatergardens.co.nz), a cleverly landscaped "wilderness" of bush and blooms, punctuated by lily ponds and a trickling stream. Against a backdrop of bush and threaded by numerous paths, the gardens tap into the Coromandel ethos with philosophical messages urging you to stop and think awhile, and it's easy to spend half a day doing just that – though you could get around in an hour. There are a few picnic areas, and excellent cream teas are served in the **café**. You can enjoy the gardens at night in luxury accommodation: an enchanting cottage for two (⑥) or a serene two-bedroom house lined with rimu ($250 for two, $320 for three to four).

The road continues for 3km on to the (easily missed) "square kauri" signpost near the road's summit, opposite a rough lay-by and just before a small bridge. Steep steps through bush (175m; 10min) lead to this giant of a tree (1200 years old, just over 41m high and 9m wide), whose unusual, angular shape saved it from loggers. From here it's another rough and twisty 19km across the peninsula to Coroglen, linking with the main road between Whitianga and Whangamata, or 9.5km back to Tapu and the continuation of SH25 north.

Back on **SH25** the road lurches inland soon after Kereta (about 12km north of Tapu), snaking over hills to the roadside **Manaia–Kereta Lookout** (206m), which has great views of the northern peninsula, the majestic Moehau Range and Coromandel Harbour. Beyond, Great Barrier Island may be visible on a clear day – a giant block of rock with vertical cliffs. Ducking and diving along the rocky shoreline and the blue-green vistas of the Firth of Thames, SH25 continues for 20km to the turn-off to 309 Road, 3km south of Coromandel, which cuts across to Whitianga by way of a few roadside attractions, all within 8km of Coromandel (see "East to Whitianga", p.389).

Coromandel

The northernmost town of any substance is the pretty little **COROMAN-DEL**, 58km north of Thames, huddling beneath high, craggy hills at the head of Coromandel Harbour. It's known to many simply as the jumping-off point for the **Coromandel Walkway** (see p.389), 57km away amid the jagged landscape of the northern peninsula, but it's worth taking time to soak up the atmosphere of this old gold town and ride its **scenic railway** into the local hills.

The town and peninsula took their name from an 1820 visit by the British Admiralty supply ship *Coromandel*, which called into the harbour to obtain kauri spars and masts, and to extend Captain Cook's brief survey of the Hauraki Gulf.

A more mercenary European invasion was precipitated by the 1852 discovery of **gold**, near Driving Creek, in the northern part of town. The subsequent boom left a string of fine wooden buildings along the main street, though these days the town just ticks by as a local service centre and minor tourist hub.

There are a couple of supermarkets and petrol stations, a BNZ bank, a cluster of cafés and a broad range of accommodation.

Moving on you've a choice of striking **east to Whitianga**, via the continuation of SH25 (see p.390) past the deserted beaches of Whangapoua and Kuaotunu, or taking the more rugged 309 Road (see p.390).

Arrival, information and transport

The combined **visitor centre** and **DOC office**, 355 Kapanga Rd (Nov–Easter daily 9am–5pm, Easter–Oct Mon–Sat 9am–5pm, Sun 10am–2pm; ☏07/866 8598, ⓦwww.coromandeltown.co.nz), is at the northern end of town, just over the bridge. It supplies **tide times** for Hot Water Beach, and **Internet access**. Daily InterCity and Turley-Murphy **buses** pull into the car park opposite the visitor centre. The only **car rental** firm in town is Fureys Creek Motors at the BP garage, 226 Wharf Rd (☏07/866 8736), which allows its cars onto the unsealed roads north of Colville.

Accommodation

For a small place, Coromandel offers a good range of **places to stay**, from a campsite in the town centre to a luxurious lodge in an idyllic setting a few kilometres north. Most are within easy walking distance of the town centre.

Buffalo Lodge Buffalo Rd, signposted north of town and past the Gold Stamper Battery ☏07/866 8960, ⓦwww.buffalolodge.co.nz. Luxurious, modern accommodation in a specially designed house high up in the bush, with superb views across the Hauraki Gulf. It offers two elegant en-suite doubles with private decks; and a separate cottage for two with its own sundeck. Give two days' notice for superb three-course dinners at $85 a head excluding wine. Reserve well in advance; closed May–Sept. Rooms ❽, cottage ❾

Celadon Cottages Motel & B&B Alfred St, about 1km north of town ☏07/866 8058, ⓦwww.celadonmotel.com. Four attractive places tucked away on a bush-clad hillside, with town and harbour views. Choose between a self-catering cabin for two, a large chalet for 2–8, a 2-bedroom unit, and a cottage for four. ❹–❻

Coromandel Colonial Cottages 1737 Rings Rd, 1.5km north of town ☏0508/222 688 & 07/866 8857, ⓦwww.corocottagesmotel.co.nz. Good-value luxury cottages (one- and two-bedroom) in tranquil gardens. Excellent facilities include a big solar-heated swimming pool and BBQ area. One-bedroom ❹, two-bedroom ❻ plus $15 each extra adult.

Coromandel Town Backpackers 732 Rings Rd ☏07/866 8327, ⓔcorobapa@hawknet.co.nz. Modern, spick-and-span hostel three mins' walk north of town with budget bunks and several attractive places; luggage and bike storage. Dorms ❶, rooms ❷

Jacaranda Lodge 3km south on Tiki Rd/SH25 ☏07/866 8002, ⓦwww.jacarandalodge.co.nz. A

modern house in farmland offering B&B in extremely comfortable and spacious rooms (two are en suite). The single room rate (around $50) makes it good value for lone travellers. ❺

Lion's Den 126 Te Tiki Rd ☏ & ⓕ07/866 8157. A super-relaxing hostel beside a stream. Stay in the villa or in a pretty, former house-truck ideal for a couple; order in advance for cooked breakfast and seafood meals. Four-shares ❶, rooms & truck ❷

Long Bay Motor Camp 3200 Long Bay Rd, 3km west of town ☏07/866 8720, ⓦwww.longbaymotorcamp.co.nz. Attractive beachfront campsite with safe swimming and good facilities such as kayak, dinghy and fishing-tackle rental. There are bunkhouse units, and additional tent sites at the secluded Tucks Bay, less than 1km away through the bush or a five-minute walk around the headland. Tent sites $10, caravans & units ❷, cabins ❸

Tidewater Tourist Park 270 Tiki Rd ☏07/866 8888, ⓦwww.tidewater.co.nz. Combined motel and associate YHA set in large, leafy grounds 300m from the town centre and near the harbour, with barbecue area and low-cost bike rental. Tents $12, dorms ❶, rooms ❷, units ❹

Tui Lodge 60 Whangapoua Rd, just off SH25 ☏07/866 8237, ⓔtuilodge@paradise.net.nz. Good-value and relaxing hostel ten minutes' walk south of town (and on the InterCity bus route), set in a big rambling house by an orchard, with plenty of doubles and twins. Perks include free linen, laundry, tea and coffee, fruit (in season), BBQ and use of bikes. Tent sites $11, dorms ❶, rooms ❷, en-suite rooms ❸

The Town and around

The town centre spreads along the main road, with a few old buildings left from gold-mining days. From the south, SH25 becomes Tiki Road and then splits into two: to the left is Wharf Road, which skirts the harbour; to the right you immediately enter the heart of the town, on Kapanga Road, lined with shops and cafés. A couple of blocks further on, it becomes Rings Road, before heading northwards out of town as Colville Road.

About 300m north of the visitor centre is the small volunteer-run **Coromandel Historical Museum**, at 841 Rings Rd (usually Nov–Feb Mon–Fri 10am–1pm, Sat & Sun 10am–4pm; rest of the year Sat & Sun only 1–4pm; $2). Based in the old School of Mines (1898), this is a mishmash of domestic items and mining memorabilia, including evocative black-and-white photographs from early mining days. The original jailhouse is around the back.

The main attraction in the immediate vicinity is **Driving Creek Railway and Potteries**, Driving Creek Road, 3.5km north of town (daily; check times with visitor centre or phone ☎07/866 8703, ⓦwww .drivingcreekrailway.co.nz). Built mostly by hand over twenty-seven years, this is the country's only narrow-gauge hill railway, the brainchild of Barry Brickell, an eccentric local potter and rail enthusiast who wanted access into the clay-bearing hills. Today the railway (which runs through bush where native saplings have been planted) mainly carries visitors on a delightfully shambolic **train trip** (daily 10.15am & 2pm; 1hr return $15; book ahead). The track is only 381mm wide and carries specially designed, articulated diesel trains, which climb 120m over a distance of about 3km. The rewards of this leisurely, commentated trip are spectacular views, extraordinary feats of engineering and quirky design; at the end of the line are panoramic views from a lookout point, the Eyefull Tower. The journey starts and ends at the **workshops**, where you can see various types of **pottery**: stoneware and earthenware items, and sculptures made from terracotta.

Around 1.5km north of town is the turn-off to the **Coromandel Goldfields Centre & Stamper Battery**, another 300m or so along Buffalo Road (daily: 10am–4pm; guided 1hr tour, at half-past each hour; $6, or $5 if combined with Driving Creek Railway), where the peninsula's goldmining history is explained. The fully functional 1899 stamper battery is also briefly operated to demonstrate the intriguing processing of gold. Outside, a stroll around the building reveals the water-wheel that still drives the machinery. The streamside garden is scattered with picnic tables and, for an extra $5, you can try your hand at gold panning. A ten-minute return bush walk climbs to a lookout with views over the town and to the Hauraki Gulf.

Three kilometres west of town, along Wharf Road, lies the beach of **Long Bay** and a pleasing **walk** through a scenic reserve (40min loop). A hundred metres inside the Long Bay Motor Camp a signpost marks the track, which climbs gently through bush to an ancient kauri tree and on to a small grove of younger ones. Beyond that, at the junction with a gravel road you can turn right to Tucks Bay and follow the coastal track back to the motor camp.

Eating and entertainment

For a small town, Coromandel is surprisingly well endowed with decent places to eat, with several good **cafés** touting for your business and a couple of fancier restaurants, nearly all of them on Kapanga Road. Evening **entertainment** is restricted to occasional live music (summer weekends only) at *Driving Creek Café* or the pubs.

△ Driving Creek Railway

Assay House Café cnr Tiki Rd and Kapanga Rd. Brightly coloured café and wine bar serving great hot chocolate, good coffee, loose-leaf tea and cakes. More substantial dishes include an ostrich burgers and a delicious eggs Benedict (free range). There's sunny courtyard seating, and tapas on busy Fri & Sat nights in summer. Closed Tues in summer; Mon & Tues in winter.

Driving Creek Café 180 Driving Creek Rd, 3.5km north of town (07/866 7066). Classic Coromandel, a laid-back and welcoming vegetarian hideaway for great coffee, snacks and meals (from 10am; and dinner Fri and Sat, till 7.30pm), with beautiful hill views from the veranda and garden. Talented guest musicians play fortnightly on summer Fri nights. BYO only; closed Tues, and Easter–Nov.

Peppertree 31 Kapanga Rd ⓣ07/866 8211. A popular bar and restaurant open from breakfast to dinner, with main courses for $20–25 and an all-day snack menu; eat indoors or in the garden. Licensed and BYO; book ahead on summer weekends.

The Success Café & Restaurant 102 Kapanga Rd ⓣ07/866 7100. An intimate café that turns into a restaurant bar in the evening, serving plenty of seafood and steak, and superb garlic mussels, mostly around the $10 mark for lunch, $20 for dinner. Sunny afternoon street dining; licensed & BYO.

Top Pub *Coromandel Hotel*, 611 Rings Rd. A pleasant evening bistro, good for its seafood, but also serving steaks and other meat dishes; open for lunch in summer too.

Umu 22 Wharf Rd ⓣ07/866 8618. Coromandel's most sophisticated café and restaurant, popular with locals for its well-prepared and reasonably priced dishes and pizzas. Open from breakfast till dinner.

North to Fletcher Bay and Port Charles

The landscape **north of Coromandel** is even more rugged than the rest of the peninsula, its green hills dropping to apparently endless beaches, clean blue sea and white surf. The tourist authorities have dubbed the area the **Pohutukawa Cape**, and indeed the dirt roads are lined with ancient pohutukawa trees, blazing red from early November until just after Christmas. With its dairy farms long deserted it is a virtually uninhabited land and there are **few facilities**: so replenish your supplies in Coromandel town. As elsewhere on the peninsula, signs have sprung up to deter freelance **camping** and the Department of Conservation has responded by opening five waterside campsites around the northern peninsula. For the two weeks after Christmas the campsites are full, but for most of the rest of the year you can have this unspoilt area to yourself.

From Coromandel, the road snakes for some 20km along the coast, then cuts inland to the tiny settlement of **COLVILLE**, little more than a post office, a petrol pump and the Colville General Store, set in a quiet green valley that appealed to counter-culture aspirants in the 1970s. The store is a good place to stock up on dry goods for the Coromandel Walkway (see box opposite) and check on the state of the road north of Port Jackson. If you fancy **staying** up this way, you can't go far wrong with *Colville Farm*, Colville Road, 1.5km south of Colville (ⓣ& ⓕ07/866 6820; camping $5–9, dorms ❶, rooms ❷, bush lodges ❸, houses sleeping 6 or 8 ❺ plus $8 each extra person), a soothing spot on a sheep and cattle farm with the opportunity to go **horse trekking** (1hr $20, 2hr $30). Accommodation ranges from campsites to backpacker dorms in a cottage, a couple of bush lodges, and two self-contained houses with fabulous views. Or opt for the tranquil *Mahamudra Centre*, Colville Rd, 1.5km south of Colville (ⓣ07/866 6851, ⓦwww.mahamudra.org.nz; tents $8, dorms ❶, single rooms $20, twins ❷), a simple Buddhist retreat centre in attractive grounds with a communal kitchen. Visitors of all denominations are welcome, as are members of WWOOF (see p.66). To be closer to the beach, try *Colville Bay Lodge*, Wharf Road, off Colville Road (ⓣ & ⓕ07/866 6814; camping $8, units ❹), the peninsula's northernmost motel and campsite, two minutes' walk from Colville Bay.

Beyond Colville the road is unsealed, and becomes narrower, rougher and dustier the further north you go, though it's not that difficult to drive if taken

The Coromandel Walkway and cycle route

Other than a bit of swimming, fishing or lolling around on the beaches, the only activity in the far north of the peninsula is to hike from Fletcher Bay to Stony Bay along the **Coromandel Walkway** (11km; 3hr one way), a gentle and clearly route-marked path with lovely sea views. The walk starts at the far end of the beach in Fletcher Bay and heads off into a no-man's-land, first following gentle coastal hills that alternate between pasture and bush, then giving way to wilder terrain as you head further south past a series of tiny bays. Several hilltop **vantage points** yield spectacular vistas of the coast and Pacific Ocean beyond. **Stony Bay** is a sweep of pebbles with a bridge across an estuary that's safe for swimming. The DOC leaflet *Coromandel Recreation Information* ($1) briefly describes the walk and shows a map but you're unlikely to need it.

A **shuttle bus** runs day-trips between Coromandel town and Fletcher Bay (T07/866 8175, W www.coromandeldiscoverytours.co.nz; $85 return; $110 including food and drink; three people minimum), dropping off walkers and collecting them at Stony Bay before returning to Coromandel. It also picks up from Fletcher Bay Backpackers.

Serious **mountain bikers** can make a circuit of the northern peninsula by going off-road from Fletcher Bay to Stony Bay using a longer, fairly extreme route further inland, which starts and finishes at the same points as the walkway.

at a steady pace (allow an hour to reach Fletcher Bay from Colville in fine weather), all the better to fully appreciate the tiny bays flanked by shelves of volcanic grey rock. Three kilometres north of Colville the road splits, with the right fork heading east over the hills to Stony Bay and the southern end of the Coromandel Walkway. The left fork runs 35km north to Port Jackson and Fletcher Bay at the very tip of the peninsula, following the coast all the way. An abandoned **granite wharf** marks the halfway spot. A couple of kilometres beyond, you'll find the diminutive and lovely *Fantail Bay Recreation Reserve* ($7), the first of the DOC **campsites**, which come equipped with basic toilets and a water supply. The road then cuts briefly inland, over hills rising straight from the shore, to reach **PORT JACKSON**, just two houses and a one-kilometre sandy crescent of beach. It's safe for swimming and backed by a grassy DOC reserve, where you can **camp** ($7) with views across to Great Barrier and Little Barrier islands. From here the road deteriorates further for the final 6km to **FLETCHER BAY**, probably the best beach of all, safe for swimming, its eastern end marking the start of the **Coromandel Walkway**. The beach is backed by another DOC **campsite** ($7), with flush toilets and cold showers; and the small and comfortable *Fletcher Bay Backpackers* (T07/866 6712, E js.lourie@xtra.co.nz; ●), set on a hill 400m away from the beach, with four-bed dorms and free kayaks.

Stony Bay, at the southern end of the Coromandel Walkway, is reached by two perilously twisty gravel roads – one across the Coromandel Range from Coromandel, the other traversing the Moehau Range from just beyond Colville. The latter runs 14km from Colville to the small holiday settlement of **Port Charles**, and a further 6km to Stony Bay, where there's another DOC campsite ($7), also with flush toilets and cold showers.

East to Whitianga

The drive east from Coromandel to Whitianga can be done in under an hour, but you could easily spend much of a day on either of two highly **scenic** roads that cross the mountains: the more direct, snaking **309 Road** (33km, of which 20km are gravel; no public transport) spends much of its time in the bush, while the main (and mostly sealed) **SH25** climbs through forested hills before switchbacking down to the coast, 46km away.

Coromandel to Whitianga: the 309 Road

From the junction with SH25, 4km south of Coromandel, the 309 Road twists 5km east to **Waiau Waterworks** (daily; Oct–March 9am till dusk; rest of the year 9am–5pm; $8; Ⓦ www.waiauwaterworks.co.nz), a rambling garden carved from the bush and dotted with whimsical water-powered contraptions and contrivances. It is quirky at every turn yet explained in enough detail to satisfy the more engineering minded. Allow a couple of hours and bring a picnic, especially if you've got kids who'll appreciate the swimming hole and two flying foxes.

One hundred metres past the waterworks, a rough access road on the left crosses a ford and climbs steeply for 3km to the trailhead for the track to **Castle Rock** (2km return; 40min–1hr 30min), the most easily accessible peak on the Coromandel Peninsula. It's a climb that gets progressively steep towards the final tree-root claw onto the 521-metre summit of this old volcanic plug, but your efforts are well rewarded by fantastic views to both coasts: on the east the Whangapoua peninsula and the Mercury Islands, and on the west Coromandel and the Firth of Thames.

A further 2.5km along the 309 Road, the **Waiau Falls** crash over a rockface into a pool below. They're not that impressive, but they are right next to the road and offer a gorgeous spot to cool off. Half a kilometre further on, a car park heralds the easy bush track to the magnificent **Kauri Grove** (1km return; 30min) and **"Siamese" Kauri** a little further on. Fortuitous gaps in the bush make this one of the best places in the country to really get a sense of the size of the kauri, and appreciate just how they stand head and shoulders above the rest of the forest trees: a boardwalk allows you to get face-to-bark with these giants.

The road tops out at the 306m saddle and descends towards Whitianga, passing a couple of relaxing riverside **accommodation** options covered under our Whitianga account (see p.393).

Coromandel to Whitianga: SH25

From Coromandel, **SH25** follows an attractive route through lush native forest passing a couple of isolated but pretty beachside settlements with campsites. About 14km from Coromandel is the 5km turn-off to the secluded village and beach of **WHANGAPOUA**, whose long stretch of white sand is lined by *baches* and a single general store/petrol station. At the end of the road (along the right fork into town) is a pleasant walk to the idyllic sandy beach of **New Chums Bay** (4km return; 1hr): from the beach, cross the estuary and follow the bushline around the headland to a saddle; on the other side is New Chums Bay (accessible at low tide only). Continuing along SH25, about 30km from Coromandel, you descend to diminutive **KUAOTUNU**, beside a lovely white-sand beach. There's a range of especially good **accommodation** here: the shady and well-equipped *Kuaotunu Motor Camp*, Bluff Road (☎07/866 5628, Ⓦ www.kuaotunumotorcamp .co.nz; tent sites $11, cabins ❷, units ❹, cottage ❹), with kayak rental; the riverside and well-equipped *Black Jack Backpackers*, SH25 (☎07/866 2988, Ⓦ www.black-jack.co.nz; tents $12, dorms ❶, doubles ❸), with free kayaks;

the highly recommended *Drift In B&B*, 16 Gray Ave, off Bluff Road (℡07/866 4321, ⓦwww.bnb.co.nz/hosts/driftinbb.html; ❹), offering fabulous sea views and dinner by arrangement ($25); and the big modern *Kuaotunu Bay Lodge*, SH25 (℡07/866 4396, ⓦwww.kuaotunubay .co.nz), set on a rise with excellent sea views, a self-contained unit (❻), B&B en-suite doubles (❼), and dinner ($45) by arrangement.

Nine kilometres north of Whitianga, on SH25, is Twin Oaks Riding Ranch, the base for extremely scenic two-hour **horse treks** (book ahead on ℡07/866 5388; daily 10am & 2pm, plus twilight trek at 6pm Nov–March; $30), giving breathtaking views of Mercury Bay and the northern Coromandel; transport from Whitianga can be arranged. From here, SH25 continues through farmland to Whitianga and the stunning expanse of Mercury Bay.

Whitianga and around

The attractive town of **WHITIANGA** clusters where the estuarine Whitianga Harbour meets the broad sweep of **Mercury Bay**. This huge bite out of the Coromandel Peninsula coastline was named by Captain Cook who stopped here in 1769 so that his party of scientists could observe Mercury pass across the face of the sun. Today a popular Kiwi summer-holiday destination, the population of about 4000 swells dramatically during January as vacationers flock to the town's **Buffalo Beach**, a long sweep of surf-pounded white sand.

Whitianga makes a good base from which to make a series of half-day and **day-trips** to some wonderfully secluded spots, so allow a couple of days here. Just across the narrow harbour mouth and strung along Mercury Bay's eastern shore are several unusual beaches, reached by passenger ferry to **Ferry Landing**, from where you can catch a **bus** or strike out along scenic coastal tracks. The area is also served by roads branching off the southbound SH25, which loops around the deeply indented harbour. Two gems here are **Cathedral Cove**, a stunning geological formation, and **Hot Water Beach**, renowned for its natural hot-water springs bubbling beneath the sand. Bordering part of the eastern shore is **Cathedral Cove Marine Reserve**, whose protected waters are a great spot for snorkelling and scuba diving. In addition, **boat trips** to the outer reaches of Mercury Bay and the volcanically formed **Mercury Islands**, 25km offshore, explore pristine waters and shoreline – and search for bottlenose **dolphins** and **whales**. Whitianga is also one of the best places in New Zealand to try your hand at **bone carving**, creating your very own *tiki* in as little as half a day, while 10km north of town you can enjoy astounding views of the whole region on a **scenic horse trek**.

Arrival, information and transport

SH25 runs through town becoming Albert Street along the main shopping thoroughfare, then Buffalo Beach Road along the shore. Virtually everything happens on these two streets or The Esplanade, which branches off to the wharf and ferry.

InterCity and Go Kiwi **buses** drop off at accommodation around town and outside the **visitor centre** at the corner of Albert Street and Blacksmith Lane (daily 9am–5pm but closes 4pm weekends March to mid-Dec; ℡07/866 5555, ⓦwww.whitianga.co.nz), which has **Internet access**, and **mountain bike**

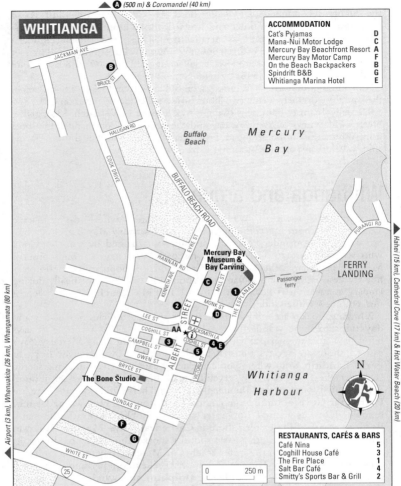

rental for $25 a day. Great Barrier Airlines (℡0800/900 600) flights from Auckland (4 days a week, twice daily) and Great Barrier Island (2–3 weekly) land at the **airport,** 4km south of the town centre and reached by a $5 ride with Mercury Bay **Taxis** (℡07/866 5643).

The surrounding **beaches** are served by ferry and buses. The **passenger ferry** to Ferry Landing (daily: 7.30am–6.30pm, 7.30pm–8.30pm & 9.30pm–10.30pm or until midnight in summer; $1 each way) takes three minutes and leaves from The Esplanade. Go Kiwi (℡07/866 0336) runs **shuttles** from Ferry Landing to Cooks Beach, Hahei and Hot Water Beach (four times daily in summer, less in winter), with services connecting with buses to Auckland and Whitianga; their all-day pass ($20) takes you to all the sights, or a trip from Ferry Landing to Hot Water Beach costs $10.

Accommodation

As one of the Coromandel's main tourist centres, Whitianga itself has plenty of **accommodation** to suit all tastes. Further out, beside the secluded **beaches** of Mercury Bay, is a small selection of perfect places to unwind, mostly at Hot Water Beach and Hahei; and it's worth considering a couple of places along the 309 Road, about 12km southwest of town, or those at Kuaotunu, 16km north (see p.390). Throughout summer you'll need to **book ahead**, and for January places get booked up about two months beforehand. Also, be prepared for **higher prices** than on the rest of the peninsula, especially anywhere with a sea view, and particularly from Christmas to the end of January when motels and campsites hike their prices.

Central Whitianga

See map on p.392

Cat's Pyjamas 4 Monk St ☏ 07/866 4663, ℮ catspjs@ihug.co.nz. Small friendly hostel with three dorms and three doubles (one en suite), just around the corner from the wharf. Perks include free linen, tea and coffee, and a BBQ. Tents $12, dorms ❶, caravan ❷, rooms ❷

Mana-Nui Motor Lodge 20 Albert St ☏ 07/866 5599, ℮ mananui@xtra.co.nz. Centrally located and comfortable motel with twelve fully self-contained units; pool and spa. ❺

Mercury Bay Beachfront Resort 111–113 Buffalo Beach Rd ☏ 07/866 5637, ⊛ www .beachfrontresort.co.nz. Luxurious motel right on the beach with eight excellent spacious units, half with great sea views and private balconies. Guests can use spa pool, BBQ, kayaks, a dinghy, fishing rods and boogie boards; and there's courtesy transport from the airport and bus depot to avoid the 35-min walk from the centre. ❻

Mercury Bay Motor Camp 121 Albert St ☏ & ℱ 07/866 5579. Large, sheltered and well-equipped site about 400m from the town centre with bargain kayak rental, a pool and spa. Camping $10–14, cabins ❷, units ❹

On the Beach Backpackers 46 Buffalo Beach Rd ☏ 07/866 5380, ⊛ www.coromandelbackpackers .co.nz. The best hostel in town, right by the bay with great views and ten minutes' walk from the centre. It's a big associate YHA, where some of the dorms are en suite and most of the doubles and twins are in self-contained units. Also offered are bikes for rent, and free use of kayaks and courtesy transport. Dorms ❶, single $46, rooms ❷

Spindrift B&B 129 Albert St ☏ 07/866 5116, ⊛ www.spindrift.co.nz. Pleasant modern B&B with views over the estuary, two en suites and a room with a private bathroom; free kayaks and bikes. ❻

Whitianga Marina Hotel The Esplanade ☏ 07/866 5818, ℮ whitiangahotel@clear.net.nz. Pleasant, old-fashioned harbourside hotel with ten well-tended rooms, most of them en suite and all with TV and washbasin. Can get noisy on Wed, Fri and Sat nights in the bar. Shared bath ❸, en suite ❹

Around Whitianga

See map on p.395

Auntie Dawn's Place Radar Rd, Hot Water Beach ☏ 07/866 3707, ℮ auntiedawn@mercurybay.co.nz. Tranquil, modern hillside house overlooking the beach with simple yet comfortable self-contained apartments for two, plus backpacker beds in summer. Backpacker $25, apartments ❺

Bushcreek Cottage 309 Rd ☏ 07/866 5151, ⊛ www.bushcreek.co.nz. Attractive backpacker-style place on a smallholding run along organic principles 10km southwest of Whitianga. Apart from a big camping field there are dorms and doubles in a kauri lodge with kitchen and sunny veranda overlooking the river and swimming holes. Bring a sleeping bag and food. Tents $12, dorms ❶, doubles ❷

Hahei Holiday Resort & Cathedral Cove Backpackers Harsant Ave, Hahei ☏ 07/866 3889, ℮ info@haheiholidays.co.nz. Located on half a kilometre of beachfront and within an easy walk of Cathedral Cove, this enormous site is close to a shop and restaurants and has options ranging from dorms in a basic backpacker lodge to luxurious self-contained villas sleeping four right on the beachfront. Tent sites $11, dorms ❶, cabins & on-site vans ❷, kitchen cabins ❹, units ❺, villas ❼ plus $18 per extra person

Hot Water Beach B&B 48 Pye Place ☏ 07/866 3991 & 0800/146 889, ⊛ www .hotwaterbedandbreakfast.co.nz. Very hospitable B&B perfectly sited close to the beach and with great sea views. The two en-suite rooms have access to sunny decks and a spa pool, and there's even a full-sized snooker table. ❼

Riverside Retreat 309 Rd ☏ & ℱ 07/866 5155, ⊛ www.riversideretreat.co.nz. A self-contained

wooden cottage ten minutes' drive southwest of Whitianga, beside a burbling stream. The bed is on a mezzanine up a steepish staircase. Optional continental breakfast is provided. ❺
Tatahi Lodge Grange Rd, Hahei ☏07/866 3992, ✉ tatahi_lodge@xtra.co.nz. Several welcoming

self-contained timber-lined units set in bush and gardens, plus pleasant backpacker accommodation in dorms and doubles, and a cottage that sleeps five. Dorms ❶, rooms ❸, units ❺, cottage ❻ plus \$10 per extra person

The Town

Much of the pleasure in hanging around Whitianga for a day or two is in getting out of town, easily done with time spent at Cathedral Cove or Hot Water Beach, or by taking boat trips on Mercury Bay (see p.396). Alternatively consider a popular **bone-carving course**, where a skilled carver helps you to produce a high-quality glossy *tiki* within a day (\$80). Ian Thorne at The Bone Studio, 6B Bryce St (book ahead on ☏07/866 2158, ⓦ www.carving.co.nz), gives just the right amount of guidance, encourages self-expression and offers longer courses. If you lack patience check out the ready-carved pieces: those at Bay Carving, The Esplanade (☏07/866 4021), are reasonably priced, but The Bone Studio has the finer specimens.

In an old butter factory on The Esplanade is the big **Mercury Bay Museum** (Oct–Dec & Feb–April daily 10am–3pm; Jan daily 10am–4pm; May–Sept Tues–Thurs & Sat & Sun 11am–3pm; \$3), which won't detain you for long. Its focus is mainly colonial history with a slight nod to Maori artefacts. Points of interest are an extensive exhibition on Captain Cook and his visit to the peninsula, and informative displays on kauri-gum digging (note the polished blackjack gum), minerals and local shipwrecks.

Ferry Landing and the beaches

The beaches across the estuary are accessible by passenger ferry (see p.392) to **Ferry Landing**, where buses continue on to the beaches; by boat (see p.396); or by car from Whitianga. The longer **road route** travels south along SH25, skirting the harbour and cutting inland through hill country to a signposted turn-off at Whenuakite, 26km from Whitianga, which strikes north towards Mercury Bay. **Facilities** at Ferry Landing are limited to a store and a café; there are no banks or liquor stores on this side, so stock up if you're planning to stay more than a day.

From Ferry Landing the first point of interest is **Shakespeare Lookout** atop a cliff that, when viewed from the sea, is said to resemble the Bard's profile. From the lookout – signposted 1.5km along the road, and reached after another kilometre uphill to a car park – panoramic views stretch east to Cooks Beach and across Mercury Bay, west to Buffalo Beach, and north towards Mount Maungatawhiri. A memorial plaque commemorates James Cook's anchorage in Mercury Bay in 1769. Signposted tracks lead from the car park to the secluded Lonely Bay and on to the popular family holiday spot of **Cooks Beach** (2km one way; 20min), which is also accessible from the main road 2km further east.

About 4km southeast of Cooks Beach along the main road lies the junction with Hahei Beach Road, leading 6km to the tiny beachside community of **HAHEI**, an easily viable place to stay if you don't fancy the bustle of Whitianga. It has a store and several eating places, and is the launch site for trips on the water (see p.396). The main attraction here is **Cathedral Cove**, reached along a hilly **coastal track** that starts at a car park at the western end of the village (30–40min to Cathedral Cove), or you can begin at Hahei Beach (1hr

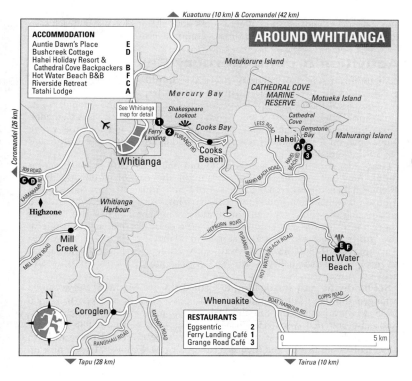

AROUND WHITIANGA

ACCOMMODATION
Auntie Dawn's Place	**E**
Bushcreek Cottage	**D**
Hahei Holiday Resort & Cathedral Cove Backpackers	**B**
Hot Water Beach B&B	**F**
Riverside Retreat	**C**
Tatahi Lodge	**A**

Motukorure Island

Mercury Bay

Motueka Island

CATHEDRAL COVE MARINE RESERVE

Cathedral Cove

Gemstone Bay

Mahurangi Island

Shakespeare Lookout

Cooks Bay

LEES ROAD

Hahei

Ferry Landing

PURANGI RD

Cooks Beach

Whitianga

See Whitianga map for detail

309 ROAD

KAIMARAMA RD

HAHEI BEACH ROAD

BEACH RD

Highzone

Whitianga Harbour

Mill Creek

MILL CREEK ROAD

HEPBURN ROAD

PURANGI ROAD

HOT WATER BEACH ROAD

Hot Water Beach

Whenuakite

BOAT HARBOUR RD

CLIPPS ROAD

Coroglen

KAPOWAI ROAD

RANGIHAU ROAD

N

RESTAURANTS
Eggsentric	**2**
Ferry Landing Café	**1**
Grange Road Café	**3**

0 _____ 5 km

5

THE COROMANDEL, BAY OF PLENTY AND THE EAST COAST | Whitianga and around

Tapu (28 km)

Tairua (10 km)

20min to Cathedral Cove) for a more strenuous walk. The walk is steep in places, with patches of pine-dominated bush, and affords great views out to sea. Five minutes' walk from the car park, a 5min track descends to the rocky **Gemstone Bay**, where DOC has set up a snorkelling course around three buoys to show off the undersea wonders of the **Cathedral Cove Marine Reserve**. Most visitors continue on to Cathedral Cove itself; striking white cliffs hug a long, sheltered and sandy beach bisected by an impressive rock arch that vaults over the strand like the nave of some great cathedral. A walk through the arch reveals another delightful beach on the other side (unsafe for swimming), while offshore the remains of several arches are stranded at sea. Bring a towel and a picnic, sink into the sand and relax.

If there is one place hereabouts that trumps Cathedral Cove, it's **Hot Water Beach**, reached along Hot Water Beach Road (5km), which branches off the main road. This is the last place you'll reach from Ferry Landing and the first you'll arrive at by road from Whitianga via SH25. The beach is split in two by a rocky outcrop that creates dangerous tidal rips (read our surf warning, see box p.131), but also provides the setting for the hot springs that give the beach its name. Be sure to visit an hour and a half either side of **low tide** (check tide times at Whitianga visitor centre or in the local paper), then dig a hole near the outcrop and sit in the hot water refreshed by waves of incoming sea water. In summer, the springs area will be pockmarked by other visitors' diggings, but otherwise you'll need to **rent a spade** from the **café** (daily; 26 Dec to mid-Feb 9am–7pm; rest of the year 9am–5pm; $4 for 2hr, plus $20 deposit), which also sells snacks and tea and coffee. There's little else at Hot Water Beach save for a few houses, some of which offer accommodation (see p.393).

Activities around Mercury Bay

The abundant waters of Mercury Bay make **dolphin sightings** a common event, and you may well see them on **scenic trips** run by Cave Cruzer Adventures (℡07/866 2275, ⓦwww.cavecruzer.co.nz). The most popular of its excursions is the two-hour Scenic & Sounds trip ($65), which visits Cathedral Cove, the nearby marine reserve, blowholes, a waterfall, and sea caves where guides put on a resonant performance with didgeridoo, African drums and Maori instruments.

Great boat trips are also run **from Hahei**, the best being Hahei Explorer (book previous evening or before 9am on the day on ℡07/866 3910, ⓦwww.haheiexplorer.co.nz; $55), a rigid-hull inflatable that takes small groups on exhilarating hour-long sea-cave trips, visiting Cathedral Cove and an amazing blowhole, with an entertaining commentary. They also rent out snorkel gear for use at Gemstone Bay ($40 a day). Alternatively, join one of the **guided sea kayak trips** run from Hahei by Cathedral Cove Sea Kayaking (℡07/866 3877, ⓦwww.seakayaktours.co.nz), who take up to twenty people: their half-day trip ($65) visits Cathedral Cove and they also organise sunset trips.

Scuba diving and snorkelling in Cathedral Cove Marine Reserve can be arranged through Hahei-based Cathedral Cove Dive & Snorkel (℡07/866 3955, ⓦwww.hahei.co.nz), in the Hahei shopping complex near the cafés. Snorkel-gear rental costs $15 a half-day. A one-dive trip costs $85 with full gear, two dives $160, less if you have your own gear. **Non-divers** can learn basic scuba skills ($130), and they also run other PADI courses. They'll pick up from Ferry Landing.

If the water's not for you, there's pleasure to be had **horse riding** 8km north of Whitianga at Twin Oaks Riding Ranch (see p.391). For more adrenalin, sign up for the jumps, swings and balance exercises at the High Zone **ropes course**, 49 Kaimarama Rd, 7km south off SH25 (℡07/866 2113, ⓦwww.highzone.co.nz; $10–60) – there are nine activities to choose from.

Eating and entertainment

Whitianga and its environs are well supplied with places to **eat**, many of the best places clustered along The Esplanade near the marina. Entertainment options are more limited though live **bands** occasionally play the *Whitianga Marina Hotel* (see below) in summer.

Whitianga

See map on p.392

Café Nina 20 Victoria St. Great coffee at this excellent daytime café. The food is carefully made to order, with vegetarian and vegan options. Try the signature seafood chowder ($8) or a delicious homemade fruitcake.

Coghill House Café 10 Coghill St. Relaxing, licensed daytime spot for high-quality snacks (great pies) or generous portions of fine food. Ease yourself into the lounging area or outdoor seating.

The Fire Place 9 The Esplanade (07/866 4828). Big-city-style restaurant for lunch and dinner, with a lovely deck overlooking the water. Coromandel oysters are a speciality, as are wonderful gourmet pizzas ($18), with mains costing $18–27. Closed Sun in winter.

Salt Bar Café *Whitianga Marina Hotel*, The Esplanade. An airy lunch and dinner café bar with decking onto the marina. Especially good for à la carte mains ($18–22.50), and specializes in Thai dishes. Discounted drinks on backpacker nights every Wed.

Smitty's Sports Bar & Grill 37 Albert St. Popular sports bar with two big screens. Great for a few beers but also serving good-value grilled meats and excellent burgers (plus a few concessions to vegetarians). Dine in the barn-like interior, or out on the covered deck.

Around Whitianga

See map on p.395

Eggsentric 1047 Purangi Rd, Ferry Landing ☏ 07/866 0307. A relaxing quirky place for a daytime meal or coffee but best in the evening when there's always live music (or poetry, or theme evening) to accompany the broad range of moder-

ately priced dinners. Closed Mon & mid-July to end Aug; licensed & BYO.

Ferry Landing Café 1134 Purangi Rd, Ferry Landing. About 100m up the hill from the wharf, this attractive, licensed garden café is a pleasant spot for light meals, coffee, and a rest among flowers and greenery. Closed Tues & Wed in winter.

Grange Road Café 7 Grange Rd, Hahei. Restful licensed spot for brunch, lunch and dinner, serving mainly seafood and simple food with a twist. The most expensive dish is whole snapper at $25; or go for fish and chips to take to the beach. Closed Mon & Tues in winter, and all of May.

South to Whangamata

The run along SH25 from Whitianga **south to Whangamata** is a pleasant enough journey, though the brief glimpses of the coast often show over-development. To some degree this is true of **Tairua**, the midway point, and especially so of its neighbour across the harbour, the luxury retirement and holiday resort of **Pauanui**; reminiscent of the worst excesses of Florida. All is not lost though – unspoilt beaches can be found, particularly the delightful **Opoutere**, a tiny harbourside retreat at the foot of a mountain, with a wild sweep of beach and a beautifully located hostel. From there, you're best off making a beeline for Whangamata.

Tairua

The small but overdeveloped beachside town of **TAIRUA** lies on SH25, 16km south of the turn-off to Hot Water Beach and 42km from Whitianga. It huddles between pine-forested hills and the calm estuary of the Tairua River, separated from the crashing Pacific breakers by two opposing and almost touching peninsulas. One is crowned by the imposing volcanic Mount Paku and the other is entirely covered by the suburban sprawl of exclusive **Pauanui**, accessible by a five-minute passenger **ferry** ride from Tairua (around 9am–5pm; Sept–Nov roughly hourly; Dec to end Jan continuous; rest of the year twice daily; $4 return), or a 25km drive. The combination of surf and sheltered waters makes Tairua popular in summer with holidaying Kiwis, who also find it a good base for Hot Water Beach, more easily reached by car from here than from Whitianga.

You could stop briefly for a dip or to climb **Mount Paku** (15min up) for spectacular views over the town, its estuary and beaches; the track starts at the end of Paku Drive, reached by following the estuary around to the north. Otherwise contact Tairua Dive & Fishinn, The Esplanade (☏07/864 8054, ✉tairuadiveandfishinn@xtra.co.nz), who deal with just about anything to do with the sea hereabouts, or hook up with Kiwi Dundee Adventures (see p.399), for one of their extremely informative and light-hearted **eco-tours**; or try your hand at windsurfing (see p.399).

InterCity **buses** from Thames and Auckland drop off at the stationery shop, a few steps from the tourist office; buses from Whitianga stop opposite the **tourist office**, 223 Main St (Mon–Sat 9.30am–3.30pm, extended hours in summer; ☏07/864 7575, ✉info.tairua@xtra.co.nz). Go Kiwi buses pass through once a day in each direction dropping off at the numerous motels and at *Tairua Beach Villa Backpackers*, 200 Main Rd, south of the centre across the river bridge (℗07/864 8345, ℮tairuabackpackers@xtra.co.nz; tents $14, dorms ❶, rooms ❷), the best hostel in town. Set among trees near the water's edge, it offers free use of kayaks, cheap bikes for rent and windsurfers (tuition available). There's even a free car to Hot Water Beach.

For **eating**, try the daytime *Out of the Blue Café*, on the corner of Main Road and Marquet Place and in the evening head to the base of Mount Paku for the moderately priced *The Upper Deck*, 1 The Marina (℗07/864 7499; summer daily; April–Nov Thurs–Mon only), located on the *SS Ngoiro*, a restored ferry that once plied Auckland's Waitemata Harbour.

Opoutere

Around twenty kilometres south of Tairua is a 5km side road to **Opoutere**, barely a settlement at all, but a gorgeous and usually deserted 4km-long surf beach backed by pines – and behind them a campsite, YHA and a few houses. The pohutukawa-fringed road hugs the shores of the Wharekawa Harbour where wetlands make good bird-watching spots, mudflats yield shellfish and the relatively calm waters are good for kayaking.

From a signposted parking area at the end of the sealed road a footbridge leads to two paths, both reaching the beach in ten minutes or so: the **left-hand fork** runs straight through the forest to the beach; the **right-hand track** follows the estuary to the edge of a protected sandspit where endangered New Zealand dotterels breed from November to March. The white-sand Opoutere Beach can have a strong undertow and there are no lifeguards, so swim with caution.

For a wider view over the estuary and the coastline out towards the Mayor and Aldermen islands, tackle the track up **Mount Maungaruawahine** (2km return; 40–50min), which climbs through gnarled pohutukawa and other native trees to the summit.

The summit track begins by the gate to the relaxing and old-fashioned **YHA** (℗07/865 9072,℮yha.opoutere@yha.org.nz; tent sites $12, dorms ❶, rooms ❷), set beside the estuary in a 1908 schoolhouse in mature grounds, with free kayaks and the chance for nocturnal glowworm spotting. The attractive **campsite**, *Opoutere Motor Camp* (Dec 1 to end April only; ℗ & ℗07/865 9152; tent sites $12, flats ❹ plus $15 per extra person, chalet ❺ plus $20 per extra person), is about 700m towards the beach from the hostel.

There's no regular **bus** service, but drop-offs can be arranged – call the YHA in advance – and bring all your food as both places have only basic **provisions** for sale.

Whangamata and the Wentworth Valley

The long, straggling resort of **WHANGAMATA**, on SH25 towards the southern end of the Coromandel Peninsula, is bounded on three sides by estuaries and the ocean, and on the fourth by bush-clad hills: nowhere else on the Coromandel do bush and beach sit so closely together. This single-storey town of 4500 grows tenfold in January, when holiday-makers flock to its four-kilometre **Ocean Beach**, a crescent of white sand that curves from the harbour entrance to the mouth of the **Otahu River**. The bar at the harbour end has an excellent break, making this one of New Zealand's true **surfie** meccas.

Arrival, information and accommodation

Whangamata's layout is initially confusing, but the **main street**, Port Road, runs straight through the small town centre, linking it with the highway. **Buses** drop off next door to the centrally located **visitor centre**, 616 Port Rd (Mon–Sat: 9am–5pm, Sun 10am–4pm & 9am–5pm in summer; ☎07/865 8340, ⊛www.whangamatainfo.co.nz), and most places are within easy walking distance of here. **Internet access** is at Bartley Internet & Graphics, 706 Port Rd (☎07/865 8832).

Kiwis flock to this small town from Christmas until the middle of January when **accommodation** is very scarce and already high prices are jacked up by as much as fifty percent. For the rest of the year it's pretty quiet.

Brenton Lodge 2 Brenton Place ☎ & ⓕ07/865 8400, ⊛www.brentonlodge.co.nz. Beautiful retreat in pretty gardens on the edge of Whangamata with sea views from two cottages (sleeping four) and one suite. Understated decor, pool, spa, and delicious breakfasts, all costing $295 for two. ❾

Bushland Park Lodge 7km southwest of town in the Wentworth Valley ☎07/865 7468, ⊛www.bushlandparklodge.co.nz. An appealing hideaway with a classy restaurant in private grounds close to the start of the track to Wentworth Falls. Four immaculate en-suite doubles, with on-site therapies such as hydrotherapeutic spa and massage at extra cost. Rooms ❼, suites ❾

Garden Tourist Lodge cnr Port Rd & Mayfair Ave ☎07/865 9580, ✉gardenlodge@xtra.co.nz. An immaculate motel and hostel. The well-equipped hostel section has four-shares, double rooms, free

use of boogie boards and transport to walks. The motel has smart and spacious units, some with full kitchen. Four-shares ❶, rooms ❷, units ❹

Palm Pacific Resort 413 Port Rd ☎07/865 9211, ⊛www.palmpacificresort.co.nz. A big motel, equipped with fairly modern, spacious units sleeping up to eight. Facilities include a barbecue, several bars, a bistro, tennis courts, large pool, spas and sauna. ❺

Pinefield Top 10 Holiday Park 207 Port Rd ☎07/865 8791, ⊛www.pinefield.co.nz. An excellent, big shady site that fills over summer. On-site accommodation comes well-equipped; there's also a barbecue and a large swimming pool. Camping $11; cabins ❷, flats & units ❹

Wentworth Valley Campground end of Wentworth Valley Rd. Lovely DOC campsite with streamside pitches, barbecues and cold showers right by the start of the track to Wentworth Falls, 7km southwest of Whangamata. $7.

The Town and around

Surfies should make straight for the Whangamata Surf Shop, 634 Port Rd (☎07/865 8252; daily 9am–5pm), heaped with designer gear. It's the only place in town where you can **rent a surfboard** ($20 half-day, $40 full-day) or a **boogie board** ($20 full-day); wetsuits ($15 per day) and fins ($10) are also available. The shop also offers surfing tuition ($40 per hour).

Aside from the surf, there are only a couple of other diversions in the foothills of the Coromandel Range, on the edge of town. One is a pleasant **walk to Wentworth Falls** (10km return; 2hr) in the nearby Wentworth Valley. Take SH25 south for 2km to the signposted turn-off to Wentworth Valley Road; at its end (4km) is a campsite (see above) and the start of the track through regenerating bush past numerous small swimming holes. The track continues into the heart of the mountains, but most turn around at the two-leap Wentworth Falls, best viewed from a small deck from where it's possible to scramble steeply to the pool at the bottom of the falls. The other reason to come here is to join one of the extremely popular **eco-tours** run by Kiwi Dundee Adventures (☎07/865 8809, ⊛www.kiwidundee.co.nz; book as far ahead as possible). For thirty years, the dedicated conservationist Doug Johansen (popularly known as "Kiwi Dundee") has been getting his message across in his own distinctive way, with the help of his wife Jan and guides, using warmth and humour. Year-round the company offers a variety of tours including the full-day Nature Experience, Gold Mines & Coastal trip ($195), taking small groups off the beaten track for a day or more to explain history, geology, Maori medicines and natural history. Their magical Wilderness Hike (full-day, $195) takes you into a hidden valley of ancient rainforest; and private tours can also be arranged. Departures are from Tairua, Pauanui and Whangamata.

Eating and drinking

Port Road is lined with **tearooms**, takeaways and **restaurants**, but few stand out, so you might want to venture further afield for more inspiring fare.

Caffe Rossini 646 Port Rd. Modern café serving the town's best range of panini, cakes, good coffee and pizzas, either inside or on tables on the street.

Nero's Port Rd, near northern junction with SH25. Evening venue for the best pizzas in town (around $17), mostly gourmet style with combinations like salmon and shrimp, and chicken and mango. They also have a small selection of mains for around $24. Closed Sun & Mon.

Nickel Strausse 7km southwest of town on the Wentworth Valley Rd ☏07/865 7468. Excellent

and good-value dining in a small restaurant in rural surroundings. A charming German couple serve typical Black Forest lunches from Christmas to the end of Jan ($15–25) and three-course dinners all year (around $65). Booking essential for lunch and dinner.

Whangamata Ocean Sports Club Harbour-end of Port Rd. Private club and home of the Whangamata Boat & Gamefishing Club, open to non-members when they're not busy; ask at the bar. It's worth the effort for great harbour and sea views, cheap drink and hearty good-value fare.

Waihi and Waihi Beach

SH25 continues 30km south from Whangamata to **WAIHI**, where it meets SH2 at the entrance to the Karangahake Gorge (see p.373). Gold was first discovered at Waihi in a reef of quartz in 1878, but it was not until 1894 that a boom began with the first successful trials in extracting gold using cyanide solution at Karangahake. By 1908 Waihi was the fastest-growing town in the Auckland Province, and remains a mining district some five-thousand strong. Although underground mining stopped in 1952, extraction was cranked up again in 1987 in the opencast but well-hidden Martha Mine. You can visit the mine, learn about its past in a good **museum**, or hop on a 1930s train for a scenic ride into the nearby **Karangahake Gorge**.

For light relief, the popular surf beach of **WAIHI BEACH** lies 12km east of town, off SH2: its long, thin strip of golden sand stretches for 8km and is one of the safest ocean beaches in the country.

The Town

At the eastern end of town, **Martha Mine** still produces gold (and silver) to the value of about one million dollars a week, and, until it's proposed closure in 2006, is one of the few working mines in the country that you can visit. **Guided tours** (book a couple of days ahead, ☏07/863 9880, ⓦwww .marthamine.co.nz; Mon–Fri, according to demand; 75–90min; donation) take visitors around the opencast gold mine and processing areas, providing background history and details of the environmental work the company is doing. Even if you decide against the gold-mine tour, it's worth heading a couple of hundred metres up Moresby Avenue from the main street to the mine

viewing platform, reached from the Golden Legacy Centre (see below). The platform allows you to peer into the vast pit where the laden trucks are dwarfed by the sheer scale of the earthworks. Meanwhile, out of sight, a two-kilometre-long conveyor belt transports about 30,000 tonnes of ore a day through a tunnel to the treatment plant just outside town. In the **Golden Legacy Centre** (Mon–Fri 9am–4.30pm) staff give a brief talk explaining more about the whole process.

For even more background visit the **Gold-mining Museum & Art Gallery**, 54 Kenny St (Mon–Fri 10am–4pm, Sat & Sun 1.30–4pm, but closed Sat in winter; $3). This is a showcase for the fine and intricately detailed models on mining themes that were made between 1976 and 1986 by ship's engineer, Tom Morgan, in his spare time. There are also some evocative dioramas depicting miners at work, and a short historical account of the violent Waihi Strike of 1912 that helped galvanize the labour movement and eventually led to the creation of the Labour Party.

At the western end of town, the ramshackle wooden station at the end of Wrigley Street is home to the **Goldfields Railway**, which operates scenic 6km rail trips year-round to Waikino in the Karangahake Gorge (trains daily 11am, 12.30pm & 2pm, with extra services as required, returning from Waikino 45min later; 20min each way; $7 one way; ☎07/863 8640). A diesel engine (or sometimes steam) pulls 1930s carriages over a stretch of track built between 1900 and 1905 by gold-mining companies; travelling alongside SH2, you get spectacular views of the Ohinemuri River.

Practicalities

InterCity **buses** pull up at Rosemont Road Service Station, 500 metres from the **visitor centre** (daily: Oct–April 9am–5pm, May–Sept 9am–4.30pm; ☎07/863 6715) on Upper Seddon Street in the centre of town. **Internet access** is at the library on Seddon Street, 100m from the visitor centre (Mon–Thurs 10.30am–4.30pm, Fri 10am–5pm, Sat 10am–noon) and the *Farmhouse Café* (see below). There's a smattering of accommodation and eating places at both Waihi and at the beach.

Accommodation

Beaches Motel, 40 Seaforth Rd, Waihi Beach ☎07/863 5439, ⓔ beachesmotel@xtra.co.nz. Small and reliable waterfront motel near the shops. ❹

Bowentown Beach Holiday Park Seaforth Rd, Bowentown Beach ☎07/863 5381, ⓔ beachholiday@xtra.co.nz. Secluded site right at the southern end of the beach, with kayaks and boogie boards for rent. Tents $13, cabins ❷, flats ❹

Chez Nous B&B, 41 Seddon St, Waihi ☎07/863 7538, ⓦ www.bnb.co.nz/cheznous.html. Central B&B offering two quiet rooms in a pleasant modern house, and dinner by arrangement. ❸

Waihi Motel, Tauranga Rd (SH2), Waihi ☎07/863 8095, ⓔ garybrown@actrix.co.nz. A mere 2mins' walk south of the town centre, this friendly motel has spacious units with kitchens. ❹

Waihi Motor Camp, 6 Waitete Rd, off Seddon St (SH2), Waihi ☎07/863 7654, ⓕ07/863 7659. A

pretty site enjoying a creekside setting only 10mins' walk from town. Tents $12, dorm bunks ❶, cabins ❷, flats ❹

Eating

20 Turner Emerton Rd, Waihi Beach. Daytime café for good coffee till 4pm or so, serving all-day breakfast, plus cakes and pizza. BYO; closed Tues.

Cactus Jack's 31 Wilson Rd, Waihi Beach. An evening BYO sit-in and takeout burger-bar perfect for a chilli burger and shake (closed Tues–Thurs).

Farmhouse Café 14 Haszard St, Waihi. Small, cheerful and licensed spot for daytime eating (till 3.30pm) all week, plus dinner at weekends; and a pretty garden.

Waitete Orchard Orchard Rd, Waihi. Café and ice-creamery in a former winery at the western end of town, offering great-value, freshly cooked organic snacks, light meals and fresh fruit juices. Try their authentic samosas ($9) and the fruit ice cream. Closed Mon.

Katikati and around

Waihi and the Karangahake Gorge mark the southern limit of the Coromandel Peninsula. From here on the coast begins to curl eastwards into the Bay of Plenty, leaving behind the bush-clad mountains and taking on a gentler, more open aspect of rolling hills carved up by tall evergreen shelter belts protecting valuable hectares of kiwifruit vines. In summer, numerous roadside stalls spring up selling ripe fruit straight from the orchards, often at knockdown prices. It takes less then an hour to drive from Waihi to Tauranga, but you may be induced to pause a while over the **murals** of Katikati or press on to the swimming beach at **Omokoroa**.

Although, strictly speaking, **Rotorua** lies in the Bay of Plenty, it is covered along with the rest of the volcanic plateau region in Chapter Four, starting on p.303.

Katikati

Some twenty kilometres south of Waihi you arrive in **KATIKATI**, an ordinary little town that was dealt a devastating economic blow when the price of kiwifruit collapsed in the late 1980s. The town reacted by fashioning itself as "Mural Town", to catch passing tourist traffic. Colourful and well-painted murals have sprung up on buildings all over town, many reflecting the heritage of the original settlers from Ulster and the growth of the town: a couple of the best are "Waitekohe No. 3", on a block wall on the right as you enter the main street from the north, and the photo-realist "Central Motors", a little further along on the left. More information on the town is available in the **visitor centre**, 36 Main Rd/SH2, in the council building (daily 9am–4pm; ☎07/549 1658, ⓦwww.katikati.co.nz), where InterCity **buses** from Auckland stop. **Internet access** is 50 metres from the visitor centre, at the *Village Fare* café, Main Road (Mon–Sat 8am–4.30pm).

A soothing interlude can be spent strolling the contemplative **Haiku Pathway** (20min return), which meanders along the river, the route punctuated by boulders inscribed with haiku poetry. The pathway is signposted on the main road 200 metres south of the visitor centre and begins at a small green beside the main road or from the car park at the bottom of the hill. Return via the road or retrace your steps.

For something to **eat** day or evening try *The Landing*, an airy café-bar on Main Road that does a good range of mains and wood-fired pizzas. The daytime, licensed *One Wild Chook* deli café, on Main Rd, about 50 metres from the visitor centre, does good snacks including sushi and has a garden bar.

If you fancy **staying overnight** in these parts, head 6km south and turn up Thompson's Track to *Jacaranda Cottage*, 2.3km along at #230 (☎07/549 0616, ⓔjacaranda.cottage@clear.net.nz; cottage ❺ plus $25 per extra person, B&B ❺), a homestay and self-catering cottage sleeping 3 to 4 with extensive Kaimai Range views. Alternatively you might want to experience one of New Zealand's only **naturist parks**, the peaceable and well-managed Katikati Naturist Park, 149 Wharawhara Rd, off SH2 and 3km south of Katikati (☎07/549 2158, ⓦwww.katikati-naturist-park.co.nz; tents $11, on-site caravans ❷, cabins ❸, units ❹), a secluded riverside campsite with excellent facilities including a pool, sauna and spas.

Around 8km south of Katikati on SH2 the South African **Cape Dutch-style** architecture of the *Morton Estate* winery (sales and tastings daily 9.30am–5pm) hoves into view. It's a charming place ringed by mountains and standing at the foot of a sloping vineyard with roses planted at the end of each row, in classic French tradition. All the grape juice is tankered here from their more extensive plantings in Hawke's Bay and Marlborough, so that they can produce their extensive range of quality wines and offer free **tastings**. You can also **eat** lunch or dinner at *The Vineyard* (reservations advised ☎07/552 0620; closed Sun eve & Mon), where dishes for $20–26 are served in an airy conservatory or outside by the vines.

Omokoroa Beach

A further 19km on, and still 17km short of Tauranga, a dead-end road spurs 5km to pretty **OMOKOROA BEACH** (no bus service), a safe swimming beach backed by a grassy reserve. From the point you can gaze across to Matakana Island, accessible from here by **ferry** (3 daily; foot passengers $4 return, cars $25 return; visitor permit required for access to forest or beach (free but limited number available, book well in advance through the forestry company on ☎07/579 5331), but with limited access there's little point making the journey except on an organized tour with Matakana Island Tours (see p.410).

You can **stay** at the quiet well-kept *Omokoroa Tourist Park*, 165 Omokoroa Rd (☎07/548 0857, ⓦwww.omokoroatouristpark.co.nz; tent sites $14, cabins ❷, tourist flats ❸), which has hot thermal pools on site. From here it's a fifteen-minute drive into Tauranga, reached through Te Puna (home of the Paparoa Marae; see p.412), and the satellite community of **Bethlehem** (see p.414).

The western Bay of Plenty: Tauranga and Mount Maunganui

The western end of the **BAY OF PLENTY** centres on the prosperous port city of **TAURANGA** ("safe anchorage"), and its beachside acolyte, **Mount Maunganui**, effectively a suburb. This amorphous settlement, sprawled around the numerous glittering tentacles of Tauranga Harbour, is one of the **fastest-growing cities** in the land and is overtaking Dunedin as New Zealand's fifth-largest urban area. A combination of warm dry summers and mild winters initially attracted retirees, followed by telecommuters and folk running their profitable small businesses from home. The result is a wealthy community that has fuelled increasing expansion and helped create a vibrant café society.

Visit outside the peak weeks of summer madness and the region's charms quickly become apparent – though you'll do best if you have access to the surrounding area. Beyond the beach and a couple of walks around the extinct volcano, Mount Maunganui's appeal runs only to a flourishing **restaurant** and **bar scene**. This it shares with Tauranga, which is best used to get out on the water: trips primarily head to **Matakana Island**, which acts as a barrier to Tauranga Harbour, and **Tuhua (Mayor) Island**, a bush-clad retreat in the Bay of Plenty. Boats also take clients to **swim with dolphins**, cruise the harbour, or on excellent full-day **sailing trips**.

Beyond the city limits are opportunities to go **kayaking**, scale an outdoor climbing wall, ride horses, and wrangle quad bikes at a couple of adventure parks, or engage in more peaceful pursuits like **wine tasting** or picnicking beside some delightful swimming holes at **McLaren Falls**.

Tauranga is in a major **kiwifruit-picking region**, but be warned, it's tough and prickly work and you must commit yourself to a minimum of three weeks (if this doesn't put you off, check out "Listings" on p.413).

Tauranga and Mount Maunganui

Once through the protecting ring of suburbs, it's apparent that rampant development hasn't spoilt central **Tauranga**, which occupies a narrow peninsula with several city parks and gardens backing a lively waterfront area. Progress has been less kind to the over-commercialized beach resort of **Mount Maunganui**, which huddles under the extinct volcanic cone of the same name – a landmark visible throughout the western Bay of Plenty. "The Mount", as hill and town are often known, was once an island but is connected to the mainland by a narrow neck of dune sand (a tombolo) covered with apartment blocks, shops, restaurants and houses. The Mount's saving grace is a 20km-long golden strand of Ocean Beach that's wonderful for swimming and surfing. No surprise, then, that the area's a big draw for Kiwi **holiday-makers** from mid-December to Easter (March or April) and on summer weekends, when Tauranga and Mount Maunganui can be rather overwhelming and accommodation hard to come by.

Arrival, information and transport

The **airport** receives daily Air New Zealand flights from Auckland and Wellington, and lies midway between Tauranga and Mount Maunganui, roughly 3km from each: a taxi to either costs around $14. Tauranga no longer has a train service, but InterCity, Newmans, Supa Travel and Go Kiwi **buses** stop at the visitor centres in both towns. The Tauranga **visitor centre**, 95 Willow St (Mon–Fri 7am–5.30pm, Sat & Sun 8am–4pm; ☎07/578 8103, ⓦwww.tauranga.govt.nz), handles transport and accommodation bookings, as well as selling maps. There is a **DOC office**, 253 Chadwick Rd, Greerton (Mon–Fri 8am–4.30pm but closed for a half-hour from noon; ☎07/578 7677), inconveniently sited some 6km south of central Tauranga. For topographic **maps** try Absolute Adventure, 94 Willow St, by the visitor centre. The Mount Maunganui **visitor centre** is on Salisbury Avenue, just off Maunganui Rd (Mon–Fri 9am–5pm, Sat & Sun 8am–4pm; ☎07/575 5099). You can avoid Tauranga's **metered parking** by choosing streets just outside the city centre.

Local transport

Visitor centres stock timetables for the local **Bay Hopper Bus** (☎0800/422 9287, ⓦwww.hopper.citynews.co.nz), which runs Monday to Saturday services that cover most places in the immediate vicinity, including a half-hourly Tauranga–Mount Maunganui run ($6 all-day ticket from driver). These dry up

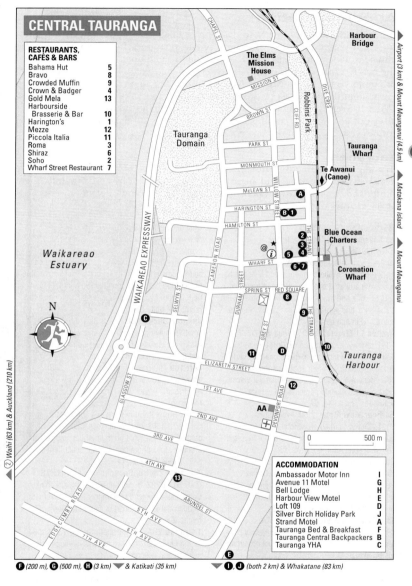

CENTRAL TAURANGA

RESTAURANTS, CAFÉS & BARS

Bahama Hut	5
Bravo	8
Crowded Muffin	9
Crown & Badger	4
Gold Mela	13
Harbourside Brasserie & Bar	10
Harington's	1
Mezze	12
Piccola Italia	11
Roma	3
Shiraz	6
Soho	2
Wharf Street Restaurant	7

The Elms Mission House

MISSION ST

Harbour Bridge

Robbins Park

Tauranga Domain

PARK ST

MONMOUTH ST

Tauranga Wharf

Te Awanui (Canoe)

McLEAN ST

HARINGTON ST

HAMILTON ST

Blue Ocean Charters

THE STRAND

WHARF ST

Coronation Wharf

SPRING ST RED SQUARE

ELIZABETH STREET

1ST AVE

2ND AVE

AA

3RD AVE

4TH AVE

Waikareao Estuary

WAIKAREAO EXPRESSWAY

Tauranga Harbour

500 m

ACCOMMODATION

Ambassador Motor Inn	I
Avenue 11 Motel	G
Bell Lodge	H
Harbour View Motel	E
Loft 109	D
Silver Birch Holiday Park	J
Strand Motel	A
Tauranga Bed & Breakfast	F
Tauranga Central Backpackers	B
Tauranga YHA	C

Airport (3 km) & Mount Maunganui (45 km)

Matakana Island

Mount Maunganui

Waihi (63 km) & Auckland (210 km)

F (200 m), G (500 m), H (3 km) & Katikati (35 km)   I, J (both 2 km) & Whakatane (83 km)

at around 5.30pm; after that you'll have to shell out for a taxi ($15–20), either from the **taxi** stand in Hamilton Street (between The Strand and Willow Street) in Tauranga or by calling one of the radio-cab companies (see p.413). During summer, there's also a daytime **ferry** (Christmas–Easter; $6 each way) to Salisbury Wharf in Mount Maunganui from the pontoon at Coronation Wharf on The Strand in Tauranga. For **bike and car rental** see p.413.

Accommodation

On arrival, your first move is to decide on which side of the water you want to stay. If you've got a car you might prefer to stop in **Tauranga**, where the choice is wider and prices tend to be a little lower, though you're further from the beach. Without your own transport, you need to balance the advantages of proximity to the surf in **Mount Maunganui** against the wider range of restaurants, nightlife and access to offshore islands that Tauranga offers.

Alternatively, you might like to stay further afield at the **beachside campsites** out of town and commute as necessary. Likely candidates are Omokoroa to the west (see p.403) or Papamoa Beach to the east (see p.414).

Tauranga

Tauranga has numerous **hostels**, **motels** and **B&Bs** all within walking distance of the centre, and plenty more in the suburbs and out into the hinterland. A plethora of motels line 15th Avenue, some offering good deals at slack times of year.

Motels & B&B

Ambassador Motor Inn 9 15th Ave ☏07/578 5665 & 0800/735 294, ⓦwww .ambassador-motorinn.co.nz. Well-appointed motel a short drive from the city centre and near the harbour, with a heated pool. Popular, well-equipped budget units and more luxurious ones, others with a spa bath, and some with water views. Studios just ❺, with spa bath ❻

Avenue 11 Motel 26 11th Avenue ☏07/577 1881, ⓦwww.avenue11.co.nz. Great-value boutique motel in a central yet quiet location overlooking the harbour, with four spacious and sumptuously decorated units (most with harbour views). Extra touches include personalized service, bathrobes and a spa. ❺

Harbour View Motel, 7 5th Ave East ☏07/578 8621, ⓦwww.harbourviewmotel.co.nz. Small, quiet and homely place a stone's throw from the bay, with spa and free kayaks. ❹

Strand Motel cnr The Strand & McLean St ☏ & ☏07/578 5807, ⓦwww.strandmotel.co.nz. Budget, central and near the waterfront, but on a fairly noisy corner. Sea views from the decks of most of the fully equipped units. ❹

Tauranga Bed & Breakfast 4 9th Ave ☏07/577 0927, ☏577 0954. Fairly central homestay near Memorial Park, with an en-suite double room and full breakfast. ❹

Hostels & campsites

Bell Lodge 39 Bell St, off Waihi Rd (take Otumoetai exit off SH2) ☏07/578 6344, ⓦwww.bell-lodge.co.nz. A clean, modern and comfortable hostel in a peaceful spot 3km from the centre, with spacious dorms, comfortable en-suite rooms and some motel units. Excellent facilities include barbecue, free pick-up and daily shuttle to Mount Maunganui. Tent sites $14, dorms ❶, rooms ❷, units ❸

Just the Ducks Nuts 6 Vale St ☏07/576 1366. A small friendly hostel 1.5km from the city centre, with great views of the harbour and the Mount, and free bikes. Dorms ❶, rooms ❷

Loft 109 109 Devonport Rd ☏07/579 5638, ⓦwww.loft109.ac.nz. Small yet central, clean and friendly hostel with a roof deck. Dorms ❶, rooms ❷

Silver Birch Holiday Park 101 Turret Rd ☏07/578 4603, ⓔsilverbirch@xtra.co.nz. Fairly central campsite right on the harbour's edge with a family atmosphere and thermal pools. Tent sites $11, cabins ❷, units ❹

Tauranga Central Backpackers 64 Willow St ☏07/571 6222, ⓔcentralbackpack@xtra.co.nz. Comfortable hostel that primarily benefits from its location right in the heart of Tauranga. Dorms ❶, rooms ❸

Tauranga YHA 171 Elizabeth St ☏07/578 5064, ⓔyha.tauranga@yha.org.nz. Well-equipped, modern and welcoming hostel in secluded grounds a 5min walk from the centre, with BBQ, volleyball and minigolf. Tent sites $12, dorms ❶, rooms ❷

Mount Maunganui

Mount Maunganui is close to the surf and although much of the accommodation is geared towards **long-staying** Kiwi holidaymakers, you'll also find several motels and a couple of hostels.

Belle Mer 53 Marine Parade ☎07/575 0011 & 0800/100 235, ⓦwww.bellemer.co.nz. Plush apartments for 4–6 with modern decor, just across the road from the beach. Most have sea views, all have spa baths, luxurious kitchens, stereo and access to a heated lap pool. ❼

Links Motel 209 Valley Rd ☎07/575 5774, ⓕ575 6495. Peaceful low-cost motel close to the beach, with Sky TV, spa pool, free newspaper and breakfast served in your room if required. ❹

Mount Backpackers 87 Maunganui Rd ☎07/575 0860, ⓔmountinternet@xtra.co.nz. Small and somewhat cramped hostel right in the thick of things – close to restaurants, bars and the beach. Low-cost bike and boogie-board rental. Dorms ❶, rooms ❷

Mount Maunganui Domain Motor Camp 1 Adams Ave ☎07/575 4471, ⓔmtdomain@xtra.co.nz. A sizeable, terraced campsite very close to the beach in a pleasant spot beside the hot saltwater pools and right at the foot of the Mount. Camping $24 per site.

Ocean Waves Motel 74 Marine Parade ☎07/575 4594, ⓦwww.oceanwaves.co.nz. Well-sited motel, as close as you'll get to the popular end of the beach and with ocean views from some units. ❺

Pacific Coast Lodge 432 Maunganui Rd ☎07/574 9601 & 0800/666 622, ⓦwww .pacificcoastlodge.co.nz. Vast hostel with good facilities (spacious dorms, large kitchen, games room, barbecue area) and a strong recycling ethic. Only a good option if you don't mind being away from the restaurants and the fashionable end of the beach. Dorms ❶, rooms ❸

The city centre

Tauranga's flat **city centre** is concentrated between Tauranga Harbour and Waikareao Estuary. It's a dense kernel of shops, restaurants and bars where you'll find just about everything you need, but little of abiding interest other than boat trips onto the bay and its islands (see p.409). Downtown Tauranga is a pleasant spot though, and you can easily spend half a day strolling along the waterfront or mooching around the couple of minor sights.

First stop should be the ornately carved traditional **war canoe**, *Te Awanui*, which stands proudly in a shelter on the corner of Dive Crescent and McLean Street, and is used on ceremonial occasions on the harbour. About one block up and entered from Cliff Street is **Robbins Park** (dawn–dusk; free), an attractive swathe of green equipped with a rose garden and begonia house, and yielding fine views across to Mount Maunganui. At the northern end of town, on Mission Street, is **The Elms Mission House** (Wed, Sat & Sun 2–4pm, and by appointment on ☎07/577 9772; $5). One of the country's oldest homes, it was built from kauri between 1835 and 1847 by an early missionary, Archdeacon A.N. Brown, who tended the wounded of both sides during the **Battle of Gate Pa** (see box below). The house has maintained its original form complete with dark-wood interior and a dining table at which Brown entertained several British officers on the eve of the Battle of Gate Pa, little suspecting that over the next few days he would bury all of them. If

The Battle of Gate Pa

In 1864 the tiny community of Tauranga became the scene of the **Battle of Gate Pa**, one of the most decisive engagements of the **New Zealand Wars**. In January the government sent troops here to build two redoubts, hoping to prevent supplies and reinforcements from reaching the followers of the Maori King (see p.247), who were fighting in the Waikato. Most of the local Ngaiterangi hurried back from the Waikato and challenged the soldiers from a *pa* they quickly built near an entrance to the mission land, which became known as Gate Pa. In April, government troops surrounded the *pa* in what was New Zealand's only naval blockade, and pounded it with artillery. Nonetheless, the British lost about a third of their assault force and at nightfall the Ngaiterangi slipped through the British lines to fight again in the Waikato.

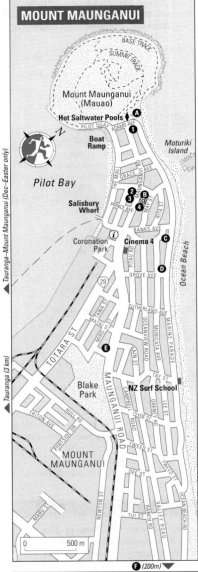

you miss the opening hours of the house you can still enjoy a picnic in the pretty **gardens** (dawn–dusk; free), boasting an English oak planted by Brown in 1838 and a reconstruction of the original chapel.

Mount Maunganui

From the eastern end of the 3.5km-long Tauranga Harbour Bridge, you are still 3km short of the heart of **Mount Maunganui**, reached through a big industrial estate: not an auspicious start. Things improve as you head to the northern tip where the 232-metre Mount itself (*Mauao* in Maori) rises above the golden **beach**, an unbroken sweep stretching more than 20km east to Papamoa (see p.414) and beyond. Habitually sun-kissed in the summer, condos and apartments have colonized the beach's fashionable northern kilometre in an unusual fashion for New Zealand. The Mount also has a reputation as something of a party town, especially at New Year. The beach is still great, perfect for a day or two playing volleyball and swimming while still within easy reach of good restaurants and bars where everyone gravitates for sundowners.

If you fancy trying your hand at **surfing**, wander along Marine Parade to the junction with Tay Street, where teachers at the New Zealand Surf School (☎07/574 1666, @nzsurfschool @yahoo.com) conduct two-hour **lessons** ($80) on specially designed longboards; they guarantee you'll stand up. After your lesson you're free to practise for as long as you like; others can rent a board and wetsuit for two hours for $20. For other gear and advice on **surf conditions** call at any of the surf shops along Maunganui Road. For **sea**

ACCOMMODATION		RESTAURANTS	
Belle Mer	C	Astrolabe	3
Links Motel	F	Hasan Baba	2
Mount Backpackers	B	Sidetrack	
Mount Maunganui		Café Pacifica	1
Domain Motor Camp	A	Volantis	4
Ocean Waves Motel	D		
Pacific Coast Lodge	E		

kayaking contact Oceanix (℡0274 942677, ⓦwww.oceanix.co.nz; from $75 for half-day).

Apart from the beach, the big draw is the mountain itself, which has a fine **walking track** around the base (3km loop; 45min), mostly level and offering a great sea and harbour outlook from under the shade of ancient pohutukawas. The base track links with a **hike to the summit** (2km one way; 1hr), which is tough going towards the top but well worth the effort for views of Matakana Island and along the coast. Both tracks start at the northern end of the beach, right by the outdoor, chlorinated **Hot Saltwater Pools**, Adams Avenue (Mon–Sat 6am–10pm, Sun 8am–10pm; public pool $5, private $6 per half hour; use of towel $2, togs $2), which form Mount Maunganui's other main attraction.

Cruises and day-trips

It would be a shame to come to the western Bay of Plenty and not get out **on the water**, something easily done from the Tauranga Wharf, with many trips also picking up at Salisbury Wharf in Mount Maunganui. A full range of boats is ready to take you cruising, fishing, sailing, parasailing and **swimming with dolphins**.

The island retreats of Matakana and Tuhua (Major) are both prime Bay of Plenty boat-trip destinations. Strictly speaking Matakana is, in fact, two islands: the tiny **Rangiwea** and the long sheltering sweep of **Matakana**, nestled close to Tauranga Harbour and used primarily for farming and forestry. **Mayor Island** is the cone-shaped dormant volcano, protruding from the Bay of Plenty 40km off the coast of Tauranga and increasingly geared towards eco-tourism.

Boat trips on the bay

About the cheapest way to get on the water is on a six-hour **harbour cruise** aboard the 1938 line-fishing boat *Ratahi* (℡07/578 9685; $40 including afternoon tea) as it chugs across the bay to Omokoroa and back.

An equally leisurely day out at sea, but with the option of **swimming with dolphins**, is run by The Tauranga Dolphin Company on its yacht *Gemini Galaxsea* (book a day ahead ℡0508 288537 & 0800/836 574; $95, take your own lunch). The skipper, Graham Butler, is a good-natured sea dog and militant greenie who has a high success rate of finding dolphins. He allows plenty of time, so don't be surprised if you're out well into the afternoon. Trips run most of the year, but only in good weather conditions. If you're on a tight schedule and still want to swim with dolphins, try the Mount Maunganui-based Dolphin Seafaris, 90 Maunganui Rd (℡07/575 4620 & 0800/326 8747; $100), which runs half-day trips in the morning and afternoon in its launch.

Scores of boats are available for **fishing charters**, many through Blue Ocean Charters, Tauranga Wharf (℡07/578 9685, ⓦwww.blueoceancharters.co.nz): game fishing for marlin, tuna and kingfish (Dec–April) is likely to cost about $250 a day per person, but if you go out for the bottom fish (snapper and tarakihi) it's cheaper at around $50 per half day.

Matakana Island

MATAKANA ISLAND has 24km of beach and great surfing on its eastern side, as well as a general store and pub for more mundane requirements. However, much of the island is Maori land with limited access, so even if you take your own wheels on the ferry from Omokoroa (see p.403), you will be fairly restricted. The ferry lands at Opurereroa Point, where most of the residents live. You can view the *marae* and laid-back island way of life, but need a permit if you wish to go through the forest or to the beach. The best way to see the island is on a **guided tour** with Matakana Island Tours (☏0800/276 391, ✉clydesdales4tour@ihug.co.nz) who offer two options: an afternoon driving tour across the island (2hr 30min, $35 including afternoon tea), and a full-day tour ($69 including ferry and lunch) in a group of 15 minimum, which includes a *marae* visit, the ocean beach, and a crossing over tidal flats on a restored horse-drawn wagon.

Tuhua (Mayor) Island

Dormant volcano, **TUHUA (Mayor) ISLAND**, has a crater virtually over-grown and a third of its coast designated a **marine reserve** in readiness for low-key eco-tourism. There are some great **walking tracks** around the island's base and through its centre, and boats coming out here will rent snorkelling gear ($10 per day) so you can explore the aquatic world. The area, however, is abundant with **wasps** and anyone allergic to stings should pack medication or just not risk it.

Since the island is privately owned by the Tuhua Trust Board, day visitors are charged a **landing fee** of $5, which is included in commercial boat fares. Several boats operate regular services from Tauranga from Nov to mid-April (from $80 return), but the rest of the year you may need to charter a boat. Check with Tauranga visitor centre for all details. The island's only landing site is Opo Bay, at the south end – though sailings are often cancelled in rough weather. The **crossing** usually takes two to three hours depending on boat and conditions. Marine-reserve **diving** trips are run by Dolphin Seafaris (see p.409; two dives, $110).

Your only **accommodation** option on the island is the *Tuhua Campsite* at Opo Bay (booking ahead essential ☏07/579 5655; tent sites $5, 4 & 6-bed dorms ❶), which sits beneath pohutukawa trees behind an idyllic bay. It has showers and toilets, but you'll need to bring a cooking stove, all utensils and food.

Eating

Tauranga and Mount Maunganui have fully embraced modern café/bar cul-ture, Tauranga in particular rating as something of a regional culinary hotspot. As elsewhere, distinctions between eating and drinking places are blurring and you may well find yourself enjoying a drink at one of the places listed below. There's also a Saturday morning farmers **market** from 8am, at the Compass Community Village, 17th Avenue West in Tauranga.

In **Tauranga**, most of the cafés and restaurants are right in the centre – a slew of them strung along Devonport Road with a bunch more lining The Strand and the streets running back from it. A little further afield, the western suburb of Bethlehem is home to a popular winery restaurant. **Mount Maunganui** doesn't have Tauranga's selection, but you can find something appealing on the half-dozen blocks of Maunganui Road that make up the centre. It also has an excellent **ice-cream parlour,** at Copenhagen Cones, Adams Avenue (open daily all year), opposite the Salt Water Pools.

Tauranga and Bethlehem

Bravo cnr Red Square and Willow St ☏07/578 4700. Cool urban café and dinner restaurant that spills onto the pedestrianized Red Square. An energizing spot for breakfast, gourmet snacks and pizzas, or dinner mains for around $26, plus a tan-talizing range of freshly squeezed juices. Book ahead for a lunchtime table outdoors in summer. Closed Sun & Mon eve.

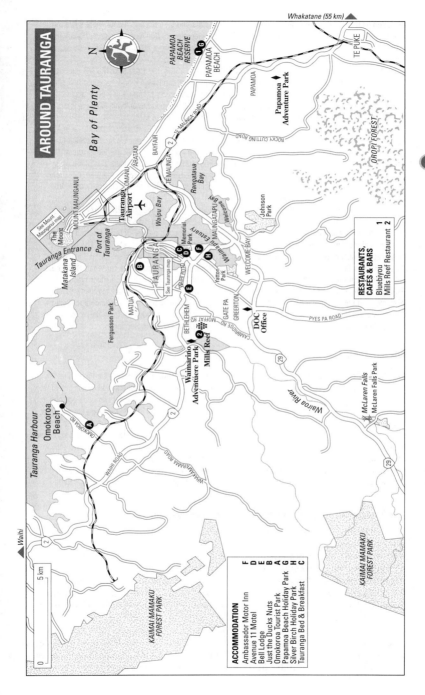

AROUND TAURANGA

N

Whakatane (55 km)

Bay of Plenty

PAPAMOA BEACH RESERVE

1 G

PAPAMOA BEACH

TE PUKE

PAPAMOA

Papamoa Adventure Park

PAPAMOA

ROCKY CUTTING ROAD

TE MAUNGA ROAD

OROPI FOREST

2

BAYFAIR

OMANU / ARATAKI

MOUNT MAUNGANUI

See Mount Maunganui map

The Mount

Tauranga Entrance

Matakana Island

Port of Tauranga

Tauranga Harbour

Omokoroa Beach

A

Waihi

OMOKOROA RD

WAIHI ROAD

WHAKAMARAMA ROAD

KAIMAI MAMAKU FOREST PARK

0   5 km

KAIMAI MAMAKU FOREST PARK

Tauranga Airport

Waipu Bay

Rangataua Bay

TE MAUNGA

Johnson Park

MAUNGATAPU

Welcome Bay

WELCOME BAY

Waimapu Estuary

TAURANGA

See Tauranga map

MATUA

Ferguson Park

BETHLEHEM

Waimarino Adventure Park

Mills Reef

CAMBRIDGE RD

MOFFAT RD

C D

E

F

H

Memorial Park

Yatton Park

GATE PA

GREERTON

PYES PA ROAD

DOC Office

29

Wairoa River

McLaren Falls

McLaren Falls Park

29

KAIMAI MAMAKU FOREST PARK

RESTAURANTS, CAFES & BARS

Bluebiyou 1
Mills Reef Restaurant 2

ACCOMMODATION

Ambassador Motor Inn F
Avenue 11 Motel D
Bell Lodge E
Just the Ducks Nuts B
Omokoroa Tourist Park A
Papamoa Beach Holiday Park G
Silver Birch Holiday Park H
Tauranga Bed & Breakfast C

Crowded Muffin 22 Devonport Rd. Daytime joint with excellent, cheap muffins to enjoy over a coffee; and good breakfast and brunch. Closed Sun.

Gold Mela cnr 4th Ave and Cameron Rd ☎07/578 1197. Authentic and good-value Mediterranean dishes for evening dining in an intimate mellow setting (advisable to book ahead). The wine list includes several French and a few Italian options. Licensed & BYO; closed Sun.

Harbourside Brasserie & Bar under the railway bridge at the southern end of The Strand. A big, airy restaurant bar right on the harbour, with great views and a covered deck over the water. Lively cosmopolitan ambience and food, with lunch and dinner mains averaging $28, as well as cheaper light meals and weekend breakfast. Book ahead for a table on the deck.

Mezze 130 Devonport Rd. Laid-back, groovy little daytime café ideal for reading the paper over breakfast or a snack, including several vegetarian options. Closed Sun.

Mills Reef Restaurant Moffat Rd, Bethlehem ☎07/576 8844. Highly regarded winery restaurant in an elevated position that's Tauranga's favourite brunch and lunch spot, open till 5pm; or you can just pop in for coffee and a cake. Great gourmet

pizzas and an à la carte menu. There's live music outdoors every Sun lunchtime and at quiet times you can ask for a 20min winery tour ($5 including tasting).

Piccola Italia 107 Grey St ☎07/578 8363. Good-value northern Italian dinner café and restaurant with wonderfully prepared authentic dishes ($17–30) served with aplomb. Takeway pizza and pasta, too. Closed Mon.

Shiraz 12 Wharf St ☎07/577 0059. Tasty Middle Eastern and Mediterranean food, excellent service and reasonable prices for lunch (under $15) and dinner (under $20) make this place often packed; reservations recommended. Leisurely eating in a small café and covered courtyard. Closed Sun.

Soho 59 The Strand ☎07/577 0577. Relaxing reasonably priced dinner restaurant that has brought French provincial (and assorted European) dining to the Tauranga waterfront. The menu is supplemented by a bistro set menu. Closed Sun.

Wharf Street Restaurant cnr Wharf St & The Strand ☎07/578 8322. Upper-floor brasserie and bar with great views over the harbour and a seafood-dominated menu for lunch and dinner – including a sumptuous seafood platter for two ($140). Closed Sat & Sun lunch.

Mount Maunganui

Astrolabe 82 Maunganui Rd. A large and popular diner-cum-drinking hole, with a beachy and slightly upmarket tenor and some late-night dancing. Open for brunch, lunch and dinner, with salads and pasta, char-grilled steak and fish, and a large range of beers.

Hasan Baba 16 Pacific Ave. Well-prepared Middle Eastern dishes, delicately flavoured and served in relaxing surroundings at moderate prices. Licensed & BYO.

Sidetrack Café Pacifica Marine Parade, under the Twin Towers. A great place to go for breakfast or morning coffee, when you can gaze across the beach to the ocean in the warming early sun. Also open for lunch.

Volantis 105 Maunganui Rd. One of the best spots on the strip for a casual coffee, or snacks along the lines of Thai chicken soup ($10.50) and gourmet burgers, with several vegetarian options. Dinner mains are $22 or so. Licensed & BYO.

Drinking, nightlife and entertainment

In both Tauranga and Maunganui the restaurants double as **bars**: neither town is especially jumping in the off-season, but come summer the evenings hot up, with Mount Maunganui having earned a reputation for boisterous behaviour. Of the two only Tauranga boasts a couple of dedicated watering holes and a **nightclub** or two, all in the same downtown area. **Films** are shown at Cinema 6 on Elizabeth Street in Tauranga (infoline ☎07/577 0800) and at Cinema 4 on Maunganui Road at The Mount (infoline ☎07/577 0900). Screening times are listed in Friday's *Bay of Plenty Times*, which is the best general source of entertainment **listings** every day of the week.

For something completely different, consider a visit to **Paparoa Marae**, Paparoa Road, 15km west of Tauranga (contact Karen Nicholas ☎ & ℱ07/552 5796), which puts on professional yet low-key cultural performances complete with traditional *wero* (challenge), a visit to the simple meeting-house, where the carvings are explained, and a display of Maori crafts. Performances are only put on for groups (or when there's a cruise ship in town), but you may be able to tag along (around $40), and evening events may also include a *hangi*.

Tauranga clubs and bars

Bahama Hut 19 Wharf St. Popular surf bar-cum-club with pool tables. A DJ plays nightly, building up to the big shindigs of Thurs–Sat.

Crown & Badger cnr The Strand & Wharf St. Lively (sometimes frenetic) English pub with a good range of beers and pub-style meals mostly for under $15.

Harington's 10 Harington St. A bar-cum-night-club, usually packed by midnight and open until 5am, with mostly dance music. Oct–April nightly; May–Sept Thurs–Sat.

Roma 65 The Strand. One of the more upmarket clubs, open from 8pm till 5am or so, with DJs on Fri & Sat nights. Closed Mon–Wed May–Sept.

Listings

Automobile Association cnr First Ave & Devonport Rd, Tauranga ☎07/578 2222.

Bike rental Around $20 a day from Underground Cycles, 111 Grey St, Tauranga (☎07/578 0208) and Bike and Pack Warehouse, 1 Dee St, Mount Maunganui (☎07/575 2189). Several of the hostels have cheaper bikes – some available to non-guests.

Books Quality Second-Hand, 26 Wharf St.

Buses InterCity and Newmans (both ☎07/578 8103) run several daily services to Auckland, Hamilton, Rotorua, and Thames (via Katikati, Waihi and Paeroa). Go Kiwi (☎0800/446 549) run daily services in summer to Auckland, Hamilton and Rotorua, with limited services in winter.

Car rental Budget deals from Johnny's Rentals, at the airport (☎07/575 9204) as well as international companies in Tauranga, notably Budget (☎07/578 5156) and Rite Price at Mount Maunganui (☎0800/250 251 & 07/575 2726).

Internet access Tauranga Library, in the Civic Shopping Centre behind the visitor centre, has Internet access at reasonable rates (Mon–Fri 9.30am–5.30pm, Sat 9.30am–4pm, Sun 12.30–4pm); and at Tauranga Central Backpackers

(see p.406). In Maunganui, head for *The Mount Backpackers* (see p.407).

Kiwifruit picking The best time for picking is late April to mid-June, but pruning is also necessary from mid-June to early Sept and again from end of Oct to Jan. For picking, you're paid by the bin or by the kilo, so speed is of the essence; an average rate is $70 a day, but quick workers can earn $100 plus. The best sources of up-to-date information are the backpacker hostels, which will often help you to find work.

Medical treatment After-hours medical care and an emergency pharmacy is available at the Baycare Medical Service Centre, cnr Edgecumbe Rd & Tenth Ave ☎07/578 8111; Mon–Fri 5pm–8am, Sat & Sun 24hr.

Post office 17 Grey St, Tauranga; Mon–Fri 8.30am–5.30pm, Sat 9am–4pm, Sun 10am–3pm; poste restante facilities.

Taxis Citicabs ☎07/577 0999; Coastline ☎0800/505 555 & 07/571 8333; Tauranga Taxis ☎07/578 6086; Mount Taxis ☎0800/829 448 & 07/574 7555.

Thomas Cook 63 Devonport Rd ☎07/578 3119.

Around Tauranga

Unless you are happy spending days on the beach, or are keen to explore the Bay of Plenty and its islands, you'll soon exhaust the temptations of Tauranga and Mount Maunganui. Help is at hand in the hinterland, where **Mills Reef winery** drapes across fertile countryside backed by the angular peaks of the Kaimai-Mamaku Forest Park. Rivers cascading down the slopes and across the coastal plain supply water for assorted activities at **Waimarino Adventure Park**, and periodically fire up **McLaren Falls**, where shallow rock pools make great swimming holes. At the coast, the great sweep of Mount Maunganui's Ocean Beach extends to **Papamoa Beach**, great for surfing and swimming away from the glitz of the Mount.

Bethlehem: Mills Reef winery and Waimarino Adventure Park

The suburb of **Bethlehem** to the west justifies a little of your time, particularly if you fancy a visit to the Art Deco-style **tasting rooms** at *Mills Reef*, 143 Moffat Rd (daily 10am–5pm; ⓦwww.millsreef.co.nz), where you can sample for free, and of course buy, bottles: the Reserve Chardonnay and Elspeth Chardonnay are usually very good, and they also produce Rieslings, Sauvignons, some sparkling wines and plenty of reds. There's a classy on-site restaurant open for brunch and lunch (see p.412).

All this eating and wine tasting could work as a perfect finale to a half-day spent at the riverside **Waimarino Adventure Park**, 34 Taniwha Place (daily 10am–6pm; ☏07/576 4233, ⓦwww.waimarino.com), which conducts a huge range of mainly water-based courses and activities. The most accessible are the **activity sessions** around the centre (passes for $9–27 per person depending on what you opt for), which all include rope swings, a hydro-slide, thermal pool, ropes course and trampolines and can include water-bikes and kayaks ($20) and the climbing wall ($9 per hour). **Kayaking** trips start with the Wairoa River Trip (3hr; $35), a tide-assisted and unguided flatwater paddle down a lower stretch of the Wairoa River to the adventure park; a three-hour moonlit version costs $60 and booking is essential. If whitewater rafting isn't thrilling enough for you, try the Extreme Boating (3hr; $150) in a double kayak and guided down either the Wairoa (certain Sundays only; Grade IV+) or the Kaituna (Grade III–IV).

McLaren Falls

Most summer Sundays, **McLaren Falls**, signposted 11km south of Tauranga off SH29, becomes the scene of frenetic activity as hundreds of rafters and kayakers congregate to run the Grade IV+ rapids of the Wairoa River. The ten-metre cataract itself is only worth viewing on the Sundays when the upstream dam releases its charge (Dec–March every Sun; Sept–Nov & April–May every second Sun) but pretty much every day of the summer locals flock here to wallow in a lovely series of shallow pools hewn out of the bedrock. It can get crowded, but a few minutes' rock-hopping should secure you a pool to yourself: bring a picnic and sunscreen.

Papamoa Beach

Mount Maunganui's stunning Ocean Beach stretches 20km east to **Papamoa Beach**, a burgeoning community accessed off SH2. Backed by the dramatic Papamoa Hills, it makes a pleasant spot for a beach break away from the city, facilitated by the outstanding *Papamoa Beach Top 10 Holiday Park*, in the domain at the eastern end of Papamoa Beach Road (☏07/572 0816, ⓦwww.papamoabeach.co.nz; camping $15, cabins ❸, units ❹ plus $15 per extra person, 4-bed villas ❻ plus $20 per extra person), where accommodation ranges from beachfront campsites to gorgeous waterside villas, all near the shops. The licensed, nautically themed *Bluebiyou* café/restaurant next door has a covered deck overlooking the sand and surf just metres away, and serves light meals, lunch, dinner and Sunday brunch.

In the hills a couple of kilometres back from the beach, there's fun to be had at **Papamoa Adventure Park**, 1162 Welcome Bay Rd, off SH2 (☏07/542 0972, ⒺPapamoa.adventure.park@xtra.co.nz; daily 9.30am–4.30pm), where they'll take you **horse trekking** ($30 per hour) over open hill country with

360-degree views. Or you can test your skills at target shooting ($30) or go for a **paintball** game in the forest (from $25).

The eastern Bay of Plenty

Moving away from Tauranga toward the **eastern Bay of Plenty**, along the Pacific Coast Highway, the urban influence wanes noticeably; the pace slows and everything seems much more rural, with orchards and kiwifruit vines gradually giving way to sheep country. You'll also find a gradual change in the racial mix, for the Eastern Bay of Plenty is increasingly Maori country; appropriate since some of the first **Maori** to reach New Zealand arrived here in their great *waka* (war canoes). In fact Whakatane is sometimes known as the birthplace of Aotearoa, for it was here that the Polynesian navigator **Toi te Huatahi** first landed.

The westernmost town, **Te Puke**, is very much New Zealand's kiwifruit capital, and is well inland, but the sea is still the focus of the region. The heyday of its port has long passed, but **Whakatane** remains the largest town, prettily set between cliffs and a river estuary. It makes a great base for forays out to volcanic **White Island**, or the bird reserve of **Whale Island**. Further east, **Opotiki** is the gateway to the East Cape in one direction and to Gisborne in the other, as well as providing access to some interesting walks in the hills to the south and to trips on the remote and scenic **Motu River**.

Te Puke

Te Puke, 31km southeast of Tauranga on SH2, is justifiably billed as the "kiwifruit capital of the world", a claim driven home at **Kiwifruit Country**, 6km east of Te Puke (daily 9am–5pm; 30–40min guided tours $12), a massive orchard and processing plant that also operates as a horticultural theme park. A surreal, giant slice of kiwifruit stands near its gateway. The complex is as tacky and commercialized as you would expect, but it's the only place to go if you're curious about how these little green, furry fruits (and their gold counterparts) grow and are harvested. The "Kiwi Kart" guided tours tell you everything you ever wanted to know about them (and much more besides).

Next door to Kiwifruit Country is the **Vintage Auto Barn** (daily 9am–5pm; $8), literally a big barn of some ninety-odd veteran, vintage and classic cars from 1906 to 1970, all kept in exceptional condition. Among the older models is a 1912 Model C Renault in pristine condition, complete with wooden-spoked wheels. Car fanatics might easily lose a few hours in the extensive motoring library.

From Te Puke it's 66km along SH2 to Whakatane, the road hugging the coast for some of the way, but with little worth breaking your journey for. The one possible exception is **Longridge Park**, SH33, 3km south of its junction with SH2 (daily 9am–5pm; ☎07/533 1515), where kids can feed farm animals and see captive eels ($1.50), and adults can take a highly scenic **jetboat** ride up the

Kaituna River ($65), spend 45 minutes self-driving an **off-road 4WD** Hill Hopper through all manner of devious mud traps and bogs ($60), or take a more sedate tour of the kiwifruit vines and working farm ($15).

Whakatane and around

The main settlement of the Eastern Bay of Plenty is **WHAKATANE**, a 14,000-strong town sprawled across flat farmland around the last convulsions of the Whakatane River, before it spills into the sea. The dull suburbs surround a genuinely attractive centre wedged between the river and bush-clad hills that rise steeply from the town. Here, the **Pohaturoa** rock outcrop provides a focal point, and the **museum/gallery** provides wet-day distraction. Whakatane's real appeal lies off the coast, either swimming with **dolphins**, or on trips to the bird sanctuary of **Whale Island**, and to the active, volcanic **White Island**, billowing white plumes of steam into the sky. Back on land, there are walks along the spine of hills above the town out to the viewpoint at **Kohi Point**, and body surfing and sunbathing to be done at the broad expanse of **Ohope Beach**.

The Whakatane area seems to have had more than its fair share of dramatic events. The **Maori** word Whakatane means "to act as a man" and comes from a legendary incident when the women of the *Mataatua* canoe were left aboard while the men went ashore; the canoe began to drift out to sea, but touching the paddles was *tapu* for women. Undeterred, the high-spirited Wairaka took matters into her own hands and paddled back to the safety of the shore, shouting *Ka Whakatane Au i Ah au* ("I will act as a man"), and a statue at Whakatane Heads commemorates her heroic act. The first **Europeans** to set foot in the area, apart from a brief sortie by Cook, were flax traders in the early 1800s and a trader called Philip Tapsell, who established a store in 1830. The next turning point in Whakatane's history came in March 1865, when missionary **Carl Volkner** was killed at Opotiki, and a government agent, **James Falloon**, arrived to investigate. At this unwelcome intrusion, supporters of a fanatical Maori sect, the Hau Hau, attacked Falloon's vessel, killing him and his crew. In response, the government declared **martial law**, and by the end of the year a large part of the Bay of Plenty had been confiscated and Whakatane was being peopled by military settlers. The memory of this led **Te Kooti** (see p.449) to choose Whakatane as his target for a full-scale attack by his Maori force in 1869, burning and looting buildings before being driven back into the hills of Urewera. In more **recent times**, Whakatane has led a relatively quiet life as a trading area and service town for the surrounding regions, and as a tourist attraction with access to many areas of natural beauty.

Arrival, information and transport

Long-distance **buses** running between Rotorua and Gisborne (along SH2) stop once a day in each direction outside the **visitor centre**, corner of Quay Street and Kakahoroa Drive (Christmas–Feb Mon–Fri 8am–6pm, Sat & Sun 9am–4pm; March–Christmas Mon–Fri 8.30am–5pm Sat & Sun 10am–4pm; ☎07/308 6058, ⑩www.whakatane.com), which is well-stocked with DOC leaflets for the local area. **Internet access** is cheapest at the visitor centre and at *Lloyds Lodge* hostel (see p.418) for use by non-guests. The **post office**, corner of Commerce Street and The Strand (☎07/307 1155), has poste restante facilities. Whakatane **airport** receives several flights daily from

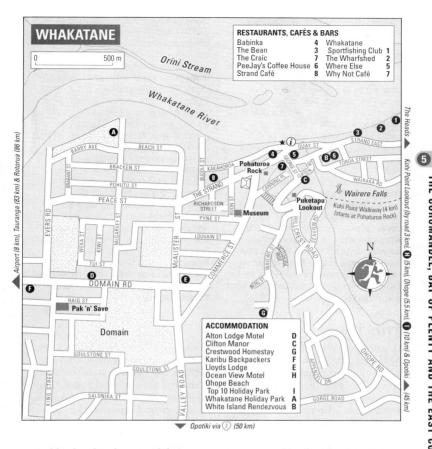

Auckland and is about ten kilometres west, connected by the town's **taxi** shuttle (☎0800/342 522; around $12). A **local bus** service is run by Eastern Bay (☎0800/422 9287, ⓦwww.baybus.co.nz) to Tauranga and Mount Maunganui (Mon–Fri), Ohope (Mon–Fri), Opotiki (Tues & Thurs) and Kawerau (Wed & Fri). Quality **bike rental** is at Pacific Adventures in nearby Ohope (☎07/312 5219; $30 half-day), who deliver to accommodation in Whakatane and run guided trips.

Accommodation

There's a reasonable selection of **accommodation** in Whakatane, much of it firmly mid-range with a preference for motels and campsites. Luxurious places are fairly thin on the ground and there are two hostels. You might prefer a campsite or motel at Ohope Beach.

Alton Lodge Motel 76 Domain Rd ☎07/307 1003 or 0800/500 468, ⓔaltonlodge@wave.co.nz. Comfortable modern motel with eleven spacious kitchen units and a heated indoor pool; good value. ⑤

Clifton Manor 5 Clifton Rd ☎ & ⓕ07/307 2145, ☎0800/307 214, ⓔcliftonmanor@xtra.co.nz. Friendly 1930s home with two adequate guest rooms (both with private bathrooms) let on a B&B

basis, and two spacious self-contained motel units. **⑤**

Crestwood Homestay 2 Crestwood Rise ☏07/308 7554, ⓦwww.crestwood-homestay .co.nz. Attractive B&B in a quiet hilltop setting with scenic views, a 20min walk from the town centre. Either rent the well-appointed self-contained upstairs floor (sleeps 5; $130 for 2) or rent a B&B room with shared bathroom. Self-contained **⑤** plus $20 per extra person; B&B **⑤**

Karibu Backpackers 13 Landing Rd ☏ & ⓕ07/307 8276. A suburban house converted into a big, well-maintained and welcoming hostel 1.5km from the town centre, with a supermarket nearby, an attractive garden for camping, free bikes and free pick-up from the bus stop. Tent sites $11, dorm & four-share rooms **①**, rooms **②**

Lloyds Lodge 10 Domain Rd ☏07/307 8005, ⓔlloyds.lodge@xtra.co.nz. Intimate and extremely welcoming hostel in a centrally located 1930s house. The couple who run it offer an inspiring introduction to Maori culture: learn songs, join an in-house *hangi* or guided forest tours with a Maori elder. Dorms **①**, doubles **②**

Ocean View Motel West End, Ohope Beach ☏07/312 5665, ⓦwww.oceanviewmotel.co.nz. Relaxing beachfront motel at the western end of the beach, with safe swimming, bush walks and fully self-contained units. **④**

Ohope Beach Top 10 Holiday Park Harbour Rd, Ohope, 10km east of Whakatane ☏ & ⓕ07/312 4460, ⓦwww.ohopebeach.co.nz. Upscale holiday park right behind Ohope Beach at the eastern end of Ohope, with a pool complex, camping ($14) and a range of cabins **③**, kitchen cabins **③**, self-contained units **④**, motel units **⑤**

Whakatane Holiday Park McGarvey Rd ☏07/308 8694, ⓔwhak@xtra.co.nz. A reasonable, sheltered campsite ten minutes' walk from The Strand. Tent sites $11, cabins **②**

White Island Rendezvous 15 Strand East ☏07/308 9500 & 0800/242 299, ⓦwww .whiteisland.co.nz. Smart, big modern motel in a quiet yet central location. Some rooms have spa baths, and all are equipped with Sky TV and microwave. There's also a peaceful cottage in a renovated villa, sleeping five (and at the lower end of the price bracket). Units **⑤**, cottage **⑥** plus $20 per extra person.

The Town

Driving into Whakatane, Commerce Street hugs cliffs that were once lapped by the sea. The junction with The Strand is effectively the town centre, marked by Whakatane's defining feature, a large rock outcrop called **Pohaturoa** ("long rock"). The place is sacred to Maori and the small park surrounding the rock contains carved benches and a black marble monument to Te Hurinui Apanui, a great chief who propounded the virtues of peace and is mourned by *pakeha* and Maori alike. This site was once a shrine where rites were performed by Maori priests, and the seed that grew into the karaka trees at the rock's base are said to have arrived on the *Mataatua* canoe. From here, it is a three-minute walk along Canning Place, then Clifton Road and Toroa Street to the base of **Wairere Falls** (see p.419) from where you can rejoin The Strand and stroll a 1km section of the 4km **river walk** to the heads, a lovely late-afternoon walk that passes a replica of the *Mataatua waka* in a reserve (also reached by car along Muriwai Drive), and a sprightly bronze statue of Wairaka on a rock.

Back in town, the **Whakatane District Museum and Gallery** (Mon–Fri 10am–4.30pm, Sat & Sun 11am–3pm; donation; ⓦwww.whakatanemuseum .org.nz) lies on Boon Street with a steam engine from a sawmill outside. Travelling exhibitions occupy the small gallery section, while the main museum is just one room packed with well-conceived displays on geological, Maori and European history. The collection is rich and varied with over 30,000 photographs and an important collection of Maori *taonga* (treasures) from the local *iwi*, tracing their descent from the *Mataatua* canoe.

Activities

You can get out on the local **Rangitaiki River** with Kiwi Jetboat Tours (☏ & ⓕ07/307 0663 or ☏0800/800 538, ⓔkiwijet@xtra.co.nz; 1hr

Kohi Point Lookout walk

There are several interesting **walks** in the area, all detailed in a free map or the more detailed *Discover the Walks Around Whakatane* booklet ($2) from the visitor centre. Easily the best is to **Kohi Point Scenic Reserve** (5.5km one way, 3hr 30min; or 18km loop, 13hr), combining part of the Whakatane Town Centre Walk with the Nga Tapuwae o Toi ("Sacred Footsteps of Toi") Walkway, which traverses the domain of the great chieftain Toi, and continues to Kohi Point giving panoramic views of Whakatane, Whale and White islands, and Te Urewera National Park.

The walk starts in two places, either from the car park at the bottom of Mokorua Gorge on Commerce Street or from the car park on Seaview Road. From the Mokorua Gorge car park head north along Commerce Street and turn right just before Pohaturoa to climb the steps to Hillcrest Road. Turn left to Seaview Road, where the track leads to **Kapu-te-rangi**, which passes the head of the **Wairere Falls**, a cool and peaceful spot. From here you walk through regenerating bush to the **Toi pa**, reputedly the oldest in New Zealand. The track continues along the cliff top past a number of other *pa* sites and food pits through more bushland, including honeysuckle and pohutukawa, before emerging onto flax and scrub towards the Kohi Point. Either return the same way for a shorter walk or continue along the headlands to **Otarawairere Bay**, an excellent swimming and picnic spot (unreachable one hour either side of high tide); the steep descent to the bay is quite beautiful. From here you press on to **Ohope Beach**, but the scenery doesn't get any better and continuation of the loop makes for a long and tiring day.

15min; $65), run by an ex-world champion jetboat racer who will take you from the Matahina Dam, 25km south of Whakatane, to the beautiful Aniwhenua Falls over a number of modest whitewater sections. There are also innumerable **fishing** guides, mostly working on a charter basis from the local marina; the visitor centre stocks a free leaflet listing the charter boats. Rewarding **guided forest walks** focusing on Maori medicine and bush survival skills are led by an elder, Peho Tamiana (℡07/312 9176; from $100–160 for 2–5 hours).

Whale- and dolphin-watching on the Bay

The rich waters around Whakatane give abundant opportunities for **whale and dolphin-watching**. The best trip from Whakatane is run year-round by the excellent Whale and Dolphin Watch, 96 The Strand (℡07/308 2001, Ⓦ www.whalesanddolphinwatch.co.nz; 3–4hr, $100 including swimming, $80 without), who runs three trips a day and gives the added opportunity of **swimming** with the dolphins in the right conditions, and live underwater scenes are played onscreen by a hi-tech onboard camera.

Ohope

Seven kilometres east of Whakatane, the tiny settlement of **OHOPE** extends along the beach in a thin ribbon to the entrance of **Ohiwa Harbour**. Ohiwa ("a place of watchfulness") is the site of a natural shell-fishery for pipi and cockles, and a place of numerous *pa* sites, signifying the importance of a convenient and renewable food source to the Maori way of life. Its fecund waters can be explored on two-and-a-half-hour **eco-tours** with Ohiwa Harbour Tours (℡027/206 6689 & 07/312 4993, Ⓔ ohiwaharbourtours@xtra.co.nz; $60), with an extremely knowledgeable guide imparting much of the area's history and giving an insight into the

Whale Island (Motohora), 10km offshore from Whakatane, is a DOC-controlled haven where considerable efforts were made decades ago to eradicate goats and rats. Native bush is rapidly returning and the island has become a bird reserve and safe environment for saddlebacks, grey-faced petrels, sooty shearwaters, little blue penguins, dotterels, oystercatchers, as well as three species of lizard – geckos and speckled and copper skinks – and the reptilian tuatara; occasional visits are made by the North Island kaka and falcon, as well as fur seals.

Access to the island is on one of only half a dozen full-day **guided tours** a year (between Dec and mid-Feb), which depart from Whakatane and can be arranged through the visitor centre for around $50 per person.

White Island

Many people ignore Whale Island in favour of the more obvious and spectacular attractions of **White Island** (Whaakari), so named by Cook for its permanent shroud of mist and steam. Over twice the size of Whale Island, White Island lies 50km offshore, sometimes a rough ride. Neither this nor its seething vulcanism deters visitors, who flock to appreciate its desolate, other-worldly landscape, with its billowing towers of gas, steam and ash, spewing from a crater lake sixty metres below sea level. They marvel at the smaller fumaroles surrounded by bright yellow and white crystal deposits that re-form in new and bizarre shapes each day. The crystal-clear and abundant waters around the island make this one of the best **dive** spots in New Zealand.

Whaakari is a living embodiment of the ongoing clash between the Indo-Australian Plate and the Pacific Plate that has been driven beneath it for the last two million years. This resulted in the upwards thrust of super-heated rock through the ocean floor creating a massive **volcanic** structure. **Sulphur**, for use in fertilizer manufacture, was sporadically mined on the island from the 1880s, but all enterprises were plagued by catastrophic eruptions, landslides and economic misfortune. The island was abandoned in 1934, and these days is home only to 60,000 grey-faced **petrels** and 10,000 **gannets**.

Two excellent **guided boat trips** to White Island are run from Whakatane. White Island Tours, also known as PeeJay, 15 The Strand East (☏07/308 9588 & 0800/733529, ⊛www.whiteisland.co.nz; daily 8.30am; 6hr; $130, including lunch) operate big boats – book at least a couple of days in advance if you can and allow a week in mid-summer. Their two-hour tour of the island begins at the site of a 1923 sulphur-processing factory, which is gradually being eaten away by the high sulphur content of the atmosphere, and the tour progresses to an open-sided crater. Here, amid pools of bubbling mud and pillars of smoke and steam, you get the chance to study sulphur deposits and stand in the wind-driven clouds (with a gas mask on). White Island Adventures (☏0800/377 878, ⊛www.whiteislandadventures.co.nz; 7hr, of which 1hr 30min is spent on the island, $130 including lunch) take smaller groups and are more flexible – arrange beforehand if you want to **snorkel** or **dive** – and have a licence for **swimming with dolphins**.

With plenty of cash and clement weather, you can also visit White Island by **helicopter** with Vulcan Helicopters (☏0800/804 354 & 07/308 4188, ⊛www.vulcanheli.co.nz; 2hr 30min; $375, including a walking tour of the island). Scott Air (☏0800/535 363 & 07/308 9558, ⊛www.scottair.co.nz) operates a **scenic flight** over White Island (55min; from $135) from Whakatane Airport.

Committed undersea explorers should approach the excellent Dive White Island, at Sportsworld, 186 The Strand (☏0800/348 394, ⊛www.divewhite.co.nz) who offer **dive trips** (usually with 2 dives) in the waters off White Island where visibility is commonly around 20m. Costs range from $155 with your own gear, to $225 for full rental and $350 for a one-to-one beginner's dive with an instructor. They'll also take you **snorkelling** on a sightseeing trip (full day, $120 including lunch).

birdlife and estuarine ecology. Trips depart from the wharf at the eastern end of Ohope, generally around high tide, and pickups can be arranged. A range of guided **kayaking trips** on the harbour are run by KG Kayaks (℡07/315 4005, ⓦwww.kgkayaks.co.nz; from $50), who depart from the same wharf and rent kayaks from $15 per hour.

Otherwise, this is very much a beach resort, and when you've had enough of the surf and sand you'll want to press on, though Ohope makes a pleasant enough base from which to explore Whakatane and its surroundings.

If you're after cheap supplies of fresh **seafood** including mussels, oysters and smoked fish, stop off at the *Ohiwa Oyster Farm* (daily 8am–8pm Nov–March, 9am–7pm rest of the year), a shack beside Ohiwa Harbour, 1km south of the beach and on the road to Opotiki, with a couple of picnic tables at the water's edge. For more formal **eating**, you're restricted to the stylish café bar *Café Addiction*, 19 Pohutukawa Avenue (eve only, closed Tues); or the licensed harbourside *Stingray Café*, Fisherman's Wharf, off Harbour Road and at the eastern end of the beach – a relaxing modern spot with deck seating for drinks, lunch or moderately priced dinners (closed Thurs in winter). The popular attached fish-and-burger takeaway (daily 4pm–9pm) has a few outdoor tables for BYO dining.

Eating, drinking and nightlife

Whakatane is gradually coming up to speed with café culture, so you'll find decent espressos and a couple of appealing waterside **restaurants** doubling as good spots for an evening tipple. A couple of cafés at **Ohope Beach** are listed above. There's virtually no entertainment, except for the **Cinema 5** multiplex, 99 The Strand (℡07/308 7623) and a couple of bars in the Whakatane Hotel, one of them a dance venue.

Babinka Kakahoroa Drive ℡07/307 0009. Very popular, specially built restaurant bar with big windows, a marine theme and versatile menu for brunch, lunch and dinner. Book ahead for dinner. Licensed & BYO.

The Bean 54 Strand East. Laid-back, groovy daytime café and coffee roastery, so you can be sure of a good hit, or opt for a juice or one of their speciality teas. Closed Sun.

The Craíc Whakatane Hotel, cnr The Strand & George St. Atmospheric Irish bar refurbished in mellow dark wood to include booths, and serving tasty fare such as potato pancakes and wood-fired pizzas. Most of the town's nightlife happens here, with live bands every Fri & Sat night, and dancing in the next-door Boiler Room bar.

PeeJay's Coffee House 15 Strand East. The best espresso in town helps wash down daytime snacks and light meals. Early opening hours (6.30am) make it a good spot for breakfast before a morning boat trip. Located in the *White Island Rendezvous Motel* building.

Strand Café 214 The Strand. A relaxing daytime café serving good coffee and a variety of tasty breakfasts, snacks and main courses,

plus takeaway shakes and smoothies. There's also a suntrap of a courtyard. Closed Sun in winter.

Whakatane Sportfishing Club Strand East. Spacious smoke-free public bar with huge windows overlooking the boats and river, great for cheap drinks, good-value bar meals at lunch and dinner, and a Friday and Saturday evening smorgasbord ($20). It is a private club, but visitors can call in.

The Wharfshed Strand East ℡07/308 5698. Excellent all-day café-cum-restaurant, with a mellow riverside setting in a converted, wooden butter store. Good-value and fun for a late breakfast, lunch or watching the sun set over the water while tucking into seafood, lamb or venison. Book ahead for dinner.

Where Else 62 The Strand. A big, popular family restaurant and bar, serving Mexican dishes and burgers for lunch and dinner.

Why Not Café in the *Whakatane Hotel*, cnr The Strand & George St. A friendly little eatery and bar, serving snacks, lunches and dinners ($17–24), including pizzas, seafood and steaks. Daily 11am–midnight (closed Sun dinner in winter).

Opotiki

The small settlement of **OPOTIKI**, 60km east of Whakatane, is the eastern-most town in the Bay of Plenty and makes a useful stopping-off point for exploring its beautiful surroundings. Though it doesn't amount to much in itself, it does act as an effective gateway to the East Coast and is your last place to stock up on supplies and petrol before heading on.

From Opotiki, **SH2** strikes inland **to Gisborne**, while **SH35** meanders along the more circumspect roads around the perimeter of **the East Coast**, never straying far from its rugged and windswept coastline.

Arrival, information and accommodation

InterCity **buses** from Whakatane and Gisborne drop off on Bridge Street near its junction with Opotiki's main drag, Church Street. From here it's five blocks to the combined **visitor centre** and **DOC office**, on the corner of St John and Elliott streets (Mon–Fri 8am–5pm, plus mid-Dec to end Jan Sat & Sun 10am–3pm; ☎07/315 8484, ⓦwww.eastlandnz.com), a good place to pick up information and advice for Opotiki and the whole of the East Coast region. The Eastern Bay **local bus** (Tues & Thurs only; ☎0800/4229287) links Opotiki with Whakatane and Tauranga.

For **accommodation** Opotiki has a couple of good **hostels**: the somewhat cramped yet friendly *Central Oasis Backpackers*, 30 King Street (☎07/315 5165, Ⓔcentraloasis@hotmail.com; camping $17, dorms ❶, rooms ❷), in a renovated kauri villa right in town; and the laid-back beachside *Opotiki Backpackers Beach House*, 7 Appleton Rd, off SH2 and 5km west of Opotiki (☎07/315 5117; tents $17, dorms ❶, room ❷), with free use of kayaks, body boards and so forth. *Eastland Pacific Motor Lodge*, 44 St Johns St (☎07/315 5524 & 0800/103 003, ⓦwww.eastlandpacific.co.nz), is probably the best of the **motels**, with comfortable modern units (❺), some with spa baths; but *Fantail Cottage* **B&B**, 318 Ohiwa Harbour Rd, 9km west of Opotiki (☎07/315 4981; ❺, dinner by arrangement), is a more peaceful and intimate place to stay, in a house with panoramic harbour views and an outdoor spa. Heading 15km south on SH2,

---

The Hau Hau

Missionaries encouraged many Maori to abandon their belief structure in favour of a zealous **Christianity** but, as land disputes with settlers escalated, the Maori increasingly perceived the missionaries as agents for land-hungry Europeans.

When **war** broke out and the recently converted Maori suffered defeats, they felt betrayed not only by the Crown but also by their newly acquired god, and some formed the revivalist **Hau Hau** movement, based on the Old Testament. Dedicated to routing the interlopers, disciples danced around *nui* **poles**, chanting for the *pakeha* to leave the country. The name is derived from the **battle cry** of the warriors, who flung themselves at their enemies with their right arms raised to protect them from bullets, believing that true faith prevented them from being shot. The movement began in 1862 and by 1865, having capitalized on widespread Maori unrest at the land situation, there was a *nui* pole in most villages of any size from Wellington to the Waikato. The Hau Hau were some of the most feared **warriors** and involved in the bloodiest and bitterest battles, but the movement began to fade after their **leader** and founder, Te Ua Haumene, was captured in 1866. Some of the sect's ideas were **revitalized** when the infamous rebel **Te Kooti** (see p.449) based parts of his **Ringatu** movement on Hau Hau doctrine.

you'll find *Riverview Cottage* (☎07/315 5553, 🌐www.nzsbestspot.com; ❼), a modern and spacious two-bedroom cottage on a property that runs down to the Waioeka River where the hosts run kayak trips.

Campers wanting to stay centrally should try the small, sheltered and riverside *Opotiki Holiday Park* (☎ 07/315 6050, 📧opotiki.holidays @xtra.co.nz; tents $10, on-site caravans & cabins ❷, units ❸), a YHA associate on the corner of Potts Avenue and Grey Street: follow King or Elliott Street west to Potts Avenue. For a seaside setting, head 10km west to *Ohiwa Holiday Park* (☎07/315 4741, 🌐www.ohiwaholidays.co.nz; camping $12, cabins ❷, units ❹), right on the beach on Ohiwa Harbour Road, off SH2, with kayaks for rent.

The Town

Opotiki has few sights of interest to delay your departure for the wilds of the East Coast or the bright lights of Gisborne, but it does have some lush countryside and beaches around it. All the significant historic buildings cluster around the junction of Church and Elliot streets, including the **Opotiki Museum**, 123 Church St (Mon–Sat 10am–3.30pm, Sun 1.30–4pm; $3), which occupies the site of the livery stables once used by the overland stagecoach to Whakatane. At the time of writing its collection was having a revamp. Opposite, the innocent-looking white clapboard **St Stephen's Church** was once the scene of a notorious murder, for it was here, in March 1865, that local missionary **Carl Völkner** was allegedly killed by a prophet, Kereopa Te Rau, from the militant Hau Hau sect. The case is far from clear-cut, however: at the time, many Maori believed that missionaries doubled as spies, duly reporting their findings to the settlers and military, and it appears that Völkner had indeed written many letters to Governor Grey espousing the land-grabbing ambitions of settlers. Local Maori claim Völkner was justly executed after being confronted with the evidence and denounced as a traitor. Whatever the truth, the settlers used the story as propaganda, fuelling intermittent skirmishes over the next three years. The museum will usually let you have a key so that you can nip in and see the gorgeous *tukutuku* panels around the altar and Völkner's grave beside it.

Around town

A welcome retreat into the bush is given by the small and unspoiled **Opotiki (Hukutaia) Domain** (dawn–dusk; free), full of native palms, lianas and trees, including a puriri tree thought to date from 500BC and once used as a burial tree by local Maori. The bush also contains a good lookout over the Waioeka Valley and a series of short yet interesting rainforest tracks. To get here, head south from the centre of town on Church Street as far as the Waioweka River Bridge, cross it and bear left along Woodlands Road for 7km.

Getting a little more active, consider the water-based activities either on the **Waioeka River** south of town, or on the **Motu River**, which surges through the hills to the east of Opotiki and meets the sea 45km to the northeast. On the former, Waioeka River Kayak Trips (☎07/315 5553, 📧nzsbestspot@xtra.co.nz) run gentle three-hour paddles down a beautiful stretch of river for $39, and also offer the semi-remote *Riverview Cottage* near the river (❼). There are superb backcountry **rafting trips** (see box, p.424) on the Motu River, and scenic flat-water **jetboating** on the lower 50km with either Motu River Jet Boat Tours (☎07/325 2735; 2hr 30min, $85; booking essential) or Motu AAA (☎025/686 6489; 1hr $65; early Dec to end of April;

⑤

Wilderness rafting on the Motu River

Some of the best **wilderness rafting** trips in New Zealand are on the Grade III–IV **Motu River**, which is hidden deep in the mountain terrain of the remote Raukumara Ranges, with long stretches of white water plunging through gorges and valleys to the Bay of Plenty coast. In 1981, after a protracted campaign against hydro-dam builders, the Motu became New Zealand's first designated "wild and scenic" river. Access by 4WD, helicopter and jetboat makes one- and two-day trips possible, but to capture the essence of this remote region you should consider one of the longer trips when you'll see no sign of civilization for three days – a magical and eerie experience.

Rotorua-based Wet 'n' Wild Rafting (☎0800/462 723, ⊛www.wetnwildrafting .co.nz) starts trips from Opotiki, generally using 4WD vehicles to get you in there. On all but the dedicated wilderness trips, the final flat drift to the coast is skipped in favour of a jetboat ride. Trips range from a two-day trip (with helicopter access, $690), to the full four-day adventure (without helicopter access, $635) from the headwaters to the sea. In all cases transport, camping equipment and food are provided, though you may need to supply your own sleeping bag.

daily 8.30am–4pm, just turn up; the rest of the year book ahead). Both operate from the Motu River Bridge on SH35, and Motu AAA do shorter trips on demand.

Eating

There are a few small daytime **cafés** in town, the best being the *Flying Pig*, right in town at 95 Church St (closed Sat & Sun, but open Sat in Jan), and the *Hot Bread Shop Café*, on the corner of Bridge and St John streets, which does the town's best coffee, yummy cakes and pastries, brunch and snacks. Once these close, things get pretty sketchy with only a handful of burger bars, some doing sit-in steak and egg dinners until around 7.30pm. Traditional **meals** are served day and evening at *Honey's* in the *Opotiki Hotel*, on the corner of Church and Kelly streets, but in fine weather you could do a lot worse than **fish and chips** from *Ocean Seafoods Fish and Chips* at 88 Church St, to eat in or take away.

The Inland Route to Gisborne

From Opotiki, **SH2** strikes out south to **Gisborne** (137km away), dotted with tiny settlements as it twists its way through the scenic and bush-clad **Waioeka Gorge**. Following the river for 30km, the route becomes increasingly narrow and steep before emerging onto rolling pastureland on the Gisborne side and dropping to plains. From there it runs straight as an arrow through orchards, vineyards and sheep farms to Gisborne (covered in Chapter Six; see p.435). The only part of the route worth breaking your journey for, or exploring from Opotiki, is the first 72-kilometre stretch to Matawai, along which a number of interesting **walks** branch off either side of the road. Ten scenic tracks through forest, ranging from fifteen minutes to ten hours one way, are described in the DOC leaflet *Walks in Waioeka and Urutawa* ($1), available at Opotiki visitor centre. This is also where you'll find *Riverview Cottage* and Waioeka River Kayak Trips (see both on p.423).

The East Coast

The East Coast (also known as the East Cape or Eastland), the nub of land jutting into the South Pacific northeast of Opotiki and Gisborne, is one of the most sparsely populated areas in New Zealand, rarely visited and something of a backwater lost in time. Between Opotiki and Gisborne, the Pacific Coast Highway (SH35) runs 330 scenic kilometres around the peninsula, hugging the rugged coastline much of the way and providing spectacular sea views on a fine day.

As soon as you enter the region you'll notice a change of pace, epitomized by the occasional sight of a lone horseback rider clopping along the road. This is one of the most unspoiled parts of the North Island, steeped in **Maori** history and not to be rushed. Contemporary Maori, who make up a significant percentage of the East Coast's population, draw on their strong culture to cope with the hardships of this untamed landscape and uncertain economic prospects. Over eighty percent of land tenure here is in Maori hands, something that sits well with the people: most feel in greater control of their destiny than Maori do elsewhere.

The East Coast is a reminder of how New Zealand once was, and the response to strangers splits into two camps: generally people are warm, friendly

Legends of the East Coast Maori

According to legend, a great *ariki* (leader) from the East Coast was drowned by rival tribesmen, and his youngest daughter swore vengeance: when she gave birth to a son called **Tuwhakairiora**, she hoped he would make good her promise. As a young man, Tuwhakairiora travelled and encountered a young woman named **Ruataupare**; she took him to her father, who happened to be the local chief. A thunderstorm broke, signalling to the people that they had an important visitor among them, and Tuwhakairiora was allowed to marry Ruataupare and live in Te Araroa. When he called upon all the *hapu* of the area to gather and avenge the death of his grandfather, many warriors travelled to Whareponga and sacked the *pa* there. Tuwhakairiora became renowned as a warrior, dominating the area from **Tolaga Bay** to Cape Runaway, and all Maori families in the region today trace their descent from him.

Ruataupare, meanwhile, grew jealous of her husband's influence. While their children were growing up, she constantly heard them referred to as the offspring of the great Tuwhakairiora, yet her name was barely mentioned. She returned to her own *iwi* in **Tokomaru Bay**, where she summoned all the warriors and started a war against rival *iwi*; victorious, Ruataupare became chieftainess of Tokomaru Bay.

Another legend that has shaped this wild land is one of rivalry between two students – **Paoa**, who excelled at navigation, and **Rongokaka**, who was renowned for travelling at great speed by means of giant strides. At the time, a beautiful maiden, Muriwhenua, lived in Hauraki and many set off to claim her for their bride. Paoa set off early but his rival took only one step and was ahead of him; this continued up the coast, with Rongokaka leaving huge footprints as he went – his imprint in the rock at Matakaoa Point, at the northern end of Hicks Bay, is the most clearly distinguishable. En route, they created the **Waiapu Mountains**: Paoa, flummoxed by Rongokaka's pace, set a snare for his rival at Tokomaru Bay, lashing the crown of a giant totara tree to a hill; recognizing the trap, Rongokaka cut it loose. The force with which the tree sprang upright caused such vibration that Mount Hikurangi partly disintegrated, forming the other mountain peaks. Finally, Rongokaka stepped across the Bay of Plenty and up to Hauraki, where he claimed his maiden.

and extremely welcoming, but sometimes it can feel as if they're standoffish, a slightly intimidating experience. In fact this is either a misinterpretation of Maori shyness (a characteristic in these parts) or a natural response on their part to the grating speed and demands of urban culture. Whatever the reason, this feeling usually evaporates with a little openness and acceptance on your part, and especially if you simply slow down. Help is always near at hand – the Ngati Porou, for example (who people the region from Lottin Point to Gisborne) are the first in New Zealand to see the sun and are known for their warmth and hospitality. As for the **climate**, it tends towards extremes – hot in summer, wet in winter, and extremely changeable at any time of year.

The **coast** is very much the focus here, and whatever time isn't spent gazing out of the car or bus window is likely to be consumed on the beach or in the water. That said, there are limited hiking opportunities, and just about everywhere you go there will be someone happy to take you **horse trekking**, either along the beach or into the bush. In general, the **towns**, such as they are, don't have much to recommend them and you're better off planning to stay between towns, though at weekends you might like to find a pub if you fancy a country-music jukebox singalong.

Inland, a central core of mountains runs through the area: the inhospitable **Waiapu Mountains**, encompassing the northeastern Raukumara Range and the typical native flora of the Raukumara Forest Park. The isolated and rugged peaks of Hikurangi, Whanokao, Aroangi, Wharekia and Tatai provide a spectacular backdrop to the coastal scenery, but are only accessible through **Maori land** and **permission** must be sought (further information is available at the DOC offices in Gisborne and Opotiki).

East Coast practicalities

The road is sealed all the way round the coast, but twists in and out of small bays so much that driving right around takes a full six hours – though three or four days is better. The further around you go, the fewer the **services**, including food stores, which are small and close at around 5pm or 6pm, and petrol pumps, some of which even run out from time to time.

Public transport on the East Coast is supplied by two **shuttle-bus** companies, each travelling halfway around the coast – one from Whakatane and back, the other from Gisborne – so you'll need to switch from one to the other to make the full circuit (around $80), breaking your journey in Hicks Bay or Te Araroa. Although booking agents encourage people to buy a full-circuit ticket, which allows only one night's stay on the way, you'll have more flexibility by buying the second portion when you need it. Note that Saturday services are limited and none run on Sunday. Timetables also change frequently so call to check: Eastland Couriers (☎07/315 6350 & 025/842 453) or Matakaoa Couriers (☎0800/628 252), or contact the Gisborne or Opotiki visitor centres. Both shuttles will pick up and drop off anywhere en route, so you can manage half a dozen stops in three or four days.

Campsites are the staple accommodation along much of the route, though free beachside camping (once the norm) is prohibited just about everywhere. **Hostels** are scattered along the route with the occasional motel and B&B, but upscale accommodation is almost non-existent.

Apart from a couple of steak-and-chips places attached to pubs and motels, there isn't anywhere on the East Coast that you'd describe as a real **restaurant**. Unless you've arranged to stay in B&Bs that serve meals you need to be prepared for self-catering, or accept a diet of toasted sandwiches and fish and chips.

Opotiki to Waihau Bay

The road from Opotiki to **Waihau Bay** covers 103km, generally sticking close to the sea, but frequently twisting up over steep bluffs only to drop back down to desolate beaches heavy with driftwood. The logs have been washed down from the Raukumara Range by the numerous rivers that reach the sea here, typically forming delightful fresh-water swimming holes. This is probably the section of the East Coast where you'll want to spend most of your time. You'll find family campsites every few kilometres, none of them far from the beach but never right beside it either. Nonetheless, most make the best of their proximity to the sea with a wealth of aquatic activities offered to guests – from boogie boards and canoes to half-day fishing and dive trips – along with horse riding and bikes to search out your own secluded cove.

Omaio and Te Kaha

Leaving Opotiki you soon hit a section of the coast that sets the scene for the next couple of hours' driving. Swimming beaches are scarce initially and, once past Tirohanga, the only place you are likely to want to **stay** is the hillside *Oariki Farm House*, Maraenui, almost 40km east of Opotiki (T & F 07/325 2678, E oariki@clear.net.nz; B&B ❺, cottage ❻), a secluded B&B and separate self-catering cottage for four surrounded by gardens and native bush, and overlooking the sea. Call for directions or pick up a printed description at Opotiki visitor centre, and either cook your own meals or eat three-course dinners ($30) made largely from organic produce. There are opportunities to go jet-boating, fishing and diving.

Continuing, you soon cross the Motu River and after 11km reach **Omaio** where there is a store with a petrol pump, and one of the few places in these parts where you can **camp** for free: turn sharp left onto Omaio Marae Road by the store. A further 13km on, **Te Kaha** spreads 7km along the highway in a beautiful crescent shape, with spectacular headlands and a deserted beach strewn with driftwood, where you can swim safely. Its beginning is marked by the super-relaxing *Te Kaha Homestead Lodge* (T 07/325 2194; dorm ❶, room ❸), a hostel at the water's edge, with an outdoor spa, access to the beach, and opportunities for kayaking and fishing. You can self-cater or pay for breakfast and dinner ($20 includes both meals). A little further along the main road is the beachside *Te Kaha Hotel* (T 07/325 2830, E tekahahotel@xtra.co.nz; ❸), providing units with sea views, some of them self-catering, and a reasonable lunch and dinner restaurant (and takeaway), plus a small store. Striking inland just after the hotel, along Loop Road to Copenhagen Road, leads to *Tui Lodge* (T & F 07/325 2922; ❺), a secluded and spacious B&B with en-suite rooms and dinner for $30. Back on the main road, 2km past the hotel lies the well-run *Te Kaha Holiday Park & Motels* (T 07/325 2894, E tekahahp@xtra.co.nz; tent sites $10, dorms ❶, cabins ❸, units ❹), a **campsite** with a store, post office and takeaway food as well as kayak rental and access to the beach.

Whanarua Bay

Te Kaha is about the closest land to White Island, 50km offshore, which remains in view as you continue 6km to the tranquil *Waikawa B&B* (T 07/325 2070, W www.waikawa.net; B&B or cabin ❺), a pretty spot above a rocky cove with a couple of en-suite **rooms** with their own access and an attractive cabin for two, plus dinner for $30. The adjacent communities of **Whanarua Bay** and **Maraehako Bay**, 10km further on, make another ideal opportunity to stop and enjoy the beaches and rugged countryside. At Whanarua Bay foodies will want to stop at the peaceful **Pacific Coast Macadamias** (daily 9am–5pm or later in high summer) set back from the main road, which has a small shop amid the nut orchards, selling delicious home-made macadamia products, and a simple café (closed April–Sept). There's **budget accommodation** at Maraehako Bay: the idyllic *Maraehako Bay Retreat* (☏07/325 2648, ✉maraehako@xtra.co.nz; tents $13, dorms ❶, singles $30, rooms ❸), signposted off the main road, is an intimate waterside hostel in a rocky cove with a safe, private swimming beach and opportunities to go kayaking, fishing, diving and on trips to White Island. The beachside *Maraehako Camping Ground* (☏07/325 2942; camping $7), discreetly signposted off the main road at the far end of Maraehako Bay, has toilets and solar-heated showers, and organizes horse treks.

Waihau Bay

Still hugging the coast, SH35 winds 13km to **Ruakokore**, where a picture-perfect, white clapboard Anglican church stands on a promontory framed by the blue ocean. From here it's five minutes' drive to **Waihau Bay**, another sweeping crescent of sand and grass that's ideal for swimming, surfing and kayaking. The abundance of shellfish and flat fish here might encourage you to sling a line for a tasty supper from the wharf beside the *Waihau Bay Lodge & Restaurant*, which serves pub meals and takeaways for lunch and dinner. You'll also find a store, post office and petrol station, and 3km further on, the *Waihau Bay Holiday Park* (☏07/325 3844, ☏325 3980; camping $10, dorm & on-site vans ❶, cabins ❷, units ❺), which has another store and the closest thing to a modern daytime **café** between Opotiki and Gisborne, popular for its latte, snacks, takeaways and light meals (also open evenings in Dec & early Jan). The best places to **stay** are the hospitable and friendly *Waihau Bay Homestay* (☏07/325 3674, ✉n.topia@clear.net.nz; ❹), 2km on at the far end of the bay, with two self-contained units and an en-suite room in a house overlooking the beach (book in advance for a superb $30 seafood dinner) and, at Oruaiti Beach 5km further on, *Oceanside Apartments* (☏07/325 3699, ✇www.waihaubay.co.nz; ❺ plus $15 per extra person), whose suites sleep 4 to 7 and there's dinner for $30, as well as diving and fishing trips.

Cape Runaway to Te Puia Springs

Beyond Waihau Bay the highway continues close to the water for a few more kilometres before veering inland at **Cape Runaway**, the East Coast's north-ernmost point. For the next 125km you hardly see the coast again, with the significant exception of Hicks Bay, Te Araroa and East Cape. Further on, the church at Tikitiki, the East Coast's largest community of Ruatoria and the hot springs at Te Puia are points of interest. In the Cape Runaway area a range of worthwhile **guided walks** are led by the vibrant Maori elder, June McDonald (☏07/325 3697, ✉tikirau@xtra.co.nz; from 1hr $30 to 4hr $75), exploring the area's history, culture, landscape and medicinal uses of native plants.

Hicks Bay and Onepoto Bay

The small coastal township of **HICKS BAY** (*Wharekahika*), 44km from Waihau Bay, shelters between headlands and coastal rock bluffs almost halfway along SH35 and makes a good base from which to visit the East Cape Lighthouse and enjoy water-based activities. Next door are the secluded sands of Onepoto Bay, a safe swimming beach also popular for kayaking and surfing. Hicks Bay was named after Lieutenant Zachariah Hicks of Cook's *Endeavour* expedition, who was the first onboard to sight it. Take time to explore the Hicks Bay region if you're interested in the numerous *pa* sites in varying states of repair, some of which were modified for musket fighting during the 1860 Hau Hau uprising.

Entering the community along Wharf Road, off SH35, you'll find a general store and a takeaway. Self-catering beachside **accommodation** is provided by *Mel's Place*, Onepoto Beach Rd (☎06/864 4694, ✉eastcapefishing@xtra.co.nz; tents $15, dorm ❶, caravan ❷), in a simple bunkroom and caravan by a rocky bay, with Maori cultural interaction and hospitality, and kayaks for rent. They can also guide you to other accommodation in Onepoto Bay, and run **dolphin-watching trips** (4hr $50) and sightseeing boat trips (half-day $50).

Alternatively continue 2km east of Hicks Bay along SH35 to the big *Hicks Bay Motel Lodge* (☎06/864 4880 & 0800/200 077, ℻864 4708; ❹), set high above both bays and where several units have cooking facilities; the motel also has a licensed **restaurant**, a **bar** and offers access to a glowworm grotto.

Te Araroa

From Hicks Bay SH35 climbs over a hill and drops back to the coast, 6km on, at the well-run *Te Araroa Holiday Park* (☎06/864 4873, ℻864 4473; tent sites $8.50, caravan & dorms ❶, cabins ❷), which has a handy shop, a takeaway van in summer, and a small indoor summer **cinema** that screens recent releases during the summer and Easter school holidays; ask at the shop for programme details and tickets.

From here it is 4km to **East Cape Manuka Oil** on SH35 (🅦www.manuka-products.com; daily 9am–4.30pm), a producer of essential oils extracted from the manuka trees grown in the surrounding hills (twigs are used) by steam distillation. Highly valued for its healing abilities the oil is exported all over the world. Manuka-oil products such as soaps and medicinal creams are on sale in the small shop and a visitor centre explains the process.

A further 2km on, the broad surf-washed shore of Kawakawa Bay is graced by the drab village of **TE ARAROA** ("long pathway"), which marks the midway point between Opotiki and Gisborne. Te Araroa was once the domain of the famous Maori warrior Tuwhakairiora and of the legendary figure of Paikea, who is said to have arrived here on the back of a whale. Ironically, the first Europeans in the area occupied a **whaling station** not far from the present township. These days the settlement contains little more than a hotel/pub, petrol station, two stores and a takeaway selling spanking fresh **fish and chips**. In the grounds of the local school on Moana Parade stands a giant pohutukawa tree, reputedly the largest in New Zealand. You can **stay** at the beachfront *Kawakawa Hotel* (☎06/864 4809; ❹), where some of the rooms are en suite.

East Cape Lighthouse

The New Zealand mainland's easternmost point is marked by the **East Cape Lighthouse**, reached by a good, partly sealed 21km road from Te Araroa: follow the sign east along the foreshore. It's a dramatic coastal run that ends in a car park, from where you climb seven-hundred-odd steps to the lighthouse perched atop a 140m hill – an atmospheric spot with views inland to the Raukumara Range, and seaward towards East Island, just offshore.

If you're relying on public transport along SH35, you can still get there at sunrise with East Cape 4WD **trips** (☎06/864 4775; 2–3hr $50), which pick up at accommodation in Te Araroa and Hicks Bay before dawn. Or contact *Mel's Place* (see p.429) to make other arrangements.

Tikitiki, Ruatoria and Te Puia Springs

From Te Araroa SH35 cuts inland through 24km of sheep-farming country, before reaching **TIKITIKI**, a village that will only delay you long enough to peek inside the modest and recently restored Anglican **church**, on a rise as you enter the town. The plain wooden exterior hides a treasure-trove of elaborate and fine Maori design, *tukutuku* and carving; unusually, the stained glass is also in Maori designs, and the rafters are painted in the colours of a Maori meeting-house. You can **stay** at *Eastender Farmstay*, Haha Road, off SH35 (☎06/864 3820; dorms ❶), with beds in dorms and cabins. They also offer **bone carving** (2–3hr \$30) and some of the best **horse treks** in the region including a gallop along a beach. You can also take the same route on **quadbike**.

Inland **RUATORIA**, 19km south of Tikitiki, is the largest town since Opotiki, though that's not saying much. The main highway skirts the town, yielding a petrol station, pub, grocery shop, and the biggest supermarket on the Cape. Also on the main road is the *Kai Kart* takeaway (4.30pm–8pm, later on Fri & Sat). Alternatively, stay on SH35 for the combined *Mountain View* café and *Blue Boar* tavern, in a peaceful setting 2km south of town where you can tuck into snacks and simple meals for lunch and dinner (till 8pm), before losing to the locals at pool.

The hill country to the west of Ruatoria comes under the jurisdiction of the Raukumara Conservation Area, which includes the upper catchments of several rivers that drain into the Bay of Plenty. The desolate terrain and limited access discourage most visitors from exploring the park, but it is possible to tackle the four-hour trek up the 1754m **Mount Hikurangi** (the highest peak in the range), offering the early riser the opportunity of being among the first in New Zealand to see the sunrise. The local Ngati Porou control the land and you should consult the visitor centres in Opotiki and Gisborne for the latest access details.

At Kopuaroa, around 15km south of Ruatoria, a loop road heads 6km to the broad sweep of **Waipiro Bay**, a busy port in its heyday, but now a beautiful and secluded inlet. Phone ahead for instruction if you want to **stay** at the welcoming *Waikawa Lodge* (☎06/864 6719, ⓦwww.waikawalodge.co.nz; ❸), which has two double rooms in a self-catering lodge with stupendous views in a unique bush setting, and two-hour **horse treks** for \$40.

The loop road to Waipiro Bay rejoins SH35 at the small settlement of **TE PUIA SPRINGS**, where a small lake is picturesquely surrounded by deciduous trees. The mineral-rich **hot springs** (roughly daily 6am–8pm; 30min \$5; book ahead from Christmas to end of Jan) have seen better days, today comprising just one pool that accommodates around six people, but you can book it for a private soak. The pool continuously fills with fresh water and lies behind the *Te Puia Hot Springs Hotel* (☎06/864 6755; ❸), which has a bar and café, simple rooms, and a basic campsite (\$5).

Tokomaru Bay to Gisborne

At **Tokomaru Bay** the road emerges from the inland bush and pastoral country to reveal the North Island's east coast in all its glory. For the remaining 80km to **Gisborne** you stay mostly inland but catch frequent glimpses of

5

yawning bays and crashing surf, accessed either on SH35 itself, or by taking short side roads to little-visited coves. In the days before a decent road was put in, this was a thriving area with coastal traders calling to drop off supplies and pick up sheep (or their dressed carcasses). The subsequent decline is most evident at Tokomaru Bay, though things pick up progressively as you approach Gisborne.

Tokomaru Bay

TOKOMARU BAY (or just "Toko"), 11km south of Te Puia Springs, makes a pretty decent place to idle away a couple of relaxed days exploring the steep green hills, rocky headlands and the broad expanse of **beach**, dotted with driftwood and pounded by surf. The Maori who settled here trace their descent to Toi te Huatahi, the great navigator and the first to arrive from the ancestral home of Hawaiki. In 1865 the Mawhai Pa was the scene of several attacks by a party of Hau Hau, but they were repulsed by a small garrison of old men and women.

At the far northern end of town, a long wooden wharf and ruined buildings of a freezing works (abattoir) testify to the former prosperity of this once-busy port, which thrived until improved road transport forced the factory's closure in 1953. The town now gets by on the merest hint of a craft industry; call at the **craft shop** on Waitangi Street (usually Mon–Fri 10am–3pm), near the general store to see flax goods, possum-fur hats, pottery and more.

There isn't a great deal to do here except surf, swim or take long walks on the beach. If you tire of the water, you can **explore on horseback** with a series of gorgeous bush and beach treks in small groups (from $40 for 2hr) available at *Brian's Place* (see below).

Budget **accommodation** starts with the *Mayfair Camping Ground*, Waitangi St (☏ & ⓕ 06/864 5843; tent sites $8.50, caravans & cabins ②), just across from the beach and beside the general store and petrol station. **Backpackers** should head up the hill to *Brian's Place*, Potae St (☏ & ⓕ 06/864 5870; tents $10, dorms ①, rooms ②), a small and welcoming place with two secluded tent sites, a couple of doubles and two twins.

Te Puka Tavern on Beach Road serves inexpensive pub **meals** in hefty portions but, as elsewhere in Eastland, self-catering is the way to go, and Toko even has a supermarket, open daily, on Waitangi Street. The pub is the only place in town for a drink and can be quite boisterous at the weekend. The summertime **Internet café** at the beach end of Potae Street (Tues–Sat 8am–2pm) does good coffee.

Anaura Bay

Some 22km south from Tokomaru, a 6km long sealed side road runs to rugged **ANAURA BAY**, a prized surf spot with a broad sweep of sand and jagged headlands. At the north end of the bay the **Anaura Scenic Reserve** harbours a large area of mixed broadleaf bush noted for its large puriri trees and abundance of native birds. Starting near the end of the road, and signposted to the west by the reserve, is the **Anaura Bay Walkway** (3.5km loop; 2hr), which follows the course of the Waipare Stream into thick green bush, up a gently climbing valley and then out into scrubland before turning back towards the bay and a lookout point with magnificent views.

Beside the beach immediately beyond the start of this walk there's a very basic DOC **campsite** (free, with water but no shower), and at the opposite end of the bay, superbly sited just back from the beach, the simple *Anaura Bay*

Motorcamp (☎ & ℱ 06/862 6380; tents $10), which has a relaxing feel. Facilities are in the former schoolhouse and there's a store selling essentials.

Tolaga Bay to Gisborne

TOLAGA BAY (*Uawa*), 36km from Tokomaru, is the first place since Opotiki with the tenor of a thriving, viable town; six hundred strong and one of the better-serviced communities on the East Coast. Once again, rugged headlands enclose the bay that was the scene of a 1769 visit by Captain Cook and his crew. They are commemorated in the town's street names: Banks, Solander, Forester and, of course, Cook.

Cook, anchoring to replenish his stocks of food and water, named the bay "Tolaga", owing to a misinterpretation of the Maori name for the prevailing wind (correctly called *teraki*). One character who stayed a little longer – and may well have provided the historical basis for the character played by Harvey Keitel in the film *The Piano* – was an early flax trader called Barnet Burns. He wore full *moko*, and stayed in the bay for three years, marrying a Maori woman and fathering three sons, before decamping; his wife, Amotawa, went on to marry the great Maori chief Te Kani-a-Takirau.

Just over 1km south of town, Wharf Road cuts seaward past the start of **Cooks Cove Walkway** (2.6km; 45min), which involves a steep and often muddy climb through bush and birdlife, rewarding the effort with good views across the bay. Another 300m along Wharf Road you'll find the 660m-long concrete **wharf** itself, the longest concrete jetty in the southern hemisphere, jutting out past steep sandstone cliffs. Built in the late 1920s to service coastal shipping, it soon became redundant and is now in a near-ruinous state, and with no safety rails. It hasn't been used commercially since 1963, and is no longer strong enough for vehicles, though you can wander to the end, which makes a picturesque spot for a picnic. A determined bunch of local residents are now trying to raise $5 million to preserve the structure and a collection vault is located by the entrance to the wharf.

Having seen the sights there's little reason to linger, but there is **accommodation** at the incongruous mock-Tudor *Tolaga Bay Inn*, on the corner of Solander and Cook streets (☎06/862 6856, ✉anne.prabah@xtra.co.nz; ❸), with simple yet cheerful rooms, meals served to guests, and a bar that occasionally sees live bands at weekends. There's also self-contained **homestay** at *Papatahi*, SH35, 3km north (☎ & ℱ06/862 6623; ❹), and beachfront accommodation at *Tolaga Bay Holiday Park*, Wharf Road (☎06/862 6716, ✉tolagabayholidaypark@msn.com; tent sites $10, caravans & cabins ❷), which has a store and great views.

The 47km stretch from Tolaga Bay to Gisborne becomes both tamer and bleaker the further south you travel, the land despoiled by clearance for farming. The road climbs in and out of more small bays, occasionally providing panoramic vistas of sea and close-ups of the slate-grey rock shelves that characterize this coast. The road passes through the modest settlement of **Whangara**, where the film *Whale Rider* was shot, but there's not much to see here apart from a sweep of sand and an offshore island said to be the fossilized remains of the whale that the legendary Paikea rode all the way from Hawaiki (for guided tours of Whangara, see p.443).

At the surf mecca of **Wainui Beach**, 9km from Gisborne, is one of the best hostels in New Zealand, the big beachside *Chalet Surf Lodge*, 62 Moana Rd/SH35 (☎0800/787 359 & 06/868 9612, ⓦwww.chaletsurf.co.nz; dorms ❶, rooms ❸, apartments ❹), where all dorms are en suite and most of the

5

doubles have sea views. Other services are free transport to the bus depot and airport, surfing lessons, surfboard rent and free bikes.

Travel details

Buses

From Coromandel to: Thames (2–3 daily; 1hr 15min); Whitianga (1 daily; 1hr)

From Opotiki to: Gisborne, via SH2 (1 daily; 2hr); Hicks Bay via SH35 (2 daily; 3hr); Rotorua (1 daily 2hr 10min); Whakatane (1 daily; 40min).

From Paeroa to: Auckland (3 daily; 2hr 30min); Hamilton (1 daily; 1hr 30min).

From Tauranga to: Auckland (4–6 daily; 3hr 40min); Hamilton (1–2 daily; 2hr); Rotorua (4 daily; 1hr 30min); Taupo (4 daily; 2hr 30min).

From Te Aroha to: Hamilton (1 daily; 1hr 10min).

From Thames to: Auckland (5 daily; 2hr); Coromandel (2–3 daily; 1hr 15min); Hamilton (2 daily; 1hr 30min); Mount Maunganui (3 daily, 2hr); Tauranga (3 daily; 1hr 45min); Whitianga (3 daily; 1hr 40min).

From Whakatane to: Gisborne (1 daily; 3hr); Kawerau (2 daily; 45min); Opotiki (1 daily; 40min); Rotorua (2 daily; 1hr 30min).

From Whitianga to: Coromandel (1 daily; 1hr); Thames (3 daily; 1hr 30min).

Flights

From Tauranga to: Auckland (5–7 daily; 40min); Wellington (2–3 daily; 1hr 20min).

From Whakatane to: Auckland (3–5 daily; 45min).

From Whitianga to: Auckland (2 daily; 30min), Great Barrier Island (3 weekly; 30min).

Poverty Bay, Hawke's Bay and the Wairarapa

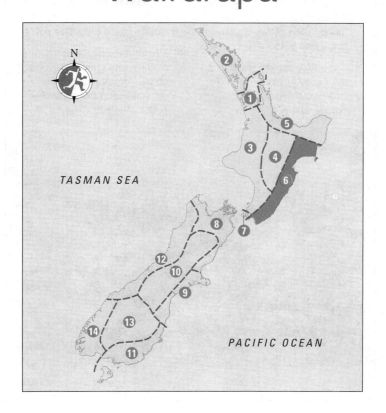

CHAPTER 6

Highlights

* **Whale Rider Tours** Head from Gisborne into the depths of Maori legends and stories with unparalleled access to a working *marae*. See p.443

* **Lake Waikaremoana** Great bush scenery and a superb round-the-lake tramp. See p.448

* **Art Deco Napier** The world's finest collection of small scale Art Deco architecture is to be found in this pleasant seaside town. See p.458

* **Cape Kidnappers** Head along the sands to visit the world's largest mainland gannet colony. See p.463

* **Hawke's Bay Wine Country** Taste some of New Zealand's finest wine and break the day at one of the great vineyard restaurants. See p.465

* **Rush Munroe's** Long-standing purveyor of rich and supremely fruity ice cream. See p.471

* **Mount Bruce** The National Wildlife Centre performs conservation heroics giving you the chance to glimpse some of the world's rarest birds. See p.474

* **Martinborough** Compact wine country with great restaurants and accommodation for a sybaritic couple of days. See p.477

△ Gannet colony, Cape kidnappers

6

Poverty Bay, Hawke's Bay and the Wairarapa

From the tip of Eastland, the North Island's mountainous backbone runs 650km southwest to the outskirts of Wellington, defining and isolating the **East Coast**. A region comprising the characteristically dry and sunny provinces of Poverty Bay, Hawke's Bay and the Wairarapa, this is sheep country. Large stations command the rich pastures of the expansive Heretaunga Plains around central Hawke's Bay and the sharp-ridged hill country to the north, the land frequently contoured into small terraces, the hallmarks of a young land eroded by overgrazing. But the region isn't all pastoral: the contiguous Raukumara, Kaweka, Ruahine, Tararua and Rimutaka mountain ranges protect much of the coast from the prevailing westerlies and cast a long rain shadow, the bane of farmers who watched their land become parched dirt, the grass leached to a dusty brown. Increasingly, these rain-shadow pastures are being given over to viticulture, and all three provinces are now noted **wine** regions. Any tour of the wineries would have to take in **Poverty Bay**, a major grape-growing region, where the main centre of **Gisborne** is both the first city in the world to see the light of the new day and was the first part of New Zealand sighted by Cook's expedition in 1769. Finding little but apparently hostile natives, he named it Poverty Bay and sailed off south across Hawke's Bay – named after Admiral Sir Edward Hawke, a boyhood hero of Cook's – to a second disastrous encounter with Maori at **Cape Kidnappers**.

The surrounding region of **Hawke's Bay** has long been dubbed "the fruit bowl of New Zealand", famed for orchard boughs sagging under the weight of prime apples, pears and peaches. In recent years the torch has passed to grapes, which have been producing the sort of fine vintages that enhance the Hawke's Bay wine country's reputation as one of the foremost in the country. The district is best visited from **Napier**, the single most appealing city on the East Coast, as much for its seafront location and range of minor attractions as for the wealth of Art Deco buildings constructed after the city was flattened by a massive

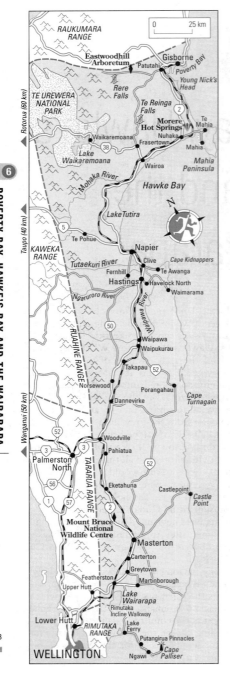

Map labels:

RAUKUMARA RANGE
0   25 km
Eastwoodhill Arboretum   Gisborne
Patutahi   Poverty Bay
Young Nick's Head
Rere Falls
TE UREWERA NATIONAL PARK
Te Reinga Falls   2   Te Mahia
Morere Hot Springs
Waikaremoana   Nuhaka
Frasertown
38   Mahia
Lake Waikaremoana   Wairoa   Mahia Peninsula
Mohaka River   Hawke Bay
N
LakeTutira
5   Te Pohue
KAWEKA RANGE
Tutaekuri River   Napier
Clive   Cape Kidnappers
Fernhill   Te Awanga
Hastings   Havelock North
Ngaruroro River   Waimarama
RUAHINE RANGE
50   Waipawa
Waipukurau
Takapau   52
Norsewood   Porangahau   Cape Turnagain
Dannevirke
52   Woodville
3   3   Pahiatua
Palmerston North   52
56   Eketahuna   Castlepoint   Castle Point
1   57   2
Mount Bruce National Wildlife Centre   Masterton
Carterton
Greytown   Martinborough
Featherston
Upper Hutt   Lake Wairarapa
Rimutaka Incline Walkway
Lower Hutt   Lake Ferry
RIMUTAKA RANGE   Putangirua Pinnacles
WELLINGTON   Cape Palliser
Ngawi
TARARUA RANGE

Rotorua (60 km)
Taupo (40 km)
Wanganui (50 km)

6

POVERTY BAY, HAWKE'S BAY AND THE WAIRARAPA

earthquake in 1931. Nearby **Hastings** suffered much the same fate and wove Spanish Mission-style buildings into the Art Deco fabric, though this won't delay you long from pressing on south through the uninspiring "Scandinavian" towns of southern Hawke's Bay. These run almost seamlessly into the similarly lack-lustre settlements in the sheep lands of the **Wairarapa**, which takes its name from Lake Wairarapa ("glistening waters"), the eye in the fish that is the North Island, according to Maori legend. Unless you've a taste for the competitive sheepmanship of the Golden Shears competition in **Masterton**, the main goal in this region is **Martinborough**, sur-rounded by another collection of fine vineyards, most of which can be visited on foot.

Access to the mountainous **interior** of this region is limited, with only six roads winding over or cutting through the full length of the ranges. The most tortuous and one of the most scenic of these is SH38, which forges northwest from the small town of **Wairoa**, midway between Gisborne and Napier, to Rotorua. En route it wends its way through the remote wooded mountains of **Te Urewera National Park**, past beautiful Lake Waikaremoana, which is encircled by the four-day **Lake Waikaremoana Circuit** tramp-ing route, as well as many appeal-ing shorter lakeside strolls. Alternatively you could try the twisting backroad from **Taihape** (see p.364) to the outskirts of Hastings and Napier – an atmos-pheric, partially sealed journey through lush green valleys that ascends wind-swept tussock covered hills with spectacular sphincter-clenching results, before dropping to the coast.

The East Coast is privileged to have the North Island's most appealing summertime **climate**: the grape-ripening heatwaves come with just enough sea breeze to make vigorous activity tolerable. The slight chill of spring and autumn mornings has its advocates, but winter can be cold and damp. As elsewhere, the **Christmas and January** madness packs out the motor camps and motels, but even Napier, the most visited destination, is manageable at this time.

Gisborne and around

The small city of **GISBORNE**, is New Zealand's easternmost city – and as such the first to catch the sun each new day. It is also one of New Zealand's more relaxing and gently appealing places, not overly endowed with entertainments, but easy-going enough for peaceful beach lounging with the chance to try various water activities, including viewing sharks in their natural habitat. Broad streets come lined with squat weatherboard houses, which are warmed by long hours of sunshine, and are interspersed with parkland hugging the flanks of the Pacific, the harbour and three rivers – the Taruheru, Turanganui and Waimata.

Gisborne holds a special place in the European history of New Zealand, for it was here in October 1769 that **James Cook** first set foot on the soil of

Aotearoa, commemorated by a shoreside statue, where he immediately ran into conflict with local Maori, killing several before sailing away empty-handed. He named the landing site **Poverty Bay**, since "it did not afford a single item we wanted, except a little firewood". The fertility of the surrounding lands belies the appellation, but the name stuck and looks set to prevail, despite the wishes of some **Maori** who would rename it Turanganui a Kiwa – in honour of a Polynesian navigator, rather than continually harking back to that unfortunate first Maori–*pakeha* encounter. Early nineteenth-century Poverty Bay remained staunchly Maori and few *pakeha* moved here, discouraged by both the Hau Hau rebellion and Te Kooti's uprising (see p.449). It wasn't until the 1870s, when these had been contained, that **Europeans** felt safe enough to head here in numbers to farm the rich alluvial river flats. A decent port wasn't constructed until the 1920s, after which sheep farming and market gardening really took off, activities only recently challenged by the ascendant grape harvest and the rise of plantation forestry.

Arrival and information

Gisborne sits near the junction of the region's two main highways, SH35, which skirts the rugged coast of Eastland, and the inland SH2, which straddles the Raukumara Range and continues south to Napier. **Buses** along these routes all converge on the **visitor centre**, 209 Grey St (daily Labour Day–Easter 9am–5pm, otherwise 10–5pm; ☎06/868 6139, ⓦwww .gisbornenz.com), which is heralded by a Canadian totem pole donated to the town in 1969, on the bicentennial of Cook's landing. The visitor centre has Internet access and helpful displays on walks in Te Urewera National Park and the Waioeka Gorge, but those needing specialist outdoor info should head to the **DOC office** at 63 Carnarvon St (☎06/867 8531; Mon–Fri 8am–4.30pm). More **Internet access** is available at Cyberzone, 83 Gladstone Rd, beside the Odeon cinema.

Flights arrive at Gisborne **airport**, on the edge of town about 2km west of the town centre, which can be reached by **taxi** (around $10) – try Gisborne Taxis (☎06/867 2222) or Eastland Taxis (☎06/868 1133). **Getting around** most of the city is easily done on foot, though **rental bikes** from Maintrax Cycles, on the corner of Gladstone and Roebuck roads (☎06/867 4571; $15–20 per day), are good for a spin around the wineries.

Accommodation

Despite the huge number of motels, chiefly along the main Gladstone Road and the waterfront Salisbury Road, **accommodation** can sometimes be hard to come by, particularly during the month or so after Christmas, when booking is advisable and prices rise a little from their normally modest levels. Campsites also tend to be full of holidaying families at this time, but you should be able to get into one of Gisborne's clutch of below-par hostels. B&Bs are relatively rare, but there are a few good places around the city.

Motels, B&Bs and homestays

Blue Pacific Beachfront 90 Salisbury Rd ☎06/868 6099, ⓦwww.seafront.co.nz. Presentable beachfront motel with fully equipped units, a sauna and spa pool. ⑤

Cedar House 4 Clifford St ☎06/868 1902, ⓦwww.cedarhouse.co.nz. Extremely appealing boutique B&B in a large Edwardian house with spacious, well appointed and tastefully decorated rooms. Breakfasts are great and last all day, and the hosts are both welcoming and knowledgeable. ⑧

Endeavour Lodge Motel 525 Gladstone Rd
ⓣ06/868 6075, ⓔ endeavourlodge@telstra.co.nz.
One of Gisborne's cheapest motels, but maintained
to a high standard and equipped with an attractive
pool. ❸
Pacific Harbour Motor Inn Cnr Reads Quay and
Pitt St ⓣ06/867 8847 ⓦ www.pacific-harbour.co
.nz. Clean lines and large open windows overlooking the harbour characterize this motel addition to
the now increasingly developed harbourside. Large
fully equipped rooms, some with balconies and
harbour views. ❻
Sea View 68 Salisbury Rd ⓣ06/867 3879 &
0800/268 068, ⓔ raewyn@regaleggs.co.nz.
Attractive, modern beachfront B&B, a 10min walk
from central Gisborne run by a very friendly
couple who can't do enough for their guests.
There's one double upstairs and a twin plus a
self-contained unit on the ground floor. ❺
Whispering Sands 22 Salisbury Rd
ⓣ06/867 1319 & 0800/405 030,
ⓔ whisperingsandsmotel@xtra.co.nz.
Luxurious beachfront motel with 14 large
modern units, all with great sea views. ❻

Hostels and campsites

Flying Nun 147 Roebuck Rd ⓣ06/868 0461,
ⓔ yager@xtra.co.nz. Reasonable hostel, if a little
rough around the edges, a 15min walk from town
in a former convent, with a pool table in the
chapel, where confessionals have become phone
booths. Some of the spacious dorms front onto
verandas, and singles cost little more than dorm
beds; doubles tend to be a bit cramped. Campsites
are available in the extensive grounds and there's
Sky TV. Tent sites $12, dorms ❶, rooms ❷
Sycamore Lodge 690 Gladstone Rd ⓣ06/868
1000, ⓔ gisbornebp@xtra.co.nz. Somewhat sterile
former orphanage but with good, clean facilities
just a 15min walk from the centre. Doubles
especially spacious, dorms less so, and there's
plenty of camping space in the grounds. Camping
$10, dorms ❶, rooms ❷
Waikanae Beach Holiday Park Grey St
ⓣ06/867 5634, ⓔ motorcamp@gdc.govt.nz.
Wonderfully sited motor park right by Gisborne's
main beach and five minutes' walk from town,
with tennis courts and comfortable cabins and
flats. Camping $12, cabins ❷, kitchen cabins ❸

The Town

Almost everywhere in this compact city an easy stroll from Gisborne's excellent and popular swimming and sunbathing strand of **Midway Beach**.
Elsewhere, pleasant parks and green spaces run along the three rivers that converge at the harbour – which is currently the centre of much redevelopment
– below the steep hummock of Kaiti Hill.

Most of Gisborne's sights are connected in some way to the historical accident
of Cook's landing and the dynamic between Maori and *pakeha* cultures it
engendered. The first of James Cook's crew to spy the mountains of *Aotearoa*, a
couple of days before the first landing, was the twelve-year-old surgeon's boy
Nick Young, who thereby claimed the gallon of rum Cook had offered as a
reward. Honouring a second pledge, Cook recorded this white-cliffed promontory, 10km south of Gisborne across Poverty Bay, on his chart as Young Nick's
Head. Young's keen eyes are commemorated with a pained-looking statue on
the western side of the rivermouth in Gisborne, next to a modern **statue of
Cook** looking commanding in a tricorn hat atop a stone hemisphere.

Three long blocks to the northeast in Heipipi Park, early Maori explorers are
commemorated with **Te Tauihu Turanga Whakamana** – a striking wooden
sculpture depicting a Maori *tauihu* (canoe prow) carved with images of
Tangaroa (god of the sea), the demi-god Maui, and Toi Kai Rakau (one of the
earliest Maori to settle in New Zealand).

Five minutes' walk north of here, the **Tairawhiti Museum**, 18 Stout St
(Mon–Fri 10am–4pm, Sat & Sun 1.30–4pm; gold coin donations;
ⓦ www.tairawhitimuseum.co.nz), sits on the bank of the Waimata River.
Frequently changing shows augment extensive displays on East Coast Maori
and a strong line in contemporary Maori arts including beautiful *kete* (flax baskets) and greenstone finely carved into *tiki*. There is also a maritime wing that
neatly incorporates the original wheelhouse and captain's quarters of the

12,000-tonne *Star of Canada*, which ran aground on the reef off Gisborne's Kaiti Beach in 1912. Most of the ship was scuttled but the bridge was turned into Gisborne's most distinctive house, a role it fulfilled for seventy years before being bequeathed to the city and moved to its present site. The rest of the maritime section is devoted to exhibits on Cook's arrival, the role of shipping, coastal wrecks and a devotional shrine of the local surfing.

Several disused buildings from around the region are clustered outside the museum, notably the six-room 1872 **Wyllie Cottage**, the oldest extant house in town, and the **Sled House**, built on runners at the time of the Hau Hau uprising (see p.422) so that it could be hauled away by a team of bullocks at the first sign of unrest.

Those who want to see a modern take on Maori tradition will be mightily impressed by the **Toihoukura School of Contemporary** ten minutes' walk away on the southwest side of the river, on Cobden Street (Oct–Jan Mon–Fri 9am–5pm; Feb–Nov by appointment ☎06/868 0347; free). Housed behind a striking triangular entrance – beside a modern metal and wood whale-tail sculpture – the school, which is also involved in the restoration of existing carvings, instructs students in the oral history and traditions of Maori design and encourages modern interpretation using contemporary materials and techniques. The results are vibrant and stunning pieces, which are often for sale. If available, tutors will walk you round the gallery explaining the background and intention intrinsic in the work. Rather more ordinary and conservative **The Stone Studio**, west at 237 Stanley Rd (Mon–Fri 8.30am–5.30pm, Sat 9am–2pm; free), offers the opportunity to watch three carvers produce beautiful greenstone pendants and other pieces in a variety of traditional shapes, which are also for sale at reasonable prices.

For the less artistically minded a visit to the small but utterly captivating **Sunshine Brewery**, 109 Disraeli St (Mon–Sat 9am–6pm), just a five-minute walk back toward town from Stanley Street is a worthy diversion. The award-winning boutique brewhouse sells its Pilsener-style Gisborne gold, delectable bitter and malt stout Black Magic all over town and particularly in Wellington. Brief tours are available and the shop prices are the best around.

Kaiti Hill and around

On the eastern side of the rivermouth, an obelisk marks **Cook's landing site**, now a couple of hundred metres inland following reclamation for the harbour facilities where mountains of logs now await export. Meanwhile Cook's botanist gets recognition near the obelisk at the waterfront in **Banks' Garden**: a locale of species – especially low-growing varieties such as ngaio, tutu, karo and puriri – that he and his accomplice Solander collected here and at Anaura Bay and Tolaga Bay as they sailed north. Behind, Titirangi Domain climbs the side of **Kaiti Hill** to the Cook Bicentenary Plaza, designed around another statue of Cook who is unusually decked out in Italian naval regalia. The highest point of the hill is occupied by the **James Cook Observatory**, which runs public stargazing nights on Tuesdays (Nov–March 8.30pm; April–Oct 7.30pm; $2).

On the eastern side of the hill lies **Te Poho-o-Rawiri Meeting House**, one of the largest in the country. The interior is superb, full of fine ancestor carvings, interspersed with wonderfully varied geometric *tukutuku* (woven panels). At the foot of the two support poles, ancient and intricately carved warrior statues provide a fine counterpoint to the bolder work on the walls. This is one of the most easily accessible working *marae*, but it is still necessary to arrange permission to enter the site (☎06/868 5364), preferably a day or two in advance. You will pretty much be left to your own devices, so remember to remove your shoes before entering the meeting house and photographs should only be taken if you have asked permission; a *koha* (donation) is appreciated. Access to the small and decorative **Toko Toru Tapu Church** next door, is prohibited until restoration work has been completed.

Outdoor activities

Gisborne offers one of New Zealand's few opportunities for heart-pounding **shark encounters**. Surfit Shark Cage Experience (T06/867 2970, Wwww.surfit.co.nz; $200) take small groups about 15km offshore from where, two at a time, people climb into a tough metal cage, which is partly lowered into the water where **mako sharks** lurk. Standing chest deep, you get around half an hour in the water – quite long enough – ducking down with a mask and snorkel or regulator to observe these curious three-metre-long, eighty-kilo killing machines. There's a fifty-percent refund in the unlikely event of not seeing any sharks. It's worth remembering that although the trip organizers aim to impact on the environment as little as possible, the trips do alter the natural balance in the waters and, as the sharks are attracted with food thrown into the water, this food–people connection can have more worrying implications for local surfers.

One of the two really worthwhile **Maori tours** in New Zealand runs from Gisborne Information Centre (see p.440 for the other). Historically Maori tours, unlike the cultural experiences of Rotorua and Taupo, are fraught with difficulty as the entire *marae* must agree to the plans if it involves *iwi* land. Whale Rider Tours (T06/868 5878; $50; minimum 3), inspired by the internationally acclaimed book and film (see p.984), pick up at the information centre and introduce travellers to a few film locations in Gisborne before heading north up the coast to Whangara to the highlight of the tour. The Taumaunu family show you round a working *marae* and relate Maori stories and legends including that of the Whale Rider, Paikea.

Around Gisborne

Winery visits with free tasting, gentle walks and a smattering of specific attractions make a day or so spent around Gisborne an agreeable prospect. If you don't have a car, your best bet is to rent a bike (see p.440) and head out on the flat roads to the wineries before retiring to one of the **short walks** just north of the city. Alternatively join one of the various Trev's Tours (T06/863 9815, Etrevs.tours@voyager.co.nz), around the wineries ($50, minimum of two), out to Eastwoodhill Arboretum ($50, minimum two) or south to Morere Hot Springs ($100, minimum of two).

About 8km out of town, just off the SH2, on Bell and Saleyards Road, lies the diminutive wooden **Matawhero Presbyterian Church**, the only building left standing after Te Kooti's Poverty Bay Massacre in the early hours of 1868. It's easily found by following the signs from the tiny settlement of Matawhero.

The wineries

Occupying a free-draining alluvial plain, in the lee of the Raukumara Range and blessed with long hours of strong sun with warm summer nights, Poverty Bay wineries have made Gisborne the country's self-professed Chardonnay capital. The region has earned itself a reputation as a viticultural workhorse, churning out vast quantities of Chardonnay, Riesling, Müller-Thurgau and Gewürztraminer grapes to be blended into cheerful wines for everyday glugging. Out in the highly fertile wine country, roadside windbreaks of poplars are a common sight, protecting the vines beyond. Most of the wineries you can visit are small concerns that open according to demand; hours given below are a guideline only, and you'd do well to call in advance.

The national giants of Corban's and Montana account for over eighty percent of the regional production, but tours of their factory-style operations are only available to groups by appointment. Still, you might call in to **The Lindauer Cellars**, 11 Solander St, around 1km west of downtown (daily 10am–5pm; $5; ☎06/868 2757), for an historic tour followed by tasting (there's also good quality food available), before heading further afield to the more interesting boutique wineries.

One of the closest and longest-established wineries is **Matawhero**, Riverpoint Road, 8km west of Gisborne, where via the Coliseum Cafe (Oct–April Mon–Sat 10am–5pm; rest of year times vary; tastings $1; ☎06/868 8366), renowned for its Gewürtztraminer and beginning to produce some fine reds. There is more of interest at **Millton Vineyard**, Papatu Road, Manutuke, 2km west (call before visiting ☎06/862 8680; tastings free), which is one of New Zealand's few fully certified organic wineries, and possibly the only one to apply the bio-dynamic principles espoused by Rudolf Steiner to all aspects of wine production. The timing of planting, harvesting and bottling are dictated by the phases of the moon, which combines to produce some delicious wines (especially Riesling, Chenin Blanc and late-harvest dessert wines) that, they claim, can be enjoyed even by those who experience allergic reactions to other wines. Considering the intricacy of such wine making, prices are surprisingly reasonable, so grab a bottle, indulge in a picnic among the vines and a leisurely game of petanque. One of the few wineries that is open daily all year is **Pouparae Park**, Bushmere Road, 10km west of central Gisborne on Bushmere Road, 4km off the southbound SH2 (☎06/867 7931, tastings free), where a parkland garden provides a lovely setting for sampling their noted Chardonnay, Merlot and Riesling – all sold at very reasonable prices.

Eastwoodhill Arboretum

A bottle of wine tucked under your arm and a groaning picnic hamper is the most conducive way to enjoy New Zealand's largest collection of northern-hemisphere vegetation at **Eastwoodhill Arboretum**, Ngatapa–Rere Road, 35km northwest of Gisborne (daily 9am–5pm; ⓦ www.eastwoodhill.org.nz; $8). The parched hills surrounding the Poverty Bay plains stand in stark contrast to the arboretum's lush glens and formal lawns. Planting began in 1910, inspired by William Douglas Cook, who had grown to love British gardens and parks. Numerous trails thread through a unique mixture of over 3500 species – magnolias, oaks, spruce, maples, cherries – brought together in an unusual microclimate in which both hot- and cold-climate trees flourish.

Te Kuri Farm Walkway and Gray's Bush

Walks are not Gisborne's strong suit, but there are a couple detailed in DOC leaflets available from the visitor centre. The closest is **Te Kuri Farm Walkway** (5.6km; 2hr; closed during lambing season mid-July to Oct), off Shelley Road, 4km north of the centre of Gisborne. Apart from a lovely panorama over the city from a ridge-top section of pastoral land, this isn't a particularly exciting route – though you do get to walk the land owned by cartoonist Murray Ball, who immortalized this terrain in his archetypal Kiwi cartoon, *Footrot Flats*, which features "the Dog", or Te Kuri. On a hot day, a better bet is the short walk through the cool kahikatea, puriri and nikau woodlands of **Gray's Bush** (30min return), 9km northeast of the city, and the largest remnant of the tall forests that once covered the Poverty Bay flats.

Eating, drinking and nightlife

For its size, Gisborne is surprisingly well supplied with decent **cafés** and **restaurants** to suit all budgets, many of them making good use of their locations on the city's beach, rivers or harbour. This makes the restaurants the best bet for an evening drink, though there are several traditional **pubs** for straightforward beer consumption.

A rough-and-ready **farmers' market** is held each Saturday morning (6.30am to around 8.30am) in the park next to the visitor centre, where you can snap up some bargain ingredients in a bustling atmosphere – keep an eye out for some of the subtropical and citrus fruits that grow here all year for the export market. Unusually for New Zealand, where local catches of **fish** are often immediately exported or transported to other parts of the country, excellent prices for fish straight off Gisborne's boats can be had at the Moana Pacific Fisheries shop (Mon–Fri 8.30am–5.30pm & 8.30am–12.30pm), on The Esplanade and opposite the Tatapouri Sports Fishing Club. Adjacent to the fishing club is the new No3 Wharf Shed Market (daily 9am–6pm), in a massive old corrugated shed which also sells fish, local cheese, vegetables, wine and fresh baked bread from a series of delis.

Movies are shown at the Odeon **cinema**, 79 Gladstone Rd (☎06/867 3339).

Cafés and restaurants

Café Verve 121 Gladstone Rd. Gisborne's grooviest all-day café and restaurant, with sofas and magazines at the back, Internet access, and gorgeous moderately priced food that extends from smoked salmon to English muffins via Scotch fillet with roast garlic.

Café Villaggio 57 Ballance St. Award-winning casual restaurant set in a suburban Art Deco house and spilling over into the courtyard. A great place for weekend brunch, lunches or simple yet delicious evening meals from around $28. Closed Sun & Mon evenings.

Fettuccine Brothers 12 Peel St ☎06/868 5700. Relaxing and long-standing Italian restaurant (with adjacent bar) serving a full range of dishes from pasta ($18) to substantial meat and fish dishes ($24–32). May–Oct closed Sun.

The Marina Marina Park, Vogel St ☎06/868 5919. One of Gisborne's smartest restaurants, with a glass-sided dining room bedecked in crisp white linen and overlooking the confluence of the Taruheru and Waimata rivers. Food is of the modern Kiwi persuasion, using fresh, local produce, at around $30 for a main course. Bookings essential for evenings. Closed Sunday.

Ruba 14 Childers Rd. Modern artsy, cool and sophisticated café away from the main drag serving all-day breakfasts, including veggie ones, terrific vermicelli salads, mussels, local wines, wonderful coffee, and chocolate brownies to write home about. Mains $10–25.

Something Fishy 61 Gladstone Rd ☎06/867 7457. Low on pretension and light bulbs but still one of the best licensed seafood restaurants in the town with great-value meals daily from 6pm, including wonderful crayfish and thick juicy steaks in mammoth portions.

Shades of Green cnr of Low St & Reads Quay. Central little café overlooking the river, serving generous omelettes, salads, filo wraps and steak sandwiches as well as good coffee and wine by the glass.

Wharf Café Shed 1, The Esplanade ☎06/868 4876. Light and airy harbourside café with a relaxed approach and a varied and well-priced menu: try the massive antipasto platter ($25) or knock back a dozen oysters ($18). Book ahead.

The Works cnr The Esplanade & Crawford Rd ☎06/863 1285. Airy, stylish Mediterranean-style café in a former freezing works set back from the wharf that's always abuzz with folk in for a coffee and a snack, or with serious diners here for seafood paella or the catch of the day ($26). Bottled wine drinkers have plenty of choice but by-the-glass drinkers only have the house's own somewhat variable range.

Pubs and bars

The Irish Rover 69 Peel St. A place of simple charms and warm atmosphere: Guinness, the natural Gisborne Gold, bar snacks and occasional live bands.

Scotty's Bar & Grill 33 Gladstone Rd. Probably the liveliest bar in town, certainly the longest established, occupying an ornate ex-bank. This is a great all-rounder, open daily with good-value food, plenty of outdoor seating, and a DJ or live band on Fri & Sat nights.

Smash Palace Wine Bar 24 Banks St. Wonderfully oddball bar and boozing garden, under the management of a couple of ex-punters, where overalls from the surrounding industrial area rub shoulders with suits in a corrugated-iron barn. Food basically comprises snacks – favourites being flaming pizzas and the nachos that have been flame-toasted with a blow torch.

Tatapouri Sports Fishing Club The Esplanade. When they're not too busy, visitors ($1 day membership, free if there's a fishing competition) are welcome to this barn-like pub/club right on the wharf. There's veranda seating for the consumption of simple generous portions of a "wharfie's plate", all imaginable seafood, steaks or gourmet burgers (all under $20), while watching the sun set behind the hills beyond the dock.

Gisborne to Wairoa

All roads south from Gisborne involve lengthy travel through vast swathes of farmland, which are sparsely scattered with nowhere villages that offer little incentive to linger. There are two routes: the faster SH2, which sticks close to the coast before veering around Hawke Bay; and the inland SH36, which sees very little traffic – and no public transport.

Following the alternative coastal route of **SH2** from Gisborne along the southern continuation of the Pacific Coast Highway, the Poverty Bay vineyards soon give way to the hill country of the Wharerata State Forest, where the first real diversion is provided by **Morere Hot Springs** (daily: Christmas–Jan 10am–9pm; Feb–Christmas 10am–5pm; $5, private pools an extra $2 for 30min), 60km south of Gisborne. Ancient sea water has been heated and concentrated along the fault line deep underground to form highly saline, iron-rich waters that well up along a small stream as it trickles down through one of the East Coast's last remaining tracts of native coastal forest. Grassy barbecue areas surround the pools and form the nucleus of numerous trails that radiate out through stands of tawa, rimu, totara and matai; a short streamside walk (10min) takes you to the Nikau Plunge Pools, where steel soaking tanks are surrounded by groves of nikau palms.

The adjacent settlement of **MORERE** has a shop-cum-tearoom and a couple of **places to stay**, both on SH2 as it passes through the village. The eccentrically managed *Moonlight Lodge* (℡ & ℻ 06/837 8824, ℮ moonlight@xtra.co.nz; dorms ❶, rooms ❷; closed June–Aug) is a spacious and broad-verandaed house, tucked away amid trees, with small dorms and doubles; there's also accommodation at *Morere Springs Tearooms & Camping Ground* (℡ 06/837 8792, ℻ 837 8790; camping $12, dorms $30, cabins ❸).

Mahia Peninsula

At Nuhaka, 8km south of Morere, the road flirts briefly with the sea before turning sharp right for Wairoa. A side road spurs east to the pendulous **Mahia Peninsula** – a popular kiwi holiday destination – a distinctive high promontory that separates Hawke's Bay from Poverty Bay, linked to the mainland by a narrow sandy isthmus. Surfers make good use of the rougher windward side, while the calmer beaches on the leeward side offer safe bathing and boating for the hundreds of families who descend each summer to swim, fish for snapper and hapuku, dive and generally chill out. Outside the mad month after Christmas it makes a relaxing place to break your journey, or to stretch your legs on the 4km looped track through the **Mahia Peninsula Scenic Reserve**.

At the northern end of the Hawke's Bay side of the isthmus is **Opuatama**, little more than a shop and the extraordinary pine-surrounded *Blue Bay Holiday Resort* (☎06/837 5867, ⓔbluebay.co.nz; camping $11, excellent backpacker buses ❶ kitchen cabins ❸, units ❹), one of the best kept and most imaginative campsites on the North Island, with a little something for everyone.

The peninsula's main settlement of **Mahia Beach** lies at the southern end of the five-kilometre strand, where there are takeaways, a café in the holiday park and a great pub, as well as the *Mahia Beach Motels & Holiday Park* (☎06/837 5830, ⓔmahia.beach.motels@xtra.co.nz; camping $12, cabins ❷, units ❺) with spacious camping, simple tourist cabins and flashier motel units. You can also stay just over the hill, closer to the surf beaches, at tiny **Te Mahia**, in the log-built *Cappamore Lodge*, 435 Mahia East Coast Rd (☎06/837 5523, ⓦwww.cottagestays.co.nz/cappamore/cottage.htm; ❺), a self-contained two-storey house. Even if you are not staying for the sandcastle competition you have to drop into the bold and lively **Sunset Sports Bar and Bistro** the only place with Internet access for miles. There are also bikes and surf boards for hire ($25 & $35 respectively), plentiful supplies of tasty grub – fresh crayfish $40, steaks $22 –free flowing booze, particularly on Fridays and through the weekend when live bands and DJs rule the roost; free condoms provided.

From Wairoa to Napier

The apparently sleepy one-horse town of **WAIROA**, some 40km west of the Nuhaka junction, hugs the banks of the broad willow-lined Wairoa River a couple of kilometres from its mouth, where ships once entered to load the produce of the dairy and sheep-farming country all around. There's little to delay you here, if you are stuck between buses stroll along the waterfront past the 1877 kauri-wood **lighthouse** beside the bridge at the town centre, which was relocated here in 1961 from Portland Island, off the southern tip of the Mahia Peninsula.

Nearby, the **Wairoa Museum**, on Marine Parade (Mon–Fri 10am–4pm, Sat 10am–1pm; donation), deserves thirty minutes for its small but well-presented displays on local history (including the devastating cyclone Bola, which swept through the region in 1988) and the beautifully carved Maori figure dating back to the eighteenth century, as well as the changing exhibitions in its gallery. The **visitor centre**, located on the corner of SH2 and Queen Street (Nov–March daily 9am–5pm; April–Sept Mon–Fri 9am–5pm; ☎ & ⓕ06/838 7440, ⓔweavic@xtra.co.nz), organise a supervised but unguided visit to the town's highly decorative **Takitimu Marae**.

Buses to Waikaremoana (see p.448), and InterCity buses to Gisborne and Napier pick up near the visitor centre and are well co-ordinated so you shouldn't need a **place to stay**. If, however, you're really stuck try the *Riverside Motor Camp* at 19 Marine Parade (☎06/838 6301, ⓕ838 6341; tent sites $10, cabins ❷), or the *Vista Motor Lodge*, on SH2 north of the Wairoa bridge (☎06/838 8279, ⓕ838 8277; ❹), that has an on-site **restaurant** (Mon–Fri 6pm–10pm).

Travelling by bus, or even by car, there is little to justify stopping in the inland farming country that lines the highway between Wairoa and Napier, though cyclists may want to break this 120km stretch. A hidden gem along this stretch is about three-quarters of the way at *Glen-View Farm Hostel*, Aropaoanui Road, 2km east off SH2 (☎06/836 6232, ⓔglenviewhostel@xtra.co.nz), a small and well-organized backpackers with Internet access, tent sites ($10), bargain four-shares (❶) and self-contained rooms (❷), plus a farm shop and tasty home-cooked meals; a separate homestay section, 2km down the road, features an elaborate breakfast – and there's **riding** ($40, 2hrs) that includes swimming the horses in the river.

A few kilometres further south, the highway passes the small **Lake Tutira** and its diminutive neighbour, Lake Waikopiro, neither worthy of much attention though if you want a breath of air you could tackle one of three farmland loop walks (1km, 20min; 3.5km, 2hr; and 9km, 5hr; all closed Aug & Sept for lambing season), which start at the roadside car park, the shortest walk encircling Lake Waikopiro and the longest incorporating a lookout over both lakes; (DOC leaflet *Napier–Tutira Highway*; $1). On a hot day you might prefer the shade offered by **White Pine Bush Scenic Reserve**, 10km south, a dense clump of kahikatea, rimu and other podocarps, where loop tracks (650m, 30min; and 3km, 1hr) thread through the bush alongside the Kareaara Stream. From here it is just 25km to central Napier.

Te Urewera National Park

Te Urewera National Park, 65km northwest of Wairoa, straddles the North Island's mountainous backbone and encompasses the largest untouched expanse of native bush outside of Fiordland. Unusually for New Zealand, it is almost completely covered in vegetation; even the highest peaks – some approaching 1500m – barely poke through this dense cloak of primeval forests whose undergrowth is trampled by deer and wild pigs, and whose cascading rivers are alive with trout. One road, SH38, penetrates the interior, but the way to get a true sense of the place is to go tramping. For hardy types, this means the **Lake Waikaremoana Track**, which is among the finest four-day tramps on the North Island, encircling a steep-sided lake at the southern end of the park. Created little more than two thousand years ago, **Lake Waikaremoana**, the "Sea of Rippling Waters", is the undoubted jewel of the park, its deep clear waters fringed by white sandy beaches and rocky bluffs making it ideal for swimming, diving, fishing and kayaking.

Habitation is very sparse. The Tuhoe people, the "Children of the Mist", still live in the interior of the park (the largest concentration around the tramping base of **Ruatahuna**), but most visitors make straight for **Waikaremoana**, which is barely a settlement at all, just a motor camp and a visitor centre right on the lake shore. Immediately to the south, the *Big Bush Holiday Camp* and the quiet former hydro-electrical development town of **Tuai** provide some additional basic services, but otherwise you're on your own.

Lake Waikaremoana

The magnificent, bush-girt **Lake Waikaremoana** fills a huge scalloped bowl at an altitude of over 585m, precariously held back by the Panekiri and Ngamoko ranges which, at the slightest opportunity, seem ready to part and spill the contents down the pastoral valley towards Wairoa. The lake came into being around 2200 years ago when a huge bank of sandstone boulders was dislodged from the Ngamoko range, blocking the river that once drained the valleys and thereby forming the lake. Maori have a more poetic explanation of the lake's creation, pointing to the work of Hau-Mapuhia, the recalcitrant daughter of Mahu, who was drowned by her father and turned into a *taniwha*, or "water spirit". In a frenzied effort to get to the sea, she charged in every direction, thereby creating the various arms of the lake. As she frantically ran

Te Kooti Rikirangi

Te Kooti Rikirangi was one of the most celebrated of Maori "rebels", a thorn in the side of the colonial government throughout the New Zealand Wars of the late 1860s and early years of the 1870s. Depicted, at least in *pakeha*-biased school books, as a ruthless guerrilla leader and the wildest outlaw in Maori history, in truth he was a mild-mannered man with a neatly trimmed beard and moustache rather than the more confrontational *moko* (traditional tattoos). An excellent fighter and brilliant strategist, Te Kooti kept the mountainous spine of the North Island on edge for the best part of a decade, eluding the biggest manhunt in New Zealand's history.

Though not of chiefly rank, Te Kooti could trace his ancestry back to the captains of several *waka* (canoes) that brought the Maori to New Zealand, and was born near Gisborne into a respected family around 1830, though little else is known of his early years. By the middle of the 1860s, he was fighting for the government against the **Hau Hau** (see box on p.422), a fanatical, pseudo-Christian cult that started in Taranaki in 1862. The cult spread to the East Coast where, in 1866, Te Kooti was unjustly accused of being in league with its devotees. Denied the trial he so often demanded, he was subsequently imprisoned on the Chatham Islands, along with 300 of his supposed allies. In 1867, he was brought close to death by a fever, but rose again, claiming a divine revelation and establishing a new religion, **Ringatu** ("the uplifted hand"), which still has some ten thousand believers today. Ringatu took its cues from the Hau Hau, but developed into a uniquely Maori version of Catholicism, drawing heavily on the Old Testament. Some say Te Kooti saw himself as a Moses figure, called to lead his people to freedom, and he was certainly charismatic in his approach – apparently given to dousing his uplifted hand in phosphorus so that it glowed in the dim meeting houses.

After two years on the Chathams, Te Kooti and his fellow prisoners commandeered a ship and engineered a dramatic escape, returning to Poverty Bay. Te Kooti sought the rugged safety of the **Urewera Range**, with the Armed Constabulary in hot pursuit. Nonetheless, Te Kooti conducted successful campaigns, exacting revenge against government troops at Whakatane on the Bay of Plenty, Mohaka in Hawke's Bay and at Rotorua. The government posted a reward of £1000 on his head, but he was always able to stay ahead of the game and it was never claimed. With the end of the New Zealand Wars in 1872, Te Kooti took refuge in the Maori safe haven of the **King Country**. He was eventually pardoned in 1883, and in 1891 was granted a plot of land near Whakatane, where he lived out the last two years of his life.

south towards Onepoto, the dawn caught her, turning her to stone at a spot where the lake is said to ripple from time to time, in a watery memory of her titanic struggle.

One of the beauties of the lake is that there is no town nearby, just the DOC-operated Aniwaniwa visitor centre (see p.452), and a motor camp, both well set-up for helping hikers tackle the Lake Waikaremoana Track (see p.450). Short visits are repaid with the opportunity to see the **Papakorito Falls**, a twenty-metre-wide curtain of water located 2km east of the visitor centre. To really see and get a feel for the place you'll need to walk, preferably armed with DOC's *Lake Waikaremoana Walks* leaflet ($2), which details the region's shorter hikes such as the stroll to the double-drop **Aniwaniwa Falls** (1km; an easy 20min return), starting from beside the visitor centre, or the **Black Beech Track** (2km; 30min one way, easy), which follows the old highway from the visitor centre to the motor camp. With the best part of a day to spare, take on the **Waipai–Ruapani–Waikareiti Round Trip** (15km; 6hr), which starts 200m north of the visitor centre and winds up through dense beech forest past

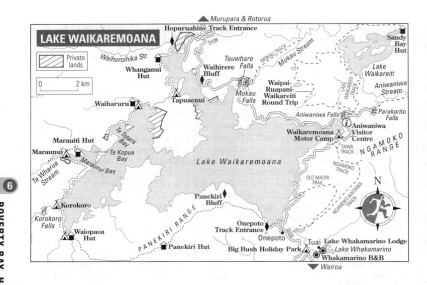

the grassy-fringed Lake Ruapani to the beautiful and serene **Lake Waikareiti**, where you can rent row-boats (around $15 per half day, $40 deposit), though you'll need to plan ahead, as the key is held at Aniwaniwa visitor centre. Return down the Waikareiti Track or head on around to the northern side of the lake (3hr one-way) and stay at **Sandy Bay Hut** (18 bunks; $14).

You can also explore the lake with watercraft rented from the Waikaremoana Motor Camp by two companies, both offering **kayaks** for about $40 a half-day and **canoes** for $30.

The Lake Waikaremoana Track

The **Lake Waikaremoana Track** (46km; 3–4 days; 900m ascent) is one of New Zealand's "Great Walks", and undoubtedly ranks among the finest multi-day tramps in New Zealand. It is also the most popular such tramp in the North Island and is often compared with the South Island's Routeburn and Milford tracks, but with the exception of an exhausting climb on the first day, this is a much gentler affair. Well-paced and mostly hugging the lakeshore, the tramp offers plenty of opportunities to fish and swim, as well as to simply admire the majestic scenery and listen to the cacophonous birdlife.

All the **information** you need to walk the track is on DOC's *Lake Waikaremoana Track* leaflet ($1), though **map** enthusiasts may fancy the detailed 1:100,000 *Urewera Parkmap*. Though three days is enough for fit individuals, the walk is normally done in four days, spending nights in the five "Great Walk" **huts** ($14) and five designated **campsites** ($10) scattered around the lakeshore. Throughout the year, huts and campsites must be **booked in advance** through the Aniwaniwa visitor centre or DOC offices nationwide; your chances of getting a place are much better outside the busy month or so after Christmas and the week of Easter. The winter months (June–Sept) can be cold and wet, making spring and autumn the best times. Each hut is supplied with drinking water, toilets and a heating stove, but a cooking stove, fuel and all your food must be carried.

About sixty percent of walkers prefer to travel clockwise around the lake, getting the challenging but panoramic ascent of Panekiri Bluff over with on the first day, though if the weather looks bad there's no reason why you shouldn't go anti-clockwise in the hope that it will improve; if you are relying on buses it makes for an easier first day if you walk anti-clockwise.

Trailhead transport

You can **drive** to the trailheads at either end of the tramp, but neither are safe places to leave your vehicle, so most people leave their clobber either at *Big Bush Motor Camp* (free); in the car park beside the Waikaremoana Motor Camp store (free); or for extra security, inside the motor camp itself ($3 per night). From the latter, **access** to the start and finish of the Waikaremoana Circuit is either by shuttle bus or by boat: whichever way you walk, you can be on the track by 9am, and you need to finish your last day's walk by 2pm.

Two **ferry services** now operate from the Waikaremoana Motor Camp to Onepoto, the long established Hopuruahine: Waikaremoana Guided Tours (☎06/837 3729 & 0800/469 879) and Big Bush Water Taxi (☎06/837 3777). They offer virtually identical services, both running several times a day to the ends of the track and charging $25 for a joint drop-off and pick-up package. Both will also run a **water taxi** service to anywhere else you might want to start or finish enabling you to walk shorter sections of the circuit by means of pre-arranged pick-ups from specified beaches – prices are dependent on numbers, but are broadly comparable with the regular ferries.

The route

When tackled clockwise, the first leg from **Onepoto to Panekiri Hut** (9km; 5hr; 600m ascent) is the toughest; carry plenty of drinking water and start at a shelter by the lakeshore close to SH38. The track climbs steeply past the site of a redoubt set up by soldiers of the Armed Constabulary in pursuit of Te Kooti (see box on p.449) to the Pukenui trig point, from where the track undulates along the ridge top. Steps up a rocky bluff bring you to the Panekiri Hut (36 bunks), magnificently set on the brink of the cliffs that fall away to the lake far below. Even if you've the energy to push on, it would be a shame not to stay here, though camping in this fragile environment is prohibited, so the hut is your only option. Committed campers must press on to Waiopaoa, a whopping nine hours' walk from the start.

From **Panekiri Hut to Waiopaoa Hut** (7.5km; 3–4hr; 600m descent) you lose the height gained the previous day, slowly at first along the descending ridge, then very rapidly through an often-muddy area where protruding tree roots provide welcome hand-holds. Occasional lake views and the transition from beech forests to rich podocarp woodlands make this an appealing, if tricky, section of track down to the hut (21 bunks) and campsite.

Pressing on from **Waiopaoa Hut to Marauiti Hut** (11km; 4–5hr; 100m ascent), you largely follow the lakeshore, initially across grassland and through kanuka scrub where a side track leads to the impressive 20m Korokoro Falls (25min return) and, just beyond the junction, the Korokoro campsite (1hr 30min from Waiopaoa Hut). Meanwhile, the main track climbs slightly above the lake past barely accessible bays, eventually reaching the Maraunui campsite and, after climbing the low Whakaneke Spur, descends to the waterside Marauiti Hut (22 bunks). From **Marauiti Hut to Waiharuru Hut** (6km; 2hr; 100m ascent) the track passes the lovely white-sand Te Kopua Bay and climbs an easy saddle, before dropping down to Te Totara Bay and following the lake to Waiharuru Hut (40 bunks) and campsite. It is a short hike from **Waiharuru**

Hut to Whanganui Hut (5.3km; 2–3hr; 50m ascent) across a broad neck of land to the Tapuaenui campsite and beyond, following the shore to the pleasantly sited hut (18 bunks).

The last easy section, from **Whanganui Hut to Hopuruahine** (5km; 2–3hr; 50m ascent), skirts the lake and follows grassy flats beside the Hopuruahine River. The trail then crosses a suspension bridge to the access road where there's another camping area (free).

Waikaremoana practicalities

The only **public transport** into the region is run by *Big Bush Holiday Camp* (bookings essential on ☏06/837 3777; $25 from Wairoa, $60 from Rotorua), who operate a daily bus service to the *Holiday Camp* from Wairoa, where it connects with InterCity buses and a service to Waikaremoana from Rotorua (departs 1.30pm Mon, Wed & Fri only). The Rotorua service runs around the eastern side of Lake Waikaremoana past the **Aniwaniwa visitor centre** (daily 8am–4.45pm; ☏06/837 3803, ✉urewerainfo@doc.govt.nz), the main source of information on Lake Waikaremoana and Te Urewera National Park. There are a stack of brochures detailing the numerous walks in the area plus excellent and extensive displays on the geology and ecology of the region, details of local social history, and the opportunity to view Colin McCahon's controversial *Urewera Mural* (see box below) which though interesting in its history is a disappointment artistically. Slightly more rewarding is the remarkable story of *Rua: The Prophet*. Rua believed himself to be leader of the Canaan, the lost tribe of the Jews and in 1905 began a Maori migration here, more than 1,000 people left their homes, to a Maori storey roundhouse surrounded by a village where he welcomed converts to his independent state until his death in 1937.

As is so often the case, places get booked out in summer so it's wise to phone ahead. The only **accommodation** inside the park is at the well-equipped *Waikaremoana Motor Camp*, on SH38, 2km south of the visitor centre

---

The Urewera Mural

The Aniwaniwa visitor centre is the unlikely permanent home of one of New Zealand's finest and most (in)famous pieces of modern art, the epic 1976 *Urewera Mural* by Colin McCahon, one of New Zealand's most celebrated artists. A large, dark triptych with boldly delineated hills emblazoned with Maori text, the painting was intended to be non-judgemental, symbolizing Tuhoe stories of time, place and spirit on each of the three panels. It immediately became contentious as some Tuhoe disputed the relevance and historical accuracy of the Maori text McCahon had used, adding to the general feeling that McCahon – a *pakeha* with a very limited understanding of the Maori language – was appropriating indigenous property. In the spirit of compromise McCahon changed some elements of the painting before it was hung in the Aniwaniwa visitor centre, but disquiet continued to simmer until June 1997 when the painting was "liberated". After a few months the Tuhoe activist **Te Kaha** was convicted of the theft and fined, but not until after he and fellow activist **Tame Iti** had struck up a friendship with Auckland arts patron Jenny Gibbs, who had stepped in to broker the return of the work. The painting had been damaged during its ordeal, but was subsequently repaired and returned to the Aniwaniwa visitor centre. Meanwhile Tame Iti has fashioned his own arts career, for a time running an art dealership specializing in Maori (specifically Tuhoe) art, and even picking up the brushes himself. At least one of his works is now held at Te Papa in Wellington.

($\textcircled{T}$ 06/837 3826, $\textcircled{W}$ www.lake.co.nz; bunkhouse ❶, cabins ❷ & units ❸), with a compact but grassy camping area ($10); showers are available for non-guests at $2 a time. Just outside the park on SH38 16km south of the Aniwaniwa visitor centre, the best bet is the ever-improving *Big Bush Holiday Park* ($\textcircled{T}$ 06/837 3777, $\textcircled{W}$ www.lakewaikaremoana.co.nz), which is fully set up for track trampers and offers camping ($10), backpacker beds (❶) and some comfortable self-contained units (❸) with TV and a small sunny deck. A further kilometre south in Tuai, former construction workers' quarters are now the less than impressive *Lake Whakamarino Lodge* ($\textcircled{T}$ 06/837 3876, $\textcircled{W}$ www.lakelodge.co.nz; rooms ❹, self-contained units ❺), which is rather short on character, despite being wonderfully sited right on the shores of the trout-filled Lake Whakamarino. Alternatively and adjacent to the lodge is the tiny Whakamarino B&B ($\textcircled{T}$ 06/837 3701; ❺) where accommodation is offered as well as a vehicle-watch service, home-cooked dinners $25 and a spa bath for $5. There are also a couple of DOC **campsites** along SH38: *Mokau Landing* ($4), 11km north of the visitor centre, and *Taita a Makora* ($3), 11km further north. You'll largely have to fend for yourself when it comes to **eating**, with the only food in the park being the limited range of groceries at the *Waikaremoana Motor Camp*. Tuai's *Big Bush Holiday Park* has reasonably priced meals and decent coffee in its characterful cowboy-style bar and restaurant, *Rangers Café*, and expensive meals are available on request at the *Lake Whakamarino Lodge*.

Beyond Lake Waikaremoana: the heart of the park

Beyond Lake Waikaremoana, SH38 twists and turns for over two hours before regaining the tar seal at Murupara, almost 100km northwest of the lake and just an hour (62km) short of Rotorua. The road, which took 45 years to build and wasn't completed until 1930, makes a tortuous journey through the heart of Te Urewera National Park, the ancestral home of the Tuhoe people.

Historically, the Tuhoe had limited contact with Europeans; even today, they live in relative isolation in ramshackle roadside villages such as **RUATAHUNA**, 48km from Waikaremoana, which has the road's only store, takeaway and petrol supplies. Ruatahuna also serves as a base for a couple of little-used tracks into beautiful and remote country north of SH38. These are most often used by anglers and hunters, but are excellent for tramping, too, with backcountry huts ($5) at regular intervals. Two DOC leaflets ($1 each) cover these tramps, the easiest of which is the **Whakatane River Round Trip**, a three-to-five-day walk suitable for most levels of fitness through varied scenery encompassing river valleys, native forest, grassy flats and farmland. For tougher specimens, there's the **Upper Waikare River Guide**, an amalgam of several tracks, many of them following riverbeds (seek local advice on the likelihood of flooding) and enabling various route combinations (2–4 days).

Napier and around

The port city of **NAPIER** is Hawke's Bay's largest, with its beautiful seafront position, a Mediterranean climate and a population barely touching 50,000, it is an easy place to come to terms. The relaxed tone is somewhat disturbed by the two-lane highway that separates the town from its beaches, but it does have one of the world's finest collection of Art Deco buildings, heaps of amusements

During January and February, Napier and nearby Hastings flip into festive mode. Small-time events take place in January, but the first of the major events is the **Harvest Hawke's Bay** (first weekend in February; W www.harvesthawkesbay.co.nz), when food and wine lovers from around the country flock to the Hawke's Bay Racing Centre, Prospect Rd, Hastings, for music, food and wine. Proceedings reach fever pitch for the Charity Wine auction, which is followed by a Sunday drive around the wineries. The **Mission Vineyard Concert** usually takes place in early February (the precise dates are dependent on artists' bookings, and announced in November), when an internationally famous vocalist – Kiri Te Kanawa, Ray Charles and Dionne Warwick have attended in recent years – performs outdoors at the Mission Estate Winery to an audience of around 20,000.

No sooner has the Hawke's Bay summer festival wound up, than Napier gears up for the **Art Deco Weekend** (T 06/835 1191, W www.artdeconapier.com, see p.458 above), usually held on the second or third weekend in February and extending to five light-hearted days of merriment, extending to guided walks, open-house tours of domestic Art Deco, bicycle tours, Thirties-dress picnics, champagne breakfasts, dress balls, silent movies and the like.

for kids and a burgeoning café society. There are other good reasons for staying around namely the trip out to the gannet colony at Cape Kidnappers and the barrel-load of excellent **wineries** on the surrounding plains.

In 1769, James Cook sailed past **Ahuriri**, the current site of Napier, noting the sea-girt Bluff Hill linked to the mainland by two slender shingle banks and backed by a superb saltwater lagoon – the only substantial sheltered mooring between Gisborne and Wellington. Nonetheless, he anchored just to the south, off what came to be known as Cape Kidnappers, on account of a less-than-cordial encounter with the native Ngati Kahungunu people. Some thirty years later, when early whalers followed in Cook's tracks, Ahuriri was all but deserted, the Ngati Kahungunu having been driven out by rivals equipped with guns – the dubious contribution of European settlers in the Bay of Islands. During the uneasy peace of the early colonial years, Maori returned to the Napier area, which weathered the **New Zealand Wars** of the 1860s relatively unscathed and profited from the peace sustained by the guiding hands of men like the missionary printer William Colenso and Land Commissioner Donald McLean, both staunch supporters of sheep farming in Hawke's Bay. The port boomed, but by the early years of the twentieth century all the available land was used up and Napier had begun to stagnate.

Everything changed in two-and-a-half minutes on the morning of February 3, 1931, when the city was rocked by the biggest **earthquake** in New Zealand's recorded history, measuring a massive 7.9 on the Richter scale. More than six hundred aftershocks followed over the next two weeks, hampering efforts to rescue the 258 people who perished throughout the Bay area, 162 of them in Napier alone. The centre of the city was completely devastated: almost all the brick-built shops and offices crumbled into a heap of smouldering rubble; the more flexible wooden buildings survived the initial tremor only to be consumed by the ensuing fire, which was fanned by a stiff sea breeze. The land twisted and buckled, finding a new equilibrium more than two metres higher; the sea drained out of the Ahuriri Lagoon, leaving trawlers high and dry and fish floundering on the mud flats. Three hundred square kilometres of new land were wrested from the grip of the ocean – enough room to site the Hawke's Bay airport, establish new farms and expand the city; cast your eye inland and you can still pick out a stranded line of sea cliffs a couple of kilometres away.

All this happened in the midst of the Great Depression, but Napier grasped the opportunity to start afresh: out went the trams; telephone wires were laid underground; the streets were widened; and buildings had to have cantilevered verandas, obviating the need for unsightly support poles. In the spirit of the times, almost everything was designed according to the precepts of the **Art Deco** movement, the simultaneous reconstruction giving Napier a stylistic uniformity rarely seen – and ranking it alongside Miami Beach as one of the largest collections of Art Deco buildings in the world.

Arrival, information and transport

Flights touch down at Hawke's Bay Airport, 5km north of town on SH2, where they are met by the Super Shuttle (☎06/844 7333), which charges $15 into town; a taxi between two costs about the same. Long-distance **buses** pull in at the Napier Travel Centre, Munroe St (☎06/834 2720), some ten minutes' walk from the large, modern **visitor centre**, 100 Marine Parade (Mon–Fri 8.30am–5pm, Sat & Sun 9am–5pm, often until 6pm or 7pm in summer; ☎06/834 1911, ⓦwww.hawkesbaynz.com). A few steps along the seafront on the landward side of the road, Napier's former courthouse houses the **DOC office**, 59 Marine Parade (☎06/834 3111, ⓕ834 4869; Mon–Fri 9am–4.15pm), where you can consult tide tables for the Cape Kidnappers walk (see p.465), pick up some mildly diverting heritage trail leaflets, and find out about walks into the remote Kaweka and Ruahine ranges to the west. For **Internet access** try Cybers Internet Café, 98 Dickens St; the **post office** is on the corner of Hastings and Dickens streets and you can glean local listings from the weekday-only *Hawke's Bay Today* newspaper, especially the Friday listings pull-out.

Getting around Napier's central sights is easily done on foot, which is fortunate as the Nimbus **local bus** services (Mon–Fri only) is of little use except for visits to Hastings, or the Mission Estate Winery (where they drop off within walking distance). To venture further afield, either join a **winery tour**, **rent a car** (try Avis ☎06/835 1828; Hertz ☎06/835 6169; or Rent-a-Dent ☎06/834 1420), **rent a bike** from Marineland on Marine Parade ($20 a half day), or grab a **taxi** with Napier Taxis (☎06/835 7777).

Accommodation

Apart from the usual shortage of rooms during the month or so after Christmas, and to a lesser extent during February and March, you should have little trouble finding accommodation in Napier. In Kiwi-seaside fashion, there are dozens of **motels** around town, the greatest concentration being in Westshore, a beachfront suburb a few kilometres from the centre beside SH2 heading north. Right in the thick of things, Marine Parade has low-cost backpacker **hostels** and classy **B&Bs**, but for homestays look no further than Bluff Hill. Predictably, none of the **campsites** are especially central.

Hotels and motels

Albatross Motel 56 Meeanee Quay, Westshore ☎06/835 5991 & 0800/252 287, ⓔalbatrossmotel@xtra.co.nz. Large and good-value motel close to Westshore Beach, with a pool, spa, studio units and self-catering family rooms but a long haul from town. ❸

Beach Front Motel 373 Marine Parade ☎06/835 5220 & 0800/778 888, ⓔbeachfrontmotel@xtra.co.nz. High standard motel of luxury suites all having balconies, sea

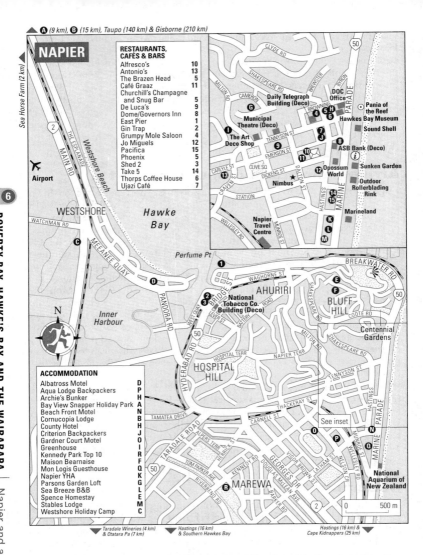

NAPIER

(A) (9 km), (B) (15 km), Taupo (140 km) & Gisborne (210 km)

Sea Horse Farm (2 km)

RESTAURANTS, CAFÉS & BARS

Alfresco's	10
Antonio's	13
The Brazen Head	5
Café Graaz	11
Churchill's Champagne and Snug Bar	5
De Luca's	9
Dome/Governors Inn	8
East Pier	1
Gin Trap	2
Grumpy Mole Saloon	4
Jo Miguels	12
Pacifica	15
Phoenix	5
Shed 2	3
Take 5	14
Thorps Coffee House	6
Ujazi Café	7

ACCOMMODATION

Albatross Motel	D
Aqua Lodge Backpackers	P
Archie's Bunker	H
Bay View Snapper Holiday Park	A
Beach Front Motel	N
Cornucopia Lodge	B
County Hotel	H
Criterion Backpackers	J
Gardner Court Motel	O
Greenhouse	I
Kennedy Park Top 10	R
Maison Bearnaise	F
Mon Logis Guesthouse	Q
Napier YHA	K
Parsons Garden Loft	G
Sea Breeze B&B	L
Spence Homestay	E
Stables Lodge	M
Westshore Holiday Camp	C

Airport

WESTSHORE

Hawke Bay

Perfume Pt

Inner Harbour

AHURIRI

BLUFF HILL

Centennial Gardens

HOSPITAL HILL

MAREWA

National Aquarium of New Zealand

See inset

Daily Telegraph Building (Deco)

DOC Office

Pania of the Reef

Hawkes Bay Museum

Municipal Theatre (Deco)

Sound Shell

The Art Deco Shop

ASB Bank (Deco)

Sunken Garden

Opossum World

Outdoor Rollerblading Rink

Nimbus

Marineland

Napier Travel Centre

National Tobacco Co. Building (Deco)

0   500 m

Taradale Wineries (4 km) & Otatara Pa (7 km) — *Hastings (16 km) & Southern Hawkes Bay* — *Hastings (16 km) & Cape Kidnappers (25 km)*

views, full kitchen, in-room spa pool or spa bath and breakfast supplied. **6**

The County Hotel 12 Browning St ☎06/835 7800 & 0800/843 468, ⊛www.countyhotel.co.nz. Elegant, beautifully decorated business and tourist hotel in the Edwardian former council offices building, one of the few to survive the earthquake. Rooms all come with en-suite facilities and Sky TV. **8**

Gardner Court Motel 16 Nelson Crescent ☎06/835 5913 & 0800/000 830, Ⓔgardencourtmotel@xtra.co.nz. Quiet and

reasonably central motel with a solar-heated outdoor pool and standard motel rooms at bargain prices. **4**

B&Bs and homestays

Cornucopia Lodge 361 SH5, Eskdale ☎06/836 6508, ⊛www.cornucopia-lodge.com. A little rural luxury amid orchards and vineyards 15km north of Napier (on the road to Taupo), with two en-suite rooms, each with open fire and sun deck. There's also a fully equipped kitchen for guests' use. A wonderful breakfast is included, and a two-course dinner and wine costs $35. **7**

Mon Logis Guesthouse 415 Marine Parade ℡06/835 2125, @monlogis@xtra.co.nz. Classy and sumptuously furnished boutique hotel with a French theme. Some rooms in this lovely two-storey wooden house overlook the sea, the tariff includes a delicious breakfast. **6**

Parsons Garden Loft 29 Cameron Rd, Bluff Hill ℡06/835 1527. Smallish en-suite room set in the leafy grounds of a fine homestead on Middle Hill, five minutes' steep walk up steps from Dalton Street, beside the Municipal Theatre. **4**

Sea Breeze B&B 281 Marine Parade ℡06/835 8067, @seabreeze.napier@xtra.co.nz. Reasonable B&B with three individually decorated rooms, Indian, Turkish and Chinese in style, and a self-service continental breakfast. **4**

Spence Homestay 17 Cobden Rd, Bluff Hill ℡06/835 9454, @ksspence@actrix.gen.nz. Friendly self-contained room in a modern house, set in a quiet area. **6**

Maison Bearnaise 25 France Rd, Bluff Hill ℡06/835 4693, @chrisgraham@xtra.co.nz. Two charming open and airy doubles in a century-old villa with a lovely garden and tasty breakfasts. **6**

Greenhouse 18 Milton Rd, Bluff Hill ℡06/835 4475 @www.the-green-house.co.nz. Extremely friendly vegetarian household surrounded by trees halfway up a hidden urban hill. Breakfasts are inventive and the three rooms quiet and comfortable, one is en suite. **4**

Hostels

Aqua Lodge Backpackers 53 Nelson Crescent ℡06/835 4523, @aquaback@inhb.co.nz. Home-style hostel with dorms and doubles shoehorned into two suburban houses in a quiet area close to the train and bus station. The good facilities include a pool, free bikes and tent sites for $10. Dorms **1**, rooms **2**

Archie's Bunker 14 Herschell St ℡06/833 7990, @www.archiesbunker.co.nz. Modern office conversion downtown, with good facilities (including a huge TV and pool lounge) and a matriarchal owner who'll help out with most things. Bike rental for $10. Dorms **1**, rooms **2**

Criterion Backpackers 48 Emerson St ℡06/835 2059, @cribacpac@yahoo.com. Napier's biggest hostel, right in the centre in an Art Deco former hotel with large communal areas. Accommodation is in 6- to 10-bed dorms, triples and four-shares and double rooms (one en suite) plus there's also a newish bar, *The Cri*, which is part of a push to attract the major tour-bus companies like Kiwi Experience. Free pick-up from bus station. Dorms **1**, rooms **3**

Napier YHA 277 Marine Parade ℡06/835 7039, @yhanapr@yha.org.nz. Well-run hostel that rambles across three houses right on the waterfront with some sea views. There are four-shares, doubles, singles, twins and a 5-bed family room, and a suntrap at the back with barbecue. Dorms **1**, rooms **2**

Stables Lodge 370 Hastings St ℡ & ℗06/835 6242, @stables@ihug.co.nz. Small, friendly and relaxed hostel with free Internet access, stereo, hammocks, a book exchange and good cooking facilities along with a barbecue area in the central courtyard. Dorms **1**, rooms **2**

Campsites

Bay View Snapper Holiday Park 10 Gill Rd, Bay View ℡06/836 7084 & 0800/287 275, @jimc@xtra.co.nz. Beachfront yet sheltered campsite 9km north of Napier, beyond the airport and 200m from a market garden for fresh vegetables. Offers excellent units, a BBQ and an on-site bar. Camping $12, on-site vans **2**, s/c units **4**

Kennedy Park Top 10 Storkey St, off Kennedy Rd ℡06/843 9126, @www.kennedypark.co.nz. Well-appointed site that's the closest to town, 3km from the city centre, and with a pool and barbecue area. Camping $10–12, cabins **2**, kitchen cabins **2**–**3**, units **5**

Westshore Holiday Camp 1 Main Rd, Westshore ℡06/835 9456, @ann.david@xtra.co.nz. Located midway along Westshore Beach, 3km north of town, this site is a little less formal than *Kennedy Park*, but still has all the facilities you're likely to need. Camping $10, cabins **2**, kitchen cabins **3**, flats **5**

The Town

Napier is blessed with a fine location, neatly tucked under the skirts of **Bluff Hill** (Mataruahou), a three-kilometre-long outcrop festooned with the twisting roads of the eponymous and highly desirable suburb. At its eastern summit is **Bluff Hill Domain Lookout** (daily 7am–dusk), offering views of Cape Kidnappers to the west, and right across to the distant Mahia Peninsula in the east.

Pania of the Reef

Local Maori tell the tale of **Pania**, a beautiful sea-maiden who, each evening, would swim from the watery realm of Tangaroa, the god of the ocean, to quench her thirst at a freshwater spring in a clump of flax close to the base of Bluff Hill, then return to her people each morning. One evening, she was discovered by a young chief who wooed her and wanted her to remain on land. Eventually they married, but when Pania went to pay a final visit to her kin they forcibly restrained her in the briny depths, and she turned to stone at what is now known as **Pania Reef**. Fishers and divers still claim they can see her with her arms outstretched towards the shore.

On Bluff Hill's southern flank, steep roads and even steeper steps switch back down to the grid pattern of the Art Deco **commercial centre** where, at the whim of mid-nineteenth-century Land Commissioner, Alfred Domett, streets were given the names of literary luminaries – Tennyson, Thackeray, Byron, Dickens, Shakespeare, Milton and more. Bisecting it all is the partly pedestrianized main thoroughfare of Emerson Street, whose terracotta paving and palm trees run from Clive Square, one-time site of a makeshift "Tin Town" while the city was being rebuilt after the earthquake, to the pine-fringed **Marine Parade**. The long strip of grey shingle flanking Marine Parade is Napier's main **beach**, where treacherous undertows and powerful surf make it unsafe for swimming.

Around the northeastern side of Bluff Hill lies the original settlement site of **Ahuriri**, now experiencing somewhat of a renaissance with several warehouses being smartened up and a handful of trendy café/bars taking their chances.

The commercial centre: Art Deco Napier

If the dark cloud of the 1931 earthquake had a silver lining, it was the chance it gave Napier to rebuild from scratch, not just with more quake-resistant materials but to completely re-invent itself. Drawing on contemporary themes, Napier fell for **Art Deco** in a big way. A reaction against the organic and naturalistic themes of Art Nouveau, Deco embraced modernity, glorifying progress, the machine age and the Gatsby-style high-life. The onset of the Great Depression at the end of the 1920s pared down these excesses, not least

Art Deco Napier tours and trails

Keen observers will find classic Art Deco everywhere, but for a systematic exploration of Napier's Art Deco revival, begin at **The Art Deco Shop**, 163 Tennyson St (daily 9am–5pm), where you can watch a free twenty-minute introductory video and buy a leaflet for the **self-guided "Art Deco Walk"** ($4), outlining a stroll (1.5km; 1hr 30min to 2hr) through the downtown area. Dedicated Deco buffs meet here for the two-hour **Art Deco Afternoon Walking Tour** (2pm: Oct–June daily; July–Sept Sat, Sun & Wed 2pm; $12), which brings 1930s Napier to life through anecdote-laden patter, and gives you the chance to gaze around the interiors of shops and banks without feeling quite so self-conscious. The shorter **Art Deco Morning Walking Tour** (daily 10am; 1hr; $8) starts at the visitor centre. For those wanting to place the Art Deco buildings in context the **Earthquake Historical Walk and Gallery Tour**, will fit the bill. Starting from the visitor centre (9.30am & 2pm; 2hrs; $10), and taking in the sights accompanied by anecdotes on the 1931 devastation before ending at the earthquake gallery – where photographs show the extent of the quake damage.

because key American exponents were restrained by Chicago and New York statutes which dictated that tall buildings like the Chrysler building had to be stepped back to let the sun penetrate the dark canyons below. Necessity became the mother of invention, and the recurring theme of ziggurats was introduced.

Napier's version of Art Deco was informed by the privations of this austere era. At the same time, the architects looked for inspiration to California's similarly sun-drenched and earthquake-prone Santa Barbara which, just six years earlier, had suffered the same fate as Napier, and had risen from the ashes. They adopted fountains (a symbol of renewal), sunbursts, chevrons, lightning flashes and stylized fluting to embellish the highly formalized but asymmetric designs. In Napier, what emerged was a palimpsest of early-twentieth-century design, combining elements of the Arts and Crafts movement, the Californian Spanish Mission style, Egyptian and Mayan motifs, the stylized floral designs of Art Nouveau, the blockish

△ Pania of the Reef

forms associated with Charles Rennie Mackintosh, and even Maori imagery. For the best part of half a century, the city's residents went about their lives, oblivious to the architectural harmony all around them and merrily daubing everything in grey or muted blue paint. Fortunately this meant that when a few visionaries recognized the city's potential in the mid-1980s and formed the **Art Deco Trust**, everything was still there. The trust continues to promote the preservation of buildings and provides funding for shopkeepers to pick out distinctive architectural detail in pastel colours close to their originals.

Visitors with only a passing interest in architecture can get a sense of what the fuss is about by wandering along the half-dozen streets in the city centre, notably **Emerson Street**, with its particularly homogeneous run of upperfloor frontages. Worth special attention here is the **ASB Bank**, on the corner of Hastings Street, its exterior adorned with fern shoots and a mask form from the head of a *taiaha* (a long fighting club), while its interior has a fine Maori rafter design. On Tennyson Street, look for the flamboyant **Daily Telegraph** building with stylized fountains capping the pilasters; and the **Municipal Theatre**, built in the late 1930s in a strikingly geometric and streamlined form.

The only building to merit a foray outside the centre is the **National Tobacco Company Building** (interior Mon–Fri 9am–5pm only), on the corner of Bridge Street and Osian Street, in Ahuriri, whose entrance is probably the single most frequently-used image of Deco Napier and exhibits a decorative richness seldom seen on industrial buildings. The facade merges Deco asymmetry and the classic juxtaposition of cubic shapes and arches with the softening Art Nouveau motifs of roses and raupo (a kind of Kiwi bulrush).

Along Marine Parade

Napier's Art Deco finery may earn it a place on the world stage, but its defining feature is undoubtedly **Marine Parade**, a 2km-long boulevard lined with stately Norfolk pines and fashioned in the British seaside tradition. Currently faintly elegant and restrained, it boasts a string of attractions – chiefly Marineland and the National Aquarium of New Zealand – linked by the promenade.

Marine Parade starts by Napier's port at the northern end of town and passes the foot of Bluff Hill, where native and exotic trees have been cultivated in **Centennial Gardens** (unrestricted entry), a former prison quarry backed by a picturesque waterfall cascading down the cliff face.

Pushing south you stroll past the **Ocean Spa**, 42 Marine Parade (☎06/835 8553), a lavish hot-pool complex overlooking the beach where you can take a bath and have a swim; $6, private spas $8, or indulge in one of the many beauty treatments, massage $35 for half an hour. A little further south is a floral clock and the ornamental Tom Parker Fountain, to the bronze cast of the curvaceous **Pania of the Reef**, a siren of Maori legend (see box on p.458).

Opposite Pania of the Reef is the **Hawke's Bay Museum**, 65 Marine Parade (daily: Oct–April 9am–6pm; May–Sept 10am–5pm; $7.50), a small but well chosen collection including *taonga* (treasures) of the Ngati Kahungunu, featuring some exquisite clubs and fish-hooks. Downstairs there's detailed coverage of Hawke's Bay's colonial history, a photo display of the damage wrought by the 1931 earthquake, and a poignant and thirty-five-minute audiovisual of survivors' stories. These are accompanied by a manageable trawl through a century of design, from Art Nouveau and Art Deco to the Philippe Starck-influenced 1990s and a history of Herbert Gutherie Smith – a Scottish farmer who managed to write one of the greatest tomes of natural history, *Tutira: The Story of a New Zealand Sheep Station*, while running the Tutira Station. There's also a small yet intriguing display about paleontologist Joan Wiffen's 1979 discovery of a Megalosaur's tail bone in a creekbed northeast of Napier. Significantly, which proved dinosaurs had existed in New Zealand when it broke away from the supercontinent of Gondwana eighty-five million years ago, despite earlier scientific beliefs that they never lived here.

Assorted seafront constructions line the next piece of the promenade: the curving colonnade of the Veronica Sun Bay and the stage known as the Sound Shell give way to a putting course and some attractive sunken gardens. Opposite, at 157 Marine Parade, **Opossum World** (daily 9am–5pm; free) presents all you ever need to know and more about New Zealand's greatest pest. Well-considered displays recount the struggle against the voracious destroyer of native bush, and a small shop sells all sorts of possum products – including pelts, fur hats and garments knitted from opossum fur blended with merino wool – with the motto that every item bought saves a tree.

Continuing beyond the sunken gardens and popular outdoor **rollerblading/skating** rink you reach **Marineland** (daily 10am–4.30pm; dolphin & seal shows 10.30am & 2pm; $4, $9 to include shows, $15 for a behind-the-scenes tour; ⓦwww.marineland.co.nz), a small marine zoo that houses a leopard seal, sea lions and penguins – many of them recovering from injuries sustained in the wild. During the outdated shows performing dolphins and seals are put through their paces. In the summer months you should try to book a couple of days in advance (a couple of weeks immediately after Christmas) if you fancy **feeding the dolphins** or an hour-long **swim with the dolphins** in the pool (ⓣ06/834 4027; $50, plus $10 for the near-essential wetsuit); they can usually be persuaded to play ball.

Further along the seafront, past the go-karts and boating lake, lies the **National Aquarium of New Zealand** (daily: Boxing day to Jan 31 9am–9pm; Feb–Easter 9am–7pm; Easter to Dec 24 9am–5pm; $12; ⓦwww.nationalaquarium.co.nz). Constantly revamped, it is consolidating its position as the finest such establishment in the country with distinct marine environments from Africa, Asia and Australia, plus a substantial New Zealand section. The most spectacular section is the **ocean tank** (hand-feeding at 2pm), with its Perspex walk-through tunnel giving intimate views of rays and the odd shark. There's more hand-feeding at the **reef tank** at 10am, plus Behind the Scenes tours ($20) at 9am and 1pm and the chance for qualified scuba divers to take a dip in the ocean tank ($40, plus $30 for gear and a full oxygen tank). It is not all aquatic and there are interesting sections on New Zealand's reptilian *tuatara*, and a nocturnal **kiwi house**.

A new addition to the canon of ocean-based activities is **The Sea Horse Farm** (daily tours at 10am, 1pm and 3pm $9; ⓣ06/834 0998, ⓦwww.theseahorsefarm.co.nz) about 4km north of town along Main Road. Beyond the understated shop-foyer entrance, the tour takes about an hour and delves into the farming, harvesting and interim life cycle of the sea horse, the life and times of Crayfish, plus a few tanks of New Zealand paddle crabs. Note that flash photography is prohibited as it kills the little critters.

Eating, drinking and entertainment

As elsewhere in New Zealand, Napier's dining scene has improved markedly over recent years and, while no match for larger centres, there are enough places to keep you well fed and watered for a few days. It is worth eating at least one lunch at one of the **wineries** around about, but there are plenty of **cafés** and **restaurants** scattered around the centre, and several more in the upper price bracket in waterside Ahuriri.

It is rare to find any really exciting entertainment, unless you hit town at **festival time** (see box on p.454), but a couple of the **bars** host live music at weekends and when touring bands pass through. Straightforward drinking happens along Hastings Street, mostly the short stretch between Browning and Emerson streets, where packs of youthful revellers surge between any of half a dozen popular bars.

There are mainstream **movies** at Downtown Cinema 4, at the corner of Station and Munroe streets (⊕06/831 0600), and more arthouse films at Century Cinema, 65 Marine Parade (⊕06/835 9248), in the Hawke's Bay Museum building.

Restaurants and cafés

Alfresco's 65 Emerson St. Somewhat barn-like upper-level café and restaurant, which is worth a visit for good-value lunches and evening mains such as beef fillet and syrah sauce or chicken grilled with Mexican beans ($19.50–26).

Antonio's cnr Carlyle St & Craven St ⊕06/835 5814. Unpretentious and good-value eat-in and takeaway pizzeria with some budget pasta dishes. Closed Mon.

Café Graaz 82 Dalton St. Great snack spot, from giant toasted sandwiches to their own specialized cakes, quiches and breakfasts. Get stuck into their potato cakes with sour cream and relish or, on the sweeter side, their scroggan slices, carrot cake or chocolate mud cake. Closed Sun.

De Luca's 180 Emerson St. Italian café-style food and good coffee during weekdays as well as tasty and filling breakfasts, bagels and formidable salads. Closed Tues.

East Pier Hardinge Rd, nr Perfume Point. Modern and breezy waterfront café/bar that's great for relaxing by the water or dining on marinated rack of lamb, seafood salad or fish and chips, with all mains mostly $26–30.

Thorps Coffee House 40 Hastings St. Solid eat-in and takeaway build-your-own sandwich place also serving good breakfasts, a lovely selection of breads, lunches, cakes, shakes and coffee; the interior features fine Art Deco details. Closed Sun.

Pacifica 208 Marine Parade ⊕06/833 6335. Newish sophisticated restaurant where, primarily, the gifts of the sea are presented to diners in imaginative and delicious combinations at a price.

Take 5 185 Marine Parade ⊕06/835 4050. Wonderful restaurant and jazz bar where the food is delicious – particularly the wild venison and Moroccan lamb – and the music just makes the experience. Probably the coolest place to eat and a must even if you're only in town for a couple of days.

Ujazi Café 28 Tennyson St. Small daytime café with a vaguely alternative feel, serving largely vegetarian snacks for breakfast and lunch: quiches, sandwiches and salads, plus scrumptious juices and good strong coffee, though the service is sometimes slower than the tide.

Bars and clubs

Churchill's Champagne and Snug Bar cnr Browning & Herschell Sts (daily). This tiny cocktail lounge gets busy on Fridays and Saturdays after about 9pm and is locally regarded as a pick-up joint for people over 21.

The Dome/Governors Inn cnr Marine Parade & Emerson St. Prominently sited wooden-floored restaurant with attached coffee shop, and intimate corner bar; a good haunt for any time of the day or night. Straightforward fare includes devilled sausages and mash, wood-fired pizzas ($12–18) and some tempting locally brewed beers.

Gin Trap West Quay, a block down from *Shed 2*, Ahuriri. Better, cooler, classier of the two warehouse-based eateries overlooking the harbour entrance, offering tasty snacks and main meals from the kiwiana recipe book ($7.50–30) and some tempting brunches at weekends. Middle-of-the-road chart music prevail in the shenanigans that take place on Friday and Saturday nights.

Grumpy Mole Saloon cnr Hastings St & Tennyson St. Napier's most jumping party bar, styled in Wild West mode and offering nightly drinks specials, plus big-screen TV sport, pool tables and a quieter cigar bar next door. On Fri & Sat nights a DJ keeps the place pumping till the small hours. Closed Mon.

Jo Miguels 193 Hastings St. The glazed-tile bar gives a Spanish feel to this tapas bar where there's a daily blackboard of a dozen or so tapas to be washed down with a glass of chilled fino or local wine. Also has pizzas, cocktails, live music at weekends and occasionally something acoustic in the week.

Phoenix 43 Hastings St. A real night club (Wed–Sat), with live bands and DJs, and very popular with locals and travellers alike.

Shed 2 cnr West Quay & Lever St, Ahuriri ☏06/835 2202. Fashionable bar, with a formal restaurant next door in a former wool store, that's fine for a beer or gourmet pizza while the restaurant dishes up more imaginative mains ($20–$25) like pan-fried calamari and twice-cooked lamb shanks. The bar comes alive at weekend evenings but can be a little too much.

The Brazen Head 21 Hastings St. A big improvement on the towns other Irish-style bars with good-value grub, outdoor seating and a lively, boozy, slightly blousy atmosphere on Fridays and throughout the weekend.

Cape Kidnappers and the wineries

No visit to Napier or Hastings is complete without spending some time exploring the surroundings: the threatened gannet colony at **Cape Kidnappers** and the forty or so **wineries** around Napier and Hastings. Heading from Napier towards Cape Kidnappers, Marine Parade (SH2) trawls through an industrial sprawl on the outskirts of Napier until 9km south it passes the windswept **Waitangi Mission site**, where a plaque records the establishment of Hawke's Bay's first mission station by William Colenso in 1844. From here it is a couple of kilometres to the village of **Clive**, where a signed turn leads to the beachside settlements of Te Awanga and Clifton, starting point for trips to Cape Kidnappers.

Cape Kidnappers

After James Cook's ill-starred initial encounter with Maori at Gisborne, he sailed south to the southern limit of Hawke's Bay and anchored off the jagged peninsula known to the Ngati Kahungunu as Te Matua-a-maui, "the fishhook of Maui" – a reference to the origin of the North Island, which was – so legend has it – dragged from the oceans by Maui. Here, Cook experienced a second unfortunate meeting. This time Maori traders noticed two young Tahitian interpreters aboard the *Endeavour*, believing them to be held against their will, the traders captured one of them and paddled away. The boy escaped back to the ship, but Cook subsequently marked the point on his chart as **Cape Kidnappers**.

Neither James Cook nor Joseph Banks, both meticulous in recording flora and fauna, mentioned any gannets on the peninsula's final shark-tooth flourish of pinnacles. However, a hundred years later, twenty or so pairs were recorded, and now there are over five thousand pairs – making this the world's largest mainland **gannet colony**. At the time of writing, however, planning permission had been granted for a huge luxury hotel on the cape. It remains to see to what extent the birds will react to the construction work and subsequent increase in visitors.

Gannets are big birds, members of the booby family distinguished by their gold-and-black head markings and their apparent lack of fear of humans. The birds start arriving at Cape Kidnappers for nesting in June, laying their eggs

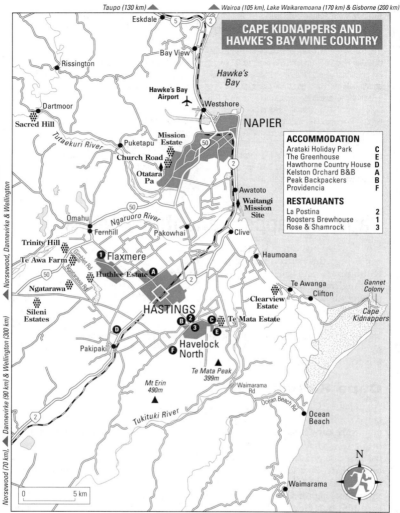

CAPE KIDNAPPERS AND
HAWKE'S BAY WINE COUNTRY

ACCOMMODATION

Arataki Holiday Park	C
The Greenhouse	E
Hawthorne Country House	D
Kelston Orchard B&B	A
Peak Backpackers	B
Providencia	F

RESTAURANTS

La Postina	2
Roosters Brewhouse	1
Rose & Shamrock	3

from early July through to October, with the chicks hatching some six weeks later. Once fledged, at around fifteen weeks, the young gannets embark on their inaugural flight, a marathon and as-yet-unexplained 3000-kilometre journey to Australia, where they spend a couple of years before flying back to spend the rest of their life in New Zealand, returning to their place of birth to breed each year.

During the **breeding season** (June–Oct), the cape is closed to the public, and one colony, The Saddle, is always reserved for scientific study. At other times you can get within a metre or so of the remaining two sites: The Plateau, a few hundred metres back from the saddle, where two thousand chattering pairs nest beak-by-jowl; and the beachside Black Reef, the largest colony, a couple of kilometres back from the tip of the peninsula, where there are a further 3500 pairs.

Practicalities

There are several ways to visit the gannets, all starting from well-signposted points in the adjacent settlements of **Clifton** and **Te Awanga**, 20km southeast of Napier, both reached from the Napier or Hastings visitor centres with Kiwi Shuttle (℡06/843 3330; booking essential; $25 return, tour $50). Most tours are tide-dependent, travelling to the colony along the beach below unstable hundred-metre-high cliffs. The least expensive way to get to the gannets is simply to walk the 11km along the beach from Clifton (roughly 5hr return); no permits are needed, but you'll need to check **tide tables** with DOC or the Hastings or Napier visitor centres and plan to leave between three and four hours after high tide; the useful DOC Guide to Cape Kidnappers ($1) contains a **map** and a few tips.

Gannet **trips** come and go, but the traditional and best way is aboard tractor-drawn trailers along the beach with Gannet Beach Adventures (Oct to late-April daily; 4hr; $28; ℡06/875 0898 & 0800/426 638, ⓦwww.gannets .com), whose pace and approach give plenty of opportunities to appreciate the geology along the way and observe the birds at close quarters. These end at a DOC shelter, from where you face a twenty-minute uphill slog to The Plateau, where you'll have half an hour to admire the birds. A worthwhile alternative, which takes you right to the gannets with almost no walking, is with Gannet Safaris (Sept–April daily 9.30am & 1.30pm; $45; ℡0800/427232 & 06/875 0893, ⓦwww.gannetsafaris.com) which gains access **overland** through Summerlee Station on three-hour trips in air-conditioned 4WD minibuses.

Hawke's Bay wine country

Napier and Hastings are almost entirely encircled by the **Hawke's Bay's wine country**, one of New Zealand's largest and most exalted grape-growing regions threaded by the **Hawke's Bay wine trail**, which wends its way past thirty-odd wineries, most offering free tastings. Many places are now fashioning themselves as "destination wineries" where tasting is almost an adjunct to eating lunch at one of the vineyard restaurants, enjoying a picnic in the landscaped grounds, maybe looking through a small museum, and even appreciating the architectural style designed to catch the eye of discerning wine tourists.

Hawke's Bay is largely the province of boutique producers, with an unshakeable domestic reputation and an international standing challenged only by the South Island's Marlborough region. One of New Zealand's most well-suited areas for viticulture, with a climatic pattern similar to that of the great Bordeaux vineyards, Hawke's Bay produces fine **Chardonnay** and **Cabernet Sauvignon**. As scientific studies unravel the complexity of the local soils and microclimates, growers have begun to diversify into **Merlot**, which has gained a foothold north of Napier along the Esk Valley, while others predict that Hawke's Bay may one day topple Marlborough's **Sauvignon Blanc** primacy. Hawke's Bay is New Zealand's longest-established wine-growing region: vines were first planted in 1851 by French Marist missionaries, ostensibly to produce sacramental wine. The excess was sold, and the commercial aspect of the operation continues today as the Mission Estate Winery. Some fifty-odd years later, other wineries began to spring up, initially favouring the fertile plains, but as tastes became more sophisticated, such sites were forsaken for the

With over forty **wineries** in the region, it would be hard to give comprehensive coverage of them all, but listed below are a few favourites, concentrating on those that make good lunch spots or feature some sort of attraction other than the obligatory wine tasting. Be warned though, the very fact that a winery has either a café or restaurant does seem to encourage high dining prices. Napier's closest wineries are 8km to the southwest in the suburb of **Taradale**, en route to a couple more wineries in the western foothills of the Kaweka Range along Dartmoor Road. Closer to Hastings, there are clusters outside **Havelock North**, 9km east of Hastings, and 10km west near **Fernhill** – the fastest-growing wine district in Hawke's Bay.

Church Road Winery 150 Church Rd, Taradale ☎06/844 2053, ⓦwww.churchroad .co.nz. A tolerably interesting wine-making museum ($7.50), some excellent bottles to sample – notably the Church Road Chardonnay – and a restaurant using fresh local produce, that spills out into the gardens, serving Mediterranean-style dishes at reasonable prices.

Clearview Estate Winery 194 Clifton Rd, Te Awanga ☎06/875 0150, ⓦwww.clearviewestate.co.nz. Some of New Zealand's most highly rated wines are produced here, in tiny quantities and sold only from the vineyard. You pay a premium for the attention to detail, but the wines are superb, especially when enjoyed with the restaurant's classy Mediterranean lunches. Can be combined with a visit to Cape Kidnappers (see p.463).

Huthlee Estate 84 Montana Rd, Bridge Pa ☎06/879 6234. A small and very welcoming winery west of Hastings where the emphasis is on reds, notably Merlot and Pinot Grigio, but their Sauvignon Blanc has done well, too. They will take you on a free vineyard walk and there's a picnic area, plus petanque.

Mission Estate Winery 198 Church Rd, Taradale ☎06/844 6025. Worth a visit for its pivotal position in the development of the Hawke's Bay's wine industry alone, but it hasn't rested on its laurels, offering well-organized, free guided tours (Mon–Sat 10.30am & 2pm). There's an à la carte restaurant on site.

Ngatarawa Wines 305 Ngatarawa Rd, Bridge Pa ☎06/879 7603, ⓦwww.ngatarawa.co.nz. An excellent first stop, a small winery with free tastings of

open-textured gravel terraces alongside the Tutaekuri, Ngaruroro and Tukituki rivers, which retain the day's heat and are free from moist sea breezes. In this area the vineyards of the **Gimblett Road** area produce increasingly praiseworthy wines.

Practicalities

If you have your own transport, head out with a copy of the *A Guide to the Wineries* leaflet (free from Napier and Hastings visitor centres), which lists wineries open to the public – see box above for the pick of the bunch – along with their facilities and current opening hours (generally daily 10am–5pm in summer but sometimes closed early in the week). Much of the country covered by the wine trail is also part of the region's **art and food trails**. The free *Hawke's Bay Art Trail* booklet directs you to the workshops and galleries of some of the best painters, sculptors, potters and craftspeople hereabouts; while the *Hawke's Bay Wine Country Food Trail* leaflet (also free) includes a map showing the whereabouts of all manner of places selling quality produce, along with cafés, wineries and restaurants.

If you can't find an abstemious driver, take a **wine tour**, most of which visit four or five wineries over the course of a morning or afternoon. They're all Napier-based but will pick up in Hastings and Havelock North, either free or

quality tipples (notably Chardonnay, Sauvignon Blanc and Cabernet Merlot, as well as highly acclaimed dessert wines from Riesling) in a century-old stable complex with attractive picnic areas and a petanque court.

Sacred Hill Wines 1033 Dartmoor Rd, 20km west of Taradale ☎06/844 0138. A lengthy excursion rewarded by a few sips of their albeit superb wine, and a tasty meal served on rustic tables under olive trees (Dec–April only; booking essential).

Sileni Estates 2016 Maraekakaho Rd, Bridge Pa ☎06/879 8768, ⓦwww.sileni.co.nz. A relative newcomer that has brought a new level of professionalism to the area with landscaped grounds (complete with culinary garden), and striking buildings that house a classy café (mains $25), a fine restaurant (four-course degustation menu $85), a gourmet food store, a culinary school and, of course, a winery with tastings ($5 for seven wines). Their first vintage was in 1998 and they're already gaining an international reputation.

Te Awa Farm Winery 2375 SH50, Fernhill ☎06/879 7602, ⓦwww.teawafarm.co.nz. Sited near the famed Gimblett Road, this winery produces exceptional reds (Merlot, Cabernet Merlot and Pinotage) that are more aromatic and livelier than many of their Hawke's Bay contenders; and their Chardonnays are pretty good too; tastings $2 for six. An indoor and outdoor lunchtime restaurant is highly regarded and serves excellent platters and daily specials that are reasonably priced.

Te Mata Estate Winery 349 Te Mata Rd, Havelock North ☎06/877 4399, ⓦwww.temata.co.nz. New Zealand's oldest winery on its existing site, now making a fairly small volume of premium hand-made wines, notably their Coleraine blend of Cabernet Sauvignon, Merlot and Cabernet Franc. Free tasting, winery tours at 11am, and the added bonus of architecturally controversial house among the grapes designed by Ian Athfield (see box on p.493).

Trinity Hill Winery 2396 SH50, Fernhill ☎06/879 7778 ⓦwww.trinityhill.com. Strikingly modern winery in the Gimblett Road area, where you can taste ($5; refunded with purchase) some of their excellent reds as well as the Chardonnay.

for a small fee. Vince's Vineyard Tours ($40; ☎06/836 6705) are great fun with an entertaining and knowledgeable guide and a flexible schedule. Other good bets include the popular Bay Tours & Charters (☎06/843 6953, ⓦwww.bay-tours.co.nz), who offer a basic five-stop lunch tour (daily 10.30am; $55, food not included); and the more intimate Vicky's Wine Tours (☎06/843 9991), who offer a number of morning and afternoon tours ($40–55).

Hastings and around

As little as ten years ago, inland **HASTINGS**, 20km south of Napier, was a rival to its northern kin as Hawke's Bay's premier city, buoyed by the wealth generated by the surrounding farmland and orchards. In recent years, shifting economic patterns, the closure of Hastings' two huge freezing works (abattoirs) and Napier's ascendancy as a tourist destination have put Hastings firmly in second place. The city's attempts to catch-up are evident in the smartened up central streets, though little else has changed. Unfortunately it doesn't completely disguise the presence of warehouse-style shops in among the far more handsome central buildings that were erected after the same

1931 earthquake that rocked Napier. Hastings was saved from the worst effects of the ensuing fires, which were quenched using the artesian water beneath the city before they could take hold. Nonetheless, the centre had to be rebuilt. As in Napier, **Art Deco** predominates and, though Hastings lacks the flamboyance and overall exuberance of its neighbour, there are some unusually harmonious townscapes along Russell, Eastbourne and Heretaunga streets. Hastings also enthusiastically embraced the **Spanish Mission** style, and two exemplary buildings warrant a brief visit, though in truth after you've perused them there's little else to keep you here unless your planning a winery binge.

Hastings is at the heart of the wonderful Hawke's Bay wine country (see p.465), and most of the vineyards are easier to reach from here than Napier. Long before grapes were big business, Hastings relied on apples, pears and peaches, all still grown in huge quantities. The harvest, which begins in February and lasts three or four months, provides casual, hard, low-paying **orchard work** for those willing to thin, pick or pack fruit; the hostels are the best sources of work and up-to-the-minute information.

If there is little reason to stay in Hastings' there is no reason to stay in its eastern neighbour, upmarket **Havelock North**, 3km east and at the foot of the striking ridge-line of **Te Mata Peak**. The only diversion is a drive or walk up the peak. In the last few years this village has become the favoured,

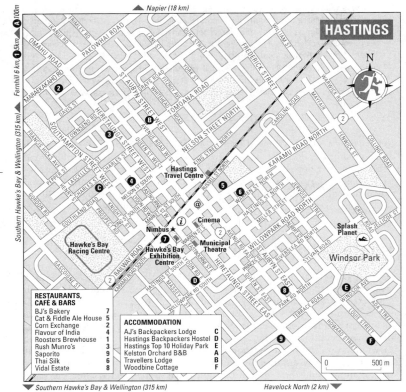

▲ Napier (18 km)

HASTINGS

N

Hastings Travel Centre

Splash Planet

Cinema

Nimbus ★

Municipal Theatre

Windsor Park

Hawke's Bay Racing Centre

Hawke's Bay Exhibition Centre

RESTAURANTS, CAFÉ & BARS	
BJ's Bakery	7
Cat & Fiddle Ale House	5
Corn Exchange	2
Flavour of India	4
Roosters Brewhouse	1
Rush Munro's	3
Saporito	9
Thai Silk	6
Vidal Estate	8

ACCOMMODATION	
AJ's Backpackers Lodge	C
Hastings Backpackers Hostel	D
Hastings Top 10 Holiday Park	E
Kelston Orchard B&B	A
Travellers Lodge	B
Woodbine Cottage	F

0   500 m

▼ Southern Hawke's Bay & Wellington (315 km)   Havelock North (2 km) ▼

second-home haunt of New Zealand's young well-to-do and as a result acquired a disproportionate number of restaurants and bars charging high prices and frequented, at weekends, by folk wearing one-strap rucksacks with mobile phone pouches over their hearts.

Arrival and information

Passenger trains no longer rumble right through the centre of town, but long-distance **buses** continue to pull up outside the Hastings Travel Centre on Caroline Road. Local bus operator Nimbus (℡06/877 8133) runs to Napier, Havelock North and Flaxmere (Mon–Fri only) from the corner of Eastbourne Street East and Russell Street.

Buses stop opposite the public toilets on Russell Street while the **visitor centre**, cnr Russell & Heretaunga streets (Mon–Fri 8.30am–5pm, Sat 9.30am–4pm, Sun 9.30am–3pm; ℡06/873 5526, Ⓦwww.hawkesbaynz.com) located inside the Westerman's Building, acts as a ticket agent. There's **Internet** access at Internet World Cyber Café, 102 Queen Street East.

Accommodation

Hastings' **accommodation** is greatly affected by the harvest: from mid-February to May, there is precious little chance of finding a bed at any of the cheaper places, which meet the demand for self-catering and longer stays. If you're hoping to secure a bed for the **fruit-picking season**, plan to arrive early in February and expect to pay around $100 a week for a bunk in a cramped room. Occupancy in the more expensive places is dictated by the normal summer-holiday pattern, and it's advisable to make **reservations** a few days ahead if you'll be here between December and February. The Havelock North market is dominated to no small degree by exclusive **B&Bs** and swanky self-catering houses so don't expect to find many bargains.

Hastings

AJ's Backpackers Lodge 405 Southland Rd ℡06/878 2302, Ⓔajslodge@xtra.co.nz. Basic hostel in an Edwardian villa that's popular with orchard workers, although there is usually a bed or two for overnighters. Dorms only ❶
Hastings Backpackers Hostel 505 Lyndon Rd East ℡06/876 5888, Ⓦwww.medcasa.co.nz. Comfortable house near the centre, with good facilities and Internet access, but full of pickers in the season. Dorms ❶, rooms ❷
Hastings Top 10 Holiday Park 610 Windsor Ave ℡06/878 6692 & 0508/427 846, Ⓔholidaypark@hastingstourism.co.nz. Appealing campsite on the edge of Windsor Park, with tent sites, a range of modern units and good facilities, though it does get busy over the fruit-picking season. Camping $12, cabins ❸, kitchen cabins ❹, motel units ❺
Kelston Orchard B&B 49 Ormond Rd ℡06/879 7301, Ⓔkelston.orch@xtra.co.nz. Attractive and extremely relaxing homestay in a big beautiful rose garden attached to an apple orchard about 3km from the town centre. In the house are two twin

rooms, sharing a bathroom, and in the garden is a self-contained en-suite double. ❹
Travellers Lodge 606 St Aubyn St West ℡06/878 7108, Ⓔtravellers.lodge@clear.net.nz. Hostel in a pair of suburban houses, with a sauna, garden and off-street parking. There is a range of rooms, all with comfy beds, but these are often full from November to May. Dorms ❶, rooms ❷
Woodbine Cottage 1279 Louie St ℡06/876 9388, Ⓔnshand@xtra.co.nz. B&B in an attractive cottage on the outskirts of Hastings with a large and lovely garden, tennis court and pool, and pleasant sunny rooms. ❺

Havelock North and around

Arataki Holiday Park 139 Arataki Rd ℡06/877 7479, Ⓔarataki.motel.holiday.park@xtra.co.nz. Rurally sited and well-appointed campsite that benefits from being one of the few inexpensive places around here that doesn't take fruit pickers. Camping $11, cabins ❷, motel units ❺
The Greenhouse 228 Te Mata Rd ℡06/877 4904, Ⓔthe.greenhouse@xtra.co.nz. Superbly

|

equipped self-catering cottage, surrounded by beautiful vineyards and sleeping up to four. ❽
Hawthorne Country House 420 SH2, 7km south-west ☎06/878 0035, ⓦwww.hawthorne.co.nz. Beautiful and very welcoming B&B in a grand Edwardian villa surrounded by croquet lawns and farmland. Five en-suite rooms are decorated with understated elegance and the breakfasts are delicious. ❽
Peak Backpackers 33 Havelock Rd ☎06/877 1170, ⓕ877 1175. Small and relaxed hostel close to the centre of Havelock North but with free

Hastings pick-up and a weekday bus service outside. Dorms ❶, rooms ❷
Providencia 225 Middle Rd, 3km south of town ☎06/877 2300, ⓦwww.providencia.co.nz. Very comfortable rural B&B with one queensize and one kingsize room in a beautifully preserved homestead built in 1903. Delicious breakfasts are served either in the guest lounge or out on the veranda, and there are complimentary drinks on arrival. Also comfy, modern self-catering cottages in the grounds with breakfast supplied. Cottages ❼, queen ❼, king ❽

The Town

After the 1931 earthquake, Hastings looked to the Californian-inspired **Spanish Mission** style of architecture. A couple of key buildings set the tone, with rough-cast stucco walls, arched windows, small balconies, barley-twist columns and heavily overhung roofs clad in terracotta tiles. All the finest examples can be seen in an hour or so, using the self-guided *Heritage of Hastings* walk leaflet (free from the visitor centre), but if time is short, limit your wanderings to Heretaunga Street East, where the visitor centre is located inside the **Westerman's Building**, recently restored to show off its gorgeous bronzework and sumptuous lead lighting. The **Municipal Theatre**, on the corner with Hastings Street, was actually built fifteen years before the earthquake, but was remodelled to create the region's finest Spanish Mission facade. Also worth a quick look is the **Hawke's Bay Exhibition Centre**, opposite the junction of Eastbourne Street and Karamu Road (Mon–Fri 10am–4.30pm, Sat & Sun 11am–4pm; free except for special exhibitions), which hosts all manner of local, national and international art shows, and has a relaxing café with good coffee.

Families may well find themselves at **Splash Planet**, Grove Road (daily 10am–6pm; $25 per person or $85 for a family; ☎06/876 9856, ⓦwww.splashplanet.co.nz), centred on a replica Disney-like castle and offering a welter of waterpark amusements from a double-dipper dual-tube ride and a "Never Ending River Ride" to hot pools ($8 without a park-wide ticket) and boating lake. Togs, towels and armbands can be rented.

Foodies in town at the weekend should make for the **Hawke's Bay Farmers Market** (Sun 8.30am–12.30pm), at the Hawke's Bay Showgrounds on Kenilworth Road, where they can enjoy a delicious selection of fresh local produce.

Te Mata Peak

Driving from Hastings to Havelock North, the long ridge of limestone bluffs which make up the 399m **Te Mata Peak** looms into view. The ridge is held to be the supine form of a Maori chief, Rongokako, who choked on a rock as he tried to eat through the hill – just one of many Herculean feats with which he attempted to woo the beautiful daughter of a Heretaunga chief. The long and winding Te Mata Peak Road climbs the hill to a wonderful vantage point overlooking the fertile plains, north across Hawke's Bay and Cape Kidnappers, and east to the surf-pounded strands of Ocean Beach and Waimarama, the main swimming **beaches** for Hastings and Havelock North.

The peak is encompassed by the Te Mata Peak Trust Park, entered 3.5km up Te Mata Peak Road, where there is a parking area and a number of **walking** tracks through the hill's patches of parkland. These are outlined in the $1 brochure on the park available at visitor centres and can be combined to create a route through groves of native trees and redwoods, and a wetland area before reaching the summit (2–3hr return).

According to legend, overcome with grief at her father's death, Rongokako's own daughter threw herself off the peak – something you can emulate by **tandem paragliding** with Peak Paragliding (℡06/843 4717 & 025/512 886; from $120), an activity that uses the thermals and winds off the Pacific to carry you along the ridge and back for at least fifteen minutes.

Eating and drinking

For a town of its size, Hastings is relatively poorly supplied with good **places to eat**, while Havelock North bumps up the quota of flashy, expensive cafes and bars. Lunches at the **wineries** are a good option, though they too may prove a strain on the wallet. Keep an eye out for Hawke's Bay summer festival happenings (see box on p.454).

Drinkers will find a smattering of welcoming places in both towns, with **beer** fans well served at *Roosters Brewhouse* (see below).

Hastings

BJ's Bakery 305 Karamu Rd South (Mon–Sat 6.30am–5pm). Something to shout about, an award-winning pie maker producing sumptuous pies at rock bottom prices, including seafood and veg, corn beef and mustard, kumara, chicken and veg' and, the most popular locally, bacon, steak and cheese.

Cat & Fiddle Ale House 502 Karamu Rd. A traditional English-style pub with a decent range of tap and bottled beers, as well as bargain chips-with-everything meals. Wednesday night is locally famous for jam sessions and every month they have a poetry night.

Corn Exchange 118 Maraekakaho Rd. Stylish restaurant and bar converted from an attractive 1930s grain store on the western fringes of the city, serving $10–15 brasserie lunches and $20–25 dinners, Thurs–Sat.

Flavour of India cnr Lyndon Rd & Nelson St ℡06/870 9992. Tasty curry dishes served up in a central Hastings house with most mains around the $15–20 mark.

Roosters Brewhouse 1470 Omahu Rd, 7km west of central Hastings. Brilliant, welcoming micro brewery, offering traditional natural brews, best supped in their pleasant café or outdoors at garden tables, while tucking into straightforward hearty dishes at reasonable prices. There's also free tasting of their English ale, lager and dark beers, and you can buy a flagon to take away, which is a wise move considering the prices elsewhere. Closed Sun.

Rush Munro's 704 Heretaunga St West. A small ice-cream garden and takeaway that's been packing in the locals for years. Its sumptuous and intensely fruity ice cream include coffee, chocolate and nut concoctions are available, but it is hard to beat the traditional fruit flavours – feijoa is particularly scrumptious, though something of an acquired taste.

Saporito 1101 Heretaunga St ℡06/878 3364. Quality take away; try one of the meat or veg lasagnes ($10) or something from the carvery ($10–20). Closed Sun & Mon.

Thai Silk 601 Karamu Rd. Standard Thai restaurant, but welcoming and with a good range of traditional Thai dishes cooked to perfection, takeaway available. Mains $15–22.

Vidal Estate 913 Aubyn St East; book at weekends ℡06/876 8105. Popular formal restaurant attached to a winery with the linen and polished glassware set amid huge wine barrels. Lunch dishes (each matched with a Vidal wine) might be duck terrine or mussel and coriander cakes ($18–25), and dinner mains run from $25–30.

Havelock North

La Postina cnr of Havelock Rd & Napier Rd ℡06/877 1714. Classy Mediterranean restaurant with minimal decor, outside seating and a strong local wine list. Expect to pay $25–30 for a main course.

Rose & Shamrock 15 Napier Rd. A fair attempt at an English/Irish pub, with Guinness and a broad range of Irish beers, draught ales, guest beers from Kiwi micro breweries, well-priced bar meals and occasional Irish folk bands.

Southern Hawke's Bay

South of Hastings, the main road (SH2) gives the coast a wide berth, taking you through the relentless sheep stations of **Southern Hawke's Bay**, a region uncluttered by places of genuine interest. Small farming towns stand as fitting memorials to the steadfast pioneers who tamed the region, spending the latter half of the nineteenth century clearing the huge totara trees of Seventy Mile Bush, pushing through communication links, and then establishing sheep runs on the rich plains.

None of the towns are especially interesting and if time is short you'd do as well to push straight on through, but with a little more leisure, the "Scandinavian" settlements of **Norsewood** and **Dannevirke** warrant half an hour each. The New Zealand Wars of the 1860s had discouraged British immigrants and, as new areas were opened up for colonization, the authorities took their search for settlers elsewhere. In 1872, Danes, Norwegians and a few Swedes answered the call for rugged folk with strong ties to the land, arriving in Napier ill-prepared for the hardship ahead of them. Their promised plots of land turned out to be tracts of impenetrable bush; the wages paid to construction workers who toiled to build road and rail links barely covered exorbitant food costs; and when the government demanded that the settlers repay their passage, many promptly upped sticks for North America, leaving little trace of their brief sojourn.

Almost all traffic follows SH2, but visitors in search of more rugged scenery might want to stray along **SH52**, which loops east towards the rugged coastline from dull **Waipukurau**, 50km south of Hastings, re-emerging at Masterton in the Wairarapa (see p.474). Thirty-five kilometres south of Waipukurau (and 6km south of Porangahau), a sign marks the hill known as **Taumatawhakatangihangakoauauotamateaturipukakapikimaunga-horonukapokaiwhenuakitanatahu**, which, unsurprisingly, rates as the world's longest place name; roughly, this mouthful translates as "the hill where Tamatea, circumnavigator of the lands, played the flute for his lover".

Whichever way you head south, the coastline is almost entirely inaccessible, apart from at Castlepoint (see p.476), reached by a sixty-five-kilometre road from Masterton.

Norsewood

Some 85km south of Hastings, SH2 enters a cutting which bisects the hilltop village of **NORSEWOOD**, invisible from the highway and easily missed. Predominantly settled by Norwegians, it manages to retain a mildly Scandinavian tenor. Like most southern Hawke's Bay towns, it was carved out of the forest, but in 1888 the bush bit back, and a raging bushfire virtually razed the place. Some regarded the devastation as an act of God precipitated by a local plebiscite that ended temperance – but, as the local paper noted, "the church was burnt down and the pub was saved".

The village is in two parts. Upper Norsewood is basically just one short, quaint and deathly quiet main street (Coronation Street) that runs past a glassed-in boathouse containing the fishing boat *Bindalsfareing*, a gift from the Norwegian government on the occasion of Norsewood's centenary, and a small **visitor centre** cum gift shop called The Barn (℡06/374 0991; roughly daily 10am–4pm). Opposite is the **Pioneer Museum** (daily 8.30am–4.30pm; $2), a cottage museum and green garage full of reminders of pioneering days housed in an 1888 house. Kiwis are more familiar with Lower Norsewood, 1km to the south, which is mainly strung along Hovding Street and home to Norsewear, a company famed for its hard-wearing woollen garments in rustic

Scandinavian designs; the socks in particular last for years. If a chill wind is swooping down from the Ruahine Range, check for bargains in the **factory shop** (Mon–Fri 8.30am–5pm, Sat & Sun 9am–5pm).

Dannevirke

There's no reason for more than the briefest of stops in **DANNEVIRKE**, a small farming town 20km south of Norsewood, that struggles to play up its heritage, with little more than a rather unpleasant modern windmill in Copenhagen Square on the main street to support its cause. Records and artefacts amassed in the **Gallery of History**, Gordon Street (Mon–Fri 9.30am–4pm; $2), provide comprehensive coverage of the founding of the town in 1872, when the forest was hacked away to create Dannevirke ("Dane's Work") – a name recalling both the ninth-century defensive earthwork constructed across the waist of the Jutland peninsula in their homeland and the task ahead, the forging of a road from Wellington to Napier. Early photos give a sense of the hard life that drove away many of the Danes, their place taken by British migrants lured by the opening of the Napier–Wellington railway in 1884. The few Danes who remained were soon outnumbered; only a flick through the telephone directory or a glance at some of the shops and street signs betray Dannevirke's Scandinavian heritage.

Napier–Wellington **buses** stop in town not far from the **visitor centre**, 156 High Street (Mon–Fri 9am–5.30pm, Sat & Sun 10am–2pm; ☎06/374 4167), where you can buy a "Take a Liking to a Viking" bumper sticker. If you are **hungry** try either *State of the Art*, 21 High Street, a reputable **café** and espresso bar or the *Barrel House*, Ward Street, behind the off-licence, where you can enjoy a pint and some generous, well-prepared and presented Kiwi staples at bargain prices. Should you need to **stay** the night here, check out the *Dannevirke Holiday Park*, Christian St (☎06/374 7625; tent sites $12, cabins ❷, flats ❸) or the *Viking Lodge Motel*, 180 High St (☎06/374 6669, ℱ374 6686; ❹).

South of Dannevirke, SH2 runs 25km to Woodville, the junction of SH3, which strikes west through the Manawatu Gorge to Palmerston North (see p.290), and SH2, which continues south into the Wairarapa.

The Wairarapa

Most of the **Wairarapa** is archetypal Kiwi sheep country, with white-flecked green hills etched sharply behind towns that share much in common with the workaday service centres of southern Hawke's Bay. In recent years, however, the southern half of the region has increasingly aligned itself with Wellington, a source of free-spending day-trippers and weekenders just an hour away over the hills.

The Wairarapa is separated from the capital by the Rimutaka Range, a persistent barrier to communication that kept the region relatively isolated for decades, until the spell was broken by the establishment of New Zealand's earliest sheep station close to present-day Martinborough. Soon the rich alluvial lands were selected for development by the **Small Farm Association** (SFA), brainchild of Joseph Masters, a Derbyshire cooper and long-time campaigner against the "Wakefield Scheme" of settlement that promoted the separation of landowner and labourer. Aided and abetted by liberal governor George Grey, Masters founded the progressive association, which had the express aim of giving disenfranchised settlers the opportunity to become smallholders. At Grey's suggestion, SFA representatives sallied forth in 1853, persuading Maori to sell land for the establishment of two towns – Masterton and Greytown.

Initially **Greytown** prospered, and it retains an air of antiquity rare in New Zealand towns, but the routing of the rail line favoured **Masterton**, which soon became the main town, famed chiefly for the annual Golden Shears shearing competition. North of Masterton, the **Mount Bruce National Wildlife Centre** provides a superb opportunity to witness ongoing bird conservation work; to the south, **Featherston** is a base for walks up the bed of the Rimutaka Incline Railway.

The goal of many Wellingtonians and visitors is **Martinborough**, the region's wine capital and far-and-away its most appealing town. Back on the coast, the holiday settlement of **Castlepoint** is the place for swimming, and **Cape Palliser** is an equally good destination for blustery mind-clearing walks and dramatic coastal scenery.

Cross the **Rimutaka Range** towards Wellington and you're into the Hutt Valley, full of commuter-belt communities none of which really warrant a stop until you reach Petone on the outskirts of the capital.

Mount Bruce

The northern half of the Wairarapa is very much a continuation of southern Hawke's Bay, but instead of speeding through this pastoral country, leave a couple of hours aside for the award-winning **Mount Bruce National Wildlife Centre**, in majestic forest 50km south of Woodville (daily 9am–4.30pm; $8; ⓦ www.mtbruce.doc.govt.nz). This is one of the best places in the country to view endangered native birds and a pioneer in the field of captive-breeding programmes. Visitors have the chance to see some of the world's rarest birds – kokako, kakariki, Campbell Island teal, hihi, kiwi and takahe – in spacious aviaries set along a one-kilometre trail through part of the last remnant of the Forty Mile Bush, lowland primeval forest which once covered northern Wairarapa. Beyond the trail several thousand hectares of forest are used for reintroducing birds to the wild. The generous size of the cages on the trail and the thick foliage often make the birds hard to spot, so you'll need to be patient (Jan & Feb are the best times); more immediate gratification comes in the form of a stand of Californian redwoods, a nocturnal kiwi house, reptilian *tuatara*, and a closed-circuit camera trained on the birds' nests in the breeding season (Oct–March). A twenty-minute audiovisual in the visitor centre gives a moving account of the decline of birdlife in New Zealand; while at 3pm each day a flock of kaka come to feed, eels are fed at 1.30pm, ducks ten minutes later. Visitors can make use of the picnic area or relax in the café, which serves good coffee and snacks. The centre relies heavily on donations, so give if you can. **Buses** between Palmerston North and Masterton pass the centre, but none at convenient times for a stop-off.

Masterton and around

As the Wairarapa's largest town, workaday **MASTERTON**, crouched at the foot of the Tararua Mountains some 30km south of Mount Bruce, is a disappointing base from which you can explore a few minor sights. The town's major event offers the dubious pleasures of the annual **Golden Shears** shearing competition, effectively the Olympiad of all things woolly, held on the three days leading up to the first Saturday in March. Contestants flock from many lands to demonstrate their prowess with the broad-blade handset; a top shearer can remove a fleece in under a minute, though for maximum points it must be done with skill as well as speed and leave a smooth and unblemished, if shivering, beast.

Central Masterton is bounded on its eastern side by the large **Queen Elizabeth Park**, and walking around the formal gardens is a pleasant way to pass an hour or so, but the town's only real sight is **Aratoi**, at the corner of Bruce and Dixon streets, opposite the park entrance (daily 10am–4.30pm; free; Ⓦwww.aratoi.co.nz), a recently revamped art and history museum concentrating on the Wairarapa region. There are no permanent exhibits, but the airy modern spaces deserve an hour of your time.

Draped over the hills to the west of town, the **Tararua Forest Park**, while not among New Zealand's tramping hotspots, offers some excellent walking through beech and podocarp forests to the sub-alpine tops, where the notoriously fickle weather can be dangerous. For details of tramps, pay a visit to the Masterton DOC field centre (see below), where you should also buy hut tickets. Serious walkers should consider the **Holdsworth–Jumbo Tramp**, a twelve-hour circuit that can be broken down into two or more manageable days by staying at some of the **huts** (two at $10 and one at $5) evenly spaced along the route. The track starts at the backcountry-hut style *Holdsworth Lodge* (tent sites $4, lodge $8), 25km west of Masterton at the end of Norfolk Road, off southbound SH2 (accessible only by taxi ☎06/378 2555; about $25), where day-trippers can undertake easy riverside walks (1–2hr) and bathe in the cool waters.

Practicalities

Masterton's commercial heart is strung along the parallel Chapel, Queen and Dixon streets. Tranzit **buses** (☎06/377 1227) pull up at the Transit Coach Building, 316 Queen St that doubles as the new **visitor centre** (Mon–Fri 9am–5pm & Sat–Sun 10am–4pm; ☎06/378 7373, Ⓦwww.wairarapanz.com). Tranz Metro (☎04/801 7000) run commuter services from Wellington to the **train station**, at the end of Perry Street, a fifteen-minute walk from the centre, or call Masterton Radio Taxis (☎06/378 2555). For trampers, DOC maintain a **field centre** (☎06/377 0700; Mon–Fri 8am–5pm), opposite the aerodrome at the western end of South Road, the continuation of Queen Street.

Masterton's doesn't have a lot of budget **accommodation** except for the spacious and attractive *Mawley Park Motor Camp*, 15 Oxford St (☎06/378 6454, Ⓔjclarke@contact.net.nz; camping$10, cabins ❷). There's quality budget B&B accommodation in a central two-storey residence at *Victoria House*, 15 Victoria St (☎06/377 0186, Ⓔparker.monks@xtra.co.nz; ❹), and relaxing motel accommodation at the well-appointed *Cornwall Park*, 119 Cornwall St (☎06/378 2939, Ⓔcormnwall@wise.net.nz; ❹), in a quiet suburb a five-minute drive from central town, with a pool and spa. For a bit of luxury try the *Copthorne Resort*, High St, about 2km out of town (☎06/377 5129 Ⓦwww.solway.co.nz; ❺) a complex of rooms, restaurants, pools and other facilities.

Masterton's range of eateries is not vast but what they have is of a decent standard, try the café at Aratoi for simple snacks or the coffee at *Russian Jack's Café*, 78 Queen St (closed Sat & Sun). The more stylish *Café Cecille* (☎06/370 1166; closed Sun & Mon eve), in Queen Elizabeth Park, is a modern café in the genteel former aquarium building with wide verandas where you can dine while watching the miniature train chug by the boating lake. For a good all-rounder head for the *Café Strada*, Regent Theatre Building (the **cinema**), cnr Queen & Jackson streets, a lively spot serving good value imaginative grub from breakfast through to dinner.

Drinkers should head for *Burridges*, corner of Queen Street North and Shoe Street, a **micro-brewery** with a choice of three beers made on site, or join the smart young things at *Stellar*, 109 Chapel St, in a former Masonic Lodge and with outside seating, or the *Cornwall Steak and Ale House*, 7 Perry Street, where massive steaks are cooked on heated stone platters and live bands strike up on Friday nights.

Castlepoint

The 300km of coastline from Cape Kidnappers, near Napier, south to Cape Palliser is bleak, desolate and almost entirely inaccessible – except for **CASTLEPOINT**, 65km east of Masterton, where early explorers found a welcome break in the "perpendicular line of cliff". A commanding lighthouse presides over the rocky knoll, which is linked to the mainland by a thin hour-glass double **beach** that encloses a sheltered pool known as The Basin. Nearby is a small settlement where Wairarapa families retreat for summer fun in the calm **lagoon**, walking to the lighthouse or the cave at its foot, riding the break-ers. Castlepoint is at its most frenetic around the third or fourth Saturday in March, when there's an informal **horse race** along the beach – a somewhat unorthodox betting set-up requires punters to bet "blind" on numbers before they are allocated to particular horses.

In the absence of a visitor centre, ask for **information** at the Castlepoint Store (℡06/372 6823). The store holds a list of *baches* which can be rented (some by the night), or you can **stay** here at the *Castlepoint Holiday Park & Motels* (℡06/372 6705, ⓦwww.castlepoint.co.nz; camping $12, dorm ❶, cabins ❷, kitchen cabins ❸, units ❹) and a garden cottage (❹). There are no restaurants at Castlepoint, but the store has a daytime **café** and sells **takeaways**.

Carterton

Once you've shaken free of the outskirts of Masterton, a string of small towns guide you towards the Rimutaka Range and over into the Hutt Valley towards Wellington. Staunchly conservative **CARTERTON**, 15km south of Masterton, is mainly known to Kiwis as the unlikely place where Georgina Beyer rose to prominence as New Zealand's first transsexual mayor. In 1999 she resigned the post when she became the world's first transgender member of Parliament. Being Maori and fairly flamboyant, it is perhaps appropriate that she should be associated with the home of the **Paua Shell Factory**, 54 Kent St (Mon–Fri 8am–5pm, Sat & Sun 9am–5pm; free; ⓦwww.pauashell .co.nz), an Aladdin's Cave of objects fashioned from this beautiful rainbow-swirled seashell. It is a treat for lovers of kitsch souvenirs, with superbly polished exam-ples of the shells themselves retailing for up to $50, but other extraordinary items can be yours to treasure for a much more modest sum. The factory sup-plies just about every tourist knick-knack shop in the country and, if you can't resist, you can even take a brief, free tour to see how the stuff is made.

Some 5km south of Carterton, a road runs 15km west into the foothills of the Tararua Range to **Waiohine Gorge**, a picturesque chasm that's ideal for picnics but hard on vehicles.

Greytown

There's a more traditional appeal to **GREYTOWN**, 9km south of Carterton. Laid out in 1853, the town still retains something of its Victorian feel, despite the traffic that now trundles between the rows of two-storey wooden buildings. Until the end of the nineteenth century, this was the Wairarapa's main settlement, but railway planners diverted the new line around the flood-prone environs and set the seal on a gradual decline that was only arrested by the development of prof-itable orchards and market gardens in the latter half of the twentieth century.

The real appeal here is the selection of **cafés** and **restaurants** along Main Street, notably the excellent and moderately priced *Main Street Deli*, at no. 88 (℡06/304 9022; licensed & BYO), which provides reason enough to stop in Greytown to stock up on unusual breads and cheeses, or tuck into more substantial fare in the attached café, including great breakfasts and dinners (daytime, Fri & Sat evenings).

If you feel you need to earn your lunch, take a historical **walk** guided by the *Heritage Trails of Wairarapa* booklet ($2) from the volunteer-run **visitor centre** (hours vary) in the Public Services building on Main Street, which is practically self-service.

Featherston and the Rimutaka Incline

The last of the Wairarapa towns before SH2 climbs west over the Rimutakas is **Featherston**, 13km south of Greytown, where the **visitor centre**, in the Old Courthouse on Fitzherbert Street (generally 10am–3pm; ℡ & ℱ06/308 8051), stands in front of the **Fell Locomotive Museum** on Lyon Street (Mon–Fri 10am–3.30pm, Sat & Sun 10am–4pm; $4 donation) which contains what, to the casual observer, appears to be an ordinary old railway engine. Steam buffs cross the country to this last surviving example of the locos that, for 77 years (until the boring of a new tunnel in 1955), climbed the 265-metre, one-in-fifteen slope of the Rimutaka Incline over the range into the Hutt Valley, gaining purchase by gripping a central rail. Alternatively try the **Heritage Museum**, adjacent to the Loco Museum (Wed–Sun 10am–4pm; gold coin donation) a pretty typical mix of odds and ends that is enlivened by the artifacts from the Japanese prisoner of war camp (1942–45) that existed just 2km up the road.

The rails have long been pulled up, but you can follow the trackbed on the **Rimutaka Incline Walkway** (17km; 4–5hr; 265m ascent), which starts 10km south of Featherston at Cross Creek, passes old shunting yards and shuffles through the 576-metre summit tunnel, before descending to Kaitoke. A free leaflet from the visitor centre details the route, provides background information and pinpoints three basic, grassy campsites along the way. Many walk just an hour or two from either end and back, but if you fancy the full trek, contact South Wairarapa Tours (℡06/308 9352, minimum of two; $60), who will organize pick-ups. There's no public transport to Cross Creek, but Masterton–Wellington buses pass within 1km of the Kaitoke end of the walkway.

There's not much point in **staying** in Featherstone but, if you need to, try the homestead B&B and backpackers combo, *Fareham House*, Underhill Road (℡06/308 9074; dorms ❶, backpacker rooms ❷, B&B rooms; ❸). The best of the **eating** options is the *Lady Featherstone Café*, 31 Fitzherbert St, a surprisingly sophisticated eatery serving home-grown and high-quality food at reasonable prices.

Martinborough

Tiny **MARTINBOROUGH**, 18km southeast of Featherston, has been transformed from a small and obscure farming town into the centre of a compact wine region synonymous with some of New Zealand's finest red wines. Being within easy striking distance of Wellington, weekends see the arrival of the smart set to lunch at the appealing cafés and restaurants and load up their shiny 4WDs at the two-dozen wineries that are within a kilometre or so of town (see p.466). On Mondays much of the town simply shuts down to recover.

The town was initially laid out in the 1870s by patriotic landowner John Martin, who named the streets after cities he had visited on his travels and

For visitors, Martinborough has the edge over other wine regions in that ten of its wineries are accessible on foot, and a dozen more are easily reached by car or a bike rented locally. The best **guide** is the widely available and free *Martinborough and Wairarapa Wine Trails* brochure, which details the hours and facilities of the 26 wineries that conduct **tastings**, most of which charge a couple of dollars especially if there are reserve wines on offer. Throughout the summer places generally open 10am–4pm at weekends and shorter hours midweek, some of the smaller places closing if they've sold their year's stock. Here's our pick of the wineries to kick-start your explorations.

Ata Rangi Puruatanga Rd ☎06/306 9570, ⓦwww.atarangi.co.nz. A great place to start as it's central and increasingly well known for its Pinot Noir and Chardonnay, as well as its Pinot Gris and Rosé.

Margrain Vineyard Ponatahi Rd ☎06/306 9292. A solid production of good quality wine, a café and some accommodation in a pleasing setting.

Martinborough Vineyard Princess St ☎06/306 9292, ⓦwww.martinboroughvineyard.co.nz. A Martinborough original and still one of the largest, producing top-quality Pinot Noir and Chardonnay. Picnicking is encouraged. Open all year.

Muirlea Rise Princess St, across the road from Martinborough Vineyard ☎06/306 9332. Top-quality Pinot Noir to go with a ploughman's lunch and lovely coffee. Open all year.

Nga Waka Kitchener St ☎06/306 9832, ⓦwww.nzwine.com/ngawaka. One of the small, young boutique wineries known for their bone-dry whites with elegant fruit.

Palliser Kitchener St ☎06/306 9019, ⓦwww.Palliser.co.nz. This pioneering Martinborough winery limits its impact on the environment while producing premium wines – Pinot Noir, Chardonnay, Sauvignon Blanc and Riesling; picnics are encouraged in the pleasant formal garden. Open all year.

Te Kairanga Martins Rd, 5km southeast ☎06/306 9122, ⓦwww.tkwine.co.nz. A consistent award-winner, open all year, which produces some delicious small-volume reserve wines. Tours on Sat & Sun at 2pm.

arranged the core in the form of a Union Jack centred on a leafy square. Martinborough languished as a minor agricultural centre for over a century until the first four wineries – Ata Rangi, Dry River, Chifney and Martinborough (all of which produced their first vintages in 1984) – re-invented Martinborough as the coolest, driest and most wind-prone of the North Island's grape-growing regions. With the aid of shelter belts that slice the horizon, the wineries produce some outstanding Pinot Noir, very good Cabernet Sauvignon, crisp and fruity Sauvignon Blanc and wonderfully aromatic Riesling.

Martinborough is no slouch at promoting its viticultural prowess, and the best time to visit is during one of its **festivals**. The first of the summer is Toast Martinborough (third Sun in Nov), a specifically wine-orientated affair with all the vineyards open, free buses doing the rounds, and top Wellington and local restaurants selling their produce; it is an exclusive event and tickets (sold from first Mon in Oct through Ticketek ☎04/384 3840 & ☎09/307 5000, ⓦwww.ticketek.co.nz; around $65) are hard to obtain. There's a considerably more egalitarian feel to the two Martinborough Fairs (first Sat in Feb & March) – a huge country fête – during which the streets radiating from the central square are lined with stalls selling all manner of arts and crafts.

Outside these times, the best starting point is **Martinborough Wine Centre**, 6 Kitchener St (ⓦwww.martinboroughwinecentre.co.nz), where you can taste local wines, or just sit in the café and enjoy a break (see p.479).

Practicalities

Tranzit Coachlines **buses** (℡0800/471 227), shuttling between Featherston, Masterton and Martinborough, meet the TranzMetro commuter **trains** from Wellington (℡0800/843 596; Mon–Fri, plus weekend day-trips in summer) and drop off at the small but informative **visitor centre**, 18 Kitchener St (Mon–Fri 9am–5pm, Sat & Sun 10am–4pm; ℡06/306 9043, ℮martinborough @wairarapanz.co.nz). **Internet access** is available at the library on Jellicoe Street, five minutes' walk from the town centre.

The range of **accommodation** leans heavily towards mid- and upper-price B&Bs and homestays, most of them in rural surroundings out of town, or self-contained cottages starting at around $100 midweek, $120 at weekends. Those on a budget should try the scruffy but cheap *Martinborough Camping Ground*, Princess St (℡06/306 9336; $5 per person), or the central *Martinborough Motel*, 43 Strasbourg St (℡06/306 9408, ℱ306 8408; ❸). With a bit more cash in your pocket it is worth stepping up to *Oak House*, 45 Kitchener St (℡06/306 9198, ℮chrispolly.oakhouse@xtra.co.nz; ❺), a homestay run by a local wine-maker with attractive rooms in a Californian-style bungalow and substantial breakfasts. Tempting alternatives include *The Old Manse*, at the corner of Grey and Roberts streets (℡06/306 8599, ⓦwww.oldmanse.co.nz; ❼), 1km from town in a wonderful old villa among the vines; the centrally located and stylish straw-bale-built *Straw House*, 24 Cambridge Road (℡06/306 8383, ⓦwww.thestrawhouse.co.nz; ❻); but by far the finest place to stay, is the sumptuously refurbished two-storey colonial *Martinborough Hotel*, The Square (℡06/306 9350, ⓦwww.martinboroughhotel.co.nz; ❽).

Martinborough caters to discerning diners. There are almost a dozen **restaurants**, with smarter and more varied places opening all the time, usually charging city prices; just wander around and see what takes your fancy. Accolades are rightfully heaped on the *Martinborough Bistro*, at the *Martinborough Hotel*, with beautifully prepared and presented dishes drawing on European cuisines and excellent local produce, at around the $26 mark. *The Flying Fish Café & Bar*, at the corner of The Square and Jellicoe Street (closed Mon–Wed in winter), is one of the best all-day **cafés** for great coffee, snacks, all-day brunches, light meals and takeaways in an attractive old building with a garden bar, while the café in the Wine Centre, see p.478, provides tasty snacks and main meals in a relaxing setting, dinners Sat, for around $15. If you want a break from all the vintner-speak in these parts head for Martinborough Brewery, on New York St ℡06/306 8310. Established in 2002 this **microbrewery** produces some truly delicious beers, with free tastings including a rich dark beer, some rewarding ale and bright sparkling lager, as well as a few light snacks (Dec–March Wed–Sun 11am–7pm; rest of the year 2pm–7pm).

Cape Palliser

The low-key cosmopolitanism of Martinborough stands in dramatic contrast to the bleak and windswept coast around **Cape Palliser**, 60km south. The southernmost point on the North Island, the cape was named in honour of James Cook's mentor, Rear Admiral Sir Hugh Palliser. Apart from a few gentle walks and the opportunity to observe fur seals at close quarters, there's not a lot to do out here but kick back, especially since swimming is unsafe and the weather changeable owing to the proximity of the Tararua Range.

From Martinborough, a sealed road leads 25km south to **Lake Ferry**, a tiny laid-back surfcasting settlement on the sandy shores of Lake Onoke, which once had a ferry service on the coastal route to Wellington before the

Rimutaka Road was completed. Here, the *Lake Ferry Hotel* (℡06/307 7831, Ⓔamtipoki@xtra.co.nz; ❶–❸) – the southernmost of the North Island – has fairly ordinary rooms and backpacker dorms; passable **meals** are also served. Three kilometres to the north, the *Gateway Holiday Park* (℡06/307 7780, Ⓕ307 7783; camping $9.50, cabins ❸, self-contained units ❹) has a pool.

From a road junction just before Lake Ferry, the Cape Palliser road twists for 13km through the coastal hills until it meets the sea near the **Putangirua Pinnacles**, dozens of grey soft-rock spires and fluted cliffs up to 50m high, formed by wind and rain selectively eroding the surrounding silt and gravel. The pinnacles lie within the little-visited Aorangi (Haurangi) Forest Park, and can be reached along an easy streambed path (1hr return) from the roadside Putangirua Scenic Reserve, where there are barbecue areas and a primitive **campsite** ($7); longer walks of up to 5hr are outlined on a map in the car park.

From here, the partly metalled road hugs the rugged, exposed coastline for 15km to **NGAWI**, a small fishing village where all manner of bulldozers grind out their last days, hauling fishing boats up the steep gravel beach. It is five rough kilometres on to the Cape proper, where the **fur-seal colony** lies right beside the road, overlooked by the century-old Cape Palliser **lighthouse**, standing on a knoll 60m above the sea at the top of a long flight of some 250 steps, worth climbing only at sunrise or sunset. It is easy enough to get within 20m of the seals, but you should keep your distance from any pups – and their protective parents – and don't get between any seal and the sea.

Travel details

Trains

There are no longer any passenger trains to Hawke's Bay, but Wellington commuter services reach out into the Wairarapa.
From Masterton to: Carterton (2–5 daily; 15min); Featherston (2–5 daily; 40min); Wellington (2–5 daily; 1hr 30min).

Buses

InterCity and Newmans run most of the bus services through the region, with a service connecting Gisborne with all the Hawke's Bay towns, Palmerston North and Wellington; one linking Gisborne to Rotorua via Whakatane; one running from Napier and Hastings to Auckland via Taupo; and another joining Palmerston North, Masterton and Wellington. Tranzit connect Wellington with the main Wairarapa towns.
From Gisborne to: Auckland (1 daily; 9hr); Hastings (1 daily; 5hr); Napier (1 daily; 4hr); Opotiki, via SH2 (1 daily; 2hr); Rotorua (1 daily; 4hr 30min); Wairoa (1 daily; 1hr 25min); Whakatane (1 daily; 3hr).

From Hastings to: Auckland (3 daily; 7hr 30min); Dannevirke (3 daily; 1hr 30min); Gisborne (1 daily; 5hr); Napier (Mon–Fri hourly or better, Sat–Sun 4–5 daily; 30–45min); Norsewood (3 daily; 1hr 10min); Taupo (3 daily; 2hr 30min); Wellington (3 daily; 4hr 45min).
From Masterton to: Carterton (2 daily; 25min); Greytown (2 daily; 40min); Featherston (2 daily; 1hr); Palmerston North (2 daily; 1hr 35min); Wellington (2 daily; 2hr).
From Napier to: Auckland (4 daily; 7hr); Dannevirke (3 daily; 2hr); Gisborne (1 daily; 4hr); Hastings (Mon–Fri hourly or better, Sat–Sun 4–5 daily; 30–45min); Norsewood (3 daily; 1hr 30min); Palmerston North (3 daily; 3hr); Taupo (3 daily; 2hr); Wellington (4 daily; 5hr 15min).
From Wairoa to: Gisborne (1 daily; 1hr 25min); Napier (1 daily; 2hr 30min).

Flights

From Gisborne to: Auckland (3–6 daily; 1hr); Wellington (3–5 daily; 1hr 10min).
From Napier to: Auckland (7–12 daily; 1hr); Wellington (4–6 daily; 55min).

Wellington and around

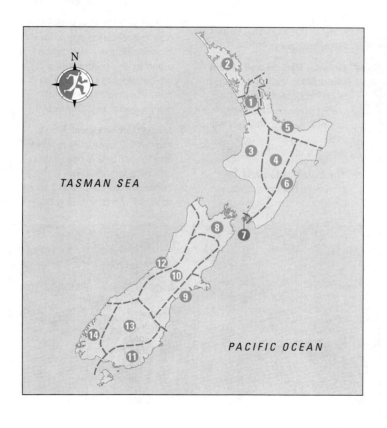

N

TASMAN SEA

PACIFIC OCEAN

CHAPTER 7   # Highlights

* **Te Papa** The national museum has quickly become Wellington's premier attraction, full of pre-European Maori culture, as well as a virtual bungy jump. See p.496

* **Cuba Street** People watching and window shopping along Wellington's "alternative" street gives a distinct taste of the city's divergent lifestyles. See p.497

* **Oriental Parade and Mount Victoria** No visit to Wellington is complete without an ice cream consumed along Oriental Parade, then taking in the panoramic views from Mount Victoria. See p.497

* **The Botanic Gardens** Take the Cable Car up and stroll back down through the gardens for great views in the city, beautiful roses and the lovely Begonia House. See p.499

* **The Parliamentary District** Visit the country's seat of power and associated national institutions, including a chance to see the original Treaty of Waitangi. See p.500

* **Karori Wildlife Sanctuary** Native birds once again flock around suburban Wellington aided by the predator-free environment and regenerating native bush at this superb wildlife sanctuary. See p.503

* **Matiu/Somes Island** A boat trip out to this wildlife reserve and former quarantine station can be augmented by continuing to the beach and café at Days Bay. See p.507

△ Beehive and Parliament House

Wellington and around

The North Island finishes with a flourish at **Wellington**, New Zealand's capital city, and, with around 400,000 residents, its second most populous. Wedged between steep hills, the glistening waters of Port Nicholson (usually known simply as **Wellington Harbour**) and the turbulent seas of Cook Strait, Wellington is arguably New Zealand's most attractive large city. As the principal departure point for the South Island it is sometimes only afforded a fleeting glimpse, but definitely warrants a stay of a couple of nights, more if you can manage it.

Tight hills restrict the city to a compact core mostly built on reclaimed land which sprouts a stimulating blend of historical and modern architecture that spills down to the bustling waterfront with its beaches, marinas and restored warehouses. All this is overlooked by weatherboard villas and bungalows climbing the steep hillsides to the encircling belt of parks and woodland which provides a natural barrier to unbridled development. Houses are accessed by narrow winding roads, or sometimes just a precipitous stairway which may be flanked by a small funicular railway to haul groceries and just about anything else up to the house. As if this weren't enough to contend with, Wellington is famously New Zealand's **windy city**, buffeted most days by air funnelled through Cook Strait, its force amplified by the wind tunnelling effect of the city's high-rise buildings.

As if to escape the inclement weather Wellingtonians have cultivated the nation's most sophisticated **café society** and a buzzing arts scene. While Auckland seems to grow ever more important (and self-important in the eyes of much of the rest of the country) Wellington reaches for higher ground promoting itself as the nation's **cultural capital**. It is certainly a cosmopolitan place, especially in late summer when the city hosts a series of arts and fringe **festivals** (see "Listings", p.517). High levels of investment in recent years have returned the city to a condition worthy of its capital status. The beacon in this rejuvenation is **Te Papa**, New Zealand's modern and inventive national museum, dramatically sited on the waterfront.

Central Wellington is easily walkable and, if the weather behaves, it is a pleasant stroll from Te Papa along the waterfront past the civic square to Queens Wharf and the **Museum of Wellington City & Sea**, which recounts the city's development and seafaring traditions. Politicians and civil servants

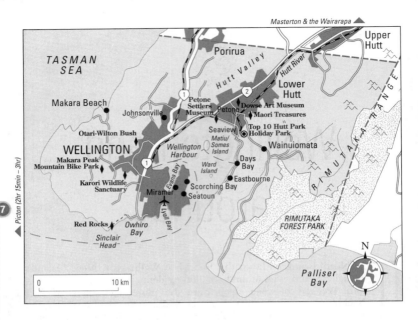

populate the streets of the **Parliamentary District**, where a brief tour of the Parliament building sets you up for viewing the **original Treaty of Waitangi** in Archives New Zealand. Nearby, New Zealand's most famous short story writer (see box, p.503) was born at **Katherine Mansfield's Birthplace**, now suitably furnished in period style.

Enticing though the indoor sights may be, it is certainly worth venturing beyond the central city. Wellington's unpredictable weather dictates you make the best of the good days when you should ride the stately **Cable Car** to Kelburn and either wander down through the **Botanical Gardens**, or continue further out to the ambitious **Karori Wildlife Sanctuary**. Take time, too, for the simple pleasures of strolling along **Oriental Parade** and up to one of the city's hilltop viewpoints, such as Mount Victoria.

Further afield you can **hike** to the seal colony at Red Rocks or wander one of the city's many trails, notably the **Southern Walkway**. Bikers are also spoilt for choice, but at some stage you should really get out on the water, either sailing or simply taking the ferry to **Matiu/Somes Island**, another wildlife sanctuary with a history as an internment camp and a quarantine station. Out in the commuter belt, Lower Hutt barely warrants a special trip, except for the excellent gallery, **Maori Treasures**, where you can learn about Maori artistic tradition.

Beyond the bounds of this chapter, Wellington can also be used as a base to explore **Kapiti Island** (see p.299) and even the **Wairarapa** (see p.473) with its windswept coastline and compact wine district around Martinborough.

Some history

Maori oral histories tell of the first Polynesian navigator, **Kupe**, discovering Wellington Harbour in 925 AD. While camped here for some time on the Miramar Peninsula near the harbour mouth, he named the harbour's islands Matiu (Somes Island) and Makaro (Ward Island) after his daughters. Several *iwi* settled around the harbour over the centuries, including the Ngati Tara people, who enjoyed the rich fishing areas and the protection that the bay offered. Both Abel Tasman (in 1642) and Captain Cook (in 1773) were prevented from entering Wellington Harbour by fierce winds and, apart from a few whalers, it was not until 1840 that the first wave of **European settlers** arrived, not long after the New Zealand Company had purchased a large tract of land around the harbour. The first settlement, named Britannia, was established on the northeastern beaches at Petone; shortly afterwards, the Hutt River flooded, forcing the settlers to move around the harbour to a more sheltered site known as Lambton Harbour (where the central city has grown up) and the relatively level land at Thorndon, at that time just north of the shoreline. They renamed the settlement after the Iron Duke and, finding flat land scarce, began **land reclamations** into the harbour in the 1850s, a process that continued at intervals for more than a hundred years.

By the turn of the century the original shoreline of Lambton Harbour had all but disappeared, replaced largely by wharves and harbourside businesses. The growing city, at the hub of coastal shipping, became a thriving import and export centre, and in 1865 it succeeded Auckland as the **capital** of New Zealand, largely because of its central location and fine harbour. Wellington has prospered ever since, and these days around seven million tonnes of cargo pass through the wharves each year. Parts of the waterfront no longer needed by the modernized shipping industry have been redeveloped for public use, while along the coast a number of shipwrecks are further testament to the city's maritime history, victims of the region's notorious high winds. Sailing ships of the 1800s were particularly susceptible, but even as late as 1968 a modern roll-on roll-off ferry, the *Wahine* (see p.498), foundered at the harbour entrance in the worst storm of the century.

Arrival and information

Wellington International Airport (🌐 www.wlg-airport.co.nz) is about 10km southeast of the city centre and has one terminal. It is an important domestic hub linking around twenty airports across New Zealand, and also handles international flights from Australia. There's a small **visitor centre** (daily 7am–7pm; ☎04/385 5123), as well as left-luggage lockers ($5) and a bureau de change (Mon–Fri 4am–6pm, Sat noon–5pm, Sun 8.30am–5pm, also open for night arrivals). To get into town, either grab a taxi (see p.518) for about $25, or walk out of the terminal and hop in the Stagecoach Flyer city bus (roughly daily 7am–8pm; $4.50), which runs about every half hour and takes fifteen minutes to Courtenay Place. Alternatively use one of the shuttle bus companies such as Super Shuttle (☎0800/748 885) who charge $12 for the first passenger to a particular destination and $4 for each extra.

Wellington's **train station**, on Bunny Street, contains little more than a small café and a rail booking office but remains the hub of the Wellington's public transport network. Tranz Scenic **trains** on the main line from Auckland (see p.519), and commuter services (see p.489) from the Kapiti Coast and the Hutt Valley all terminate here, city buses (see p.489) pull up outside, and Newmans and InterCity **buses** (see Basics, p.28) terminate alongside Platform 9.

Arriving by **car** is fairly painless. State Highway 1 through Porirua and SH2 through Lower Hutt both turn into short urban motorways which merge, run scenically along the harbourside, then drop you right downtown. It can be a problem finding cheap parking close to the centre of the city (for more

CENTRAL WELLINGTON

Matiu/Somes Island & Days Bay ▲

ACCOMMODATION

Abel Tasman		Museum Hotel	I
Apollo Lodge Motel		Rawhiti	P
base Backpackers		Richmond Guesthouse	O
Booklovers B&B		Rowena's Lodge	W
Cambridge Hotel		Shepherd's Arms	Q
Carillon Motor Inn		Talavera	V
Downtown Backpackers		The Mermaid	C
Duxton		Tinakori Lodge	D
Halswell Lodge		Wellington City YHA	K
Ibis		Wellington Motel	R
Intercontinental		Wildlife House	F
Lodge in the City		Worldwide	G
Majoribanks Apartments	S		

RESTAURANTS, CAFÉS & BARS

Angkor	18	Matterhorn	17
Asian Food Market	13	Midnight Espresso	38
The Backbencher Pub	3	Molly Malone's	19
The Blue Note	41	Motel	35
BNZ Centre Food Court	6	Nicolini's	8
Bodega	21	Nikau Gallery Café	31
The Catch	30	Olive	36
Chow	34	Pandoro	24
Coyote	28	Pound/Sovereign	14
Crumbs the Bakers	2	Roti Chenai	12
Deluxe	43	Sahara Café	34
Dockside	5	Stamp and Go	39
Dorothy	27	Strawberry Fare	45
Espressoholic	23	StudioNine	11
Eva Dixon's Place	22	Sushi of Japan	25
The Fat Ladies Arms	20	Uncle Chang's	42
Felix	9	Valve	40
Fidel's	46	The Vegetarian Café	37
Hummingbird	32	Vista	16
Kopi	10	Wellington Sports Café	29
Leuven	4	Wellington Trawling	44
Maria Pia's	1	Sea Market	
Masala	26	The White House	15
		Zico	33

Westpac Stadium

Container Terminal

WATERLOO QUAY

THORNDON QUAY

HOBSON ST

THORNDON

MURPHY ST

MULGRAVE ST

Old St Paul's Cathedral

Archives New Zealand

Local Buses

Long Distance Buses

Train & Bus Station

National Library

Lambton Interchange

DOC Office

Old Government Buildings

Parliamentary Library

Parliament House

The Beehive

St Paul's Cathedral

Bluebridge Ferry Terminal

Lynx Ferry Terminal

Dominion Post Ferry Terminal

Academy Galleries

Ferry Terminal

Queens Wharf

Ferg's Kyaks

Queens Wharf Events Centre

Plimmer's Ark Gallery

Museum of Wellington City & Sea

Cable Car Lower Terminal

LAMBTON QUAY

THE TERRACE

AURORA TERRACE

CLIFTON TERRACE

CLERMONT

WELLINGTON MOTORWAY

PARK ST

Otari-Wilton Bush (6 km) ▲

Town Belt

Botanic Gardens

Begonia House

Lady Norwood Rose Garden

Carter Observatory

Cable Car Museum

Bolton Street Memorial Park

WESLEY ROAD

GLENMORE ST

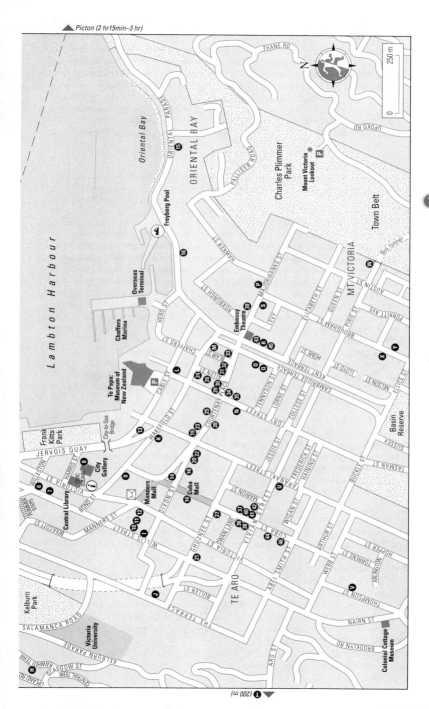

Picton (2 hr15min–3 hr)

N

250 m
0

Lambton Harbour

Oriental Bay

ORIENTAL BAY

Picton (2 hr15min–3 hr)

THANE RD

ORIENTAL PARADE

PALLISER ROAD

Charles Plimmer
Park

Mount Victoria
Lookout

Town Belt

UPOKO RD

Freyberg Pool

Overseas
Terminal

Chaffers
Marina

HERD ST

HAWKER ST

MAJORIBANKS ST

ROXBURGH ST

Embassy
Theatre

LEVY

ELIZABETH ST

QUEEN ST

BROUGHAM ST

PIRIE ST

AUSTIN ST

MT VICTORIA

Bus tunnel

PORRITT AVE

HOME ST

KENT TERRACE

Te Papa:
Museum of
New Zealand

CABLE ST

CHAFFERS ST

BLAIR ST

ALLEN ST

COURTENAY PLACE

TENNYSON ST

LORNE ST

CAMBRIDGE TERRACE

COLLEGE ST

TORY STREET

LLOYD ST

NELSON ST

ELICE ST

Basin
Reserve

Frank
Kitts
Park

City-to-Sea
Bridge

WAKEFIELD ST

JERVOIS QUAY

City
Gallery

Central Library

CIVIC
SQUARE

HARRIS ST

VICTORIA ST

WILLISTON ST

BOULCOTT ST

BOND ST

MANNERS ST

Manners
Mall

Cuba
Mall

DIXON ST

GHUZNEE ST

WILLIS STREET

SWAN LANE

VIVIAN ST

VICTORIA ST

ABEL SMITH STREET

CUBA STREET

MARION ST

JESSIE ST

TARANAKI STREET

FREDERICK ST

HAINING ST

WIGAN ST

BUCKLE ST

TASMAN ST

SUSSEX ST

ARTHUR ST

WEBB ST

TORRENS ST

HOPPER ST

ARLINGTON

THOMPSON ST

NAIRN ST

ARO ST

BROOKLYN RD

Colonial Cottage
Museum

TE ARO

BUTLER ST

THE TERRACE

Kelburn
Park

SALAMANCA ROAD

Victoria
University

KELBURN PARADE

GLASGOW ST

CENTRAL TERR

RAWHITI TERR

UPLAND RD

7

WELLINGTON AND AROUND

487

To travel between the bottom of the North Island and top of the South Islands you need to cross **Cook Strait**, either using a vehicle ferry or catamaran between Wellington and Picton, or flying. Timewise, there is little to be gained going by plane from Wellington to Picton though you might still make that journey to escape a choppy ferry crossing. The scenic way between the islands is by sea. Around half the journey is across open water, but the southern half is spent negotiating the narrow channels of the Marlborough Sounds where you cruise past barely inhabited bays and might catch sight of dolphins. The ferries even offer an audio tour about Cook Strait on most services.

By sea

Two companies run passenger and vehicle ferry services. **Interisland Line** (℡04/498 3302 & 0800/802 802, ⓦwww.interislandline.co.nz) operate two modern **Interislander ferries** (all year 3–5 daily; 3hr) and the faster **Lynx catamaran** (late Aug–Nov sporadically, Dec–April 1–2 daily, 2hr 15min). Ferries leave from Wellington's Interisland Ferry Terminal, just over a kilometre north of the train station, and linked by the free shuttle bus which leaves the train station 35 minutes before each sailing. The Lynx leaves from Waterloo Quay, opposite the train station.

Interisland Line offers a wide range of prices in three fare categories: **Ultra Saver** is the cheapest but the least flexible and non refundable; the mid-range **Saver Change** allows bookings to be amended up to the time of departure (depending on space) and offers a 50 percent refund if cancelled; **Easy Change** is the most expensive and most flexible, allowing changes right up until departure and is fully refundable. In general, expect to pay $30–50 one way for a single passenger, $150–230 for a car and driver, and $10–15 for bicycles. For detailed fares and information visit the Interline website.

In summer it is often cheaper travelling with **Bluebridge** (℡0800/844 844, ⓦwww.bluebridge.co.nz) who run a ferry on the same route (1–3 daily; 3hr 20min) from their terminal opposite Wellington's train station. All bookings are non-refundable but fully transferable, and they charge a flat fare all year: passengers ($40 one way); car up to 6 metres ($110); bicycles $10.

By air

Soundsair (℡03/520 3080 & 0800/505 005, ⓦwww.soundsair.co.nz) fly between Wellington and Picton (7–8 daily; 25min; $79 one way, $139 return), and offer small backpacker discounts and $55 special fares on some flights. Foot passengers keen to get directly to Nelson, Christchurch or Queenstown will find it quicker and possibly cheaper if they fly direct from Wellington though you'll miss a lot of the scenery.

see p.489), so if you are planning to relinquish your rental car here you might as well get rid of it as soon as you arrive. If arriving from the **South Island**, you'll be coming either by plane or by ferry (for details see box, above).

Information

Wellington's well-stocked and efficient **visitor centre**, cnr Wakefield and Victoria streets (Mon–Fri 8.30am–5.30pm, Sat & Sun 9.30am–4.30pm; longer hours in summer, often until 7pm; ℡04/802 4860, ⓦwww.wellington.nz.com), shares a glass-fronted section of the Civic Centre with a café and an Internet-access business. The info desk sells city maps ($1) and provide the handy free *Wellington: Official Visitor Guide* booklet.

The **DOC office** is in the Old Government Buildings (see p.500) at the corner of Lambton Quay and Whitmore Street (Mon–Fri 9am–4.30pm, Sat

10am–3pm ☎04/472 7356), with stacks of information on walks in the Wellington region. They also sell hut tickets and issue permits to visit Kapiti Island (see p.299).

City transport

If you are staying centrally, you'll have little need for public transport and can see almost everything on foot. But when you do need public transport it is pretty good. As well as the bus and train discounts mentioned below, you may find use for the **Capital Explorer** ticket ($15) which gives unlimited bus and train travel throughout the Wellington region from 9am on weekdays and all day at weekends. For Wellington region **train and bus information** pick up the free *Wellington Bus & Train Guide* at the visitor centre or train station, or call Ridewell (☎04/801 7000) anytime.

Wellington's extensive network of **buses and trolley buses** (Mon–Sat 7am–11pm, Sun 8am–11pm) operates from Lambton Interchange just west of the train station, and has an After Midnight service (Sat & Sun hourly 1–3am) centred on Courtenay Place to get revellers home safely. The most useful service downtown is the **City Circular** (every 15min; $2) which makes a loop along the major shopping and eating streets between Parliament and Te Papa calling at, or near, all points of interest. There's also the airport Flyer discussed on p.485.

One-way **fares** are $2 within the inner city, beyond which a zone system comes into operation: Karori Wildlife Sanctuary costs $3. After Midnight services also cost upwards of $3. Buy from the driver who can also sell you a **Star Pass** ($8) giving all-day travel on the buses, including the airport Flyer, but not After Midnight buses.

With little flat land, super-steep hills and a reputation for fierce winds, **cycling** around Wellington may not be your first choice, though on a fine day there is little to beat renting a bike (see p.512) for a spin around the bays east of the city. There's also some excellent **mountain biking** covered on p.511.

Suburban trains

If you plan to explore Wellington's northern hinterland – especially the Hutt Valley (p.508) and Kapiti Coast (p.299) – you may want to use the fast and efficient **suburban train service** run by Tranz Metro (☎04/498 3000, ⓦwww.tranzmetro.co.nz). Trains on both main lines leave the train station roughly every half hour for Waterloo (for Lower Hutt; 20min; $3.50); Porirua (20min; $4); Plimmerton (30min; $5); and Paraparaumu (1hr; $8). There's also a line to Johnsonville that provides handy access for hiking the northern walkway (see p.510).

Rover tickets (1 day for $10, 3 days for $15) give you the run of the train network after 9am weekdays and all weekend. Bikes cost the same as the adult fare up to a maximum of $4. Tickets can be bought at the Tranz Rail Travel Centre at the main train station or on the train.

Driving and parking

With a compact city centre and good public transport there is little value in having a car in the city. Still, a car is good for exploring the bays and outer suburbs, and **driving** around the inner city is simple enough once you get used to the extensive one-way system and remember to avoid the rush-hour traffic (roughly 7–9am & 4.30–6.30pm). There is little free **parking** downtown, but numerous car parks charging $2–3 an hour often with a one-day maximum of

$8–10 and typically only $4–5 after 6pm or at weekends. There's a convenient one right by the Te Papa museum which is suitable for campervans ($7 all day), and several others nearby. If you don't want to bother with moving the vehicle all the time, some places charge around $20 to leave it for the full 24hr day.

Most downtown streets have **parking meters** (usually Mon–Thurs 8am–6pm & Fri 8am–8pm $2/hr; otherwise free) which limit you to a two-hour stay during the metered hours. A little further out you get **coupon parking** (Mon–Fri 8am–4pm) where the first two hours are free, but to stay longer you have to display a coupon ($4 all day) available from dairies and petrol stations: ask locally.

City tours

4WD Seal Coast Safari ☎0800/732 527 & 04/802 4860. Two-hour tours out to the Red Rocks seal colony (see p.510), charging $59 for a lift out there and some commentary.

Hammond's Scenic Tours ☎04/472 0869, ⓦwww.WellingtonSightseeingTours.com. Slightly more staid feel to trips which range from a City Sights Tour (2 daily; 2hr 30min; $40) to extended tours to the Kapiti Coast (2 daily; 4hr; $65) and the Wairarapa (daily; 8hr; $130).

Flat Earth ☎0800/775 805, ⓦwww.flatearth.co.nz. Upmarket tours who take very good care of you on their three full-day tours (each $210): Capital Arts, Wild Wellington,Inspiration and Lord of the Rings.

Walk Wellington ☎04/384 9590, ⓦwww.wellingtonnz.com/walkwellington. Operate entertaining ninety-minute walking tours of the downtown area (Nov–March Wed, Fri, Sat & Sun at 10am and Mon–Fri at 5.30pm; April–Oct Sat & Sun 10am; $20) leaving from the visitor centre (which is where you book).

Wellington Rover ☎021/426 211, ⓦwww.wellingtonrover.co.nz. Operate a **hop-on-hop-off minibus service** with an interesting commentary making a loop around the city's outer sights – Mount Victoria, Red Rocks, Karori Wildlife Sanctuary, Scorching Bay, the zoo and a couple of LOTR locations – four times a day and offering a day pass (Mon–Sat; $35) that allows you to get on and off as often as you wish and offers small discounts for entry to various sights along the way. There's also a Twilight Rover ($30) visiting the south coast, Otari-Wilton Bush and Mount Victoria, a Karori Wildlife Rover ($10) getting you to the sanctuary and back, and a Rings tour (see p.507).

Accommodation

With so much of Wellington easily accessible on foot, most visitors plump for **accommodation** in the city centre, close to all the action. There's plenty of choice at all levels, not least a pretty decent selection of **backpacker hostels**, several of them recently opened or substantially revamped. **B&Bs** are also in abundant supply, many in beautifully preserved Victorian villas with a concentration in Thorndon, close to Parliament. Bear in mind though that Wellington is a great place to breakfast or brunch out so you might not want a place where breakfast is included in the tariff. Centrally sited **motels** are in short supply, but there are plenty of downtown **hotels** which cater mostly to the business crowd but can offer good deals, especially at weekends.

Unusually for New Zealand, the city has no **campsite** – instead you have to head all the way out to the Hutt Valley on the harbour's northeastern shore for the *Hutt Park Holiday Park* (see p.492). There are other reasons to stay **outside the centre**, not least the problem of parking: if you've got a vehicle be sure there'll be somewhere to leave it before you commit yourself to staying anywhere. Vehicle or not, you might want to stay north of Wellington at beachy places like **Paekakariki** and **Plimmerton** (see p.300), both of which have excellent backpackers with good train access for forays into Wellington.

Availability anywhere in the inner city is limited during the busiest part of the summer (mid-Dec to Feb), so it pays to book as far ahead as possible: at least a week for the more popular places. **Prices** are a touch above average: in hostels, most dorms are four- to six-bed and rates hover in the $20–25 range, while doubles and twins go for $50–60. At the other end of the scale, hotels offer good weekend specials, and B&Bs charge at least $20 more than you would elsewhere.

Hotels and motels

Abel Tasman 169 Willis St at Dixon St ⓣ 04/385 1304 & 0800/843 827, ⓦ www.abeltasmanhotel.co .nz. This extremely central hotel may lack character but it makes up for it with low prices. All rooms are en suite with phone and sky TV and minibar. ⑤

Apollo Lodge Motel 49 Majoribanks St ⓣ 04/385 1849, ⓦ www.apollo-lodge.co.nz. Central, medium-sized motel, 400m from Courtenay Place with modern decor. There's off-street parking and many units have fully equipped kitchens. Studios ⑤, suites ⑥

Carillon Motor Inn 33 Thompson St ⓣ 04/384 8795, ⓕ 385 7036. Slightly run-down, old-fashioned hotel about a kilometre south of Courtenay Place. Rooms are en suite and have a TV and tea-making facilities, plus there's a simple communal kitchen with a microwave and fridge. About as cheap as you'll find outside the hostels and they have parking. ④

Duxton 170 Wakefield St ⓣ 04/473 3900 & 0800/655 555, ⓦ www.duxton.com. A gleaming modern corporate hotel on the waterfront near Civic Square, with an à la carte restaurant and brasserie. Weekday rates start around $280 but weekend specials include a deluxe room, breakfast for two and a bottle of bubbly for $200. ⑨

Halswell Lodge 21 Kent Terrace ⓣ 04/385 0196, ⓦ www.halswell.co.nz. Comfortable, central and welcoming establishment with plain but good-value hotel rooms, relatively pricey motel units and some lovely deluxe rooms (some with spa) in a lodge set back from the street. Limited first-come-first-served off-street parking. Hotel ⑤, motel ⑥, deluxe ⑥, spa ⑦

Intercontinental cnr Grey St & Featherston St ⓣ 04/472 2722 & 0800/442 215, ⓦ www .interconnental.com. Geared chiefly towards businesspeople this is one of the pricier international hotels in town, and comes complete with gym, pool, a classy restaurant and an airport limousine service. Weekend rates (around $200) including breakfast, weekdays start around $250 without breakfast. ⑨

Ibis 153 Featherstone St ⓣ 04/496 1880 & 0800/444 422. Cut-price modern hotel that has pleasantly furnished en suite rooms with cable TV, two restaurants and a bar. Book online for the best deals. No parking. Weekends ⑤, weekdays ⑥

Majoribanks Apartments 38 Majoribanks St ⓣ 04/385 1849, ⓦ www.apollo-lodge.co.nz. Run by Apollo Lodge, these recently renovated apartments in a modern block close to the heart of the city are mostly let long-term, though it is worth asking for shorter stays; off-street parking. ⑤

Museum Hotel 90 Cable St ⓣ 04/802 8900 & 0800/994 335, ⓦ www.museumhotel.co.nz. Big, black business hotel locally famous for having been trundled across the street from the Te Papa construction site, hence its nickname, the Hotel de Wheels. It makes up for a lack of style with reasonable rates for this standard, and some of the better rooms have harbour views. Good weekend reductions. Rooms ⑦, harbour view ⑧

Shepherd's Arms 285 Tinakori Rd, Thorndon ⓣ 04/472 1320 & 0800/393 782, ⓦ www .shepherds.co.nz. Near the Parliamentary District, this small 1870 hotel (reputedly New Zealand's oldest) with bar and restaurant is tastefully renovated in period style, but also has all mod cons. Fifteen percent discounts at weekends. Rooms ⑦, suites ⑧

Wellington Motel 14 Hobson St ⓣ 04/472 0334, ⓔ wellington.motels@clear.net.nz. Not really a motel at all, but quiet self-catering rooms with TV and phone, in a large house in the diplomatic quarter close to ferries and Parliament. Family rooms $110, studios $100.

B&Bs and guesthouses

Booklovers B&B 123 Pirie St ⓣ 04/384 2714, ⓦ www.booklovers.co.nz. Literary flavoured B&B in an Edwardian villa close to Courtenay Place an Mount Victoria Park. There are books in every room and they even encourage you to take one away to read on your travels. ⑥

Edge Water 459 Karaka Bay Rd, Karaka Bay, Seatoun ⓣ 04/388 4446, ⓦ www .edgewaterwellington.co.nz. One of Wellington's finest B&Bs, once popular with *Lord of the Rings* cast and crew, a 15min drive from downtown. Simply but beautifully decorated rooms either overlook the harbour entrance or an internal courtyard and breakfasts are delightful. Room ⑦, suites ⑧

Koromiko Homestay 11 Koromiko Road, Highbury ⓣ 04/938 6539, ⓦ www.adventureout.co.nz. City homestay for "gay men and their friends" in a quiet street overlooking the botanical gardens. There are great harbour views, free Internet and meals ($25) on request. ⑤

The Mermaid 1 Epuni St, cnr with Aro St ⓣ 04/384 4511, ⓦ www.mermaid.co.nz.

A luxurious guesthouse for women only, set in a restored century-old house among bush-covered hills, a ten-minute walk from downtown. Four tastefully furnished rooms (one with private bathroom), each with a view of the garden or hills. Kitchen and lounge. Room ⑤, en suite ⑥

Rawhiti 40 Rawhiti Terrace, Kelburn ☎04/934 4859, ⓦwww.rawhiti.co.nz. Gorgeous and peaceful B&B right by the upper cable car terminus in a classic century-old home with two casually but elegantly decorated rooms (one en suite, one shared bath), both getting the morning sun. Breakfasts are delicious and there's a nice garden out the back. ⑦

Richmond Guesthouse 116 Brougham St ☎04/385 8529, ⓦwww.richmondguesthouse.co.nz. Simple and welcoming 14-room guesthouse an easy walk from town and with free on-street parking. Plain rooms are all en suite and there's a guest TV lounge, and a guest kitchen where a continental breakfast is served. ④

Talavera 7 Talavera Terrace, Kelburn ☎04/471 0555. An 1897 villa on a quiet, leafy hill above the central business district, ten minutes' walk from Lambton Quay and on the cable-car route. Sweeping views from a self-contained flat with a veranda. ⑦

Tinakori Lodge 182 Tinakori Rd, Thorndon ☎04/939 3478, ⓦwww.tinakorilodge.co.nz. A modest but comfortable B&B in a big, well-appointed Victorian villa, a short walk from the Parliamentary District, with nine airy rooms and a conservatory that looks onto a bushland reserve. Rooms ⑤, en suites ⑦

Hostels and campsites

base Backpackers 21–23 Cambridge Terrace ☎03/801 5666 & 0800/227 369, ⓦwww.basebackpackers.com. Slick and well-organised 300-bed hostel recently converted from an office building. Everything is nicely decorated, beds all come with sheets, and there's a women-only "Sanctuary" floor ($2 a night extra) with towel and lotions provided. The place comes with all the big-hostel facilities including cheap Internet access, budget café, lockable cupboards and a bar in the basement with theme nights. Dorms ①, en-suite rooms ④

Cambridge Hotel 28 Cambridge Terrace ☎04/385 8829 & 0800/375 021, ⓦwww.cambridgehotel.co.nz. The muddy brown exterior belies the nicely renovated decor of this 1930s colonial hotel that now operates as a combined backpackers and hotel. Spacious 4- to 8-bed dorms come with made-up bunks and there's a good café and bar, but there's only one common area used for cooking, eating and TV watching. Hotel rooms aren't huge but are en suite, well-appointed and good value. Dorms ①, rooms ④

Downtown Backpackers 1 Bunny St ☎04/473 8482, ⓦwwww.downtownbackpackers.co.nz. Large and ageing hostel in the Art Deco Waterloo Hotel that's very convenient for train, bus and ferry arrivals. Dorms and rooms are adequate but unexciting, though there's a good bar with cheap beer, a café serving low-cost breakfasts and dinners. Dorms ①, rooms ③, superior en suite doubles ④

Lodge in the City 152 Taranaki St ☎04/385 8560 &0800/257 225, ⓦwww.lodgeinthecity.co.nz. Rambling former student lodgings that now offers a good range of rooms – plus free off-street parking, on-site bar, a roof garden with good views over the city, and free shuttle to the ferry, bus and train. Somewhat blighted by long-stay residents whose demands are at odds with those of tourists. Dorms ①, rooms ③, self-contained units ④

Rowena's Lodge 115 Brougham St ☎04/385 7872 or 0800/801414, ⓦwww.wellingtonbackpackers.co.nz. A decaying hostel well past its best, though it is the only place in town with tent camping ($12.50 including use of hostel facilities). Free shuttle to ferry and train. Dorms ①, rooms ②

Top 10 Hutt Park Holiday Park 95 Hutt Park Rd, Lower Hutt ☎04/568 5913 or 0800/488 872 , ⓦwww.huttpark.co.nz. Located 12km north of Wellington on the harbour's northeastern shore, this is the capital's closest campsite. It is close to beaches, shops and bush walks and can be accessed on buses #81–#85 from Lambton Interchange. Camping $13, cabins ②, self-contained units ③, motel units ④

Wellington City YHA 292 Wakefield St, cnr Cambridge Terrace ☎04/801 7280, ⒺYha.wellington@yha.org.nz. One of the best urban hostels in the country, great value and right in the heart of the city. It has spacious and comfortable common areas, well-equipped kitchen, bike storage, travel desk and a full day and evening activities programme. Many of the doubles, twin, four- and six-share dorms have en suites, and there are great harbour views from some of the top-floor rooms. Book at least a week in advance in summer. Dorms ①, rooms ③, en suites ④

Wildlife House 58 Tory St ☎04/381 3899, ⓦwww.wildlifehouse.co.nz. An excellent zebra-stripe painted high-rise hostel converted into comfortable and roomy accommodation. Also offers free Internet access, travel desk, job find service and its own bar. Dorms ❶, twins & doubles ❸, en suites ❸ **Worldwide** 291 The Terrace ☎ 04/802 5590, ⓦ www.worldwidenz.co.nz. Bright and cheerful

hostel in an attractive house with singles, doubles and twins, four-shares and 6-bunk dorms, plus free local calls and Internet access. All beds have sheets. Dorms ❶, rooms ❸

The City

Wellington's **city centre** is compact and easy to cover on foot, with most of the major attractions within a two-kilometre radius. The heart of the city stretches from the train station in the north to Cambridge and Kent Terraces at the eastern end of Courtenay Place, taking in the waterfront along the way, while the central business district runs along The Terrace and Lambton Quay; the latter is also the principal shopping thoroughfare. The main districts for eating, drinking and entertainment are Courtenay Place, Cuba Street, Willis Street, and down to the waterfront at Queens Wharf. **Cuba Street** is also the "alternative" shopping district with secondhand bookshops, record stores, retro clothes retailers and quirky cafés.

It's best to start at the **Civic Square**, the nearest thing to a real centre that Wellington has. From there, points of interest run both ways along the waterfront. The area south of Civic Square contains New Zealand's national museum, **Te Papa**, the city's number one attraction, its cerebral pleasures nicely balanced by shopping and entertainment districts around **Courtenay Place** and **Cuba Street** to the south. For further contrast, take a stroll along **Oriental Parade** and up to **Mount Victoria** beyond for some excellent views of the city. North of the Civic Centre, Jervois Quay runs past the well-executed **Museum of Wellington City & Sea** and a couple of minor

The architecture of Ian Athfield

The work of New Zealand's most influential and versatile living architect, **Ian Athfield**, generates the kind of love-hate reaction usually associated with the Lloyd's Building in London and the Pompidou Centre in Paris. His principal motif is the juxtaposition of old and new, regular and irregular, as seen in the facade of the **Palmerston North Public Library** (see p.292). However, many of the finest examples of Athfield's work are in his home town of Wellington, where the facade of the **Moore Wilson Building** from 1984 (a food warehouse at the corner of College and Tory streets) explores fractures, while the **Oriental Parade Apartments**, built in 1988 near the start of the Southern Walkway on Oriental Parade (see p.497), have an almost Egyptian facade. Athfield also likes artwork to appear as part of his buildings, as demonstrated by the sculptural forms of the **Wellington Public Library** (see p.494). Perhaps the best example of his work is **Logan House** at Windy Point in Eastbourne, across the bay from Wellington (see p.508), where he has cleverly combined an old structure with a new one, making full use of the natural surroundings and revitalizing a disused building. However, many people's favourite Athfield building is a house-cum-office on a hillside in the northern suburb of **Khandallah** (at 105 Amritsar St; closed to the public). Visible from the Wellington motorway and – at some distance – from the ferry to Days Bay, it seems to grow organically down the hill, showing a respect for the environment and a willingness to engage with it that's often lacking in New Zealand architecture. In contrast, the house adjoining the **Te Mata Estate Winery** in Havelock North (see p.467) is a sly backhanded tribute to the modernists of the 1930s and an expression of the architect's humour, though it still manages to look perfectly placed in its surroundings.

attractions on Queens Wharf. A couple of blocks inland, **Lambton Quay** forms the backbone of the central business district with its **cable car** running up to the leafy suburb of Kelburn. Lambton Quay runs to Thorndon and the **Parliamentary District**, seat of New Zealand's government and home to institutions like **Archives New Zealand**, the national library, the new and old **cathedrals** and Katherine Mansfield's birthplace.

Heading out from the centre, the lovely **Botanic Gardens** lead west towards a couple of sylvan sites: **Karori Wildlife Sanctuary** with its growing population of native birds; and **Otari-Wilton's Bush**, one of the last remnants of virgin bush in the area. These form part of the **Town Belt**. A band of greenery across the hills that encircle the city centre, it was originally set aside in 1839 by the New Zealand Company for aesthetic and recreational purposes, and contains several good walks and many of the city's best lookout points. Further south the Town Belt runs past the Wellington Zoo and east where it cuts the city off from the quiet suburbs and beaches of the **Miramar Peninsula**.

Civic Square

The city's main visitor centre backs onto **Civic Square**, a fairly compact open space which was extensively revamped in the early 1990s by Wellington architect Ian Athfield (see box, p.493). Now, a popular venue for outdoor events, it is full of interesting sculptures including Neil Dawson's Ferns, interlinking metal fern fronds formed into a ball that seems to float above the square.

A couple of buildings are worth a quick visit. The most immediately arresting is the big and refreshingly bold **Central Library** (Mon–Thurs 9.30am–8.30pm, Fri 9.30am–9pm, Sat 9.30am–5pm, Sun 1–4pm), another Athfield design opened in 1991. It's a far cry from the fustiness of most libraries, a spacious high-tech environment of steel, stone and timber with its inner workings – air ducts, water pipes, etc – exposed to form an integral part of the design, the whole enhanced by strong sculptural forms, colour and plenty of light flooding in. Athfield also created the supporting steel nikau palms which ring the building and provide a link to the rest of the Civic Square by continuing out beyond the building itself.

An adjacent 1939 Art Deco building houses the **City Gallery** (☎04/801 3952, ⓦ www.city-gallery.org.nz; daily 10am–5pm; free, except $5–10 for special exhibitions), a contemporary art gallery that hosts touring shows of national and international works. Attached is the small arthouse **City Cinema** often showing works relating directly to exhibits elsewhere in the gallery but also used in conjunction with some of the city's many specialist film festivals. There's also the stylish *Nikau Gallery Café* (see "Eating", p.512), opening onto an outdoor terrace.

Across the square, the striking modern **City-to-Sea Bridge**, was intentionally made broad in an attempt to make access from downtown to the long-ignored waterfront as seamless as possible. So successful has it been that a second crossing is planned nearby. The original comes decorated with timber sculptures of birds, whales and celestial motifs. The work of Maori artist Para Matchitt, completed in 1993, these symbolize the arrival of Maori and European settlers and, by extension, that of present-day visitors from the sea to city.

South of Civic Square

You're likely to spend much of your time south of the Civic Square either at **Te Papa** or eating and drinking around Courtenay Place and Cuba Street.

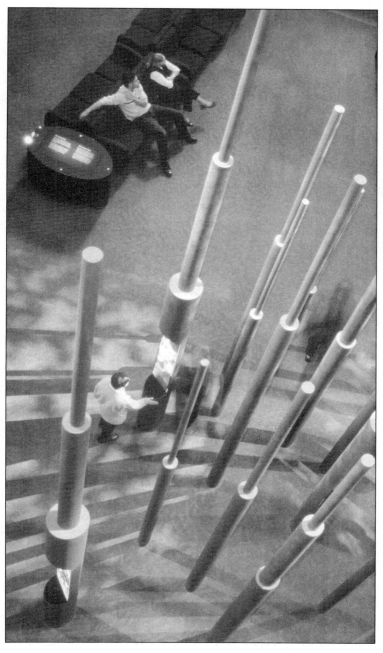

△ Te Papa

But don't miss out on **Oriental Parade**, a lovely stroll with great harbour views, a small city beach and the chance to hike up to the summit of **Mount Victoria**.

Te Papa

Universally known as **Te Papa**, the **Museum of New Zealand**, Cable Street (daily 10am–6pm & Thurs till 9pm; free; map $2, audio tour $5, parking $2 per hr; ☎04/381 7000 ⓦwww.tepapa.govt.nz), is Wellington's star attraction. Unlike the dusty old buildings that house national museums elsewhere in the world, Te Papa occupies a purpose-built, $350 million five-storey building right on the waterfront. After considerable consultation with *iwi* (tribes) the museum opened to great fanfare in early 1998. You'll need half a day to explore this celebration of all things New Zealand, but may prefer a series of short visits to avoid information overload. A couple of **cafés** help sustain one long visit, and **kids** are well catered for with Discovery Centres dotted throughout.

Aimed equally at adults and children it combines state-of-the-art technology and bright active exhibits with plenty of opportunity to dig deeper, though detractors criticise Te Papa for hiding away much of its collection. Still, there's heaps to see, so it is well worth buying the *Te Papa Explorer* guide ($2), outlining routes such as "Te Papa in a Hurry" or "Te Papa for Kids"; or calling ahead to join one of the **guided tours** (daily 10.15am & 2pm; 45min; $9).

The hub of Te Papa is **Level 2**, with its interactive section on earthquakes and volcanoes, where you can experience a mild quake in a house, watch Mount Ruapehu erupt on screen and hear the Maori explanation of the causes of such activity. The interesting "X-Ray Room" houses the skeletons of great sea creatures such as whales, dolphins and seals. Kids (of all ages) will be drawn to the Time Warp zone, with a series of **rides** (every 15min; all $6–8) including a virtual bungy jump, and the opportunity to be jolted forwards to Wellington 2055 ("Future Rush") or back to a prehistoric New Zealand to witness the extraordinary formation of the land ("Blastback") while getting jerked about watching a screen and listening to the sound effects. Buy tickets early during school holidays. Level 2 also provides access to **Bush City**, an outdoor synthesis of New Zealand environments complete with native plants, a small cave system and its own weeny swing bridge.

The main collection continues on **Level 4**, home to the excellent main Maori section including a thought-provoking display on the Treaty of Waitangi dominated by a giant glass image of this significant document. There's also an active *marae* with a modern meeting house painted in a rainbow of pastel colours, mirrored by a stunning stained-glass window and protected by a sacred boulder of *pounamu* (greenstone); you are not allowed to enter the meeting house unless invited. High quality temporary and touring exhibitions include one of which concentrates on the art and culture of Maori people of a particular region. The Whanganui Iwi Exhibition on the people associated with the Whanganui River runs until May 2006 when it will be replaced by that of another *iwi*.

As you walk around adjacent displays on New Zealand's people, land, history, trade and cultures look out for playful pieces of modern art such as Michel Tuffery's bullock made from corned beef cans, Jeff Thomson's Holden station wagon clad in corrugated iron, and Brian O'Connor's *paua* shell surfboard.

There's more art on **Level 5** where the Boulevard gallery displays a changing roster of works on paper, oils and sculpture typically representing all the luminaries of the New Zealand art world past and present.

Courtenay Place and Cuba Street

A couple of blocks south of Te Papa and you're into the heart of Wellington's dining and entertainment district centred on **Courtenay Place**. You'll continually find yourself here for a coffee, a few drinks, a meal or a movie, or just passing through. For mooching around during the day, there's more interest along **Cuba Street**, traditionally Wellington's alternative quarter with tattoo parlours, secondhand book and clothes shops. Towards the southern end it gets slightly seedier though it is becoming less so as groovy shops and cafés spill over from nearby streets. Between Dixon and Ghuznee streets you can't miss Wellington's colourful and iconic **Bucket Fountain**, first installed in 1969 and still splashing unsuspecting passers-by.

There's little specific to see beyond the southern end Cuba Street, though heritage fans could press on a couple of hundred metres to the **Colonial Cottage Museum**, 68 Nairn St (Christmas–April daily noon–4pm, May to Christmas Wed–Sun noon–4pm; $5) central Wellington's oldest building, dating from 1858 and beautifully presented in Victorian style.

Oriental Parade and Mount Victoria

Immediately east of Te Papa, a fairly grotty patch of parkland is now in the process of being remodelled as **Waitangi Park**, named after a long-culverted stream which will be restored to its natural course, creating a small urban wetland. It should provide a welcome link to the start of **Oriental Parade**, Wellington's most elegant section of waterfront. Skirting **Oriental Bay**, this Norfolk-pine lined road curls past some of the city's priciest real estate and even flanks a **sandy beach** installed here in 2003 with sand brought across Cook Strait from near Takaka. On a fine day it is hard to beat a stroll along the promenade, ice cream in hand, admiring the city across the harbour. Apart from the Freyberg pool (see "Swimming", p.518) and a couple of restaurants there are no sights as such, but your stroll can be extended out into a full afternoon by continuing to Charles Plimmer Park and joining the Southern Walkway (see p.510) to the summit of **Mount Victoria**.

At 196m, **Mount Victoria Lookout** is one of the best of Wellington's viewpoints, offering sweeping panoramic views of the city, waterfront, docks and beyond to the Hutt Valley; all particularly dramatic around dusk. Next to the summit car park stands the **Byrd Memorial**, a triangular construction faced with multicoloured tiles and intended to simulate an Antarctic expedition tent, with the Southern Lights playing across it. The memorial honours the American aviator and Antarctic explorer Richard E Byrd (1888–1957), who mapped large areas of the Antarctic and was the first man to fly over the South Pole, using New Zealand as a base for his expeditions. Though less rewarding than walking, you can also reach the summit by bus (#20; Mon–Fri), using the Wellington Rover (see p.490), or by car following Hawker Street, off Majoribanks Street, then taking Palliser Road, which twists uphill eventually to the lookout.

North of Civic Square

In recent years the northern waterfront has become more lively as the city progressively reconnects itself to the harbour. Much of the action goes on around **Queens Wharf** where a couple of museums, some bars and fine restaurants attract a lively throng. Redevelopment is now moving further north and the imaginatively named North Queens Wharf is about to undergo major renovation with yet more cafés, shops and apartments.

The business heart of Wellington beats along Lambton Quay which runs north to the **Parliamentary District** where apart from the Parliament Buildings themselves you can see the original Treaty of Waitangi in **Archives New Zealand** and visit the city's ecclesiastic heart. Parliament marks the southern edge of **Thorndon**, Wellington's oldest suburb and home to the **Katherine Mansfield Birthplace**, first home of New Zealand's most famous writer.

All this is manageable on foot, though you could seek assistance from the City Circular bus (see p.489).

Queens Wharf and around

North of the Civic Centre Square a waterfront stroll past the slender Frank Kitts Park and the barn-like Events Centre brings you to **Queens Wharf**, a T-shaped affair dating from 1862, its timber warehouses now rejuvenated and always bustling (at least on fine days). Come to soak up the atmosphere, eat at one of the restaurants (see "Eating", p.512), shop, inline skate (see p.511) and visit a couple of worthwhile sights.

At the entrance to Queens Wharf sits the **Museum of Wellington City & Sea** (daily 10am–5pm; free; ⓦ www.museumofwellington.co.nz), which, by taking a more traditional approach and being housed in a Victorian bond store, nicely balances the modernity of Te Papa. Wellington's social and maritime history unfolds through well-executed displays on early Maori and European settlement and the city's strong seafaring heritage.

For many, particularly Kiwis of a certain age, the star attraction is the display on the **Wahine disaster** remembering the inter-island ferry *Wahine* which sank with the loss of 51 lives on 10 April 1968. The ferry, with 734 people on board, foundered in one of New Zealand's most violent storms ever. Rescue attempts were repeatedly thwarted until the weather calmed enough for passengers to start abandoning ship, only to find that the ship had so much that the lifeboats on the upper side were unusable. The tale is so powerfully told in a short movie (run continuously) that a broken walking stick and damaged lifeboat propeller displayed nearby seem particularly moving. The ship's mast is displayed in nearby Frank Kitts Park.

Elsewhere an impressive holographic projection tells the Maori legends of the creation of Wellington Harbour, and a tall screen features a roster of short films.

The museum also looks after the nearby **Plimmer's Ark Gallery** (daily 10.30am–4.30pm; free), a slender corridor alongside the Events Centre where the remains of the good ship *Inconstant* are kept in soggy perpetuity. After delivering a load of female refugees from the Irish potato famine to Adelaide, the ship was Peru-bound and called at Wellington to pick up water. It hit rocks and was towed to Te Aro Beach where it lay until bought for £80 by John Plimmer, a Shropshire carpenter. He turned it into a trading store on the wharf – hence Plimmer's Ark – where it became part of his growing empire. Plimmer became known as the Father of Wellington for his devotion to the growing community, but the boat eventually fell into disrepair; the remains were only rediscovered in 1997.

The majority of the scant remains were transported here where they rest in glass cases constantly sprayed with water, to prevent them drying out and disintegrating, surrounded by information boards describing its history and the characters involved.

By the entrance to Queens Wharf, the **Academy Galleries** (daily 10am–5pm if there is something on; generally free, temporary exhibits $2–5) offer changing exhibits of mostly Kiwi artists but with occasional foreign exhibits.

Lambton Quay and the Cable Car

Traditionally Wellington's main shopping and business street, **Lambton Quay** formed the original waterfront but was cut off by the docks formed by reclamation. Many of the more interesting shops have moved elsewhere, but the street remains the heart of the CBD becoming more formal and businesslike as you head north to the Parliamentary District. Lambton Quay starts at its junction with Willis street where glass floor panels in the basement of the Old Bank Arcade reveal the remains of the bow of **Plimmer's Ark** (see p.498). At the northern end you reach Old Government Buildings (see p.500) and beyond it the bus interchange and the stately 1937 **Wellington Railway Station**. It is a little run down and due for imminent restoration, but still worth a glance for its unashamedly self-important Doric-columned entrance, and Beaux Arts booking hall.

Even if you never use the rest of Wellington's public transport system, be sure to take the short and scenic ride up to the leafy suburb of Kelburn and the upper section of the Botanic Gardens on the **Cable Car** (Mon–Fri 7am–10pm, Sat & Sun 9am–10pm; $1.80 each way). It's shiny red cars depart every ten minutes from the lower terminus on Cable Car Lane, just off Lambton Quay and climb a steep, one-in-five incline, making four stops on the way and giving great views over the city and harbour. Operational since 1902, the cars were originally driven by steam but were converted to electricity in 1933, and in 1978 the current Swiss-designed system was installed. At the upper terminus on Upland Road the **Cable Car Museum** (Mon–Fri 9.30am–5pm, Sat & Sun 10am–4.30pm; free) contains the electric drive motor and a cat's cradle of cables along with a century-old example of the original cars and plenty of background on this and other cable cars around the world. A **lookout** by the upper terminus gives spectacular views over the city, matched only by those from inside the adjacent *Skyline Café*. Unfortunately the food isn't that great, and if you're after a decent lunch or coffee, then walk for ten minutes along Upland Road to the Kelburn shopping area and *Caffè Mode* (see p.513).

The Botanic Gardens and observatories

At the top of the Cable Car you're also at the highest point of Wellington's **Botanic Gardens** (daily dawn–dusk; free), a huge swathe of green on peaceful rolling hills with numerous paths that wind down towards the city. You could easily while away a couple of hours here visiting the observatory, begonia house and rose garden, or simply strolling through stands of pohutukawa, remnants of dense native forest and ornamental flower beds. Pick up the useful free map from the Wellington visitor centre or at the main entrances. Apart from using the Cable Car, you can access the Botanic Gardens on Glenmore Road (bus #12, 13 or 21 from downtown), and by crossing the footbridge from Bolton Street into the Bolton Street Memorial Park.

It's a two-minute walk from the upper Cable Car terminus to the 1941 **Carter Observatory** (Mon–Fri 10am–5pm, Sat & Sun noon–5pm; ☎04/472 8167, ⓦ www.carterobs.ac.nz) where entry ($5) entitles you to see astronomy displays, computers and a historic telescope. Add $5 and you can also see one of their half-hour planetarium shows. Weather permitting, they also have evening programmes which include a chance to view the southern night sky (Tues, Thurs & Sat from 6.30pm; $20): call to reserve a place and to check the likelihood of a viewing. Within sight of the Carter Observatory is the recently renovated 1912 **Thomas King Solar Observatory** (daily 11am–4pm; $7.50), where on fine days you can look directly at the safely filtered sun complete with corona, flares and sunspots. One of the first observatories, it played a vital role in navigation and time-keeping.

The *tour de force* of the Botanic Gardens and their most visited section is the **Lady Norwood Rose Garden**, on flat ground at the Glenmore Road entrance. The fragrant garden blooms throughout the summer, with 300 varieties of roses laid out in a formal wheel shape around a fountain and the whole enclosed by a colonnade of climbing roses. The adjacent, large **Begonia House** (daily: Oct–March 10am–5pm; April–Sept 10am–4pm; free) is divided into two areas: the tropical, with an attractive lily pond and a small cage containing carnivorous plants; and the temperate, which has seasonal displays of begonias and gloxinias in summer, changing to cyclamen, orchids and impatiens in winter. Further down from the rose garden, a monolithic memorial to New Zealand's most lauded politician, Richard Seddon, marks the entrance to **Bolton Street Memorial Park**, an atmospheric Victorian cemetery where many of the city's early pioneers are buried. The main pathway through the memorial park crosses the motorway by a footbridge to an isolated remnant of the cemetery and a pretty weatherboard chapel (daily 10am–4pm) containing burial records. Here you're up against the high-rise buildings of The Terrace only a short walk from the Parliamentary District. Old-fashioned roses clamber over the ageing headstones and twist through ironwork in the shade of mature trees. Established in 1840 as three separate cemeteries (Anglican, Jewish and public), the cemetery was closed in 1892 except for burials in existing plots. In the 1960s, amid public outcry, it was abandoned altogether, and over 3500 bodies were exhumed and relocated to make way for the motorway that now bisects it.

Parliamentary District

The northern end of Lambton Quay marks the start of the **Parliamentary District** and is dominated by the grandiose **Old Government Buildings** (Mon–Fri 9am–4.30pm, Sat 10am–3pm; free). At first glance an opulent Italian Renaissance construction of cream stone, it is in fact built from wood, its entrances decorated with grand timber columns and porticoes. Designed by Colonial Architect William Clayton (1823–77) to mark the country's transition from provincial to centralized government, it was supposed to be built in stone but cost cutting forced a rethink. When completed in 1876 it was the largest building in New Zealand, and except for an ornamental palace in Japan remains the largest timber building in the world. Built on reclaimed land, it was physically isolated from the rest of the city and dominated Lambton Harbour. It housed government ministers and most of the Wellington-based public service for many years, and the Cabinet regularly met in the room immediately above the main entrance until 1921. As departments grew, they moved to other buildings and by 1975 only the Education Department remained. Fully restored, it is now the home of Victoria University's Law Faculty. At the entrance, the DOC **visitor centre** (see p.488) contains coverage of the extensive mid-1990s restoration and provides maps for a free self-guided **tour** through part of the building, including the Cabinet Room. Compared to the exterior, the interior is quite a restrained affair of honey-coloured kauri panelling, except for two carved rimu staircases that are among the finest in the country. Upstairs, look out for the photos of the building as backdrop to various demonstrations and protests.

The Parliament Buildings

Visible across Lambton Quay are the **Parliament Buildings**, the seat of New Zealand's government, a trio of highly individual structures which somehow manage to sit quite harmoniously together. The most distinctive is the modernist **Beehive** (officially the Executive Wing), a seven-stepped truncated cone which houses the cabinet and the offices of its ministers. Designed by British (and Coventry Cathedral) architect Sir Basil Spence in 1964, it wasn't started until 1969 and was finally completed in 1982, six years after Spence's death. The story goes that Spence designed this curiosity on a napkin after dinner, having been inspired by the label on a box of matches. With its lack of square corners and disorienting circular design the building is apparently impractical to furnish and clean, and a pig to work in. The Beehive is connected directly to the Edwardian Neoclassical **Parliament House**. This looks suitably solid and reliable for a seat of government, which is more than can be said for the almost frivolous Victorian Gothic **Parliamentary Library** next door.

For security reasons, the Beehive is off limits, but you can visit the other two buildings on a free hour-long **guided tour** (departing on the hour Mon–Fri 10am–4pm, Sat 10am–3pm, Sun noon–3pm; ℡04/471 9053, ⓦwww.parliament.govt.nz), which starts at the visitor centre in the ground-floor foyer of Parliament House. Informative and anecdotal, the tour begins with a short video on the extensive and detailed restoration work that was carried out after a fire in 1992, which began in the library and swept through parts of Parliament House. With a major faultline just 400m away, the building had to be protected from earthquakes, calling for some ingenious retrofitting of special isolating foundations. After a glimpse of these you're into the buildings proper, with its formal meeting rooms seemingly at odds with the modern artworks. If it is not in use, the tour includes the highly decorative **Maori Affairs Select Committee Room**, and undoubted highlight with its specially commissioned carvings and woven *tukutuku* panels from all the major tribal groups in the land. An all too brief look at the ornate and beautifully restored Victorian Gothic library gives a sense of its ecclesiastical feel; no accident as it was designed in 1899 by Thomas Turnbull, who was famous for his work on churches. Finally, if Parliament isn't sitting, you are led through the Debating Chamber; when the house is in session you are able to watch proceedings from the public gallery after the tour.

MPs mostly drink at the private *Bellamy's* in the basement of the Beehive, but occasionally venture across Molesworth Street to the 1893 **Backbencher Pub** (see p.515), which is worth visiting to admire the satirical cartoons and outsized latex puppets of notable local politicians since the late 1970s.

The National Library and Archives

Opposite Parliament on Molesworth Street, the **National Library of New Zealand**; Mon–Fri 9am–5pm, Sat 9am–1pm; free), the most comprehensive research library in New Zealand. It is home to the **Alexander Turnbull Library**, a vast collection of volumes, documents, paintings and so on, mostly relating to New Zealand and the Pacific, which was assembled by a wealthy Wellington merchant and gifted to the Crown in 1918. Much of the collection is off limits to the general public, and unless you are here with research in mind you can probably skip the public reading room, though it is worth sticking your head into the library's large **gallery** (Mon–Fri 9am–5pm, Sat 9am–4.30pm, Sun 1–4pm), which regularly hosts free exhibitions, lectures and events.

A stone's throw east along Aitken Street, **Archives New Zealand**, 10 Mulgrave St (Mon–Fri 9am–5pm, Sat 9am–1pm; free), is the country's repository of all things sacred. Again, much of the building is devoted to research, but you can visit the **Constitution Room**, effectively a dimly lit, climatically controlled vault containing documents pertinent to the nation's social and constitutional development. The prize exhibit is the original Maori-language **Treaty of Waitangi** (see p.187), which barely survived a long spell lost in the bowels of the Old Government Buildings, suffering water damage and the gnawings of rodents before it was rescued in 1908. Various copies of the Treaty which did the rounds collecting Maori chiefs' signatures give a sense of how haphazard the whole process was. Other archives highlight important milestones on the country's road to independent nationhood, notably the 1835 Declaration of Independence of the Northern Chiefs and **Maori petitions** dating back to 1909, which complain of broken treaty promises. Look also for the facsimile of the 1893 **petition for women's suffrage**, put together by New Zealand's iconic suffragette, Kate Sheppard – who features on the $10 note. At this third attempt she managed to amass 32,000 signatures, a quarter of the adult female population of the country at the time, so ushering in legislation which made New Zealand the first country to give women the vote. Outside the Constitution Room is a small container of water, to help Maori neutralize *tapu* (ill-effects caused by a taboo action or object) after viewing the treaty.

The Cathedrals – old and new

Long before the houses of the Parliamentary District were taken over by government departments and foreign delegations, this area of Thorndon was a thriving suburb and its religious needs were served by the modest **Old St Paul's**, at the corner of Mulgrave Street and Pipitea Street (daily 10am–5pm; free). Possibly the finest European timber church in the country, it operated as the parish church of Thorndon from 1866 to 1964 and was only saved from demolition in the 1960s by sustained public protest. It remains a consecrated building popular for weddings. You'll understand why when you see its beautiful wooden interior, crafted in early English Gothic style (more commonly seen in stone) from native timbers which have since darkened with age to a rich mellow hue. The ranks of arches, the pews, pulpit and choral area are all highlighted by lovely stained-glass windows and the sheen of polished brass plaques on the walls. The church was the major work of an English ecclesiastical architect, Reverend Frederick Thatcher, who designed it for Bishop Selwyn and was vicar here for a few years.

Old St Paul's could hardly stand in greater contrast to it's modern successor, **St Paul's Cathedral** (Mon–Fri 7.30am–5pm, Sat 10am–5pm, Sun 8am–6pm; free), a block away on Molesworth Street. A curious mix of Byzantine and Santa Fe styles, it was designed in the 1930s by Cecil Wood of Christchurch, a renowned ecclesiastical architect. Queen Elizabeth II laid the foundation stone in 1954 but the cathedral wasn't finally complete until 1998. The interior is cavernous, dwarfing the dark wood choir stalls which look completely out of place amongst all the powder-pink concrete. Note the distinctive pipe organ that was built in London and first installed in Old St Paul's.

Katherine Mansfield Birthplace

Walk north from Parliament for about ten minutes, crossing the bridge over the motorway to reach the **Katherine Mansfield Birthplace**, 25 Tinakori Rd (daily 10am–4pm; $5.50; bus #14 stops at nearby Park Street). A modest wooden house with a small garden, this was the childhood home of Katherine Mansfield (see p.503) and comes stuffed with antiques and ornaments. The house has a cluttered Victorian/Edwardian charm and unusual decor, which was avant-garde for its time, inspired by Japonisme and the Aesthetic Movement. This has been beautifully restored and the walls are bright with colour and reprints of original wallpapers. In the kitchen is a doll's house, reproduced from the story of the same name, while an upstairs room is set aside to recount a history of the author's life and career, with some black-and-white photos of Wellington and the people that shaped her life, and an excellent 50-minute video, *A Woman and a Writer*.

The suburbs

Wellington's suburbs offer a relaxing escape from the bustle of the city. The groundbreaking **Karori Wildlife Sanctuary** is within easy striking distance of the centre and is nicely complemented at a couple of other sites: the fine stand of native bush a few kilometres north at **Otari–Wilson's Bush**, and the **Wellington Zoo**, just south of downtown. A number of good walks thread through the greenery of the Town Belt or head beyond to the quiet pleasures of **Scorching Bay** on the Miramar Peninsula.

Karori Wildlife Sanctuary

The **Karori Wildlife Sanctuary**, 31 Waiapu Road (Nov–Feb daily 10am–8pm; March–Oct Mon–Fri 10am–4pm, Sat & Sun 10am–5pm; $6; ☎04/920 9200, infoline ☎04/920 2222, ⊛www.sanctuary.org.nz), 3km west of downtown, is an ambitious project to restore a sliver of New Zealand native bush (and attendant wildlife) to 253 hectares of urban Wellington. Designed around two century-old reservoirs which formerly supplied Wellington's drinking water, the managing trust first designed and constructed an 8.6km-long **predator-proof fence** which is intended to keep out all introduced mammals. As well as restocking the area with native trees and eradicating weeds, the trust is introducing native birds – kiwi, weka, saddleback, kaka, tuatara, morepork, tui, bellbird, whitehead and North Island robins – and the grasshopper-like weta to the sanctuary from the overspill of the successful conservation and restocking programme on Kapiti Island (see p.299). Started in the late 1990s, it is a far-reaching project which won't be entirely complete until the forest has matured in around 500 years. There's a long way to go, but already you can walk the 35km of paths (some almost flat, others quite rugged) listening to birdsong heard almost nowhere else on the mainland. All of a sudden you can understand why early European arrivals to New Zealand were so impressed with the birdsong.

It is worth spending half a day here (preferably towards sunset to catch the evening chorus) wandering past viewing hides, areas noted for their fantails or saddleback, and even the first few metres of a gold mine tunnel from the 1869 Karori gold rush. Alternatively join one of the **guided tours** which take place daily in summer and on winter weekends. Day tours ($10) last about ninety minutes, or go for the nocturnal tour ($15) which starts just before dusk and gives you a chance to hear (and maybe see) kiwi.

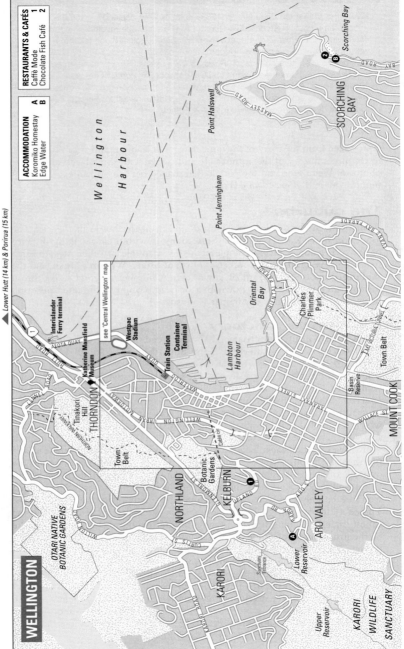

WELLINGTON

RESTAURANTS & CAFÉS
Caffé Mode   1
Chocolate Fish Café 2

ACCOMMODATION
Koromiko Homestay   A
Edge Water   B

▲ Matiu/Somes Island & Days Bay

▲ Picton (2 hr15min – 3 hr)

▲ Lower Hutt (14 km) & Porirua (15 km)

▲ Makara (10 km)

Wellington Harbour

Scorching Bay

SCORCHING BAY

MASSEY ROAD

BAY ROAD

Point Halswell

Point Jerningham

EVANS BAY PARADE

Interislander Ferry terminal

Katherine Mansfield Museum

Tinakori Hill

THORNDON

AOTEA QUAY

HUTT ROAD

THORNDON QUAY

see 'Central Wellington' map

Westpac Stadium

Train Station

Container Terminal

WATERLOO QUAY

WELLINGTON URBAN MOTORWAY

Lambton Harbour

Oriental Bay

Charles Plimmer Park

Town Belt

THE TERRACE

WILLIS STREET

Basin Reserve

WALLACE ST

MOUNT COOK

Town Belt

Botanic Gardens

Cable car

NORTHLAND

KELBURN

GLENMORE STREET

BOWEN ST

SALAMANCA RD

UPLAND RD

KELBURN PDE

ARO VALLEY

Lower Reservoir

Southern entrance

KARORI

Upper Reservoir

KARORI WILDLIFE SANCTUARY

OTARI NATIVE BOTANIC GARDENS

WILTON RD

CURTIS ST

KARORI RD

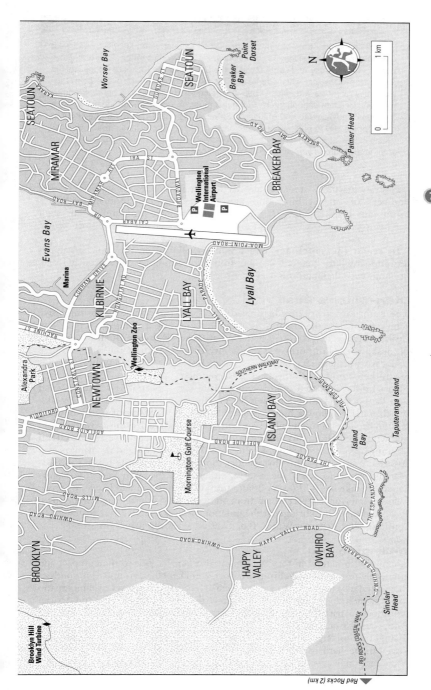

◀ *Red Rocks (2 km)*

Brooklyn Hill
Wind Turbine

N

0   1 km

SEATOUN

SEATOUN

Worser Bay

Breaker
Point
Dorset

Bay

MIRAMAR

BREAKER BAY

Palmer Head

BAY ROAD

BROADWAY

CALABAR

Wellington
International
Airport

P   P

MOA-POINT-ROAD

BREAKER ROAD

Evans Bay

Marina

COBHAM DRIVE

KILBIRNIE

LYALL BAY

PARADE

Lyall Bay

Wellington Zoo

NEWTOWN

Alexandra
Park

RIDDIFORD ROAD

ADELAIDE ROAD

SOUTHERN WALKWAY

THE ESPLANADE

Taputeranga Island

Mornington Golf Course

ISLAND BAY

ADELAIDE ROAD

THE PARADE

Island
Bay

BROOKLYN

MILLS ROAD

OWHIRO ROAD

OWHIRO ROAD

HAPPY
VALLEY

HAPPY VALLEY ROAD

OWHIRO
BAY

THE ESPLANADE

O BAY PARADE

Sinclair
Head

RED ROCKS COASTAL WALK

The best view in Wellington

If the city panorama from Mount Victoria isn't an extensive enough view, head west to **Brooklyn Hill**, easily identified by its crowning 32m **wind turbine**. Fantastic views unfold across the city and south towards the South Island's Kaikoura Ranges as the giant propeller blades whirr overhead. This demonstration turbine has been harnessing Wellington's wind since 1993, providing energy for up to a hundred homes but failing to ignite enough interest to install more. To reach the turbine by car, take Brooklyn Road from the end of Victoria Street, turn left at Ohiro Road, then right at the shopping centre up Todman Street and follow the signposts (the road up to the turbine closes at 8pm Oct–April and 5pm May–Sept). Bus #7 running along Victoria street in town drops you within walking distance.

The sanctuary's existence is already having a wider effect with increasing numbers of tui, bellbirds and kaka spotted in neighbouring suburbs. Profits are mainly fed back into the conservation programme, but such has been the success that plans are advanced for a big new visitor centre and restaurant.

To reach the sanctuary, either walk the 2km from the cable car upper terminus, catch the frequent #12 bus from Lambton Quay or Courtenay Place, or come with Wellington Rover (see p.490).

Otari–Wilton's Bush

The Karori Sanctuary may be predator free and is undoubtedly an impressive achievement, but the flora is far from mature. For a glimpse of the New Zealand bush as it was, you're better off at **Otari–Wilton's Bush** (daily dawn till dusk; free), 6km northwest of the city centre. Much of the area's original podocarp–northern rata forest was set aside in 1860 by one Job Wilton, and this forms the core of the 80 hectares preserved here.

Start by the unstaffed visitor centre (daily 9am–5pm) at 160 Wilton Road near its junction with Gloucester Street. Here you'll find a map of the walks, which initially follow a hundred-metre **Canopy Walkway** of sturdy decking high in the trees across a gully. This leads to the **Native Botanic Garden**, laid out with plants from around the country, and the informative **Nature Trail** (30min), a good introduction to the New Zealand forest and its many plants. Assorted trails (all 30min–1hr) wander through the bush, one passing an 800-year-old rimu. To reach the reserve, either walk the 3km from the Karori Sanctuary, take bus #14 (every 30min from the Lambton interchange) or drive: follow Moleworth Street north from the centre, which becomes Wadestown Road and then Blackbridge. At the junction with Churchill Drive turn left and continue till it becomes Wilton Road, off which is the main entrance.

Wellington Zoo

Sticking with natural history, you might also fancy a visit to the compact and eminently manageable **Wellington Zoo**, 200 Daniell St, around 4km south of the central city (daily 9.30am–5pm; $9; ☎04/381 6755, ⓦwww.wellingtonzoo .com), which does a nice line in exotics – the Malaysian sun bear and African wild dogs in particular – but excels with its native collection. Kaka, kea and Antipodes Islands parakeets squawk, a great contrast to the peace of The Twilight, an underground nocturnal house for morepork, tuatara and kiwi. The kiwi can be hard to see, but the bush environment with no walls or glass encourages reflective lingering…which increases your chances.

Around the Miramar Peninsula

Around 10km southeast of the city centre, Wellington's airport occupies a narrow isthmus between Evans Bay and Lyall Bay. Beyond is the **Miramar Peninsula** a lumpy chunk of suburbs and beaches, some overlooking the channel where Cook Strait ferries head off to the South Island. The area is mostly of interest for *Lord of the Rings* fans: Peter Jackson lives out this way, and Miramar is where much of the non-location footage was shot and digitally processed. Cast and crew often stayed out here too, many favouring visits to **Scorching Bay**, a crescent of white sand 13km east of the city centre, which has safe swimming and a play area. It is very popular on sunny weekends, not least for the *Chocolate Fish Café* (see p.513) where you can sit right by the water and watch the ferry glide by. At peak times you can take bus #30 all the way there; otherwise, catch the frequent, daily bus #11 and walk around 4km north along the coast; or get here with Wellington Rover (see p.490).

The harbour

The sight of multicoloured sails scudding across the water should be enough to convince you that it's impossible to come to Wellington and ignore the lure of the harbour. With its reliable winds **Wellington Harbour** (or Port Nicholson to give it its official but barely used title) offers excellent sailing experiences and entertaining kayaking (see both on p.511), or simply hop on the ferry to **Matiu/Somes Island** and **Days Bay**.

Matiu/Somes Island

Isolated in the northern reaches of Wellington Harbour, the diminutive and hilly **Matiu/Somes Island** (daily 8.30am–5pm; free) has long held spiritual significance to Maori, spent over a century as a quarantine station and is now a scenic and historic reserve. Kupe is said to have named it Matiu (meaning "peace"), when he sailed into the harbour in the tenth century. Early Maori settled here and continued in residence until deposed by European settlers in the late 1830s. They renamed the island after Joseph Somes, then deputy governor of the New Zealand Company which had "bought" it. For eighty years it was a quarantine station where travellers carrying diseases such as

WELLINGTON AND AROUND | The City

Doing the Rings thing

Many of the scenes from the *Lord of the Rings* trilogy were shot in and around the city and loads of the stars based themselves here for the duration. Director Peter Jackson even felt "incredibly proud that this country, and especially this town, is responsible for what we have done". Jackson still lives in the Wellington suburb of Seatoun, the Weta studio used for all the masses of digital manipulation is in Miramar, and the *Return of the King* had its world premier at the Embassy Theatre.

With all the sets dismantled, Wellington locations lack the interest and scenic grandeur of the more dramatic South Island sites, but for Rings geeks interest in the capital is high. You can still pick out places where scenes were shot – the gardens of Isengard, and the race to the ferry, Helm's Deep – and re-enact them should you wish.

Wellington Rover (see p.490) offer a relatively low-cost full day **Rover Ring Tour** ($150) including six locations, a picnic at "Rivendell" and a stop at the *Chocolate Fish Café* (see p.513) on the Miramar Peninsula, once a cast favourite. For something more upscale, try Flat Earth Tours (☏04/977 5805 & 0800 775 805, ⊛www.flatearth.co.nz) who do a full-day **Middle Earth Tour** ($245) hitting the main locations in the region and including a gourmet lunch.

smallpox were held until they recovered or died. During both world wars anyone in New Zealand considered even vaguely suspect – Germans, Italians, Turks, Mexicans and Japanese – were interned until the end of the war, after which it became an animal quarantine station for a number of years.

In the early 1980s its conservation value was recognised and the place is now managed by DOC who oversee continued efforts to revitalize **native vegetation** and restore several historic buildings. Introduced mammalian predators have now all been eradicated and threatened native species are being introduced in an effort to save them from extinction. Already there are three types of lizard, kakariki (the red-crowned parakeet), the grasshopper-like weta, and the ancient reptilian tuatara. About fifty of these ancient lizard-like beasts were captive-bred at Wellington's Victoria University and released in 1998. They seem to like the place and numbers are increasing.

Views back towards the city are excellent from the **Dominion Post Ferry** (2–3 daily, weather permitting; $16.50 return) which stop here enabling you to explore the island for a couple of hours or so before catching a later ferry on to Days Bay (see below) or back to Wellington. From the wharf at the island's northeastern end, a sealed road runs uphill for 500m to the **DOC field centre**, in an old hospital, which has maps of the island, although you can save time by picking one up in advance from the city DOC office (see p.488). A popular option is to take a picnic lunch onto the island. Note that this is a protected reserve and smoking is not allowed.

Days Bay

The Matiu/Somes Island ferry continues to the mainland commuter suburb of **Days Bay**, little more than a single road wedged between sheer bush-clad hills and Wellington's favourite beach. Come to laze on the beach, rent out windsurfers, kayaks and canoes from Days Bay Boatshed beside the wharf (late Oct–Easter Sat & Sun from 10am; ☎04/562 8150), and refuel at the excellent daytime *Chocolate Dayz Café* (☎04/562 6132), a hundred metres south of the ferry wharf. Architecture fans will want to stroll a further 400m south to see the unusual Ian Athfield-designed **Logan House**, which is built around and within two big old stone chimneys, whose thick walls are punctured by arrow-slit windows, like medieval towers. Athfield then designed the rest of the house to link with not only the chimneys but also the cliff-face directly behind them, so that the new structure fully interacts with its natural surroundings. Best viewed from the main road, which runs in front, it can also be seen from the ferry as you approach.

The nearest shops are at **Eastbourne village**, a kilometre further south along the coast, which also has a few cafés and restaurants.

The easiest access is on the speedy **Dominion Post Ferry** (Mon–Fri up to 8 daily 6.30am–6.30pm, Sat & Sun 5 daily 10am–5pm; 30min; $7.50 each way; ☎04/499 1282, timetable ☎04/499 3339, ⓦwww.eastbywest.co.nz), which departs for Days Bay from Queens Wharf. Alternatively, drive or cycle around the head of the Wellington Harbour, or catch **buses** numbered #81 to #85 from the Lambton Interchange in Wellington.

The Hutt Valley

Crouched on the northeastern shore of Wellington Harbour, 15km from the city centre, the Hutt Valley is essentially commuterland bisected by SH2 and easily accessible by suburban train. The suburb of **Lower Hutt** barely contains enough interest to merit a trip – unless you happen to be staying locally at

Wellington's closest campsite (see p.492) – though you may call in on the way to the **Rimutaka Forest Park**, prime picnicking and tramping territory for weekending Wellingtonians.

The northern shore of Wellington Harbour is occupied by the suburb of **Petone**, the site of the first, short-lived European settlement in the Wellington region: the **Petone Settlers Museum**, The Esplanade, Petone (Tues–Fri noon–4pm, Sat & Sun 1–5pm; $2), tells the tale of the early settlement. Across the alluvial plains north of Petone sprawls **LOWER HUTT**, home to the **Dowse Art Museum**, 45 Laings Rd (Mon–Fri 10am–4pm, Sat & Sun 11am–5pm; free; ☎04/570 6500), which admirably showcases high-calibre contemporary New Zealand art, with a strong leaning towards jewellery, ceramics, textiles and glass. The art theme continues 3km southeast at **Maori Treasures**, 58 Guthrie St (daily 9am–4pm; ☎04/939 9630, ⓦ www.maoritreasures.com) a classy Maori art studio, gallery and shop with carving in wood, greenstone and bone, painting, basketry, fibre arts, clay works and stone sculpture. Informative tours (3hr; $85) include a chance to watch artists at work, learn something of Maori artistic traditions and customs, touch a kiwi-feather cloak and make a flax souvenir.

By car, exit the SH2 motorway at the Petone off-ramp; by train, take one of the regular daily Tranz Metro commuter services from Wellington train station to Waterloo. From the station, the Dowse Art Museum is a 1.5-kilometre walk northwest down Knights Road; the Maori Treasures complex is ten-minutes' walk from the station in the opposite direction, along Guthrie Street off Cambridge Terrace.

Rimutaka Forest Park

Due south of Lower Hutt is the main entrance to the **Rimutaka Forest Park**, popular among city-dwellers for its series of easy short and **day-walks** in the attractive Catchpool Valley; there's also picnic and barbecue facilities, and a well-maintained **campsite** ($5), the nearest DOC site to Wellington. Some 20km from Wellington along the Coast Road, a signpost marks the park **entrance** (gates open 8am–dusk), from where Catchpool Road winds a further 2km up the valley to the car park, the starting point for most of the walks. Keen walkers/campers will want to get as far as the braided Orongorongo River, from where a startlingly grand landscape begins; you can camp for free along the riverbanks. There is no really convenient bus service, so you'll probably want to drive. Two hundred metres beyond the park entrance is a well-equipped **DOC field centre** (Dec–Feb daily 11am–4pm; March–Nov Sat & Sun 11am–4pm; ☎04/564 8551), which stocks the useful *Catchpool Valley/Rimutaka Forest Park* leaflet (50¢), detailing walks in the vicinity.

Activities

Being the capital city, Wellington isn't perhaps the sort of place you would expect to get into the outdoors much, but there are a number of worthwhile **activities**. Walking along the waterfront (particularly Oriental Parade) is great, and there are more arduous **hikes** through the encircling Town Belt (see box, p.510). **Bikers** can make use of much the same territory, and then there's the harbour.

Oriental Bay has a small, handy beach but if you're making an afternoon of it, head out to Scorching Bay (see p.507). To get out **on the water** there's a choice of gentle sailing or more active pursuits like windsurfing, kiteboarding and kayaking.

With its encircling wooded Town Belt, great city views from nearby hills and the temptation of watching seals along the southern coast, Wellington offers some excellent and easily accessible walking. Pick up relevant free leaflets from the visitor center.

Red Rocks Coastal Walk

Understandably popular, the easy **Red Rocks Coastal Walk** (4km each way; 2–3hr return) traces Wellington's southern shoreline to Sinclair head, where a colony of bachelor New Zealand **fur seals** takes up residence from May to October each year. The walk follows a rough track along the coastline from Owhiro Bay to Sinclair Head, passing a quarry and the eponymous **Red Rocks** – well-preserved volcanic pillow lava, formed about 200 million years ago by underwater volcanic eruptions and coloured red by iron oxide. Maori variously attribute the colour to bloodstains from Maui's nose or blood dripping from a *paua*-shell cut on Kupe's hand, while another account tells how Kupe's daughters cut themselves in mourning, having given up their father for dead.

The track starts around 7km south of the city centre at the quarry gates at the western end of Owhiro Bay Parade, where there's a car park. To get there by **bus** either take the frequent #1 to Island Bay, get off at The Parade at the corner of Reef Street and walk 2.5km to the start of the walk; or at peak times, catch #4 which continues to Happy Valley, only 1km from the track. Both leave downtown on Courtenay Place heading east. Alternatively join the Wellington Rover hop-on-hop-off bus or come with Seal Coast Safari (see p.490 for both).

The Southern Walkway

The **Southern Walkway** (11km; 4–5hr, or as shorter segments) cuts through the Town Belt to the south of the city centre, between Oriental and Island bays. Despite a few steep stretches it is fairly easy going overall. The walk offers plenty of variety, yielding excellent views of the harbour and central city (particularly from the summit of Mount Victoria and Mount Albert), shade, tranquillity, and rich scents in the pines of the Town Belt, and exposed coastline between Houghton and Island bays. Fantails, grey warblers and wax-eyes provide company, and Island Bay offers some of the city's best swimming.

The walk can be undertaken in either direction and is clearly marked by posts bearing orange arrows. To start at the city end, simply walk along Oriental Parade (or take **bus** #14 or #24) to the entrance to Charles Plimmer Park just past 350 Oriental Parade. To begin at the southern end, take the #1 bus to Island Bay and follow the signs from nearby Shorland Park.

The Northern Walkway

Extending through tranquil sections of the Town Belt to the north of the city centre, the **Northern Walkway** (16km; 4–5hr, or tackled in sections) offers spectacular views. Stretching from Kelburn to the suburb of Johnsonville, it covers five distinct areas – Botanic Garden, Tinakori Hill, Trelissick Park, Khandallah Park and Johnsonville Park – each accessible from suburban streets and served by public transport. Highlights are the **birdlife** on Tinakori Hill (tui, fantails, kingfishers, grey warblers, silver-eyes); the regenerating native forest of **Ngaio Gorge** in Trelissick Park; great views across the city and the harbour and over to the Rimutaka and Tararua ranges from a lookout on **Mount Kaukau** (430m); and, in **Johnsonville Park**, a disused road tunnel hewn through solid rock.

Start either at the top of the cable car and head north through the Botanic Garden, or join the walk at Tinakori Hill by climbing St Mary Street, off Glenmore Street, and following the orange arrows through woodland. To begin at the northern end, take a **train** to Raroa station on the Johnsonville line.

Sailing and windsurfing

Apart from Dominion Post Ferry out to Matiu/Somes Island and Days Bay (see p.508) Wellington makes only limited use of its harbour. For real **sailing** engage the services of the Dolphin Sailing Academy (☎04/586 0699, ⓦwww.dolphinsailing.co.nz) who take up to eight people on a 28-foot yacht letting passengers lend a hand or sit back and take in the atmosphere. The cost is $150 for the whole yacht so it is cheaper the more you can get along, though they'll help match up groups. Lunch and dinner cruises are also available.

Wellington's reliable winds make the harbour a great place for windsurfing and kiteboarding, with most action centred on Kio Bay, to the east of Oriental Bay and around the point towards Evans Bay. Unless you have your own gear, **windsurfers** should visit H2O Watersports, 251 Marine Parade, Seatoun (☎9463787 & 04/388 6164, ⓦwww.h2osports.co.nz). They rent gear by the hour ($25, $35 or $50 depending on quality) or by the day ($89, $109 or $135). They also do lessons at $35 an hour including all equipment and wetsuit. Get there on bus #11 or with Wellington Rover who offer a small saving on the windsurfing and tour combo.

For **kiteboarding** lessons, try Wildwinds, Chaffers Marina, Overseas Terminal (☎04/384 1010, ⓦwww.wildwinds.co.nz), just east of Te Papa, who offer a series of two-hour lessons to get you going: land-based at first ($80), then water-based ($100) and finally with the full rig ($120).

Kayaking, skating and rock climbing

If the sun's out and it's not too windy, **kayaking** along the waterfront is a great way to spend a couple of hours. Nip down to Queens Wharf and Ferg's Kayaks in Shed 6 (☎04/499 8898, ⓦwww.fergskayaks.co.nz; Oct–April Mon–Fri 9am–10pm, Sat & Sun 9am–8pm; May–Aug daily 10am–8pm) for **rental kayaks** (sit-on-top kayaks $12 for 2hr; singles $18 for 2hr, $40 per day; double $35/$80), or join one of their **guided trips** such as their Night Trip in double kayaks on calm nights, with romantic city–illuminated views, for a minimum of four people including a light supper (6–9pm; $45, book at least a week in advance).

Ferg's Kayaks also rent out **in-line skates** ($15 for 2hr including pads), perfect for use at nearby Frank Kitts Park or around Oriental Parade; and have a popular indoor **climbing wall** ($12 per person for 1hr including introductory lesson; equipment and shoes $6). They have discounts such as weekdays between 11am and 2pm, and do a proper Introduction to Rock Climbing session (3hr; $30). Groups of two or three work best so you can belay each other.

There's also indoor climbing on New Zealand's highest wall at Hang Dog Indoor Rock Climbing Cavern, 453 Hutt Road, Lower Hutt (daily 9am–9pm; ☎04/589 9181): contact the same folk for half a day abseiling down waterfalls ($50) or a full day **climbing and abseiling** ($75).

Cycling

Wellington is blessed with some great biking close to the city. Leisurely riders will want to avoid the hills inland, but riding the **coastal roads** can be a very pleasurable way to see the city. Start by heading east from Te Papa along Oriental Parade and follow the coast as far as you want; even right past the airport and around the northern tip of the Miramar Peninsula to Scorching Bay (see p.507) and Seatoun (25–30km one way).

For something more energetic there's a stack of **off-road riding**, much of it outlines in the *Mountain Biking in Wellington City* leaflet (available free from the visitor centre) which contains maps of key areas all a short ride from the city. Rides to consider include the coastal track out to Red Rocks (see "Walks around Wellington" box, p.510), the perimeter fence of the Karori Wildlife Sanctuary, and the singletrack trails around Mount Victoria. Committed mountain bikers flock to **Makara Peak Mountain Bike Park** (Ⓦwww .makarapeak.org.nz) an area of forest and farmland centred on the 412m Makara Peak, up behind Karori some 10km west of downtown Wellington. There's no entry fee and you'll have the run of 40km of tracks suitable for all abilities.

Bikes can be rented in town from Penny Farthing Cycle Shop, 89 Courtenay Place (Ⓣ04/385 2279) who charge $35 a day for a hardtail mountain bike, and right by Makara from Mud Cycles, 1 Allington Road, Karori (Ⓣ04/476 4961 Ⓦwww.mudcycles.co.nz) who charge $25 a half-day and $40 a day. The latter will also do guided bike tours ($35 for 3hr) and one-on-one lessons ($25 for two-hours).

Eating, drinking and entertainment

There's not much chance of going hungry or thirsty in Wellington, at least in the centre where you're spoilt for choice. In fact there's little need to venture much beyond the bounds of the CBD, though we've picked a couple of reasons to stray. It's a cosmopolitan scene, not least because Wellington is New Zealand's **coffee** capital, with the good stuff served up at numerous spots from the down-home to the *trés* chic.

Downtown, there's a plethora of ethnic restaurants – Malaysian and Indian places being particularly abundant – and a number of fancier places trying to lure the crowds around **Courtenay Place** and Cuba Street (and the adjacent Allen, Blair, Cuba and Dixon streets). The same area is home to some of the best **nightlife** in the country with a huge array of late-night cafés, bars and clubs, all within walking distance of each other. New places constantly spring up as tired ones just quietly drop off the perch or, after a lick of paint reinvent themselves under a different name. The partying goes on late into the night, and pumps hardest from Thursday to Saturday, when more secluded places nearby offer a less frenetic setting.

The **arts** are also strong with several theatres, and a healthy festival season.

Eating

During the day budget-minded visitors should make for one of the **food courts** which offer bargain grazing from an array of international outlets, though there are also budget lunch specials at many of the city's ethnic restaurants. For **groceries** head to New World Metro, 68 Willis St or the larger New World, at the eastern end of Wakefield Street near Te Papa.

Food Courts and takeaways

Asian Food Market Cable Street. Rather dowdy surroundings but good for authentic Indian, Chinese, Malaysian, Middle Eastern and Bengali food. Open Fri–Sun 10am–5.30pm.
BNZ Centre Food Court in the basement at 1 Willis St. The standard setup with counters selling sushi, Thai, Chinese, Mexican, Indian, and Turkish plus a bakery and the licensed café. Closed evenings and all day Sun.

The Catch 48 Courtenay Place. Inexpensive sushi bar with dishes revolving on the countertop conveyor belt (plates are colour-coded according to price), to take away or eat in; also does side orders and bigger meals ($10–20) from a set menu. Closed Sun lunch.
Pandoro on the corner of Wakefield & Allen Sts. Excellent specialist bakery supplying all manner of loaves, as well as sandwiches for $6 or under, to eat at one of their two tables, washed down with a coffee.

Wellington Trawling Sea Market 220 Cuba St. An absurdly long name for the best fish-and-chip shop in the city, eat in or takeaway, which also sells wet fish. Closed Sun eve.

Cafés

Caffè Mode 86a Upland Road ☎ 04/939 0090. Relaxed little café less than ten minutes walk from the top of the cable car and the Botanical Gardens. Pop in for coffee, cakes, quiches ($5) or lunch, which might include a roasted vegetable stack ($14).

Chocolate Fish Café 497a Karaka Rd, Scorching Bay ☎ 04/388 2808. Bustling waterside café in Wellington's eastern suburbs that's typically popular with locals (especially at weekends) and was a regular haunt of *Lord of the Rings* cast and crew. Along with the usual café fare they do a good bircher muesli breakfast and a popular kidney, bacon and mushroom mix. Suitable for kids too.

Crumbs the Bakers Aiken St ☎ 04/499 2898. Rub shoulders with breakfasting or lunching civil servants in this modern bakery/café, great for coffee and cake or meals like chicken udon noodles ($12) or panini and salad ($8).

Deluxe 10 Kent Terrace ☎ 04/801 5455. Great coffee and low-cost cakes and savouries, much of them vegetarian, served in a slightly off-beat café that's popular with the post-cinema and theatre crowd.

Dorothy 136 Cuba St ☎ 04/385 7324. Perch in little booths in this small patisserie and chocolaterie where hot chocolate drinks, handmade chocolates and French pastries supplement the usual menu of espresso coffees.

Espressoholic 128 Courtenay Place. Long-standing Wellington favourite famed for its sinful desserts and hot chocolates at virtually any hour (especially at weekends). Come for breakfast, panini, cakes, pasta dishes ($15), mains ($18–20) and assorted beers and wine. Also plenty of newspapers and magazines for perusing and some backyard seating.

Eva Dixon's Place 35 Dixon St, above *The Fat Ladies Arms*. Overlooking but oddly removed from the bustle of Courtenay Place, this relaxed café with a devoted local (and gay) following serves breakfast all day, has good coffee, homemade cakes a tasty $12 Caesar salad and larger meals (around $18).

Felix cnr Cuba St & Wakefield St. A happening all-day café bar where you can enjoy pasta or udon noodles for under $20, or their famous copper-pan breakfast/brunch of eggs, bacon sausage, toms and hash browns ($15), while sipping strong coffee and browsing the newspapers.

Fidel's 234 Cuba St. Located at the off-beat end of Cuba Street, with clientele to match, this café/restaurant comes plastered with revolution-era pics of Castro and includes a camouflage–netted, open-air seating area at the back for smokers. Come for coffee and smoothies, or a great chicken laksa ($12).

Kopi 103 Willis St. Something of an antidote to Wellington coffee-houses. Good-value Malaysian dishes such as roti and chicken korma (from 10am till late; $15) in a cosy café on two floors, with smoking allowed on a small balcony upstairs. Licensed & BYO.

Masala 2–12 Allen St ☎ 04/3852012. Snazzy modern Indian that feels like a big friendly café serving good quality lunches and dinners daily. They do $6 lunch specials with free rice and naan and some hot steamy curries.

Midnight Espresso 178 Cuba St. A caffeine junkie's heaven, this mellow coffee-house peddles beans for all palates. Sip a cup on its own, with breakfast or alongside a cheap snack (good toasted sandwiches, focaccia and pizza, plus vegetarian and vegan food), while poring over their reading material. Open until around 3am.

Nikau Gallery Café City Gallery, Civic Square. Stylish, contemporary daytime café/bar with an airy setting, an outdoor terrace, excellent coffee and a reasonably priced menu: try the kedgeree made with smoked warehou.

Olive 170 Cuba St ☎ 04/5266. Relaxed and spacious bare-boards café that's great for coffee and cakes, but also does delicious breakfasts (organic porridge $7; French toast with bacon and banana $13) and full meals like their antipasti plate ($18) and lamb shanks in a red wine sauce ($23). Closed Sun & Mon evenings.

Roti Chenai 120 Victoria St ☎ 04/3829807. Tiny, simple South Indian and Malaysian café with an open kitchen in the middle where roti are prepared in front of your eyes, as well as delicious *dosai*, *murtabak*, curries and *rendang*. Lunch specials ($6–8) are great value, dinner mains cost $14–17. Licensed & BYO.

Sahara Café 39 Courtenay Place ☎ 04/385 6362. Not to be confused with the kebab takeaway next door, this is an intimate venue for quality Middle Eastern dinners (mostly $15–18), plus belly dancing and live music on Sat. Book ahead at weekends. Licensed & BYO.

Stamp and Go 21 Marjoribanks St. A refreshing addition to the café scene is this lively Caribbean-style eat-in and takeaway that specializes in wraps and baps filled with spicy sausage and Jamaican Pepperpot (slow-simmered shin beef), Jamaican patties, Jerk chicken and char-grilled vegies, salted cod fritters and fresh mango lassi. Closed Mon.

Sushi of Japan 189 Cuba St. One of a national chain that do excellent value sushi and miso soups. Daytime only, closed Sun.

The Vegetarian Café 179 Cuba St. Calming, mostly vegan spot with a broad-ranging menu that includes meals in a bowl ($7–13). Closed Wed & Sat evening and all day Sun; no alcohol allowed.

Restaurants

Angkor 43 Dixon St ☎04/384 9423. An affordable, spacious Cambodian restaurant with a fine line in delicious curries and spicy grilled dishes complemented by a good range of local wines. Go for the chicken tamarind soup ($9) or pumpkin-seed salad ($9) followed by lamb grilled with lemongrass and garlic ($22). Closed Sun.

Chow 45 Tory St. Hip restaurant serving tasty and beautifully presented Southeast Asian dishes in a stylish, modern setting. The noodle soups ($16–19) are great and there's a wide selection of "long plates" ($11–14) ideal as side dishes or in combination as a banquet – go for the Thai chicken wrapped in banana leaf with sweet chilli jam, or the Cantonese roasted duck with stewed shitaki & fresh egg noodles. Linked to *Motel* (see p.515).

Dockside Shed 3, Queens Wharf ☎04/499 9900. Classy place-to-be-seen restaurant and bar in a vast converted wooden warehouse with a glass frontage and deck area overlooking the harbour, serving lunch and dinner, plus brunch at weekends. Hot on seafood – try the Dockside Fish and Chips, $22, and other fish dishes for $20–40. Book if you want a window seat.

Maria Pia's 55 Mulgrave St ☎04/499 5590. Maria Pia is passionate about her food, and it shows in this cosy southern Italian trattoria and wine bar. The menu varies seasonally and almost everything is cooked from scratch using mostly organic ingredients. Stop in for lunch while touring the Parliamentary District, or make a special effort and come for dinner and expect to pay $20–25 for a main course. A must. Closed Sat lunch plus all day Sun & Mon.

Matterhorn 106 Cuba St ☎04/384 3359. Glam bar and restaurant accessed down a narrow corridor which opens into a beautiful haven of cream concrete, dark wood panelling and red velvet. It is always popular with the beautiful people but welcoming enough to pop in for a beer or a cocktail (try the basil and manuka honey martini; $15) perhaps with a selection of their $5 bowls of tapas. Food is served all day and is beautifully done: try the breakfast avocado on toast with grilled lime ($10), the pan fried *tarakihi* with broccolini ($23) and the vanilla rice pudding with roasted pear ($10).

Nicolini's 26 Courtenay Place. A genuine no-fuss, inexpensive Neapolitan restaurant, small, bustling and full of divine smells and colourful food. Delicious pork scaloppine, fish marinara, reasonably priced wine and a friendly atmosphere. Mains $15–20.

Strawberry Fare 25 Kent Terrace ☎04/385 2551. A sweet-lovers delight, this restaurant is principally known for its fabulous range of two dozen sumptuous desserts (mostly $12–15).

Uncle Chang's 72 Courtenay Place. The best Chinese in town, for lunch and dinner daily. Great rice noodle soups and combination menus for $23–39 per person. Licensed & BYO. Closed Mon.

Vista 106 Oriental Parade ☎04/385 7724. Welcoming and casual wood-floored café handily sited five minutes walk from Courtenay Place, serving a wide range of breakfasts (including black & white pudding; $15), a great seafood laksa ($14) and dinner mains such as twice-cooked pork loin with baby bok choy ($22). Daily 9am–11pm.

Zico 8 Courtenay Place ☎04/802 5585. Young, exuberant, authentic Italian that won't break the bank, with veal scaloppini, creamy risotto, calamari and seafood laksa mostly around $18–20 mark. Daily for lunch & dinner.

The White House 232 Oriental Parade ☎04/385 8555. Great harbour views and exquisite food makes *The White House* one of Wellington dining's picks. Expect the likes of mushroom risotto with truffle oil ($16), followed by chargrilled tuna with tamari sauce and wasabi infused mash ($32) with crème caramel with strawberries in balsamic dressing ($16) to finish. Open nightly & for lunch Wed–Fri.

Drinking and nightlife

Most **pubs** and **bars** are open daily, from around eleven in the morning until around midnight or later. Those closest to the business district, The Terrace and Lambton Quay, tend to be the most expensive. The distinction between bars and **clubs** is often blurred with many of the bars having free live music and dancing in the evenings, especially at weekends. Guest and celebrity DJs mix broad-ranging styles to create a party- or club-style atmosphere. Live **bands** (usually Kiwi but sometimes international) are a regular fixture, playing in bars, dedicated smaller venues or bigger halls like the Queens Wharf Events Centre

The scene in Wellington is focused in the inner city, particularly around **Courtenay Place**, and woven into the general café/bar mainstream; and though smaller than that of Auckland, it tends to be less cliquey and judgemental. In the centre, at least, gays openly express affection in public, and gays, lesbians, transgender and bi-folk mix freely together. You're unlikely to find hostility anywhere downtown but **venues** worth checking out are *Eva Dixon's, Pound/Sovereign* and *Valve*, all listed separately in the appropriate sections on p.513 & p.516. There are a couple of **cruise clubs** make good sources of information on what's happening: Club Wakefield, 15 Tory St (☎04/385 4400), and Sanctuary, 3rd floor, 39 Dixon St (☎04/384 1565).

For **information** on venues and events at other times, check out Wellington's free gay monthly *UP*, the national gay fortnightly **newspaper** *Express* ($2.50; ⓦwww.gayexpress.co.nz), available free from the YHA and Unity Books (see "Bookshops", p.517); or the national *OUT* magazine. Other contacts are the Gay Switchboard (☎04/473 7878; daily 7.30–10pm), the Lesbian Line (☎04/499 5567, ⓔwgtnlesbianline@hotmail.com; Tues, Thurs & Sat 7.30–10pm), and the Lesbian and Gay Advisory Group which produces a free *Guide to Groups in Wellington*: good for longer stayers.

(☎04/472 5021) and occasionally in **free concerts** in the waterfront Frank Kitts Park or at the Civic Square.

Pubs and bars

The Backbencher Pub cnr Molesworth St & Kate Sheppard St, opposite the Parliament Buildings. A favourite with MPs not just for the satirical cartoons and puppets (see p.501) but for the cosy atmosphere, the dozen or more draught beers and good unpretentious food such as chicken tostadas ($12) and fish and chips ($13). At its busiest on Fri night, when there's often free live music.

Coyote 63 Courtenay Place. Urban Santa Fe-style bar that pulls in the dance crowds on Fri & Sat nights with its own brand of commercial and hard house. Reasonably priced drinks and with a low-key crowd.

The Fat Ladies Arms 35 Dixon St. A no frills, studenty sort of bar that's good for a drinking session. Gets loud at weekends.

Hummingbird 22 Courtenay Place ☎04/801 6336. Predominantly a chic but relaxed bar with dark wood panelling and large windows opening out onto Courtenay Place. Come for a feijoa martini or something from the extensive wine list, and stick around for tapas ($12–15) such as duck sausage, peppered fillet steak, and saffron risotto or full meals ($25–30). Live music on Sun. Open until 3am most nights.

Leuven 135–137 Featherston St ☎04/499 2939. Belgian-style beer café in the heart of the business district, good for breakfasts of Belgian pancakes ($13) and full meals – 1kg of mussels in curried cream, apple and coriander with fries and mayo for $17 – but especially popular for early evening tie-loosening sessions over a Hoegaarden or three.

The Malthouse 47 Willis St. Airy first-floor bar with table service and a pleasant balcony over the street where over thirty high-quality naturally brewed Kiwi beers are on tap, swilled by a mixture of businesspeople and discerning ale-heads, especially on Fri evening.

Matterhorn 106 Cuba St. An eternally cool spot for a beer or a cocktail anytime. See p.514.

Molly Malone's cnr Taranaki St & Courtenay Place. Hugely atmospheric, loud and in-your-face Irish pub, with foot-tapping live Irish music every evening (jam sessions on Mon night). Upstairs is the quieter *Dubliner* restaurant and bar, serving snacks, $10–12 lunches, reasonable dinners and weekend brunches, though Sat nights a musician plays up here too.

Motel Foresters Lane ☎04/382 8585. Once so exclusive it reputedly turned away Liv Tyler when she was in town shooting *The Lord of the Rings*, this retro chic bar still cuts it with its white-jacketed waiters, semi-private booths and cool sounds (mostly jazz). It is notoriously difficult to find: head up Tory St from Courtenay Place and take the first alley on the left. Open until late nightly.

Clubs and gigs

The Blue Note cnr Cuba St & Vivian St ☎04/801 5007. Dark club open every night from 4pm (till 6am Sun–Fri, till 3am Sat) regularly hosting live jazz or acoustic bands; usually free midweek with occasional cover charge of $5–15 at weekends.

Bodega 101 Ghuznee St. Now around the corner from its original home, but still Wellington's longest-running musical institution. Every Kiwi band worth its salt has played here; DJs also visit, and it sometimes hosts dance parties. Great atmosphere is the draw in this small bar aimed at a slightly older drinking crowd.

Pound/Sovereign Level One, Oaks Complex, Dixon St ℡ 04/384 8445, ⓦ www.pound.co.nz. A big dance venue (Fri & Sat 11pm–5am) with a gay following; also works as a bar called *Sovereign* (from 5pm) with pool table, juke box and early evening happy hours.

StudioNine Upstairs at 9 Edward St ℡ 04/384 9976. Wellington's premiere dance locale that draws the young and hip with DJs playing house, dance, techno, high NRG and jungle. Cover charge $15–20, depending on the DJ; also has rave-style parties some weekends.

Valve 154 Vivian St ℡ 04/385 1630. Lively venue with gigs or DJs almost every night with the emphasis on hardcore, garage punk, Drum 'n' Bass and the like. Occasional gay Boyznite from 8.30pm on Wednesdays.

Wellington Sports Café cnr Courtenay Place & Tory St. Late-night post-pub dancing in a sports bar. Live music every other Thurs, DJs playing middle-of-the-road dance and chart music Thurs–Sat, and expensive drinks. Nightly until late.

Performing arts and festivals

Performing arts are strong in Wellington: it is home to four professional theatres, the Royal New Zealand Ballet, the New Zealand Symphony Orchestra, and assorted opera and dance companies. The best introduction to what's on is the *Wellington – What's On* booklet, free from the visitor centre and from accommodation around the city. There are also weekend **listings** in *The Dominion Post*, while bland reviews and more useful listings appear in both of the city's free ad-ridden weekly *Capital Times*, which you can pick up at the visitor centre and from racks around town.

Classical music, theatre and cinema

The city regularly hosts **orchestral** and other performances, while four professional **theatres** stage Kiwi and international shows. Tickets normally cost $30 upwards (average $40), but the visitor centre sells theatre tickets cheaper depending on availability. In addition to its quota of multiplexes, Wellington also has a smattering of arthouse **cinemas**: you can usually save a couple of dollars by going during the day or any time early in the week.

Book **tickets** direct at venues or, for a small fee, through Ticketek (℡ 04/384 3840, ⓦ www.ticketek.co.nz), who have outlets at the St James Theatre, 77–87 Courtenay Place.

Theatres and concert halls

Bats Theatre 1 Kent Terrace ℡ 04/802 4175, ⓦ www.bats.co.nz. Lively theatre concentrating on developmental works served up at affordable prices.

Circa cnr Taranaki St & Cable St ℡ 04/801 7992, ⓦ www.circa.co.nz. One of the country's liveliest and most innovative professional theatres, which has fostered the skills of some of the best-known Kiwi directors and actors. At either of the two spaces in this new complex (the main house and a 100-seater Studio) you can count on intimate, imaginative productions.

The Downstage cnr Courtenay Place & Cambridge Terrace ℡ 04/801 6946, ⓦ www .downstage.co.nz. Stages both its own productions and the best touring shows: a mix of mainstream and new drama, dance and comedy, with the emphasis on quality Kiwi work. Cheaper gallery seats available.

Opera House 111–113 Manners St ℡ 04/384 3840, ⓦ www.stjames.co.nz. Hosts touring opera, ballet and musicals.

Town Hall (Michael Fowler Centre), 111 Wakefield St ℡ 04/801 4325, ⓦ www .wellingtonconventioncentre.com. Wellington's major venue for orchestral and other performances.

Westpac St James Theatre 77–87 Courtenay Place ☎04/802 4060, ⓦwww.stjames.co.nz. This refurbished theatre in a fine 1912 building, is the major venue for the Royal New Zealand Ballet and host to opera, dance, musicals and plays. It also has a licensed café for pre- and post-performance drinks.

Westpac Stadium Between Aotea Quay and Waterloo Quay. Dubbed "the cake tin" by its detractors for its iron-clad design, this modern purpose-built stadium near the ferry terminal is the venue for all things rugby and cricket (although cricket tests are still played at the Basin Reserve), and acts as an occasional rock concert venue.

Cinemas

Embassy 10 Kent Terrace ☎04/384 7657, ⓦwww.deluxe.co.nz. Recently revamped for the December 2003 world premiere of *The Return of the King*, the Embassy shows mainstream and

independent movies on a single giant screen in the city centre.

Regent on Manners 73 Manners Mall ☎04/472 5182, ⓦwww.hoyts.co.nz. Mainstream movies for $10 ($8.50 on Tues): the cheapest in town.

Paramount 25 Courtenay Place ☎04/384 4080, ⓦwww.paramount.co.nz. A central venue showing both arthouse and mainstream movies on three screens, which you can watch while sipping a glass of beer or wine.

Reading Cinemas 100 Courtenay Place ☎04/801 4610, ⓦwww.readingcinemas.co.nz. Mostly mainstream movies ($13) with the option of going for their plush Cinélounge seats ($28) which come with unlimited free pop and popcorn plus in-seat food and drink service.

Rialto cnr Cable St & Jervois Quay ☎04/385 1864, ⓦwww.rialto.co.nz. Independent and avant-garde productions, plus special screenings of New Zealand films.

Festivals

Whenever you visit Wellington there's a good chance there'll be some sort of arts-related festival happening. The visitor centre has full details, but the following are the biggest occasions, listed chronologically.

New Zealand International Arts Festival ☎04/473 0149, ⓦwww.nzfestival.telecom.co.nz. Month-long festival held in March of even-numbered years, which draws the top performers from around the world to the country's biggest cultural event. Fashioned along the lines of the Edinburgh Festival, it celebrates the huge diversity of the arts, performances include classical music, jazz and pop, tragic opera, puppet shows and the Grotesque, cabaret, poetry readings, traditional Maori dance, modern ballet and experimental works – and most of the venues are within easy walking distance of one another.

Wellington Fringe Festival ⓦwww.fringe.org.nz. Originally part of the Arts festival, this vibrant affair

is now run as a separate and roughly concurrent event filling the inner city with street and indoor theatre.

Wellington Film Festival ⓦwww.enzedff.co.nz. Typically held from mid-July to early August, with less mainstream offerings playing at cinemas around town.

Wellington International Jazz Festival ⓦwww.jazzfestival.co.nz. A two-week festival in October bringing some of the world's best performers primarily to the *Jazz Club*, 107 Cuba Street. As well as official mid-evening concerts there are free performances in restaurants and bars, and improvised sessions in Civic Square, on the waterfront and all over the city.

Listings

Airlines and flights Details of Wellington's international and domestic flights (including airline contact details) are given in the appropriate section of Basics. For details of transport to the airport see p.485, and remember there is a $25 airport tax when leaving the country that is not included in your ticket price.

American Express Client mail and emergency cheque cashing are now handled by Holiday Shoppe (see "Travel Agents" p.518).

Automobile Association 342–352 Lambton Quay ☎04/931 9999.

Banks and foreign exchange Banks are dotted all over the CBD, but to change money head along the southern end of Lambton Quay to: ANZ at 215–229 Lambton Quay ☎0800/180 925; BNZ at 1 Willis St ☎04/474 6000; and Travelex at 108 Lambton Quay ☎04/473 5167, 358 Lambton Quay ☎04/472 2848, and at the airport ☎04/801 0130.

Bike rental See "Cycling" on p.511.

Bookshops The best selection of New Zealand and special interest (especially gay and lesbian) books is Unity Books, 57 Willis St ☎04/499 4245.

It is also good for more mainstream fare, as are the majors: Whitcoulls, 312 Lambton Quay ☎04/472 1921 and 91 Cuba St ☎04/384 2065; and Dymocks, 360 Lambton Quay ☎04/472 2080. For good secondhand and book exchanges try Arty Bee's Books, 17 Courtenay Place ☎04/385 1819; Bellamy's, 105 Cuba St ☎04/384 7770; and Crossroads, 110 Featherston St ☎04/499 5212.

Buses InterCity and Newmans (both ☎04/472 5111) run services all over the North Island. See Travel Details (p.519) for frequencies and route durations.

Camping and outdoor equipment Mainly Tramping, 39 Mercer St ☎04/473 5353 are conveniently sited; Bivouac, 138 The Terrace ☎04/473 2587 have the top brands and knowledgeable staff; Ski & Camp, 52 Taranaki St ☎04/801 8704 also provide a repair service for tents, backpacks, stoves and lights; and Kathmandu, 57 Willis St ☎04/472 0113 are great for cheap clothing when they have their frequent sales.

Car rental As well as the companies covered in Basics (see p.32) various local firms offer good deals: Nationwide, 37–39 Hutt Rd ☎04/473 1165 & 0800/803 003, ⓦ www.nationwiderentals.co.nz; Rent-a-Dent, 50 Tacy St, Kilbirnie ☎04/387 9931, ⓔ wellingtonairport@rentadent.co.nz; and Wellington Carhire, 138 Adelaide Rd, Newtown ☎04/389 2983, ⓦ www.carrentalcentrre.co.nz.

Embassies and consulates Australia, 72 Hobson St, Thorndon ☎04/473 6411; Canada, 61 Molesworth St ☎04/473 9577; Germany, 90 Hobson St, Thorndon ☎04/473 6063; Netherlands, Investment House, Featherstone St ☎04/471 6390; Thailand, 21 Cook St ☎04/476 8618; UK, 44 Hill St (☎04/472 6049); USA, 29 Fitzherbert Terrace, Thorndon (☎04/472 2068); for other countries, look in Yellow Pages, under "Diplomatic and consular representatives".

Internet access Plenty of places, mostly along Courtenay Place, generally charging $4 an hour. Try: Em@il Shop, inside the visitor centre (all Macs); or @Internet, 97 Courtenay Place.

Library Wellington's Central Library (Mon–Thurs 9.30am–8.30pm, Fri 9.30am–9pm; Sat 9.30am–5pm, Sun 1–4pm; ☎04/801 4060) is on Victoria Street, where it backs onto Civic Square.

Market James Smith's Market is a popular flea market on cnr Cuba St & Manners St, second floor. Open to 6pm, and 9pm on Friday.

Medical emergencies For emergencies call ☎111. If less critical call the Free Ambulance (☎04/472 2999) for the nearest on-duty doctor; for 24hr emergency treatment, the After-Hours Medical Centre, 17 Adelaide Rd, Newtown, near Basin Reserve ☎04/384 4944. Wellington Hospital is on Riddiford St, Newtown ☎04/385 5999. For dental care, try Symes deSilva & Associates, Second Floor, 97 Courtenay Place ☎04/801 5551 or check the Yellow Pages under Dentists.

Newspapers *The Dominion Post* is the local morning paper, its influence spreading over much of the southern half of the North Island. Events and entertainment listings are best on Thursday and Saturday. The free weekly *Capital Times* has a round-up of events and plenty of listings: pick it up in cafés and the like.

Pharmacy Unichem Eddie Fletcher Pharmacy 204 Lambton Quay ☎04/472 0362 is handy, but for late service go to After Hours Pharmacy, 17 Adelaide Rd, Newtown ☎04/385 8801 (Mon–Fri 5–11pm, Sat, Sun & public holidays 8am–11pm).

Photographic supplies Wellington Photographic Supplies, 11–15 Vivian St ☎04/384 3713. The place for digital and film needs.

Police Wellington Central Police Station, cnr Victoria St & Harris St ☎04/381 2000.

Post office There are several throughout the downtown area. For poste restante go to the Post Shop, 43 Manners St (Mon–Fri 8.30am–5pm, Sat 10am–1.30pm; ☎04/473 5922).

Swimming Freyberg Pool and Fitness Centre, 139 Oriental Parade ☎04/801 4530 (daily 6am–9pm, Fri closes 5.30pm), has a 33-metre indoor pool ($3.50 to swim), plus gym, spas, saunas, steam-room, fitness classes and massage therapy.

Taxis The biggest company is Wellington Combined Taxis ☎04/384 4444 & 0800/384 444. Also try Central City Taxis ☎04/499 4949; Gold & Black Taxis ☎04/388 8888; or Wellington City Cabs ☎0800/2580 2580. Authorized stands are located at the train station; on Whitmore St (between Lambton Quay & Featherston St); outside the *James Smith Hotel* on Lambton Quay; off Willis St on the Bond St cnr; outside Woolworths on Dixon St; and at the junction of Willis & Aro streets.

Travel agents Air New Zealand Travel Centre, cnr Lambton Quay & Panama St ☎04/474 8950; branches of Holiday Shoppe at 99 Willis Street (☎04/473 1230), 184 Lambton Quay (☎04/473 1199), and 101 - 103 Courtenay Place (☎04/382 8747); STA Travel at 130 Cuba St ☎04/385 0561 and 100 Courtenay Place ☎04/385 4917.

Travel details

Unsurprisingly, Wellington is a major transportation hub with trains and buses homing in on the ferries which cross Cook Strait to Picton and the South Island (see p.525). Here we've only listed direct buses and flights but there are numerous connections to further flung places.

Buses

Wellington to: Auckland (2–3 daily; 11hr); Masterton via the Hutt Valley (4 daily; 2hr); Napier (3 daily; 5hr 15min); New Plymouth (2 daily; 6hr 30min); Palmerston North (5–6 daily; 2hr); Paraparaumu (9 daily; 50min); Rotorua (3 daily; 7hr); Taupo (5 daily; 6hr).

Trains

Wellington to: Auckland (2 daily; 11hr); Hamilton (2 daily; 9hr); Hutt Central/Waterloo (every 30min; 20 min); Levin (2–3 daily; 1hr 30min); Masterton (2–6 daily; 1hr 30min); National Park (2 daily; 5hr 30min); Otaki (2–3 daily; 1hr 20min); Otorohanga (2 daily; 8hr); Palmerston North (2–3 daily; 2hr 20min); Paraparaumu (every 30min; 1hr); Taihape (2 daily; 4hr).

Ferries

Wellington to: Picton (5–10 daily; 2hr 15min–3hr).

Flights

Wellington to: Auckland (25–30 daily; 1hr); Blenheim (15 daily; 25min); Christchurch (25–30 daily; 45min); Dunedin (4–6 daily; 1hr 15min–2hr 15min); Gisborne (4–5 daily; 1hr); Hamilton (10–12 daily; 1hr); Napier/Hastings (6–8 daily; 50min); Nelson (15–20 daily; 35min); New Plymouth (6–8 daily; 55min); Palmerston North (3 daily; 30min); Picton (8 daily; 25min); Rotorua (5 daily; 1hr 15min); Taupo (3 daily; 1hr); Tauranga (5 daily; 1hr 15min); Timaru (3 daily; 1hr 15min); Westport (1 daily; 55min); Whangarei (1 daily; 1hr 30min).

Marlborough, Nelson and Kaikoura

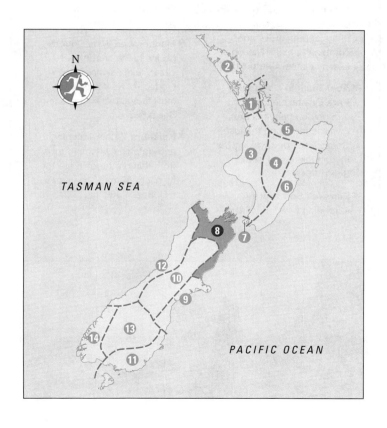

CHAPTER 8

Highlights

✳ **The Queen Charlotte Track** Staying in great backpackers and B&Bs, and having your bags carried for you makes tramping this beautiful track far easier than most. See p.534

✳ **Nelson** A vibrant arts community, vineyards on the doorstep, a laidback atmosphere and great weather combine to make Nelson an essential stop. See p.542

✳ **Abel Tasman National Park** Crystal clear water and golden beaches are rewards for hiking the lush Coast Track or kayaking the myriad inlets and islands. See p.554

✳ **Farewell Spit tours** A surprising array of wildlife can be seen on four wheel-drive tours along this thin strip of ocean-girt desert. See p.571

✳ **Heaphy Track** The huge range of dramatic scenery and final sense of achievement make this Great Walk worth the effort. See p.575

✳ **Marlborough Wine Country** No trip to this area is complete without sampling the produce of New Zealand's most famous wine region. See p.582

✳ **Kaikoura** Whale watching and dolphin swimming trips from this pretty town are the highlight of many a visitor's trip. See p.589

△ Abel Tasman National Park

Marlborough, Nelson and Kaikoura

T he South Island kicks off spectacularly. The whole northern section is supremely alluring from the indented bays and secluded hideaways of the Marlborough Sounds and the sweep of golden beaches around Nelson to an impressive array of national parks, sophisticated wineries around Marlborough and the natural wonders of Kaikoura. In fact, if you had to choose only one area of New Zealand to visit, this would be a strong contender.

Most visitors travel between the North Island and the South Island by ferry, striking land at the town of **Picton** – drab in the winter, lively in the summer and surrounded by the rugged and beautiful **Marlborough** Sounds. Here, bays full of unfathomably deep water lap at tiny beaches each with its rickety boat jetty, and the land rises steeply to forest or stark pasture.

To the west, the lively yet relaxed city of **Nelson**, is the starting point for forays to wilder spots further north. Some of the country's most gorgeous walking tracks and dazzling golden beaches populate the **Abel Tasman National Park**, while yet further north the relatively isolated **Golden Bay** offers peaceful times in relaxed settings. The curve of the Golden Bay culminates in a long sandy bar that juts into the ocean, **Farewell Spit**, an extraordinary and unique habitat. It borders the Kahurangi National Park, through which the rugged and spectacular **Heaphy Track** forges a route to the West Coast.

The most neglected of the region's preserved areas is the sparsely populated **Nelson Lakes National Park**, principally a spot for tramping to alpine lakes with relatively little company, though the nearby **Buller River** also lures raft rats.

South of Picton, you can slurp your merry way through **Marlborough**, New Zealand's most renowned wine-making region centred on the modest towns of **Blenheim** and **Renwick**. A night or two in one of the rural B&Bs and some time spent sampling the wares happily balances the more energetic activities of the national parks, and sets you up nicely for a few days of ecotourism in **Kaikoura**. **Whale watching** and **swimming with dolphins** and seals are the main draws, but there's also pleasure in local walks or just relaxing outside one of the cafés.

The region's **weather** is some of the sunniest in the land, particularly around Blenheim and Nelson which regularly compete for the honour of the greatest number of sunshine hours in New Zealand. The climate is mild throughout the year though the **peak season** is December to February when the Abel Tasman

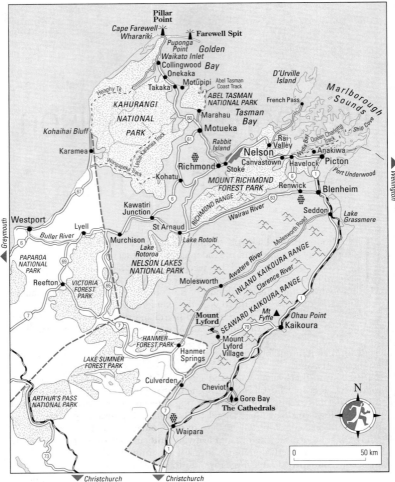

National Park and Queen Charlotte Track are enormously popular. For more solitude and the chance to travel without having to book everything in advance, it makes more sense to visit either side of high season if you can.

The Marlborough Sounds

The **Marlborough Sounds** are undeniably picturesque, whetting the appetite for the rest of the South Island and providing a lingering first impression for those travelling by ferry from the North Island. The Sounds' coastline is a stimulating filigree of bays, inlets, islands and peninsulas rising abruptly from the water to rugged, lush green wilderness and cleared farmland. Large parts are only accessible by sea, which also provides the ideal vantage point for witnessing its splendour. The area is part working farms, including salmon or mussel farms, and part given over to some fifty-nine reserve areas – a mixture of islands, sections of coast and land-bound tracts. The Sounds' nexus, **Picton**, is the jumping-off point for **Queen Charlotte Sound** where cruises and water taxi provide access to the rewarding and very manageable **Queen Charlotte Track**. Heading west, Queen Charlotte Drive winds precipitously to the small community of **Havelock**, which is well worth a stop to explore the delightful **Pelorus Sound** and maybe tramping the **Nydia Track**. Most then carry on to Nelson and the Abel Tasman National Park, but if you've got time to spare consider exploring the road to the swirling waters of **French Pass**.

Picton and around

Cross-strait ferries from Wellington arrive at **PICTON**, a nicely set small town sandwiched between the hills and the deep, placid waters of Queen Charlotte Sound. In between ferry arrivals it is a fairly sleepy place where you'd be forgiven for having a coffee looking out over the water and pressing on. But there's interest in the shape of the historic *Edwin Fox* ship, a few local walks and, of course, the proximity of Queen Charlotte Sound. **Cruises and kayak trips** help you get out on the water, dive trips explore the depths, and the water taxis buzz across to access the lovely **Queen Charlotte Track**. Picton also makes a decent base for exploring the **wine region** around Blenheim, half an hour's drive to the south. Companies offering trips around the wineries mostly pick up in Picton (see p.585).

There was a European settlement in the region as early as 1827 when John Guard established a whaling station, but Picton itself didn't come into being until the New Zealand Company purchased the town site for £300 in 1848. Picton flourished as a port and **service town** for the Wairau Plains to the south but predominantly as the most convenient port for travel between the islands. It will probably keep this status for years to come, but the desire for ever faster transport keeps alive the proposal to establish a new ferry terminal at Clifford Bay southeast of Blenheim.

Arrival and information

Ferries dock in Picton Harbour, 600m from the town centre and just steps away from the **train station** which is perfect for transfers to the daily TranzCoastal **train** to Christchurch: one-way fares start at $35. Interislandline ferry and Fast Cat schedules work in well with train times in both directions. **Buses** stop outside the passenger ferry terminal and again at the visitor centre (see below). **Vehicles** crossing Cook Strait travel on the same ferries but disembark on the western side of town about 1km from the centre. Koromiko **airport**, 9km south of town, is served by Soundsair flights from Wellington (☎03/520 3080 & 0800/505 005; see p.582). Their own free bus meets flights and runs into Picton.

The combined **visitor centre** (daily: Jan–Feb 8am–6pm; Oct–Dec & March–Sept 8.30am–5pm; ☎03/520 3113, ⓦwww.picton.gen.nz) and **DOC office** (daily 8.30am–5pm; ☎03/520 3002) is on the foreshore, five minutes' walk from the ferry terminal. It is packed with leaflets on the town and the rest of the South Island, including several worthwhile maps: the free *Picton and Waikawa Street*

For details of **transport** between the **North and South islands**, see "Listings" on p.518.

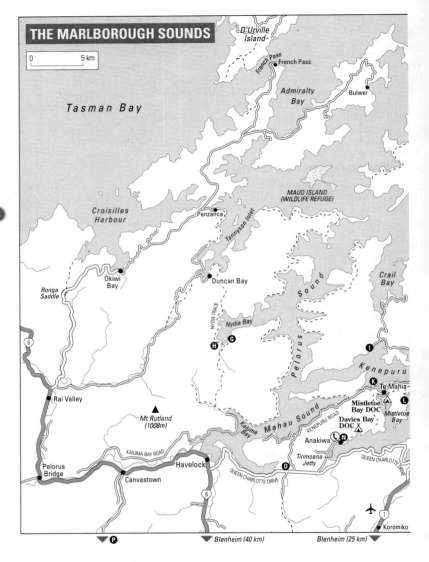

THE MARLBOROUGH SOUNDS

0 _____ 5 km

D'Urville Island

French Pass
French Pass

Admiralty Bay

Bulwer

Tasman Bay

MAUD ISLAND
(WILDLIFE REFUGE)

Croisilles Harbour

Penzance

Tennyson Inlet

Crail Bay

Okiwi Bay

Duncan Bay

Ronga Saddle

NYDIA TRACK

Nydia Bay

H **G**

Sound

Pelorus

I

Kenepuru

K Te Mahia

Rai Valley

Mistletoe Bay DOC

L

Mt Rutland (1008m)

KENEPURU ROAD

Davies Bay DOC

Mistletoe Bay

KAIUMA BAY ROAD

Kaiuma Bay

Mahau Sound

Anakiwa

M

Pelorus Bridge

Canvastown

Havelock

Tirimoana Jetty

QUEEN CHARLOTTE DRIVE

6

QUEEN CHARLOTTE DRIVE

O

6

1

Koromiko

P   Blenheim (40 km)   Blenheim (25 km)

Map, detailing walks close to town; DOC's detailed *Marlborough Sounds* leaflet ($1);
the DOC *Queen Charlotte Track* map ($1); and the free *Marlborough Wine Region*
map detailing wineries around nearby Blenheim (see p.582).

Accommodation

As a major **transit centre**, Picton is disproportionately well endowed
with accommodation, ranging from backpacker hostels to upscale lodges.
You should have no difficulty finding somewhere to suit your needs within

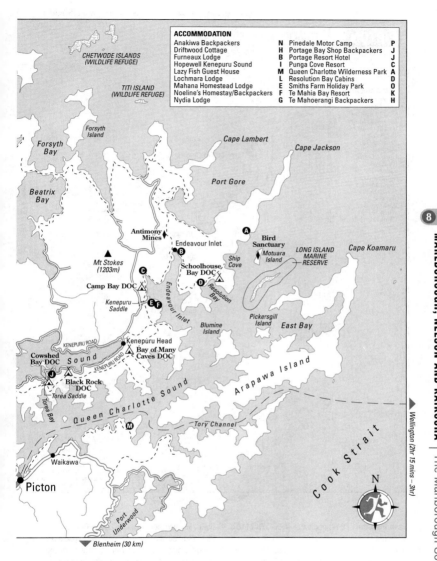

ACCOMMODATION

Anakiwa Backpackers	N	Pinedale Motor Camp	P
Driftwood Cottage	H	Portage Bay Shop Backpackers	J
Furneaux Lodge	B	Portage Resort Hotel	J
Hopewell Kenepuru Sound	I	Punga Cove Resort	C
Lazy Fish Guest House	M	Queen Charlotte Wilderness Park	A
Lochmara Lodge	L	Resolution Bay Cabins	D
Mahana Homestead Lodge	E	Smiths Farm Holiday Park	O
Noeline's Homestay/Backpackers	F	Te Mahia Bay Resort	K
Nydia Lodge	G	Te Mahoerangi Backpackers	H

walking distance of the gangplank for most of the year, although from mid-December to the end of February you should definitely **book** in advance.

Motels

Broadway Motel 113 Picton High St
☎03/5736563 & 0800/101 919, ⓦwww
.broadwaymotel.co.nz. Attractive modern motel
units in the centre of town with good views from
the 1st floor balcony. ➎

Harbour View Motel 30 Waikawa Rd
☎03/573 6259 & 0800/101 133, ⓦwww
.harbourviewpicton.co.nz. Twelve brand new, and
tastefully appointed, fully self-contained units with
great views over the harbour. All have a balcony or
a small deck. ➎

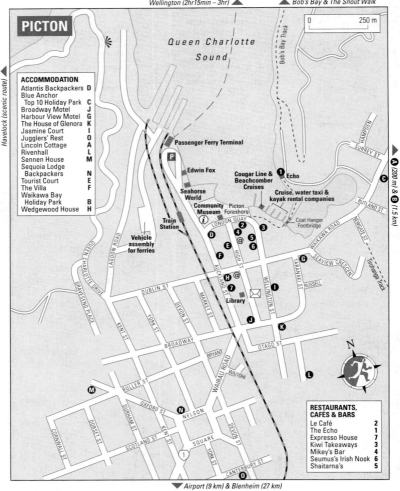

PICTON

0   250 m

Queen Charlotte Sound

Havelock (scenic route) ◄

ACCOMMODATION

Atlantis Backpackers	**D**
Blue Anchor	
Top 10 Holiday Park	**C**
Broadway Motel	**J**
Harbour View Motel	**G**
The House of Glenora	**K**
Jasmine Court	**I**
Jugglers' Rest	**O**
Lincoln Cottage	**A**
Rivenhall	**L**
Sennen House	**M**
Sequoia Lodge	
Backpackers	**N**
Tourist Court	**E**
The Villa	**F**
Waikawa Bay	
Holiday Park	**B**
Wedgewood House	**H**

Passenger Ferry Terminal

Edwin Fox

Cougar Line & Beachcomber Cruises

Echo

Cruise, water taxi & kayak rental companies

Seahorse World

Community Museum

Picton Foreshore

Coat Hanger Footbridge

Train Station

Vehicle assembly for ferries

Library

N

RESTAURANTS, CAFÉS & BARS

Le Café	**2**
The Echo	**1**
Expresso House	**7**
Kiwi Takeaways	**3**
Mikey's Bar	**4**
Seumus's Irish Nook	**6**
Shaitarna's	**5**

MARLBOROUGH, NELSON AND KAIKOURA | The Marlborough Sounds

8

528

Jasmine Court 78 Wellington St ☎03/573 7110 & 0800/421 999, ⓦwww.jasminecourt.co.nz. Top-of-the-line modern motel with beautifully kept, non-smoking, luxury units fitted with DVDs, CD players and each with a sunny verandah. There is also access to a day room where you can hang out if you have a late departure or early arrival. ❻

Tourist Court 45 High St ☎03/573 6331, ⓦwww.tourist-court.co.nz. Small but tolerable en-suite doubles at low prices. ❹

B&Bs and homestays

The House of Glenora 22 Broadway ☎03/573

6966, ⓦwww.glenora.co.nz. Lovely B&B in Picton's original magistrate's house, a spacious 1860 building with a pleasant en-suite room and an excellent self-catering suite with large verandah. A smorgasbord breakfast includes Swedish-style porridge, and unusual dietary requirements are a speciality. Room ❺, suite ❼

Lincoln Cottage 19 Lincoln St ☎03/573 5285, ⓦwww.pictonstay.com. A traditional B&B in a sky-blue Art Deco house with two pleasant rooms sharing a terrace and kitchen with the house and a small garden cottage, all about 1.5km from the town centre. ❺

Staying out in the Sounds

The best way to soak up something of the spirit of the Marlborough Sounds is to stay in some of the swanky lodges, modest resorts and superb backpacker hostels inaccessible (or barely accessible) by road. Many of the best dot the Queen Charlotte Track but there's no need to go tramping as water taxis will get you there in a few minutes from Picton (and to a lesser extent Havelock; see p.538). As well as those listed below, consider staying at *Lochmara Lodge* and *Furneaux Lodge* (for both see pp.536–537).

Christopher Grey (covered on p.534). Bunk accommodation onboard this boat with daily access to Queen Charlotte Track tramping.

Hopewell Kenepuru Sound ℡03/573 4341, ⓦwww.hopewell.co.nz. A gorgeous backpacker hostel in a dreamy setting where even a couple of nights isn't enough to fully appreciate the relaxing setting, wonderfully welcoming hosts, waterside hot tub, kayaks, fishing and opportunities to visit the local mussel farm or go water skiing. Access is either on a tortuous 2–3hr drive along Kenepuru Road, or by a sequence of water taxis from Picton ($65 return per person): call the hostel for details. Four shares ❶, rooms ❷, en suites ❸, self-contained cottage sleeping 4 $110

Lazy Fish Guest House ℡03/573 5291, ⓦwww.lazyfish.co.nz. Romantic and rejuvenating hideaway right by the water in Kahikatea East Bay. Rooms and cottages are luxurious and all come with four-poster bed, a candle-lit terrace and an outdoor bath. Rates ($345 a room; 2-night minimum stay) include all meals and free use of kayaks, windsurfer and row boat. Access in 20min with The Cougar Line from Picton $40 return per person. ❾

Queen Charlotte Wilderness Park Port Jackson ℡03/579 9025, ⓦwww .truenz.co.nz/wilderness. A resort set amid farmland northeast of Ship Cove and accessible from the northern end of the Queen Charlotte Track. A two-night stay ($285) gets you an en-suite room with dinner provided and free use of canoe and dinghy. Self-catering is available and each extra night costs $85. Transport from Picton is $80 return and the morning boat can drop you at Ship Cove allowing you to walk from there to the lodge without having to carry bags.

Rivenhall 118 Wellington St ℡03/573 7692, ⓔrivenhall.picton@xtra.co.nz. On the left-hand side up the hill, this is a charming, historic homestay with big rooms grand views and a warm welcome from the hosts. ❺

Sennen House 9 Oxford St ℡03/573 5216, ⓦwww.sennenhouse.co.nz. Gorgeous 1886 grand villa ten minutes' walk from town that has been tastefully converted into a B&B with three suites each with kitchen facilities where breakfast fixings are supplied. After a glass of wine with the owners on the back deck you are left to yourselves in considerable comfort. Large suite with fireplace and verandah just ❾, smaller suites ❽

Hostels and campgrounds

Atlantis Backpackers cnr Auckland St & London Quay ℡03/573 7390, ⓦwww.atlantishostel.co.nz. Central hostel close to ferry with the town's cheapest bunks, if you're prepared to share with 30 others, though there are also smaller dorms,

twins and doubles plus free breakfast and the use of an indoor heated pool shared by the local dive school (See p.532). Dorms ❶, rooms ❷

Blue Anchor Top 10 Holiday Park 70–78 Waikawa Rd ℡03/573 7212 & 0800/277 299, ⓦwww.blueanchor.co.nz. Centrally located campsite with a swimming pool, children's playground, cabins (bedding $5) and motel-style units, in a pleasant spot with trees providing shelter. Camping $13, cabins ❷, kitchen cabins ❸, motel units ❹

Jugglers' Rest 8 Canterbury St ℡03/573 5570, ⓔjugglers-rest@xtra.co.nz. Picton's smallest hostel, a fun place run by jugglers who are usually happy to try to pass on some skills. There are a couple of 6-bed dorms and some rooms plus a small swimming pool and the "celestial bathroom" with stars on the ceiling. Dorms ❶, rooms ❸

Sequoia Lodge Backpackers 3 Nelson Sq ℡03/573 8399 & 0800/222 257, ⓦwww.sequoialodge.co.nz. The pick of the Picton hostels, ten minutes walk from the centre and with excellent, free home-made bread each night. Attention to detail shows with bedlights and side tables for all beds (including bunks), heated towel rails in the doubles and twins, and the inclusion of a covered barbecue area, hammocks and off-street parking. There's also a separate female dorm, and free ferry, bus and train pick-up. Dorms ❶, rooms ❸

The Villa 34 Auckland St ☎03/573 6598, ⓦwww.thevilla.co.nz. Well-regarded central hostel with a youthful feel based around a century-old house and a more modern one next door. When busy it can feel a little cramped, but it works well and there are all manner of inducements such as free breakfast, free bikes, apple crumble in winter and a hot tub. They also rent

out camping packs ($15 for 3 days) ideal for ill-equipped Queen Charlotte Track hikers. Dorms ❶, rooms ❸

Waikawa Bay Holiday Park 302 Waikawa Rd ☎03/573 7434 & 0800/924 529, ⓔhiyah@ihug.co.nz. Five minutes' drive from the ferry terminal, this large, sheltered site has views over the water and a good range of accommodation. Camping $10, cabins ❷, motel units ❹

Wedgewood House 10 Dublin St ☎03/573 7797, ⓔwedgewoodhouse@xtra.co.nz. Uninspiring associate YHA hostel in a small house, with restricted office hours (8–10am, 1–2pm, 5–6.30pm, 8–10pm), but there are extra, larger rooms next door. Dorms ❶, rooms ❷

The Town

Pretty much everything of interest in Picton is along the waterfront, close to **Picton Foreshore**, a strip of park which has recently been spruced up with brick paving and native plantings around the line of phoenix palms. At its western end, close to the ferry terminal, a large steel shed houses the hulk of the 1600 tonne **Edwin Fox** (daily 9am–5pm; $6), the sole survivor of the fleets that once brought migrants to New Zealand and the last of some four thousand "Indiamen" built in India through the nineteenth century. This 1853 example operated as a troop carrier in the Crimean War and transported convicts to Australia, before bringing free settlers to New Zealand. After years working as a merchant vessel and helping to establish the frozen meat trade in New Zealand, it was towed into Shakespeare Bay (just west of Picton) in 1967. Vandalised and weather beaten for twenty years, but still afloat, it was finally moved to Picton Harbour where in 1999 it was finally dry-docked and preserved. A small but well designed museum explains the life and significance of the ship, preparing you for the age-blackened hull itself. Standing on the small part of the deck that remains gives a sense of what it must have been like to sail, but the best bit is below decks in the large open hold, all heavy planking partly rotted away to reveal the teak ribs.

Beside the Edwin Fox, **Seahorse World** (daily 9am–5pm; $12) offers an insight into the lives of seahorses and has a few jellyfish, small sharks and a preserved giant squid. Twenty-minute narrated tours include a little of the significance of sea creatures to Maori.

Heading further east around the bay onto London Quay, the **Picton Community Museum** (daily 10am–4pm; $3) contains displays devoted to the Perano Whaling Station, which operated in Queen Charlotte Sound until 1964. There are photographs of the station in its heyday, and a harpoon gun from one of the steamboat chasers as well as some excellent examples of carved whalebone. Smaller displays deal with Maori and *pakeha* local history, and there is a finely carved chair inlaid with *paua* shell, as well as a large collection of brightly coloured shells from all over the world.

The maritime theme continues further around the harbour and across the Coat Hanger footbridge where the **Echo** is permanently moored in the marina. Built in 1905, the *Echo* was a top-sail schooner, with a square bilge scow-type hull, developed to take cargo from the sea upriver to the remote

Hiking around Picton

The best of the local **trails** run through Victoria Domain, a mostly bush-clad peninsula immediately east of Picton. As most trails link up at some point it can be a little confusing, though several free and widely available maps of town show the way.

Bob's Bay Track (1km one way; 30min; gently undulating). Starting at Shelly Beach near the *Echo*, this extends along the shoreline to a safe swimming and picnicking beach at Bob's Bay providing great views across the water to the ferry terminal and up the Queen Charlotte Sound. From Bob's Bay a short steep path climbs away from the bay to the **Harbour View** parking area.

The Snout (5km one way; 1hr 15min; 200m ascent on return). From the Harbour View parking area (see above) follow the top of ridge past the self-explanatory Queen Charlotte View to the tip of the promontory, The Snout, whose evocative Maori name, *Te Ihumoeone-ihu*, translates as "the nose of the sand worm".

Tirohanga Track (3km one way; 1hr 15min; 300m ascent). Fairly strenuous walk up the hills behind Picton passing the lovely Hilltop Viewpoint. The track starts on Newgate St.

communities of New Zealand. From 1920 it ran river services out of Blenheim, and was the last ship to trade commercially under sail in New Zealand waters. Retrieved from a ships' graveyard, she was used by the US Navy as a supply ship for the New Hebrides, Solomon Islands and New Guinea area. It now operates as a **café/bar** where for the price of a coffee or a beer you can sit surrounded by evocative black and white photos of New Zealand's early coastal traders.

Eating and entertainment

Picton isn't a great place to eat but there are enough decent **restaurants** to satisfy for a couple of days and plenty of tearooms and **cafés**. Entertainment is similarly limited though, on summer weekends, *Mikey's Bar* often has **bands** trying to scrape together enough money to escape to somewhere bigger.

Le Café 14 London Quay. A good quality, café and bar with pavement seating just across from the Sound serving mouth-watering steak sandwiches with home-made chutney, and all sorts of seafood at reasonable prices. Occasional live music also peps up the atmosphere. Daily for breakfast & lunch, plus dinner in summer.

The Echo East Harbour. This permanently moored ship is a fine place for beer in the sun on deck perhaps tucking into their cheese and seafood platter for two ($28) or something from their low-cost all-day menu.

Expresso House 58 Auckland St 03/573 7112. A Picton secret that's easy to miss; the casual minimalist surroundings are relieved by rimu flooring, New Zealand oak tables and the odd Native American photograph on the walls. Great food includes the likes of pumpkin satay noodles ($12), lemon and salmon fettuccine ($14), and rare beef fillet with wasabi cream and Drambuie

mustard ($24). Great desserts too, and plenty of wines by the glass. Often closed June–Aug & Wed off-season.

Kiwi Takeaways 14 Wellington St ☎03/573 5537. Grab some local fish and chips, or maybe some scallops, and wander down to Foreshore Park as the sun sets on the Sound.

Mikey's Bar 18 High St. Popular bustling modern bar in Tex/Mex-style with alfresco seating, pool table and bands playing fairly frequently in summer. DJs fill in the gaps in the barn-like nightclub out back.

Seumus's Irish Nook Wellington St. Fairly authentic Irish bar with a great atmosphere and decorated with Irish instruments.

Shaitarna's 19 Wellington St ☎573 6365. Dinner-only seafood restaurant which spills outside on warm summer evenings serving the likes of warm chicken salad ($15), baked smoked hoki ($19) and pan-seared scallops ($27).

Listings

Banks Picton has branches of a couple of the major banks (BNZ and Westpac), both on High Street.

Bike and boat rental Buzzy Bikes and Boats, The Foreshore (☎03/573 7853) have bikes for $40 a day along with canoes (single $15 a day; double $25), dinghies ($35) and fishing tackle ($10). Marlborough Sounds Adventure Co rent bikes for use on the QCT for $40 a day and kayaks (see p.534).

Bookshops Take Note, 28 High St (Mon–Sat 9am–5pm; ☎03/573 6107).

Buses You can book all the buses through the information centre or directly. Atomic Shuttles (☎03/322 8883) run to Christchurch, St Arnaud, Nelson and Greymouth; Deluxe Travel Line (☎03/578 5467) go to Blenheim; East Coast Express (☎0508/830 900) run down the coast to Christchurch; InterCity (☎03/379 9020) run to Nelson, Blenheim and Christchurch via Kaikoura; K Bus (☎0800/881 188) go Takaka via Blenheim, Havelock, Nelson and Motueka; and South Island Connections (☎03/366 6633) heads for Dunedin with a change in Christchurch. The cheapest onward connections to Blenheim are with K Bus who charge just $5.

Car rental Most of the major international and Kiwi companies have offices at the Ferry Terminal or scattered around town: over thirty in total. The visitor centre has a free sheet listing them all, but local numbers for the most commonly used companies are: Ace ☎03/573 7157; Avis ☎03/573 6363; Avon ☎03/573 6009; Budget ☎03/573 6081; Hertz ☎03/573 7224; National ☎03/573 8800; NZ Rent A Car ☎03/573 7282; Pegasus ☎03/573 7733; Rent-a-Dent ☎03/573 7787; Thrifty ☎03/573 7387.

Diving Divers World, cnr London Quay & Auckland St (☎03/573 7323, ⓦwww.pictondiversworld .co.nz), offers gear rental ($77 for full kit and one tank), wreck dives ($159–190 including gear) and runs 4-day SSI courses ($425).

Internet access The Creek Pottery, 26 High St, has speedy machines at $2 for 20min, as does United Video, 60 High St, which stays open daily until 9pm.

Library 67 High St (Mon–Thurs 8am–5pm, Fri 8am–5.30pm, Sat 10am–noon).

Luggage storage Most lodgings store luggage while you walk the Queen Charlotte Track. Cars can be left unsecured on the streets around Picton, or safely with Sounds Storage (☎03/573 5136) who will pick up and drop off your vehicle anywhere in Picton and charge $10 for the first night then $6 for each subsequent night.

Medical treatment Picton Medical Centre, 71 High St ☎03/573 6092.

Pharmacy Picton Healthcare, 3 High St Mon–Fri 9am–6pm, Sat 9am–1pm.

Post office The main post office is in the Mariners Mall on High Street Mon–Fri 8.30am–5pm, plus Oct–April Sat 9.30am–12.30pm.

Rural Mail Bus Service You can ride the Rural Mail Bus Service (☎03/573 7389), essentially a minivan serving remote spots linking the main post offices in Havelock and Picton, and the southern end of the Queen Charlotte Track at Anakiwa. There are several runs: Picton to Anakiwa (8am & 12.40pm, the latter meeting the ferry from Wellington; $8); Anakiwa to Picton (6am & 11am by arrangement; $8); Anakiwa to Havelock (9.30am; $5) and Havelock to Anakiwa (10.30am; $5).

Taxis Blenheim Taxis ☎03/578 0225; see also "Water taxis" below.

Water sports Sunnyvale Motels, 384 Waikawa Rd (☎03/573 6800), rents out kayaks (singles $40 a day, doubles $80), laser yachts ($50 per half day), and dinghies ($15 per hour).

Water taxis Arrow Water Taxis ☎03/573 8229; Beachcomber Fun Cruises ☎0800/624 526 & 03/573 6175, ⓦwww.beachcombercruises.co.nz; Cougar Line ☎0800/504 090 & 03/573 7925, ⓦwww.cougarlinecruises.co.nz; Endeavour Express ☎03/573 5456, ⓦwww.boatrides.co.nz; The Sounds Connection ☎0800/742 866 & 03/573 8843, ⓦwww.soundsconnection.co.nz; and West Bay Water Transport ☎03/573 5597, ⓦwww.westbay.co.nz.

Winery tours Tours of the Marlborough wine country are covered in detail in "Listings" on p.586, and most companies do Picton pick-ups. Marlborough Wine Tours and Picton-based Sounds Connection don't charge any extra for their tours and Deluxe Wine Tour only charge an extra $5 for Picton pickup for their morning tour and meet the 10am Lynx ferry arrival from Wellington. Wine Tours by Bike charge $15 extra to pick up from Picton.

Exploring Queen Charlotte Sound

Picton is a pretty spot, but you've barely touched the region's beauty until you've explored **Queen Charlotte Sound**. This wildly indented series of drowned valleys encloses moody picturesque bays, small deserted sandy

Several companies run great cruises around Queen Charlotte and Pelorus sounds, but there is something special about the **Rural Mail Runs**, pulling up at a lonely wharf and having some farmer's wife (or the whole family) coming out to receive their first mail delivery for a week. Chances are there'll also be perishable groceries to deliver and perhaps coursework for kids doing correspondence schooling. Golden beaches and bush-clad shorelines abound, and you might even be escorted by dolphins. It may not be many years before these trips cease delivering mail, so grab the chance while you can.

Altogether there are six mail runs, all operated by Beachcomber Fun Cruises (℡03/573 6175 & 0800/624 526, ⊛www.beachcombercruises.co.nz), and all providing tea and coffee, though you'll need to bring lunch and clothing suitable for the conditions.

Three routes in **Queen Charlotte Sound** operate as the *Magic Mail Run* (daily except Sun at 1.30pm; $66). All leave from Picton and take four hours, but different routes are followed on different days. There isn't much difference between them so hop on whichever is convenient, maybe calling at bays in Queen Charlotte Sound, the Regal Salmon Farm and the Perano Whaling Station, or heading into Endeavour Inlet, Resolution Bay and Ship Cove.

A further three routes around **Pelorus Sound** are collectively known as the *Pelorus Mail Boat* (Tues, Thurs & Fri; $95) and take around eight hours. These are most comprehensively done from Havelock (leaving at 9.30am), though a shortened version can be done from Picton (leaving 10.15am). Friday's route to the Outer Sounds is perhaps the pick, though Tuesday's Western Run is also very good.

beaches, headlands with panoramic views and cloistered islands while grand lumpy peninsulas offer shelter from the winds and storms in Cook Strait and solitude for the contemplative fisherman, kayaker or tramper. For a taste of these labyrinthine waterways, take one of the many **day-cruises** from Picton, but to really appreciate their tranquil beauty you're far better off **kayaking** round the bays or **tramping** the Queen Charlotte Track. The relatively calm waters of the Sounds also give the opportunity for **scuba diving**, either checking out the wrecks and rich marine life or just doing an open-water qualification (see p.532).

The Sights

The principal pleasure in exploring Queen Charlotte Sound is just being out on the water, but there are a couple of sights which crop up on most itineraries. One is Motuara Island, a DOC managed predator-free wildlife sanctuary that is home to the saddleback, South Island bush robin, bellbird and a few Okarito brown kiwi. All the birds are quite fearless and will rest and fly startlingly close to you. A steep trail climbs to the island's higher reaches where the best birdsong can be heard. Little blue penguins choose to nest in boxes provided rather than build their own. In spring (Oct–Dec) you can gently lift the top of the box and see the baby penguins inside.

Just across a channel from Motuara Island, Ship Cove marks the bay where Captain Cook spent considerable time on his three trips to New Zealand. A large white concrete monument commemorates his various visits.

Cruises and tours

Water taxis are always flitting about Queen Charlotte Sound taking hikers to the Queen Charlotte Track or delivering guests to some swanky lodge. If you just want to get out on the water for a few minutes this may be all you need, but several companies also run **cruises** on the Sounds. The cheapest are Nellie Harbour Trips ($20; ☏021/333 661) which leave from the Town Wharf several times a day for a one-hour inshore jaunt.

Along with their rural mail runs (see p.533) Beachcomber Fun Cruises offer twice-daily trips around the bays (2hr; $40), some including Ship Cove (3hr; $53), or Motuara Island (3hr; $53). For four-hour **dolphin and bird watching** trips join Dolphin Watch, Town Wharf (daily 8.30am & 1.30pm; $85; ☏03/573 8040 & 0800/945 354, ⊛www.naturetours.co.nz) who combine a half-day cruising with observing dolphins (Duskys in winter and spring, Hector's in spring and summer, and bottlenose all year) for $70 including spending 45min exploring Motuara Island. They also do a Birdwatcher's Special ($88), also visiting Motuara Island, and team up with Endeavour Express to offer their trip with Ship Cove drop off and full Queen Charlotte Track pack transport for $89.

One particularly fine way to get out on the water is with Myths and Legends **Eco Tours** (☏03/573 6901, ⊛www.eco-tours.co.nz) who take out their 1930 kauri launch (4hr for $100 or 8hr for $150 including lunch) for a tour around the bays explaining all about the history and culture of the region from the perspective of a sixth generation local *pakeha* and his Maori wife. They also run a Stargazer BBQ ($100) which usually rolls in pretty late.

To stay out on the water longer, go on the *Christopher Grey*, the so-called **Track and Tramp Boat** (☏0800/287 267, ⊜fosshome@ihu.co.nz) which runs three-day trips from Picton with two nights bunk-style B&B onboard, and the opportunity to hang out on board reading, fishing or swimming, walk the entire QCT or take along bikes for riding the track. Trips ($160) typically leave Monday and Friday and there is a kitchen for packing lunches and preparing evening meals.

Kayaking

Visitors dashing across to Abel Tasman National Park often overlook the uncrowded waters and breathtaking views to be had kayaking in Queen Charlotte Sound. The large and professional Marlborough Sounds Adventure Company, Town Wharf (☏03/573 6078 & 0800/283 283, ⊛marlborough-sounds.co.nz) offer a huge range of **guided kayaking** trips including a lovely twilight paddle around Picton (3hr; $50), a gentle one-dayer (7hr; $85), a two day trip ($145) on which you join the one-day trip then camp out by yourselves and paddle home the next day, and a fully-guided three-dayer in the outer sounds ($445).

Smaller, but in many respects just as good, is Sea Kayaking Adventure Tours (☏03/574 2765 & 0800/262 549, ⊛www.nzseakayaking.com), based at Anakiwa by the end of the Queen Charlotte Track. They have one-day guided trips ($75) as well as a three-day trip along the length of the track either camping ($280) or upgrading to fancier accommodation.

Both companies have **rental kayaks** ($40–45 per day), reducing to $35 for three days or more.

The Queen Charlotte Track

The **Queen Charlotte Track** (QCT: 71km one way; 3–5 days; open all year; ⊛www.qctrack.co.nz) is a spectacularly beautiful walk partly tracing skyline ridges with brilliant views across dense coastal forest to the waters of Queen Charlotte and Kenepuru sounds on either side. It is broad, relatively easy going and is distinguished from all other multi-day tramps by the **abundant**

accommodation along the way. There are no DOC huts and no fees to hike the track, but with the temptation of some lovely places to stay it may cost you more than you bargained for. Access and egress is generally by boat from Picton, and your water taxi will **transport your bags** to your next destination each day making hiking the Queen Charlotte Track a thoroughly pleasurable (if not completely relaxing) experience. Since boats call at numerous bays along the way, less ambitious walkers can tackle shorter sections, do day hikes from Picton or tackle the track as part of a guided walk (see p.536). Though the track is less crowded than some, its popularity is rapidly increasing.

Queen Charlotte Sound was an important trade route and provided good shelter and bountiful food for **Maori**, who carried canoes over the low saddles of the walkway to avoid long, unnecessary and hazardous sea journeys around the full length of the sounds. **Captain Cook** stopped at Ship Cove on five occasions and made it his New Zealand base, spending over 100 days there between 1770 and 1777. The shelter and fresh water made it an ideal spot and its plentiful supplies of (what became known as) Cook's scurvy grass were particularly valued for the vitamin C content.

The changing seasons are reflected by splashes of colour: karaka groves are laden with bright yellow berries in the summer; native clematis (puawanga) is festooned with creamy-white **flowers** in the spring; and supplejacks and kohia (Kiwi passion fruit) produce red and orange fruits in the autumn. As a result, there is no shortage of **birds**, with tui and bellbirds in profusion, as well as the ever-friendly fantails and little piebald robins. The forests also contain the morepork (a native owl named for its "more pork" call), while the rocky shorelines boast an abundance of shags, gannets, terns and shearwaters, as well as the stooping oystercatchers patrolling in pairs. If you're lucky, you may spot a little blue penguin making its way to the fishing grounds in the morning or on its way home in the evening, and on rare occasions you can see the odd kiwi, endangered and embattled but still clinging obdurately to survival.

Information and Access

First stop should be Picton's visitor centre where you'll be given a free leaflet detailing all the latest transportation costs and frequencies, and outlining the accommodation options. They'll also talk you through organising your trip and sell you DOC's *Queen Charlotte Track* leaflet ($1). **Mountain bikers** will want the free leaflet detailing special regulations. Most of the track is open to bikers year-round, though the northern quarter is off limits from December to February.

Trampers and bikers normally **travel north to south** from Ship Cove to Anakiwa, using **water taxis** to drop them off and pick them up. Sections of the track are also **accessible from Kenepuru Road** (see p.538), but there is no public transport and hitching or using your own vehicle seems counter to the spirit of the whole enterprise.

Water taxi companies (see p.532 for details) do variations on a basic theme offering transfer to Ship Cove, bag transfers and pick up at Anakiwa or the nearby Tirimoana Jetty for $55–65. You can save $10 by carrying your own bag, but you might as well save your energy for tougher walks down south where you don't have the option. **Bikes** are usually charged at $5 per journey.

Beachcomber Fun Cruises and Endeavour Express both only charge $55 for the full package and have extensive timetables with drop-offs at Ship Cove (the northern end of the track), Endeavour Inlet, Torea Bay, Mistletoe Bay and Anakiwa (the southern end of the track). This allows great flexibility if you only want to walk part of the track. Beachcomber only have 9.30am Picton departures for Ship

Cove so late starters might prefer to go with Endeavour who have departures at 9am, 10.30am (Dec–Feb only), 1.15pm and 6pm (on demand).

Most water taxis run a late-afternoon service back to Picton from Anakiwa, which is also accessible using the Rural Mail Bus Run, see Picton listings (p.532).

Guided walks, combos and day-trips

All sorts of companies around Picton offer organised encounters with the QCT with varying degrees of assistance. Marlborough Sounds Adventure Company offers **freedom walks** (4-day $445; 5-day $535) with nights spent at *Furneaux Lodge*, *Punga Cove Resort* and *Portage Resort Hotel*, though apart from the convenience of having all the booking done for you, you might as well do it yourself for less money. Their **guided walks** (4-day $965; 5-day $1250) add in a knowledgeable guide accompanying you the whole way. Better still, try their 4-day Paddle and Walk ($965) which includes a visit to Moturua Island with Dolphin Watch (see p.534), the first two days of the guided walk from Ship Cove to *Punga Cove*, a day kayaking on Kenepuru Sound, a night at *Portage Cove Resort* then a final day paddling back to Picton. Perhaps their most appealing trip of all is the 3-day Ultimate Sounds Adventure ($410–595 depending on accommodation) combining a day each of hiking, kayaking and cycling.

Most of the water taxis will drop you off and pick you up later in the day so you can arrange a one-day walk on any bit of track that suits for about $40 but some companies put together specific packages. Beachcomber Fun Cruises offer a series of one-day walks ($32–45) some with afternoon tea at Furneaux Lodge, and the Cougar Line (T0800/504 090, Wwww .queencharlottetrack.co.nz) offer walks from one to five hours ($53).

You should also consider the Tramp the Track Boat (see p.534) which allows you to sleep afloat and tramp during the day.

Accommodation

A hot shower, a good meal and a comfy bed are three things seldom encountered on long tramps but the Queen Charlotte Track offers comfort in spades plus a good deal of more modest accommodation, though even hostels charge $25–30, some going up a couple more dollars if you want sheets. **Booking** is essential, not just to guarantee a bed for the night but to ensure your water taxi company knows where to deliver your bags. Many of the cheaper places don't accept EFTPOS or credit cards, so **take plenty of cash**. The seven DOC **campsites** (all marked on the map on p.526) cost $5 and have water and toilets but generally don't have water taxi access.

The following are listed geographically from north to south, with hiking distances measured from Ship Cove.

Resolution Bay Cabins Resolution Bay Km5 T03/579 941, E reso@xtra.co.nz. The closest accommodation to Ship Cove, in a pretty and atmospheric spot offering swimming, canoes and comfortable rooms in a 1920s-style resort. Meals available on request. Camping $10, dorms $25–30, cabins ❹, cottages ❺

Furneaux Lodge Endeavour Inlet, Km14 T03/579 8259, W www.furneaux.co.nz. One of the region's bigger lodges built around a century-

old homestead set in attractive gardens. Still fairly rustic in style but with a restaurant, a couple of bars, Internet access and gear hire shop. Dorms $28, chalets ❻, new en-suites ❼

Punga Cove Resort Endeavour Inlet Km26 T03/579 8561, W www.pungacove.co.nz. A large resort straggling from the boatshed bar by the wharf up a hillside to the classy restaurant with panoramic views. Guests have the use of the pool, spa, sauna, kayaks and a lot more. Dorms $30, budget rooms ❸, chalets ❼, deluxe ❽

Mahana Homestead Lodge Endeavour Inlet, Km27 T03/579 8373, W www.mahanahomestead.com.

Modern and functional 12-bed hostel with four-shares and twin/family rooms all with sea views. There's a good kitchen but they also serve home-cooked dinners and it is only a ten minute stroll to the restaurant and bar at Punga Cove. Dorms ❶, rooms ❸

Noeline's Homestay / Backpackers Nr Punga Cove, Km27 ☎03/ 579 8375. There's a friendly welcome to this comfortable accommodation in a relaxing atmosphere at the best place to stay in the cove – you may not want to leave. Linen available. ❶

Portage Resort Hotel Kenepuru Road, Km51, ☎03/573 4309, ⓦwww.portage.co.nz. Stylish hotel beside Kenepuru Sound, ten minutes' walk from the QCT at Torea Bay. Recently remodelled with bold coloured rooms and designer bathrooms, the place comes with a classy restaurant, good café and bar, swimming pool and great views. The dorms have a full kitchen. Access is by car along Kenepuru Road, or by water taxi from Picton ($15). Dorms $25, with linen $35, non-view rooms ❼, view rooms ❽

Portage Bay Shop Backpackers Kenepuru Road, Km51 ☎03/573 4445, ⓦwww .portagecharters.co.nz. Handily located beside the Portage Resort Hotel this 14-bed hostel has comfortable beds ($30, made-up $35), TV and lovely views of Kenepuru Sound. There's a store and takeaway attached and they rent out bikes and all manner of aquatic toys. Dorms $30–35

Lochmara Lodge Lochmara Bay, Km58 ☎03/573 4554, ⓦwww.lochmaralodge.co.nz. Comfortable, waterside eco retreat where a portion of your bill goes to fund predator control and tree planting aimed at getting kakariki (native parakeets) to breed here. It is a great place to relax in hammocks, soak in the hot tub, kayak, fish, snorkel or read but there's no TV and you'll have to cook your own meals. Non-hikers should call the lodge to arrange a water taxi ($15 each way) which generally leaves Picton daily at 1.45pm and 4.00pm. Dorms ❶, budget rooms ❸, self-contained units & en-suite rooms ❻

Te Mahia Bay Resort Te Mahia Bay, Km59 ☎03/573 4089, ⓦwww.temahia.co.nz. Just off the QCT, this resort is nicely sited overlooking Kenepuru Sound and has a store and kayaks and rowboats for rent. Accessible by road from Picton. Camping and hookups $13, dorms $30, family units ❺, waterview units ❻

Anakiwa Backpackers Anakiwa, Km73 ☎03/574 1388, ⓦwww.anakiwabackpackers.co.nz. A clean, simple and relaxed homestay hostel with all made-up beds. There are a couple of nice doubles, and dorms, one en-suite that's good as a family room. Dorms ❶, rooms ❷

Smiths Farm Holiday Park Queen Charlotte Drive ☎03/574 2806, ⓦwww.smithsfarm.co.nz. Pleasant campsite an easy 4km walk beyond the Anakiwa end of the track. Camping $9–10, cabins ❷, kitchen cabins ❹, motel units ❺

The route

The track passes through some grassy farmland and bleak gorse-covered hills, but both ends of the track are forest reserves with lush greenery, including nikau palms and climbing keikie, right down to the shoreline. There are a number of **detours** off the main track to places of interest, including a short walk from Ship Cove to a pretty forest-shrouded waterfall where Cook frequently bathed, a scramble down to the Bay of Many Coves, or a foray to the Antimony Mines (where there are exposed shafts – stick to the marked tracks). The most spectacular **views** are to be had en route to the mines and at Torea Saddle and Kenepuru Saddle.

To do the whole track in three days, get an early start from Ship Cove and plan to hike to Punga Cove. From there you have a fairly long day to Portage or Lochmara, then a relatively easy finish.

Ship Cove to Resolution Bay (4.5km; 2hr; 200m ascent). The track climbs steeply away from the shore through largely untouched forest to a lookout with great views of Motuara Island, before dropping down to Resolution Bay, where there's a DOC campsite and *Resolution Bay Cabins*.

Resolution Bay to Endeavour Inlet (15km; 5hr; 200m ascent). Follows an old bridle path over the ridge to *Furneaux Lodge* and *Endeavour Resort*.

Endeavour Inlet to Punga Cove (11.5km; 4hr; 100m ascent). Coastal track through regenerating forest thick with birdlife. DOC campsite and several lodges.

Punga Cove to Portage (24.5km; 8hr; 650m ascent). The longest stretch without convenient roofed accommodation (just two DOC campsites) is

also the most rewarding mostly following a ridge with views down to the Sounds on both sides. **Portage to Mistletoe Bay** (7.5km; 4hr; 450 ascent). A steep initial climb is followed by a pleasant ridge walk through manuka, gorse and shrubs with the chance to break the journey at *Lochmara Lodge*, some 2km off the track or continue to *Te Mahia Bay Resort.*
Mistletoe Bay to Anakiwa (12.5km; 4hr; 100m ascent). Follows an old bridle path well above the water with great views, then finishes off through some lovely beech forest.

Queen Charlotte Drive and Kenepuru Road

With water taxis providing convenient access to fabulous out of the way spots, it seems a little perverse to try to see the Marlborough Sounds by car; doubly so when you start weaving your way around the mostly paved but **narrow and twisting roads**. Don't expect to average more than 40km/hr. In compensation, the views through the ferns to turquoise bays are magic.

The 35km Queen Charlotte Drive between Picton and Havelock is a picturesque and spectacular back-road sliding past the flat plain at the head of Queen Charlotte Sound and climbing up the hills overlooking Pelorus Sound before descending to SH6 and Havelock itself. It is a slow and winding drive, but you may want to take it even slower by stopping to wander down to a couple of sheltered coves.

Around 18km west of Picton, a narrow road heads north to **ANAKIWA**, the southern end of the Queen Charlotte Track. Here you'll find a card phone for calling water taxis (though you should have something already arranged), a wharf used by water taxis taking hikers back to Picton, and *Anakiwa Backpackers* (see p.537).

A couple of kilometres further along Queen Charlotte Drive, **Kenepuru Road** cuts right and begins its 75km journey out along the shores of Kenepuru Sound. There are no real sights along the way though Kenepuru Road provides access to several points along the Queen Charlotte Track, a handful of DOC campsites, and runs past several places to stay – *Te Mahia, Portage Resort Hotel, Portage Shop* and *Punga Cove* – all listed on pp.536–537. The road ends at the wonderful *Hopewell* **backpackers** (see p.529).

Havelock and Pelorus Sound

Nestled in the heart of the Sound, **HAVELOCK**, 35km west of Picton, comprises little more that a thin ribbon along the main road linked to a newly expanded and gentrified marina. The town won't detain you long, but it is an excellent base for hiking, kayaking or cruising the stunning **Pelorus Sound**, an exciting maze of sunken seaways with high mountain peaks.

A hundred years ago Havelock was a boom town, revelling in the wealth created by an inland gold rush and rampant logging, before slowing to a sleepy fishing village. In recent years its fortunes have revived with an influx of travellers here to discover the fun to be had in these quiet environs, and feast on **green–lipped mussels**. Havelock is the world capital for these choice morsels and you simply can't leave without tucking into a plateful or buying some from the wharf.

A complex of small cream wooden buildings near the Shell Garage on Main Road houses the **Havelock Museum** (sporadic but generally open daily 9am–5pm; donation), a miscellaneous collection of bric-a-brac plus a wood-milling display and the honour rolls from Havelock School which feature pioneering atom-splitter, **Ernest Rutherford**, who went to school here for two years from 1882 in what is now the YHA. There's a memorial in the centre of town detailing Rutherford's life story along with that of local boy **William Pickering**, to a NASA scientist during the Cold War.

The town's other famous son is the itinerant author **Barry Crump**. Crumpy, as he was affectionately known, began life as a hunter and bushman, culling deer and pigs in some of New Zealand's roughest country – a way of life he described in a series of humorous, poignant and superbly descriptive novels until his death in 1996.

If you feel like filling your lungs, ask at Rutherford Travel (see below) for directions to the **Takorika Ridge Track** (5km return; 3–5hr; 700m ascent) which heads steeply up the hill opposite the *Havelock Hotel*. It is easy as far as the waterfall (about 35min) then steepens until two-thirds of the way up when great views over Havelock and the sounds are revealed.

To see something of Pelorus Sound, either get aboard the Pelorus **Mail Boat** (covered on p.533), or go for a more personal and flexible all-day cruise with the *Foxlady* ($65) on which they typically cook up mussels and you can take your own wine. The sheltered nooks and crannies of Pelorus Sound are a perfect environment for uncrowded exploration by **kayak**. Sounds Natural do an excellent all-day trip ($79; min 2) involving a shuttle to Tennyson Inlet where you spend about five hours paddling, including a stop for lunch. They also do camping-based overnight trips ($140 a day per person), and rent kayaks ($45 first day then $35) to the suitably experienced. All the above trips are booked through Rutherford Travel (see below).

Practicalities

Buses between Picton and Nelson all stop at Havelock, while local bus and **water-taxi** operators offer services to Kenepuru and Pelorus sounds. There is no official **visitor center**, but information and booking needs are met by Rutherford Travel, 46 Main Rd, inside the *YHA* (daily 8am–10pm; ☎03/574 2114 & 0800/742 897, ⓦ www.rutherfordtravel.co.nz), who also act as the local DOC agent. Just down the street, Soundz Interesting, 60 Main Rd (Dec–March Mon–Fri 8.30am–5pm, Sat & Sun 9am–4pm; April–Nov Mon–Fri 8.30am–5pm, Sat 9am–4pm; ☎03/574 2633), also book trips and have good local knowledge.

Accommodation options include *Havelock Garden Motel* at 71 Main Rd (☎03/574 2387, ⓦ www.gardenmotels.com; ❹), with nine fully self-contained units and helpful hosts; and *Havelock Motor Camp*, 24 Inglis St (☎03/574 2339) just off Main Road in the heart of town with $10 camping, basic cabins at $15 per person, and on-site vans (❸). The traditional *Rutherford YHA Hostel*, 46 Main Rd (☎03/574 2104, ⓔ enquiries@rutherfordtravel.co.nz; camping $11, dorms ❶, rooms ❷), is centrally located in the characterful old schoolhouse which has been much improved in recent years, and has a sunny garden out back. The small *Blue Moon Backpackers*, 48 Main Rd (☎03/574 2212, ⓔ cruisinon@xtra.co.nz; dorms ❶, rooms ❷) is a welcoming spot with made-up beds, and a nice deck with long views of the marina.

Food in Havelock is surprisingly good, especially if you like mussels. The place to eat them is *Mussel Boys Restaurant*, 73 Main Rd (closes 6–7pm outside the summer season), where they dish up green-lipped mussels in myriad different sauces ($16), excellent chowder and a farmer's platter ($13) for those who don't like shellfish. Around the restaurant are details about mussels and a step-by-step guide on the best way to eat them. Otherwise, try the simple cuisine in massive portions at the *Havelock Hotel*, 54 Main Rd, where for under $20 Shirley makes sure you stock up on carbohydrates before attempting any

If you are looking for excellent bush walking with few fellow travellers, consider the **Nydia Track** (27km one way; 2 days), best tackled from Havelock and explained on DOC's *The Nydia Track* leaflet (50¢). It follows a series of bridle paths, making its way through pasture, shrubland and virgin forest, with great views from the Kaiuma Saddle (387m) and Nydia Saddle (347m), as well as along the head of Nydia Bay. The first day (5–6hr) is pleasant, but the second (4–5hr) is the real gem. **Mountain biking** is allowed on the track, but it is a fairly tough proposition in the dry, and near impossible when wet.

Maori called Nydia Bay *Opouri* – "place of sadness" – because when a *hapu* (subtribe) was preparing to migrate from the North Island to the Sounds, their leader sacrificed a young boy to Tangaroa the sea god to ensure a safe journey. When the boy's father found out, he sought revenge, storming across to Pelorus Sound and slaughtering the disgraced *hapu*.

Start at **Kaiuma Bay**, most easily accessed by water taxi from Havelock, but also driveable in around an hour and a half: turn off SH6 12km west of Havelock onto Daltons Road. The track finishes at Duncan Bay, in **Tennyson Inlet**, about an hour's drive from Havelock. The most convenient approach is to buy a package from Rutherford Travel ($45) which includes water taxi to the start and shuttle bus pickup from the end back to Havelock. They'll also organise **accommodation** somewhere around Nydia Bay, roughly halfway along the track. Groups are best served by DOC's *Nydia Lodge* ($15 per person) which will only open if there are four or more people. Otherwise go for a couple of places nearby: *Driftwood Cottage* (☎03/579 8454; $30 per person), a cosy homestay with doubles and twins; or the small and relaxed *Te Mahoerangi Backpackers* ($18, including linen). There is also a **campsite** ($5) at the northwestern end of Nydia Bay, and a waterside one at the Duncan Bay end of the track (dusk to dawn only; $5).

Southern Wilderness (☎03/520 3095, ⓦwww.southernwilderness.com) offer a two-day guided walk on the Nydia for $400 including lodging, meals and transport.

of the local walks; or *The Clansman*, 72 Main Rd (☎03/574 1170), a cosy and welcoming pub with café food during the day and good meals ($15–20) taking a Kiwi slant on Celtic classics. On a warm evening, wander down to the marina and the *Slip Inn* for a sundowner or a full meal.

Pelorus and the road to Nelson, French Pass

Following SH6 from Havelock towards Nelson, you soon pass through **Canvastown**, 9km west, a large tent city in the mid-nineteenth century but now only of note as the turn off for *Pinedale Motor Camp*, 8km south of the main road (☎03/574 2349; camping $9–10 cabins ❷), a delightful spot to relax for a few days, with bushwalks, glowworms, gold-panning and 1km of river frontage with swimming holes.

Three kilometres further along SH6 a twisting mostly-dirt road heads to the start of the Nydia Track. Carry on along SH6 to reach the **Pelorus Bridge Scenic Reserve**, 18km west of Havelock, a gorgeous forested spot run through by the crystal-clear trout-filled Pelorus River with its sandy beaches and abundant swimming holes. Superb examples of black beech trees and golden green rimu, as well as kahikatea, miro and the blue-green foliage of matai trees provide shelter for an abundance of tui, grey warblers and bellbirds. This fertile area saw a succession of Maori settlements, which prospered until Te Rauparaha conquered the north of the South Island in the 1820s. The misery caused by the war and the encroachment of European settlers drove most of the Maori away – the few that remained produced flax that Te Rauparaha could trade for rifles.

The place is understandably popular in summer. Facilities include a basic DOC **camping** area (T03/571 6019; tent sites $8, cabins $30), and a **DOC office** adjoining a small **café** (daily: Nov–March 8.30am–7pm; April–Oct 8.30am–4.30pm) purveying delicious home-made muffins, pastries, quiches and a selection of light meals.

The **walking tracks** in the reserve are fairly flat, well maintained and well marked: the **Totara** (1.5km return; 30min) and **Circle** (1km return; 30min) routes pass through the low-lying woodland for which the area is famous, while the **Trig K** (2.5km one way; 2hr), after a steady climb to 417m, offers stunning views of the whole area. From the summit you can head straight down or follow the **Beech Ridge Track** (3km; 90min), via two waterfalls, which takes the scenic route back to the start of the Trig K track.

The road west then continues past the turn off to French Pass (see below) at the small settlement of **Rai Valley** and climbs the hills past Happy Valley Adventures (see p.548) to Nelson.

Duncan Bay and French Pass

Just west of Rai Valley, almost 40km west of Havelock, a side road tempts you with signs to Tennyson Inlet and French Pass. Both are off the main tourist circuit, but if you have the time it is worth braving the narrow and winding roads: the 60km drive to French Pass takes two hours. **Duncan Bay**, 30km off the highway at the northern end of the Nydia Track (see box, p.540), is the easier of the two destinations reached initially through farmland then climbing over a bush-clad hill and dropping down to the hamlet of a couple of dozen houses. It is a gorgeous and peaceful spot with turquoise waters of Tennyson Inlet lapping the golden fringes of the bush. Bring all you need for a picnic lunch and plan to walk along the Nydia Track, perhaps to Pipi Beach (15min one way), a narrow strip of swimming beach steeply shelving into the sound.

The road to French Pass winds its way 22km to **Okiwi**, a small settlement set on a wide open bay with no facilities except for a summer-only café and *Okiwi Bay Holiday Park & Lodge* (T03/576 5006, Wwww.okiwi.co.nz; camping $12–14, lodge $28 per person, on-site vans ❷). For another 40km you drive through pockets of bush locked in sheep country and plantation pines with occasional tantalizing glimpses of inaccessible bays and coves. Just when you're beginning to wonder whether the whole expedition was worth it, you emerge from a tunnel of regenerating bush to expansive views and – when you look closer – a load of mussel farms. French Pass itself is a narrow channel between the mainland and D'Urville Island where nineteenth-century French explorer Dumont d'Urville was spun by tumultuous whirlpools. If you're here at mid-tide it is easy to understand why these seething waters were so feared. The maelstrom is best seen from a couple of short tracks in **French Pass Scenic Reserve**, 1km before the road end at **French Pass**. This tiny settlement is little more than a wharf, a petrol station and shop, DOC's basic *French Pass* **campground** ($5) and *Sea Safaris & Beachfront Villas* (T03/576 5204, Wwww.seasafaris.co.nz; camping $11–13, on-site vans ❷, B&B ❹) with a good range of accommodation and meals available on request. They also run all manner of dive trips, tank refills, boat charters, rent sea kayaks ($45 a day) and take groups over to D'Urville Island for the exemplary mountain biking, though you'll need to bring your own bike.

Nelson and around

The thriving, small city of **NELSON**, set on the coast in a broad basin between the Arthur and Richmond ranges, is a beguiling place. Initially it is not much to look at, but on longer acquaintance it gets its hooks into you. A warm, sunny climate, access to good beaches and a cluster of worthwhile wineries in the hinterland are powerful lures, but Nelson is also supremely placed for accessing Golden Bay and three national parks – Abel Tasman, Kahurangi and Nelson Lakes. It is also a haven for **artists** who are drawn by the sunlight, the landscape and the unique raw materials for pottery and ceramic art that lie beneath the rich green grass.

It will come as no surprise that the Nelson region is one of the most popular visitor destinations in New Zealand, but the appeal isn't lost on Kiwis who are moving to the region in droves pushing up property prices ridiculously: in 2003 house prices rose seventy percent, five times the national average.

You'll probably end up staying and doing much of your eating and socialising in central Nelson, particularly along the busiest **thoroughfares** of Trafalgar Street and Bridge Street. The **Suter Gallery** and the lively **Saturday Market** are good reasons to hang around Nelson, but you'll soon want to venture further, notably to **Tahunanui Beach** and the western suburb of **Stoke** for the fascinating **World of WearableArt** museum. Further west, the satellite town of **Richmond**, 14km out, is the starting point for the arts, crafts and wine district to the north. To get further away from it on a short day-trip, head for the beaches of **Rabbit Island**, which are accessible at low tide.

Some history

Nelson is one of the oldest settlements in New Zealand, a place where many early European immigrants got their first taste of the South Island. By the middle of the sixteenth century, the Ngati Tumatakokiri occupied most of the Nelson area, providing a reception committee for **Abel Tasman**'s long boats at Murderer's Bay (now Golden Bay), where they killed four of his sailors. By the time Europeans arrived in earnest, Maori numbers had been decimated by internecine fighting and the nearest *pa* site to Nelson was at Motueka, although this did little to prevent land squabbles, culminating in the **Wairau Affray** in 1843. Despite assurances from Maori chiefs Te Rauparaha and Te Rangihaeata that they would abide by the decision of a land commissioner, the New Zealand Company went ahead regardless, sending surveyors south to the Wairau Plains. A skirmish ensued, during which Te Rangihaeata's wife was shot. The bereaved chief and his men slaughtered twenty-two people in retaliation. The settlers continued their land acquisition undeterred but due to illness and hardship the community was dying on its feet when the arrival of industrious German immigrants saved it from complete dissolution.

Arrival, information and transport

Flights arrive at Nelson **airport**, 8km west of the centre, and are met by Super Shuttle Nelson (☎03/547 5782; $10) or **City Taxis** (☎03/528 8225; around $15). All **buses** drop you near the centre of the city, within easy walking distance of most accommodation. InterCity pulls in at 27 Bridge St, while the other companies all stop outside the **visitor centre**, on the corner of Trafalgar Street and Halifax Street (daily: Nov–March 8.30am–5pm; Oct–April

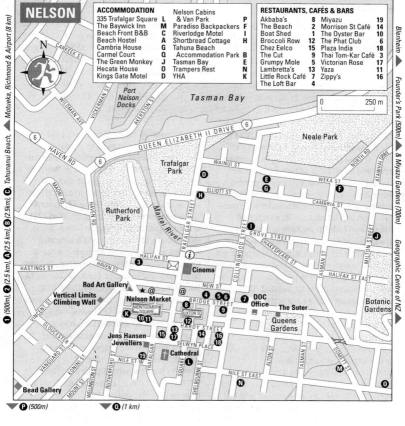

NELSON

ACCOMMODATION		
335 Trafalgar Square	L	Nelson Cabins
The Baywick Inn	M	& Van Park	P
Beach Front B&B	C	Paradiso Backpackers	F
Beach Hostel	A	Riverlodge Motel	I
Cambria House	G	Shortbread Cottage	H
Carmel Court	Q	Tahuna Beach
The Green Monkey	J	Accommodation Park	B
Hecate House	O	Tasman Bay	E
Kings Gate Motel	D	Trampers Rest	N
		YHA	K

RESTAURANTS, CAFÉS & BARS			
Akbaba's	8	Miyazu	19
The Beach	2	Morrison St Café	14
Boat Shed	1	The Oyster Bar	10
Broccoli Row	12	The Phat Club	6
Chez Eelco	15	Plaza India	18
The Cut	9	Thai Tom-Kar Café	3
Grumpy Mole	5	Victorian Rose	17
Lambretta's	13	Yaza	11
Little Rock Café	7	Zippy's	16
The Loft Bar	4		

9am–5pm; ☎03/548 2304, ⓦ www.nelsonNZ.com). The centre stocks heaps of leaflets on Nelson and the surrounding region, books onward travel, sells hut passes and has all the details on local national parks including Abel Tasman tide tables. Consequently you probably won't need to go to the main **DOC office**, 186 Bridge St (☎03/546 9335; Mon–Fri 8am–4.30pm), in the Munro Building next to the Courthouse.

SBL **buses** (☎03/548 0285; Mon–Fri 8am–6pm, Sat 8am–12.30pm; $2 a ride) run two routes between Nelson and its satellite communities from the terminal at 27 Bridge Street, while numerous smaller **shuttle buses** run further afield to Golden Bay, the Abel Tasman, Kahurangi and Nelson Lakes national parks. There's also **The Summertime Bus** ($5 per ride, $10 all day), a red double-decker that visits most of the key sights including Tahunanui Beach and the World of WearableArt on a fairly frequent basis.

Otherwise, you can get around most of the sights in the immediate vicinity with the help of a **rental car** or **bike**, while plenty of **tours** take in the highlights of the city and its surroundings (see p.550, for details of all these).

Accommodation

Most of the best places to stay are in Nelson where you have a choice of relaxing **beachside** locations or the bustling **centre** within reach of cultural diversions and nightlife. The range is broad, but those seeking out **B&Bs** might prefer to stay 14km to the southwest in Stoke where some classy establishments are well placed for accessing the wine and crafts trails immediately to the north.

With numerous good backpacker hostels you may want to save your **camping** for the prettier areas around Motueka, the Abel Tasman National Park or Golden Bay, but there are a couple of options close to town.

Nelson hotels and B&Bs

The Baywick Inn 51 Domett Street ☎03/545 6514, ⓦwww.baywick.com. Lovely restored two-storey villa from 1885 peacefully set overlooking the Maitai River and with luxuriously appointed rooms. An enthusiastic welcome includes afternoon tea, and the full cooked breakfasts are excellent. Room with private bath ❻, en suites ❼

Beach Front B&B 581 Rocks Rd ☎03/548 5299, ⓦwww.bnb.co.nz/beachfrontbb.html. Not quite on the beach front but with great views of the beach and sea from the deck out front. Just two pleasant rooms (one en suite, the other with private bathroom), very helpful hosts and a hearty full breakfast. ❺

Cambria House 7 Cambria St ☎03/548 4681, ⓦwww.cambria.co.nz. This 140-year-old weatherboard house boasts a lovely back deck and garden, beautiful fireplaces, and a wide choice of breakfasts – all just ten minutes' walk from town on a quiet road. Suites ❼, deluxe ❽

Carmel Court 50 Waimea Rd ☎03/548 2234, 1-800/18 33 18, ⓔcarmel.court@xtra.co.nz. This motel offers twelve fully self-contained units in a well-kept modern building with off-street parking, but it's a fifteen- to twenty-minute walk from the main drag. ❺

Kings Gate Motel 21 Trafalgar Street ☎03/546 9108, ⓔstay@kingsgatemotel.co.nz. Central motel with comfortable well-kept rooms including full kitchens and a pool. ❺

Riverlodge Motel 31 Collingwood St ☎03/548 3094, ⓦwww.riverlodgenelson.co.nz. One of the better motels, giving value for money in range of new and older units, all clean and comfortable. ❺

Nelson hostels

335 Trafalgar Square 335 Trafalgar Square ☎03/548 4335, ⓦwww.trafalgaraccommodation .co.nz. Newly opened Backpackers partly in a restored nineteenth-century house and keeping the Victorian theme throughout. Cheaper dorms have unusual three-tier bunks but there are pricier dorms, a range of doubles and twins, and a bar downstairs. Dorms ❶, rooms ❸

Beach Hostel 25 Muritai St ☎03/548 6817, ⓔnelsonbeachhostel@xtra.co.nz. A pleasant hostel three minutes' walk from Tahunanui Beach, with a maximum of four beds in dorms, free bikes and local phone calls, a lounge with deck and good views, free bus pick-up and frequent shuttle service to and from the city. Dorms ❶, rooms ❸

The Green Monkey 129 Milton St ☎03/545 7421, ⓦwww.thegreenmonkey.co.nz. An English-owned, converted villa, this boutique hostel is very quiet, well-kept and has a relaxed atmosphere. It has all the usual amenities and is about 1km from the town centre. Book well in advance. Dorms ❶, doubles ❷

Hecate House 181 Nile St East ☎03/546 6890, ⓔhecatehouse@xtra.co.nz. A relaxing, tucked–away women-only guesthouse in a Californian-style bungalow. The decor is restful and the garden an organic delight. The name, appropriately enough, is that of a Greek god who watched over travellers. Twins or 3-bed dorms ❶, doubles ❸

Paradiso Backpackers 42 Weka St ☎03/546 6703, ⓦwww.backpackernelson.co.nz. Based in a large, century-old converted villa and assorted purpose-built outbuildings this is a lively hostel that tends to pack out in summer, though the pressure is eased by being able to relax around the outdoor pool. Dorms ❶, rooms ❸

Shortbread Cottage 33 Trafalgar St ☎03/546 6681. Charming boutique hostel with polished wood floors and just 12 beds, so book ahead. It is a 500m walk from central Nelson and offers free pick up and drop off, free bedding, free tea and coffee and nightly shortbread. Dorms ❶, doubles ❸

Tasman Bay 8–10 Weka St ☎03/548 7950, ⓕ548 7897. A purpose-built hostel ten minutes' walk from the town centre with enthusiastic management, lively decor and a friendly welcome. Good-sized dining and kitchen areas, a large lounge, and clean spacious rooms make this a sound choice. Dorms ❶, rooms ❷

Trampers Rest 31 Alton St ☎03/545 7477. A cosy backpackers and wheelpackers haven, with home-style accommodation in comparatively small rooms in a pleasing, no-smoking villa, shared with a real

...and paradise

Pacific Islands - away from it all

Air New Zealand offers the largest range of international flights with stopovers in the South Pacific Islands.
It's easy to discover these true paradise islands by stopping off along Air New Zealand's famous Coral Route.

Dreaming about it is one thing, being there is everything. For a great trip to New Zealand at a great fare contact us at:

 0800 028 4149
24 hours a day

 www.airnewzealand.co.uk

 or visit the
Air New Zealand Travelcentre at Upper Ground Floor, New Zealand House, 80 Haymarket, London SW1Y 4TE.

AIR NEW ZEALAND
A STAR ALLIANCE MEMBER

tramping enthusiast. There's a tiny garden with hammock, bike storage and the host is an absolute mine of information. Dorms ❶, doubles ❷

YHA 59 Rutherford St ☏ 03/545 9988, ✉ yha.nelson@yha.org.nz. This purpose-built hostel in a central location remains the best in town, with a wide range of accommodation, including connecting rooms for families and two disabled-accessible units. One big and one smaller kitchen take the strain, the staff are very helpful and there are discounted rates in winter. Dorms ❶, rooms ❸

Nelson campsites

Nelson Cabins & Van Park 230 Vanguard Rd ☏ 03/548 1445, ✉ nncabins@quicksilver.net.nz. A very small, well maintained and well sited van park (no tents) that comes complete with cabins and tourists flats. Camping $10, cabins ❷, flats ❸

Tahuna Beach Accommodation Park 70 Beach Rd, Tahunanui ☏ 03/548 5159 & 0800/500 501, ⓦ www.tahunabeachholidaypark.co.nz. Enormous estuary-side campground and holiday park five minutes walk from Tahunanui Beach with a wide range of quality accommodation from tent and campervan sites through assorted cabins and units to full motel units. There's also a minigolf course, kids' playgrounds and TV room. Camping $11, cabins and units ❷–❸, motels ❹

Richmond and Monaco

Althorpe 13 Dorset St, Richmond ☏ 03/544 8117, ⓦ www.althorpe.co.nz. A pretty B&B in the tranquil neighbourhood of Richmond, with just two neat bedrooms in an 1880s homestead surrounded by roses and with a pool and spa out back. ❻

The Honest Lawyer 1 Point Rd, Monaco ☏ 03/547 8850 & 0800/921 192, ⓦ www.honestlawyer.co.nz. A surprisingly accurate reconstruction of an English pub in all elements except that, for guests who can't drag themselves away, it has some luxuriously comfortable en-suite rooms and a particularly nice cottage. Rooms ❼, cottage ❽

Kershaw House 10 Wensley Rd, Richmond ☏ 03/544 0957, ⓦ www.kershawhouse.co.nz. A large, welcoming B&B in a 1929 house which has been authentically restored – a highlight is the gorgeous dark-stained rimu staircase. All rooms are smartly decorated and have private facilities and the owners are German speakers. Mostly ❾, one room ❼

Mapledurham 8 Edward St, Richmond ☏ 03/544 4210, ⓦ www.mapledurham.co.nz. The best place to stay out of town, a beautiful rimu villa encircled by a wide, grey-floored veranda and well tended garden. The house is light and airy, dressing gowns are provided, and the breakfasts are superb. ❽

The City and around

The grid pattern streets of Nelson are dominated by the glowering, greystone **Christ Church Cathedral**, perched on a small hill peering down Trafalgar Street towards the sea. Fortunately, the cathedral's interior is nowhere near as grim as its exterior. Dazzling stained-glass windows illuminate the building, with ten particularly noteworthy examples tucked away in a small chapel to the right of the main altar. The cathedral has had a chequered history, which may account for its ugliness. English architect Frank Peck's original 1924 design was gradually modified over many years due to lack of money; World War II further intervened, and even now the cathedral tower looks as if it's still under construction.

The modern city architecture and well-disguised older buildings of Nelson are enlivened by the temporary presence of the renowned **Nelson Market** (Sat 7am–1pm), which takes over nearby Montgomery Square. Artists are flushed out of their rural boltholes and stalls are groaning with hand-dipped candles, turned wooden bowls, bracelets made from forks and all manner of produce from the crafts community. Food stalls with mounds of fruit, endless varieties of fresh bread and fish, Thai and vegetarian dishes, preserves, coffee and cakes sustain you while you browse.

Just east of the centre on Bridge Street, the pretty Victorian **Queens Gardens** (daily 8am–dusk; free), with its mature trees and well-populated duck pond, hosts **The Suter**, 208 Bridge St (daily 10.30am–4.30pm; $3; ⓦ www.TheSuter.org.nz). This small public art museum is one of the finest in the South Island, built in 1899 as a memorial to Andrew Burn Suter, Bishop of Nelson from 1866 to 1891. It hosts visiting exhibitions and shows relating to the local area, as well as changing displays from the gallery's own collection. During the summer there's usually something from their stock of **water-colours** – especially those of John Gully, a friend of the bishop whose works here largely depict scenes from the surrounding area. Look out too for oils by **"Toss" Woollaston**, a founder of the modernist movement in New Zealand art and one of a group of artists and writers who, during the 1930s and 40s, began exploring notions of a New Zealand culture independent of colonial Britain. Particular significance in the gallery is given to a famous 1909 portrait by Gottfried Lindauer of Huria Matenga, a Maori woman who, with her husband and friends, saved many lives from the wreck of the *Delaware* in 1863. Her status is indicated by traditional *moko* tattoos, feathers, bone, greenstone jewellery and the ceremonial club she holds; in the background is the foundering American ship. The other significant part of the permanent collection is devoted to ceramics and the work of local potters; the Nelson area is rich in raw materials for potters and ceramic artists.

Continue further west along Bridge Street, across the Maitai River, to the lacklustre **Botanic Gardens**, where New Zealand's first ever rugby game was played in 1870. It is mainly of interest for a small hill which, it is claimed, marks the **geographical centre of New Zealand**. The spot is appropriately marked and commands a good view over the town and its surroundings.

About 1km north of the Botanical Gardens, **Founders Park**, 87 Atawhai Drive (daily 10am–4.30pm; $5), presents relocated and replica buildings to give a somewhat sanitized version of early colonial history. It is all quite pleasant on a sunny day and good for kids, though adults might prefer the organic brewery and café, where you can sample some tasty locally brewed ales and lagers.

For a relaxing half-hour, continue 200m north along Atawhai Drive to the delightful Japanese-style **Miyazu Gardens** (daily 8am–dusk; free), a quiet oasis of reflective pools, ornamental cherry trees and restrained statuary; the gardens are at their best during December and January.

Arts and crafts

Many of the region's artists and craftspeople display at galleries outside Nelson (see account from p.551) but you can get an idea of what's in store by visiting galleries in town. A good starting point is Red Art Gallery, 1 Bridge St (T03/548 2170) which specializes in contemporary New Zealand fine art, glass and jewellery plus imported rugs.

Just southeast of the centre, the **Bead Gallery**, 18 Parere St (Mon–Sat 9am–5pm plus Sept–April Sun 10am–4pm; W www.beads.co.nz) packs a small 1920s cottage to the rafters with a heady collection of over 2000 bead styles, all for sale. The idea is simple: you can either design your own bead-piece or have one custom made for you using anything from 10¢ baubles to some of the most exotic anywhere in the world (up to $500 a piece). They have a particularly fine range of psychedelic century-old Venetian glass trade beads from West Africa at relatively modest prices.

There's another opportunity to put your creativity to work **hand-painting ceramics** at Sunshine Ceramics, 26 Gloucester St (Mon–Fri noon–5pm, Sat 10am–3pm; T03/545 9958, W www.sunshineceramics.co.nz), where you can decorate any of eighty designs of platters, cup bowls, pet dishes, etc. Aspiring **bone carvers** should try one-day workshops with Stephan ($55; T03/546 4275) which should see you with an attractive pendant by the end of the day.

If you're committed to exploring your creative potential while getting closer to local artists then contact Creative Tourism New Zealand (T03/526 8812,

The highlight of the festival calendar occurs over the middle two weeks of September when the **Nelson Arts Festival** (Ⓦwww.nelsonfestivals.co.nz) presents all manner of arts, theatre, music, writers' readings and street entertainment, much of it either free or costing just a few dollars. Headline events such as rock gigs and major plays command $15–30 ticket prices. It conveniently coincides with the **World of WearableArt Awards Show**, which has become an international event, staged every year over the second and third weekends in September (currently Fri–Sun & Thurs–Sun). This unique catwalk show combines elements of sculpture, performance art, theatre, choreography and dance to create an extraordinary spectacle. The best of the costumes subsequently go on display at the World of WearableArt museum (see below). Tickets for this bizarre two-hour extravaganza cost $65–95, but usually sell out months in advance: either advance purchase from the museum website or turn up at the museum on spec hoping for a cancellation.

Nelson also hosts the **Nelson Jazz Festival** (Ⓦnelsonjazz.co.nz) which attracts musicians from around the country for 5–6 days leading up to the New Year's Day finale; and **Hooked on Seafood** (in late March), a demonstration of seafood expertise by chefs working at stalls and dishing up food for passers-by.

Ⓦwww.creativetourism.co.nz) who coordinate **creative workshops** with topics ranging from harakeke (flax) weaving and woolcraft to bone carving, bronze casting and seafood cookery.

Lord of the Rings fans will, of course, want to visit the jewellers Jens Hansen, cnr Church St & Selwyn Place (Mon–Fri 9am–5pm, Sat 10am–1pm; Ⓦwww.jenshansen.com) who Peter Jackson got to make "**The one ring to rule them all**", or a few dozen of them to suit various cast members. Replicas are available, but remember what happens to the owner of such a ring.

Southwest Nelson and Stoke

Haven Road (SH6) runs northwest out of central Nelson and, after a kilometre, becomes **Wakefield Quay**, a popular spot for strolling along the waterfront but primarily known for the *Boat Shed Café* (see p.549) jutting picturesquely out over the water. Continue 3km along SH6 to reach **Tahunanui Beach Reserve**, a long golden strand backed by grassland and drifting dunes. It is where Nelson comes to relax on sunny weekends, with safe swimming, a fun park, zoo and children's playgrounds: buses run here frequently along SH6 from the city.

A further 3km out along SH6, follow signs to the **World of WearableArt and Collectable Cars** (WOW; daily: Nov–Easter 10am–6.30pm; Easter–Oct 10am–5pm; $15; Ⓦwww.worldofwearableart.com), the undoubted new jewel in Nelson's crown. It is primarily a purpose built showcase for the best designs from the WearableArt shows (see above) combined with some highly desirable shiny automobiles, both old and fairly new. The fashion show with a difference, first put on by Suzie Moncrieff outside a cobb cottage in 1987, has grown into an international event and now attracts participants from all over the world, the criteria being sculptures or pieces of art that can be worn as clothes – in many cases made from the most unusual materials such as household junk, food, metal, stone, wood and tyres. It is all highly imaginative, but only the best get displayed here in a manner that owes more to glitzy fashion shows and colourful theatre productions than static gallery or museum exhibitions. Footage of past events brings the whole thing to life. To get there take an SBL bus to Stoke, getting off at the *Black Cat* bar, five minutes' walk from the gallery, or join The Summertime Bus (see p.543) which comes to the door.

Nelson's suburban spread seamlessly becomes **Stoke**, 8km southwest of Nelson city centre. Main Road runs right through the centre passing one of the best diversions around, **Mac's Brewery**, 660 Main Rd (daily: Oct–April 10am–6pm; May–Sept 10am–5.30pm; ☎03/547 0526, ⓦwww.macsbeer .co.nz) which conducts hour-long **tours** (11am & 2pm; $8). These take you through the completely natural brewing process – the brewery sits on its own spring, and uses local Motueka hops – and includes tasting of superior brews.

Activities

Nelson is the sort of place that lying on the beach at Tahunanui might be as active as you want to get, though there is no shortage of energetic diversions. On a wet day retreat to Vertical Limits, 34 Vanguard St (☎0508/837 84225, ⓦwww.verticallimits.co.nz; $15) for some indoor **rock climbing** and when the weather improves you can join their full-day climbing trips ($130) to Payne's Ford in Takaka.

Another good destination, in the wet or dry, is Happy Valley Adventures, 194 Cable Bay Rd, 17km northeast of Nelson off SH6 (☎03/545 0304, ⓦwww.HappyValleyAdventures.co.nz), a large forested farm explored on **quadbikes**. Assorted **safaris** explore their 40km of track, climbing hills, passing monstrous matai trees, stopping to learn a little about the forest and its stories and eventually reaching a high spot with expansive views of Cable Bay and the ocean. The most popular trips are the Bayview Circuit (2hr; rider $90, passenger $30), and the Skyline Special (3hr; $125, no passengers) designed for the more skilled and ambitious rider. Some rides visit the site of the **Skywire** ($85), a four-seater cablecar chair that swoops almost a kilometre across a forested valley then back to their hilltop café with its panoramic deck. A ride on this can be combined with a quadbike ride for $160.

For **horse riding** you'll have to head 17km southwest of Nelson through Richmond to Stonehurst Farm Horse Treks, Haycock Rd (☎0800/487 357, ⓦwww.stonehurstfarm.co.nz). The majority of the shorter treks (1hr $35, 2.5hr $69, 4hr $85) take place in the foothills of the Richmond ranges and offer great views of the coast and beyond; there are horses to suit all abilities, the routes are challenging but not frightening and there's a full safety briefing.

Visiting Abel Tasman National Park from Nelson

Most people visiting the Abel Tasman National Park base themselves at Motueka, Kaiteriteri or Marahau (for all see p.554), but it is quite possible to visit the park directly from Nelson. K Bus (☎03/525 9434, ⓦwww.kahurangi.co.nz) and Abel Tasman Coachlines (☎03/548 0285, ⓦwww.abeltasmantravle.co.nz) both have early morning departures and late afternoon return buses giving you enough time for a water taxi ride and a few hours walking along the Coast Track. Depending on what you want to do, your day's transport will cost $50–75.

A speedy alternative is to ride the Exhilarator ($80 return; ☎03/548 8066, ⓦwww.exhilarator.co.nz), a super-fast jetboat that whisks you from Nelson to the park in double-quick time. It meets water taxis and Abel Tasman Sailing Adventures for further exploration.

To get airborne try **tandem paragliding** with Richmond-based Nelson Paragliding (☎03/544 1182, ⓦwww.nelsonparagliding.co.nz): a hair-raising drive up the hill to the launch site reveals a spectacular landscape, before you run like hell then glide off into the quiet up draughts for 15–20 minutes of eerily silent flight. Tandem flights go for $110 and a one-day introductory lesson costs $150. For more of a birdlike quality to your flying experience, go with Nelson Hang Gliding (☎03/548 9151; $140).

Eating

Nelson's enviable lifestyle is reflected in the **broad choice** of eating options within easy reach of the town centre. And when you tire of these, there's always fine food and wine in gorgeous settings at the **wineries**. If fast food beckons, try out one of the small **ethnic cafés** which offer everything from sushi to kiwi burgers via kebabs and pasta. Don't forget Nelson's pubs and bars (see p.550) for a quick snack either.

Akbaba's Turkish Kebabs 130 Bridge St. Plenty of cheap kebabs and salads ($5–11) to take away, munch in the courtyard out back, or in booth seating on low floor cushions; Turkish decor and music create a lively and casual atmosphere for lunch and supper. Closed Sun.

The Beach Tahuna Beach Reserve. Handy spot close to Tahunanui Beach with espresso and all your Kiwi café favourites.

Boat Shed 350 Wakefield Quay ☎03/546 9783. A converted boat shed perched out over the water with unimpeded views of spectacular sunsets over Tasman Bay. Exceptional seafood (mains $25–35) and a bustling ambience mean that it suffers somewhat from its own popularity at weekends. Make the effort to come on one of the quieter nights and save room for the fab desserts.

Broccoli Row 5 Buxton Square ☎03/548 9621. Generous portions of frittata, excellent soups and salads (all $8–10) make up the daytime fare at this vegetarian and seafood restaurant which also does more formal dinners with blackboard specials ($19–22). Dine inside or out, and book for dinner at weekends. Closed Sun; BYO only.

Chez Eelco 296 Trafalgar St. Nelson's first real café opened in 1961 and long maintained a European hippy tenor, though it is now a fairly standard but perfectly decent café and bar made more interesting by the frequently changing artworks on the walls.

The Cut 94 Collingwood St ☎03/548 9874. A swish but relaxed café/restaurant in an historic villa with a broad menu including steaks, pan-roast pork, peppered tuna and at least one veggie option. The wine list is extensive and mains range around $25.

Lambretta's 204 Hardy St. Lambretta scooters lord it over this cavernous and bustling restaurant which does good coffee and specializes in exotic

pizzas (all named after Lambretta models), pasta dishes (around $18), plus the likes of pork and apple sage pie ($21).

Miyazu *Rutherford Hotel*, Nile St near Trafalgar Square ☎03/548 2299. Predictably expensive but excellent dinner-only Japanese restaurant in stylish surroundings. Perfect when nothing but sashimi will do.

Morrison St Cafe 244 Hardy St. Modern café and gallery with tasty brunches, lunches, snacks and pleasing decor liberally hung with local art. Plenty of outdoor seating too.

Plaza India 132 Collingwood St ☎03/546 9344. An authentic and reasonably priced Indian restaurant serving tasty lunches and dinners. Eat inside or in the tiled courtyard.

Thai Tom-Kar Café 70 Achilles St ☎03/545 9998. It doesn't look much – just three tables and a cash register – but this place does the best Thai in town, by far. It is all good, but the Penang curry ($15) and seafood white noodles ($16) are outstanding. Takeaways available. BYO only.

Victorian Rose 281 Trafalgar St. Good just for a drink (see p.550) or a coffee in the late afternoon sun but also dishes up straightforward chicken-and-chips style meals at reasonable prices, made even more affordable with a discount voucher available at many of the town's backpackers.

Yaza Montgomery Sq. A hip little licensed coffee house selling excellent breakfasts, lunches, snacks, coffees and various teas. It's very reasonably priced and turns into an alternative night spot late in the week with various advertised events – poetry, music, talks. Well worth seeking out.

Zippy's 276 Hardy St. If you're looking for home-baked veggie or wheat-free food, wicked vegan curries, tofu burgers and coffee that bites back, and you can bear the purple and orange walls, then this is the place for you. Mon–Sat 9am–6pm.

Drinking, nightlife and entertainment

While most of its neighbours retire early to sip their cocoa, Nelson stays up all night and has a party – at least on Friday and Saturday. For raucous boozing and a little dancing head for the half dozen bars on Bridge Street between Trafalgar and Collingwood streets. Pubs and **bars** of all sorts dominate, many with **live music**, karaoke and DJ **nights**; check out the Friday edition of the *Nelson Mail* ($0.80) to find out **what's on**.

Mainstream **movies** play at the State Cinema 6 (℡03/548 3885), opposite the central post office while flicks of more minority interest turn up at the Suter Cinema, at the Suter Art Gallery, 208 Bridge St (Thurs–Sun only; ℡03/548 0808).

Grumpy Mole 141 Bridge St. Always open late with DJs playing top 40 and pop in all the bars including the garden. They have early evening happy hours, big video screens and free pool from 7–9pm (Mon–Thurs only). There are half a dozen broadly similar places within a short stagger if this place doesn't suit.

The Honest Lawyer 1 Point Rd (See p.545). A comfortable, country pub with a great beer garden overlooking the beach. They have a wide range of local and foreign beverages, wholesome grub – Nelson Bay scallops, steak and Guinness pie (both $19) – and live music late in the week, often Irish folk or covers.

Little Rock Cafe 165 Bridge St. Very lively and popular dance venue on Fri and Sat when they have a broad-ranging DJ-led party.

The Loft Bar 123a Bridge St. Upstairs late night bar and club with a balcony overlooking the excesses of Bridge St. They get a lot of live music and like to play a little hip hop and high NRG from time to time.

The Oyster Bar 115 Hardy St. A tiny, chic, no-smoking bar serving the best gin and tonic in town and dishing up Californian-style sushi to discerning customers. The best bet for a quiet drink and cool sounds. Closed Sun & Mon.

The Phat Club 137 Bridge St ℡03/548 3311. The place you'll catch any touring bands or DJs that happen to be around.

Victorian Rose 281 Trafalgar St. Olde English-style pub with a good range of beer and plenty of live music with jazz on Tuesday and Thursday and a variety of styles at the weekend. Happy hours from 4–7pm

Listings

Automobile Association 45 Halifax St ℡03/548 8339.

Bike rental Natural High, 52 Rutherford St (℡03/546 6936, ⊛www.cyclenewzealand.com) offer bikes at around $20 for half a day, $30 a day, and run a range of small-group escorted rides such as a four-day Nelson/Marlborough circuit for $1200. They're also a great resource for bike tourers, selling used bikes and renting panniers, tandems, kids' trailers, touring trailers and camping gear.

Buses and shuttles Abel Tasman Coachlines (℡03/548 0285, ℮atc@nelsoncoaches.co.nz) leaves Nelson at 7.15am daily for Marahau or Totaranui, via Motueka, connecting with launch services deeper into the park, and operates a service to the head of the Heaphy Track; Intercity (℡03/548 1538) offers daily services to Picton, Blenheim and Christchurch or to Richmond, Motueka, Takaka and Totaranui; K Bus (℡03/525 9430 & 0800/173 371) goes to Abel Tasman, Totaranui, Golden Bay and the Heaphy, Havelock ,

Blenheim and Picton; Lazerline (℡0800/220 001) runs between Christchurch and Nelson via Maruia Springs and Hanmer; Nelson SBCL (℡03/548 3290) runs buses to Stoke, Richmond and small communities thereabouts, as well as to the Abel Tasman National Park; and Southern Link Shuttles (℡03/758 3338) goes to Westport, Christchurch, Hanmer Corner and Reefton. Atomic does daily runs to the Nelson Lakes, Picton and beyond.

Camping and outdoor equipment Wet-weather clothing and camping gear can be bought from Rollo's BBQ and Camping Centre, 12 Bridge St, or Basecamp, 295 Trafalgar St.

Car rental Avis ℡03/547 2727; Budget ℡03/547 9586; Hardy Cars ℡03/546 1681; Hertz ℡03/547 2299; and Rent-a-dent ℡03/546 9890. Daily rates start at about $60–70; $50 a day for week-long rentals.

Diving gear Scuba gear can be rented from Richmond Sportsworld, 213 Queens St, Nelson.

Internet access Aurora Tech Ltd, 161 Trafalgar St, between New St and Bridge St daily 9am–10pm;

Internet Outpost in the Megabyte Café, 35 Bridge
St, Mon–Sat 10am–6pm; and Discount Internet at
Boots-off Travel Centre, 53 Bridge St, Mon–Sat,
10am–5pm.
Left luggage $2 a day at Nelson visitor centre.
Medical treatment Nelson Public Hospital,
Waimea Rd ☎03/546 1800.

Pharmacy Prices Pharmacy, cnr Hardy &
Collingwood St, open daily till 6pm.
Post office Cnr Trafalgar St and Halifax St, oppo-
site the visitor centre (Mon–Fri 7.45am–5pm, Sat
9.30am–12.30pm).
Taxis Nelson City Taxis ☎03/548 8225; Sun City
Taxis ☎0800/422 666.

West of Nelson and the road to Motueka

Much of the pleasure in hanging around Nelson is what lies on its doorstep, particularly to the west where what at first looks just like standard New Zealand farmland turns out to harbour some excellent **wineries**. Here the vines appreciate the combination of natural spring water, New Zealand's sunniest climate and either the free draining alluvial gravels of the Waimea Plains or the clay gravels of the Moutere Hills. Wineries are interspersed with the studios of a number of contemporary artists working in the Nelson region, many of whom exhibit in their own small **galleries**, showcasing ceramics, glass-blowing, woodturning, textiles, sculpture and painting.

Most places are located on or just off SH60 which runs north from Richmond towards Motueka through some lovely scenery big on sea views. You can sample the best of the region on an extended drive from Nelson to Motueka but the region is appealing enough to warrant a couple of leisurely days perhaps basing yourselves in Richmond (see p.553) or one of the places closer to the wineries (see below). At the heart of the region is the burgeoning settlement of **Mapua** with its excellent restaurants, galleries and kayaking trips.

What follows is only an introduction to some of the best (and better known) places, and for more thorough investigations equip yourselves with leaflets such as *Winemakers of Nelson*, *Nelson's Creative Pathways*, *Nelson Wines Trailmap*, the *Tourist Guide to Nelson Potters*: all free and available from visitor centres and most of the places listed below.

Driving or cycling is probably the best way to get around, though you may want to join a **guided tour** some of which combine the wineries and art galleries. Some of the cheapest are Nelson Excursions (☎03/544 4744) who offer an afternoon tour ($50) and a slightly extended variation with platter lunch ($60). Alternatively, go with Bay Tours (☎0800/229 868, Ⓦwww.baytoursnelson.co.nz) either on an afternoon trip (5 wineries; $60) or a full-day tour (6 wineries; $135) which includes an excellent lunch. Bay Tours also do combination wine, art and craft tours (half-day $50, full day $72).

Around Waimea Inlet

Highway 6 runs some 17km southwest of Nelson to Richmond where SH60 cuts north towards Motueka around the shores of **Waimea Inlet**. A couple of kilometres along SH60, the *Grape Escape* makes a good starting point for a wine tour of the region (see p.553). Craft fans are better off 3km further along at **Höglund Art Glass**, Lansdowne Road (daily 9am–5pm; ☎03/544 6500, Ⓦwww.nelson.hoglund.co.nz), New Zealand's only inter-national-standard glass centre with a gallery (free) displaying an amazing array of their work. The style of the glassware (mostly tableware) is Scandinavian-influenced, which works best in the bigger, bolder pieces with clean lines and bright, unusual colours. Some pieces are valued at several thousand dollars, but there is also a "seconds" shop where minor blemishes earn large discounts. They also run a 45min **tour** (3–5 daily; $15) introducing you to the history and techniques of handblown glass manufacture – partly through early works by Swedish owners Ola and Marie Höglund – then you're taken out into the main workshop to watch these beautiful works in production. On full-day beginner glassblowing classes ($580) you should manage a paperweight, and there are two-day hands-on sessions ($990) for those with some experience.

A couple of kilometres north along SH60, the Moutere Highway cuts left for **Upper Moutere** and a cluster of excellent wineries. Almost opposite the Moutere Highway junction, Redwood Road runs past the Nelson area's largest winery, *Seifried*, and on to picture-book pretty **Rabbit Island**, one of Nelson's most popular beaches with golden sands backed by trees: note that the access road is barred at dusk each day.

Back on SH60 it is another 5km north to the **Bronte Gallery**, Bronte Road East, recommended for the highly individual work by internationally recognized ceramic artist, Darryl Robertson, all done on site. He also does notable abstract oils, a medium used by his partner, Lesley Jacka Robertson, whose work is on display. There's appealing **accommodation** next door in the form of the delightful *Atholwood* (T03/540 2925, W www.atholwood.co.nz; **7**), with garden and bush running down to Waimea Inlet, swimming pool and spa, and breakfast included.

Mapua and the Motueka road

Mapua, a couple of kilometres off SH60 and some 34km from Nelson, overlooks the northwestern end of Rabbit Island and the picturesque Waimea Estuary. The wharf was once legendary for producing smoked fish from a quirky jumble of old buildings, but in recent years it has turned into a fashionable dining retreat with several restaurants and assorted minor attractions. The original operation still makes excellent manuka-smoked fish (of several species), great mussels and a widely acclaimed fish paté, but the transformation came with the opening of the waterside *Smokehouse* restaurant (book for dinner on T03/540 2280), a polished affair with mains around $25. This remains one of the best places to eat throughout the day, challenged by the adjacent and stylish *Flax* (T03/540 2028).

A meal or a beer by the water and a stroll around the small galleries – notably The Cool Store Gallery right by the wharf – is justification enough to visit, but you could also visit the surprisingly interesting **aquarium** (daily Oct–April 9.30am–8pm; May–Sept 9am–5pm; $5), with its touch-tanks full of fish and some informative video and static exhibits. Much more fun is to be had with Mapua Adventures (T03/540 3833) whose **jetboat** at the wharf does a $55 zoom around Rabbit Island (45min), stopping off along the way to identify some of the rare birds that inhabit the shores. They also do guided kayak tours (2.5hr; $55) and rent bikes ($20 a half-day).

North of Mapua, SH60 runs 7km to the tiny settlement of **Tasman**, and the *Jester House* (T03/526 6742, W www.jesterhouse.co.nz), an excellent daytime café popular with Motueka residents for its garden seating, rose arbours, and **tame eels** to keep the kids entertained. The food is all home-baked and reasonably priced, and the coffee is strong. It is all very tempting and for $250 there's even fairytale **accommodation** around the back in *The Boot* (B&B; **9**), an enormous red Mother Hubbard boot with a luxurious lounge area, a romantic bedroom upstairs and its own little garden patio.

A pleasant day can be spent touring Nelson's wineries, perhaps stopping for lunch at one of several good restaurants, or picking up picnic requisites and heading for Neudorf. *Seifried* and the *Grape Escape* are signposted off SH60 just a few kilometres north of its junction with SH6; the rest of the wineries listed below are clustered around Upper Moutere, around 5km west of SH60. To get there follow signs for the Moutere Highway. Core **hours** in summer are typically daily 10am–4.30pm and are much reduced in winter: call ahead.

Glover's Gardner Valley Rd ☎03/543 2698, ⓦ www.glovers-vineyard.co.nz. Small-output winery run but the slightly eccentric Dave Glover, once renowned for tucking a Wagner CD into every package destined for overseas. Wagner usually plays in the background while you taste (free) European-structured wines crafted to produce highly tannic reds (Pinot Noir and Cabernet Sauvignon) and acidic whites (Sauvignon Blanc and Riesling) which stand up to food and age well. Open Oct–April daily 10am–5pm.

Grape Escape cnr SH60 and McShanes Rd ☎03/544 4054. Growing complex with several specialty food shops and a wine tasting room where you can sample the wares of three wineries, Te Mania, Holmes and Richmond Plains. Between them there's a pretty wide range of styles to taste.

Kahurangi Estate Sunrise Rd ☎03/543 2980, ⓦ www.kahurangi.com. Well-respected winery with a chance to taste their wares ($2, refunded with purchase), particularly the Riesling and Gewürztraminer. The place is always popular for its modern, stylish café with alfresco dining on the likes of an antipasto platter for two ($28), warm chicken salad ($15) or bruschetta topped with vine–ripened tomato and the estate's own olive oil ($12). They have the region's best coffee, too. Sept–May daily 11am–5pm.

Moutere Hills off Sunrise Valley Rd, Upper Moutere ☎03/543 2288, ⓦ www.moutterehills.co.nz. Follow signs off the Moutere Highway to this family-run winery and relaxed garden café serving their "Woolshed Platter" ($17) complete with Blackball salami, Kapiti cheese and assorted pickles, a cheeseboard ($12) and the likes of smoked chicken vol-au-vents ($15). Tastings are free and everything is available by the glass and bottle: their rosé goes down nicely on a sunny day. Open Oct–April daily 11am–6pm.

Neudorf Neudorf Rd, Upper Moutere ☎03/543 2643, ⓦ www.neudorf.co.nz. Relaxed winery in a low-slung wooden building covered by vines with simple outdoor seating in the shade of some tall ancient trees. It is a lovely spot for sampling some of their superb wines (free) some produced from their 30-year-old vines on site, some of the oldest in the region. Everything is available by the bottle and glass, so bring a picnic and relax in the garden. Open Sept–May Mon–Sat 10.30am–5pm and Sun in Jan.

Seifried Estate cnr SH60 and Redwood Rd ☎03/544 5599, ⓦ www.seifried.co.nz. The area's largest winery, which free tasting from their wide range of wines, and good dining in their large restaurant which does the usual platters, great desserts and has a kids' menu. Tasting daily 10am–5pm; restaurant open for lunch daily, dinner at weekends.

A few hundred metres towards Motueka, the Tasman Store marks the turn off for the **Fullmer Gallery**, Baldwin Rd (daily 10am–5pm), one of the best galleries in the region notable for Steve Fullmer's brightly coloured ceramic art and tableware (starting around $25 for a cup and saucer), and oils by other artist such as Blenheim-based John Porter Parker.

Motueka is just 10km ahead.

Abel Tasman National Park and around

The **Abel Tasman National Park**, 60km north of Nelson, is a stunningly beautiful area with an international reputation. This results in large crowds of trampers, kayakers and day-trippers all through the summer: indeed as the busy season gradually extends into spring and autumn it may be necessary to impose some limitations to preserve the unique experience the park now provides. Some contend it is better to come in early spring, mid-autumn, or even winter, but if you have to come in summer, don't be put off. Despite being New Zealand's smallest national park – just 20km by 25km – the Abel Tasman absorbs the crowds tolerably well and packs in some real beauty: golden sandy beaches lapped by crystal-clear waters and lush green bushland, all interspersed with granite outcrops and inhabited by abundant wildlife.

The goal of most visitors is the coastline. Some come to hike the **Abel Tasman Coast Track** with its picturesque mixture of dense coastal bush-walking, gentle climbs to lookouts and walks across idyllic beaches. There are even abundant water taxis allowing you to pick the sections you want to hike, or get a lift back if you've had enough. Others come for the wonderful **kayaking** around the mercurial coastline spending leisurely lunchtimes on golden sands before paddling off in the late afternoon sun to some campsite or hut. The two can be combined and you might even tack on **sailing** the limpid waters and **swimming with seals** to round out the experience.

Wherever you go you'll likely hear birdsong and the gently soporific lapping of the waves on the shore, but the park isn't entirely devoid of habitation with a few dozen private residences scattered around the more popular bays. Most only have access by foot or boat but that doesn't stop a handful of places operating as B&Bs making overnighting in the park a comfortable experience. Of course there are also DOC huts and campsites for hardier specimens.

The main base for forays into the southern section of the park is the service town of **Motueka**, a pleasant if unexciting place where you'll likely organise hiking or kayaking trips. Most Abel Tasman tourism operators are based right at the southern entrance to the park in tiny **Marahau** where virtually everything is focused on catering to visitors. This is where most people start, though with ever greater crowds, the kayaking companies have had to devise new ways to keep the kayaks from forming a brightly coloured traffic jam just off the park shores. To ease the pressure, a few of the cruises and paddling trips start a little further south from the diminutive beach community of **Kaiteriteri** which also has limited accommodation and can make a relaxed place to spend a night or two.

The northernmost parts of the park are accessed from **Takaka** (see p.566) where Abel Tasman Drive leads to Awaroa and Totaranui, both on the Coast Track. **Totaranui** comprises just a huge campground and a lovely beach from where water-taxi operators head back to their Marahau and Kaiteriteri bases, stopping in the bays on the way home.

Some history and natural history

Since around 1500, Maori made seasonal encampments along this coast and some permanent settlements flourished around the mouth of the Awaroa River. In 1642, **Abel Tasman** anchored his two ships near Wainui in Golden Bay and promptly lost four men in a skirmish with the Ngati Tumatakokiri, after which he departed the shores remarking "There be giants" in his journal. Frenchman **Dumont d'Urville** dropped by in 1827 and explored the area between

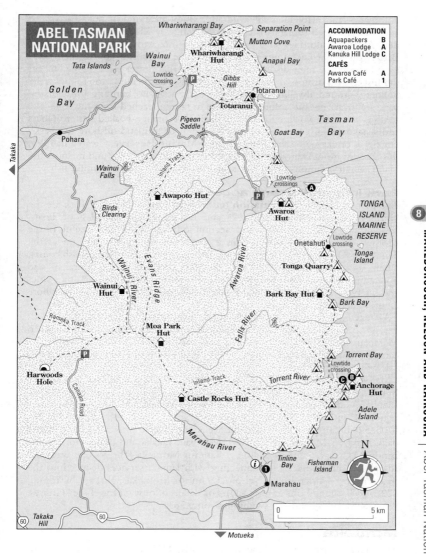

ABEL TASMAN
NATIONAL PARK

Whariwharangi Bay   Separation Point
                                    Mutton Cove
Tata Islands   Wainui   Whariwharangi
                      Bay   Hut
                                    Anapai Bay
                      Lowtide   Gibbs
Golden   crossing   Hill
Bay   Pigeon   Totaranui
                      Saddle   Totaranui
Pohara
                                          Goat Bay   Tasman
                                                          Bay
Wainui
Falls   Inland Track
                      Awapoto Hut
Birds   Awaroa   TONGA
Clearing   Hut   ISLAND
                      Evans Ridge   Awaroa River   MARINE
                                          Onetahuti   RESERVE
                      Wainui   Tonga
                      River   Lowtide   Island
Wainui   crossings
Hut   Tonga Quarry
                      Rameka Track
                                          Bark Bay Hut   Bark Bay
                      Moa Park   Falls River
                      Hut
Harwoods   Torrent Bay
Hole   Lowtide
                      Inland Track   crossing
                      Castle Rocks Hut   Torrent River   Anchorage
                                                          Hut
                                          Adele
                      Marahau River   Island
                                          Tinline   Fisherman
                      Takaka   Bay   Island
                      Hill   Marahau   N

                      Motueka

ACCOMMODATION	
Aquapackers	B
Awaroa Lodge	A
Kanuka Hill Lodge	C
CAFÉS	
Awaroa Café	A
Park Café	1

0   5 km

MARLBOROUGH, NELSON AND KAIKOURA | Abel Tasman National Park

Marahau and Torrent Bay, but it was not for another 23 years that **European settlement** began in earnest. The settlers chopped, quarried, burned and cleared until nothing was left but gorse and bracken. Happily, few obvious signs of their invasion remain and the vegetation has vigorously regenerated over the years. Named after the first European explorer to experience its shores, the Abel Tasman National Park was **gazetted** in 1942, following the tireless campaigning of one **Perrine Moncrieff**, a determined woman by all accounts.

With a range of habitats from sea level to 1000m, Abel Tasman is full of rich and varied **plant life**. In the damp and torpid gullies, beech trees and shrubs dominate, kanuka tolerates the wild and windy areas and manuka thrives on land that has been subject to repeated burnings by Maori and European settlers. At higher altitudes, silver and red beech mix with rata, miro and totara. **Birds** you might encounter include tui, native pigeons, bellbirds (their presence betrayed by their distinctive call), fantails that flutter close by feeding off the insects you disturb as you walk through the bush, and if you're lucky the bobbing, ground–dwelling weka. The fresh waterways burbling through the park are invariably the colour of tea due to tannin leached from the soil.

Along the coast you might see the distinctive orange-beaked oystercatchers and shags who dive to great depths in search of fish; and offshore the park's sanctity is preserved by the **Tonga Island Marine Reserve**. Created in 1993, this extends from Awaroa Head to just beyond Mosquito Bay and includes the island which is famous for its **fur seal colony**, seabirds and plentiful fish.

Park information and access

The main sources of **information** on the Abel Tasman National Park are the visitor centres at Nelson, Motueka and Takaka which will all book boats, kayaks, hut passes, transport and accommodation. The most useful is the Motueka visitor centre which runs a centralised booking system under the banner of Abel Tasman Green Rush (Ⓦwww.AbelTasmanGreenRush.co.nz). There are also **unmanned** DOC **display shelters** at the Marahau and Totaranui **park entrances**, with general information about the park, tide times and safety precautions – including intentions books you should fill in before entering and after leaving the park.

Access into the park is generally on foot or by boat, but a couple of roads extend to the park entrances: in the south you can drive on a sealed road to Marahau; and in the north a partly gravel road leads from Takaka to the large campground at Totaranui. A rough spur off the latter runs down to the north side of the Awaroa Estuary.

Major **bus** lines like InterCity and Atomic will get you to Nelson but only K Bus (Ⓣ03/525 9434, Ⓦwww.kahurangi.co.nz) does a run from Picton via Blenheim and Nelson to Motueka and on to Takaka. The best service in the region is with Abel Tasman Coachlines (Nelson Ⓣ03/548 0285, Motueka Ⓣ03/528 8850; Ⓦwww.abeltasmantravel.co.nz), which runs two to three times daily between Motueka, Kaiteriteri, Marahau, Takaka and points north. One handy ATC service leaves Nelson at 7am for Motueka (1hr; $9 one way) and Marahau (1hr 40min; $14) connecting with launch services deeper into the park; another service leaves Nelson at 7am for Motueka, Takaka (2hr 15min; $22) and Totaranui (3hr 15min; $33). For details of onward travel see "Cruises, water taxis, sailing and seal swimming" on p.561.

Motueka

The once sleepy hop-growing town of **MOTUEKA**, 47km northwest of Nelson, is now firmly established as the base for exploring the Abel Tasman National Park. You don't have to start here, but with a complete booking service, a range of accommodation and places you can rent hiking gear it is the obvious choice.

The name Motueka means "land of the weka", a reference to the abundance of these edible birds. Maori dined on them, grew kumara in the fertile soil and exploited the plentiful marine life until the arrival of European settlers in 1842 heralded the demise of the community-based traditional lifestyle in the region. Nonetheless, horticulture has long been the mainstay of the Motueka economy, and with all those orchards and vineyards around, it makes a good place to get **seasonal work**. Work is most plentiful from December to March and workers can often get free accommodation: contact the Motueka visitor centre for details.

The town and activities

Motueka is strung along SH60, with quieter streets spurring off from the main highway. Head a kilometre down Old Wharf Road or Tudor Street to reach **Motueka Quay**, where the ghost of this once-busy port lingers among the scant remains of the old jetty and store houses. Here lies the rusting hulk of the Scottish-built *Janie Seddon* – named after the daughter of Richard Seddon, premier of New Zealand from 1893 until his death in 1906. Having served in both world wars and as a Wellington pilot vessel it was ignominiously beached here in 1955.

The tiny **Motueka District Museum** (Nov–May Mon–Sat 10am–3pm, Sun 10aam–1pm; June–Oct Tues–Fri 1–3pm; $2) delves into the area's history through a few Maori and European artefacts, as well as the *Motueka Carvings*, a modern four-panel frieze tucked away in the records room that skilfully depicts the livelihoods that have traditionally sustained Tasman Bay.

People are usually too desperate to get to the Abel Tasman National Park to bother with other activities around Motueka, but there's excellent **hiking** in the hills to the west (see below) and the opportunity to get a preview of where you might tramp by going **tandem skydiving** with Skydive Abel Tasman (℡0800/422 899 & 03/528 4091, Ⓦwww.skydive.co.nz). Based at Motueka airport, 3km southwest of town, they offer all the usual jumps ($210 from 9000ft; $260 from 12,000ft; $360 from 15,000ft) plus excellent scenery and helpful, friendly parachuting "buddies".

A less intense but no less rewarding experience is **adventure horse riding** with Western Ranges Horse Treks (Oct–May only; ℡03/522 4178, Ⓦwww.thehorsetrek.co.nz), located around 40km southwest of Motueka on SH61: call for directions. They take you to wild and challenging places often involving river crossings: half a day ($90; no credit cards) gives you a taster but for the full experience you really need a full day ($130), two days ($350) overnighting in a comfy hut with meals cooked outdoors over a wood fire, or even the monstrous ten-day trek ($2000).

Walks around Motueka

Some of the best sub-alpine hiking in the north of the South Island is around the 1795m **Mount Arthur** and the associated uplifted plateau, the **Mount Arthur Tablelands**, all detailed in DOC's *The Cobb valley, Mount Arthur and the Tablelands* leaflet ($1) available from the visitor centre in Motueka. Traditionally, few visitors have bothered coming up this way, so what company you find will mostly be Kiwis.

The principal starting point is the Flora car park, on the Graham Valley Road, which leads off SH61 south of Motueka. From here there are commanding views of the lowlands, with Mount Arthur dominating the southern skyline. It is only an hour from the car park to the **Mount Arthur Hut** ($10), from where you can continue on to the top of Mount Arthur in another 3 hours; or head up from the car park to the 1448m summit of Mount Lodestone (2hr).

Penetrating the moor-like **Tablelands** requires a little more effort though you can stay at Salisbury Lodge around 4hr from the Flora car park.

Practicalities

Buses pick up and drop off on the corner of High Street and Parker Street, and there are regular **flights** from Wellington to the grass airfield at 16 College Street, about 3km southwest of the centre; Motueka Taxis (☏03/528 1031) will take you into town for around $7. The **visitor centre**, Wallace St (daily: Christmas–Feb 8am–7pm; March–Christmas 8am–5pm; ☏03/528 6543, ⓦwww.AbelTasmanGreenRush.co.nz), is the first point of call for organising your visit to the Abel Tasman National Park and the Heaphy Track. Consequently you don't really need to visit the **DOC office**, cnr High and King Edward streets, 2km south of the visitor centre (Mon–Fri 8am–4.30pm; ☏03/528 9117), though it also gives out information on the local national parks, and sells tickets for the track.

Camping and tramping **gear** can be **rented** by the day from most hostels and from Coppins, 255 High St (☏03/528 7296), and SportsWorld, 201 High St (☏03/528 6710). Expect to pay around $10 a day for a pack, $10 for a two-person tent, $10 for a stove and pots, and $5 for a bedroll; and there are discounts for rentals over three or four days. There's **Internet access** at CyberWorld, 15 Wallace St, opposite the visitor centre.

For a small town Motueka has a fairly decent range of **accommodation** and there are enough **places to eat** for the couple of nights you might spend here. You might even want to catch a **movie** at the intimate Gecko Theatre, 78 High St (☏03/528 4272).

Accommodation

Abel Tasman Motel and Lodge 45 High St ☏03/528 6688 & 0800/845 678, ⓦwww.motuekamotel.co.nz. Clean and well-maintained budget motel with fully self-catering units plus a range of lodge rooms with access to a large communal cooking area and lounge. Basic lodge rooms ❸, en-suite lodge rooms ❹, units ❹

Baker's Lodge 4 Poole St ☏03/528 0102, ⓔbakers@motueka.co.nz. Very comfortable, spacious and welcoming associate YHA hostel in a clean, modern building with the added bonus of nightly homebaked mini-muffins. Dorms ❶, rooms ❷

Equestrian Lodge Motel Tudor St ☏03/528 9369 & 0800/668 782, ⓦwww.equestrianlodge.co.nz. Well-kept and renovated upscale motel with units backing onto a large grassy area with a pool. ❺

The Laughing Kiwi 310 High St ☏03/ 528 9229, ⓔmarknwendy@xtra.co.nz. Attractive and centrally sited backpackers with a convivial atmosphere plenty of outdoor seating and a hot tub. Accommodation is in four shares and doubles and there are plans for imminent expansion with more doubles. Camping $12, dorms ❶, rooms ❷

Motueka Top 10 Holiday Park 10 Fearon St ☏03/528 7189, ⓦwww.motuekatop10.co.nz. Verdant campground with plenty of trees for shelter and clean, well-kept facilities just 1km from the town centre. Camping $12.50, cabins ❷, self-contained units ❸, motel units ❺

Rowan Cottage 27 Fearon St ☏03/528 6492, ⓦwww.rowancottage.net. Tastefully styled cottage with two polished-floor rooms set in an attractive garden where chickens lay eggs for the full breakfast. One room comes with its own secluded deck with sunken bath. ❻

Treedimensions Organic Farmstay Shaggery Rd, 10km west of Motueka ☏03/528 8718, ⓦwww.treedimensions.co.nz. Wake up to birdsong then breakfast on the deck of these attractive, modern self-contained units with polished wood floors, very comfy beds and stereo. They overlook an organic orchard with 45 types of fruit and 700 species and you can usually try whatever's ripe. There's also an older apartment ideal for families. Apartment & units ❺

The White Elephant 55 Whakarewa St ☏03/528 6208, ⓔwhite.elephant.clear.co.nz. Spacious hostel in a big house set in mature grounds. They're well set up to cater to Abel Tasman visitors and are only a short walk from town. Camping $12, dorms ❶, rooms ❷

Eating and drinking

Bakehouse Café and Pizzeria 21 Wallace St. The best place to get a pizza or anything remotely Italian. Everything is home-baked and tasty and they have superb Havana coffee. Eating inside or al fresco.

Gothic Gourmet Café 208 High St ☏03/528 6699. Good, old-fashioned restaurant in a neo-Gothic 1920s former Methodist church. The food is pretty good (mains around $25) with imaginative French and Italian touches. Lunch & dinner daily.

Hot Mama's 105 High St. Motueka's pick for simply hanging out over a beer or a coffee either in the breezy, bright interior or in the patio garden. The music's always interesting and at weekends it is usually live with occasional appearances by touring New Zealand folk, jazz, acoustic and rock acts. The food's nothing startling but the pizza, Moroccan fish and Tandoori chicken (all $15–20) are OK. Daily until late. Licensed and BYO.

Muses Café Beside the Museum Building, High St. A charming little daytime café with some of the best coffee in town, some reasonably priced breakfasts and lunches and tasty snacks. Try the smoked fish chowder.

Swinging Sultan 172 High St ☏03/528 8909. Kebab takeaway with just a couple of tables out on the pavement where you can tuck into chicken and beef kebabs and felafel (all $6–9) plus good coffee.

T.O.A.D. Hall 502 High St, 3km south of the town centre. An organic fruit-and-veg vendor serving delicious home-made ice-cream and good coffee which can be drunk out in the attractive garden.

Kaiteriteri

The tiny resort settlement of **KAITERITERI**, 15km north of Motueka and just south of the Abel Tasman National Park, ranks highly in the pantheon of Kiwi summer holiday destinations and is consequently packed to its limited gills from Christmas through to mid-January, and is busy well into March. There's an understandable appeal, with a golden arc of safe swimming beach looking out towards Tasman Bay where a couple of small islands add texture. With Marahau (see p.560) becoming too congested for some tastes, Kaiteriteri has fashioned itself as an alternative embarkation point for Abel Tasman cruise and kayaking trips. Temporary-looking shacks on the beach-front are starting points for trips with Kaiteriteri Kayaks, Wilson's Experiences, a couple of water taxi companies and **Waka Tours** (4hr; $135 including lunch; ☏03/527 8160, ⓦwww.wakatours.co.nz),who offer a chance to paddle a replica Maori war canoe, swim relax and learn something of the local culture.

Accommodation is very limited. Kiwi families flock to the beachside *Kaiteriteri Motor Camp* (☏03/527 8010, ⓦwww.kaiteriteribeach.co.nz; camping $10, cabins ❷, bedding $5 per person); but there is now the option of staying at *Kaiteri Flashpackers*, just back from the beach on Inlet Rd (☏03/643 8281, ⓦwww.kaiteriflashpackers.co.nz; dorms $30, rooms ❹, deluxe ❻), something between a motel and an upscale backpackers with modern four-share rooms with made-up beds, tasteful en-suite doubles and all the expected hostel accoutrements.

Bellbird Lodge, Sandy Bay Rd (☏03/527 8555, ⓦwww.bellbirdlodge.com; ❺) offers two floral suites, welcoming hosts and great breakfasts, but for something comfortable and very relaxing, stay at *Kimi Ora Spa Resort* (☏03/527 8027, ⓦwww.kimiora.co.nz; rooms ❼, suites ❽), a hillside complex set in pine forest on Martin Farm Road, signposted 1km back from the beach road with heated indoor and outdoor pools. You can just stay in one of their spacious rooms or suites, but the emphasis is on fitness, therapy and indulgent massage sessions such as water jet massage ($60), algae detox slimming wrap, or getting wrapped in German peat (both $90). There are also accommodation packages (extra $70 per couple) which include dinner at the *Lemon Tree* (see below) and one treatment (though of course you can stump up for more).

The *Shoreline* café restaurant and bar does decent **food** served on its terrace with great sea and beach views, or there's à la carte dining ($23–27) and gourmet pizza to go ($20–23) at the *Beached Whale* on Inlet Rd (☏03/527 8114). The wood-lined summer-only *Lemon Tree Café* at Kimi Ora (☏03/527 8668) is open to all and serves healthy, vegetarian **lunches** and à la carte **dinners** (mains $22–28), rounded off by a range of coffees, teas and juices.

Marahau

About 8km further north along the beach road from Kaiteriteri, tiny **MARAHAU** is poised right at the southern entrance to the Abel Tasman National Park, something that affects almost everything that happens here. Most of the tours, water taxis and kayak operators working in the park are based here, and a selection of backpackers, campgrounds and a couple of restaurants makes this a very popular last or first night of civilisation. There's even a proposal to build a large new hotel in this ecologically fragile spot, though there's considerable resistance from those who believe it will destroy Marahau's charm.

The beach road runs through the settlement before petering out at its northern end right by the **park entrance**, marked by an unstaffed DOC display shelter with an intentions book. From here, a long boardwalk across marshland leads into the national park itself.

Next to the shelter, the licensed *Park Café* (Sept–May daily 8am–late) is legendary among appreciative walkers emerging from the park for its extensive range of fine, wholesome food, home-made cakes and excellent coffee.

A dirt road called Harvey Road runs opposite the *Park Café* to two of the most convenient **places to stay**. Closest is *The Barn* (T03/527 8043; camping $10, dorms ❶, rooms, tipis & truck ❷), a well-kept and peaceful combined campground and backpackers with a rather public general dorm, a separate women's dorm, and doubles and the "Barn" plus tipis, a twin housetruck and plenty of camping. Two minutes' walk down Harvey Road is *Old MacDonald's Farm* (T03/527 8288, W www.oldmacs.co.nz; camping $10, dorms ❶, cottages ❸), a family-run farm with a spacious campsite plus a few cabins. You share the grounds with llamas, alpacas and a host of other animals (day visitors $2), and there's secure parking ($4 a night), along with a well–stocked shop and gear storage, and an open-air fish-and-chip shop in the summer months. Back down the beach road from the park entrance is the Marahau Valley Road, where about 200m along is *Abel Tasman B&B* (T03/527 8181; ❺), the best and most comfortable spot close to the park, offering a friendly welcome, seriously good cooking.

Exploring the Park

There is an almost infinite variety of ways to explore the Abel Tasman National Park. It is beyond the scope of this guide to cover every permutation, but no matter what combination of activities you'd like to try there is bound to be an operator who can oblige. Relatively few people tramp the **Inland Track**, most keen to stick to the park's **coastline**, with its long golden beaches, clear water, spectacular outcrops and the constant temptation to snorkel in some of the idyllic bays. This is also where you'll find a good array of **accommodation** ranging from beachside campsites to swanky lodges. **Water taxis** can take you virtually anywhere along the coast, and they usually give a bit of a commentary along the way, though there are also dedicated **cruises** some visiting the seal colony on the **Tonga Island Marine Reserve** and **Split Apple Rock**, a large boulder that split and has fallen into two halves.

The intricate details of the coast are best explored by **kayak**, either on a guided trip or by getting a group together, renting kayaks and setting your own itinerary. This is enormously popular, but even more people **tramp the Coast Track**, though this can easily be combined with sections of kayaking, water taxi rides and even a little sailing in a combo to suit.

Accommodation and food

Unlike many of New Zealand's national parks, the Abel Tasman offers a range of accommodation, most of it on or close to the coast where it can be accessed either by boat or by the Abel Tasman Coast Path. We've listed the best below, but you might also consider 3–5 day guided walking and kayaking holidays ($900–1400) run by Wilson's Experiences (℡0800/223 582, ⓦwww.AbelTasmanNZ.com) with accommodation at their two lodges at Torrent Bay and Awaroa.

Many people stay at the four **DOC huts** (Oct–April $14; May–Sept $10) which are spaced around four hours' walk apart along the coast. These come with potable water, heating, good toilets, basic but comfortable bunks and most have showers, but there are no cooking facilities: bring a sleeping bag, cooking stove, pans, and food. Hardened trampers will want to camp at some of the twenty-one **DOC campgrounds** (all year $7) strung along the coast, all either beside beaches or near the DOC huts (whose facilities you are not allowed to use); all sites have a water supply and toilets, but it means carrying more gear and you'll need an ocean of sandfly repellent. Huts and campsites both have a two night maximum stay in summer but huts are still booked well in advance: the Whariwharangi Hut is the most likely to have space.

Huts and campsites must always be paid for in advance, but during the summer season (Oct–April) you must also **book huts**: it pays to reserve at least a week ahead. Book from July 1 through the Motueka Information Centre, Wallace St, Motueka (℡03/528 0005, ℻03/528 6563), or by visiting any DOC office. Booking forms can be downloaded from ⓦwww.abeltasmangreenrush.co.nz, and hut users must state where they want to stay each night.

In the off-season (May–Sept) huts are first-come-first-served but a hut or camping pass must still be pre-purchased.

The following are listed from south to north through the park.

Kanuka Hill Lodge Anchorage ℡03/5482863, ⓦwww.kanukalodge.co.nz. All the comforts of home but in a gorgeous bush setting. The price (around $400 a double in summer) includes a superb three-course dinner, en-suite room (most with gorgeous views) and a cooked breakfast. Closed May–Sept. ❾

Aquapackers Anchorage ℡0800/430 744, ⓦwww.aquapackers.co.nz. Relaxed backpacker accommodation in made-up dorms and doubles aboard two converted boats moored for the summer just off the beach in Anchorage Bay: there's a free ferry from beach to boat. The package includes barbecue dinner, B&B, free use of sit-on kayaks, access to a pay bar and a cut lunch for the next day. It can be a little cramped but the quiet of the park at night and sound of the lapping sea make it worthwhile. Dorms $60 per person, doubles $175.

Awaroa Lodge Awaroa ℡03/528 8758, ⓦwww.awaroalodge.co.nz. Nestled in the bush with great wetland views, this recently upgraded lodge has a number of stylish and comfortable units and en-suites along with the classy *Awaroa Lodge Café* which uses ingredients from their organic garden. Hikers and casual visitors can still drop in for a coffee or a drink by their enormous fireplace, but it is increasingly aimed at well-healed guests arriving by water taxi ($30 from Marahau) or plane ($105 from Motueka) and staying in their en-suite rooms or lovely studio suites. Rooms ❼, suites ❾

Totaranui Campground Totaranui. The only car-accessible accommodation on the Able Tasman coast, this huge campground (room for 850; $9) is so busy in summer that places are obtained by lottery for December and January. A form can be downloaded from ⓦwww.doc.govt.nz. There's a separate section for track hikers which should have space, though you might want to press on.

Cruises, water taxis, sailing and seal swimming

Kayaking and hiking may be the bread and butter of the Abel Tasman National Park, but you don't have to be quite so energetic. Many are quite happy taking a cruise or perhaps hoping on a water taxi in Kaiteriteri, Marahau or Totaranui, riding to some gorgeous beach and getting a later water taxi back. You might even include a little walking along the track or stay overnight in one of the water-access lodges mentioned above.

Wilson's Experiences (℡0800/223 582 & 03/528 7801, ⓦwww .AbelTasmanNZ.com) offer pleasant launch **cruises** (Oct–late April) from Kaiteriteri such as one to Bark Bay and back (3hr; $44), all the way to Totaranui and back (5hr; $58), or Seals, Bush 'N' Beach (7hr; $49) with the chance to walk from Torrent Bay to Onetahuti. The launch calls 2–5 times daily at the beaches along the way on a regular schedule allowing you to plan your own escape. One-way fares from Kaiteriteri or Marahau are: Anchorage $24, Onetahuti $30 & Totaranui $35.

If their timetable doesn't work for you, try a **water taxi**. Aqua Taxi (℡0800/278 282 & 03/527 8083, ⓦwww.aquataxis.co.nz) are fast, efficient run their trips from Marahau to coincide with incoming buses and include a commentary along the way. They also have a fixed schedule and charge slightly less than Wilson's.

If you'd rather let the gentle zephyrs of this coast propel you along, contact Abel Tasman Sailing Adventures (℡0800/467 245, ⓦwww.sailingadventures .co.nz) who do bare-boat **yacht rentals** for 2–4 people ($200–250 a day), and for those without the experience, offer small group trips along the coast for up to six people (4hr $275; full day $445, two days $795).

Lastly, Kaiteriteri Kayak (see p.563) offer an hour of **swimming with seals** ($120) accessed by a 45min water taxi trip. Swimming with seals can be a lot more fun than swimming with dolphins simply because seals are more manoeuvrable and curious. The water is usually crystal clear and the impact on the seals is minimised by ensuring that you wait for the seals to come and swim with you rather than just leaping in and splashing about among them.

Kayaking

One of the best ways to explore the park's remoter shores is by **sea kayak**. It is hard to beat gently paddling along exploring little coves (and possibly being accompanied by seals or dolphins), stopping on a golden beach for a dip then continuing to your nearly-deserted campsite where you cool your beer in a stream for sundowners. Of course, you're not the first to discover such pleasures, and in the height of the summer over one hundred kayaks may be on the water at any one time.

Most kayak operators are based at Marahau at the southern end of the park: the initial stretch north of here is known as the "Mad Mile", but congestion quickly eases further north. Only Golden Bay Kayaks (see p.563) works the quieter north end of the park. All companies offer a similar range of one- to five-day guided trips, and "freedom rentals" where you are typically accompanied by an instructor/guide for the first few hours then let loose (though you are not allowed to go solo nor to venture north of Abel Head at the north end of the Tonga Island Marine Reserve). One-way hires are available with a fee ($30–35) for returning the kayak to base by water taxi. **Prices** vary little and are quoted per person regardless of whether you paddle a single or double kayak. The price structure for **freedom rentals** varies between companies and you may need to shop around to find the best deal for your itinerary, but expect to pay $100 for the first two-days, $35–40 for the third then $25–30 for each subsequent day. There is an enormous range of **guided trips** combining paddling with walking, water taxi rides, overnight stays visiting seals and more. Consider a basic 4hr paddle ($70), step up to a full day on the Mad Mile ($100–130), ride a water taxi to get further north then paddle back ($150) or indulge in a three-day fully catered camping and kayaking trip ($400–550).

Most companies have a range of camping equipment for rent and will store your vehicle and/or gear while you're away. Companies operate year-round though the range of trips is much reduced in winter.

For a Marahau-based trip with one of the larger companies go with Ocean River (☎0800/732 529 & 03/537 8266, ⓦwww.seakayaking.co.nz), who offer Beaches and Islands (1 day; $115) paddling the Mad Mile, swimming and putting up sails for the cruise back to Marahau; Beaches and Seals (2 days; $330) visiting the Tonga Island Marine Reserve and camping on a beach; and a two-day paddle-and-walk combo ($165). Slightly cheaper rates are offered by Kaiteriteri-based Kaiteriteri Kayak (☎0800/252 925 & 03/527 8383, ⓦwww.seakayak.co.nz) with whom you might do a Sunset Paddle (Dec to mid-Feb; 3hr; $65), or a one-day trip that visits the distinctive Split Apple Rock ($95).

Better still head over the hill to Takaka and kayak in relative isolation of the northern end of the national park with Pohara-based Golden Bay Kayaks (☎03/525 9095, ⓦwww.goldenbaykayaks.co.nz). They offer rentals off the beach and elsewhere in the park and have half-day guided tours.

Hiking the Coast Track

The **Abel Tasman Coast Track** (51km; 2–5 days) is one of the **easiest** of New Zealand's Great Walks – one for people who wouldn't normally think of themselves as trampers. You should obtain DOC's *Abel Tasman Coast Track* leaflet ($1), but the track is clear and easy to follow. Lack of fitness is no impediment as you can use water taxis to skip some sections or just pick the bits you fancy walking. Entry and exit to the beach sections are clearly marked and you are never more than four hours from a hut or campsite. In dry conditions you don't even need strong boots – trainers will do fine. All this combines to make the Coast Track extremely popular, especially from December to the end of February when the more popular sections seem like some hikers' highway: heading for the section north of Totaranui can deliver a less frenetic experience.

The **route** traverses broad golden beaches lapped by emerald waters, punctuated by granite pillars silhouetted against the horizon and zigzagging gentle climbs through valleys. The main planning difficulty is coping with two **tide-dependent** sections at Onetahuti and across the Awaroa Estuary. Tide times will help you decide which way you're going to do the track – if there are low tides in the afternoon you'll probably want to head south, if they're in the morning, north. Before setting off you should also arrange your transport drop-offs and pick-ups (see "Park information and access" on p.556).

Marahau to Anchorage (11.5km; 4hr). The track follows a wooden causeway across the Marahau estuary to the open country around Tinline Bay before rounding a point overlooking Fisherman and Adele islands just off the coast. As the track winds in and out of gullies, the surroundings are obscured by beech forest and tall kanuka trees until you emerge at Anchorage, with its B&B, hut, campsite and summertime offshore backpackers.

Anchorage to Bark Bay (9.5km; 3hr). Aim to cross Torrent Bay two hours either side of low tide or be prepared to skirt the bay (adding an hour) to reach the few dozen houses that constitute the settlement of Torrent Bay. Climb out of the bay through pine trees then meander through valleys to reach the gorgeous Falls River, crossed by a long swingbridge. The Bark Bay hut and campsites lie 30min ahead.

Bark Bay to Awaroa (11.5km; 4hr). After crossing (or skirting) Bark Bay Estuary you cut away from the coast only to return at Tonga Quarry where there's a campsite and views out to Tonga Island and its associated Marine Reserve. You soon reach the golden beach at Onetahuti. The stream at its northern end is tidal (cross 3hr either side of low tide). The track then climbs to the Tonga Saddle and descends to Awaroa Inlet and the settlement of two dozen houses and a DOC hut with a campsite alongside; *Awaroa Lodge* and its café are also within easy walking distance.

Awaroa to Totaranui (5.5km; 1hr 30min). You must cross the Awaroa estuary (2hr either side of low tide) to reach Goat Bay then up to a lookout above Skinner Point before reaching Totaranui with its extensive campground.

Totaranui to Whariwharangi (7.5km; 2hr). After rounding the Totaranui Estuary, press on over and around rocky headlands as far as Mutton Cove then wander through alternating shrubland and beaches to the hut at Whariwharangi. From here it's possible to take a short hike to Separation Point, where there is a fur seal colony and a good lookout, or to tackle the strenuous climb up Gibbs Hill for even better views.

Whariwharangi to Wainui (5.5km; 1hr 30min). It is an easy walk to the road on the eastern side of Wainui Bay where buses pick up, but it is also possible to cross Wainui Bay (2hr either side of low tide) or following the road around the bay. If you follow the road, you can also take in the short hike up to the Wainui Falls which heads off the road at the base of Wainui Bay.

Inland Track

The **Inland Track** (42km; 3–5 days) between Marahau and Totaranui is far less popular than the Coast Track and is strenuous enough to require moderate fitness and decent tramping gear. The route climbs from sea level to **Evans Ridge** past many granite outcrops and views of the coast: highlights include the **Pigeon Saddle**, the moorlands of Moa Park and the moon-like Canaan landscape. The track can be combined with the Coast Track to make a six- to seven-day loop or you could link up with Rameka Track on Takaka Hill and the Harwoods Hole track (see p.565) along the way.

Camping is not permitted on the Inland Track, but there are **four DOC huts** ($5; annual hut passes valid) mostly spaced less than five hours' walk apart. They are first-come-first-served but there is rarely competition for bunks. Water supplies and toilets are provided, but you'll need to take a cooking stove.

Starting **from Marahau** in the south, the Inland Track splits away from the Coastal Track at Tinline Bay and climbs steadily through regenerating forest to the **Castle Rocks Hut** (11.5km; 4hr 30min; 12 bunks), which is perched near rocky outcrops and has great views of the Marahau Valley and Tasman Bay. From **Castle Rocks to Moa Park Hut** (3.5km; 2hr; 4 bunks) you climb steeply, followed by an undulating section over tussock. Most trampers continue on from **Moa Park** to the **Awapoto Hut** (14.5km; 6–7hr; 12bunks) trekking along **Evans Ridge** and descending to the hut. Accommodation is also available at **Wainui Hut** (4 bunks) an hour's walk off the main track. The last day involves topping **Pigeon Saddle** then dropping down before ascending to the summit of **Gibbs Hill**, from where you get some of the most expansive views across the park, and meet up with the select few Coast Track walkers who had the energy to make the arduous climb from Totaranui. Afterwards, it is an easy descent to the **Wainui carpark** (10km in all; 3hr 30min).

Golden Bay

Occupying the northwestern tip of the South Island, **GOLDEN BAY** curves gracefully from the northern fringes of the Abel Tasman National Park to the encircling arm of **Farewell Spit**, all backed by the magnificence of the Kahurangi National Park. A relatively flat area hemmed in by towering mountains on three sides and with waves lapping at its exposed fourth side, its inaccessibility has kept it outside the mainstream. The coastline is washed by clear, sparkling water, creating excellent conditions for windsurfing, while its hinterland is home to the country's largest freshwater springs,

Te Waikoropupu Springs, as well as a number of other curious geological phenomena.

Wainui Bay, just east of the main town of **Takaka**, is most likely the spot where Abel Tasman first anchored, guaranteeing his place in history as the first European to encounter Aotearoa and its fierce inhabitants. The isolating presence of **Takaka Hill** and lack of any road access from the West Coast keep today's bayside communities small and very manageable. This isolation goes some way to explaining the region's spirit of **independence** and self-reliance, and also why the bay has lured such a cross section of alternative lifestylers, craftspeople and artists. Sunny, beautiful and full of fascinating sights, Golden Bay deserves a few days of your time and has a knack of inducing you to stay a few more.

For some insight into the events, places to visit, entertainment listings and general tittle-tattle, pick up the local newspaper, *The G.B. Weekly* ($0.50).

Takaka Hill

The only way to get to Golden Bay by road is on SH60 over the historically feared **Takaka Hill** which skirts the inland border of the Abel Tasman National Park. It twists and turns endlessly to get up to 791m and then down again, but it is paved all the way, and taken steadily is no problem. Along the way, viewpoints provide glorious mountain and seascapes from Nelson north to D'Urville Island.

After climbing Takaka Hill, some 20km out of Motueka, a short bumpy track leads to the **Ngarua Caves** (Oct–April daily 10am–4pm; 35min guided tours on the hour; $11, cash only), a celebration of tackiness with illuminated stalactites and stalagmites formations such as the Wedding Cathedral, including some with musical accompaniments. Tour guides also point out *moa* bones and regale you with an informative commentary on the caves' history and geology.

Half a kilometre further north, the twisting, unsealed Canaan Road runs 11km to a car park (longdrop and water supply) with access to **Harwoods Hole** a huge vertical shaft 176m deep and over 50m in diameter, which links up to a vast cave system below. Its lip is reached by an enchanting trail (6km return, 1hr 30min; mostly level) through silver beech forest then follows a dry rock-strewn riverbed to a point with an amphitheatre of cliffs above and the hole dropping away in front. There is no viewing platform, so only the brave and foolhardy get much of a look down the hole. About 30min along the trail a side trail (20min return) leads to a **clifftop viewpoint** with views down towards the Takaka Valley and the coast. The marble under foot has been eroded into what looks like micro-mountain ranges. A spot beside Canaan Road 3km back from the car park is one of several sites in the area used by the **Lord of the Rings** crew, in this case a scene with Strider leading the hobbits from Bree through Chetwood Forest.

At the Harwoods Hole trailhead on Canaan Road, you can join the clearly signposted **Rameka Track** (5km; 3hr one way; 750m descent), which follows one of the earliest surveyed routes down into the Takaka Valley with superb views of the granite outcrops and the surrounding country. The Rameka Track is particularly popular with downhill **mountain bike** fans who can complete a Rameka Track loop from Takaka (65km, 4–6hr) using SH60 and Canaan Road.

Back on SH60, it is another 4km to the **Takaka Hill Walkway** (1–4hr; donations appreciated) several undulating loop trails which link together across open farmland, beech forest and karst landscape pocked with sinkholes.

SH60 then twists its way across the mountain before descending rapidly into Golden Bay and Takaka.

Takaka and around

The small town of **TAKAKA**, almost 60km north of Motueka, is set slightly inland turning its back on the crook of Golden Bay. Still, it is an attractive rural town that's increasingly pitching itself to summer tourists while continuing to cater for the local farming community and barefoot crusties who emerge from their shacks and tipis to sell their crafts and healing services. Immediately north, **Te Waikoropupu Springs** emerge from their underground lair, while to the north yawns a considerable stretch of beautiful bay, running parallel to SH60 as it rolls into Collingwood and Farewell Spit. To the east, Abel Tasman Drive winds past the safe swimming beach at **Pohara** and a few minor sights before heading into the northern section of the Abel Tasman National Park (see p.569).

Arrival and information

Only charter flights from Nelson or Wellington land at Takaka's **airstrip**, 5km north of town. Golden Bay Coachlines (☎03/525 8352) and K Bus (☎03/525 9434, ⓦ www.kahurangi.co.nz) both run from Motueka and continue north to Collingwood and the Heaphy Track, and east to Totaranui. Both **bus** companies drop off outside the **visitor centre** (daily 9am–5pm; ☎03/525 9136, ⓦ wwwgoldenbay.net.nz), on SH60 as you enter town from the south. It carries all DOC information, handles bookings and hut tickets for the national parks and tracks, and stocks material on local attractions. The free and comprehensive *Golden Bay Visitors Guide* booklet is pretty much essential, and if you're into the arts pick up the *Guide to Artists in Golden Bay* (also free) pinpointing major artists and craftspeople who open their studios to the public.

There is usually someone who **rents cars**: ask at the visitor centre. Most of the hostels have free bikes for guests, and The Quiet Revolution, 11 Commercial St (closed Sat afternoon & Sun; ☎03/525 9555, Ⓔquietrev@hotmail.com), **rents mountain bikes** for \$25 a day and can sell you *Fat Tyre Fun* (\$2) containing over a dozen great mountain bike rides in Golden Bay. **Internet access** is available at the Library, 63 Commercial St (Mon–Thurs 9.30am–5pm, Fri 9.30am–6pm, Sat 9.30am–12.30pm; \$2 for 20min), and Unlimited Copies, 37 Commercial St.

Accommodation

Golden Bay is a popular holiday spot with both Kiwis and foreign visitors; as a result there is a lot of good quality accommodation from backpackers to some fairly swanky lodges. Camping ranges from the enormous DOC campground at Totaranui to wayside spots where you can park your campervan overnight. The local council allows fully self-contained campervans to park free in the region as long as you observe any No Camping signs: the same lenient approach doesn't apply to tenters and those wanting to sleep in their car.

Takaka

Anatoki Lodge Motels 87 Commercial St ☎03/525 8047, Ⓔanatoki@xtra.co.nz. Modern, fully self-contained units close to the centre of town, with an indoor pool, great service and helpful staff. ⑤
Autumn Farm Lodge 3km south of Takaka off

SH60 ☎03/525 9013, ⓦwww.autumnfarm.com. A charming gay-friendly lodge on a six hectare plot, with comfortable rooms, a big bathhouse and a laidback (clothing optional) atmosphere. Also hosts a 10-day annual summer camp over New Year. Camping \$10, backpackers \$30, B&B ⑤

Golden Bay "Barefoot" Backpackers 114
Commercial St ☎0508/525 700, ⊛www.bare-foot
.co.nz. Pleasant low-cost backpackers in a house
with dorms, one sunny double and camping out
the back where there's a hot tub. Camping $10,
bunks ❶, rooms ❷
Golden Bay Motel 132 Commercial St ☎0800/401
212 & 03/525 9428, ⊛www.goldenbaymotel.co.nz.
A pretty, well-kept little motel with off-street parking
and spacious rooms. ❹
Kiwiana 73 Motupipi St ☎0800/805 494 &
03/525 7676. Beautifully kept and well-run hostel
in a large villa where the Kiwiana theme runs to
the labelling of the airy rooms – paua, jandals, tiki,
etc – and collection of books in the games room
where they have table football, pool and table
tennis. Space for tents ($12–14) still leaves room
for a free hot tub and barbecue area. Closed July
& Aug. Dorms ❶, rooms ❷
Nirvana Lodge 25 Motupipi St ☎03/525 8766,
⊛www.nirvanalodge.co.nz. Comfortable and
friendly associate YHA right in town with a homely
atmosphere, a nice garden, a spa pool, free use of
bikes, a few private rooms and limited space for
tents. Camping $10, dorms ❶, rooms ❷
Rose Cottage Motel and B&B SH60, 5km south of
Takaka ☎03/525 9048, ⊛www.nzmotels.co
.nz/rose.cottage. Three beautifully maintained motel
units set in a large, lovingly tended garden (complete
with indoor pool), plus a homestay option, all with
friendly and helpful hosts. Very good value. ❹
Waitapu Bridge Pleasant riverside freedom
camping site with toilets and river water 4km
north of town on SH60. Free

Around Takaka

Golden Bay Lodge and Garden Tukurua, signposted off SH60 17km north of Takaka ☎03/525
9275, ⊛goldenbaylodge.co.nz. Two fully self-contained units plus two B&B rooms overlooking a
lovely garden and the sea, with easy beach
access. Self-catering ❻, B&B ❼

The Nook Abel Tasman Drive, Pohara, 9km east
☎03/525 8501, ✉thenook@paradise.net.nz. A
relaxed backpackers in a lovely wood-floored
house where TV and the Internet are intentionally
absent. Apart from the comfy dorms and doubles
there's a fairly luxurious, straw-and-plaster extension, rented as a self-contained unit or two doubles. Free pick–up from Takaka by arrangement
and free bikes once you're here. Dorms ❶,
doubles ❷, units ❸
Sans Souci Inn Richmond Rd, Pohara Beach,
10km east ☎03/525 8663, ⊛www.sanssouciinn
.co.nz. Endearing B&B in a building reflecting the
Mediterranean atmosphere of the bay, constructed
of mudbricks, with sods as the roofing material,
and distinctive floor tiles. Rooms all share one
large bathroom with a bath and shower stalls, and
self-composting toilets. There's also an excellent
restaurant (see p.570). ❹
Shambhala SH60,18km north at Onekaka
☎03/525 8463, ⊛www.shambhala.co.nz.
Welcoming backpackers with a slightly spiritual
bent located 2km down a track almost opposite
the *Mussel Inn* (see p.570), from where a free
pick-up can be arranged. Dorms are in the main
house, or there are spacious twins and doubles
with good views in a separate block, with solar-
heated showers and composting toilets. Camping
$14, dorms ❶, rooms ❷
River Inn Backpackers SH60, 3km north
☎03/525 9425, ⊛www.riverinn.co.nz.
Mostly backpackers in the former hotel rooms
in this 1870s pub just out of town (but with
free pickups from Takaka). Rooms are clean
and comfortable and there's an array of rentals:
kayak ($10/hr), bike ($25/day), and all you need
to snorkel at Te Waikoropupu Springs (wetsuit,
mask & fins for $45). Camping $10, dorms ❶,
rooms ❷.
Totaranui Campground (see p.570). Large
and popular beachside campground, 26km east
of Takaka.

The Town and around

Despite being the bay's largest settlement, Takaka is a low and architecturally
barren affair where three roads, SH60 (Commercial Street as it passes through
town), Motupipi Road and Meihana Street, form a triangle. Close to the
centre of town the 1899 former post office now houses the **Golden Bay
Gallery**, 67 Commercial St (Oct–April daily 10am–4pm; May–Sept closed
Sun; free), an art and gift store with wonderful silk paintings by Sage Cox and
a bizarre wooden sculpture built by Arnold Gustafson known as The Dresser.
Like some Daliesque melting chest of drawers it is for sale, but with a tag of
$150,000 is could be there for some time. The adjacent **Golden Bay
Museum** (entry through the Gallery; donation) is well worth a look even
if it's only for the breathtakingly detailed diorama depicting Abel Tasman's

△ Waterfall

ill-fated trip to Wainui Bay in 1642. The rest of the museum houses Maori artefacts, some fascinating geological and natural history material, as well as the usual mish-mash of bits and bobs rooted out of attics or accumulated during travels abroad (usually to wars).

Most of the rest of the diverting sights are east of town along Abel Tasman Drive (see below) but be sure to nip 4km north along SH60 to a turnoff for **Te Waikoropupu Springs** Scenic Reserve (unrestricted access), the site of what are usually known simply as "Pupu Springs". The largest in New Zealand, they're set amid old gold workings, regenerating forest and a vestige of mature forest. There are at least sixteen crystal clear freshwater springs here, with two major vents at the main pool, one major and several minor vents at Dancing Sands (where the sands, pushed by the surging water, appear to dance), and about twelve springs along Fish Creek. The colourful aquatic plant life can be seen by means of a large reverse periscope on one of the boardwalks, and there is some recreational scuba diving, though because of the springs' cultural significance DOC are trying to dissuade people. This task is not helped by the *River Inn* a local backpackers which hires out wet suits for a snorkelling/drifting river swim that begins near the falls.

Abel Tasman Drive

East of Takaka, **Abel Tasman Drive** threads its way past the small waterside settlement of Pohara then splits into three, each road ending at a trailhead for the Abel Tasman Coast Track: Awaroa, Totaranui and Wainui Bay. Many of the features are shown on the Abel Tasman National Park map on p.555.

The first point of some interest, just over 2km out of Takaka, is **Labyrinth Rocks Park** (daily noon to an hour before dark; $7), a family-oriented maze of naturally sculpted limestone formations in a garden setting. "Master of Rocks", Dave, encourages a light-hearted approach and bakes wonderful rock cakes.

There are more impressive sights ahead in the form of **Rawhiti Cave**, its cavernous mouth hung with myriad pendulous stalactites stained by the earth and rain to hues of dirty brown and brightened by the rich green of the moss that covers some of them. Carefully descend a few steps into the entrance to see the fascinating formations, including transparent stone straws full of water, a discarded billy can now encrusted in rock deposited from the dripping ceiling and rock pools containing perfectly round stone "marbles". The cave is unprotected so it is doubly important not to touch or damage any of the formations. To reach the cave drive 5km along Abel Tasman Drive from Takaka, turn right into Glenview Road then left into Packard Road and follow it to the end. A poorly signed trail (1hr 20–2hr return) leads beside a (usually) dry stream bed then up into the bush to the cave mouth. For some company, cultural significance and natural history enlist the services of Kahurangi Guided Walks (℡03/525 7177, ⊛www.kahurangiwalks.co.nz; $25), who run a 3hr **tour** leaving from the visitor centre.

Two kilometres further along Abel Tasman Drive from the Rawhiti Caves turning, a signposted side road leads 800m to the wonderful **Grove Scenic Reserve** (unrestricted access), a mystical place in grey-green that could have been transplanted straight from Arthurian legend, where massive rata trees sprout from odd and deformed limestone outcrops. A ten-minute walk from the car park takes you to a narrow slot between two enormous vertical cliffs where a lookout reveals expansive views of the coast and beaches around Pohara. Self-caterers should drop in to the nearby Golden

Salami (℡03/525 9385), which produces a variety of delicious, totally natural **salami** from their own aggressively healthy Sussex beasts and a handful of secret ingredients.

Pohara, 10km from Takaka, has a couple of places to stay and eat (see below) but otherwise you'll soon want to press on east past the former site of a cement factory, a jarringly industrial ruin in such a wonderfully scenic spot. The ugly **Abel Tasman Memorial** at least offers great views of the coast ahead: Ligar Bay and **Tata Beach** with the Tata Islands picturesquely set offshore.

Beyond Tata Beach signs guide you half a kilometre inland to a trailhead for **Wainui Falls**. The falls themselves are a forty-minute return walk, heading up through dense bush with the roar of the falls growing ever louder. Nikau palms shade the banks of the river, and a curtain of spray swathes the rather lovely falls – a great place to just sit and dream.

The road now splits and deteriorates to winding gravel. The Wainui Bay road runs past the **Tui commune** (the last of several started in Golden Bay in the 1970s), and ends at the northernmost access point to the Coast Track. Other roads go to a car park at Awaroa Estuary, and the wonderful golden arc of **Totaranui Beach**. This is a common place to finish the Coast Track, right by the *Totaranui Campground* (see p.567)

Eating and entertainment

Takaka has a surprising number of good places to **eat**, a couple on Commercial Street and more a few kilometres out that easily justify the journey. **Drinking** and music tend to be confined to the big old hotels/pubs, the *Wholemeal Café* or *Mussel Inn* some way out of town. Entertainment is mostly self-made, but it is worth catching a recent release at the atmospheric **Village Cinema**, 34 Commercial St (℡03/525 8453 or see *The G.B. Weekly* for programme details), where the seating includes bean bags and there are cups of tea to sip during the films.

Takaka

Beach Park 1 Commercial St. Combination eat-in and takeaway joint serving low-cost Asian dishes – pad Thai, nasi goreng, laksa, etc – for $9 plus burgers and fish & chips. BYO.

The Dangerous Kitchen 48 Commercial St (℡03/525 8686 for takeaway orders). This peculiarly named little café spilling out onto the pavement specializes in exotic pizzas and good coffee. Try the breakfast pizza with bacon, egg, grilled tomato and pesto. Daily until late.

Wholemeal Café 60 Commercial St. A Takaka institution that's endearingly sloppy at times, but always good to hang out over a coffee and cake. Return for pizza, colourful and healthy salads, assorted fish dishes and a good range of curries (all $14–18) in the cavernous interior or on the back deck. In the evenings there's sometimes live music. Daily until 7pm, and later in summer.

Around Takaka

Mussel Inn SH60, 18km north of Takaka. Do not miss this place – whether you want to eat, enjoy

wine or ale (they brew their own), sit and read, play chess or soak up the lively atmosphere of a live band. The wooden building is adorned with local art and some clumpy but comfortable wooden furniture. You can always get a simple, fresh and wholesome meal; try a plate of the local mussels for around $10. Open daily until late.

Penguin Café Abel Tasman Drive, Pohara. Spacious modern, café restaurant and bar that's worth the drive out from Takaka if only to sip a beer or coffee on the roadside deck which catches the sun most of the day. Well presented dishes might include seafood chowder ($10), a gourmet bacon burger ($17), or seafood mornay pie ($18) finished off with a lime sorbet and fresh fruit ($9).

Sans Souci Inn see p.567. This simple summer-only licensed restaurant has a daily set menu which can include hot smoked fish or beef fillet with spätzle (traditional Swiss pasta) and a veggie option each night. There's also a choice of sumptuous freshly made desserts. Expect $10–15 for breakfast, and $20–24 for dinner which must be booked in advance.

The Road to Collingwood: arts and crafts

Many of the region's best **artists and craftspeople** live and work between Takaka and Collingwood, so the winding roads offer endless opportunities for meandering around country galleries. The free *Artists in Golden Bay* leaflet should help you decide where to focus your attentions, but a few places can be sampled without going far off the main road.

Following SH60 north out of Takaka look for roadside signs for Onekaka Arts, 13km north (☎03/525 7366) a gallery containing hand-crafted jewellery and scrimshaw created by Peter Meares, and jade carved by Geoff Williams. A little further along, Tim Jessep Pottery (generally daily all year; ☎03/524 8663) specialize in large courtyard pieces and water features. Next up, Rosie Little and Bruce Hamlin run Estuary Arts (Dec–April Wed–Sun 10am–5pm; ☎03/524 8466), one of the best pottery galleries in the bay, with brightly coloured table-ware and handmade low-relief art tiles, plus a gallery of some of Rosie's evocative paintings all prettily set high on a hill overlooking the bush and parts of the bay.

Collingwood and around

Golden Bay's northernmost settlement of any consequence is **COLLING-WOOD**, a quiet kind of a town occupying a thread of land wedged between the sea and Ruataniwha Inlet. It is really just a couple of short streets with one store, a couple of cafés, a friendly pub, a tiny museum and a few places to stay, but during the 1850s' gold rush the site of Collingwood was briefly championed as the nation's new capital. Street plans were drawn up but as the gold petered out, so did the enthusiasm. It is an attractive and peaceful spot to relax for a few days, but is mainly of interest for the tours to **Farewell Spit** (see below) and as a base for the **Heaphy Track** (see p.575).

The Town and around

Over the years, many of the town's older wooden edifices have burned down, leaving only a few buildings of note on Tasman Street, where the small

---

Farewell Spit tours

Only two companies are licensed to run tours to **Farewell Spit**, 22km north of Collingwood. Both operate year round, but departure times are dependant on tides: check the websites for expected departure times up to several months ahead.

Since 1946 tours have been run by Original Farewell Spit Safari (☎03/524 8257 & 0800/808 257, ⓦwww.farewellspit.co.nz) from their office on Tasman Street in Collingwood. They use characteristic ex-army trucks adapted to this unique environment, as well as a bunch of newer and more plush vehicles. The pick of their trips are the **Lighthouse Safari** (5hr 30min; $60) which heads out along the sands of the spit to the historic Farewell Spit lighthouse, all with bright commentary, peppered with local lore. During the day, you'll see vast numbers of birds, seals and fossils, climb an enormous sand dune and maybe see the skeletons of wrecked ships if the sands reveal them. To see the massive gannet colony towards the very end of the spit you'll need to take the more eco-oriented **Gannet Colony Tour** (6hr 30min; $85) which includes most of the above plus a 20min walk to the gannets. On both these trips lunch ($8) is optional.

The other operator is Kahurangi Nature Experiences (☎03/524 8188 & 0800/250 500, ⓦwww.farewell-spit.co.nz), whose **Nature Tour** (6hr 30min; $75, including lunch) starts from the Farewell Spit visitor centre (see p.573) and runs along the spit to the lighthouse and also visits Pillar Point lighthouse.

Collingwood Museum (daily 9am–6pm; donation) is devoted to the history of the early settlers and the impact of gold mining on the area.

Some 7km southwest of Collingwood in the Aorere Valley, on the road to the Heaphy Track trailhead, is the turn-off for a striking natural sculpture: two plinths of limestone on either side of the road support bulbous overhangs – dubbed the **Devil's Boots** for their resemblance to two feet protruding from the ground with tree and shrubs growing on their soles. Just before the Boots the road forks 1km to **Te Anaroa Caves**, where informal guided tours take you over the slippery surfaces to some stunning limestone formations. Make sure your footwear is both sturdy and waterproof ($20; advisable to book on ☎03/524 8131).

As the heart of the Golden Bay gold rush the Aorere Valley is packed with history, though one piece is still living in the form of **Langford's Store** at Bainham, a further 10km inland. A combined general store and post office it was built in 1928 by the grandparents of the current owner, Lorna Langford. She has worked here since 1947 and has been postmistress for over fifty years during which time little looks to have changed. Wooden shelves are stacked with ageing goods, you can still get an assorted bag of sweets for 50¢ and the hand-cranked Burroughs adding machine is used to tally up your bill. The store is usually open in the afternoons, but even if it is closed Lorna is unlikely to be far away and may open up.

Practicalities

Buses from Takaka drop-off in the centre of Collingwood, near the **general store** on Tasman Street. There are a few **places to stay** in town, all within a couple of minutes stroll of the centre, plus a couple of excellent places on the road to Farewell Spit (see p.573). Right in town the *Collingwood Motor Camp*, William Street (☎03/524 8149; camping $10, cabins ❷, motels ❺), is a pretty, sheltered site with a wide range of cabins; and the superb *Old Post Office*, Tasman St (☎03/524 8963, ✉jacklee@xtra.co.nz; ❶/❷) offers boutique backpacker accommodation with room for just six in three large, white, wooden floored rooms, minimally furnished with original artworks and all with sea or estuary views. Rent bikes ($15 a day) to explore locally, take out kayaks on sheltered waters nearby ($20 a half day) or join one of Jock's adventure caving trips ($45).

Also consider *Beachcomber Motels*, Tasman St (☎03/524 8499 & 0800/270 520; ❹), which back onto the river estuary with lovely views and clean, self-contained units; or *Collingwood Homestead*, just off Elizabeth St (☎03/524 8079, ✇collingwoodhomestead.co.nz; just ❾), one of the best homestays in Golden Bay in a beautiful 1904 colonial-style homestead with spacious comfortable rooms, excellent breakfasts and dinner by arrangement ($50 including wine).

All the eating options are within 50m of each other along Tasman St. There's cheap, simple **food** at *Collingwood Café*, and pub meals at the *Collingwood Tavern and Bistro*, but undoubtedly the best place to eat in Collingwood, and one of the best in Golden Bay, is the licensed *Courthouse Café* (closed Mon in winter; ☎03/524 8572), based in the atmospheric 1901 courthouse where they serve excellent coffee, good cakes and have a reasonably priced and imaginative blackboard menu.

North to Farewell Spit

Heading north out of Collingwood the road skirts Ruataniwha Inlet, and after 10km, passes *The Innlet* (☎03/524 8040, ✇www.goldenbayindex.co.nz /theinnlet.html; camping $15, dorms ❶, rooms ❸, self-contained cottages ❺), an excellent **hostel** offering spacious dorms and doubles in the main house and three delightful cottages nearby, plus a barbecue area and several heated outdoor baths. Ride the low-cost rental bikes to the base of Farewell Spit, go caving, rent kayaks ($35 a day), hike up through the on-site bush track or simply relax in the garden. Decent inexpensive meals are available 2km north in the hamlet of **Pakawau** at *The Old School Café & Restaurant*.

The road now follows the coast 11km to Puponga, another tiny place chiefly of interest for **Puponga Farm Park**, a coastal sheep farm open to the public at northern tip of the South Island. From here **Farewell Spit** – named by Captain Cook at the end of a visit in 1770 – stretches 25km east, curling slightly south to follow the tidal flows which formed it. Debris sluiced out of flooding West Coast rivers is carried by coastal currents and deposited here to form an uninterrupted desert of sand which curls back towards Golden Bay, whose shores capture much of the windblown sand from the spit's exposed side. The whole vast sand bank is a **nature reserve** of international importance, with saltmarshes, open mudflats, freshwater brackish lakes and bare dunes providing habitats for over a hundred **bird species**: bartailed godwit, wrybill, long-billed curlew and Mongolian dotterel all come to escape the Arctic winter, and there are breeding colonies of Caspian terns and gannets, and large numbers of black swans. Sadly, the unusual shape of the coastline seems to fool whales' navigation systems and beachings are common. If you follow one of the tracks around the base of the spit, you might well come across the wasting carcass of a stranded pilot whale – a sobering sight amid such wild beauty.

To protect shipping, the original **Farewell Spit Lighthouse** was erected in 1870, from materials carried along the spit, and trees were transplanted to the area to provide shelter for the keepers' dwellings. Since rebuilt of steel and now automated, the lighthouse (and most of the rest of the spit) can only be accessed on guided tours from Collingwood (see p.571).

The Puponga Farm Park contains the combined Farewell Spit **visitor centre** and *Paddle Crab Kitchen* café (Sept–June daily 9am–5pm, closed July & Aug; ☏03/524 8454), beautifully set on a hill overlooking the spit. Along with a viewing room with binoculars trained on the spit, there are some evocative photographs that recount the history of the area and the story of a mass whale-stranding in 1991. Obtain leaflets on local walking tracks, including some to a complex of middens over 50m wide and running for almost 1km along the base of the spit. Composed mostly of burned shell they provide evidence of **Maori settlement** over a period of at least 700 years. Puponga Point was the site of a defended *pa*, with the ditches and house terraces clearly visible, and at Whau Creek there are deep pits and extensive midden spilling down to the stream, indicating a *kainga*, or undefended living area. In 1846 explorer Charles Heaphy reported seeing *waka* heading to the ocean beach and down the West Coast, and in 1867 Edmund Davidson collected two *waka*, adorned with elaborate artistic designs.

Short **walks** head to the outer beach (2.5km) and the inner beach (4km); both provide good views of the spit and its wading bird population and offer an undiluted experience of this rather odd landscape. Away from the spit, walks head through the farm park to Cape Farewell (the northernmost point on the South Island), to the strikingly set **Pillar Point Lighthouse**, and even to Wharariki Beach

North to Wharariki Beach

Around 1km before the Farewell Spit visitor centre, a gravel road runs 2km west to the excellent Cape Farewell Horse Treks (☏03/524 8031,

@www.horsetreksnz.com), offering some of the most visually spectacular **horse riding** in the South Island – with Mount Beale on one side, views of Farewell Spit, and the Burnett Range forging away down the West Coast. Although they don't actually go onto Farewell Spit this is a good way of becoming familiar with the area through horseback trips: Pillar Point (90 min; $35); Triangle Valley (2hr; $35), Wharariki Beach (3hr; $55); overnight to Pakawau, along beaches and to Kahurangi and the lighthouse (around $150); and any number of customized longer excursions. They can also accommodate you in a self-contained cabin that sleeps four (❹) in regenerating bush near a babbling brook. There's no electricity, gaslight, cooking facilities or shower, just solitude and the sound of birds and running water.

Continue 4km beyond the stables to a road-end parking area, the beginning of a twenty-minute walk across farmland and sand dunes to **Wharariki Beach**. The beach is a startling introduction to the rigours of the West Coast; exposed to the harsh winds and waves, and backed by striking cliffs gouged with caves. Rock bridges and towering arches are stranded just offshore, while deep dunes have blocked rivermouths, forming briny lakes and islands where fur seals and birds have made a home. Though too rough for safe swimming, the beach is a superb place to explore, watch seals in the rock pools at half-tide and lounge around.

Kahurangi National Park

The huge expanse of **Kahurangi National Park** was created in 1996, and encompasses 40,000 square kilometres of the northwestern South Island; appropriately enough, its name means "treasured possession". The park enfolds the exposed western side of the Wakamarama Range (among the wettest mountains in the country) and the peaks of Mount Owen and Mount Arthur. A remote and beautiful place with relatively few visitors, the best way to appreciate its extraordinary landscape is on foot. In fact, this is the only way to get to much of the park and most people come here to walk the **tracks**, primarily the **Heaphy Track**, though its lesser-tramped cousins offer equal rewards and more solitude. The best bases for visiting the northern section of the Kahurangi National Park are **Collingwood** and **Takaka**, from where buses run to the head of the Heaphy Track (summer only). **Motueka** provides access to the Tablelands, Mount Arthur and the Leslie–Karamea Track from the Flora Saddle car park; and the southern reaches of the park are best approached from Murchison (see p.580).

Some natural history and history

Geologically Kahurangi is an incredibly diverse area, comprising sedimentary rocks faulted and uplifted from an ancient sea leaving limestone and marble riddled with deep caves, bluffs, natural bridges and arches, sink holes and strange outcrops. Over half of New Zealand's native **plant species** are represented in the park, as are most of its alpine species, while the remote interior is a haven for birds and **animals**, including rare carnivorous snails and giant cave spiders.

Around 800 years ago, the area was well travelled by **Maori**, as they made their way to central Westland in search of *pounamu* for weapons, ornaments and tools. From Aorere, they traversed the Gouland Downs, crossed the Heaphy rivermouth and headed down the coast, constantly at risk of being swept away.

8

The first **Europeans** to arrive were Australian sealing gangs in the 1820s, who within twenty years had almost wiped out the entire seal population. In 1856 the first **gold rush** ignited interest in the area and although it had petered out three years later, prospectors tarried on at the Aorere Gold Fields (now a reserve) and deeper into the interior. Ironically, now the area is protected it faces its greatest test as millions of **possums**, which invaded the area in the late 1960s, obliviously munch their way through the native plants and devastate the snail population.

The Heaphy Track

The **Heaphy Track** (82km; 4–6 days) is one of New Zealand's Great Walks. It can be walked year-round and links Golden Bay with Kohaihai Bluff on the West Coast by way of the northern reaches of the Kahurangi National Park. It is appreciably tougher than the nearby Abel Tasman Coast Track but compensates with its beauty and the diversity of the landscapes it covers: the confluence of the turbulent Brown and Aorere rivers, broad tussock downs and forests, and nikau palm groves at the western end. The track is named after Charles Heaphy who, with Thomas Brunner, became the first Europeans to walk the West Coast section of the route in 1846, accompanied by their Maori guide Kehu. Currently there is no reservation system though peak season crowds mean there is always the possibility of one being instituted at short notice.

Information, accommodation and guided walks

DOC's *Heaphy Track* **brochure** ($1) is available from visitor centres and DOC offices, and includes a schematic map that is satisfactory for hiking, though it is always wise to carry the detailed 1:150,000 Kahurangi ParkMap ($16). Along the route, there are seven **huts** (Oct–April $14; May–Sept $10), with heating, water and toilets: all except Brown and Gouland Downs have cooking stoves, but it is sensible to carry your own along with pots and pans. There are also seven designated **campsites** (all year $7), mostly close to huts. Before setting off, you must purchase a hut or camp **pass** from a DOC office or visitor centre, though this does not guarantee a bunk: there is a two-night limit in each hut. There is nowhere along the track to pick up **supplies** so you must take all provisions with you, and go prepared for sudden changes of weather and a hail of sandflies.

Guided walks along the track (and elsewhere in the park) are handled admirably by the ecologically caring Bush and Beyond Guided Wilderness Treks (☎03/528 9054, ⓦwww.naturetreks.co.nz) who run five-day trips either driving back from Karamea ($850), or flying back ($1025).

Trailhead transport

The Heaphy Track is particularly awkward in one respect: the western end is over 400km by road from the eastern end, so if you leave gear at one end, you'll have to re-walk the track, undertake a long bus journey, or fly back to your base at Nelson, Motueka or Takaka.

The Heaphy starts at **Brown Hut**, 28km southwest of Collingwood. Abel Tasman Coachlines and Golden Bay Coachlines (☎03/525 8352) jointly run there from Nelson (departing 7am; $42), Motueka (8am; $35), Takaka (9am; $20) and Collingwood (9.30am; $10). K Bus (☎03/525 9434, ⓦwww.kahurangi.co.nz) run a directly competing service at virtually the same times.

At the West Coast end you'll arrive at Kohaihai shelter, 10km north of Karamea (see p.782). Shuttle buses (see p.783 for details) run you into Karamea where you'll need to spend the night (unless you are flying back). To get back from Karamea **by bus** you'll have to catch the Karamea Express (at 7.50am; ☎03/782 6757) and change in Westport to Atomic Shuttles (9.40am; ☎03/322 8883). This reaches Nelson at 3.30pm, just in time to catch the Abel Tasman Coachlines bus to Motueka and Takaka (3.40pm; ☎03/548 0285). All up that will cost $50 to Nelson, $59 to Motueka and $72 to Takaka.

A better solution is to go with Nelson-based Drive Me Wild Expeditions (☎03/5468876, ⦿www.drivemewild.co.nz) who run you direct from Nelson to Brown Hut then, several days later, pick up at Kohaihai Shelter and run you back to Nelson that evening, all for $115.

Flying also gives you the chance to return to your car the same day you finish the track: it is obviously more expensive but if you can get four or more people together the price can be very competitive. Flight Corporation (☎0800/359 464, ⦿www.flightcorp.co.nz) and Abel Tasman Air (☎0800/304 560 & 03/528 8290, ⦿www.flytasmanbay.co.nz) both fly from Karamea to Nelson ($145 per person, minimum 2), Motueka ($155) or Takaka ($155) on demand. Karamea Helicopters will take you from Karamea straight to your vehicle at the eastern end of the Heaphy Track in fifteen minutes ($600 for 2, $700 for 3; ☎03/782 6111)

Track transport only runs from late October to late April: in **winter** months everything becomes more difficult requiring taxis to reach trailheads.

The route

The most popular approach is to walk the Heaphy Track from east to west, thereby getting the tough initial climb over with and taking it relatively easy on subsequent days. From **Browns Hut to Perry Saddle Hut** (17km; 5hr; 800m ascent) it is a steady climb all the way passing the Aorere campsite and shelter, and Flanagans Corner viewpoint – at 915m, the highest point on the track. It's then a very easy walk from **Perry Saddle Hut to Gouland Downs Hut** (8km; 2hr; 200m ascent) across Perry Saddle through tussock clearings to the valley before crossing limestone arches to the hut. You now cross the Gouland Downs, an undulating area of flax and tussock, to **Saxon Hut** (5km; 1hr 30min, 200m descent). From Saxon Hut to **Mackay Hut** (14km; 3hr; 400m ascent) involves crossing grassy flatlands, winding in and out of small streams as they tip over into the Heaphy River below. If you have the energy, it is worth pressing on to **Lewis Hut** (13.5km; 3–4hr; 700m descent), a haven of nikau palms – and less welcome sandflies. It is possible to get from here to the track end in a day but it is more enjoyable to take your time and stop at the **Heaphy Hut** (8km; 2–3hr; 100m ascent), near where you can explore the exciting Heaphy river-mouth: its narrow outlet funnels river water into a torrid sea, resulting in a maelstrom of sea and fresh water. The final stretch (16km; 5hr; 100m ascent) is a gentle walk through forest down the coast until you reach Crayfish Point, where you can cross the beach if you are within two hours of low tide; other-wise, take the high-tide track. Once you reach Scott's Beach, you have only to climb over Kohaihai Bluff to find the **Kohaihai Shelter** car park on the other side – and hopefully your pre-arranged pick-up from Karamea (see p.782).

The rest of the park

The Heaphy Track is all that most people see of Kahurangi, but there are a number of other worthwhile **walking** tracks, all of which offer a taste of this unusual and still relatively unknown area. Visitor centres in Takaka, Motueka and Nelson have plenty of **information** on the area and can advise on the limited transport to trailheads.

Two quite arduous but rewarding and uncrowded tracks are the **Wangapeka Track** (60km; 4–5 days), usually walked from Little Wanganui, just south of Karamea on the West Coast (see p.782 for details), and the **Leslie–Karamea Track** (90km; 5–7 days), which links the Wangapeka Track with Mount Arthur and the Tablelands above Motueka. The Leslie–Karamea Track starts at the Flora Saddle car park near Motueka (see p.586) and heads south along the Leslie and Karamea rivers and through beech forest before joining the Wangapeka Track near the Luna Hut. There are seven main huts (all $5–10) along the track, which is quite rough in places and should only be attempted by reasonably fit and well equipped trampers. A track brochure ($1) is available from DOC offices and visitor centres but you should also carry the appropriate topographic maps.

Nelson Lakes National Park and around

The **Nelson Lakes National Park**, around 120km southwest of Nelson, is characterized by its two glacial lakes, **Rotoiti** ("little lake") and **Rotoroa** ("long lake") nestled in the mountains at the northernmost limit of the Southern Alps. Both are surrounded by tranquil mountains and shrouded in dark beech forest, and jointly form the headwaters of the Buller River. Tramping is undoubtedly the main event and you could easily devote a week to some of the longer circuits, though short lakeside walks reward a shorter visit.

The main base for forays into the park is tiny **St Arnaud**, on SH63 draped around the northern shores of Lake Rotoiti 100km southwest of Blenheim. Anglers, kayakers and yachties mostly base themselves here. It is possible to stay in the mixed beech and podocarp forest beside the deep blue waters of Lake Rotoroa in rather more seclusion hemmed in by mountains, but track access is poorer from here unless you take a water taxi across the lake.

The park's sub-alpine rivers, lakes, forests and hills are full of bird life, but it has offered little solace to humans: Maori passed through the area and caught eels in the lakes, but the best efforts of European settlers and gold prospectors yielded meagre returns. Now, recreation is all.

St Arnaud

ST ARNAUD (pronounced Sn-AR-nard) is a speck of a place scattered around the north shore of Lake Rotoiti, with around a hundred residents but over four hundred houses, mostly used by holidaying Kiwis. It is where you'll come to stay and eat, though the choice is fairly limited. Aside from beautiful lake and mountain vistas and a heap of walks (see box p.578) there's little to detain you except the DOC **visitor centre**, on View Rd (daily: Christmas–Feb 8am–6pm; March–Christmas 8am–4.30pm; ☎03/521 1806), guarded by a red statue depicting Rakaihautu, creator of the lakes. The centre has all the hiking, biking, fishing and ecology information you could need as well as local accommodation and transport listings. There is also a short audio-visual display ($1; shown on demand) on Maori history and the ecology of the Nelson Lakes and Buller River region, an area which supports giant eels that can be over 100 years old. They also provide intentions sheets for those planning major hikes: be sure to sign in (or call) on your safe return.

Rotoiti **Water Taxis** ($15pp, min 3 or 4; ☎03/521 1894) operate on Lake Rotoiti from Kerr Bay, so if you fancy sections of hiking at the southern end of the lake there's no need to walk the whole way. Alternatively, you can pay them to take you on a scenic cruise around the lake, or they'll rent **kayaks**, canoes, row boats ($30 half day, $40 per day).

Practicalities

The only **buses** that come direct to St Arnaud are Cain Road Service (☎03/522 4044) which runs from Nelson (Mon, Wed & Fri only), and Atomic Shuttles on their daily run between Nelson to Westport and their summer-only daily express run between Picton and Greymouth. Other services (including InterCity) only come as close as Kawatiri (on SH6, 25km away) from where you'll need the services of Nelson Lakes Shuttles ($15pp, min 2; ☎03/521 1900).

The hub of St Arnaud is the **Nelson Lakes Village Centre** (daily 7.30am–6.30pm) a combined petrol station, post office, store and takeaway. Opposite, *Alpine Lodge and* Alpine *Chalet* (☎03/521 1869, ⓦalpinelodge.co.nz; dorms ❶, budget rooms ❷, hotel rooms ❺) has **accommodation** in modern wooden buildings plus a licensed restaurant, bar and spa pool. About 150m up the street is the combined *Yellow House* and *St Arnaud Log Chalets* (☎03/521 1887, ⓦwww.nelsonlakes.co.nz; dorms ❶, rooms ❷, chalets ❹): the former is a small, neat hostel with doubles, twins and shared rooms, kitchen, TV and a wealth of information; the latter is a cluster of comfortable fully self-contained log-built chalets next door. Both have access to a hot tub ($4) and there's camping out back ($13). Most of the year holiday homes are available for rent by the night through St Arnaud Holiday Cottages (☎03/521 1900, ⓦwww.starnaudholidaycottages.co.nz), and costing $65–120 for up to four people. There's a one-night surcharge of $10 and you'll need your own bedding and towels. For sumptuous B&B amid beech forest and rhododendrons, try *Avarest*, 1 Kerr Bay Rd (☎521 1864, ⓦwww.avarestbnb.co.nz; ❽).

Nelson Lakes hikes

With 270km of track served by twenty huts there is no shortage of walking options. Arm yourself with the *St Arnaud Short Walks* and *St Arnaud Day Walks* leaflets (both $0.50 from DOC) or consider the two excellent **longer tracks** listed below. These are alpine tracks so you must be equipped with good boots, and warm, waterproof clothing – it can snow in almost any month up there – as well as the relevant DOC maps and leaflets, and hut tickets from the DOC office in St Arnaud. Both tracks start from the upper Mount Robert car park, 5km from St Arnaud, which can be reached on foot, by car, or by bus with Nelson Lakes Shuttles ($10pp, min 2; ☎03/521 1900, ⓦwww.nelsonlakesshuttles.co.nz).

The following hikes are listed in approximate order of difficulty.

Bellbird Walk Kerr Bay, St Arnaud (10–15min loop; flat). Easy meander through beech forest alive with the sound of tui, bellbirds and fantails thanks to the Rotoiti Nature Recovery Project, an attempt to replicate the successful offshore island pest clearances by concerted trapping and poisoning. Several of these "mainland islands" have been set up across New Zealand since the late 1990s with apparent success. Visit in the early evening when the birds are particularly noisy and frisky.

Honeydew Walk Kerr Bay, St Arnaud (30–45min loop; flat). An extension of the Bellbird Walk, named for the sweet excretions of the scale insect which burrows into the bark of the beech trees. It is this that the nectar-loving tui and bellbirds come for.

Whisky Falls Mt Robert trailhead (3–5hr return, 10km; 100m ascent). From a parking area on the Mount Roberts Road, follow the Lakeside Trail to these 40m falls. Almost always shrouded in mist and fringed by hanging ferns, the falls are particularly grand after heavy rain.

Finally, there are two DOC **campsites** (☎03/521 1806; $8–10), both close to town overlooking the lake with toilets and pay showers. *Kerr Bay* is open all year and also has cooking facilities and a barbecue area; *West Bay* is only open from December to March.

Eating is limited to average takeaways, and meals at the *Alpine Chalet and Lodge*, whose licensed **restaurant** offers breakfast and dinner (daily 8–9.30am & 7–9pm; mains $22–28), plus bar meals (daily 5–6.15pm) of burgers, soups, salads and grills.

Mountain biking

Off-road biking is not allowed within the national park, but there is a number of mountain biking possibilities nearby, the best of them listed in the two *St Arnaud Area Mountain Bike Trails* leaflets ($0.50 each) available from the visitor centre. Locally, the short and mostly flat **Teetotal Trails**, about 1.5km west of St Arnaud off SH63, are perfect for beginners and families. For something a little more challenging try the ride from St Arnaud up the gravel **Mount Robert Road** to the Mount Robert car park (8km return; 1hr 15min; 200m ascent), or the occasionally steep but scenic **Porika Road**, the old 4WD track between Lakes Rotoiti and Rotoroa, which can be ridden from St Arnaud, though the offroad section (4km one way; 1hr; 300m ascent) starts from SH63 13km northwest of town.

Energetic bikers can tackle the spectacular **Rainbow Road** (1–2 days; generally open Christmas–March) that connects St Arnaud to Hanmer Springs, 112km to the southeast. The road crosses some private land, for which keys and permission must be arranged at the DOC offices at either end: there's a fee of $20 for the privilege. The highest point on the route is **Island Saddle**

Mount Roberts Circuit (4–5hr loop; 9km; 600m ascent) An excellent loop around the visible face of Mount Roberts starting at the Mount Robert car park, ascending the steep Pinchgut Track to edge of the bush then traversing across to Bushline Hut ($10) before zig-zagging down Paddy Track to the start.

Angelus Hut Loop Mt Robert trailhead (2 day loop; 28km; 100m ascent). One of the most popular overnighters from St Arnaud following **Robert Ridge** to the beautiful Angelus Basin with its welcoming hut ($10) and alpine tarn, a legacy of glaciers that retreated over 10,000 years ago, leaving the characteristic steep-sided valley walls, bluff-ringed creeks, and sharp ridges. Two common routes complete the loop: the relatively easy Cascade Track and the tougher Speargrass Track.

Travers-Sabine Circuit (80km; 4–7 days; 1200m ascent). This major tramp is the scenic equal of several of the Great Walks, but without that status it is far less crowded. The track probes deep into remote areas of lakes, fields of tussock and 2000-metre mountains, of which the highlight is the Travers Saddle (1780m) and a deep bowl fed by a 20-metre cascade and subject to freezing conditions at any time of year. At the height of summer, the track verges are briefly emblazoned with yellow buttercups, white daisies, sundew and harebells. According to Maori legend, the area's fecundity and peppering of lakes is due to Rakaihautu, a famous chief who travelled the great mountains with his *ko* (digging stick), digging enormous holes that he filled with water and food for those that followed. The circuit requires a good level of **fitness**, but is fairly easy to follow with bridges over most streams. There are six huts along the track ($10) and **camping** is allowed – but fires aren't, so carry a stove and fuel. Obtain **hut tickets** and the *Sabine-Travers Circuit* leaflet ($1) from DOC in St Arnaud and stock up on food and water.

(1347m), with panoramic views of the Tarndale Lakes, Lake Tennyson and the surrounding countryside. For accommodation en route, there are two back-country huts at Connors Creek and Island Gully ($5) and a campsite at Lake Tennyson, with a cold water supply and toilets ($5); treat water before use. The route is also followed by the annual **Rainbow Rage** bike race: the website (Ⓦ www.rainbowrage.co.nz) has some images of the route.

Lake Rotoroa

Lake Rotoroa feels a good deal more remote than the area around St Arnaud. Approached along the Gowan Valley Road which veers off SH6 some 20km northwest of St Arnaud, it ends near a self-registration DOC **campground** (non-powered sites only $8; no showers), and the exclusive, 1920s *Lake Rotoroa Lodge* (Ⓣ03/523 9121, Ⓦ www.lakerotoroalodge.com; ❾), the preserve of dedicated anglers and stressed-out executives who can afford almost $600 each per night.

The lake itself is pretty and there are a few short walks but nothing like the range at St Arnaud. It is possible to follow the Lakeside Track all the way to Sabine hut and hook up with the Travers–Sabine Circuit, but the walk along the lake is dull and you're better engaging Lake Rotoroa Water Taxis ($30pp, min 3; Ⓣ03/523 9199) who ply the length of the lake). Nelson Lakes Shuttles (Ⓣ03/521 1900) run here on demand from St Arnaud to Lake Rotoroa ($20, minimum 3).

Murchison and around

MURCHISON, 125km southwest of Nelson and 60km west of St Arnaud is a small farmers service town much favoured by hunting and fishing types as well as rafters and kayakers. Numerous rivers feed the Buller nearby providing excellent whitewater and plenty of opportunities for bagging trout.

A couple of colonial hotels stand as testimony to Murchison's glory days during a series of **gold rushes** in the district between 1862 and 1915. Though the workings were in rugged hard to reach areas, prospectors flocked here, some paddling up the Buller River in Maori canoes.

Tales of the gold days fill the **Murchison Museum**, 60 Fairfax St (daily 10am–4pm; donation requested), in the 1911 former post office with newspaper clippings, photographs and various oddities. Next door, the barn-like annex contains ancient telephone exchanges, gold-rush era Chinese pottery and opium bottles, and a bike belonging to Bob Bunn, local pioneer, long-time saw-miller and avid cyclist.

Murchison is surrounded by mountains and river valleys, in a district dominated by rugged escarpments, bush-clad ranges, lakes and many rivers. A good way to explore the area is by **bike**, which can be rented from *Riverview Holiday Park* ($15 for 2hr). A $5 booklet details several mountain bike trails (16–85km) and is available at the visitor centre; all routes begin and end in Murchison. If you want to try your hand at **gold panning**, pick up a pan ($5) and the *Recreational Gold Panning* leaflet ($0.50) from the visitor centre: this lists the likely places to strike it rich – Lyell Creek, Ariki Falls and the Howard Valley – and advises on technique. Pans rent for $5

The **Skyline Walk** (6km return; 2hr) makes a pleasant diversion and is listed on DOC's handy *Murchison Day Walks* leaflet ($0.50). The route starts from the car park 500m west of the bridge crossing the Matakitaki River, at the junction of SH6 and Matakitaki West Bank Road. Climbing up through the native forest to the skyline ridge above Murchison, the walk yields views of the township and the confluence of the Buller, Matakitaki, Maruia and Matiri rivers.

Rafting

There's considerably more fun to be had getting wet on excellent **rafting** and inflatable **kayak** trips on the Buller, Mokihinui and Karamea. Wherever you go the scenery is breathtaking, the water swift – and the sandflies omnipresent, so don't forget the insect repellent. The biggest operator is **Ultimate Descents**, 51 Fairfax St (℡03/523 9899 & 0800/748 377, ⓦwww.rivers.co.nz), whose year-round bread and butter trips run the Buller (Gd III–IV; 4hr 30min; $105) spending two hours on the water and including lunch and a post-trip hot tub. There are also gentler family rafting trips (Gd II; 4hr 30min; $95), inflatable kayaking trips (Gd II–III; 4hr 30min; $115) and combo trips (Gd II–IV; 9hr; $185) rafting the tougher bits then paddling down some easier sections. Multi-day affairs include the Mokihinui (Gd III–IV; 2 days; $650), the Karamea (Gd IV–V; 3 days; $995) and custom trips to order.

White Water Action Rafting Tours, behind the Visitor Centre on Main Road (℡0800/100582, ⓦwww.whitewateraction.co.nz), offer similar trips (all followed by a barbecue. Go for either half a day on any of the three main rafted sections ($95) or a full day combining two sections ($165).

Once clear of Murchison, SH6 romps alongside the Buller River through the Buller Gorge to the **West Coast** town of Westport, a route covered in Chapter Twelve (see p.779). If you're heading for the **east**, you can retrace your route along SH6, then cut across to Blenheim, 160 scenic kilometres away on SH63.

Practicalities

Everything of note is on SH6 (Waller Street in Murchison), or Fairfax Street which crosses it. **Buses** drop off at several places around town, none more than 100m from the **visitor centre**, 47 Waller St (daily: Oct–May 9am–6pm; June–Sept 11am–3pm; ℡03/523 9350, ⓦwww.murchisonnz.co.nz), which stocks a number of leaflets on activities in the area. Like many small towns Murchison has **no bank** or ATM.

Campers have two choices. Kayakers and rafters tend to frequent, the *Riverview Holiday Park*, SH6 1km east (℡03/523 9315; camping $16 for two, cabins ➋, tourist flat ➌, motel unit ➍) a delightful, bird-filled, shady campsite by the gurgling Buller River. Families prefer *Kiwi Park*, 170 Fairfax St, 1km south of the town centre (℡03/523 9248, ⓔkiwipark@xtra.co.nz; camping $9, cabins ➋, cottages ➍, motel units ➎), which has a broad range of accommodation. There's also the small and comfortable *Lazy Cow* **backpacker**, 37 Waller St (℡03/523 9451, ⓦhomepages.paradise.net.nz/lazycow; dorm ➊, doubles & twins ➌).

Clearly signposted about 1km from town, *Mataki Motel*, 34 Hotham St (℡03/523 9088; ➌) is clean and quiet; some units have a full kitchen, others make do with a kettle and toaster. If you don't mind being 16km south of Murchison, try *Awapiriti Farmstay*, SH65 (℡03/523 9466, ⓔawapiriti @ihug.co.nz; ➎), with plenty of local bush walks, plus a full breakfast.

Murchison's **eating** options include several tearooms and takeaways, but the best bets for decent food and coffee are: the *Commercial Hotel*, 47 Fairfax St (closed Mon in winter), with stuffed bagels ($8) and mains like butter chicken ($18); and the *River Café*, 51 Fairfax St (in the Ultimate Descents Centre; closed May–Sept), which does some imaginative and reasonably priced snack and good coffee during the day, as well as more substantial main meals ($18–23) on summer evenings.

Our account of the Buller Gorge and the road west continues on p.779

Blenheim and the Marlborough wine country

In the early 1970s, **BLENHEIM**, 27km south of Picton, was a fairly sleepy service town set amid pastoral land: now it is a fairly sleepy service town completely surrounded by some of the most fecund and highly regarded vineyards in the land – the **Marlborough wine country**. In the intervening years Marlborough Sauvignon blanc has helped put the New Zealand wine industry on the world map, and increased plantings have now edged the region ahead of Hawke's Bay as the country's largest producing region with over forty percent of the national grape crop.

In recent years, the wineries have been going all out to attract visitors using distinctive architecture, classy restaurants, art and gourmet foodstuffs as lures. The profusion of weekend visitors from Nelson, Wellington and further afield has spawned a number of classy B&Bs throughout the district, all trying to out-luxury one another. If this is the sort of experience you're after, there's little need to bother with Blenheim itself, particularly since most of the vineyards are closer to the small, unremarkable town of **Renwick**, 10km to the west. But Blenheim works well enough as a base, both for the wine country and for hikes in the nearby **Richmond Range**.

To get here from Picton you can either drive the direct SH1, or opt for the circuitous and **scenic coastal route**, which takes in the sights of old whaling stations via Port Underwood, as the road winds tightly up and down the bluffs. The two routes meet at Koromiko where the cheese factory has a tasting room.

Arrival, information and accommodation

Trains and long-distance **buses** all stop outside the **visitor centre**, in the train station on Sinclair Street (Dec–March daily 8.30–5.30pm; April–Nov Mon–Fri 8.30am–5pm, Sat & Sun 9am–4pm; ☎03/577 8080, ⓦwww .destinationmarlborough.com), which stocks an assortment of **leaflets** and rents bikes (see "Listings", p.587). Remember to pick up a local walks map, the *Marlborough Wine Region* map, the *Art and Craft Trail* brochure (all free) and perhaps the snazzy, detailed *Wines of Marlborough Map* ($2). The **airport** is 7km south of town, and flights are met by Airport Super Shuttle (☎03/572 9910; about $10).

As befits a major wine region there's an abundance of luxury **accommodation** scattered around the district, plus more modest places in town and one stunning **hotel**. Budget places are thinner on the ground and most cater to seasonal workers, though there are a couple of good hostels, especially *Watson's Way* in Renwick.

During the first full week of February almost all accommodation is booked up far in advance for the **festival season** (see box, p.584): either plan well ahead or steer clear at this time.

Blenheim

Beaver B&B 60 Beaver Rd ☎03/578 8401, ⓔrdhopkins@xtra.co.nz. Attractive self-contained unit ten minutes' walk from central Blenheim, and a continental breakfast is supplied. ❹

Honi-B Backpackers 18 Parker St ☎03/577 8441, ⓔhoni-b-backpackers@xtra.co.nz. The pick of Blenheim's fairly poor crop of hostels; modern with a well-equipped kitchen and barbecue area, and close to the centre. Dorms ❶, rooms ❷

Hotel d'Urville 52 Queen St ☎03/577 9945, ⓦwww.durville.co.nz. This former bank right in the centre of town has been turned into a world-class, highly individual hotel and restaurant, with each room thematically and colourfully decorated. The best, and some say the only, place to stay in town and a good place to eat and party. Rooms cost $300 in summer. ❾

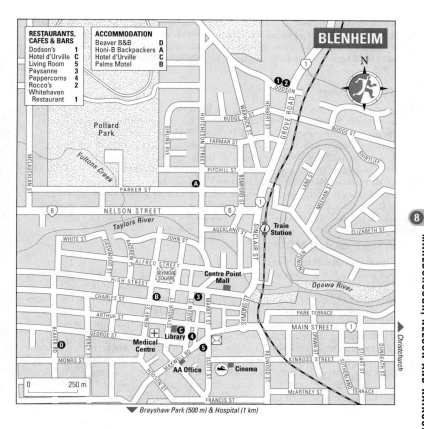

Palms Motel cnr Henry & Charles sts ☎03/577
8845 & 0800/256 725, ⓦwww
.blenheimpalmsmotel.co.nz. New, central motel
with Sky TV and a range of units including one
with a courtyard and outdoor spa. ⑤

The wine region

Charmwood Rural Retreat 158 Murrays Rd
☎03/570 5409, ⓦwww.charmwood.co.nz.
Wonderfully hospitable homestay on a beef
farm, with large rooms, tennis court, swimming
pool and hearty breakfasts of home-grown
produce. ⑤

Cranbrook Cottage 145 Giffords Rd, about 9km
northwest of town ☎03/572 8606, ⓦlodgings
.co.nz/cranbrook.html. Handy for the wineries,
this superb self-contained picture-book cottage
has the added bonus of breakfast delivered to
your door from the main house. Romantic and
quiet. ⑦

Old Saint Mary's Convent Rapaura Rd,
close to the junction with Hammerich's Rd
☎03/570 5700, ⓦwww.convent.co.nz. A
grand two-storey house among the vines built
in 1901 for the Sisters of Mercy and now a
gorgeous lodge with delightful rooms
including a honeymoon suite with stained
glass windows. Rates start at $350;
honeymoon suite $450. ⑨

Uno Più 75 Murphys Rd ☎03/578 2235,
ⓦwww.geocities.com/unopiu. Run by
friendly, former Italian-restaurant owner, Gino,
who makes this homestay magical. It's hard to
imagine being better looked after, either in the
1917 homestead or out in the new mudbrick
self-catering cottage. Breakfasts are great and
excellent dinners are available by arrangement.
Book in advance. ⑧

Watson's Way Backpackers 56 High St,
Renwick ☎03/572 8228,

@www.watsonswaybackpackers.co.nz. Easily Marlborough's best hostel: a very comfortable spot in the shade of large trees in a wonderful garden, with a public tennis court over the fence, snug rooms, three made-up doubles, easy access to the wineries, low-cost bikes, a safari bath, barbecue and owners who can't do enough for you. Closed Sept. Tents $10, dorms ❶, rooms ❷

The town

With the exception of the wineries, Blenheim has no **sights** to speak of. **Seymour Square**, in the centre of the town, has pretty flowerbeds and a distinctive stone clock tower, and **Pollard Park**, accessed off Parker Street, ten minutes' walk north, is pleasant with its rose gardens, rhododendrons and native rock garden. Other than that, there's a lacklustre reconstruction of an early settlers' community and a collection of vintage farm machinery and vehicles out in **Brayshaw Park**, off New Renwick Rd, 2.5km south of the town centre (roughly daily 10am–4pm; museum $2), and the tiny 1860s **Cobb Cottage**, on SH1, 3km southeast of town (Sat 10am–4pm, Sun 1–4pm; donations requested), which has been restored to house yet more displays on the lives of early settlers.

Wine country

The gravel plains that flank the Wairau River around the towns of Blenheim and Renwick make up some of New Zealand's most prized **wine country**. The region, sheltered by the protective hills of the Richmond Range, basks in around 2400 hours of sunshine a year making it perfect for ripening the grapes for its esteemed Sauvignon Blanc. Chardonnay and Pinot Noir grapes also grow well (almost guaranteeing tasty bubbly), and the region is gaining a reputation for its light and golden olive oil.

Over fifty wineries call this home, most of them accessible for cellar-door sales and **tasting** (either free or for a small charge, which is often deducted from any subsequent purchases). Some add a short tour, tack on a restaurant or even link up with outlets hawking olive oil, fruit preserves and the like. Most of the notable wineries are around Renwick or immediately north along Raupara Road, all listed on the free *Marlborough Wine Region* sheet (along with their opening hours and facilities), and most also feature on the more detailed *Marlborough Wineries and Wines* fold-out map ($2). **Opening hours** are generally 10am–4pm daily, though often much reduced in winter.

Marlborough festivals

Blenheim springs to life during the first full week of February. On the first Saturday, the **Blues, Brews and BBQ Festival** kicks off proceedings at the Blenheim A&P Showground with a combination of musicians and brewers parading their wares from all over the country. This is mixed in a heady cocktail with some good old-fashioned kiwi snags, kebabs and burgers, as well as some more adventurous fare. Well worth a look if you're in party mode.

Various arts and crafts demonstrations, exhibitions, markets and special events pad out the next week, but Blenheim's big event is the annual **Wine Marlborough Festival** ($35, includes a glass for slurping; noon–8pm; @www.bmw-winemarlborough-festival.co.nz) on the second Saturday. Around 10,000 people flock to the Montana Brancott winery, where a vast field full of marquees offering local wines and food for purchase, with live music and general revelry.

Deluxe Travel Line run **buses** ($6) to the festival site from the town and the airport, as well as from Picton ($14).

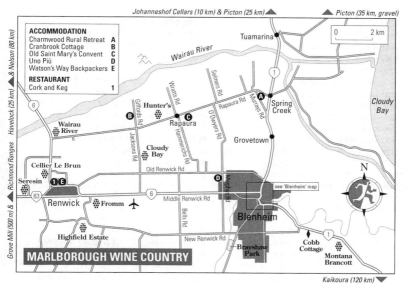

Johanneshof Cellars (10 km) & Picton (25 km) ▲   ▲ Picton (35 km, gravel)

ACCOMMODATION
Charmwood Rural Retreat   **A**
Cranbrook Cottage   **B**
Old Saint Mary's Convent   **C**
Uno Più   **D**
Watson's Way Backpackers   **E**

RESTAURANT
Cork and Keg   **1**

0   2 km

Tuamarina

Wairau River

Havelock (25 km) ▲ & Nelson (80 km) ▲
Richmond Ranges ▲
Grove Mill (500 m) ▲

Watts Rd
Selmers Rd
Rapaura Rd
Murrays Rd
O'Dwyers Rd
Hammericks Rd
Jacksons Rd
Giffords Rd
Bells Rd
Murphis Rd

Hunter's
Rapaura
Wairau River
Cloudy Bay
Cellier Le Brun
Seresin
Renwick
Fromm
Highfield Estate

Spring Creek
Grovetown

Cloudy Bay

Old Renwick Rd
Middle Renwick Rd
New Renwick Rd

see 'Blenheim' map

Blenheim

Brayshaw Park

Cobb Cottage
Montana Brancott

MARLBOROUGH WINE COUNTRY

N

Kaikoura (120 km) ▼

Armed with these you're ready for a day among the vines, preferably with lunch at one of the winery restaurants. Few wines are available for much under $20 a bottle, and wineries like to show off with their restaurants, so although it will almost certainly be a pleasurable experience it won't be cheap. And don't be tempted to cram too many into a day; most are more suited to leisurely vineyard tastings than whistle-stop tours.

You'll seldom have to go more than 5km to get to the next winery of interest, but touring the wineries by car has an obvious downside for the driver. The main alternative is an organized **wine tour** with someone like Marlborough Travel (℡0800/990 800) who offer budget half-day ($45) and good value full day ($55) tours of the region. Deluxe Wine Tour (℡0800/500 511, ⓦ www.deluxetravel.co.nz) runs a morning tour ($49 including all tasting fees) visiting three wineries including a tour of Montana Brancott, and an afternoon tour ($40) which skips the Brancott. Sounds Connection (℡0800/742866 & 03/573 8843, ⓦ www.soundsconnection.co.nz) offers a half day tour visiting 4–5 wineries ($49), a full day circuit of 6–7 wineries ($65, lunch at your own expense), and a full-day gourmet tour ($125) including a five-course lunch at *Cellier Le Brun* with matched wines. Tours pick up at accommodation around Blenheim.

Rental bikes are also a possibility (see "Listings", p.587), though the wineries are fairly spread out and you may find that after a couple of visits your desire to cycle diminishes rapidly. To travel at a more leisurely pace, go with Wine Tours by Bike (℡03/572 9951, ⓦ www.winetoursbybike .co.nz) who charge $60 for the day's bike rental and $120 for a guide for the day.

Most of the wineries will **ship cases** of wine anywhere in the world, but shipping costs and high import duties mean that it seldom works out good value: expect $120 a case to Australia, more like $160 a case to the UK or US. Buy what you can drink and carry, and when you know what you like, enquire as to who distributes their wine in your home country.

The wineries

Cellier Le Brun Terrace Rd ☎03/572 8814, ⓦwww.lebrun.co.nz. Producer of extremely high-quality Daniel Le Brun Methode Champenoise offers tastings ($3) of vintage and non-vintage wines. Also a good restaurant where you might expect monkfish on chargrilled ciabatta or caramelized pork loin (both $18) at lunch. Dinner mains go for $28–30.

Cloudy Bay Jacksons Rd ☎03/520 9140, ⓦwww.cloudybay.co.nz. Marlborough Sauvignon Blanc put New Zealand on the world wine map in the late 1980s and the Cloudy Bay Sav was its flagship. It is still drinking well today and can be tasted (free) along with a range of their other top notch offerings.

Fromm Godfrey Rd ☎03/572 9355, ⓦwww.frommwineries.com. A vineyard that is turning winemakers' heads with a very hands-on approach and producing predominantly red: excellent Pinot Noir, and peppery Syrah as well as a Riesling with echoes of the best German efforts. Visit if you're serious about the subject and you'll taste (free) a product that's a match for anywhere in the world, at a price.

Highfield Estate Brookby Rd ☎03/572 9244, ⓦwww.highfield.co.nz. Easily recognizable by its Tuscan-inspired tower, which you can climb for excellent views, Highfield offers free tastings and lays on some of the best food in the region, with $15–20 mains, antipasto platters ($30) that will easily feed two and delectable desserts ($10).

Hunter's Rapaura Rd ☎03/572 8489, ⓦwww.hunters.co.nz. Jane Hunter is recognised as one of the world's top women winemakers. Drop by to taste, visit the art gallery or eat in the classy restaurant.

Johanneshof Cellars SH1, 20km north of Blenheim ☎03/573 7035. Famous for its historic underground cellars carved out of the face of the hill. Tours (30min; $8) include tastings of their good quality wines (otherwise $3).

Montana Brancott 5km south of Blenheim on SH1. Montana effectively kicked off the wine region in the early 1970s and now operate the country's largest winery here, a favourite with coach parties. They run a winery tour (daily 10am–3pm; 1hr; $10), teach a little wine appreciation and offer tastings (some free, others for a small fee). There's a good café too.

Seresin Bedford Road ☎03/572 9408, ⓦwww.seresin.co.nz. Stylish winery with a distinctive primitivist "hand" logo perched on a rise overlooking the vines. Wines are produced from largely organic, estate-grown grapes often using wild yeast to produce world-class food wines. Free tastings, and samples of good local olive oil.

Wairau River Rapaura Rd ☎03/572 9800, ⓦwww.wairauriverwines.com. At the foot of the Richmond Range, this splendid rammed earth and rimu timber construction by the river deals with wine from both the *Wairau River* and *Foxes Island* wineries. They offer free tastings and very good quality lunches and snacks, including spicy Thai-style mussels and Manuka smoked salmon salad.

The Richmond Range

Twenty-six kilometres southwest of Blenheim, the **Richmond Range** of mountains is well supplied with **walks** and Scenic Recreation Areas. The DOC leaflets *Central Marlborough Recreation Areas* ($0.50 from the visitor centre) and *Mount Richmond Route Guide* ($1) are useful guides to the facilities and trails. For further information you can also try the DOC Field Centre, Gee Street, Renwick (Mon–Fri 9am–12.30pm & 1.30–5pm).

Mount Richmond itself is 1760m high, with expansive views from its summit, taking in the entire Wairau Valley, the Kaikoura and St Arnaud ranges. Easily accessible from the Top Valley and Timms Creek routes, it's possible to tackle the summit on a day-trip from the wineries. The **Top Valley route** (7.5km; 3hr 30min one way) is ideal for a single-minded assault on the **summit**, whereas **Timms Creek** (10km; 4hr 30min) provides access to the backcountry **Mount Richmond Hut** ($5) and longer, more ambitious tramps into the park. Both routes **start** from the **Northbank Road** (16km from Blenheim on SH6) and, if you don't have your own car, you'll need to arrange **drop-off** and **pick-up** with a local shuttle company, such as Deluxe Travel Line (☎03/578 5467), or talk to the visitor centre in Blenheim.

Of numerous other walks in the area, the **Wakamarina Track** (details in the DOC's *Richmond Ranges* leaflet, $0.50) is a useful short cut for trampers and mountain bikers, crossing the Richmond Range from the Wairau Valley to the Wakamarina Valley near Havelock. There are two backcountry **huts** along the track ($5), which is best walked or ridden from south to north: trampers should allow one or two days to cover the 12-kilometre track; bikers should be able to manage it in an afternoon.

Eating, drinking and entertainment

A few hours spent visiting vineyards should be accompanied by lunch at one of the wineries: we've mentioned several worth trying (see p.586). Few are open in the evenings so you may need to head into Blenheim for dinner. The choice is pretty reasonable though the presence of free-spending wine fans keeps prices high. If you've had enough of the wineries and all the hot air that circulates about them then a truly refreshing alternative can be found with good **beer** at a couple of pubs, one in Blenheim, one in Renwick. **Entertainment listings** can be found in the Friday edition of the daily *Marlborough Express* ($0.80).

Cork and Keg Inkerman St, Renwick. Comfortable English-style pub with a warming stone hearth and traditional games like dominoes. The beer is made to order in Westport and includes some excellent natural brews, including dark, draught, lager and old English Hurricane. They also serve inexpensive bar meals.

Dodson's 1 Dodson St. Bar and microbrewery with a pleasant garden in which to sup one of their six preservative- and additive-free beers (plus guest beers). They even do a five-beer tasting rack ($7) and you can soak it all up with the likes of bangers and mash and lambs' fry and bacon.

Hotel d'Urville 52 Queen St ☎03/577 9945. Classy restaurant with stylish modern decor and exemplary cuisine making the best of seasonal produce. Expect something special – perhaps venison osso bucco or turmeric roasted fish – and be prepared to pay around $30 for mains.

Living Room 2 Scott St. An absolute delight and real favourite with locals and travellers alike. You can have stonking coffee, delicious cakes, a glass of wine or some finely presented light meals – perhaps char-grilled field mushrooms on mesclun salad ($14.50) or the daily pasta, risotto or pizza ($14–18).

Paysanne 1st floor, The Forum, High St. A stylish café/wine bar with views of shopping locals. Serves good cakes and coffee during the day and some excellent main meals from $16, including very passable wood-fired pizza. Occasional live music in the evening but essentially a place to chill.

Peppercorns 73 Queen St. Small deli-cum-eatery where they serve the best gourmet pies in town as well as some tasty panini, calzone and quiches.

Rocco's 5 Dodson St ☎03/578 6940. This enjoyable Italian restaurant, which makes its own fresh pasta daily is the undoubted pick of the bunch. For a blow-out, order the awesome chicken Kiev alla Rocco – chicken breast filled with ham, garlic butter and cheese, all wrapped in a veal schnitzel ($23). Dinner only, closed Sun.

Whitehaven Restaurant 1 Dodson St ☎03/577 6634. Stylish mid-range restaurant and wine tasting cellar, specializing in fresh, high-quality New Zealand produce – bacon-wrapped scallops ($17) or Stewart Island cod ($26) – rounded off with rich desserts and excellent wines – served in a comfortable and atmospheric building.

Listings

Airlines Soundsair (☎04/388 2594) operates daily scheduled flights to Wellington.
Automobile Association 23 Maxwell Rd ☎03/578 3399.
Bike rental Bikes are available from the visitor centre ($30 half day, $40 full day).
Cinema 3 Kinross St ☎03/577 5559.

Medical treatment Medical Centre, 24 George St (☎03/578 2174), about 100m from junction with Queen St.
Post office Central post office, cnr Scott St & Main St (Mon–Fri 9am–5pm, Sat 9am–1pm).
Taxis Marlborough Taxis ☎03/577 5511; Red Band Taxis ☎03/577 2072.

South from Blenheim: the Kaikoura Coast

From Blenheim it is a 130km run down between the coast and the brooding Seaward Kaikoura Range to the next place of any consequence, Kaikoura. It can be done in an hour and a half, but is best if allotted more time for frequent stops along some gorgeous stretches of coastline. Around 20km south of Blenheim a sign points inland along the Awatere Valley, mostly of interest for the few weeks each year when it provides access through **Molesworth Station** to Hanmer Springs (see box, below).

Immediately after the junction, SH1 crosses the Awatere River on a single-lane bridge shared by the train line which runs overhead. The road then continues 10km, through the small town of Seddon, to Lake Grassmere, a vast shallow salt lake put to use producing much of New Zealand's table salt. Dominion Salt Ltd offers tours of the salt works (Tues & Fri 1.30pm; free) where over the summer months the region's long sunshine hours and low rainfall combine to provide excellent evaporation conditions.

Drivers will probably want to press on, but **cyclists** may want to overnight 20km south of the salt works on at *Cycle Packers Hostel* (☎03/575 6708, Ⓔpedallers@xtra.co.nz; ❶): it is 1.5km off SH1; look for the water tank and sign beside the road. You're now following the coast with grey gravel beaches all the way, accessible at various points. Almost 90km out of Blenheim, the rocky Kekerengu Point juts out and makes a great place to stop, both for the coastal views and *The Store* (☎03/575 8600), an excellent **café** and restaurant.

Another 35km on and you hit the best stretch of coastline, signalled by **Ohau Point**, a great roadside parking area right beside the South Island's largest seal colony with (usually) dozens of seals lolling on the rocks not more than twenty metres away. Along the final 30km into Kaikoura, the shoreline is dotted with craggy rocks making this a perfect habitat for **crayfish**, which are sought by the locals and sold at good prices from roadside shacks, notably at Rakautara, 22km before Kaikoura.

Driving the Molesworth Road

Timing is everything if you want to drive the Molesworth Road through **Molesworth Station**, at 180,000 hectares New Zealand's largest farm. The central 59km section has traditionally only been open for a few weeks each summer (late Dec to mid-March) but as of July 2004 it became a high-country park under DOC management and access may improve. It is an impressive run through New Zealand's most accessible high country passing historic cob houses with towering mountains all around. The drive from Blenheim to Hanmer Springs (190km) takes over five hours, a couple of them on gravel, and since there are no services make sure your rig is in good nick and the tank topped up. The cost is $15 per vehicle plus $5 per adult, and bicycles go for $5: fees are collected along the road. **Camping** is only permitted at Molesworth Homestead and Acheron Historic Homestead (both $5). For the latest information obtain DOC's *Molesworth* leaflet ($1) and check the DOC website, Ⓦwww.doc.govt.nz.

Access is also possible from October to May with Molesworth Backcountry Safaris (☎03/575 7525 & 0800/104 532, Ⓦwww.backcountrysafaris.co.nz) who explore the region on one-day trips ($240), overnight expeditions ($390) and a three-day experience ($695).

Kaikoura and around

The small town of **KAIKOURA**, 130km south of Blenheim and 180km north of Christchurch, is prettily set in the lee of the Kaikoura Peninsula. Offshore, the sea bed drops away rapidly to the Kaikoura Canyon – 1000 metres deep a kilometre from land – a phenomenon that brings sea mammals in big and varied numbers. **Whale watching** and **swimming with dolphins** have become big business here, and the presence of expectant tourists has spawned a number of eco-oriented businesses offering swimming with seals, sea kayaking, scuba diving, hiking and even sky watching. If you happen to be in the

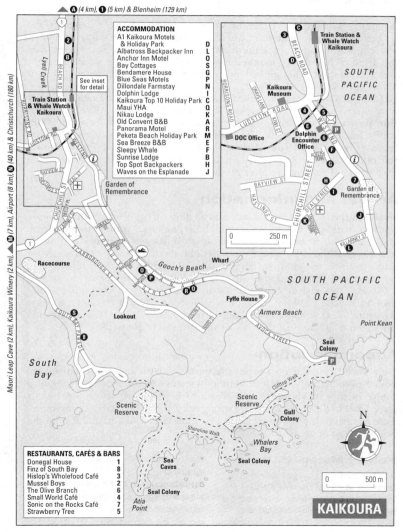

ACCOMMODATION

A1 Kaikoura Motels & Holiday Park	D
Albatross Backpacker Inn	L
Anchor Inn Motel	O
Bay Cottages	S
Bendamere House	G
Blue Seas Motels	P
Dillondale Farmstay	N
Dolphin Lodge	I
Kaikoura Top 10 Holiday Park	C
Maui YHA	Q
Nikau Lodge	K
Old Convent B&B	A
Panorama Motel	R
Peketa Beach Holiday Park	M
Sea Breeze B&B	E
Sleepy Whale	F
Sunrise Lodge	B
Top Spot Backpackers	H
Waves on the Esplanade	J

RESTAURANTS, CAFÉS & BARS

Donegal House	1
Finz of South Bay	8
Hislop's Wholefood Café	3
Mussel Boys	2
The Olive Branch	6
Small World Café	4
Sonic on the Rocks Café	7
Strawberry Tree	5

KAIKOURA

area in the **winter**, the newest and one of the most diverse of New Zealand's skiing areas at **Mount Lyford** is worth investigating.

Whale watching and dolphin swimming are very popular and visitors often book well in advance to be sure of getting a place. Unfortunately, being open ocean the sea easily chops up in **bad weather** and trips are often cancelled. If you don't want to miss out, allow yourself a couple of days flexibility here.

Kaikoura was named by an ancient **Maori** explorer who stopped to eat crayfish and found it so good he called the place *kai* (food) *koura* (crayfish). Maori legend also accounts for the extraordinary coastline around Kaikoura. During the creation of the land, a young deity, Marokura, was given the job of finishing the region: first he built the Kaikoura peninsula and a second smaller peninsula (Haumuri Bluff), then he set about creating the huge troughs in the sea between the two peninsulas, where the cold waters of the south would mix with the warm waters of the north and east. Tuterakiwhanoa (a god), realizing the depth of Marokura's accomplishment, said that the place would be a gift (*koha*) to all those who see its hidden beauty – and it is still known to local Maori as Te Koha O Marokura.

The Ngai Tahu people harvested the wealth of the land and seas until they were decimated by the warrior Te Rauparaha around 1830. The first **Europeans** to settle in the area were whalers who came in the early 1840s, swiftly followed by farmers. The trials and tribulations of their existence are recorded in the **Kaikoura Museum** and the more evocative **Fyffe House**. Kaikoura ticked on pretty quietly until the late 1980s when whale watching really took off and put the place on the tourism map.

Arrival and information

Buses on the Picton–Christchurch run all drop off on Westend Parade, in the town car park near the visitor centre. The TransCoastal **train** between Picton and Christchurch arrives at the station on Whaleway Station Road, while scenic flights land at the grass Peketa **airfield**, about 8km south of town. Most places in town are within walking distance, though as the town now spreads out along SH1 you may find a bike or taxi useful when you're weary; see p.595.

The log cabin **visitor centre** on Westend Parade (daily: Dec–Jan 9am–6pm; Feb–April 9am–5.30pm; May–Nov 9am–5pm; ☎03/319 5641, Ⓦwww .kaikoura.co.nz), is full of helpful information, handles all **DOC** enquiries and has a 20min audio-visual show about the area (every 30min; $3).

Accommodation

For a small town, Kaikoura seems overburdened with **accommodation**, but from November to March it is splitting its seams and you'll do well to book a couple of days in advance, longer if you have your heart set on a particular place. Most of the places to stay are strung out along SH1 (Beach Road) immediately north of the centre, or along The Esplanade which head out onto the peninsula east of town.

Hotels, Motels B&Bs and homestays

Anchor Inn Motel 208 Esplanade ☎03/319 5426 & 0800/720 033, Ⓦwww.anchor-inn.co.nz. One of the country's most luxurious motels and with prices to match. Modern, air conditioned and with

every con-venience. Standard ➐, with view and spa bath ➑
Bay Cottages 29 South Parade ☎03/319 5506, Ⓔbaycottages@xtra.co.nz. Excellent value accommodation in five purpose-built, well-equipped, self-contained units in a quiet spot at a

silly price. The owner is exceptionally friendly and sometimes takes guests out crayfishing for breakfast in the morning. The only disadvantage is being 2km from town in South Bay. ❹

Bendamere House 37 Adelphi Terrace ☎03/319 5830 & 0800/107 770, ✉bendamerehouse@xtra .co.nz. A house on the hill overlooking the bay, with old-fashioned hospitality, comfy rooms and hearty home-cooked breakfasts. ❹

Blue Seas Motels 222 Esplanade ☎03/319 5441 & 0800/507 077, ✉blue.seas@xtra.co.nz. Small, simple and good value older motel units which are close to the sea but don't have great views. ❺

Dillondale Farmstay 188 Stag & Spey Rd ☎03/319 5205, ✉acton.adams@actrix.co.nz. Forty minutes' drive inland from Kaikoura is this very professionally run farmstay far away from all the world's worries. Rates are for B&B, and hearty two-course dinners (on request) cost $40. ❻

Nikau Lodge 53 Deal St ☎03/319 6973, ⓦwww.nikaulodge.com. Most of the six tastefully decorated en-suite rooms in this lovely, wooden, 1925 house have great mountain or sea views. There's also satellite TV with in-room movies, free Internet access and a good breakfast. ❼

Old Convent B&B Cnr Mount Fyffe Rd & Mill Rd, 4km northwest of town ☎03/319 6603, ⓦwww.theoldconvent.co.nz. Something of a curiosity, this French-styled 1912 ex-convent is set in spacious grounds and has a quiet rural atmosphere. Bright, en-suite rooms are atmospheric, if relatively modest, and there's a restaurant and bar on site. ❻

Panorama Motel 266 Esplanade ☎03/319 5053, ✉panorama.motel@xtra.co.nz. There are superb views from these stripped-pine, clean units with a chalet feel; you'll pay $10 extra for the better view from the upper floor. ❺

Sea Breeze B&B 2 Adelphi Terrace ☎03/319 5549. Cheerful and central B&B that offers few frills but is great value. ❹

Waves on the Esplanade 78 The Esplanade ☎03/319 5890, ⓦwww.KaikouraApartments .co.nz. Luxurious two-bedroom motel-style apartments all with excellent sea views. ❽

Hostels, campsites and motor parks

A1 Kaikoura Motels & Holiday Park 11 Beach Rd ☎03/319 5999 & 0800/605 999, ✉kaikouramotel@xtra.co.nz. Very central motor park offering a variety of somewhat ageing accommodation from motel units through four different types of cabin, to backpacker bunks and campsites, all on a smart site that backs onto the

river. Tent sites $10, dorms ❶, cabins ❷–❸, motels ❹

Albatross Backpacker Inn 1 Torquay St ☎03/319 6090, ⓦwww.albaross-kaikoura.co.nz. A friendly, spacious and beautifully cared for converted post office and telephone exchange with unusual Turkish-style decor in some rooms. A BBQ and well tended grounds make it especially good on fine days. Cash only. Dorms ❶, rooms ❷

Dolphin Lodge 15 Deal St ☎03/319 5842, ✉dolphinlodge@xtra.co.nz. Boutique hostel with lovely gardens (complete with spa) overlooking the sea and pleasant little doubles but no twins, all at modest rates. Dorms ❶, rooms ❷

Kaikoura Top 10 Holiday Park 34 Beach Rd ☎03/319 5362, ⓦwww.kaikouratop10.co.nz. This central, shaded award-winning park maintains high standards and offers a range of accommodation, including cabins and motels, and has an outdoor private spa. Camping $12, cabins ❷–❸, self-contained unit ❹, motel ❺

Maui YHA 270 Esplanade ☎03/319 5931, ✉yha.kaikoura@yha.org.nz. Comfortable, if slightly dowdy, hostel which compensates with tremendous sea and mountain views, particularly from the lounge and kitchen. Dorms ❶, rooms ❷

Peketa Beach Holiday Park SH1, 7km south of Kaikoura ☎03/319 6299, ✉peketabeach@xtra.co .nz. A peaceful beachside campsite that's very popular with surfers who make use of the excellent waves on the doorstep. Camping $9, cabins ❷

Sleepy Whale 86 Westend ☎03/319 7014, ✉sleepywhale@xtra.co.nz. Comfortable, spacious and slightly clinical hostel right opposite the visitor centre with all beds made up and a great deck with BBQ overlooking the sea. Some rooms are en-suite. Dorms ❶, rooms ❸

Sunrise Lodge 74 Beach Rd ☎03/319 7444, ⓕ319 7445. Well-kept purpose-built boutique hostel with a fully equipped kitchen and comfortable, if somewhat spartan, twin rooms (no doubles) all with made-up beds. Free laundry and shonky bikes. Closed June–Aug. Dorms ❶, rooms ❷

Top Spot Backpackers 22 Deal St ☎03/319 5540, ✉topspot@xtra.co.nz. Tucked away 200m up a signposted track (the Lydia Washington Walkway) from the visitor centre, this very friendly and well-run hostel has good views over Kaikoura and the coast, a log-burning fire, mountain bikes, BBQ and sundeck and offers seal swimming trips. It is consequently popular with the backpacker tours buses. Dorms ❶, rooms ❷

The Town and the peninsula

Most visitors are dead-set on seeing whales or swimming with dolphins, and the smattering of other sights and activities are often treated as ways of filling in the time until their turn comes, or a means of waiting out bad weather.

Some distraction is provided by the **Kaikoura Museum**, 14 Ludstone Rd (Mon–Fri 12.30–4.30pm, Sat & Sun 2–4pm; $3), where exhibits cover the period from the early moa hunters, through the various groups that have occupied the land since. Along with a large number of argillite and greenstone artefacts and a daunting collection of old photos, there are bits of the fossilized Plesiosaur and Mosasaur, two monstrous sea creatures of the Cretaceous period, kept near the front of the museum in a large glass case.

Out on the peninsula, don't miss the town's oldest building, **Fyffe House**, 62 Avoca St (daily 10am–6pm, excellent 30min guided tours; $5), an old whaler's cottage occupying a great site with views up and down the coast. Still on its original whalebone foundations, the house began life as part of the Waiopuka Whaling Station which was founded by Robert Fyffe in 1842. Originally an unprepossessing two-room cooper's cottage, it was extended by George Fyffe in 1860, and looks now much as it did then.

Across the road, a single chimney is all that remains of the old customs house, which looks remarkable perched in front of the upright layer-cake rock strata that lead to the sea. The road itself follows the edge of the peninsula round to a car park (the start of the Kaikoura Peninsula Walkway; see box below) where fur **seals** often lounge on flat, sea-worn rocks watching the plentiful bird life, gulls, shags, and black oystercatchers, who in turn explore the rock pools full of rich tidal detritus.

South of town, SH1 runs 2km to **Maori Leap Cave** (℡03/319 5023; 35min tours daily at 10.30am, 11.30am, 12.30pm, 1.30pm, 2.30pm & 3.30pm; $10), which contains some remarkable limestone formations. Stalagmites and stalactites sprout from the floor and ceiling of the cave, and translucent stone straws seem to defy gravity by maintaining their internal water level. There are also examples of cave coral and algae that survive in the dank cave by turning darkness into energy – a kind of skewed photosynthesis. There are two rival explanations for the cave's name: one has it that a Maori warrior jumped to his death

---

Kaikoura Peninsula Walkway

On a fine afternoon or evening it is well worth walking part or all of the **Kaikoura Peninsula Walkway** (11km full length; 3–4hr) which is outlined on DOC's *The Peninsula Walkway* leaflet ($1 from the visitor centre). The Kaikoura Peninsula is made up of limestone and siltstone laid down beneath the sea sixty million years ago, with a backdrop of rugged mountains and abundant wildlife. The shoreline section of the walkway from Point Kean to South Bay is particularly fine, revealing gaping sea caves, folded limestone rocks in thin layers and stacks at Atia Point.

Starting at a car park 3km east of town, out beyond Fyffe House, the walkway loops around the peninsula, past a seal colony and rejoins the road system at South Bay (see map, p.589). With just an hour or two to spare, drive to the car park and follow the Shoreline Walk as far as Whalers Bay then follow the path up the hill and take the Clifftop Walk back to the start – about 5km in all. Chances are you'll see red-billed and black-backed gulls, oystercatchers, herons and shags, as well as a number of fur seals, rejoicing in being away from the crowds back at the car park. Be warned that gulls nesting during September and October are likely to attack if they feel threatened: steer well clear.

from the hills above the cave after he was captured by another tribe; the other has two thwarted lovers from different tribes plunging to their deaths.

Roughly 300m further south, a steep driveway leads to **Kaikoura Winery** (daily 10am–5.30pm; tastings $3; ⓦ www.kaikourawines.co.nz), perched on the steep hillside overlooking South Bay. Its seaside location flies in the face of conventional viticultural wisdom, but since the 2004 crop will produce their first full vintage it is hard to say how successful they've been. Be here on the hour to join one of their tours ($7.50) into the specially designed cellars, which concludes with a tasting session.

Marine life and activities

Less than a kilometre off the Kaikoura Peninsula the coastal shallows plummet into the Kaikoura Canyon and the 1000-metre-deep Hikurangi Trench, a network of undersea troughs and canyons that funnel warm sub-tropical waters and cold sub-Antarctic flows into a nutrient rich upwelling. This provides an unusually rich habitat supporting an enormous amount and variety of marine life. Marine mammals come for an easy meal, and tourists come to watch. You can expect to see gigantic sperm **whales** (all year), **dolphins** (all year), migratory humpback whales (Jun–July) and **orca** (Dec–Feb), all at relatively close quarters.

Whale watching

Kaikoura's flagship activity is **whale watching**, conducted by the Maori-owned and operated Whale Watch Kaikoura (ⓣ03/319 5045 & 0800/655 121, ⓦ www.whalewatch.co.nz) who run up to fifteen sailings a day (2hr 30min; $110), each with an excellent introductory video and safety demonstration. You meet at the train station and are bussed around to South Bay where a speedy catamaran whisks you a couple of kilometres offshore (much closer than similar trips elsewhere in the world). Hopefully there'll be several whale sightings along with dolphins and sea birds before you head back.

An alternative is **aerial whale watching** with Wings Over Whales (ⓣ03/319 6580 & 0800/226 629, ⓦ www.whales.co.nz) who have 30min flights for $135; and Kaikoura Helicopters (ⓣ03/319 6609, ⓦ www.worldofwhales.co.nz) who offer a 25min flight for $165. Obviously you don't get as close to whales as you would by sea, so bring a good pair of binoculars.

Swimming with dolphins and seals

The other main reason people visit Kaikoura is to go **swimming with dolphins**, an experience many find vaguely spiritual. The only operator is Dolphin Encounter, 58 Westend (ⓣ03/319 6777 & 0800/733 365, ⓦ www.dolphin.co.nz) who do three trips a day (6am, 9am & 1pm; $115 to swim, $55 to watch). Places fill quickly so book three weeks in advance in summer, though standbys sometimes become available at short notice. You'll get most out of it if you're a reasonably confident swimmer; the more you duck-dive and generally splash around, the more eager the dolphins will be to investigate. They seem to find it attractive listening to you humming through your snorkel – any tune will do – and they love pregnant women. Don't get too carried away though: dolphins have a penchant for swimming in ever-decreasing circles until lesser beings are quite dizzy and disorientated.

Seals tend to be even more curious than dolphins, often coming closer to check you out. Consequently you may prefer **swimming with seals**, something done either from shore or by boat. Topspot Seal Swim ($50; ⓣ03/319 5540; Nov–April only) involves bach entry and a fair bit of swimming so it helps if you've snorkelled before. If you'd prefer something boat-based try three-hour trips with Dive Kaikoura, 94 Westend ($65; ☎0800/728 223, Ⓦwww.scubadive.co.nz). Dive Kaikoura also run **scuba diving** tours with the chance to see a temperate reef with kelp forests, nudibranches and sponges. Experienced divers are catered for (1 dive $95, two dives $130), and novices can do a "resort" dive with an instructor ($120).

Bird watching and sea kayaking

Fans of sea birds won't be able to resist **Albatross Encounter**, 58 Westend (2–3 trips daily; 2–3hr; $60; ☎0800/733 365 & 03/319 6777, Ⓦwww .oceanwings.co.nz), a chance to get a kilometre or two offshore in a small boat as bait is laid to attract all manner or seabirds – shags, mollymawks, gannets, petrels and a couple of varieties of albatross. They come amazingly close, but be warned, the sharks' livers used to attract the birds have an evil stench and if you get downwind of it you may lose your breakfast to the sea.

Another way to see the wildlife is **sea kayaking** with Sea Kayak Kaikoura (☎03/319 5641 & 0800/452 456, Ⓦwww.seakayakkaikoura.co.nz) who offer half-day guided trips ($70) and full-day kayak rentals ($70) with the option of also renting snorkel and dive gear.

Other activities

If you'd rather stay on dry land, and learn something of the Maori culture here-abouts, join **Maori Tours** (☎03/319 5567 &0800/866 267, Ⓦwww .maoritours.co.nz) who offer a selection of trips organized and guided by an ex-whale watch boat driver and give a real taste of *Maoritanga* and the genuine hospitality it demands. Three hour tours ($75) take in various local sights, story telling, explanations of cultural differences and involve learning a song.

There's great **horse riding** around 13km inland at Fyffe View Horse Treks (from $45; ☎03/319 5069), and aspiring fliers might like to **Pilot a Plane** ($85; ☎ & Ⓕ03/319 6579), a chance to take the controls for thirty minutes: an adrenaline buzz with great scenery to boot.

Once the sun goes down, clear nights offer a great chance to experience **Kaikoura Night Sky** (1–1.5hr; $35; ☎03/319 6635, Ⓔstarskaikoura @xtra.co.nz), with small groups clustered around a mobile eight-inch telescope in the fields away from the Kaikoura lights. The chance planets, moon craters and distant galaxies come alive with tales of celestial navigation and what the southern sky means to Maori.

Eating and drinking

The least expensive way to sample the local **crayfish** is to buy them ready-boiled from one of the shacks and caravans alongside SH1 north of town. You can buy good quality **fresh fish** from the Pacifica Seafoods (Kaikoura) Ltd, near the wharf at the eastern end of Gooch's Beach. There are also a number of chip shops in town producing excellent fried-fish **takeaways**; try the *Continental*, 47 Beach Rd. The **restaurants** and **cafés** in town are all a bit pricey, safe in the knowledge that you're not exactly spoilt for choice, particularly near the town centre. But there are notable exceptions where the cooking is good, the prices fair and the atmosphere pleasing.

Donegal House Mt Fyffe Rd ☎03/319 5083. A local legend, this purpose-built Irish bar and restaurant in the middle of a farm works surpris-ingly well with a wide ranging, modestly priced menu and a very lively atmosphere. It is ten minutes drive north of town (follow SH1 for 4km then 2km west along left School House Road) so you may want to go by cab or arrange to stay at the on-site B&B ($120). Daily 11am–whenever.

Finz of South Bay Bay Parade ☎03/319 6688. An excellent fine-dining restaurant and bar offering a broad range of well-prepared and wonderfully presented evening dishes made from local ingredients with new world panache, also the best seafood in town. Dinner only. Closed Mon & Tues in winter.

Hislop's Wholefood Café 33 Beach Rd ☎03/319 6971. Excellent wooden-floored café that's fine for coffee and cakes inside or out, but specializes in organic meals (some vegetarian) including toothsome daily fresh-baked bread to eat in with their lovely chowder. Wine by the glass including vegan varieties.

Mussel Boys 80 Beach Rd ☎03/319 7160. The delightful cousin of the Havelock restaurant where you can get wonderful mussels, a variety of other seafood delights and thick tasty chowder, washed down with wines from the Kaikoura vineyard at reasonable prices.

Olive Branch 54 Westend. A light and airy upmarket eatery and wine bar offering panini, mussels and fish all prepared imaginatively with either an Asian influence or a soupçon of French style.

Small World Café Cnr Westend & SH1. Atmospheric and low-key café, serving the best java in town and some juicy souvlaki, chicken and falafel. This place also acts as alternative night spot and venue when there's a good travelling band or DJ around.

Sonic on the Rocks Café Westend & The Esplanade. Lively modern café/bar that becomes the town's main nightspot as the evening wears on, often with occasional live music or a DJ. The wide menu runs from plates of nachos ($10) to gourmet pizza ($15 & $20) to lamb shanks with field mushrooms ($25).

Strawberry Tree Westend. Loosely Irish-styled bar that's almost always busy, often spilling out into the beer garden.

Listings

Bike rental West End Motors 50 Westend ☎03/319 5065 charge $27 a day.

Buses InterCity and Atomic run frequently to Christchurch and Picton via Blenheim; South Island Connections (03/366 6633) do much the same with connections to Dunedin; and the Hanmer Connection (☎0800/377 378) run three days a week to Hanmer Springs via Mount Lyford.

Car rental BP Car Rental, Beach Road ☎03/319 5036 and limited km deals from $35 a day.

Internet access Internet Outpost, 19 Westend, have stacks of machines.

Medical treatment Kaikoura Hospital and Doctors Surgery, Deal St, 50m from cnr Churchill St ☎03/319 5040.

Pharmacy Kaikoura Pharmacy, 37 Westend (Mon–Fri 9am–5pm, Sat 9am–1pm).

Post office 41 Westend (Mon–Fri 9am–5pm, Sat 9am–1pm).

Taxis Kaikoura Taxis (☎03/319 6214) operates taxi services, sightseeing and trailhead transport.

Around Kaikoura

The Seaward **Kaikoura Ranges** and Mount Fyffe dominate Kaikoura's western horizon: bleak and foreboding in heavy cloud but inspiring when snowy peaks catch the spring sun. Some of the walks close to town are outlined in DOC's *Mount Fyffe and the Seaward Kaikoura Range* leaflet ($0.50) the most immediately appealing being the hike to the 1602m summit of **Mount Fyffe** (16km return; 6–8hr; 1400m ascent). Starting at a poorly signposted car park 12km northwest of town the route climbs steadily up a 4WD road to the summit with its glorious views over the Kaikoura Peninsula and coast.

It is also possible to access the Inland Kaikoura Range and the huts of the **Clarence River Conservation Area** from Kaikoura, a journey of about 25km. Head south out of Kaikoura on SH1, then turn inland on SH70 to the reserve car park at the Kahutara Bridge. The Clarence River Conservation Area offers the opportunity to explore some uncrowded walking tracks in an area with some of the highest mountains outside the Southern Alps and some stunning geological formations. Should you decide to explore, go well-equipped as the weather in this area can change in an instant.

Some 60km southwest of Kaikoura off SH70, **Mount Lyford** (mid-June to mid-Oct, 9am–4pm; general information ℡03/315 6178, premium-rated snowphone 0900/34 444, Ⓦwww.mtlyford.co.nz) offers some of the upper South Island's best **skiing** and New Zealand's newest skifield. It is small and has limited lift facilities ($45 a day), but Mount Lyford caters for a broad range of abilities and is rarely crowded. **Mount Lyford Village**, 3.5km from the field, has comfortable **accommodation** at the *Terako Lodge B&B* (℡03/315 6059; ④) and back on SH70 there's *Mount Lyford Lodge* (℡03/319 6182, Ⓦwww.mtlyfordlodge.co.nz; dorms ①, rooms ⑤), which has a welcoming restaurant and bar.

South from Kaikoura

South of Kaikoura it is a two- to three-hour run down SH1 to Christchurch with only relatively minor points of interest along the way. The road initially follows a 20km stretch of delightful rocky coastline then ducks inland through farming country for most of the rest of the way to Christchurch.

Glenstrae Farm, almost 30km south of Kaikoura (℡0800/004 009 & 03/319 7021) make a good journey break for their **quadbike rides** (3hr; $80) across farmland with coastal views.

There are opportunities to see more of the coast, one of the best being the excellent privately owned **Kaikoura Coast Track** (43km; 3 days; 600m ascent), a manageable way to explore the area. The trail climbs through farmland and native bush across the Hawkeswood Range and along beaches, with spectacular views of the Seaward Kaikoura mountains and the Southern Alps, starting and ending at *The Staging Post*, 2111 Parnassus Rd, Hawkeswood, 50km south of Kaikoura. Only a limited number are allowed to walk the track at any one time so you must **book in advance** (℡03/319 2715, Ⓦwww.kaikouratrack.co.nz) and pay the fee of $130. In return you get bag transport (so you only need carry a day pack), and three nights' **accommodation** in warm, clean cottages with fully equipped kitchens, baths and showers as well as fresh farm produce, milk, bread and home-cooked meals by arrangement. The track is now also open to **mountain bikers**, who pay $70 for a two-day ride, one nights' accommodation and bag transport.

Continuing south, SH1 runs winds through the coastal hills to quiet **Cheviot**, to the up and coming **wine district of Waipara**, which warrants a couple of hours for lunch and a tasting or two. Eventually the land flattens into the Canterbury Plains for the run into Christchurch.

Cheviot and Gore Bay

The only significant town between Kaikoura and Christchurch is the sleepy farming town of **CHEVIOT**, 70km south of Kaikoura, which held a pivotal role in changes to colonial land distribution. In the early years of settlement most agricultural land was in vast estates, but in 1893 one Sir John McKenzie (see p.663) parcelled the land into small farms and holdings, so the same land could support 650 people, rather than just 80 – a process that was to be replicated across New Zealand, breaking up the enormous landholdings of a few rich and powerful men (as recounted in John Wilson's book, *Cheviot: Kingdom to Country*). The story is detailed in the **Cheviot Museum**, 6 Main St (Sat 10am–noon, Sun 2–4pm, or by arrangement with Pat Robinson ☎03/319 8308; donation requested), which also provides some interesting insights into the origins of the town and its surroundings along with moa bones and a display devoted to local son, George Forbes, who became prime minister from 1930 to 1935.

To dispel driving fatigue or museum ennui, take a walk by the sea at **Gore Bay**, a small collection of homes, 8km east of Cheviot. There's a lovely beach with safe swimming and a couple of simple campgrounds that might warrant an overnight stop. Even if you've only got a few minutes, drive 500m up the hill at the southern end of the beach to a viewpoint overlooking **The Cathedrals**, some dramatic examples of badland erosion where siltstone cliffs have weathered into huge stalagmite-like fingers that resemble the pipes of a cathedral organ.

Waipara Valley

Some 50km south of Cheviot, paddocks full of newly planted vines announce your arrival in the **Waipara Valley**, one of New Zealand's fastest growing wine regions. Thanks to its long warm days, combination of alluvial gravels and lime-stone clays, and protection from cooling sea winds, the Waipara Valley has begun producing some notable Pinot Noirs, Rieslings, Chardonnays and Sauvignon Blancs, but as a wine destination it is very much in its infancy. Half a dozen places offer tastings and several have restaurants on site but there is virtually nothing else.

The region is centred on the hamlet of **WAIPARA** at the junction of SH1 and SH7 to Hanmer Springs and the Lewis Pass. Everywhere is within 5km radius of here. Around 4km north on SH1, Waipara Springs (daily 11am–5pm; ☎03/314 6777, ⓦwww.waiparasprings.co.nz) was first planted in 1982 and offers tastings of their latest vintages though they are perhaps best appreciated in their modestly-priced daytime **café** which always has wholesome fresh-baked bread to go with their daily specials. There's a considerably more upscale tenor to Pegasus Bay, Stockgrove Rd, 4km south of the junction along SH1 then 3km east (daily 10.30am–5pm, ☎03/314 6869, ⓦwww.pegasusbay.com) with contemporary artworks surrounding diners in their **restaurant** (daily noon–4pm). Nip in to taste some of their delicious wines or stay for lunch which might be creamed leek and scallop tart ($13) followed by beef sirloin with celeriac and horseradish puree ($29). Each course is matched with an appropriate wine (which costs extra).

More workaday needs are satisfied by *The Corner Cupboard*, cnr SH1 & SH7 which does light **meals** and sells ice creams, and there is intriguing backpacker **accommodation** just around the corner at *Waipara Sleepers*, 12 Glenmark Drive (☎03/314 6003, ⓔwaipara.sleepers@inet.net.nz; dorms ❶, rooms ❷) where disused railway guards' vans have been converted into dorms and dou-bles, and an old station functions as a kitchen.

Travel details

Ferries and fast catamarans cross Cook Strait and link up with the region's only train, from Picton to Christchurch. Buses fill in the gaps, many doing the same Picton–Christchurch run via Kaikoura with others running to Blenheim and Nelson where there are connections for the Abel Tasman National Park and Golden Bay. Flights listed are non-stop direct flights; there are many others which stop or require changes in Wellington or Christchurch.

Ferries

From Picton to: Wellington (5–10 daily; 2hr 15 min–3hr).

Trains

From Picton to: Blenheim (1 daily; 30min); Christchurch (1 daily; 5hr 30min); Kaikoura (1 daily; 2hr 30min).

Buses

From Blenheim to: Christchurch (5 daily; 4hr 30min–5hr); Greymouth (1 daily; 4hr 30min); Murchison (1 daily; 2hr 10min); Nelson (5 daily; 1hr 40min); Picton (12–-14 daily; 30min); St Arnaud (1 daily; 1hr 15 min).
From Kaikoura to: Christchurch (5 daily 2hr 30min); Picton (5 daily; 2hr 15min).
From Motueka to: Kaiteriteri (5–6 daily; 20min); Nelson (5–6 daily; 1hr); Takaka (2–3 daily; 1hr).
From Murchison to: Blenheim (1 daily; 2hr 10min); Greymouth (1 daily; 2hr 15min); Nelson (2 daily; 2–4hr); Westport (2 daily; 1hr 15min).
From Nelson to: Blenheim (5 daily; 1hr 40min); Christchurch (2 daily; 7–8hr); Greymouth (2 daily; 6–8hr); Kawatiri Junction, for Nelson Lakes (1 daily; 1hr 5min); Motueka (5–6 daily; 1hr); Murchison (2 daily; 2–4hr); Picton (5 daily; 2hr); Takaka (2–3 daily; 2hr–2hr 30min); Westport (2 daily; 3hr).
From Picton to: Blenheim (12–14 daily; 30min); Christchurch (5 daily; 5hr–5hr 30min); Kaikoura (5 daily; 2hr 15min); Nelson (5 daily; 2hr); St Arnaud (1 daily; 1hr 40min).
From St Arnaud to: Blenheim (1 daily; 1hr 15 min); Picton (1 daily; 1hr 40min).

Flights

From Blenheim to: Auckland (4 daily; 1hr 20min); Christchurch (1 daily; 50min); Wellington (15 daily; 25min).
From Kaikoura to: Christchurch (1–2 daily; 1hr 20min); Wellington (1–2 daily; 1hr).
From Motueka to: Takaka (2 daily; 30min); Wellington (2 daily; 45min).
From Nelson to: Auckland (10–12 daily; 1hr 15min); Christchurch (11 daily; 50min); Palmerston North (2 daily; 50min); Wellington (15–20 daily; 35min).
From Picton to: Wellington (8 daily; 25min).

Christchurch and south to Otago

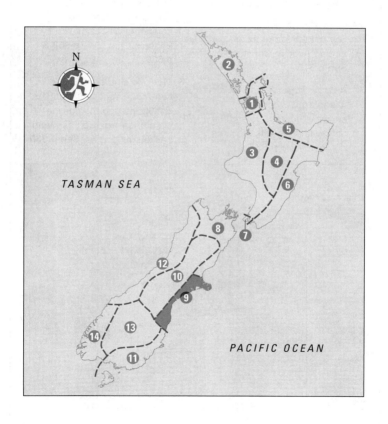

N

TASMAN SEA

PACIFIC OCEAN

✳ **Christchurch Art Gallery**
New Zealand's newest major
gallery with a fine collection
of Kiwi art. **See p.614**

✳ **The Arts Centre** Head down
to the markets and food stalls
around the Arts Centre to
check out arts, crafts and
great ethnic food. **See p.614**

✳ **Take a punt** Pick a sunny
day to punt along the willow-
fringed Avon in Christchurch.
See p.615

✳ **Akaroa** Stay in a fine B&B in
this relaxed French-influenced village and spend the
day swimming with Hector's
dolphins. **See p.637**

✳ **Maori rock art** Maori rock art
dates back hundreds of years
and offers a window into the
culture that existed before
European settlement. **See
p.652**

✳ **Oamaru** Break your stroll
around the historic district
with a spell in the Victorian
Criterion Bar, and finish up
down the road at the kooky
Penguin Club. **See p.653 &
p.659**

✳ **Moeraki Boulders** These
two-metre spherical boulders
artfully littering the tideline
were once regarded as Maori
baskets or gourds. **See p.660**

△ Oamaru

9

Christchurch and south to Otago

ncompassing some stunning and varied scenery, the South Island's east coast perhaps comes closer to most visitors' expectations of New Zealand than any other part of the country. The main hub of the region is New Zealand's third city, **Christchurch**, stretched out between the Pacific Ocean and the agriculturally rich flatlands of the Canterbury Plains, and with the Southern Alps acting as a distant backdrop to the west. A relaxed city where parks and gardens rub shoulders with some fine Victorian architecture, it boasts its fair share of urban thrills, provided largely by the cafés, bars and pubs which crowd a busy downtown area. It's also a seaside resort in its own right, with **beach suburbs** like New Brighton and Sumner within easy reach of the centre.

Immediately southeast of Christchurch rise the **Port Hills**, providing welcome relief from the flat Canterbury Plains. Beyond them, **Banks Peninsula** is a popular escape for city residents, its coastline indented by numerous bays and harbours. Perched beside these harbours are the two main communities of the peninsula, the brusque port of **Lyttelton** and the attractive, if slightly twee, town of **Akaroa**.

South of Banks Peninsula the main road and rail lines forge across the Canterbury Plains, a patchwork of rich fields and vineyards bordered by long shingle beaches littered with driftwood. Further south the countryside again changes character, with undulating coastal hills and crumbling cliffs announcing the altogether more rugged terrain of **North Otago**. The historic settlements dotted along the coast are a testament to the wealth that farming and mineral extraction brought to the region. The main centres here are the lively port of **Timaru**, close to a series of **Maori rock paintings** that indicate the region has a longer history than the imposed European feel would have you believe; and the quieter **Oamaru**, with an engaging nineteenth-century centre and some captivating **penguin colonies** just outside town. Beyond routes lead on towards Dunedin and the south, passing the unearthly **Moeraki boulders**, perfect spherical rocks formed by a combination of subterranean pressure and erosion.

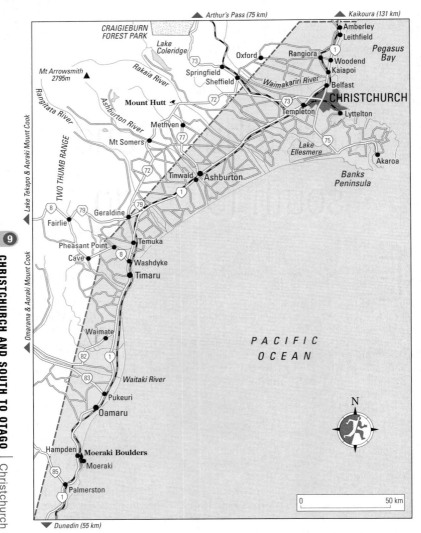

Map labels:

▲ Arthur's Pass (75 km)   ▲ Kaikoura (131 km)

CRAIGIEBURN
FOREST PARK
Lake
Coleridge
Oxford
Rangiora
Amberley
Leithfield
Woodend
Kaiapoi
Pegasus
Bay
Mt Arrowsmith
2795m
Rakaia River
Springfield
Sheffield
Waimakariri River
Belfast
CHRISTCHURCH
Rangitata River
Ashburton River
Mount Hutt
Templeton
Lyttelton
Methven
Mt Somers
Lake
Ellesmere
Akaroa
Tinwald
Ashburton
Banks
Peninsula
Geraldine
Fairlie
Temuka
Pheasant Point
Cave
Washdyke
Timaru
Waimate
PACIFIC
OCEAN
Waitaki River
Pukeuri
Oamaru
N
Hampden
Moeraki Boulders
Moeraki
Palmerston

TWO THUMB RANGE

Lake Tekapo & Aoraki Mount Cook
Omarama & Aoraki Mount Cook

0   50 km

▼ Dunedin (55 km)

Christchurch

Capital of the Canterbury region and the largest city on the South Island, **CHRISTCHURCH** (population 300,000) exudes a palpable air of gentility and a connectedness with the mother country. After all, it was perceived as an outpost of Anglicanism by its first settlers, was named after an Oxford college, and has some of the feel of a traditional English university town, with its neo-Gothic architecture and gently winding river. To some degree it pursues an archetype – the boys at Christ's College still wear striped blazers, and punts course along the Avon – but the Englishness is largely skin deep. Modern Christchurch is both multicultural and sophisticated, and those who regard Christchurch as a quiet place in which to sleep off jet lag or take a break from the long journey across the South Island will be pleasantly surprised by the city's contemporary face. In recent years its traditional conservatism has gained a more youthful, bohemian edge, with an explosion of lively bars and restaurants and a burgeoning of the visual arts, theatre, music and street entertainment. Such urban pursuits are nicely balanced by the Pacific Ocean suburbs of New Brighton and Sumner, both of which line excellent beaches.

The city can also be used as a base for exploring further afield with a plethora of city-based companies offering **activites** involving rafting, paragliding, ballooning, mountain biking in the surrounding countryside (see box p.616). The city is also within a two-hour drive of several good **skifields** to the west, making it possible to combine a day on the pistes with an evening in Christchurch's numerous watering holes.

Some history

Located in what was historically a dry and windswept area populated only sparsely by Maori, Christchurch came into being as the result of a programmatic policy of colonization by the **Canterbury Association**. Formed in 1849 by members of Christ Church College Oxford, and with the Archbishop of Canterbury at its head, the association had the utopian aim of creating a new Jerusalem in New Zealand: a middle class, Anglican community in which the moralizing culture of Victorian England could prosper. The site of the city was chosen by the association's surveyor Captain Joseph Thomas, who was quick to recognize the agricultural potential of the surrounding plain. A few Europeans were already farming the area (notably the Scottish Deans brothers, who had arrived here in 1843; see p.617), although the main centre of white settlement at the time was the port of Lyttelton to the southeast, a base for whalers since the 1830s. It was at Lyttelton that four ships containing nearly 800 settlers arrived in 1850, bound for the new city of Christchurch – by this stage little more than an agglomeration of wooden shacks. Descent from those who came on the "four ships" still carries social cachet among members of the Christchurch elite. The earliest settlers weren't all Anglicans by any means, and the millenarian aspirations upon which the city was founded soon faded as people got on with the exhausting business of carving out a new life in unfamiliar terrain. Nevertheless, the association's ideals had a profound effect on the cultural identity of the city. The elegant neo-Gothic architecture which still characterizes Christchurch's public buildings oozes with the self-confidence of these nineteenth-century pioneers, while the symmetry of the city's grid-iron street plan hints at the order the planners hoped to impose upon the community.

Arrival and information

Christchurch Airport, 10km northwest of the city centre, has one terminal divided into domestic and international sections. It stays open day and night so you may well find yourself arriving at some ungodly hour. Fortunately there

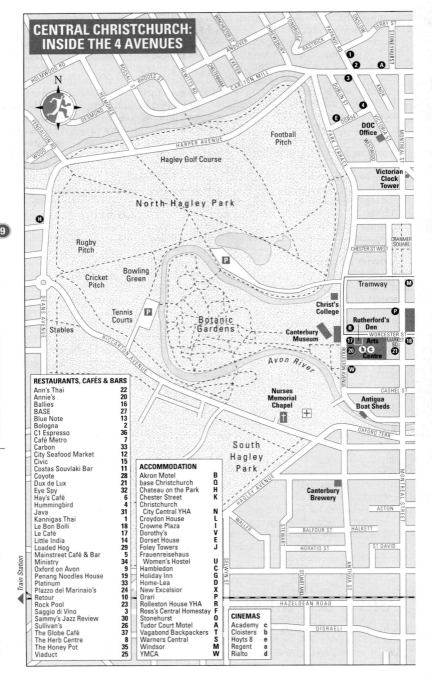

CENTRAL CHRISTCHURCH: INSIDE THE 4 AVENUES

North Hagley Park

Hagley Golf Course

Football Pitch

Rugby Pitch

Cricket Pitch

Bowling Green

Tennis Courts

Stables

Botanic Gardens

Christ's College

Canterbury Museum

Avon River

Nurses Memorial Chapel

South Hagley Park

Antigua Boat Sheds

Canterbury Brewery

Victorian Clock Tower

DOC Office

Tramway

Rutherford's Den

Arts Centre

Cranmer Square

Chester Street West

RESTAURANTS, CAFÉS & BARS

Ann's Thai	22
Annie's	20
Ballies	16
BASE	27
Blue Note	13
Bologna	2
C1 Espresso	36
Café Metro	7
Carbon	33
City Seafood Market	12
Civic	15
Costas Souvlaki Bar	11
Coyote	28
Dux de Lux	21
Eye Spy	32
Hay's Café	6
Hummingbird	4
Java	31
Kannigas Thai	1
Le Bon Bolli	18
Le Café	17
Little India	14
Loaded Hog	29
Mainstreet Café & Bar	5
Ministry	34
Oxford on Avon	9
Penang Noodles House	19
Platinum	33
Plazzo del Marinaio's	24
Retour	10
Rock Pool	23
Saggio di Vino	3
Sammy's Jazz Review	30
Sullivan's	26
The Globe Café	37
The Herb Centre	8
The Honey Pot	35
Viaduct	25

ACCOMMODATION

Akron Motel	B
base Christchurch	Q
Chateau on the Park	H
Chester Street	K
Christchurch City Central YHA	N
Croydon House	L
Crowne Plaza	I
Dorothy's	V
Dorset House	E
Foley Towers	J
Frauenreisehaus Women's Hostel	U
Hambledon	C
Holiday Inn	G
Home-Lea	D
New Excelsior	X
Orari	P
Rolleston House YHA	R
Ross's Central Homestay	F
Stonehurst	O
Tudor Court Motel	A
Vagabond Backpackers	T
Warners Central	S
Windsor	M
YMCA	W

CINEMAS

Academy	c
Cloisters	b
Hoyts 8	e
Regent	a
Rialto	d

Train Station

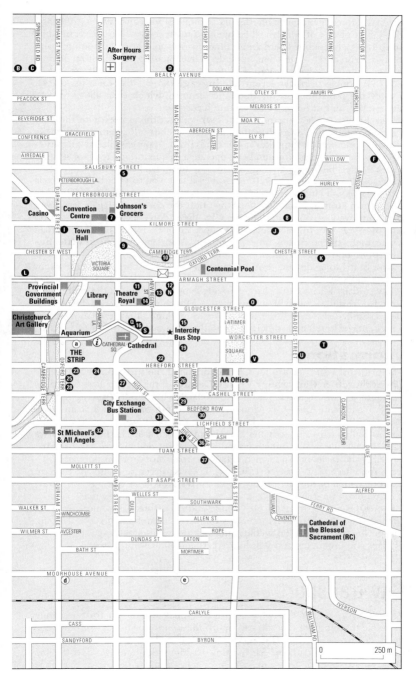

9

are ATMs, foreign exchange booths and a couple of **visitor centres** (☎03/353 7774), at least one of which will be open no matter when you arrive. In addition, there's a freephone board for accommodation and car rental bookings, and many Christchurch hotels will provide a free pick-up service from here if you've already booked a room. Failing that, there is one airport hotel (see p.607). A couple of places accept **left luggage** ($5–8 a day for a backpack), notably the post office in the domestic terminal, which even allows you to retrieve bags out of hours by contacting security.

City buses (see "City transport" below) connect the airport with the City Exchange bus station every 20–30 minutes on weekdays (6.30am–11.30pm; $5 one way), and every 30 minutes at weekends (8am–11pm); while various **shuttle** buses (see "Listings" for numbers) operate a frequent door-to-door service. There'll often be several waiting outside the terminal: hop in and once there is a viable load (usually under 10mins) they'll take you to your lodging. **Taxis** wait outside and charge around $30 into town: otherwise call (see p.628).

The **train station** is on Clarence Street near the corner of Hagley Park, over 2km southwest of Cathedral Square. City buses don't serve the train station directly – you have to walk almost 1km up Clarence Street to Riccarton Road where there are numerous buses into town. Alternatively get a **shuttle bus** ($8–10) or **taxi** ($12–19) from the station into the centre.

Most of the long-distance **bus** companies conveniently drop off at the major hostels and some hotels around town as well as near the visitor centre (see below) usually for no extra charge provided you are staying in the central area bounded by the so-called "Four Avenues" – Moorhouse, Fitzgerald, Bealey and Deans. Cathedral Square itself is within easy walking distance of most of the hostels, major hotels and some of the B&Bs and motels.

Information

The principal visitor centre for Christchurch and the surrounding area is the **Christchurch & Canterbury Visitor Centre**, in the former Post Office on the south side of Cathedral Square (Nov–March Mon–Fri 8.30am–6pm, Sat & Sun 8.30am–5pm; April–Oct Mon–Fri 8.30am–5pm, Sat & Sun 8.30am–4pm; ☎03/379 9629, ⓦwww.christchurchnz.net). You can book all forms of transport as well as trips and activities here; be sure to pick up the free *Christchurch City Centre Walks* leaflet, which provides a good introduction to local history, as well as the *Tramway* map, which details the main stops on this popular sightseers' route (see "City transport" below). The visitor centre is also the place to find out which of the city's many excellent **festivals** (see "Listings" on p.627) is currently in progress.

The **DOC** (Department of Conservation) **office**, 1km northwest of Cathedral Square at 133 Victoria St (Mon–Fri 8.30am–5pm; ☎03/379 9758), has specific information on wildlife and walking routes, stocks a good selection of maps and brochures, and sells hut tickets and annual hut passes.

City transport

You can easily see most of what Christchurch has to offer **on foot**, resorting to public transport for the odd trip out to the suburbs or to get from one side of the centre to another. **Bus** services are operated by several companies all unified under Metro (Mon–Sat 6.30am–10.30pm, Sun 9am–9pm; ☎03/366 8855, ⓦwww.metroinfo.org.nz) which operates a smart new City Exchange bus station on the corner of Colombo and Lichfield streets. In the immediate vicinity along Colombo Street between the Town Hall and Moorhouse Avenue there's the free, yellow **Shuttle** which runs every 10–15mins, though unless you have heavy bags you may find it quicker to walk. With the exception of this and the Airport Bus (see opposite) the **fare** anywhere in the city (including Sumner and Lyttelton) is $2, which entitles you to two hours of unlimited travel. If you're here for a few days, savings can be made by obtaining a **Metrocard** (minimum purchase $10) which entitles you to ride for $1.50 and can be recharged when it runs low: get one from the City Exchange bus station. Most routes run from 6am until around midnight (slightly longer in the case of more popular routes).

Perhaps the best way of familiarizing yourself with the central city area is to hop on the **Tramway** (daily: Nov–March 9am–9pm; April–Oct 9am–6pm; Ⓦ www.tram.co.nz), which weaves a 2.5km circuit past many of the central sights, including the Arts Centre and Cathedral Square and comes with a rudimentary commentary. The tramway was only installed in 1995, but the rolling stock is largely made up of lovingly restored 1905 originals. Your ticket ($12.50) is valid for two days and you can get on and off as often as you like.

Several key sights – the Antarctic Centre, Willowbank Wildlife Reserve and Christchurch Gondola – have joined forces and offer a **Best Attractions shuttle** ($15 for 24hr) which may be worthwhile if you're intent on bagging these on one hectic day. Contact the visitor centre for further information.

Driving in Christchurch is pretty straightforward providing you avoid morning and evening rush hours. Most central parking spaces are metered from Monday to Saturday between 7am and 6pm (otherwise free). If you have to drive into town, there's convenient **parking** in the centre of Hagley Park (Armagh Street entrance): free for the first 3hr and all day at weekends.

Given the city's relatively quiet roads and flat terrain, **cycling** is an ideal way of appreciating some of the more out-of-the-way suburbs. Expect to pay around $25–30 a day for **bike rental** (see "Listings", p.627, for details of outlets).

Accommodation

As the largest city in the South Island and a major port of entry, Christchurch has one of New Zealand's broadest ranges of accommodation, and although prices are by no means extortionate, they're understandably higher than in the South Island's smaller towns and cities.

Most of the **business hotels** and backpacker **hostels** are situated within the city centre, as are a number of the better **B&Bs**, though there are also several fine B&Bs out in the leafier suburbs. Probably the best value for money is found at the hostels, none too far away from the action and most offering good deals on rooms and ensuites. The majority of the **luxury hotels** are close to Victoria

---

Airport accommodation

With efficient shuttle services into the city, and establishments geared towards late arrivals and early departures, you are unlikely to need **airport accommodation**. If pushed you can stay five minutes' walk from the terminal at the *Sudima Hotel Grand Chancellor*, corner Memorial Avenue and Orchard Road (☏ 0800/100 876, Ⓦ www.sudimahotel.co.nz; ⑥), a modern business hotel with assorted restaurants and bars. It's especially pleasant if you can land a poolside room.

Square, with **motels** strung out along Papanui Road to the northwest, and on Riccarton Road which runs west from Hagley Park. Predictably, **campsites** are scattered outside the city centre, mostly within walking distance of a bus stop.

Christchurch is a very manageable city and staying in the centre is by no means unpleasant, but there is something about waking up close to the beach. Staying in beachside **Sumner** is an appealing prospect particularly if you've got your own vehicle, though city buses (#30 and #31) are fast and frequent.

With Christchurch operating a 24-hour airport, most places are well used to accommodating **late arrivals** and early departures: when making a reservation it pays to double check the dates, especially if you're arriving around midnight.

Hotels and motels

Central Christchurch has plenty of large, flashy **hotels** often with rooms overlooking Hagley Park, Cathedral Square or Victoria Square. On the whole, these represent the most expensive option, and there are cheaper **motel** rooms not far away. The best hunting ground is around fifteen minutes' walk northwest of the Square: upwards of a dozen highly competitive places line **Papanui Road** which leads to the classy suburb of Merivale. Alternatively, try **Riccarton Road**, again just outside the Four Avenues and only twenty minutes' walk from the city through Hagley Park. Rates are pretty competitive, so you shouldn't have any trouble finding a studio for around $90, and many establishments offer **special deals** for weekend and long-term stays.

City centre

Akron Motel 87 Bealey Ave ☎ 03/366 1633 & 0800/778 787, ⓦ www.akronmotel.co.nz. A small motel in a quiet area set back off the road with plain but functional units, some of which open out onto a small garden; about ten minutes' walk from Cathedral Square. ④

Cashel Court Motel 457 Cashel St ☎ 03/389 2768 & 0800/389 270. Very reasonably priced motel, fifteen minutes' walk east of the city centre and with an outdoor pool. Small but comfortable. ④

Chateau on the Park 189 Deans Ave ☎ 03/348 8999 & 0800/808 999, ⓦ www.chateau-park.co.nz. Two-hundred-room hotel, memorable for its lovely surroundings on the edge of Hagley Park, with an outdoor pool, restaurants and cocktail bar. Fifteen minutes' walk from the Square. ⑦

Crowne Plaza cnr Kilmore St & Durham St ☎ 03/365 7799 & 0800/801 111, ⓦ www.crowneplaza.com. This spectacular hotel is an outstanding feature of the city – a sort of Maya temple with a glass atrium. Overlooking Victoria Square, it has a magnificent lobby and foyer and standard international rooms. There are three bars and three restaurants, and it's well worth dropping in for a drink or afternoon tea even if you're not staying here. ⑧

Holiday Inn 356 Oxford Terrace ☎ 03/379 1180 & 0800/801 111, ⓦ www.christchurch.holiday-inn.com. Lovely business hotel on the edge of the CBD but beside the Avon River and with relaxing courtyard

gardens. High-standard rooms and all the expected facilities including indoor pool, restaurant and bar. ⑦

Tudor Court Motel 57 Bealey Ave ☎ 03/379 1465 & 0800/488 367, ⓦ www.tudorcourt.co.nz. Very small motel in a peaceful environment with simple, comfy units. Cooked and continental breakfasts are available; 12mins walk to Cathedral Square. ④

Papanui Road

Colonial Inn Motel 43 Papanui Rd, Merivale ☎ 03/355 9139 & 0800/111 232, ⓦ www.colonialinnmotel.co.nz. A modern well-appointed motel about fifteen minutes' walk from Cathedral Square. Clean and comfortable units. ⑤

Diplomat Motel 127 Papanui Rd, Merivale ☎ 03/355 6009 & 0800/109 699, ⓔ diplomatchch@xtra.co.nz. Situated in the heart of Merivale, 2km from Cathedral Square, this smart motel has large self-contained units with separate kitchens, where the extra few dollars is justified by a nice outdoor pool and spa. ⑤

Randolph 79 Papanui Rd ☎ 03/355 0942 & 0800/537 366, ⓦ www.randolphmotel.co.nz. Excellent brand new motel in grounds overshadowed by a huge copper beech tree. Rooms with bold modern decor are extremely well equipped with cooking facilities, TV/DVD, stereo and in-room laundry. Deluxe rooms come with double spa bath and there's even a small gym for guests. Rooms ⑤, deluxe ⑥

Strathern Motor Lodge 54 Papanui Rd, Merivale
☎03/355 4411 & 0800/766 624, ⓦwww.strathern
.com. Spacious and well-presented modern units all
with either kitchenette or full kitchen, and one with
its own spabath, located fifteen minutes' walk from
Cathedral Square with its own spa pool. ⑥

Riccarton Road
Aalton Motel 19 Riccarton Rd ☎03/348 6700 &
0800/422 586, ⓦwww.aalton.co.nz. Very
spacious, slightly ageing rooms represent good
value and there's an indoor spa and poorly sited
outdoor pool that's just about OK for a cooling dip.
Close to Hagley Park. ④

Annabelle Court Motel 42 Riccarton Rd
☎03/341 1189 & 0800/775 577,
ⓦwww.annabellecourtmotel.co.nz. Attractive
modern motel with spacious and well appointed
units, some with spa baths. ⑤

Sumner
Sumner Bay Motel 26 Marriner St ☎03/326
5969 & 0800/496 949,
ⓦwww.sumnermotel.co.nz. Brand-new, stylish
motel a block back from the beach with a range of
studios and apartments all with a balcony or
courtyard, Sky TV and DVD player. There's also
bike and board rental. ⑥

B&Bs and guesthouses

As elsewhere in New Zealand, the standard of **bed and breakfast** accommodation in Christchurch is very high. There's a sprinkling of excellent B&Bs in
the centre and in the nearby, easily reached suburbs, and another concentration
of places in the seaside community of Sumner. All represent good value for
money, and are invariably comfortable and friendly.

City centre
Croydon House 63 Armagh St ☎03/366 5111 &
0800/276 936, ⓦwww.croydon.co.nz. Very pleasant and well-run B&B with smallish modernized
rooms in the main house and a couple of lovely
cottages in the compact but appealing garden.
There's a guest lounge with TV and chess, 24hr tea
and coffee, and a cooked breakfast is served. ⑥
Dorothy's 2 Latimer Sq ☎03/365 6034,
ⓦwww.dorothys.co.nz. Boutique hotel with six
lovingly restored en-suite rooms plus a separate
apartment and an appreciable gay following.
There's a generous continental breakfast plus a
fine on-site restaurant serving á la carte inside or
alfresco; the *Rainbow Bar* (open to all) follows the
Wizard of Oz theme. Rooms ⑦, suites (just) ⑨
Hambledon 103 Bealey Ave ☎03/379 0723,
ⓦwww.hambledon.co.nz. Luxurious B&B with rich
Victorian furniture in one of the city's oldest and
grandest houses, built in 1856 for one of the early
city fathers – but with a homey feel with family
photos dotted about. Choose from an array of
high-standard, spacious suites; all come with
complimentary port and sherry, and delicious
breakfasts. ⑧
Home-Lea 195 Bealey Ave ☎03/379 9977 &
0800/355 321, ⓦwww.homelea.co.nz.
Comfortable and recently refurbished B&B in a
two-storeyed wooden house, built in the 1900s.
There's a quiet family atmosphere, the cosy bedrooms mostly have TVs, and continental breakfast
is served; 10mins walk from the city centre ⑤

Orari 42 Gloucester St ☎03/365 6569,
ⓦwww.orari.net.nz. Informally run and elegantly
styled B&B inn in a large 1893 home just steps
from the Arts Centre. Ten bright, sunny rooms all
have TVs, phones, artworks and either ensuites or
private bathrooms (one with a tub). Delicious
breakfasts. Closed June & July. ⑦
Ross's Central Homestay 410 Oxford Tce
☎03/366 0962 ⓔrossed@xtra.co.nz. Gay, lesbian
and mixed homestay on the banks of the Avon. ④
Windsor 52 Armagh St ☎03/366 1503 &
0800/366 1503, ⓦwww.windsorhotel.co.nz.
A traditional guesthouse with forty rooms in a
1907 former student hall of residence. Nothing
flash and none of the rooms have ensuite bathrooms, but the rooms are comfortable, clean and
mostly quiet, the staff are friendly and the cooked
breakfast keeps you going all day. They also offer
a winter special of a two-course meal at the
Oxford on Avon for half price and an all-day tram
transport pass. ⑤

Outside the Four Avenues
The Charlotte Jane 110 Papanui Rd ☎03/355
1028, ⓦwww.charlotte-jane.co.nz. Very elegant
boutique hotel named for one of Canterbury's
founding "Four Ships", and transformed from a
grand 1890 family home-cum-school. This is one
of the most desirable places to stay in the city with
beautiful wood-panelled rooms, twelve ensuites,
breakfast when you want it and an atmospheric

restaurant attached (dinner only), with a wine cellar. Standard rooms ($275) are gorgeous but the next level up ($375) have spa baths and working fireplaces. ❾

Elm Tree House 236 Papanui Rd, Merivale ☏03/355 9731, ⓦwww.elmtreehouse.co.nz. A very welcoming B&B fashioned out of a listed historic building in Merivale, just 2km from the Cathedral Square. Largely built from dark native timbers with clean lines and plain colours, all rooms are en suite, there is a spa bath, a conservatory and courtyard for evening drinks, and a hearty breakfast. Evening meals by arrangement ($45). ❽

Fendalton House 50 Clifford Ave, Fendalton ☏03/355 4298 & 0800/374 298, ⓦwww .fendaltonhouse.co.nz. Lovely upmarket homestay located in leafy Fendalton – a pleasant 25min walk from the city through Mona Vale and Hagley Park. There are three spacious ensuites, a spa and an outdoor swimming pool. ❼

Highway Lodge 121 Papanui Rd, Merivale ☏03/355 5418, ⓔhighway.lodge@xtra.co.nz. Attractive Tudor-style home that is modest compared to the palaces all about, but is ten minutes' walk from the city centre, close to restaurants, shops and Hagley Park, and has clean, well-equipped rooms. Rooms ❸, ensuites ❹

Sumner

Abbott House 104 Nayland St ☏03/326 6111 & 0800/020 654, ⓦwww.abbotthouse.co.nz. An attractively restored 1870s villa set a block back from the beach and offering accommodation in either a studio with kitchenette, a suite with large lounge and kitchen, and a separate three-bedroom house around the corner sleeping up to eight. All have TV/VCR or DVD, private entrances and continental breakfast ingredients are supplied. Studio ❺, suite ❻, house just ❾

Villa Alexandra 1 Kinsey Terrace, Clifton Hill ☏03/326 6291, ⓦwww.villaalexandra.co.nz. An excellent-value homestay in a spacious villa overlooking Sumner Bay with a sunny veranda and turret, offering three bedrooms and one spacious loft apartment all en suite or with private bathroom. Welcoming hosts prepare meals using garden vegetables and their own free-range eggs (dinner $35, including wine) and there's a full cooked breakfast. They also run a modern self-contained apartment overlooking the beach let with a 3-night minimum. Rooms ❹, loft ❺, apartment ❻

Hostels

Most **backpacker hostels** in Christchurch are within the Four Avenues, or just beyond, and almost all representing excellent value for money. We've picked a range of the best: modern quieter hostels; party oriented downtown places where a night on the tiles is pretty much the norm and sleep is something of a luxury; and those a few blocks out with gardens and a homely atmosphere (something Christchurch specializes in). Prices don't vary a great deal, generally just over $20 for dorm beds and around $50 for doubles and twins, a little more for doubles with sheets and towels. None of the hostels listed here have tent sites.

During the peak summer months try to book accommodation a few days in advance to be sure of getting a bed; most hostels are prepared for late plane arrivals, and many have long-term storage for bike boxes and gear you won't need while in the South Island.

City Centre

base Christchurch 56 Cathedral Sq ☏03/982 2225, ⓦwww.basebackpackers.com. Modern 300-bed hostel in a 1880 building in the heart of the city that has recently undergone a transformation under the "base" brand bringing card swipe entry, new café and bar, made-up beds and a separate women's section known as "Sanctuary". It is a fun place to stay with plenty of lounges, pool table and an Indian restaurant on the doorstep. Dorms ❶, rooms & ensuites ❸, queen en-suite ❹

Chester Street 148 Chester St East ☏03/377 1897, ⓔchesterst@free.net.nz. With just 14 beds (no bunks) this is the city's smallest hostel and feels more like a shared house with made-up doubles and 3-bed dorms. Separate TV lounge, limited off-street parking and a pleasant garden. Dorms ❶, rooms ❷

Christchurch City Central YHA 273 Manchester St ☏03/379 9535, ⓔyha.christchurchcity@yha.org.nz. Large and very central, purpose-built hostel with lots of high-quality rooms, two kitchens, two common rooms and well-informed staff that run the travel, events and booking office. If you're staying in the older wing go for one of the exterior doubles. Dorms ❶, rooms ❸, ensuites ❹

Dorset House 1 Dorset St ☎03/366 8268, ⓦwww.dorsethouse.co.nz. Renovated, small and spacious hostel in an 1871 house located in a quiet area and firmly pitched at the upper end of the backpacker market, with firm beds (no bunks) and sheets and duvets. There's Sky TV and pool in a huge lounge fitted with stained glass windows, off-street parking and free tea and coffee. Dorms ❶, rooms ❸

Foley Towers 208 Kilmore St ☎03/366 9720, ⓔfoley.towers@backpack.co.nz. Fairly large hostel built around a couple of old houses, that manages to maintain an intimate feel aided by attractive gardens and an abundance of doubles and twins. Good low rates too. Dorms ❶, rooms & ensuites ❷

Frauenreisehaus Women's Hostel 272 Barbadoes St ☎03/366 2585, ⓔjesse-sandra@quicksilver.net.nz. Wonderfully relaxed and superbly well-equipped women-only hostel in an old and fairly central wooden house. Much loved by those looking for scented candles, mood music, spring water direct from the garden and non-violent videos. Spacious rooms have beds rather than bunks; there's also a games room, free local calls, free laundry and Internet access. Dorms ❶, twins ❷

New Excelsior cnr Manchester St & High St ☎03/366 7570 & 0800/666 237, ⓦwww .newexcelsior.co.nz. This central and well-managed hundred-bed hostel in a large former hotel is nicely decorated and features a spacious deck with rooftop views. Two-bunk rooms at dorm prices are a boon. Dorms ❶, rooms ❸

The Old Countryhouse 437 Gloucester St ☎03/381 5504. If you are prepared to be fifteen minutes' walk from the Square (bus #30) then this lovingly restored suburban house has to be one of Christchurch's finest small hostels. It's all polished wood and bold decor, the dorms are spacious and the kitchen well equipped. Dorms ❶, rooms ❷–❸

Rolleston House YHA 5 Worcester Blvd ☎03/366 6564, ⓔyharollestonhouse@yha .org.nz. The best-located hostel in Christchurch:

opposite the Arts Centre and full of character. Plenty of dorms but a limited number of twins and no doubles, so book ahead for a room. Dorms ❶, rooms ❸

Stonehurst 241 Gloucester St ☎03/379 4620 & 0508/786 633, ⓦwww.stonehurst.co.nz. Central and very popular accommodation with a wide range of accommodation, 24hr reception, a basic restaurant and outdoor pool and barbecue area. All beds are made up and private rooms have TV and phone. There's off-street parking and even campervan hookups. Dorms ❶, backpacker rooms & ensuites ❷, motels ❺, apartments ❼

Vagabond Backpackers 232 Worcester St ☎03/379 9677, ⓔvagabondbackpackers @hotmail.com. Very friendly place with only thirty beds, some in an annex at the back of the house; all are well kept, quiet, clean and recently redecorated – the kitchen even has a dishwasher. There's off-street parking, barbecue and a lovely garden area. Dorms ❶, rooms ❷

Warners Central 50 Cathedral Sq ☎03/377 0550, ⓔballie@xtra.co.nz. With only 45 beds this hostel is small and intimate for a place so centrally sited. There's never more than four to a room and it is all tastefully decorated. Dorms ❶, rooms & ensuites ❸

YMCA 12 Hereford St ☎03/365 0502 & 0508/962 224, ⓦymcachch.org.nz. Very central, state-of-the-art YMCA with dorms, singles, basic doubles and deluxe en-suite doubles with phone, tea and coffee, and TV. Guests get significant discounts at the fitness centre, gym, squash courts, climbing wall and sauna, and there's an on-site café. Dorms ❶, rooms ❸, ensuites ❹

Sumner

The Marine 26 Nayland St ☎03/326 6609, ⓦwww.themarine.co.nz. Old pub and hotel recently converted into a bright and cheerful backpackers with spacious four-share rooms and several doubles all with doors opening out onto a upstairs verandah at the front of the building. Beds are all made up, toast is provided for a light breakfast and there's a sunny deck. Four-shares ❶, rooms ❸

Campsites

Given the low cost of hostel accommodation in Christchurch, **camping** saves little money, and most of the sites are in any case some distance away from the city centre. There are some well-equipped motor camps within the city limits which are fine for campervans, offer tent sites and have good deals on cabins, but they tend to have a holiday–camp atmosphere.

All Seasons Holiday Park 5 Kidbrooke St, off Linwood Ave, Linwood ☎03/384 9490, ℱ384 9843. This modern park has a swimming pool, spa pool and large children's playground. Easy access to the beach (good for windsurfing), Linwood shopping centre and Sumner, and only ten minutes' drive from the city centre. Camping $10, cabins and tourist flats ❷

Amber Park 308 Blenheim Rd, Upper Riccarton ☎03/348 3327, ⓦ www.amberpark.co.nz. Spacious, grassy site with all the expected features just 4km south of the city (bus #21 stops right outside), and handy for the train station, Addington Raceway and Canterbury University. Camping $12, cabins ❷–❸

Meadow Park Top 10 39 Meadow St, St Albans ☎03/352 9176, ⓦ www.meadowpark.co.nz. Situated 5km north of Cathedral Square on SH74 (and reached by bus route #4) this campsite, close to supermarkets and restaurants, covers a large area and has a full range of facilities. Camping $13, on-site vans, cabins & cottages ❷–❸, flats & motels ❹

South New Brighton Motor Camp Halsey St, South New Brighton ☎03/388 9844, ⓦ www.holidayparks.co.nz/southnewbrighton. Handily sited near the beach 7km east of the city centre this medium-sized site had good facilities and a limited range of cabins and flats. Camping $9, flats ❷–❸

The City

The low-rise, gridplan city centre, together with many of its more compelling sights, is encased within the **Four Avenues** – Moorhouse, Fitzgerald, Bealey and Deans. They define a useful border round the downtown area, in the very centre of which is **Cathedral Square** with its landmark spire. Scattered in the streets around the square are the city's most attractive buildings, predominantly nineteenth-century Gothic, though with some outstanding modern structures such as the new **art gallery**. Beyond the art gallery on the western edge of the city centre lies **Hagley Park**, a focal point for leisure activities at weekends. It is threaded by the placid River Avon, and there's no more relaxing way to experience some of the prettier parts of the city than by **punt**.

Outside the Four Avenues you pass into suburban districts like Riccarton, Fendalton, Merivale and St Albans, each characterized by one- and two-storey residential housing and beautifully kept gardens. Further west lie the coastal suburbs of New Brighton and Sumner, which provide access to the Pacific Ocean **beaches**.

Within the Four Avenues

Christchurch is dominated by its **Cathedral** (Nov–March Mon–Fri 8.30am–7pm, Sat & Sun 9am–5pm; April–Oct Mon–Fri 9am–5pm; free: $5 for guided tours Mon–Fri 11am & 2pm, Sat 11am, Sun 11.30am) and the square that surrounds it. Designed by George Gilbert Scott, architect of London's St Pancras Station, the cathedral was begun in the 1860s and completed in 1904 – a Gothic revival Anglican church with a cool and spacious interior and a 63-metre spire ($4 to ascend the 134-step claustrophobic staircase) with the best panoramic views of the city. On the left-hand side from the main entrance, look out for the Maori contribution of *tukutuku* panels made of leather and rimu wood, celebrating the Maori proverb: "What is the most important thing in life? It is people, people, people". Visitors and worshippers contributed many of the stitches. To sample the marvellous acoustics of the building, drop by for choral evensong (Tues & Wed 5.15pm for the full choir, Fri 4.30pm for boys' choir only); note that this doesn't take place during school holidays, principally Christmas to early February.

Christchurch's grid of streets spreads out from **Cathedral Square** (or just "the Square") – a large, open, paved area typically abuzz with lunching office workers, skateboarders and tourists. The Italianate 1879 **Old Post Office** and adjacent 1901 Palladian-style former **Government Building** on the southeast corner of the square together provide a pleasing contrast to the predominantly Neo-Gothic architecture on show elsewhere. The former contains the visitor centre and the **Southern Encounter Aquarium** (daily 9am–4.30pm; $10; Ⓦwww.southernencounter.co.nz), a fishy extension of Orana Wildlife Park (see p.617), that mimics many of the damper habitats of the South Island. Although it's on a small scale, many native saltwater and freshwater species of fish are represented, with touch tanks fashioned after rock pools consigning a number of wee creatures to a life of being picked up and fondled, plus artificial eel and salmon runs and a mock-up of a fly fishing lodge. As well as three short melodramatic films, there are opportunities to watch **feeding** (11am, 1pm & 3pm) and be guided through a nocturnal house to view North Island **brown kiwi**.

Outside stands the 1867 **Statue of Robert Godley**, the founding father of Christchurch and agent of the Canterbury Association. It is said to be the earliest public sculpture in New Zealand and is the work of Pre-Raphaelite Thomas Woolner, who was briefly in New Zealand after failing on the Australian goldfields. Nearby, the **Memorial of the Four Ships** shows the vessels sent by the Canterbury Association in 1850 to create a model Anglican community here; and Neil Dawson's **Chalice** sculpture takes the shape of a monstrous ice-cream cone, coloured silver on the outside and metallic blue on the inside, with leaf and fern patterns cut out of its higher reaches. It was unveiled just before September 11, 2001, after which it became a focal point for flowers, messages and public grief. Since then, it has taken a place of affection in most locals' hearts and is now climbed quite regularly by people with something to protest about.

A less permanent occupant of the square is the **Wizard** (usually Mon–Fri 1–1.45pm in summer; Ⓦwww.wizard.gen.nz), a local eccentric and former English lecturer who has been lambasting bemused audiences with muddle-brained but occasionally interesting rantings for over a quarter of a century. Variously regarded as a national treasure and a harmless fool, he arrives in a red VW Beetle (made from two front ends welded together), then pontificates on the nature of the world, god and women. The visitor centre stocks his Upside Down Map ($5) with New Zealand rightly placed near the top.

The area **south of Cathedral Square** has the greatest concentration of shops, restaurants and bars, and you'll continually find yourself back here in the evening. There are no sights to speak of, but one area to make for is **High Street**, lined with the more off-beat music and clothes shops as well as the cooler end of the café scene. Parts of this area (particularly along Lichfield Street) can be pretty seedy at night, but it is seldom intimidating.

North of Cathedral Square

A grid of shopping streets spreads north from the Square, the most interesting section being around **New Regent Street** two minutes' walk east along Gloucester Street. Built in 1932, and home to some of the city's more interesting upmarket cafés and stores, it's one of Christchurch's most attractive streets, with pastel-coloured buildings and trellised balconies recalling the Spanish Mission style of architecture which flourished in eighteenth-century California and New Mexico.

One block west, the manicured Victoria Square is bounded to the north by the languid River Avon and Christchurch's starkly modern **Town Hall** which is linked by footbridge to the glass-fronted Convention Centre on the opposite side of Kilmore Street. Epicureans should nip around the corner to the venerable **Johnson's Grocers**, 787 Colombo St, a tiny treasure trove stacked to the rafters with just about every packaged gourmet product imaginable.

Following the river a few steps to the southwest you find the **Provincial Government Buildings**, corner of Durham Street and Armagh Street (Mon–Sat 10.30am–3pm, also Oct–May Sun 2–4pm; donation requested; built between 1858 and 1865. These are the only provincial government buildings left in New Zealand and are widely regarded as the masterpiece of Christchurch's most renowned early architect, **Benjamin W. Mountfort**. Built in neo-Gothic style, the older wooden portion of the chambers has a fine flagstone-paved corridor. The Great Hall, built in 1869 as the council chamber, is magnificently decorated with an intricate ceiling and elaborate stonework. Masks of the two craftsmen responsible for all this finery appear in the stonework: on the east wall near the fireplace on the ground floor and on the east wall of the public gallery.

Head north from here past the **casino** and along Victoria Street to reach the Victorian **clock** tower, which houses a clock originally imported from England in 1860 to adorn the government buildings.

Christchurch Art Gallery

With so much neo-Gothic architecture in Christchurch it is refreshing to come face to face with the brand-new **Christchurch Art Gallery**, on the corner of Worcester Boulevard and Montreal Street (daily 9am–5pm & until 9pm on Wed; free; Ⓦ www.christchurchartgallery.org.nz), with its striking frontage of curving glass intersecting at odd angles. Natural light floods into the large atrium – all grey concrete slabs and pale wood – from where a grand staircase leads up to the main galleries. International works are displayed, but the Gallery is strongest on New Zealand creations, particularly those by Christchurch and Canterbury artists.

An interconnected series of large rooms contains the historical, twentieth century and contemporary collections. The European landscape tradition comes through strongly in nineteenth-century paintings by Charles Goldie and those by émigré, Petrus van der Velden, such as *Mountain Stream Otira Gorge*. More recent works of note include Tony Fomison's compellingly dark *No!*, and Bill Hammond's primordial *The Fall of Icarus*, liberally scattered with his iconic bird-headed humanoids.

Elsewhere the ceramics and glass collection contains superb pieces by Ann Robinson and Shona Firman, especially the latter's blue canoe prow, *Te Waka Taniwha*. Lastly, check out the assortment of "Works on Paper" which includes a Rembrandt etching, Goya aquatint, Blake engraving, a Warhol screenprint of *Chairman Mao* and Bill Frizell's *From Mickey to Tiki Tu Meke*, a seven-head transformation from Mickey Mouse to a Maori Tiki.

The Arts Centre

The **Arts Centre**, diagonally across from the Art Gallery, was built in 1874 as the University of Canterbury and Christchurch Girls' and Boys' High Schools. The university decamped to suburban Ilam in 1975 and, after a period of uncertainty, the Arts Centre, with its restaurants, food stalls, galleries, cinemas and the Court Theatre (see p.626), moved in. Benjamin Mountfort, the architect of the Christchurch Museum, Christ's College and the Provincial Chambers, was at his Gothic best here using volcanic "bluestone" and Oamaru limestone, and inscribing the subject – biology, zoology, etc – above the appropriate entrances. Today the leafy courtyards and grassy quadrangles make a great place to watch the world go by: it is especially active at weekends when the Market Square on the east side is turned over to a lively **craft market**, complete with buskers and musicians. Much of what's on sale is made in the Arts Centre's stores and workshops dotted throughout the building. To the rear of the arts centre, via the *Dux de Lux* pub and courtyard, a collection of ethnic food stalls (Sat & Sun 10am–4pm) offer Czech, Lebanese, Thai, Korean, Chinese and a planet-load of other national dishes dirt cheap. The **information centre** (daily 10am–5pm ☏03/366 0989, ⓦ www.artscentre.org.nz) runs free 20min **tours** of the buildings on demand, and provides access to **Rutherford's Den**, which honours Nobel Prize winning atom-splitter **Ernest Rutherford** – he on the $100 banknote. It is an appropriately reverential place with thoughtful displays, a look at the tiny basement laboratory where he did post-graduate research, and a fine old lecture theatre with sumptuously graffitied benches.

Canterbury Museum, Hagley Park and around

Across Rolleston Avenue from the Arts Centre stands the **Canterbury Museum** (daily: Oct to mid-March 9am–5.30pm; mid-March to Sept 9am–5pm; donation appreciated), a neo-Gothic structure founded in 1870 and initially directed by archaeologist Julius Haast (who gave his name to the Haast Pass, see p.817). One of the best exhibits is the "Exploration of Antarctica", covering the many expeditions that have used New Zealand as their jumping-off point. The exhibits of Maori treasures have undergone a fair bit of restructuring and are also well worth a look. Other rooms deal with Moa hunters, European settlers, native birds and mammals, fossils and geology. Over the next few years the museum is revamping and expanding, and the plan is for visitors to be able to watch the whole process as it takes place.

Next door stands **Christ's College**, the city's most elite private school. There are no tours, but you are free to wander round the grounds and admire yet more Victorian architecture.

The Museum and Christ's College block off the city from **Hagley Park** which, it is whispered by the mischievous priest of St Michael's, was put here in order to protect the solidly Anglican districts within the Four Avenues from the Presbyterians in the suburbs beyond. The park contains the spectacular Botanic Gardens, a golf course and playing fields, and at weekends it seems like the entire population of Christchurch is here strolling around or playing some form of sport.

One corner is devoted to the **Botanic Gardens** (Rolleston Ave gate; daily 7am until 1hr before sunset; conservatories 10.15am–4pm; free), which does all it can to live up to Christchurch's Garden City moniker. It has an astonishing collection of indigenous and exotic plants and trees that's unrivalled on the South Island. Throughout summer and autumn the perennials give a constant and dazzling display of colour. There is also a herb garden, containing a variety of culinary and medicinal plants; a rose garden with over 250 types of roses; and the Cockayne Memorial Garden, an area of native bush named after one of New Zealand's greatest botanists. Best of all, though, it is just a great place to hang out on a sunny day with picnicking families, studying students and couples flattening the grass.

The gardens are enclosed by a loop of the River Avon which you can explore by heading along to the **Antigua Boat Sheds**, 2 Cambridge Terrace (☏03/366 5885, ⓦ www.boatsheds.co.nz) and renting a paddleboat ($14 per half hour for two), canoe ($7 per hour), or rowboat ($20 per hour for 3). Better still, get **punted** along the river by a guide nattily dressed in striped blazer and straw boater ($15 per person for 30min).

On the southern borders of Hagley Park, Christchurch Hospital almost engulfs the tiny brick-and-slate 1928 **Nurses' Memorial Chapel**, Riccarton Ave (Mon–Sat 1–4pm, Sun 10am–4pm; free), dedicated to nurses who served in World War I. It was constructed after the death of three Christchurch-trained nurses aboard a torpedoed troopship in 1915, and contains four stained-glass windows by the English glass artist Veronica Whall, with an uneven texture and a variety of colours set off by the otherwise dark, low-ceilinged interior.

Heading back into town along Oxford Terrace, the eye-catching stand-alone **belltower** houses a bell from one of the first four migrant ships and once served as a timepiece for the settlers and was rung on the hour. The belltower belongs to the adjacent 1875 **St Michael and All Angels Church** (Nov–April Mon–Fri 10am–5pm, Sat & Sun 2–5pm; guided tours on demand; April–Oct open for regular church services only), done in French and English medieval Gothic styles. The stained-glass windows covering both east and west wings are particularly beautiful, their bright colours contrasting with the dark hues of the surrounding timber. Look out also for the **Te Tapenakara o te Ariki** ("The Tabernacle of the Lord") hung from the ceiling over the central aisle, traditionally a container used by Maori chiefs to store *taonga* (treasure) such as ceremonial feathers.

Two blocks southwest of St Michael's, the fifty-minute **Canterbury Brewery Heritage Tour**, 36 St Asaph Street (Mon–Thurs 10am & 12.30pm, Sat 1pm; $12; reservations advised ☏03/379 4940), gives you a brief history of brewing in the region, a glimpse of the working brewery itself, and the usual reward at the end.

Beyond the Four Avenues

Inspired by a couple of hours spent in the Botanic Gardens, you might fancy a stroll across North Hagley Park to their logical extension, the beautiful precincts of **Mona Vale** at 63 Fendalton Rd (grounds open daily 8.30am to just before dusk; free). Originally part of the Deans' estate (see p.617), the site Horticultural Society. The gardens have majestic displays of roses, dahlias, fuchsias and irises, as well as magnolias, rhododendrons and herbaceous perennials.

Activities in and around Christchurch

Christchurch isn't really the sort of place you think of coming to get physically active, but as the the country's capital there's plenty to keep the energetic entertained, either in town or further afield.

A gentle way to get airborne is with Up Up And Away (☏03/381 4600, ⓦwww .ballooning.co.nz) who offer peaceful and eye-bulging hour-long **balloon flights** over Christchurch for around $220. Aoraki Balloons (☏0800/256 837, www.nzballooning.co.nz) also offer good trips from $230, or $285 for a longer trip including bubbly. Alternatively, get your adrenal gland pumping with Nimbus Paragliding (☏0800/111 611, ⓦww.nimbusparagliding.co.nz) or Paragliding NZ (☏0508/727 245, ⓦwww.paragliding.co.nz), who both offer 20-minute **tandem paragliding** flights on the Port Hills from around $120; pick-ups available.

Apart from Sumner and New Brighton beaches (see p.620) there is **swimming** at Centennial Leisure Centre, Armagh St (Mon–Thurs 6am–9pm, Fri 6am–7pm, Sat & Sun 7am–7pm; ☏03/366 8917; $5), and at QEII Leisure Centre in New Brighton (see p.620; Mon–Fri 6am–9pm, Sat & Sun 7am–8pm; $5) which has an Olympic-sized pool, diving pool and wave area.

You'll get just as wet going **whitewater rafting**. There are no big rivers near here, but Rangitata Rafts (see p.689) run one of the best trips in these parts on the Grade IV+ Rangitata River and they pick up from Christchurch.

became the property of the city in 1969 and is now tended by the Canterbury The Bath House has been converted for use as a greenhouse and the old homestead is open for lunch daily. You can rent a **punt** and enjoy the gardens from the river ($16.50 per person for 30min).

You could hardly make a greater botanical leap than to wander ten minutes to the southwest to the suburb of Riccarton and **Deans Bush** (aka Riccarton Bush; daily dawn–dusk; free), an area of native forest containing several 500-year-old kahikatea trees. The survival of this valuable area of forest is largely due to Scottish brothers William and John Deans, who came to farm the area in 1843 and somehow resisted the temptation to put all their property to immediate agricultural use. Today a concrete path navigates the bush, with signs pointing out the species that still grow here. By the northern entrance off Kahu Road you'll find the black pine **Deans Cottage** (daily 9am–dusk; free), the oldest structure on the Canterbury Plains, built by the Deans brothers upon their arrival in 1843. This tiny affair is furnished as it would have been until the deaths of William (1851) and his brother (1854). Their descendents later built the adjacent, grand Victorian **Riccarton House** (guided tours Mon–Fri 10am & 2pm, Sun 2pm; $10; ⓦ www.riccartonhouse.co.nz), all oak panelling and stags heads.

The International Antarctic Centre

Beyond Deans Bush, Memorial Avenue runs northwest to the airport and the **International Antarctic Centre**, 38 Orchard Rd (daily: Oct–April 9am–8pm; May–Sept 9am–5.30pm; $20; ⓦ www.iceberg.co.nz), a well-presented and dynamic exhibit concentrating on New Zealand's involvement on the world's coldest, highest and driest continent. Since the mid-1950s, Christchurch airport has been the base of the US Antarctic programme which sponsors over 140 flights a year to their base at McMurdo Sound, and the neighbouring New Zealand outpost at Scott Base. There's stacks here on Antarctic exploration and the fragile polar ecosystem with video presentations, daily digital photos emailed from the ice at Scott Base, recordings of the current weather conditions, traditional and interactive displays and innovations such as the Snow & Ice Experience where you can don a down jacket and experience a snowy environment at −5°C, cooled further by a fan giving a wind chill of −25°C. Antarctic enthusiasts should leave time for the hourly **Hägglunds Ride** ($12, combined ticket including the museum $30), a 15-minute jaunt in a five-tonne tracked buggy. The centre also has the *60° Antarctic Cafe and Bar* and one of the country's more imaginative gift shops. True fans of all things Antarctic can even pick up a free *Antarctic Heritage Trail* leaflet detailing connected sites around Christchurch and Lyttelton.

Orana Park and beyond

Drivers can skirt around the northern perimeter of the airport – follow Russley Road then McLeans Island Road – to **Orana Wildlife Park**, within the McLeans Island Recreational Area (daily 10am–5pm; $14; ⓣ 03/359 7109, ⓦ www.oranawildlifepark.co.nz), a well-organized zoological park containing a wide variety of native and imported animals. Volunteer guides are on hand, and highlights include endangered New Zealand species like kiwi and tuatara, and the chance to observe the feeding of lions and tigers from a treetop viewing balcony. The only public transport is the Sunshine Shuttle (ⓣ 03/379 1699; $20 return), which leaves from the visitor centre at 10.30am and 1.10pm.

Although nowhere near as exciting as Orana Park, the smaller and more intimate **Willowbank Wildlife Reserve**, 60 Hussey Rd (daily 10am–10pm; $16, ⓣ 03/359 6226, ⓦ www.willowbank.co.nz), has some

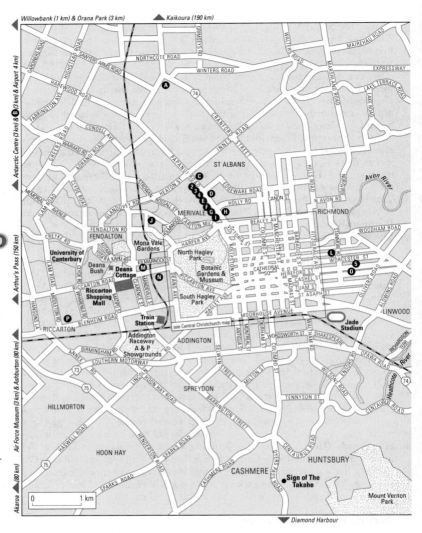

Willowbank (1 km) & Orana Park (3 km)   ◄ Kaikoura (190 km)

good displays of native birds including a kiwi house (11.30am–10pm). This is also the site of the Kotane Maori Experience (see p.626). To get here use the Best Attractions shuttle (see p.607), the Sunshine Shuttle (☎03/379 1699; $15 return), or bus #4: catch it from Cathedral Square as far as the junction of Harewood Road and Gardiners Road, then walk northeast up Gardiners Road for fifteen minutes or so before turning right into Hussey Road.

Around twenty minutes' drive southwest of Hagley Park and accessible via Blenheim Road and Great South Road is the **Air Force Museum** (☎03/343 9532, ⊛ www.airforcemuseum.co.nz; daily 10am–5pm; $15), located beside the former RNZAF base at Wigram. Among the two dozen aircraft you'll see the

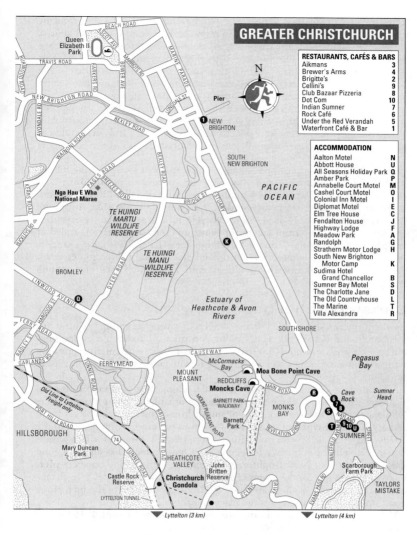

RESTAURANTS, CAFÉS & BARS

Aikmans	3
Brewer's Arms	4
Brigitte's	2
Cellini's	9
Club Bazaar Pizzeria	8
Dot Com	10
Indian Sumner	7
Rock Café	6
Under the Red Verandah	5
Waterfront Café & Bar	1

ACCOMMODATION

Aalton Motel	N
Abbott House	U
All Seasons Holiday Park	Q
Amber Park	P
Annabelle Court Motel	M
Cashel Court Motel	O
Colonial Inn Motel	I
Diplomat Motel	E
Elm Tree House	C
Fendalton House	J
Highway Lodge	F
Meadow Park	A
Randolph	G
Strathern Motor Lodge	H
South New Brighton Motor Camp	K
Sudima Hotel Grand Chancellor	B
Sumner Bay Motel	S
The Charlotte Jane	D
The Old Countryhouse	L
The Marine	T
Villa Alexandra	R

Dakota converted for use on the British Queen's state visit in 1953, and several World War II veterans including a Spitfire. Three flight simulators will keep the (big) kids happy, particularly the one simulating the World War II Mosquito as it engages in very realistic combat in the Norwegian fjords. Enthusiastic volunteer guides conduct free tours of the restoration and storage hangars (daily 11am, 1pm & 3pm).

The Christchurch Gondola

The **Christchurch Gondola**, 10 Bridle Path Rd (daily 10am–10pm or later; $17 return; ⓦ www.gondola.co.nz), is a scenic and gentle way of seeing the surrounding countryside from the top of the Port Hills, which lie to the southeast of Christchurch centre. The Gondola terminal is located right by the entrance to the Lyttelton tunnel 15 minutes' drive from Cathedral Square, and is serviced by the Lyttelton bus (#28) and the Best Attractions shuttle (see p.607). The Gondola cable cars climb to the 945-metre summit of **Mount Cavendish**, providing views of Christchurch, the Canterbury Plains, the volcanic outcrops of the Banks Peninsula and the Southern Alps. The station at the top contains a "heritage time tunnel" museum (same hours; free), which covers the geology and geography of the area as well as Maori legends, life aboard early migrant ships and a video about modern-day Canterbury. Also in the station are a viewing deck, souvenir shop, café, and an indifferent restaurant where you can eat while enjoying fantastic views of the city below – especially at night.

From the summit, you can take one of the footpaths that explore the hills or head straight back down – either by cable car, or tandem **paragliding** with Nimbus (☎03/326 7922, Ⓦwww.nimbusparagliding.cjb.net; $120; reservations essential). Alternatively visit the gondola with the Mountain Bike Adventure Company (☎0800/424 534, Ⓦwww.cycle-hire-tours.co.nz; reservations essential) who pick up from the visitor centre and offer a number of guided or self-guided descents: the "Mount Cavendish Experience" ($40), for example, allows two hours to explore the station and tackle one of three routes down the surrounding Summit Road system with bird's-eye views of Sumner's beaches, Lyttelton and Banks Peninsula.

Christchurch's beaches

As the summer sun bakes the city streets it's very tempting to head for the beach, and Christchurch has plenty on offer all accessible by frequent buses. The area around **Redcliffs** and **Sumner** is particularly appealing with a choice of places to stay and eat if you fancy spending some time out there.

Around eight kilometres east of the centre, a long swathe of sand runs from Waimari Beach south along a spit to the mouth of the Avon estuary – the whole area is a great place to swim or simply lounge on a towel. The centre of activity is **New Brighton** (bus #5 or #40 from the city), locally famed in the 1970s and early 1980s for its Saturday shopping in the days when almost nowhere else in the country was open at weekends. Its tenor has slipped a good deal since then, but New Brighton is resplendent with its long concrete **pier**, built seemingly just for the scores of anglers hanging over the sides. The chance of a beer or a coffee at the *Waterfront Café & Bar*, at the base of the pier, plus a good stretch of sand make this the place to hang out.

Marine Parade runs north from here towards **Queen Elizabeth II Park**, a stadium and pool complex (for details see p.616) built for the 1974 Commonwealth Games. It is sited around 500m inland at the corner of Travis Road and Bower Avenue.

South of New Brighton, a spit of land provides shelter for the waters of the Avon and Heathcote river estuary, which is backed by the quiet suburb of **Bromley** and the Te Huingi Manu and Te Huingi Martu **wildlife reserves** (daily dawn–dusk; free), great spots for bird watchers. The estuary basin is excellent for windsurfing and dinghy sailing.

Redcliffs and Sumner

On the whole, you are better off on the southern side of the river estuary where Redcliffs, and particularly Sumner (both accessed by bus #30 or #31

Walks around Sumner

The best selection of short walks in the area lace **Scarborough Head**, the eminence that marks the southeastern end of Sumner Beach and accessed along Nayland Street from the centre of the village.

Where Nayland Street becomes Herberden Avenue, just inland from the beach, the **Edwin Mouldey Track** climbs sharply up then eases off and continues for about fifteen minutes before being crossed by a track to the Boat Shed. Head down this for a great view across Pegasus Bay, stretching away to the northwest (the bay is named after the *Pegasus*, in which Captain Chase sailed the coast looking for sealing grounds), and then join the **Boat Shed to Sumner Head Track**. This ploughs uphill again for about fifteen minutes, skirting the cliff edge and giving increasingly spectacular views.

From **Sumner Head** you can see the Kaikoura Peninsula in the north, and Godley Head and Banks Peninsula to the east. At this point you have two alternatives for reaching the botanical reserve of **Nicholson Park**: either head straight inland along a clay track to the park ten minutes away; or, more interestingly, continue around the cliffs, hiking up quite steeply, for views down the eastern side of the head (20min). On entering Nicholson park the latter track leads onto a small point, from which you can see **Whitewash Head** (so named because of the large number of seabirds that nest on its cliffs), and the **Giants Nose**, a small finger of land behind which is the surf beach of **Taylor's Mistake**.

the City Exchange bus station), have developed into tight beachside communities with plenty going on and a number of good places to stay and eat.

Redcliffs lies at the mouth of the estuary below (and increasingly on top of) some fractured dull red cliffs which give the community its name. The sea has eroded the base of the cliffs to leave a series of caves, the largest of which once contained moa bones and shellfish remnants indicating Maori habitation up to 700 years ago. As you drive along Main Road, look out for the large entrance to **Moa Bone Point Cave** a much graffitied recess later used by European settlers. Half a kilometre further along the smaller **Moncks Cave** heralds Barnett Park, the starting point for the **Barnett Park Walkway** (5km loop; 1hr 45min), a well-formed track which climbs through grassland onto rock outcrops, with steps giving access to a large rock shelter and several caves. The walkway then bisects a copse of native bush and passes a seasonal waterfall, before crossing a creek and descending via bluffs past **Paradise Cave**, home of a Maori family in the 1890s.

As you follow the coast around from Redcliffs you pass the river mouth, and estuary beaches become sea beaches, the best being at **SUMNER**, a Norfolk Pine-backed strip of craft shops, restaurants, cafés, wine bars, surf shacks and a cinema, all fronting a broad patch of golden sand. Named after Dr J.B. Sumner, Archbishop of Canterbury and president of the Canterbury Association in the 1850s, it's now one of Christchurch's more desirable suburbs. It is a popular destination on summer weekends and a great place just to hang out anytime. The highlight of the beach is **Cave Rock**, a geological anomaly of honey-combed rock – its underside is peppered with little caves like an enormous Swiss cheese and is accessible at low tide. The lifeguard's lookout point on top can be reached by clambering up the rock. Elsewhere, you can stroll the clifftop paths around Sumner Head (see box above) or visit Urban Surf, 25d Marriner St in the heart of the village (℡03/326 6023) which rents boards ($20 for 2hr, $60 a day) and wetsuits ($5 & $15) and gives twenty percent BBH discount.

They also deal with **surf coach** Aaron Beaumont (☎326 7830) who charges $45 for a ninety minute lesson complete with board and wetsuit.

The best **surfing** is 2km south at **Taylor's Mistake** (reached along Nayland Street), a narrow beach and small community named, according to local lore, for a captain who ran aground here after mistaking the bay for the entrance to Lyttelton Harbour.

Drivers can continue beyond Sumner following the extension of Wakefield Street inland and over Evens Pass to Lyttelton, only 6km away.

Eating

Christchurch has the largest number and widest range of **restaurants** in the South Island, with yet more opening every week and more culinary styles added to the old favourites. Top-quality gourmet cuisine is increasingly well represented, and now nicely balances the selection of ethnic restaurants on offer. There's also a growing number of fun, themed establishments featuring live music, and for a more down-to-earth atmosphere, many of the city's **pubs** serve hearty food to soak up their brews.

With more and more **cafés** and **bars** offering substantial food, distinctions between eating and drinking venues are increasingly blurred, and many of the establishments listed under "Drinking" (p.625) are perfectly good places in which to enjoy a main meal, as well as a bit of a bop afterwards. For something different, you could always try à la carte dining as you clunk around the streets on Christchurch Tramway's **dinner tram** (☎03/366 7511), which operates from 7.30pm offering local delicacies as well as a broader selection of New Zealand cuisine: mains around the $30 mark.

If you're **self-catering**, you'll probably want to make use of the New World **supermarket** at 555 Colombo Street.

Central Christchurch

For **eating** there is little reason to venture beyond the Four Avenues; in fact you'll find most of what you need in the grid of downtown streets close to Cathedral Square, notably along Colombo Street, Cashel Street, Manchester Street and High Street. One area which deserves special mention is Oxford Terrace between Cashel and Gloucester streets, which has become known as "**The Strip**" with almost a dozen restaurant/bars bang next to one another, all spilling out onto the pavement. They appear to be morphing into clones of each other with little to chose between them, though you're assured of good dining, and as the evening wears on the lights go down, the music cranks up and booze flows freely. The clubbing set usually pops in for a couple of hours around 10.30pm before drifting off to livelier dancefloors.

Cafés and takeaways

C1 Espresso 150 High St. Tardis-like, red-brick, young and funky café where you get filling gourmet sandwiches (around $10), omelettes, pizza, flat breads, smoothies and dynamite coffee, all of which can be enjoyed as you browse their selection of mags and papers. Old rucksacks hang from a metal rack, there's a mishmash of furniture and thumpy music.

City Seafood Market 277 Manchester St. An extraordinary range of reasonably priced fresh fish, including the best fish and chips in the centre of the city (takeaway only). Mon–Fri 9am–6pm.

Costas Souvlaki Bar 150 Armagh St. Unpretentious and cheap little kebab, falafel, Greek salad and, obviously souvlaki café that has been around since time began. Closes 8pm & all day Sun.

The Globe Café 171 High St. Wonderful coffee spot and lunchtime hangout for students from the jazz school across the road, which turns into a slightly more sophisticated eatery on Fridays after 5.30pm. The spacious interior and pavement seating are both great for enjoying their huge selection of teas, or tucking into all manner of panini, salads, quiches and stunning cakes. The evening menu varies taking a particular country as the theme and producing its signature dishes. Licensed.

The Herb Centre 225 Kilmore St. Daytime eat-in and take-out café specializing in vegetarian and vegan cuisine served up with a range of caffeine-free drinks, smoothies and organic coffee. For the dedicated, there's *Piko Healthfoods*, two doors up at no. 229, which sells great bread and self-catering supplies and has a good noticeboard. Closed Sun.

Hummingbird 165 Victoria St. Great little café serving delicious light snacks, salads and cakes plus some of the finest organic coffee in town: you'll see the Hummingbird brand all over the region.

Java cnr High St & Lichfield St. Young and very groovy coffee bar with options on the strongest coffee in town and very loud music at the more challenging end of the spectrum. Low-cost meals start with breakfast and continue with hot snacks, salads, sandwiches, specialty burgers ($6–12) and cakes until the small hours. A mezzanine floor for smokers. Open 24hr at weekends.

Le Café in the Arts Centre, Worcester St ☎03/366 7722. This relaxed café is open from 7am to at least midnight daily and is always popular for breakfast specials, club sandwiches ($12), a selection from their broad-ranging main menu (under $15), including fruit crumble ($8) and excellent coffee. BYO & licensed.

Mainstreet Café & Bar 840 Colombo St ☎03/365 0421. Very good vegetarian restaurant open from breakfast until late with a wide selection of dishes (some vegan) served in huge portions at low prices. Come with a big appetite and the capacity for $2.50 bottomless coffee.

Café Metro cnr Colombo St & Kilmore St. One of the best cafés in this part of town, right by the town hall with great coffee, a good range of quiches, pies, muffins and cakes, and a varied stack of up-to-date mags.

Under the Red Verandah 502 Worcester St. Delightful suburban, daytime café twenty minutes' walk east of the centre, but worth the effort for its predominantly vegetarian fare – pumpkin and corn cakes, bacon and kumara frittata, organic breads and good coffee served in the bare-boards interior or out in the sunny courtyard. Closed Sun & Mon.

Restaurants

Ann's Thai 165 Hereford St ☎03/379 9843. Classic Thai cooking in a simple, clean-lined evening-only restaurant with a pleasant little bar and broad wine list. Try the spicy salad, roast duck or whole fish.

Annie's The Arts Centre ☎03/365 0566. Superb wine bar and restaurant within the polished wood-floor confines of the Arts Centre and spilling outside into the courtyard. Lunches ($13–16) might include a summer frittata or Cajun baked chicken, though if there are a few of you order the antipasto plate ($20), groaning with mussels, squid, smoked salmon and salami. Dinner mains are usually $23–30 and include aubergine tofu ratatouille and baked Canterbury ostrich.

Blue Note 22 New Regent St ☎03/379 9674. Restaurant and bar where diners spill out onto the pedestrianized street as they tuck into $18–25 mains such as warm lamb and feta with cashews and salad or chicken stuffed with leek and feta accompanied by zingy new-world wines. Live jazz Thurs–Sat with no cover. Closed Sun. Licensed.

Le Bon Bolli cnr Worcester St & Montreal St ☎03/374 9444. Don't let the modern brick exterior fool you – inside you could imagine you're in France. Lunchtime attracts the business crowd to dine in the café downstairs. Upstairs is more formal (booking essential) with beautifully presented French cuisine.

Dux de Lux cnr Hereford St & Montreal St. Excellent restaurant and microbrewery (see p.625) that's one of the most popular places in town, with outdoor and indoor seating and a longstanding reputation for superb seafood and vegetarian meals at moderate prices : Thai red mussel curry or gourmet pizza for under $20

Hay's Café 63 Victoria St ☎03/379 7501. A must for lamb aficionados, though the fairly spartan interior gives little indication of the exceptional quality and presentation of the succulent dishes prepared using lambs reared on the owners' Banks Peninsula property. Mains $25–30; closed Mon lunch & Sun.

The Honey Pot 114 Lichfield St (no reservations). Brilliant restaurant and all-day café with funky decor and rustic wooden tables, where you can enjoy all-day breakfasts, pizzas on naan bread, char-grilled marinated lamb, fantastic steaks and imaginatively presented veggies. Snacks under $10 and mains $17–26.

Little India cnr of Gloucester & New Regent St. Café-style, reliable Indian restaurant, part of a chain, with quite expensive but still authentic curries and an extensive veggie menu ($16–26). Best value are the set menus, for lunch and dinner.

Oxford on Avon 794 Colombo St ☎03/379 7148. Pub on the banks of the Avon, famed for its enormous portions of straightforward nosh. Always busy with the food-bargain hunters and open for breakfast, lunch and dinner.

Penang Noodles House 172a Manchester. Cheap, cheerful and authentic, with a menu that never strays over $13. Try the pan-fried noodles with any two mains or one of the noodle soups and/or the specials. Lunch Mon–Fri only, dinner daily.

Plazzo del Marinaio's 108 Hereford St (2nd floor of Shades Arcade) ☎03/365 5911. If you've been saving up for a week then this is the place to treat yourself to some of the best seafood and steaks, plus the finest wine, port, brandy and malt whisky.

You'll be lucky to get change from $100 for two. Open daily for lunch and dinner.

Retour cnr Cambridge Terrace & Manchester St ☎03/365 2888. Beautifully located dinner-only restaurant in a glass-sided bandstand on the banks of the Avon. The award-winning European chefs melt influences from the world over with fresh and wholesome local ingredients to create a real eating experience to remember (mains $25–30).

Saggio di Vino 185 Victoria St ☎03/379 4006. Classy Italian restaurant where dishes such as chicken and artichoke salad ($25) or fresh grouper fillet ($27) can be accompanied by wine from an extensive award-winning cellar; all available by the glass. Servings are not overly generous but they are delicious. Dinner nightly.

Papanui Road and Merivale

There's little culinary reason to leave the city centre and head out to the suburbs, but the villagey Merivale is well placed if you are staying along Papanui Road or in the northern reaches of the city, and is increasingly packed with excellent places to eat.

All the following places are marked on the map on p.618.

Aikmans 154 Aikmans Rd, Merivale. A moderately priced café/bar with a laid-back atmosphere, and serving all-day breakfast, a broad range of salads, pasta dishes and curries for lunch and dinner. Plenty of outdoor seating, and it becomes more of a bar as the evening wears on.

Bologna 6 Papanui Rd ☎03/379 7497. Tiny country Italian restaurant with a short menu of traditional and gourmet pizzas plus pasta dishes and Italian desserts, all served without fuss for around $18–20. There's a bottle store across the road – handy since it is BYO only.

Brigitte's Hawkesbury Building, Aikmans Rd, Merivale. Relaxed restaurant and wine bar with an open courtyard at the back, and good-quality Mediterranean and Kiwi-style food as well as some wonderful New Zealand–Thai combinations, all at moderate prices.

Kannigas Thai 18a Papanui Rd ☎03/355 6228. Great Thai food served in a fairly soulless interior or out in the courtyard – try the chicken pad Thai ($13) or ginger prawn and rice ($16). BYO.

Sumner

You won't starve during your day at the beach as Sumner sports at least a dozen decent places to eat and drink with more opening all the time. Even if you are staying in the city it is worth coming out here for the evening, especially considering the #31 bus back to the city runs until gone 11pm.

All the following places are marked on the map on p.618.

Cellini's 32 Nyland Rd ☎03/326 6720. Bright, bustling and modestly priced café serving a wide range of dishes from Indonesian sweet beef curry and Akaroa smoked salmon salad to Mediterranean vegetable-stuffed pita, smoothies and coffee. Closed Tues evening.

Club Bazaar Pizzeria 15 Wakefield Ave ☎03/326 6155. Bar and elaborate balcony where you can sample cheap pasta dishes and good pizzas in a distinctive atmosphere of Kiwi nostalgia. Licensed.

Dot Com 42 Marriner St ☎03/326 4000. Sleek modern café with good coffee, a range of light and tasty meals and Internet access.

Indian Sumner 11a Wakefield Ave ☎03/326-4777. Good name, great curries. Dine outside on the pavement, take away or hope to get into their cramped but atmospheric interior for something from their small but well chosen selection of mains ($12–14). Dinner only; closed Mon. Licensed & BYO.

Rock Café 22a The Esplanade ☎ 03/326 5358. Excellent and very popular restaurant with pavement tables just across the road from the sea. Come for breakfast, great muffins, a coffee or a full meal, though you'll probably need to book on summer evenings.

Drinking, nightlife and entertainment

Gone are the days when evenings in Christchurch revolved around decaying, male-dominated Edwardian pubs. The modern city harbours enough traditional hostelries, late-night cafés and throbbing music bars to suit most tastes, and many of these offer more than just booze: live music, resident DJs and good food are increasingly taken for granted. After about 10pm the restaurants of The Strip (see below) metamorphose into rowdy bars and clubs: just follow the crowds.

Serious music and drama are centred on venues like the Town Hall and the Arts Centre, while less cerebral entertainment is offered by a concentration of downtown clubs and a clutch of city-centre cinemas. Entertainment **listings** are published in Christchurch's daily newspaper *The Press*: the "What's On" section on Fridays is best for live music and clubbing.

Drinking

Most drinking venues are to be found within the Four Avenues, with Colombo and Cashel streets harbouring a particularly dense concentration of watering holes. These areas, along with **The Strip** along Oxford Terrace, are probably the best place to stroll at weekends, when a variety of establishments use loud music and late licences to pull in the crowds.

Pubs and bars

Ballies 50 Cathedral Sq. Lively renovated old Irish-style bar with live local jazz and rock bands and plenty of tap beers.

Brewers Arms 177 Papanui Rd, Merivale. Northwest of the centre, this is a suburban pub with a range of beers and English-style pub food in large portions at moderate prices. Open from 11am until late.

Coyote 126 Oxford Terrace. The heart of The Strip which, around 10pm, becomes one of the main gathering places before a night's clubbing with a mixture of commercial chart-toppers and house music. Still no excuse for the imitation adobe walls and fake beams.

Dux de Lux cnr Hereford St & Montreal St. Ever popular restaurant (see p.623) that doubles as a great bar with several award-winning beers brewed on the premises. Live music Thurs–Sat and generally no cover charge.

Eye Spy 56 Lichfield St. A late-night bar full of mellow music and intimate DJ action Thurs–Sat. Known mainly for its stylish decor, padded walls, lovely cocktails and a higher-rolling crowd.

Loaded Hog cnr Manchester St & Cashel St. Comfortable but ever-busy city-centre boozer with ales brewed on the premises, and good bar meals in the $10–15 range served all day and substantial breakfasts at weekends. Jazz on Tues, Latin dancing on Thurs and DJs Fri and Sat.

Mainstreet Café & Bar 840 Colombo St (see "Cafés" p.622). Ever popular bar with six beers on tap (plus guest microbrews), live music Thurs–Sun usually with no cover. Expect singer-songwriters, folk and indie, plus open-mic every second Tues.

Rock Pool 85 Hereford St. A broad spectrum of imported beers, cocktails and 22 pool tables to choose from, as well as a PA rarely turned below ear-splitting level. Daily 9am till late.

Sammy's Jazz Review 14 Bedford Row. Live jazz in hepcat surroundings from 5pm till late Mon–Sat. Good Kiwi food to boot, and the electric-blue glass revolving door will fascinate.

Sullivan's 150–152 Manchester St. Fairly traditional Irish bar with pictures of the old country, gallons of beer, live Irish-style bands from Wed–Sat, and late-night dancing towards the end of the week.

Viaduct 136 Oxford Terrace. One of almost a dozen near-identical restaurant/bars along "The Strip" and so good a starting point as any. Its Greek-column-and-Spanish-tile interior help create a cocktail atmosphere midweek, though weekends are always rowdy.

Clubs and gigs

Christchurch may not be the clubbing capital of the southern hemisphere, but there's a sprinkling of places within the Four Avenues offering a range of dance-music styles. Some of these are full-on **club venues**, although there's a growing number of bars which transform themselves into dancing venues at weekends by drafting in a DJ or two. There's a surfeit of bars offering **live music**, although most places content themselves with a meagre diet of cover bands or minor local rock acts. If you want to just stroll around and see where the crowds are going, make for Lichfield Street, home to a heady mix of cutting-edge dance clubs and seedy massage parlours.

BASE 674 Colombo St ☎03/377 7149. Dark and sweaty, high-energy club with guest DJs mainly spinning platters from the UK dance scene. Open until late Thurs–Sat. Cover charge $5–15.

Carbon downstairs at 76 Lichfield St. Currently top of the dance pile with the good stuff – drum 'n' bass, hip-hop and all manner of house styles – happening from Wed–Sun until very late. Entry free–$10.

Civic 186 Manchester St ☎03/374 9966. Popular, large clubbing venue offering a range of themed nights (eg funk, hip-hop, rare groove, house,

techno), some headline live acts and Latin dancing on three weeknights; check listings in *The Press* to see what's on. 10pm–6am.

Ministry 88–90 Lichfield St ☎03/379 2910. One of the biggest and liveliest of the clubs, with two dance floors; deep, dark and with a thumping drum'n'bass till sun up.

Platinum 76 Lichfield St ☎03/377 7891. Well-respected, gay cellar bar with an even mix of men and women. Thumping dance music in the main room and a quieter cocktail bar out the back.

Concerts, theatre, cinema and spectator sports

Apart from in Rotorua, one of the best places to experience a Maori concert and sample a hangi is here in Christchurch at **Ko Tane: The Maori Experience** held at the Willowbank Wildlife Reserve (see p.617; ☎03/359 6226, ⓦwww.willowbank.co.nz/kotane). The basic package is the cultural performance and tour of Willowbank (several times nightly; $25) complete with powhiri greeting, Maori cultural performance and a look at the animals; or step up to the full Maori Experience (dining at 6.30pm & 7.30pm; $65) with added *hangi* dinner.

The shining star in Christchurch's **drama** firmament is the Arts Centre's Court Theatre, 20 Worcester Blvd (bookings ☎0800/333 100 & 03/963 0870, ⓦwww.courttheatre.org.nz), home to one of New Zealand's longest-standing and most highly reputed professional theatre companies. Their performances are well advertised around town and in *The Press*. Touring shows frequently play in the James Hay Theatre at the Town Hall on Victoria Square (contact Ticketek on ☎03/377 8899), which also has a programme of **classical music** and ballet in the main auditorium.

Concerts by touring **jazz** and **rock** acts take place either at the Arts Centre or at the Theatre Royal, 145 Gloucester St (☎03/377 01000), a fine old Edwardian venue which attracts the glitzier, more mainstream acts. There is also a varied programme of music events in Hagley Park throughout the summer (☎03/941 6840 ⓦwww.summertimes.org.nz).

If it is first-run international **movies** you are after, head for the city-centre multiplexes: the Regent, 94 Worcester St (☎ 03/366 0140), right by Cathedral Square; Hoyts 8, Moorhouse Ave (☎0900/33303 & 03/366 6367), at the southern end of Manchester Street; and the Rialto, 250 Moorhouse Ave

(☎03/374 9404) on the corner of Durham Street. **Arthouse** movies are shown at the Academy and Cloisters cinemas (☎03/366 0167, ⓦwww .artfilms.co.nz) in the Arts Centre.

Jade Stadium, southeast of the centre near the junction of Moorhouse Avenue and Ferry Road, is the main venue for the big spectator **sports**, hosting **cricket** in the summer and **rugby** on weekends throughout the autumn and winter: visit ⓦwww.jadestadium.co.nz for **information** and Ticketek (☎03/377 8899, ⓦwww.ticketek.co.nz) for **tickets**.

Listings

Automobile Association 210 Hereford St ☎03/379 1280.

Banks and exchange Most banks have branches and ATMs on or near Colombo St and Hereford St. American Express operate through Holiday Shoppe, 683a Colombo St (Mon–Fri 8.30am–5.30pm, Sat 10am–1pm; ☎03/366 6032); Thomas Cook is at the corner of Armagh St & Colombo St (Mon–Fri 8.30am–5pm, Sat 10am–4pm; ☎03/379 6600); and there's Travelex, 730a Colombo St (☎ 03/365 4194).

Bike rental The most convenient bike rental is Wheels 'n' Deals Cycles, 159 Gloucester St between Manchester and Colombo (Mon–Fri 8am–6pm, Sat 10am–4pm; ☎03/377 6655) who rent out mountain bikes and tourers for $15 a half-day and $20 a day. You can also call City Cycle Hire (☎0800/343 848) who deliver bikes to your accommodation or to the visitor centre.

Bookshops The majors, Whitcoulls and Dymock's, are both in Cashel Street Mall. Otherwise try: Scorpio Books, 79 Hereford St; Liberty Books, 151 High St, which is good for secondhand paperbacks; Map World, 173 Gloucester St, which has the best range of maps and guides; and *Madras Cafe Bookshop*, 165 Madras St, which stocks quality books and has a good little café on site.

Car rental There are dozens of car rental places in Christchurch and yet from January to March you may have trouble landing anything if you don't book ahead; for more on car hire and contact details for international and nationwide companies, see "Basics", p.32. The following are reputable local agencies: Avon Percy ☎0800/736 828 & 03/379 3822, ⓦwww.avonrentacar.co.nz; Better ☎0800/269 696 & 03/365 2979, ⓦwww .betterrental.co.nz; McDonalds ☎0800/164 165 & 03/366 0929, ⓔinfo@mcdonaldrentacar.co.nz; Nationwide ☎0800/803 003 & 03/357 2314, ⓦwww.nationwiderentals.co.nz; Renny Rent-a-Car ☎0800/944 466 & 03/366 6790, ⓦwww .rennyrentals.co.nz; Scotties ☎0800/777 766 &

03/338 0997, ⓦwww.scotties.co.nz; U–Save ☎0800/582 299 & 03/358 2299, ⓦwww .rental-car.co.nz).

Festivals The local city council enthusiastically backs a number of summer festivals, most of them much better than you'd expect to find elsewhere. Look out particularly for the Jazz Festival (mid-Oct); the World Buskers Festival (late Jan), which is lots of fun and free and mostly takes place around the Arts Centre and in front of the *Dux De Lux*; and the Festival of Romance (early to mid-Feb) on the lead up to Valentine's Day. Check at the information centre for more details or consult ⓦwww.bethere.org.nz.

Internet access Christchurch is littered with places offering Internet access, but none are bigger and more centrally sited than Vadal (daily 8am–10pm) on the north side of Cathedral Square, with fast connections, low prices and cheap international phone calls as well as a left luggage facility.

Left Luggage Vadal (see "Internet access" above) store luggage from $3 per item for the first day and 50¢ a day thereafter. Also lockers at the public toilets on Cathedral Square.

Library Christchurch Central Library, Gloucester St (Mon–Fri 10am–9pm, Sat 10am–4pm, Sun 1–4pm).

Medical treatment In emergencies call ☎111. For a doctor at any time call The 24 Hour Surgery, cnr Bealey Ave & Colombo St (☎03/365 7777, no appointment necessary). Biggest of the hospitals is Christchurch Hospital, cnr Oxford Terrace & Riccarton Ave (☎03/364 0640).

Pharmacies After hours pharmacy at the 24 Hour Surgery (see "Medical Treatment" above; ☎03/366 4439), stays open daily until 11pm.

Police Central Police Station ☎03/379 3999.

Post office The main post office on Cathedral Square (☎03/353 1814) has poste restante facilities.

Shuttle buses For airport and train station transfers, shuttle buses offer a cheaper alternative to taxis. Try Super Shuttle (☎0800/748 885) or Falcon

Christchurch is the hub of air, road and rail routes for the South Island: see Travel Agencies in "Listings" (below) for bookings.

There are direct **flights** to Blenheim, Dunedin, Hokitika, Invercargill, Nelson, Queenstown, Wanaka, and several North Island cities. After retrenchment in recent years, there are now only two very scenic passenger **trains**: the TranzCoastal to Picton (meeting ferries to the North Island) and the TranzAlpine to Greymouth (covered fully on p.675).

Most inter-city journeys are best attempted by **bus** or **shuttle bus**, which are reasonably frequent to major destinations, though it is worth bearing in mind that journeys from, say, Christchurch to Nelson or Queenstown are likely to take up most of the day. Almost all companies now operate a door-to-door policy picking up and dropping off at the visitor centres, main hostels, some hotels and airports where applicable. Usually there's no additional cost, though there is sometimes a charge if you are being picked up outside Christchurch's central Four Avenues area, and for being dropped off around Queenstown. The main exception to this rule is the nationwide InterCity/Newmans. These companies run the following services:

Akaroa French Connection ℡0800/800 575: to Akaroa twice daily.

Akaroa Shuttle ℡0800/500 929: to Akaroa 2–3 times daily.

Alpine Coaches ℡ 0800/274 888: to Greymouth and Hokitika via Arthur's Pass.

Atomic Shuttles ℡ 03/322 8883: north to Kaikoura, Blenheim, and Picton; south to Ashburton, Timaru, Oamaru and Dunedin; west to Greymouth, then down the West

Shuttles (t0800/859 898), who all run from Cathedral Square to the airport (#15 for one, $8 each for three). They'll also pick you up from your accommodation. If you're catching a morning flight you should book your transfer the evening before.

Taxis Blue Star (℡03/379 9799), Arrow Taxis (℡03/379 9999) and Gold Band (℡03/379 5795) all have heaps of cabs.

Tours Guided walking tours (daily: Oct–April 10am & 1pm; May–Sept 1pm; 2hr; $8; ℡03/365 8480), led by local volunteers who really know their stuff, start from a kiosk in Cathedral Square near the cathedral entrance. Christchurch Sightseeing Tours (℡0508/669 660, ⓦwww.christchurchtours.co.nz)

offer 3 tours and combinations which save $5–10: City Gardens (mid-Sept to early Dec & mid-Jan to March Tues–Sat 9.30am–12.30pm; $30) visits 4 of their roster of 20 gardens each day; Heritage Homes (Wed & Sat 1.30–4.30pm; $30) calls at 3 homes not normally open to the public; and City sightseeing (mid-Sept to mid-April daily 9am & 1.30pm, mid-April to mid-Sept 1.30pm; $35) spends 3–4hr touring the vicinity including Mona Vale, Sumner, Lyttelton and the Summit Road.

Train information ℡0800/802 802.

Travel agencies Your best bets are Flight Centre, 116 Cashel St (℡03/3666371) and STA, 90 Cashel St (℡03/379 9098).

Banks Peninsula

Flying into Christchurch only the least observant could fail to be struck by the dramatic contrast between the flat plains of Canterbury and the rugged, f issured topography of **Banks Peninsula**, a volcanic thumb sticking out into the Canterbury Bight. When James Cook sailed by in 1769 he erroneously charted it as an island and named it after his botanist Joseph Banks. His error was only one of time, as this basalt lump initially formed as an island, one only

Coast to Queenstown; and inland through Geraldine and Twizel to Wanaka and Queenstown.

Budget Buses and Shuttles Timaru ℡03/615 5119: daily to Timaru

Catch-a-Bus ℡03/363 1122: south to Ashburton, Timaru, Oamaru and Dunedin.

Coast to Coast ℡ 0800/800 847: to Greymouth and Hokitika via Arthur's Pass.

Daylight Express ℡0800/800 904: daily to Queenstown via Lake Tekapo and Wanaka

East Coast Express ℡0508/830 900: north to Kaikoura, Blenheim and Picton.

The Hanmer Connection ℡0800/377 378: daily to Hanmer Springs

InterCity/Newmans ℡03/379 9020: north to Kaikoura, Blenheim, Picton and Nelson; south to Ashburton, Timaru, Oamaru, Dunedin and Invercargill; and inland to Methven, Aoraki Mount Cook, Wanaka and Queenstown. Services depart from the outside Christchurch visitor centre and from the Christchurch Travel Centre at 123 Worcester Street.

Knightrider ℡03/342 8055: evening/night trips to Dunedin and Invercargill.

Larry's Shuttles ℡0800/684 4891: daily to Timaru

Lazerline ℡ 0800/220 001: to Nelson via the Hanmer Springs turn-off and Murchison.

Methven Travel ℡03/302 8106: to Methven.

South Island Connections ℡ 03/366 6633: south to Ashburton, Timaru, Oamaru and Dunedin; and north to Kaikoura, Blenheim, and Picton.

Southern Link Shuttles ℡ 03/358 8355: north over the Lewis Pass to Murchison and Nelson; and southwest to Wanaka and Queenstown via Geraldine and Twizel.

joined to the land as silt sluiced down the rivers of the eastern flanks of the Southern Alps has accumulated to form the plains.

The fertile **volcanic** soil of the peninsula's valleys sprouted totara, matai and kahikatea trees which, along with the abundant shellfish in the bays, attracted early Maori around a thousand years ago. The trees soon succumbed to the fire stick, a process accelerated with the arrival of European timber milling interests. The lumber yards ground to a halt when the trees ran out in the late 1880s and the peninsula is now largely bald, with large areas of tussock grass on the rolling hills, and tiny pockets of regenerating native bush.

Today, the two massive drowned craters which form Banks Peninsula are key to the commerce of the region. Lyttelton Harbour protects and nurtures the port town of **Lyttelton**, disembarkation point for many of the fledgling provinces' migrants and now the South Island's major port. It is a workaday town, but interesting for its historic timeball station, harbour cruises and a couple of entertaining places to eat and drink. The various pleasure trips include swimming with dolphins. There's an altogether more refined and prestigious tone to the town of **Akaroa**; picturesque and French-influenced on account of its first of batch settlers who arrived from France at the same time as northern Maori and the British were signing the Treaty of Waitangi. Elsewhere on the peninsula, a network of narrow, twisting roads – not least the ridge-crest-hugging Summit Road – wind along the crater rims and dive down to gorgeous, quiet bays once alive with whalers, sealers and shipbuilders, but now seldom visited except during the peak of summer.

Despite the denuded and parched nature of much of the landscape, Banks Peninsula is very popular for relatively easy scenic **walks**, with panoramic views, ancient lava flows, relics from the earliest Maori and European settlers, and great beaches. A number of tracks cross private land and there are folk

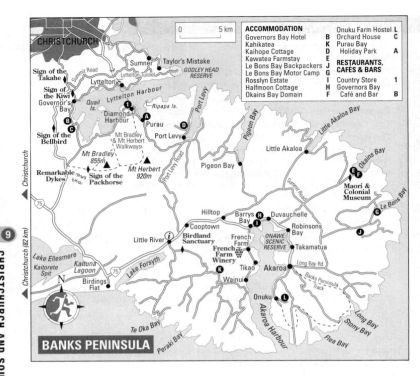

Map text:

CHRISTCHURCH

0   5 km

ACCOMMODATION
Governors Bay Hotel   B
Kahikatea   K
Kaihope Cottage   D
Kawatea Farmstay   E
Le Bons Bay Backpackers   J
Le Bons Bay Motor Camp   G
Rosslyn Estate   I
Halfmoon Cottage   H
Okains Bay Domain   F

Onuku Farm Hostel   L
Orchard House   C
Purau Bay
   Holiday Park   A

**RESTAURANTS,
CAFÉS & BARS**
Country Store   1
Governors Bay
   Café and Bar   B

Sumner   Taylor's Mistake
Sign of the Takahe
Summit Road   GODLEY HEAD RESERVE
Lyttelton Tunnel
Sign of the Kiwi   Lyttelton
Governor's Bay   Lyttelton Harbour
Quail Is.
Diamond Harbour   Ripapa Is.   Port Levy
Purau
Sign of the Bellbird   Mt Bradley & Mt Herbert Walkways   Port Levy
Mt Bradley 855m
Remarkable Dykes   Sign of the Packhorse   Mt Herbert 920m
Port Levy Road
Pigeon Bay
Little Akaloa
Little Akaloa Bay
Okains Bay
Maori & Colonial Museum
Le Bons Bay
Summit Road
Hilltop   Barrys Bay   Duvauchelle
Cooptown   Robinsons Bay
Little River   Birdland Sanctuary
French Farm
French Farm Winery   ONAWE SCENIC RESERVE   Takamatua
Lake Ellesmere
Kaituna Lagoon
Lake Forsyth
Tikao   Akaroa   Long Bay Rd
Kaitorete Spit
Birdings Flat
Wainui   Banks Peninsula Track
N
Onuku
Te Oka Bay   Akaroa Harbour   Long Bay   Stony Bay
Peraki Bay   Flea Bay

BANKS PENINSULA

Christchurch

Christchurch (82 km)

9

630

---

offering their services to deliver your pack to your destination. As befits a city playground, the peninsula is also well endowed with country-style B&Bs and farmstays, and Akaroa has a host of fine restaurants.

The peninsula merits at least a day-trip from Christchurch. With more time on your hands, you could enjoyably spend two to three days exploring the quieter nooks and crannies. From Christchurch, the main route to Akaroa is **SH75**, via Lake Ellesmere and Little River, but a more picturesque route follows the **Summit Road** from Sumner via Lyttelton, along the Port Hills and ridges of the peninsula. **Buses** from Christchurch serve only the main towns of Lyttelton and Akaroa, and to reach the smaller communities tucked into the bays you'll need your own transport, whether motorized or pedal-powered (see Christchurch listings, p.627, for car and bike rental details). If you're planning on cycling, bear in mind that the peninsula is extremely hilly, and the routes linking the summit road with the various bays below can be very steep. A good alternative is to join the Akaroa mail run (see p.642), as the long-suffering mail van winds in and out of the tiny bays.

Lyttelton

Just 12km from Christchurch city centre, **LYTTELTON** is a world apart, hemmed in by the rocky walls of the drowned volcanic crater that forms **Lyttelton Harbour**. Attractive though its setting is, Lyttelton is foremost a port, one where countless European migrants disembarked to start their new

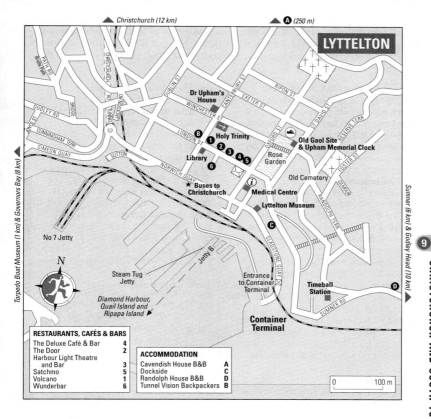

Christchurch (12 km)   ▲ ⓐ (250 m)

LYTTELTON

Dr Upham's House

Holy Trinity

Library

Old Gaol Site & Upham Memorial Clock

Rose Garden

Old Cemetery

★ Buses to Christchurch

Medical Centre

Lyttelton Museum

No 7 Jetty

N

Jetty B

Steam Tug Jetty

Entrance to Container Terminal

Timeball Station

Diamond Harbour, Quail Island and Ripapa Island

Container Terminal

Torpedo Boat Museum (1 km) & Governors Bay (8 km)

Sumner (6 km) & Godley Head (10 km)

RESTAURANTS, CAFÉS & BARS
The Deluxe Café & Bar	4
The Door	2
Harbour Light Theatre and Bar	3
Satchmo	5
Volcano	1
Wunderbar	6

ACCOMMODATION
Cavendish House B&B	A
Dockside	C
Randolph House B&B	D
Tunnel Vision Backpackers	B

0   100 m

CHRISTCHURCH AND SOUTH TO OTAGO | Banks Peninsula

lives. It still retains a raffish air: rowdy clanking from the docks, rumbustious waterfront bars, and plenty of overheard snippets of Polish, Russian and Filipino. Boats servicing the New Zealand and the US bases in Antarctica leave from here, and cruise ships even visit a few dozen times a year, though the passengers are mostly bussed off to Christchurch as soon as they arrive.

The town itself overlooks the docks and quays, climbing up the Port Hills behind and spreading southwest along the coast toward Governors Bay. Running parallel to the waterfront, the main road of Norwich Quay is fringed by a series of down-at-heel pubs designed to attract dockers, ships' crews and truck drivers. The web of streets behind are primarily residential, although it's here that the best bars, restaurants, shops and accommodation possibilities are found.

Arrival, information and accommodation

The quickest way from Christchurch to Lyttelton is through the 2km Lyttelton Tunnel, which ejects you right in the heart of town, just twenty minutes after leaving Christchurch. The #28 **bus** from Cathedral Square leaves about every 15–30min (35min; $2 each way) and can drop you right by the **visitor centre**, 20 Oxford St (daily 9am–5pm; ☎03/328 9093, ✉lyttinfo@ihug.co.nz). The staff will hand out a leaflet describing a self-guided **walk** around Lyttelton's many historic sites and help you learn what lurks behind Lyttelton's workaday facade.

631

Accommodation right in Lyttelton is somewhat limited, though there is an excellent backpackers and a couple of B&Bs. Most of the best places are some way out of town around Lyttelton Harbour, along with the only campsite that is remotely close.

Cavendish House B&B 10 Ross Terrace ☎03/328 9505, Ⓔcavendish@clear.net.nz. Set high in the hills with great views over the town and the port is this luxurious B&B, occupying an Edwardian villa, with two en-suite guest rooms. It was named after one of the original members of the Canterbury Association and boasts the sort of care visitors in those days would have been thrilled to receive. ❻

Dockside 22 Sumner Rd ☎03/328 7344. Well-run, self-catering B&B apartment with a sunny en-suite room and a deck with panoramic harbour views plus one very pleasant bed-sit. Continental breakfast is available. Bed-sit ❸, apartment ❹

Governors Bay Hotel Main Road, Governors Bay ☎03/329 9433, Ⓦwww.governorsbayhotel.co.nz. A large colonial hotel that has been entirely renovated but retains simple bathless rooms above the bar but with great harbour views. ❸

Orchard House Governors Bay ☎03/329 9622, Ⓔn.j.wilkinson@xtra.co.nz. Pleasant accommodation 8km from Lyttelton in a house surrounding by farmland and with views of the harbour. The double room has French doors that open onto a deck where breakfast is served. ❺

Purau Bay Holiday Park Diamond Harbour ☎03/329 4702 & 0800/468 678, Ⓦwww .holidayparks.co.nz/purau/. Pleasant campsite situated among tall sheltering trees and across the road from the bay, 2km from Diamond Harbour and half an hour's drive from Lyttelton. There are cabins, a bunkhouse, a shop, pool and a kitchen. Camping $11, dorms ❶, on-site vans ❷, cabins ❷, kitchen cabins ❸

Randolph House B&B 49 Sumner Rd ☎03/328 8877, Ⓔgabby@exi.co.nz. Set in a nineteenth-century wooden villa, this guesthouse has a double attic bedroom, plus other comfortable rooms with shared facilities, grand views over the harbour and tasty breakfasts. ❺

Tunnel Vision Backpackers 44 London St ☎ & Ⓕ03/328 7576. A brightly decorated, well-maintained, first-class backpackers occupying a renovated old hotel in a central location with a good selection of double and twin rooms, some with harbour views. Often closed July & Aug. Dorms ❶, rooms ❷

The Town

There is one attraction above all others for which Lyttelton is famous – the **Timeball Station**, Reserve Terrace (Nov–March daily 10am–5pm; April–Oct Wed–Sun 10am–5pm; $2.50), a steep 1km climb up Sumner Road from the centre. Built by prisoners in 1876, it looks for all the world like a Gothic tower that has carelessly lost its castle. It is clearly visible from all over town and harbour, and for over fifty years mariners recalibrated their on-board chronometers – critical for accurate navigation – on the descent of a large black ball down the pole on the roof. Radio signals replaced the timeball in 1934 and the station fell into disrepair, but progressive restoration since the 1970s has left it in immaculate condition. Once again, the ball is hoisted up its pole every day at precisely 12.57pm, then on the stroke of 1pm (to the nearest half-second) it begins its descent. Inside the station are a number of exhibits explaining the importance of the timeball to navigational techniques, plus the oily mechanism itself. The view from the roof is superb, and you can see the freshly restored ball close up.

There's an overall air of a long-neglected attic at the **Lyttelton Museum**, Norwich Quay (Tues, Thurs, Sat & Sun 2–4pm; donations appreciated), a former Seaman's Institute where you are greeted by a penguin. The nautical flavour lingers in a display of ancient telescopes, which straightfacedly informs visitors that the size and elaborateness of a sailor's telescope denoted his rank. Other exhibits reflect the town's history, while the Antarctic display spotlights Scott and Shackleton, both of whose expeditions set out from Lyttelton. Other curious artefacts have been salvaged from the small shelters built during the nineteenth century on various islands off the New Zealand shore, which were supplied with provisions to cater for unfortunate shipwrecked souls.

Prettiest of the town's churches is the 1860 **Holy Trinity Anglican Church**, on the corner of Winchester Street and Canterbury Street, which was originally earmarked as the Cathedral of the Diocese, a status never afforded it once building started in Christchurch. Diagonally opposite stands **Dr Upham's** 1907 house: for over fifty years the two-storey house served as the home for this saintly doctor, remembered for his devotion to the lepers of Quail Island and his refusal to accept money from patients who could not afford to pay. The good doctor is also commemorated at the end of Winchester Street by the **Upham Memorial Clock**, which stands in the Rose Garden on the site of the old jail – the remains of a couple of the cells can be seen on the northern side of the gardens. Built in 1851, the jail became the South Island's major penal institution, even accommodating sheep rustler James McKenzie (see p.694) for a time. Above the jail site is the **Old Cemetery**, full of gravestones dating back to the earliest settlers, except for the seven who were hanged at the jail between 1868 and 1918 – they did not merit a stone.

Boats and harbour cruises

To get a sense of Lyttelton's maritime importance, particularly in time of war, visit the **Torpedo Boat Museum** (Tues, Thurs, Sat & Sun 1–3pm; $2) reached by a five-minute shoreline walk from a car park on Charlotte Jane Quay about 1km west of town. After the 1885 Russian invasion of Afghanistan the fear of further Russian expansionism spread around the western Pacific, and New Zealand responded by building a Torpedo Boat to protect Lyttelton Harbour. Designed to charge up to an invading ship, detonate a charge below the waterline then scarper before it could be attacked itself, the boat was never used in anger and has only recently been restored after spending years abandoned and later buried. Its remains (principally the bow, stern and a fully restored engine) are now displayed in a former powder magazine along with a good video.

For a piece of living history, visit the **Steam Tug Lyttelton**, the older of only two steam tugs still operating in the country. It is docked at the wharf opposite Norwich Quay, over the Overhead Bridge, and on most summer Sundays the tug fires up for round-trip **cruises** (booking required ☎03/322 8911; 2.30pm, 1hr 30min; $12), steaming all the way to the head of the harbour. Built in Glasgow by the Ferguson brothers in 1907, this beautiful antique boat is maintained in full working order by an impassioned bunch of volunteers. If you climb aboard, one of the volunteers will escort you on an unofficial and extremely informative tour, which includes a museum occupying the captain's cabin, officers' quarters, saloon and other cabins. The boiler room is particularly impressive: all burnished brass and oily pistons, it was cutting edge in its heyday, with steam-power-assisted steering.

A variety of other **cruises** depart from Lyttelton offering a splendid sea-level perspective on the harbour. If you can do without a commentary or simply want more time to explore, check out the regular ferry services to Diamond Harbour and Quail Island (see p.635) run by Black Cat Cruises (☎03/328 9078 & 0800/436 574, ⓦ www.blackcat.co.nz) who depart from Jetty B opposite Norwich Quay: most sailings link with the #28 bus from Christchurch. Black Cat also offer a Wildlife Cruise (2.30pm daily; $45), departing from jetty B, which includes the prospect of seeing Hector's dolphins up close. **Hector's dolphins** are also the target of The Dolphin Adventure run by Canterbury Sea Tours (☎03/326 5607), who run flexible tours pretty much to order, though you'll need half a dozen people to make the price manageable.

Eating and drinking

Lyttelton has a well-founded reputation for quality food and a nightlife that's way livelier than you'd expect for such a small town. In fact, a trip to Lyttelton is justified solely on the intention to dine at the *Volcano Café* and then troop over the road to sample the pleasures of the *Wunderbar*.

The Deluxe Café & Bar 18 London St. Polished wooden furnishings and floors provide a relaxing setting for high-quality moderately priced lunches and dinners.

The Door 36 London St ☎03/328 8855. Good café combined with a boutique **cinema** (generally Thurs–Sat; $11) with old aircraft seating and sofas draped with scarlet sheepskins and the chance to snack, drink or have a full meal served while you watch.

Governors Bay Café and Bar 79 Main Rd, 8km west of Lyttelton ☎03/329 9825. A little gem perched upon a hill overlooking the water and serving simple, inexpensive, home-baked dishes available from about 10am daily, and later into the evenings on Thurs, Fri & Sat in summer.

Governors Bay Hotel Main Rd, 8km west of Lyttelton ☎03/329 9433. A large colonial hotel that has been entirely renovated and contains a wonderful long wooden bar and veranda seating where you can enjoy straightforward but tasty fare such as fish and chips ($15), chicken risotto ($15) and lemon tart with berry coulis ($9). They also have rooms available (see "Accommodation" p.632).

Harbour Light Theatre and Bar 22 London St. Old theatre that still hosts some pretty lively gigs,

usually advertised on the door or in the local press, with a functional little bar that opens when someone's playing.

Satchmo 8 London St. Casual restaurant and bar with a good line in salads, gourmet pizzas (from $12) and pasta dishes ($14) served in a peaceful garden or inside with background jazz.

Volcano 42 London St ☎03/328 7077. A Lyttelton institution fashioned out of a former fish-and-chip shop with bright, eclectic decor and meals served on Formica tables all with fresh flowers. Cuisine draws on Cajun, Mexican, Spanish and Italian influences, with all sorts of home-made treats in substantial portions (mains $20–25). Licensed and BYO.

Wunderbar London St. An idiosyncratic late-night drinking-hole and club with decor ranging from crushed velour to a gruesome doll's-head light-shade. There's pool, table football and a wonderful deck overlooking the harbour that's great for a peaceful drink if you can't take the clamour within. Entertainment ranges from 1940s and 50s cabaret nights, through poetry, live bands, stand-up comics, club and disco music, to film noir evenings. Entry is down steps beside the super-market, and up an iron fire escape. Mon–Fri 5pm–late, Sat & Sun 3pm–even later.

Around Lyttelton Harbour

Lyttelton would be nothing without its harbour, and it would be a shame to spend time here without venturing along its shores. Boats reached Lyttelton through "the heads", best seen from Godley Head – a moody, grass- and rock-covered promontory with steep sea cliffs offering excellent views. On the water, the main destinations are the small community of **Diamond Harbour**, and two islands: **Quail Island** in the centre of Lyttelton Harbour and the tiny **Ripapa Island** just east of Diamond Harbour. Both are havens for birds, as well as offering solitude and superb views; for access to the islands, see the p.635.

Godley Head

At the northernmost tip of the harbour, **Godley Head** stands guard – a spectacular piece of land with high cliffs and excellent views, administered by DOC. Follow the signs east out of Lyttelton to the Summit Road, which takes you out onto Godley Head (about 10km) and the **Godley Head Reserve**, a delightfully scenic spot for walks and picnics. The walkway network is extensive, in places stumbling across installations left behind after World War II, including dark warren-like tunnels and searchlight emplacements perched like birds' nests on the cliffs. From here, you can also walk down to the tiny coastal settlements of Boulder Bay and Taylors Mistake (see box on p.621).

Diamond Harbour

In bright sunlight the harbour sparkles like a million gems at **Diamond Harbour**, directly across the water from Lyttelton. Black Cat Cruises (see below) operate passenger **ferries** (sailings every 1–2hr: Mon–Fri 6.15am–6.50pm, Sat & Sun 6.55am–7.10pm; $3.60 each way) across the harbour making a handy shortcut to Camp Bay, the Mount Herbert Walkway and the rest of Banks Peninsula. Arriving at the Diamond Harbour wharf you can generate a thirst with a 500-metre walk uphill, then slake it at either the *Country Store*, which does coffee, muffins and toasted sandwiches, or at **Godley House**, a popular vantage point with gardens and lawns overlooking Diamond Harbour which have attracted visitors from Christchurch and beyond for more than a hundred years. The house has been taken over by the conference market in recent years, but on summer weekends you can still buy a beer or lunch and sprawl out on the grass. If you want to stay over this way there's the *Purau Bay Holiday Park* (see p.632) at Purau 2km east.

Quail and Ripapa islands

Set in mid-harbour, **Quail Island** was known by the local Maori as *Otamahau* because it was the place where children collected seabirds' eggs. It was used as a leper colony between 1907 and 1925 (when the afflicted were transported to Fiji), Shackleton and Scott quarantined their dogs here before venturing to the South Pole, and the wrecks of several ships can sometimes be spied at low tide. These days it's a venue for day-trips, swimming and walking; it makes a relaxing and fascinating place to spend a day: pack provisions, plenty of drinking water and rain gear. Travel with Black Cat Cruises (Sept–April daily 9.30am & 1.30pm boats leaving Quail at 1.40pm & 4.40pm; May–Aug daily 12.30pm plus Sat & Sun 9.30am; $10 return), and pick up the *Quail Island Walkway* leaflet (50¢) from the Christchurch DOC office or the Lyttelton visitor centre, which details two circular **walking tracks** (1hr & 2hr 30min), both starting from the island's wharf.

Historically the defensibility of **Ripapa Island**, just off the southern shore of the Harbour near Diamond Harbour, has been its key feature. Successively a Maori *pa*, then the site of an 1880s fort built as a measure against a feared Russian invasion that never materialized, it later became a prison camp for Count Felix Von Luckner, a German "sea raider". The island now enjoys some peace as a historic reserve administered by DOC, which can only be visited on **guided tours** run by Black Cat (bookings essential ☎03/328 9078).

Christchurch to Akaroa

With ample time on your hands and a taste for exploration consider approaching Banks Peninsula on the **Summit Road** (see box on p.636), which winds around the crater rim of Lyttelton Harbour then around the northern bays before finally dropping you down to Akaroa.

A much faster and more convenient way of covering the 85km run **from Christchurch to Akaroa** is along SH75 which heads south from the city before curling southeast along the southern shore of the peninsula, then over the hills to Akaroa: it takes around an hour and a half, though there are reasons to pause along the way, notably the cheese factory at **Barry's Bay**.

Lake Ellesmere and Little River

Around 30km from Christchurch SH75 tracks the water's edge of **Lake Ellesmere** (*Waihora*), a vast expanse of fresh water separated from the Pacific Ocean by the 30km-long Kaitorete spit, which juts southeastwards

Drivers – and particularly **cyclists** – should consider passing up the fast and relatively straight SH75 from Christchurch to Akaroa, in favour of the **Summit Road**, actually a sequence of connecting backroads which forms a giant S-shaped circuit around the peninsula's two crater harbours. Designed with pedestrians and wagons in mind, it keeps as close as possible to the ridge tops marking an undulating course – with few sustained ascents – and offering stupendous views all around. For cyclists, **traffic** is fairly sparse, but what there is tends to hare around blind corners, so keep your wits about you.

The Summit Road was the consuming passion of the public-spirited **Harry Ell**. He dreamed of building a highway with **walking tracks** and fourteen rest stations along the summit of the Port Hills and right around the peninsula. The project got under way at the beginning of the twentieth century, and when Ell died in 1934 only four rest stations (mostly named after native birds) had been built. The first, sited at what was the southern limit of Christchurch trams (now bus #10), the junction of Dyers Pass Road and Takahe Drive, was the **Sign of the Takahe** – a Gothic-style baronial house distinguished by enormous kauri beams, salvaged from a bridge that once spanned the Hurunui River. This house is now a daytime **café** so for the price of a coffee you can still take a look at some unique friezes fashioned from old packing cases and stone quarried from the peninsula, which are kept in a memorial room. Look out for the heraldic embellishments relating to early governors of New Zealand, coats of arms of local families and shields portraying significant events in British history. In the evening the place becomes a formal **restaurant** (☎03/332 4052) serving mostly Pacific Rim cuisine with mains around the $28 mark: an excellent spot for that special night out.

From the *Sign of the Takahe*, Dyer's Pass Road runs 4km uphill to the Summit Road and the second rest station, the **Sign of the Kiwi**, now a reasonable café with excellent views from the car park. This is perhaps the best place to start following the Summit Road. However, enthusiasts needing a sense of completeness should start at the true beginning by Godley Head, near the Lyttelton Harbour entrance.

From the *Sign of the Kiwi* the Summit Road follows the ridgetops 9km southwest to the single remaining room of the third of Ell's structures, the **Sign of the Bellbird**, a stone picnic shelter with exceptional views. The last of the rest stations, the **Sign of the Packhorse**, is a trampers' hut off the Summit Road which can also be accessed on the **Mount Herbert Walkway** (13km return; 6hr). This starts from the Summit Road near Gebbie's Pass and heads through open country past the **Remarkable Dykes** – fissures created by the heat of volcanic activity, forming a receptacle for molten rock. As the molten rock cooled and solidified, it proved more resistant to erosion than the surrounding material, thereby creating the protruding ridges which were subsequently dubbed "dykes". The Walkway then skirts Mount Bradley through very old native bush and heads down to Diamond Harbour.

Harry Ell's main rest stations can also be reached as part of the worthwhile **Crater Rim Walkway** (18.5km one way; 4hr), a magical path along a part of the crater of the extinct Lyttelton volcano. The track starts on Dyers Pass Road near the Sign of the Takahe and climbs past pretty reserves to the Sign of the Kiwi from where you turn southwest and follow the crater-rim ridge to the Sign of the Bellbird.

The Summit Road completes its circuit of Lyttelton Harbour by dropping down to Diamond Harbour and over to Port Levy, a tiny valley with a beach that once supported the largest Maori population in Canterbury. The Summit Road returns to follow the ridgetops, occasionally throwing spurs down the valleys to secluded coves such as **Pigeon Bay**, the lovely **Okains Bay** (see p.645) and **Le Bons Bay** (see also p.644) before descending to Akaroa.

from Banks Peninsula to rejoin the mainland. It's a picturesque area popular with fishermen, although other visitors will probably content themselves with the fine views of the lake to be had from the road. At the base of the spit is **Birdlings Flat**, a narrow shingle bank that has traditionally been a rich source of food for local Maori, who were granted protected fishing rights here in 1896; the accumulated shingle of the sheltering bank also provides a fossicking ground for greenstone and gems. Birdlings Flat separates the sea from **Lake Forsyth** (*Wairewa*), a long finger of water skirted by SH75 on the way to the tiny community of **LITTLE RIVER**, 53km from Christchurch. The place is primarily of interest for the excellent café, bar and bakery of the *Little River Store*, and the **Old Railway and Craft Station** on Main Road, which houses a small **visitor centre** (Oct–April daily 9am–5pm; May–Sept daily 10am–4pm; ☎03/325 1255). There's also a reminder of the area's Maori heritage – a statue of Tangatahara, the famous chief of the ultimately unsuccessful defence of the Onawe Peninsula, which stands in the town, alongside a lengthy Maori inscription describing many of his battles.

Barry's Bay

From Little River, SH75 starts climbing the hills which separate Akaroa Harbour from the rest of Banks Peninsula. The road tops out at the *Hilltop Tavern* from where there is a great view of what is still to come, including the steep descent to **BARRY'S BAY**, right at the head of Akaroa Harbour. This is home to the settlers' original dairy factory, **Barry's Bay Cheese**, SH75 (Mon–Fri 8.30am–5pm, Sat & Sun 9.30am–5pm; ☎03/304 5809), where all the cheeses are sold on the premises: try the cheddar, Barry's Bay Sharp, Havarti, Akaroa Mellow or Port Cooper, with one of the locally made chutneys or mustards on a piece of fresh bread for lunch. It is a bit of a tourist trap visited by all the coaches, though it is worth nipping in for the free samples. Accounts of early cheese-making go back to 1844, when chessets (the traditional cheese moulds still in use today) were brought from Europe and the region became one of the first in New Zealand to export cheese to Europe.

There's **accommodation** nearby at *Rosslyn Estate*, just off SH75 (☎03/304 5804, ✉rosslyn@xtra.co.nz; ❻), with very comfortable ensuite B&B in a large 1860s country house set in extensive grounds. There's home baking on arrival and evening meals on request ($30). For something cheaper, stay at *Halfmoon Cottage*, SH75 (☎03/304 5050, ✉halfmoon.co@clear.net.nz; shares ❶, rooms ❸), a lovely small hostel in a colonial house set in a pretty garden just across from the beach. It can be as relaxing as you want, or sign up for a few hours on a 28-foot keeler ($30).

Almost opposite, the **Onawe Peninsula Scenic Reserve** (daily dawn–dusk) juts out into Akaroa Harbour. The peninsula once offered a highly defensible sanctuary for local Maori, and remains of the *pa* fortifications, deep ditches and ramparts are still distinguishable, despite years of farming. From here it is only 10km to Akaroa, reached through the tiny but pretty settlements of Duvauchelle, Robinson's Bay and Takamatua – originally known as German Bay after the first settlers who arrived with Akaroa's French.

Akaroa

The small waterside town of **AKAROA** ("Long Bay"), 82km from Christchurch on the eastern shores of Akaroa Harbour, comes billed as New Zealand's **French settlement**. Certainly the initial settlers came from France, some of their architecture survives and the street names they chose have stuck,

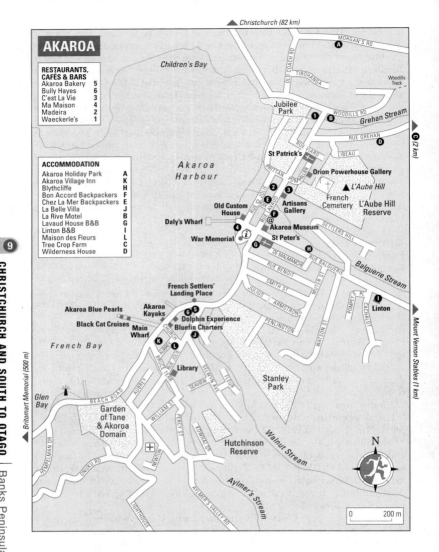

AKAROA

Christchurch (82 km)

RESTAURANTS, CAFÉS & BARS

Akaroa Bakery	5
Bully Hayes	6
C'est La Vie	3
Ma Maison	4
Madeira	2
Waeckerle's	1

ACCOMMODATION

Akaroa Holiday Park	A
Akaroa Village Inn	K
Blythcliffe	H
Bon Accord Backpackers	F
Chez La Mer Backpackers	E
La Belle Villa	J
La Rive Motel	B
Lavaud House B&B	G
Linton B&B	I
Maison des Fleurs	L
Tree Crop Farm	C
Wilderness House	D

Children's Bay

Jubilee Park

Akaroa Harbour

St Patrick's

Orion Powerhouse Gallery

L'Aube Hill

French Cemetery

L'Aube Hill Reserve

Artisans Gallery

Old Custom House

Daly's Wharf

Akaroa Museum

War Memorial

St Peter's

French Settlers' Landing Place

Akaroa Blue Pearls

Akaroa Kayaks

Dolphin Experience

Black Cat Cruises

Bluefin Charters

Main Wharf

French Bay

Library

Glen Bay

Garden of Tane & Akaroa Domain

Stanley Park

Hutchinson Reserve

Britomart Memorial (500 m)

Mount Vernon Stables (1 km)

N

0   200 m

but that's about as French as it gets. Nonetheless, the town milks the connection with a couple of French-ish restaurants, some French-sounding boutique B&Bs and a tricolour fluttering over the spot where the first settlers landed.

Still, it is a pretty place with attractive scenery all around, a smattering of low key activities to keep you occupied – including the **Banks Peninsula Track**, which starts and finishes nearby (see box on p.643) – and, most of all, a very relaxed air well suited to gentle strolls followed by quality cuisine and a comfy bed. These factors combine to make Akaroa a popular Kiwi holiday destination; a full two-thirds of its houses are *baches*, leaving only around 750 permanent residents.

Once the domain of the Ngai Tahu paramount chief, Temaiharanui, the site of Akaroa attracted the attention of some of Canterbury's earliest migrants. In 1838 a French Commander, Jean Langlois, purchased what he believed to be the entire peninsula for goods to the value of 1000 French francs, and returned to France to encourage settlers to sail with Captain Lavaud and populate a new French colony. However, while the French were making their way to New Zealand, the British sent Captain William Hobson to assume the role of lieutenant-governor over all the land that could be purchased; and just six days before Lavaud sailed into the harbour, the British flag was raised in Akaroa. Lavaud's passengers decided to stay, which meant that the first formal settlement under **British sovereignty** was comprised of sixty-three French – and six Germans who had come along for the ride.

You can treat Akaroa as a day-trip from Christchurch, although you'll only have time to scratch the surface of this beguiling spot; far better to spend a night or two in order to appreciate the town and its surrounds.

Arrival and information

Buses run by Akaroa Shuttle (Dec–March 3 daily; April–Nov 2 daily; $20 return; ℡0800/500 929, ℮info@akaroashuttle.co.nz) and Akaroa French Connection (2 daily; $20 return; ℡0800/800 575) leave the Christchurch visitor centre for the 1hr 30min run to Akaroa. They drop off outside the combined **post office** and **visitor centre**, 80 rue Lavaud (daily 10am–5pm; ℡03/304 8600, ⓦwww.akaroa.com), which has pack storage ($1/hr, $4 a day), stocks free brochures, various walks leaflets ($0.50 each) and the *Akaroa Historic Village Walk* booklet ($5). Several places have **Internet access** including Bon-e-mail, a shack beside *Bon Accord Backpackers* with several machines. There is a BNZ **bank** (Mon–Fri 9.30am–4.30pm) with ATM opposite the visitor centre on rue Lavaud.

Accommodation

Akaroa's best **accommodation** caters to the weekend getaway set and there are some gorgeous B&Bs and lodges. Staying in one of these seems to suit the spirit of Akaroa, and it is worth stretching the budget if you can. Otherwise, try the excellent backpacker hostels – a couple in town, one in Onuku (see all below), a fourth at Le Bons Bay (see p.644) and *Halfmoon Cottage* (see p.637) back towards Christchurch.

B&Bs, Lodges and hotels

Akaroa Village Inn 81 Beach Rd ℡03/304 7421 & 0800/695 2000, ⓦwww.akaroa.co.nz. Rambling hotel complex built around the town's original 1842 hotel, complete with heated outdoor pool. Rooms are all tastefully decorated, self-catering and many come with good harbour views. Studio units ⑤, apartments ⑥, luxury apartments, just ⑨

La Belle Villa 113 rue Jolie ℡ & ℮03/304 7084. B&B in a lovely wooden house with spacious light rooms, a large swimming pool and alfresco breakfasts in summer. Shared bath ⑤, ensuite ⑥

Blythcliffe 37 rue Balguerie ℡03/304 7003, ⓦwww.blythcliffe.co.nz. One of Akaroa's finest B&Bs in a grand old house – equipped with a full-size billiard table – surrounded by semi-formal gardens and bush. There are a couple of lovely rooms with private bathrooms and a delightful garden cottage. ⑦

Kahikatea Wainui Valley Rd, nr Akaroa ℡03/304 7400, ⓦwww.kahikatea.com. If you want to treat yourself and you've got some dosh ($325 a night) to spare then try this delightful B&B/homestay where the level of care is exceptional, the food delicious, the accommodation luxurious, and the views are stunning. *Kahikatea* is on the other side of the harbour from Akaroa, best accessed from Barry's Bay (see p.637). ⑨

Lavaud House B&B 83 rue Lavaud ℡03/304 7121, ℮lavaudhouse@xtra.co.nz. Historic home overlooking the main swimming beach, with fresh flowers and antique furniture in every room. A comfortable and friendly place, with four bedrooms and a choice of cooked or continental breakfast. ⑥

Linton B&B 68 rue Balguerie ☎ 03/304 7501, ⓦ www.linton.co.nz. Stay in a living art gallery (see p.641) built in and around this 1881 house known locally as the *Giant's House*. Large rooms are all shared-bath but come wildly decorated, with say, a boat bed or a greenhouse conservatory. A delicious continental breakfast is served. **❼**

Maison des Fleurs 6 Church St ☎ 03/304 7804, ⓔ maison.des.fleurs@xtra.co.nz. Boutique accommodation in a modern two-storey cottage (you get all of it), built from peninsula-milled timbers. It's superbly appointed with allergy-free linen, natural fibre beds and so on, plus there's a sunny balcony, wood stove for winter, and always a heap of fresh flowers, complimentary port and current magazines. **❽**

La Rive Motel 1 rue Lavaud ☎ 03/304 7651 & 0800/247 651, ⓔ larive@paradise.net.nz. Large, curiously shaped motel (its open-sided, two-storey conical tower is an allusion to French chateau architecture) in a tranquil garden setting, with a white picket fence at the front and eight units, all containing full kitchens and TVs. **❹**

Tree Crop Farm 2km up rue Grehan ☎ 03/304 7158. Romantic retreat in one of three rustic huts (two without electricity) set on a private farm (see p.641), where they believe in "hot bush baths under the stars and late, late breakfasts on the veranda". Afternoon tea and brunch provided. **❽**

Wilderness House 42 rue Grehan ☎ 03/304 7517, ⓦ www.wildernesshouse.co.nz. Lovely and welcoming B&B in a fine old home with four tastefully decorated rooms, each with ensuite or private bath (one with a deep tub). There's a sumptuous guest lounge with port, and a delicious breakfast is served, perhaps on the terrace overlooking semi-formal grounds with English roses. They even have their own small vineyard. **❼**

Hostels and camp-grounds

Akaroa Holiday Park Morgan's Rd, off the Old Coach Rd ☎ 03/304 7471, ⓔ akaroa.holidaypark @xtra.co.nz. Sprawling across a terraced hillside overlooking the harbour and the main street running through town, this site has modern facilities, including a swimming pool. Camping $10–11; cabins & on-site vans **❷**, tourist flats **❸**

Bon Accord Backpackers 57 rue Lavaud ☎ 03/304 7782, ⓦ www.bon-accord.co.nz. Small, upscale hostel fashioned from two tiny houses knocked into one. Beds come with sheets and towels, and there's off-street parking. Four-shares **❶**, rooms **❷**

Chez La Mer Backpackers 50 rue Lavaud ☎ 03/304 7024, ⓔ chez_la_mer@clear.net.nz. Historic building dating back to 1871, and offering high-quality budget accommodation in a homely environment with a nice garden out the back. The staff are helpful, offer free use of bikes and some useful hand-drawn maps of local walks and points of interest. Dorms **❶**, en-suite doubles **❷**

Onuku Farm Hostel 6km south of town on the Onuku road ☎ 03/304 7066. Beside the bay, this secluded and quiet spot on a sheep farm has accommodation in the main house or in very cheap summer-only huts. Free pick-up from Akaroa and kayaking ($25), and dolphin swimming trips ($80) run from the hostel. Closed June–Aug. Camping $10, dorms **❶**, rooms **❷**

The Town

Akaroa is strung along the shore in a long, easily walkable ribbon. In fact the best way to get acquainted with the place is by following the **Akaroa Historic Village Walk**, which pinpoints buildings of interest and architectural note.

Opposite the visitor centre, the **Akaroa Museum**, corner rue Lavaud and rue Balguerie (daily: Oct–April 10.30am–4.30pm; May–Nov 10.30am–4pm; $4), stands head and shoulders above most small-town museums. You might only spend half an hour or so inside but will come away with a good sense of Akaroa's place in New Zealand history. Several interesting Maori artefacts and a twenty-minute film account of the remarkable and sometimes violent history of Maori settlement on the peninsula are backed up by a display illustrating the differences between the English version of the Treaty of Waitangi and a literal English translation of the Maori-language document signed by Maori chiefs all over Aotearoa. Other exhibits deal with the peninsula's whaling history and settlement, including albums full of fascinating photographs of the original French and German settlers and the British that followed them. The museum also incorporates the **Langlois–Eteveneaux Cottage**, possibly the oldest house in Canterbury, partly constructed in France before being shipped over, and now filled with French nineteenth-century furniture. Also associated with the museum are the town's former **Court House**, still with its original dock and bench peopled by some unconvincing mannequins, and the tiny **Custom House**, across rue Lavaud next to Daly's Wharf, from which spy-glass-wielding officials once kept watch on the port below.

Continuing the Gallic theme is the **French Cemetery** at the northern end of town, reached by a footpath which leads from rue Pompallier into the L'Aube Hill Reserve. The first consecrated burial ground in Canterbury, the cemetery was sadly neglected until 1925, when the bodies were reinterred in a central plot marked by a single monument, shaded by weeping willows – romantically said to have been grown from a cutting taken at Napoleon's grave in St Helena. Continue about 150m up L'Aube hill for even better views over the town and harbour. At the northern end of rue Pompallier, the French-inspired **Church of St Patrick** has its origins in the mission station built here by Bishop Pompallier in 1840, but the first two church buildings were destroyed by fire and a storm respectively. The church you see today is a third-time-lucky effort, built in 1864 from large slabs of unplaned totara. The combination of totara, black pine and kauri, and the changing colours of the wood as it ages, fills the church with rich colours, complementing the bold stained glass in the east window, behind the altar.

Galleries and gardens

Also situated at the northern end of rue Pompallier is the **Orion Powerhouse Gallery** (Oct–April Mon–Fri 1.30–4.30pm, Sat & Sun 11am–4.30pm; donation requested; ☏03/304 7245), which occupies a former hydroelectric plant, and serves as a venue for national and local exhibitions of arts and crafts, as well as for concerts of various types of music on Sundays. Also worth a look is the **Artisans Gallery**, 45 rue Lavaud (daily 10am–5pm), a sales-oriented collection housed in an 1877 cottage and displaying pottery, weaving, silk, jewellery, knitwear, clothing and turned wood. Stray a little further if you like jewellery to **Akaroa Blue Pearls**, Main Wharf (daily 10am–4pm; ☏03/304 7877) where beautiful blue pearls are cultured in the harbour; renowned jeweller Murray Brereton will knock you up an individually designed piece with one of these mementoes as its centre piece, for a price.

Lastly, be sure not to miss **Linton**, 68 rue Balguerie (daily 2–4pm; $10), home of sculptor Josie Martin and a working testament to her abstract art. Every room, the garden and even the drive to the garage have become a canvas on which she can display her talents. Huge mosaics, concrete figures and sculpted seats tucked away in garden nooks all come with an overriding spirit of fun.

Drivers, and those who fancy more than just a gentle walk around town, can head out into the immediate surroundings of Akaroa. One destination that divides opinions is **Tree Crop Farm**, 2km up rue Grehan (daily 9am–5pm; $8 including a drink and a nibble), a private lifestyle farm centred on a garden area with a kind of managed overgrown look. Fans love to amble along the farm tracks and through the gardens reading aphorisms written everywhere imaginable. They're initially entertaining – "the best plastic surgery is to cut up your credit cards", "old age isn't bad when you consider the alternative" – but soon become tiresome. A small café serves berry juices and exotic coffee drinks at relatively high prices, and there is accommodation (see p.640) in simple but nicely furnished huts.

Activities around Akaroa

You may want to do nothing more in Akaroa than sip a pinot gris and mooch around the galleries, but there is no shortage of diversions, from waterfront strolls to dolphin swimming and quad-biking. One particularly good way of exploring the hinterland is to join the **Akaroa Scenic Mail Run** (Mon–Sat 8.20am; 4hr 30min; $20; booking essential through the visitor centre) which follows a 140-kilometre rural delivery run, serving the eastern bays of the peninsula, including Okains and Le Bons Bays.

Harbour cruises and swimming with dolphins

Two main companies are eager to take you out **swimming with Hector's dolphins** – the world's smallest breed of dolphins, usually 1.2–1.4 metres in length – both also offering spectator-only rates. Most go with Black Cat, Main Wharf, Beach Rd (Nov–April 6am, 9am & noon; June–Oct noon; $85, spectators $45; ☎0800/436 574, ⓦwww.canterburycat.co.nz): trips take around two hours and if you can't swim with the dolphins you can go again free of charge until you do. Dolphin Experience, 61 Beach Rd (daily: Nov–April 6am, 9am & noon; May–Oct 9am & noon; $80, spectators $35; ☎0508/365 744, ⓔdolphins.akaroa@xtra.co.nz), offers a more personal experience taking up to three hours. If you don't get to swim with the dolphins you can take a 50 percent refund or return at any time for a second try at $38.

Black Cat also runs two-hour **harbour cruises** (Nov–March at 11am & all year at 1.30pm; $39) which visit the mouth of the harbour and back via a rookery, a beautiful high-walled volcanic sea cave, colonies of spotted shags and cormorants, Penguin Caves (where blue penguins can sometimes be spotted) and a fish-feeding stop in Lucas Bay. A wonderfully atmospheric alternative is Coastline Adventures who will take you out around the outer bays on their *Fox II* (☎03/304 5048; daily 11am & 2pm; around $38), a wooden ketch built in 1922. The cruise takes a good look round Akaroa Harbour and the outer bays.

Fishing and kayaking

Bluefin Charters, 65 Beach Rd (☎03/304 7866, ⓦwww.bluefincharters.co.nz) runs all sorts of dolphin- and bird-watching cruises, but specialise in harbour **fishing trips** (3hr; $50).

Directly opposite Bluefin Charters is Akaroa Kayaks (☎03/304 8758), who will rent out their boats ($25 half-day, $35 full-day) to people with a high level of **kayaking** competence. Although the bay is sheltered, it's not worth trying to fool them if you've not done much paddling before because it can quickly get windy and the waters rough.

Seal viewing, horse riding and quad-biking

Back on land, Akaroa Seal Colony Safari (☎03/304 7255, ⓔdouble.l@xtra.co.nz) runs air-conditioned 4WD coaches to **view fur seals** from Goat Point on the eastern tip of the peninsula. Tours (daily 9.30am & 1pm; $50) last over two hours and are limited to six people. **Horse riding** can be organized with Mount Vernon Lodge and Stables, rue Balguerie (☎03/304 7180), who offer various guided treks depending on the amount of time you want to be in the saddle over hilly country ($35 per hour). **Off-road riding** is offered by 4 Wheel Bike Safaris (☎03/304 7619), who run two-hour guided cross country trips on 4WD bikes ($79; sturdy shoes required) leaving from the Akaroa Heritage Park on Long Bay Road, 5km from town.

Walks

If you lack the time or inclination to tackle the **Banks Peninsula Track** (see box on p.643), there are some equally rewarding shorter walks. The best is the

The Banks Peninsula Track

One of the most popular tracks in the area is the **Banks Peninsula Track**, a thirty-five kilometre private track which traverses spectacular volcanic coastline, verdant farmland, exposed headlands and sandy beaches, as well as the Hinewai Nature Reserve (a marine reserve around the southeastern bays of the peninsula), before reaching the end of the track at Mount Vernon Lodge just east of Akaroa. The track is open from Oct 1 to April 30 and typically takes four days to walk (though there is a two-day option for robust hikers). Either way, a reasonable level of **fitness** is required, but because you're guaranteed a bunk at each hut you can walk at your own pace. The **fee** ($180 4-day option; $120 2-day option) includes transport to the start from Akaroa and accommodation along the way; though you'll need to bring a good pair of boots, sleeping bag and all-weather gear. You should also carry provisions for at least the first two days, although it is possible to augment your **supplies** with fresh farm produce at Stony Bay and snacks at Otanerito Beach. You can also have your pack carried in for you on the first day, or transported out on the fourth ($70 and $40 respectively).

Only twelve people are allowed to start the track each day on the 4-dayer, and four people on the 2-dayer, so **bookings** should be made well in advance through Banks Peninsula Track, PO Box 54, Akaroa (℡03/304 7612, ⊛www.bankstrack.co.nz).

The route

The trail starts at Onuku, 5km south of Akaroa, and the first night is spent in **Onuku hut** at the start of the track. There's usually enough time on the following day to explore neighbouring trails before embarking on the first stage of the walk proper from **Onuku to Flea Bay** (11km, 3hr 30min), passing three small waterfalls and providing views of the peninsula's east coast. Accommodation at Flea Bay is in a charming 130-year-old cottage with a veranda overlooking the beach, and comes complete with electric stove, lights and hot showers. The second day, **Flea Bay to Stony Bay** (8km; 2hr 30min) is an exposed hike along coastal cliffs, with a seal colony providing lunchtime distraction around the halfway point. The night is spent in one of the huts-cum-cottages in Stony Bay, where there's also a modest family museum, a bath under the stars, a small shop selling bread, tinned food and beer, and a few short tracks exploring the bay. The walk from **Stony Bay to Otanerito Bay** (6km; 2hr) takes care of the third day, with overnight accommodation provided in a farmhouse just 50m from a great swimming beach, run by New Zealand author Fiona Farrell and her partner. The fourth and final day's walk heads inland, from **Otanerito Bay to Mount Vernon Lodge** (10km; 3hr; 600m ascent), passing two waterfalls and providing a last glimpse of the ocean before descending to the calmer waters of Akaroa Harbour.

Round the Mountain Walk (10km; 4hr return) which circumnavigates the hills above Akaroa via the Purple Peak Road – the route is shown on a hand-drawn photocopied map (50¢ from the visitor centre).

For something easier, simply stroll along the waterfront Beach Road towards Glen Bay and the nineteenth-century red-and-white wooden **lighthouse**, which used to stand at Akaroa Head to guide ships into the harbour before being moved to its current location in 1980. Continuing towards Akaroa Head for about fifteen minutes, you'll come to **Red House Bay**, the scene of a bloody massacre in 1830, when the great northern chief Te Rauparaha bribed (with flax) the captain of the British brig *Elizabeth* to conceal Maori warriors about the vessel and invite Te Rauparaha's unsuspecting enemies (led by Temaiharanui) on board, where they were slaughtered. Te Rauparaha and his men then feasted on the victims on the beach.

You can also follow the inland **Onuku Road** (5km one way; 1hr 15min) which takes you to **ONUKU**, where you'll find the **Onuku Marae** and a tiny church, established in 1876–78. Onuku is even quieter than Akaroa: roughly translated, the name means "coming and going though never staying long" – and, sure enough, there's little to keep you here, except maybe more walks and the prospect of a bed for the night at the *Onuku Farm Hostel* (see p.640).

Eating and drinking

With an eager tourist market and its **French heritage**, Akaroa is a very good place to eat, making it popular with people from Christchurch, who think nothing of driving 85km for their evening meal. This does tend to push up prices a little and means that more **expensive** establishments predominate, although there are the usual takeaways and cheaper cafés to fall back on. The reliance on the summer **tourist trade** also means that many places cut back their hours, or even close completely, during winter.

Akaroa Bakery 51 Beach Rd. Excellent fresh-baked bread, plus a small café serving sandwiches, pies, cakes, pizza and bottomless cups of coffee. Daily from early morning to 5pm.
Bully Hayes 57 Beach Rd ☎03/304 7533. Named after a famous local con-man, this place serves reliable kiwi fare, including roast lamb, steaks and seafood (mostly $14–17).
C'est La Vie 33 rue Lavaud ☎03/304 7314. Probably Akaroa's best restaurant: an exceptional, intimate dinner-only establishment with relaxing live music. The fine French cuisine uses organically grown ingredients and fresh seafood, all rounded off with delicate pastries. Main courses

such as canard à l'orange and escargots in herb butter are about $25–30.
Ma Maison 6 rue Balguerie ☎03/304 7658. Classy modern café and restaurant nicely sited on the waterfront with some outside seating and a log fire for those chillier nights. Great espresso, light meals and full dinners (mains around $25) with the usually broad Kiwi range.
Madeira rue Lavaud. Spirited Kiwi pub always jumping at weekends.
Waeckerle's in the *Grand Hotel*, 6 rue Lavaud. Pleasant and reasonably priced lunch and dinner venue, with particularly tasty fish dishes and a few bar snacks. Mains $15–25.

Around Akaroa

Unless you have reached Akaroa by means of the Summit Road, you'll have missed some of the best Banks Peninsula has to offer. Fortunately it is easy enough to drive over the hills to gems such as **Le Bons Bay** and **Okains Bay**, though getting around the twisty roads will take you longer than you'd expect.

Le Bons Bay

As SH75 enters Akaroa from the north, Long Bay Road rises off into the hills giving access to the Summit Road and the verdant **LE BONS BAY**, 20km from Akaroa. It is a small peaceful community with a number of holiday homes ranged behind a gorgeous sandy **beach**, framed on two sides by cliffs, that provides safe swimming. One satisfying way to get here is via the Akaroa–Le Bons Bay walking track which winds up at the *Le Bons Bay Holiday Park*, 15 Valley Rd (☎03/304 8533, ℮lebonsholiday @xtra.co.nz; camping $11, on-site vans & cabins ❷, ensuite units ❸, motels ❹), a fairly run-down but picturesque **campsite** by a stream, with a store and swimming pool.

The only other accommodation in the area is the wonderful family-run *Le Bons Bay* **backpackers** (☎03/304 8582; closed June–Sept; dorms $18, rooms ❷), a cosy 1875 house situated 5km back from the beach, far enough up the bay to provide spectacular views. It is a little inconvenient without your own vehicle, but makes a great place to relax for a few days, lounging on the veranda or in the garden hammock, popping down to the beach to fish or gather shellfish which might be used in the communal evening dinner ($12, and well worth it), or taking long walks down the valley or across the hilltops. Breakfast is free, and you should call to arrange pick-up from Akaroa. The owners also run daily **boat trips** (1hr 30min; $22) to see penguins, dolphins, shags and seals. These are open to all; contact the hostel.

Okains Bay

The next bay north from Le Bons Bay is **OKAINS BAY**, some 20km from Akaroa, a popular holiday and picnic area with a tiny permanent population. No public buses come this far, so those without their own transport will have to use one of the Akaroa mail runs (see p.642). The beach and the placid lagoon formed by the **Opara Stream** are excellent for swimming and boating, but the real reason to visit is a remarkable museum containing one of the best collections of Maori artefacts in the South Island. A former cheese factory on the only road going into the bay now houses the **Okains Bay Maori and Colonial Museum** (daily 10am–5pm; $5), originally amassed by a local collector and very strong on Maori artefacts. Within the same compound, several outbuildings contain the more traditional exhibitions relating to European settlement, including a "slab" stable and cottage – simply constructed from large slabs of totara wood. Among the thought-provoking Maori exhibits are a god stick dating back to 1400, a war canoe from 1867 and various weapons, as well as a valuable *hei tiki* (a pendant with a design based on the human form) recovered in England and brought back to Okains Bay. Beside the Maori exhibition building, there is also a beautiful meeting house (it's *tapu* or sacred, although visitors are allowed to look around it), with fine symbolic figures carved by master craftsman John Rua.

Also on the only road descending to Okains Bay, the very welcoming *Kawatea Farmstay* (T03/304 8621, @kawatea@xtra.co.nz; ⑥) is a century-year-old **homestead** set in lush gardens bordered by 5km of scenic coastline and offering three rooms decorated with native timbers and stained glass. Dinners are available on request ($30). At the end of this road is *Okains Bay Domain* **campsite**, just behind the beach (camping $6), which has a small store with very limited stocks: bring supplies with you.

Pigeon Bay and Port Levy

The two largest bays on the northern side of Banks Peninsula are further west, closer to Lyttelton Harbour and reached by yet more narrow and steep lanes. Neither warrant a special visit though both are of some historical interest: **Pigeon Bay** was an important timber milling and shipbuilding settlement in the nineteenth century when the peninsula had trees; and **Port Levy** once held the largest Maori community in Canterbury. The main reason to come now is to rest up for a couple of days at Port Levy's lovely and historic *Kaihope Cottage* (T03/329 4679, @jhowden@xtra.co.nz; ③), situated on part of a deer and sheep farm, but right by the sea. The two-bedroom cottage sleeps six and is fully self-contained: bring bedding and food.

South to Otago

Heading south from Christchurch both the principal road, SH1, and the rail line forge across the **Canterbury Plains** in an unrelenting straight line, bisecting small service towns catering for the farms on the rich flat land. The **Southern Alps** flank the route to the west and in clear weather provide awesome views. In the main though, it is a monotonous landscape broken only by the broad gravel beds of braided rivers, usually little more than a trickle spanned by kilometre-long bridges, though they can overspill their broad gravely banks after heavy rain. The first of the bridges, the 1.8km-long structure spanning the Rakaia River 58km south of Christchurch, was the longest in the southern hemisphere at the time of its construction in 1939. It leads into the tiny salmon-fishing and sheep-shearing settlement of **Rakaia**, where a minor road called Thompson's Track heads inland to link with SH77, which in turn grants access to Methven, Mount Hutt and Mount Somers (see pp.683–689), on the western fringes of the Canterbury Plains. A further 27km south is the larger though equally quiet settlement of **Ashburton**, where SH77 joins SH1.

As the road (and the parallel rail line) passes the pottery town of **Temuka** and reaches the southern end of the Canterbury Plains, looming hills force it back to the shoreline at **Timaru**, a small city with a busy port. Timaru is also the point where SH8 strikes inland towards Fairlie, Lake Tekapo and Mount Cook. From here on, the trip south is a visual treat, with rolling hills inland and spectacular sea views, and yet another opportunity to cut inland. This time it is SH82 and SH83, which head along opposite banks of the Waitaki River – noted for its excellent whitebait, sea-run trout and quinnat salmon fishing – en route to Omarama, Aoraki Mount Cook and Wanaka.

The coastal highway and railway continue south to the architecturally har-monious city of **Oamaru**, and the unique and fascinating **Moeraki Boulders**. You are also heading into **penguin** country with several opportunities to stop off and spy blue and yellow-eyed penguins. From Moeraki there is little to delay you on your progress toward Dunedin, except maybe the small crossroads town of **Palmerston**, where SH85, "The Pigroot" to **Central Otago**, leaves SH1, providing another opportunity to forsake the coast and follow a histori-cal pathway to the goldfields inland.

Ashburton

The long, thin and stubbornly suburban town of **ASHBURTON** lies 87km southeast of Christchurch, perched on the north bank of the Ashburton River, with an extension, **Tinwald**, across the bridge on the opposite bank. Built on a long defunct ceramics industry and maintained as a service town for the local farms, Ashburton is off the itinerary for most visitors, but if you are heading along SH1 you'll be passing through and may care to stop and examine the smattering of minor sights.

Breaking up the dreary huddle of the town centre the **Ashburton Domain** (daily 8am–dusk), facing West Street, is fringed by stately hundred-year-old European trees and contains expertly manicured gardens and an artificial lake, created from the water race of an old mill. Just north of the Domain is the **Ashford Craft Village**, at 415 West St (daily 9am–4.30pm), which comprises a café, antique shop, the Eastside Gallery, and a massive collection of spinning wheels, looms and accessories, all of which are for sale – though bargains are few.

In the town centre, the **Historic Art Gallery and Museum**, 248 Cameron St (Tues–Fri 10am–4pm, Sat & Sun 1–4pm; donation requested), is a cool and airy place with temporary art exhibitions upstairs. The neat museum has an informative display on braided rivers and the bird life they support, such as the endangered black-fronted tern and the wrybill plover, which breeds only in this region.

The most interesting of the town's other small museums is **The Plains**, in Tinwald Domain just south of town, where there's a **Vintage Railway Museum** (every second Sun of the month 1–5pm; $6; ☎03/308 9621, ⓦwww.plainsrailway.co.nz), and the **Museum of Woodworking and Ornamental Woodturning** (Tues, Thurs, Sat & Sun 10am–4pm; ☎03/308 6611; $3). Housed in a woodturner's workshop, it contains a substantial collection of antique ornamental lathes, with plenty of intricately turned pieces on display.

Practicalities

InterCity and assorted shuttle **buses** pause outside the **visitor centre**, corner of East Street and Burnett Street (Mon–Fri 9am–5.30pm, Sat 10am–3pm, Sun 10am–1pm; ☎03/308 1064, ⓔinfocentre@ashburton.co.nz;), which stocks a local map ($0.50) and timetable information for local buses and shuttles. The **post office**, 390–408 East St (☎03/308 3184), has poste restante facilities.

Ashburton has an adequate range of **accommodation**, with many places either clustered at the south end of East Street, or across the river in Tinwald. In winter many cater to skiers from Mount Hutt just a short drive away. **Campers** and budget travellers should head for *Coronation Park*, 780 East St, adjacent to the Domain (☎03/308 6603; tents $11, dorms ❶, on-site vans & units ❷–❹), though you might prefer the relative comforts of the nearby *Academy Lodge Motel*, 782 East St (☎03/308 5503; ❹), or the more homely environment of the pretty and secluded *Carradale Farmstay*, Ferriman's Rd, Lagmhor, 8km west of Tinwald (☎03/308 6577, ⓦwww.ashburton.co.nz/carradale; ❺), which presents the opportunity to join in farm activities and offers dinner by arrangement ($25).

Ashburton has a few decent **places to eat**. For good coffee, lunches and light evening meals, the place to go is *Kelly's Café and Bar* on East Street, though later on you might be tempted by *Tuscany*, opposite the visitor centre, a café/bar offering reasonably priced snacks and meals as well as booze and coffee (daily 11.30am–10pm). Around the corner from *Tuscany*, at 264 Burnett St, lies *Lunch*, a stylish and quite pricey daytime-only place producing very tasty dishes and great coffee.

Temuka

The small town of **TEMUKA**, 60km south of Ashburton on SH1, takes its name from the Maori for "fierce oven", and a large number of Maori earth ovens have been found in the area. It continues to live up to its reputation today with the presence of kilns for the ceramic factories built by immigrants from the "Potteries" area around Stoke-on-Trent in England. Within New Zealand, Temuka has become synonymous with **pottery**, and you can visit the Temuka Homeware shop (Mon–Fri 9am–5.30pm, Sat & Sun 10am–4pm) on SH1 at the junction of Domain Avenue. Once a byword for dowdy patterns and colours, they've smartened their image in recent years, and if you are inspired enough to want to look around the factory, make sure you are here for the hour-long **factory tour** (☎03/615 9551 for information; Wed 1.30pm; free).

Across Dominion Avenue you'll find the old court house containing the **Temuka Museum** (Oct–June Fri–Sun 2–4pm, otherwise enquire at the library; donation requested) which has a fair bit on the pottery industry but, oddly, nothing on Temuka's favourite son, aviator **Richard Pearse** – locally held to be the first man to achieve powered flight in 1902, some months in advance of the Wright brothers. Pearse's plane was technically far ahead of that of his rivals, but Pearse himself did not believe his first powered flight was sufficiently controlled or sustained to justify his townsfolk's claim. He managed a rather desperate 100m, followed by an ignominious plunge into gorse bushes. He was a lifelong tinkerer and inventor, although the true gauge of Pearse's genius was his idea for an aircraft that could fly and hover like a modern Harrier jump jet. There's a memorial to Pearse at the site of the legendary flight, about 13km from Temuka on the way to Waitohi; and further reminders of his achievements in the South Canterbury Museum at Timaru (see p.651).

Practicalities

Most buses will drop off and pick up in Temuka, and onward travel can be arranged at the **visitor centre**, in the library at 72 King St (Mon–Thurs 9am–5.30pm, Fri 9am–8pm; ☎03/615 9537, ✉timlibrary@xtra.co.nz). There is really little reason not to continue on to Timaru or beyond, but you'll find **accommodation** at the clean and comfortable *Benny's Gateway Motel*, 54 King St (☎03/615 7119; ❹), or the *Temuka Holiday Park*, 1 Ferguson Drive (☎03/615 7241; camping $9, cabins ❷), a spacious, well-looked-after site in the Domain, five minutes' walk from King Street.

There are a number of **pubs** and bars along King Street and one or two **restaurants**, but none of them beats the friendly *Benny's* **café/bar** at no. 134 (daily 11.30am–2pm & 5.30pm–late), which has good coffee, cheap and imaginative food including vegetarian options, plus wine and a tempting dessert menu.

Timaru

The small port city of **TIMARU**, 18km south of Temuka, is one of the South Island's larger provincial centres, weighing in with 28,000 residents. At the end of a straight and flat two-hour drive from Christchurch, the city's gently rolling hills mark a subtle change and provide the setting for an austere streetscape partly built of volcanic "bluestone" – the local council insisted on stone and brick constructions after a devastating fire in 1868. With the possible exceptions of the **Aigantighe Art Gallery** and the **South Canterbury Museum**, there is no vastly compelling reason to stop here; though if you are looking to rest up somewhere pleasant that doesn't have much in the way of tempting demands on your cash supply, then you may just have found your spot.

The name Timaru comes from *Te Maru*, Maori for "place of shelter", as it provided the only haven for *waka* paddling between Banks Peninsula and Oamaru. In 1837 European settlement was initiated by Joseph Price, who set up a **whaling** station south of the present city at Patiti Point. A large part of today's commercial and pastoral development was initiated by Yorkshiremen **George and Robert Rhodes**, who established the first cattle station on the South Island in 1839 and founded Rhodes Town not long after, just north of the existing settlement of Government Town. The towns gradually grew together and merged to form Timaru. Despite an influx of European migrants

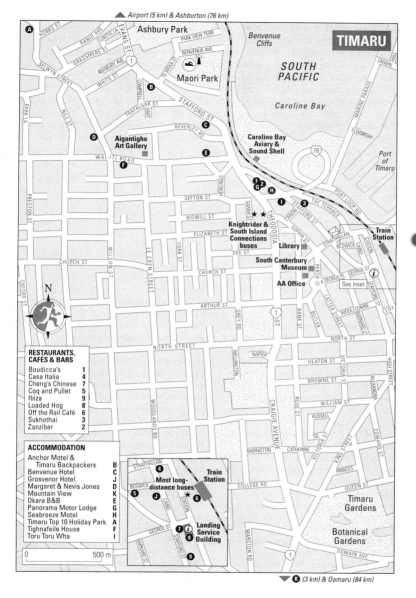

Airport (5 km) & Ashburton (76 km)

Ashbury Park

Benvenue Cliffs

TIMARU

SOUTH PACIFIC

Maori Park

Caroline Bay

Aigantighe Art Gallery

Caroline Bay Aviary & Sound Shell

Port of Timaru

Knightrider & South Island Connections buses

Library

South Canterbury Museum

AA Office

Train Station

See inset

N

RESTAURANTS, CAFES & BARS

Boudicca's	1
Casa Italia	4
Cheng's Chinese	7
Coq and Pullet	5
Ibiza	9
Loaded Hog	8
Off the Rail Café	6
Sukhothai	3
Zanzibar	2

ACCOMMODATION

Anchor Motel & Timaru Backpackers	B
Benvenue Hotel	C
Grosvenor Hotel	J
Margaret & Nevis Jones	D
Mountain View	K
Okare B&B	E
Panorama Motor Lodge	G
Seabreeze Motel	H
Timaru Top 10 Holiday Park	A
Tighnafeile House	F
Toru Toru Wha	I

Strathallan

Most long-distance buses

Train Station

Landing Service Building

College Rd

Timaru Gardens

Botanical Gardens

0   500 m

K (3 km) & Oamaru (84 km)

aboard the *Strathallan* in 1859, it was some years before a safe harbour was established on the rocky coast. A welcome by-product of the land reclamation that created the harbour in 1877 was the fine sandy beach of Caroline Bay. For a time, Timaru became a popular seaside resort, and its annual **summer carnival**, starting on Christmas Eve and running for over two weeks, is still well worth dropping in on.

Arrival and information

Timaru's **airport** (with daily flights to Wellington) is just 7km north of town; a $10 shuttle meets arrivals. The **train station** on Station Street in the centre of the city is the principal drop-off and pick-up point for all trains and most buses; Knightrider and South Island Connections drop off outside Caroline Bay Burger King on Sarah Street). For bus and train tickets go to the **visitor centre**, 2 George St (Mon–Fri 8.30am–5pm, Sat & Sun 10am–3pm; ☎03/688 6163, ⊛www.southisland.org.nz), which provides free maps of South Canterbury and Timaru, and a free booklet of historic walks about town. You probably won't need Timaru's **local bus service**, which is run by CRC (☎03/688 6497), with a flat rate of $1 for all journeys around the city and suburbs, including one transfer.

Accommodation

There's is a wide range of **accommodation**, generally in good supply except for the Christmas to mid-January period when you should book well in advance. Most places are fairly central, with motels lining Stafford Street to the north and B&Bs more widely distributed.

Anchor Motel & Timaru Backpackers 42–44 Evans St ☎03/684 5067, ⊜rotty@quicksilver.net.nz. Extremely friendly and central, if slightly run-down, 1960s two-storey building with off-street parking and ten comfortable units, some of which get put to use as part of *Timaru Backpackers*, an associate YHA run jointly with the *Anchor* to provide highly flexible accommodation – dorms, motel units and a variety of double and single rooms – along with a nice veranda that catches the afternoon sun. Free tea and coffee. Dorms ❶, rooms ❷, motel units ❸

Benvenue Hotel 16–22 Evans St ☎03/688 049 & 0800/104 049, ⊜benvenue@voyager.co.nz. Set on a hill with a good view of the bay and the town, this hotel has refurbished rooms, a bar, restaurant and heated indoor pool and spa. ❺

Grosvenor Hotel 26 Cains Terrace ☎03/688 3129 & 0800/106 102, ⊜grosvenortimaru@xtra.co.nz. Ordinary business hotel in an imposing 1875 building once known as the "Grand Old Lady of the South". The public areas are nice but the rooms are nothing special, though they come with TV, phone, mini bar and breakfast. ❺

Margaret & Nevis Jones 16 Selwyn St ☎ & ☎03/688 1400. Homestay in a lovely late-1920s house with lush gardens and its own grass tennis court. Rooms are either en suite or have private facilities, it is only fifteen minutes' walk from town and they pick up and drop off. ❺

Mountain View 200m along Talbots Rd off SH1, 3km south of Timaru ☎03/688 1070, ☎688 1069, ⊛www.bnb.co.nz/mountainview. Small farm B&B offering homely rooms with private bathrooms and a cooked breakfast. Dinner by arrangement ($25); venison a speciality. ❹

Okare B&B 11 Wai-iti Rd ☎03/688 0316, ⊛www.okare.co.nz. Relaxed and comfortable, boutique B&B run by a lovely couple who offer three rooms (one with en-suite) in their spacious 1909 mini mansion, with heart rimu floors, a balcony and excellent breakfasts. ❺

Panorama Motor Lodge 52 The Bay Hill ☎03/688 0097, ⊛www.panorama.net.nz. Excellent, striking and hospitable motel with big spacious units, and all the usual facilities plus a sauna, spa baths, gym and off-street parking, plus great views over Caroline Bay. ❺

Seabreeze Motel 28 The Bay Hill ☎0800/443 443, ⊜seabreezetim@xtra.co.nz. Comfortable, well-appointed and quiet motel close to town, Caroline Bay and a couple of good restaurants. ❺

Tighnafeile House 62 Wai-iti Road ☎03/684 3333, ⊛www.taighnafeile.com. Boutique lodge in a grand 1911 house close to the art gallery. Rooms ($295) are all sumptuously decorated – even the garage has a carpet. ❾

Timaru Top 10 Holiday Park 8 Glen St ☎03/684 7690 & 0800/242 121, ⊛www.timaruholidaypark .co.nz. Slightly pricey, high-standard holiday park close to the golf course and within walking distance of Maori Park. Camping $11, cabins & kitchen cabin $46, motel units ❹ _

Toru Toru Wha 334 Stafford St ☎03/684 4729, ⊛www.334onstafford.co.nz. Appealing, recently modernized combined hostel and hotel right in the heart of town and close to Caroline Bay. Accommodation ranges from dorms through ensuite doubles with TV and dataport; they even have their own art gallery and coffee shop on the ground floor. Dorms ❶, doubles ❷, ensuites ❸, deluxe ❺

The City

Timaru undulates over low hills, all roads eventually bringing you down to the reclaimed land of the harbour and the park-backed golden sweep of Caroline Bay, a good spot for the kids even if the beach is overlooked by the port. Nearby, at the southern end of Stafford Street, is the central business district with the train station and the visitor centre, now in part of the 1870 Landing Service Building. It was built of volcanic "bluestone" and originally used to store goods unloaded from the small boats that were winched up onto a shingle beach in front, roughly where the railway lines are now. The building is shared by *The Loaded Hog* restaurant and bar (see p.652), and hosts occasional historic maritime displays, accessible through the visitor centre.

A couple of hundred metres uphill, the **South Canterbury Museum**, Perth St (Tues–Fri 10am–4.30pm, Sat & Sun 1.30–4.30pm; donation appreciated; Ⓦwww.timaru.govt.nz), displays well-labelled local Maori artefacts, some good examples of **scrimshaw** (intricate etchings on whale teeth and bone) and other memorabilia from the whaling station that occupied Patiti Point in the late 1830s and early 1840s. Look out, too, for the wonderful **E.P. Seally collection** – drawers crammed full of butterflies, moths, eggs, minerals and rare colourful shells. A nineteenth-century naturalist, Seally collected hundreds of butterflies and moths from all over the world, each one conscientiously labelled, including the *Morpho Cypris*, a beautiful blue from Brazil; the smaller electric-aquamarine *Morpho Adonis*; and the (now sadly silent) yodelling cicada. Hanging over the main hall of the museum, and best viewed from the first-floor balcony, is a reconstruction of the 1902 **aircraft** used by Richard Pearse in his attempt to notch up the first powered flight in the world (see p.648).

Probably the best way to pass an hour or two is to visit the **Aigantighe Art Gallery**, 49 Wai-iti Rd (Tues–Fri 10am–4pm, Sat & Sun noon–4pm; donation appreciated; ☎03/688 4424), constructed around a venerable Timaru house known as Aigantighe (Gaelic for "at home") in the days before it became a gallery. Original features of the house have been preserved and provide a suitable setting for a rotating permanent collection founded on donations and bequests from Timaru's wealthier families – some works date back to the seventeenth century. A vigorous purchasing policy has produced an enviable collection of works by South Canterbury artists including relatively minor, but often intimate and personal, works by native son Colin McCahon. Other artists to look out for are Frances Hodgkins, and the prolific Austen Deans, whose luminous landscapes interpret the local countryside as well as any.

In 1990 Kiwi, Japanese and Zimbabwean sculptors came here as part of a symposium and carved thirteen works from soft Mount Somers stone (see p.687). These have weathered nicely and now sit harmoniously in the gallery's small but impressive **sculpture garden**, a great place for a picnic (bring your own). Look particularly for *Baboon*, nearest the house, carved with power tools by a Zimbabwean who had only ever hand carved. The nodules in the animal's hand represent the seeds of knowledge gained by the experience. Call the gallery for details of temporary exhibitions.

Hector's dolphins have always swum around off the coast at Timaru and Timaru Marine Cruises (☎03/686 9365; $40) have permission to run **dolphin watching** trips. They're run by the harbour master, who fits in the trips around his other duties, so be flexible. On a fine day, you could also spend a quiet hour ambling around the **Botanical Gardens**, Queen Street (daily 8am–dusk; free), or strolling along the low cliffs north of Caroline Bay past the wooden 1878 **Blackett's Lighthouse** to Dashing Rocks. Wet days are better spent on the free ninety-minute tour and sampling at the **DB Brewery**, Sheffield Street,

CHRISTCHURCH AND SOUTH TO OTAGO | Timaru

Rock art

Around five hundred years ago, Maori moa hunters visited the South Canterbury and North Otago coastal plain, leaving a record of their sojourn on the walls and ceilings of open-sided limestone rock shelters. There are more than three hundred **rock drawings** around Timaru, Geraldine and Fairlie: the faded charcoal and red ochre drawings depict a variety of stylized human, bird and mythological figures and patterns. Some of the best cave drawings can be seen in the region's museums (notably the North Otago Museum in Oamaru, see p.656). Those remaining in situ are often hard to make out (and require your own wheels), but the best examples are at Risk Shelter, Acacia Downs, Blackler's Cave and Hazelburn Shelter (15–20km northwest of Timaru), all marked on the *Pleasant Point Ward Map* available from the Timaru visitor centre. The visitor centre can also organise access across **private land** to the sites.

Washdyke, 2km north of town on SH1 (Mon–Thurs 10.30am; free; no sandals; ☎03/688 2059).

Finally, for those with a desire to see a traditional craft revived in a truly modern and totally eccentric way drive 15km northwest to the town of Pleasant Point and visit **The Artisan**, 5 Maitland St, close to the historic railway (daily 10am–5pm; ⓦ www.iron.co.nz), the shop and forge of bare-foot blacksmith, Gareth James. He'll show you around his forge ($5) and often make something you can buy, or there's plenty of ready-made handiwork to choose from in his gallery.

Eating, drinking and entertainment

Timaru's **restaurants**, though numerous, don't offer great variety in terms of decor or ambitious cuisine, but you'll find the usual cache of fish-and-chip shops, as well as a couple of Italian and Asian eateries: the best of the bunch are listed below.

Things hot up in Timaru for the three post-Christmas weeks of the **summer carnival** (ⓦ www.carolinebay.org.nz) when there's a circus, a fair, and free concerts in Caroline Bay. Otherwise, Timaru is a pretty quiet place; if there is anything going on in town, then the **entertainment** listings in the daily *Timaru Herald* (particularly the Friday and Saturday editions) will provide details. You can catch first-run Hollywood **movies** at Movie Max 3, corner of Canon and Sophia streets (☎03/684 6987).

Boudicca's 64 The Bay Hill. Good-quality, stylish café/bar specializing in Middle Eastern and Kiwi cuisine. A kebab, salad and a variety of sauces, including delicious sweet chilli, will set you back less than $10, and there's felafel and other meat-free options, as well as mouth-watering, home-made desserts, fresh fish and big steaks. Daily for lunch and dinner.

Casa Italia 2 Strathallan St ☎03/684 5528. Located in the atmospheric Victorian Customs House, this is probably Timaru's finest restaurant. The Italian chef reliably turns out authentic cuisine with pasta made on the premises ($14 & $21 portions), pizza ($19) and *segundi piatti* around the $25–30 mark. Leave room for the chocolate mousse ($10). Evenings daily.

Cheng's Chinese 12 George St. Excellent set menus, good fish dishes, and great chow mein, with main meals hovering in the $12–21 range. Open daily for lunch and dinner.

Coq and Pullet 209 Stafford St. Daytime café and deli opening early for weekday breakfast but only lunches at weekends, and offering panini, gourmet pies and reasonable coffee.

Ibiza 129 Stafford St, in the old national bank. Not much of a place but what passes for a dance club in these parts (Wed–Sun), with a late licence, table football and local and visiting DJs.

Loaded Hog 2 George St. Former brewpub that now gets its supply from a sister operation in Christchurch, this cavernous establishment occupies a wonderful stone grain store. The blackboard menu features $6 lunch specials and mains such as their famous beer-battered fish, using the Hog's Weiss beer ($12.50). Touring bands tend to play here (usually Thurs–Sun till 3am).

Off the Rails Café 22 Station St, in the train station. Fun daytime café in the 1967 former waiting room, with old booths, a jukebox with sixties tunes, white leather sofa and a selection of panini, soups, pasta and espresso all at modest prices. Try the Kiwi classic "pea, pie and pud" and Timaru's

innovative cuboid chocolate éclair called an "E Square". They also have Internet access and rent bikes.

Sukhothai 303 Stafford St ℡03/688 4843. Good Thai restaurant serving all your favourites (mostly around $16) plus $9 lunch specials.

Zanzibar 56 The Bay Hill. Bustling, modern bar and restaurant with good views over the port and Caroline Bay, serving hearty helpings ranging from Thai fish cakes ($15) to beer-battered blue cod ($14).

Listings

Automobile Association 26 Church St ℡03/688 4189.

Bike rental The Cyclery, 98 Stafford St (℡03/688 8892), rents bikes from $20 a day, and the *Off the Rails Café* has runabouts for the same price.

Buses Bus companies operating Timaru–Christchurch, Timaru–Dunedin and Timaru–Twizel routes include Atomic Shuttles (℡03/322 8883); Budget Shuttles (℡021/344 780; also run an airport service for $10); Catch-a-bus (℡03/489 4641); and South Island Connections (℡03/366 6633).

Car rental Rental Vehicles, 6 Sefton St ℡03/684 7179.

Internet access At the library and at *Off the Rails Café* (see above).

Library Timaru District Library, Sophia St (Mon, Wed & Fri 9am–8pm, Tues & Thurs 9am–6pm, Sat 10am–1pm, Sun 1–4pm).

Medical treatment Try the Medical Clinic, 5 Dee St (weekdays 24hr, Sat & Sun 9am–noon, 4–6pm; ℡03/684 8209) for an after-hours doctor. Timaru Hospital is on Queen St (℡03/684 4000).

Pharmacies Ashbury Pharmacy, Northtown Mall 2km north of the centre on SH1 (daily 9am–7pm; ℡03/688 9736).

Post office The post office in Books and More, 19 Strathallan St (℡03/686 6040), has poste restante facilities.

Taxis Budget (℡03/688 8779) and Timaru Taxis (℡03/688 8899) both offer a 24hr service.

Oamaru and around

The former port town of **OAMARU**, 85km south of Timaru on SH1, is one of New Zealand's more alluring (and undersold) provincial cities, making it a relaxed place to spend a day or two. Perhaps its most immediate appeal is the presence of two **penguin colonies** on the outskirts of town, which provide an unmissable opportunity to observe both the diminutive blue penguins and their larger yellow-eyed cousins. The town itself has attractions too, not least the well-preserved core of nineteenth-century buildings of its central **Historic District**, built of the distinctive cream-coloured local limestone, which earned Oamaru the title "The Whitestone City". At the turn of the twentieth century it had a reputation as being the most attractive city in the South Island, and with the ongoing restoration it may well regain that status. A handful of the grand edifices have scrubbed up nicely and more are scheduled for treatment, so it only seems a matter of time before the existing nub of cafés and chi-chi galleries will spread to the renovated buildings.

The limestone outcrops throughout the area once provided shelter for Maori and later the raw material for ambitious European builders. As a commercial centre for goldrush prospectors, and shored up by quarrying, timber and farming industries, Oamaru grew in wealth, giving shape to its prosperity in the elegant stone buildings that today grace the town centre. The port opened for **migration** in 1874, with three hundred ships arriving that year and a further

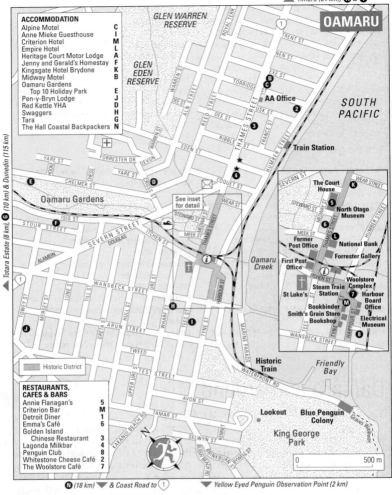

ACCOMMODATION
Alpine Motel	C
Anne Mieke Guesthouse	I
Criterion Hotel	M
Empire Hotel	L
Heritage Court Motor Lodge	A
Jenny and Gerald's Homestay	F
Kingsgate Hotel Brydone	K
Midway Motel	B
Oamaru Gardens	
Top 10 Holiday Park	E
Pen-y-Bryn Lodge	J
Red Kettle YHA	D
Swaggers	H
Tara	G
The Hall Coastal Backpackers	N

GLEN WARREN RESERVE

GLEN EDEN RESERVE

SOUTH PACIFIC

AA Office

Train Station

Oamaru Gardens

See inset for detail

Oamaru Creek

Historic District

▲ Totara Estate (8 km), **Ⓖ** (10 km) & Dunedin (115 km)

The Court House
North Otago Museum
Former Post Office
National Bank
First Post Office
Forrester Gallery
St Luke's
Steam Train Station
Woolstore Complex
Harbour Board Office
Bookbinder
Smith's Grain Store Bookshop
Electrical Museum

Historic Train

Friendly Bay

Lookout
Blue Penguin Colony

King George Park

Graves Walkway

0 — 500 m

RESTAURANTS, CAFÉS & BARS
Annie Flanagan's	5
Criterion Bar	M
Detroit Diner	1
Emma's Café	6
Golden Island	
Chinese Restaurant	3
Lagonda Milkbar	4
Penguin Club	2
Whitestone Cheese Café	2
The Woolstore Café	7

❶ (18 km) ▼ & Coast Road to ①   ▼ Yellow Eyed Penguin Observation Point (2 km)

four hundred between 1876 and 1878, although many foundered on the hostile coastline and wrecks littered the late nineteenth-century shore. After this boom period Oamaru's fortunes declined, and it's only in recent years that the town has begun to come alive again.

The writer Janet Frame (see Contexts, p.983) spent some of her childhood in Oamaru and lived here on and off in her later years. Fans of her work may want to follow the **Janet Frame Trail** (a leaflet is available from the visitor centre, see opposite) which concentrates on locations used in varying degrees of disguise in her books – the former subscription library in the Athenaeum that featured in *Faces In The Water*, or the rubbish dump that formed the symbolic centre of *Owls Do Cry* – although such sights are hardly essential for the uncommitted. Frame's death in early 2004 may well focus more attention on her legacy.

Arrival and information

Buses drop off at the corner of Eden and Thames streets, and there's a **train station** just northeast of the centre on Humber Street. There are currently no passenger services, though at the time of writing there were rumours of a daily Christchurch to Dunedin run. You can walk just about everywhere from here, but if you have heavy bags you can always call for a **taxi** (℡ 03/434 1234).

The **visitor centre**, 1 Thames St (Nov–Easter Mon–Fri 9am–6pm, Sat & Sun 10am–5pm; Easter–Oct Mon–Fri 9am–5pm, Sat & Sun 10am–4pm; ℡ 03/434 1656, ⓦ www.tourismwaitaki.co.nz), less than ten minutes' walk from the bus stop, has useful free leaflets including the *Janet Frame Trail* and *Historic Oamaru*, which focuses on the Historic District.

If you can manage it, the times to be here are from November to January when penguins are in greatest numbers, or for the **Victorian Heritage Celebrations** over the third weekend in November when the streets of the historic district become a race track for penny-farthings, cheered on by local residents in Victorian attire and accompanied by a fair.

Accommodation

Most of the accommodation is on, or near, Thames Street, though some very pleasant B&Bs and homestays are further out. Finding a place is seldom difficult though the usual recommendation to book ahead from December to February still applies.

Hotels and motels

Alpine Motel 285 Thames St ℡ 03/434 5038 & 0800/272 710, ⓔ alpine.motel.oamaru@xtra.co.nz. Modern building close to the town centre, with ten spacious studio units, some with full kitchens. ❹

Criterion Hotel 3 Tyne St ℡ 03/434 6247, ⓦ www.criterion.net.nz. Charming Victorian styled boutique B&B in a 1877 building right in the historic district. A hearty breakfast is included. Shared bath ❻, ensuite ❼

Heritage Court Motor Lodge 346 Thames St ℡ 03/437 2200 & 0800/732 200, ⓦ www .heritagecourtlodge.com. Newish, upmarket motel that's clean and spacious, and has comfortable units with cooking facilities and in-house video. ❹

Kingsgate Hotel Brydone 115 Thames St ℡ 03/434 0011 & 0800/279 366, ⓔ oamaru@kingsgatehotels.co.nz. Modernized business hotel in a nice Oamaru stone with an ornate Italian facade, dating from 1880. All rooms have phone and Sky TV. ❺

Midway Motel 289 Thames St t03/434 5388 & 0800/447 744. Opposite the fire station and close to the centre of town, this budget establishment has units with full cooking facilities. ❹

B&Bs and homestays

Anne Mieke Guesthouse 47 Tees St ℡ 03/434 8051, ⓔ anne.mieke@xtra.co.nz. A large suburban house offering B&B close to the town centre and the blue penguin viewing area. Each room has its own washbasin, bathrooms are shared and the rooms at the back of the house have views of the bay. ❹

Jenny and Gerald's Homestay 11 Stour St ℡ 03/434 9628, ⓔ geraldlb@clear.net.nz. About twenty minutes' walk from the bus stop, this attractive 1920s house contains an ornate staircase, a pleasant double with private facilities, and two singles, one with private, the other shared, facilities. Jenny and Gerald are very friendly and share an interest in local history, as well as running Slightly Foxed, a secondhand bookshop. Dinner ($35) by arrangement. ❻

Pen-y-Bryn Lodge 41 Towey St ℡ 03/434 7939, ⓦ www.penybryn.co.nz. One of the finer lodges in these parts; a splendid restored Victorian home on a hill overlooking the town, graced with hand-crafted floor-to-ceiling fireplaces, a billiard room, richly carved bookcases and a Florentine-style dining room of rimu timber and English oak. The large and luxurious rooms all have private facilities. Rates are $740 a double (May–Sept $590) and include a sumptuous four-course meal and breakfast. ❾

Tara Springhill Rd ℡ 03/434 8187, ⓦ www .tarahomestay.co.nz. Comfortable and welcoming rural homestay with just one twin room with a private bathroom 8km west of town set among rose gardens, native trees and farmland where alpacas and donkeys are kept. Breakfast includes free-range eggs and homemade bread, and there's dinner by arrangement ($30), often roast. ❺

Hostels and campsites

Empire Hotel 13 Thames St ☎ 03/434 3446, ⓔ empirehotel@hotmail.com. Well organized hostel in a restored 1867 heritage building with free Internet, free bikes, separate TV lounge, and excellent-value Sunday roast dinners. Dorms ❶, rooms ❷

The Hall Coastal Backpackers All Day Bay, 18km south of Oamaru near Kakanui ☎ 03/439 5411, ⓦ www.coastalbackpackers.co.nz. Hugely relaxing rural backpackers well off the beaten track but within easy walk of a good beach and some coastal wetlands. Doubles and dorms are in a couple of separate buildings each with lounge

and log-burning stove, and there's an on-site restaurant and bar. There's free laundry, bikes and bodyboards. Dorms ❶, rooms ❷

Oamaru Gardens Top 10 Holiday Park Chelmer St ☎ 03/434 7666 & 0800/280 202, ⓦ www .topparks.co.nz. In a lovely sheltered setting, this site offers pitches, tourist flats and cabins. Camping $10, cabins, kitchen cabins & units ❷–❸

Red Kettle YHA cnr Reed St & Cross St ☎ 03/434 5008, ⓔ yha.oamaru@yha.org.nz. Small, pleasant and well-managed hostel close to the town centre with small dorms, a couple of twin-bunk rooms and a couple of twins. Dorms $18, rooms ❷

Swaggers 25 Wansbeck St ☎ 03/434 9999, ⓔ swaggers@es.co.nz. Small, homely and bargain hostel in a suburban house with twins, four-shares and one five-bunk dorm. Dorms ❶, rooms ❷

The town

Thames Street and the knot of streets around Tyne, Itchen and Harbour streets define Oamaru's **Historic District**, a dense cluster of grand civic and mercantile buildings that sets the town centre apart from any other in the land. The key is Oamaru stone, which hardens with exposure to the elements but, when freshly quarried, is what is known in the trade as a "free stone", easily cut and worked with conventional metal hand tools. While keeping the prevailing Neoclassical fashion firmly in mind, the architects' imaginations ran riot, and the craftsmen were given free rein to produce deeply fluted pilasters, finely detailed pediments and elegant Corinthian pillars topped with veritable forests of acanthus leaves. Oamaru was given much of its character by architect R.A. Lawson and by the firm Forrester and Lemon who together produced most of the more accomplished buildings between 1871 and 1883. Incidentally, Oamaru stone is still used in modern buildings – witness the Waitaki Aquatic Centre in Takaro Park – and enthusiasts can visit its source at the **Parkside Quarry**, 7km west of town, which has ad hoc tours (around $5 per person depending on numbers; ☎ 03/433 1134, ⓦ www.oamarustone.co.nz).

Along Thames Street

The majority of civic buildings are along Thames Street. The first of the nineteenth-century edifices to command attention is the Courthouse, an elegant, classically proportioned Palladian building showing the same Forrester and Lemon hand as the adjacent Athenaeum building, that served as a subscription library before providing a home for the **North Otago Museum** (Mon–Fri 1–4.30pm, Sat 10am–1pm; free). This absorbing collection documents all aspects of North Otago life focusing on the origin of Oamaru stone and its use in the town, along with the town's role as a thriving port. The Former Post Office, a few steps further along Thames Street, originally came without the tower, which was added by the architect's son, Thomas Forrester, in 1903. This building replaced the adjacent 1864 First Post Office, which predates all the other whitestone work and is the town's only remaining example of the work of W.H. Clayton, whose simple Italianate design houses a restaurant and bar. Directly opposite the one-time post offices are two of Lawson's buildings: the imposing **National Bank** has perhaps the purest Neoclassical facade in town; while its grander neighbour now operates as the **Forrester Gallery** (Mon–Fri

10.30am–4.30pm, Sat 10.30am–1pm, Sun 1–4.30pm; donations welcome), which features touring exhibitions of contemporary and traditional art, alongside an extensive permanent collection of works by New Zealand artists.

Continuing along Thames Street, its junction with Itchen Street is dominated by **St Luke's Anglican Church**, topped by its looming 39-metre spire. The beautiful dark-wood interior boasts an 1876 Conacher pipe organ and three locally made stained-glass windows (on the left as you face the altar), depicting Christ flanked by saints Luke and Paul.

Tyne–Harbour Street Historic Precinct

Continuing towards the waterfront you enter Oamaru's original commercial quarter, again built of Whitestone and often flamboyant considering the original mercantile purpose of the buildings. It is quickly becoming the place to hang out, perhaps grabbing a coffee or a beer in between browsing the bookstore, art galleries and minor museums.

Follow Itchen Street east and round as you the corner into Tyne Street you'll spot the **Woolstore Complex**, 1 Tyne St, complete with the *Woolstore Café*, the **Oamaru Auto Collection** (daily 10am–4pm; $4), with its array of ancient and not-so-old vehicles, and upstairs, the Market Promenade where a small market is held every Sunday (10am–4pm). The Italianate-styled *Criterion Hotel*, 3 Tyne St, has a quaint bar serving fine ale and comfy rooms upstairs (see p.655).

Continuing a few steps along Tyne Street, the old **Union Offices**, at #7, is a traditional bookbinder's workshop (Mon–Fri 2–6pm; free; ℡03/434 9277), where you can watch fine book binding and repair work and see examples of old printing and letterpress machines. Next door, the elegant **Smiths Grain Store**, built in 1881 by stonemason James Johnson, now houses the **Grain Store Gallery**, usually full of challenging works. Yet further along, *Slightly Foxed*, 11 Tyne St, offers a great array of secondhand and classic **books**.

Harbour Street runs parallel to Tyne Street and is lined by more rejuvenated mercantile buildings. The 1876 Venetian Renaissance-style **Harbour Board Office** was one of the first public buildings designed by the prolific Forrester and Lemon and is now an art gallery. The adjacent **North Otago Electrical Museum**, Harbour St (Mon–Fri 10am–4pm, Sun noon–4pm; $2) is of nostalgic and passing interest, but you should press along Harbour Street to see the striking Loan and Mercantile Warehouse which, when it was built in 1882, was the largest grain store in New Zealand. Look out for the ornamental rope design garlanding the second storey.

On weekends and public holidays you can gaze at the backs of some of these buildings from the **Oamaru Historic Steam Train** (every 30min 11am–4pm; $5 return; ℡03/434 5634), if it is working, which it does for most of the summer and when the volunteers can get round to repairing it in the winter, from a platform beside the visitor centre on Itchen Street a few hundred metres along the waterfront. The engines and carriages have been lovingly restored by a friendly bunch of fanatics, who also care for the blue penguins that nest in the engine shed at the end of the line.

The Oamaru Gardens

Five minutes' walk west of Thames Street along either Severn Street or Itchen Street lies the manicured natural beauty of the **Oamaru Gardens** (daily dawn–dusk, glasshouses 9am–4pm; free). These are among the most stunning gardens in New Zealand, dating back to 1876 and indicative of the wealth the town once enjoyed. The main Severn Street entrance leads to the spectacular Craig Fountain, built from Italian marble and surrounded by packed flowerbeds. Further on is the hundred-year-old Victorian summerhouse, full of bright blooms from around the world, with an extensive collection of cacti in a nearby purpose-built glasshouse. Flanking Oamaru Creek as it flows through the gardens are a rhododendron dell and two large ponds, while a splendid red Japanese bridge spans the creek to reach the Chinese and Fragrant Gardens.

The penguin colonies

Oamaru is unique in having both yellow-eyed and blue **penguin colonies** within walking distance of the town centre. It is usually possible to see both colonies in one evening, since the yellow-eyes tend to come ashore earlier than the blues, but check at the visitor centre for expected arrival times. Penguins are timid creatures and easily distressed, so keep quiet and still; and do not encroach within ten metres of the birds. Once disturbed, the penguins may not return to their nests for several hours, even if they have chicks to feed.

First up, about fifteen minutes' walk southeast of the town centre along Waterfront Road, is the **Blue Penguin Colony** (best visited just before dusk but check for exact times at the visitor centre; $12.50, kids under 16 free). At the visitor centre there's a chance to see an infra-red 24-hour monitor in one of the nest boxes and videos on blue penguins before being deprived of your cameras and videos and led out to the 350-seat grandstand. Come during the breeding season (June–Dec) and you'll see chicks – and hear them calling to their parents out at sea, hunting for food. When the parents return around dusk, travelling in groups (known as rafts), they climb the steep harbour banks and cross in front of the grandstand to their nests. Outside the breeding season the penguins indulge in much less to-ing and fro-ing, but provide an engaging spectacle nevertheless. In the peak season (Nov–Jan) you might hope to see a hundred penguins in a night, though this might drop to a dozen or so in March, June and August. It can all be a bit of circus and if you'd prefer a less formalized penguin encounter ask locals about other good spots to see the birds. You won't see as many, but it will be free, though you should still be careful not to disturb the penguins' routine.

The much larger **yellow-eyed penguins** nest in smaller numbers but keep more sociable hours, usually coming ashore in late afternoon or early evening (best Oct–Feb). They mainly arrive on **Bushy Beach**, reached by road 2km along Bushy Beach Road, or on foot via the **Graves Walkway** (closed at the time of writing because of storm damage but due to reopen; 1.25km; 30min each way) which starts just past the blue penguin colony. The path curves round a headland at the end of Oamaru Harbour and continues to a point overlooking the small cove of Boatman's Harbour. This is worth exploring at low tide when **lava pillows** about 50cm in diameter are exposed in the cliff wall. These were formed millions of years ago when molten lava encased hard fossil-bearing limestone, producing a honeycomb effect with each cell defined by a rim of black lava. The walkway ends overlooking Bushy Beach, where a hide enables you to see the yellow-eyed penguins making their way across the beach.

To facilitate penguin watching a couple of people offer tours. Jim Caldwell's 40min **Yellow-eyed Penguin Tour**, sets out from the hide via the Bushy Beach car park in the late afternoon (Oct–Feb; $9, check with the visitor centre for exact time). Jim's been working with the penguins for years and can fill you in on anything you want to know, with the added advantage that he's allowed to take you within about 5m of the birds. To get there you can use the door-to-door **Penguin Express** ($20; ☎03/434 7744, ℮penguinexpress@xtra.co.nz) a bus tour which visits Bushy Beach giving you enough time to join Jim's tour,

Blue Penguins, the smallest of their kind, are found all around the coast of New Zealand, and along the shores of southern Australia, where they are known as fairy penguins. White on their chests and bellies, they have a thick head-to-tail streak along their back in iridescent indigo-blue. Breeding takes place from May to January, and the parents take it in turns to stay with the egg during the 36-day incubation period. The newly hatched chick is protected for the first two or three weeks before both parents go out to sea to meet the increasing demand for food, returning full of krill, squid and crustaceans, which they regurgitate into the chick's mouth. At eight weeks the chicks begin to fledge, but 70 percent will die in the first year; the juveniles that do survive usually return to their birthplace. At the end of the breeding season the birds fatten up before coming ashore to moult: over the next three weeks their feathers are not waterproof enough for them to take to the sea and they lose up to half their bodyweight.

then whips you around town with a bit of commentary and gets you to the blue penguins in time for their arrival.

Eating, drinking and entertainment

Oamaru isn't over-endowed with good places to eat and drink, though you'll do well enough for a night or two, and a range of pockets are catered for. You shouldn't have to stray too far from the central Thames Street to find what you want, though if you're planning an outing to Moeraki Boulders consider dining at *Fleur's Place* (see p.663)

Annie Flanagan's 84 Thames St. An Irish bar Oamaru-style with the usual range of draught Guinness and Kilkenny plus live music most Saturday nights and a pretty decent selection of stews, curries, soups, steaks and sandwiches mostly around the $15–20 mark.

Criterion Bar *Criterion Hotel*, 3 Tyne St. With the tenor of a Victorian English pub there's a long wooden bar some good old-fashioned beer, including London Porter and Emersons traditional ale, plus pork pies, bacon butties, fish and chips and bangers and mash.

Detroit Diner on SH1, next to the Waitaki Truck Stop 4.5km north of the centre. Retro American-style diner serving breakfasts, snacks, grills and scallops for only $15 a plate. Solid and cheap, this place is much favoured by truckies and stays open until around 10pm.

Emma's Café 30 Thames St. Hip daytime café serving great coffee, bagels, wholemeal croissants, muffins and lemon syrup cakes. Work by local artists decorates the walls.

Golden Island Chinese Restaurant 243 Thames St. Dependable and inexpensive Chinese with a good range of set menus for couples or groups, and some generous vegetarian dishes. Daily from 5pm; licensed & BYO.

Lagonda Milkbar 193 Thames St, cnr Eden St.

One of the better greasy spoons in town, open for breakfast, lunch and early dinner. Also operates as the InterCity booking office and has Internet access.

Penguin Club off Harbour St ⓦ www.penguinclub .co.nz. Cool, near-legendary back-alley bar and venue hosting Friday jam nights (from 8pm), poetry, theatre and gigs by Kiwi touring bands ($10–15 cover charge): almost everyone of note has played here. From the *Criterion Hotel*, walk down Harbour St, turn left down an unprepossessing alley. Entry price is small, and if you pick up a programme of events from the visitor centre you'll be let in at the members' price.

Whitestone Cheese Café cnr of Torridge and Humber streets. Small café associated with the Whitestone Cheese Company, mainly the place for sampling their excellent cheeses with some of the local wine. Particularly good are the Farmhouse, a semi-soft cheese with a lemongrass aroma and nutty taste, the Brie, which has a hint of mushroom, the strong Airedale and the Windsor Blue, a creamy soft cheese – all made on the premises. Mon–Fri 9am–5pm, Sat & Sun 9.30am–4pm.

The Woolstore Café 1 Tyne St ☏ 03/434 8336. A quality modern café and restaurant in one of Oamaru's recently renovated buildings serving good coffee, cakes, smoothies etc.

Listings

Car rental Smash Palace Rentals (☎ 03/434 1444) rents ten-year-old cars for as little as $30 a day. **Courtyard Rentals** (☎ 03/434 5222) have more modern vehicles and charge more like $60 a day. **Cinema** William's MovieWorld 3, 239 Thames St (☎ 03/434 1070), shows the latest movies and sells panini, snacks beer and wine, which can all be taken in to the screening.
Library Oamaru Public Library, next door to the North Otago Museum on Thames St (Mon–Thurs 9.30am–5.30pm, Fri 9.30am–8pm, Sat 10am–12.30pm).
Medical treatment Oamaru Hospital, 8 Stewart St ☎ 03/433 0290.
Newspaper The Mon–Fri only *Oamaru Mail* (75¢) has entertainment listings and emergency numbers.
Post office The post office, 2 Severn St (☎ 03/433 1190), has poste restante facilities.
Tours Book through the visitor centre for informative, guided walking tours of the town (1hr; $8).

South of Oamaru to Moeraki – and the Moeraki Boulders

South of Oamaru, most people make a beeline for the **Moeraki Boulders** and Dunedin, but is worth taking half an hour or so to look around **Totara Estate**, the home of New Zealand's first ever frozen meat shipment. Alternatively, take leave SH1 for the first 20km and follow Kakanui Beach Road on the back-roads to the coast at Kakanui. The road continues 3km to All Day Bay, the peaceful location of *The Hall Coastal Backpackers* (see p.656), then winds back to the main highway.

Totara Estate

Until the early 1880s New Zealand was a major wool exporter and its flocks were becoming huge, but no one knew what to do with all the surplus meat. The country's small population certainly couldn't consume it all, no matter how meat-loving. Meanwhile, Britain's burgeoning industrial cities were on the brink of starvation. Shippers were just beginning to experiment with refrigeration, but New Zealand wasn't on the regular steam ship routes and it fell to the Australia and New Zealand Land Company to pioneer refrigeration on a sailing ship. In 1882, the three-masted *Dunedin* was refitted with coke-driven freezers and filled with lamb from one of the most fecund and productive sheep stations, **Totara Estate**, SH1, 8km south of Oamaru (Oct–April daily 10am–6pm; May–Sept Wed–Sun 10am–4pm; $7; ⓦ www.totaraestate.co.nz). This birthplace of the New Zealand meat industry is now a grassy historic park built around solid whitestone estate buildings largely reconstructed with the original dressed stones. A small museum and video in the former workmens' quarters sets the tone for the harness room, stables, granary barn and blacksmiths forge, all appropriately equipped. The foundations and partial remains of the original slaughterhouse and carcass shed form the basis of a modern reconstruction which gives and idea of what work was like here. If your imagination isn't vivid enough, half a dozen heritage breeds of sheep are kept nearby.

Moeraki Boulders

Forty kilometres south of Oamaru on SH1 the large, grey and almost perfectly spherical **Moeraki Boulders** (some of which reach 2m in diameter) lie partially submerged in the sandy beach at the tide line. Their smooth skins hide honeycomb centres, which are revealed in some of the broken specimens. Despite appearances, the boulders did not fall from the sky, nor were they washed up by the sea, but rather lay deep in the mudstone cliffs

661

△ Moeraki Boulders

behind the beach. As the sea eroded the cliffs, out fell the smooth boulders, and their distinctive surface pattern was formed as further erosion exposed a network of veins. The boulders were originally formed around a central core of carbonate of lime crystals which attracted minerals from their surroundings – a process that started sixty million years ago, when muddy sediment containing shell and plant fragments accumulated on the sea floor. The masses formed range in size from small pellets to large round rocks, some with a small void in the middle. There were a large number of these boulders in the area, but the smaller ones have all been souvenired over the years, leaving only those too heavy to shift.

Access to this strangely compelling phenomenon is either by a 300m walk along the beach from a parking area (often used for ad hoc camping), or more immediately via a restaurant-cum-**visitor centre** (daily: Oct–April 8am–6pm; May–Nov 9am–5pm; ℡03/439 4827) which overlooks the beach, accessed on a short private trail ($2 in the honesty box at any hour).

Maori named the boulders *Te Kaihinaki* (food baskets), believing them to have been washed ashore from the wreck of a canoe whose occupants were seeking *pounamu*. The seaward reef near Shag Point (see opposite) was the hull of the canoe, and just beyond it stands a prominent rock, the vessel's petrified navigator. Some of the Moeraki Boulders were *hinaki* (baskets), the more spherical were water-carrying gourds and the irregular-shaped rocks farther down the beach were *kumara* from the canoe's food store. The survivors among the crew, Nga Tamariki, Puketapu and Pakihiwi Tahi, were transformed at daybreak into hills overlooking the beach.

Once you've had a good look at the boulders it's worth walking along the beach past Moeraki village (see below) to the Moeraki Point whalers' lookout, where there's a view south down the coast to the lighthouse, and the likelihood of seeing Hector's dolphins, which often surf in the breakers off the beach. If you're in the area in the winter (June–Aug), you might chance upon some of the thin, silvery frost fish which beach themselves along the shoreline on frosty nights for no apparent reason.

Accommodation in these parts is fairly limited, but there are places in Moeraki Village (see below), across SH1 from the boulders at *Moeraki Boulder Downs B&B* (℡03/439 4855, ⊛www.moerakiboulders.co.nz; ➎), and at Wainakarua, 12km north, at the organically-run *Olive Grove Lodge & Holiday Park*, SH1, (℡03/439 5830, ⊛www.olivebranch.co.nz). Set on a bend in a river with good swimming holes, it is a relaxing spot with a selection of nicely decorated and well appointed doubles and twins (➌), dorm bunks (➊) and plenty of space for camping and van hookups ($10).

Moeraki village

The sleepy fishing village of **MOERAKI**, 1km to the south along SH1 then 1.5km down a side road, which makes a tranquil place to break your journey.

On the right-hand side of the road just before you enter the village is the **Kotahitanga** ("One People") **Church**, built in 1862 and containing beautiful stained-glass windows, crafted in Birmingham in 1891. Considered unusual for its (at the time rather daring) portrayal of Maori alongside Jesus and Mary, the left light of the window is a portrait based on a photograph of Te Matiaha Tiramoreh of Moeraki, a respected leader of the Ngai Tahu who died in 1881. Sadly the church is almost never open, though you might get a glimpse of the stained glass through cracks in the church's frosted windows.

Of the **accommodation** available in the village, the *Moeraki Motel* (℡ & ℻03/439 4862; ➍), on the only road entering the village, is a friendly place located close to a beach with six cottages and four two-storey units facing the bay, all with fully equipped kitchens. There's also the *Moeraki Motor Camp* (T03/439 4759, @moerakimotorcamp@xtra.co.nz; tent sites $10, cabins ❷–❹), situated on a hill farther into the village, with cooking facilities (camp kitchens and outdoor barbecues) and a store. The village may not amount to much, but as well as the tolerable restaurant/bar at the boulders' visitor centre with great views of the ocean and boulders, there is also a very good **restaurant**. *Fleur's Place* (daily 7am–midnight; T03/439 5980, Wwww.fleursplace.com; lic & BYO) lures sophisticates from Dunedin (and Gwyneth Paltrow when she was filming nearby) to this converted fishing shack for great seafood meals (mains $20–25) or just a coffee.

Smaller **shuttle buses** will drop you in the village, although services run by the major companies merely drop off at the point where the side road into the village leaves SH1.

Shag Point

A number of smaller, odd-shaped boulders can be found at Shag Point Scenic Reserve, 10km south along SH1 and 3km in from the highway (or an 11km walk along Katiki beach if you're feeling energetic). The beach near the point is sometimes visited by fur seals (Oct–March) and yellow-eyed penguins, which usually come ashore between 3.30pm and nightfall – there's a small hide with a little wooden bench overlooking the beach where you can keep watch.

Palmerston

The lumber town of **PALMERSTON**, 22km south of Moeraki, marks the junction of two routes: SH1 running 55km south to Dunedin; and the "Pigroot" (SH85) inland to the Maniototo and the historic goldfield heartland of Central Otago. There's little reason to stop long in Palmerston, though on even the briefest visit you'll notice the **monument** atop Puketapu Hill. It was erected in recognition of one-time local resident **John McKenzie**, a Gaelic-speaking Scottish shepherd who arrived in the 1860s and eventually rose to become Minister of Lands, Agriculture and Immigration. In the early 1890s he pushed through a couple of land settlement acts which effectively laid the groundwork for modern farming by breaking up the vast holdings of absentee landlords and making them available to new immigrants. It was a popular move, eventually earning him a knighthood six weeks before his death in 1901. To take in the extensive view from the monument, follow signs to Goodwood Road from the central junction.

The licensed *DeRail Café and Bar*, in the former station in the centre of town, offers the best **food** in town with gourmet pizza and the typically wide range of New Zealand café fare. Simple **accommodation** is covered by *Pioneer Motels*, 56 Tiverton St (T03/465 1234; ❹), with self-contained units, or, for something considerably more luxurious, call for directions to *Centrewood*, Bobby's Head Rd (T03/465 1977, Wwww.ecostay.co.nz; ❽), a high-ceilinged 1904 homestead set amid English rose gardens well away from the road in the coastal hills and close to beaches frequented by seals and yellow-eyed penguins. The approach is low-key, but there is an effortless grace to the rooms let either separately ($200) or both rooms with use of the vast lounge with polished rimu floors and a small billiard table sleeping up to four; $400). Evening meals ($40 and up) include wine and can be taken with the family who are descended from physicist Ernest Rutherford, and keep a small collection of mementoes.

Travel details

There are no longer any passenger trains running south of Christchurch but **buses** are fast and reasonably frequent. The coastal bus route from Christchurch to Dunedin is the most hotly contested in the South Island with half a dozen companies offering a range of schedules and very competitive prices. The inland run from Christchurch to Queenstown is another hot ticket, but services running inland from the coast are sporadic to say the least: InterCity (☎03/379 9020), Atomic Shuttle (☎03/322 8883) and Southern Link Shuttles (☎03/358 8355) have the broadest networks.

Trains

From Christchurch to: Arthur's Pass (1 daily; 2hr 10min); Blenheim (1 daily; 5hr); Greymouth (1 daily; 4hr 20min); Kaikoura (1 daily; 3hr); Picton (1 daily; 5hr 30min).

Buses

From Ashburton to: Geraldine (2 daily; 40min); Timaru (10 daily; 1hr); Twizel (6–7 daily; 3hr 40min).
From Christchurch to: Akaroa (4–5 daily; 2hr 50min); Aoraki Mount Cook (1 daily; 6hr 15min); Arthur's Pass (3 daily; 2hr 15min); Ashburton (15 daily; 1hr–1hr 20min); Blenheim (5 daily; 4hr 30min–5hr); Dunedin (8 daily; 5–6hr); Fairlie (6–7 daily; 2hr 30min); Geraldine (6–7 daily; 2hr);

Greymouth (3 daily; 4hr); Hanmer Springs (1–2 daily; 2hr 30min); Hokitika (3 daily; 5–6hr); Kaikoura (5 daily; 2hr 30min); Lyttelton (every 30min 8.10am–11.25pm; 35min); Methven (2 daily; 1hr); Nelson (2 daily; 7–8hr); Oamaru (8 daily; 3hr 30min–4hr 30min); Picton (5 daily; 5hr–5hr 30min); Timaru (10 daily; 2hr 30min); Twizel (6–7 daily; 4hr); Queenstown (6–7 daily; 7–9hr); Wanaka (2–5 daily; 6hr 20min–9hr).
From Oamaru to: Aoraki Mount Cook (2–3 weekly; 2hr 45min); Christchurch (8 daily; 3hr 30min–4hr 30min); Dunedin (8 daily; 2hr); Twizel (2–4 weekly; 2hr).
From Timaru to: Aoraki Mount Cook (2–3 weekly; 3hr 15min); Christchurch (10 daily; 2hr 30min); Dunedin (8 daily; 3hrs 30mins); Oamaru (8 daily; 1hr 20min); Twizel (2–4 weekly daily; 2hr 30min).

Flights

From Christchurch to: Auckland (20–25 daily; 1hr 20min–2hr 30min); Blenheim (1 daily; 50min); Dunedin (5–11 daily; 1hr); Hokitika (1–4 daily; 35min); Invercargill (7–8 daily; 1hr 15min); Napier (2–3 daily; 1hr 30); Nelson (11 daily; 50min); Palmerston North (5–6 daily; 1hr 15min); Queenstown (6–8 daily; 1hr); Rotorua (3 daily, 1hr 15min–1hr 40min); Wanaka (1 daily; 1hr); Wellington (20–25 daily; 45min).
From Timaru to: Wellington (2–3 daily; 1hr 10min).

10

The Central South Island

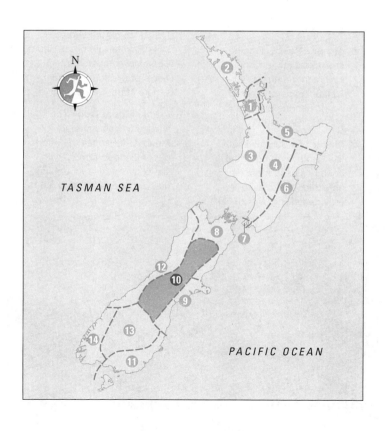

* **Hot springs** Soak your bones at the resort of Hanmer Springs, the more rustic Maruia Springs or the totally natural pool at Sylvia Flats. See p.670, p.674 & p.674

* **The TranzAlpine** Take one of the world's top rail journeys, coast to coast through the Southern Alps. See p.675

* **Arthur's Pass** Hiking here provides a jaw-dropping insight into a uniquely beautiful landscape populated by indigenous plants and animals. See p.681

* **Skiing** The Central South Island offers some of the country's best, most reasonably priced and least-crowded skiing. Mount Hutt is a great starting point. See p.686

* **Rafting the Rangitata** Raft some of the best and bounciest whitewater in the land on rafting trips from Peel Forest, or as a day-trip from Christchurch. See p.689

* **Lake Pukaki** Free camp at The Pines on the shores of Lake Pukaki with great Mount Cook views uninterrupted views of the southern hemisphere stars. See p.696

* **Aoraki Mount Cook** The short day walks around Mount Cook repay the effort of some steep climbs, with views over alpine mountains, glaciers and lakes. See p.699

△ Lake Tekapo

The Central South Island

The **Central South Island** is one of the most varied and intriguing areas in New Zealand, with extensive pasturelands, dense native forests, and a history rich in tales of human endeavour. The region's defining feature is the ice sawtooth ridge of the **Southern Alps**, which forms the South Island's central north-south spine and peaks at Australasia's loftiest summit, the 3754m-high **Aoraki Mount Cook**. A logistical nightmare to Maori and European settlers, the region is typical pioneer country, and the communities themselves are simple places, tinged with the toughness and idiosyncrasies of the early settlers. Explorers and surveyors that opened the region often lent their names to the towns – Arthur's Pass and Lewis Pass to name just two.

The mountains present a major obstacle to travel between east and west coasts, a barrier only breached in two places, both providing access to mountain scenery, walks and skifields. The most northerly of these routes is the **Lewis Pass Road**, which conveys traffic from the Canterbury Plains north of Christchurch to Westport on the west coast, passing the tranquil, forested spa resort of **Hanmer Springs**. Further west there are more low-key hot pools at **Maruia Springs**. South of here, road and rail both pass through **Arthur's Pass**, historically an important trade route connecting the coalfields of the west coast with the port of Lyttelton. The spectacular Christchurch–Greymouth **TranzAlpine** makes a particularly fitting way to approach **Arthur's Pass National Park**, with its abundance of day walks and longer trails.

South of Christchurch, roads lead across the Canterbury Plains towards the small but lively foothill settlements of **Methven** and **Mount Somers**, a popular destination for **Mount Hutt**-bound skiers and summer adventurers after some jetboating, whitewater rafting and first class tramping.

The southern half of the region leaves behind the rolling hills for the sun-scorched grasslands of the **Mackenzie Country**, an area renowned for massive sheep runs and the beautiful blues of its glacier-fed lakes, **Tekapo** and **Pukaki**. The mightiest of the Southern Alps form an imperious backdrop and are most easily accessed at **Aoraki Mount Cook Village**, huddled at the foot of Aoraki Mount Cook, and the starting point of numerous walks.

With the high prices close to the Alps, visitors to the regions mountains and lakes are increasingly basing themselves in **Twizel**, an odd former hydro-construction town now developing a more pronounced identity, as a cheaper

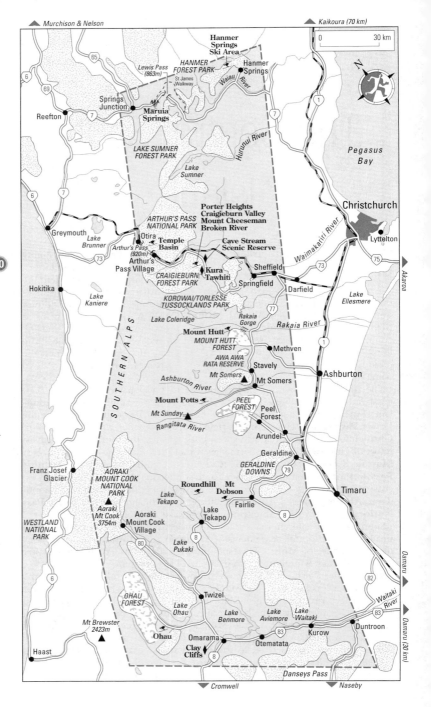

and more varied base. The Mackenzie Country hydro-electric schemes all eventually feed water down the scenic **Waitaki Valley** which threads its way to the east coast at Oamaru, though you may well be tempted to stay inland and forge south towards Wanaka and Queenstown.

The Central South Island **climate** is generally hot and dry in summer with long days that sear the grasslands to tinder dry. In winter precipitation falls as snow, feeding the numerous ski fields but also clearing to reveal clear, calm, if chilly, days. It is a climate that fosters rare alpine plants and wildlife, including the famous Mount Cook lily, the largest white mountain daisies in the world, and that most mischievous of birds, the kea, the world's only alpine parrot.

Road **transport** around the area is plentiful, with most places easily accessible by bus, while the single rail track from coast to coast, via Arthur's Pass, provides a viable and entertaining alternative.

Hanmer Springs and Lewis Pass

Most northerly of the cross-mountain routes, SH7 crosses the **Lewis Pass** following the course of a track that provided both Maori and early Pakeha with a necessary link between the east and west coasts. Travelling from the east coast the route starts at Waipara (see p.597), 80km north of Christchurch, then crosses the coastal plain and begins its gradual climb between foothills of the Southern Alps. Lying just off this route in a side valley, the spa resort of **Hanmer Springs** acts as a base for summer walks and adventure activities, and as a convenient resting place for winter sports enthusiasts who enjoy the nearby **Hanmer Springs Ski Area**. It also offers the best range of accommodation hereabouts, a wooded mountain hinterland, and one of the top ten golf courses in the country. Some 60km further west, the **Lewis Pass** itself is set amidst some exhilarating subalpine terrain and deep forest; while **Maruia Springs**, just beyond the summit of the pass, is another appealing, though minute, resort

St James Walkway

For a complementary blend of pastoral land, riverside path, forest and subalpine tussock country it is hard to beat the **St James Walkway** (66km; 5 days; 271m ascent). You don't need a great deal of experience or high levels of fitness, though you will need a bit of time (best Nov–April), **all-weather gear**, a plentiful supply of **food**, and tickets for the five DOC **huts** (20 bunks; $10). Buy tickets from the visitor centre in Hanmer Springs where you can also obtain the *St James Walkway* leaflet (50¢), the *Lewis Pass* leaflet (50¢), and the 1:50,000 *St James & Lewis Pass* Trackmap ($15).

The tramp is best done north to south starting at the Lewis Pass picnic area and car park 63km west of the Hanmer Springs turn-off and rejoining the highway about 16km towards Hanmer at the Boyle Shelter car park. Huts are equipped with wood stoves for heating, but be sure to carry a cooking stove and, in the peak summer season, a tent in case the huts are full.

If you can't face the whole thing, consider just the initial descent to the **Cannibal Gorge Bridge**, from the Lewis Pass end, an excellent short walk for the less adventurous (2km; 80min).

There are a couple of **bus services** – East West Coach Service and Lazerline – between Lewis Pass and Boyle, so you can get back to your car from either end of the track.

in which to soak in soothing thermal waters. There is a variety of public **transport** into the region, with several daily buses making the trip from Christchurch direct to Hanmer Springs, and other services heading from Christchurch over the pass to Greymouth and Nelson.

Hanmer Springs

About 140km north of Christchurch, a side road leaves SH7 to head 9km north towards the quaint spa resort of **HANMER SPRINGS**. Just after the turn-off from SH7, you'll cross the spectacular **Waiau Ferry Bridge**, designed by John Blackett and now set up for bungy jumping (see p.59). The bridge was considered a major feat of engineering when it was opened in 1887, and the locals threw such a party that the site of the hospitality tent became known as Champagne Flat. Hanmer Springs itself is pleasantly situated at the edge of a broad, fertile agricultural plain snuggled against the Southern Alps foothills. Only around 700 people call Hanmer home but the place is awash with holiday homes and – in-keeping the resort spirit – a preponderance of minigolf courses. The **thermal pools** are undoubtedly the main draw, but a handful of minor attractions and activities can help fill a day or two.

To most Kiwis "I'm off to Hanmer" may mean a day at the pools, but could equally refer to time spent drying out at the **Queen Mary Hospital**, New Zealand's most famous residential alcohol and drugs rehab centre, which closed in 2003.

Arrival and information

Bus transport to Hanmer is easiest with Hanmer Connection (☎0800/377 378) who run here from Christchurch, Kaikoura and Greymouth. East West

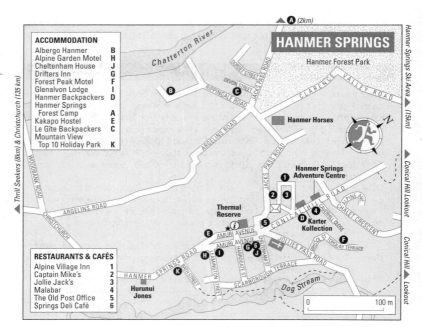

HANMER SPRINGS

Hanmer Forest Park

ACCOMMODATION
Albergo Hanmer	B
Alpine Garden Motel	H
Cheltenham House	J
Drifters Inn	G
Forest Peak Motel	F
Glenalvon Lodge	I
Hanmer Backpackers	D
Hanmer Springs Forest Camp	A
Kakapo Hostel	E
Le Gite Backpackers	C
Mountain View	
Top 10 Holiday Park	K

RESTAURANTS & CAFÉS
Alpine Village Inn	1
Captain Mike's	2
Jollie Jack's	3
Malabar	4
The Old Post Office	5
Springs Deli Café	6

Hanmer Horses

Hanmer Springs Adventure Centre

Thermal Reserve

Karter Kollection

Hurunui Jones

Chatterton River

Hanmer Springs Ski Area ▲ (15km)

Conical Hill Lookout ▲

Conical Hill Lookout

▲ Thrill Seekers (8km) & Christchurch (135 km)

Dog Stream

0   100 m

Coach Service (☎0800/142 62), Lazerline Coaches (☎0800/220 001) and InterCity also call in. All buses stop outside the **visitor centre** on Amuri Avenue, next to the hot pools (daily 10am–5pm; ☎03/315 7128, Ⓦ www.hurunui.com), which has a supply of DOC brochures and maps, sells hut tickets and includes a small **bank** (Mon–Fri 10am–2pm) with an **ATM** (daily 9am–9pm). Upstairs are illuminating displays on the Hurunui region's natural assets and journeys through the area by Maori, cattle drovers and the remarkable Park brothers who canoed across the main divide via Harper's Pass.

Notwithstanding the abundant accommodation and eating places, Hanmer is a small town and has limited **groceries**: if you're self-catering bring what you need.

Accommodation

Hanmer's reputation amongst Kiwis as an elegant little resort has attracted considerable hotel and motel development leaving a wide range of accommodation from backpacker hostels to swanky B&Bs. The town is busiest at the height of summer and during school holidays, when it's wise to book ahead.

Albergo Hanmer Rippingale Rd ☎03/315 7428 & 0800/342 313, Ⓦ www.albergohanmer.com. B&B in a modern house fifteen minutes' walk from town containing spacious rooms all with views. All come with large ensuites and a gourmet three-course breakfast is served. ❻

Alpine Garden Motel 3 Leamington St ☎03/315 7332 & 0800/335 556, Ⓔ alpinegardens @xtra.co.nz. Clean, comfortable, self-contained units, in a quiet setting three minutes' walk from the thermal pools. ❺

Cheltenham House 13 Cheltenham St ☎03/315 7545, Ⓦ www.cheltenham.co.nz. The best value B&B in town, with four large, light rooms set in a lovingly and tastefully renovated 1930s house and two cottages in the well-tended garden. ❻

Drifters Inn 2 Harrogate St ☎03/315 7554, Ⓦ www.driftersinn.co.nz. The best deal in this price range, this is a centrally located motel-cum-lodge, diagonally opposite the thermal pools. You'll get neat comfortable rooms and use of several communal areas, or ensuite rooms in a neighbouring villa. Prices include a continental breakfast. Villa rooms ❹, units ❺

Forest Peak Motel 4 Torquay Terrace ☎03/315 7132 & 0508/224 678, Ⓦ www.forestpeak.co.nz. This motel has ten clean comfortable units (some with open fires) and three attractive pine cabins all set close to town and the forest. ❹–❺

Glenalvon Lodge 29 Amuri Ave ☎03/315 7475, Ⓦ www.glenalvon.com. Luxury accommodation in

two B&B rooms (including a continental breakfast) in the main house or nine well-kept, motel units out the back. Both ❺

Hanmer Backpackers 41 Conical Hill Rd ☎03/315 7196, Ⓔ hanmerbackpackers@hotmail .com. Cosy, central chalet-style backpackers, offering mostly shared rooms, with three doubles. Dorms ❶, rooms ❷

Hanmer Springs Forest Camp 243 Jollies Pass Rd ☎03/315 7202, Ⓔ hanmer.forest.camp @xtra.co.nz. If you've got wheels, head 2.5km north of town to this sylvan campground (no powered sites) with a good collection of log cabins and a self-catering lodge. Camping $8, dorms ❶, rooms ❷

Kakapo Hostel 14 Amuri Av ☎03/315 7472, Ⓔ stay-kakapo@xtra.co.nz. Large, central and comfortable, spacious and has beds rather than bunks but completely lacks atmosphere. Dorms ❶, rooms ❷

Le Gîte Backpackers 3 Devon St ☎03/315 5111, Ⓦ www.legite.co.nz. Probably the pick of the hostels in a couple of converted houses ten minutes' walk from the centre. All beds are made up, and there's plenty of room, including a nice deck. Dorms ❶, rooms ❷

Mountain View Top 10 Holiday Park cnr Amuri Ave & Bath St ☎03/315 7113 & 0800/904 545, Ⓦ www.holidayparks.co.nz/mtnview. A range of tourist flats and cabin accommodation, in a large well-kept area. Camping $10, cabins ❷–❸, self-contained units ❹

The Resort

The oak-lined Amuri Avenue runs past the thermal reserve, visitor centre and most of the shops becoming Conical Hill Road as it heads north towards the hills. Right in the centre, the shady park that gives the town its quiet and sheltered feel marks the entrance to the **Hanmer Springs Thermal Reserve**

(daily 10am–9pm; $10, two entries on same day $13; www.hanmersprings
.co.nz), an extensive pool complex which is set to get even bigger over the next
two years. The jury remains out on whether it will manage to retain the little
Victorian charm that remains.

While searching for stray cattle in 1859, one William Jones stumbled across
the springs which are fed by rainwater that seeps down through fractures in the
rocks of the Hanmer Mountains, accumulating in an underground reservoir
some 2km beneath the Hanmer Plain. After absorbing some minerals and
being warmed by the earth's natural heat, the water rises to the surface via
fissures in the greywacke rock. Word of Hanmer's waters spread at a time when
the beneficial effects of mineral baths were much hyped, and by the 1870s
Hanmer was nationally famous for the waters' relaxing and curative powers.

The modern pool complex contains assorted artificially landscaped thermal
pools full of light-blue springwater, as well as a standard chlorinated 25m
swimming pool. There's also a toddlers' pool, a series of play pools including
a waterslide ($5 extra), volcano lava pools, and a series of more intimate
private pools ($15 each per half hour, includes general entry for as long as you
like). With a gym, health and beauty centre and the *Garden House Café* you
could stay all day, but if you have to pick a time, go in the evening when the
crowds thin.

The small, privately owned **Karter Kollection Museum** (roughly daily
8.30am–5.30pm; $2), about two minutes' walk from the Thermal Reserve on
Conical Hill, contains a mish-mash of odds and ends that barely justifies the
price of admission. There's a little more fun to be had at **Hurunui Jones**,
Amuri Avenue, 1km from the visitor centre (daily 10am–dusk; $7), a maze with
obstacles that is supposed to pay homage to the adventurous archeological
discovery scenes in *Indiana Jones* movies but barely makes the grade.

Hiking and biking in Hanmer Forest Park

By far the best and least expensive entertainment to be had around Hanmer is
hiking and biking through the Black pines, Norway spruce, Douglas firs and
assorted deciduous trees of **Hanmer Forest Park**. Located on the northern
and eastern fringe of town, it was created in 1901 using convict labour and is
now protected from logging. The excellent *Hanmer Forest Recreation* leaflet ($1)
maps out eighteen **walks** (1–6hr), notably the **Forest Walk** (2.5km; 1hr),
which leads through some of the oldest of the sycamore, oak and silver birch;
the **Woodland Walk** (2km; 45min), with its stream, flax wetland and ponds
teeming with birds; and the **Waterfall Track** (2.5km; 3hr; 400m ascent), leading to the 41m-high Dog Stream Waterfall.

Hanmer Forest is also renowned for **mountain biking** and hosts races
throughout the summer. Pick up the free *Mountain Bike Tracks* leaflet from
Hanmer Springs Adventure Centre, 20 Conical Hill Rd (03/315 7233), who
do **bike rental** ($40 a half-day). Bikes are also available from BackTrax
(0800/422 258, www.bscktrax.co.nz) who run bike safaris such as The
Summit ($79) with full day rental, a lift to the top of a long hill, and a hot-pool
pass for the end of the day.

Other activities

Thrillseekers (03/315 7046, www.thrillseeker.co.nz), an adventure centre
9km out of town at the Waiau Ferry Bridge, enjoys a near-monopoly on local
water-based activities. These include scenic 2hr **rafting** trips through the
Waiau River Canyon (grade 2–3, $85); **jetboat** rides through the steep-sided
gorges of the Waiau River (30min $69, 40min $79; 90min raft and jet combo,

$145), and **bungy jumps** ($114), from a 35m-platform midway across the Waiau Ferry Bridge.

As an alternative to pedal power, check out **Backtrax 4-wheel Motorbike Safaris** (T 0800/422 258, W www.backtrax.co.nz), which offers a River Valley Ramble (2hr 30min; $130) and an Alpine Spectacular (4hr; $245), involving tackling backcountry tracks up to some spectacular views, with a guide.

Horse riding in the area is run by Hanmer Horse, Jacks Pass Road (T 03/315 7444 & 0800/873546; 1hr $40, half day $80) which caters for people of all abilities and experience. More serious riders should contact Hurunui Horse Treks (T 03/314 4204, W www.hurunui.co.nz), based near Hawarden, off SH7 about 60km south of Hanmer, which organizes some of the best **horse safaris** in the region. Alpine Horse Safaris, based on Waitohi Downs, (T 03/314 4293; 2hr–10days; $35–$1200). Longer trips include all food and accommodation, but must be booked at least a month in advance. They'll do half-day ($90) and full day ($130) treks but what make the place special are the multi-day trips well away from roads following old gold miners trails or stock routes between stations. Book well in advance for trips such as The Overnighter ($395) including all meals and a night in a shearing shed; or the Seaward River (4 days; $995), again mostly staying in shearers quarters and eating with farming families along the way.

The Hanmer Springs Ski Area

If you're here during the limited ski season (mid-July to sometime in September) consider heading up to the small **Hanmer Springs Ski Area**, which is particularly suited to intermediate boarders and skiers. It is located on the slopes of Mount St Patrick and the St James Ranges a forty-minute drive from Hanmer up the Clarence Valley Road (free for skiers, but sightseers have to pay a $10 toll). **Transport** from Hanmer ($25 return) can be arranged through the Hanmer Springs Adventure Centre, 20 Conical Hill Rd, Hanmer (T 03/315 7233, E hbc@clear.net.nz), where you can also rent ski gear. Gear can also be rented at the ski area where there's a heated day lodge, with stoves, toasted sandwiches and tea and coffee, and comfortable backpacker accommodation ($20). There's just one poma-style lift for which you pay $35 a day.

The **Mount Lyford Skifield**, 60km to the northeast is also accessible from Hanmer via SH1.

Eating and drinking

Hanmer is booming, and though still small, new **places to eat** seem to pop up all the time. As a popular resort, value-for-money can be hard to a find, but you won't go hungry

Alpine Village Inn 10 Jacks Pass Rd. Convivial locals' bar with a range of traditional fish, steak and chicken meals ($15–18) and lighter snacks.

Captain Mike's Shop D, Hanmer Mall T 03/315 7771. The best in fish and chip takeaways.

Jollie Jack's Hanmer Mall T 03/315 7388. A good all rounder; fine for coffee or a beer but also serving Cajun battered chicken strips ($13) and substantial mains ($21–26) such as leg of venison or wild pork chops.

Malabar 5 Conical Hill Rd T 03/315 7754. Flashy Asian fusion restaurant putting a modern twist on

dishes from South and southeast Asia as well as the odd Japanese dish. Expect tempura seafood and Thai green curry along with Indian spiced rack of lamb. Mains cost $23–28 and there are lovely desserts ($10) plus cocktails.

The Old Post Office Jacks Pass Rd T 03/315 7461. The best fine dining in town is at this stylish, imaginative restaurant with starters like pumpkin and pine nut-stuffed saffron ravioli ($16), followed by oxtail-glazed fillet of beef ($29).

Springs Deli Café 47 Amuri Ave. A great spot for breakfast, salads or a coffee all at relatively modest prices.

West to Lewis Pass

West of the Hanmer Springs turn-off, SH7 continues on its climb towards the 907-metre **Lewis Pass**, 65km away. Maori had long crossed through this high country pass to trade, but it wasn't until 1860 that surveyors Christopher Maling and Henry Lewis stumbled upon the pass and so opening up a relatively easy route between the east and west coasts. In 1866 a bridle track linking Hanmer Plain with Murchison was finished, and by 1936 a spectacular highway suitable for motor vehicles was finally opened.

The land between Hanmer and the squat hills of the **Boyle Bluffs**, which herald the **Doubtful River Valley** (a one-time gold diggers' route), is a rugged area of low-yielding grassland, with broom (a blazing yellow in the summer), spiky matagouri, manuka and kanuka taking hold where the farms have failed. As you approach the pass, red and silver beech forest begins to predominate. Shortly after the tiny cluster of houses that is the settlement of **BOYLE**, 50km out from Hanmer, you will come across **Sylvia Flats**, part of the Lewis Pass National Reserve, where it is possible to park and follow a track beside the Lewis River for about 50m to pools where warm water bubbles up through the rocks, mixing with the cold river water to create refreshing thermal pools. For reasons best known to themselves, DOC has removed all signposting, and when water levels are high the spot can be hard to find. The best bet is to pick up the *Syliva Flats Rest Area* leaflet (50¢) from the Hanmer Springs Visitor Centre, and bring something to deter the sandflies.

Lewis Pass itself is just 15km further on, and offers views along the high-sided Cannibal Gorge (see p.669) towards the Spenser Mountains.

Maruia Springs and Springs Junction

Eight kilometres west of Lewis Pass, **MARUIA SPRINGS** is another thermal spa resort, grouped around a bath complex with **hot pools** (daily 9am–8.30pm; communal pool areas $10; private baths $15/hr) overlooking the Maruia River. The outside pools contain waters whose colours range from black to milky white, depending on the level of minerals they contain. The steaming waters are allegedly good for arthritis – but not so good for jewellery, which gets badly tarnished by the sulphurous fumes. **Accommodation** at the *Maruia Springs Resort* (☎03/523 8840, ✉enquiries@maruia.co.nz; camping $18, units ⑥) ranges from camping to simple en-suite units with breakfast included; guests are entitled to free use of the springs. Within the complex there's also the *Hot Rocks* **café/bar** and the Japanese-style *Shuzan Restaurant*.

Twenty kilometres west of Maruia Springs, there's a parting of the ways at **SPRINGS JUNCTION**, with the SH7 continuing west towards Reefton and the SH65 forging northwards to Murchison. Springs Junction itself has little to recommend it except an unstaffed **DOC Information Centre** and walks; and essential services such as a petrol station and village shop.

Arthur's Pass and around

The most dramatic of the three Southern Alps crossings links Christchurch with Greymouth via **Arthur's Pass**. Traversed by both a highly scenic rail line and the equally breathtaking SH73, the route is a popular excursion for city-based travellers eager for a quick taste of the high country and winter sports enthusiasts who wish to take advantage of the many and varied skifields.

When completed in 1923, the train line from Christchurch to Greymouth was a massive boon for travellers, covering in five hours what formerly took two rugged days by horse-drawn coach – a passage tough enough to shorten the average life expectancy of the draught horses to just eighteen months. The journey is now covered by the **TranzAlpine** (4hr 30min; $84 one way, $138 day return) which leaves Christchurch train station at 8.15am every morning and returns by 6.05pm. Altogether it passes through nineteen tunnels and crosses numerous viaducts, all seen from the train's large viewing windows, comfortable seats, and open-sided observation car. Complimentary morning or afternoon tea is served, and snacks are available at only slightly inflated prices. The scenic, 231km, coast-to-coast journey starts out across the Canterbury Plains as far as Springfield, after which you start gently up into the mountains. The halfway point is reached around Craigieburn, open tussock country which is dried throughout the summer by strong norwester winds which leave it crisp and golden. As you head up to Arthur's Pass the annual rainfall increases encouraging transition-zone vegetation of mossy beech forests. There's a pause at Arthur's Pass to add an extra locomotive, after which the train dives through the 8.5km-long Otira Tunnel which burrows under the 920m pass itself. The train then descends to the high-rainfall West Coast, the predominant, lush podocarp forests appearing particularly around Lake Brunner just before you trundle down the Grey Valley into Greymouth.

If you travel in December you will see red and white rata in bloom, but the trip is at its romantic, snow-cloaked best in the winter months (June–Aug).

The pass gets its name from civil engineer **Arthur Dobson**, who "discovered" it after hearing about the route from local Maori who had traditionally used it as a highway for raiding parties and for trade, sometimes *pounamu*. Dobson surveyed the pass in 1864, and by 1866 horse-drawn coaches were using it to serve the Westland goldfields. The railway was built in 1923, coinciding with the booming interest in alpine tourism worldwide.

From Christchurch to Arthur's Pass

Both road and rail routes from Christchurch to Arthur's Pass encompass great geographical contrasts, beginning in the agriculturally rich Canterbury Plains and ending in an earthquake-shaken village 735m above sea level. The 920m pass itself is 4km to the west of Arthur's Pass Village, marked by a large obelisk inscribed with the name Arthur Dudley Dobson, and is the start of many rewarding walks.

From Christchurch the route follows the course of the shingle-lined Waimakariri River, passing though a series of low-lying farm communities before beginning the gradual climb away from the neatly organized fields of the plains. The route ascends gently to **Springfield**, 70km out of Christchurch, at which point the river and the rail line veer away to the northwest, while the road continues climbing steadily past the sources of several rivers and streams to the 923m **Porter's Pass**, at the northern end of Lake Lyndon. As the route winds through increasingly dramatic gorges it passes the **Korowai/Torlesse Tussocklands Park**, the Porter Heights skifield (see p.678), lakes **Pearson**, **Grasmere** and **Sarah** to the north, which are directly opposite **Craigieburn Forest Park**, and the **Craigieburn**, **Mount Cheeseman**, and **Broken River** skifields (see p.678). About 6km beyond Lake Grasmere is the small settlement of **Cass**, where the tarmac and track routes rejoin and once again accompany the Waimakariri River along its wind-ing progress through the Southern Alps. On reaching **Bealey**, the you'll leave the river and push on to Arthur's Pass village, in the centre of the national park and wedged between the 2271m **Mount Rolleston** and the 1913m **Mount Temple**.

Just after Arthur's Pass Village the railway dives through the long glum **Otira Tunnel** while the road climbs beyond the settlement and then descends through the recently constructed **Otira Viaduct**. This spectacular piece of engineering best seen from a signed lookout point where you can snap some spectacular photographs of the road and, in one spot, the roof which keeps the cascade of mountain water off its surface. After that both road and rail slip quickly down toward the pounding seas of the West Coast.

Springfield

Although it doesn't look much, **SPRINGFIELD**, 70km from Christchurch, is the first place worth stopping, especially if you fancy a high-speed boat trip down the **Waimakariri Gorge** to blow away the cobwebs. The gorge is narrow, and the river water as clear as gin, with many waterfalls making for a safe, spectacular and beautiful ride. Waimak Alpine Jet, on Rubicon Rd, off the Kowahi Bush Road (☎03/318 4881, Ⓦ www.waimakalpinejet.co.nz; 30min $65, 1hr $85), operates 22-seater jetboats, and Springfield Jet (☎03/318 4797) do 20min runs ($50) and throw in a sheep shearing demo and afternoon tea; both operate daily but trips aren't frequent so call ahead.

In town on the northwest side of SH73 (Main Road) is the local domain where you can easily spend a relaxing twenty minutes exploring the pleasing **monument** to Springfield's best-loved son, Rewi Alley. Named after Rewi Maniapoto, the Maori leader who shouted at the battle of Orakau, *Kaore e manu te tongo. Ake! Ake!* ("We will never make peace. Never! Never!"), Alley displayed similar resilience throughout his fascinating life. After World War I he worked as a missionary in China, setting up small manufacturing co-operatives during the hazardous Japanese occupation. He went on to found schools, help with oil development, translate Chinese poetry, write poetry and prose of his own and act as an unofficial ambassador for China, despite his misgivings about the direction of the post-war communist regime and his increasing isolation within the country. The peaceful, Chinese-style garden memorial includes rock and water features, Rewi's abridged biography and a memorial to his remark-able mother, Clara, a leader in the New Zealand women's suffrage movement.

There's a small **visitor centre**, King St (daily 8.30am–5pm; ☎03/318 4000) in the train station signposted 500m off SH73. If you feel like breaking your journey, Springfield offers one of the friendliest and most comfortable affiliate YHA **hostels** on the South Island – *Smylie's*, Main St, opposite the domain (☎03/318 4740, Ⓦ www.smylies.co.nz; dorms ❶, rooms ❷, motel units ❸). Busiest in the winter when it operates as a ski lodge, *Smylie's* has great facili-ties, a refreshing Japanese influence (Japanese baths in winter), cosy rooms and Japanese meals available (from $12). For sustenance or a refreshing **drink** try the *Springfield Hotel* on Main Street, offering a selection of ales, reasonably priced snacks and substantial main courses.

Korowai/Torlesse Tussocklands Park

About 10km west of Springfield, the highway neatly bisects the undeveloped, 21,000-hectare **Korowai/Torlesse Tussocklands Park**, New Zealand's first tussock grasslands conservation park. It aims to protect the unique and quickly disappearing eastern Southern Island high country landscape typified by great swathes of treeless grassland covering mountainous knolls and ridges, seen in relief against the snow-capped Torlesse and Big Ben mountain ranges. The region is filled with endangered shrubs, unusual plants, flowers and animals adapted to the unstable screes and rock ridges. Look out for the cushion-like vegetable sheep, Haast's scree buttercup, scree lobelia, mountain daisy, and animals such as the native grasshopper, weta, butterflies and kea. The park is named after surveyor Charles Torlesse who, in 1849, was the first Pakeha to summit these mountains, led by Maori who know the region as *korowai* meaning cloak – a symbol of togetherness and prestige.

Approaching Porter's Pass along the highway, watch out for the extraordinary **Torlesse Gap** (aka Gunsight Gap), a narrow fissure 20m wide and 40m deep between the Red and Castle Hill peaks. A contrast to the otherwise rolling nature of the ridgeline, it is best seen from the Cave Stream Reserve, though if viewed from Springfield the ridgeline can resemble the outline of a woman lying on her back with the gap defining her neck. There are no marked tracks in the park, but there are several routes that are not too difficult to follow, like the climb from **Porter's Pass** (beside the road) to **Foggy Peak** (1733m). Various huts are dotted throughout the park but if you are going to explore it on foot check in with DOC and make sure you have provisions and a good map.

Another way into the park is to turn left off SH73 after Porter's Pass and head towards Lake Lyndon, between Mount Lyndon and the Big Ben Range.

Kura Tawhiti (Castle Hill Reserve)

About 30km west of Springfield, SH73 passes **Kura Tawhiti Scenic Reserve** (Castle Hill), a swathe of rolling grassland peppered by clusters of grey limestone outcrops ranging from the size of a sheep to something as big as, well, a castle. Since the mid-1990s, the place has gained an international reputation for the quantity and quality of its **bouldering**, an abbreviated rope-free form of rock climbing which doesn't generally get its adherents far off the ground, though experts might spend days perfecting their moves on a particularly hard problem. On fine days there are always boulderers out there, visible from a number of **paths** which wind among the rocks and tussock-covered hills.

Maori once stopped here on trading missions and the place retains a spiritual significance. It is also a photogenic place with mountain daisies and Castle Hill buttercups blooming in summer.

Cave Stream Scenic Reserve

A bare wild area in the same vein as Kura Tawhiti, **Cave Stream Scenic Reserve** nestles among limestone outcrops with views of the Craigieburn and Torlesse ranges. Access is from SH73 6km west of Kura Tawhiti where a dirt, oval car park and a number of DOC information boards announce this rare opportunity for unguided exploration of a limestone cave (362m; 1hr). Cave art, signs of seasonal camps and the discovery of a wooden framed flax backpack and other artefacts over 500 years old (now in the Canterbury Museum, see p.615), indicate that Maori once visited the area extensively. The cave itself contains bones, suggesting it was a burial site; it also provides a home for large harvestman spider and young eels who wriggle along the walls. This is a wet and exciting underground adventure, though the cave often hosts school outings so you're unlikely to be alone. The best time to go is from December to April, but at any time dress warmly, take a companion, plus at least one torch each with spare batteries (there's no light in the cave) and make sure you have something dry to change into afterwards. The **walk/wade** itself involves entering at the downstream end where you'll cross a deep pool (if the water is more than waist high, fast flowing, foaming and discoloured, do not attempt the walk) before gradually climbing upstream. There are only two obstacles: a 1.5m rockfall about halfway and a 3m waterfall at the very end. The latter you'll negotiate by crawling along a short, narrow ledge and up a ladder of iron rungs embedded in the rock.

Craigieburn Forest Park

The **Craigieburn Forest Park** lies on the eastern ranges of the Southern Alps, about 15km beyond Kura Tawhiti and 42km before Arthur's Pass Village. It is chock-a-block with good walking tracks, longer tramps and mountaineering opportunities in the more rugged country further west. The park is dominated by dense, moss-covered mountain beech forest, alpine scrub and tussock grasslands, which are peppered with scarlet native mistletoe flowers from December to February. A variety of native birds streak and squawk through the forest, including bellbird, rifleman, silver eye and kea, and between October and February, long-tailed and shining cuckoos join the throng. The nearby **Craigieburn Valley skifield**, within the boundaries of the forest park, is one of the most exciting in the vicinity of Arthur's Pass – see box below for details.

Skifields around Arthur's Pass

There are five accessible skifields in the area around Arthur's Pass, each offering accommodation and equipment rental. Although there is not an enormous variety of runs they are unusual and challenging with some spectacular views, as well as reliable snow and relatively deserted slopes. The **season** is generally July to September with October often good. For full details and information on snow conditions visit Ⓦwww.snow.co.nz. The fields are described from east to west, heading along SH73 from Christchurch. Many people choose to access the skifields from Christchurch, but if you want to cut down on travelling stay at *Smylie's* in Springfield (see p.676) or in Arthur's Pass Village.

Porter Heights 96km west of Christchurch, just off SH73 via a 6km unsealed road Ⓣ03/318 4002, Ⓔ ski@porterheights.co.nz. The region's main commercial field, with the longest single run in the southern hemisphere. Lift passes cost $48 per day and learners' lift $30 per day.

Mount Cheeseman 112km from Christchurch along SH73 Ⓣ03/379 5315, Ⓦwww.mtcheeseman.com. An exceedingly well-appointed club field with good facilities and a friendly atmosphere. There's a wide variety of runs for intermediates and off-piste for those with experience. Lift passes are $42 per day.

Broken River 120km out from Christchurch at the end of a 6km access road, off SH73 Ⓣ03/318 7270, Ⓔ ski@brokenriver.co.nz. A very well equipped field, offering night skiing and good snowboard terrain. Lift passes are $41 a day. Accommodation huts (②) instruction package $30 an hour. The

ski area is only about 20min walk from the car park and there's a free goods lift. It is possible to ski between Broken River and Craigieburn, which have transferable lift passes.

Craigieburn Valley 120km out of Christchurch and another 6km up a side road Ⓣ03/365 2514, Ⓦwww.craigieburn.co.nz. A challenging area whose extreme slopes (a 609m vertical drop) make it the best-kept secret in the southern hemisphere. It's only really suitable for intermediate and advanced skiers and boarders. Lift passes about $42 per day.

Temple Basin 4km west of Arthur's Pass Village Ⓣ03/377 7788, Ⓦwww .templebasin.co.nz. Right at the Arthur's Pass col, this field is superb for snowboarding with a 430m drop, floodlit for night-skiing and has a variety of runs for all abilities. There's a 1hr walk in and lift passes cost $34 a day but there's a free goods lift.

In a signposted car park just off SH73 by Cave Stream is the **Craigieburn Picnic Area** and a walkers' **shelter** with fixed maps of the local tramps. The *Craigieburn Forest Park Day Walks* leaflet (from local visitor centres; $1) details eleven of the best short and day walks in the park. From the picnic area the path up to and around the **Lyndon Saddle** (4km; 3–4hr) is worthwhile, but if you do nothing else take the **Hut Creek Walk** (2km; 1hr) beginning outside the Environmental Education Centre (closed to the public) at the top of the winding, dirt road 3km further on from the picnic site and SH73, or accessible from the Broken River Skifield Road which jags away from SH73 1km south of the picnic area turn-off. The track itself winds down to the creek and continues through mountain beeches, emerging onto a slope of native hebe, dracophyllum (whose leaves shade from green to a reddish-brown in spring and autumn), cassinia and matagouri. There are great views from the lookout, and kea (see box, p.680) are often about. To tack on a pleasant extra twenty minutes try the nature trail that also begins at the centre.

If you want to break your journey before the final assault on the pass, head for the *Flock Hill Lodge* (℡03/318 8196, 🌐www.flockhill.co.nz; dorms ❶, linen $5 extra, rooms ❺), 10km west of Cave Stream, which has basic backpacker accommodation in shearers' quarters and a range of spacious units in beautiful grounds, plus a restaurant and bar for guests. A further 27km on, and 12km short of Arthur's Pass Village, the solitary *Historic Bealey Hotel* (℡03/318 9277, 🌐www.bealeyhotel.co.nz; dorms ❶, motel units ❹), is wonderfully set on a knoll overlooking the broad expanse of the Waimakariri River. The hotel is easily recognized by the welcoming presence of a large concrete *moa*, which commemorates the owner's reputed 1993 sighting of such a beast (some three centuries after the species became extinct). Trade was boosted massively. Once a stop-off point for Cobb & Co coaches that travelled to and from the West Coast, the hotel now provides clean and simple backpacker and motel-style accommodation, beer and good **food** in the *Klondyke* bar, and more filling fare in its bistro and restaurant.

Arthur's Pass Village

ARTHUR'S PASS VILLAGE, 4km east of the pass itself, nestles at 735m in a steep-sided, forest-covered U-shaped valley. With only about forty residents it forms a thin straggle along the main road (SH73). The area receives over four metres of rainfall a year, and the village invariably hunches beneath mist or clouds: there's often a moody contrast between the white clouds that hover halfway up the valley wall, and the rich green trees and vegetation of the valley floor and slopes. The kea (see box, p.680) don't seem to mind and are often around the village, especially in the early evening.

The Arthur's Pass settlement came about in the early 1900s to provide shelter for tunnel diggers and rail workers, and nowadays ekes a living from the tourists visiting the surrounding **national park**. It's a superb base for walking and climbing, with the nearby **Temple Basin skifield** (see box on p.678) providing good skiing and snowboarding opportunities in winter.

Practicalities

Regular coast-to-coast **buses** (Coast to Coast ℡0800/800 847, Alpine Coaches ℡0800/274 888 & Atomic Shuttles ℡03/322 8883) and TranzAlpine **train** (see p.675) all stop in the centre of the settlement a short walk from everything. There is an excellent **DOC office** and **visitor centre**, on the main

Kea: New Zealand's trickster alpine parrot

One of the most enduring memories of a visit to Arthur's Pass and many other alpine areas of the South Island is the sight of a bright green **kea** (or a flock of them) mischievously getting their beaks into something. Or, more often than not, simply posing for the camera. With their lolloping sideways gait, scavenging tendencies and inexhaustible curiosity, the world's only alpine parrots are so endearing you're tempted to try to feed them. Human food does them more harm than good, but these kleptomaniacs can be persistent and frequently grab sandwiches from inattentive lunching walkers. You'll hear the ruffle of feathers, see the flash of red beneath their wings and they'll be tearing at your lunch just out of reach.

At backcountry huts you might find kea sliding down the corrugated iron roofing or pulling at the nails holding the roof on, but if they notice a carelessly abandonned pair of hiking boots they'll soon latch onto them. Trampers have been known to wake up to a pile of leather strips and shredded laces.

With these playful tendencies it is hardly surprising they traditionally got the blame for attacking sheep, and for many years were routinely shot by farmers. Recent research seems to indicate kea only attack already weakened sheep, and shooting has long since stopped as the birds are now fully protected.

street (daily: Nov–April 8.30am–5pm; May–Oct 8.30am–4pm; ☎03/318 9211, ⓦ www.apinfo.co.nz), with extensive displays on wildlife, plants, geology and local history, and a video about the trail blazed by the stage coaches and the railway is played on request ($1). The visitor centre also has a 24hr sheltered porch with a map of the village, weather information and search and rescue action cards.

The only public phones are just outside the YHA. There's a rarely open **post office** (in a shed), a **petrol station** and a shop in the village, but no banks. Everyone has EFTPOS.

There's a reasonable choice of good-value **accommodation** in the village – strung out along the main road – although places fill up quickly during the high season (Dec–Feb), when it's a good idea to book in advance. If there's no room at the inn, you could always try the *Historic Bealey Hotel*, 12km to the east, or the *Flock Hill Lodge*, 40km east, toward Christchurch (see p.679). **Eating** is limited to the three places listed, all close to each other on SH73, plus a single **shop** selling basic supplies.

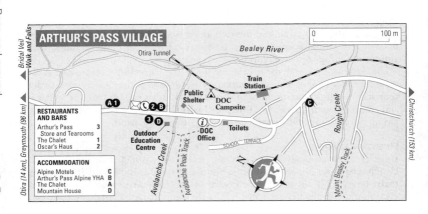

Accommodation

Alpine Motels ⊤ 03/318 9233, Ⓔ alpine.motels@xtra.co.nz. Basic motel units with private facilities, and simpler rooms at slightly cheaper rates. ❹

Arthur's Pass Alpine YHA ⊤ T03/318 9230, Ⓔ yha.arthurspass@yha.org.nz. Occupying a prime spot in the village, this 1955 hostel was the first purpose-built YHA in the country and boasts helpful staff, a large firewood-warmed common room, a bike shed and gear storage. Book early. Camping $12, dorms ❶, rooms ❷

The Chalet ⊤ 03/318 9236, Ⓦ www.arthurspass.co.nz. A relatively large alpine chalet offering B&B in ensuite and shared bath rooms (plus one room used as a small dorm) all with central heating and TV and some with mountain views. Rooms and dorm all come with continental breakfast in the café downstairs. Dorm $40, shared-bath ❺, ensuite ❻.

DOC Campsite next to Arthur's Pass Public Shelter and backing on to the railway. Basic site with cold water and toilets. Camping $5

Mountain House ⊤ 03/318 9258, Ⓦ www .trampers.co.nz. Clean bunkrooms, plus some doubles and twins, and a large comfy common room and kitchen, run in tandem with the area's best accommodation – a row of spacious, self-contained, cottages with two to three bedrooms, high on the hill over the village. Either rent a room in the cottage and share facilities or rent the whole place. Camping $10, dorms ❶, rooms ❷, cottage room ❷, whole cottage $150–250.

Eating and drinking

Arthur's Pass Store and Tearooms Traditional tearooms with recent addition that includes an espresso machine. Best for takeaways, sandwiches and cakes. Open daily 8am–7.30pm.

The Chalet The best (and most expensive) food in Arthur's Pass is found at this convivial all-day café based around an open fire, serving breakfast from 7am (cooked from 8.30am). There's a good range of salads, quiches and bistro meals ($10–20) until late, and an evening à la carte menu (mains $22–28).

Oscar's Haus Licensed café selling everything from muffins and coffee to gourmet pies ($5), roast dinners ($14) and gourmet pizza ($16–23). Daytime year-round and evenings in summer.

Arthur's Pass National Park

Despite the spectacular views you get from the pass itself, you really need to take one of the many day (or longer) walks to get a feel for this remarkable alpine landscape. The 720 square kilometres surrounding the pass were designated the **Arthur's Pass National Park** in 1929, and have exerted a powerful attraction over walkers and mountaineers ever since. The park encompasses much of the alpine flora unique to New Zealand. Otira just west of the pass gets around 6m of rain a year; Bealey, 15km to the west gets only 2m. Explore a while and you'll see the rich crimson of the southern rata trees, the broad-leaved evergreen podocarp forest of the wetter regions and the tussock grasslands stretching east.

Although easily accessible, the park can still be a hazardous place and apart from a few easy walks around Arthur's Pass Village is a place for experienced, well-prepared trampers: take simple precautions and use your common sense. The weather is highly changeable and often wet, so be sure to bring warm and waterproof clothing, sturdy footwear, a supply of drinking water and (even on the shortest walks) some energy-giving food. If you're embarking on tramps of a day or longer fill in the relevant search and rescue action card at the DOC visitor centre in Arthur's Pass Village before setting out.

Suggested **short walks** are detailed in the *Walks in Arthur's Pass National Park* leaflet ($1), stocked by the DOC office in Arthur's Pass Village, and there is an entire series of exhaustive national park guides covering day and longer walks (50¢ each); all these leaflets work best when used in conjunction with the 1:50,000 *Otira* topographic map, which covers most of the park.

Among the most popular short walks are the **Devil's Punch Bowl** (2km return; 1hr; 100m ascent), an all-weather climb and descent to the base of a 131-metre waterfall, crossing two footbridges and zigzagging up steps, and the

△ Arthur's Pass

Bridal Veil Nature Walk (2.5km return; 1hr 30min; 50m ascent), which ascends a gentle gradient through mountain beeches then crosses the Bridal Veil Creek before returning along the road.

The climb to **Avalanche Peak** (5km return; 6–7hr; 1000m ascent) is longer and more strenuous but offers wonderful views of the surrounding mountains and should only be attempted in reasonable weather. The best way is going up the Avalanche Peak track and then making a circuit of it by returning on the **Scotts Track** (total walking time 6–7hr; 1000m descent).

To include a night in a backcountry hut, go for the **Mingha–Deception** (25km; 2 days; 400m ascent, 750m descent) which traces the route used for the mountain run stage of the arduous Coast to Coast race (see p.795). Long sections are easy to follow, but there are unmarked areas requiring a little route finding, and some unbridged river crossings – so watch the water levels. If you're feeling particularly fit and travelling in the summer, add on the side a trip to Lake Mavis (500m ascent), a high mountain tarn with some lovely views. You can use either the Goat Pass Hut (20 bunks; $10) or the Upper Deception Hut (6 bunks; $5) and ponder how mad you'd have to be to run the route competitively.

One of the most demanding tramps is the **Harman Pass to Kelly Saddle** (55km; 4–5 days; 1700m ascent), a rewarding trip mostly along unmarked tracks and involving the crossing of unbridged rivers. Prospective trampers need to be fit and well-equipped; the huts along the way are $5–10 but still quite comfortable, and the best views are to be had from the ridges near Kelly Saddle. One of the slightly easier tracks that doesn't skimp on great views is **Casey Saddle to Binser Saddle** (40km; 2 days), a pleasant tramp crossing easy saddles on well-defined tracks through open beech forest, staying overnight in Casey Hut (16 bunks; $10).

The South Canterbury foothills

The **South Canterbury foothills** mark the transition from the flat Canterbury Plains to the rugged and spectacular Southern Alps. It is a region frequently ignored by visitors hurrying out of Christchurch bound for the more obvious charms of Arthur's Pass in the west or Aoraki Mount Cook and Queenstown to the south, but warrants a little of your time. The area is primarily known for the winter resort town of **Methven**, which serves the ski slopes of **Mount Hutt**. Things are relatively quiet here in summer, but there's a wealth of natural attractions in the region, with the **Mount Hutt Forest**, the **Rakaia Gorge** and **walks** around **Mount Somers** rewarding travellers who make the effort to stop. Further south, inland from Timaru, the tiny communities of **Geraldine** and **Fairlie** link the east coast with the mountains and provide bases from which to enjoy either skifields or summer adventure activities.

The main **route** through the area is SH72 which has been dubbed the "Inland Scenic Route" – follow the brown signs. InterCity and Newmans **buses** running between Christchurch and Queenstown represent the main means of getting here by public transport, though services are limited to one or two per day.

Methven and around

A hundred kilometres west of Christchurch on SH77, **METHVEN** is Canterbury's winter sports capital and the accommodation and refuelling centre for the **Mount Hutt** skifield during the June to October **ski season**. In summer

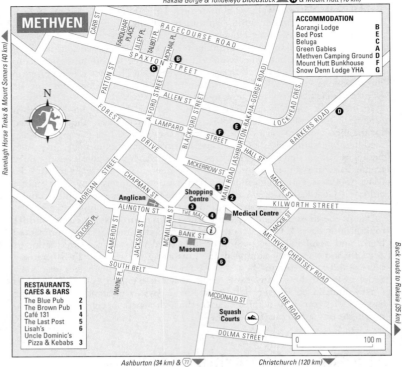

METHVEN

ACCOMMODATION

Aorangi Lodge	B
Bed Post	E
Beluga	C
Green Gables	A
Methven Camping Ground	D
Mount Hutt Bunkhouse	F
Snow Denn Lodge YHA	G

RESTAURANTS, CAFÉS & BARS

The Blue Pub	2
The Brown Pub	1
Café 131	4
The Last Post	5
Lisah's	6
Uncle Dominic's Pizza & Kebabs	3

Ashburton (34 km) & ⑦ ▼   Christchurch (120 km) ▼

the town is quiet and fairly uninspiring, but makes a good base for exploring the nearby Rakaia Gorge, Mount Somers and doing a handful of activities.

Scotsman Robert Patton bought land in the area in 1869 and named Methven after his home town. The place ticked by as a farming service town until the major development of the skifield in the mid-1970s. About the only thing of sustaining interest from the early days is the **Anglican Church**, on the corner of Chapman Street and Alington Street, and even that is an interloper. Built in 1880 in the tiny settlement of Sherwood 75km south, the church was transported to Methven by two traction engines in 1884.

Practicalities

Buses stop on Main Road (SH77), outside the **visitor centre**, 93 Main Rd (daily: Nov–May 9am–5pm; June–Oct 7.30am–6pm; ☎03/302 8955, ⓦwww.methven.net.nz), which has lots of information about Methven, the skifields and **walks** in the vicinity, and can arrange **car rental** (from around $60 per day). They also book the Methven Travel shuttle (☎03/302 8106) to Christchurch ($27 one way) and the Mt Somers. The town itself is easily explored on foot, and an array of companies offer minibus **transport to the skifields** (expect to pay $22–25 return; 1hr); the visitor centre has details of current operators.

The small shopping centre around the junction of Main Street and Forest Drive including banks, a post shop and several **ski shops** (specializing in gear rental and repairs), the best of which is Big Al's (☎03/302 8003).

Accommodation

In winter there's a huge range of **accommodation** in Methven. Much of it stays open through the summer but the disappearance of most visitors means that prices are quite competitive and there's even scope for excellent deals.

Aorangi Lodge 38 Spaxton St ☏ 03/302 8482, Ⓔ aorangi.lodge@xtra.co.nz. Excellent single-storey simple wooden building with twin, double, triple and quad rooms, all sharing bathrooms. Free and hearty continental breakfast, cooked breakfast $4–9 extra. ❸

Bed Post 177 Main St ☏ 03/302 8508, Ⓦ www.mthuttbeds.com. Bargain combination motel and hostel, all well maintained and with a separate self-contained backpacker house (complete with female dorm). Motel units are fully equipped and some have spa bath. Dorms ❶, rooms ❷, motel units ❹

Beluga 40 Allen St ☏ 03/302 8290, Ⓦ www .beluga.co.nz. Luxurious B&B accommodation much loved by skiers, in two well-kept houses which have retained their original charm and are surrounded by tranquil gardens. Bathrooms are separate but not shared, robes are provided, and home-made bread accompanies a breakfast of your choice. ❼

Green Gables 3km north of Methven on SH77 ☏ 03/302 8308 & 0800/466 093,

Ⓔ greengables@xtra.co.nz. A peaceful rural B&B partly surrounded by a deer farm. Accommodation consists of one en-suite double, and a double and single with shared facilities. Breakfasts are generous, and dinner is available by arrangement ($45). ❻

Methven Camping Ground Barkers Rd ☏ 03/302 8005, Ⓔ methvennz@hotmail.com. Conveniently sited with a mountain backdrop. Camping $9, cabins ❷

Mount Hutt Bunkhouse 8 Lampard St ☏ 03/302 8894, Ⓔ mthuttbunks@xtra.co.nz. Comfortable and welcoming backpacker accommodation in the main house or a separate self-contained house next door. Dorms ❶, rooms ❷

Snow Denn Lodge YHA cnr McMillan St & Banks St ☏ 03/302 8999, Ⓦ www .methvenaccommodation.co.nz. New, purpose-built hostel with a spacious lounge with views of the mountain, and a hot tub. Dorms ❶, rooms ❷, ensuites ❸

Eating and drinking

There are some snug little cafés and coffee houses serving thick, steaming soups to winter sportsmen or low-fat Italian salads and panini to the summer crowds, along with a smattering of pleasant if not overly lively bars. Some establishments open only in the winter but prices lean to the higher side no matter what the season. All of the places listed below are open year round.

The Blue Pub *Methven Hotel*, cnr Kilworth St & Barkers Rd. The 1918 hotel popular with the après ski crowd has two sections. The *Base Café* serves deli sandwiches, soups, cakes, light meals and full evening meals ($16–18), while *Samuel's Bar* has big screen sports plus touring bands and DJs.

The Brown Pub opposite *The Blue Pub* in the old *Canterbury Hotel*. Passable and very cheap bar meals in generous portions, this locals' drinking hole also boasts a bottle shop.

Café 131 131 Main St. The pick of the daytime cafés, good for coffee and muffins, but also serving full breakfasts ($7–15), a tasty chicken Caesar salad ($14), and a dreamy brandy cake with cream.

The Last Post Main St ☏ 03/302 8259. Classy wood-floored restaurant that's about the most formal in town, serving the likes of Thai marinated chicken ($20), followed by steamed fig and ginger pudding ($13).

Lisah's Main St. Straightforward mainstream licensed dining, but tasty and reasonably priced. Try the pasta ($15), lemongrass chicken ($21) or the Cajun fish ($21).

Uncle Dominic's Pizza and Kebabs 253 Forest Drive, in the main shopping centre. Surprisingly good pizzas and kebabs, at reasonable prices, to eat in or take away. Summer lunches and evenings, weekends only, winter daily; BYO.

Around Methven

Methven's main attraction is **Mount Hutt**, 26km to the northeast off SH72, with its excellent skifield where, in winter, they even run the **Mount Hutt Bungy** (June–Oct; Ⓦ www.mthuttbungy.com; around $100) at the ski area car park. In summer, there's little reason to visit and a gate bars the access road, though the Methven visitor centre have a key if you need access.

For most, in summer there's more appeal in horse-riding, hot-air ballooning, walking the tracks in the **Awa Awa Rata Reserve** or visiting the **Rakaia Gorge** with its walkway, jet boating and pleasant campground.

Mount Hutt Skifield

Twenty-six kilometres northeast of Methven, just off SH72, **Mount Hutt** (☏03/302 8811, ⓦwww.nzski.com; daily lift pass $72) is widely regarded as the best and most developed skifield in the southern hemisphere, with a vertical rise of 655m and a longest run of 2km. It also enjoys the longest season (roughly June–October) and offers a broad range of skiing and boarding conditions. Beginners can take advantage of a one-day starter pack (skiing $80, boarding $99), and there are assorted rental and instruction packages. There's no accommodation on the mountain, so most people stay in Methven from where there are frequent shuttle buses (roughly 1hr to the skifield). Leopard Coachlines (☏03/302 8707) run **buses** to and from Methven ($25 return) and Christchurch ($38) every day, dropping off in the morning and picking up in the afternoon.

Awa Awa Rata Reserve

Awa Awa Rata Reserve, 14km northwest of Methven, is a beautiful spot with tall mountain beech sprouting on the eastern flanks of the Southern Alps with snow tussock above the scrub line providing a home for a variety of native and introduced birds. It is all part of the Mt Hutt Conservation Area, covered by a DOC leaflet ($1 from the visitor centre) which details several **walking tracks** (30min–2hr). Most are accessed from the McLennans Bush Road entrance reached by heading north from Methven on SH77 and going straight ahead onto McLennans Bush Road at base of Mt Hutt access road. It is worth taking a little extra time to examine the Mount Hutt flora during the spring and summer: of the **alpine plants** of New Zealand, 94 percent grow only in New Zealand, of which 130 species can only be found on Mount Hutt. One such is the unique vegetable sheep (*Raoulia eximia*), which forms huge grey mounds that look not unlike sheep lying down, from a distance. There's also the *Ranunculus haastii*, a beautiful species of buttercup with blue-grey leaves and luminous yellow flowers, and ten species of mountain daisies, *Celmisias*, which form huge cushions of flowers.

Rakaia Gorge

Some 15km north of Methven the Rakaia River emerges from the **Rakaia Gorge**, a steep-sided defile created by an ancient lava flow and now lined in many places with regenerating forest. **Maori history** tells how a *taniwha* (water spirit) lived nearby, hunting and eating *moa* and *weka*; his possessions, because of his status as a spirit, were *tapu*. One cold day he went to find a hot spring, and while he was away the northwest wind demon flattened his property. To prevent this happening again, the *taniwha* collected large boulders and stones from the mountains to block the course of the demon, and in so doing narrowed the Rakaia River so that it flowed between the rocky walls. The spirit became so warm because of his exertions that the heat from his body melted the snow and ice on the mountains, and his perspiration fell on the rocks and formed crystals in the riverbed.

All this sweaty work can be seen from the **Rakaia Gorge Walkway** (15km; 3–4hr return), which starts where SH72 crosses the river beside an information shelter with maps of the area and a list of activities. The path leads through several forest stands and spectacular geological areas, past hardened lava flows of rhyolite, pitchstone and andesite, to the upper gorge lookout. The less committed might fancy just walking as far as a fenced viewpoint high on a bluff above the river (1hr return).

Below the gorge, the river fans out into a classic example of the braided rivers so common on the eastern side of the South Island. It is here you can board a **jetboat ride** with Rakaia Gorge Scenic Jets (℡03/318 6515, 🅦www.cvcanterburypages.co.nz/rakaiajet), whose tours range from twenty to fifty minutes, with a standard trip weighing in at about $65 per person. Slightly more edifying is to let them take you to the end of the **Rakaia Gorge** (around $25 per person, min of 2) and then walk back. The gorge offers a delightful and easy walk – take a picnic and it's a great way to spend an afternoon.

On SH72, over on the south side of the river the nicely sited *Rakaia Gorge* **camping** ground ($8 per site) offers peaceful camping with water supply and toilets.

Horse-riding and hot-air ballooning

Aside from skiing and jet boating on the Rakaia (see above), the two most interesting things to do around Methven are horse trotting and ballooning, but both come with a hefty price tag. **Horse trotting** happens 20km north of Methven on Lauriston Barrhill Road, off SH77 ($155 for 2hr 30min; daily by arrangement on ℡03/302 4800). Included are a tour and the opportunity to observe the usual preparations and participate in a race, riding tandem in one of the unstable-looking carts as it careers round the course behind a highly strung thoroughbred. The most spectacular activity in Methven, though, is **hot-air ballooning** with Aoraki Balloon Safaris (℡03/302 8172 & 0800/256 839, 🅦www.nzballooning.com) who offer a four-hour sunrise trip ($285) including champagne breakfast; the fine views of the patchwork quilt of the Canterbury Plains and the magnificent Southern Alps make this one of the best balloon flights on the South Island.

Mount Somers and around

The 1687m **Mount Somers** rises from the flatlands of the Canterbury Plains above the villages of Mount **Somers** and **Stavely**. On a spur protruding from the Southern Alps, it is not an especially striking sight, but the encircling **Mount Somers Walkway** is unusual in New Zealand for its high-country tramp mainly above the bushline and in the rain shadow of the mountains. When it is raining in Arthur's Pass, and Mount Cook is clagged-in there's a fair chance you'll get some hiking in here.

The landscape differs from its surroundings as it's formed from volcanic rhyolite rock, which is harder than greywacke and shows fault lines, exposing columns and fractures of darker andesitic material. As a result the terrain is generally more rugged, with outcrops of rock poking out from patches of regenerating beech forest and large areas of low-fertility soil subject to heavy rainfall turning to bog. As a result you'll find bog pine, snow totara, toatoa and mountain flax as well as (though less often) the rare whio (blue duck).

More is explained in DOC's handy *Mount Somers Conservation Area* leaflet ($1 from the Staveley Store and Methven visitor centre), which also describes the Mount Somers Walkway and several short walks.

Staveley

The northern access point for the walkway is tiny **STAVELEY**, 22km south-west of Methven, where the Staveley Village Store (daily 8am–6pm; ☎03/303 0859) stocks last minute supplies (including espresso), and can put drivers in touch with a **car shuttling** service (see below). They also hold the keys to the **Staveley Geological and Historical Centre**, in the Springburn School Building across the road (donation appreciated). The building dates back 125 years and contains displays on the unique geology of the mountain. Even if you have no intention of tackling an overnight hike, at least drive 2km to the northern trailhead at Sharplins car park and stroll to **Sharplins Falls** (1hr return). If you don't fancy exploring the area independently, you could join the excellent Tussock and Beech Ecotours (☎03/303 0880, ⓦwww.nature.net.nz) for one- to three-day eco-tours ($120–520) which are informative and entertaining. DOC fees, accommodation, food and transport from Christchurch are included or you can save $40 by finding your own way to Staveley. They also operate tours to other areas in the South Canterbury Foothills, are experts on the climbs on Mt Somers, and have lovely **accommodation** in the form of *Ross Cottage* (❺), a delightful 130-year-old self-catering cottage just outside Staveley.

Mount Somers

Access to the southern end of the walkway at Woolshed Creek is from the hamlet of **MOUNT SOMERS**, 8km south of Staveley. The Mount Somers Store sells hut tickets and a reasonable range of groceries, and there's the pleasant tree-filled *Mount Somers Holiday Park*, Hoods Road, 1km off SH72 (☎03/303 9719, ⓦwww.mountsomers.co.nz; camping $9, cabins ❷, ensuite ❸). The only real **restaurant** hereabouts is the top class *Stronechrubie*, just south of Mount Somers on SH72 (bookings essential ☎03/303 9814, ⓦwww.stronechrubie.co.nz), where the chef uses fresh local ingredients and only the best meat to produce mouthwatering dishes. Try the lamb shanks ($22), or panfried salmon ($25), and for dessert don't miss the McRae's whisky cake and whisky sabayon ($8). If you can't tear yourself away after dinner (or can't move), *Stronechrubie* also has **rooms** (❺) all with kitchens, wicker furniture and views of the mountain, and offers dinner bed and breakfast for two for $200.

From Mount Somers, Ashburton Gorge Road heads past the start of the Mount Somers Walkway (good for some short walks around some old coalmine workings) to **Lake Clearwater**, with excellent windsurfing amid superb scenery.

Mount Somers Walkway

The star attraction around these parts is the **Mount Somers Walkway** (17km one way; 9–10hr; 800m ascent), a subalpine track around the north side of the mountain which should soon be turned into a loop with the completion of a southern component. The walk passes abandoned coal mines, volcanic formations and a deep river canyon, and can be done in one long day, though it's often treated as a leisurely two-day affair.

Those without their own vehicles should base themselves in Methven where Methven Travel (☎03/302 8106; $35 return; min 2) operates a Mount Somers shuttle service on demand. Drivers will want the services of a **vehicle shuttle**, best organised through the Staveley Village Store (see above). The deal is that for $30 you drive someone to where you'll start the walk, and they then drive your car to some safe place overnight and deposit it at the other end in time for your emergence from the wilds.

The track is generally walked from the Mount Somers end from where you take Ashburton Gorge Road for 11km then follow a signpost 3km along an old tramway route to the **Woolshed Creek** car park and picnic area. From here follow the nature walk to the signposted junction and follow the poles from there to the plateau lip, from which you can make your own way to the beacon on the gently rolling top. After 2–3 hours you reach Mount Somers Hut (aka Woolshed Creek Hut; $5). From there it is 3–4hr to the Pinnacles Hut ($5) reached along a track past river-worn caves over the 1170-metre Mount Somers Saddle and through tussock. It is another 3–4hr from there down to the car park passing a side track to Sharplins Falls.

Remember that the rolling country on top of the hills is subject to fog and can be very disorienting so carry a topographical map and a compass.

Peel Forest and rafting the Rangitata

Peel Forest Park, 35km south of Mount Somers, encloses a vast expanse of beautiful forest, scrub and alpine vegetation. Follow the signs off SH72 and after 12km you'll reach the hamlet of **PEEL FOREST** about 1.5km short of the reserve entrance, a useful spot for stocking up on supplies and picking up information from the **Peel Forest Store** (☎03/696 3567; Mon–Thurs 8am–7pm, Fri & Sat 8am–7.30pm, Sun 9am–7pm), which serves as a visitor centre, campsite booking office, bottle store, post office, petrol station, takeaway and tea rooms, and stocks the DOC leaflet ($1) which describes the **Peel Forest Tracks**, thirteen walking tracks ranging from thirty minutes to six hours. Of these, the best are the **Acland Falls Walking Track** (1.5km; 1hr return), a steep climb followed by a short streamside walk to a 14m waterfall, and **Allan's Track** (4km; 2–3hr round-trip), a steady ascent past the head of Mils Stream and through podocarp forest which can be extended by joining the **Deer Spur Track** (5km; 2hr return), a steep but well-defined route which climbs above the bushline to a sparkling mountain tarn at an altitude of about 900m. Take time while you walk to admire the huge, ancient totara trees, rata and ferns, and to watch the antics of the fantails and tomtits – these little birds often hover around, feeding on the insects disturbed by trampers and picnickers.

The park is also the home to one of the best **whitewater-rafting** operators in New Zealand, the very professional Rangitata Rafts (☎0800/251 251,

ⓦ www.rafts.co.nz) at Peel Forest River Base, 8km north of Peel Forest Store. They run excellent, fun trips on the Rangitata River (Oct–May daily at 11.30am; 3hr; $135 including lunch & dinner): a maximum of six rafts take to the river at once, with a full briefing beforehand and one guide for every nine passengers. The first part of the rafting is Grade I, which gives you a chance to get used to the rafts before the thrilling trip through the Grade IV–V rapids of the high-sided Rangitata Gorge; there's also an optional ten-metre cliff jump near the end. Afterwards, your ordeal by water is rounded off with welcome hot showers and a barbecue dinner. Pickup from Geraldine or Christchurch costs $10 extra.

There is also an Outdoor Pursuits Centre based 100m north of the Peel Forest Store (ⓣ03/696 3832), which offers a sit-on (as opposed to sit-in) **kayaking trip** (half-day; $105), along the Rangitata or Orari rivers, paddling up to Grade II, all equipment provided.

To **stay** in the area there's a choice of the pleasant *Peel Forest B&B* (ⓣ03/696 3557; $40 per room) just north of the Peel Forest Store, a DOC **campground** (camping $7, cabins $15pp) 2km further on, and accommodation at Rangitata Rafts: camping ($10 per site), and very basic bunk accommodation in its lodge (dorm $18, double or twin ❷).

Geraldine and around

The pretty and prosperous farming town of **GERALDINE**, 45km south of Mount Somers and 35km north of Timaru, was traditionally a toilet and cuppa stop on the way to somewhere more interesting. Of late it has smartened its act aiming to attract visitors with its smattering of **craft shops**, **galleries** and specialist **food stores**. The pleasures and brilliant rafting of the **Peel Forest** area (see p.689) are also within easy reach.

The Town and around

In town, the tiny **Geraldine Historical Museum**, on Cox Street (Mon–Sat 9.30am–midday & 1.30–3.30pm, Sun 2–4pm; donation), has little of outstanding interest but is housed in a rather quaint blue-and-white stone building with an attractive garden. More extensive is the **Geraldine Vintage Car and Machinery Club**, 174 Talbot St (Nov–Feb daily 10am–4pm; March–Oct Sat & Sun only 10am–4pm; $5), which houses a surprising collection of old cars, tractors and planes, mostly well-kept but with a few not quite so well-loved.

To check out Geraldine's wealth of **artists, galleries and craft shops**, pick up the *Geraldine District Arts and Crafts Guide* or the *Geraldine* leaflet (both free from the visitor centre). Stained Glass Windows, 177 Talbot St (open most mornings), where you can browse among the colourful lampshades and stained-glass work, is well worth visiting. Equally good to explore is The Giant Jersey, 10 Wilson St (Mon–Fri 9am–5pm, Sat & Sun 10am–4pm; ⓣ03/693 9820, ⓦ www.giantjersey.co.nz), where amongst the usual display of jumpers you'll find the *Guinness Book of Records'* **World's Largest Jersey** (weighing 5.5kilos). There's also an array of heraldic mosaics and a 34-metre-long half-scale **tableau of the Bayeux Tapestry** (ⓦ www.1066.co.nz), made entirely from tiny pieces of spring steel broken from knitting machines. Once you've finished staring yourself bug-eyed at the tapestries you can then drive yourself batty by trying out a few of the owner's homegrown, cypher-like alphametics and magic number cubes, after which you'll probably need some fresh air.

The best place to get it is a few hundred metres away at the **Talbot Forest Scenic Reserve**, at the end of Hislop Street, the last remnant of a once extensive native forest, with the largest radiata pine in the world and plenty of other mature native trees including matai, kahikatea and totara. It's a peaceful place to spend an hour or two with a picnic.

Heading west towards Fairlie on SH79 call at Denise Bélanger-Taylor Glassblower (ring ahead ☏03/693 9041), where you may be able to see the delicate and intricate **glass working** in progress, and a home-made kiln. The bright plates, mosaics and jewellery produced by this French-Canadian artist are beautiful but extremely expensive, however. Turn onto Te Moana Road 5km from Geraldine, and follow it until it becomes a dirt road and then watch out for the signs to the studio on your right.

Practicalities

Buses drop off at the junction of Talbot Street and SH79 a few steps from Geraldine's **visitor centre**, 32 Talbot St (Oct–April Mon–Fri 8.30am–5pm, Sat & Sun 10am–4pm; May–Sept daily 10am–3pm; ☏03/693 1006, Ⓦwww.southisland.org.nz), which stocks DOC leaflets for the area and sell DOC passes.

Accommodation

There's a small concentration of **accommodation** in Geraldine, none of it too expensive, and it's rarely a problem getting a bed for the night.

Crown Hotel 31 Talbot St ☏03/693 8458, Ⓔgeraldine-crown@xtra.co.nz. Upmarket pub with eight clean and airy rooms, most with en-suite bathrooms. ❹

Geraldine Motel 97 Talbot St ☏03/693 8501. Six pleasant fully equipped units close to the town centre. Complimentary newspaper in the morning. ❹

Geraldine Motor Camp Hislop St ☏03/693 8147, Ⓔgeraldine.motor.camp@xtra.co.nz. Surrounded by sheltering trees, this spacious site is inside Geraldine Domain. Camping $9, cabins and units ❷–❸

Lilymay 29 Cox St ☏03/693 8838, Ⓔlilymay@bed-and-breakfast.co.nz. Clean and very hospitable B&B shared-bath rooms, a large garden and freshly baked cookies. ❹

The Old Presbytery Backpackers, 13 Jollie St ☏03/693 9644, Ⓔpkoelet@hotmail.com. Revamped, clean and well-kept dorm accommodation in a historic building opposite the Talbot Forest Reserve, with helpful hosts and a warm and friendly atmosphere. Dorms ❶, rooms ❷

Eating, drinking and entertainment

All Geraldine's restaurants and cafés are within a couple of hundred metres of each other along Talbot Street. If you're after **picnic supplies** try the highly individual cheeses at *Talbot Forest Cheese* 76G Talbot St, which go well with some pickle and fruit wine from the *Berry Barn*, 66 Talbot St. Round this off with handmade chocolates from *Fellmen Chocolates*, 10 Talbot St. About the only entertainment is **movies** at the wonderful Geraldine Cinema, 84 Talbot St (☏03/693 8118), a casual affair with sofas, beanbags and a very enthusiastic owner. It is the model for a few similar place springing up around the country – Wanaka and Takaka to name two – and you can bring your own wine.

The Easy Way 76F Talbot St. Stylish café/bar with a wide range of imaginative food at moderate prices including some hot, steaming curries. Daily until late.

Papillon Chinese Restaurant 40 Talbot St. A peculiar mix of East-meets-New-Zealand tea rooms: Chinese food, fish, burgers and chips. Closed Mon & Tues; licensed & BYO.

Totara Bar and Restaurant *Crown Hotel*, 31 Talbot St. A large restaurant serving reasonably priced Kiwi nosh. One of the best places in town for a drink.

The Village Inn 41 Talbot St. A broad selection of reasonably priced and fairly imaginative food for lunch or dinner in a comfortable bar setting, or on the outdoor terrace.

Fairlie and around

Heading for the wilds of the Mackenzie Country, you first pass through the small town of **FAIRLIE**, 45km west of Geraldine at the junction of SH79 and SH8. A quintessential crossroads town with a population of only six hundred, Fairlie was originally called Fairlie Creek; the name was shortened when the telegraph office opened in 1892, the creek having long since dried up. The rail link with Timaru closed in 1960, and the town has pretty much remained in stasis ever since. Your best bet is to look around quickly, and then move on.

The centre of the town is marked by the junction of Allandale Road (SH79) and Main Street (SH8), which becomes Mount Cook Road as it heads west out of town. Follow the latter 300m to **Mabel Binney Cottage and Vintage Machinery Museum** (daily 8am–5pm; $2 turnstile) heralded by a wind-powered water pump. An old railway station moved here in 1968, a cottage honouring the first European settlers through an extensive collection of early photographs, and a museum stuffed with farm machinery, wagons and traction engines make up the collection.

For a little exercise, wander along the **Fairlie Walkway** (3km; 40min one way) which starts below the Allendale Road Bridge over the Opihi River and follows the willow-shaded riverbank past open pastureland and through trees to emerge near Talbot Road.

In winter, a good deal more exercise can be had on the slopes of **Mount Dobson** skifield (℡03/685 8039, ⓦwww.dobson.co.nz), a treeless basin 26km northwest of Fairlie, reached along a 15km unsealed road off SH8. The mountain is known for its powder snow, long hours of sunshine, uncrowded fields and suitability for all levels of skiing and snowboarding. Equipment rental is available, and there is a lodge serving hot pies and drinks. Lift passes cost $45 per day, ski rental goes for $27 (board $40) and there are beginners' packages (ski $47, board $60) including lift passes, tows, rental and a group lesson. The nearest accommodation is in Fairlie, from where there are shuttle buses in season; for details call ℡03/693 9656.

Practicalities

Daily InterCity **buses** stop near the centre of town on Main Street, from where everything's easily reached on foot. The Resource Centre, 64 Main St (Mon–Fri 10am–4pm; ℡03/685 8496) acts as an ad hoc **visitor centre** and has information on local **accommodation** such as: the riverside *Fairlie Gateway Top 10 Holiday Park*, 10 Allandale Rd (℡03/685 8375 & 0800/324 754, ⓦwww.fairlietop10.co.nz; camping $11, cabins ❷, units ❸), and the quiet and comfortable *Aorangi Motels* 26 Denmark St (℡03/685 8340 & 0800/668 351, ⓦwww.aorangimotel.co.nz; ❹) which has an indoor hot tub. There are a couple of cafés and takeaways along Main Street, but your best bets for **eating** are *Wild Olive*, 64–68 Main St, with cheap breakfasts, herbal teas, good coffee and larger meals; or the comfortable *Old Library Café*, 6 Allendale Rd, originally built in 1914 and offering a broad menu and well stocked bar.

Aoraki Mount Cook and the Mackenzie Country

South of Fairlie SH8 shoots westward – lupin- and broom-flanked in the summer – through the sheep-grazed grasslands of the **Mackenzie Country**

Both the **sky father** (Raki) and the **earth mother** (Papa-tua-nuku) already had children by previous unions. After their marriage, some of the sky father's children came to inspect their father's new wife. Four brothers, Ao-raki, Raki-roa, Raki-rua and Raraki-roa, circled around the earth mother in a **canoe** called Te Waka-a-Aoraki, but once they left her shores, disaster befell them. Running aground on a reef, the canoe was turned to stone. The four occupants climbed to the higher western side of the petrified canoe, where they too were turned to stone: **Aoraki** became Mount Cook, and his three younger brothers formed flanking peaks. Aoraki towers over his brother mountains – Mount Dampier, Mount Teichelmann & Mount Tasman – in height, age and spiritual status, as an Atua (god).

More prosaically, Mount Cook was named in honour of the English sea captain by one Captain Stokes of HMS *Acheron* in 1851. Its summit was first reached in 1894, but because of the peak's sacredness to Maori, climbers are asked not to step on the summit rocks.

onto the Aoraki Mount Cook area, considered by many to be the most spectacular section of the Southern Alps. The region is dominated by New Zealand's tallest mountain, the 3754-metre **Mount Cook**, increasingly known but its Maori name, **Aoraki** – meaning "cloud piercer". The two names are used interchangeably and are often seen run together as Aoraki Mount Cook.

Approaching from the north you cross **Burkes Pass**, a low rise between the Rollesby Ranges and the evocatively named Two Thumbs Range. All of a sudden you burst out into the Mackenzie Country, a region of rolling, dry grasslands divided into high country sheep farms known as "stations" or "runs", often stocked with hardy Merino sheep which produces fine wool for classy suits.

Star billing goes to the glacier-fed **Lake Tekapo** and **Lake Pukaki**, opaque, pale blue sheets backed by the glistening peaks of the Southern Alps. Both lakes offer abundant fishing and water skiing, although it's Lake Tekapo that has the bulk of the tourist facilities. Lake Pukaki is quiet in comparison, despite the memorable view of the mountain across its still waters. Main access to the mountainous terrain is provided by **Aoraki Mount Cook Village**, which grew at the base of the mountain to cater for nineteenth-century tourists brought here by horse-drawn coaches. You can walk from Aoraki Mount Cook Village to the glaciers lurking beneath Mount Cook's flanks, notably the 27km-long **Tasman Glacier**, fed by icefalls tumbling from the surrounding heavily glaciated peaks. The unexciting, modern town of **Twizel**, 70km to the south, makes a decent base for exploring the region and spying extremely rare **black stilts**, wading birds that are protected in a reserve nearby. From the gliding mecca of **Omarama** 30km south of Twizel, SH83 runs eastwards down the **Waitaki Gorge** to Oamaru, providing a quick link between the Mount Cook area and the east coast.

Lake Tekapo and around

About 42km west of Fairlie, the small village of **LAKE TEKAPO** occupies the southern shore of, unsurprisingly, **Lake Tekapo** and comprises little more than a roadside ribbon of buildings, with a population of just 400. The name Tekapo derives from the Maori *taka* ("sleeping mat") and *Po* ("night"), suggesting that this place has long been used as a stopover, a role it maintains as an obligatory photo-snapping and expensive trinket shopping stop for tour buses. In the last few years housing developments have started to sprout on the hill behind town, and the tourist shops and new accommodation spread

James McKenzie

A Kiwi folk hero, **James McKenzie** lends his name (well close enough anyway) to the **Mackenzie Country**, a 180km crescent of rolling dry grassland between Fairlie and Kurow (to the south on SH83). A Gaelic-speaking Scottish immigrant of uncertain background, McKenzie seems to have only spent a couple of years in New Zealand but his legend lives on. He was arrested in 1855 for stealing sheep on a grand scale, amassing over 1000 in all, most of them from the Rhodes brothers' Levels Run station near Timaru (see p.648), grazing them in the basin of rich high-country pastureland which now bears his name. McKenzie escaped from prison three times during the first year of his five-year sentence, and when holding him became too much trouble he was given a free pardon. He quietly disappeared, some say to America, others say to Australia.

It is difficult to fathom why exactly McKenzie became such an important and popular figure in New Zealand lore. He was certainly a prodigious thief, somehow controlling his vast flock of rustled animals with the assistance of a single dog, Friday – a hound fondly remembered as the prototype for the many hard-working sheep dogs held in deep affection by South Islanders. McKenzie is also regarded as one of the great pioneers, opening up an area of hitherto undiscovered grazing land that contained some of the best sheep runs in the country. There is a poem in honour of the man and his dog in the visitor shelter at Lake Pukaki near the turn-off to Mount Cook.

shorewards adding nothing to its charm. To make the best of the place, stay overnight and enjoy the scenery and sunset free of the day-trippers.

At an altitude of 710m, the area is reputed to have the clearest air in the southern hemisphere, and on a good day views really do have sharp edges and vibrant colours, making this one of the best places from which to photograph the Southern Alps. The most striking thing about the **lake** itself is its colour: the light reflected from microscopic rock particles suspended in glacial melt-water lends its waters a vibrant turquoise hue. Fed by the **Godley** and **Cass** rivers, the lake covers 83 square kilometres and spills into the **Tekapo River**, which tumbles across the Mackenzie Basin.

Arrival and information

Lake Tekapo is a stop on the popular Christchurch to Queenstown **bus** run (Intercity, Atomic & Southern Link all call daily), and The Cook Connection between Timaru and Aoraki Mount Cook run three times a week. All stop outside the strip of businesses which constitute the town centre where you can make onward travel bookings at a souvenir shop called Kiwi Treasures, which also works as a small **visitor centre** (T03/680 6686; daily: April–Oct 8am–6pm; Nov–March 8am–8pm). Staff is usually busy helping tourists with the joys of retail therapy, but do have an assortment of leaflets including a free map of town which discusses local walks.

Accommodation

Most accommodation in this tourist-oriented village is on the expensive side, and the few budget options tend to be oversubscribed – it's a good idea to book ahead.

The Chalet 14 Pioneer Drive T 03/680 6774 & 0800/843 242, W www.thechalet-laketekapo.co.nz. A boutique motel with six individually decorated, self-contained apartments overlooking the lake and well away from the highway, run by a friendly Swiss couple who also rent out holiday homes for four people and will do breakfasts. 6

THE CENTRAL SOUTH ISLAND | Aoraki Mount Cook

10

Godley Resort Hotel in the centre of the village ⓣ03/680 6848, ⓦwww.tekapo.co.nz. Large hotel in the process of being revamped that lures the tour-bus crowds to its comfortable rooms, some with lake views. There's a restaurant, outdoor pool and gym, and breakfast is included. Budget ❻, lakeview ❼

Lake Tekapo Grandview B&B 32 Hamilton Drive ⓣ03/680 6910, ⓦwww.laketekapograndview.co.nz. The four luxurious en-suite rooms in this modern home overlooking the lake are all spacious, tastefully decorated and come with fresh flowers and breakfast. ❽

Lake Tekapo Motels and Motor Camp Lakeside Drive ⓣ03/680 6825, ⓦwww.laketekapo-accommodation.co.nz. Situated among trees at the southwestern end of Tekapo 1km from town, this is a large, well-

equipped campsite. Camping $11, cabins, tourist cabins and motel ❷–❺

Tailor-made-Tekapo Backpackers 9–11 Aorangi Crescent ⓣ03/680 6700, ⓦwww.tekapo-backpackers.co.nz. Off SH8, five minutes' walk from the bus stop and shops, this friendly hostel is a touch cheaper than the YHA but lacks the view. Dorms and rooms have beds (no bunks) plus there are spacious grounds with an organic vegetable garden. Dorm ❶, rooms ❷

Tekapo YHA Simpson Lane, just west of the village ⓣ03/680 6857, ⓔyha.laketekapo@yha.org.nz. An excellent place to stay with one of the finest lakeside locations of any hostel in New Zealand, its pride and joy is the common room with a floor-to-ceiling window. Doubles and twin rooms, as well as bunks. Dorms ❶, rooms ❸

The Village and around

Lake Tekapo is surrounded by heart-stopping scenery, but there is little to the settlement itself – though you should pause long enough to look inside the tiny **Church of the Good Shepherd**, on Pioneer Drive (daily: Oct–May 9am–5pm; June–Sept 11am–3pm; donation appreciated). Overlooking the lake from a small raised platform, the little stone church was built as a memorial to the pioneers of the Mackenzie Country in 1935. Behind the rough-hewn Oamaru stone altar, a square window perfectly frames the lake and the surrounding hills and mountains; in the stillness of this simple church, the sunset can be quite a moving experience. About 100m east of the church is the perky-looking **Collie Dog Monument**, erected in 1968 by the sheep farmers of the Mackenzie Country as a mark of their deep respect and affection for the dogs that make it possible to graze this harsh terrain.

Of a number of good **walks** in the area, the best is to **Mount John Lookout** (10km return; 3hr; 300m ascent), starting just past the motor camp on Lakeside Drive and climbing through a larch forest full of birds to a loop track which circles the summit of Mount John. After soaking up views of the Mackenzie Basin, Lake Tekapo and the Southern Alps, you can either return the way you came or continue on the loop path and back along the lakeshore to your starting point – well worth the extra hour it adds.

The air is so clear that organized **star gazing** (starting between 7 & 9pm depending on season; $35; ⓣ03/680 6565, ⓦwww.stargazing.co.nz) can be an educational and visually stimulating treat, but only when tour operator Hide (pronounced He–day) guides the trip himself. Other pursuits include **ice skating** at the local rink (May–Aug only) on Lakeside Drive, and guided **horse treks** with Mackenzie Alpine Trekking (Nov–April 30min–2hr; $20–60; ⓣ03/680 6760), through dramatic scenery.

Determined sightseers short of time can join Air Safaris on SH8, about 6km west of Tekapo (free transfers from town), for a "Grand Traverse of Aoraki Mount Cook". This **scenic flight** swoops across the Main Divide to the West Coast, providing views of the Franz Josef and Fox glaciers, the Hooker and Muller glaciers and, of course, Aoraki Mount Cook (ⓣ03/680 6880 & 0800/806 880, ⓦwww.airsafaris.co.nz; hourly, weather permitting; 50min; $240).

Finally, in winter, families flock to the **Roundhill** ski area (ⓣ03/680 6977, ⓦwww.roundhill.co.nz), overlooking Lake Tekapo some 30km north of SH8.

There's just one long T-bar and a learner tow but plenty of gentle slopes and undulating terrain. A lift pass costs $45 and there's the usual ski and board rental packages, plus snow tubing at $10 per hour.

Eating and drinking

On a fine day you can't do better than a picnic by the lake, but Tekapo's string of cafés and **restaurants** – all within 200m along SH8 – are decent enough, if a little pricey. Most places have great lake views, though this is traded for a cosy fireside setting at *Pepe's Pizza and Pasta* (T03/680 6677), which does good pizza and has a fair range of wines by the glass. To get the view, and great sushi and sashimi without breaking the bank head to *Kohan* (T03/680 6688).

Towards Lake Pukaki

From Tekapo, SH8 heads southwest towards **Lake Pukaki** some 47km distant. The opaque, pale blue waters of this 30km-long lake provide a perfect foreground for views north to the Aoraki Mount Cook and its icy attendants. When the weather is clear the views can be breathtaking, so it is worth lingering on this stretch, perhaps detouring along the paved Tekapo–Pukaki Canal road which follows one of the canals of the Waitaki hydro scheme (see p.707).

The road then rejoins SH8 on the southern shores of Lake Pukaki. Skirting the southern shore of the lake brings you past an unsigned **free camping area** locally known as *The Pines*. There are longdrop toilets and a water tap, fabulous lake and mountain views from spots along the waterfront, and place among the pines protected from occasional lake winds. Around 1km further on there are similarly wonderful views of Aoraki Lake Pukaki **visitor centre** (daily: May–Oct 10am–4.30pm; Nov–April 9.30am–5pm; T03/435 3280, W www.mtcook.org.nz) which stands beside a display with tales of Maori and Pakeha history, plus a poem to Mackenzie and his dog (see p.648).

Another kilometre on, SH80 branches north towards Aoraki Mount Cook Village, while SH8 continues 6km to Twizel (see p.702).

Aoraki Mount Cook Village

A good, fast road leads from the Lake Pukaki junction along the tussocklands of the western shore of Lake Pukaki to Aoraki Mount Cook Village, 55km distant. Twelve kilometres in you'll pass **Peters Lookout**, a popular viewing point on the lake side of the road, and at 33km the *Glentanner Park Centre* (T03/435 1855 & 0800/453 682, W www.glentanner.co.nz) offers accommodation (see p.698) and has its own restaurant and helicopter pad.

On hot days, an atmospheric white mist rises from the plain at the base of the mountain, as you approach the diffuse collection of buildings that make up **AORAKI MOUNT COOK VILLAGE**. At a height of 760m in an encircling horseshoe of mountains it is a spectacular spot, and though the village is nothing special it blends in tolerably. It is dominated by **The Hermitage**, a swanky alpine-style hotel that has been modernized and expanded in recent years, and is certainly a far cry from the original 1884 hostelry. Mount Cook is something of a company town with *The Hermitage* owning just about everything – and employing most of the summer population of 300 who work for them. With this near monopoly on services and an almost captive market it should come as no surprise that prices are higher than elsewhere in the region. If you're watching the pennies, either plan to commute in from Twizel or Lake Tekapo, or stock up on groceries before you arrive and then camp or sleep in one of the self-catering lodges. If money is less of an issue, then sit back and enjoy good food and lodging in beautiful mountain surroundings.

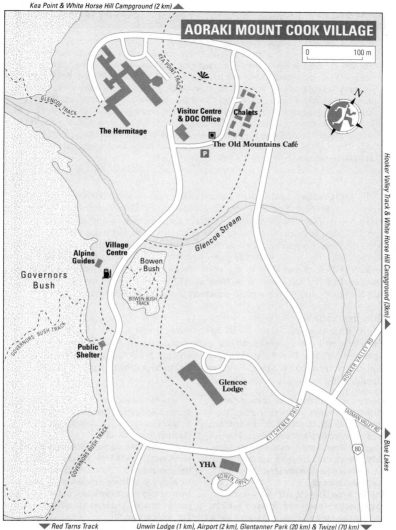

AORAKI MOUNT COOK VILLAGE

0   100 m

GLENCOE TRACK

KEA POINT TRACK

Visitor Centre & DOC Office

Chalets

The Hermitage

The Old Mountains Café

P

N

Glencoe Stream

Hooker Valley Track & White Horse Hill Campground (3km) ▶

Village Centre

Alpine Guides

Bowen Bush

BOWEN BUSH TRACK

Governors Bush

GOVERNORS BUSH TRACK

Public Shelter

Glencoe Lodge

KITCHENER DRIVE

HOOKER VALLEY RD

TASMAN VALLEY RD

▶ *Blue Lakes*

80

YHA

BOWEN DRIVE

GOVERNORS BUSH TRACK

▼ *Red Tarns Track*   *Unwin Lodge (1 km), Airport (2 km), Glentanner Park (20 km) & Twizel (70 km)* ▼

10

THE CENTRAL SOUTH ISLAND | Aoraki Mount Cook

Practicalities

Most **bus** services stick to SH8 dropping off in Twizel where you can hop on The Cook Connection (☏0800/266 526) or High Country Shuttles (☏0800/435 050) for the shuttle up to Aoraki Mount Cook Village ($15 each way). Direct services to the village from Christchurch and Queenstown are run by Newmans (☏03/379 9020). All the buses drop off in the car park near *The Hermitage*, from where everything is within walking distance. Shuttles also stop at *Glentanner Park Centre*, *Unwin Lodge* and the *YHA* on request

Sir Edmund Hillary

Surveys seeking to find the most admired New Zealander frequently find **Sir Edmund Hillary** near the top of the pile. Being one of the first pair to summit Mount Everest in 1953 is undoubtedly a noteworthy achievement, but the veneration lies more in his conduct. Hillary embodies the qualities Kiwis hold most dear: hardworking, straight-talking, honest and, most of all, modest. As he said on his return from the successful summit attempt "Well George, we knocked the bastard off". That's what gets your face on every $5 note in this country.

Though he grew up near Auckland, Ed did much of his early climbing around Aoraki Mount Cook Village where a **bronze statue** of a youthful Hillary stands outside *The Hermitage*. Now in his mid-80s he doesn't come back often, but returned in 2003 to officially open the *Old Mountaineers' Café*.

The **DOC office and visitor centre** (daily: mid–Nov to March 8.30am–6pm; April to mid–Nov 8.30am–5pm; ☏03/435 1186, ✉mtcookvc@doc.govt.nz), located near *The Hermitage* is the best place for information and advice on walks and activities. It stocks everything from leaflets to detailed maps and displays of Mount Cook memorabilia. Buy petrol before you get here, otherwise you'll have to cope with the single unstaffed **petrol pump** which requires a NZ credit card or EFTPOS card and PIN to use it, or phone the hotel desk and pay them $5 extra to do it for you. There is no bank or ATM but everyone accepts credit cards and EFTPOS, and there's a **post office** in the *Hermitage* gift shop.

Accommodation

With the exception of the YHA hostel, the Alpine Club's *Unwin Hut, Wyn Irwin Hut* and the campground, all accommodation in Aoraki Mount Cook is operated by *The Hermitage*. Wherever you stay, book early from October to April. Conversely, the village is deserted for the rest of the year and prices drop considerably, especially at *The Hermitage*.

Glentanner Park Centre 22km south on SH8 ☏03/435 1855, ⓦ www.glentanner.co.nz. Well-equipped, site with shop, camping, new dorm-like accommodation (Oct–April only) and cabins with panoramic views of the mountains and the Tasman Valley. There's also a fairly poor restaurant, though it is cheap and the views are great. Camping $10, dorms ❶, cabins ❸

The Hermitage ☏03/435 1809, ⓦwww.mount -cook.com. Large modernized complex of buildings approached through an impressive foyer and with a welcoming lounge, all leather chairs and fabulous mountain views. Rooms in the main building vary in luxury ($265–410) but all come with a balcony (though not necessarily much of a view) plus dinner and breakfast. The complex also includes self-contained A-frame chalets (B&B ❼), assorted motel units (B&B ❽) and the separate *Glencoe Lodge* (D, B&B ❽; closed in winter) with fairly standard hotel rooms. ❼–❾

Mt Cook YHA cnr Bowen Drive & Kitchener Drive ☏03/435 1820, ✉ yha.mtcook@yha.org.nz. Excellent hostel with 72 beds in a wooden building and modern, well-kept facilities. Free videos are shown in the evenings, there are free evening saunas, bargain pizzas, and a well-stocked shop. It's nearly always full so book well in advance. Dorms ❶, rooms ❸–❹

Unwin Lodge near the airport turn-off, 4km from the village ☏03/433 1102. An Alpine Club hut that gives priority to NZAC members and climbers but is open to all (handy if the YHA is full), offering basic bunk-room accommodation and the use of a massive common area with kitchen. Members $10, non-members $25

White Horse Hill Campground Hooker Valley Rd. A serene and informal first-come-first-served DOC camping area with stony ground and running water in summer (which is not treated and so should be boiled for 3min before use). The campground is 2km north of *The Hermitage*, accessible by road or a 20min walk along the Kea Point Track. Camping $5.

Wyn Irwin Hut Hooker Valley Rd ☏03/942 9188, ⓦ www.cmc.net.nz. Base hut with 16 bunks, solar lighting, gas cooking and shower run by the Canterbury Mountaineering Club who keep the place locked. You must book ahead; $15.

Groceries don't come cheap here and the range is very limited, but *The Hermitage* has a small supply and the *YHA* a slightly wider selection: bring what you need from Twizel or further afield. The best place to eat is undoubtedly *The Old Mountaineers'* (℡03/435 1890), a relaxed spot to hang out on inclement days, but perfect for its wonderful mountain views on clear days. With a log fire, comfy chairs, pool table, Internet access, café-style food, great coffee, beer and wine it can't be beat.

The Hermitage offers a wider range of places: a reasonable coffee shop with a nice sunny terrace; the buffet style *Alpine Restaurant* serving all-you-can-eat breakfast ($12–27), lunch ($38), dinner ($48); and the swanky à la carte *Panorama Restaurant* (℡03/435 1809) which is only open to hotel guests at busy times. There are also decent bar meals (and a bar) at *Glencoe Lodge*.

Exploring the Aoraki Mount Cook National Park

The 700 square kilometres surrounding the peak and extending to the north and east forms the **Aoraki Mount Cook National Park**, which was designated a **world heritage site** by UNESCO in 1986. With twenty-two peaks over 3000m, the park contains the lion's share of New Zealand's high mountains, mostly made of greywacke laid in an ocean trench 250–300 million years ago.

About 2 million years ago the Alpine Fault began to lift, progressively pushing the rock upwards and creating the Southern Alps. These days the process continues at about the same rate as erosion, ensuring that the mountains are at least holding their own, if not getting bigger. Aoraki Mount Cook is at the heart of a unique mountain area, where the rock of the Alps is easily shattered in the cold, leaving huge amounts of gravel in the valley floors. The inhospitable ice fields of the upper slopes are contrasted by the tussock-cloaked foothills, where Mount Cook lilies, summer daisies and snow gentians thrive. The weather here is changeable, often with a pall of low-lying cloud liable to turn to rain, and the mountain air is lung-searingly fresh.

There are **walking opportunities** catering for a wide range of abilities, with a variety of scenic trails beginning on the edges of Aoraki Mount Cook Village itself. Walking as far as the Hooker and Tasman glaciers is well within the capability of the moderately fit, and longer walks for the more ambitious branch out from these basic routes. Don't walk on the surface of any of the glaciers unless you've already had prior experience and you've sought advice on conditions from DOC, or you're in the company of a qualified local guide.

Although walking is an unbeatable way of exploring the park, the **scenic flights** on offer can provide you with glimpses of areas that you could never dream of reaching on foot. Such flights are extremely popular, and must be booked as far in advance as possible. Remember that flights are cancelled in high winds or if visibility is poor – and the weather can change by the hour, so if you get the chance to go, jump at it. The peak season for flights is from November to March, but in winter (June & July) the weather's often clearer, with better visibility. Fly-in skiing is also a possibility, as is **heli-hiking**, which involves hopping on a helicopter and getting delivered three-quarters of the way along one of the walks, climbing to a summit and then walking back. If none of this appeals then one of the most entertaining experiences is a **boat ride** (see p.701) up the Tasman Lake, which gets you within touching distance of the terminal moraine and the honeycomb ice of the Tasman Glacier.

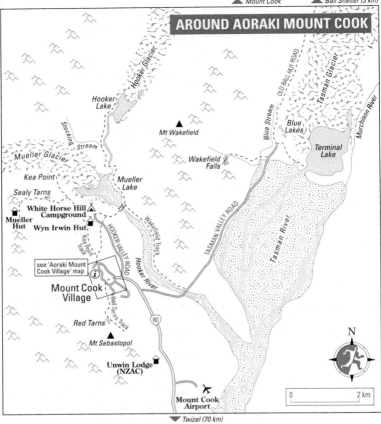

AROUND AORAKI MOUNT COOK

Hooker Glacier

Hooker Lake

Mt Wakefield

Stocking Stream

Mueller Glacier

Kea Point

Sealy Tarns

Mueller Lake

Wakefield Falls

Blue Stream

OLD BALL HUT ROAD

Blue Lakes

Tasman Glacier

Terminal Lake

Murchison River

White Horse Hill Campground

Mueller Hut

Wyn Irwin Hut

HOOKER VALLEY ROAD

Kea Point Track

Wakefield Track

TASMAN VALLEY ROAD

Tasman River

see 'Aoraki Mount Cook Village' map

ⓘ

Mount Cook Village

Red Tarns Track

Red Tarns

Mt Sebastopol

80

N

Unwin Lodge (NZAC)

Mount Cook Airport

0   2 km

Walking, heli-hiking and guided trekking

For most visitors, the principal activity around Aoraki Mount Cook Village is hiking the numerous trails which range from gentle day-hikes to arduous and spectacular alpine treks. Consult DOC for the latest information and get their *Walks in Mount Cook National Park* leaflet ($1), which lists ten excellent shorter walks (10min–5hr), all of which can be extended by those with relevant experience. All start in the Village except for the Blue Lakes walk. Alpine Guides, adjacent to the petrol pump (daily 8am–5pm; Ⓦ www.alpineguides.co.nz), offer experienced **climbing guides** and **rent equipment** such as walking poles, tents, crampons and axes.

To experience high altitude hiking (and spectacular views) without the uphill struggle, go guided **heli-hiking** with Cloud 9 HeliHiking (☏03/435 1077, Ⓦ www.glacierexplorers.co.nz) who will take you up Mount Dark and guide you back down on foot for $285 (minimum two people). This is still a fairly energetic activity and you'll need appropriate clothing, though they provide trekking poles, waterproof over-trousers, hiking boots and jackets.

It is an appreciable step up to **guided trekking** with Alpine Recreation (℡0800/006 0996, www.alpinerecreation.com) who run the Ball Pass Trek ($625), a three-day alpine crossing close to Aoraki Mount Cook reaching 2130m at Ball Pass. Crampons may be required, but it is essentially just a strenuous walk staying in comfortable huts.

Blue Lakes and Tasman Glacier View (1km return; 40min; 100m ascent). A fairly gentle walk with good views of the lower sections of the Tasman Glacier which is 600m deep at its thickest, 3km across at its widest, and moves at a rate of 20cm a day. One Harry Wigley landed an Auster aircraft on the glacier in 1955, paving the way for easier access for mountaineers. The walk starts at the Blue Lakes car park, 3km north of the village (8km drive) up the Tasman Valley Road.
Governors Bush Walk (1hr return; 2km). Easy walk through a stand of silver beech with good views and abundant birdlife. Sheltered in poor weather.
Hooker Valley Track (9km return; 4hr; 200m ascent). A popular and superb hike which crosses a couple of swingbridges, passes the pretty Mueller Lake, and climbs opposite the western side of Aoraki Mount Cook past the viewpoint at the Alpine Memorial, ending at the Hooker Lake. Starting at the White Horse Hill campground saves 45min.

Kea Point Walk (2hr return). Rewarding hike to a lookout over Mueller Lake with the hanging glaciers and icefalls of Mount Sefton above. Starting at the White Horse Hill campground saves 45min.
Mueller Hut Route (10km return; 6–8hr; 1000m ascent). You'll need to be fairly fit for the slog up to the Mueller Hut, which leaves the Kea Point Track just before its arrival at the glacier and climbs steeply westwards up the **Sealy Tarns Track**. From the tarns the route to the hut is marked by orange triangles which guide you up the final assault on loose gravel to a skyline ridge and the **Mueller Hut** (28 bunks; $20). At 1800 metres the views are quite startling and you are engulfed by almost perfect silence, interrupted only by the murmur of running water and squawking kea.
Red Tarns Track (4km return; 2hr; 300m ascent). This excellent and very achievable walk has one short, steep section but rewards with two tarns named after the red pondweed that grows in them. Uninterrupted views of Aoraki, the village and along the Tasman Valley make it well worth the sweat.

Boating

One of the most fun trips available is the Glacier Explorer (Oct–April daily; $105; ℡03/435 1077, www.glacierexplorers.co.nz) an eerie **boat ride** on the glacial lake at the base of the Tasman Glacier. Here icebergs, recently detached from the glacier itself, drift around in the lake which is turned grey but the presence of ground-down rock, or rock flour, that mixes with the water and reflects the light. Chunks of ice fall off the glacier and can be examined up close, revealing a mixture of beautiful honeycombed ice cells and the detritus that has been picked up and carried along its course. The guides are a mine of information, and the three hours will pass quickly providing you had the good sense to wrap up warmly. Trips involve a 15min drive from the Village, a half hour walk then the one hour boat ride.

For more involvement, go **kayaking** among icebergs on the lake below the Mueller Glacier on three-hour trips with Glacier Sea-Kayaking ($70; ℡03/435 1890, www.mtcook.com).

Skiing Aoraki Mount Cook

There are no developed skifields in the Aoraki Mount Cook area but planes and helicopters open up the Tasman Glacier and surrounding mountains for guided **fly-in skiing and snowboarding**. None of this comes cheap, but during the **season** (July–Sept), steep, exhilarating and untouched runs open up for those with strong intermediate skills or better. Alpine Guides (℡03/435 1834, www.heliskiing.co.nz) will take you onto the Tasman Glacier for two guided 10km runs ($650); while all-day skiing with helicopter transfers to a range of different runs starts at around $735 and advances into orbit, with equipment rental extra.

Scenic flights

Fixed-wing **scenic flights** from the Mount Cook Airfield are operated by Mount Cook Ski Planes (T03/435 1026 & 0800/800 702, Wwww .mtcookskiplanes.com) who offer flights from as little as $180 (for 25min), ranging up to the mammoth Grand Circle (55min; $350) which loops around Aoraki, briefly crosses the Main Divide, then lands and takes off from the Tasman Glacier in a heart-stoppingly short distance. The glaciers are silent once the plane engine splutters off and wandering around on the footprint-free snow is almost as exhilarating as the landing and take-off.

From *Glentanner Park Centre* (see p.698), 20km south of the village, the Helicopter Line (T03/435 1801 & 0800/650 651, Wwww.helicopter.co.nz) fly three scenic **helicopter trips** with opportunities to hover along the valley walls and peaks, or viewing the tumbling blocks of the Hochstetter Icefall; all include brief snow landings. Choose from the Alpine Vista (20min; $185), Alpine Explorer (30min; $280) and the Mountain high (45min; $390) which circumnavigates Aoraki.

Twizel-based Glacier Southern Lakes Helicopters (T03/435 0370, Wwww.heli-flights.co.nz) offer similar flights ($205 to $510) but covering greater distances, with the longer you spend in the air adding to the amount you pay.

Twizel and around

Nine kilometres south of the junction of SH8 and SH80 from Aoraki Mount Cook, you'll come upon **TWIZEL** (rhymes with bridle), a leafy island surrounded by seas of pasture with a backdrop of alpine scenery. The modest settlement of around 1300 began life in 1966 as a construction village for people working on the Waitaki hydro scheme (see box on p.707), and was supposed to have been bulldozed flat after the project was finished in 1985. Some thought this would have been a kinder fate but residents had got used to the cold dry winters and hot arid summers, and enough wanted to stay that their wishes were granted. Long ridiculed as dull and featureless, the town is now making modest claims as a service town for the Mackenzie region and as a base for forays to Mount Cook National Park (a 45min drive away) and the scenic Lake Ohau.

The Town and the Black Stilt visitor hide

This two-storey town erupts into a brief summertime frenzy when tourists flock to visit Mount Cook and attend the various boat races on the surrounding lakes, before lapsing back into its mundane existence as an administrative centre.

You're best off heading straight out to the **Kaki/Black Stilt visitor hide**, which occupies a wetland area 3km south of Twizel on SH8. The colony is attempting to preserve the world's rarest wading bird from extinction – an urgent task as only 125 adults are left in the wild, about half of them female, and 75 adults in captivity. Access is by guided tour only (Oct–March daily 9.30am & 4.30pm; 1hr; $12.50; book in advance T03/435 0802, Einfo @twizel.com), but there is a hide where you can watch the birds without disturbing them; binoculars are provided. The long-red-legged kaki once thrived on the banks of braided rivers, feeding mainly on mayfly and exhibiting the endearing post-coital behaviour of walking cross-billed as if indulging in upright pillow talk. All this changed due to habitat loss as a result of introduced plant species, the Waitaki hydroelectric project and the introduction of mammalian predators such as cats, ferrets, rats and stoats.

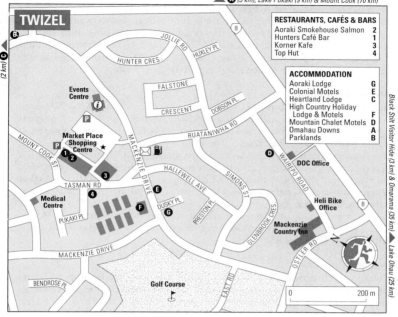

TWIZEL

Ⓑ

Ⓒ

(2 km)

JOLLIE RD

HUXLEY PL

HUNTER CRES

FALSTONE

Events Centre ⓘ

P

CRESCENT

DOBSON PL

Market Place Shopping Centre ★

P

MOUNT COOK ST

MACKENZIE DRIVE

RUATANIWHA RD

Ⓓ DOC Office

HALLEWELL AVE

SIMONS ST

WAIRERO ROAD

Ⓒ

TASMAN RD

Medical Centre

PUKAKI PL

DUSKY PL

PRESTON PL

GLENBROOK CRES

Heli Bike Office

Mackenzie Country Inn

OSTLER RD

MACKENZIE DRIVE

BENDROSE PL

Golf Course

0   200 m

EAST RD

RESTAURANTS, CAFÉS & BARS	
Aoraki Smokehouse Salmon	2
Hunters Café Bar	1
Korner Kafe	3
Top Hut	4

ACCOMMODATION	
Aoraki Lodge	G
Colonial Motels	E
Heartland Lodge	C
High Country Holiday Lodge & Motels	F
Mountain Chalet Motels	D
Omahau Downs	A
Parklands	B

Black Stilt Visitor Hide (3 km) & Omarama (35 km) ▲ *Lake Ohau (25 km)*

⑩

THE CENTRAL SOUTH ISLAND | Aoraki Mount Cook

The centre operates by incubating clutches from all the wild and captive kaki pairs, hatching the eggs in captivity and raising the chicks to three or nine months before releasing them into the wild. Thankfully there is currently an eighty-plus percent survival rate. Given that the majority of your tour fee goes into the project you can both enjoy the education and get to feel good about it. If you want to know more about the kaki or other braided-river species and their habitat then get copies of the informative *Conservation of Braided River Birds*, *Braided River Care Code* and *Project River Recovery* leaflets, available at the visitor centre.

Activities

There are plenty of ways of getting out of unlovely Twizel into the beautiful surroundings. *Lord of the Rings* fans won't be able to resist a quick look at the spot used for the filming of battle scenes on the Pelennor Fields, only done by joining the **LOTR Tour** (1hr 30min; $50) run by Discovery Tours (☎0800/213 868, ⓦwww.discoverytours.co.nz).

Mountain bikers can engage Heli Bike (☎03/435 0626 & 0800/435 424, ⓦwww.helibike.com) to fly you and the bikes somewhere spectacular and guide you on the pedal back. Routes take in such diverse places as the Benmore Range (1300m descent; $190); the fast descent Ridge (100m descent; $150); and the gentler Pyramid ($150); all with bike rental $25 extra. Heli Bike also organizes the annual Helibike Challenge (second Sat in Feb) which is generally an excuse for groups to spend a day riding for fun, although there's always someone who takes it seriously. A more sedate way to enjoy the area is to join Big Sky Adventure (☎0800/236 667, ⓔbigskyadventure@xtra.co.nz) for a little **kayaking** on Lake Benmore (half-day $59; full day $90), or follow some of the picturesque walks around lakes Aviemore, Ohau and Tekapo using

DOC's *Day Walks of the Mackenzie Basin and Waitaki Valley* leaflet ($1). If you are intending to **climb** any of the peaks in the area, contact Shaun Norman (☏03/435 0622), a skilled and experienced guide who also offers introductory, intermediate and advanced mountaineering instruction. There are also Mount Cook **scenic flights** operating from Twizel (see p.702 for details) and **skiing** at Mount Cook or Ohau (see p.701 & p.705).

Practicalities

The most convenient **bus** links are Cook Connection (☏0800/266 526) from Mount Cook, Timaru and Oamaru; and both Atomic and InterCity on their Queenstown–Christchurch runs. They disgorge beside the **visitor centre**, in the Events Centre, Mackenzie Drive (daily 9am–6pm; ☏03/435 3124, ⓦwww.twizel.com), which has local info, stocks DOC leaflets and has fast Internet access. For further information try the free monthly *Mackenzie Mail*, an insight into the community's collective psyche. Across the road, the **Market Place Shopping Centre** provides the town's focal point, and contains a small supermarket, restaurants and a **bank**.

Almost everything of interest is within walking distance from the Market Place; for exploring further afield, *Mackenzie Country Inn*, Warepo Road, offers **bike rental** ($10 a day).

Accommodation

Twizel's **accommodation** is a reasonable value, but being just a 45-min drive from Mount Cook it pays to **book ahead** around Christmas, New Year, the second week in February and Easter, when the town is packed with holidaying New Zealanders.

Aoraki Lodge 32 Mackenzie Drive ☏03/435 0300, ⒺⒶ aorakilodge@xtra.co.nz. A luxurious B&B with individually decorated rooms, wheelchair access, en-suite bathrooms, the use of a large comfortable lounge and tastebud-tingling breakfasts and dinners (3-course dinner from $30; BYO). ❻

Colonial Motels 36–38 Mackenzie Drive ☏03/435 0100, ⓦwww.twizel.com/colonialmotel. Superior ground-floor units with full kitchens and facilities, and conveniently close to shops and restaurants. ❺

Heartland Lodge 19 North West Arch ☏03/435 0008 & 0800/164 666, ⓦwww.heartland-lodge.co.nz. Spacious and nicely decorated B&B a couple of kilometres west of town with mountain views and full breakfast. Rooms have huge beds and under-floor heating, and there's a separate self-contained apartment sleeping up to six. B&B ❼, apartment $100 for two plus $15 each extra.

High Country Holiday Lodge & Motels 23 Mackenzie Drive ☏03/435 0671, ⓦwww.twizel.com/highcountrylodge. The former

hydroelectric workers' camp, this has retained some of its institutional character, with barracks-like bunk rooms. Hotel and motel rooms are a better bet, with a communal kitchen and there is also a restaurant on site. Dorms ❶, budget rooms ❸, motel ❹

Mountain Chalet Motels Wairepo Rd ☏03/435 0785, ⓦwww.mountainchalets.co.nz. Ten spacious, light-filled, self-contained A-frame chalets. The adjacent lodge section offers simple clean and comfortable backpacker accommodation in dorms. Dorms ❶, chalets ❺

Omahau Downs SH8, 3km north of Twizel ☏03/435 0199, Ⓔ lyons.accord@xtra.co.nz. Recently opened hostel, rurally set with views of Mount Cook and accommodation in chalets around the main house, and access to an outdoor wood-fired bath. Dorms ❶, rooms ❷.

Parklands 122 Mackenzie Drive ☏03/435 0507, Ⓔ parklands1@xtra.co.nz. A rejuvenated backpackers with spacious doubles, dorms and cosy cabins with breakfast included. Camping $9, dorms ❶, cabins ❷, ensuite cabins ❹

Eating and drinking

Twizel's **eating and drinking** options are fairly limited. For simple dining head for *Korner Kafe*, 20 Market Place, which serves good breakfasts and meals all day, or, for some unexpected big-city style, wander around the corner to *Hunters Café*

Bar, 2 Market Place (☎03/435 0303), who serve espressos, generous lunches ($10–15) and dinners such as beer-battered fish, locally farmed salmon ($16–20) and occasionally have live music. Bar meals and takeways are good at the *Top Hut* café and bar, 13 Tasman Rd, also the best for straightforward drinking with outdoor seating. Self-caterers will want to drop in at *Aoraki Smokehouse Salmon*, 3 Market Place, for locally smoked salmon and one or two other delicacies.

Lake Ohau

Lake Ohau, 25km west of Twizel along a narrow service road, is famed for its beech forest, river and **skifield** (see below). Renowned for the purity of its water, the lake surrounds boast some distinctive natural features, such as kettle lakes (small depressions left when blocks of glacial ice melt) and the terracing on its banks that reflects the light of summer sunsets. Although it lacks the colour of Lake Tekapo, it is popular for fishing and kayaking, as are the Dobson and Hopkins rivers that flow into the lake's northern end (contact Twizel's visitor centres for details of boat rental). Ohau ("the place of the wind") was a seasonal food gathering stop-off for Maori making their way to and from the West Coast via Brodrick Pass and was the scene of many battles between rival *iwi*.

The **Ohau Forests** lie northwest from the lake, their stands of mountain beech and subalpine scrub criss-crossed by numerous tracks; DOC's *Ohau Conservation Area* ($1 from the Twizel visitor centre), details various walks (30min–4hr). The forests flank wide valleys cut by surging rivers, which are now a little more gentle unless in flood and separated by narrow mountain ranges, with short tussock grasslands predominating around the lakes and lowlands. It's a pretty area but lacks any real points of interest so unless you're planning to head up to the backcountry huts to get away from it all you'll probably find more worthwhile entertainment and sights around Mount Cook or along the well-beaten roads running south.

The community near the lake is made up almost entirely of holiday homes and has no amenities except for camping and the *Lake Ohau Lodge* (☎03/438 9885, ⓦwww.ohau.co.nz/index.cfm/lodge; dorms $20, rooms & chalets ❺–❻), which offers a wide variety of **accommodation**. Breakfast and dinner are available here, too. The huts on the tramps ($5) offer bunks and nothing else.

Ohau skifield

Ohau Skifield, about 42km southwest of Twizel, off SH8 (☎03/438 9885, ⓦwww.ohau.co.nz; July–Oct), is a small high-country (1033m) field with reliable powder snow and uncrowded slopes. Especially good for intermediate skiers and boarders, the field has the longest T-bar in New Zealand and great views from the **Ohau Ski Lodge** with its sun deck and café.

Equipment rental is available at the field and lift passes cost $48 per day, with access provided by **bus** from the Lake Ohau Lodge ($15 return); otherwise, transport can be arranged by phoning the skifield information number. Learners' **packages**, with gear rental and passes thrown in, start at $35 for ninety minutes.

South from Twizel

South of Twizel, SH8 runs past the Kaki Aviary (see p.702) and a couple of water channels for the Waitaki hydro scheme then traverses tussock and sheep county to the junction settlement of **Omarama** – New Zealand's gliding capital – 30km on. The only other thing of interest is the **Clay Cliffs Scenic Reserve** just north of Omarama.

Travelling south from Omarama towards Wanaka, Cromwell and Queenstown (see Chapter 13), SH8 crosses the **Lindis Pass**, a rewarding scenic drive on narrow roads through predominantly tussock and grassland, though in bad weather it can feel distinctly foreboding. Eastbound, you follow SH83 past the reservoirs of the Waitaki Valley (see p.707).

Clay Cliffs Scenic Reserve

Some 25km south of Twizel and 5km north of Omarama, a signposted, rough side road runs 10km west to **Clay Cliffs Scenic Reserve** ($5 per vehicle in the honesty box), which can be inaccessible after very wet weather. The braided Ahuriri River provides a picturesque backdrop to these eerie badlands of bare pinnacles and angular ridges separated by narrow ravines and canyons. They were created when a 100m uplift caused by the Ostler Fault exposed gravels, which became differentially weathered.

The Maori name for the clay cliffs is *Paritea*, meaning white or light-coloured cliff, and they were so named by Araiteuru, who brought *kumara* (sweet potatoes) from Hawaiki. The cliffs provided natural shelter for moa hunters, with several surviving earth ovens indicative of early Maori settlement.

For a distant view, continue on SH8 some 7km south of Omarama and the pinnacles can be clearly seen off to the west.

Omarama

Buses travelling through the Mackenzie Country all stop briefly at **OMARAMA** (Maori for "place of light"), little more than a road junction with a couple of petrol stations, a few cafés, some places to stay and a small **visitor center** (daily 8.30am–6.30pm; ☏03/438 9818) in Glencraig's Souvenirs.

Flat land and mountains all around provide some of the best conditions in the southern hemisphere for **gliding**, and one-time playground of **Dick Georgeson**, pioneer of New Zealand aviation and the South Island's first glider pilot back in 1950. In the 1960s he held all manner of world gliding records attaining almost 11,000m in 1960 using unusual air-wave patterns to catapult himself right along the island. Now retired, he still returns to Omarama to help American billionaire pilot **Steve Fossett** in his springtime attempts to ride the "polar vortex" to a record 19,000 metres. Alpine Soaring (☏03/438 9600, ⊛www.soaring.co.nz; 20–60min; $185–$285) takes advantage of the beneficial conditions to provide spectacular flights in two-seater gliders, with a turn at the controls on the longer flights. The land and rivers around Omarama are also prime territory for hunting chamois and red deer, and fly fishing for trout and salmon. The fish and the venison are delicious, but no one seems to know what to do with the chamois – except hang their heads on walls. Bookings for **fly fishing** can be made through Omarama visitor centre who organize guides and can point you to somewhere to buy licences ($17 for 24hr).

The most conducive **place to stay** is *Buscot Station*, about 8km north of Omarama on SH8 (they'll arrange pick-ups if you book ahead; ☏03/438 9646; closed June & July; dorms ❶, rooms ❷), a merino sheep farm where backpacker accommodation is provided in the old shearers' quarters, surrounded by a beautifully kept garden. Otherwise, there's the sheltered *Omarama Top 10 Holiday Park*, at the junction of SH8 and SH83 (☏03/438 9875, ⊛www.omaramatop10.co.nz; camping $10, cabins ❷, motel ❹), and the *Ahuriri Motel*, 500m north on SH8 (☏03/438 9451 & 0800/435 945; ❹–❺).

The only eating place really worth seeking out is the *Clay Cliffs Estate*, 500m south on SH8 (☏03/438 9654, ⊛www.claycliffs.co.nz), a Tuscan-style

café/bar (daily 11am until late) with a selection of platters (around $20), light meals and a full à la carte menu in the evening (mains $20–30). This is New Zealand's highest **vineyard**, growing pinot gris and muscat on site, plus making pinot noir and others from imported grapes. A tasting flight of five ($5) is a perfect accompaniment to a meal.

The Waitaki Valley

The route from Omarama **east to Oamaru** follows SH83 passing through a string of small settlements evenly spaced along the **Waitaki Valley**, a region irrevocably changed by a mammoth hydroelectric scheme and the lakes it created (see box below).

At **OTEMATATA**, 26km from Omarama, a side road runs 5km to the huge earth-built **Benmore Dam** where you can walk or drive to the top, and take a short loop track with distant views of Mount Cook. **Tours** of the power station (1hr 15min; Oct–April daily 11am, 1pm & 3pm, May–Sept Sat & Sun only; $5; ℡03/438 9212, ℮benmorecentre@meridianenergy.co.nz) leave from a small **visitor center** (daily 10.30am–4.30pm) near the base of the dam and visit the control room, generators and lots of gushing water. You can stay in town at the *Otematata Lakes Hotel* (℡03/438 7899, ℗www.otematatalakeshotel.co.nz; ❹), which overlooks Lake Aviemore and has a dining room and bar.

KUROW, 30km further along SH83, is regarded as a fisherman's paradise. Twin wooden bridges (dating from 1880) span the salmon- and trout-filled Waitaki River, and there are a few limestone buildings of some minor grandeur in the settlement itself. Another 19km on, at the side of the road, you'll see the remains of some Maori **rock paintings** (see box, p.652) sheltered beneath a bird-infested rock overhang right beside the road. Many of the best have been removed to museums for safekeeping and those that remain aren't that impressive to the untrained eye. **DUNTROON**, 4km on, is full of Gothic revival

---

The Waitaki Hydro Scheme and Project Aqua

The Waitaki Hydro Scheme currently provides over a fifth of the nation's power from twelve power stations scattered along the Waitaki River and into its headwaters around lakes Tekapo, Pukaki and Ohau. The scheme has its origins in the work of the engineer Peter Seton Hay, who in 1904 submitted a report to the New Zealand government indicating the extraordinary hydro-electric potential of the region. Construction began with the Waitaki power station in 1935 and continued through to 1985 when the commissioning of the Ohau C station completed one of the largest construction projects in New Zealand.

Throughout the region water is diverted along a confusing network of canals to fill a long sequence of storage lakes held back by impressive dams, particularly the 100m-high earth-built Benmore Dam.

National power demands continue to increase, and the government-owned Meridian Energy recently proposed a new sequence of canals and small powerhouses along the Waitaki Valley which would rob the river of much of its flow. After much opposition from locals, boaters and environmentalists the project was recently cancelled and the country is fretting about how future energy needs will be met. The gas fields off the coast of Taranaki are running out, no one wants nuclear power and large hydro schemes are no longer popular. The government does little to encourage more energy-efficient living so energy managers are increasingly looking to new power stations exploiting New Zealand's abundant stocks of coal, though this seriously threatens the country's commitment to the Kyoto Protocol on greenhouse gases.

architecture, the *Duntroon Tavern* (good for cheap snacks), and a **Vanished World Centre**, 7 Campbell St (Mon–Sat 10am–4pm, often closed in winter; ☎03/431 2024, ⓦwww.vanishedworld.co.nz) whose primary exhibit, "The Valley of the Disappearing Whale", tells the story of the fossilized whale skeleton recently discovered in Dansey's Pass, and provides the visitors with a chance to go and see it in the hills: a brochure ($8), with photos and maps, is available here. The road continues over the hills towards **Naseby** (see p.891) in the Central Otago gold country.

Just off the road, after about 1.5km, a winding narrow road climbs for 4km to the weird limestone formations of **Elephant Rocks**, popular with rock climbers of modest ability. The unmissable stand-alone rocks look like a small herd of elephants, in shape and colour, making their way through a grassy bowl. They were formed by hard limestone subjected to chemical erosion similar to the tor process that occurs in schist, where vertical cracks have eroded the stone around them with the remaining harder rocks becoming solid pachyderms. Back in Duntroon, a road beside the alarmingly cream church leads, after 6.5km, to the poorly signed **Earthquakes**, a collapsed cave where you can walk up the gently sloping roof and peer through dark crevices to the floor many feet below, flanked by the cave walls, which in place extend a sheer 20m above you.

Pressing on from Duntroon, the junction with the main east-coast highway (SH1) is just 35km away, and Oamaru is a further 8km south.

Travel details

The only **train** through the region is the TranzAlpine from Christchurch to Greymouth which stops at Arthur's Pass. **Buses** head north from Christchurch to Hanmer Springs, over the Lewis Pass to Nelson; and southwest towards Wanaka and Queenstown passing Tekapo and Twizel. InterCity buses also visit Methven, but most services avoid the there-and-back run into Aoraki Mount Cook. Apart from local shuttles from Twizel the only buses are the Newmans service between Christchurch and Queenstown, and The Cook Connection linking Timaru and Oamaru.

Trains

From **Arthur's Pass** to: Christchurch (1 daily; 2hr 10min); Greymouth (1 daily; 2hr).
From **Christchurch** to: Arthur's Pass (1 daily; 2hr 10min).

Buses

From **Aoraki Mount Cook** to: Christchurch (1 daily; 6hr 15min); Oamaru (2–3 weekly; 2hr 45min); Queenstown (1 daily; 4hr); Tekapo (1–2 daily; 1hr 15min); Timaru (2–3 weekly; 3hr 15min); Twizel (4 daily; 1hr).

From **Arthur's Pass** to: Christchurch (3 daily; 2hr 15min); Greymouth (3 daily; 1hr 30min–2hr); Hokitika (3 daily; 2hr).
From **Christchurch** to: Aoraki Mount Cook (1 daily; 6hr 15min); Arthur's Pass (3 daily; 2hr 15min); Fairlie (6–7 daily; 2hr 30min); Geraldine (6–7 daily; 2hr); Hanmer Springs (1–2 daily; 2hr 30min); Maruia Springs (2 daily; 3hr 15min); Methven (2 daily; 1hr); Tekapo (6–7 daily; 3–4hr); Twizel (6–7 daily; 4hr).
From **Fairlie** to: Christchurch (6–7 daily; 2hr 30min); Tekapo (6–7 daily; 1hr); Timaru (1–2 daily; 50min).
From **Geraldine** to: Christchurch (6–7 daily; 2hr); Fairlie (6–7 daily; 30min).
From **Hanmer Springs** to: Christchurch (1–2 daily; 2hr 30min); Kaikoura (3 weekly; 2hr).
From **Methven** to: Christchurch (2 daily; 1hr); Geraldine (2 daily; 1hr 30min).
From **Omarama** to: Oamaru (2–3 weekly; 2hr); Queenstown (6–7 daily; 2hr 15min); Twizel (6–7 daily; 30min).
From **Tekapo** to: Aoraki Mount Cook (1 daily; 1hr 15min); Christchurch (6–7 daily; 3–4hr); Fairlie (6–7 daily; 1hr); Twizel (6–7 daily; 30min).
From **Twizel** to: Aoraki Mount Cook (4 daily; 1hr); Omarama (6–7 daily; 30min).

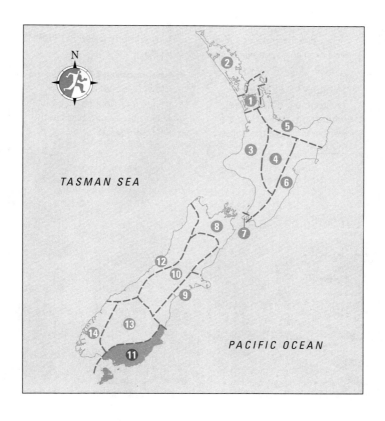

11

Dunedin to Stewart Island

N

TASMAN SEA

PACIFIC OCEAN

CHAPTER 11

Highlights

* **Dunedin Public Art Gallery** An airy and beautifully designed gallery. See p.718

* **The Otago Museum** A fascinating insight into the southern end of the South Island and the people who inhabit it. See p.721

* **Kayaking** Explore the Otago Peninsula by kayak and see a rich variety of landscape and wildlife in an atmospheric, sheltered environment. See p.737

* **Penguin Place** A unique environment of trenches where you, rather than the penguins, are in the cages.

You could hardly get closer. See p.734

* **Curio Bay** Visit a petrified forest, a yellow-eyed penguin colony and watch as Hector's dolphins surf in the waves of the Catlins Coast. See p.745

* **Ulva Island** Not so much bird watching as bird meeting – when you step into the bush, they come to greet you. See p.760

* **Kiwi-spotting** Mason Bay, on Stewart Island's west coast offers your best chance of seeing these rare birds in the wild. See p.762

△ Dunedin Public Art Gallery

Dunedin to Stewart Island

T
he southeastern corner of the South Island contains some of the least-visited parts of New Zealand, yet, hidden away here are a couple of real gems. The first is the darkly attractive city of **Dunedin**, some 400km south of Christchurch. Once the commercial and cultural centre of the country, this harbourside city was made prosperous by the discovery of **gold** in the craggy mountains of Otago's hinterland in 1861. Though it is now only New Zealand's fifth largest city, its dominant position in the southern half of the South Island means that Dunedin is still regarded as the country's fourth city, and remains a seat of learning and culture, influenced by its university and strong Scottish tradition. From here down to Stewart Island, local accents are marked by a distinctive Scots "burr", the only true regional variation in the country. Within easy reach of the city is the inviting **Otago Peninsula**, an important wildlife haven where you can observe at close range a variety of marine life and seabirds, including penguins and even rarer albatrosses. South of Dunedin stretches the second highlight, the wild **Catlins Coast**, a large protected reserve reaching towards New Zealand's southernmost city of Invercargill. This is a magical, virtually forgotten region, home to several rare species and offering dramatically varied scenery, from hills covered with dense native forest to a shoreline vigorously indented with rocky bays, long sweeps of sand and unusual geological formations.

On the South Island's southern tip lies **Invercargill**, bordered by the rich pastureland of Southland's prosperous farming communities. The city acts as the springboard to the country's third island, the comparatively small **Stewart Island**. Relatively few visit, but the island is a growing tourist destination, its blanket of virgin rainforest offering a tramper's paradise. Others come for the abundant birdlife, particularly on **Ulva Island**, and to unwind in the restful setting, have a drink in New Zealand's southernmost pub, or to spot kiwi in the wild.

To do the region justice you need to ease into the slower pace of life, allowing a minimum of three days for Dunedin and the Otago Peninsula, two or more days in the Catlins and at least a couple on Stewart Island. Generally, the best time to visit the region is during the **summer** months (Oct–April), when you're most likely to enjoy warm, though changeable, weather, with mid-summer temperatures averaging around 19°C in Dunedin. You'll also catch the best of the wildlife, coinciding with the breeding season of many species.

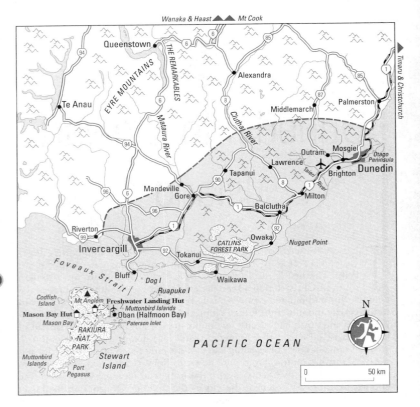

Kiwis from more northern parts take great delight in condemning the **climate** of the southern South Island, describing a permanently harsh, cold and rain-lashed landscape. Though this is an exaggeration, it is true that the further south you go, the wetter it gets. The Catlins and Invercargill get their highest rainfall in the spring (Sept & Oct), while Stewart Island has showers most days in between bursts of sunshine.

Getting around is a straightforward business, with regular bus services linking all the major towns as well as crossing the island to Queenstown and the West Coast. Stewart Island is served by ferries and planes from Invercargill.

Dunedin

DUNEDIN (pronounced Dun-EEdin) is New Zealand's **Scottish city**, the "Edinburgh of the South", its name is a Gaelic translation of its Scottish counterpart, with which it shares street and suburb names. Founded by Scottish settlers it was soon at the commercial centre supplying the gold rush towns of nearby Central Otago. The legacy is a central kernel of imposing Gothic-Revival buildings surrounded by closely packed, but often grand, villas climbing the hills that hem in the town. With a population of only around

115,000 it is a manageable place and comes blessed with numerous parks and gardens, a temperate, if changeable, climate, and pleasant beaches.

Hard, volcanic bluestone and soft, creamy limestone from Oamaru were imaginatively combined to create a streetscape of **iconic buildings** designed to assert the city's importance. Assorted civic structures and churches are out-done by the Dunedin Railway Station and, finest of all the registry building for the **University of Otago**. Founded in 1871, the university is the oldest such institution in New Zealand, and it still occupies a substantial area near the city centre. The presence of eighteen thousand students contributes to a lively **arts scene**, helping to consolidate Dunedin's long-held reputation as a cultural and intellectual centre, but also contributes to the slightly tatty nature of certain areas where there are concentrations of student housing. To see the city at its busiest, visit during term time (mid-Feb to mid-June & July–Nov) when the **nightlife**, in particular, takes off.

Dunedin sits at the head of **Otago Harbour**, a long and sheltered body formed ten million years ago by a series of volcanic eruptions and now virtu-ally encircled by rugged hills. It is home to two working ports: a small one in the heart of Dunedin; and **Port Chalmers**, a down-at-heel container-port town whose prospects seem to be on the rise.

Otago Harbour is protected from the Pacific Ocean by the lovely **Otago Peninsula**, with its wealth of wildlife, principally penguins, seals and alba-trosses. The peninsula is commonly visited on a day-trip from the city, but rural accommodation only half an hour from the city allows you to stay out of town and drive into Dunedin as needed.

Some history

From around 1100 AD, **Maori** fished the rich coastal waters of nearby bays, travelling inland to hunt moa, ducks and freshwater fish, and trading with other *iwi* further north. Eventually they formed a settlement on both sides of the harbour, calling it Otakou (pronounced "O-tar-go") and naming the headland at the harbour's entrance after their great chieftain, Taiaroa. Today a well-developed *marae* occupies the Otakou site. By the 1820s European whalers and sealers sought shelter in the only safe anchorage along this stretch of coast unwittingly introducing foreign diseases which decimated the local population. It reached a minimum of 110 but subsequent intermarriage bolstered numbers and formed a resilient cultural mix.

The New Zealand Company selected the Otago Harbour as a suitable site for a planned **Scottish settlement** as early as 1840 and purchased land from local Maori for a meagre sum, but it wasn't until 1848 that the first migrant ships arrived. Some 344 people, mostly staunch Scots Presbyterians arrived on the *John Wickliffe* and the *Philip Laing*, led by Captain William Cargill and the Reverend Thomas Burns, nephew of the Scottish poet, Robert Burns. With the arrival of seven hundred English and Irish the following year, the Scots were soon in the minority, but Scottish fervour was sufficient to stamp a distinct character on the growing town, bequeathing some fine churches, as well as a passionate enthusiasm for education.

In 1861, a lone Australian prospector discovered **gold** at a creek near modern-day Lawrence, about 100km west of Dunedin. Within three months, diggers were pouring in from Australia, and as the main port of entry Dunedin suddenly found itself in the midst of a gold rush. The population doubled in six months, the port was expanded, then the population treble in the next three years making Dunedin New Zealand's most important city. This was Dunedin's period of unbridled construction, with the new-found wealth used to establish

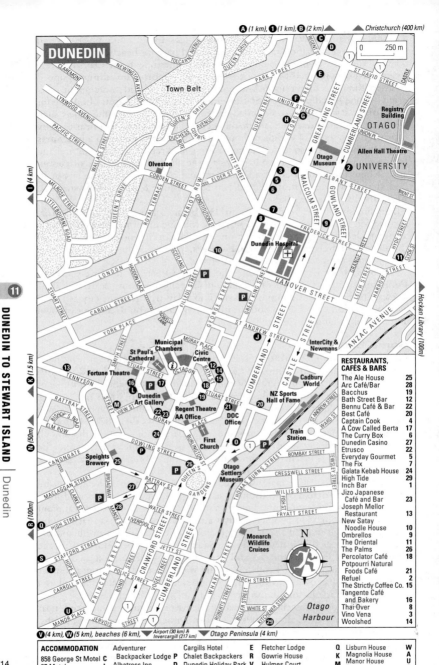

the university, Otago Boys' High School as well as Otago Girls' High School. By the 1870s gold mania had largely subsided, but Otago sustained economic primacy through **shipping**, railway development and the efforts of thousands who stayed on to farm. Decline set in during the early years of the twentieth century, when the opening of the Panama Canal in 1914 made Auckland a more economic port for British shipping. In the 1980s, the improvement in world gold prices and the development of equipment enabling large-scale recovery of gold from low-yielding soils re-established **mining** in the hinterland. Today you can visit massive mining operations, including the one at Macraes, an hour's drive from Dunedin (see p.893).

Arrival, information and city transport

Dunedin **airport**, 5km off SH1 some 30km south of town, is served by domestic flights from Auckland, Christchurch, Queenstown, Invercargill and Wellington, as well as international flights direct from Sydney, Melbourne and Brisbane with Freedom Air (see p.17). Shuttle bus companies (see p.727) meet each flight and run into the city centre (from $15) dropping off at accommodation along the way; a taxi ride to the city centre will set you back about $40.

Dunedin has no mainline passenger train service, but the tourist-oriented services along the Taieri Gorge Railway (see p.728) leave from the Dunedin Railway Station on Anzac Avenue. This is also the terminus for Atomic Shuttles. InterCity **buses** drop off in the city centre at 205 St Andrew St; and South Island Connections terminate at the visitor centre (see below).

Information

You can't miss Dunedin's **visitor centre** (Nov–March Mon–Fri 8.30am–6pm, Sat & Sun 9am–6pm; April–Oct Mon–Fri 8.30am–5pm, Sat & Sun 9am–5pm; ☎03/474 3300, ⓦwww.CityofDunedin.com) in the grand stone Municipal Chambers that dominate the Octagon, a grassy area at the centre of the city. The visitor centre handles all the usual transport, accommodation and trip bookings and can furnish various walk leaflets including *Walk the City* ($2.50) which details points of interest along a gentle stroll round central Dunedin. The **DOC** office is at 77 Lower Stuart St (Mon–Fri 8.30am–5pm; ☎03/477 0677), and has plenty of information on Otago, Fiordland and Mount Aspiring.

City transport

All the central sights, hostels, hotels and places to eat and drink are easily accessible on foot. To get further out you'll want to use the efficient **bus** system, operated by several companies all orchestrated by the Otago Regional Council (ⓦwww.orc.govt.nz) which publishes the free Dunedin Bus Timetable. Pick it up from the Dunedin City Council on the ground floor of the Civic Centre on the corner of the Octagon and George Street.

Most lines run Monday to Saturday from around 7.30am to 11pm with limited services on Sunday and public holidays. Buses are not numbered but are identified by their route: the most useful is the Normanby–St Clair run which goes from the beach right through the city past the Botanic Garden to the foot of Baldwin Street and beyond. **Fares** are calculated according to the number of zones crossed: the central city is one zone ($1.20), to Baldwin St is two zones ($1.60), to St Clair is three zones ($2), and to Port Chalmers is four zones ($2.30). On the Normanby–St Clair service there's a $5 **all-day pass**: buy it from the driver. Buses all start from or pass through the centre of town, most stopping at different stands around the Octagon.

You might also want to join the hop-on-hop-off **guided tour** of the city with Dunedin City Explorer ($15; ☎0800/322 240) which makes an hour-long loop of the central city sights, Olveston, the Botanic Gardens and Baldwin Street with the chance to get off for around ninety minutes at up to four of those places. Alternatively, try the **double-decker bus tour** with Newton Citisights (☎03/477 5577; 1hr; $15), which departs from the visitor centre five times daily.

There are several **taxi** ranks in the city centre (see p.728 for locations and details of taxi companies). **Drivers** will soon discover the one-way system running north–south through the city and affecting Cumberland, Castle, Great King and Crawford streets. **Parking** is seldom a problem with inexpensive meters and restricted zones in the centre but free long-term street parking a few hundred metres outside.

Accommodation

There's a broad choice of accommodation in Dunedin, most of it in or near the city centre. With a couple of exceptions, the **hotels** in the heart of town are bland affairs designed to attract business people. Several **motels** line George Street, with others dotted around the city, while the best **B&Bs and home-stays** are in the hillside suburbs 2–5km from the centre. The handful of **hostels** are generally good value and closer to the city centre. Three well equipped **campsites** are no more than three kilometres out of town and two are on bus routes. As in all New Zealand's major cities, **booking ahead** in summer is advisable, wherever you're staying. If you prefer to stay somewhere more rural and travel in to the city, check out the collection of places on the **Otago Peninsula** (see p.737).

Hotels

Bentley's 137 St Andrew St ☎03/477 0572 & 0800/266 336, ⓦ www.bentleyshotel.co.nz. A fairly luxurious, modern, business hotel in the heart of the city offering rooms, suites and a family unit, plus an airy restaurant, bar and café. ⓖ

Cargills Hotel 678 George St ☎03/477 7983 & 0800/737 378, ⓦ www.cargills.co.nz. Adjacent to the business district and university, this recently refurbished place offers a peaceful garden setting and a variety of well-appointed rooms equipped with minibars and fridges. The on-site licensed restaurant serves Kiwi and international cuisine. ⓖ

Leviathan 27 Queens Gardens ☎03/477 3160 & 0800/773 773, ⓦ www.dunedinhotel.co.nz. The most atmospheric hotel in Dunedin, and the best value. Built in 1884, it is grand yet comfortable in the style of a classic railway hotel, and just a short stroll from both the Octagon and the train station. Off-street parking available. Budget rooms ④, standard ⑤, suites ⑥

Motels

858 George St Motel 858 George St ☎03/474 0047 & 0800/858 999, ⓦ www.858george streetmotel.co.nz. Unusual, new and well-executed design by Dunedin architects, based on Victorian

houses divided into big luxurious units. Studios ⑤, suites ⑥

97 Motel 97 Moray Place ☎03/477 2050 &0800/909 797, ⓔ info@97motel.co.nz The best-located, friendliest motel in town, with spacious, gleaming units, each equipped with a microwave. ⑤

Allan Court 590 George St ☎03/477 7526 & 0800/611 511, ⓦ www.nzmotels.co.nz/allan.court. Central, modern, upmarket and comfortable, with full kitchens in all units, guest laundry and a choice of breakfasts for an extra charge. ⑤

Farrys 575 George St ☎03/477 9333 & 0800/109 333, ⓔ farrys@farrysmotel.co.nz. An excellent family motel next to the main shopping area offering one-, two- and three-bedroom units, all fully self-contained, plus a free laundry and small playground. Studios ④, units ⑤

B&Bs and homestays

Albatross Inn 770 George St ☎ & ⓕ03/477 2727 & 0800/441 441, ⓦ www.albatross .inn.co.nz. Extremely hospitable B&B in a characterful Edwardian house close to the university and city centre. Rooms are comfortable and well appointed and come either en suite or with a private bathroom. Doubles are fine but larger rooms are better and some spacious examples have a kitchenette. A substantial continental breakfast is served. Rooms ⑤, with kitchenette ⑥

Fletcher Lodge 276 High St ☏ 03/477 5552, ⓦ www.fletcherlodge.co.nz. Extremely luxurious and central boutique lodge in an English baronial-style home built in 1924 for a leading Kiwi industrialist, Sir James Fletcher, with a secluded garden. The living room is richly oak-panelled, everything is kept spotless and all rooms are en-suite. There's also a large suite ($550), off-street parking, a laundry service and a sumptuous breakfast. ⑧

Gowrie House 7 Gowry Place, Roslyn ☏ 03/477 2103, ⓔ gowriehouse.bnb@xtra.co.nz. Excellent rural and city views from this small, cosy, turn-of-the-century house set on a hill five minutes' drive from the centre and on the Octagon to Maori Hill–Prospect Park bus route. Two double rooms, both light and airy with big windows and shared facilities. ⑥

Hulmes Court 52 Tennyson St ☏ 03/477 5319 & 0800/448 563, ⓦ www.hulmes.co.nz. A pair of characterful homes (one a grand 1860 Victorian affair) just off the Octagon yet quiet. Rooms are big and individually themed, several of them ensuite, and there's off-street parking, free bus and rail pick-up, free mountain bikes and Internet access. Rooms ⑤, ensuites ⑥

Lisburn House 15 Lisburn Ave, Caversham ☏ 03/455 8888, ⓦ www.lisburnhouse.co.nz. Luxurious and beautifully preserved Victorian-Gothic house run by very friendly hosts, in a suburb ten minutes' drive south of the city. Each of the three distinctly styled and spacious rooms has a four-poster bed, fine linen, fresh flowers and a private bathroom. Not suitable for children. ⑧–⑨

Magnolia House 18 Grendon St, Maori Hill ☏ 03/467 5999 & ⓔ mrsuth@paradise.net.nz. A spacious Victorian villa, set in a large garden in the leafy suburb of Maori Hill, 2km north of the Octagon (courtesy car available). One ensuite and two well appointed doubles with shared facilities, and two house cats. ⑤

Sahara Guesthouse & Motel 619 George St ☏ 03/477 6662, ⓦ www.dunedin-accommodation .co.nz. Spacious, central 1863 guesthouse where most rooms have shared facilities. TV lounge, off-street parking. They also have a motel section with ten standard self-contained units. ④

Hostels

Adventurer Backpacker Lodge 37 Dowling St ☏ 0800/422 257, ⓔ adventur@es.co.nz. A convivial hostel in the heart of the city, with dorms ranging from 2-bed to 9-bed and a few singles,

doubles and twins; off-street parking and free Internet access. Dorms ①, rooms ②

Chalet Backpackers 296 High St ☏ 03/479 2075 & 0800/242 538, ⓔ kirsti@paradise.net.nz. Central, comfortable hostel with a great atmosphere and excellent kitchen and dining facilities. Four-shares have beds rather than bunks and there are nice single and double rooms plus a pool and piano room. Dorms ①, rooms ②

Elm Lodge 74 Elm Row ☏ 03/477 1872 & 0800/356 563, ⓦ www.elmwildlifetours.co.nz. An airy, clean, 1930s house on a hill near the centre. The dorms are 4- or 6-bed. Free linen and pick-up service. Dorms ①, rooms ②

Manor House 28 Manor Place ☏ 03/477 0484 & 0800/477 0484, ⓦ www.manorhousebackpackers .co.nz. Well-equipped and beautifully kept colonial house on a hill fifteen minutes' walk south of the Octagon. Dorms are 4-bed to 8-bed; free pick-up service. Dorms ①, rooms ②

Ramsay Lodge 60 Stafford St ☏ 03/477 6313, ⓔ ramsay.lodge@xtra.co.nz. Upscale backpackers in a spacious, high-ceilinged nineteenth-century villa with stained-glass windows. Beds are made up and they only accommodate around twenty. Dorms ①, twins ②, doubles ③

Stafford Gables YHA 71 Stafford St ☏ 03/474 1919, ⓔ yha.dunedin@yha.org.nz. Characterful YHA in a large, 1902 homestead ten minutes' walk from the Octagon. The best bit is the roof garden with excellent views over the city. The dorms are 3- to 7-bed, double and twin rooms are generally large, some doubles come with balconies and there are also family rooms. Office hours from 8am–9pm. Dorms ①, rooms ③

Campsites and motorparks

Aaron Lodge Top 10 Holiday Park 162 Kaikorai Valley Rd ☏ 03/476 4725 & 0800/879 227, ⓦ www.aaronlodgetop10.co.nz. A sheltered, fairly spacious and well-tended site, in the hills 2.5km west of the city centre. Facilities include a heated pool and playground. Camping $12–13, cabins ②, flats ③, motel units ④

Dunedin Holiday Park 41 Victoria Rd ☏ 03/455 4690 & 0800/945 455, ⓦ www.dunedinholidaypark .co.nz. Lying alongside St Kilda Beach, this well-appointed park is five minutes' drive from the city centre and served by the Brockville–St Kilda bus: pick it up at Octagon Stand 3. Well appointed and with a seven-day camp store, it has standard and more comfortable en-suite cabins. Camping $10–11, cabins ②, en-suite units ③, tourist flats ③

Leith Valley Touring Park 103 Malvern St ☏ 03/467 9936, ⓔ lvtpdun@southnet.co.nz. A small, pleasant campsite beside a creek at the foot of bush-clad hills, 3km north from the centre. The site is served by the Octagon to Garden Village bus

on weekdays and there's a 24hr grocery within walking distance. Camping $11, on-site vans ❷, flats ❸

The City

Day or night, the hub of Dunedin's activity is the **Octagon**, a green, tree-filled space in the heart of the city, bordered by historic buildings and circled by Moray Place. Restaurants, offices, banks, bars, clubs and most of the sights are concentrated around it, and the **shopping district** stretches immediately north and south along George Street and Princes Street. Further north lies the **university area** and the expanse of the **Botanic Garden**. To the east is the head of **Otago Harbour**, a sheltered inlet 22km long and no wider than a river in places. The waters are shared by windsurfers, yachts and sightseeing boats, and occasionally dolphins and whales. Two sandy **beaches** lie a short bus ride south from the city centre in the suburbs of St Clair and St Kilda. For an overview of the city, head for the **lookout points** on the hills around Dunedin (see p.729)

The Octagon

The **Octagon** was originally laid out in 1846 by Charles Kettle, the Chief Surveyor of the New Zealand Company, who subsequently died in a typhoid epidemic that swept the city during the 1862 gold rush. Today, it's a mixture of modern and beautifully preserved buildings overlooking grassland and trees, presided over by a statue of Robert Burns, a potent symbol of Dunedin's Scottish origins and literary associations. Every Friday (10am–4pm), the area spills over with **market** stalls selling locally made crafts, such as stained glass, pottery, woodwork and jewellery, while in summer live bands provide free entertainment.

Dominating the Octagon is the 1880 **Municipal Chambers** building, a grand, classical structure with a clock tower, all constructed from limestone dramatically offset against volcanic bluestone. It's a fine example of a recurring combination of materials that's seen throughout the city and also of the handiwork of Scottish architect **Robert A. Lawson**, whose hand can be seen in the design of many of Dunedin's public buildings. Beside the Municipal Chambers rise the twin white stone spires of **St Paul's Cathedral**, one of Dunedin's finest buildings and the seat of Anglican worship in the city. This impressive Gothic Revival edifice, entirely constructed from Oamaru stone, was designed by English architect Edmund Harold Sedding and consecrated in 1919. Inside, the twenty-metre-high stone-vaulted ceiling is the only one of its kind in New Zealand, and much of the stained glass in the impressive windows is original; the stark chancel and altar were added in 1971.

Continuing anticlockwise around the Octagon, the spacious and gleaming **Dunedin Public Art Gallery**, 30 The Octagon (daily 10am–5pm; donation, plus charges for special exhibitions) was completed in 1996, breathing new life into the area. Dunedin City Council architects fashioned the new gallery out of six Victorian buildings, elegantly refurbished to create an airy, modern, split-level space of several exhibition areas – a contrast to the original public art gallery, founded in 1884 and the oldest in the country. The foyer of polished wooden floors, ironwork and a hundred-year-old spiral staircase is worth a look in itself. The gallery's main strength is a rotated collection of early and contemporary New Zealand works, including Van der Velden's powerful *Waterfall in the Otira Gorge*, William Goldie's well-known *All 'e same t'e Pakeha*, and a small gallery devoted to the works of Frances Hodgkins. There's also an assemblage of relatively minor works by Old Masters and more recent

△ Lonekers Beach, Stewart Island

practitioners with Turner, Gainsborough, Monet and Constable all represented. The space also regularly hosts temporary shows of international standard.

Further around at 17 The Octagon is the 1874 facade of the **Regent Theatre**, a one-time hotel that was transformed into a cinema in 1928 then subsequently into a theatre. Today it's a venue for international shows and the Royal New Zealand Ballet, as well as live music (see p.727). Inside, elaborate nineteenth-century plasterwork and marble staircases juxtapose colourful 1920s stained-glass windows and geometric balustrades. During the 24hr **Regent Theatre Book Sale** (around mid-May or June) the theatre is filled with all manner of books, from 50-cent copies to collector's items.

Behind the Regent Theatre on Moray Place, the 54-metre stone spire of the **First Church of Otago** stands as a landmark throughout the city. The church, generally recognised as the most impressive of New Zealand's nineteenth-century churches, was designed in neo-Gothic style by Robert A. Lawson. Two other small, wooden churches had already occupied this site, and when Lawson's version was consecrated in 1873 it was the first Presbyterian church to open in Otago. Of particular interest inside are a wooden gabled ceiling and, above the pulpit, a brightly coloured rose window, while another large window commemorates those who fell in World War I.

South and east of the Octagon

A five-minute walk southeast of the Octagon, the **Otago Settlers Museum**, 31 Queens Gardens (daily 10am–5pm; $4), catalogues two hundred years of social history in Dunedin and Otago, drawing from an exhaustive collection of artefacts, paintings and photographs. Highlights include the "Portrait Gallery", whose walls are plastered with black-and-white photographs of the region's early settler families, and "Window on a Chinese Past", which provides an insight into the lives of the legions of Chinese who left their families behind to seek a fortune in the Otago Goldfields, many of them staying for years. Among the exhibits over in the transport wing there's a stylish and beautifully appointed 1940s caravan, a restored double-ended Fairlie steam engine, the chance to sit on a penny-farthing and a hilarious early 1950s cycling road safety film featuring chimp "actors".

The **Dunedin Railway Station**, 200m northwest on Anzac Avenue, is an imposing building faced with pale Oamaru stone. Constructed on reclaimed swampland and opened in 1906, the station was designed by George A. Troup who produced a grand exterior complete with towers, turrets and minarets. But the real surprise lies inside the main foyer, which has been preserved in its original state and gleams with gentle-toned green, yellow and cream majolica wall tiles made especially for New Zealand Rail by Royal Doulton. A fine, classical, china frieze of cherubs and foliage encircles the room, and elaborate tilework decorates the ticket booths. The mosaic floor celebrates the steam engine and consists of more than 700,000 tiny squares of Royal Doulton porcelain. Upstairs on the balcony, a stained-glass window at each end depicts an approaching train, whose headlights gleam, no matter from which angle you look at them.

The upper floor also houses the **New Zealand Sports Hall of Fame** (daily 10am–4pm; $5), a collection of memorabilia relating to those 150-odd New Zealand sports people lucky or talented enough to have been inducted. Hagiographic displays are devoted to: sainted rugby loose forward, Colin Meads; 1954 world record long jumper, Yvette Williams; late 1950s world champion sheep shearer, Godfrey Bowen; mountaineer, Edmund Hillary; fast-bowler, Richard Hadlee; yachtsman, Peter Blake; middle distance runners Jack Lovelock, Dick Quax, Rod Dixon and John Walker; and many, many more.

Further east beyond the train station is the **Hocken Library** at 90 Anzac Ave, near the junction with Parry Street (Mon–Fri 9.30am–5pm, Tues also 6–9pm, Sat 9am–noon; free), an extensive university research library that opened on campus in 1910, before moving here in the late 1990s. Its impressive collection of books, manuscripts, paintings and photographs relating to New Zealand and the Pacific was originally assembled by Dr Thomas Morland Hocken, a Dunedin physician and one of the country's first historians. Details of exhibitions held in the library gallery (Mon–Fri 9.30am–5pm, Sat 9am–noon, Sun check on ℡03/479 5600; free) are regularly advertised in the *Otago Daily Times*.

North of the Octagon

Around a kilometre north of the Octagon the **Otago Museum**, 419 Great King St (daily 10am–5pm; $5) can easily absorb half a day. Much expanded and renovated in recent years it is packed with well considered displays ranged around an airy atrium. Star attraction is the fascinating Southern Land, Southern People gallery, which covers virtually all aspects of life and natural history in the southern half of the South Island and the sub-Antarctic islands but, understandably enough, concentrates on Otago. Large boulders give an idea of the rock that underlies the region in displays which also draw in a fossilised plesiosaur skeleton and material on Oamaru stone and its influence on the region's architecture. Everything is knitted neatly together, discussion on climate being illustrated by a Maori flax rain cape, and coverage of the regions fish calling on the experience of whitebaiters.

Elsewhere in the building, look out for the Animal Attic, a deeply Victorian amalgamation of macabre skeletons and stuffed beasts some literally strung up among the skylights where some wit has secreted a monkey and a couple of chickens, and even painted droppings on the rafters beneath them. The special exhibitions gallery is usually worth a look, and on level one there's **Discovery World**, an interactive science museum-within-a-museum (extra $6) that's perfect for the six to elevens.

Guided tours ($10) take place at 11.30am and 3.30pm, there's a free lecture presentation at 2pm each day, and for a break there's a good café.

Olveston

Dunedin's showpiece historic home is **Olveston**, 42 Royal Terrace (1hr guided tours only: daily 9.30am, 10.45am, noon, 1.30pm, 2.45pm & 4pm; $14; book a day ahead in summer ℡03/477 3320), ten minutes' walk northwest of the Octagon. Contained within the walls of this fine Edwardian house is a treasure trove of art and exquisite antiques collected from all over the world by one family and left just as they were when the last of the lineage passed away. The collection was gradually assembled by a wealthy, Jewish mercantile family, the Theomins, who lived here from 1906 and were passionately interested in travel, art and music. On her death in 1966, the longest-surviving member of the family, Dorothy, bequeathed the house and its contents to the City of Dunedin.

Built in 1904–06, the Jacobean-style house itself is reminiscent of the English Arts and Crafts Movement. London architect Sir Ernest George filled the house with extraordinary decorative detail, incorporating polished wooden floors, stained-glass windows, wood panelling, fine brass fittings and stairways leading to mezzanine galleries. A particularly striking piece of craftsmanship is the oak staircase in the Grand Hall, made in England and constructed without the use of nails. The house was also a masterpiece of modernity for its time, being among the first to be fitted with the conveniences of central heating, heated towel rails and an in-house telephone system.

The University

Less than ten minutes' walk north of the city centre lies New Zealand's oldest university, founded by Scottish settlers in 1869. Based on the design of Glasgow University, the **University of Otago** quickly expanded into a complex of imposing Gothic bluestone buildings, foremost among them the registry building at the heart of the campus. With its Gothic **clock tower**, it is an academic icon and is one of the most-photographed landmarks in Dunedin. Today the campus sprawls over several blocks northeast of Cumberland and Albany streets, strung along the Water of Leith, a small river, winding through it. The **Student Enquiries Office** (Mon–Fri 9.30am–4.30pm) in the registry building has simple free campus maps for visitors, and a stroll through the campus from Union Street to Leith Street will take you past the key buildings.

The Botanic Garden and Signal Hill

Established in 1863 in the far northern reaches of the inner city, the well-tended **Dunedin Botanic Garden** (sunrise–sunset; free) lies at the foot of Signal Hill. The hilly Upper Garden contains an expansive Rhododendron Dell, where well-established specimens grow among native bush, flowering trees and plants. This is the star attraction during the city's annual **Rhododendron Week** in the third week of October. On the hills there's also an arboretum, a native plant collection and a modern aviary complex, home to native birds such as kea and kaka, as well as exotic birds from all over the world. The flat Lower Garden features exotic trees, Winter Garden conservatories (daily 10am–4pm), an Alpine House (daily 9am–4pm), a rose garden and a well-equipped playground. A volunteer-run information centre (daily 10am–4pm) lies between the tea kiosk and the Winter Garden, stocked with maps and displays on the Botanic Garden. The garden's tea kiosk (daily 9.30am–4.30pm) serves inexpensive snacks and meals. Access to the Lower Gardens car park is from Cumberland Street, while the Upper Gardens car park is on Lovelock Avenue.

Just north of the Botanic Garden, Opoho Road leads up to the 393m summit of **Signal Hill**, a scenic reserve with a magnificent view over Dunedin, the upper harbour and the sea from the Centennial Memorial. This is apparently the nation's only monument commemorating one hundred years of British sovereignty (1840–1940) following the signing of the Treaty of Waitangi, and flanked by two powerful bronze figures symbolizing the past and the future. Embedded in the podium is a tribute to Scotland: a chunk of the rock upon which Edinburgh Castle was built.

Apart from driving up here you can ride the Opoho **bus** (from Octagon Stand 7) to within 1km of the summit, or make the fairly gentle walk (6km return; 1hr 30min) from the Botanic Garden.

Baldwin Street

Dunedin rejoices in containing the world's steepest street, **Baldwin Street**, which with a Guinness Book of Records-verified maximum gradient of 1 in 2.66 has a slope of almost 19 degrees, impressive indeed though a good deal less than the 38 degrees widely quote around town. No one comes for the modest views from the top of this dead-end street, but everyone wants to walk up, something achieved in about five minutes. The honestly titled Baldwin Street Tourist Shop, 282 North Rd (daily 8.30am–6pm), in a former post office near the bottom of Baldwin Street, sells much needed drinks as well as T-shirts and a certificate ($2) marking your achievement. During the annual "Gutbuster" event in mid-February (part of the Dunedin Summer Festival) contestants run to the top and back down again – the current record is one minute 56 seconds.

Baldwin Street is 5km north of the city centre: follow Great King Street until it becomes North Road then look for the tenth road on the right. The Normanby–St Clair bus from Stand 2 on Princes Street drops you at the foot of Baldwin Street.

Dunedin's beaches

Four kilometres south of the city centre, the suburbs of St Kilda and St Clair culminate in a long wild sweep of creamy sand enclosed by two volcanic headlands (served by buses from the corner of the Octagon and Princes Street). **St Clair Beach** is excellent for surfing and is patrolled by lifeguards during the summer. For swimming in calmer waters, head to the western end to the **St Clair Hot Salt Water Pool**, The Esplanade (Oct–March Mon–Fri 6am–7pm, Sat & Sun 8am–7pm; $4.50; ☎03/455 6352), a large, outdoor, heated saltwater pool beside the rocky point. The pool acts as a contact point for Southern Coast Surf Clinic (☎03/455 6007, ⓦwww.surfcoachnz.com), which offers **surfing lessons** (1hr for $40, min two people) with wetsuit and board supplied.

About halfway along the strip, St Clair merges with **St Kilda Beach**, which is reasonably safe for swimming as long as you keep between the flags; it is also patrolled in summer. At the beach's eastern end, a headland separates St Kilda from the smaller **Tomahawk Beach** (not safe for swimming), often dotted with horses and buggies preparing for trotting races at low tide. The best swimming beach in Otago is the blend of sand and rocky outcrops at **Brighton**, 15km south of Dunedin: catch the Brighton bus from Stand 5 on Cumberland St between Hanover and St Andrew streets ($2.80).

Cadbury World and Speight's Brewery

Stand in the sweet vapours downwind of Dunedin's downtown chocolate factory and it is hard to resist a visit to **Cadbury World**, 280 Cumberland St (daily 9am–4pm; $14; ☎0800/223 287, ⓦwww.cadburyworld.co.nz). Enthusiastically-run tours (around 1hr 15min) start with diverting displays and the history of chocolate, a film about the factory, and a chance to nibble on cacao beans – bitter and highly caffeinated but not unpleasant. Then it is into the factory to see lines producing Crunchie, chocolate buttons, Easter eggs and the like, though if you're here on a weekend or from Christmas to mid-January many of the lines may be shut down. A rather gratuitous "chocolate waterfall" set up for visitors will entertain the kids, and everyone gets liberally showered with free samples. Bookings are recommended, especially during school holidays.

A few blocks to the southwest, the **Speight's Brewery Tour**, 200 Rattray St (daily 10am, 11.45am, 2pm, plus Mon–Thurs at 7pm, and Sat & Sun at 4.30pm; $15; ☎03/477 7697, ⓦwww.speights.co.nz), offers a similar experience in one of New Zealand's oldest breweries. The tall, brick chimney topped by a barrel crafted from stone is visible from across the city and guides you to the hour-long tours (best booked in advance), essentially a light-hearted journey through the alchemy of traditional brewing. Much restored in recent years it is all burnished copper mash tuns and kauri gyles, and there's the chance to sniff some of the raw materials.

Of course, you get to try six samples of the product, and you shouldn't miss the tongue-in-cheek *Southern Man TV* ads that run continuously. The entry is beside a **water spigot** fed by the same sweet-tasting artesian water that is used to brew the beer: you'll usually see locals filling water bottles and containers.

The two factories offer a **combined ticket** ($25) giving access to both plus a ten percent discount on merchandise.

Eating

In a city that's undeniably enthusiastic about food, with cuisine from around the world, you'll never be at a loss for somewhere to satisfy your appetite, plus you'll seldom need to stray far from the **city centre**. Restaurants and cafés ring the Octagon and are strung along George Street, particularly between Hanover and Albany streets to the north. You'll find there's an excellent range, across the board from classic espresso cafés to fine dining restaurants, and in recent years there's been an explosion in cheap ethnic cafés – Cambodian and Filipino as well as the usual Thai and Indian. Some of the city's **pubs** also serve reasonably priced food (see p.726). Useful spots for **stocking up** are *Tangente Café and Bakery* for organic bread and the *Everyday Gourmet* deli (both listed below). For simpler needs visit the Night 'n' Day, cnr George and Regent streets, a 24-hour food store (locally known as the two-four) that's a Dunedin institution and handy after the pubs have closed for sandwiches, pies and snacks. Eating places on the **Otago Peninsula** are listed separately on p.737.

Cafés and snack bars

Arc Café/Bar 135 High St. Excellent, big and groovy cyber café/bar serving well-priced gourmet vegetarian and vegan snacks as well as eye-opening coffee and a good range of herbal teas, plus free Internet access. Music most nights (see p.726).

Best Café 30 Stuart St. Spartan and unprepossessing, this local legend (here since the 1950s) offers some of the city's best traditional fish and chips, served in a time warp in this location with bread and butter and the constant background yap of the television. You are liable to be greeted by the sort of smile last seen on a recently deceased blue cod. Mon–Fri 11.30am–7pm.

Everyday Gourmet 466 George St. A cosy deli-cum-café stuffed with specialist cheeses, salami, fine meat pies and other imported speciality foods. Also bagels, substantial sandwiches, take-home meals, great Anzac biscuits and excellent coffee. Generally closed Sun.

The Fix 15 Frederick St. Small, daytime student-haunt for cheap but very good coffee and juices, with a garden terrace where you can eat your own food. Closed weekends

Galata Kebab House 126 Princes St. Authentic, cheap Turkish food to eat in or take away, offering the usual mix of vegetarian dishes, falafels and kebabs, from 11am till late. Licensed & BYO.

Jizo Japanese Café and Bar 56 Princes St. Inexpensive sushi, rice dishes, miso and noodle soups to take away or eat in at this small, split-level café. Licensed & BYO, closed Sun.

New Satay Noodle House 16 Hanover St. A cheap-and-cheerful all-day spot for noodle soups, satay Thai and Indian dishes (all around $7) from 11am. All the Asian students come here.

Percolator Café 142 Stuart St. A well-established inexpensive espresso bar just down from the

Octagon, open from 9am till the early hours Fri & Sat, till 10pm the rest of the week. Brunch is served on Sat & Sun morning, and there are light meals anytime.

Potpourri Natural Foods Café 97 Lower Stuart St. Established veggie venue got up to look like a church. Wholemeal baking, a big salad bar and great frozen yoghurt to eat in or take away. No alcohol and no smoking, closed Sun.

The Strictly Coffee Co 23 Bath St. The best coffee in town, sold by the cup or the kilo in an elegantly simple café. They also do a variety of homemade cakes and some simple sandwiches. Mon–Fri 8am–4.30pm.

Tangente Café and Bakery 111 Moray Place. Mellow central spot using organic grains and flours, free-range eggs and filtered water to produce gourmet snacks and meals from breakfast onwards. Try a home-baked organic bread cup – a bowl made of bread filled with the concoction of your choice – while browsing their magazines. Dinner, Fri & Sat nights only; licensed & BYO.

Restaurants

A Cow Called Berta 199 Stuart St ☎03/477 2993. Swiss-style country dinners of simple strong flavours based on French cuisine, in the cosy yet classy ambience of a converted Victorian terraced house. Expect vegetable-stuffed fillo with rösti ($23), or Moroccan-spice dusted blue cod ($25). Closed Sat lunch and Sun.

Bacchus 1st floor, 12 The Octagon ☎03/474 0824. Restaurant and wine bar with a great vantage point overlooking the Octagon from a prestigious historic building. Over fifty wines, accompanied by moderately priced lunches ($14–16) and dinners ($24–28). Popular office workers' lunch spot Mon–Fri; dinner Mon–Sat.

The Curry Box 442 George St ☎03/477 4713. Café-style restaurant dishing up good curries, tandoori breads, chicken balti, rogan josh and a whole lot more, many in vegetarian versions (all $12–14). Weekday lunches and nightly for dinner. No alcohol.

Etrusco 1st floor, 8 Moray Place ☎03/477 3737. Authentic dinner-only Italian fare presented in an airy and lovingly restored building. Moderate prices and friendly service. Good wine list, also BYO.

High Tide 29 Kitchener St ☎03/477 9784. A quietly romantic and friendly waterside hideaway for excellent evening meals, complemented by great views over the harbour and peninsula. The moderately priced menu consists of imaginative seafood, vegetarian and meat dishes, as well as homemade soups and desserts. Licensed & BYO.

Joseph Mellor Restaurant 1st floor, Otago Polytechnic, cnr York Place & Tennyson St, entrance directly opposite Kavanagh College ☎03/479 6172. Unbelievably cheap, high-quality French/New Zealand cuisine prepared by world-class chefs and their students in a bustling restaurant with one of the best city views in Dunedin. Book a few days ahead. Open March–Oct Tues–Thurs only for a set lunch (noon–1.30pm; $11) and dinner (6.30–9pm; $21). Licensed and BYO.

Ombrellos 10 Clarendon St ☎03/477 8773. An attractive Mediterranean-style courtyard café/bar in the heart of the university area. Open all day, offering breakfast through to dinner (mostly around $15–20) and an affordable wine list. Closed Mon lunch; bar open 4pm–late with occasional live music.

The Palms 18 Queens Gardens ☎03/477 6534. Something of an institution among locals and very popular, this semi-formal place has picture windows overlooking Queens Gardens and a menu of modestly priced dishes such as jumbo ravioli ($21), lentil curry ($23) or rack of lamb ($27). Dinner only; licensed & BYO.

Thai Over 388 George St. Authentic Thai food in a modern, bright and open café-style space, where you can sample larb gai, tom kar and tom yum, green, yellow and red curries and peanut sauce with satay or stir fry, all for around $16. Open daily for lunch and dinner; licensed.

Vino Vena 484 George St ☎03/479 0110. Swish Italian-style spot on the first floor and set back from the main road, where you can sip some very smooth coffee and taste some delightful smoked warehou with poached eggs and hollandaise sauce, linguini with smoked salmon or pansotti with pumpkin lasagna, all for under $25.

The Dunedin Sound

In the late 1970s and early 1980s an idiosyncratic style of rock music began to emerge from Dunedin's local pub scene. Musicians of the era claim there never was a movement as such, but the scene was quickly tagged the **Dunedin Sound**. Isolated from the commercial mainstream the bands produced a kind of jangly garage sound and indulged in songwriting for the sheer hell of it. They were championed by indie Christchurch label Flying Nun (now based in Auckland; ⊛flyingnun.co.nz) who put out early records but by bands like The Chills, The Clean and the Verlaines. All saw some success in New Zealand and found a receptive (if underground) audience in Europe and the States.

As late as 1992, the *Chicago Tribune* called Dunedin the "Rock Capital of The World", but then the scene had moved on. Some of the bands are still going (in one form or another), and the spirit survives with musos and fans the world over still celebrating the era. In 2002 Flying Nun released its 21st birthday CD of Flying Nun covers called *Under The Influence*: ex-Pavement frontman Stephen Malkmus covered The Verlaines' wonderful *Death and the Maiden*.

The songs have certainly stood the test of time, and as the rock 'n' roll wheel turns, you can hear an updated version of the same kind of sound coming from bands like The Strokes and their imitators.

If you want to dig deeper, check out Records Records, 213 Stuart St (☎03/474 0789, ⊛www.recordsrecords.co.nz), a new- and secondhand-**music shop** that's particularly strong on Kiwi bands.

Drinking, nightlife and entertainment

As the evening draws in, Dunedin shifts into a higher gear, especially during term time or one of its many festivals. Drinking is taken seriously here and there's no shortage of **pubs** and **bars** some serving the produce of Dunedin's premier microbrewery, Emerson's, which produces half a dozen excellent English- and German-style beers. Many pubs are student hangouts where local **bands** play at weekends: once the students go home for the holidays some of the dance floors can look pretty sad. For entertainment and events **listings**, pick up the free and widely available weekly *Fink* (ⓦwww.fink.net.nz), a complete guide to music, exhibitions and movies predominantly aimed at students. The *Otago Daily Times* also has a listings section, best on Thursday.

The city is also well served with **theatres**, **cinemas** (both arthouse and mainstream) and **concert halls**.

Events can be **booked** through the venue or through the Ticketek office in the Regent Theatre in The Octagon takes bookings for a selection of national and local events (ⓣ03/477 8597, ⓦwww.ticketek.co.nz; Mon–Fri 8.30am–5pm, Sat 10.30am–1pm).

You might also consider going to a **rugby match** as Carisbrook Stadium on Burns Street, 2.5km southwest of the Octagon. Games are usually held every second weekend during the season (roughly the end of Feb to end of Oct). A free schedule of games is available from the Champions of the World shop right by the Octagon at 8 George St, and tickets can be booked through Otago Rugby Football Union (ⓣ03/455 1191, ⓦwww.otagorugby.co.nz).

Pubs, bars and clubs

The Ale House 200 Ratray St ⓣ03/471 9050. Very popular Speight's-owned pub with excellent brews and very good quality food, even if under all the wood and antique memorabilia it's just a glorified sports bar with a big screen TV, that borrows heavily on the Loaded Hog theme of urban/arable chic. Open daily from 11.30am.

Arc Café/Bar 135 High St (see p.724). Café with a separate club section at the back featuring live bands or DJs play most nights, with top Dunedin acts at weekends.

Bath Street Bar 1 Bath St (between the Octagon & Moray Place). Intimate and stylish studeny nightclub tucked away on a quiet road just below George St, where DJs play underground stuff. Usually $3–5 cover; closed Mon.

Bennu Café & Bar 12 Moray Place. Young professionals are drawn to this elegant venue in one of Dunedin's finest buildings, decorated with a skylight right over the bar, and palm trees. Daily until late.

Captain Cook cnr Albany St & Great King St. A favourite with young students, the Cook is reputed to have the highest beer consumption of any pub in New Zealand and can be seedy. The downstairs bar has pool tables and cheap bar snacks, and there's a pleasant garden bar.

Casino cnr Princes St & High St. Men need to wear a collared shirt, and trainers and jeans are banned in this ornate restoration of what was the Grand Hotel of 1883. You don't have to play the tables or slot machines to enjoy the gold-leaf plasterwork, a drink or a meal at their Grand Bar and Café.

Inch Bar 8 Bank St. Tiny hip watering hole with plenty of special beers on tap (including the locally brewed Emerson's) and a wide range of imported brands. Bar snacks available.

Oriental Tavern 157 Frederick St. "The Ori" is a student institution and something of a pick-up joint, with dance floor and occasional live acts.

Refuel Student Union Building. Venue with old vinyl stuck on the ceiling. It is only open term times when it is alive to the sounds of hard house, trance, drum 'n' bass and dub reggae. There's a gay and lesbian night called *Funk* on the last Saturday of every month.

Woolshed 318 Moray Place. A long, thin bar stretching back from the road that looks like it's been decorated with the leftovers from a number of clearance sales, and offering some simple, wholesome blackboard specials for lunch and supper. Invariably there are live bands or loud music and a good atmosphere, concentrated mostly around the end of the week.

Theatre, cinema and classical music

Dunedin has a lively theatre scene and several movie houses along with a healthy **classical music** and **opera** scene. Regular concerts are given by the New Zealand Symphony Orchestra, the Dunedin Sinfonia (a semi-professional orchestra), and chamber music groups at the Town Hall or the Glenroy Auditorium at the Dunedin Centre (T03/477 4477). The Dunedin Opera Company stages two or three productions a year at the Mayfair Theatre, 100 King Edward St (T03/455 4962), and regular public recitals are held by the music department of the University of Otago (see posters around town or T03/479 1100 during office hours).

There are also a number of **festivals** during the year: we've listed them chronologically.

Cinemas

Hoyts 6 33 The Octagon T03/477 7019. Mainstream multiplex.

Rialto 11 Moray Place T03/474 2200. Refurbished and good for mainstream movies.

Metro Town Hall, Moray Place T03/474 3350, W www.metrocinema.co.nz. With only 56 seats this is one of the smallest public cinemas in New Zealand and is a delightful place to watch arthouse movies. Popcorn is out, but you're welcome to take your coffee in with you. Book ahead, and there are discounted tickets before 5pm on weekdays.

Theatres

Allen Hall Clyde Street T03/479 8896. Campus theatre that showcases the talents of the university's drama students. Shows are often on the fringe.

Fortune Theatre 231 Stuart St T03/477 8323, W www.fortunetheatre.co.nz. Converted from a neo-Gothic church, the Fortune divides its pro-gramme between new works by Kiwi playwrights, fringe theatre, popular Broadway-style plays and occasional musicals. Tickets around $25; closed Jan.

Globe 104 London St T03/477 3274. This small and intimate venue features contemporary plays, classical drama and experimental works.

Regent 17 The Octagon T03/477 8597. The city's largest and most ornate theatre, hosting musicals, ballets, touring plays and performances by popular singers, comedians and groups.

Festivals

Dunedin Summer Festival. All manner of local events a trolley derby, street races and the Baldwin Street Gutbuster. Mid-February

Scottish Week Daily concerts, pipe bands, Highland dancing enliven this celebration of the city's cultural roots in March

Dunedin Film Festival W www.enzedff.co.nz. The usual mix of oddball and pre-release mainstream movies. Late July to early August.

Fringe Festival W www.dunedinfringe.org.nz. A ten-day arts and culture festival typically happen-ing in late September and early October every even year.

Rhododendron Festival W www.rhododunedin.co.nz. Four days' celebrat-ing Dunedin's myriad blooms as the city's parks explode with colour. Thursday to Sunday at the end of October.

Listings

Airport transport Airport Direct Shuttle Service T03/471 4101; Airport Shuttle City Taxis T03/477 1771; Dunedin Airport Shuttle T03/477 6611; and Super Shuttle T0800/748 885.

Automobile Association 450 Moray Place (T03/477 5945).

Banks and foreign exchange The major banks are clustered on George and Princes streets, all with ATMs. The only place to change money at weekends is the Thomas Cook agent, Brooker Travel, 346 George St (T03/477 1532) which is open on Saturday morning.

Bike rental There's a handy cluster of bike shops around the junction of Lower Stuart St and Cumberland Stand: first up try The Cycle Surgery, 67 Stuart St (T03/477 7473, W www.cyclesurgery.co.nz) who do repairs, rents bikes from $25 per day, rent panniers and can help organise self-guided trips on the Otago Central Rail Trail.

Bookshops University Bookshop, 378 Great King St, opposite the Otago Museum (☎03/477 6976, ⓦwww.unibooks.co.nz; Mon–Fri 8.30am–5.30pm, Sat 9.30am–3pm, Sun 11am–3pm), is a comprehensive independent bookshop on two floors, stocking a broad range of New Zealand and international fiction and non-fiction – bargains upstairs.

Buses Dunedin is a local hub with several services daily to Christchurch. Atomic Shuttles (☎03/477 4449) run to Christchurch, Wanaka, Queenstown and Invercargill; InterCity (☎03/474 9600) links Dunedin with Christchurch, Queenstown, Te Anau, Wanaka and Invercargill; and Catch-a-Bus (☎03/479 9960) have a handy service to Queenstown and Wanaka via the Maniototo.

Camping and outdoor equipment R & R Sport, 70 Lower Stuart St, has the biggest range of camping, skiing, cycling and all sporting equipment; also mountain bike and pack rental. Bivouac, 171 George St (☎03/477 3679), has mountaineering, skiing and kayaking gear for rent and for sale; also tramping and alpine gear for sale.

Car rental As well as all the international and nationwide car rental agencies (for details, see p.33) there are good local companies such as Rhodes, 124 St Andrew St (☎0800/746 337, ⓦwww.rhodesrentals.co.nz) and Reliable Rentals (☎03/488 3975).

Horse riding There's excellent horse riding to be done on a harbourside farm at Hare Hill Horse Treks (☎0800/437 837, ⓦwww.horseriding-dunedin.co.nz), some 15km northeast of Dunedin

beyond Port Chalmers. They do anything from a harbour trek (1hr 30min; $40) and a half-day trail ride ($50) to an overnight escape ($175) staying in a romantic cottage.

Internet access *Arc Café* (see p.724) offers 25 minutes of free but slow access. For something more convenient head to The Internet Depot, 18 George St, right by The Octagon, which has a stack of fast machines.

Library Dunedin Public Library, cnr John St & Stewart St (☎03/474 3690; Mon–Fri 9.30am–8pm, Sat 10am–4pm, Sun 2–6pm), has excellent facilities, newspapers and Internet access.

Medical treatment Dunedin Hospital, 201 Great King St (☎03/474 0999). After-hours' doctors are available at 95 Hanover St (☎03/479 2900).

Pharmacy After-hours service at Urgent Pharmacy, 95 Hanover St (☎03/477 6344; Mon–Fri 6–10pm, Sat & Sun 10am–10pm).

Police In an emergency call ☎111.

Post office The post shops at 243 Princes St and 233 Moray Place are most convenient. The former holds poste restante (Mon–Fri 8.30am–5.30pm).

Taxis You'll find taxi ranks in the Octagon, between George St & Stuart St; on St Andrew St, between George St & Filleul St; and on Frederick St, between George St & Filleul St. Radio cabs include United (☎03/455 5282 & 0800/829 411) and Otago Taxis (☎03/477 3333).

Travel agents Brooker Travel, cnr St Andrew St & George St ☎03/477 3383; and STA, 207 George St ☎03/474 0146 & 0508/782 872.

Around Dunedin

Attractive though Dunedin is, you'll soon be keen to get out of town to explore its wider environs, most likely on day-trips. The most popular outings are the scenic foray into the dry hillcountry inland aboard the **Taieri Gorge Railway**, and a trip to the dealers galleries and antique shops of Dunedin's harbourside acolyte, **Port Charmers**.

Set more time aside for the **Otago Peninsula** where you can get incredibly close to all sorts of animal and birdlife that is either hard or impossible to see anywhere else in the world. An impressive array of tours by bus, boat and kayak leave from Dunedin, though there's also enough places to stay and eat for longer sojourns.

Taieri Gorge Railway

The **Taieri Gorge Railway** (services daily; ☎03/477 4449, ⓦwww.taieri.co.nz) stretches 77km northwest from Dunedin into the high country of Otago, penetrating rugged mountain scenery that is only accessible by train. Constructed between 1879 and 1921, the line once carried supplies from

From the city, a variety of walks (1–3hr) lead up to and along the skyline ridges surrounding the harbour, giving spectacular views of tussock-covered hilltops, fine bushland, river valleys and beaches. Get DOC's factsheets for each walk ($0.50 each) from the DOC office or visitor centre, and go prepared for Dunedin's notoriously changeable weather.

If these suggestions whet your appetite for tramping, see "Walks on Otago Peninsula" (p.733) for more routes in the vicinity.

Tunnel Beach (1.5km return; 1hr). One of the best local walks is also the shortest and least strenuous, yet offers breathtaking coastal views of creamy sandstone cliffs and islets weathered into curious shapes. Untouched by lava flows, it gives a glimpse of Dunedin's geology before the volcanic eruptions that changed the landscape. A steep path drops through bush and pasture to impressive sandstone clifftops and a magnificent sea-arch. Additionally, at low tide, you can walk down the steps of a short tunnel carved through the cliff in the 1870s, which leads to a pretty sandy beach on the other side with sandstone buttresses towering above – a pleasant spot for a picnic. The walk crosses private land and is closed during the lambing season (Aug, Sept & Oct).

The route starts from the car park at the end of Green Island Bush Road, some 16km southwest of the centre. The Corstophine bus (Octagon Stand 1) will drop you within a kilometre of the start of the walk – get off at Stanhope Crescent.

Mount Cargill Unrivalled panoramic views of the Dunedin area are the reward for making it to the windy summit of Mount Cargill on the city's northeastern outskirts. There are in fact three peaks – Cargill, Holmes and Zion – which to Maori represent the petrified head and feet of an early Otakou princess. European settlers named the dominant peak after their lay leader, Captain William Cargill.

You can either drive to the summit car park – twenty-minutes from the city centre along Pine Hill Road – and just tackle the network of easy tracks around the summit area, or walk the whole track from Bethunes Gully picnic ground, about 7.5km northeast of the Botanic Garden (8km return; 3hr). This skirts the mountain's northern flank and climbs steadily to 550m before sidling around to the saddle and onto the summit. To reach the picnic ground by bus catch the Normanby bus from Stand 8 on George Street and get off at the junction of North Road and Norwood Street. From here it's about 2km northeast along Norwood Street to the picnic ground.

On the slopes of nearby Mount Holmes, an intriguing ancient rock formation called the **Organ Pipes** can be reached on foot, either from the Mount Cargill summit – following the peaks and saddles of Cargill, Buttar and Holmes (3km return; 90min) – or from a steep track starting at the car park on Mount Cargill Road (3km return; 1hr), on the mountain's eastern side (not accessible by public transport). Either way, the route passes through colourful remnant forest to a series of rock columns, formed about ten million years ago by molten lava that cracked as it cooled.

Dunedin 235km to the old gold town of Cromwell, returning with farm produce, fruit and livestock back to the port and points north. Commercial traffic stopped in 1990, and the bulk of the route was turned into the Otago Central Rail Trail (see box, p.889), but the most dramatic section – through the schist strata of the Taieri Gorge – continues, now almost exclusively for tourists.

The train itself is comfortable and air-conditioned, made up of a mix of modern steel carriages with large panoramic windows, and nostalgic, refurbished 1920s wooden cars. Storage space is available for backpacks and bicycles, and there's a licensed snack bar on board. The train is mostly run by enthusiasts, so if you ask ahead you might even be able to ride with the driver for a spell. The journey is rewarding at any time of year, from the snow in winter to the searing heat of summer, and rainy days encourage the waterfalls.

The most frequent trip is known as the Taieri Gorge Limited (4hr return; April–Sept daily 12.30pm; Oct–March daily 2.30pm, plus late Dec–March 9.30am on Sundays and holidays; $39.50 one way, $61 return) which runs to **Pukerangi** – a peaceful spot 58km from the city near the highest point of the track (250m), where pause briefly before heading back. On summer Sundays the train continues a further 19km to the old gold town of **Middlemarch** (5hr return; Oct–March; $45 one way, $69 return) in the fertile Strath Taieri Plains (see p.808).

Apart from these day-trips, the Railway makes an excellent way to start your journey inland towards Wanaka and Queenstown. The Track and Trail bus service meets the train at Pukerangi or Middlemarch and heads through the Maniototo (see p.888) to Alexandra ($95 one way) and Queenstown ($110): book through the Taieri Gorge Railway.

It makes even more sense if you're biking. **Cyclists** can ride the train (bikes go free) then hop straight onto the Otago Central Rail Trail. If you don't have your own bike, look into the Rail-Trail-specific deals offered by Dunedin's bike rental companies (see "Listings", p.727).

Port Chalmers

With a few hours to spare, head 12km northeast of Dunedin along the western shore of Otago Harbour to **PORT CHALMERS**, a small historic town arranged around a modern container port. Its fine nineteenth-century buildings may look a little run down but the place is on the cusp of gentrification on the back of a thriving artistic community. This is headed by celebrated painter and sculptor **Ralph Hotere**, one of the most respected (and most expensive) artists in the land. Already the main George Street has more galleries and antique/bric-a-brac emporia than real shops: come at the weekend to see everything at its best.

The site was chosen in 1844 as the port to serve the proposed Scottish settlement of New Edinburgh, later called Dunedin. The first settlers arrived on the *John Wickliffe* in March 1848 and named the port after the Reverend Dr Thomas Chalmers, who had led the split between the Presbyterian and Free churches of Scotland. Development was slow until the Otago **gold rush** of the 1860s, which heralded a boom for Port Chalmers. Later, it served as the embarkation point for several **Antarctic expeditions**, including those of Captain Scott, who set out from here in 1901 and again for his ill-fated attempt on the pole in 1910. The first trial shipment of **frozen meat** to Britain was sent from Port Chalmers in 1882 and today the export of wool, meat and timber is its chief business.

The Town

Port Chalmers crawls up the hills on either side of **George Street** which runs down a short hill to the port where two pale green container cranes loom over the town. Two late Victorian churches dominate: the elegant stone-spired Presbyterian **Iona Church** on Mount Street; and the nuggety bluestone Anglican **Holy Trinity**, another Robert A. Lawson design.

George Street meets the port at its junction with Beach Street, where you'll find the small and atmospheric **Museum** (Mon–Fri 9am–3pm, Sat & Sun 1.30–4.30pm; donations appreciated) in a 1877 former post office. Brimming with maritime artefacts and some local settler history, museum highlights include a history of navigational equipment with splendid models and photographs. Downstairs is a large working electric model of a

gold dredge, built in 1900 by a boilermaker apprentice. Staff can fill you in on local walking trails, and can also arrange escorted historical walks along the nearby beaches.

The rest of George Street is lined with **art galleries** and **craft shops** such as the Crafty Banker, 16 George St (Thurs–Sun), a pleasant gallery and craft shop, or Portfolio, 52 George St (Thurs–Sun or by appointment ☎03/472 7856) which has a good selection of rugs, kilims and objets d'art.

Practicalities

By **car** from Dunedin, it's a ten-minute harbourside drive along SH88, or you can take the longer scenic route, following Mount Cargill and Upper Junction roads. From the north on SH1, take the road to Port Chalmers from Waitati. **Buses** from Dunedin to Port Chalmers leave from Stand 4 opposite Countdown supermarket in Cumberland Street, dropping you off in George Street about 25 minutes later (sporadic service on Sunday).

Pick up the "Port Chalmers" map either at the Dunedin visitor centre or at one of the George Street galleries. This highlights the more historically significant buildings and outlines three road walks, the best being the **coastal walk** (4km; 1hr; mostly flat), which predominantly follows gravel roads and offers great views of the harbour and Otago Peninsula beyond. Terns, oystercatchers, shags, gulls, herons and ducks can often be seen as you pass Back Beach.

Eating options are limited to cafés and takeaways, the best being *The Port Royale*, 10 George St, which serves reasonably priced soups, bagels, quiches and salads either inside or out in their compact garden. Alternatively, you'll find scenic picnic spots along Peninsula Beach Road, just around from the harbour.

The Otago Peninsula

A 35km-long crooked finger of land running northeast from Dunedin, the **OTAGO PENINSULA** divides Otago Harbour from the Pacific Ocean and offers outstanding **marine wildlife viewing**. This lightly populated land of undulating grass- and sheep-covered hills affords excellent views of the harbour, open sea and the spread of Dunedin against its dramatic backdrop of hills.

The winding but smooth harbourside road – Portobello Road and later Harington Point Road – makes the peninsula easily accessible, a drive from the city to the tip at **Taiaroa Head** taking less than an hour. This road passes a few places to stay and eat (the best covered on p.737), and strings together most of the sights.

The chief reason for visiting the peninsula is to appreciate the intriguing variety and abundance of **marine wildlife** that is drawn to its shores year round. At its tip is the small headland of **Taiaroa Head**, a protected area where several colonies of sea mammals and sea birds congregate. Unique among these is the majestic **royal albatross**, which breeds here in the only mainland colony of albatross in the world. Also concentrated on the headland's shores are **penguins** (little blue and the rare yellow-eyed) and **southern fur seals**, while the cliffs are home to other sea birds including three species of **shag**, **muttonbirds** (sooty shearwaters) and various species of gull. The peninsula's other beaches and inlets play host to a great variety of wading and waterfowl and, occasionally, New Zealand **sea lions** (while offshore, orca and other **whales** can sometimes be spotted).

Although there's ample opportunity to see much of the wildlife without having to pay for the privilege, it's well worth forking out for one or more of

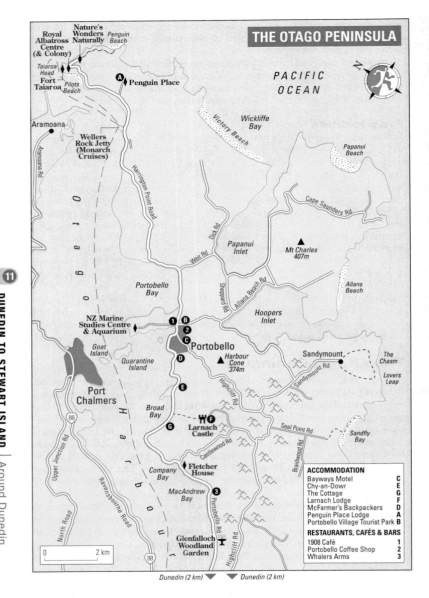

THE OTAGO PENINSULA

PACIFIC OCEAN

ACCOMMODATION

Bayways Motel	C
Chy-an-Dowr	E
The Cottage	G
Larnach Lodge	F
McFarmer's Backpackers	D
Penguin Place Lodge	A
Portobello Village Tourist Park	B

RESTAURANTS, CAFÉS & BARS

1908 Café	1
Portobello Coffee Shop	2
Whalers Arms	3

0   2 km

Dunedin (2 km) ▼   ▼ Dunedin (2 km)

the several official **wildlife tours**, since they are informative and take you up close, yet cause minimal disturbance to the animals.

On the way to Taiaroa Head there are a handful of other sights, including the large woodland gardens and walks of **Glenfalloch**, particularly renowned for their rhododendrons, azaleas and camellias; the bizarre **Larnach Castle**, which is little more than an overblown folly; **Fletcher House**, a delightfully restored

The *Otago Peninsula Tracks* leaflet (free from the Dunedin visitor centre or DOC office) briefly describes several walks on the peninsula. Bear in mind that they cover hill country and that though most tracks are well defined, some are pretty steep. Also, the weather here can turn cold or wet very quickly, even on the sunniest days.

The most rewarding walks include the easy loop track to **Lovers Leap and the Chasm** (3km; 1hr; closed Aug–Oct) which crosses farmland to sheer cliffs dropping 200m to the sea, with collapsed sea caves and rock faces of layered volcanic lava flows visible. The track begins from the end of Sandymount Road, a 25-minute drive from the centre of Dunedin. Also good is the track along **Sandfly Bay** (3km; 80min) which leads to sweeping dunes visited by yellow-eyed penguins and, occasionally, New Zealand sea lions (see box on p.746). There's a penguin hide at the far end of beach. This walk begins at the end of Seal Point Road, a twenty-minute drive from the city.

small Edwardian villa; and the excellent Marine Studies Centre **aquarium**. A number of **scenic walks** cross both public and private land to spectacular views and unusual land formations created by lava flows.

Listings for **accommodation**, **restaurants**, **transport** and **tours** can be found under Peninsula Practicalities from p.736.

The road to Portobello

Around the head of Otago Harbour, **Portobello Road** quickly shakes off Dunedin's scrappy southern suburbs and begins to weave its way along the harbour shoreline past little bays as often as not dotted with stilts on which perch boathouses in various states of disrepair.

Eleven kilometres from Dunedin, the peaceful **Glenfalloch Woodland Garden**, 430 Portobello Rd (daily dawn–dusk; $3 donations requested), contains 12 hectares of rambling mature garden and bush, surrounding a homestead built in 1871. The garden is at its best between mid-September and mid-October, when it is resplendent with rhododendrons, azaleas and camellias and, to a lesser extent, magnolias, fuchsias and roses. Near the entrance, a licensed café (generally daily 11.30am–3.30pm) serves snacks and drinks.

Around 3km further on at **Company Bay**, Castlewood Road runs 4km inland to Larnach Castle (see below), while Portobello Road sticks to the coast past Broad Bay to **The Fletcher House**, 727 Portobello Rd, Broad Bay (Christmas–Easter daily 11am–4pm; Easter–Christmas Sat & Sun 11am–4pm; $3), an attractive small Edwardian villa, lovingly restored to its original state and furnished in period style. Built entirely of native wood in 1909, it was the family home of the Broad Bay storekeeper. Inside the house, the absence of restricting ropes allows you to appreciate fully the furniture and fine woodwork, including the tongue-and-groove panelling in the small kitchen and richly coloured rimu ceilings and floors.

Next up is the village of **Portobello**, 17km from Dunedin, with Hatchery Road which leads 2km along a headland to the **NZ Marine Studies Centre & Aquarium** (daily noon–4.30pm; $6; ☏03/479 5826, ⓦwww.otago.ac.nz/MarineStudies), which is perfect for anyone wanting to find out more about marine life here and around New Zealand. This is a working marine laboratory (run by the University of Otago) and there are always staff about to answer questions, but it is also set up with numerous interactive displays. The fun part is sticking your hands into the several shallow "touch tanks" to feel the small sea creatures, or participating in **fish feeding** (Wed & Sat 2pm). There's also a free, one-hour **behind-the-scenes tour** (daily 10.30am).

Larnach Castle

The nineteenth-century Gothic Revival **Larnach Castle** (daily 9am–5pm; grounds only $8, grounds & castle $15; @ www.larnachcastle.co.nz) sits high on a hill commanding great views across the harbour to Dunedin. More chateau than castle, it is a dramatic place that was the sumptuous residence of Australian-born banker and politician, William Larnach, who spent a fortune on its construction and decoration. Designed by Robert A. Lawson (yes, him again) and completed in 1871, it was a gargantuan project. Materials were shipped from all over the world – including glass and marble from Italy and tiles from England – then punted across the harbour and laboriously dragged up the hill by ox-drawn sleds before the very best local and overseas craftsmen pieced together the family home.

After years of neglect the castle was rescued by the Barker family in the late 1960s and has since been progressively restored while remaining their home. The effect is engaging: grand in design but never overwhelming with few prohibitive signs, photos on the sideboards, and no audio tours.

Unless you have your own transport (or are on a tour), you'll have to take the Portobello **bus** either to Company Bay, from where it's a five-kilometre (signposted) walk, uphill all the way, or to Broad Bay, from where you'll have an even steeper but shorter walk (2km). Once here, at least you can **stay** (see p.737).

Around Taiaroa Head

The peninsula's marine wildlife is mostly concentrated 10km east of Portobello around **Taiaroa Head**, 33km from Dunedin, where cold waters forced up by the continental shelf provide a rich and constant food source. Other than taking a tour, the best opportunities for seeing animals are on the beaches and inlets on either side of the headland. Southern fur seals can be seen at **Pilots Beach**, on the western side (follow the main road to the shore as it snakes past the Royal Albatross Centre) and from the **cliff tops** on the eastern side of the headland. Pilots Beach is also home to a small colony of little blue penguins, which are best visited around dusk but be sure to keep your distance and stay quiet or they'll turn tail. A short signposted walk from the Royal Albatross Centre car park to a **cliff-edge viewing area** unfolds spectacular scenes of a spotted shag colony, while royal albatross in flight can be spied all year round from anywhere on the headland.

When **observing wildlife**, respect the animals by staying well away from them (at least 5m), and keeping quiet and still. **Penguins** are especially timid and easily frightened by people getting too close. They will be reluctant to come ashore (even if they have chicks to feed) if you are on or near the beach and visible. In summer, stay well away from them and keep to the track as they're extremely vulnerable to stress while nesting and moulting. Never get between a **seal** and the sea; these animals can be aggressive and move surprisingly quickly.

The Penguin Place

For the rare privilege of entering a protected nesting area of around a hundred yellow-eyed penguins get along to the **Penguin Place**, Harington Point Road, and award-winning penguin-conservation project about 3km south of Taiaroa Head. Carefully-controlled and informative guided 90min

The yellow-eyed penguin (hoiho)

Considered the most ancient of all living penguins, the endangered **yellow-eyed penguin**, or *hoiho*, is found only in southern New Zealand and numbers around four thousand birds. It evolved in forests free of predators, but human disturbance, loss of habitat and the introduction of ferrets, stoats and cats have had a devastating effect. The small mainland population of just a few hundred occupies nesting areas dotted along the wild southeast coast of the South Island (from Oamaru to the Catlins); other smaller colonies inhabit the coastal forest margins of Stewart Island and offshore islets, and New Zealand's sub Antarctic islands of Auckland and Campbell.

Male and female adults are identical in colouring, with pink webbed feet and a bright yellow band that encircles the head, sweeping over their pale yellow eyes. Standing around 65cm high and weighing 5–6kg, they have a **life expectancy** of up to twenty years. Their **diet** consists of squid and small fish, and hunting takes them up to 40km offshore and to depths of 100m.

Maori gave this rare penguin the name of **hoiho**, meaning "the noise shouter", because of the distinctive high-pitched calls (an exuberant trilling) it makes at night when greeting its mate at the nest. Unlike other penguins, the yellow-eyed does not migrate after its first year, but stays close to its home beach, making daily fishing trips and returning as daylight fails.

The penguins' **breeding season** lasts for 28 weeks, from mid-August to early March. Eggs are laid between mid-September and mid-October, and both parents share in the duties of incubation, a period lasting about 43 days. The eggs hatch in November and for the next six weeks the chicks are constantly guarded against predators. By the time the down-covered chicks are six or seven weeks old, their rapid growth gives them voracious appetites and both parents must fish daily to satisfy them. The fledglings enter the sea for the first time in late February or early March and journey up to 500km north to winter feeding grounds. Fewer than fifteen percent of fledged chicks reach breeding age, but those that do return to the colony of their birth.

tours (Oct–early April 10.15am–dusk; early April–Sept 3.15–4.45pm; every 15–30min; $30; bookings essential on ☎03/478 0286, ⓦwww.penguin-place .co.nz) begin with a talk about penguins and their conservation, then a guide takes you to the beachside colony, where well-camouflaged trenches and hides among the dunes allow an extraordinary proximity to the penguins and excellent photographic opportunities. Proceeds from the tours are used to fund the conservation work and a unit that looks after injured penguins. The Penguin Place is a major part of the itinerary of The Twilight Wildlife Tour (see p.737), and you can even stay overnight in budget accommodation on the farm (see p.737).

The Royal Albatross Centre and Historic Fort Taiaroa

Serving as the gateway to the only mainland colony of albatrosses in the world, the **Royal Albatross Centre** (daily: Nov–April 9am–7pm; May–Oct 10am–4pm; $2 donation requested) contains a café with panoramic windows, and galleries with interesting displays on local wildlife and history. Buy tickets here for the centre's excellent and frequent **Royal Albatross Tour** (60min; 24 Nov–16 Sept $25; 17 Sept–23 Nov closed for breeding season; booking essential on ☎03/478 0499) which includes an introductory film and plenty of time to view the birds from an enclosed area in the reserve (binoculars provided). Non-birders

The royal albatross

The majestic and mysterious **albatross**, one of the world's largest seabirds, has long been the subject of reverence and superstition: the embodiment of a dead sea captain's soul, condemned to wander the oceans forever. A solitary creature, the albatross spends most of its life on the wing or at sea.

The largest of all the albatross family is the **royal albatross** – a stunning sight, with an impressive **wing span** of up to 3.5 metres. They can travel 190,000km a year, at speeds of 120kph, and have a **life expectancy** of 45 years. The albatross mates for life, but male and female separate to fly in opposite directions around the world, returning to the same **breeding** grounds once every two years, and arriving within a couple of days of one another. The female lays one egg (weighing up to 500g) per breeding season, and the parents share incubation duty over a period of eleven weeks. Once the chick has hatched, the parents take turns feeding it and guarding it against stoats, ferrets, wild cats and rats. Almost a year from the start of the breeding cycle, the fledgling takes flight and the parents leave the colony and return to sea only to start the cycle again a year later.

may find it a little pricey for what you get, but where else can you get so close to these great birds.

Adult birds arrive for the new season in September. Courting and mating takes place in October, eggs are laid and incubated from November to December, and the chicks hatch in January and February. The **best months** for viewing are from April to August, when parent birds leave the nests and return towards the end of the day to feed their chicks. By September the chicks and adults are ready to depart and new breeding pairs start to arrive.

The Centre is also the starting point for visits to the **Historic Fort Taiaroa**, a warren of tunnels and gun emplacements originally built in 1885 when an attack from Tsarist Russia was feared, and rearmed during World War II. The main attraction is the restored Disappearing Gun, visited on either the basic 30min tour (all year; $12) or the Unique Taiaroa Tour (90min; $25–30), which combines it with the Royal Albatross Tour

Nature's Wonders Naturally

The road beyond the albatross colony doubles back 1.5km to **Natures Wonders Naturally** (T0800/246 446, Wwww.natureswondersnaturally .com) who offer personalized adventure conservation tours, which involve a lively ride around the head on specially constructed tracks in modified 8WD amphibious vehicles. The tours (1hr; $35) run with unstinting good humour and exhausting enthusiasm, take in penguin-viewing areas, New Zealand fur seals, sea lions and old World War II relics. Although you might wonder what the animals will make of these odd, noisy little vehicles speeding around this working sheep farm, it doesn't seem to stop them going about their business.

Peninsula practicalities

With your own transport, access to the peninsula from Dunedin is easy, either via the snaky **Portobello Road**, which hugs the western shoreline overlooking the harbour, or the inland **Highcliff Road**, which heads up and over the hills. Dunedin visitor centre supplies the handy free *Visitor's Guide to the Otago Peninsula*. The public Peninsula **bus** (3–7 daily) from Stand 5 on Cumberland Street in Dunedin runs halfway along the peninsula, as far as Portobello (35min), from where it's still another 14km to Taiaroa Head.

Exploring the peninsula: cruises, tours and kayaking

Even if you have your own wheels there's a lot to be said for exploring the Otago Peninsula on a guided tour, almost certainly learning a lot more than you would going under your own steam. Mini-bus tours give the most flexibility, but it is hard to pass up seeing the peninsula from the water either on a harbour cruise or by kayak.

Elm Wildlife Tours ☏03/474 1872, ⓦwww.elmwildlifetours.co.nz. Guided bus tours with afternoon trips (5–6hr; $62) which visit the Penguin Place and Albatross Centre. Trips can include an Albatross Centre tour ($87) or a one-hour Monarch Cruise ($92).

Monarch Wildlife Cruises & Tours Wharf St, Dunedin ☏03/477 4276, ⓦwww.wildlife.co.nz. A comfy converted fishing boat with heated cabin and licensed galley is put to good use spending much of the day out at Taiaroa Head running one-hour cruises ($30) from the Wellers Rock jetty. These are worthwhile if you're driving out along the peninsula but it is worth considering their Peninsula Cruise (9am; $70), which leaves from the wharf in Dunedin, cruises around Taiaroa Head then drops you at Wellers Rock (where you can visit the penguins or albatrosses; $30 extra) then returns to Dunedin by bus.

Twilight Wildlife Tour ☏03/474 3300, ⓦwww.wilddunedin.co.nz. Excellent small-group, conservation-minded bus tours (5–6hr; $55, students and backpackers $47) which leave daily from the Dunedin visitor centre and tour the peninsula visiting plenty of birding sites, and spending quality time at the Penguin Place.

Wild Earth Adventures ☏03/473 6535, ⓦwww.wildearth.co.nz. For a different, often magical, perspective on the coast and its wildlife, go sea kayaking on 4hr tours with this Dunedin-based company whose trips ($79) go around Taiaroa Head and spend around two hours on the water.

Accommodation and eating

There's a limited amount of **accommodation** on the peninsula and much of what exists is pricier than in Dunedin, though there are some budget places. **Eating** is more problematic with very few restaurants (though it isn't that far to drive back into Dunedin.

Accommodation

Bayways Motel 697 Highcliff Rd, Portobello ☏03/478 0181, ⓔbyways@clear.net.nz. Four fully self-contained motel units with sundecks and harbour views. ⑤

Chy-an-Dowr 687 Portobello Rd, Broad Bay ☏03/478 0306, ⓔhermanvv@xtra.co.nz. A spacious harbourside 1920s house midway along the peninsula, with three doubles (two en suite, one with separate but private bath) and a sunroom giving a panoramic view of the harbour. ⑥

The Cottage 748 Portobello Rd, Broad Bay ☏03/476 1877, ⓔthecottage@xtra.co.nz. A cosy 1905 harbourside cottage with real charm, lots of little luxuries, and no TV. There's just one ensuite double and a breakfast hamper for two costs $35. ⑥

Larnach Lodge ☏03/476 1616, ⓦwww.larnachcastle.co.nz. Boutique lodging in buildings in the tranquil grounds of Larnach Castle high above the harbour. The converted stables contains six basic shared-bath rooms, while the Lodge, refurbished to imitate a two-storey colonial farm building, has twelve en-suite rooms, each individually decorated in period style. Everyone gets free castle admission, rates include breakfast and you can also book for dinner in the castle's dining room (around $45 per head plus wine). Stables ⑤, lodge ⑧, premium rooms ⑨

McFarmer's Backpackers 774 Portobello Rd ☏03/476 0389, ⓔmcfarmersbackpackers@hotmail.com. Excellent harbourside backpackers with a relaxed atmosphere, nice four-shares, plus rooms and a self-contained unit that's ideal for families. Shared ①, rooms ②, cottage ③

Penguin Place Lodge Harington Point Rd ☏03/478 0286, ⓔpenguin.place@clear.net.nz. Simple budget accommodation with single, double and twin rooms, shared showers and kitchen located at the Penguin Place (see p.734). Linen hire is $5, if required. Single ①, room ②.

Portobello Village Tourist Park 27 Hereweka St, Portobello ☏03/478 0359, ⓔportobellopark@@xtra.co.nz. Campground, well-sited centrally for Larnach Castle and the albatrosses with a range of accommodation. Camping $10–12, self-contained units ③

Eating

1908 Café 7 Harington Point Rd Portobello ☏03/478 0801. Elegant restaurant, café and bar in a 1908 house with an intimate interior and outdoor seating with views of the harbour. Open three times daily for breakfast, lunch and dinner serving a varied range of dishes from $6–26, plus enormous desserts. Licensed & BYO.

Portobello Coffee Shop 699 Highcliffe Rd, Portobello. Handy spot for a quick bite to eat during the day, reasonable coffee and Internet access.

Whalers Arms 494 Portobello Rd Macandrew Bay ☎03/476 1357. Café and bar with well-priced food and great views across the harbour.

South from Dunedin: Balclutha and the Catlins Coast

The dramatic, rugged coastal route linking Dunedin and Invercargill is one of the least travelled highways in New Zealand, and traverses some of the country's wildest scenery along the **Catlins Coast**. It is part of the **Southern Scenic Route** that continues on to Te Anau in Fiordland.

Within this significant region is the largest area of native forest on the east coast of the South Island, most of it protected as the **Catlins Forest Park**, and consisting of rimu, rata, kamahi and silver beech. Roaring southeasterlies and the remorseless sea have shaped the coastline here into plunging cliffs, windswept headlands, white sand beaches, rocky bays and gaping caves, much of this accessible on a number of short bushwalks. Not surprisingly, this relatively untouched area abounds with **wildlife**, including several rare species of marine bird and mammal, and the whole region rings with birdsong most of the year, though the **birds** are at their most active during June to August when breeding. The Catlins have something to offer at any time of the year, but from mid-November to mid-December you benefit from spring/summer weather and avoid the busy season during and after Christmas. The only stop-off point of any size between Dunedin and the Catlins Coast is **Balclutha**, which is a good place to stock up before entering the relative wilderness beyond. At Balclutha, SH1 turns inland, skirting the Catlins region before turning south to Invercargill at the town of **Gore**, a centre for brown-trout fishing.

Maori hunters once thrived in the Catlins region, one of the last refuges of the flightless moa, but by 1700 they had moved on, to be supplanted by European **whalers and sealers** in the 1830s. Two decades later, having decimated marine mammal stocks, they too moved on. Meanwhile, in 1840, Captain Edward Cattlin arrived to investigate the navigability of the river that bears his (misspelt) name. He purchased a tract of land from the chief of the Ngai Tahu and soon after, boatloads of **loggers** began to arrive, lured by the great podocarp forests. Cleared valleys were settled, bush millers supplied Dunedin with much of the wood needed for housing and, in 1872, more timber was exported from the Catlins than anywhere else in New Zealand. From 1879, the rail line from Balclutha began to extend into the region, bringing with it sawmills, schools and farms. Milling continued into the 1930s, but gradually dwindled and today's tiny settlements are shrunken remnants of the once-prosperous logging industry.

The 126-kilometre stretch of road through the Catlins should present no problems for vehicles especially now that the final gravel sections are being sealed. Until now only small bus/tour companies have run through the area, but access is likely to improve. Without your own transport, or if you just want to make a day-trip, you can take one of several **guided tours** (see p.741), which operate from Dunedin, Balclutha and Invercargill.

The **western continuation** of the **Southern Scenic Route**, from Invercargill to Te Anau via Tuatapere, is covered in the Fiordland chapter, p.897.

Balclutha

The farming service town of **BALCLUTHA**, 80km southwest of Dunedin on SH1, lies amid rich pastures in the heart of South Otago. The **Clutha River** which divides the town in two, was once a source of alluvial gold but today is used to generate hydroelectricity and provides substantial stocks of brown trout and salmon for anglers.

There's little reason to stop longer than it takes to glean information on the Catlins or Dunedin from the helpful **Clutha visitor centre**, 4 Clyde St (Nov–March Mon–Fri 8.30am–5pm, Sat & Sun 9.30am–3pm; April–Oct Mon–Fri 8.30am–5pm, Sat & Sun 9.30am–2pm; ℡03/418 0388, ⒺClutha.vin@cluthadc.govt.nz), which has **Internet access**. **Buses** stop right outside and almost everything else is within a couple of blocks along Clyde Street.

There's a limited selection of **accommodation** in town. The best campsite is the small *Naish Park Motor Camp*, 56 Charlotte St (℡03/418 0088, Ⓔnaishparkmotorcamp@xtra.co.nz; camping $9, cabins ❷), five minutes' walk from the town centre and set in pleasant parkland with excellent modern facilities. *Balclutha Backpackers*, 89 Clyde St (℡03/418 1164; dorms ❶, rooms ❷) offers simple but comfortable and welcoming hostel accommodation, and there are fully self-contained motel units at the friendly *Helensborough Motor Inn*, 23 Essex St (℡0800/444 778 & 03/418 1948, Ⓦwww.helensborough motorinn.co.nz; ❺). Twelve kilometres north of Balclutha is the luxurious *Garvan Homestead B&B* (℡03/417 8407, Ⓦwww.garvan-homestead.co.nz; ❺), a large Tudor-style retreat in rambling gardens with a good licensed restaurant.

Places to eat are strung along Clyde Street: the daytime *Gate Café*, at #47, is good for espresso, cakes and light meals; *The Captain's*, #13, serves reasonable and well-priced bar food, from snacks to steaks; and there's good BYO Chinese at *Gins*, at #27.

The Catlins Coast

The best way to enjoy the **CATLINS COAST** is to take it slowly, absorbing its unique atmosphere over at least a couple of days. There's plenty to see at any time of year, but, in summer, if you visit during the week you'll avoid most of the day-trippers from Dunedin. From Nugget Point in South Otago (just southeast of Balclutha) to Waipapa Point in Southland (60km northeast of Invercargill), the wild scenery stretches unbroken, with dense rainforest succumbing to open scrub as you cut through deep valleys and past rocky bays, inlets and estuaries. The coast is home to **penguins** (both little blue and yellow-eyed), **dolphins**, several types of sea bird and, at certain times of year, migrating **whales**. Elephant **seals**, fur seals, and increasingly, the rare New Zealand **sea lion** are found on the sandy beaches and grassy areas, and within the mossy depths of the forest are abundant **birds**: tui, resonant bellbirds, fantails, grey warblers and colourful tree-top dwellers such as kakariki and mohua.

Scenic splendour peaks at **Nugget Point**, a rugged, windswept promontory favoured by fur seals and sea lions; **Purakaunui Falls**, among the most photographed in New Zealand; the impressive **Cathedral Caves**, their high "ceilings" and deep chambers carved out of the cliffs by the sheer force of the sea; and **Curio Bay**, where an intriguing forest has been captured in stone.

THE CATLINS COAST

RESTAURANTS, CAFES & BARS

Catlins Diner	C
The Lumberjack	C
Niagara Falls Café	I
Owaka Pub	C
The Point	A

ACCOMMODATION

Blowhole Backpackers	C	Hill Top Backpackers	G
Catlins Farmstay	J	Kereru Cottage	I
Catlins Lodge Motel	C	Nugget Lodge	B
Catlins Retreat Guesthouse	C	Nugget View	A
Curio Bay Accommodation	M	& Kaka Point Motel	
Curio Bay Camping Ground	M	Papatowai Motels	H
Falls Backpackers	E	Slope Point Backpackers	L
Fernlea Backpackers	A	Surat Bay Lodge	D
Greenwood Farmstay	K	Waikawa Holiday Lodge	F

Gore (94 km) & Invercargill (159 km)

Dunedin (80 km)

Invercargill (40 km)

PACIFIC OCEAN

N

By the time you read this, the final section of gravel road through the Catlins should be sealed, and interest in the area is likely to increase. Facilities will follow suit, but for the moment you really need to come prepared. The Catlins' main settlement is **Owaka** (Place of the Canoe), a farming village of around two hundred souls some 38km from Balclutha. It has a small selection of accommodation, services and shops, including a pub, supermarket, store/diner/backpackers, pharmacy and a 24–hour medical centre.

Outside Owaka you'll find a smattering of places to stay but very few places to eat or stock up with supplies. There are general stores at **Kaka Point** and Papatowai, and limited supplies at **Curio Bay** campground. **Petrol** stations are few and far between, so fill up before you set off, then at Kaka Point, Owaka, Papatowai or Tokanui (pumps close at around 5pm). There are **no banks** within the Catlins, and bear in mind that **theft from cars** is on the increase

Tours of the Catlins

If you don't have your own transport, **guided tours** are really the only way of exploring the Catlins. The closest thing to a bus service is the no-frills **Catlins Coaster** minibus (daily mid-Nov to April; ☎0800/304 333, ⓦwww.catlinscoaster.co.nz) which does a complicated series of shuttles between Queenstown, Dunedin and Invercargill collectively allowing you to tour the Catlins with plenty of time off the bus for bush and beach walks, wildlife encounters and the major scenic sights.

The routes are designed so that you can whisk through the area in a day – Invercargill–Dunedin ($95); a loop from Dunedin ($100), Queenstown ($130) or Te Anau ($130) – but for an extra $25–30 you buy the freedom to get off and pick up a later bus. A popular optional extra on all trips is an overnight farmstay including a full day on a working sheep, beef and deer farm ($100 extra).

There's a similarly laid-back atmosphere to **The Bottom Bus** (☎03/442 9708), which supplements the Kiwi Experience bus trips in Southland using in small buses though without the booze-bus approach. It runs from Dunedin through the Catlins to Invercargill on its clockwise loop to Riverton, Te Anau and Queenstown. Choose from Dunedin to Invercargill (minimum 1 day; $95), Dunedin to Te Anau (2 days; $149), or several longer options. Departures from Dunedin are on Monday, Wednesday, Thursday & Saturday mornings.

Catlins Natural Wonders (☎0800/353 941, ⓦwww.catlinsnatural.co.nz) run more intimate and flexible, small-group **day-trips** ($130 ex-Dunedin; $85 ex-Balclutha) taking in most of the main sights along the coast and a few hidden treasures, with plenty of time for walking. It is possible to take in their **yellow-eyed penguin evening trip** ($25 when added to a day-trip, otherwise $30 with pick-up in Owaka) or even extend it into a two-day trip ($200 ex-Dunedin; $150 ex-Balclutha) including the tour, penguin trip and time spent hiking the Catlins River Track, but not accommodation (though this can be arranged). Trips run roughly every second day in summer and less frequently in winter, so be sure to call ahead.

Lastly, Papatowai-based **Catlins Wildlife Trackers** (☎03/415 8613, ⓦwww .catlins-ecotours.co.nz; advance bookings essential), run an entertaining and inspirational **eco-tour** sharing in-depth knowledge about the local ecology, history and geology. The organizers are committed to conservation and offer an intimate two- or four-day tour ($295 & $590 respectively) for groups of up to eight, which explores remote beaches and rich rainforest from their secluded coastal home. You can drive there or be picked up from Balclutha on Mon, Thurs & Sat mornings. All meals, accommodation, transport and equipment are provided and a shuttle service to and from Dunedin can be arranged for an extra fee. You stay in their tranquil house – overlooking native forest, an estuary, beach and ocean – in a separate section containing double and twin rooms sharing a bathroom.

in the region, especially in the remoter spots: don't leave valuables in the car and be sure to lock it.

Throughout the Catlins we have mentioned what restaurants exist, though few can be wholeheartedly recommended, so it may pay to bring your own supplies and self-cater where possible.

Kaka Point and Nugget Point

First stop inside the Catlins is **KAKA POINT**, 22km south of Balclutha, a tiny holiday community with golden sands that are patrolled by lifeguards in summer making this a good swimming and surfing spot. Just behind the township a fine scenic reserve of native forest is accessible on an easy loop track (2.5km; 30min; signposted from the top of Marine Terrace).

The Point, on the waterfront, is the spot to go for a coffee, a decent meal or a beer by the fire, but with Kaka Point's proximity to Nugget Point you may also want to **stay**, perhaps at *Fernlea Backpackers* (T03/412 8834; ❶) on Moana St but accessible from behind *The Point*, has great sea views from the sunny balcony; bring a sleeping bag. Alternatively there's the extremely well-appointed *Nugget View & Kaka Point Motel*, 11 Rata St (T0800/525 278 & 03/412 8602, e nugview@catlins.co.nz; budget ❸, standard ❺, spa units ❼) which has a wide range of spacious units almost all with decking and ocean views. The motel also runs **boat trips** around Nugget Point (weather permitting) and fishing trips. Another friendly spot offering charming, self-contained accommodation by the beach is *Nugget Lodge* (T03/4128783, W www.nuggetlodge.co.nz; ❺), 5km around along the coast towards Nugget Point, run by a wildlife photographer and ranger who share their enthusiasm for the area with their visitors.

Nine kilometres south along the coast from Kaka Point, a car park marks the start of a 15min track to **Nugget Point**, a steep-sided, windswept promontory rising 133m above the sea. Just offshore lie **The Nuggets**, jagged stacks of rock whose layers have been tilted vertical over time. The track ends at a still functioning 1870 lighthouse from where you can gaze down on lively groups of honking southern fur seals, supplemented from October to March by the world's only mainland breeding colony of **elephant seals**. Gannets, spoonbills and three species of shag wheel overhead and nearby Roaring Bay has a hide from where you can watch **yellow-eyed penguins** (see p.735) as they leave their nests at sunrise and descend the steep grassy cliffs to the sea or as they return two hours before dark. Their progress is slow, so you need plenty of patience, and binoculars are handy.

You'll need to backtrack to a few kilometres then head out to the coast again to reach the long crescent of sand known as **Cannibal Bay**, a haul-out spot for rare New Zealand sea lions (see p.746) which, from a distance, look like logs. Stroll along the beach for a closer look, but keep at least five metres away from them and back off quickly if they rear up and roar.

Owaka and Jack's Blowhole

The only settlement of any size in the Catlins is the farming town of **OWAKA**, 18km southwest of Kaka Point, little more than a crossroads where you'll find the **Catlins visitor centre**, cnr Main Rd & Ryley St (Oct–April Mon–Fri 9am–4pm; T03/415 8371, W www.catlins-nz.com), which has plenty of leaflets, DOC information, tide tables to help you plan for a couple of the sights only accessible at low tide, and a heap of useful bumf in the foyer for when it is closed.

Nearby there the tiny **Catlins Museum**, 10 Main Rd (Dec–Feb daily 1–4pm; March–Nov Sun 1.30–4.30pm or by arrangement T03/415 8490; $1 donation), focuses on local pioneer history, early settlement, sawmills, dairy factories and shipwrecks.

There isn't a great deal else except a couple of shops, petrol station, a pub and a few **places to stay**. The very comfy *Blowhole Backpackers*, 24 Main Rd (℡03/415 8998, ℮catlinsbb@xtra.co.nz; dorm ❶, room ❷) offers excellent budget accommodation; *Catlins Lodge Motel*, 12 Ryley St (℡03/415 8728, ℮owakalodgemotel@xtra.co.nz; ❹) has straightforward but comfy units; and the friendly and nicely decorated *Catlins Retreat Guesthouse*, 27 Main Rd (℡03/415 8830, ℮retreat@catlins-nz.com; twin ❺, ensuite doubles ❻) offers African- and French-themed rooms and a hearty breakfast. Tucked away in a peaceful spot at the coast 5km east of Owaka is the well-kept *Surat Bay Lodge*, Surat Bay Rd, Newhaven (℡03/415 8099, ⓦwww.suratbaylodge.co.nz; dorm ❶, rooms ❷), overlooking the Catlins Estuary, with free pick-up from Owaka and kayaks for rent.

For **meals**, your best bet is the *Owaka Pub*, 21 Ryley St (daily but meals only Thurs–Sat), where the food is great value, mostly arriving with chips. There are also snacks and takeaways from the *Catlins Diner*, 3 Main Rd, and upscale but not especially good meals at the central *The Lumberjack*, 3 Saunders St.

A pleasant waterside drive runs 10km southeast from Owaka to Jack's Bay from where a farmland track (20–30min each way; closed for lambing in Sept & Oct; $1 donation appreciated) leads to **Jack's Blowhole** an impressive 55m-deep hole in the ground which connects though a 200m tunnel to the sea. Effectively the collapsed roof of cave, the bottom of the hole is washed by surf at high tide, though few people seem to have ever seen it actually spout.

Southwest to Papatowai

A couple of minor waterfalls lie to the southwest, both accessed along pleasant nature trails. The three-tiered **Purakaunui Falls** lie in a scenic reserve of silver beech and podocarp, signposted off the main road 14km from Owaka. There's a picnic area here and an easy track (10min) through the forest to a viewing platform. Near the falls, *Greenwood Farmstay* (℡03/415 8259, ℮greenwood -farm@xtra.co.nz; ❺), occupies a nicely kept house on a sheep, cattle and deer farm, and there's dinner on request ($40). Opposite, lies the comfortable *Falls Backpackers* (℡03/415 8724, ℮sparx@es.co.nz; dorms ❶, rooms ❷).

Five kilometres south of the Purakaunui turn-off, the pretty **Matai Falls** (15min return) are reached along an easy trail through ten-metre-high fuschia trees, easily identified by their pealing pinkish bark and, in early summer, small red and blue trumpet flowers.

Across the estuary of the McLennan River, the small settlement of **PAPATOWAI** offers a general store, several forest and beach walks and an excellent **eco-tour** with the Catlins Wildlife Trackers (see p.741) and the start of the **Catlins Top Track** (see p.744). In a cheerful old bus beside the main road The **Lost Gypsy Gallery** (hours vary, closed June–Aug; cash only) makes a quirky stop if only to play with the handmade automata built on site from recycled materials and old electrical components. Everything is for sale from teabag dunkers to dancing penguins and oddball gizmos that light up and make noises.

There are also a few good **places to stay** including the small and wonderful *Hill Top Backpackers*, 77 Tahakopa Valley Rd (℡03/415 8028, ⓦwww.catlins-nz.com: dorms ❶, rooms ❸), set on a farm signposted 1km inland from Papatowai, which occupies a pair of delightful, well-kept cottages with astounding panoramic views. Back on the main road, *Papatowai Motels* (℡03/415 8147, ℮b.bevin@paradise.net.nz; ❹), next to the general store, has

The longest and most varied walk in the region is **Catlins Top Track** (22km loop) which begins and ends at Papatowai and crosses sweeping beaches, privately owned bush, and farmland, delivering fascinating geology, a great variety of flora and fauna, and true tranquillity. It can be walked in a day (9–10hr; $15) but most people of moderate fitness walk it leisurely in two days ($35 including accommodation). The track is managed by Catlins Wildlife Trackers (℗03/415 8613 & 0800/228 5467, ⓦwww.catlins-ecotours.co.nz), who offer pack transfer for $30 per group. All walkers are given an excellent booklet that details each section of the walk accompanied by a map. Catlins Wildlife Trackers can help with accommodation, or take your pick from the range at Papatowai (see p.743).

The first day takes about six hours, starting with a walk along one of the finest open beaches in the Catlins, then following an old coach road and climbing to weathered sandstone cliffs and the night's accommodation beyond. The second day takes half the time and is very different: you pass through bush containing ancient trees and emerge at the walk's highest point (just over 300m) to spectacular views before following a former railway line to the McLennan River and then continue to the pre-arranged pick up point.

Numbers are limited to six overnight walkers, who stay in a converted 1960s trolley bus high up on a spectacular viewpoint, which has one double bed and four single bunks, electric lighting, a gas camping stove with cutlery and dishes, a wood-burning stove for heat in winter, and its own water supply. There's even a separate loo with a view. Bring your own food, drinking water and sleeping bag.

Catlins Wildlife Trackers also offer the **Beach to Beech walk** (Nov–March Thurs & Fri; 26km, 6 people maximum; $375 including two nights accommodation, all food and transport to starting point), a two-day trek for the moderately fit with only light packs. The walk starts by following the Catlins River Track through beech forest, spotting wildlife and listening to stories before arriving at the comfortable *Mohua Lodge*. The second day the route follows the beautiful old Catlins train line then over farmland to the estuary and beach at Papatowai for a welcome drink back at base where you spend the night.

three newish units with fully equipped kitchens; the modern self-contained *Kereru Cottage* (book through Catlins Wildlife Trackers, see p.741; ❻) offers great ocean and estuary views and a queen-sized en-suite bedroom, plus bunks and a sofabed; the same people offer a couple of lovely self-catering cottages nearby (❺ & ❻).

Porpoise Bay and Waikawa

On the main road 2.5km southeast of Papatowai, **Florence Hill Lookout** presents a fabulous panoramic view of Tautuku Bay, a magnificent crescent of pale sand backed by extensive forest. For a closer look, call in at the **Tautuku Boardwalk** (20–30min return), with a raised walkway nature trail over some lakeside marshes.

Some 11km southeast of Papatowai you'll have to turn off to reach, **Cathedral Caves** ($3), the grandest and most accessible of the fifteen-or-so caves that punctuate this part of the coast. They were formed by two connecting caverns with massively high walls created by furious sea action against the cliffs, and can only be entered one hour either side of low tide. Times are published by the entrance from where it is a pleasant, easy forty-minute walk to the caves. A kilometre or so further along the main road, Rewcastle Road runs 3km to the car park for the picturesque **McLean Falls** (30min return), reached along a pleasant forest walk. Easily the most impressive of the falls hereabouts, it is best in the late afternoon when sun strikes the main cascade.

One of the few restaurants in these parts, the *Niagara Falls Café*, some 20km on, serves good coffee and sophisticated homemade café food. At the fishing village of **WAIKAWA**, 40km from Papatowai, there's the **Waikawa District Museum** (Oct–May daily 10.30am–4.30pm; June–Sept Thurs & Sun 10.30am–4.30pm; donation appreciated), whose chief attraction in a higgledy-piggledy exhibition is a display on seafarers and logging. Opposite, an old church houses a small coffee shop and the **Dolphin Information Centre** (Sept–May daily 9am–6pm; ℡03/246 8444) which has stacks of material on the Hector's Dolphins (see p.746), which come in close to the shore at nearby **Porpoise Bay** to rear their young from November to April. This is the only place in the world where dolphins live permanently so close to shore, and there are about twenty resident, with others coming and going near the long arc of golden sands. Dolphin Magic Cruises (℡03/246 8444 & 0800/377 581, ℮dolphinmagic@xtra.co.nz) operate sensitive, regular dolphin encounter trips (1hr 30min for $50; 2hr 30min for $75; departures at 10am, 2pm & 5pm) for small groups. On the longer trips you'll also see some spectacular geology and colonies of seals and yellow-eyed penguins. Since the dolphins are extremely shy and easily upset, swimming is not allowed on any of their trips.

Accommodation in the area includes *Waikawa Holiday Lodge* (℡03/246 8552, ℮niagarafallscafe@xtra.co.nz; dorm ❶, rooms ❷), a clean friendly hostel in a renovated cottage beside the museum, with a four-bed dorm, a twin and a double; and *Catlins Farmstay*, 174 Progress Valley Rd (℡03/246 8843, ℮catlinsfarmstay@xtra.co.nz; ❼), a comfortable homestead on a large, sheep, deer and cattle farm, offering home-cooked meals ($40). They also have four-bed backpacker cabin (❶), hidden in the bush a couple of kilometres away, and equipped with a pot-bellied stove and cooker, but no electricity; bring your own sleeping bag.

Curio Bay and Slope Point

At the western end of Porpoise Bay, a headland is occupied by the *Curio Bay Camping Ground* (℡03/246 8897; camping $5 per site, powered sites $15), a popular campsite with a tiny store, sites sheltered by clumps of flax, and wonderful views on all sides – east along Porpoise Bay and west into **CURIO BAY**. Most come to watch Hector's dolphins cavort in the surf of Porpoise Bay, but take note of the beach signs that warn you to keep your distance (see p.746). Yellow-eyed penguins can be viewed on the Curio Bay side, from the top of McColgan's Loop, but again keep your distance (at least 10m) and stay hidden; most activity is at sunrise and towards the end of the day, and if they spy you they will not come ashore in the evenings, thus depriving their young of an eagerly awaited meal.

A few hundred metres west along Curio Bay a wave-cut platform reveals evidence of a **petrified forest**, a particularly fine example of fossilized Jurassic trees that are clearly visible at low tide. Over 180 million years ago, when most of New Zealand still lay beneath the sea, this would have been a broad, forested floodplain. Today, the seashore, composed of several layers of forest buried under blankets of volcanic mud and ash, is littered with fossilized tree stumps and fallen logs.

Apart from the campground, you can stay nearby at *Curio Bay Accommodation*, 501 Curio Bay Rd (℡03/246 8797, ₩www.curiobay.com; dorm ❶, room ❸, ensuite ❹) a beautifully sited hostel with one room and the common area overlooking the sea.

Two extremely rare species – the New Zealand or **Hooker's sea lion** (*Phocarctos hookeri*) and **Hector's dolphin** (*Cephalarhynchus hectori*) – are found only in New Zealand waters.

Hooker's sea lion mostly live at the subantarctic Auckland Islands, 460km south of the South Island, but a small amount of breeding also takes place on the Otago Peninsula, along the Catlins Coast and around Stewart Island. The large, adult male sea lions are black to dark brown, have a mane over their shoulders, weigh up to 400kg and reach lengths of over 3m. Adult females are buff to silvery grey and much smaller – less than half the weight and just under 2m. Barracuda, red cod, octopus, skate and, in spring, paddle crabs together make up their diet, and although Hooker's sea lions usually dive less than 200m for four or five minutes, they're capable of achieving depths of up to 500m. Pups are born on the beach, then moved by the mother at about six weeks to grassy swards, shrubland or forest, and suckled for up to a year.

Sea lions prefer to haul out on sandy beaches and in summer spend much of the day flicking sand over themselves to keep cool. Unlike seals they don't fear people. If you encounter one on land, give it a wide berth of at least five metres (30m during the December to February breeding season) and if it rears up and roars, back off quickly – they can move surprisingly swiftly. When swimming or diving near haul-out sites, be aware that the sea lions can be boisterous and don't antagonize or attempt to feed them.

The **Hector's dolphin**, with its distinctive black and white markings, is the smallest dolphin in the world and with a population under 4000 it is also one of the rarest. It's only found in New Zealand inshore waters – mostly around the coast of the South Island – with eastern concentrations around Banks Peninsula, Te Waewae Bay and Porpoise Bay, plus western communities between Farewell Spit and Haast. In summer they prefer shallow waters within 1km of the shore to catch mullet, arrowsquid, red cod, stargazers and crabs; they seldom venture beyond 8km from shore in winter. Female dolphins are typically a little larger than the males, growing to 1.2–1.4m and weighing 40–50kg. They give birth from November to mid-February, and calves stay with their mothers for up to two years.

In summer and autumn, the tiny resident population at Porpoise Bay regularly enters the surf zone and even comes within 10m of the beach. Hector's Dolphins are shy creatures and being disturbed can impact on feeding, which in turn affects their already threatened breeding rate. If you're spending time around them, be sure to follow DOC rules (posted locally), which essentially forbid, touching, feeding, surrounding and chasing dolphins and encourage you to keep a respectful distance. Swimming around pods with juveniles is also forbidden.

From Curio Bay it is 16km along unsealed roads to **Slope Point**, the southernmost point in the South Island, where a ten-minute farmland walk finds you at a sign marking the distances to the South Pole and the Equator. Some 3km back from Slope Point, *Slope Point Backpackers* (T03/246 8420, E justherb@xtra.co.nz; dorms ❶, rooms ❷) offers pleasant if fairly simple accommodation and pet sheep.

Continuing west, it is a ten-minute drive to **Waipapa Point**, 22km beyond Curio Bay, the site of New Zealand's worst civilian shipwreck, in 1881, when 131 lives were lost on *SS Tararua*. The lighthouse that now stands on the point was erected soon after and you may now see fur seals and sea lions on the golden beach and rocky platform at its foot.

Back on the main road, once past the windswept trees of Fortrose, it's a clear run of 60km along a bland inland stretch of SH92 to Invercargill.

Gore and around

Seventy-one kilometres west of Balclutha the quiet, Southland farming town of **GORE** is a pleasant enough transit point at the intersection of routes from Dunedin to Te Anau and Invercargill. Dominated by the Hokonui Hills, Gore spans the Mataura River ("reddish swirling water"), and claims to be the **brown trout capital** of the world – celebrated by an enormous fish statue in the town centre. During the fishing season (Oct–April), pit your wits against a wily brown trout with tackle rented from B&B Sports, 65 Main St (℡03/208 0801) and a licence from the visitor centre (around $17 for 24hr, $34 for a week).

Gore is also New Zealand's home of **country music** and for eight days in autumn it attracts hundreds of would-be country stars and a few established performers for the Gold Guitar Awards (late May & early June; ℡03/208 1978, Ⓦwww.goldguitars.co.nz).

While here, pop along to the **Hokonui Heritage Centre**, cnr Norfolk St & Hokonui Drive (Mon–Fri 8.30am–5pm, Sat & Sun Oct–March 10am–4pm, April–Sept 1–4pm) which contains the **visitor centre** (℡03/203 9288, Ⓦwww.goredc.govt.nz), a small local **history museum** (donation requested), and the entertaining **Hokonui Moonshine Museum** ($5), detailing decades of illicit whisky distillation deep in the local bush-covered hills, which began in 1836 and reached a peak during a regional fifty-year-long local Prohibition from 1903. Among notable distillers were the Scottish McRae family, who settled in this area during the 1870s. Despite the best efforts of police and customs, the only people caught in the act were the Kirk brothers, whose cow shed and stills are on display.

Across the street, the opening of the **Eastern Southland Art Gallery** (Tues–Fri 10am–4.30pm, Sun 1–4pm; free) has recently put Gore on the New Zealand art map. Much of what's on show was bequeathed by ex-pat Kiwi sexologist, Dr John Money, who over half a century amassed a wonderful collection of works including some majestic African carvings, notably some Dogon horsemen and a pair of life-size Bambara ancestral figures. Local interest focuses on: richly-coloured oils by Rita Angus; works by Dutch émigré, Theo Schoon, who incorporated Maori iconography into his painting long before it was fashionable; and career-spanning pieces from the private collection of arguably New Zealand's top living painter, Ralph Hotere. Temporary exhibitions, usually by notable Kiwi artists, justify repeat visits.

Fans of vintage aircraft should head 17km west along the road to Queenstown (SH94) to the **Old Mandeville Airfield**, where you can take to the air on joyrides (from $60 for 10min to $270 for 1hr; contact Croydon Air Services ℡03/208 9755, Ⓦwww.themoth.co.nz) in Tiger Moth, Fox Moth, Dominie or Dragonfly. You're welcome to have a look around the hangar, where renovation is constantly in progress on all sorts of aircraft, and there's a restaurant/bar here, too (see below). The eighth weekend of every year sees the Mandeville Fly-in, a two-day celebration of vintage and modern aircraft, classic cars, joyrides and so on (for more details contact the Gore visitor centre).

Practicalities

Gore lies on the major bus route between Dunedin, Invercargill and Te Anau. Buses drop off at the visitor centre (see above) near the giant trout, where you can book accommodation and transport and pick up information on the town and surrounding area.

Accommodation

Croydon Hotel cnr SH94 & Waimea St ☎03/208 9029, ✉reservations@scenic-circle.co.nz. A modern hotel-cum-motel with two bars and restaurants, set in extensive grounds, including a golf course. On the outskirts of town. ⑤

Dellmount Woolwich Street, East Gore ☎03/208 1771, ✉bnjross@hotmail.com. A super-friendly country-stay on a small Arabian horse stud 2km northeast of Gore town centre on the banks of the Mataura River. Dinner on request $25. ④

Esplanade Motels 35 Railway Esplanade, SH1 ☎03/208 0888 & 0800/285 050, ✉esplanademotelsgore@hotmail.com. Comfortable, spacious, well-maintained units in a compound run by friendly hosts, about 1.5km northeast of the centre of town. ⑤

Gore Motor Camp 35 Broughton St ☎03/208 4919, ✉gorecamp@xtra.co.nz. Well-run and fairly central campsite 1km south off SH1. Camping $10–11, cabins ②

Old Firestation Backpackers 19 Hokonui Drive ☎03/208 1925, ✉oldfirestation@ispnz.co.nz. Small, clean, central and welcoming hostel with a spacious living room and pool table. Dorms ①, rooms ②

Riverlea Motel 46–48 Hokonui Drive ☎03/208 3130 & 0508/202 780, ✉riverleamotel@xtra

.co.nz. Snazzy and slightly more expensive, but worth it for the well-equipped, plush white units and breakfast on request. ⑤

Eating

Croydon Hotel cnr SH94 & Waimea St. There are two licensed restaurants in this hotel on the outskirts of town, serving moderately priced lunchtime grills, à la carte dinners and a popular Sunday-night smorgasbord ($30).

Da Vinci's 78 Medway St ☎0800/727 476. Cheap and cheerful café-style pizza house where you can eat in or take away.

Green Room 59 Irk St. The nicest of the town's cafés and the locals' choice. Good coffee, snacks and Internet access.

Howl at the Moon 2 Main St. Airy all-day café/bar with a subdued, Kiwi cowboy feel, serving a good range of snacks and bigger meals for under $25. The bar hots up Fri & Sat nights.

The Moth Restaurant and Bar Old Mandeville Airfield, 17km northwest of Gore on SH94 ☎03/208 9662. Good-quality food and coffee at reasonable prices in a sumptuous, airy 1920s-style restaurant and bar kitted out with nostalgic aircraft mementoes, Lunch from noon, dinner from 6pm, & open all day for coffee and drinks. Closed Mon.

Invercargill and around

For most visitors, the southern city of **INVERCARGILL** is little more than a waystation en route to Stewart Island or the Catlins Coast. Southland's thriving economic and cultural centre, with a population of around 50,000, it was settled in the mid-1850s, and has, like Dunedin, a predominantly Scottish character. Here the legacy is evident in streets named after Highland rivers, and a few fine old stone buildings in the city centre, ornately carved from white Oamaru stone transported here from north of Dunedin.

Regularly lashed by harsh winds and rain yet occasionally blessed with bright days, Invercargill sprawls over an exposed, broad expanse of flat land at the head of the New River Estuary, the monotony compounded by a low skyline, but much relieved by the city's huge parks and its friendly people. To the south, a small nub of land just out into Foveaux Strait, and at its tip lies **Bluff**, the departure point for ferries to **Stewart Island** (see p.756). The town is worth an hour or two of your time for a handful of sights and a couple of short coastal walks.

Arrival, information and city transport

Direct domestic flights from Christchurch, Dunedin and Stewart Island land at Invercargill's **airport**, 2.5km southwest of the city centre. Blue Star taxis (☎03/218 6079; $10–15) provide transport into town. Knightrider **buses** from Christchurch pull up at their depot on Tay Street, but all others (see p.752) stop outside the excellent **visitor centre**, 108 Gala St, in the foyer of the Southland

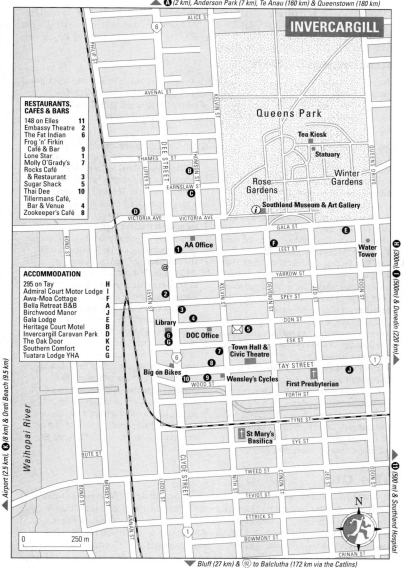

INVERCARGILL

ALICE ST

PHILIP STREET

AVENAL ST

Queens Park

Tea Kiosk

Statuary

Winter Gardens

Rose Gardens

Southland Museum & Art Gallery

RESTAURANTS, CAFÉS & BARS

148 on Elles	**11**
Embassy Theatre	**2**
The Fat Indian	**6**
Frog 'n' Firkin Café & Bar	**9**
Lone Star	**1**
Molly O'Grady's Rocks Café & Restaurant	**3**
Sugar Shack	**5**
Thai Dee	**10**
Tillermans Café, Bar & Venue	**4**
Zookeeper's Café	**8**

DEE STREET
THAMES ST
LIFFEY ST
EARNSLAW ST
THOMSON ST
KELVIN ST

VICTORIA AVE

QUEENS DRIVE
GALA ST

D
B
C
i

AA Office **1**
F LEET ST

Water Tower
E
H (300m), **I** (500m) & Dunedin (220 km) ▲

BOND ST
LEVEN ST
KELVIN ST
DEVERON ST
SPEY ST
JED ST
DOON ST

@
YARROW ST

2
3
Library
DOC Office **4**
5
7 Town Hall & Civic Theatre
8
DON ST
ESK ST

Big on Bikes **10** **9** Wensley's Cycles
WOOD ST
First Presbyterian
J
TAY STREET
FORTH ST
1

St Mary's Basilica
TYNE ST
EYE ST

ACCOMMODATION

295 on Tay	**H**
Admiral Court Motor Lodge	**I**
Awa-Moa Cottage	**F**
Bella Retreat B&B	**A**
Birchwood Manor	**J**
Gala Lodge	**E**
Heritage Court Motel	**B**
Invercargill Caravan Park	**D**
The Oak Door	**K**
Southern Comfort	**C**
Tuatara Lodge YHA	**G**

Waihopai River

◄ Airport (2.5 km), **K** (8 km) & Oreti Beach (9.5 km)

BUTE ST
MERSEY ST
BOND ST
LIDDEL ST
CLYDE STREET
NITH ST
TWEED ST
TEVIOT ST
CONON ST
JED ST
DOON ST

ETTRICK ST
ANNAN ST
BOWMONT ST
CRINAN ST

1

N

0 ————— 250 m

11 DUNEDIN TO STEWART ISLAND | Invercargill and around

▲ **I** (500 m) & Southland Hospital

Museum (daily: Dec–April 8am–7pm; May–Nov 8am–5pm; ☎03/214 6243, Ⓦwww.invercargill.org.nz) where you can pick up the *Southlands Events Calendar* (good for local events listings) and get **Internet access**. While here, pick up the Invercargill Bus Timetable, which outlines the city's ten **bus** routes ($1.50, all-day pass $3.50; timetable information ☎03/218 2320), which mostly make loops out from the centre.

The city's **DOC office**, in the State Insurance Building, Level 7, on Don Street (Mon–Fri 9am–4.30pm; ☎03/214 4589), is the best place to go for information on walks and wildlife in the Catlins, Stewart Island and Fiordland.

Accommodation

Accommodation prices this far south are very reasonable, and there's a good choice in the centre close to the transport links, mostly on or near Tay Street. Motels are plentiful and good quality, starting at around $65. Bluff also has a couple of places to stay if you want to avoid Invercargill altogether on your way to or from Stewart Island.

295 on Tay 295 Tay St ☎0800/295 295 & 03/211 1295, ⓦ www.295ontay.co.nz. Modern and palatial motel with all mod cons including broadband Internet access and spa baths. ❻
Admiral Court Motor Lodge 327 Tay St ☎0800/111 122 & 03/217 1117, ⓔ nicebeds@xtra.co.nz. Ten spotless, fully self-contained units with extras including breakfast delivered to your door and transport to and from the airport, train and bus stations. ❺
Awa-Moa Cottage 110 Leet St ☎03/214 3164, ⓔ mgmiller@southnet.co.nz. Extremely central B&B/homestay offering double rooms that share a guest bathroom. Good rates for singles. ❺
Bella Retreat B&B 70 Retreat Rd ☎03/215 7688, ⓦ www.bellaretreat.co.nz. About as swanky as Invercargill gets with spacious, taste-fully decorated ensuite rooms in a modern home on the edge of town. ❼
Birchwood Manor 189 Tay St ☎0800/888 234 & 03/218 8881, ⓦ www.birchwoodmanor.co.nz. A well-run new complex with 35 spacious units just beyond the city centre offering spa baths and a courtesy vehicle to and from public transport. ❺
Gala Lodge 177 Gala St ☎03/218 8884, ⓔ charlie.ireland@xtra.co.nz. A welcoming, large and central homestay overlooking Queens Park,

with extensive gardens and a double and a twin room sharing a bathroom; courtesy car. ❺
Heritage Court Motel 50 Thomson St ☎0800/243 748 & 03/214 7911, ⓦ www.heritagecourt.co.nz. The most reasonably priced motel just outside the centre in a quiet sunny spot near Queens Park and the visitor centre. ❹
Invercargill Caravan Park 20 Victoria Ave ☎03/218 8787. Central and fairly basic but comfortable campsite. Camping $8–12, cabins ❷
The Oak Door 22 Taiepa Rd, Otatara ☎03/213 0633, ⓔ blstuart@xtra.co.nz. A modern, airy B&B in a tranquil bush setting, three minutes' drive west of the centre, close to Oreti Beach. ❹
Southern Comfort 30 Thomson St ☎03/218 3838, ⓔ coupers@xtra.co.nz. Very good city hostel in a beautifully kept Art Nouveau villa set among manicured lawns. Pleasant, clean dorms and double rooms, an excellent kitchen, large dining room and free luggage storage for those tramping on Stewart Island. Dorms ❶, rooms ❷
Tuatara Lodge YHA 30 Dee St ☎03/214 0954, ⓔ tuataralodge@xtra.co.nz. Very central and recently refurbished, this friendly and spacious hostel has all the amenities you could wish for, including good security. Dorms ❶, rooms ❷, ensuites ❸

The City

Invercargill's chief attraction is the large **Southland Museum and Art Gallery**, at the southern entrance to Queens Park on Victoria Avenue (Mon–Fri 9am–5pm, Sat & Sun 10am–5pm; $2 donation requested). Capped with a big white pyramid, the building houses a well laid out collection, over two storeys. Upstairs, the extensive and imaginative "Beyond the Roaring Forties" focuses on New Zealand's **subantarctic islands**, the tiny windswept clusters lying thousands of kilometres apart between New Zealand and the Antarctic. These are the only obstacles in the path of the westerly gales that rage through these latitudes, earning them the names Roaring Forties and Furious Fifties. In a region mostly made up of ocean, the islands provide a vital breeding ground for marine wildlife, including albatrosses. Displays cover shipwrecks through the ages, wildlife, climate and so on. Downstairs, there's coverage of a successful breeding programme of **tuatara**, reptilian relics from the dinosaur age found nowhere else in the world. You can observe several of the small, well-camouflaged tuatara in simulated natural environments, but you'll need to peer hard to spot them (they usually come out of hiding on sunny days in the early afternoon). The remainder of the museum covers Southland's history, both human and natural, with exhibits ranging from moa bones to Maori artefacts and Victoriana. The **Art Gallery** displays international and national works, with exhibitions changing every few weeks.

The huge public gardens of **Queens Park** stretch north behind the museum from Gala Street and have been a public reserve since 1869. Today there are showhouses, a formal rose garden, a rhododendron dell, a walk-through aviary, a small animal park and a statuary, as well as an eighteen-hole golf course, various sports grounds and **Splash Palace** – a multi-million-dollar aquatic centre with a fifty-metre sports pool and hydroslide. There's access behind the museum, but the park's main entrance is on Queens Drive.

At the southeastern corner of the park, the top of the forty-metre-high brick **water tower** (1889), cnr Doon & Leet streets (Sun & public holidays 1.30–4.30pm; outside these times collect a key from the Water Works office next door; $1) offers the best views over the city.

In the city centre, Tay Street has some distinctive **architecture**. At the junction with Jed Street is the 1915 **First Presbyterian Church** (usually closed) is actually the second on the site, built in Romanesque style in 1915 with impressive ornamental brickwork. Near the corner with Deveron Street stands the magnificent **Civic Theatre**, completed in 1906 in English Renaissance style with its plasterwork, pediments and ornamental parapets carved from white Oamaru stone. The elegant copper dome of the Roman Catholic **St Mary's Basilica**, two streets south, is visible for miles around, but you'll need to wait for a church service to see the sumptuous Oamaru stone interior.

Anderson Park, Oreti Beach and Tiwai Point

On the outskirts of Invercargill, 7km north of the city centre, the beautiful grounds of **Anderson Park** provide the setting for the atmospheric **Anderson Park Art Gallery** (daily 10.30am–5pm; by donation except during special exhibitions), housed in a 1925 neo-Georgian mansion built for a local businessman. Designed by Christchurch architect Cecil Wood, it was constructed from reinforced concrete and set against a backdrop of forest. The delightful gallery displays a permanent collection of traditional and contemporary New Zealand art. During the month of October, a spring exhibition of recent Kiwi art replaces the permanent collection, and there are recitals each Sunday, when classical music drifts around the gardens. Behind the gallery, **The Maori House**, also built in the early 1920s, was used for dances, its doorway and porch decorated with carvings by Tene Waitere, a renowned Rotorua carver. Anderson Park is a 3km drive along McIvor Road, via North Road/SH6, or during daylight hours through Donovan Park, off Bainfield Road. There is no bus service out to here; a taxi will cost you about $15–20 one way.

Oreti Beach, 9.5km west of the city centre, is a beautiful broad expanse of fine sand, sweeping 30km right around to the seaside resort of Riverton to the west, and giving great views of Stewart Island and Bluff. In summer, it's popular for swimming (surf patrols operate), yachting and waterskiing, but windy days cause violent sandstorms. Use the entrance off Dunns Road (the others are pretty rough going); there's no bus service to the beach.

Lastly, fans of big industry will want to see Southland's biggest employer, the sprawling Tiwai Point **aluminium smelter**, 25km south of town. You can join a surprisingly interesting **free tour** which goes most weekdays at 10am (booking essential ☏03/218 5494).

Eating and drinking

Invercargill certainly has enough decent places to eat to keep you sated for the short time you're likely to be here, though there are few really special treats. The bulk of cafés and **restaurants** are on Dee Street, with a few on Tay Street. Look out for local **seafood**, including excellent blue cod and Bluff oysters (fresh April–Oct). Another local delicacy is **muttonbird**, though the oily and rather fishy flavour is something of an acquired taste: if you are interested try the deli at Woolworth, cnr Tay St & Queens Drive.

Several lively **bars** transform into dance venues as the evening wears on, though the town is usually quiet until Thursday night. **Local bands** play at several of the city's hotels (check *The Southland Times* for details) and there are also a handful of **nightclubs**; hardly the epitome of cool, but full of enthusiasm especially during university term time.

The five-screen Movieland **cinema** at 29 Dee St (☎03/214 1110) has reduced ticket prices on Tuesday and any weekday before 5pm.

148 on Elles 148 Elles Rd ☎03/216 1000. An elegant and upmarket dinner restaurant, serving local seafood, steak, venison and ostrich, at a price, in a restored 1912 building.

Embassy Theatre 112 Dee St ☎03/214 0050. This onetime hotel and former cinema is now a dance venue with a spectacular interior hosting live bands, comedy, poetry readings and DJ-led grooving with big-screen videos: check the posters or local listings for upcoming events.

The Fat Indian Piccadilly Lane, 38 Dee St ☎03/218 9933. One of the best licensed restaurants in town. Modern decor, friendly and prompt service, and best of all, authentic Indian-via-the-north-of-England grub. BYO wine only.

Frog 'n' Firkin 31 Dee St. This good café/bar for economical pub food transforms into a popular weekend dance spot; mostly DJs playing chart favourites but occasionally with a live band.

Lone Star cnr Leet St & Dee St. Tex-Mex dinner venue in a big old building with a bar at one end and café at the other. One of the dance spots in town, with a DJ on Thurs–Sat nights.

Molly O'Grady's 16 Kelburn St. Open from 11am until late, this first-floor pub has DJs on Friday and Saturday and a live band once a month.

Rocks Café & Restaurant Courtville Place, 101 Dee St ☎03/218 7597. The small café-cum-wine bar always comes up trumps with some of the best food in town from a varied menu. A little pricey but worth it.

Sugar Shack 77 Don St. Garish night club and late-night bar with lots of DJs but rarely anything live. The play list is mostly middle of the road and chart-oriented, with banks of video screens to entertain the 300-plus crowd.

Thai Dee 9 Dee St ☎03/214 5112. Modern, authentic Thai restaurant where the food strikes an exotic balance between salty, spicy, sweet and sour, with many Kiwi variations on Thai favourites. Closed Sun lunch.

Tillermans Café, Bar & Venue 16 Don St ☎03/218 9240. A relaxed local institution offering high-quality cosmopolitan food (lunch around $15, dinner around $25). Upstairs is a popular bar with pool tables, a focal point for live music on Sat nights, often fairly offbeat. Closed Mon & Tues evenings, Sat lunch and all day Sun.

Zookeeper's Café 50 Tay St. Very popular, zany, inexpensive, split-level café and bar easily identified by the corrugated ironwork elephant on the outside roof. Open 10am till late, they serve brunch, bar food, snacks (great seafood chowder) and meals from a wide-ranging menu with generous portions – nothing over $20. Best for brunch and lunch, coffee or a drink.

Listings

Automobile Association 47 Gala St ☎03/218 9033.

Bike rental Big on Bikes, 2 Dee St ☎03/214 4697), $20–25 a day depending upon the state of the bike; Wensley's Cycles, cnr Tay St & Nith St (☎03/218 6206), $20 a day.

Buses InterCity (☎03/214 6243) operate daily from the visitor centre to Dunedin, Christchurch, Queenstown & Te Anau. Shuttle bus services include Atomic Shuttles (☎03/214 6243) to Gore, Queenstown and Wanaka, and to Dunedin and Christchurch; Catch-a-Bus (☎03/214 5652) to Dunedin; and Scenic Shuttles (☎0800/277 483) to Te Anau, via the Southern Scenic Route.

Campbelltown Passenger Service (☎03/212 7404) run regular buses to Bluff for the ferry to Stewart Island.

Internet access At the visitor centre and Global Byte Café 150 Dee St.

Left luggage At visitor centre ($2 a day).

Library Invercargill Public Library is at 50 Dee St (Mon–Fri 9am–8.30pm, Sat 10am–1pm; ☎03/218 7025).

Medical treatment Southland Hospital, on Kew Rd (☎03/218 1949), has a 24hr accident and emergency department. For illness and minor accidents outside surgery hours, contact the Urgent Doctor Service at 103 Don St (☎03/218 8821; Mon–Fri 5–10pm; Sat, Sun & public holidays 24hr).

Pharmacy Inside the Countdown supermarket (Mon–Fri 8.30am–10pm, Sat & Sun 9am–7pm).

Police The central police station is at 117 Don St (☎03/211 0400).

Post office The main post office is at 51 Don St, near the junction with Kelvin St (Mon–Fri 8.30am–5pm, Sat 10am–1pm).

Bluff

Twenty-seven kilometres south of Invercargill, perched at the tip of a peninsula with great views across Foveaux Strait, is the small run-down fishing town of **BLUFF** and its man-made harbour. This is the departure point for ferries to **Stewart Island** (see p.754), and you may choose to avoid Invercargill altogether and stay here in the local B&B or hotel. You won't need more than a couple of hours to get a good look at the place, but without a car this involves a good deal of walking as the town spreads along the shoreline for about 6km.

Bluff is the oldest European town in New Zealand, having been continuously settled since 1824. It is showing its age, and is a little ragged around the edges, but the **harbour** flourishes, exporting Southland's meat, timber, aluminium, fish and wool, and importing a variety of goods from overseas. In addition Foveaux Strait yields a highly sought-after delicacy – the **Bluff oyster**. This deepwater shellfish has a sweet and succulent taste, and is usually dredged from the end of March until October then processed in local oyster sheds before being sent all over the country. Between June and August you can buy direct at factory prices from Johnson's Oyster Factory on the waterfront (daily 8am–5pm; ☎03/212 8665). An annual **Bluff Oyster and Southland Seafood Festival** (ⓦwww.bluffoysterfest.co.nz) celebrates these slimy little bivalve molluscs on the middle weekend in April at the Bluff Events Centre (tickets $20) with cook-offs, oyster opening competitions and street entertainment.

Across the harbour is the Tiwai Point **aluminium smelter**, which can be visited from Invercargill (see p.751).

The town

Bluff's small **Maritime Museum** (Mon–Fri 10am–4.30pm, Sat & Sun 1–5pm; $2), on Foreshore Road as you enter town from Invercargill, has historical displays focusing on whaling, the harbour development, oyster harvesting and shipwrecks. Pride of place is given to a vast triple-expansion steam engine, taken from a steam tug, *Monica*, which spent most of its life working the harbour. Back on the main road, you'll pass the ferry wharf and, three streets further, on the corner with Henderson Street, the kitsch **Paua Shell House** (daily 9am–5pm; donation). This was the home of Myrtle and Fred, a couple who, until their respective deaths in 2000 and 2001, spent years amassing a collection of shells from all over the world. The major spectacle is the living room which is plastered with iridescent paua shells gathered from local beaches and creating a wall-to-wall shimmer in blue and green.

From here it's another 1.5km to the end of the road at **Stirling Point**, where a multi-armed signpost – balancing the one at the other end of the country at Cape Reinga – marks the distance to major cities around the world. On a clear day, you can see as far as Stewart Island, 35km away. From the car park at the end of the road you can set out on a couple of easy walks: the **Foveaux Walkway** (6.6km; 2hr one way; mostly flat) which follows the coast back to town; and the **Topuni Track** (2km one way; 45min; 265m ascent) which climbs to **Bluff Hill Lookout**, with its 360-degree view encompassing Stewart Island, Foveaux Strait and Bluff Harbour. The lookout is also accessible by road from Bluff: follow Lee Street, opposite the ferry wharf for 3km.

Practicalities

Bluff is a twenty-minute drive down SH1 from central Invercargill. Campbelltown Passenger Service (T03/212 7404) runs a regular bus service from Invercargill ($10 each way), to connect with the ferry. For details on ferry sailings to Stewart Island, see p.756.

Good **accommodation** in Bluff is limited. In town try the *Foveaux Hotel*, 40 Gore St (T03/212 7196, W www.foveauxhotel.com; B&B ④, ensuite ⑤), which has an in-house bar; or *The Lazy Fish*, 35 Burrows St (T03/212 7245, E thelazyfish@es.co.nz; ⑤), a self-contained unit with a sunny courtyard. Alternatively, drive 2km south to Sterling Point and *Land's End* (T03/212 7575, W www.landsend.net.nz; ⑤) four attractive ensuite rooms above the **wine bar and café** of the same name. Breakfast (included) is served in the café, which is also the best place for lunch or dinner: specialities include pan-fried blue cod ($25).

Stewart Island

New Zealand's third main island is the small, rugged triangle of **STEWART ISLAND**, separated from the mainland by Foveaux Strait and until recently largely ignored by tourists. With the creation of **Rakiura National Park** in 2002 a full 85 percent of the island is now protected, and though little has actually changed, the designation has enhanced the island's pulling power. While the island is never crowded, if you come during the summer peak (mid-Dec to mid-Feb) you should book most things in advance. The climate is temperate, but unpredictable, so come prepared for all weathers.

Most of the island is uninhabited and characterized by bush-fringed bays, sandy coves, windswept beaches and a rugged interior of tall rimu forest and granite outcrops. Stewart Island's Maori name is Rakiura ("The Land of Glowing Skies") and the jury is still out on whether this refers to the aurora australis (southern lights) occasionally seen at these high latitudes or the fabulous sunsets. Captain Cook came by in 1770 and erroneously marked a peninsula on his charts. The island was later named after William Stewart, the first officer on a sealing vessel that visited in 1809. With the arrival of Europeans, felling rimu became the island's economic mainstay supporting three thousand people in the 1930s. Now almost all Stewart Island's four hundred residents live in the sole town, **Oban**, surviving on **fishing** (crayfish, blue cod and paua), **fish farming** (salmon and mussels) and tourism.

With the expense of getting over here, Stewart Island justifies taking a little time over; indeed the slow island ways can quickly get into your blood and you may well want to stay longer than you had planned, especially if you're drawn to some of the serious wilderness **tramping**. Other people come for the unspoilt nature: perhaps sea kayaking the vast flooded valley of **Paterson Inlet**, visiting the open, predator-free bird sanctuary of **Ulva Island**, just off the shore of Oban, or kiwi-spotting in the wild at **Mason Bay** on Stewart Island's west coast.

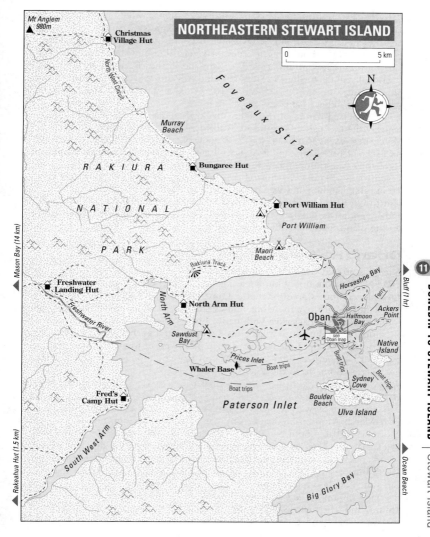

Mt Anglem 980m

Christmas Village Hut

North West Circuit

F o v e a u x   S t r a i t

Murray Beach

R A K I U R A

Bungaree Hut

N A T I O N A L

Port William Hut

Port William

P A R K

Maori Beach

Rakiura Track

Mason Bay (14 km)

Freshwater Landing Hut

North Arm

North Arm Hut

Freshwater River

Sawdust Bay

Prices Inlet

Whaler Base

Boat trips

Boat trips

Oban

Halfmoon Bay

Horseshoe Bay

Ackers Point

Native Island

Boat trips

see Oban map

Fred's Camp Hut

Rakeahua Hut (1.5 km)

South West Arm

Paterson Inlet

Boulder Beach

Sydney Cove

Ulva Island

Big Glory Bay

Bluff (1 hr)

ferry

Ocean Beach

11

Getting to Stewart Island

Foveaux Straight has a reputation for trying the stomachs of even the hardiest sailors so many people choose to **fly** from Invercargill with Stewart Island Flights (3 daily; $80 one way, $145 return; ☎03/218 9129, ⓦwww .stewartislandflights.com) who sometimes offer standby discounts (around $55 one way, $95 return). Getting out to Invercargill airport will cost $10–15, and the transfer between Oban's airfield and the centre of town is included in the price of your ticket. Note that a strict **luggage allowance** of 15kg per person applies and camping gas canisters are not allowed.

If you have a lot of luggage, want to carry camping stove fuel or just need to save money, take one of the **ferries**. Foveaux Express (2 daily; $45 one-way, $84 return; ☎03/212 7660, ⓦwww.foveauxexpress.co.nz) run a fast catamaran which makes the hour-long journey between Bluff and the wharf in Oban. Boats typically leave Bluff around 9.30am and in the late afternoon. They are fractionally undercut by the Stewart Island Adventures (1 daily; $45 one-way, $80 return; ☎0800/000 511 & 03/212 8080, ⓦwww.stewartislandnz.co.nz) who leave Bluff at 10am.

The dispersed nature of the sights on Stewart Island make it well suited to being visited as part of a **guided walking trip**, such as those run by Kiwi Wilderness Walks (☎03/442 6017, ⓦwww.NZwalk.com). Their Invercargill- or Te Anau-based four-night Stewart Island trips ($1495) involve a night at Riverton's Guesthouse (see p.934), a flight to Mason Bay with a walk along the beach to the Mason Bay hut where there's a chance to spot kiwi, a hike to Freshwater Landing and water taxi to Oban where there's guided kayaking, a visit to Ulva Island and a bit of free time. They run roughly weekly in summer and are entirely guided so you'll be well looked after. If you want to stay longer on the island that can easily be arranged.

Oban (Halfmoon Bay)

Nicely scattered around Halfmoon Bay and enclosed by bush-clad hills, **OBAN** (also commonly known as Halfmoon Bay) comprises little more than a few dozen houses, a visitor centre, a tiny museum, a couple of stores and cafés, and a hotel with a pub. More houses straggle away up the hills often surrounded by bush that's alive with native birds.

Coming from the South Island, this is where you'll **arrive**, either at the wharf right downtown or at the tarmac airstrip 3km west of town. If you're arriving by water taxi, perhaps after visiting Mason Bay, you'll pull up at **Golden Bay** just over a kilometre to the southwest.

Information

The combined Stewart Island **DOC office** and **visitor centre**, Main Rd (late Dec–March Mon–Fri 8.30am–7pm, Sat & Sun 9am–7pm; rest of the year Mon–Fri 8.30am– 5pm, Sat & Sun 10am–noon or later; ☎03/219 0009, DOC ☎03/219 0002, ⓦwww.stewartisland.co.nz), has excellent displays on the island's tracks and natural history, supplies local maps and information, and sells DOC hut passes. There's a stock of free videos about Stewart Island that you can watch at the visitor centre, the best being *Beyond the Mainland* (a general overview; 50min), *The Underworld of Paterson Inlet* (focusing on the marine life; 15min) and *The Other Side* (a tongue in cheek TV programme about out-of-the-way places and their inhabitants; 45min). The centre also has **luggage lockers** (small $2.50 for as long as you like; large $5).

It is usually best to contact trip operators directly, but Oban Tours & Stewart Island Travel on Main Rd (☎03/219 1456), the Stewart Island Flights office on Elgin Terrace (☎03/219 1090) act as **booking agencies**.

Bear in mind that there are **no banks** or bureaux de change on Stewart Island. Most businesses take credit cards and visitors with New Zealand bank accounts can use EFTPOS, but it is wise to bring plenty of cash.

The **post office** is in the Stewart Island Flights depot, Elgin St on the waterfront, near the junction with Ayr Street (daily: Oct–March 7.30am–6pm; April–Sept 8.30am–5pm), where stamps are still cancelled by hand. For **Internet access** try *Justcafé* on Main Rd (see p.759) and the hotel.

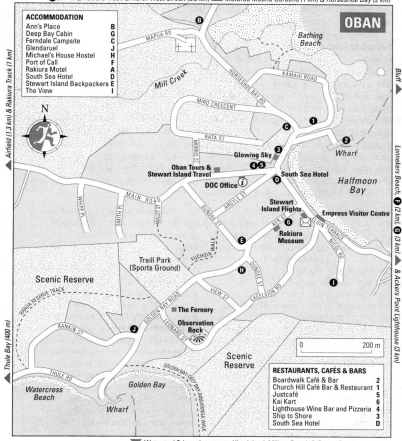

ACCOMMODATION

Ann's Place	B
Deep Bay Cabin	G
Ferndale Campsite	C
Glendaruel	J
Michael's House Hostel	H
Port of Call	F
Rakiura Motel	A
South Sea Hotel	D
Stewart Island Backpackers	E
The View	I

RESTAURANTS, CAFÉS & BARS

Boardwalk Café & Bar	2
Church Hill Café Bar & Restaurant	1
Justcafé	5
Kai Kart	6
Lighthouse Wine Bar and Pizzeria	4
Ship to Shore	3
South Sea Hotel	D

Water taxi & launch routes to Ulva Island, Millars Beach & Ocean Beach

Local transport

Oban is a pleasant place to **walk** around and unless you are staying in one of the more distant lodges you won't need any land transport. To get a feel for the lay of the land on a **general tour** join Billy the Bus (2 daily; 1hr 30min; $20; book ahead on ☏03/219 1269) run by the irrepressible Sam, a naturalist and historian who imparts his intimate knowledge of local history, flora and fauna and the islanders' way of life.

Oban Tours & Stewart Island Travel (☏03/219 1456) operate what amounts to a **taxi** service and rent cars ($75 a day) and motor scooters ($35 for 2hr, $50 for 24hr). **Mountain bikes** are rented out by Innes Backpackers on Argyle Street (☏03/219 1080; $10 per day including helmets).

Once away from the road system you'll need the aid of **water taxis**, typically speedboats with powerful outboard motors carrying 6 to 10 passengers. Half a dozen companies all offer a broadly similar service: try Seaview Water Taxi (☏03/219 1014) and Stewart Island Water Taxi (☏03/219 1394). As well as regular trips to Ulva Island and Freshwater Landing, they will all run **charter trips**.

Accommodation

Despite its diminutive size, Oban's range of **accommodation** is surprisingly broad with everything from campsites and hostels to swanky lodges. Even places in town feel pretty rural, but there are also some beautiful bush and seaview locations just a short distance away. Increased tourism is raising standards and beginning to moderate the traditionally **high summer prices**, but finding a place in high season can be difficult: it always pays to have something **booked** before you arrive. If you fancy self-catering, enquire through the visitor centre about **holiday cottages** for rent. You should be able to get a place with a couple of bedrooms for under $100 a night.

Finally, a word of **warning** to women travellers: repeated reports on the grapevine suggest you should avoid the massage "therapy" advertised at *Andy & Jo's B&B* and steer clear of *Innes Backpackers*.

Ann's Place 55 Horseshoe Bay Rd ⊕03/219 1065. Great little hostel in a self-contained cottage set in bush and gardens with just three twin rooms. There are no advance bookings and you'll need a sleeping bag, but it is only $14 each. Closed June–Aug. ❶

Deep Bay Cabin Deep Bay ⊕03/219 1219, Ⓔewanjengell@xtra.co.nz. Snug private self-contained wooden cabin hidden in the bush with four bunks, kitchen and shower. Roughly a 20min walk from town and a great spot for resting after the longer tracks. There's a pot-bellied stove in winter. ❷

Ferndale Campsite Horseshoe Bay Rd ⊕03/219 1176. Campsite handily sited 200m north of the wharf in central Oban. Facilities include coin-operated showers, a covered cooking area with hotplates and a washing machine. Camping $8.

Glendaruel 38 Golden Bay Rd ⊕03/219 1092, Ⓦwww.glendaruel.co.nz. Comfortable and welcoming B&B a 10min walk from town, surrounded by native bush that's alive with kaka. Rooms are all ensuite, guests get their own lounge, and Ronnie and Raylene will do their best to ensure you have a great time on the island. ❼

Michael's House Hostel Golden Bay Rd ⊕03/219 1425. Simple house with just one double and one twin at $20 per person. ❶

Port of Call Jensen Bay ⊕03/219 1394, Ⓦwww.portofcall.co.nz. A boutique B&B in a large, beautifully designed sun-filled contemporary house overlooking the bay 2.5km east of town, plus a gorgeous separate self-catering cottage sleeping three comfortably. Everything is beautifully appointed and there's free transport to and from town. Cottage ❽, B&B just ❾

Rakiura Motel Horseshoe Bay Rd ⊕03/219 1096, Ⓦwww.rakiuraretreat.co.nz. Great views over Halfmoon Bay from a hill just outside Oban, 2.5km from the wharf (a 25-minute walk, or $10 taxi ride). Five well-maintained units sleeping four to six. Courtesy transfers. ❻

South Sea Hotel 26 Elgin Terrace ⊕03/219 1059, Ⓦwww.stewart-island.co.nz. Century-old waterfront pub with good clean rooms upstairs all sharing bathrooms and a nice lounge overlooking the wharf. Some rooms have sea views but others are directly above the noisy bar: pick carefully. There are also more modern motel units out the back. Rooms ❹, seaview ❺, units ❻

Stewart Island Backpackers cnr Ayr St & Dundee St ⊕03/219 1114, Ⓦwww.stewart-island.co.nz/shearwater. Central, large and fairly basic hostel with loads of pleasant shared-bath doubles and twins and a backpacker section of four-bed dorms plus camping ($8) with use of hostel facilities. Everyone shares the kitchen and sizeable lounge, and a BBQ area and breakfast are available. Rooms ❸, dorms ❶

The View Nichol Rd ⊕03/219 1328. Friendly, warm, spacious and clean, this backpackers is just 500m from the wharf, its double room ($60) just nudging into this code. Closed May–Sept. Four-share ❶, rooms ❸

The town

Oban's sights are fairly limited though you should devote a few minutes to the **Rakiura Museum** on Ayr Street (Mon–Sat 10am–noon, Sun noon–2pm; $2) with its adequately displayed artefacts imparting some local history. The small Maori collection boasts a rare necklace of dolphin teeth,

⑪

while the whaling display has two individual giant teeth from a sperm whale. Around the corner at 45 Elgin Terrace, the **Empress Visitor Centre** is mainly there to promote the blue Empress Pearl (artificially grown in a paua) but also contains a small **aquarium** (daily 10am–5pm; $8.50) concentrating on the sealife around Stewart Island and comes complete with touch tanks where you can handle sea slugs, starfish and even a small carpet shark. You might also want to look in **Glowing Sky**, cnr Main Rd and Elgin Terrace (Ⓦ www.glowingsky.co.nz), a local designer clothing company that produce hand-printed T-shirts and hoodies emblazoned with designs inspired by nature or Maori sculptural forms.

Less than ten minutes' walk up the hill along Ayr Street, you'll find **The Fernery** (Oct–March daily 10am–5pm; winter by arrangement ☏ 03/219 1453), a cornucopia of souvenirs and gifts, all inspired by the island and handmade by New Zealand artists and craftspeople. A little further uphill, Leonard Street leads to **Observation Rock** (15min), with its hilltop panorama of Paterson Inlet and beyond to the island's highest peak, Mount Anglem. An evening visit here is an Oban ritual, and as the sun dips down you may well be treated to perhaps a dozen kaka screeching and flying about.

North of Halfmoon Bay, twenty-minutes' walk along Horseshoe Bay Road, are the attractive and secluded **Moturau Moana gardens**, which were donated to the island in 1940 by a longtime local resident. Picnic tables, barbecues and a viewing platform looking out across the bay to Oban are set amid lawns, native plants and dense virgin forest.

Eating and drinking

Oban only has a few **places to eat** and even these close early when the town is quiet. If you book ahead, most places will organise to pick you up from your accommodation if necessary. **Drinking** is confined to the bar at the *South Sea Hotel* and the *Boardwalk* on the wharf. For self-caterers, grocery prices compare well with the mainland but, surprisingly, fresh fish can be hard to come by as direct sales from the boats are illegal. Ask locals if this is what you're after. **Ship to Shore**, near the wharf, is a general store with basic foodstuffs, fruit and vegetables plus a selection of prepared lunch boxes ($8–10) ideal for trips to Ulva Island; closes around 7pm in summer.

Boardwalk Café & Bar On the wharf ☏ 03/219 1470. Non-smoking place above the ferry terminal with great sea views but little character. Expect the likes of blue cod kebabs with lemon and garlic butter ($14) or panini ($8) then full evening meals like muttonbird fillets ($25) or smoked salmon with avocado tossed salad ($17).

Church Hill Café Bar & Restaurant 36 Kamahi Rd ☏ 03/219 1323. Fine views of Halfmoon Bay from the deck of this century-old house help make this one of the best places to eat in town. Come for cake and espresso or their good-value lunches and dinners: perhaps an entrée of steamed mussels ($12) followed by chargrilled butterfish with a aioli and salad garnish ($24) unsalted muttonbird ($27) or crayfish (seasonal).

Justcafé 6 Main Rd. Tiny café with decent espresso, toasted sandwiches, light meals, cakes and pricey Internet access.

Kai Kart Ayr St. Very good fish, chips, toasted sandwiches, burgers and the like to eat in, at the tables outside or at the adjacent beach, from an old Pie Kart from Gore, a glorified caravan shipped to the island a few years back.

Lighthouse Wine Bar and Pizzeria 10 Main Rd ☏ 03/219 1208. Tasty pizzas to eat in or out from the only pizzeria on the island.

South Sea Hotel Elgin Terrace. Very much Oban's social centre and the island's main pub, serving Roaring Forties ale, once brewed on the island and now brought over from Invercargill. Also has a café and restaurant offering lunches and early evening meals (closes 9pm in summer) such as pan-fried haloumi with Mediterranean vegetables ($15) or grouper steak in a wine and caper sauce ($23).

Paterson Inlet and Ulva Island

While on this side of Foveaux Strait, almost everyone finds their way to **Ulva Island**, an open wildlife sanctuary 2km south of Oban set in **Paterson Inlet**, a flooded valley cutting deep into Stewart Island. The birdlife in Oban is pretty special, but Ulva Island goes one better with cacophonous birdsong, the chance to see endangered saddleback and rare red-fronted parakeets on a series of easy walks through rich native vegetation to secluded beaches. The former Norwegian **Whalers Base** is another popular destination, and can be included on guided **kayaking trips**.

Ulva Island

Clearly visible from Oban, just two kilometres to the north, the long, low **Ulva Island** (daylight hours; free) has largely escaped the effects of introduced predators and is now an open **sanctuary** where you'll see more native birdlife than almost anywhere else in New Zealand. The place is full of birdsong, its dense vegetation alive with weka, bellbirds, kaka, yellow- and red-crowned parakeets, tui, fantails and pigeons, who fearlessly approach visitors out of curiosity. In 2000 saddlebacks were reintroduced after an absence of 140 years.

Access is mainly by **water taxi** (10min each way; $20 return from Golden Bay), and armed with DOC's *Explore an Island Paradise: Ulva Island* booklet ($1) you can root at your leisure through ferns and orchids on easy trails across a forest floor covered in mosses and liverworts. Allow half a day and bring a picnic.

Water taxis arrive at **Post Office Bay** with its hundred-year-old former post office, a remnant from the days when the island was the hub of the local community. A web of trails leads first to nearby **Sydney Cove** where there's a pleasant picnic shelter on the beach.

For a **guided tour** of the island with a little Maori culture thrown in, join Ulva Amos of Ulva's Guided Walks (☎03/219 1216, ⓦwww.ulva.co.nz) who runs excellent trips for small groups (3hr; $75, including water taxi fees).

Whalers Base

One of the more interesting historical sites on the shores of Paterson inlet is **Whalers Base**, an over-wintering spot for Norwegian whalers near **Millars Beach** about 7km west of Oban. It is only accessible by water taxi ($40 return), and most operators will leave you there for a few hours and pick you up later. From Millars Beach, an easy twenty-minute coastal walk heads north from the beachside picnic shelter through native bush to the whaling base. Several eerie relics remain from 1923–33, when a fleet of Antarctic whaling ships was repaired here, and the beach is littered with objects left behind: old drums, cables, giant iron propellers, a boiler out in the water and, at the far end, a wrecked sailing ship deliberately sunk by the whaling company to create a wharf.

Activities

Though Ulva Island and Whalers Base can easily be visited by water taxi, both also form part of various **tours** which explore Paterson Inlet and beyond. There's also a chance to see **kiwi in the wild** without crossing the island to Mason Bay, and some great sea **kayaking** and short **walks**. Longer hikes are covered on p.762 & p.763.

Paterson Inlet tours

The sheltered waters of Paterson Inlet can be explored on numerous yacht and speedboat tours, some of the best outlined below.

Aurora Charters ☎ 03/219 1126, ✉ vaila@ihug.co.nz. Particularly good trips on a comfortable 25-passenger boat costing $60 for a half-day of fishing and scenic touring.

Bravo Adventure Cruises ☎ 03/219 1144, ✉ philldsmith@xtra.co.nz. Evenings around Oban can be well spent on cruises geared around spotting the Stewart Island brown kiwi (a sub-species of the mainland birds) in remote areas around the shores of Paterson Inlet. Four-hour trips ($90) go every other night, leaving from the wharf in Halfmoon Bay around dusk. You'll need warm clothing, sturdy footwear and a torch, as the outing entails a short boat trip and a brief uphill bushwalk in the dark to a windswept beach, where the kiwi feast on tiny crustaceans. Great care is taken to avoid disturbing these timid birds.

Seabuzz ☎ 03/219 1282, ⊛ www.seabuzzz.co.nz. Water taxi operator who, when conditions are clear, run short trips ($25) to see life below the surface using their glass-bottom boat. Underwater viewing also forms part of the visit to a mussel farm ($50).

Talisker Charters ☎ 03/219 1151, ⊛ www .taliskercharter.co.nz. Excellent half-day trips ($55) aboard the 17m motor ketch *Talisker* head around the inlet visiting either Ulva Island or Whalers Base. Enjoyable though these are, the yacht comes into its own on full-day trips ($100) which usually venture about two hours south of Paterson Inlet to Port Adventure (sailing if the winds are favourable) the itinerary largely set by the group. You'll need a bit of advance planning to get on their wonderful longer trips which head into remoter parts of Stewart Island and beyond to New Zealand's sub-Antarctic Islands sleeping and eating on board.

Thorfinn Charters ☎ 03/219 1210, ⊛ www.thorfinn.co.nz. Tours of Paterson Inlet (half-day $65; full day $90) sometimes including Ulva Island in their itinerary.

Kayaking

Adventurous visitors are seldom content with water taxis and will want to explore more thoroughly by **sea kayaking** around the scattered inlet's and islands. On extended trips you could even paddle out to one of the four water-accessible **DOC huts** around the inlet. Bottle-nosed dolphins and fur seals are frequent visitors to these waters, and the tidal flats attract wading birds including herons, oystercatchers, godwits and the New Zealand dotterel. Bear in mind that the waters around Stewart Island can be changeable and May to August brings the most settled weather; only extremely experienced kayakers should venture into these waters unaccompanied.

Rakiura Kayaks (☎ 03/219 1160, ⊛ www.rakiura.co.nz) run excellent guided trips: a half-day sticking fairly close to base ($45); a full day ($70) perhaps taking in Whalers Base; and overnight trips with the option of staying in a house on an offshore island (price negotiable). They're not permitted to guide on Ulva Island but you can paddle there in **rental kayaks** (single $40 a day; double $80). They also have sit-on-top kayaks for messing about ($10 first hour, then $5 each extra).

Short walks around Oban

Over a dozen short **walks** around Oban are covered DOC's *Day Walks* leaflet ($1), and a couple of the nicest are right in town.

Fuchsia Walk/ Raroa Reserve Track (2km one way; 30min). A pleasant way to Watercress Beach without walking on the road, this walk initially winds through fuchsia forest alive with tui, bellbirds and pigeons then comes out at Traill Park. Cross this and head down through rimu forest to the beach.

Golden Bay–Deep Bay–Ringaringa (6km loop; 1hr 30min–2hr). Skirting east from Golden Bay the track follows the coast to Deep Bay and then over the hill to Ringaringa Beach where you can follow the shore to Ringaringa Point and the graves of early missionaries Reverend Wohlers and his wife.

Harold Bay and Ackers Point Lighthouse (3km return; 40min). Easy and well-graded coastal walk with a chance to see little blue penguins and muttonbirds returning to their nests at dusk (Nov–Feb). Near the start of the track, you can follow a brief diversion to Harrold Bay, the site of a simple stone house built in 1835, making it one of the oldest European buildings in New Zealand. The main track continues through coastal forest to a lighthouse and lookout point from where you can watch the penguins arduously climbing to their nests hidden in the bush. You'll need a torch to find your way around after dusk, but it's important to keep the beam pointed to the ground to avoid disturbing the birds, which are easily distressed. The track starts at the end of Leask Bay Road, 2.5km east of town.

The rest of Stewart Island

There are no roads outside the immediate vicinity of Oban, so straying further afield requires some planning. Essentially you have to fly, take a water taxi or walk. One of the most popular destinations is the DOC hut at **Mason Bay** from where visitors venture out seeking foraging kiwi. You can fly there or walk using part of the island's two main walking tracks.

As ever, **trampers** need to be ready for whatever the New Zealand weather conjures up, and this is doubly so on Stewart Island which is exposed to winds coming straight across the southern ocean from Antarctica. Take several layers of clothing to cope with sun and rain (often at almost the same time), and don't forget sandfly repellent. Both tracks are usually deserted except for the Christmas to mid-January period.

Mason Bay

In the last few years, Stewart Island has become synonymous with **kiwi spotting** in the wild, something that is virtually impossible to do anywhere on mainland New Zealand. Tours from Oban (see box, p.756) include kiwi spotting, but most people are keen to get to **Mason Bay**, on the west coast, where they stay overnight in the DOC hut ($5) and head out after dark in the hope of seeing these elusive beasts. You'll almost certainly hear them, and have a fair chance of seeing them provided you don't go crashing about in the bush: just pick a spot and wait for them to come to you. Take a torch, plus all your camping gear except for a tent.

The cheapest way to visit is to **walk there** (37km one way; 13–15hr) along the southern leg of the North West Circuit (see below), probably staying overnight at Freshwater Landing Hut ($5). You can save a lot of time by catching a **water taxi** from Oban to Freshwater Landing Hut ($35 one-way; $45 return) then walking to Mason Bay (14km; 3–4hr; flat). Better still, Stewart Island Flights and one of the water taxi companies work together allowing you to complete a **loop**, flying from Oban to the beach at Mason Bay, staying a night or two there, walking to Freshwater Landing then getting a water taxi back to Oban (or visa versa). It costs $145 for the flight and water taxi with a three-person minimum. They charge the same price if you fly direct to Mason Bay from Invercargill then complete the circuit to Oban.

Rakiura Track

Stewart island's most popular overnight track is the relatively gentle **Rakiura Track** (36km loop; 2–3 days), one of New Zealand's Great Walks. This makes a circuit starting and finishing in Oban, though you can shave 7km off the route by getting someone to drop you off and pick you up at the road-ends. DOC's *Rakiura Track* leaflet ($1) is adequate for route finding, and you'll need to pre-purchase a **Great Walks Pass** from DOC for the two huts ($10 a night) and three campsites ($6) along the track. The huts are equipped with mattresses, wood stoves for heating only, running water and toilets, but you'll need your own stove. You can walk in either direction at any time of the year, and there is no limit on the number of nights you stay at each place.

The Rakiura Track makes an excellent introduction to the island's history, forest and birdlife, and the presence of long boardwalks keeps your feet dry much of the time. Starting through bush, the track follows the coastline before climbing over a three-hundred-metre forested ridge and traversing the shores of Paterson Inlet. The highlight is a lookout tower on the summit ridge, which provides excellent views of Paterson Inlet and beyond to the Tin Range.

North West Circuit

It is a very big step up from the Rakiura Track to the **North West Circuit** (130km; 8–12 days) around the island's northern arm: only the hardiest (masochistic) trampers should consider attempting it. With few boardwalks covering the boggy terrain it quickly becomes energy sapping even in good weather: thigh-deep mud is not uncommon. And unless you organise a boat to drop food for you at one of the coastal huts, you'll have to carry all your supplies.

The track itself alternates between open coast and forested hill country, offering highlights of a side trip to the 980-metre summit of Mount Anglem (5.5km; 6hr return) and the chance to see kiwi in the wild at Mason Bay. DOC's *North West and Southern Circuit Tracks* leaflet ($1) gives a good overview, pinpointing the ten huts (mostly sited on the coast: there are no campsites). Most huts cost $5 a night (annual hut pass valid), but Port William and North Arm huts are both Great Walks huts ($10) so it will probably pay to buy a **North West Circuit Pass** ($38) which entitles you to a night in each hut on the circuit.

Travel details

Trains

From Dunedin to: Middlemarch (summer Sundays only 1 daily; 2hr 30min); Pukerangi (1 daily, 2hr).

Buses

From Dunedin to: Alexandra (4–5 daily; 3hr); Balclutha (4–5 daily; 1hr 30min); Christchurch (8 daily; 5–6hr); Cromwell (4–5 daily; 3hr 15min); Gore (4–5 daily; 2hr 30min); Invercargill (4–5 daily; 3hr 30min); Lawrence (4–5 daily; 1hr 30min); Oamaru (8 daily; 2hr); Queenstown (4–5 daily; 4–5hr); Ranfurly (daily except Sat; 1hr 30min); Te Anau (1 daily; 4h 30min); Wanaka (2 daily; 4hr).
From Invercargill to: Balclutha (4–5 daily; 2hr 30min); Dunedin 4–5 daily; 3hrs 30 mins);

Gore (4–5 daily; 1hr); Queenstown (2 daily; 3–4hr); Te Anau (1 daily; 4hr); Wanaka (1 daily; 4hr 15min).

Ferries

From Bluff to: Stewart Island (2–3 daily; 1hr).
From Stewart Island to: Bluff (2–3 daily; 1hr).

Planes

From Dunedin to: Auckland (2–5 daily; 1hr 45min–2hr 40min); Christchurch (5–11 daily; 1hr); Wellington (4–6 daily; 1hr 15min–2hr 15min).
From Invercargill to: Christchurch (7–8 daily; 1hr 15min).
From Stewart Island to: Invercargill (3 daily; 20min).

The West Coast

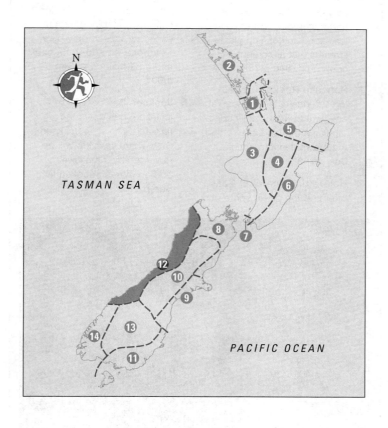

* **Formerly The Blackball Hilton** Meet the real West Coast in the hotel bar in the tiny former coal town of Blackball. See p.774

* **Oparara Basin** Set a day aside to explore caves still harbouring moa bones, vast limestone arches and placid streams that are great for cooling off. See p.784

* **Pancake Rocks** This geologic curiosity is gorgeous at any time but especially spectacular with high seas setting the blowholes into action. See p.788

* **Heli-rafting** The West Coast offers rafting down some of New Zealand's finest wild rivers, made all the more enticing by a helicopter flight into the headwaters. See p.802

* **The Franz Josef glacier** Hiking out onto the glacier is an awe-inspiring experience, surpassed only by a helicopter ride up to its back and a hike along it. See p.807

* **Jackson Bay** For real isolation, ride down the remote highway to Jackson Bay, where your trip will be rewarded by a massive portion of fresh-cooked fish. See p.816

△ Franz Josef glacier

The West Coast

he Southern Alps run down the backbone of the South Island, both defining and isolating **the West Coast**. A narrow, rugged and largely untamed coastal strip of turbulent rivers, lush bushland and crystal lakes that's seldom more than 30km wide, it comes fringed by astonishing surf-pounded beaches backed by the odd tiny shack or, more frequently, nothing at all. What really sets "the Coast" apart is the interaction of settlers with their environment. **Coasters**, many descended from early gold and coal miners, have long been proud of their ability to coexist with the wild primeval landscape – a trait mythologized in their reputation for independent-mindedness and intemperate beer-drinking, no doubt fuelled by a heavy mixture of Irish drawn to the 1860s gold rushes. Stories abound of late-night drinking sessions in pubs way past their closing times, and your fondest memories of the West Coast might well be chance encounters one evening in the pub, rather than the sights.

Cook sailed up this way in 1770, when he described the Coast as "an inhospitable shore, unworthy of observation, except for its ridge of naked and barren rocks covered with snow. As far as the eye could reach the prospect was wild, craggy and desolate". Little here then for early **European explorers** such as Thomas Brunner and Charles Heaphy, who made forays in 1846–47, led by Kehu, a Maori guide. They returned without finding the cultivable land they sought, and after a shorter trip in 1861 Henry Harper, the first Bishop of Christchurch, wrote, "I doubt if such a wilderness will ever be colonized except through the discovery of **gold**". Prophetic words: within two years reports were circulating of flecks of gold in West Coast rivers and a year later Greymouth and Hokitika were experiencing full-on gold rushes. The boom was soon over, but mining continued into the twentieth century, with huge dredges littering the landscape, looking like beached galleons as they worked their way up the gravel riverbeds, scuttling through spent tailings.

As gold was worked out, longer-lasting **coal** took its place, laying the foundation for more permanent towns. Many of these have since foundered (although the West Coast still produces a third of the country's coal) and a shrinking economy has tapped the resourcefulness of the people – you'll still find individual miners hacking away at a single coal seam or running a sawmill in the bush single-handed. Alongside are people taking advantage of the abundant open space and low land prices and nurturing a thriving **alternative culture** – you may well spot the smoke stack of some purple bus sticking out from behind the trees. In the last fifteen years or so, however, everything has been turned upside down by the challenge of increasing **tourism** and a greater awareness of the Coast's fragile **ecosystems**, a situation that has given rise to tension between the Coasters and the government, particularly regarding native timber felling and its detrimental effect on the unique environment.

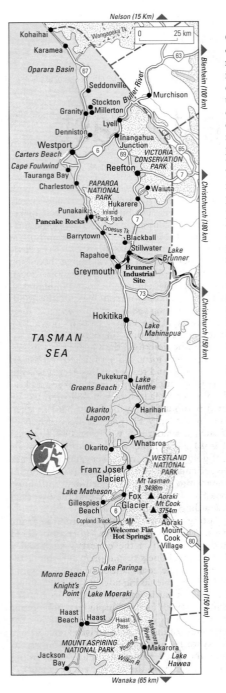

Nelson (15 Km) ▲

Kohaihai
Karamea
Oparara Basin (67)
Seddonville
Stockton
Granity ● Millerton
Lyell
Denniston
Westport
Carters Beach
Cape Foulwind
Tauranga Bay
Charleston
PAPAROA
NATIONAL
PARK
Punakaiki
Pancake Rocks
Barrytown
Rapahoe
Greymouth
Brunner
Industrial
Site
Hokitika
TASMAN
SEA
Pukekura
Greens Beach
Okarito
Lagoon
Okarito
Franz Josef
Glacier
Lake Matheson
Gillespies
Beach
Fox
Glacier
Copland Track
Welcome Flat
Hot Springs
Monro Beach
Knight's
Point
Haast
Beach
Haast
MOUNT ASPIRING
NATIONAL PARK
Jackson
Bay

Wangapeka Tk
0   25 km
(63)
Buller River
Murchison
Inangahua
Junction (69)
VICTORIA
CONSERVATION
PARK (65)
Reefton
(7)
● Waiuta
Hukarere
Inland
Pack Track
(7)
Croesus Tk
Blackball
Stillwater   Lake
Brunner
(73)
Lake
Mahinapua
Lake
Ianthe
Harihari
Whataroa
WESTLAND
NATIONAL
PARK
Mt Tasman
3498m
Aoraki
Mt Cook
3754m
Aoraki
Mount
Cook
Village (80)
Lake Paringa
Lake Moeraki
Haast
Pass
Makarora
River
Makarora
Lake
Hawea
Young R
Wilkin R

Blenheim (100 km) ▶
Christchurch (180 km) ▶
Christchurch (150 km) ▶
Queenstown (150 km) ▶

N

Wanaka (65 km) ▼

No discussion of the West Coast would be complete without mention of the torrential **rainfall**, which falls with tropical intensity for days at a time; every rock springs a waterfall and the bush becomes vibrant with colour. Such soakings have a detrimental effect on the soil, retarding decomposition and producing a peat-like top layer with all the minerals leached out. The result is **pakihi**, scrubby, impoverished and poor-looking paddocks that characterize much of the West Coast's cleared land. But the abundant sunshine that alternates with the downpours produces excellent conditions for **marijuana**-growing, a significant component of the local economy. Enthusiasm for dope-growing is matched only by the springtime rush to catch **whitebait**, when fishers line the tidal riverbanks on rising tides trying to net this epicurean holy grail.

The boom-and-bust nature of the West Coast's gold- and coal-mining past produced scores of ghost towns, but also spawned its three largest towns – the harbour town of **Westport**, and the former ports of **Greymouth** and **Hokitika**. The real pleasure of the West Coast, though, lies in smaller places more closely tied to the countryside, where the Coasters' indomitable spirit shines through: places such as **Karamea**, on the southern limit of the Kahurangi National Park, the strike town of **Blackball** at the foot of the Croesus Track on the Paparoa Range, the gold town of **Ross** and windswept **Okarito**. With the exception of a couple of decent museums and a handful of sights, the West Coast's appeal is in its scenic beauty. The **Oparara Basin**, near Karamea, and the **Paparoa National Park**, south of Westport, exhibit some of the country's finest limestone formations, including huge arched spans and the famous Pancake Rocks, while in the Westland National Park the frosty white tongues of the **Franz Josef** and **Fox glaciers** career down the flanks of the Southern Alps into dense emerald bush almost to sea level.

Since this is New Zealand, there's no lack of activities, particularly the matchless fly-in **rafting** trips down the West Coast's steep rivers. The limestone bedrock makes for some great adventure **caving**, and there's plenty of **hiking** with the Heaphy Track in the north, the Inland Pack Track near Punakaiki and the stack of steep tramps around the glaciers.

Most people visit from November to April, and you might expect that a place with such a damp reputation is a bad place to visit in **winter**, but temperatures are not as low as you might think and the greater number of clear days make for cloud-free viewing. Pesky sandflies are also less active in the winter. The West Coast never feels crowded but in the off-season you'll have even more room to move and accommodation will be cheaper; the downside is that adventure trips and scenic **flights**, which require minimum numbers to operate, may be harder to arrange.

Getting around

The simplest way to get around the West Coast is with your own **vehicle**. Likewise, **cycling** isn't such a chore: the coast road is undulating but the distances between towns aren't off-putting and you can always find somewhere to camp in between. Public transport, on the other hand, is fairly restrictive. **Trains** only penetrate as far as Greymouth; **bus services** are infrequent and, though they call at all the major towns, they won't get you to most of the walks. Having said that, with patience and a degree of forward planning it is possible to see much of interest, especially if you are prepared to walk a little. For details of transport routes see "Travel Details" on p.820.

The northern approaches: along the Buller and Grey rivers

Stretching 169km from its source at Lake Rotoiti in the Nelson Lakes National Park to its mouth at Westport, the **Buller River**'s blue-green waters reflect sunlight dappled through riverside beech forests as they swirl and churn through one of the grandest of New Zealand's river gorges between the Lyell and Brunner ranges. The Maori name for the Buller is *Kawatiri*, meaning "deep and swift", a fitting description of its passage through a region which, in the national consciousness, is associated with two devastating **earthquakes**. The first, registering 7.8 on the Richter Scale, was centred on Murchison in 1929; the other had its epicentre near Inungahua and struck in 1968. Landslides associated with these catastrophic events have combined with the natural geology to soften the curves of rocky bluffs that shelter white-sand beaches inaccessible from the road but frequently used by rafting parties. Gold was discovered along the Buller in 1858, sparking a gold rush centred on **Lyell**, now a ghost town whose outlying remains can be visited on the **Lyell Walkway**.

The Buller is traced by SH6 from Kawatiri Junction to Westport through Inungahua Junction, where Greymouth-bound travellers turn south towards **Reefton**. From Reefton, SH7 hugs the **Grey River**, a far less dramatic watercourse than the Buller, as it flows through a wide valley to the east of the granite tops of the Paparoa Range past more evidence of long-dead gold and coal industries, principally at laidback **Blackball** and the **Brunner Industrial Site**.

The Buller Gorge

SH6 from Nelson passes through Murchison (see p.580) and follows the Buller River 11km to **O'Sullivan's Bridge** where you turn right to remain on SH6 as it enters the Upper Buller Scenic Reserve. After 6km, the road passes the **Buller Gorge Swingbridge** (☎03/523 9809, ⓦwww.bullergorge.co.nz; $5), a kind of heritage park accessed by a 110-metre swing bridge, New Zealand's longest example of these swaying pedestrian footbridges. It crosses high above the Buller River parallel to a fun 160-metre-long **flying fox** (zipwire), on which you can ride sitting ($25), tandem ($25 each), or prone (Superman-style) for $35. On the far side of the swift flowing water, the heritage park has a variety of **bush walks** (ranging from 15min to over 2hr) taking in a waterfall, where White's Creek joins the river, the White's Creek faultline, epicentre of the 1929 earthquake, and the miner's workings that took advantage of the 4.5-metre rise in the ground caused by the quake. You can also pan for gold ($10) or if you've a mind push on into the bush to lookouts and the Ariki Falls (1hr round trip). In summer there are also exciting **jetboat** rides ($65; 40min) up river to the Ariki Falls and then spinning round back to the bridge along the gorge.

Westland's endangered forest

If gold and coal built the West Coast's foundations, then the **timber industry** supported the structure. Ever since timber was felled for sluicing flumes and pit props, Coasters relied on the seemingly limitless forests for their livelihood. As coal and gold were worked out, miners became loggers, felling trees which take from three hundred to six hundred years to mature and which, according to fossil records of pollen, have been around for 100 million years.

Few expressed any concern for the plight of Westland's magnificent stands of **beech** and **podocarp** until the 1970s, when the magnitude of the threat to the forests became clear. Environmental groups rallied around a campaign to save the Maruia Valley, east of Reefton, which became a touchstone for forest conservation, but it wasn't until the 1986 **West Coast Accord** between the government, local authorities, conservationists and the timber industry that some sort of truce prevailed. In the 1980s and 1990s most of the forests were selectively logged, often using helicopters to pluck out the mature trees without destroying those nearby. While it preserves the appearance of the forest, this is little comfort for New Zealand's endangered **birds** – particularly kaka, kakariki (yellow-crowned parakeet), morepork (native owl) and rifleman – and long-tailed **bats**, all of which nest in holes in older trees.

With the benefit of hindsight, many considered the accord far too weak: felling off the south Westland rimu forests stopped in 1994, but continued apace in Buller until the election of the left-leaning Labour–Alliance coalition government in 1999. Though torn between their commitment to jobs and to the environment, Labour leader Helen Clark honoured her election pledge and almost immediately banned the logging of beech forests by the State-owned Timberlands company. Precious West Coast jobs were immediately lost and the government stepped in with the $100 million West Coast Development Trust, which has helped kick start the local economy. Several communities remain threatened, and thousands still feel betrayed in this traditionally Labour-voting part of the world, but with a strong farming sector, rampant property prices and booming tourism the future looks brighter.

Fifteen kilometres on, a lay-by provides the **View of Earthquake Slip** which, thirty-odd years after the Inungahua earthquake, is gradually being recolonized but still bears the scars of the huge landslide that completely dammed the Buller River for several days. Following a four-kilometre bend in the river, the road passes the grassy site of **Lyell**, a former gold-mining town named after the great geologist Charles Lyell. The town sat high above the Buller on flats beside Lyell Creek and, in its 1890s heyday, supported five hotels, two banks, two churches and even its own newspaper, all serving a population of three thousand spread between here, Gibbstown and Zalatown, further up the Lyell Creek. Fires and the gradual decline in gold mining saw off all three settlements, but a few mementoes remain. These can be visited via the short but fairly strenuous **Lyell Walkway**, which passes terraces where huts once stood, the sobering slabs that stand askew in the cemetery (15min return), and the ten-hammer Croesus quartz stamping battery (1hr 30min return). The roadside site of the former township itself is now a peaceful DOC **campsite** ($5).

The next town, 17km to the west, is **INUNGAHUA JUNCTION**, which is little more than a service station attached to a café and grocery shop, an excuse for a brief stop only, unless you want to stay at the bargain *Inwoods Farm Backpackers* (℡03/789 0205; closed July–Sept; ❶), a well-maintained house with just a twin, a triple and a quad, signposted 400m down Inwoods Road which spurs off beside the general store which closes early: bring what you need.

West of Inungahua Junction the river approaches Westport through the **Lower Buller Gorge**, the narrowest and most dramatic section. The road hugs the cliff-face in places, most notably at **Hawks Crag**, where the rock has been hewn to form a large overhang – the fact that the water level rose several metres above this carved-out section during a 1926 flood will give you some idea of the volume of water that can surge down the gorge.

Reefton and around

Located beside the Inungahua River at the intersection of roads from Westport, Greymouth and Christchurch, **REEFTON**, as its name suggests, owes its existence to rich gold-bearing quartz reefs. These were exploited so heavily in the 1870s that Reefton was considered by some "the most brisk and businesslike place in the colony". This frenzy of financial speculation put Reefton in the vanguard, and it became the first place in New Zealand, and one of the first in the world, to install electric street lighting powered by a hydroelectric generator. Such forward-looking activity soon abated and, despite decades as an important coal-mining town, Reefton weathered poorly. However, things are now looking up: a couple of interesting galleries and even a good café opening in recent years, together with a couple of pleasant strolls on the outskirts of town, mean you may want to tarry a while. After a couple of hours, though, you'll probably want to explore the nearby Victoria Conservation Park or press on down the Grey Valley.

Specific points of interest around town are linked by two walks, both the subject of brochures available from the visitor centre (see "Practicalities", below). The elegiac **Historic Walk** (40min; brochure $1) meanders around Reefton's grid of streets, visiting once-grand buildings – the Masonic Lodge, the School of Mines and the Court House – some ripe for preservation, others part way there. The pleasant **Powerhouse Walk** (40min; 20¢) is slightly more uplifting in recalling an illustrious past, perhaps because of its course along the Inungahua River. In the centre of town, on the corner of Walsh and Broadway, the so-called "Bearded Miners" entertain visitors at an old **miner's cottage** and smithie (daily, pretty much when they feel like it; donation) and will fire up the forge and let you pan for gold.

The water for Reefton's original hydroelectric scheme was diverted 2km from Blacks Point, where the **Blacks Point Museum**, SH7 towards Springs Junction (Oct–April Wed–Fri & Sun 9am–noon & 1–4pm, Sat 1–4pm; $2), occupies a former Wesleyan Chapel. The museum charts the district's cultural and mining history through engaging photos and a large collection of lamps, moustache cups, clunky old typewriters and the like. Outside, parts from two ancient stamper batteries have been knitted together to form one five-hammer battery hydro-driven by a Pelton wheel; the whole ensemble is cranked into action on Sunday afternoons and during school holidays. **Walks** along mining trails through the regenerating bush to the mine shafts and stamping batteries of the Murray Creek Goldfield start from behind the museum and range from half an hour to a day; pick up the informative *Walks in the Murray Creek Goldfield* leaflet from the visitor centre or museum.

Coal- and gold-mining heritage combines with a vast area of bushland in the **Victoria Conservation Park**, which cloaks the ranges right around the western side of Reefton. The park is well off the traditional tourist itinerary and is consequently little-visited, making it all the more appealing for wilderness devotees. Day-walks are possible, but most require overnight stays in DOC huts; the visitor centre in Reefton can fill you in on all the options.

Practicalities

Buses all stop on Broadway, Reefton's main street, within sight of the helpful combined **visitor centre** and **DOC office**, 67–69 Broadway (daily: Dec–Feb 8.30am–6pm; March–Sept 8.30am–4.30pm; Oct–Nov 8.30am–5.30pm; ☏03/732 8391, ⓦwww.reefton.co.nz), which has **Internet access**, a small replica goldmine ($0.50), rents out gold pans for $2 a day and bikes for $25 a day.

Almost all Reefton's **accommodation** is on, or just off, Broadway; the cheapest place is the *Old Bread Shop Backpackers*, 155 Buller Rd (☏03/732 8420; ❶), a small well-run hostel of just eleven beds. The best place in town is *Reef Cottage B&B*, 51–55 Broadway (☏03/732 8440 & 0800/770 440, ⓦwww.reefcottage.co.nz; ❹), where they offer beautiful, individually decorated Victorian- and 1920s-style ensuites and a friendly welcome. **Motels** units are available in the *Bellbird*, 93 Broadway (☏03/732 8444; ❹), and at the *Dawson's on Broadway*, 74 Broadway (☏03/732 8406, ❹); while **campers** should make for the *Reefton Domain Motor Camp*, 1 Ross St, at the top of Broadway (☏03/732 8477; camping $8–9, cabins ❷), where there's good swimming in the Inungahua River, or head 10km south down the Grey Valley to the DOC's primitive *Slab Creek* campsite ($5).

Good **eating** options are few. Culinary relief from rural tearoom hell comes in the form of the daytime *Reef Café*, a bright and comfortable spot serving muffins, sandwiches, pasta, soup, good coffee and specializing in particularly luscious desserts (menu ranges from $5–15; BYO). For something more substantial try *Alfresco Outside Eatery*, on Upper Broadway (☏03/732 8513), with light meals, good coffee and lovely pizza served at lunch, and in evenings during the summer; or head along to the *Hotel Reefton*, 75 Broadway, for its enormous $8 roast dinners (not Sun).

The Grey Valley

Southwest of Reefton, SH7 follows the Grey Valley, cut off from the Tasman Sea by the rugged Paparoa Range and hemmed in by the Southern Alps. From both sides, the bush is gradually reclaiming the mine workings that characterized the region for a century. Nothing has stepped in to replace them, and the small communities tick over, a few eking a living from inquisitive tourists keen to explore the former mining towns of **Waiuta** and **Blackball**, and to walk the **Croesus Track**.

Waiuta

The first diversion of any consequence lies 21km south of Reefton where **Hukarere** marks the junction for **WAIUTA**, a ghost town seventeen partly-sealed kilometres east. This was the last of the West Coast's great gold towns, attaining a population of 6000 in the 1930s.

The end came for Waiuta when a mine shaft collapsed in 1951, burying large deposits of gold-bearing reef-quartz almost 900m down, where it was uneconomic to extract them. Miners left for jobs on the coast, much of the equipment was bought by Australian mining companies – many houses were even carted off – but the town wasn't completely abandoned; four of the remaining five cottages are occupied and there are several more buildings scattered around, including the original post office. The rolling country pocked by waste heaps is slowly being colonized by pioneer species like gorse and bramble, but the cypresses and poplars that once delineated gardens and the fruit trees that filled them remain; the rugby field, whippet track, croquet lawns and swimming pool are faring less well.

The whole place is wonderfully atmospheric for just mooching around, guided by the invaluable *Waiuta* leaflet ($1 from Reefton visitor centre) and strategically placed interpretive panels. You can see the lot in a couple of hours, but Waiuta is an ideal **place to stay** for well-equipped campers, who can pitch their tent just about anywhere. For the less hardy, there's the open-plan thirty-bunk *Waiuta Lodge* (book through the Reefton visitor centre; $15), with a fully equipped kitchen, TV and video and a public phone. There's no other accommodation, no public transport and nowhere to buy food, so come prepared.

Blackball

Both the Grey River and SH7 meander through inconsequential small towns until they reach **Stillwater**, 11km short of Greymouth, where side roads lead to Blackball and Lake Brunner.

Refugees from the blistering pace of Greymouth gravitate to languid **BLACKBALL**, a former gold- and coal-mining village spread across a plateau at the foot of the Paparoa Range, 11km northeast of Stillwater. Here, commuters, neo-hippies and gnarled folk still hunting and prospecting in the bush seem to coexist fairly harmoniously. Blackball owes its existence to alluvial gold discovered in Blackball Creek in 1864, but gold returns diminished by the early twentieth century and it was left to coal, also mined from 1893, to save the day. Coal supported Blackball until the mine's closure in 1964, along the way staking the town's place in New Zealand's history as the birthplace of the **labour movement**.

During the first three decades of the twentieth century, the whole of the Grey Valley was a hotbed of doctrinaire socialism, as organizers moved among the towns, pressing unbending mine managers to address the atrocious working conditions. Anger finally came to a head, resulting in the crippling 1908 "cribtime strike", when Pat Hickey, Bob Semple and Paddy Webb requested an extension of their "crib" (lunch) break from fifteen to thirty minutes. Management's refusal sparked an illegal ten-week strike – the longest in New Zealand's history – during which the workers' families (already suffering enormous sacrifice and deprivation) were fined £75 for their action. None had the money to pay and although the bailiffs tried to auction their possessions, the workers banded together, refusing to bid – one then bought all the goods for a fraction of their worth and redistributed them to their original owners. It is this spirit which eventually won the day: the workers returned to the mine and crib time was extended, but the £75 was extracted from subsequent wages.

The struggle led to the formation of the Miners' Federation, which later transformed itself into the Federation of Labour, the country's principal trade union organization. Eric Beardsley's historical novel *Blackball 08* (see p.982) gives an accurate and passionate portrayal of the 1908 strike, but the most powerful evocation of the labour spirit is in the TV room at *Formerly the Blackball Hilton* (see below), with its relics and press cuttings from the strike and red flags bearing rousing slogans.

These days Blackball's rustic tranquillity is the main draw, abetted by excellent walking through the gold workings of Blackball Creek and up onto the wind-blasted tops of the Paparoa Range along the **Croesus Track** (see p.775). Jane at the *Hilton* has a hatful of other suggestions including gold panning, evening possum shooting with Bob ($25) and even heli-hiking and heli-biking from the top of the range (around $100).

Practicalities

Blackball's social life revolves around the welcoming and wonderfully low-key *Formerly The Blackball Hilton*, Hart Street (☎0800/425 225, ⓦwww .blackballhilton.co.nz; camping $10, dorms ❶, rooms ❺), the last of the mining-era **hotels** which opened as the *Dominion* in 1910 and subsequently operated as the *Hilton* – ostensibly named for the former mine manager remembered in Hilton Street nearby – until challenged by the international hotel chain of the same name. Apart from lively drinking with locals the hotel offers accommodation in shared-bath double and twin rooms (and one 6-bed dorm) all brightly decorated. The emphasis is on character rather than creature comforts, but guests have use of an indoor hot tub, small gym and table tennis, but there's no kitchen. Breakfast is included in the room price and the restaurant is open for good lunches ($8–15) and dinners ($15–22) which might include Blackball sausages or steak.

For picnic supplies, call in at the excellent *Blackball Salami Co* up the street from the *Hilton*, and feast on venison sausages, salami, delectable morsels; or pop across the road for fish and chips from the dairy.

There is no public transport but the hotel can organize a ride from Greymouth ($20 per group).

Lake Brunner

From the SH7 near Blackball, a good sealed road runs 55km south to link up with SH73 between Greymouth and Arthur's Pass. Along the way it passes Lake Brunner (Moana Kotuku), a filled glacial hollow celebrated for its trout fishing. The shoreline village of **MOANA** is popular with holidaying Kiwis but unless you have your own rod or aquatic playthings it is not brimming with things to do. By late summer the lake is surprisingly warm and makes for good **swimming**, or head out on foot along a couple of easy paths. At the end of town beyond the motor camp (see opposite) a slender swingbridge over the fledgling

Prospectors seeking new claims gradually pushed their way up Blackball Creek, cutting paths to get their reef-quartz rock down to stamping batteries and to get supplies back up to their shelters in the bush. The scant remains of decades of toil now provide the principal interest on the **Croesus Track**, the first half easily explored in a day from Blackball, the whole track over the 1200m Paparoa Range to Barrytown on the coast north of Greymouth taking two relatively gentle days or one eight-hour slog. DOC's informative *Central West Coast* leaflet (50¢) shows adequate detail for walkers, and the NZMS's 1:50,000 *Ahaura* topomap is the one for map enthusiasts.

Access and accommodation

The track **starts** at Smoke-ho car park, at the end of a rough but passable road 7km north of Blackball, and **finishes** opposite the Barrytown Tavern on SH6, where buses pass twice daily in each direction. The only hut is the first-come-first-served **Ces Clarke Hut** (24 bunks; $10), with panoramic views, pots and a good coal-burning stove; the adjacent Top Hut is now abandoned.

The track

Much of the track was designed to accommodate tramways and the requirements of a gentle, steady grade characterizes today's track. The route wends through hardwood and native podocarps interspersed with ferns and mosses and vines, gradually giving way to hardier silver beech and eventually alpine tussock and herbfields above the tree line. Sea mist commonly cloaks the tops during the middle of the day.

The trail from **Smoke-ho** begins along a well-graded track, gradually descending to cross Smoke-ho Creek then rising gently to a clearing (reached in half an hour), from where a ten-minute return path leads to the former site of the **Minerva Battery**. Immediately after the clearing, the path crosses Clarke Creek on a new wire bridge above the remains of an old wooden bridge. Another half hour on, a side track leads to two more clearings that once contained **Perotti's Mill** (10min return) and the **Croesus Battery** (50min return), respectively. After almost an hour, another side path leads to the primitive **Garden Gully Hut** (5min return) and the **Garden Gully Battery** (40min return). The main track turns sharply west before reaching the **Ces Clarke Hut** on the tree line in around an hour: fill your water bottles here, there is no supply beyond. The top of the ridge near Mount Ryall (1220m) lies two undulating hours beyond, a little more if you run off to climb **Croesus Knob** (1204m) along the way. If it isn't cloaked in cloud, the broad ridge offers wonderful views down to the coast, which is reached in under three hours by a steep but well marked path that dives down into the bush.

An alternative for experienced and fit trampers is to follow a loop that joins the Croesus Track with **The Moonlight Track**, marked on the *Arahau* topomap.

Arthur River provides access to the riverside **Rakaitane Track** (30min return) and the **Lake Side Track** (20–60min return) with good mountain views.

The TranzAlpine **train** makes a regular daily stop at Moana. Facilities here are limited, but there's **accommodation** at the *Moana Hotel Motel*, Ahau Street (☎03/738 0083 & 0800/525 327, ⓦwww.moanahotelmotel.co.nz; cabins ❶, rooms ❸, units ❹), and the well-run neighbouring *Lake Brunner Motor Camp* (☎03/738 0600, ⒺLake.brunner@paradise.net.nz; camping $8–10, cabins ❷). The licensed *Station House Café*, Koe Street (☎03/738 0158), offers the best **eating** around about, with lunches from $15, dinners from $22 and views across the lake.

Brunner Industrial Site

Back on SH7, a couple of kilometres past Stillwater, a tall chimney marks the **Brunner Industrial Site** (unrestricted access). Roadside information panels mark the path to a fine old suspension bridge (recently strengthened and refurbished but still only open to foot traffic), which crosses the swirling river to the few remaining buildings and the largely intact ruins of distinctive beehive cooking ovens.

On his explorations in the late 1840s, Thomas Brunner noted the seam of riverside coal. By 1885, the mine site was producing twice as much coal as any other mine in the country and exporting firebricks throughout Australasia, but in 1896 New Zealand's worst mining disaster (with 69 dead) heralded its decline. The site was finally abandoned in the 1940s, and only exhumed from dense bush in the early 1980s. Half an hour wandering around the foundations and the fifty-minute bushwalk to some of the old mine sites evoke a long-gone era.

Westport and around

WESTPORT is one of the West Coast's more dispiriting towns, a drab place of wide streets and slim opportunities which nevertheless warrants a visit for the access it provides to the surrounding area. Fresh walks to the seal colony at **Cape Foulwind** and the ghostly former coal towns of the **Rochford Plateau** compete with the lure of the limestone country and the Heaphy Track, accessed from Karamea 100km north. Besides, as this is a principal transport interchange, you may well end up spending a night or two here, which is made tolerable by good-value accommodation, an interesting museum and a couple of adventure activities.

Westport was the first of the West Coast towns, established by one **Reuben Waite** in 1861 as a single store beside the mouth of the Buller River. He made his living provisioning the few Buller Gorge prospectors in return for gold, but when the miners moved on to richer pickings in Otago, Waite upped sticks and headed south to help found Greymouth. Westport turned to the more dependable coal and, while the mining towns to the north were becoming established, engineers channelled the river to scour out a **port**, which fast became the largest coal port in the country but now lies idle. Westport battles on, with a respectable-sized fishing fleet and the odd ship laden with the produce of New Zealand's largest cement works at Cape Foulwind, which is fuelled by coal from open-cast Stockton, the only large mine left.

Arrival, information and transport

Almost everything of consequence in Westport happens around Palmerston Street. The helpful **visitor centre**, 1 Brougham St (daily: Christmas–Jan 9am–7pm; rest of year 9am–5pm; ☎03/789 6658, Ⓦwww.westport.org.nz), is the place to go for your Heaphy Track info and **hut tickets**, but for the low down on less popular tracks visit the **DOC office**, at 72 Russell St (Mon–Fri 8am–noon & 1–5pm; ☎03/788 8008, Ⓔbulao@doc.govt.nz). There's **Internet access** at The Web Shed, 204 Palmerston St and less conveniently (though cheaper) at the *Denniston Dog* (see p.780).

Bus stops are scattered around town. Atomic and the Mainlander service to Christchurch (☎0800/836 969) stop outside the visitor centre; Cunningham's Coaches from Karamea pull up at their depot at 179 Palmerston St; and InterCity stop outside the Caltex service station at 197 Palmerston St. The

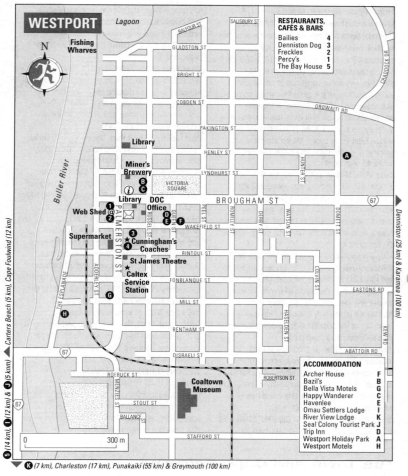

airport, with direct flights to Wellington (1–2 daily except Sat), is 8km south of the centre: Buller **Taxis** (☎03/789 6900) will run you into town for $12. Westport is compact enough for you to **get around** on foot, though to reach the nearby attractions you'll need your own transport or a taxi. **Bike rental** is available from Becker's Sports World, 204 Palmerston St ($20 a day; ☎03/789 8787).

Accommodation

Accommodation is surprisingly abundant in Westport, so it isn't hard to find somewhere to stay. **Backpackers** are well catered for, and there's a cluster of decent **motels** along Palmerston Street, though the choice of more luxurious places is limited. Budget travellers might want to consider a couple of excellent hostels around 20km south towards Punakaiki (see p.788).

Archer House 75 Queen St ☎03/789 8778, ⓦwww.archerhouse.co.nz. Classy B&B in a spacious, heritage home offering ensuite or private facilities, and a large sunny lounge. ❼

Bazil's 54 Russell St ☎03/789 6410 & 0800/303 741, ⓔbazils.backpackers@xtra.co.nz. An attractive, airy house converted to backpacker accommodation, with a pleasant garden, some nice modern doubles and twins, a separate self-contained house with three doubles, and bike rental for $5 a day. It is the favoured destination of Kiwi Experience buses, the occupants of which descend upon the place en masse. Camping $12, dorms ❶, rooms ❷.

Bella Vista Motels 314 Palmerston St ☎0800/493 787 ⓔbella.vista.westport@xtra .co.nz. Ugly but modern and well-appointed motel with Sky TV. The studios are small and have limited cooking facilities, but larger ones are much more spacious and some have spa baths. Studios ❹, spa units ❺

Happy Wanderer 56 Russell St ☎03/789 8627, ⓔhappywanderer@xtra.co.nz. Large, comfortable and sprawling associate-YHA hostel that has rooms in three buildings, the dorms all having TV, toilet, shower and their own kitchen. Many of the newer doubles are particularly luxurious. Non-guests can make use of the showers ($3). Camping & powered sites $10, dorms ❶, rooms ❷

Havenlee 76 Queen St ☎03/789 8502 & 0800/673 619, ⓦwww.havanlee.co.nz. One comfortable twin and two doubles, with shared facilities, in a very friendly homestay where you're plied with a continental breakfast and helpful information each morning. ❺

Omau Settlers Lodge 1054 Cape Rd, 12km west of Westport ☎03/789 5200 & 0800/466 287,

ⓔthecape@xtra.co.nz. Brand-new luxury units with beautiful recycled-wood-floored bathrooms, kettle and fridge, and continental breakfast included. Just a short drive from *The Bay House* restaurant. ❻

River View Lodge Buller Gorge Rd, 7km south of Westport ☎03/789 6037, ⓦwww.rurallodge.co.nz. Attractive lodge overlooking the Buller River with four en-suite rooms each with a veranda. Three-course dinners by arrangement ($45, which also gets you a glass of wine). ❼

Seal Colony Tourist Park Marine Parade, Carters Beach, 5km west ☎03/789 8002 & 0508/937 876, ⓦwww.sealcolonytouristpark.co.nz. Spacious, fully equipped Top 10 site with some very comfortable motel units fronting onto a broad beach on the way to Cape Foulwind. Camping $12, cabins ❷, motel units ❹–❺

Trip Inn 72 Queen St ☎03/789 7367, ⓔtripinn@clear.net.nz. Small dorms, doubles and some family units in a big old rambling back-packers that discourages the backpacker tour buses. There's a barbecue area and all the usual features, including plenty of videos, though no quiet lounge. Camping $12, dorms ❶, rooms ❷

Westport Holiday Park 31–37 Domett St ☎03/789 7043, ⓔwestportholidaypark @xtra.co.nz. Smallish, low-key site partly hemmed in by native bush and ten minutes' walk from the town centre. Camping $9–10, dorms ❶, cabins & ensuite chalets ❷, motels ❸–❹

Westport Motels 32 The Esplanade ☎03/789 7575, ☎0800/805 909, ⓔwestportmotel@xtra.co.nz. These older motel units are all well-appointed and come complete with modern kitchens. Cooked ($12) or continental ($9) breakfast is also served. ❹

The Town and Cape Foulwind

Anyone with even the vaguest interest in Westport's coal-mining past should visit **Coaltown**, Queen Street (daily 9am–4.30pm; $7), an imaginatively presented museum concentrating on the Buller coalfield. Scenes of the workings in their heyday pack an interesting video, which complements remnants salvaged from the site – a coal wagon on tracks angled as it was in situ, at an unsettling forty degrees, and a huge braking drum – and a mock-up of a mine tunnel, complete with musty smells and clanking sound effects. Fascinating photos of the tramways in operation, a scale model of the plateau and a collection of miners' hats and lamps round out this engaging exhibition. The museum also tries to fulfil the role of a pioneer museum, with less compelling exhibits on gold dredging, the Buller earthquakes, brewing and the town's maritime history.

Before leaving town, try the preservative- and chemical-free beers made by the co-operatively run **Miner's Brewery**, 10 Lyndhurst St (Mon–Sat 10am–5.30pm; ☎03/789 6201), which distributes its beers throughout the northern half of the South Island and offers free tasting of their draught, dark, Pilsner and the organic "Green Fern" lager.

Cape Foulwind

Once again we have Captain Cook, battling heavy weather in March 1770, to thank for the naming of Westport's most dramatic and evocatively titled stretch of coastline, **Cape Foulwind**, 12km west of town. Cook's name has stuck, and also lends itself to the undulating four-kilometre **Cape Foulwind Walkway**, which runs over exposed headlands, airing superb coastal views. It is perfect for sunset ambling between the old lighthouse, a replica of Abel Tasman's astrolabe and the **Tauranga Bay Seal Colony**, where platforms overlook New Zealand's most northerly breeding colony of fur seals. The seals are at their most active and numerous from October to January, often numbering three hundred or more, a sign of the welcome recovery from the decimation of 150 years of sealing.

The quickest access to the seals is from the sandy but treacherous beach of Tauranga Bay, accessible by road and at the southern end of the walkway, ten minutes along from the seals. To save retracing your steps all the way back, look for a marker around the halfway point, indicating an alternative route around the foot of the cliffs.

Activities

As the largest town hereabouts, Westport has become the base for a couple of adventure companies, both operating trips some distance from town. The bread-and-butter trip for Norwest Adventures (℡0800/116 686, Ⓦwww.caverafting.com) is **Underworld Rafting** (4–5hr; $120), which starts with a minibus trip 28km south to the Charleston Tavern (see p.787): you can also join the trip here for the same price. A short train ride and a bushwalk through a dramatic valley of limestone bluffs within the Paparoa National Park gets you to the trip proper. This involves an informative guided walk through the Metro cave system; you'll be decked out in wetsuit and caver's helmet, and lugging a rubber inner tube, which comes into play for the final drift down a flooded glow-worm cave and out through a gorgeous ravine into the Nile River. None of it is tremendously arduous; if you like caves and water, you'll like this. For the more timid there's the **Glowworm Cave Tour** (3hr; around $60), and they also run a trip for experienced cavers.

Rafting and jetboating are run by Buller Adventure Tours (℡03/789 7286 & 0800/697 286, Ⓦwww.adventuretours.co.nz), located some 8km east of Westport on SH6, heading into the Buller Gorge. Throughout the year they run the six major rapids of the Grade IV "Earthquake Slip" section of the **Buller River**, around Lyell, spending over two hours on the water for $95. Trips to more isolated rivers reached by helicopter are run less often and are dependent on numbers, so booking in advance is recommended. They also offer **jetboat rides** through the Lower Buller Gorge (1hr; $65), **horse trekking** through bush and along a river beach (from $50) and forty-minute rides in an eight-wheeled all-terrain vehicle ($30).

Eating, drinking and nightlife

Westport has fewer decent **places to eat** than the other towns on the West Coast, and if you want anything flasher than tearoom fare and pub meals you'll have to drive out to *The Bay House*. **Pubs** are plentiful, most following the West Coast tradition, with those towards the northern end of Palmerston Street exhibiting a raw edge. **Nightlife** is limited to occasional bands at *Bailies* or the *Denniston Dog* and **movies** at the fine St James Theatre, 193 Palmerston St (℗03/789 8936), where in the interval you can slurp one of their glorious ice creams.

Bailies 187 Palmerston St. Westport's best attempt at an Irish pub – only Guinness, pint glasses and the odd folk-music CD distinguishing it from the others. Pretty lively though, and with decent bar lunches, a cook-it-yourself barbecue, and occasional live music at weekends. Popular with the Kiwi Experience bus.

The Bay House Tauranga Bay ℗03/789 7133. Superb restaurant/café out towards the seal colony at the southern end of the Cape Foulwind Walkway. Coffee, lunch and excellent dinners (mains around $28) – such as fillet of beef with potato and parsnip rosti, locally caught turbot, at least one veggie option and mouth-watering desserts – are served in the cosy interior or on the terrace, where you can watch the surfers on the bay. Open for lunch and dinner daily plus weekend brunch.

Denniston Dog 18 Wakefield St ℗03/789 7640. Sophisticated (for Westport) café/bar with a good range of beers and excellent meals including Cajun fillets and green-lipped mussels. Occasional DJs and live music.

Freckles 216 Palmerston St. Simple breakfasts, hearty sandwiches, quiches and cakes, and a few tasty treats such as Thai beef burgers ($9). There's also peaceful seating out at the back. Closed Sun.

Percy's 198 Palmerston St ℗03/789 6648. Modern, licensed café open for snacks, lunch and dinner, offering steaks, venison, veggie stacks and heavenly bananas mixed with caramel, rum, pecan nuts and vanilla ice cream.

Around Westport

Westport's role as a service town was entirely dependent on trade from the coal-mining towns to the north, towns often sited in such inhospitable spots that fresh vegetables were hard to grow and sheep were almost impossible to raise. Foremost among them was **Denniston**, for years New Zealand's most productive coalfield, located high on the Rochford Plateau. Coal hasn't been mined here in any quantity since the late 1960s; houses have been carted away and the bush is rapidly engulfing what remains of the mining machinery. It makes an intriguing place to explore for half a day, or longer if you want to tackle the **Denniston Incline Walk**. All the other deep mines have gone the same way, leaving a legacy of inclines, tramways and rusting machinery that can be visited on a number of walks, the **Charming Creek Walk** being the best.

Denniston

The Karamea Road runs north from Westport 17km to Waimangaroa, the junction for a steep 9km road that wends its way 600m up to the semi-ghost-town of **DENNISTON**, the best-preserved example of a mining community.

The Coalbrookdale Seam was first discovered by one John Rochford in 1859, and the plateau was soon humming with activity, though the difficult access slowed development until the construction of the **Denniston Self-acting Incline** in 1879. Regarded as something of an engineering marvel in its time, and still impressive today, this gravity-powered tramway was the steepest rail-wagon incline in the world, lowering coal-filled wagons 518m over 1.7km, while hauling up empty wagons. Throughout its 88-year lifespan, over a thousand tonnes of coal a day would rattle at a prodigious 70km/hr down to Conn's Creek, where they would be marshalled onto rail tracks for the trip into Westport. Initially everything destined for Denniston – goods, machinery and people – also came up the incline but after four people were flung to their death from careering wagons, a path was constructed in 1884 and sixteen years later the road was put in, finally easing some of the hardship of living up on the plateau.

Denniston was joined by Coalbrookdale and Burnett's Face, the three jointly peaking at around 2500 inhabitants around 1910 when they were served by a post office, six hotels and numerous shops. The accessible coal eventually played out and the incline closed in 1967. After limping by on a skeleton staff for several years, the last coal was extracted in 1997, leaving the post office, a fire station, half a dozen scattered houses, occupied by thirteen people and a treasure trove of industrial archeology centred on a gaunt winding derrick.

The coastal views from up here are impressive, but the greatest pleasure is in just rambling about (exercising care not to disappear down mine shafts), especially when bad weather brings a blanket of cloud and damp fog down over the town, adding a suitably ethereal quality to this desolate landscape.

The old schoolhouse here has been turned into a small "Friends of the Hill" **museum** and **visitor centre** (Sun only 10am–3pm; free), containing historical photos and old mining machinery. It all comes alive when you talk to curator, Gary James (℡03/789 9755), who is usually happy to open up at any time.

Fit and ambitious visitors to Denniston can tackle the **Denniston Walk** (2km one way; 2–3hr; 520m ascent), starting at Conn's Creek, 2km inland from Waimangaroa. The route follows the 1884 path roughly parallel to the incline, but the most interesting section is close to the top and can more easily be reached from Denniston. From Denniston to Middle Brake (1hr 30min return), the incline can still be seen in the bush, as can the midway point where wagons were disconnected from one hauling cable and connected to another for the lower half of the journey.

Minor roads continue beyond Denniston to the sites of Burnetts Face and Coalbrookdale, neither of which have much to detain you, but you can pass a day exploring the backroads and walkways then repair to *The Railway Tavern* in Waimangaroa to admire the photos of Denniston.

North of Waimangaroa

The road north of Waimangaroa, SH67 runs 7km to **Granity**, where you can break your journey with a coffee from the daytime *Drifters Café and Bar*, then continues 2km to **Ngakawau**. Here, a coal depot signals the start of the lovely **Charming Creek Walk** (5km one way; 2hr; 100m ascent), which follows an old railway that was used for timber and coal extraction between 1914 and 1958. The first half hour is the least diverting, but things improve dramatically after the S-shaped Irishman's Tunnel, with great views of the boulder-strewn river below and, after a swingbridge river crossing, the Mangatini Falls. From here to the picnic stop by the remains of Watson's Mills is the most interesting section of the walk and is commonly the furthest people get (2–3hr return). The walk finishes among the manuka and gorse scrub and post-industrial wasteland of Charming Creek Mine, which is also accessible by 12km of mostly dirt road through the hamlet of Seddonville, just beside the Mokihinui River.

Ngakawau merges imperceptibly with **Hector**, notably mainly for *The Old Slaughterhouse*, 2km north of the village on the SH67, a small **hostel** (℡03/782 8333; dorms ❶, rooms ❸) in a lovely wooden house perched on the hillside with vast ocean views, a couple of big, soft dogs and welcoming hosts. There are good bush walks all about, and Hector's dolphins regularly play in the surf. Access is by a steep ten-minute walk off SH67, though if you call ahead they'll meet you with a quad-bike.

There's more accommodation and some good meals 15km further north at the *Gentle Annie Coastal Enclave* (℡03/782 1826, ⓦwww.gentleannie.co.nz; camping $8, dorms ❶, rooms ❷, cottages sleeping 6–9 $90–120 per couple), a very relaxed place beautifully sited near the mouth of the Mokihinui River, beside

Gentle Annie Beach; turn left off the highway on the Karamea side of the bridge and head 3km west of SH67 on an unsealed road. Accommodation ranges from camping and a budget lodge to spacious and well-equipped self-catering cottages all with either sea or river views; swimming, horse riding and canoeing can all be organised. The adjacent *Cow Shed* (Nov–April daily 9am–5pm) presents fresh, wholesome and moderately priced meals in a converted cow shed or outside in the extensive grounds – well-worth a diversion from the highway.

Karamea and the Oparara Basin

The northwestern corner of the South Island competes with Fiordland as the least developed and most inaccessible region in the country, a distinction acknowledged by the formation of the **Kahurangi National Park** in 1996. The second-largest park in the country, it embraces a vast wilderness of spectacular hill country supporting alpine meadows, the high Matiri ("Thousand Acre") Plateau, New Zealand's finest karst landscape, dramatic windswept beaches and a coastal strip warm enough to support extensive stands of nikau palms. Charles Heaphy and Thomas Brunner surveyed the region in 1846, paving the way for European and Chinese goldminers, who came a couple of decades later and sporadically took thin pickings as late as the Depression years of the 1930s. Pioneers followed, establishing themselves at **Karamea**, now the base for visiting the fine limestone country in the southern half of the park – and the first sign of civilization for walkers coming off the Heaphy Track (see p.784); other activities in the area are concentrated in the **Oparara Basin** and the final straight of the track.

The road north from Westport initially runs parallel to the coast, pinched between the pounding Tasman breakers and bush-clad hills as it passes through meagre hamlets with barely a shop or a pub. The journey takes almost two hours if you don't stop, though there are plenty of opportunities to do so, not least at the coal towns around Westport (see p.780). North of the **Mokihinui River**, the road leaves the coastal strip, twisting and climbing over **Karamea Bluff** before descending again into a rich apron of dairying land. Rainfall begins to drop off and humidity picks up, promoting more subtropical vegetation, characterized by marauding cabbage trees and coastal nikau palms. At the foot of the bluff, **Little Wanganui** marks the turn-off for the start of the **Wangapeka** and **Leslie-Karamea** tracks (jointly 52km; 3–5 days), which traverses the southern half of the Kahurangi National Park to Matariki, 50km west of Nelson. Though they lack the coastal scenery of the more famous Heaphy Track, they easily compensate with dramatic mountain terrain. Trampers searching for something quieter than the Heaphy should pick up the DOC's *Wangapeka Track* leaflet ($1), and be prepared for backcountry huts.

Karamea

Diminutive **KARAMEA**, 100km north of Westport, is one of those places where doing nothing seems just right. This peaceful and isolated spot is virtually at the end of the road; to continue any distance north, you'd have to go on foot along the Heaphy Track. At the same time there is no shortage of things to do in the vicinity, the southern section of the Kahurangi National Park easily justifying a day or two of exploration.

Back in 1874, when land grants lured pioneers to a dense and isolated patch of bush at the mouth of the Karamea River, this was very much

frontier territory, with the port providing the only link with the outside world. Settlers on the south shore of the Karamea River eked a living from **gold** and **flax**, but after a couple of fruitless years realized that the poorly drained *pakihi* soils wouldn't support them. Haunted by ill fortune, they moved upstream and north of the river to the current town site which, sure enough, soon after their move, was devastated by **floods**. Determinedly they pushed on, opening up the first road to Westport just in time for the upheavals of the 1929 Murchison **earthquake**, which altered the river flow and permanently ruined the harbour. Life hasn't been much better since and logging finally ceased in 2000 leaving **tourism** and agriculture as the town's lifeblood.

Only devoted fans could spend more than ten minutes among the pioneering and sawmilling paraphernalia inside the **Karamea Centennial Museum** (Christmas–Feb Mon, Tues & Thurs–Sat 10.30am–5pm; other times by arrangement ☏03/782 6652; $2), on the SH67 just by the *Last Resort*. Otherwise there's **swimming** and **fishing** in the Karamea River, or **canoeing** through the beautiful and fairly gentle Karamea Gorge. Canoes are best organised through the *Karamea Holiday Park* (see below) who charge $20 for a drop off and float back; *The Last Resort* do similar but charge a few dollars more.

Karamea is also a base for some top class, fly-in **whitewater rafting** on the Karamea River though most trips (see box, p.802) are run from Murchison or Greymouth.

Practicalities

The **visitor centre** at Market Cross, 2km east of the centre (Jan–April daily 9am–5pm; May–Dec Mon–Fri 9am–5pm & Sat 9am–1pm; ☏03/782 6652, ⓦ www.karameainfo.co.nz), has information about exploring the local area, **Internet access**, and issues **hut passes** for the Heaphy Track, as do *The Last Resort* and the *Karamea Village Hotel*. The **Heaphy Track** is generally walked from north to south and is covered on p.575.

Two scheduled **bus** services ply the Westport–Karamea route: Cunningham's Coaches (in Westport ☏03/789 7177) run to Westport in the morning (Mon–Fri only; $15 each way, bikes $7), returning in the afternoon; Karamea Express (Nov–Easter Mon–Sat; Easter–Oct Mon–Fri; $20 each way; ☏03/782 6757) also run to Westport in the morning and set off around 11.30am for the return journey. Both buses connect with ongoing services in Westport. Karamea Express also serves the **Heaphy Track** trailhead at Kohaihai (late-Oct to Easter daily around 2pm; $8 each way; in winter on demand), as do Cunningham's, who also run to the Wangapeka ($8 each way).

In recent years Karamea has begun to gear itself for tourism and there are now quite a few **places to stay**, and some good **camping** spots (see below). The only **places to eat** are the daytime *Saracens Café*, opposite the visitor centre, which serves coffee, pies, enormous sausage rolls and sandwiches in a craft gallery; the *Karamea Village Hotel*, which dishes up cheap takeaways, straightforward bar meals and a good selection of "Wild Food" dishes including renowned whitebait meals ($30); and *The Last Resort*, with pub snacks and meals at the *LR Café & Bar* (licensed), and the *à la carte* main restaurant, where you can get good-quality meat and fish for around $25.

Accommodation

Bridge Farm Motels SH67, 600m south of the visitor centre ☏03/782 6955 & 0800/527 263, ⓦ www.karameamotels.co.nz. Modern motel units on a deer and alpaca farm with spacious, well-

appointed units, some with full kitchens and spa bath, and all with continental breakfast included. ❹

Karamea Domain on SH67 in between *The Last Resort* and the *Karamea Village Hotel*; no phone, enquire at adjacent caravan. Fairly primitive site utilizing the showers and toilets for the town's sports field but with a good kitchen. Camping & hookups $8–10 per site, dorms ❶

Karamea Holiday Park SH67, 3km south of town ⓣ03/782 6758, ⓦwww.karamea.com. Commercial campground on a neat and well-kept site with ageing cabins and motel units. They also run canoe trips down the Karamea gorge (see above) and rent canoes ($16 for 4hr). Camping $9–10, cabins ❷, motels ❸

Karamea Lodge SH6, 5km south of town ⓣ03/782 6034, ⓦwww.bnb.co.nz/karamealodge.html. Luxury units with decks, sea views and a common kitchen and lounge. ❻

The Last Resort SH67 ⓣ03/782 6617 & 0800/505 042, ⓦwww.lastresort.co.nz. Modern salvaged-timber-and-turf-roofed complex that has lost some of its charisma but still offers good accommodation: dorm rooms (no bunks but also no kitchen); simple but attractive lodge rooms; unimaginative motel-style studios; and well-appointed "cottages" sleeping four. They also have a restaurant, café and bar on site, a spa ($7 per half-hour for two), rent bikes ($25 a day) and have Internet access. Dorms ❶, lodge ❸, ensuite lodge ❹, studios ❺, cottages ❻

Punga Lodge SH67 ⓣ03/782 6667. Welcoming and comfortable hostel that some might find overly casual in its approach. Expect four-to-eight bed dorms, made-up doubles and a lounge with big stereo and TV. Dorms ❶, rooms ❷

The Oparara Basin and Kohaihai

Kahurangi's finest limestone formations lie east of the Karamea–Kohaihai Road in the **Oparara Basin**, a compact area of **karst** topography characterized by numerous sinkholes, underground streams, caves and bridges created over millennia by the action of slightly acidic streams on the heavily jointed rock. This is home to New Zealand's largest native **spider**, the harmless, 15cm-diameter gradungular spider (found only in caves in the Karamea and Collingwood area, where it feeds off blowflies and cave crickets), and to a rare species of ancient and primitive carnivorous **snail** that grows up to 70mm across and dines on earthworms. Tannin-stained rivers course gently over bleached-white boulders and, in faster-flowing sections, the rare whio (blue duck) swims for its supper. If your interest in geology is fleeting, the Oparara Basin still makes a superb place for an afternoon **swim** or a **picnic** by one of the rivers.

Ten kilometres north of Karamea, North Beach marks the turn-off for the steep and narrow 16km dirt road to the **Honeycomb Caves**, only discovered in the 1970s and a valuable key to understanding New Zealand's fauna. The lime-rich sediment on the cave floor has helped preserve the ancient skeletons of birds, most of them killed when they fell through holes in the cave roof. Bones of over fifty species have been found here including those of the Haast Eagle, the largest eagle ever known with a wingspan of up to four metres. In total there are 15km of passages through the cave system, some of which can only be visited on the excellent and educational **Honeycomb Hill Cave Tour** ($65; ⓣ03/782 6111, ⓦwww.adventurenz.co.nz). Tours depart from the end of McCallums Mill car park, close to the cave and takes three hours: call for reservations and they may be able to organise a ride out there. Cave trips can be combined with the **Honeycomb Arch Kayak Tour** (separately $85), a gorgeous float among organic forms.

As is common in limestone areas, the watercourses alter frequently, leaving behind dry caves such as the **Crazy Paving and Box Canyon caves** (about 10min return), just near the Honeycomb Caves. Both are accessible by a five-minute track from the road-end car park and are good for spider- and fossil-spotting: take a torch each, and watch out for slippery floors.

The two most spectacular examples of limestone architecture lie at the end of beautiful, short bushwalks signposted from a car park 3km back down the road towards Karamea. The largest is the **Oparara Arch** (40min return), a vast two-tiered bridge 43m high, 40m wide and over 219m long, which appears magically out of the bush but defies any attempt at successful photography. The **Moria Gate Arch** (1hr return) is a little more distant, though the untouched, high-canopy native forest and a magnificent cavern make it all worthwhile. A short path to the deep black reflections in **Mirror Tarn** (20min return) spurs off the road close to the start of the Moria Gate Arch walk.

Kohaihai

Visitors with no aspirations to tramp the full length of Heaphy Track can sample the final few coastal kilometres from the mouth of the Kohaihai River, 17km north of Karamea, where there is good river (but not sea) swimming, a beautifully-sited, toilets-and-water DOC **campsite** ($5) and an abundance of sandflies. In the heat of the day, you're much better off across the river in the cool of the **Nikau Walk** (30–40min loop), which winds through a wonderfully shaded grove dense with nikau palms, tree ferns and magnificent gnarled old rata trees dripping in epiphytes. When it cools off, either continue along the Heaphy to **Scott's Beach** (1hr 30min return), or stick to the southern side of the Kohaihai River and the **Zig-Zag Track** (35min return), which switchbacks up to an expansive lookout.

Paparoa National Park and around

South of Westport lies the Paparoa Range, a 1500m granite and gneiss ridge inlaid with limestone that separates the dramatic coastal strip from the valleys of the Grey and Inungahua rivers. In 1987, the limestone country of the South Island's western flank was designated the **Paparoa National Park**, still one of the country's smallest and least-known parks. The highlight is undoubtedly the **Pancake Rocks**, where crashing waves have forced spectacular blowholes through a stratified, pancake-like stack of weathered limestone. But to skip the rest would be to miss out on a mysterious world of disappearing rivers, sinkholes, caves and limestone bluffs best seen on the **Inland Pack Track**, but also accessible on shorter walks up river valleys close to Punakaiki.

Fertile limestone soils always support distinctive flora and fauna, a trait exaggerated here by the Tasman Convergence, a current warmed in the Coral Sea off Queensland, Australia. Striking this stretch of coast, the current creates a balmy microclimate favoured by the **Westland black petrel** and some of New Zealand's largest and noisiest native **cicadas**.

The mild climate provided a sustaining bounty for **Maori**, who often stopped here while travelling the coast in search of *pounamu* (greenstone). Early **European explorers** followed suit seeking agricultural land. Charles Heaphy, Thomas Brunner and two Maori guides came through in 1846, finding little to detain them, but within twenty years this stretch of coast was alive with **gold** prospectors at work on the black sands at the towns of **Charleston** and **Brighton**, the former barely hanging on, the latter long gone.

Visitor interest is centred on **Punakaiki**, close by the Pancake Rocks, where bus passengers get a quick glimpse and others pause for the obligatory photos. A couple of days spent here will be well rewarded with a stack of wonderful walks, horse riding, canoeing up delightful limestone gorges and just slobbing about.

Westport to Punakaiki

South of Westport, SH67 crosses the Buller River and picks up SH6, the main West Coast road. There's little reason to stop except for a couple of good **places to stay**. Around 17km south of Westport, *Beaconstone Eco Lodge* (☎027/431 0491; closed June–Sept; shares ❶, rooms ❷) is one of the best places to stay on this part of the coast, a great-value and welcoming backpacker lodge, with a few doubles and one triple. Eco-friendly features include composting toilets and solar power, and it's set in 120 acres of native bush threaded by various trails. Continue 4km south to reach *Jack's Gasthof* (☎03/789 6501, ✉jack.schubert@xtra.co.nz; ❸), just a couple of colourful, budget **rooms**, basic **camping** ($5) and a café and bar serving great pizza and the likes of Thai curry, Greek salad and fruit shakes: many of the ingredients are fresh from the garden and are organic. The whole set-up is pretty laid-back, with a sauna, swimming in the creek and loads of great bush walking.

A couple of kilometres further along SH6 is **Mitchells Gully Gold Mine** (usually 9am–4pm; $5; ☎03/789 6553), a family-run mine working dating back to 1866, which has been reopened mainly to demonstrate the time-honoured methods used to extract fine gold held in a cement-like mass of oxidized ironsand. Along with a predictable collection of mining

Paparoa walks and the Inland Pack Track

The 1:50,000 Paparoa National Park map ($15) covers the region in great detail, but DOC's Inland Pack Track leaflet (50¢) provides enough information for that tramp.

The best way to truly appreciate the dramatic limestone scenery of the Paparoas is on the **Inland Pack Track** (27km; 2–3 days). Most of the terrain is easy going with only one low hill to negotiate, but there are no bridges for river crossings, and while the water barely gets above your knees in dry periods, you need to be aware of the possibility of flash floods. With less time or greater demand for comfort, some of the best can be seen on two day-walks. The delightful **Punakaiki–Pororari Rivers Loop** (12km; 3hr 30min; 100m ascent) follows the initial stretch of the Inland Pack Track as far as the Pororari River, which is then followed downstream between some magnificent limestone cliffs to return to Punakaiki. The **Fox River Cave Walk** (10km; 2hr 30min; 100m ascent) traces the last few kilometres of the Inland Pack Track from the Fox Rivermouth as far as the caves and returns the same way.

Practicalities

The Inland Pack Track can be walked in either direction, though by going from south to north you eliminate the risk of missing the critical turn-off up Fossil Creek. There are no huts along the way and you're advised to carry a **tent**. This isn't absolutely necessary, as trampers can shelter under the rock **bivvy** known as the Ballroom Overhang at the end of a long first day; by carrying full **camping gear**, though, you get protection from bugs, earn the freedom to break the walk into more manageable chunks and, perhaps most importantly, avoid a wet night in the open if the rivers flood. Choose a spot well away from flood risk areas and take care off the main track, as there are unmarked sinkholes. **Campfires** are permitted at the Ballroom Overhang, but DOC recommends carrying a stove as most of the usable wood has already been burned. All tracks can become difficult or even hazardous in some weather conditions, so check the latest **weather forecast**, available from the visitor centre in Punakaiki, where you should fill out an **intentions form**, remembering to check in on your return.

Drivers should leave their vehicle at the end of the walk and either hitch or catch one of the infrequent **buses** to get to the start. Alternatively, base yourself in Punakaiki and call *The Rocks* **homestay** (☎03/731 1141) who run a drop-off and pick-up service for around $25 per run (max 4 people.)

paraphernalia, you can see a restored overshot wheel driving a stamping battery, and water races and tunnels that are still in use.

The most intensive mining went on 3km to the south at **CHARLESTON**, then a rollicking boom town of around 18,000 people, but now with a mere thirty residents. Apart from a pretty bay and a couple of short coastal walks, there really isn't much to see, though the *Charleston Tavern* acts as a meeting point for Westport-based Underworld Rafting (see p.779). For a less boisterous look at the local features, join their **Nile River Rainforest Train** (3–4 daily; $20) a 25-minute interpretive journey on a modern narrow-gauge train through some nice limestone country. The *Charleston Tavern* dishes up suitably modern fare of nachos and grills, and you can stay nearby either at the modest *Charleston Motel* (☎ & ℱ 03/789 7599; ❹), or at the *Charleston Motor Camp* (☎ & ℱ 03/789 6773; camping $8–10, cabins ❷).

Some 20km south of Charleston, the Fox River marks the site of the classic boom-and-bust town of **Brighton**, which experienced just four months of frantic activity in 1867, temporarily eclipsing Charleston for gold exports. Immediately to the south rise the 50m cliffs of Te Miko – tagged Perpendicular

---

The Inland Pack Track

The starting point of the Inland Pack Track is 1km south of the Punakaiki visitor centre at the end of a 1.5-kilometre track that follows the south bank of the Punakaiki River to a car park. From **Punakaiki River to Pororari River** (3.5km; 2hr 30min; 120m ascent, 100m descent), the track crosses to the true right bank then cuts northeast, gradually rising to a low saddle then descending to the ford of the Pororari River. From **Pororari River to Bullock Creek** (6km; 2hr; 100m ascent) it stays pretty level with views inland to the Paparoa Range before reaching Bullock Creek, which should be forded with some care – in flood conditions a wall of water courses down the creek's usually dry lower section. Camping is possible on the DOC-owned farm by the Bullock Creek crossing. From **Bullock Creek to Dilemma Creek** (8km; 2hr 30min; 100m ascent, 100m descent), the farm track soon becomes a path, skirting swampland then climbing to a ridge. Descend gradually to Fossil Creek, where you wade downstream from pool to pool, occasionally clambering over fallen tree trunks. After half an hour of this, Fossil Creek meets the main tributary of the Fox River, Dilemma Creek, by a small sign – keep your eyes peeled. Heading **downstream to Fox River** (2km; 1hr; gradual descent) is the most dramatic section of the trip but potentially the most dangerous, with 18 fords to cross between gravel banks in the bed of Dilemma Creek: if you have any doubts about the first crossing, turn back, as they only get worse. The lower river carves out a deep canyon between gleaming white vertical cliffs and, if you can find a patch of sun, this makes a great place to rest awhile. The track resumes by a sign on the true left bank just above the confluence with the Fox River; a steep bluff on the right makes a useful landmark.

Even if you don't plan to stay, the vast limestone **Ballroom Overhang** (1km; 30min each way; negligible ascent) is worth a look. A signposted track crosses to the true right bank of the Fox River below the confluence, then crosses several more times higher up. There's no chance you'll miss the 100m-long lip, which could easily provide shelter for a hundred or more campers; a long-drop toilet has been installed and a huge fire pit has developed. Return the same way to **the confluence**, from where the track runs **to the Fox Rivermouth** (5km; 2hr; 100m descent). A short distance along, a sign points across the river to the interesting **Fox River Cave** (30min). Meanwhile, the Inland Pack Track crosses to the car park by the Fox Rivermouth, some 12km by road from your starting point; the southbound InterCity **bus** currently passes around noon, or you can walk back to Punakaiki along SH6.

Point by Charles Heaphy, who in 1846 recorded climbing the cliff on two stages of ladders constructed of shaky and rotten rata vines while his dog was hoisted on a rope. The vines were later replaced by a chain ladder, but Te Miko remained an impenetrable barrier to pack animals until 1866, when the combined needs of traders and the new Westport–Greymouth telegraph line prompted the forging of the **Inland Pack Track**, a path now followed by the tramp of the same name (see p.787).

The coast road, finally completed in 1927, now climbs over Te Miko, passing the **Iramahuwhero Point Lookout**, with stupendous views along the coast past the layered rocks of the Te Miko cliff.

Punakaiki and the Pancake Rocks

The **Pancake Rocks** and blowholes at **PUNAKAIKI** are often all visitors see of the Paparoa National Park, as they tumble off the bus outside the visitor centre opposite the ten-minute long paved track which leads from the road to Dolomite Point. Here layers of limestone have weathered to resemble an immense stack of giant pancakes created by **stylobedding**, a chemical process in which the pressure of overlying sediments creates alternating durable and weaker bands. Subsequent uplift and weathering has accentuated this effect to create wonderfully photogenic formations. The edifice is undermined by huge sea caverns where the surf surges in, sending spumes of brine spouting up through vast **blowholes**: high tide with a good swell from the south or southwest sees the blowholes at their best.

More shapely examples of Paparoa's karst landscape are on show on a number of walks. The **Punakaiki Cavern Track** (5min return), 500m to the north, leads into a glow-worm cave (go after dark: torch essential), and 2km beyond that, the **Truman Track** (30min return) runs down from the highway to a small beach hemmed in by wave-sculpted rock platforms.

No matter how slight your interest in birds, you could hardly fail to be impressed by the sight of **Westland black petrels** (*taiko*) bundling through the trees at dusk to the world's only breeding colony of this, the largest of the burrow-nesting petrels. These relatives of the albatross glide effortlessly at sea, where they live most of their lives, but are less gainly when they leave their offshore rafts to crash land at their burrows. Birds arrive nightly from April to November, but activity reaches fever pitch from April to June, when the eggs are laid and hatched. Unfortunately there are no longer any tours, but if you're really keen contact Paparoa Nature Tours in Christchurch (℡03/322 7898), who visit a viewing platform right in the middle of a sub-colony.

Kiwa Sea Adventures run excellent nature trips (Dec–Feb daily; 2–3hr; $110; ℡768 7765, ⓦwww.raclay.co.nz), taking to the ocean in search of Hector's, dusky and common dolphins with a maximum of five onboard. They make no promises, but usually find something and offer the opportunity to go **dolphin swimming**. More conventional swimming spots are rare along the West Coast but relatively abundant here, with good **river swimming** in the Pororari and Punakaiki rivers, and **sea bathing** at the southern end of Pororari Beach, a section also good for point-break **surfing**.

Keeping with aquatic pursuits, Punakaiki Canoes (℡03/731 1870, ⓦwww.riverkayaking.co.nz) rent out **kayaks** ($30 for 2hrs, $50 per day) from their base beside the Pororari River; and run guided trips from $80. There's also excellent **horse riding** with Punakaiki Horse Treks (Oct–April; ℡03/731 1839), who charge $95 for two and a half hours trekking through bush, rivers and along the beach; and a range of **caving** and **environmental tours** with

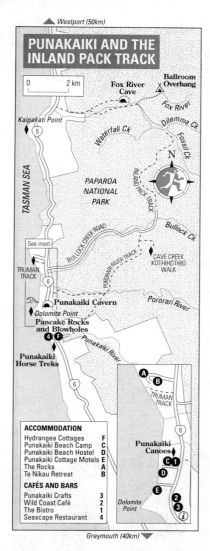

PUNAKAIKI AND THE INLAND PACK TRACK

▲ Westport (50km)

0   2 km

Ballroom Overhang

Fox River Cave

Fox River

Kaipakati Point

6

Dilemma Ck

Waterfall Ck

Fossil Ck

N

TASMAN SEA

PAPAROA NATIONAL PARK

INLAND PACK TRACK

Bullock Ck

See inset

TRUMAN TRACK

6

BULLOCK CREEK ROAD

PORORARI RIVER TRACK

CAVE CREEK KOTHIHOTHIO WALK

Punakaiki Cavern

Pororari River

Dolomite Point

Pancake Rocks and Blowholes

4 F

Punakaiki River

Punakaiki Horse Treks

6

A
A   B

TRUMAN TRACK

6

ACCOMMODATION

Hydrangea Cottages	F
Punakaiki Beach Camp	C
Punakaiki Beach Hostel	D
Punakaiki Cottage Motels	E
The Rocks	A
Te Nikau Retreat	B

Punakaiki Canoes

C 1

D

E

CAFÉS AND BARS

Punakaiki Crafts	3
Wild Coast Café	2
The Bistro	1
Seascape Restaurant	4

Punakaiki Canoes

Dolomite Point

2
3

i

Greymouth (40km) ▼

Green Kiwi Tours (☎0800/474 733, ⓦwww.greenkiwitours.co.nz), costing around $60 per hour for the whole group.

Practicalities

North- and south-bound **buses** run by InterCity and Atomic stop for around half an hour outside the Paparoa National Park visitor centre, giving enough time for a quick look at the Pancake Rocks across the road. Both InterCity services pass in the middle of the day, but the northbound Atomic service arrives at 8.30am making it possible to treat Punakaiki as a day-trip from Greymouth with eight free hours before the south-bound Atomic comes through around 5pm. DOC's **Paparoa National Park visitor centre** (daily: Dec–Easter 9am–6pm; Easter–Nov 9am–4pm; ☎03/731 1895, ⓦwww.punakaiki.co.nz), has excellent displays on all aspects of the park, information on activities, walking maps and leaflets and extremely helpful staff.

Punakaiki is a tiny place, but its popularity is growing, spawning a slew of new places to stay (see below). Unfortunately, the **restaurant** scene hasn't kept pace and there's no decent shop for buying supplies. Daytime eating options are limited to the coffee shop at *Punakaiki Crafts*, by the visitor centre, where you can sit on the deck under nikau palms and munch counter-food and organic chocolate; and the appealing though expensive *Wild Coast Café* (licensed & BYO) next door, which serves "blow-hole" breakfasts (a mass of bacon, eggs and hash browns), bagel brunches, panini, salads and snack foods until around sunset. The *Bistro*, 500m north of the visitor centre, offers the best value, but for something more fancy head a few hundred metres south of the visitor centre for the classy *à la carte* dining at the *Seascape Restaurant* at the *Punakaiki Rocks Hotel* (☎03/731 1167).

Accommodation

Hydrangea Cottages SH6 ☎03/731 1839, ⓦwww.pancake-rocks.co.nz. Four gorgeous

cottages set above the road most with sea views. The real appeal though is the self-catering cottages themselves (studio, 1- & 2-bedroom), all very tastefully decorated and using native timbers and local stone. Small discount for two night stays. Studios ❼, suites ❽–❾

Punakaiki Beach Camp SH6 ☏03/731 1894, ✉beachcamp@xtra.co.nz. Attractive, grassy campground close to the beach and pub. Camping $10–12, cabins & kitchen cabins ❷

Punakaiki Beach Hostel Webb Street ☏03/731 1852, ✉punakaiki.beachhostel @ihug.co.nz. There's a relaxed atmosphere to this vibrantly painted hostel where guests can buy freshly baked wholemeal bread, surf the Net and use the outdoor spa pool. Camping $14, dorms ❶, rooms ❸

Punakaiki Cottage Motels Mabel Street ☏03/731 1008, ✉punakaikicottagemotels @xtra.co.nz. Comfortable motel units with full kitchens, some overlooking the breakers. ❺

The Rocks Hartmount Place ☏03/731 1141, ⓦwww.therockshomestay.com. Comfortable and welcoming homestay with three en-suite rooms all with bush or sea views, and a lounge with a broad seascape. Dinners are available on request ($35–45), and the same folk manage the adjacent, self-catering *Te Puna Bush Haven*, a well-appointed and nicely designed modern home surrounded by bush and sleeping four. B&B ❻, Haven ❻ then $20 each extra adult.

Te Nikau Retreat Hartmount Place ☏03/731 1111, Ⓕ731 1102. Associate YHA hostel which must rank as one of the most relaxing backpackers in the country, carved out of bush that's peppered with nikau palms and occasionally reveals a building with small dorms, rooms and rustic huts for couples. Fresh bread and muffins are sold, and there's Internet access. Dorms ❶, rooms ❷

Punakaiki to Greymouth

The road from Punakaiki to Greymouth is a spectacular drive, sometimes pushed onto the sea-cliffs by intrusive ramparts of the Paparoa Range, but there's little to stop for until you get close to Greymouth. The former gold town

△ Pancake Rocks

of **BARRYTOWN**, 15km south of Punakaiki, is no more than a scattered shock of houses and the *All Nations Hotel* (☎03/731 1812; dorms ❶), opposite the end of the **Croesus Track** (see p.775), which has bunks, a kitchen, and sells bar meals. A better bet is to continue 4km south to the simple *Hexagon* backpackers, on Golden Sands Road (☎03/731 1827; dorms ❶, rooms ❷), a nice little **hostel** with beds in a glassed-in hexagon, and a couple of lovely cabins; one twin, and one double with a grapevine-strung sunhouse. Guests can help themselves to organic produce from the garden. The best eating hereabouts is the licensed *Rata Café*, 2km south of Barrytown (☎03/731 1151) with long views over the Tasman as you down a good coffee and a bite.

The next settlement of any consequence is **RAPAHOE**, which has about the safest bathing beach on the coast and a reputation for gemstones. Seven Mile Creek meets the sea here, by the beginning of the **Point Elizabeth Track** (5km; 3hr return; 100m ascent), a lovely and little-used walk along former gold-miners' trails and through dense bush that ends 5km north of Greymouth at the end of Domett Esplanade. It is simple just to hike as far as the excellent vantage of Point Elizabeth (2hr return), then back. If you want **to stay** near here, try the basic *Rapahoe Beach Motor Camp*, 10 Hawken St (☎ & ℱ03/762 7025; camping $8, on-site vans & cabins ❷), which has a swimming pool and volleyball court, and is only a short stagger from the local pub.

Greymouth and around

The Grey River forces its way through a break in the coastal Rapahoe Range and over the treacherous sand bar to the sea at workaday **GREYMOUTH**, which ranks as the West Coast's largest town but still claims under ten thousand residents. Greymouth is hardly going to be a highlight on most visitors' itineraries, though there's some high quality greenstone carving in evidence, a bunch of worthwhile **adventure activities**, while the kids will get a kick out of **Shantytown**, a replica gold town to the south. Best to do what you need to and move on, especially in winter when you might be plagued by **The Barber**, a razor-sharp cold wind that whistles down the Grey Valley and envelops the town in a thick icy fog.

The town began to take shape during the early years of the **gold rush** on land purchased in 1860 by James Mackay, who bought most of Westland from the Poutini Ngai Tahu people for 300 gold sovereigns. The deal was finalized on the site of their Mawhera *pa*, where the river bridge across to the suburb of Cobden now stands; a plaque beneath the bridge marks the spot. Several respectably grand buildings from the prosperous later decades of the nineteenth century pepper Greymouth's gridplan streets but there's nothing to give the place any defining character except for the river, which is deceptively calm and languid through most of the summer, but awesome after heavy rains. Devastating **floods** swept through Greymouth in 1887, 1905, 1936, 1977 and 1988; since the last great flood, the Greymouth Flood Protection Scheme, completed in 1990, has successfully held back most of the waters.

Arrival, information and transport

The stylish way to arrive in Greymouth is on the daily TranzAlpine **train** from Christchurch (see p.675), which pulls in at the station on Mackay Street and is met by InterCity and Atomic **buses** (tickets from the visitor centre or the agency inside the station; ☎03/768 7080) running south to Hokitika and

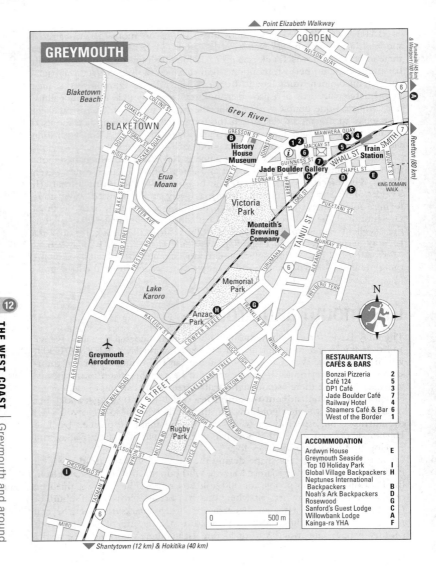

GREYMOUTH

Point Elizabeth Walkway

COBDEN

Punakaiki (45 km) & Westport (100 km)

NELSON QUAY

Blaketown Beach

BLAKETOWN

Grey River

COALEY ST
COLLINS ST
DOYLE ST
O'GRADY ST
RIGG ST
PACKERS QUAY

GRESSON ST

JOHNSTON ST

MAWHERA QUAY

MACKAY ST

Train Station

WHALL ST
SMITH ST
MOUNT ST

Reefton (80 km)

Erua Moana

BLAKE STREET
REID STREET
STEER AVE

ANNEY ST
GUINNESS ST
LEONARD ST
HERBERT ST

History House Museum

Jade Boulder Gallery

KING DOMAIN WALK

Victoria Park

LORD ST
TAINUI ST

PUKETANI ST

Monteith's Brewing Company

TURUMAHA ST

MURRAY ST
ALEXANDER ST

PRESTON ROAD

Lake Karoro

Memorial Park

FREYBERG TERR

Anzac Park

COWPER STREET
RALEIGH ST
FRANKLIN ST
WINNIE ST

N

AERODROME RD

Greymouth Aerodrome

WATER WALK ROAD

BUCKLEUGH ST

SHAKESPEARE STREET
PALMERSTON ST
LYDIA ST
MARSDEN RD

HIGH STREET

MARLBOROUGH ST

Rugby Park

NELSON ST
BYRON ST
MILTON RD
JOYCE CR

CHESTERFIELD ST

TASMAN ST

MIRO

0   500 m

RESTAURANTS, CAFÉS & BARS

Bonzai Pizzeria	2
Café 124	5
DP1 Café	3
Jade Boulder Café	7
Railway Hotel	4
Steamers Café & Bar	6
West of the Border	1

ACCOMMODATION

Ardwyn House	E
Greymouth Seaside Top 10 Holiday Park	I
Global Village Backpackers	H
Neptunes International Backpackers	B
Noah's Ark Backpackers	D
Rosewood	G
Sanford's Guest Lodge	C
Willowbank Lodge	A
Kainga-ra YHA	F

Shantytown (12 km) & Hokitika (40 km)

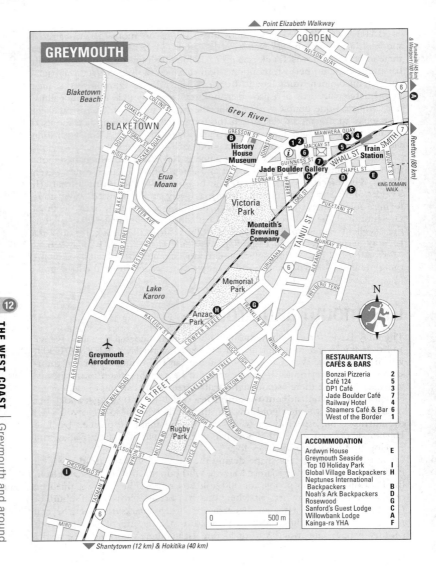

Franz Josef, and north to Westport and Nelson. Greymouth's nearest **airport** is at Hokitika, 40km down the coast; Greymouth Taxis (☎03/768 7078) charge about $20 each way and will meet planes.

The **visitor centre**, inside the Regent Cinema on the corner of Mackay Street and Herbert Street (Nov–Easter Mon–Fri 8.30am–7pm, Sat 9am–6pm, Sun 10am–5pm; Easter–Oct Mon–Fri 8.30am–5.30pm, Sat & Sun 10am–4pm; ☎03/768 5101, ⑩www.westcoastbookings.co.nz), will provide the *Grey District* leaflet which contains a good street map. **Bike rental** is available from *Wildside Café*, 121 Mackie St (☎03/768 5959) for $15 a half-day. You might also want to check out **tours** to the Pancake Rocks (9am & 2.15pm; 2hr 30min; $50) run by Kea Tours (℗0800/532 868, ⓦwww.keatours.co.nz).

Folk planning to **rent a car** in South Island are increasingly riding the TranzAlpine train then picking up a rental in Greymouth; Avis, National and Budget all have **car rental** offices at the train station, though you may find it cheaper to go with one of several local outfits for long-term rentals, who often charge little or no fee for vehicles dropped off in Queenstown or Christchurch. Short-term rental starts around $70 a day, but drops to $50 a day for anything over four days. Try Value Rentals (℗03/762 7503, ℗762 7500) or NZ Rent a Car (℗03/768 0379, ℗greenfield@minidata.co.nz). At the time of writing, no companies currently offer campervan rentals from Greymouth.

Accommodation

Visitor demands seldom put much pressure on Greymouth's modest collection of **places to stay**, except during the Coast to Coast Race (around the second weekend in Feb; see p.795), when everything is packed to the gills. At other times there is a fair choice of hostels, moderately priced motels and a couple of comfortable B&Bs.

Ardwyn House 48 Chapel St ℗03/768 6107, ℗ardwynhouse@hotmail.com. Appealing and very welcoming homestay in a comfortable 1920s house, surrounded by a quiet garden and close to the town centre. No ensuites, but broad views across the town from many rooms. ❹

Global Village Backpackers 42–54 Cowper St ℗03/768 7272, ℗globalvillage@minidata.co.nz. Light and spacious hostel backing onto parkland and a river. The rooms are imaginatively decorated in tribal themes with artefacts the owner has collected around the world and there's a range of tempting activities: free bikes and kayaks, low-cost sauna and small gym, and a barbecue out back most fine evenings. All beds are made-up and there are some single-sex dorms. Camping $15, dorms ❶ rooms ❷

Greymouth Seaside Top 10 Holiday Park 2 Chesterfield St ℗03/768 6618 & 0800/867 104, ⓦwww.top10greymouth.co.nz. The more central of the two motor parks, right by the beach and with very good facilities. Camping $11–12, cabins ❷, units ❸, motels ❹

Kainga-ra YHA 15 Alexander St ℗03/768 4951, ℗yha.greymouth@yha.org.nz. Former priests' residence, now a relaxed, central hostel with all the usual facilities, including a well-informed booking facility, a selection of dorms, twins and doubles, and sea views over the town. Dorms ❶, rooms ❷

Neptunes International Backpackers 43 Gresson St ℗03/768 4425. Excellent hostel in a former pub with nautical decor and a free hot tub and two baths supplied with free bubble bath. Dorms and rooms all have made-up beds (no bunks) and there's a big-screen TV, pool and Internet access in the lounge. Free train pick ups. Dorms ❶, rooms ❷

Noah's Ark Backpackers 16 Chapel St ℗03/768 7272 & 0800/662 472, ℗noahsark@xtra.co.nz. Large and comfortable hostel occupying a two-storey villa originally built as a monastery, with great verandas and a spacious lounge with Sky TV. Rooms and dorms are all lavishly decorated with animal themes. Dorms ❶, rooms ❷

Rosewood 20 High St ℗03/768 4674 & 0800/185 748, ⓦwww.rosewoodnz.co.nz. Appealing B&B in a characterful 1920s home – all wood panelling, lead-light windows and floral decor. Rooms are mostly ensuite and a cooked breakfast is included. ❻

Sanford's Guest Lodge 62 Albert St ℗ & ℗03/768 5605. Excellent-value small hotel with simple, fresh and airy rooms, complete with colour TV and the option of a bargain continental or cooked breakfast. ❹

Willowbank Lodge SH6, 3km north of town ℗03/768 5339 & 0800/668 355, ℗ted.lois .willowbank@xtra.co.nz. Sprawling motel with a good range of modern and older en-suite rooms and use of a small indoor swimming pool and spa. ❺

The Town and around

Greymouth has a long heritage of greenstone carving, and a few outlets around town offer carved pieces of varying qualities and prices. Some of the finest pieces are found at the **Jade Boulder Gallery**, 1 Guinness St (Oct–April Mon–Fri 8am–9pm Sat & Sun 9am–9pm; May–Sept daily 8.30am–5pm; Ⓦ www.jadebouler.com), including works by master carver, Ian Boustridge. Even if you have no intention of buying, pop in to watch the cutting, grinding and polishing processes in the workshop, and to visit the **Jade Boulder Trail** ($10, by guided tour), which tells the parallel stories of jade from a Maori mythological, and geological perspective. Especially impressive five-tonne boulders of raw nephrite lead through to a room lined with ancient and modern carved pieces, put into a world context by the presence of Chinese and Meso-American works: look out for the Ming goddess figure and the eighth-century, grotesque bat figurine from Copan in Honduras. Simple Maori adzes could hardly contrast greater with the exquisite modern museum pieces.

Another gallery worth a gander is the tiny **Shade of Jade**, 16 Tainui St (Mon–Fri 9am–5pm, Sat 10am–2.30pm, Sun noon–2.30pm) a reasonably priced spot – the local carvers can keep the prices down because they own the shop and make their own stock.

Greymouth's **History House Museum**, Gresson Street (Mon–Fri 10am–4pm, Sat & Sun times vary; ℡03/768 4028; $3), is hidden in the former Grey County Chambers out towards the fishing harbour. It makes a good shot at relating the Grey District's history through piles of maritime memorabilia and a stack of photos depicting the town's heyday. The towns-people's long struggle to combat the floods is also given a thorough and diverting treatment.

Rainy and sweltering days both provide equally good excuses to join the tastings and brewery tours at **Monteith's Brewing Company**, corner of Turumaha Street and Herbert Street (℡03/768 4149 ext 1; Mon–Fri 10am, 11.30am & 2pm, Sat & Sun 11.30am & 2pm; $10), where age-old recipes have recently been revived to produce some deep-brown, flavoursome brews popular all down the Coast. Sample them at the end of a brief tour.

Greymouth also makes a good base for the **Point Elizabeth Track** (see p.791), beginning over the river north of the suburb of Cobden and returning from Rapahoe by one of the twice-daily buses.

If you're looking for a short walk and somewhere to watch the sun go down, try the **King Domain Walk** (1hr return) starting on Mount Street near the Cobden Bridge and meandering through the bush to a panoramic viewpoint over the city and the Southern Alps.

Shantytown

The replica 1880s West Coast gold-mining settlement of **Shantytown** (daily 8.30am–5pm; $12, entry plus gold panning $15; Ⓦ www.shantytown.co.nz), 8km south of Greymouth and 4km off the main highway, is squarely aimed at the stream of visitors who pile off tour buses, and makes a good place to bring kids. Most of it has been constructed since the early 1970s, but the complex incorporates rescued older buildings, mostly fairly tastefully restored. Look out for the 1902 Coronation Hall from Ross, the 1865 church originally from No Town in the Grey Valley, and the hotel cobbled together from parts. Notice, too, the printing shop with its faded billboards advertising the latest films; the wonderful 1837 Colombian Press, which found its way here from Philadelphia via London, Auckland and Napier; the hospital, identical to one built in Greymouth; and the Gem Hall, with its collection of minerals. At the replica train station, your entry ticket entitles you to a two-kilometre round-trip ride behind the 1887 steam engine *Kaitangata*, calling at a mine site and sawmill, where boards are cut on summer days and, of course, sage prospectors will help

Kiwis are mad on multisport. Every weekend from early spring to late autumn you'll see scores of people toning their muscles and honing their biking and paddling skills. The ultimate goal of all true multisporters is the gruelling 239km **Coast to Coast Race** (ⓦwww.coasttocoast.co.nz) which began in 1983 when it was the world's first major multisport event. It is held annually between the West Coast and Christchurch in mid-February on the weekend after Waitangi Day (6 February).

The course requires a pre-dawn start from the beach near Kumara Junction, 15km south of Greymouth. A 3km run leads to a 60km cycle uphill to Otira where jelly-kneed contenders tackle the most gruelling section, a run up and down the boulder-strewn creek beds of the Southern Alps before kayaking for several hours down Canterbury's braided Waimakariri River and then cycling the final stretch to Sumner.

The event is actually two races in one. Most competitors take two days, but around 150 elite tri-athletes compete in "The Longest Day", the same course in a time frame of less than 24 hours. Mere mortals – though admittedly extremely fit ones – can also compete by forming two-person teams sharing the disciplines.

From humble beginnings in 1983 the whole event has blossomed into a very professional affair with competitors training for months and serious contenders engaging the services of a highly organized support crew. The equipment too has become highly specialized; only the lightest and most high-tech of bikes will do and designers build racing kayaks especially for Waimakariri conditions.

Women compete in increasingly large numbers, but the event remains largely a macho spectacle that draws considerable press interest – with one journalist for every seven competitors – and correspondingly generous sponsorship. As an incentive to record-breaking, a vehicle manufacturer is usually coaxed into offering a car or truck to the winner if they break a certain time. Several have gone to Kiwi super-athlete, Steve Gurney, who won his ninth title (aged 39) in 2003, but failed to round out his tally in 2004. The course record is an astonishing 10hr 35min.

you pan for "colour" in salted tanks. As if that weren't more than enough schmalz, a mock hotel serves beer in saloon surroundings.

No public **transport** runs to the site, but Kea Tours (see p.793) finish their Goldstrike Tour (2 daily; 2hr 30min; $38) around various gold rush sites at Shantytown.

Activities

Activities around Greymouth are predominantly aquatic or subterranean, or both. Some of the best trips are run by Wild West Adventures (☎0800/223 456, ⓦwww.nzholidayheaven.com), notably their Dragons Cave Rafting (5hr; $120), a challenging **caving** trip into the Taniwha cave system; wetsuits and cavers' lamps are the order of the day for scrambling down a fairly steep underground streambed, floating along deep sections on inner tubes and, for the adventurous, squeezing through some tight sections. They also have the gentler **Jungle Boat Cruising** (3hr; $95) plying placid waterways using rafts and pontoons made to look like a Maori *waka*. This is partly aimed at those hopping off and then back on the TranzAlpine.

Wild West also run a bunch of rafting and **heli-rafting** trips (see p.802) and offer a money-back guarantee if you don't enjoy yourself.

Eco-Rafting, at the *DP1 Café*, 108 Mawhera Quay (☎03/768 4005, ⓦwww.ecorafting.co.nz) take a slightly different approach to their trips, using the rafting as a vehicle for introducing customers to the nature and social history of the places visited. The half-day trip (4hr; $80) runs the Grade II Arnold

River, while the full-day offering ($130, including lunch) takes on Grade III sections of the Buller or Grey rivers.

Wild Cat Fishing Charters (☎03/762 6680, ⓦwww.wildcatcharters.co.nz) will take you out for a little speculative **dolphin watching** (1hr; $50), and Scenic West Jet (☎0800/293 785) will take you jetboating up the Grey River (30–40min; $60). The latter mostly runs in the evenings providing an alternative to hanging out in Greymouth's bars.

Eating and drinking

You'll soon exhaust Greymouth's scope for **eating and drinking**, but there are enough places serving tasty and hearty dishes to last the night or two you're likely to stay. For evening entertainment there are numerous pubs and mainstream **movies** at the Regent Theatre, cnr Herbert & Mackay streets.

Bonzai Pizzeria 31 Mackay St. Cheerful licensed restaurant with tearoom staples through the day, including some good pastries and quiches and a broad range of reasonably priced and tasty pizzas served daytime and evening.

Café 124 124 Mackay St. Modern licensed café with a fine range of light meals and a good brunch menu, muffins and good coffee served inside or at outdoor seating suitably sheltered from the West Coast weather. Evening meals ($16–26) could include chicken and coconut curry.

DP1 Café 108 Mawhera Quay. Greymouth's coolest café serving snacks and excellent coffee, with Internet access and regular gigs.

Jade Boulder Café 1 Guinness St. Excellent, daytime café specializing in wild foods. Expect the likes of goat curry, whitebait sandwiches, thar and ostrich burgers as well as less exotic fare: the Tandoori chicken burger ($13) is excellent.

Railway Hotel 120 Mawhera Quay. Basic pub chiefly notable for its nightly $3 all-the-sausages-you-can-eat barbecue, which can be upgraded to rump steak ($8).

Steamers Café & Bar 58 Mackay St. High-quality, low-priced licensed carvery ($15) that also has a full menu.

West of the Border 19 Mackay St. A Kiwi-style Tex-Mex dinner restaurant serving groaning plates of barbecued chicken, buffalo wings, Cajun fish fillets and the like for $20–28.

Hokitika and around

South from Greymouth, SH6 hugs a desolate stretch of coast that's fine for long moody beachcombing walks, but there's little of abiding interest until **HOKITIKA**, 40km away. On initial acquaintance "Hoki", as it is known to its friends, appears only marginally more interesting than Greymouth – its jumble of mundane modern buildings interspersed with gussied up edifices from the town's golden days. Still, it is a long way to the next place of any size, and its proximity to the beach and good bushwalks, and a couple of quality restaurants, give it the edge.

Like the other West Coast towns, Hokitika owes its existence to the **gold rushes** of the 1860s. Within months of the initial discoveries near Greymouth in 1864, fields had been opened up on the tributaries of the Hokitika River, and Australian diggers from Ballarat and Bendigo and Irish hopefuls all flogged over narrow passes from Canterbury to get their share. Hokitika boomed and within two years it had a population of 6000 (compared with today's 4000), streets packed with hotels, and a steady export of over a tonne of gold a month, mainly direct to Melbourne. Despite a treacherous bar at the Hokitika Rivermouth, the **port** briefly became the country's busiest, with ships tied up four deep along Gibson Wharf. As gold became harder to find and more sluicing water was needed, the enterprise eventually became uneconomic and was

Maori revere **pounamu** (hard nephrite jade) and **tangiwai** (the softer, translucent bowenite), usually collectively known as **greenstone**. In Aotearoa's pre-European culture, it took the place of durable metals for both practical, warfaring and decorative uses: adzes and chisels were used for carving, *mere* (clubs) were used for hand-to-hand combat, and pendants were fashioned for jewellery. Charles Heaphy observed a group of Maori producing a *mere* in 1846, and noted the process by which they "saw the slab with a piece of mica slate, wet, and afterwards polish it with a fine sandy limestone which they obtain in the vicinity. The hole is drilled with a pointed stick with a piece of Pahutanui flint. The process does not appear so tedious as has been supposed; a month sufficing, apparently, for the completion".

In Maori, the entire South Island is known as **Te Wahi Pounamu**, "the place of greenstone", reflecting the importance of its sole sources, the belt from Greymouth through the rich Arahura River area near Hokitika south to Anita Bay on Milford Sound – where the beautifully dappled tangiwai occurs – and the Wakatipu region behind Queenstown. When the Poutini Ngai Tahu arranged to sell most of Westland to James Mackay in 1860, the Arahura River, their main source of pounamu, was specifically excluded.

Its value has barely diminished. Mineral claims are jealously guarded, the export of raw greenstone is prohibited and no extraction is allowed from national parks; penalties include fines of up to $200,000 and two years in jail. **Price** is heavily dependent on quality, but rates of $100,000 a tonne are not unknown in the raw state – and the sky's the limit when the stone is fashioned into sculpture and jewellery. Many of the cheaper specimens are quite crude, but pricier pieces (and we're talking a minimum of $100 for something aesthetically pleasing, and over $1000 for anything really classy) exhibit accomplished Maori designs executed to perfection; at the other end of the scale, simple pendants can be picked up for as little as $20.

Hokitika is the main venue for greenstone shoppers: bear in mind that the larger **shops** and **galleries** are firmly locked into the tour-bus circuit so prices (and standards) are consequently high. They are fine for learning something about the quality of the stone and competence of the artwork, though it is worth checking out the smaller places which often have more competitive deals. Specific **recommendations** are given on p.800.

replaced by dairying and the timber industry. The **railway** started to transport the region's produce and the port closed in 1954, only to be smartened up in the 1990s as the focus for the town's Heritage Trail.

In the last decade or so, Hokitika has become synonymous with the annual **Wildfoods Festival**, on the second Saturday in March (℡03/755 8322, Ⓦ www.wildfoods.co.nz; all tickets are presold for $20, no gate sales). The town quadruples its population for this celebration of bush tucker, which takes place around Cass Square, where up to fifty stalls sell such delicacies as stir-fried possum, golden-fried huhu grubs, marinated goat kebabs and smoked eel wontons, all washed down with home-brewed beer and South Island wine. The gorging is followed by an evening hoe-down, the Wildfoods Barn Dance ($10).

Arrival and information

Air New Zealand Link **fly** daily to Hokitika from Christchurch, arriving 2km east of the centre, and though a rail line comes as far as Hokitika, there are no passenger services. Coast to Coast run **buses** from Christchurch and terminate here, InterCity offer a southbound **bus** service in the afternoon as far as Fox

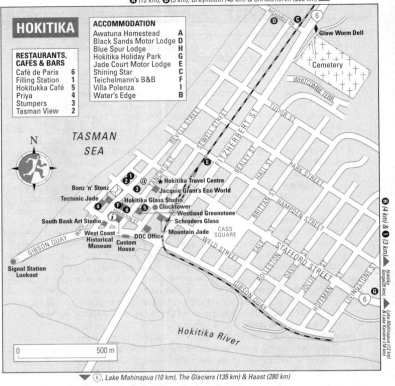

HOKITIKA

ACCOMMODATION

Awatuna Homestead	A
Black Sands Motor Lodge	D
Blue Spur Lodge	H
Hokitika Holiday Park	G
Jade Court Motor Lodge	E
Shining Star	C
Teichelmann's B&B	F
Villa Polenza	I
Water's Edge	B

RESTAURANTS, CAFES & BARS

Café de Paris	6
Filling Station	1
Hokitukka Café	5
Priya	4
Stumpers	3
Tasman View	2

TASMAN SEA

N

Bonz 'n' Stonz
Tectonic Jade
Hokitika Travel Centre
Jacquie Grant's Eco World
Hokitika Glass Studio
Clocktower
Westland Greenstone
Schroders Glass
South Bank Art Studio
West Coast Historical Museum
Custom House
DOC Office
Mountain Jade
CASS SQUARE

Signal Station Lookout

GIBSON QUAY

Glow Worm Dell
Cemetery

Hokitika River

0   500 m

⑫

THE WEST COAST | Hokitika and around

Glacier, while Atomic come through in the morning making for Queenstown and run a service to Nelson.

All buses stop outside the Hokitika Travel Centre, 65 Tancred St (☎03/755 8557), and all except InterCity also stop at the **visitor centre**, cnr Hamilton & Tancred streets (Dec–March daily 8.30am–6pm; April–Nov Mon–Fri 8.30am–5pm, Sat & Sun 10am–4pm; ☎03/755 6166, ✉hkkvin@xtra.co.nz). Just a few paces away, the **DOC office**, on Sewell Street (Mon–Fri 8am–4.45pm; ☎03/755 8301), is stocked with leaflets on local walks. **Internet access** is available at Video Ezy, 110 Revell St, and at the public library.

While here, you may need to make some preparations for the long drive south. Though there is an ATM at Franz Josef, the **banks** here are the last before Wanaka, more than 400km away over the Haast Pass. **Cyclists** can obtain spares at the well-stocked Hokitika Cycles and Sports, 33 Tancred St (☎03/755 8662).

Accommodation

Apart from during the Wildfoods Festival (second weekend in March), **accommodation** is seldom hard to find. There are good places to stay right in town, but many of the better places (at both end of the scale) are some way out.

Awatuna Homestead SH6, 13km north of Hokitika ☎03/755 6834 & 0800/006 888, ⓦwww.awatunahomestead.co.nz. Very welcoming B&B with 3 comfortable, tasteful rooms and 1 self-catering apartment. It is a place to relax with canoes to paddle on the creek, assorted animals, plenty of books, outdoor bath and evening storytelling sessions; evening meals on request ($50). Rooms ❼, apartment sleeping 5 ❺ plus $30 each extra

Black Sands Motor Lodge 252 Revell St ☎03/755 8773 & 0800/755 222, ⓦwww .blacksands.co.nz. Spacious motel offering a range of comfortable units ten minutes' walk from the centre, plus swimming pool, spa, kids' playground, Internet access and campervan hook-ups. $20 per van, cabins ❷, units ❺

Blue Spur Lodge Cement Lead Rd ☎03/755 8445, Ⓔbluespur@xtra.co.nz. Spacious, modern and airy pine house, plus a new house with lovely en-suite doubles, all in a tranquil setting 5km from town and close to bushwalks; they do pick-ups from town and offer free use of bikes. They'll also drop off and pick up at trailheads, and rent out kayaking and fly-fishing gear at very reasonable rates. Dorms ❶, rooms ❷

Hokitika Holiday Park 242 Stafford St ☎03/755 8172, Ⓔholidaypark@hokitika.com. Outwardly scruffy-looking but actually decent and well-priced campground with clean and tidy cabins plus a good kids' playground. Camping $9–10, cabins ❷, self-contained units ❸, motels ❹

Jade Court Motor Lodge 85 Fitzherbert St ☎03/755 8855 & 0800/755 885, ⓦwww .jadecourt.co.nz. Modern and very well-equipped motel five minutes' walk from town with in-house video and pleasant gardens. Some rooms have private spa baths. Units ❺, spa units ❻

Shining Star 11 Richards Drive ☎03/755 8921 & 0800/744 646, ⓦwww.accommodationwestcoast .co.nz. Close to the beach with tent and campervan sites plus an extensive range of classy log cabins most with good self-catering facilities. Camping $10, cabins ❷, ensuite cabins ❸, self-contained cabins ❹, motel units ❺

Teichelmann's B&B 20 Hamilton St ☎03/755 8232 & 0800/743 742, ⓦwww.teichelmanns .co.nz. Comfortable, well-appointed and central B&B, with friendly hosts, a range of upgraded ensuite rooms and a small studio out the back with double spa bath. A hearty cooked breakfast is served. ❼

Villa Polenza Brickfield Rd ☎03/755 7801 & 0800/241 801, ⓦwww.villapolenza.co.nz. Luxurious boutique lodge in a gorgeous Italianate mansion high on a plateau above Hoki where you can watch the sun set amid lavender or bathe under the stars in a pair of tubs. Everything is stylishly modern with swathes of colour and well-chosen furniture. Rooms cost $400–550; sumptuous dinners are $90 extra. ❾

Water's Edge SH6, 4km north of town ☎03/755 6349, Ⓔwatersedge@snap.co.nz. Small and relaxed hostel right by a driftwood-strewn beach where the owners light a campfire on fine nights. Accommodation is in a four-share or twins and doubles, there's free Internet access, and you're encouraged to find some greenstone on the beach which they'll then polish into a pendant ($20). Share ❶, rooms ❷

The Town

Hokitika's leading role in the West Coast gold rushes rightly occupies much of the **West Coast Historical Museum**, entered through the visitor centre (daily: Dec–Easter 9.30am–5pm; Easter–Nov Mon–Fri 9.30am–4pm, Sat & Sun 10am–2pm; $5, gold panning $5 extra) and which, along with greenstone and pioneering life, forms the focus for an interesting audio-visual presentation every half hour. The photos of the submerged horrors of the Hokitika River bar and the pleasures of the hundred or so bars of another kind that once lined Tancred Street are highlights among a predictable collection of fire-fighting and shipping paraphernalia.

With interest suitably kindled, grab the free **Hokitika Heritage Walk** leaflet, which details the remaining landmarks from the town's past, including the centrepiece **clock tower** commemorating the Boer War, a statue of **Richard Seddon**, local boy made good to become prime minister from 1893 to 1906, and the Gibson Quay area. This restored former riverside dock makes a pleasant place for an evening stroll from the 1897 **Custom House**, past an ugly concrete memorial to ships lost on the bar, to the spit-end **Signal Station Lookout**, where coloured flags and raised balls used to help guide ships into the rivermouth. The Heritage Walk also crosses the river to a plaque marking the site of the Southside Aerodrome where, in 1934, one Bert Mercer started New Zealand's first licensed air service to the glaciers, using a de Havilland Fox Moth, a replica of which stands outside Hokitika Airport.

Those with kids to entertain will welcome **Jacquie Grant's Eco World**, 60 Tancred St (daily: 9am–5pm; $12), a combined aquarium and nocturnal house with the chance to see kiwi, tuatara, huge fat eels (fed at 10am, noon & 3pm), a large shark tank and an area with possums: at last a chance to see one that isn't flattened on the road.

Arts and crafts

Hokitika is crafts mad. Everywhere you look there is someone trying to sell you carved wood, blown glass, woven wool or a greenstone pendant, preferably with gold embellishments; and for those in buying mode, there are quality pieces to be found. The southwestern end of Revell Street is becoming a bit of an artists' enclave. **Greenstone** (see p.797) is big business, with shops all over town. For some of the finest work, visit Tectonic Jade, 67 Revell St, or stroll down to the Traditional Jade Company, 2 Tancred Street, for pendants at middling prices. If you want to work a piece for yourself, pop along to Bonz 'n' Stonz Carving Studio, 83 Revell St (☏0800/214 949) where Steve Gwaliasi will guide you through the design and execution in greenstone (5hr; $150) or bone (3hr; $60).

Glass blowing is another longstanding Hoki tradition, and there are currently two exponents, both with working artisans on show: the Hokitika Glass Studio, 25 Tancred Street, is the more venerable; while Schroder's Glass, 41 Weld St, goes for more contemporary designs. And don't miss the **copper art** at the South Bank Art Studio, cnr Revell and Camp Sts, where Ian Phillips creates wonderful hand-crafted sculptures out of heat-treated copper sheet: small pieces go for under $200 but larger works, often combining polished driftwood, greenstone and paua are more like $2000.

Activities

Hokitika isn't just about watching glass being blown. Riverplay (see box, p.802) would love to take you **whitewater rafting** on some of the excellent local rivers. Canoe Safaris (☏0800/383 937, ⓦwww.duewest.co.nz) generally head out to Lake Mahinapua (see below) for half a day **canoeing** ($80) with morning, afternoon and evening departures, and even a moonlit paddle when conditions are right: if it is windy they'll stick up sails. Lastly, Wilderness Wings, out at the airport (☏03/755 8118), do a number of **scenic flights** (from 45min; $180), principally around Mount Cook and the glaciers (1hr 15min; $260) reached by flying past all the big, snowy peaks of the Southern Alps.

Eating and drinking and entertainment

Hokitika offers some of the best **eating** on the Coast, and it's reasonably priced too – reason enough to make this an overnight stop before heading south. The most pleasant places to **drink** are the restaurants, though Hokitika has its share of beer barns. Evening entertainment is limited to a stroll to an attractive **Glow Worm Dell** (free) about a kilometre north of the centre beside SH6; and the Regent **cinema**, 15 Weld St, which shows mostly mainstream releases.

Café de Paris 19 Tancred St ☏03/755 8933. This fine restaurant is tastefully decorated and has a relaxed atmosphere. An extensive selection of moderately priced breakfasts gives way to café lunches and more formal evening dining with a Mediterranean theme (mains around $25).

Licensed & BYO; booking advisable in the evenings.

Filling Station 111 Revell St. Good licensed, all-day café serving omelettes, panini, sandwiches, salads and soups, plus decent coffee.

Hokitukka Café 15 Weld St. Great lunch and coffee spot in the same building as the Regent cinema, and open in the evenings when the pro-jector is turning. Serving breakfast, muffins, cakes and excellent coffee all day.

Priya 79 Revell St ☏03/755 7225. Reliable curry restaurant serving all the usual suspects (around $17) and doing takeaways for a few dollars less.

Stumpers 2 Weld St, cnr of Weld and Revell sts. Modern swish sports bar and day-time café with live bands and some passable grub.

Tasman View 111 Revell St ☏03/755 8344. Classy *à la carte* evening dining specializing in seafood and lamb (mains $25–28), served with great views over the sea from inside or out on their deck.

Around Hokitika

Some of the best bush scenery and the finest **walks** hereabouts lie among the Taharoa Forest, where the dairying hinterland turns into the foothills of the Southern Alps some 30km inland along Stafford Street. Minor roads make a good seventy-kilometre scenic drive (shown in detail on the DOC's *Central West Coast* leaflet, available from the visitor centre for $1), passing the fishing, water skiing and tramping territory of **Lake Kaniere**, a glacial lake 18km from Hokitika with several picnic sites and primitive camping ($5) along the east-ern side. The most popular walk is the **Kaniere Water Race Walkway** (9km one way; 3hr; 100m ascent), which starts from the lake's northern end and fol-lows a channel that used to supply water to the goldfields, through stands of regenerating rimu. Close by is the **Lake Kaniere Walkway** (13km one way; 3–4hr; flat), which traces the western lake margin by way of the basic Lawyer's Delight Hut – more of a lunch stop than a place to stay. The eastern-shore road passes the attractive **Dorothy Falls** and continues to a spur leading to the **Hokitika Gorge**, 35km from Hoki, where a short path leads to a swingbridge over the tranquil Hokitika River as it eases through a deep gorge.

Immediately south of Hokitika, SH6 runs inland for 15km before meeting the old coastal Rautapu Road near Lake Mahinapua. Take the old road to visit the **Lake Mahinapua Recreation Reserve**, from where there are a number of short walks plus the easy **Mananui Walkway** (16km return; 4hr; mainly flat), detailed in a free leaflet available from the Hokitika DOC office. Gentle paddle-boat **cruises** along the Mahinapua Creek to the lake (☏03/755 7239; Dec–April 2pm; 90min; excellent value at $25) start 5km south of Hokitika.

From Hokitika to the glaciers

The main highway leaves the coast **south of Hokitika** and snuggles in close to the Southern Alps for most of the 135km to the glacier at Franz Josef, the next town of any size. The journey through pakihi and stands of selectively logged native bush is broken by a series of insignificant settlements such as **Ross**, **Pukekura** and **Harihari**, none of which warrant stopping long. There's more fun to be had visiting herons from Whataroa, and **Okarito** may just seduce you with the relaxed charms of its lagoon.

Ross

The tiny village of **ROSS**, 30km south of Hokitika, lies right on top of one of New Zealand's richest alluvial **goldfields**. The mining company is still chew-ing away at the large hole on the edge of town and would dearly love to get

Rafting the wild West Coast rivers

The production line rafting trips out of Rotorua and Queenstown are fun and don't cost that much, but kayakers and rafters are realising that some of the most thrilling and scenic whitewater trips in the world are here on New Zealand's West Coast. Dramatically steep rivers spill out of the alpine wilderness fed by the prodigious quantity of rain that guarantees solid flows most of the time. The steepness of the terrain means you're in Grade IV–V territory – constantly thrilling if not downright scary.

Few of these rivers had been kayaked or rafted until the 1980s when helicopters were co-opted to reach them. Rafting trips still require **helicopter access**, so costs are relatively high, and what you pay will often depend on numbers. Getting, say, six people together will save you a packet.

Though their popularity is increasing, trips are still relatively infrequent and you should **book** as far in advance as possible. The main **season** is November to April.

The **most commonly run rivers** are (from north to south) the Karamea (Gd III+), the Mokihinui (Gd IV), the Arahura (Gd IV), the Whitcombe (Gd V), the Hokitika (Gd III–IV), the Wanganui (Gd III), the Perth (Gd V), the Whataroa (Gd IV), Landsborough (Gd IV), and the Waitoto (Gd III).

Several rafting companies dot themselves along the coast, most claiming they run all (or most of) the above rivers. In practice it makes sense to go with the company running local rivers – they know them best. In general, there is a minimum age of 16 years for the Grade IV & V trips; 13 for the Grade III trips. We've listed the principal companies and their areas of expertise below.

Riverplay Hokitika ☎03/755 5339 & 0800/116 348, ⓦwww.riverplay.co.nz. Though experienced on many of the local rivers, these guys specialize in trips on the Arahura River, sacred to Maori as the source of *pounamu*, and equally revered by kayakers and rafters for its great rapids. Either four-wheel-drive in and raft out ($195) or go for one of the Coast's cheapest heli-rafting trips, flying in then rafting out ($280). For something a little tamer, try their Adventure Kayaking, tackling Grade II water in stable inflatable kayaks ($175).

Rivers Wild Franz Josef ☎0800/469453, ⓦwww.riverswild.co.nz. Very professional operation with experienced guides concentrating on the southern rivers, principally the fabulously scenic and exciting Whataroa and the hair-raising Perth (though only for parties that can demonstrate above average ability). Also multi-day trips on the Landsborough and the Waitoto. One-day trips start at $600 each for two people but drop rapidly (as it were) to $390 for groups of seven to ten. Two-day trips cost $860–1200 per person with everything included. Operates Nov–April.

Ultimate Descents 51 Fairfax St, Murchison ☎03/523 9899 & 0800/748 377, ⓦwww.rivers.co.nz. Primarily concentrating on the Buller River (see p.770), but also offering one-day heli-rafting on the Karamea ($295), three-day trips on the same river ($995), and two-day trips on the Mokihinui ($650).

Wild West Adventures 8 Whall St, Greymouth ☎03/768 6649 & 0800/147 483, ⓦwww.nzholidayheaven.com. These guys offer a wide range of trips from hard-man descents of the Whataroa and Perth rivers ($565) and the Frisco Canyon on the Hokitika River ($355) to relatively gentle drive-in trips on the Taipo (Gd III; $155), and their so-called Love Adventure on the relatively tame Wanganui involving time spent in hot pools with a bottle of bubbly.

at the gold-bearing gravels underneath. The government have given consent provided all the townspeople agree to move off the land: around half are adamant they'll stay.

Though Ross had over 3000 residents at its gold rush peak, things had slowed considerably by 1909 when a couple of diggers prospecting less than 500m from the current visitor centre turned up the largest gold nugget ever found in New

Zealand, the 3.1-kilo **"Honourable Roddy"**, named after the then Minister of Mines. The nugget was bought by the government and given as a coronation gift in 1910 to Britain's George V, who melted it down to make royal tableware. A replica of the fist-sized lump of gold resides in the 1885 **Miner's Cottage**, Bold Street (daily 9am–4pm; free), surrounded by gold-rush photos.

The visitor centre (see below) has details of several good walks, notable the easy and popular **Water Race Walk** (DOC leaflet available), which passes the remains of fluming designed to supply water for gravel washing. Before leaving the area, check out the Jade Studio at 23 St James St (daily noon–5pm), one of the best small **jade** galleries in the region.

Practicalities

The **visitor centre**, 4 Aylmer St (daily: Dec–March 9am–5pm; April–Nov 9am–4pm; ☎03/755 4077), presents an interesting **multi-media** show (free) on the 1865 gold rush and subsequent sawmilling and farming history, and stocks DOC leaflets on local walks ($0.50 each).

The best **accommodation** in town is at the *Bellbird Bush B&B*, 4 Sale St (☎03/755 4058; ❹), about 200m off SH6, which offers a separate unit with a good view and a continental breakfast. Otherwise, you're limited to the *Historic Empire Hotel*, 19 Aylmer St (☎03/755 4005, ✉empire_gold@paradise.net.nz; camping $8–10, cabins ❷, rooms ❸), which has spacious verandahed doubles (some en suite), four-person cabins and tent and campervan sites, and the basic but functional *Ross Motel*, 10 Gibson St (☎03/755 4153, ✉anneandterry @xtra.co.nz; ❹). If there's nobody at the motel, ask at Manera's General Store.

Backpackers may want to continue almost 20km south to *The Old Church Lodge*, SH6 (☎03/755 4000, ⓦwww.theoldchurch.co.nz; dorms ❶, rooms ❸), a wonderfully relaxing little spot, though bush walks, kayaking, fishing and horse trekking can all be arranged.

For sustenance in Ross, the *Empire Hotel* does good bar **snacks** and **meals**, and the *Roddy Nugget Café*, on the SH6, does tearoom staples and has what passes for a restaurant in this town.

Pukekura

A giant sandfly at the hamlet of **PUKEKURA**, 25km south of Ross, marks the **Bushman's Centre** (daily 9am–5.30pm; free; ☎03/755 4008, ⓦwww.pukekura .co.nz). The centre's **museum** ($4) takes a light-hearted approach to showing how people make a living from the forest through timber milling, possum trapping and growing sphagnum moss for east Asian orchid growers, as well as housing several huge eels. You can **stay** across the road at the welcoming *Puke Pub and Lodge* (☎03/755 4144; camping & powered sites $7.50–10, dorms ❶, cabins ❷, holiday home ❸), where they have artificial hot pools out back. The bar has a pool table amongst all the rough-hewn country decor, and they serve filling breakfasts, and wild foods: wild boar sandwiches, rabbit, possum, hare and chamois.

The rest areas around beautiful **Lake Ianthe**, 4km south, make good picnic stops, and you can board the cute, little, century-old *Tamati* for a forty-minute lake tour ($15; ☎0800/119 494). For the committed, an unsealed road winds 10km through the Lake Ianthe Forest to the exposed **Greens Beach**, from where it is an hour and a half's walk south to a seal colony.

Harihari

Some 20km further south, tiny **HARIHARI** was once the marshy landing site of **Guy Menzies'** who flew from Sydney to New Zealand in 1931, becoming

THE WEST COAST | From Hokitika to the glaciers

the first to do the trip solo. Menzies' plane, the *Southern Cross Junior*, crash-landed in the La Fontaine swamp, leaving Menzies strapped in upside down in the mud. There's little reason to actually stop in Harihari but you might want to turn onto Whanganui Flat Road and drive 20km coastwards to the start of the **Harihari Coastal Walkway** (8km; 2–3hr; negligible ascent), which follows a track used by miners heading south in the 1870s. The route runs through kahikatea forest to a spectacular piece of coastline, a sandy beach and the Doughboy Lookout, with great views of the Southern Alps.

Harihari **accommodation** is limited to a couple of places on the main road (SH6): the old but pleasant and cycle-friendly *Tomasi Motel* (☎0800/753 311; beds ❶, cabins ❷, motel rooms ❹) and the *Harihari Motor Inn* (☎0800/833 026, ✉hhmi@xtra.co.nz; dorms ❶, rooms ❹), which also has space for camping and vans ($7.50) and a spa; and the excellent *Wapiti Park Homestead* (☎03/753 3074 & 0800/927 484, ⓦwww.wapitipark.co.nz; ❼), a farmstay on the southern exit from town. Best **eating** option is the *Harihari Motor Inn*, where there are good bar meals.

Whataroa

From mid-October to late February, New Zealand's entire population of the graceful white heron (*kotuku*) arrives to breed at the Waitangiroto Nature Reserve, by the northern end of the Okarito Lagoon. The sanctuary is near **WHATAROA**, 35km south of Harihari, but access is strictly controlled and the only way to visit is with the DOC-sanctioned **White Heron Sanctuary Tours** (Nov–Feb 3–7 daily; 2.5hr; $89; booking advised ☎0800/523 456, ⓦwww.whiteherontours.co.nz), which include a twenty-minute bus journey, a twenty-minute jetboat ride on the narrow Waitangiroto River, and half an hour observing the birds from a well-placed hide. Outside the heron season, the Rainforest Nature and Jetboating Tours ($89) follow essentially the same route but concentrate on what's appropriate to that season – tui and bellbirds feeding on flowering kowhai from August to October for example. In town, take a look in the Kotuku Gallery, which contains some local, one-off greenstone, bone and wood carvings and some hand-woven flax items, all at reasonable prices.

The White Heron Sanctuary Tours office on the main highway acts as the local **visitor centre** (no set hours; ☎03/753 4120) and also has **motel** units (❹) and cabins (❷). The *Whataroa Hotel* (☎03/753 4076, ✉whataroahotel@xtra.co.nz; ❹) has B&B, as well as a bit of wasteland out the back for campervans ($15). The *Whataroa Hotel* serves evening **meals** and is the focal point of the town, while the *White Heron Tearooms* caters to daytime snackers.

Okarito

In 1642, Abel Tasman became the first European to set eyes on Aotearoa at **OKARITO**, a hamlet scattered around the southern side of its eponymous lagoon and reached by a ten-kilometre side-road, 15km south of Whataroa. Two centuries later, the discovery of gold sparked an eighteen-month boom that saw fifty stores and hotels spring up along the lagoon's shores. Timber milling and flax production stood in once the gold had gone but the community foundered, leaving a handful of holiday homes, a few dozen permanent residents, and a lovely beach and lagoon used as the setting for much of Keri Hulme's Booker Prize-winning novel, *The Bone People*.

The best of the **Okarito Lagoon** is hard to fully appreciate from the shore, but Okarito Nature Tours (☎ & ℻03/753 4014, ⓦwww.okarito.co.nz) run excellent-value and well-organized guided **kayaking trips**, either going for a couple of hours ($65; minimum two), or overnight staying in an old hut ($250). Most people simply **rent double sea kayaks**, either for a two-hour paddle around the sheltered lagoon ($35), or for longer trips up to a full day ($55) or even going overnight ($85), and camping at a remote beach. Call first to check tide conditions, but plan to go out early in the morning when the water is calmest and the birds are most abundant.

Worth a look for its interpretation of the local ecology are gentle two-hour birdwatching-oriented **boat trips** with Okarito Boat Tours (either 8am or 9am; $65; ☎03/753 4017) around the lagoon, which can be booked through Okarito Nature Tours but are run by a separate group.

Boating aside, Okarito seems to draw people in, mainly just to laze about and take long strolls along deserted beaches, the most popular being the **Okarito Trig Walk** (1hr 30min return; 200m ascent) at the southern end of town, which climbs to a headland with fabulous mountain and coastal views. An extension to the Trig Walk, the **Coastal Track Walk** (3hr return from Okarito; negligible ascent), should only be tackled on a receding tide.

Practicalities

Okarito only has one street, The Strand, and the community's limited accommodation is all on it: there is **no shop** or café, so bring provisions with you. A memorial commemorating Tasman's sighting stands next to the associate *Okarito YHA* (☎03/753 4151, ✉yha.franzjosef@yha.org.nz; ❶), a simple two-room affair in an 1860 former schoolhouse, with twelve made-up bunks and a spacious and well-appointed kitchen/living area. There is no shower so you'll need to wander across the street to the shady **campsite** ($7.50; no powered sites) where showers take $1 coins. For something less primitive, try the *Royal Hostel* (☎03/753 4080, ✉info@okaritohostel.com; dorms ❶, doubles ❸, cottage ❹) a huddle of buildings with a good range of accommodation including comfy rooms and a romantic little cottage. Up the street *Kotuku Lodge* (☎03/753 4151, ⓦwww.thestrandhostel.com; triple-share ❶, room ❷), is small, attractive, welcoming and has made-up beds with towels. The owners also manage a couple of **holiday houses** which can be rented by the night (❹ plus $20 each extra); and there's *Debbie's Apartment* (☎03/753 4019, ✉okarito@minidata.co.nz; ❺) a self-contained flat with breakfast and optional extra.

Back on SH6 just south of the Okarito junction, there's a fine DOC **campsite** ($5) at Lake Mapourika.

The glaciers

Around 150km south of Hokitika, two blinding white rivers of ice force their way down towards the thick rainforest of the coastal plain – ample justification for inclusion of this region in Te Wahipounamu, the South West New Zealand World Heritage Area. The glaciers are stunning viewed from a distance, but are even more impressive close up, generating a palpable connection between the

---

The glacial name game

To avoid confusion between the villages and the glaciers from which they derive their names, we've used a capital "G" for the Franz Josef Glacier (Waiau) village, and a lower-case "g" for the Franz Josef glacier; the same goes for the village of Fox Glacier (Weheka), which lies close to the foot of the Fox glacier.

Glaciers for beginners

The existence of a **glacier** is always a balancing act between competing forces: snow-fall at the **névé**, high in the mountains, battles with rapid melting at the **terminal** lower down the valley, the victor determining whether the glacier will advance or retreat. Snowfall metres thick gradually compacts to form clear **blue ice**, which accumulates to the point when it starts to flow downhill under its own weight. Friction against the valley walls slows the sides while ice in the centre charges headlong down the valley, giving the characteristic scalloped effect on the surface, which is especially pronounced on such vigorous glaciers as Franz Josef and Fox. Where a riverbed steepens, the river forms a rapid: under similar conditions, glaciers break up into an **ice fall**, full of towering blocks of ice known as **seracs**, separated by **crevasses**.

Visitors familiar with grubby glaciers in the European Alps or American Rockies will expect the surface to be mottled with **rock debris** which has fallen off the valley walls onto the surface; however, the glaciers here descend so steeply that the cover doesn't have time to build up and they remain pristine and white. Rock still gets carried down with the glacier though, and when the glacier retreats, this is deposited as **terminal moraine**. Occasionally retreating glaciers leave behind huge chunks of ice which, on melting, form **kettle lakes**.

The most telling evidence of past glacial movements is the location of the **trim line** on the valley wall, caused by the glacier stripping away all vegetation. At Fox and Franz Josef, the advance associated with the Little Ice Age around 1750 left a very visible trim line high up the valley wall, separating mature rata from scrub.

coast and the highest peaks of the Southern Alps. Within a handful of kilometres the terrain drops from over 3000m to near sea level, bringing with it **Franz Josef glacier** and **Fox glacier**, two of the largest and most impressive of the sixty-odd glaciers that creak off the South Island's icy backbone, together forming the centrepiece of the rugged **Westland National Park**. Legend tells of the beautiful Hinehukatere who so loved the mountains that she encouraged her lover, Tawe, to climb alongside her. He fell to his death and Hinehukatere cried so copiously that her tears formed the glaciers, known to Maori as Ka Riomata o Hinehukatere – "The Tears of the Avalanche Girl".

The park is equally characterized by the West Coast's prodigious **precipitation**, which here reaches its greatest expression, with five metres being the typical yearly dump. These conditions, combined with the rakish angle of the western slopes of the Southern Alps, produce some of the world's fastest-moving glaciers; stand at the foot for half an hour or so and you're bound to see a piece peel off. But these phenomenal speeds haven't been enough to completely counteract melting, and both glaciers have receded over 3km since Cook saw them at their greatest recent extent, soon after the Little Ice Age of 1750. In 1985 the process reversed, but after fifteen years of bucking the world trend by advancing, the glaciers have been backtracking once again.

Art critic and arbiter of public taste in Victorian England, John Ruskin, once postulated that glaciers retreat "on account of the vulgarity of tourists", and Franz Josef and Fox had certainly turned their tail when contemporary travellers battled their way down the coast to observe these wonders of nature, initially named "Victoria" and "Albert" respectively. In 1865, geologist Julius von Haast renamed Franz Josef after the Austro-Hungarian emperor, and following a visit by prime minister William Fox in 1872, the other glacier was bestowed with his name.

Activity in the glaciers focuses on two small **villages**, which survive almost entirely on tourist traffic. Both lie close to the base of their respective glacier and offer a comparably wide variety of plane and helicopter **flights** and **guided glacier walks** (see p.810). Franz Josef has marginally better facilities, while Fox Glacier is the quieter, more rural; with your own transport, it makes sense to base yourself in one of the two villages and explore both glaciers from there.

Franz Josef Glacier

Historically there has been little to choose between the two glacier villages, but in recent years **FRANZ JOSEF GLACIER** has edged ahead, with a wider range of places to stay and an improving culinary scene. The Franz Josef glacier almost licks the fringes of the village, the Southern Alps tower above and developers have done what they can to create an alpine character with steeply pitched roofs and pine panelling. It is an appealing place though, and small enough to make you feel almost like a local if you stay for more than a night or two — something that's easily done, considering the number of fine walks, the proximity of the glaciers and the excellent heli-rafting trips.

Arrival and information

Daily InterCity **buses** run in both directions along the coast, their schedule forcing you to spend the night in one of the glacier villages. The southbound bus drops off around Franz Josef then continues to Fox Glacier; in the morning it picks up in both villages and continues south: the northbound bus does

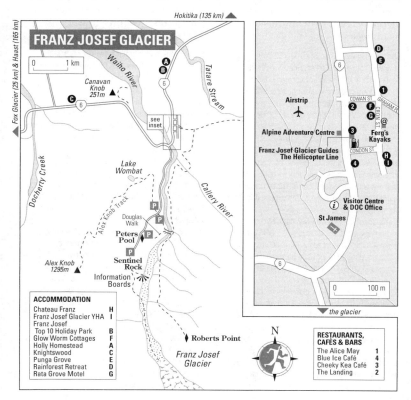

FRANZ JOSEF GLACIER

Hokitika (135 km)

Fox Glacier (25 km) & Haast (165 km)

0   1 km

Waiho River

Tatare Stream

Canavan Knob 251m

see inset

Docherty Creek

Lake Wombat

Callery River

Alex Knob Track

Douglas Walk

Peters Pool

Alex Knob 1295m

Sentinel Rock

Information Boards

ACCOMMODATION

Chateau Franz	H
Franz Josef Glacier YHA	I
Franz Josef	
Top 10 Holiday Park	B
Glow Worm Cottages	F
Holly Homestead	A
Knightswood	C
Punga Grove	E
Rainforest Retreat	D
Rata Grove Motel	G

Airstrip

Alpine Adventure Centre

Franz Josef Glacier Guides
The Helicopter Line

COWAN ST

GRAHAM PL

CRON ST

Ferg's Kayaks

CONDON ST

Visitor Centre & DOC Office

St James

0   100 m

the glacier

Roberts Point

Franz Josef Glacier

N

RESTAURANTS, CAFÉS & BARS

The Alice May	1
Blue Ice Café	4
Cheeky Kea Café	3
The Landing	2

the reverse. Atomic buses in both directions come through in the middle of the day on their Greymouth–Queenstown run.

First stop in Franz Josef should be the excellent combined **DOC office** and **visitor centre** on SH6 (daily: Nov–April 8.30am–6pm; May–Oct 8.30am–5pm; ℡03/752 0796, ✉franzjosefvc@doc.govt.nz), which has stacks of leaflets on walks in the area and first-class displays on every aspect of glaciation and the region's geology. Every half hour they show a documentary film ($3) discussing the whole South West New Zealand World Heritage Area with limited coverage of the glaciers. The centre also gets up-to-the-minute **weather reports** so check with them before starting any of the serious walks.

Pretty much everything else you are likely to need is within a couple of hundred metres along, or just off, SH6, including the region's sole **cash machine**: there are no banks hereabouts. There's fast and efficient **Internet access** at several places, including Ferg's Kayaks on Cron Street.

Getting around the region without your own transport can be a pain, but Glacier Valley Eco Tours (℡03/752 0699, ⓦwww.glaciervalley.co.nz) offer a **shuttle service** to the glacier road end ($10 return) and a series of local tours such as Lake Matheson (3hr: $55) and a Lake Matheson combo with Fox glacier ($80)

Accommodation

Despite a considerable expansion in what is available both here and in Fox Glacier, accommodation is still tight throughout the summer. Between December and March, you should aim to make **reservations** at least a week in advance.

Chateau Franz 8 Cron St ℡03/752 0738, ⓦwww.chateaufranz.co.nz. Heavily renovated hostel with a wide range of accommodation from budget dorms and smaller en-suite dorms, to full-blown motel units. There's a free spa, free soup nightly and TVs and VCRs everywhere. Dorms ❶, ensuites ❹, units ❺

Franz Josef Glacier YHA 2–4 Cron St ℡03/752 0754, ✉yha.franzjosef@yha.org.nz. After a large investment this is now the best budget accommodation in the area; very modern, well-run and airy, with a spacious kitchen, clean comfortable rooms, barbecue area and all the expected facilities. Dorms ❶, rooms ❷, ensuites ❹

Franz Josef Top 10 Holiday Park SH6, 1km north of town ℡03/752 0735 & 0800/467 897, ⓦwww.mountainview.co.nz. Rural campground with a good range of tent and powered sites, cabins and units. Camping $13, cabins ❷, units ❺

Glow Worm Cottages 27 Cron St ℡03/752 0172 & 0800/151 027, ⓦwww.glowwormcottages.co.nz. Small and homely hostel with a well-equipped kitchen, slightly cramped 6-bed dorms and four-shares with their own bathrooms, plus comfy doubles, and motel-style ensuites. Free soup, spa and bike rental ($20 a day). Dorms ❶, rooms ❷, ensuites ❺

Holly Homestead SH6, 1km north of town ℡752 0299, ⓦwww.hollyhomestead.co.nz.

Upscale B&B in an attractive two-storey 1920s home just outside town with four rooms, all with private facilities, and including a full breakfast. ❼

Knightswood SH2, 3km south of town ℡03/752 0059, ⓦwww.knightswood.co.nz. Comfortable en-suite B&B rooms in a spacious modern native-timber house surrounded by bush and a deer farm. Hearty breakfasts put you in good stead for glacier hiking. ❼

Punga Grove Cron St ℡03/752 0001 & 0800/437 269, ⓦwww.pungagrove.co.nz. Stylish, modernized luxury motels all nicely furnished and with Sky TV. Luxury units back onto the bush and come with DVD, underfloor heating and spa bath. ❼

Rainforest Retreat Cron St ℡03/752 0220 & 0800/873 346, ⓦwww.rainforestretreat.co.nz. Beautiful, bush-girt lodge and campervan park with gravel pads (good for campervans; OK for tents) and access to a communal lodge. Also spacious kitchen cabins, atmospheric log cabins on stilts, lovely luxurious lodges, Internet access, and spa pool. Camping $12–15, cabins ❹–❺, log cabins & lodges ❼

Rata Grove Motel 25 Cron St ℡0800/101 933, ⓦwww.ratagrove.co.nz. Central and fairly simple motel with studios (some with kitchens), and spacious fully equipped self-catering units sleeping up to six. Studios ❺, units ❻

THE WEST COAST | The glaciers

⑫

Walks and activities around town

Top of everyone's list of **walks** is the one from the glacier car park, 5km south of the village, to the face of the Franz Josef glacier (6km return; 1hr 30min; flat), a roped-off and ever-changing wall of ice where the Waiho River issues from beneath the glacier. The rough track crosses gravel beds left behind by past glacial retreats, giving you plenty of opportunity to observe small kettle lakes, the trim line high up the valley walls and a fault line cutting right across the valley (marked by deep gullies opposite each other). One of the best viewpoints is from the top of the glacier-scoured hump of **Sentinel Rock**, a ten-minute walk from the car park.

Worthwhile walks off the access road include the circular **Douglas Walk** (1hr) past Peter's Pool, a serene lake left by a retreat in the late eighteenth century, and the **Alex Knob Track** (12km; 8hr return; 1000m ascent), which climbs high above the glacier through several vegetation zones and offers fine views up the valley. The first few metres of the Douglas Walk are shared with the spectacular **Roberts Point Track** (9km; 5hr return; 600m ascent) which climbs up through dripping rainforest on the opposite (northern) side of the valley, high above the glacier. Slippery stream crossings and occasional rock staircase make this an entertaining though not especially strenuous walk. The only way to actually walk on the glacier surface is with a guide (see box on p.810).

The shortest walk from town follows SH6 for a couple of hundred metres south to **St James Church**, which once framed the glacier in the altar window. The ice retreated from view in 1953, and the church itself nearly did the same in 1995, when the flooded Waiho River scoured away the alluvial bank and left the church precariously poised on a cliff. The authorities have since constructed protective stop banks which also serve to ensure the town doesn't get flooded: the glacier's advance in recent years has pushed forward so much gravel that the riverbed is now higher than most of the town.

Glacier hikes go in most weathers, but on misty and **wet days** you may well find that scenic flights and helihikes are called off and alternatives are limited. There's always the twenty-minute *Flowing West* wide-screen film (3–5 showings daily; $10) at the Alpine Adventure Centre, an over-produced journey around the region with all the spirit of a failed soft-drink commercial. A better bet might be to join a **guided kayaking** with Ferg's Kayaks, The Red Bus, Cron St (℡0800/423 262, ⓦwww.glacierkayaks.com), with relaxing and informative trips on the rain-forest fringed Lake Mapourika ("Flower of the Dawn"), 8km north of town. Trips run in the morning, afternoon and early evening, last about 3.5hrs (2.5hrs on the water; $55), offer an insight into the local plant- and bird-life, loads of photographic opportunities and are, of course, equally enjoyable in fine weather.

Further afield, there's excellent **heli-rafting** on local rivers with Franz Josef-based Rivers Wild (see p.802).

Eating and drinking

Franz Josef is a small place with a surprisingly decent range of **places to eat** and drink. The relatively remote location keeps prices high though, and even if you are self-catering you can expect to pay over the odds for a limited stock of **groceries**.

The Alice May cnr Cowan St & Cron St. Intimate and convivial restaurant and bar with good beer and a range of bistro meals for $17–$27, including some tasty pizzas ($20); justifiably a favourite with the locals.

Blue Ice Café SH6. The modern and airy restaurant at street level serves imaginative and tasty mains for around $25 and a range of gourmet pizzas from $20, which can also be ordered to take away or eaten in the upstairs bar where the free pool table

The range of flights and glacier walks available from Franz Josef Glacier and Fox Glacier are almost identical.

Flightseeing

On any fine day the skies above both villages are abuzz with choppers and light planes. Safety demands that specific **flight paths** must be followed, limiting what can be offered and forcing companies to compete on price; ask for youth, student, YHA, BBH, senior or just-for-the-sake-of-it **discounts**, most readily given if you can band together in a group of four to six and present yourselves as a ready-to-go plane or chopper load.

Plane flights (mostly from Franz Josef) give you a longer flight with grater range for less money, and a skiplane landing on a snowfield can be quite exciting. The only company doing landings is Mount Cook Ski Planes (℡03/752 0714 & 0800/800 702, ＠www.mtcookskiplanes.com) who run overflights of both glaciers (30min; around $190) and circuits of Mount Cook (55min; $265): both can add landings (conditions permitting; extra $50–65) on a glacier where the silence is deafening. Air Safaris (℡03/680 6880 & 0800/723 274, ＠www.airsafaris.co.nz) are usually a smidgen cheaper but don't do landings.

Increasingly, **helicopters** are taking over, with all operators regularly landing on a snow field high above the glacier where the rotors are left running – hardly a serene setting. Three companies all charge similar prices for flights, including snow landings: one glacier (20min; $165), two glaciers (30min; $220), and two glaciers plus Mount Cook (40min; $310): Fox and Franz Josef Heliservices (℡03/751 0866 & 0800/800 793, ＠www.scenic-flights.co.nz) are as good as any.

Walking on glaciers

Two companies are licensed to take visitors on **Franz Josef glacier walks** including the venerable Franz Josef Glacier Guides, SH6 (℡03/752 0763 & 0800/484 337, ＠www.franzjosefglacier.com), who undertake a **half-day trip** (2–4 daily; $65) that involves a trudge across the braided riverbed below the glacier in boots fitted with mini-crampons then an hour or so on the ice, snaking up ample ice steps cut by your guide. Occasional bridges span deep blue crevasses but it can still be unnerving for vertigo sufferers. For a more tangible sense of adventure, fork out for the **full-day trip** ($110) which gives around five hours on the ice, and gives you a chance to use an ice axe, though it is mostly for show. **Heli-hiking** (2–3 daily; 2hr 30min; $260) combines a short helicopter flight with a couple of hours on a fascinating section of ice caves, pinnacles and seracs that you couldn't hope to reach on foot in a day: well worth saving up for. Try to be clear about your aspirations and abilities and you can be matched up with a party of like-minded folk. The Guiding Company (℡0800/800 102, ＠www.nzguides.com) offer an almost identical selection of trips, plus ice climbing ($200) – an instructional roped-up day in plastic boots with crampons and ice tools on steep ice.

Glacier walking is perhaps more rewarding (and cheaper) on the **Fox Glacier**, where entry is from the side, giving more immediate access to crevasses and seracs. Alpine Guides (℡03/751 0825 or 0800/111 600, ＠www.foxguides.co.nz) lead half-day walks (2–4 daily; $49), with around an hour on the ice, and full-day trips ($79), giving over three hours on the ice, and helihikes ($235) with three hours of icy hiking. For serious ice addicts, they also offer **Ice Climbing Instruction Days** ($190), which give you a chance to get vertical, and **Heli-ice Climbing** ($435) throwing in a scenic flight that gets you higher on the glacier.

and rowdy music draws in a lively, sometimes back-packer heavy, crowd nightly; another local favourite. **Cheeky Kea Café** SH6. Cheerful and inexpensive café serving a middle-of-the-road selection of grills, burgers, steaks, chicken, fish, sandwiches and lots of chips. BYO.

The Landing cnr of SH6 and Condon St. All day licensed café and bar serving naan plat-ters ($8), feta salad ($12) and chicken wraps ($15), plus more substantial fare in the evenings (mains around $24); all available indoors or out.

Fox Glacier

FOX GLACIER, 25km south of Franz Josef, lies scattered over an outwash plain of the Fox and Cook rivers, and supports the local farming community, as well as sightseers. Everything of interest is beside SH6 or Cook Flat Road, which passes the scenic Lake Matheson on the way to the former gold settlement and seal colony at Gillespies Beach. The foot of the Fox glacier lies around 6km away.

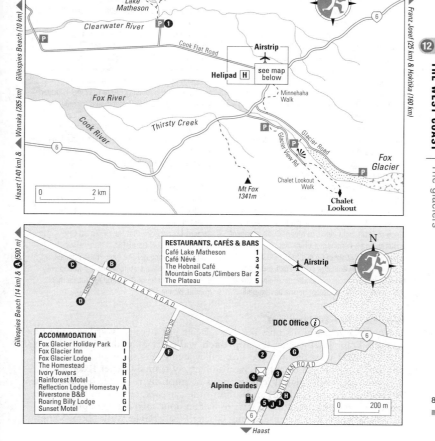

Arrival and information

The village of Fox Glacier experiences the same **bus** schedule as Franz Josef (see p.807) and consequently has similar problems with accommodation through the summer months. If you come unstuck, seek help at the combined **DOC office** and **visitor centre**, SH6 (Dec to mid-April daily 9am–4.30pm; mid-April to Nov Mon–Fri 9am–4.30pm; ℡03/751 0807, Ⓔflxglaciervc@doc.govt.nz) which, besides providing information about the region, has displays concentrating on lowland forests.

Accommodation

Fox Glacier's range of places to stay is more limited than Franz Josef's but is generally pretty good; **booking** as far ahead as you can is a good idea and be prepared for resort prices.

Fox Glacier Holiday Park Kerrs Rd ℡03/751 0821, Ⓦwww.holidayparks.co.nz/fox. Fairly basic campsite with tent sites, a bunkhouse, cabins and self-contained units. Camping $10, dorms ❶, cabins ❸, units ❹

Fox Glacier Inn Sullivan Rd ℡03/751 0022 & 0508/369 466, Ⓦwww.foxglacierinn.co.nz. Combination backpackers and lodge complete with booking centre, bar and café. Four-shares and simple made-up doubles are in the older block, and there are 16 spacious rooms with small ensuites. Four-shares ❶, backpacker rooms ❸, ensuites ❺.

Fox Glacier Lodge Sullivan Rd ℡03/751 0888 & 0800/369 800, Ⓔfoxglacierlodge@hotmail.com. A pine-lined alpine chalet and associated cabins with attractively furnished en-suite rooms (some with spa baths) all sharing communal kitchen and lounge area. A buffet breakfast is included, and there are campervan hook-ups outside. Bikes can be rented for around $25 a day. Powered sites $12 per person, rooms ❼

The Homestead Cook Flat Rd, 700m off SH6 ℡03/751 0835, Ⓔfoxhmstd@xtra.co.nz. Friendly homestay in a nice old house within walking distance of town, with views of Mount Cook, pleasant ensuites and a continental breakfast. ❻

Ivory Towers Sullivan Rd ℡03/751 0838, Ⓦwww.ivorytowerslodge.co.nz. Fox's only genuine backpackers in town; a friendly, clean and colourfully decorated hostel. Most dorms having beds rather than bunks and some rooms (all with sheets) share a separate lounge area. The kitchen is spacious, there's a spa, and bikes can be rented for $24 a day. Dorms ❶, rooms ❸, ensuites ❹

Rainforest Motel Cook Flat Rd, 200m off SH6 ℡03/751 0140 & 0800/724 636, Ⓦwww.rainforest.co.nz. Log cabin exteriors belie the clean interior lines of attractive and well-priced studios and larger one-bedroom units. ❺

Reflection Lodge Homestay Cook Flat Rd, 1.5km off SH6 ℡03/751 0707, Ⓦwww.reflectionlodge.co.nz. So named because of the reflection of the mountains in the large garden pond, this neat homestay offers reasonably priced accommodation in comfortable and friendly surroundings. ❻

Riverstone B&B 33 Pekanga Drive ℡03/451 0048, Ⓦwww.fox-glacier.co.nz. Nice, modern two-room B&B with continental breakfast included. Shared bathroom ❺, ensuite ❻

Roaring Billy Lodge SH6 ℡03/751 0815, Ⓔkathynz@xtra.co.nz. Friendly homestay in the centre of Fox Glacier with simple rooms, a comfortable lounge area and a cooked vegetarian breakfast. ❺

Sunset Motel Cook Flat Rd, 800m off SH6 ℡03/751 0062 & 0800/751 006, Ⓦwww.sunsettourism.co.nz. The best of the upscale motels, brand new, tastefully decorated and with great views of Mount Cook and Mount Tasman from all rooms. ❼

Walks and activities

It would be a shame to miss the Fox glacier just because you have already seen the Franz Josef glacier: the **approach walks** are quite different and their characters are very distinct, the Fox valley being less sheer but with more impressive rock falls. The approach, imaginatively named Glacier Road, crosses the wide bed left by glacial retreats and is occasionally re-routed as "dead" ice under the roadway gradually melts. From the car park, 6km from the town, a track leads to the foot of the glacier in half an hour, crossing a couple of small streams en route. Part way back along Glacier Road, **River Walk** (2km; 30min) crosses a historic swingbridge to the Glacier Valley Viewpoint on Glacier View Road, which runs along the south side of the Fox River. From here, the **Chalet Lookout Walk** (4km; 1hr 15min return) climbs moderately for stupendous glacier and mountain views.

It's difficult to imagine a New Zealand calendar or picture book without a photo of Mount Cook and Mount Tasman mirrored in **Lake Matheson**, 6km west of town along Cook Flat Road. A well signposted lakeside boardwalk through lovely native bush encircles the lake, which was formed by an iceberg left behind when the Fox glacier retreated 14,000 years ago. It takes around an hour and gives everyone, but particularly those who venture out before breakfast, a chance for that perfect image. The *Café Lake Matheson*, by the Lake Matheson car park, is beautifully located.

Continue 15km along Cook Flat Road to reach **Gillespies Beach**, a former gold-mining settlement where a small cemetery, the remains of a dredge and piles of tailings can be seen. A **walk** from here (3–4hr return) takes you north, parallel with the beach, before reaching Galway Beach and a colony of **fur seals**.

Back in Fox, fill an empty half hour with a stroll around the flat **Minnehaha Walk** (1km; 20min loop), which winds through lush bush that's cool and shady on a summer day, or dank and brooding in the rain. Come after dark to see **glow-worms**.

Finally, if all this leaves you unruffled then try a **tandem skydive** (☎03/751 0080) either from 9000ft ($225) or 12,000ft ($265).

Eating and drinking

For its diminutive size, Fox Glacier does a reasonable job of catering to hungry walkers coming off the glacier-side paths, with a small selection of reasonably priced **cafés**, a restaurant and a couple of lively **bars**.

Café Lake Matheson Cook Flat Rd
☎03/751 0878. Good café at the start of the walk around Lake Matheson, made special by its mountain views. Their $10 all-day breakfast rewards an early walk, or come later for the $25 sunset barbecue (6–9pm; call for a free pick-up in town).

Café Névé SH6. Great café serving excellent food and coffee throughout the day both inside and out. Try the smoked chicken and pinenut salad ($15), BLT on Turkish flatbread ($14), a range of evening main courses (around $28), and something from their broad range of wines by the glass. The vegetarian gourmet pizza ($14–28) comes particularly recommended.

The Hobnail Café SH6. Adequate café in the same building as Alpine Guides, with a standard range of pies, sandwiches, cakes and coffee in alpine-chalet surroundings.

Mountain Goats/Climbers Bar at the *Fox Glacier Resort Hotel*, SH6. Straightforward drinking bar with pool table attached to a room where equally straightforward bar meals ($8–18) are served.

The Plateau SH6. Newish café and bar serving classy lunches and dinners at what are quite modest prices for these parts. Try the chicken, avocado and brie burger ($16), spinach and ricotta pasta ($15) or one of the nightly special mains ($22–27). The desserts blackboard always has something tempting.

South Westland and Makarora

South from the glaciers, the West Coast feels remoter still. There wasn't even a road through here until 1965 and the final section of tarmac wasn't laid on the Haast Pass until 1995. SH6 mostly runs inland, passing the start of the hike to the **Welcome Flat Hot Springs** (see p.814), through kahikatea and rimu forests as far as **Knight's Point**, where it returns to the coast along the edge of the Haast Coastal Plain, with its stunning **coastal dune systems** sheltering lakes and some fine stands of kahikatea. The plain continues south past the

Welcome Flat Hot Springs and the Copland Track

The most popular two-day hike in the region is the in-and-back jaunt to the **Welcome Flat Hot Springs**, a series of open-air pools where you're bound to find a spot that's just the right temperature for easing those bones. Almost everyone spends the night at DOC's adjacent **Welcome Flat Hut** ($10; 30 bunks) or camping nearby ($5). Be warned that during the summer the hut is very popular and you may just get a mattress on the floor or worse.

The track from **SH6 to Welcome Flat** (17km; 6–7hr; 400m ascent), is a fairly tough tramp (far less defined than any of the Great Walks) following the true right bank all the way to Welcome Flat, crossing numerous creeks by hopping from rock to rock or wading. If the creeks are high, as they commonly are, you may have to use the flood bridges, which will add an hour or so. After heavy rain, the track becomes impassable: take plenty of extra supplies in case you get held up by a day or two.

The track starts by a car park on SH6, 26km south of Fox Glacier: Atomic and InterCity **buses** will drop-off, and pick up pre-booked customers.

The track to Welcome Flat is part of the three-to-four-day **Copland Track** over the spectacular 2150m Copland Pass to Aoraki/Mount Cook Village. It has long been regarded as the pinnacle of tramping achievement, on the cusp of real mountaineering. It always requires competent use of an ice axe and crampons but is currently highly dangerous on account of unstable rock rubble beside the Hooker Glacier on the Mount Cook side. If you're still keen, talk to one of the guiding companies in Fox Glacier or Aoraki/Mount Cook Village.

scattered township of **Haast** to the site of the short-lived colonial settlement of **Jackson Bay**. From Haast, SH6 veers inland over the Haast Pass to the former timber town of **Makarora**, not strictly part of the West Coast but moist enough to share some of the same characteristics and a base for the excellent **Gillespie Pass** Tramp.

South to Haast

Many visitors do the run from the glaciers to Wanaka or Queenstown in one day, missing out on some fine country that makes up for its relative lack of comforts with its sheer sense of remoteness. Facilities aren't completely absent: the majority of the accommodation and eating places are clustered around Haast, but there are a few pitstops along the way. One place you might like to break your journey is **Bruce Bay**, 45km south of Fox Glacier, where the road briefly parallels a long driftwood-strewn beach perfect for an atmospheric stroll. Some 17km further south, the road crosses the **Paringa River**, where a plaque marks the southern limit of Thomas Brunner's 1846–48 explorations. He recorded in his diary the desire to "once more see the face of a white man, and hear my native tongue". Buses all stop nearby at the *Salmon Farm* for an expensive snack or light lunch on a wooden deck overlooking salmon-rearing ponds. A better bet is to pick up some delicious hot- or cold-smoked salmon to take away and continue 7km south to the northern shores of **Lake Paringa** and the *Heritage Lodge Lake Paringa* (☎03/751 0894 & 0800/727 464; rooms ❹, units ❺), where there's a good café and accommodation in basic rooms and self-contained units. If plans go ahead, the café should be moved lakeside in 2005 and a completely new hotel will be build on the site. The lodge sells fishing licences and has fishing tackle for guests' use, handy if you are planning to fish for Quinnat salmon (Oct–March) and brown trout (all year) from the DOC's simple but beautifully sited Lake Paringa **campsite** ($5), a further kilometre to the south.

Around 18km south of Lake Paringa, the **Monro Beach Walk** (5km; 1hr 30min return) leads through lovely forest to one of the best places for spotting rare **Fiordland crested penguins** – mainly during the breeding season (July–Dec), but also occasionally in February, when they come ashore to moult. Nature lovers with ample wallets can gain a deeper appreciation of the fragile ecosystems of south Westland by staying nearby at the exclusive *Wilderness Lodge Lake Moeraki* (T03/750 0881, Wwww.wildernesslodge.co.nz;) where, for around $250 per person per day, you get lodge **accommodation**, all meals, free canoe use and all manner of guided nature walks and safaris.

The highway finally returns to the coast 5km on at **Knight's Point**, where a roadside marker commemorates the linking of Westland and Otago by road in 1965; a dog belonging to one of the surveyors lent his name to this dramatic bluff fringed by magnificent seascapes where, with binoculars, seals can often be picked out on the rocks below. Ahead lies the **Haast Coastal Plain**, which kicks off at the tea-coloured **Ship Creek**, where a picnic area and information panels by a beautiful long surf-pounded beach mark the start of two lovely walks: the twenty-minute **Kahikatea Swamp Forest Walk** up the river through kahikatea forest to a lookout and the **Mataketake Dune Lake Walk** (2km; 30min return) along the coast to the dune-trapped Lake Mataketake.

From Ship Creek it is only another 15km to the 700m-long Haast River Bridge, the longest single-lane bridge in the country, immediately before Haast Junction.

Haast

HAAST is initially a confusing place, with three tiny communities all taking the name: Haast Junction, at the intersection of SH6 and the minor road to Jackson Bay; Haast Beach, 4km along the Jackson Bay Road (see p.816) and Haast Township, the largest settlement 3km along SH6 towards the Haast Pass and Wanaka.

The first stop is Haast Junction, site of the distinctive **Haast Visitor Centre** (daily: early Nov to April 9am–6pm; rest of year 9am–4.30pm; T03/750 0809, Ehaastvc@doc.govt.nz), which serves as the local visitor centre but is much more, with highly informative displays on all aspects of the local environment, and the short *Edge of Wilderness* film shown every half hour ($3). Time spent in here may well induce you to spend longer in what they are at pains to point out is part of the Southwest New Zealand World Heritage Area. To explore deeper into this region, consider joining a **jetboat safari** with Waiatoto River Safaris (T03/750 0780 & 0800/538 723, Wwww.riversafaris.co.nz; daily on demand; $125), an excellent two-hour wilderness ride from the coast into the heart of the mountains with the emphasis firmly on appreciation of the area's history and scenery. Alternatively, try the extremely knowledgeable pilots at Heliventures (T03/750 0866, Wwww.heliventures.co.nz), who offer **flights** to the Hidden Valley (30min; $245, minimum 3) and Mount Aspiring (1hr; $395, minimum 3) including a snow landing.

Even if you're just passing through you'll probably want to **eat**, but shouldn't expect too much. At Haast Township the *Fantail Café* does adequate teas, snacks and takeaways; and *Smithy's Tavern* is good for the likes of BLT and chips ($10), fish and chips ($18), a humungous mixed grill ($20), and a lively night at the bar with the locals. There's a small and fairly expensive supermarket for supplies. Up the road at Haast Junction, *McGuires Lodge* has a handy café and restaurant.

Those wanting to **stay** have an increasing range of choices, but Haast still gets busy from Christmas to the end of February and you should book ahead.

Accommodation

Collyer House, Okuru, 13km south of Haast Junction ☎03/750 0022, ⓦwww
.collyerhouse.co.nz. Very appealing luxury accommodation with four modern ensuites decorated in a nice mixture of antique and modern furnishings and all with distant sea views. A sizeable cooked breakfast is served and there are evening meals by arrangement ($45). **❼**

Haast Beach Holiday Park Okuru, 15km south of Haast Junction ☎03/750 0860. ⓔhaastpark
@xtra.co.nz. Simple but comfortable holiday park close to the beach and the Hapuku Estuary Walk. Tents $11, dorms **❶**, cabins **❷**, motel units **❹**

Haast Highway Accommodation Haast Township ☎03/750 0703, ⓔhaastway
@xtra.co.nz. Inferior associate YHA hostel and associated motel that's handy for its campervan hook-ups and does take tents, though if it is raining or the manager decides the hostel facilities are already stretched you'll be forced to either travel 17km to the *Haast Beach Holiday Park* (see

below), or use a little discreet imagination. Camping $11, dorms 1, rooms **❷**, motel units **❺**

Heritage Park Lodge Haast Township ☎0800/526 252, ⓦwww.heritageparklodge.co.nz. Friendly motel offering probably the best value rooms around: modern, comfortable studios with TV and video, and some units with self-catering facilities. Studios **❹**, units **❺**

Kenmure House Hannah's Clearing, 22km south of Haast Junction ☎0800/750 087, ⓔkenmure2
@hptmail.com. Fully equipped three bedroom house sleeping up to six and let for just $80 for the first two adults plus $15 for each extra. This is the closest accommodation to Jackson Bay. The hosts live nearby and can even arrange breakfast. **❹**

Wilderness Accommodation Haast Township ☎03/750 0029. Comfortable and welcoming spot combining a backpacker hostel with four-shares and made-up doubles, and a series of motel studio units, all with access to a common area and kitchen. They also have scooter rental for $40 a half-day, ideal for trips to Jackson Bay. Dorms **❶**, backpacker rooms **❷**, units **❹**

The road to Jackson Bay

A real sense of isolation soon sets in on the 50km dead-end road south to the fishing village of Jackson Bay, a long thin strip of tarmac hemmed in by verdant prehistoric bush and tall trees. A modest number of inquisitive tourists make it down this way, to discover a place hanging on by its fingernails. Leaving Haast Junction, the canopies of windswept roadside trees are bunched together like cauliflower heads down to and beyond **Haast Beach**, 4km south, where there's a small shop and petrol supplies. The one-time Maori fishing and greenstone-gathering settlement of **Okuru**, 10km further south, dates back to around 1300, and now comprises a strip of beach housing set back from a wild coastline. There's accommodation in the form of *Collyer House* (see above) and, a couple of kilometres on, *Haast Beach Holiday Park* (see above). Opposite, the **Hapuku Estuary Walk** (20min loop), which follows a raised boardwalk over a brackish lagoon and through kowhai forest that gleams brilliant yellow in October and November. Old sand dunes support rimu and kahikatea forest, and there are occasional views out to the **Open Bay Islands**, noted by Cook in 1770 and later gainfully employed as a sealing base away from the sandflies of the coast. They are now a **wildlife sanctuary** and a major breeding colony for fur seals and Fiordland crested penguins.

The road continues 35km to **JACKSON BAY** (Okahu in Maori), a former sealing station tucked in the curve of Jackson Head, which protects it from the worst of the westerlies. In 1875 it was chosen as the site for a "Special Settlement", a significant port and commercial centre to rival Greymouth and Hokitika. Assisted migrants – Scandinavians, Germans, Poles, Italians, English and Irish – were expected to carve a living from tiny land allocations, with limited and irregular supplies. Sodden by rain, crops rotted, and people were soon leaving in droves; a few stalwarts stayed, their descendants providing the core of today's residents, who eke out a meagre living from lobster and tuna fishing.

Try the **Wharekai Te Kau Walk** (40min return) across the low isthmus behind Jackson Head to a beach where Fiordland crested penguins can sometimes be seen from July to November. Also consider the **Smoothwater Track** (3hr return), with great coastal views on the way to the Smoothwater River, or the longer **Stafford Bay Walk** (8–10hr return), with the possibility of a night at the basic Stafford Bay Hut (free). Details and tide tables are available from the Haast Visitor Centre.

There are no **facilities** in Jackson Bay except for *The Craypot*, a kind of diner on wheels where you can get fantastic fresh-cooked fish and chips, big mugs of tea and various meat options, away from the sandflies while gazing at the sea-tossed fishing boats through fake leadlight windows and listening to the roar of the surf. Occasionally, you'll even see hungry local hunters dropped off at the beach by helicopter.

Haast Pass and Makarora

From Haast it is nearly 150km over the **Haast Pass** (at 563m, the lowest road crossing of the Southern Alps) to Wanaka – a journey from the verdant rain-soaked forests of the West Coast into the parched, rolling grasslands of Central Otago. Ngai Tahu used the route as a greenstone trading route and probably introduced it to gold prospector Charles Cameron, who became the first Pakeha to cross in 1863; he was closely followed by the more influential **Julius Von Haast**, who modestly named it after himself. The pass was finally opened as a vehicular road as far as Haast in 1960, linked through to Fox Glacier in 1965 and completely sealed in 1995.

The road starts beside the broad **Haast River** which, as the road climbs, narrows into a series of churning cascades. Numerous short and well signposted walks, mostly to waterfalls on tributaries, spur off at intervals. The most celebrated include the **Thunder Creek Falls** (10min), the roadside **Fantail Falls**, and the **Blue Pools Walk** (30min return), where an icy, aquamarine stream issues from a narrow gorge: swim if you dare. Though there are few specific sights, it is a great area to linger a while, **camping** in one of the DOC's toilets-and-water sites (all $5 per person) along the way: first up is Pleasant Flat, 45km from Haast, followed by Cameron Flat, 8km over the Pass and 10km short of Makarora.

Makarora

The hamlet of **MAKARORA** lies roughly midway between Haast and Wanaka, on the northern fringe of the Mount Aspiring National Park. If you're aching for the comforts of Wanaka and Queenstown there's little reason to stop, but casual hikers, and keen trampers with a few days to spare should consider tackling the local walks, some aided by flights and jetboat rides.

In the nineteenth century the dense **forests** all about and the proximity of Lake Wanaka made Makarora the perfect spot for marshalling cut logs across the lake and coaxing them down the Clutha River southeast to the fledgling North Otago **gold towns** of Clyde and Cromwell. The creation of the national park in 1964 paved the way for Makarora's increasing importance as the main northern access point to a region of majestic beauty, alpine vegetation and dense beech-filled valleys.

About all you'll find here is a motor camp, a shop and a **DOC office** (late Dec to April Mon–Fri 8am–5pm Sat & Sun 8.30am–4.30pm; May to late Dec Mon–Fri 8am–5pm; ☎03/443 8365, ☎443 8374), the place to go for information and hut tickets for tramps. The main justification for stopping here is

Gillespie Pass: the Wilkin and Young valleys circuit

This tramp over the 1490m **Gillespie Pass** links the upper valley of the **Young River** with that of the **Siberia Stream** and the **Wilkin River**. The scenery is superb, the match of any of the more celebrated valleys further south, but is tramped by a fraction of the folk on the Routeburn or the Greenstone tracks; perhaps the biggest gripe for the tramping purist is the disturbance caused by **planes** flying into the Siberia Valley. The tramp can be divided up into smaller chunks, using Siberia Experience's planes and jetboats (see below), but the full circuit (60km) takes three days.

The DOC's *Tramping Guide to the Makarora Region* ($3.50) has all the detail you need for this walk, though the *Mount Aspiring National Park* and the 1:50,000 *Wilkin* **maps** are useful.

Access and accommodation

All the **huts** ($10) in the Wilkin and Young valleys are equipped with mattresses and heating (but not cooking) stoves; hut **tickets** and annual hut **passes** are available from the DOC office in Makarora (see p.817). The walk is typically done up the Young Valley and down the Wilkin – the way we've described it here. **Access** at both ends of the walk is a question of **wading** the broad, braided **Makarora River**. The river changes course frequently, rains bring up the level and in spring and early summer snowmelt increases flows in the afternoon: consult DOC about the best approach. Expect the water to be between knee and thigh level. It may pay to band together with other trampers and get a **jetboat** to drop you at the confluence of the Young and Makarora rivers ($25, minimum 3); it's also a good idea to arrange a **pick-up** by jetboat ($50) from Kerin Forks at the far end of the walk, unless you want to take your chances with river crossings or a stand-by flight out of Siberia Valley. The DOC leaflet indicates which operators are providing access and pick-up services at any given time of the year.

The route

The walk proper starts on the northern bank of the confluence of the Young and Makarora rivers; from Makarora, walk 3km upstream, find a good crossing place upstream of the confluence then walk down the true right bank of the Makarora to the bush-side marker. From the **confluence to Young Hut** (15km; 7–9hr; 700m ascent), the easy-to-follow track traces the true left bank through beech forest then, after a fork, follows the true left bank of the South Branch, climbing steeply with some

to head out on the Gillespie Pass tramp (see above) or to join Southern Alps Air's four-hour **Siberia Experience** (☎0800/345 666, ⊛www .siberiaexperience.co.nz; $225), an excellent combination of flying into the remote Siberia Valley, three hours of tramping to the Wilkin River and jetboating back to Makarora. The same operator also offers flights around Mount Aspiring (around $170, min 3 people). The **jetboating** section can also be tackled separately with Wilkin River Jet (☎03/443 8351; 1hr; $72), as good value a jetboat ride as you'll find anywhere in New Zealand. Ask about their **Jumboland Wonderwalk** ($225) involving a helicopter flight, six hours of walking along the Wilkin River, and the jetboat out.

Finally, if the longer hikes seem a little daunting, there are a couple of **shorter walks** close to Makarora, the **Makarora Bush Nature Walk** (20min), which starts near the visitor centre and, branching off this, the **Mount Shrimpton Track** (5km return, 4–5hr, 900m ascent), which climbs very steeply up through silver beech to the bushline, then to a knob overlooking the Makarora Valley.

difficulty over a bad slip. It eases after a while and the track continues, sometimes indistinctly, through ever more stunted bush and occasional clearings to the tree line. Collect firewood here – you're now less than half an hour from the Young Hut (10 bunks), which is wonderfully sited in a magnificent avalanche-scoured rock cirque crowned by 2202m Mount Awful, apparently named in wonder rather than horror.

Suitably rested, you've another fairly strenuous day ahead from **Young Hut to Siberia Hut** (9km; 6–7hr; 500m ascent, 800m descent) over the Gillespie Pass. Keep to the true right bank until you reach a rock cairn, which marks the start of a steep and lengthy ascent, following snow poles to a saddle; it'll take two or three hours to reach this fabulous, barren spot with views across the snow-capped northern peaks of the Mount Aspiring National Park. Grassy slopes marked by more snow poles lead steeply down to Gillespie Stream, which is followed to its confluence with the Siberia Stream, from where it's a gentle, undulating hour downstream to Siberia Hut (20 bunks), though keen types might tag on a side-trip to **Lake Crucible** (4–5hr return) before cantering down to the hut. Those with more modest aspirations can spend two nights at Siberia Hut and do the **Lake Crucible side trip** (13km; 6–7hr return; 500m ascent) on the spare day. From the Siberia Hut, retrace your steps to the confluence of the Siberia and Gillespie streams, ford the Gillespie Stream and continue along the true left bank of the Siberia Stream a short distance until you see Crucible Stream cascading in a deep gash on the far side. Ford Siberia Stream and ascend through the bush on the true right bank of the stream. It is hard going, and route-finding among the alpine meadows higher up can be difficult but the deep, alpine lake tucked under the skirts of Mount Alba and choked with small icebergs is ample reward.

Planes fly in and out of the **Siberia Valley airstrip**, and you can take your chance on "backloading" **flights out** ($45). To continue tramping from **Siberia Hut to Kerin Forks** (6km; 2–3hr; 100m ascent, 300m descent), enter the bush at the southern end of Siberia Flats on the true left bank of Siberia Stream and descend away from the stream then zigzag steeply down to the Wilkin River and the **Kerin Forks Hut** (10 bunks), where many trampers arrange to be met by a jetboat. If it has rained heavily, fording the Makarora lower down will be impossible, so don't forgo the jetboat lightly. The alternative is to walk from **Kerin Forks to Makarora** (17km; 6–7hr; 100m ascent, 200m descent), following the Wilkin River's true left bank, then crossing the Makarora upstream of the confluence.

InterCity and Atomic buses pass through, and backpacker **buses** stop overnight at Makarora; everyone **stays** at the *Makarora Tourist Centre*, SH6 (☏03/443 8372, ⓦwww.makarora.co.nz; camping $9, dorms ❶, chalets ❸–❺), a collection of self-catering and simple A-frame chalets in a clearing. It is all very peaceful and there's a pool, making it a good place to hole up for a day or two, provided you are well supplied and prepared to self-cater – the tearooms are only open until around 4.30pm, and the shop has very limited supplies. The only alternative is *Larrivee Homestay*, SH6 (☏03/443 9177, ⓦwww.lariveehomestay.co.nz; ❻), a lovely house hidden behind the DOC office, offering B&B, plus BYO dinners for $35.

Continuing towards Wanaka, the only place you are likely to want to break your journey is *Kidds Bush*, a DOC **campsite** ($5) beside Lake Hawea, 6km down a side road off SH6 at The Neck, where lakes Wanaka and Hawea almost meet.

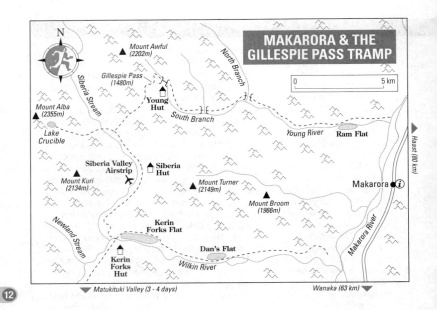

MAKARORA & THE GILLESPIE PASS TRAMP

N

Mount Awful
(2202m)

Gillespie Pass
(1480m)

North Branch

Siberia Stream

Young
Hut

Mount Alba
(2355m)

South Branch

Young River   Ram Flat

Lake
Crucible

Haast (80 km)

Siberia Valley
Airstrip

Siberia
Hut

Mount Kuri
(2134m)

Mount Turner
(2149m)

Makarora

Mount Broom
(1966m)

Newland Stream

Kerin
Forks Flat

Makarora River

Dan's Flat

Kerin
Forks
Hut

Wilkin River

Matukituki Valley (3 - 4 days)   Wanaka (63 km)

0   5 km

Travel details

The only passenger **train** services to the West Coast are from Christchurch over Arthur's Pass to Greymouth. InterCity **buses** in both directions on the West Coast run meet the train and continue either to Nelson or to Fox Glacier. The other main bus operator on the coast is Atomic who base themselves in Greymouth and run daily services north to Picton and south down the coast to Queenstown.

Trains

From Greymouth to: Arthur's Pass (1 daily; 2hr); Christchurch (1 daily; 4hr 20min).

Buses

From Fox Glacier to: Franz Josef (3 daily; 30min); Hokitika (2 daily; 3hr); Makarora (2 daily; 4hr 15min); Wanaka (2 daily; 5hr 15min).
From Franz Josef Glacier to: Fox Glacier (3 daily; 30min); Haast (2 daily; 3hr); Hokitika (2 daily; 2hr 30min); Makarora (2 daily; 4hr 30min); Queenstown (2 daily; 8hr); Wanaka (2 daily; 6hr).
From Greymouth to: Arthur's Pass (3 daily; 1hr 30min–2hr); Blenheim (1 daily; 4hr 30min); Christchurch (3 daily; 4hr); Fox Glacier (2 daily; 3hr 30min-4hr 15min); Franz Josef (2 daily; 3-4hr); Hokitika (2 daily; 30min); Murchison (1 daily; 2hr

15min); Punakaiki (2 daily; 45min); Queenstown (1 daily; 10hr 15min); Reefton (1 daily, 1hr); St Arnaud (1 daily; 3hr 15min); Wanaka (1 daily; 9hr); Westport (2 daily; 2hr–2hr 30min).
From Hokitika to: Arthur's Pass (3 daily; 2hr); Christchurch (3 daily; 5-6hr); Fox Glacier (2 daily; 3hr); Franz Josef (2 daily; 2hr 30min); Greymouth (2 daily; 30min); Ross (2 daily; 25min); Whataroa (2 daily; 1hr 30min).
From Westport to: Greymouth (2 daily; 2hr–2hr 30min); Karamea (2 daily; 1hr 30min); Murchison (2 daily; 1hr 15min); Nelson (2 daily; 3hr 30min–6hr); Punakaiki (2 daily; 1hr).

Flights

From Hokitika to: Christchurch (1–6 daily; 35min).
From Westport to: Wellington (1 daily; 50min).

Queenstown, Wanaka and the Gold Country

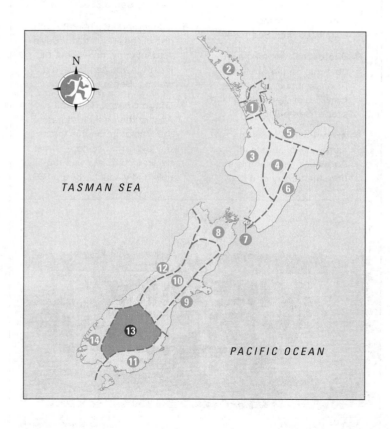

CHAPTER 13

Highlights

* **Wineries** Central Otago is the world's most southerly wine growing area, creating conditions for sublime pinot noir and tastings at over twenty wineries. See p.836

* **Parabungy** The newest and highest bungy in the land, where you launch from a parachute over the waters of Lake Wakatipu. See p.840

* **Shotover River** Take a jet-boat ride on the Shotover River, an iconic part of the New Zealand adventure landscape. See p.840

* **Arrowtown** Wander the narrow, leafy streets of Arrowtown and sample a pie from the bakery or a beer from one of the bars, the ideal antidote to the pace of Queenstown. See p.847

* **The Routeburn Track** Lush bush, alpine scenery and the camaraderie of backcountry huts combine to make this one of New Zealand's best tramps. See p.860

* **Canyoning** Get intimate with one of the Matukituki Valley's verdant canyons – about the most fun you can have in a wetsuit. See p.869

* **Otago Central Rail Trail** Absorb the rural pleasures of the Maniototo on this three-day cycle ride along a former rail line, complete with tunnels and viaducts. See p.889

△ Wine tasting, Wanaka

Queenstown, Wanaka and the Gold Country

Wedged between the sodden beech forests of Fiordland, the fertile plains of south Canterbury, the city of Dunedin and the sheep country of Southland lies Central Otago, a region encompassing **Queenstown**, **Wanaka** and the surrounding **gold country**. Rolling, deserted hills to the east give way to the sharper profiles of the mountains around Queenstown and Wanaka, which rub shoulders with the final glaciated flourish of the Southern Alps. Meltwater and heavy rains course out of the mountains into the seventy-kilometre lightning bolt of **Lake Wakatipu**, which in turn drains through the Kawarau River, carving a rapid-strewn path through the Kawarau Gorge. Along the way it picks up the waters of the Shotover River from the goldfields of Skippers and Arrowtown. To the north, the pristine, glassy lakes of Wanaka and Hawea feed the **Clutha River**, which joins forces with the Kawarau at Cromwell and high-tails it to the coast through the heartland of the Otago gold country.

Queenstown is undoubtedly the region's jewel, with a legendary setting looking across Lake Wakatipu to the craggy heights of The Remarkables range. New Zealand's self-proclaimed adventure capital, it can take on the atmosphere of a high-priced theme park, offering the chance to indulge in just about every adrenalin-fuelled activity imaginable: numerous competing operators have honed bungy jumping, jetboating, rafting and paragliding into well-packaged, forcefully marketed products – although they're no less exciting for it. All this wonderful scenery and adventure has gained something of an international profile of late, providing some of the background for major feature films such as Martin Campbell's *The Vertical Limit*, in which the mountains stood in for Pakistan's Karakorams, and numerous scenes from *The Lord of the Rings* trilogy.

No matter how abiding the appeal of Queenstown, you'll soon be looking for a break, something easily done in neighbouring **Arrowtown**, an extremely popular day-trip destination from Queenstown, which wears its gold heritage well. Visit the intriguing remains of a former Chinese settlement and take a day-long walk to the defunct gold mines around the nearby ghost town of **Macetown**.

For details on visiting Milford sound from Queenstown, see box on p.916"

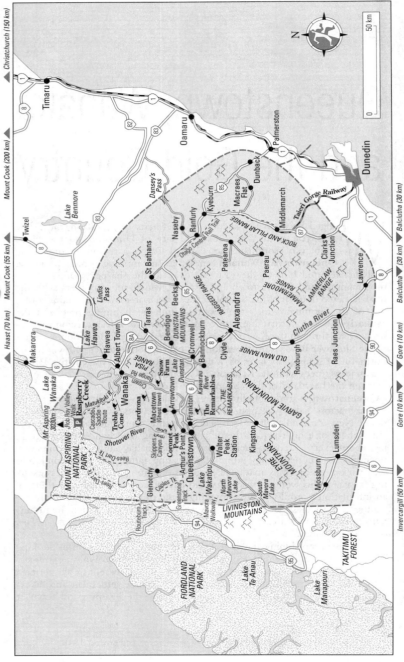

Perhaps the perfect antidote to the rigours and flash of Queenstown is the great outdoors, and some of the country's most exalted multi-day tramps start from the nearby town of **Glenorchy** at the head of Lake Wakatipu. Well-organized track transport will drop you at the trailheads of the magnificent **Routeburn Track**, the match of any in the country; the less challenging **Caples** and **Greenstone** tracks, which can be combined with the Routeburn to make a satisfying five-day circuit; and the rugged **Rees–Dart Track**, which opens up the arduous Cascade Saddle Route towards Mount Aspiring.

The glacially scoured, three-sided pinnacle of "the Matterhorn of the South" forms the centrepiece of the **Mount Aspiring National Park**. This permanently snow-capped alpine high country is linked by the Matukituki valley to the upcoming resort of **Wanaka**, slung around the placid waters of its eponymous lake. Wanaka's laid-back atmosphere stands in marked contrast to the frenetic bustle of Queenstown, though there's no shortage of operators keen to take you canyoning, stunt flying, rock climbing or on any number of other pursuits.

Queenstown and Wanaka lie on the fringe of the **Otago Goldfields**, which stretch east towards the coast at Dunedin. Most of the gold has long since gone and the area is largely deserted, but there are numerous interesting reminders of New Zealand's gold-rush days, including old workings set amidst rugged scenery. Queenstown and Arrowtown were two of the biggest gold towns, but to the east lie the more modest centres of **Cromwell**, **Alexandra** and **Roxburgh**, scattered along the banks of the Clutha River which once provided Maori with the easiest path to the greenstone fields of the West Coast. Gold miners subsequently used the same paths, fanning out to found tiny towns such as **St Bathan's** and **Naseby**, the most enjoyable places in which to idle among the mouldering boomtime remains.

From June to October the region's focus switches to **skiing**, with Queenstown acting as a base for the downhill resorts of Coronet Peak and The Remarkables, while Wanaka serves the Cardrona and Treble Cone fields, as well as the **Snow Farm** Nordic field.

Getting around the region is easily done on the reasonably frequent buses linking the main towns, supplemented by shuttle buses to trailheads, and minibuses transporting you from your hotel out to the various adventure activities. For more detailed coverage of route frequencies and times, consult "Travel details" on p.895.

Queenstown

QUEENSTOWN is in many ways a victim of it own popularity. Kiwis and visitors seduced by New Zealand's tranquil rural beauty can often be overheard complaining that the country's main centre for adventure sports is getting overcrowded and too big for its boots. There is no doubt that it is one of New Zealand's most popular and commercialized year-round resorts, but it remains an idyllic spot, attractively set beside the deep blue Lake Wakatipu and hemmed in by craggy mountains. Furthermore, it offers the best selection of restaurants outside of the bigger cities, and some of the flashiest (and most highly priced) accommodation in the country.

For details on visiting Milford sound from Queenstown, see box on p.916.

Ring things

Without Queenstown and its immediate surrounds, **The Lord of the Rings** trilogy would have looked quite different. Numerous scenes from all three films were shot in the area, though some were digitally manipulated to the point where you really need to stand there with a still from the film to work out just what was and wasn't used.

More than anywhere else in the land, an entire industry has been built up to show the visitors where it all happened, and if you really want to stand where Frodo stood you need to join one of the **specialist tours**. Apart from these, just about anyone who runs adventure trips into the countryside (even if they had nothing to do with the making of the movies) will tag on "as seen in The Lord of the Rings" or "venturing into Middle-Earth" in their promotional material. Bandwagon-jumping perhaps, but there's no doubting the demand.

Locations

Arrow River, near Arrowtown. A spot around 200 metres upstream from the town centre was where Arwen helped Frodo across the Ford of Bruinen with the Nazgûl in pursuit.

The Deer Park, Kelvin Heights (daily 9am–dark; $20 per vehicle). A scenic hilltop park where you can feed the highland cattle, bison, llamas, miniature horses etc. Signs point to half a dozen locations from all three movies including the site for Gandalf riding towards Minas Tirith, the spot where Gimli was thrown from his horse, and the lakeshore where the Rohirrim were led to refuge.

Glenorchy Saruman's Tower of Orthanc was digitally inserted into the plain at the head of Lake Wakatipu with the Dart Valley behind.

Kawarau River, beside the AJ Hackett bungy site. The river stood in for the River Anduin in the first movie and the gorge walls here were digitally enhanced with the Argonath, the Pillars of the Kings.

Paradise, near Glenorchy. The beech-forest edge of Dan's Paddock, just north of

Unfortunately, a haphazard attitude to local planning and a hands-off approach to development has allowed hotels to appear on the foreshore and more and more lavish residences to climb into the hills, spreading out towards Arrowtown. However, the place still retains a semblance of its original character, thanks in part to the inventive renovation the centre received after being heavily flooded in the late 1990s.

Queenstown is best taken in small doses, either as a base from which to plan lengthy forays into the surrounding countryside, or as a venue for sampling the many outdoor activities on offer. The most prominent of these is undoubtedly **bungy jumping**. The town's environs now boast five of the world's most gloriously scenic bungy sites (including one from a parachute over Lake Wakatipu), visited either in isolation or as part of a multi-thrill package, perhaps including **whitewater rafting** and **jetboating** on the Shotover River, or a helicopter flight into the dilapidated former gold workings along the **Skippers Road**.

Visitors after a more sedate time are equally spoilt for choice, with **lake cruises** on the elegant TSS *Earnslaw*, the last of the lake steamers; the **gondola ride** to Bob's Peak, which commands magnificent vistas from a cable car over Queenstown and The Remarkables range; and a choice of **wine tours** around some of the world's most southerly wineries. Formal lakeshore gardens and hillside viewpoints provide the focus for easy local **walks**, with heartier multi-day tramps starting at Glenorchy (p.857) at the head of the lake.

Even the frantic summers are nothing in comparison to winter, when Kiwi and international skiers descend on **Coronet Peak** and **The Remarkables**,

the Arcadia Homestead, is where Gandalf rode to Isengard. The forests a little further north briefly stood in for Lothlórien.

The Remarkables. From the top of the skifield road you can hike up to Lake Alta, where Aragorn, Frodo and Co headed down Dimrill Dale toward Lothlórien

Skippers Canyon. Around 12km along the Skippers Road the gravel riverbanks were used (along with the Arrow River, above) for shooting the Ford of Bruinen.

Twelve-Mile Delta, 11 km west of Queenstown. DOC campground that stood in for Ithilien in *The Fellowship of the Ring*.

Tours

Dart River Safaris ☎03/442 9992 & 0800/327 853, ⊛www.dartriver.co.nz. Glenorchy-based jetboat trips with a significant LOTR component (see p.857).

Heliworks ☎03/441 4011 & 0800/464 354, ⊛www.heliworks.co.nz. These folk did much of the flying for the cast and now run a wide range of LOTR Scenic Flights starting from around $200 for half an hour including one landing.

Glenorchy Air ☎03/442 2207, ⊛www.trilogytrail.com. Queenstown Airport-based small planes flew cast and crew during filming and now offer a One Ring Trail (3hr; $125) offering a minibus tour of sites around Queenstown; a Two Ring Trail (2–3hr; $285) flying past locations around Arrowtown, Glenorchy and Mavora Lakes; and a Three Ring Trail (6hr; $665) with landings at three more distant major locations including Edoras (see p.689).

Nomad Safaris ☎03/442 6699 & 0800/688 222, ⊛www.nomadsafaris.co.nz. Specialist *Safari of the Rings* tours in 4WD vehicles with frequent stops to envisage scenes being shot. Good background from drivers who were often involved as extras. The Wakatipu Basin trip (4hr; $120) focuses on the area immediately around Queenstown, while the Glenorchy trip (4hr; $120) heads up to the head of Lake Wakatipu around Glenorchy and Paradise.

two fine ski fields within half an hour of Queenstown, which are at their peak during the annual **Queenstown Winter Festival** in late June and early July.

Arrival, information and city transport

Buses all arrive in the centre of Queenstown around the junction of Camp Street and Shotover Street, from where it's less than fifteen minutes' walk to hotels and hostels. Generally, buses no longer drop you off outside your accommodation though some of the smaller operators will if it isn't out of their way; others may charge a small fee (say $5) for the service. For route details, see "Listings" on p.846.

Queenstown's **airport** is just outside Frankton, 7km northeast of central Queenstown; the Shopper Bus runs roughly hourly to the top of Shotover St (9am–3.30pm; 20min; $6), and the door-to-door Super Shuttle (around $10 for one, cheaper for two) meets most flights. **Taxis** (☎03/442 6666 or 442 7788) charge around $20 for the ride into town. Most of the major car rental companies also have offices at the airport.

Information

Queenstown's main downtown area is concentrated around Rees Street, Shotover Street, Camp Street and the pedestrianized Mall, which runs from the Main Town Wharf northeast to Ballarat Street. Shotover Street is awash with visitor centres-cum-booking offices for local and national activities as well as for travel. The official **visitor centre** (cnr Camp & Shotover streets; daily:

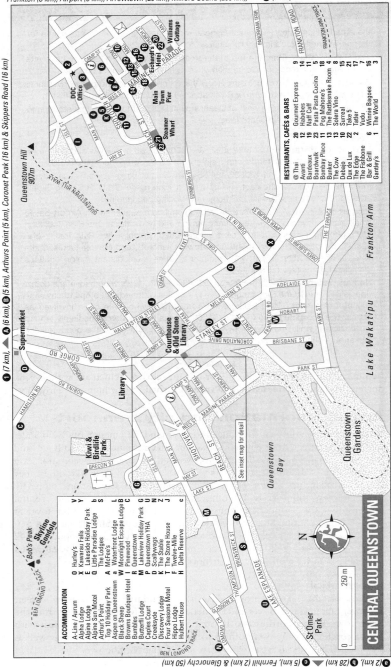

Dec–April 7am–6.30pm; May–Nov 7am–6pm; ☎03/442 4100, ✉qvc @xtra.co.nz, ⓦwww.queenstown-nz.co.nz), also does bookings and offers less partisan advice than the others.

For outdoors information visit the **DOC office**, 37 Shotover St (Oct–Nov daily 9am–5pm, Dec–April daily 9am–6pm; ☎03/442 7933, ✉queenstownvc@doc.govt.nz), which is stacked with leaflets on DOC activities and operates a Great Walks Booking Desk (Oct–April daily 9am–5pm) for aspiring Routeburn, Kepler and Milford track walkers.

Of the main booking offices, perhaps the most prominent is **The Station** on the corner of Camp and Shotover streets, which acts as the nerve centre and the main pick-up spot for AJ Hackett bungy and the Shotover Jet. A few steps along Shotover Street the **Info & Track Centre** (37 Shotover St, ☎03/442 9708, ⓦwww.infotrack.co.nz) is a particularly handy backpacker-oriented booking office, offering useful track advice when the DOC office is closed. It is also the main stopping point for Kiwi Experience and offers various day and overnight trips to Glenorchy and the Routeburn Track, though you can do it cheaper independently.

Tourist **publications** worth seeking out include the free *itag visitor guide* (ⓦwww.itag.co.nz), which is packed with information and the latest prices, and *Kidz Go!* (ⓦwww.kidzgo.co.nz) with good guidance on how to keep the nippers entertained and full listings of minimum ages for various activities. Also look out for the local *Mountain Scene* newspaper for an insight into what is currently making Queenstown tick.

City transport

Pretty much everywhere you are likely to want to go in central Queenstown can be reached **on foot**. Most of the activities – bungy jumping, whitewater rafting and the like – take place out of town, although all operators run courtesy buses from the centre of town to the site, usually picking up from accommodation en route. There's a **taxi rank** on Camp Street at The Top of the Mall and one on Shotover Street, or call ☎03/442 6666 or 442 7788.

The only useful bus services are those to Arrowtown (see p.848) and the Shopper Bus, from Camp Street near the visitor centre (☎03/442 6647; daily departures every hour 6.30am–11pm), which runs out to Frankton and the airport.

More personalized transport comes in the form of **rental cars** and **bikes**, which are available from several outlets around town (see "Listings", p.846). The common practice of renting a car for a day to drive to Milford Sound isn't encouraged, with most companies that rent out vehicles for such a short period charging per kilometre on top of the rental fee. Still, for three or four of you it can work out a good deal if you don't mind the long and tiring drive.

Drivers will have no problem negotiating Queenstown's streets; although **parking** can be tight in the centre of town you only need to go a few streets away to find free all-day parking.

Accommodation

Queenstown has the widest selection of **places to stay** in this corner of New Zealand, but such is the demand in the middle of summer and at the height of the ski season that rooms can be hard to come by and prices are correspondingly high.

With a few exceptions, all the accommodation is packed into a compact area less than fifteen minutes' walk from the centre of town. Good deals are sometimes offered by the big **hotels** in what passes for Queenstown's off season (essentially April, May & Nov) but in general you'll do better in smaller places, particularly the **B&Bs**, **homestays** and **lodges**, of which there are some fine examples. Families, groups and keen self-caterers might consider **motels**, which match the Kiwi standard but tend to charge a little more than in less popular resorts. The best budget deals are to be found at the many **hostels**, which compete fiercely for trade, offering activity booking, free luggage storage and the like. The Queenstown district also has abundant **campsites** with attendant cabins, though only a couple of these are within walking distance of town.

If a less frantic atmosphere – and lower prices – appeal, it's also worth considering **Arrowtown** as a base for exploring the Queenstown area (see pp.847–852), or **Glenorchy** (see p.853).

Hotels

A-Line / Aurum 27 Stanley St ☎03/442 7700 & 0800/696 963, ⓦ wwwscenic-circle.co.nz. Effectively two hotels in one, the cheaper rooms in a cluster of nicely furnished rooms in A-frames with good lake views. Newer studios and one-bedroom apartments all have lakeview balconies, kitchens and the full range of luxury appointments. Prices drop considerably when business is slow. Rooms ❼, apartments ❽

Aspen on Queenstown 139 Fernhill Rd ☎03/442 7688 & 0800/427 688, ⓦ www.queenstownhotel .com. A sprawling hotel with a small indoor pool and great lake views. The well-equipped rooms and apartments are overpriced in high season but can be an off-peak bargain – especially the two-bedroom apartments, whose rates drop by as much as a third. The hotel is around 2km from the centre of Queenstown. Rooms ❻, apartments ❽

Hurley's Cnr Frankton Rd & Melbourne St ☎03/442 5999 & 0800/589 879, ⓦ www .hurleys.co.nz. Tasteful, luxuriously appointed apartments and studios close to the centre of Queenstown, each equipped with a full kitchen, TV, CD and cassette player, spa baths and with free access to two saunas and a full gym. Studios ❻–❼, apartments ❾

Motels

Alpha Lodge 62 Frankton Rd ☎03/442 6095 & 0800/661 668. Good value, low-cost motel close to town with all basic amenities and a range of budget and studio units. ❺

Alpine Sun Motel 18 Hallenstein St ☎03/442 8482 & 0800/101 914, ⓔ alpine.sun@xtra.co.nz. Good-value basic motel units with Sky TV, kitchenettes, free spa and off-road parking. ❺

Caples Court 20 Stanley St ☎03/442 7445, ⓦ www.caplescourt.co.nz. Appealing motel with more spirit to its decor than most with each room done in a different style. Most have a kitchen and a balcony with views over the town. ❻

Four Seasons Motel 12 Stanley St ☎03/442 8953, ⓦ www.queenstownmotel.com. Reasonable downtown motel with off-street parking, good kitchens, mountain views, an outdoor swimming pool and a spa. Studios ❺, apartments ❼

The Lodges 8 Lake Esplanade ☎03/442 7552 & 0800/284 356, ⓦ www.thelodges.co.nz. Top-quality lakeside studio units, and three-bedroom apartments with full kitchens, laundry and parking that are good value for groups of four or more. ❼–❾

B&Bs, homestays and lodges

Browns Boutique Hotel 26 Isle St ☎03/441 2050, ⓦ www.brownshotel.co.nz. Very appealing ten-room downtown lodge with spacious, well-appointed rooms ($250) all with small balconies overlooking the town and a luxurious guest lounge with an open fire where a continental breakfast is served. ❾

Hulbert House 68 Ballarat St ☎03/442 8767, ⓦ www.zqn.co.nz/hulbert.house. In a rambling century-old Victorian villa built on the hill behind Queenstown Bay, this opulent but tasteful B&B has a large library, idyllic gardens and great breakfasts. ❽

Little Paradise Lodge Meilejohn Bay, 28km along Glenorchy Rd ☎03/442 6196, ⓦ www .littleparadise.com. An idyllic homestay close to the lake where almost everything is made from logs cut or stone hewn by the Swiss owner, Thomas, including the non-chlorinated swimming pool fed by its own stream and complete with water lilies. Accommodation is in standard rooms and a charming en-suite chalet. You can cook for yourself and there is free use of kayaks, a dinghy and fishing gear. ❺

Moonlight Escape Lodge Arthur's Point, 5km north of Queenstown ☎03/441 3110, ⓦ www.moonlightescape.com. This luxurious, modern, stone and timber lodge on the site of some early gold workings is a remarkably peaceful getaway: just six beautiful rooms and dinner available on request. Prices start at $300 for two including drinks on arrival, full cooked breakfast and airport pick up and drop off. ❾

The Stable 17 Brisbane St ☎03/442 9251, ⓦwww.thestablebb.com. Cosy and welcoming homestay stacked with books with just two rooms, the best in a former stable. Cooked or continental breakfasts are served. ➐

The Stone House 47 Hallenstein St ☎03/442 9812, ⓦwww.stonehouse.co.nz. Lovely four-room B&B in a stone-built 1874 house surrounded by roses. Rooms ($250) are comfortable and tastefully furnished, evening drinks are served in a spacious, sunny lounge, breakfast is excellent and there's a hot tub outside. ➒

Hostels

Alpine Lodge 13 Gorge Rd ☎03/442 7220, Ⓔalpinelodge@xtra.co.nz. Small, welcoming and central hostel which can be a little cramped when full but has an additional self-contained building known as *Turner Lodge* with spacious en suites, made-up doubles, a large lounge and off-street parking. It's more like a B&B without the breakfast. Dorms ➊, hostel rooms ➌, en suites ➍

Black Sheep 13 Frankton Rd ☎03/442 7289, ⓦwww.blacksheepbackpackers.co.nz. Converted motel that's spacious enough to cope with the backpacker tour-bus crowd who frequently pack out the three- to seven-bed dorms. Can be rowdy, but everything is well organized, and there's a barbecue near the spa pool, a bar (4–10pm only), free luggage storage and you can book just about everything at the 24hr reception. Dorms ➊, rooms ➌

Bumbles 2 Brunswick St ☎03/442 6298 & 0800/428 625. Among the best hostels in town and justly popular. Well-sited across the road from the lakefront with great views from most rooms and common areas, spacious well-equipped kitchens, abundant washing facilities, barbecue area, off-street parking and attentive management. Dorms ➊, made-up twins & doubles ➌

Butterfli Lodge 62 Thompson St ☎03/442 6367, ⓦwww.butterfli.co.nz. A small house overlooking the lake that provides a friendly atmosphere and cosy accommodation for a limited number of people. Book early. Dorms ➊, rooms ➌

Discovery Lodge 47 Shotover St ☎03/441 1185, ⓦwww.dlq.co.nz. We haven't seen it in operation, but with four hundred beds (all made-up) and a promised range of excellent facilities this purpose-built hostel (owned by Auckland Central Backpackers) is sure to become a big player. Dorms ➊, rooms ➌, en suites ➍, premium lakeview ➐

Hippo Lodge 4 Anderson Heights ☎03/442 5783, ⓦwww.hippolodge.co.nz. A couple of suburban houses imaginatively converted into four sections

each with its own bathroom, kitchen and living area. Several of the rooms and lounges have fabulous views over Queenstown, and there are even a few cramped tent sites ($12). At peak times, there's overflow accommodation at the *Hippo Hideaway* bolt-hole at Arthur's Point, 5km from Queenstown (➎). Dorms ➊, doubles and en suites ➌

McFee's Waterfront Lodge 48a Shotover St ☎03/442 7400, ⓦwww.megalo.co.nz/mcfees. Large hostel recently taken over by the YHA, with good communal areas overlooking the lake. Accommodation is in four-bed dorms, budget doubles with TV, and flashier en-suite rooms. Dorms ➊, rooms ➌–➍

Pinewood 48 Hamilton Rd ☎03/442 8273, ⓦwww.pinewood.co.nz. An extensive collection of new and older renovated self-contained buildings (all surrounded by lawns) jointly making up some of the best budget accommodation in Queenstown. Located on the edge of town ten minutes' walk from the centre, they have great facilities including a spa bath ($10 per half-hour) and bike rental (around $20 a half-day). Dorms ➊, rooms ➌, en suites & family units ➍

Queenstown YHA 88 Lake Esplanade ☎03/442 8413, Ⓔyha.queenstown@yha.org.nz. Always bustling, this is one of New Zealand's flagship YHAs with accommodation in spacious, mostly six-bed dorms and doubles, many with good lake views. Plans are afoot to rebuild this hostel in the near future so be sure to call first. Dorms ➊, rooms ➌

Scallywags 27 Lomond Crescent ☎03/442 7083, Ⓕ442 5885. Pitched as an upmarket backpackers' hostel, this suburban house is a steep ten-minute walk up from town. It has stupendous views and a very laid-back muck-in atmosphere, with use of a kitchen and free tea and coffee. Four-shares ➊, made-up rooms ➌

Campsites and motorparks

Arthur's Point Top 10 Holiday Park Close to the Shotover Jet site at Arthur's Point ☎03/442 9311 & 0800/462 267, Ⓔtop10.queenstown@xtra.co.nz. Smallish, quiet and fully equipped site with a small pool. Camping $11–12, standard cabins ➋, kitchen cabins ➌, motel units ➎

Creeksyde 54 Robins Rd ☎03/442 9447, ⓦwww.camp.co.nz. Highly organized and spotlessly clean Top 10 holiday park ten minutes' walk from town comes with shaded sites, many of them used by campervanners. A central building houses a spa bathroom ($5 per half-hour for two), sauna ($10), ski store and drying rooms. Camping $12–14, rooms ➌, en suites & units ➍–➎

Kawarau Falls Lakeside Holiday Park 7km northeast of Queenstown on SH6, near Frankton airport ☎ 03/442 3510, ⓦ www.campsite.co.nz. Very attractive lakeside campsite with excellent facilities that extend to spacious tent sites, a back-packer-style lodge and three different grades of cabins, some with their own facilities. In peak season, the Shopper Bus comes to within 500m; within 1km out of season. Camping $12–13, dorms ❶, cabins ❷–❺
Queenstown Lakeview Holiday Park Brecon St ☎ 0800/482 735, ⓦ www.holidaypark.net.nz.

Enormous site that sprawls over the base of Bob's Peak and seems to swallow just about all of Queenstown's campers. Recently revamped it has all new facilities done to a high standard and accommodation runs from grassy, though not well shaded, tent sites (showers cost extra) to self-contained motel units. Camping $12–14, cabins & units ❸–❺
Twelve-Mile Delta Reserve 5km west of Queenstown towards Glenorchy. Lakeside DOC campsite with facilities limited to basic toilets and water. $5

The Town

Central Queenstown has very little to show for its gold-rush past. At the Top of The Mall, Ballarat Street crosses a small stream spanned by an 1882 stone bridge to reach the **Courthouse** and **Old Stone Library** (now offices) both built in the mid 1870s and since dwarfed by century-old giant sequoias. At the opposite end of the Mall, the waterfront **Eichardt's Hotel** dates partly from 1871 when the Prussian Albert Eichardt replaced the Queen's Arms, a bar William Rees created from a woolshed in 1862. Around the corner on Marine Parade is the 1866 **Williams Cottage**, which retains many original features and now operates as a gallery shop and café.

Marine Parade continues east past Williams Cottage to **Queenstown Gardens** (unrestricted entry), an attractive parkland retreat which covers the peninsula separating Queenstown Bay from the rest of Lake Wakatipu. Two English oaks were planted when the land was first designated as a reserve in 1867; they're still going strong, as are sequoias and a stack of other exotics – ornamental cherry, maple, sweet chestnut and the like – lavished around the rose gardens and bowling lawns.

Across town, Brecon Street heads for Bob's Peak past Queenstown's **cemetery** – the final resting place of Queenstown pioneer Nicholas von Tunzelmann, as well as Henry Homer, discoverer of the Homer Saddle – on the Milford Road. Almost opposite, the **Kiwi & Birdlife Park** (daily: Nov–Feb 9am–7pm; March–Oct 9am–6pm; $15.50; ⓦ www.kiwibird.co.nz), is an expanse of ponds, lawns, stands of bush and aviaries that are home to some of New Zealand's rarest birds. The effect is more zoo than wildlife park but it does a good job of presenting morepork, kea, kereru (native pigeons), kakariki (native parakeets) and black stilt (one of the world's ten most endangered bird species), alongside the products of captive breeding programmes for the North Island brown kiwi. Time your visit to coincide with the twenty-minute **Conservation Show** (daily 11am & 3pm; free), when you get close and personal with kereru, kea and tuatara, or the tour of the **Maori Hunting Village** (daily 10am & 2pm; free) to learn something of early Maori life in the bush.

Bob's Peak

The best all-round views of Queenstown, Lake Wakatipu, The Remarkables and Cecil and Walter peaks are from **Bob's Peak**, which rises up immediately behind the town and can be reached on one of Queenstown's gentler rides. The **Skyline Gondola**, Brecon Street (daily 9am–midnight; $17 return), deposits you at the Skyline Complex, where a fair proportion of passengers are herded into **Kiwi Magic** (daily 10am–8pm; 30min; $9), a well-produced and engagingly corny promotional film that's beginning to show its age, not least because the lead, comedian Billy T. James, died well over a decade ago.

The magnificent vistas may induce you to dine at the café or buffet restaurant (lunch $46, dinner $59; both including gondola ride), probably best left until after you've tried The Ledge bungy and swing (see p.840), or The **Luge** (1 ride $6, 5 rides $20, 5 rides & Gondola $32), a twisting concrete track negotiated on a wheeled plastic buggy with a primitive braking system – take it easy on your first run.

Throughout the day paragliders launch themselves from the conifer-clad slopes; if you're overcome by a sudden impulse to join their ranks, you can book a tandem paraglide for around $185 at the booth just outside the Skyline Complex.

The complex can also be reached on foot in under an hour by following Kent Street up from town.

Cruising on Lake Wakatipu

The coal-fired steamship **TSS Earnslaw**, the last of the lake steamers, is one of Queenstown's most enduring images. Wherever you are, the encircling mountains echo the haunting sound of the steam whistle as this beautifully restored relic slogs manfully out from Steamer Wharf. Before the lakeside roads were built, almost all commerce in and out of Queenstown was conducted by boat, with a fleet of four steamers serving the large sheep stations at the top of the lake and the southern railhead at Kingston.

Prefabricated in sections in Dunedin, the *Earnslaw* was transported on the now defunct railway to Kingston, where its steel hull was riveted together. Launched in 1912, the 51-metre-long craft was the largest steamer to ply the lake – and surely one of the most stately. Burnished brass and polished wood predominate even around the gleaming steam engine which is open for inspection. Crowds usually cluster around the piano at the back of the boat for a surprisingly popular music-hall sing-song that can make the return journey seem much longer.

The *Earnslaw* is operated by Real Journeys (☎0800/656 503, ⓦwww.realjourneys.co.nz) and runs from Queenstown across the lake to **Walter Peak High Country Farm** (4–6 daily; 90min; $36 return), a tourist enclave nestling in the southwestern crook of Lake Wakatipu. The Walter Peak homestead, a convincing replica of an original building which burnt down in 1977, is beautifully sited among lawns that sweep down to the lakeshore, and plays host to a **farm tour** – an entertaining if sanitized vignette of farm life, with demonstrations of dog handling and sheep-shearing. Visit for the farm tour, tea and scones (3.5hr; $55 including cruise from Queenstown); the farm tour and barbecue meal (3.5hr; $72); 40min horse trek, tea and scones (3.5hr; $92); a 5hr horse trek with lunch ($205); or a carvery buffet dinner (6pm; 4hr; $93). In June each year the *Earnslaw* is overhauled and replaced by a launch.

By going one way to Walter Peak ($25) and taking your own bike (free) or motorbike ($10) you'll have the freedom of the remote and unsealed 80km road up the Von River past Mavora Lakes to SH94 at Burwood, 27km east of Te Anau.

The Shotover River and Skippers Canyon

The churning **Shotover River** is inextricably linked with Queenstown. The majority of the town's adventure-based trips – bungy jumping, rafting, jet-boating, mountain biking and more (see "Activities", p.837) – take place on, in

Walks around Queenstown

All the hard-sell on adventure activities in Queenstown can become a bit oppressive, and a few hours away from town can be wonderfully therapeutic. The majority of the walks outlined below – listed in ascending order of difficulty – are well covered by the DOC's *Queenstown walks and trails* leaflet ($1), which also includes a sketch map. Serious multi-day tramps in the region are centred on Wanaka and Glenorchy (see p.878 and p.857, respectively).

One Mile Creek Walkway (90min return; 6km; 50m ascent). Fairly easy walk through a gully filled with beech forest and following a 1924 pipeline from Queenstown's first hydroelectric scheme. The route starts on the lakefront by the Fernhill roundabout and offers a good opportunity to acquaint yourself with fuchsia, lancewood and native birds – principally fantails, bellbirds and tui.

Queenstown Hill Track (2–3hr return; 5km; 500m ascent). Starting from the top of York Street, this is a fairly steep climb through mostly exotic trees to panoramic views from the 907m Queenstown Hill.

Ben Lomond Summit Track (6–8hr return; 11km; 1400m ascent). A full-day, there-and-back tramp scaling the 1748m Ben Lomond, one of the highest mountains in the region and consequently subject to inclement weather, especially in winter when the track can be snow-covered. Start by the One Mile Creek Walk or use the Skyline Gondola and walk up past the paragliding launch site to join the track, which climbs through alpine tussock to reveal expansive views. Gentler slopes approach Ben Lomond Saddle, from where it's a steep final haul to the summit.

Ben Lomond–Moonlight Track (8–10hr one way; 16km; 1400m ascent). A demanding and occasionally difficult-to-follow route which combines the ascent to Ben Lomond Saddle (see above) with a poled sub-alpine route to the site of the former gold town of Sefferstown and the eastern section of the Moonlight Track to Arthur's Point. Organize someone to pick you up at Arthur's Point or be prepared for a 5km slog back to Queenstown.

---

or around the river and, if you are prepared to drive the treacherous Skippers road, there's also a stack of gold-rush relics to explore.

The Shotover rises in the Richardson Mountains north of Queenstown and picks up speed to surge through its deepest and narrowest section, **Skippers Canyon**, and into the Kawarau River downstream from Lake Wakatipu. Tributaries run off Mount Aurum, beneath which is the mother lode of the Shotover goldfields, first discovered when a couple of pioneer shearers, Thomas Arthur and Harry Redfern, found gold in 1862 at Arthur's Point (see p.836), on the banks of the Shotover 5km north of Queenstown. Word spread that prospectors were extracting over ten kilos a day, and within months thousands were flocking from throughout New Zealand and Australia to work what was soon dubbed "The Richest River in the World". The river-edge gravels had been all but worked out by 1864, necessitating ever more sophisticated extraction techniques. With the introduction of gravity-fed water chutes, mechanical sieves and floating dredges, the construction of a decent road became crucial. From 1863, Chinese navvies spent over twenty years hacking away with pick and shovel at the Skippers Road; those who stuck out the harsh conditions began building quarters more substantial than the standard-issue canvas tents. Meanwhile, entrepreneurially minded pioneers began to exploit the boom, building 27 hotels along the 40km of road, and selling fresh fruit and vegetables at extortionate prices to miners often suffering from scurvy. By the turn of the century the river was worked out, though a few stayed on. Even today a couple of die-hards make a living from gold panning and sluicing, and in

Cromwell (50 km), Wanaka (110 km) & 8

Invercargill (170 km), Te Anau (150 km) & Milford Sound (280 km)

Wanaka (20 km)

Cardrona River

Cardrona

Crown Range
Saddle (1121 m)

Peregrine

Watin Creek

Nevis
Bungy

Kawerau
Bungy

Mount
Edward

Chard
Farm

Gibbston
Valley

Ben Nevis
2240m

The Remarkables

Arrowtown

Amisfield

Lake
Hayes

THE REMARKABLES

Macetown

Arrow River

Millbrook
Resort

Frankton

Coronet Peak
1651m

Coronet
Peak

Skippers Township
(Ghost town)

Skippers Canyon

Skippers Rd

Edith Cavell Bridge
& Oxenbridge Tunnel

Arthurs
Point

Kelvin
Heights

Pipeline Bungy

Shotover River

Stony Creek

Moonlight Track

Ben Lomond
1748m

Queenstown

Earnslaw Cruise

Walter Peak
Station

Mt Aurum
2234m

Seffertown
(Ghost town)

Ben Lomond
Summit Tk

Moke
Lake

RICHARDSON MOUNTAINS

Mt Nicholas
Station

Lake Wakatipu

Mavora Lakes (25 km) & Te Anau (80 km)

Little Paradise
Lodge

Rees-Dart Track

Rees River

Dart River

Glenorchy

Paradise

Diamond
Lake

Kinloch Lodge

Caples Track

Caples River

Greenstone Track

Greenstone River

Routeburn Shelter

The Divide

10 km

0

13

QUEENSTOWN | Queenstown

1999, for a few days after flooding, happy hunters were panning up to $600 worth in a couple of hours.

The Skippers Road

The extremely narrow and winding **Skippers Road** is best left to experienced drivers. Locals who know the road like the back of their hand tend to hare around, leaving little space for oncoming traffic; besides, rental cars aren't insured for Skippers. Being driven to either the Pipeline bungy site or the start point for the Shotover rafting trips (see p.840 for more on these) gives you a good chance to see the valley. By far the best way, though, is on a four-hour **tour** with Nomad Safaris ($110; ☎03/442 6699 & 0800/688 222, ⓦwww.nomadsafaris.co.nz), who take in most of the highlights including the Skippers Bridge, the settlement and restored schoolhouse.

The Skippers Road, which follows the Shotover River only in its upper reaches, branches off Coronet Peak Road 12km north of Queenstown. It is approached along Malaghans Road through **Arthur's Point**, 5km north of Queenstown, marked by the historic *Arthur's Point Hotel*, the only one of the Skippers Road hotels still operating. Half a kilometre on, the Edith Cavell Bridge spans a gorge where the Shotover Jet performs its antics its upstream progress limited by the Mother-in-Law rapid and the 1911 **Oxenbridge Tunnel**. After three years of drilling, this 200m-long bore – designed to accommodate the flow of the Shotover while the gold-bearing riverbed was worked – reaped meagre rewards, returning only 2.5kg of gold.

Skippers Road soon begins to shadow the river, negotiating Pinchers Bluff, where Chinese and European navvies cut the road from a near-vertical cliff face. Upstream, the 1901 **Skippers Bridge** was the first high-level one built – and consequently survived the winter floods, which had swept away all past efforts. For the first time, the township of Skippers had reliable access, though this did little to prevent the exodus that saw a population of 1500 dwindle to nothing once the gold ran out. The old schoolhouse has been restored and there are the ruins of a few more buildings scattered around, but otherwise it is a bleak, haunted place. You can **camp** here at a toilets-and-water site for five bucks.

The Gibbston Valley wineries and wine tours

Grapes have been grown commercially in the **Central Otago** district – essentially Wanaka, Queenstown and the Clutha Valley – only since the 1980s, but local winemakers have already garnered a shelf-full of awards. Widely billed as "the world's most southerly wine-growing region", the vineyards lie close to the 45th Parallel in country, which detractors pooh-poohed as too cold and generally unsuitable for wine production, despite the fact that the Rhône Valley in France lies on a similar latitude. A continental climate of hot dry summers and long cold winters prevails, which tends to result in low yields and high production costs, forcing wineries to go for quality boutique wines sold at prices which might seem high ($20–30) until you taste them.

The steep schist and gravel slopes on the southern banks of the **Kawarau River** were first recognized as potential vineyard sites as early as 1864, when French miner Jean Désiré Feraud, by now bored of his gold claim at Frenchman's Point near Clyde, planted grapes from cuttings brought over from Australia. His wines won awards at shows in Australia (though standards were none too exacting at the time), but by the early 1880s he'd decamped to

Dunedin. No more grapes were grown until 1976, when the Rippon vineyard was planted outside Wanaka (see p.868). It was another five years before the Kawarau Gorge was recognized as ideally suited to the cultivation of Pinot Gris, Riesling and particularly Pinot Noir grapes. As an added bonus, the dry conditions inhibit growth of fungus and mildew; the dreaded phylloxera has been kept at bay so far and, to keep it that way, strict protocols exist about bringing vines into the district. An unexpected late frost drastically reduced yields for the 2004 vintage, but as ever the winemakers are hopeful of producing good stuff with the limited supply of grapes.

Altogether, over twenty wineries are open for tasting throughout Central Otago. There are concentrations around Bannockburn (see p.884) and Clyde (see p.885), but those closest to Queenstown are on the southern slopes above the Kawarau Gorge, along SH6 around 20km to the northeast.

You can drive to them all but you'll learn a lot more (and everyone can drink) if you join one of the **wine tours**. For expert guidance and a chance to see a fair bit of the local area, join Central Otago Wine Tours (⊤03/442 0246, ⓦ www.winetoursnz.com) who call at wineries in the Gibbston Valley but focus on those around Bannockburn and Clyde. Their afternoon Boutique Wine Tour ($125) includes lunch at one of the four wineries visited, but enthusiasts will want to go for the more leisurely, full-day Gourmet Wine Tour ($159) taking in five vineyards plus cheese tasting and lunching at *Oliver's* in Clyde (see p.886). Queenstown Wine Trail (⊤03/442 3799, ⓦ www .queenstownwinetrail.co.nz; daily 12.30pm; 5hr; $80) restricts itself to the immediate Queenstown area with tastings at four wineries.

The following are listed in increasing distance from Queenstown.

Wineries

Amisfield 10 Lake Hayes Road ⊤ 03/442 0556, ⓦ www.amisfield.co.nz. Chic, modern winery artfully combining local schist construction with big windows and recycled timbers. Kiwi art on the walls, free tastings (especially the Pinot Noir made from grapes grown on site), and they plan to sell lunch platters to eat in their lovely courtyard. Open daily: Nov–March 10am–6pm, April–Oct 11am–6pm.

Chard Farm Chard Rd ⊤ 0800/843 327, ⓦ www.chardfarm.co.nz. Free tasting of a wide range of wines most notably the Chardonnay, Pinot Noir and Pinot Gris. Reached down a precipitous 2km-dirt road off SH6 opposite the Kawarau Bungy. Daily 10am–5pm.

Gibbston Valley SH6 ⊤ 03/442 6907, ⓦ www.gvwines.co.nz. The most highly evolved of the region's wineries with a popular daytime restaurant, tasting, tours and an on-site cheesery selling a particularly toothsome wine-washed Monk's Gold, amongst others. Star attraction is the Winery & Cave Tour (hourly 10am–4pm; 30min; $9.50, refundable with a six-bottle purchase) which explores cellars burrowed into the hillside. This is not especially impressive, but the tour includes an informed and generous tasting session. Simple tastings cost $4.

Peregrine SH6 ⊤ 03/442 4000, ⓦ www .peregrinewines.co.nz. Nestled under a huge steel and plastic structure designed to mimic both the peregrine's wing and the angled layering of the local schist, this stylish winery has free tasting with views of the industrially-elegant barrel room. In summer the wing provides shelter and some shade as you tuck into beautifully prepared platters and a glass or two of their Riesling and pinots. Daily 10am–5pm.

Mount Edward Coalpit Road ⊤ 03/442 6113 ⓦ www.mountedward.co.nz. Specialist winery off the main tourist circuit run by Alan Brady, the Valley's original wine pioneer. Come for quality Pinot Noir and excellent Riesling, but it is probably best to call in advance.

Activities

Many activity companies are little more than a van and a mobile phone and don't operate an office, though most are directly associated with one of the **information** and **booking offices** that line Shotover Street. In practice,

Two skifields – **Coronet Peak** and the smaller **Remarkables** – within easy striking distance of numerous quality hotels, good restaurants and plenty of après-ski combine to make Queenstown New Zealand's **premier ski destination**. The highlight of the season is the ten-day **Queenstown Winter Festival** (ⓦwww.winterfestival .co.nz), around the end of June or early July, which, as well as all the conventional ski events, has snow sculpture, ski-golf and a great line-up of entertainment. Of the various other events, The Remarkables' family-oriented **Spring Carnival**, in the first week of the September school holidays, is one of the best.

Both fields (and Mount Hutt) are run by the same company whose website (ⓦwww.nzski.com) has contact details, snow reports, web-cams and all the latest pricing and rental availability info. One-day tow passes are specific to each field, but there are **multi-day tickets** which are valid at all three fields (3-day $204, 5-day $330, 8-day $504).

Neither field has **accommodation** on site, but frequent shuttle buses run to and from Queenstown ($20), where the supply is plentiful – except during school holidays. For **ski rental** visit the excellent Brown's (cnr Shotover & Brecon streets, ☎03/442 4003, ⓦwww.brownsnz.com), who charge $39 a day for midrange skis, boots and poles ($44 for a snowboard); or Outside Sports (cnr The Mall & Camp St, ☎03/442 8883, ⓦwww.outsidesports.co.nz), who offer similar deals.

Coronet Peak

Coronet Peak (☎03/442 4620, ⓔservice@coronetpeak.co.nz), 18km north of Queenstown, opened in 1947, making it New Zealand's first real ski destination. Sophisticated snow-making equipment extends its season into spring, when cobalt blue skies and stunning scenery earn it an enviable reputation. Its range of **runs** for skiers of all abilities, and over 400 vertical metres of skiing, only add to its popularity – get here early to avoid long waits for the tows. Throughout the season, which typically starts in early June and sometimes makes it into October, **buses** from Queenstown shuttle back and forth along the sealed access road (no toll). **Passes** for daytime skiing (9am–4pm) cost $77; floodlit skiing (July–Sept Fri & Sat 4–9pm) goes for $37.

The Remarkables

The Remarkables (☎03/442 4615, ⓔservice@theremarkables.co.nz), 20km east of Queenstown, is one of the newer commercial fields, occupying three mountain basins tucked in behind the wrinkled face of The Remarkables. It is most renowned as learner and intermediate terrain but there are also good runs for advanced skiers, and rapid access to some excellent country for off-piste ski touring. A **day pass** costs $72. Though the bottom of the tows is 500m higher than at Coronet Peak, more snow is required to cover the tussock, giving a slightly shorter season (late June to early Oct). At 320m, the total vertical descent from the tows is also less than at Coronet, but you gain an extra 120m by taking the Homeward Run – a long stretch of powder with sparkling scenery – to the 14km unsealed **access road** (no toll), where frequent buses shuttle you back up to the chairlift.

virtually every booking office will book any trip, or you could just book through your hotel or hostel. Prices don't usually vary, but it may be worth asking for **discounts** –YHA, backpacker and so forth – if you think you might be eligible. Almost all the booking offices are open daily, usually to around 9pm in summer, 8pm in winter. For more on booking offices, see p.829.

With so much on offer it is tempting to be frugal elsewhere and blow the lot when you reach Queenstown. But, most activities in Queenstown are more

expensive than in other parts of the country, so it may pay to have fun else-where. To get the most action for the least money here, check out one of the numerous **combination deals** knitting together two to five of the main activ-ities and tending to focus on either the Shotover or the Kawarau rivers: decide what you want to do and there'll probably be a combo to suit. Pack it all into one day with the **Awesome Foursome** (8hr; $455), which bundles all the top-money activities: a helicopter ride into Skippers Canyon, rafting the Shotover, joining the Shotover Jet, and leaping from the Nevis Bungy.

Photos of your jump, jetboat ride or rafting trip are pretty much de rigueur, so you'll frequently encounter **photographers** demanding a cheesy grin; the results are available for purchase almost immediately. A lot of people like to pay extra for a video or photo of themselves patently terrified while pretending not to be, while a few others buy T-shirts proclaiming their exploits and wear them proudly round town.

Bungy jumping

Even visitors who never had any intention of parting with a large wad of cash to dangle on the end of a thick strand of latex rubber find themselves **bungy jumping** in Queenstown. A combination of peer pressure, magnificent scenery and hard-sell promotion eventually gets to most people and, let's face it, historic bridges high above remote rivers beat a crane over a supermarket car park any day. AJ Hackett (☎0800/286 495, ⓦ www.ajhackett.com) cur-rently operates four fixed bungy sites around Queenstown, and then there's the massive Parabungy (see p.840).

Kawarau Bungy beside SH6, 23km east of Queenstown (daily 8.30am–6.15pm in summer, reduced hours in winter; $130). AJ Hackett's orig-inal, most famous and most frequently jumped bungy site is 43m high and is the only place around Queenstown where you can get dunked in the river. The price includes a certificate, T-shirt and transport from Queenstown if required: an extra $39 gets you a short video recording your fifteen seconds of fame. At busy times the whole scene resembles a rather ghoulish production line, as bungy initiates are trundled out, and tour buses disgorge spectators to fill sev-eral viewing platforms. The best views are from the **Kawarau Bungy Centre**, beside the bungy bridge (daily 8am–7.30pm; $5), where you can learn more than you thought there was to know about bungy jumping, eat at the café and experience the new **Bungy Dome**. Aimed at those who don't fancy jumping but want a taste of the experience, you stand in a room surrounded by TV screens, smoke and pumping music as you are walked through the whole pro-cedure (though you remain upright at all times).

Nevis Highwire Bungy (4 Queenstown departures daily; $195). Some say that with bungy jumping it is only the first metre that counts, but when it comes down to it, size does matter. AJ Hackett know this and have pulled out all the stops with this whopping 134m affair. Jumpers launch from a partly glass-bottomed gondola strung way out over the Nevis River, a tributary of the Kawarau some 32km east of Queenstown. Access is by 4WD through private property so spectators will have to fork out $35 to watch their buddies, though this does give you a ride out to the launch gondola and a wonderful view.

Same-day second jumpers often gravitate to the 47-metre **Ledge Bungy** (summer generally 4–9pm; winter 4–8pm; $130, including T-shirt and gondola ride), from the top of the Skyline Gondola, where it feels like you are diving out over Queenstown. Unlike the other sites, you are fitted with a body har-ness allowing you to do a running jump, and if they aren't too busy you may be able to jump with all manner of "toys" (surf boards, bikes and the like) to add that extra dimension. Night jumps in winter make for yet another variation for the committed.

Jumping at any of these three sites gives you the option of a cheaper **second jump** ($59 at Kawarau or The Ledge; $115 at Nevis) if taken within 24 hours; and all three can be combined in the half-day "Thrillogy" ($289 including a T-shirt) with one jump from each site.

Hackett have recently taken over the 102m **Pipeline Bungy** ($160 including T-shirt, same-day repeat jumps $102) which spans the Shotover River in Skippers Canyon, where the jumping platform is atop a reconstructed 1864 sluice-water pipeline. The freefall is almost as great as Nevis with much more of a ground rush.

The last contender in the unending "highest bungy" contest is 150–180m **Parabungy** (☎03/409 0712, ⓦwww.adventurecentre.co.nz; $229), which takes the novel approach of attaching you and a jump master to a parachute towed behind a boat on Lake Wakatipu. As the boat charges off across the water in front of Queenstown you are winched out high above the water. Then you jump, typically coming within ten metres of the water surface. With a one-hour turnaround it is quicker than the out-of-town bungy sites, and with great mountain views it is also scenic.

Swinging

Swinging presents an alternative to bungy jumping that still involves launching yourself fearlessly into the void. Along with that stomach-in-your-mouth freefall sensation you get the bonus of a massive swoop through the air and no dangling on the end of rubber cord.

Canyon Swing (☎03/442 6990 & 0800/279 464, ⓦwww.canyonswing.co.nz; $109). Reputedly the world's highest swing, on this 109m arc above the Shotover River is the pinnacle of Queenstown swinging. If you time it right you'll have rafts full of spectators below on the river as you launch –

forwards, backwards, head first, or even sat in a chair.
Ledge Sky Swing ($85 including the ride to the top of the gondola; ☎0800/286 495). Try a 43m swing above Queenstown at AJ Hackett's Ledge Bungy site.

Jetboating

Commercial **jetboating** kicked off in Queenstown way back in 1965, and it remains high in the adrenalin hierarchy. There are strong arguments for spending your jetboating dollar on better value wilderness trips elsewhere – the Wilkin River Jet, Waiatoto River Safaris and trips down the Wairaurahiri River spring to mind – but Queenstown shouldn't be overlooked.

Though it is marginally the most expensive of the local trips, the most thrilling is the **Shotover Jet** (☎0800/746 868; daily 9am–5pm; 30min; $89), a slick operation and the only company to run thrill-a-second trips down Shotover Canyon downstream from Arthur's Point, 5km north of Queenstown. Battered boats attest to a lifetime of close shaves with rocks and canyon walls, and half an hour of 360-degree turns and periodic dousings is quite enough. Courtesy minibuses run from The Station (see p.829) throughout the day.

Two operators run excellent trips along the Dart River from Glenorchy (see p.856), both offering Queenstown pick-ups for an extra $20.

Rafting

The majority of jetboat operators stick to fairly flat water, leaving the rough stuff for **whitewater rafting** on the Kawarau and Shotover rivers.

Thousands of people do these trips every year without incident, but you should bear in mind that rafting, in common with other adrenalin-charged sports, always entails a degree of risk. The most reliable of the two rivers is a seven-kilometre section of the large-volume **Kawarau River**, negotiating four Grade III rapids (exciting but not truly frightening; see "Basics", p.57, for details of river grading) and culminating in the potentially nasty Chinese Dog Leg, said to be the longest commercially rafted rapid in New Zealand. Being lake-fed, its flow is relatively steady, though it peaks in spring and drops substantially towards the end of summer.

In contrast, the fourteen-kilometre rafted section of the Grade III–IV **Shotover River** flows straight out of the mountains and its level fluctuates considerably, thereby affecting its raftability. In October and November, snow melt ensures good flows and a bumpy ride; by late summer low flows can make it a bit tame for hardened rafters, though it is still scenic and fun for first-timers. In winter the lack of sunlight reaching the depths of the canyon makes it too cold for most people though there are shorter helicopter access trips for $199.

The Shotover in particular is a demanding river: revelling in names such as Shark's Fin and The Toilet, the rapids reach their apotheosis in the Mother-in-Law rapid, often bypassed at low water by diverting through the 170-metre Oxenbridge Tunnel (see p.836).

Trips on the Kawarau River take around four hours with a little over an hour on the water; those on the Shotover last an hour longer, with most of the extra time given over to more rafting.

Although there appear to be three Queenstown rafting companies all with assorted packages and combo deals, everyone in fact goes on rafts operated by Queenstown Rafting (☎0800/723 8464, ⓦ www.rafting.co.nz) which charges $135 for the Kawarau and $145 for the Shotover.

Moving into a different league, Queenstown Rafting also runs three-day, fly-in wilderness trips on the **Landsborough River** (mostly Gd III; $1200) spending a day and a half on the river. There are usually only 3–4 trips each summer (Nov–March; call for details).

Rafting is usually limited to those over thirteen years of age, but by tackling an easier (Gd I–II) stretch of the Shotover, **Family Adventures** (☎03/442 8836 & 0800/4rafting) can take all ages. Their trips (adults $150, kids $110) include a drive into the Skippers Canyon and around ninety minutes on the water floating past a beached gold dredge and the ruins of attempts to divert the waters to get at the gravels below; with oar rafts you don't even need to paddle.

River surfing and whitewater sledging

Through the summer months (generally mid-Oct to April) two sections of the Kawarau River are used for the parallel sports of whitewater sledging and river surfing – the "Dog Leg" section used by the rafters, and the "Roaring Meg" run, a few kilometres downstream. For both sports small groups are equipped with a board or sledge, a padded wetsuit, a helmet and fins, then led downstream and encouraged to view their independence and freedom of movement as virtues rather than hazards: it works best if you are both confident in water and a decent swimmer.

River surfing involves floating downstream, grasping a foam boogie board and surfing as many as possible of the rapids' standing waves. While rafters bob around high up on their inflatable perches with little water contact, river surfers get right in the thick of it: what look like ripples to rafters become huge waves and the serious rapids can be thoroughly daunting, as froth engulfs you on all sides.

Largely the same techniques are used in **whitewater sledging**. Suited primarily to shallow, rocky rivers, this involves grasping the handles of a foam or plastic "sledge" and snuggling arms and upper body down into a streamlined shape. The extra buoyancy gives a better roller-coaster ride over the waves and greater manoeuvrability for catching eddies, though surfing is more difficult.

Frogz Have More Fun ☎0800/338 737; $119. This Wanaka-based sledging operation does double runs down the "Roaring Meg" section. They also pick up at the Kawarau Bungy, 23km east of Queenstown.
Mad Dog River Boarding ☎03/442 9708; $129. Ninety wet minutes are spent river surfing the

"Roaring Meg" run adding in rope swings and jet-skiing along the flat section.
Serious Fun (☎0800/737 468; $129). Four-hour trips spend around 90 minutes river surfing either the "Dog Leg" or "Roaring Meg" sections depending on the conditions.

Canyoning

Fans of river surfing and whitewater sledging may also be drawn to **canyoning** where small groups are led down verdant narrow canyons walking in streams, swimming across pools, sliding down rocks and jumping off cliffs all suitably protected by wetsuit, helmet and climbing harness. The closest trips are with 12 Mile Delta Canyoning (☎03/441 4468 & 0800/222 696, Ⓦwww.xiimile.co.nz; $135), who offer morning and afternoon trips and give you three hours away from Queenstown, around half that time in the water. It is great fun, but for a little more commitment and a longer day out go with Routeburn Canyoning (☎03/441 4386, Ⓦwww.gycanyoning.co.nz; Oct–April;) who'll take you up to the start of the Routeburn Track and launch you into a water-sculpted, narrow canyon full of jumps and slides – and you don't even have to do any real abseiling (7hr ex-Queenstown; $230). The pinnacle of canyoning in the area is their extended trip (9–10hr ex Queenstown $250) which covers the same ground as Routeburn Canyoning but starts higher up the canyon and throws in a few long abseils down waterfalls. You can meet both these trips in Glenorchy saving $15 and two hours of driving.

Via Ferrata

If all the mountains around Queenstown look tempting but you don't have the skills or equipment to go rock climbing, you can get a sense of the experience with **Via Ferrata** (☎03/409 0696, Ⓦwww.viaferrata.co.nz). Suitably harnessed up, you make your own way up a trail of steel rungs drilled into a series of cliff faces just above Queenstown. There is no belaying or abseiling, but you are protected by clipping yourself into a long steel cable which runs beside the rungs. Anyone unused to outdoor activities will want to start on Level 1 (3–4hr; $109), which is mostly at a gentle angle but still gets high above town. Level 2 (4–5hr; $149) is steeper and tougher, and Level 3 (3–4hr; $149) is for those who have already proved their abilities on Level 2.

Paragliding, hang-gliding, skydiving and fly-by-wire

A fine day with a little breeze is all it needs to fill the skies above Queenstown with people **tandem paragliding** from Bob's Peak, immediately above town and reached by the Skyline Gondola. It works like a taxi rank, so if you want a go, simply pay your way up the Skyline Gondola then stand in line until it is your turn. By handing over $185 you then get the next paraglider in the queue for your jump, which typically lasts ten to fifteen minutes. How many acrobatic manoeuvres are executed is largely down to you, your jump guide and the conditions. If you don't see anyone in the air during the main 9am–5pm operating times then the conditions aren't right and you don't need to trouble yourself with the Gondola ride.

There's more of a bird-like quality to **tandem hang–gliding**, where you and your instructor are harnessed in a prone position under the wing of a hang-glider and execute a number of progressively steep turns as you soar down from Coronet Peak to the Flight Park on Malaghans Road 700m below. Skytrek Hang Gliding (℡03/442 6311; $165 for 12–15min in the air) is the longest-standing operator running several flights a day throughout the year, sometimes launching from The Remarkables.

Paragliding while being towed behind a boat goes by the name of **parasailing**, an activity offered by Paraflights NZ, Main Town Pier (℡03/442 8507), who run a large motorboat saddled with a small helipad. For $75 each, you (and a buddy if you wish) are winched out on a rope until you reach a height of 100m above the lake surface and, after ten minutes admiring the scenery, winched back in again, still dry.

Queenstown is an expensive place to go **tandem skydiving** but the scenery does go some way to compensate. NZone (℡0800/376 796, Ⓦwww.nzone .biz) run jumps from 9000ft ($245; 25sec freefall), 12,000ft ($295; 45sec) and 15,000ft ($395; 65sec), all taking place over Lake Wakatipu and landing by the foot of The Remarkables. Another airborne possibility includes a fifteen-minute spin in a Pitt Special **stunt plane** with Actionflite (℡03/442 9708; $235).

Petrolheads keen to get airborne should try **Fly By Wire** (℡0800/359 299, Ⓦwww.flybywire.co.nz; $160), which involves piloting a kind of miniature plane which is tethered by a hundred-metre leash to a fixed point on a wire strung between two hills. Loaded with a six-minute charge of fuel, there's free rein to circle around, gaining height (up to almost 100m) and swooping down, perhaps reaching 140km/hr. Once the fuel cuts out you drift back to earth. Trips from Queenstown out to the site (on private property) run 2–3 times daily.

Horse riding, off-road driving and mountain biking

The scenery makes Queenstown a great place to go **horse riding**. Good-value trips are run from Shotover Stables on Malaghans Road, 7km north of town (℡03/442 9708); their treks ($60; 1hr 30min) emphasize local history, exploring gold-mining relics down by the Shotover riverbed and often visiting the old mining tunnel on St Kilda Hill. Alternatively there are a couple of horse-riding companies running out of Glenorchy (see p.857).

If you're happier with more than one horsepower then try guided **off–road driving** with Off Road Adventures (℡03/442 7858, Ⓦwww.offroad.co.nz), who offer motorbike and quad bike adventure tours (allow 3hr, 1hr 15min riding; $169).

On exhilarating **mountain-biking** trips you take the strain, though much of the riding is downhill.

Fat Tyre Adventures ℡0800/328 897, Ⓦwww.fat-tyre.co.nz. Bike trips for mountain bikers offering a variety of single-track packages (6hr; $195) with up to four hours in the saddle, including an excellent trip in the Dunstan Mountains above Cromwell. All-day helicopter-access trips ($350–475 depending on numbers) are scenic, challenging and great fun, and there are family-oriented picnic rides ($195) along gravel roads.
Gravity Action ℡03/441 1021, Ⓦwww

.gravityaction.com. Relatively cheap thrills descending almost 600m down a narrow track which, until a better road was pushed through in 1888, was the only route into Skippers Canyon. $99, with over 2hr in the saddle.
Vertigo ℡03/442 8378 & 0800/837 844, Ⓦwww.heli-adventures.co.nz. These guys offer a couple of steep rides down from the top of the gondola in Queenstown (2.5hr; $109), or fly you to the top of a 1600m downhill (4hr; $265).

Four-wheel drive tours and scenic flights

For those wishing to relinquish control completely there are a number of **4WD** vehicles on offer where the driver/guide takes a gentler more informative approach to the countryside, some focussing on *The Lord of the Rings* locations (see box, p.826). Easily the biggest operator is Nomad Safaris (T03/442 6699 & 0800/688 222, W www.nomadsafaris.co.nz) who do trips into Skippers Canyon (see p.834), cross the Arrow River over twenty times on the run into Macetown (see p.852) and offer a couple of Safari of the Rings trips (see box, p.827). They'll also let you get behind the wheel for some real off-roading ($175). To get into the backcountry with the aim of unearthing some gold, join Goldseeker Tours (T03/442 5949, W www.queenstown-goldseekers.co.nz; $95).

Much of the **flying** around Queenstown is done as part of some other adventure activity, either helibiking, skydiving, making a quick trip to Milford Sound, or as part of a combination deal alongside rafting or bungy jumping. If you have the cash to spare you might want to try helicopter landings at the top of The Remarkables (20min; $160) with Southern Lakes Helicopters (T0800/801 616), or a similar trip with the other main operator, The Helicopter Line (T0800/500 575).

Eating

You can eat well in Queenstown. There are stacks of restaurants, many of them very good and correspondingly expensive, but cheaper places can be found. Increasingly, restaurants are making the most of Queenstown's summer climate, spilling out onto the pedestrianized streets or stretching out along the waterfront, where you can sit and watch the *Earnslaw* glide in. **Breakfast** and **snack** places generally close by 6pm, though some serve early **dinners**, while restaurants often double up as bars as the evening wears on.

With the opening of Queenstown's first large **supermarket**, just five minutes' walk along Gorge Road from town, grocery prices have come more-or-less into line with city prices.

Breakfasts, cafés and snacks

Gourmet Express 62 Shotover St. About the nearest you'll get in New Zealand to a genuine American diner, with pancakes, French toast, all-day breakfasts, burgers and sandwiches at reasonable prices. Daily 6.30am until late.

Habebes Wakatipu Arcade, Beach St. Hole-in-the-wall vegetarian and Lebanese daytime café serving Queenstown's best felafel, tabouleh and Kiwi variations on Middle Eastern dishes, as well as juicy lamb and chicken kebabs.

Naff Caff 66 Shotover St. A relaxed daytime café that's great for hanging out over some of the best coffee in town, notably the "mega mucho" strong cappuccino. There's also a good range of breakfast pastries and pies, quiches and panini at lunch, and there's an open-air terrace at the back.

Take 5 Steamer Wharf, at the end away from the centre of town, Beach St. The best coffee in town, excellent juices, fine toasted bagels and sandwiches in this tiny little all-day café which spills out onto the lakefront.

Vudu 23 Beach St. One of Queenstown's groovier cafés with booths, comfy chairs and loads of magazines. The place is strong on inexpensive breakfasts, quiches, panini, scrumptious muffins and good coffee, plus more substantial fare like chicken wraps, steak sandwiches and pasta.

Restaurants

@ Thai Second floor, Air New Zealand building, Church St T03/442 3683. Probably the best of the town's Thai places and certainly authentic. Try the excellent tum yum soup ($7) and perhaps the tamarind, potato and lamb curry ($17). Takeaways available. Lic & BYO.

Avanti 20 The Mall. Cheery Italian place whose reasonable food at modest prices ($20 mains) guarantees popularity, especially on Wednesday seafood nights. Gourmet pizzas and bowls of pasta go for $15–25.

Boardwalk 1st Floor, Steamer Wharf ℡03/442 5630. Swanky, seafood restaurant that often caters to very distinguished guests. It serves some of the freshest seafood in town, imaginatively prepared and often with delicate Asian touches. Dress smartly and expect to pay $27–35 for mains and then mortgage your kidneys for a bottle from their extensive wine list.

Bombay Place 68 Shotover St ℡03/441 2886. Excellent little authentic Indian lunch and dinner restaurant serving the likes of shrimp masala or chicken pasanda (both $19) plus some wonderful veggie options. BYO and Licensed.

Bunker Cow Lane ℡03/441 8030. Behind the signless exterior is this exclusive, swish fine-dining restaurant, with a funky cocktail bar (see p.846). The food is beautifully presented and made from the best ingredients; try the prosciutto-wrapped salmon or a mezze platter ($30–35), and sample some of their sophisticated wine to wash down the bill.

The Cow Cow Lane. Long-standing and popular pizzeria in a cosy stone house. The food's pretty good and reasonably priced ($17–25 a head), and they pack 'em in so be prepared to share a table. BYO & licensed.

The Fishbone Bar and Grill 7 Beach St. Excellent value spot that's obviously doing something right. It has been round a while operating as a high-class, quirky and fun fish-restaurant and a work-a-day fish-and-chip takeaway, favoured by all the locals in the area. Open for lunch and dinner. BYO & licensed.

Gantley's Malaghans Rd, Arthur's Point ℡03/442 8999. Classy and romantic restaurant in an 1863 stone cottage 7km north of Queenstown serving award-winning Kiwi dishes with French leanings. Mains start around $30 and the wine list is extensive. Reservations are essential, and courtesy transport from Queenstown is laid on.

Tatler 5 The Mall ℡03/442 8372. One of Queenstown's most fashionable and cosmopolitan restaurant/bars right in the thick of things serving the likes of crispy duck, Thai curry and lamb shanks as well as some sticky desserts. Eat early if you want to avoid the inevitable smoke and clamour as the place transforms itself into a lively jazz and wine bar.

Pasta Pasta Cucina 6 Brecon St ℡03/442 6762. Lively and simply decorated Italian restaurant serving wonderful crisp pizza (around $22) from the *manuka*-fired oven and great pasta dishes. Try the spicy Devil's pizza or imaginative toppings such as pan-seared lemon, rocket pesto and roast capsicum. Desserts and coffee are equally superb. Evenings only.

Solera Vino 25 Beach St ℡03/442 6082. This small, licensed, elegant fine-dining restaurant offers Mediterranean dishes, which might include comfit of duck with potato rosti and pomegranate sauce ($32), and has a wine list as long as a baguette. Open daily from 6pm.

Winnie Bagoes 7–9 The Mall. Excellent gourmet pizzas and pasta, good à la carte and blackboard menu, all at reasonable prices (see also "Bars and Clubs", p.846).

Drinking and nightlife

Despite its high profile and large number of visitors, Queenstown is still essentially a small town. Touring bands are relatively rare, there isn't much in the way of highbrow culture and some of the **clubs** border on being backpacker cattle markets or are simply cheesy. Still, they can be great fun, and there is no shortage of lively **places to drink**, many doubling as restaurants early in the evening, when there are often a couple of **happy hours** to help get things going. The free *Mountain Scene* newspaper, found all over town, gives up-to-date **listings**, including the **movies** shown at the Embassy Cinemas, 11 The Mall (infoline ℡03/442 9990).

About the only regular entertainment is at the two **Maori concert and hangi** events. The traditional Maori Concert and Feast, 1 Memorial St (Wed–Sat; reservations essential ℡03/442 8878; $50), a five-course *hangi* buffet followed by an hour-long cabaret-style concert that takes a tongue-in-cheek romp through potted Maori mythology, the *haka*, *poi* dances and stick games. A modern and less corny equivalent is the **Maori Hangi and Cultural Experience** (nightly at 7pm; $95; ℡03/442 8059) at the Kiwi & Birdlife Park (see p.832), which includes kiwi viewing.

Bars and clubs

Bardeaux 5 Eureka Arcade. A funky little cocktail bar, intimate with big sofas, roaring fire, a broad selection of excellent whisky, wine and occasional jazz and blues bands. Relaxed early evening, but picks up big-time after 11pm

Bunker Cow Lane ☎03/441 8030. A funky, stylish, upstairs cocktail bar with cool music, open very late.

Debajo Cow Lane. A Catholic-icon-filled Spanish bar sitting uneasily beneath the *HMS Britannia* (an English-style pub), this could almost be Majorca. Open until 5am with DJ music, mostly funky house and sexy grooves, some killer cocktails, a real lounge feel and some affordable snacks.

Dux de Lux 14 Church St ☎442 9688. Queenstown outpost of this Christchurch institution serving vegetarian and seafood meals either inside a dark, stonebuilt cottage or out on the terrace. They brew half a dozen excellent beers and there's frequent live music.

The Edge Cnr Camp St & Robins Rd. Club that's often jumping to top-forty and mainstream dance tunes. Very cheesy but fun.

Póg Mahone's 14 Rees St. Queenstown's established Irish bar, typically crowded with folk clamouring for draught Guinness and loosely-Irish bar meals. It is even fuller for the live Irish music and Celtic rock on acid usually Fri, Sat and Sun.

The Rattlesnake Room 14 Brecon St ☎03/442 9995. This upstairs bar at the *Lone Star* pub is a rowdy spot for an early-evening drink with a happy hour (4–7pm), pool tables, and DJs Wed–Sun nights.

Surreal 7 Rees St. Early evening restaurant that soon transforms into a harder-edged club with DJs and occasional live music. The preferred sounds are house, techno, and big beat, which kick off after about 10.30pm.

Winnie Bagoes 7–9 The Mall. Italian eating joint (see "Restaurants", p.845) with jazz or other bands, pool tables and thumping DJ-inspired music, which means it progressively becomes less restauranty as the night wears on.

The World 27 Shotover St. One of the livelier clubs with a dedicated budget clientele here for the happy hours and adventure give-aways.

Listings

Airlines Air New Zealand Travel Centre, Church St ☎03/441 1900.

Banks and exchange All major banks have a branch and ATM around the centre. Best bets for exchange services are Thomas Cook, in The Station, cnr Camp & Shotover sts (☎03/442 6403; daily: Oct–May 8am–8pm; June–Sept 8am–7pm); and the ANZ Bank, 81 Beach St (☎0800/180 921; daily 9am–9pm); Travelex, in the main visitor centre (same hours), also has reasonable rates.

Bike rental Several places around town rent out low-spec bikes good for around town and the lakeside trails for around $25 a half-day or $35 a day. Try Higher Gear (☎0800/881 488) on Lake Esplanade by Steamer Wharf. For real off-road use visit Dr Bike at Outside Sports, cnr The Mall & Camp St (☎03/442 8883; 9am–9pm), who rents out hardtails ($35 half-day, $50 full day) and dual suspension mega machines ($50 half-day, $75 full day).

Buses Atomic Shuttles (☎03/442 9708) run to Christchurch, Dunedin and up the Coast to Greymouth; Catch-a-Bus (☎03/471 4120) operates a door-to-door service to Dunedin; InterCity (☎03/474 9600) operates the most extensive services to all major destinations; Southern Link Shuttles (☎03/358 8355) runs from Queenstown

to Nelson via Wanaka and Christchurch; Super Shuttle (☎0800/748 885) meets planes from Queenstown's airport; and Wanaka Connexions (☎03/443 9122) runs the most direct service to Wanaka.

Camping and outdoor equipment At Small Planet, 17 Shotover St (☎03/442 6393; daily 10am–6pm), you can pick up used gear, including snowboards, ski gear, wetsuits, bikes, camping and tramping gear and books – all at good prices and with competitive buy-back deals. If you've got something to get rid of, they'll hawk it for 25 percent commission.

Car rental You can pick up a 1.3 litre car for around $49 a day usually with the first 100km free and 20¢ a kilometre after that. For rental periods over three or four days you get unlimited free kilometres. For a two litre car expect to pay $60–90, rising to around $100 for small 4WD vehicles. Companies to try include: Apex (☎03/442 8040); Budget (☎03/442 9274); NZ Rent a Car (☎03/442 7465); Network Car Rental (☎03/442 7055); and Rent-a-Dent (☎03/442 9922).

Internet access Fierce competition means good rates, fast connections and long opening hours, often until 10pm or later. Places to look out for are *E Café*, 50 Shotover St; Budget Communications,

2nd floor, O'Connell's Mall; and Internet Outpost, 27 Shotover St.

Library Cnr Shotover St & Gorge Rd (Mon–Thurs 10am–5pm, Fri 10am–6pm, Sat 10.30am–12.30pm).

Medical treatment Queenstown Medical Centre, 9 Isle St (☎03/441 0860), and Lakes District Hospital, 20 Douglas St, Frankton (☎03/441 0015).

Pharmacy Wilkinsons Pharmacy, The Mall

(☎03 /442 7313), is open daily from 8.30am to 10pm.

Police 11 Camp St (☎03/441 1600).

Post office The main post office, cnr Camp St Ballarat St (Mon–Fri 8.30am–6pm, Sat 9am–4pm) has poste restante facilities.

Taxis Alpine Taxi ☎03/442 6666 & 0800/730 066; and Queenstown Taxis ☎03/442 7788 & 0800/477 888.

Thomas Cook Inside The Station, cnr Camp St & Shotover St ☎03/442 6403.

Arrowtown and Macetown

The former gold-rush settlement of **ARROWTOWN** seems perched on the brink of tour-bus hell as day-trippers from Queenstown, 23km to the southeast, swarm around the sheepskin, greenstone and gold of its souvenir shops. But Arrowtown manages to retain the spirit of a living community, with grocers' shops, a pub and post office fitfully coexisting alongside the gift-wrapped centre. The best way to appreciate Arrowtown is to linger on after the crowds have gone, leaving behind a peaceful town at the confluence of the Arrow River and Bush Creek. The sheltering hills give Arrowtown parched summers and snowy winters, thrown into sharp relief by autumn, when the deciduous trees planted by the mining community cast golden shadows on a central knot of picturesque miners' cottages.

Arrowtown's permanent population is only around 1200, but in summer, when holiday homes are full and tourists arrive in force, it comes close to regaining its 7000-strong peak attained during the **gold rush**. There is some debate as to whether American William Fox was actually the first to discover alluvial gold in the Arrow River in 1862, but there is no doubt that he dominated proceedings hereabouts, managing to keep the find secret while he recovered over 100kg of gold. Jealous prospectors tried to follow him to the lode, but he gave them the slip, on one occasion leaving his tent and provisions behind in the middle of the night. The town subsequently bore his name until Foxes gave way to Arrowtown. The Arrow River became known as the richest for its size in the world – a reputation which drew scores of Chinese miners (for more on which, see the box on p.848), who lived in the now partly restored **Arrowtown Chinese Settlement**. Prospectors fanned out over the surrounding hills, where brothers Charley and John Mace set up **Macetown**, now an appealing ghost town. As prospectors pushed further up the Arrow and Bush Creek, they began to populate **the valleys**; scattered communities sprang up along the banks, but were abandoned just as suddenly, leaving telltale poplar, rowan and willows to be reclaimed by nature. Where settlers' cottages once stood, **fruit** trees have colonized the riverbanks, and in autumn apples, pears and plums weigh down the branches, and bushes of blackberry, blackcurrant, gooseberry, raspberry and elderberry become rampant. There are few specific sights, but you can easily spend a lazy afternoon gorging on fruit and trying to identify the overgrown sites of houses. The surrounding hills are speckled with **rose bushes**: according to folklore, these were planted by miners seeking vitamin C (rosehips are one of the richest sources); others contend that they were planted primarily for their root systems, which could be fashioned into briar pipes.

13

QUEENSTOWN | Arrowtown and Macetown

The initial wave of miners who came to Arrowtown in the early 1860s were fortune-seekers intent on a fast buck. When gold was discovered on the West Coast, most of them hot-footed it to Greymouth or Hokitika, leaving a much-depleted community that lacked the economic wherewithal to support the businesses which had mushroomed around the mining communities.

The solution, as it had been ten years earlier on the Victorian goldfields of Bendigo and Ballarat in Australia, was to import **Chinese labour**. The first Chinese, who principally came from the Canton delta region of Guangdong, arrived in Otago in 1866, their number reaching 5000 by 1870. The community settled along Bush Creek, its **segregation** from the main settlement symptomatic of the inherent racism of the time – something which also manifested itself in working practices that forced the Chinese to pick over abandoned mining claims and work the tailings of European miners. Even Chinese employed on municipal projects such as the Presbyterian church were paid only half the wages paid to Europeans doing the same job.

A ray of light is cast amid the prevailing bigotry by contemporary newspaper reports, which suggest that many citizens found the Chinese conduct of their business "upright and straightforward" and their demeanour "orderly and sober" – perhaps surprisingly in what was an almost entirely male community. Most came with starry-eyed dreams of earning their fortune and returning home so, initially at least, few brought their families; a process of chain **migration** later brought wives, children and then members of the extended family. Few realized their dreams, but around ninety percent did return home, many in a box, driven into an early grave by overwork and poor living conditions. Many more were driven out in the early 1880s when recession brought racial jealousies to a head, resulting in the enactment of a punitive poll tax on foreign residents. There was little workable gold by this time and those Chinese who stayed mostly became market gardeners or merchants and drifted away, mainly to Auckland, though the Arrowtown community remained viable into the 1920s. Once the Chinese had left or died, the Bush Creek settlement was **abandoned** and largely destroyed by repeated flooding.

Arrival and information

Two **buses** run from Queenstown to Arrowtown, both departing from The Top of the Mall on Camp Street in Queenstown and stopping outside the library on Buckingham Street in Arrowtown. The scheduled Arrow Express (☏03/442 1900; 3–5 daily; 25min; $10 one way, $18 return) runs mostly via Frankton and Queenstown airport, though some services go via the Shotover Jet and Millbrook Resort. The Double Decker Bus Tour uses a red London bus to operate Queenstown-based **tours** (☏03/442 6067; daily 10am & 2pm; 2hr 30min; $34), visiting the Kawarau bungy bridge and Gibbston Winery en route and spending an hour in Arrowtown before heading directly back to Queenstown.

Arrowtown's **visitor centre** is in the foyer of the Lakes District Museum at 49 Buckingham St (daily 8.30am–5pm; ☏03/442 1824, ⓦwww.museumqueenstown.com), where you can pick up the *Historic Arrowtown* booklet ($2.50), and the informative *Arrowtown Chinese Settlement* booklet ($2.50).

Accommodation

To see Arrowtown at its best, you really need to **stay** the night; happily, there's plenty of accommodation, most of it at a very high standard.

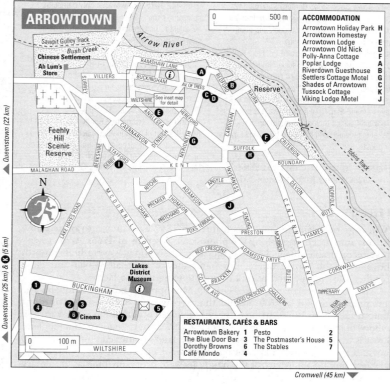

Macetown (16 km)

ARROWTOWN

0 — 500 m

Sawpit Gulley Track
Bush Creek
Chinese Settlement
Ah Lum's Store
VILLIERS
SURREY

Arrow River
RAMSHAW LANE
BUCKINGHAM
AV OF TREES
WILTSHIRE
See inset map for detail
BELFORD
NAIRN
Reserve

Feehly Hill Scenic Reserve

ANGLESEA
CAERNARVON
DENBIGH
BERKSHIRE
STAFFORD
DERBY
HEREFORD
MERIONETH
CARDIGAN
CRITERION
SUFFOLK
BOUNDARY
Tobins Track

MALAGHAN ROAD
KENT
INVERNESS
DEVON
NORFOLK

N

RITCHIE
PREMIER
THOMSON
PRITCHARD
SHAW
ADAMSON
ARGYLE
JENKINS
PRESTON
MCKIBBEN
BUTEL
THAMES
CENTENNIAL AVENUE
BUTE

LAKE HAYES ROAD
MCDONNELL ROAD
FOXS TERRACE
REID CRESCENT
ADAMSON DRIVE
COTTER AVE
BRACKEN
HOOD CRESCENT
CHALMERS
CORNWALL
TIPPERARY
DAVEYS
EVA DAWSON

Lakes District Museum

BUCKINGHAM
Cinema

0 — 100 m

WILTSHIRE

Cromwell (45 km)

ACCOMMODATION

Arrowtown Holiday Park **H**
Arrowtown Homestay **I**
Arrowtown Lodge **E**
Arrowtown Old Nick **D**
Polly-Anna Cottage **F**
Poplar Lodge **A**
Riverdown Guesthouse **B**
Settlers Cottage Motel **G**
Shades of Arrowtown **C**
Tussock Cottage **K**
Viking Lodge Motel **J**

RESTAURANTS, CAFÉS & BARS

Arrowtown Bakery	1	Pesto	2
The Blue Door Bar	3	The Postmaster's House	5
Dorothy Browns	6	The Stables	7
Café Mondo	4		

Motels

Settlers Cottage Motel 22 Hertford St ☎03/442 1734 & 0800/803 801, ⓦwww.arrowtown.co.nz /settlers. A lace-and-Laura Ashley place that has earned numerous plaudits. Studios and one- and two-bedroom units are all fitted out to a high standard, with decorations based on traditional pioneer motifs. ⑤

Shades of Arrowtown Cnr Buckingham & Merioneth sts ☎03/442 1613, ⓦwww .shadesofarrowtown.co.nz. Tastefully decorated and very well appointed modern motel set in leafy surrounds in the heart of town with a good range of units plus a self-contained cottage sleeping six. Studios ⑤, larger units ⑥, cottage ⑦

Viking Lodge Motel 21 Inverness Crescent ☎03/442 1765, reservations ☎0800/181 900, ⓦwww.vikinglodge.co.nz. One of Arrowtown's best-value motels, featuring an outdoor pool and a cluster of one- and two-bedroom A-frame chalets with well-equipped kitchens and VCRs. ⑤

B&Bs and homestays

Arrowtown Homestay 18 Stafford St ☎03/442 1747, ⓔagormack@xtra.co.nz. Comfortable, well-appointed rooms in a spacious modern homestay five minutes' walk from the town centre. Has a pool and badminton court, plus long views over the Arrow Basin. ⑤

Arrowtown Lodge 7 Anglesea St ☎03/442 1101, ⓦwww.arrowtownlodge.co.nz. Four modern, comfortable and tastefully furnished cottages built from recycled nineteenth-century mud-bricks, each with en-suite bathroom and mountain views. Breakfast can be served out on the sunny deck, and there's also free Internet access and laundry. ⑦

Arrowtown Old Nick 70 Buckingham St ☎03/442 0066 7 0800/653 642, ⓦwww .oldnick.co.nz. Tasteful, welcoming and kid-friendly B&B partly in the former police office and residence, though most of the (smallish) rooms are in a modern stone-built annex all with lovely bathrooms and heated floors. Excellent cooked breakfasts are served in the large kitchen. ⑦

Polly-Anna Cottage 43 Bedford St ℡ 03/442 1347. Homestay in a tidily restored hundred-year-old miner's cottage with a sun deck and manicured lawns; close to the centre. ❺

Tussock Cottage 48 Rutherford Rd, Lake Hayes ℡ 03/442 1449, ⓌWwww.tussockcottage.co.nz. A lovely and luxuriously equipped two-room self-contained apartment in a strawbale-constructed building with tussock covered roof, close to Lake Hayes around 5km from Arrowtown. It is decorated in a tribal/Pacifica theme, a sumptuous breakfast basket is provided and there are bikes and kayaks for guests' use. ❽

Hostels and campsites

Arrowtown Holiday Park 11 Suffolk St ℡ &

Ⓕ03/442 1876. Arrowtown's only campsite: spacious, central, with showers and laundry available to non-guests ($3 each) and a tennis court. Camping $10, standard cabins & units ❷–❹

Poplar Lodge 4 Merioneth St ℡03/442 1466, Ⓦwww.poplarlodge.co.nz. Very central backpackers in a fairly modern home plus a separate en-suite double without access to a kitchen. Dorms ❶, rooms and en suite ❸

Riverdown Guesthouse 7 Bedford St ℡03/409 8499. Delightful boutique backpackers in riverside location, currently sleeping six, but with a couple of en-suite rooms in construction. Closed May–Oct. Four-share ❶, rooms ❸

The Town

Twin rows of sycamores and oaks planted in 1867 have grown to overshadow the tiny miners' cottages along the photogenic **Avenue of Trees**, Arrowtown's most recognizable image. Most of the sixty or so cottages were built towards the end of the nineteenth century and they're unusually small and close together, the chronic lack of timber undoubtedly being a factor.

A visit to the informative Lakes District Museum (see below) is probably the best preparation for a stroll around the **Arrowtown Chinese Settlement** (unrestricted entry). This string of heavily restored buildings hugging a narrow willow-draped section of Bush Creek at the western end of Buckingham Street is easily the best-preserved of New Zealand's Chinese communities, and provides an insight into a fascinating, if shameful, episode in the country's history (see box p.848). Many of the buildings were originally built as temporary retreats from peripatetic prospecting and to provide shelter during the harsh winters, only becoming permanent homes as miners aged. With tin, sod and timber the principal building materials, little was left standing when an archeological dig began in 1983, and most of the dwellings languish in a state of graceful decay. Some schist, mortar and corrugated-iron buildings fared rather better and five of these have been restored. The best is **Ah-Lum's Store**, built in typical Canton delta style in 1883 for Wong Hop Lee and leased from 1909 to 1927 to Ah-Lum, one of the pillars of the Chinese community in its later years. By this time integration was making inroads: Ah-Lum sold European as well as Chinese goods, and operated an opium den and bank. Wood panelling divides the store into low-roofed rooms with mezzanine areas above, perhaps used for opium smoking. Beyond that it is mostly stone plinths and chimney breasts fleetingly brought back to life by interpretation panels.

Artefacts found during the 1983 Chinese Settlement dig are displayed inside the former BNZ building of 1875 that now operates as the **Lakes District Museum** (49 Buckingham St; daily 8.30am–5pm; $5), a bits-and-bobs museum which succeeds in bringing local history to life. Not surprisingly, it mainly covers the lives of the gold-miners and their families, with a particular emphasis on the Chinese community and archeological excavations. There's also a feature on opium smoking, which remained legal in New Zealand until 1901, some twenty years after games of chance – *fantan* and *pakapoo* – were proscribed. Technophiles also get a look in, with displays on the quartz-reef mining used at Macetown and on one of the country's earliest hydro schemes,

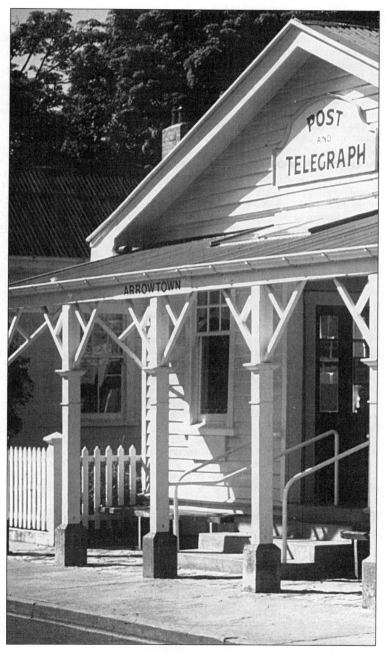

△ Post office, Arrowtown

which once supplied mining communities in Skippers and Macetown with power. Down in the basement are displays on the old brewery, a bakery, a print room with a hot metal press and a school room, which all add a little more of the community feel to the whole venture.

On a more hedonistic note, Arrowtown is also known (at least within NZ) as the home to **Millbrook Resort**, on Malaghans Road, 2km west (☎0800/800 604, ⊛www.millbrook.co.nz), a gated residential and hotel complex set around an international golf course. You might want to call in to try one of their cafés and restaurants, though there's more appeal to the Health and Fitness Centre ($30 a day) with its gym, 25m indoor heated pool, saunas, tennis courts and beautifully landscaped outdoor spa.

Around Arrowtown: Macetown

As gold fever swept through Otago in the early 1860s, prospectors fanned out, clawing their way up every creek and gully in search of a flash in the pan. In 1862, alluvial gold was found at Twelve Mile, sparking the rush to what later became known as **Macetown** (unrestricted entry), now a ghost town and a popular destination for mountain bikers, horse trekkers and trampers (see p.853). On first acquaintance, it isn't a massively exciting place, but the grassy plateau makes a great free camping spot, sheltered by low stone walls and willow, sycamore and apple trees. The only facilities are long-drop toilets and river water, but arriving with tent and provisions, and spending a day or two exploring the old mines and grubstake claims, is the best way to experience the place's unique atmosphere.

Macetown's story is one of boom and bust: at its peak, it boasted a couple of hotels, a post office and a school; but, when the gold ran out, it couldn't fall back on farming in the way that Arrowtown and Queenstown did and, like Skippers, it died. All that remains of the town itself are a couple of stone buildings – the restored schoolmaster's house and the bakery – and a smattering of wooden shacks. The surrounding creeks and gullies are littered with the twisted and rusting remains of gold batteries, making a fruitful hunting ground for industrial archeology fans; the area is covered in some detail in the *Macetown and the Arrow Gorge* booklet ($4, available from the Lakes District Museum in Arrowtown).

Macetown is a full-day (or overnight, if you want to camp among the ruins) outing either on foot (see box, p.853), by **mountain bike** (you'll need to rent one from Queenstown unless you have your own), or on a **4WD** trip with Queenstown-based Nomad Safaris (☎0800/688 222; 4–5hr; $110), who will pick you up in Arrowtown on request.

Eating, drinking and entertainment

Arrowtown's small but booming **eating** scene has plenty to offer for a few days. Further afield there is also refined dining at the *Gibbston Valley Winery*, 14km away on SH6 (see p.837); or you could splash out at one of the swanky restaurants in the *Millbrook Resort* (see above), a couple of kilometres outside Arrowtown.

Finally, if your visit is during the week leading up to Easter, you can partake in the **Autumn Festival** (enquiries to the visitor centre), with all manner of historic walks, street theatre and hoe-downs, much of it free.

Arrowtown Bakery Buckingham St. Fantastic bakery that produces a prodigious range of gourmet pies (such as lamb and kumara, or oyster), and wonderful Italian, sourdough and gluten-free breads; try their "football", a kind of soft-bread calzone.

The Arrowtown–Macetown Circuit

The sixteen-kilometre 4WD road up the Arrow Creek from Arrowtown to Macetown is the district's premier biking and trekking route, but walkers have the edge by being able to include the road as part of the fairly strenuous, full-day **Arrowtown–Macetown Circuit** (8hr loop; 32km; 700m ascent).

The walk is best done in the months from **Christmas to Easter**, after the winter snows have melted and the swollen Arrow River has subsided a little, making the 22 river crossings on the Arrow Creek a little easier – though even in summer, access can be problematic after rain. The *Macetown and the Arrow Gorge* booklet makes a good companion for the route, interpreting sights along the way.

The walk starts by the confluence of the Arrow River and Bush Creek, following the northern bank of the latter westwards, then skirting the base of German Hill and branching up Sawtooth Gully. The gully emerges through open hill country to Eichardt's Flat, a terrace named after a local farmer and brother of the Queenstown hotelier. At this point, about an hour out of Arrowtown, you can pursue the **Sawpit Gully variation** east down Sawpit Gully to meet the Arrow River road and Arrowtown, thus making a two- to three-hour circuit.

From the Sawpit Gully junction, the Macetown path contours gradually around to the **Big Hill** saddle, with its expansive views back to Lake Hayes and **The Remarkables**. The route then drops steeply towards Eight Mile Creek, the path becoming indistinct – marked by infrequent poles – as it traverses soggy and potentially ankle-twisting country. After three or four hours, you stumble across the Arrow Creek road, just a couple of kilometres short of **Macetown**.

When you've had your fill of Macetown, follow the Arrow Creek road back to Arrowtown, occasionally diverting onto paths that run parallel to the road for respite from the dust.

The Blue Door Bar Buckingham St beside *Pesto*. Stylish, intimate and very cool little bar in a 130-year-old cellar that once belonged to the general store. The bar has a cocktail feel but is informal and occasionally presents live jazz, blues and folk.

Dorothy Brown's Upstairs behind *Pesto* ☎03/442 1968, ⓦ www.dorothybrowns.com. A charming small-scale but high quality cinema and bar that's almost too good to be true. Mainstream and more arty films can be seen from stupendously comfortable seats ($15) and you take your wine and snacks in with you.

Café Mondo 4 Buckingham St. Small coffee shop and bar, tucked back off the street with courtyard seating. They do a nice line in breakfasts and the coffee is always good. Internet access.

Pesto 18 Buckingham St ☎03/442 0885. Great gourmet pizza and pasta restaurant with just the right balance of casualness and formality. Most mains are under $20 and if they're busy they'll retrieve you from the *Blue Door Bar* (see above) when your table's ready.

The Stables 28 Buckingham St ☎03/442 1818. Beautiful old stone building with outdoor seating where you can feast on classy bistro-style dishes, such as Thai chicken ($17) or tempura vegetables ($14), or just nip along for a Devonshire tea. Closed Mon.

The Postmaster's House Buckingham St. Fine dining in a lovely 1907 wooden house (or out on the verandah) tucking into the likes of tempura fish and chips ($26) or organic rack of lamb ($35), followed by crème brûlée with hazelnut and fig biscotti.

Glenorchy and the major tramps

The tiny mountain-girt town of **GLENORCHY**, at the head of Lake Wakatipu 50km northwest of Queenstown, is quiet and supremely picturesque, making it a perfect retreat for a couple of days. For the majority of visitors this still isn't remote enough, and for them Glenorchy is simply a staging post en route to some of the finest **tramping** New Zealand has to offer – a circuit of the Rees and Dart Rivers, the Routeburn Track and the Greenstone and Caples **tracks**.

Glenorchy and around

The Glenorchy region's fantastic scenery owes a debt to beds of ancient sea-floor sediments laid down some 220–270 million years ago and metamorphosed into the grey-green schists and *pounamu* (greenstone) of the Forbes and Humboldt mountains. The western and northern flanks of the Forbes Mountains were shaped by the Dart Glacier, now a relatively short tongue of ice which, at its peak 18,000 years ago, formed the root of the huge glacial system that gouged out the floor of Lake Wakatipu.

In pre-European times the plain beside the combined delta of the Rees (*Puakere*) and Dart (*Te Awa Whakatipu*) rivers was known as **Kotapahau**, "the place of revenge killing", a reference perhaps to fights between rival *hapu* over the esteemed *pounamu* which littered an area centred on the bed of the Dart River. There's still greenstone up there, but most is protected within the bounds of the Mount Aspiring National Park, including a huge, 25-tonne boulder estimated to be worth some $15 million.

The first **Europeans** to penetrate the area were gold prospectors, government surveyors, and nearby runholders in search of fresh grazing. James McKerrow finished the first reconnaissance survey in 1863, about the same time as a party of five miners led by Patrick Caples made their way up the Dart River. The fledgling community of Glenorchy served these disparate groups, along with teams of sawmillers and workers from a mine extracting scheelite, a tungsten ore used in armaments manufacture. Despite the lack of road access to Glenorchy, **tourists** began to arrive early in the twentieth century, cruising across Lake Wakatipu on the TSS *Earnslaw*, before being decanted into charabancs for the 20km jolt north to the Arcadia homestead at **Paradise**. Paradise has been deemed stunning enough to act as movie backdrops for the Rockies, the European Alps and Middle Earth, though the jury is out on whether it draws its name from its idyllic qualities or the abundance of paradise ducks.

The **road from Queenstown** was eventually pushed through in 1962, opening up a fine lakeside drive that passes **Bob's Cove**, the best place to observe the lake's seiche, an ill-understood phenomenon which causes the lake level to fluctuate by around 150mm every five minutes. Glenorchy has remained defiantly rural, and while there has been a marked increase in tourist traffic since the road was finally paved all the way in 1997, the few tourist-oriented ventures barely disturb the bucolic atmosphere.

Arrival and information

Summer-only Backpacker Express **buses** (☎03/442 9939, ⓦwww .glenorchyinfocentre.co.nz; Nov–April 3–5 daily) ply the Queenstown–Glenorchy route, charging around $15 for the one-hour run. They're based at the *Glenorchy Holiday Park* (2 Oban St ☎03/442 7171), which is also one of the best sources of general **information** and the place to go for post-tramp **transport bookings**.

For all tramping and outdoors information visit the **DOC Glenorchy Visitor Centre**, cnr Mull & Oban Sts (Nov–April daily 8.30am–4.30pm; May–Oct Mon–Fri reduced hours; ☎03/442 9937, ⓔglenorchyvc @doc.govt.nz).

Martins Bay ◄

Milford Sound (30 km) ◄

Te Anau (70 km) ◄

SKIPPERS RANGE

Lake Alabaster

BRYNEIRA RANGE

BARRIER RANGE

Cascade Saddle Route ►

Cattle Flat

Dart Hut

Snowy Ck

Quinns Flat

Rees-Dart Track

Rock Biv

Daleys Flat Hut

FORBES MOUNTAINS

Rees Saddle 1447m

Shelter Rock Hut

Alabaster Hut

Hollyford River

Dredge Flat

Sandy Bluff

Clarke Slip

25 Mile Creek

Hunter Creek

Rees-Dart Track

Hidden Falls Hut

Pluto Peak 2481m

Mt Earnslaw

25 Mile Hut

Dart River

East Peak 2830m

SERPENTINE RANGE

Lake Unknown

'Chinaman's Bluff' Chinaman's Flat

Rees River

Muddy Creek

Rockburn Chasm

Rockburn Rock Burn

Rockburn Hut

Turret Head 2341m

Hollyford Track

Roadend Shelter

Conical Hill 1515m

Routeburn Falls Hut

Sylvan-Rockburn Track

Mill Flat

Lake Harris

Harris Saddle 1277m

Harris Shelter

Routeburn Track

Lake Sylvan

Route Burn

Paradise

HUMBOLDT MOUNTAINS

Routeburn Flat Hut

Routeburn Shelter

Arcadia

Diamond Lake

Deadman's Track

Hollyford

Routeburn Station

Earnslaw Station

Lake Mackenzie

Roaring Creek

Mackenzie Hut

Routeburn Kinloch Road

RICHARDSON MOUNTAINS

Lake Marian

THE ORCHARD

Fraser Creek

Pass Creek Tk

Howden Hut

Key Summit 919m

The Divide Pass

Divide Shelter

Glenorchy Paradise Rd

McKellar Saddle 1005m

Upper Caples Hut

Key Creek

Mt Bonpland 2348m

Kinloch Lodge

Glenorchy

Lake McKellar

AILSA MOUNTAINS

Caples River

Caples Track

Lake Gunn

McKellar Hut

Mid Caples Hut

Lake Wakatipu

Greenstone River

Steele Creek Rd

Steele Creek

Pigeon Island

Greenstone Track

Greenstone Wharf

Steele Creek Bivvy

Slip Flat

Lake Rere

Elfin Bay Wharf

Bob's Cove

Greenstone Hut

Mt Crichton 1871m

N

Mavora Walkway

0   5 km

Mavora Lakes ▼

Accommodation

After the rigours of the tramp, Glenorchy is a welcome sight and, considering its size, there is a reasonable range of accommodation to suit most budgets.

Glenorchy Holiday Park & Backpackers 2 Oban St ☏03/442 7171, Ⓦwww.glenorchyinfocentre.co.nz. This well-organized campsite is the cheapest place in town, with spacious tent and powered sites ($9–10), plus bunks, basic double or twin cabins and a self-contained unit. Non-residents can shower here for $4. Dorms ❶, cabins ❷, unit ❹

Glenorchy Hotel Cnr Mull St & Argyll St ☏03/442 9902 & 0800/453 667, Ⓔrelax@glenorchynz.com. Reasonable back-packer-style dorms, with communal kitchen and lounge, are hidden behind this hotel. Also plain double rooms (some en suite) with great views up the Dart Valley. Dorms ❶, rooms ❺

Glen Roydon Lodge Cnr Mull St & Argyll St ☏03/442 9968, Ⓦwww.glenroydon.com. Good modern rooms with a nod to ski-lodge style, all sharing the comfortable guest lounge with its open fire, TV and videos. ❺

Kinloch Lodge 862 Kinloch Rd ☏442 4900, Ⓦwww.kinlochlodge.co.nz. Located 26km from Glenorchy but close to the trailheads for the Greenstone, Caples and Routeburn tracks, this combined lodge and backpackers makes a peaceful retreat and is well set up for getting you out hiking or just fishing on the lake. The original 1868 homestead houses small but comfortable rooms with shared-bathrooms, and there's a separate self-catering backpacker section. Excellent meals are served, there's a bar and they can arrange transport from Queenstown ($20). Four-shares ❶, backpacker rooms ❸, backpacker en suites ❹, lodge rooms ❼

Mt Earnslaw Motels 87 Oban St ☏03/442 6993, Ⓦwww.earnslaw.bizland.com. Glenorchy's only motel has well-kept, clean and spacious cabin-style units with a comfortable and homey feel and is run by very friendly and helpful people. ❺

The Town

While growing to meet the ever-increasing number of tourists, Glenorchy still doesn't amount to much – a petrol station, a post office, a couple of pubs and cafés, some accommodation and a grocery shop. Still, it is doing its best, with just about everyone plastering their promotional material with *The Lord of the Rings* location imagery. If you need to see specific shooting sites, join the Queenstown-based Safari of the Ring trips run by Nomad Safaris (see p.827), but for many it is enough just to be here.

To get a feel for the area and its geography, follow the 2km loop of the **Glenorchy Walkway** from the wharf at the end of Islay Street along the edge of Lake Wakatipu and through the wetlands around the town's lagoon, a pleasant way to soak up the mountain scenery at either end of the day.

Almost all the activities in and around town are pitched at the Queenstown crowd, but all can be met in Glenorchy. We've quoted times and prices from Glenorchy: most companies charge around $20 for transport to and from Queenstown and Queenstown-based trips will be two hours longer.

Jetboating

Traditionally, Glenorchy's big non-tramping lure has been **jetboating** on the **Dart River**, a two-hour journey which fully utilizes the jetboat's shallow-water capabilities, picking routes through braided riverbeds amid grand snow-capped mountains and finally entering a short gorge of dense bush before turning round on the edge of the Mount Aspiring National Park. The highlight is the brief stop to walk (or jetboat if conditions are right) into **Rockburn Chasm**, where a small tributary of the Dart has carved out a narrow, twisting canyon filled with calm, clear water.

Pure **jetboating** enthusiasts should go with Dart Wilderness Adventures (6hr; $159; ☏03/442 9939, Ⓦwww.glenorchyinfocentre.co.nz), who run trips up to the boundary of the national park and back. The appreciably slicker **Dart**

River Safaris (☎03/442 9992 & 0800/327853, ⓦwww.dartriver.co.nz) offers combination trips jetboating in only one direction. The Safari (3hr; $159) involves a ninety-minute jetboat ride, a twenty-minute bushwalk, and a ride in a 4WD coach though some magnificent scenery including spots used in *The Lord of the Rings*.

Better still, combine the upstream jetboat section of the Dart River Safaris with canoeing back downstream with **funyaks** (6hr; $235) two- or three-person inflatable canoes carried upriver in the jetboats, then paddled down. Suitable even for absolute beginners, this is a gentle trip with no rapids and very little likelihood of an enforced swim.

Other activities

If you're not here for the major tramps, and still fancy a hike, consider a day-walk along the Routeburn Track. By using the first and last Backpacker Express buses from Glenorchy you get four hours to explore, either up to Routeburn Shelter, or tackling the **Lake Sylvan Walk** (5km loop; 1hr 30min; negligible ascent), which starts at a signposted car park 3km before Routeburn Shelter. It largely crosses gravel river terraces supporting beech and totara forest then loops around Lake Sylvan, turned brown from its feeder streams leaching through the soil. You might even consider overnight on the Routeburn at the Routeburn Flats hut ($35) which usually has space even when other huts are full.

Glenorchy has always been a horsey town, and you can join in the activity at Dart Stables (☎03/442 5688, ⓦwww.dartstables.com) who run **horse riding** trips (2hr for $85; all day $160) through the surrounding countryside, often crossing rivers. The two-hour twilight rides ($95) are particularly good.

More of the local area can be seen with Mountainland Rovers (☎0800/246 494, ⓦwww.mountainlandrovers.co.nz) who run **Land Rover tours** (ex-Glenorchy 3hr for $129; ex-Queenstown 5hr for $149) up the Rees Valley across the river a couple of times to the spectacular Lennox Falls. The emphasis is on appreciating the scenery and history of the area, and driver Dick Watson spins a good yarn.

Out at the airstrip, 3km south on the road to Queenstown, Vertical Descent (☎03/409 0363, ⓔverticaldescent@xtra.co.nz) offers **skydiving** with some pretty special views, and a free pickup from Queenstown. The best deal is the popular 12,000ft jump ($295) combined with Routeburn Canyoning (see p.842) into a full-day package known as The G Spot ($495). There are also 9000ft jumps ($245) and 15,000ft jumps ($395).

Eating

Eating is fairly limited in Glenorchy, though the licensed *Glenorchy Café* in the former Post Office on Mull Street, serves soup, panini, sandwiches, cakes and espresso in the daytime. Hungry and thirsty trampers can also gravitate toward the *Glenorchy Hotel*, which serves a good selection of Kiwi staples at modest prices. Lunches and dinners are a touch more formal across the road at the *Glen Royden Lodge*, which serves substantial mains ($18–26) and a range of home-made pies, quiches, cookies and assorted treats. The widest selection of **tramping food** is to be found in Queenstown, but you can always pick up some last-minute supplies from the store at the *Glenorchy Holiday Park*.

The major tramps

The fame of the **Routeburn Track** is eclipsed only by that of its westerly neighbour, the Milford Track (see p.920). Many justly claim that the

Routeburn is superior, citing its more varied scenery, longer time spent above the bushline away from sandflies, and better spacing of huts. The Routeburn is certainly one of New Zealand's finest walks, straddling the spine of the Humboldt Mountains and providing access to many of the southwestern wilderness's most archetypal features: forested valleys rich with bird life and plunging waterfalls are combined with river flats, lakes and spectacular mountain scenery.

The nature of the terrain means that the Routeburn is usually promoted as a moderate tramp, though the short distance between huts eases the strain considerably. Fit hikers might consider doing it in two reasonably long days, though that doesn't leave much time for soaking up the scenery and wallowing in the relative solitude. To return by road from the end of the Routeburn to the start is something approaching 300km, so to avoid a lot of backtracking, anyone with an extra day or two to spare should consider returning to Glenorchy by hiking either the Greenstone or Caples tracks.

Both the **Greenstone and Caples tracks** are easy tramps, following gently graded, parallel river valleys where the wilderness experience is moderated by grazing cattle from the high-country stations along the Lake Wakatipu shore. The Greenstone occupies the broader, U-shaped valley carved out by one arm of the huge Hollyford Glacier, but despite the grandeur of the surrounding mountain scenery, it is sometimes criticized for being dull. Its detractors prefer the track over the sub-alpine McKellar Saddle and down the Caples Valley, where the river is bigger and the narrow base of the valley forces the path closer to it.

As the Routeburn reaches maximum capacity, the **Rees–Dart Track** is now being primed for wider usage with better-routed tracks and improved huts. Nonetheless, it remains the toughest of the major tramps in the area, covering some fairly rugged terrain and requiring six to eight hours of effort each day. It follows the standard Kiwi tramp formula of climbing one river valley, crossing the pass and descending into another, but adds an excellent side-trip to the Cascade Saddle and the chance of a jetboat trip to complete the final day.

In **winter** the Routeburn takes on a different character and becomes a much more serious undertaking. The track is often snowbound and extremely slippery, the risk of avalanche is high and the huts are unheated. Return day-trips from *Routeburn Shelter* to *Routeburn Falls Hut* and from The Divide to the *Lake Mackenzie Hut* are much better bets. The lower-level Greenstone and Caples tracks also make a less daunting prospect – not least because the huts are heated by wood-burning stoves which can be used throughout the year – though the McKellar Saddle is often snow-covered. The Rees–Dart Track in winter is really only for mountaineers.

Practicalities

Tramping **information** is best sought at the **DOC Glenorchy Visitor Centre** (see p.854), where you can fill in intentions forms (not required for the Routeburn), get the latest weather forecast, gen up on track conditions and either rent ($5) or buy ($15–20) maps. **DOC's leaflets** on *The Routeburn Track* (free) and *The Greenstone and Caples Tracks* ($1), together with the 1:75,000 *Routeburn/Greenstone Trackmap*, cover these three walks. For real route-finding, purchase the *Mount Aspiring National Park* map ($15). For the Rees–Dart Track the *Rees and Dart Tracks* leaflet ($1) and *Mount Aspiring National Park* map are good, but the considerably more detailed 1:50,000 *Aspiring* and *Earnslaw* Topomaps are far better.

The information below assumes you're starting from Glenorchy but it is also possible to hike the Greenstone/Caples and Routeburn combination from The Divide (north of Te Anau) with the luxury of *Kinloch Lodge* (see p.856) as your third night. They run their own transport from the Greenstone car park to the lodge ($15) then on to Routeburn Shelter ($15).

Trailhead transport

During the summer tramping season, there is little difficulty with transport to or from either end of the tracks. Most walkers base themselves at Glenorchy from where Backpacker Express (☎03/442 9939, ✉info@glenorchyinfocentre .co.nz) runs convenient **buses** to the trailheads. Routes are divided into sectors – Queenstown to Glenorchy; Glenorchy to the start of the Routeburn; Greenstone car park to Glenorchy; Glenorchy to the start of the Rees–Dart – and all cost $15. The only exception is the run from Chinaman's Bluff to Glenorchy ($20) at the end of the Rees-Dart.

Trampers wanting to be dropped off or picked up at The Divide (the western end of the Routeburn) can hop on any of the buses running between Te Anau and Milford Sound (ask visitor centres or the companies above for schedules). Perhaps the most useful is Tracknet (☎03/249 7777 & 0800/483 262, ✉tracknet@destinationnz.com) with Milford-bound buses passing The Divide at 8.30am, 10.45am and 2.15pm ($19 to Milford), and Te Anau-bound buses passing at 10.15am, 3.45pm and 5.45pm ($25).

To save backtracking, trampers may be able to arrange to have their **bags** sent from Queenstown to Te Anau with Atomic Shuttles, though carriage (and cost) is at the discretion of the driver on the day.

Hut and campsite bookings

The **Routeburn Track** has a compulsory system of booking **accommodation passes** for the four huts and two campsites for the duration of the tramping season (Nov–April). It's a reasonably flexible system, allowing people to walk in either direction, retrace their steps and stay up to two nights in a particular hut. Numbers are limited, so you'll need to book as far ahead as possible – three weeks if you can be adaptable, three months if you need a specific departure date or are part of a large group. This way you get a guaranteed bed in a hut equipped with flush toilets, running water (which must be treated), heaters and gas rings: you'll need to carry your own pans and plates. The cost is $35 per person per night; though there is a small discount if you spend three nights on the track in certain huts.

Credit-card phone or mail **bookings** are taken from July 1 for the following season: contact the Great Walks Booking Desk in Te Anau or, from November, the DOC visitor centres in Glenorchy or Queenstown. Accommodation passes can be collected from Te Anau or Glenorchy the day before you start and up to 2pm on your day of departure: those without accommodation passes will be charged $50 a night. If the track is closed due to bad weather or track conditions, full refunds are given; however, new bookings can only be made if there is space. Changes can be made to existing bookings ($10 per alteration) either before you start or with the wardens at each hut, but again only if space allows. **Outside the season** the huts revert to backcountry status ($10). Bookings are not required and annual hut passes are valid.

A limited number of simple **campsites** (with long-drop toilets and water; $15) exist close to the Routeburn Flats and Mackenzie Huts; campers are not allowed to use hut facilities.

The **Greenstone and Caples tracks** are far less popular, and bookings are not necessary at any time of year. Each trail has two $10 huts, but none of them have gas rings. One warden patrols each valley and may be inclined to sell you hut tickets, although you should really buy them in advance unless you have an annual hut pass (see "Basics", p.55). Free camping is allowed in both valleys along the fringes of the bush (though not on the open flats), but you are encouraged to camp close to (but at least 50m away from) the huts and use their free outside facilities – long-drop toilets and water. If you use the hut itself but sleep outside you pay half the hut fee.

The three **Rees–Dart** huts (all $10) cannot be booked in advance. Trampers should carry an annual hut pass or buy hut tickets in advance.

Guided walks

Routeburn aspirants who aren't confident about their level of fitness or who prefer not to lug heavy backpacks should consider joining a **guided walk**. The pace is fairly leisurely and walkers have to carry only their personal effects (no food or camping equipment); daily hikes are typically 5–6 hours, occasionally on rough terrain, so anyone unused to hill walking should still do a good deal of preparatory hiking.

Accommodation is in clean, plain huts, which are by no means luxurious, but do have hot showers, duvets on the bunks, and you'll be served cooked breakfasts and three-course dinners with wine. All you have to do is walk – but there's a **price** to pay for all this pampering: the **Routeburn Guided Walk** (T03/442 8200 & 0800/762 832, W www.ultimatewalks.co.nz; Nov–April), including return transport from Queenstown and three days' walking with two nights' accommodation in huts, costs $1090 (Nov & April $950); while the **Grand Traverse**, a five-day, six-night walk combining the Routeburn and Greenstone tracks, will set you back $1475 (Nov & April $1325).

The Routeburn can also be combined with the Milford Track Guided Walk (see p.922).

The Routeburn Track

Most people walk the **Routeburn Track** (33km; 2–3 days) westwards from Glenorchy towards The Divide; it can also be combined with the Greenstone and Caples tracks to make three- to five-day loops. The Routeburn isn't for everyone, though. The terrain is sometimes rough and the paths steep, but anyone of moderate fitness who can carry a backpack for five or six hours a day should have little trouble. That said, the track passes through sub-alpine country and snowfall and flooding can sometimes close it, even in summer.

The first day on the Routeburn is an easy one. Trailhead buses offer mid-morning and mid-afternoon start times, both leaving enough time to reach either Routeburn Flats or Routeburn Falls huts, and the earlier one giving ample opportunity to explore the North Branch of Route Burn. From **Routeburn Shelter to Routeburn Flats Hut** (7km; 2–3hr; 250m ascent) the route follows Route Burn steadily uphill on a metre-wide track, though it's never strenuous and has an even shingle surface. Because Route Burn is a tributary of the Dart River, you are following a side valley and will have

Hiking times

Note that all **times** and **distances** given in the following accounts are **one way**, unless otherwise stated.

experienced a wide variety of scenery – river flats, waterfalls and open beech forest – by the time you reach the Routeburn Flats Hut. The nearby Routeburn Flats campsite is superbly sited on the edge of wide alluvial flats at the end of a short path a couple of hundred metres beyond the hut. Only a few tents are permitted so there is plenty of space to spread out, and campers can make use of an open fireplace and a small shelter, the run-off from which provides water for cooking. Hut users are better off making the first day a little longer and tackling the next leg, **Routeburn Flats Hut to Routeburn Falls Hut** (2km; 1hr–1hr 30min; 300m ascent), which is considerably steeper and rougher, but the extra exertion is rewarded by a stay at the well-sited Routeburn Falls Hut, perched on the bushline above a precipice with eastward views looking back to Routeburn Flats and Sugar Loaf (1329m).

The second day is the longest, continuing from **Routeburn Falls Hut to Mackenzie Hut** (11km; 4–6hr; 300m ascent, 350m descent) on the most exposed section of the track. Most of the day is spent above the bushline among the sub-alpine snow tussock of the Harris Saddle (1255m) and passing through bog country, where sundews, bladderworts and orchids thrive. You might even catch sight of chamois clambering on the rocks to either side of the saddle. The track climbs gradually enough to the Harris Saddle Shelter (2–3hr), which offers respite from the wind and has toilets; on a clear day, drop your pack here and climb up to the 1515m summit of **Conical Hill** (2km return; at least 1hr; 260m ascent) for superb views down into the Hollyford Valley and along it to Martin's Bay and the Tasman Sea. Continuing from the Harris Saddle Shelter you cross from the Mount Aspiring National Park into the Fiordland National Park and skirt high along the edge of the Hollyford Valley, before switchbacking down through silver beech, fuchsia and ribbonwood to Mackenzie Hut. The bush beside the hut hides a somewhat cramped **campsite**.

From **Lake Mackenzie Hut to Howden Hut** (9km; 3–4hr; 250m descent), the track continues along the mountainside through a grassy patch of ribbonwood known as The Orchard and past the cascading Earland Falls to the Howden Hut at the junction of three tracks. The Greenstone and Caples tracks (handy for turning the tramp into a five-day Glenorchy-based circuit) head south, while the Routeburn continues from **Howden Hut to The Divide** (3km; 1hr–1hr 30min; 50m net descent), initially climbing for fifteen minutes to a point where you can make a half-hour excursion to Key Summit for views of three major river systems – the Hollyford, the Eglinton and the Greenstone. From the **Key Summit** (919m) turn-off, the track descends through silver beech to the car park and shelter at The Divide.

The Greenstone Track

Trampers starting on the **Greenstone Track** (36km; 2–3 days) at The Divide first cover the short section to Howden Hut (described in reverse, above), then walk south from **Howden Hut to McKellar Hut** (7km; 2hr–2hr 30min; 50m descent), passing (after 20min) a free primitive **campsite** where fires can be lit. The Greenstone continues beside Lake McKellar to McKellar Hut ($10; 20 bunks), just outside the Fiordland National Park.

The easy track from **McKellar Hut to Greenstone Hut** (17km; 4.5–6.5hr; 100m descent) starts by crossing the Greenstone River and follows the left bank down a broad, grazed valley mostly along river flats and through the lower slopes of the beech forests. A swingbridge then crosses Steele Creek, and the track continues for two more hours to the Greenstone Hut, a good base for exploring the gentle **Mavora Walkway** to the south. This takes two to three days through open tussock country and beech forest to Mavora Lakes (see p.864); a couple of $5 huts provide accommodation en route.

From **Greenstone Hut to Greenstone car park** (10km; 3–5hr; 100m descent), the track follows the left bank as the valley narrows and the river heads into a long gorge. The river soon meets the Caples River, an enticing series of deep pools that make great swimming holes. A swingbridge gives access to the left bank of the Caples River and the Caples Track; turn right to Greenstone Wharf (20–30min), or left to Mid Caples Hut (see below).

The Caples Track

The Caples Track (27km; 2 days) follows the Greenstone Track from **The Divide to Howden Hut** and then the first half of the section from Howden Hut to McKellar Hut, turning off an hour south of Howden Hut and beginning the very steep bush-clad zig-zag up the **McKellar Saddle** (1005m). Try to assess your capabilities beforehand as many find the walk from The Divide to Upper Caples Hut (17km; 7–9hr; 500m ascent, 550m descent) too much for one day, but are obliged to push on, as camping is neither pleasant on the saddle's bogland nor permitted on what is very fragile open tussock. The descent mostly follows snow poles, crossing and recrossing the infant Caples River before regaining beech forest and the **Upper Caples Hut** ($10; 20 bunks).

Greenstone Wharf is within a day's walk of here, though you can break it up into two sections: from **Upper Caples Hut to Mid Caples Hut** (7km; 2hr–2hr 30min; 50m descent) you mainly cross easy grassland to the hut ($10; 12 bunks). From **Mid Caples Hut to Greenstone Wharf** car park (7km; 2–3hr; 100m descent) the path reaches a short but dramatic gorge, crosses it and follows the true left bank, continuing alongside the bush edge and crossing grassy clearings before arriving at the junction with the Greenstone Track, from where it is only twenty minutes to Greenstone Wharf.

The Rees–Dart Track

The standard approach to the Rees–Dart Track is to walk up the Rees and down the Dart, an anticlockwise circuit which leaves open the option of finishing off with an expensive jetboat ride with Dart River Jet (see p.856) who charge the full $159 just for the ride out. The track from **Muddy Creek car park to Shelter Rock Hut** (17km; 6–7hr; 400m ascent) follows a 4WD track across grass and gravel flats on the true left bank of the braided lower Rees and requires a couple of foot-soaking stream crossings. Press on past the Otago Tramping Club's Twenty-five Mile Hut (pay $3 to DOC in Glenorchy), across Twenty-five Mile Creek and over more river flats for another hour or so, with Hunter Creek and the peaks of the Forbes Mountains straight ahead. Just past the confluence of Hunter Creek, the Rees valley steepens appreciably and becomes cloaked in beech forests. Soon after, the track crosses a swingbridge to the true right bank and climbs above river level, eventually coming out on the grassy flats of Clarke Slip. The track is bush-bound again up to just below the tree line where it passes the site of the old Shelter Rock Hut then continues for a kilometre until you hit tussock country. One final crossing of the Rees River, now a large stream, takes you back to the left bank and the Shelter Rock Hut ($10; 20 bunks).

The second day, from **Shelter Rock Hut to Dart Hut** (9km; 4–6hr; 600m ascent, 450m descent), is the shortest but one of the toughest, scaling the 1447m Rees Saddle. Stick to the true left bank of the Rees over sub-alpine scrub and gravel banks for a couple of kilometres before crossing the river and gradually climbing up to a tussock basin and the saddle. Descend rapidly and then more steadily across snow grass following the true left bank of Snowy Creek, which churns down a narrow gorge to your right. A kilometre or so later the track crosses a swingbridge to the true right bank, commencing a loose and rocky descent past a long series of cascades to another crossing of Snowy Creek, just above its confluence with the Dart River. Grassy areas on the true right bank provide camping spots and the Dart Hut ($10; 32 bunks) sits on the true left bank; many stay two nights here giving time to explore the Cascade Saddle route (see "Walks in the Matukituki Valley" box on p.878).

The track from **Dart Hut to Daleys Flat Hut** (16km; 6–8hr; 450m descent) initially climbs high above the river and stays there for 3km, passing through beech forest before dropping to Cattle Flat, 5km of grassed alluvial ridges traced by a winding and energy-sapping but easy-to-follow route. At the end of Cattle Flat the track returns to the bush and runs roughly parallel to the river until it reaches the beautiful grassy expanse of Quinns Flat (perfect in the late afternoon light), where the track turns inland. Within half an hour you reach the sandfly-ridden **Daleys Flat Hut** ($10; 20 bunks), redeemed by its pleasant location on the edge of a clearing.

Trampers planning to pick up a jetboat to Glenorchy at 10.30am will need to leave around 8am for the **Daleys Flat Hut to Sandy Bluff** section (6km; 2hr–2hr 30min; 100m ascent, 150m descent). The walk skips through the bush for around 4km until Dredge Flat, where you make your own track, looking for markers on the left that indicate where you re-enter the bush. The track then climbs steeply over Sandy Bluff before dropping down to river level and the jetboat pick-up point.

Most trampers continue from **Sandy Bluff to Chinaman's Bluff** (10km; 3hr; negligible descent), a fairly easy walk crossing the flats south of Sandy Bluff and following the river to Chinaman's Bluff. Backpacker Express pick up from here, though you can continue on foot from **Chinaman's Bluff to Paradise car park** (6km; 2hr; negligible descent) along the 4WD track.

Kingston and the road to Fiordland

Most people travel from Queenstown to Fiordland by road, making the 170km journey to Te Anau in under three hours. It is an attractive if unspectacular route that follows the lakeshore road, hugging the foot of The Remarkables then striking out across open Southland farming country.

As the Dart glacier retreated at the end of the last ice age, Lake Wakatipu formed behind the terminal moraine at what is now **KINGSTON**, a scattered community 46km south of Queenstown on SH6. The lake's waters formed the Mataura Valley to the south, but successive terminal moraines raised the lake level to the point at which it was able to carve out a new passage down the bed of the Kawarau, out of the Frankton Arm. In the 1860s the Mataura Valley provided a perfect route from the populated coast to new gold fields on the Shotover and Arrow rivers. Kingston became a major transit centre, accommodating up to five thousand people while they waited for boats across the lake or bullock carts to transport their spoils to Dunedin or Invercargill. By 1878, the railroad had reached Kingston, and the prefabricated parts for ever-larger steamers could be brought in and assembled on the lakeshore. The 1936 completion of the lakeside road to Queenstown drove the last nail into the coffin of the steamer freight trade, and goods trains went the same way.

However, the line has managed to struggle on thanks to the **Kingston Flyer** tourist train (Kent Street ☎03/248 8848, Ⓦ www.kingstonflyer.co.nz; daily Sept to mid-May 10am, 1.30pm & 3.45pm; $25 one way, $30 return). Initially it plied the 60km to Lumsden and was much eulogized in those halcyon days before Kiwi tourism went ballistic, but since 1982 the cut-down thirty-minutes-each-way service only runs 15km to the nowhere hamlet of Fairlight. Gleaming black steam engines haul creaky but sumptuous turn-of-the-century first-class carriages with embossed steel ceilings and brass gas lamps: arrive early to avoid being shunted down to the less exalted second-class seats, which are charged at the same rate.

The only **accommodation** in Kingston, and for some distance either side, is at the roadside *Kingston Motels & Holiday Park*, 2 Kent St (☎ 03/248 8501, Ⓔ peterm@xtra.co.nz; tents $10, dorms 1x, cabins 2x, motel units 3x–4x).

Beyond Kingston there's little to delay your progress to Te Anau. Just short of the dull Southland farming town of **Lumsden**, a signposted short cut diverts you to **Mossburn** and SH94. Some 14km west of Mossburn a narrow road cuts north towards the popular summertime retreat of **Mavora Lakes**; the southern lake is reserved for quiet pursuits like fishing and canoeing while the larger North Mavora Lake hosts rowdy boats. Trails through the surrounding beech forests make great mountain-biking territory, and trampers can head north along the Mavora Walkway (see p.861) and link up with the Greenstone Track (see p.861).

Back on SH94 you soon enter the Red Tussock Conservation Area, named for a type of grass essential to the livelihood of the takahe (see Contexts, p.973), and before long you'll find yourself in Te Anau, perched on the brink of Fiordland (see p.902).

Wanaka

WANAKA (pronounced evenly as Wa-Na-Ka), only 55 air kilometres northeast of Queenstown but an hour and a half by road, once languished in the shadow of its brasher southern sibling, though it offers a similar combination of beautiful surroundings and robust adventure activities. With extensive recent development and new housing subdivisions popping up everywhere, many regard it as the next Queenstown, albeit a more restrained version. Certainly it is one of New Zealand's fastest-growing small towns.

Wanaka is situated at the point where the hummocky, poplar-studded hills of Central Otago rub up against the dramatic peaks of the Mount Aspiring National Park. It commands a wonderful spot on the shores of the willow-girt Lake Wanaka, with the jagged summits of the Southern Alps as often as not mirrored in its waters.

Founded in the 1860s as a service centre for the local run-holders and itinerant gold miners, the town didn't really take off until the prosperous middle years of the twentieth century, when camping and caravanning Kiwis discovered its warm, dry summer climate and easy-going pace. Wanaka remains a small and eminently manageable place, with the tenor of a village and an overwhelming feeling of light and spaciousness. It continues to promote itself as an adventure destination in its own right, and it's an excellent place in which to relax for a couple of days and eat well in some fine cafés and restaurants.

A half day spent exploring Wanaka's intriguing **maze** and modest **museums** will leave plenty of time to go kayaking, jetboating, rock climbing, horse riding

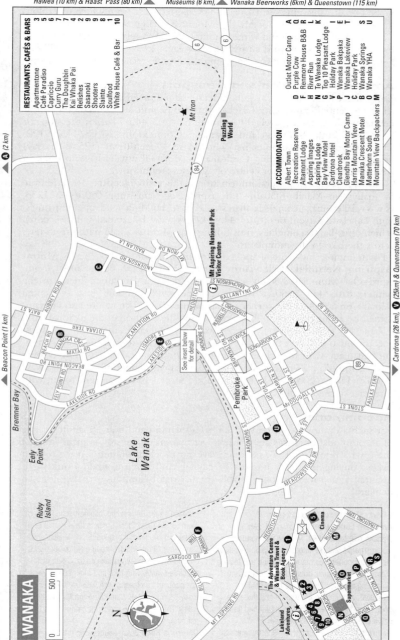

or, best of all, canyoning. Wanaka is also the perfect base from which to explore the surrounding region, notably the Mount Aspiring National Park and the Cardrona Valley. During the winter months, Wanaka's relative calm is shattered by the arrival of **skiers and snowboarders** eager to explore the downhill ski-fields of Treble Cone and Cardrona, and the Nordic terrain at the Snow Farm.

Arrival, information and transport

Daily direct **buses** from Christchurch, Dunedin, Queenstown and Franz Josef all arrive centrally: InterCity, Catch-a-Bus and Atomic stop outside the visitor centre, while United Travel (99 Ardmore St ☎03/443 7414) is the stop for Southern Link Shuttles and Wanaka Connexions (☎03/443 9122, Ⓦwww.wanakaconnexions.co.nz) who go to Queenstown ($25 each way) using the direct but winding Cardrona Road. You'll usually have to book in advance through the visitor centre or agencies around town.

The best source of general information is the **visitor centre**, 100 Ardmore St (daily: Jan–March 8.30am–7pm; April–Dec 9am–5pm; ☎03/443 1233, Ⓦwww.lakewanaka.co.nz). It shares a lakeside building (and opening times) with Lakeland Adventures (☎03/443 7495, Ⓦwww.lakelandadventures.co.nz), which rents kayaks, dinghies, runs fishing trips and has a café with great views across the lake to the mountains.

For tramping and general backcountry information, go to DOC's **Mount Aspiring National Park visitor centre** (Nov–March daily 8am–4.45pm, April–Oct Mon–Sat 8.30am–4.45pm, closed for a 1hr lunch break in the winter; ☎03/443 7660, Ⓔwanakavc@doc.govt.nz), 500m east of central Wanaka on SH84 at the corner of Ballantyne Road. The centre also contains some interesting displays on local wildlife and the creation of the national park.

Wanaka is so compact that you can **walk** everywhere in the centre, and most accommodation is less than fifteen minutes' away on foot. Longer excursions are best made with **bicycles** or **cars** rented from several outlets around town (see "Listings", p.874); for short trips into the surroundings, there's always Wanaka Taxis (☎03/443 7999). There are several **banks** around town, with foreign-exchange facilities and ATMs.

Accommodation

For such a diminutive place, Wanaka has a splendid and ever-expanding range of accommodation: **rates** are a little lower than in Queenstown but still reflect the town's resort status. You should have no problem finding a place to suit, except during the peak months of January and August, when **booking** is essential and prices in some establishments rise in response to the surge in demand.

Hotels and motels

Altamont Lodge Mount Aspiring Rd, 2km west of Wanaka ☎03/443 8864, Ⓦwww.altamontlodge .co.nz. The perfect ski lodge, with a pine-panelled alpine atmosphere, communal cooking and lounge areas, spa pool, tennis court, drying rooms, and ski-tuning facilities. Rooms are functional but attractive, with shared bathrooms and there are good rates for singles. Bring your own bed linen or pay a one-off charge of $5 per bed. ❸

Aspiring Lodge Cnr Dungarvon St & Dunmore St ☎03/443 7816 & 0800/269 367, Ⓦwww .aspiringlodge.co.nz. Spacious and attractive wood-

panelled studio units with kitchenettes and drying room for ski gear. Those upstairs have partial lake views and continental breakfasts are available. ❺

Bay View Motel Mount Aspiring Rd ☎0800/229 843, Ⓦwww.bayviewwanaka.co.nz. Quiet, well-appointed motel with lake and mountain views, a spa pool, and a pleasant site well back from the road, 1.5km west of Wanaka up the Matukituki Valley. They also have space for campervans ($31 per site). ❻

Cardrona Hotel 26km south along the Crown Range Road ☎03/443 8153, Ⓦwww .cardronahotel.co.nz. Comfortable, modern en-suite rooms, all with access to a hot tub, set behind a characterful, restored gold-rush hotel. Very popular with skiers from the nearby Cardrona and Waiorau slopes. ⑦

Clearbrook Cnr Helwick & Upton Sts ☎ 03/443 4413 & 0800/443 441, ⓦ www.clearbrook.co.nz. Classy, modern motel with tastefully decorated luxury units ranged along the burbling Bullock Creek. All units have TV, stereo, full kitchen with dishwasher, laundry and balconies with mountain views. There are also separate three-bedroom houses sleeping six. Studios ⑥, larger units ⑦, houses $350

Manuka Crescent Motel 51 Manuka Crescent ☎ 03/443 7773 & 0800/626 852, ⓦ www.manukacrescentmotel.co.nz. Pleasant, good-value motel with a mix of modern and older units, a small pool and kids' play area. It's 20min walk from town and continental breakfasts are available. ⑤

B&Bs and homestays

Aspiring Images 26 Norman Terrace ☎ 03/443 8358, ⓦ www.aspiringimages.co.nz. Comfortable suburban homestay, with nice rooms, each with a terrace, and there are mountain bikes for exploring. ⑤

Harris Mountain View 30 Mataraki Place ☎ 03/443 5115, ⓦ www.harrismountainview .co.nz. B&B in a modern, spacious home partly constructed from recycled native timbers and set on a ridge with great views. Very relaxing. ⑤

Renmore House B&B 44 Upton St ☎ 03/443 6566, ⓦ www.renmore-house.com. Large purpose-built house centrally located beside the burbling waters of Bullock Creek. The three plush en-suite rooms are all fitted out to a high standard. There are bikes for guests' use and the hosts are genial and welcoming. ⑦

River Run Halliday Rd, 7km east of Wanaka ☎ 03/443 9049, ⓦ www.riverrun.co.nz. Stylish lodge gloriously sited on ancient river flats with trails leading down to the Clutha River. The modern house built using lots of recycled timbers was thoughtfully conceived by the owners and contains five beautifully appointed en-suite rooms as well as sunny verandas and a common dining area where most guests stay for high-quality three-course meals ($85). Rates ($290 & $390) include breakfast and pre-dinner drinks. ⑨

Te Wanaka Lodge 23 Brownston St ☎ 03/443 9224 & 0800/926 252, ⓦ www.tewanaka.co.nz. One of the finer B&B inns in central Wanaka, with thirteen luxurious en-suite rooms, separate TV and quiet lounges, and a cedar hot tub. The sumptuous buffet breakfast is a mellow affair centred on a huge dining table, and there's even a house bar with a good wine selection. ⑦

Wanaka Springs 21 Warren St ☎ 03/443 8421, ⓦ www.wanakasprings.com. As far as central luxury accommodation goes, this takes the biscuit. About five minutes' walk from the lake, a purpose-built boutique lodge with a mixture of top-notch, en suites, twins and doubles decorated individually in tasteful swank. There are also comfortable communal areas, free liqueurs, and all the facilities you could wish for including a spa pool in a charming native garden and well-informed and helpful hosts. ⑧

Hostels

Matterhorn South 56 Brownston St ☎ 03/443 1119, ⓦ www.matterhorn.co.nz. Combined hostel and budget lodge, with an appealing backpacker section with 8-bed dorms and a log fire surrounded by scatter cushions. The more upmarket section has modern, en-suite four-shares with TV and fridge, and access to an excellent kitchen and comfortable lounge area. Dorms ①, rooms ②

Mountain View Backpackers 7 Russell St ☎ 03/443 9010, ⓦ www.mtnview.co.nz. New, small and fairly cosy hostel in a converted house with cheery dorms and doubles. Dorms ①, rooms ③

Purple Cow 94 Brownston St ☎ 03/443 1880, ⓦ www.purplecow.co.nz. Large and spacious hostel in a former hotel with maximum 6-bed dorms, many in separate former motel rooms with their own lounge, bathroom and TV, plus plenty of en-suite doubles. Sit and gaze at the fabulous lake view through the big picture windows or play pool in the large lounge. Bike rental is $25 a day and there are frequent bargain barbecues in the evening. Dorms ①, rooms ③

Wanaka Bakpaka 117 Lakeside Rd ☎ 03/443 7837, ⓔ wanaka.bakpaka@xtra.co.nz. Low-key hostel five minutes' walk from town and with great lake and mountain views, a peaceful atmosphere, summer barbecues and bike rental ($20 a day). Go for the nicer, newer rooms if you have a choice. Dorms ①, rooms ②

Wanaka YHA 181 Upton St ☎ 03/443 7405, ⓔ yha.wanaka@yha.org.nz. Decent hostel ten minutes' walk from the centre with small dorms and a good garden. Plans are afoot to progressively replace the hostel through to mid-2005 so call ahead. Dorms 1, rooms ③

Campsites and motorparks

Albert Town Recreation Reserve 6km northeast of Wanaka on SH6. Open, informal camping area, with water and toilets, on the banks of the swift-flowing Clutha River. $5

Glendhu Bay Motor Camp Mount Aspiring Rd, 12km west of Wanaka ℡ 03/443 7243, ℮ glendhucamp@xtra.co.nz. Popular lakeshore family campsite with fabulous views across to Mount Aspiring, boat-launching facilities, canoe and bike rental. Camping $10, bunks ❶, cabins ❷

Outlet Motor Camp Lake Outlet Rd, 6km from Wanaka ℡ 03/443 7478, ℻ 443 7471. Simple but beautifully sited campground at the point where Lake Wanaka becomes the Clutha River and in a great position for strolls along the lake or river frontage. Closed mid-April to Oct. Camping $10, on-site vans and one cabin ❷

Top 10 Pleasant Lodge Holiday Park 217 Mount Aspiring Rd, 3km west of Wanaka ℡ 03/443 7360 & 0508/926 252, ℺ www.nzsouth.co.nz /pleasantlodge. Sprawling, family-oriented site with tent sites ($10), a range of cabins and heaps of amenities, including bike rental, pool and a spa. Cabins ❷, tourist apartments ❸, motel units ❹

Wanaka Lakeview Holiday Park 212 Brownston St ℡ 03/443 7883, ℮ martini_@xtra.co.nz. The most convenient of the campsites, ten minutes' walk from central Wanaka, with $10 tent sites and all the usual facilities including rooms in a lodge which has bathrooms and kitchen under the same roof. Dorms ❶, lodge and cabins ❷, tourist flats ❸

The Town

Though central Wanaka is a pleasant place to hang out, there are no sights as such. For attractions you'll either need to head east to Puzzling World and the museums around the airport (see the following accounts) or venture 3km west to the small **Rippon Vineyard**, Mount Aspiring Road (Dec–April daily 11am–5pm, July–Nov daily 1.30–4.30pm; ℡ 03/443 8084, ℺ www.rippon .co.nz). The dry, stony and sun-soaked slopes running down to Lake Wanaka were planted in 1974 and produced their first vintage in 1987. The winery now crafts nearly ten wine styles with particularly good Pinot Noir, Sauvignon Blanc and the rare Osteiner Riesling hybrid. All are available for free sampling, and over the peak summer season (Christmas–early Jan and maybe a couple of weeks either side) outside picnic lunches are available for around $16. The best approach to the vineyard from Wanaka is on foot, along the lakefront Waterfall Creek Walk (see box on p.870), though it is easy to go too far: turn up a track after the first block of vines. Every even year, in February the vineyard plays host to the one-day Rippon **open air music festival** (℺ www.rippon festival.co.nz; tickets $65) with top Kiwi bands and a stonking after-party.

The solid lump of Mount Iron rises immediately east of town, pointing the way to **Stuart Landsborough's Puzzling World**, almost 2km away on SH84 (daily from 8.30am, last admission 5pm; $9). Star attraction is "The Great Maze", a complex wooden structure comprising 1500m of dead-end passageways packed into a dense labyrinth, with overhead bridges linking the two halves. Should you choose to accept it, your mission is to reach all four corner towers, either in any order (30min–1hr) or in a specific sequence (at least 1hr), then to find your way out again; if it all goes horribly wrong, you can cheat by using escape doors. Put aside a couple of hours to appreciate this prototype for the Eighties maze-building boom that swept New Zealand and Japan – where Stuart Landsborough briefly enjoyed a fanatical following. The ticket price includes entry to the "Hologram Hall", full of the usual 3-D images, and the "Tilted House", which revels in tricks of perspective produced by the floor being fifteen degrees off the horizontal. Zip through these to get to the "Hall of Following Faces", a large octagonal room with seven of the sides made up by arrays of moulded images of famous people – Churchill, Einstein, Van Gogh, Lincoln, etc. As you walk around the faces appear to turn towards you, aided by the lack of ears, which apparently hinder the illusion. Rooms which play with your sense of perspective and all manner of illusions delay your progress to the café where you can easily spend an hour playing with the puzzles scattered over the tables.

Wanaka's airport, 7km east of Puzzling World on SH6, is the base for a number of aerial activities (see "Activities", below) and the **New Zealand Fighter Pilots Museum** (daily: Christmas–Jan 9am–6pm; rest of year 9am–4pm; $8; Ⓦwww.nzfpm.co.nz), which honours Kiwi pilots and ground crew who fought in the two world wars. This homage to the New Zealand contingent contains hagiographic profiles of the men and blow-by-blow descriptions of the major battles and campaigns, all accompanied by rousing war anthems. Star exhibits, all airworthy, are New Zealand's oldest Tiger Moth, Spitfire, a P-51D Mustang and several rare Soviet Polikarpovs – an equivalent of the Spitfire first used in the Spanish Civil War. Younger visitors may prefer the half-dozen linked PCs allowing you to engage in interactive combat. If any of this strikes a chord, then you might want to time your visit to coincide with the biennial, three-day "**Warbirds over Wanaka**" air show (Ⓣ03/443 6819 & 0800/496 920, Ⓦwww.warbirdsoverwanaka.com). At Easter each even-numbered year over 100,000 people descend to watch all manner of airborne craft – but predominantly small and vintage planes – take to the air; details and tickets ($110 for 3 days or $50 for Saturday, the main event) are available online and locally.

A similar theme is explored in the adjacent **Wanaka Toy and Transport Museum** (daily: Nov–April 8.30am–6pm; May–Oct 8.30am–5pm; around $7), an engaging hoard of cars, trucks and bikes preserved by Wanaka's dry climate. There should be something here to titillate anyone with even a passing interest in motor vehicles. Some machines are just well-kept examples of stuff still puttering around New Zealand roads, but there's also exotica such as a Centurion tank, a ten-seater Lockhead Lodestar used by the US Army in the 1950s, Velocette and BSA bikes, and the Solar Kiwi Racer, an aluminium and glass-fibre bullet-shaped car powered by solar panels on its roof. Many of the main exhibits are replicated along the walls with all manner of other toys. If some of your party are extra-interested, others can pass the time in the adjacent **Wanaka Beerworks** (daily 9.30am–3.30pm or later; Ⓣ03/443 1865), an award-winning microbrewery which produces a golden malt, a pilsner and a dark ale, all sold through bars and restaurants around Central Otago. You can sample all three for $4.

The perfect antidote to the museums lies across the road at **Have A Shot** (daily 9am–5.30pm), where you can, well, have a shot with a golf club on the driving range ($7 for 50 balls), a gun at either the claybird range ($26 for 20 rounds), the .22 smallbore range ($12 for 30 rounds), or a bow at the archery range ($12 for 20min). There's also a crazy golf course ($7) and groups of more active combatants can join battle with spongy tennis balls in the battlefield ($6 for 20min).

Activities

Wanaka's relatively low profile and the absence of the hard sell and conveyor-belt style that characterizes some of Queenstown's slicker operations add up to a more relaxed approach – and frequently better value for money. Most accommodation and numerous agents around town handle **bookings**, or call direct.

Canyoning

If abseiling down thirty-metre waterfalls and sliding down eighty-degree polished rock chutes into deep green pools appeals, then **canyoning** should fit the bill. You don't need any special experience, just a sense of adventure and water confidence – once you start into the canyon, there is only one way out. Deep

Visitors shy of the beard-and-Gore-Tex walks in the Mount Aspiring National Park to the west might reap greater rewards from these more modest expeditions. No special gear is required, just robust shoes, wet-weather gear, sun protection and DOC's *Wanaka Walks and Trails* leaflet ($1) which has a good map of most of the following walks.

Mount Iron Track

The most accessible of Wanaka's hilltop walks is up the 549m **Mount Iron** (2km; 1–2hr; 240m ascent), a glacially sculpted outcrop, its western and northern slopes ground smooth by the glacier that scoured its southern face. The path through farmland and the bird-filled *manuka* woodland of the Mount Iron Scenic Reserve starts 1.5km east of Wanaka on SH84, climbing the steep southern face to the summit. Here you can enjoy magnificent panoramic views of Wanaka and the nearby lakes, before following the path down the east face of Mount Iron towards the entrance to Puzzling World (see p.868).

Mount Roy track

The **Mount Roy Track** (16km; 4–6hr; 1100m ascent) is a much more ambitious prospect, winding up to the 1578m summit of Roy's Peak for wonderful views over Lake Wanaka and surrounding glaciers and mountains. The path starts 7km west of Wanaka on the Mount Aspiring Road, but is closed during the lambing season (1 Oct–10 Nov).

Diamond Lake–Rocky mountain Track

The long vistas from Mount Iron and Mount Roy are only really challenged by those on the **Diamond Lake Track** (7km; 2hr 30min; 400m ascent), a community project which requests a $2 donation. From the car park 18km west of Wanaka on the Mount Aspiring Road there are a couple of short variations – but to get the views, you'll need to tackle the 775m summit of Rocky Hill.

Beacon Point–Clutha Outlet Circuit

This is a long but undemanding riverbank and lakeside walk which starts from Wanaka and follows the shore to **Eely Point** (15min), a sheltered bay popular for boating and picnics. Beyond Eely Point is Bremner Bay and the continuation of the waterfront path to **Beacon Point** (a further 30min). Either return the same way or continue along Beacon Point Road to the Outlet Motor Camp and pick up the **Outlet Track**, which runs 4km to Alison Avenue, then down to SH6 not far from the Albert Town bridge. By following SH6 this can be turned into a loop back to Wanaka (16km in all), passing Puzzling World (see p.868) and the base of Mount Iron (see above).

Waterfall Creek walk

The westbound equivalent of the Beacon Point–Clutha Outlet Circuit leaves Roy's Bay along the **Waterfall Creek Walk** (3km one way; 35min; negligible ascent), heading through Wanaka Station Park and past Rippon Vineyard to a car park at Waterfall Creek. From here the path continues as the **Millennium Walkway** (5km each way; 1hr; 100m ascent) following lakeside terraces to Ironside's Hill. Both of these are open to **bikers**.

Canyon (☏03/443 7922, ⊕www.deepcanyon.co.nz; Nov–March) take up to five canyoners with each guide, who secures all abseils with safety ropes and provides enough warm, protective clothing to ease the sense of vulnerability. First-timers usually tackle **Emerald Creek** ($195 for a full day), a narrow fissure where fern-draped verdure envelops you, in complete contrast to the parched landscape of the surrounding Matukituki valley. Half-time tea and biscuits are served on a huge slab wedged high above a cascade, and the day is rounded off with a fine picnic and strong camp-brewed coffee. The main alternative is the **Niger Stream**, which can be used for first timers ($195), though those after a more full-on experience can opt for the longer and tougher section, **Big Nige** (8hr; $260).

Rock climbing and mountaineering

Wanaka's dry, sunny climate is ideal for **rock climbing**. Tuition and guiding are offered by Wanaka Rock (℡03/443 6411, ⓦwww.wanakarock.co.nz), who run full-day introductory courses involving top-roping, seconding and abseiling for two to four people ($165 each). For the more experienced they offer guided climbing ($185); or you can get out onto the Matukituki valley schist and gneiss unsupervised with a copy of *Wanaka Rock* ($20, available from Good Sports – see p.874).

If the idea of performing gymnastics on roadside crags pales beside the prospect of getting up into the ice and snow of the Southern Alps, then you can always try one of the expensive but professional all-inclusive **mountaineering** packages offered by Mount Aspiring Guides (℡03/443 9422, ⓦwww.aspiringguides.com). Their Summit Week ($2540 per person) sees two of you and one guide exploring the upper reaches of the Southern Alps (often around the Fox glacier where ice climbing skills are honed) and bagging a number of peaks. Specific ascents include Mount Cook (Oct to mid-Feb; $3985), Mount Tasman (Oct–May; $3850), and Mount Aspiring (Oct–May) which has a five-day helicopter access option or a seven-day walk in variation (both $2195). All these require a high degree of fitness and some mountain experience. Private mountain guiding will set you back around $300–500 per person per day depending on the trip, plus the cost of hut fees, transport and food.

Bike and horse riding

Wanaka abounds with shops renting out all-terrain bikes, but for a day's guided **mountain biking**, join Alpine & Heli Mountain Biking (℡03/443 8943, ⓦwww.mountainbiking.co.nz) who specialize in **heli-biking**, whisking you up to Treble Cone (Nov–April; 5–6hr; $280) or Mount Pisa (all year; 3–6hr; $265–295) for up to 1600 vertical metres of downhill track. They also run a 4WD-supported biking day-trip (Nov–May; 4–7hr; $145–185).

Freelance riders should enquire at the bike shops (see "Bike rental" on p.874) which sell the *Lake Wanaka Cycling Map* ($2), detailing the excellent local off-road rides. The lakeside tracks (see box, p.870) are open to riders, and the "Sticky Forest" has a particularly dense knot of excellent single-track. During the first couple of weeks of January, one of the chairlifts up at Treble Cone skifield fires up turning some of the trails into a bike park (lifts $20 a day): rent a bike in town if you don't have your own.

Saddles of a different cut are employed by Backcountry Saddle Expeditions (℡03/443 8151, ✉backcountry.saddle.expeditions@xtra.co.nz; 2hr–2 days; $55–180) from their stables 25km south of Wanaka in the Cardrona Valley; they'll pick you up from Wanaka if you book in advance.

Flights, skydiving and paragliding

Magnificent scenery, clear skies and competitive prices make Wanaka an excellent place to get airborne. A twenty-minute scenic flight can be combined with 30–45 seconds of freefall on a **tandem skydive** with Tandem Skydive Wanaka, Wanaka

Airport (☎03/443 7207; $245 from 9000ft, $295 from 12,000). If you open your eyes, it is all very picturesque, and they'll even do 15,000ft jumps on request.

A less fraught approach to viewing the tremendous scenery is to go **tandem paragliding**, a kind of scenic flight and paraglide all in one with Lucky Montana's Flying Circus (Dec–March; ☎0800/247 287; $170). You and your tandem guide are attached water-skiing-style to the back of a boat as you take off from the town beach and gradually gain around 600m over 15 minutes as the boat recedes to a dot below. You then detach from the tow line and begin the normal tandem paraglide turns and wing-overs back to the beach.

New Zealand's highest tandem flight takes off from the Treble Cone skifield with Wanaka Paragliding (☎03/443 9193, ⓦwww.wanakaparagliding.co.nz), who offer three trips: Eco (100–250m descent; $90) which involves walking up; Big Mountain (800–900m descent; $170) with a drive up to the skifield; and Huge Vertical (1500m descent; $250) which only runs in mid-summer when the chairlifts are running.

Flights to Milford (see p.896) from Wanaka tend to be a few dollars more expensive than those from Queenstown, and give you more air time flying over a wider range of scenery including Mount Aspiring, the Olivine Ice Plateau and the inaccessible lakes of Alabaster, McKerrow and Tutoko. Most local accommodation receives daily bulletins on Milford weather and flight conditions. Both Aspiring Air (☎03/443 7943 & 0800/100 943, ⓦwww .nz-flights.com) and Wanaka Flightseeing (☎03/443 8787 & 0800/105 105, ⓦwww.flightseeing.co.nz) do an extensive range of flights, the most popular being a combination flight and Milford Sound cruise (4hr; $340–355).

Cruises and boat activities

With a beautiful lake, a number of decent rivers and a friendly, low-key approach, there's plenty of opportunity for getting wet in style. Lakeland Adventures, 100 Ardmore St (☎03/443 7495), lays on all manner of waterborne activities, the most leisurely being **lake cruises** ranging from the Scenic (1hr; $50) to the Mou Waho (3hr; $90) which visits a small island where you walk to Arethusa Pool, a lake within a lake. The Stephensons Island trip (2hr; $70) includes a 15min walk through the breeding territory of the buff weka. For thrills and spills, try the hour-long **jetboat rides** onto the upper reaches of the Clutha with Clutha River Jet, Main Wharf (same phone; $70). Some 500m west along the beach, Lake Wanaka Yacht Charters (☎03/443 1369) rent small yachts ($30/hr), catamarans ($40/hr), **windsurfers** ($40/hr) and **sea kayaks** ($35 a half-day, $40 for doubles).

From October to April, Alpine Kayak Guides (☎03/443 9023, ⓦwww.alpinekayaks.co.nz) will take you on a number of different full-day **kayaking** trips on the Matukituki, Clutha or Hawea rivers (all Grade II; $145), half-day trips ($99) and gentle 3hr float trips ($65). They'll pick up in Wanaka or you can visit them at 150 Main Road, Luggate, 12km east of Wanaka.

A far cry from Queenstown's boisterous Kawarau and Shotover rivers, the **rafting trips** run by Pioneer Rafting (☎03/443 1246; Sept–April; half day $115, full day $165) are pitched at families, the emphasis being on appreciating the scenery, swimming and gold panning as you drift down the Upper Clutha. No-holds-barred thrill-seekers need look no further than **whitewater sledging** on the Kawarau river with Frogz Have More Fun (see p.842).

Fishing

Wanaka and Hawea lakes and the rivers flowing into them are popular territory for quinnat salmon and brown and rainbow **trout fishing**. There's a maximum bag of six fish per day and you'll require the sport fishing licence ($17 a day, $34 a week), obtainable from tackle shops. Unless you really know your bait, you'll have a better chance of catching your supper with Lakeland Adventures who charter a cabin cruiser holding six comfortably ($250 for three hours for up to three people, plus $25 for each extra), or they'll rent you a rod, reel and lures for about $20 a day.

Eating and drinking

The sophisticated tastes and open wallets of Wanaka's skiers, combined with a healthy influx of summer tourists, have together fostered an abundance of very good places to eat. The town's drinking dens are less appealing, but you can always take refuge in the restaurant bars. Unless you strike it lucky and catch a band passing through, the only entertainment is the wonderful Paradiso **cinema** (cnr Ardmore St & Ballantyne Rd ⏊03/443 1505, Ⓦwww .paradiso.net.nz; $12), an off-beat place where you sit in sagging old sofas, armchairs, cushions and even a Morris Minor installed along one side. Unless there is a general consensus to press on through, there will be an interval when everyone tucks into cookies, ice-cream, coffee or booze from the on-site café (see below). Films range from Hollywood to arthouse.

Apartmentone 1st floor, 99 Ardmore St, entry from the car park and concrete steps at the back of the building. Hard to find but worth the effort, this chic lounge with a balcony overlooking the lake is the cruisiest drinking den in town. With occasional DJ sounds, a simple selection of antipasto platters and mellow background music, this is the perfect place to enjoy the sun going down. 6pm until late.

Café Paradiso Cnr Ardmore St & Ballantyne Rd. Groovy little licensed café attached to its cinema namesake with Formica tables and piles of old *Empire* magazines to keep you occupied over muffins, sandwiches, pasta dishes, some excellent main courses ($20–26), coffee that's freshly roasted in the basement, cookies and home-made ice-cream that's free of additives and wondrously fruity.

Capriccio 123 Ardmore St ⏊03/443 8579. A little gem of an Italian-style restaurant, which branches out into Thai and Kiwi flavours, with filling pasta dishes for lunch and more sophisticated evening meals for around $27. Go for anything with fish in it.

Curry Guru Pembroke Mall ⏊03/443 6086. Good quality and reliable curry restaurant with the usual range of north Indian favourites done well at modest prices.

The Doughbin Pembroke Mall. Home-style bakery with good cakes and pies, including vegetarian versions, from 6am–6pm and offering a late menu through a serving hatch round the side, for the hungry drinkers and clubbers midnight–6am.

Kai Whaka Pai Cnr Ardmore St & Helwick St. Undoubtedly Wanaka's essential daytime eating spot and a hot favourite with the locals, who come here for Danish pastries and croissants for breakfast, damn fine coffee and fabulous meals in gargantuan proportions through the day. Expect the likes of laksa ($14), Tandoori chicken salad ($24) and dukkah-rubbed venison ($28).

Relishes 99 Ardmore St ⏊03/443 9018. Pretension-free, swish dinner-only restaurant that has become an institution. Wonderful pasta dishes for around $22, plus the likes of seafood Tom Kha appetiser ($16), seared leg of venison ($28) and mouth-watering deserts. BYO & licensed.

Sasanoki 145 Ardmore Rd ⏊03/443 1188. Stylish and modern Japanese influenced restaurant with Western overtones where you might start with sake-steamed green-lipped mussels ($12) followed by salmon sashimi ($16) or lamb shank simmered in soy broth ($25). Great lake views too.

Shooters 145 Ardmore Rd. Big, modern drinkers' bar with sports TVs, pool tables, loud chart-oriented DJ-mixed tunes on Friday and Saturday and airy seating out front with lake views.

Slainte 21 Helwick St. Lively bar in international-Irish style with Guinness and Kilkenny on tap and a good range of low-cost Irish-Kiwi meals: expect fish and chips ($18), Irish stew ($17), Shamrock burgers ($12) and a range of hearty breakfasts.

Soulfood 74 Ardmore St ⏊03/443 7885. Organic vegetarian grocery and café with outdoor seating (front and back), serving a range of smoothies ($7), coffee, all-day breakfast ($5–10) and the likes of felafel ($11) and salads ($11).

White House Café & Bar 33 Dunmore St ☎ 03/443 9595. One of Wanaka's best: a classy yet casual restaurant in a flamboyantly nautical open-plan house with a sunny patio (or a raging fire in winter). The cuisine is Mediterranean with strong Mahgrebi and Middle Eastern leanings, accompanied by wonderful fresh breads and great strong coffee. Mains are $20–30, and can be washed down with something from the extensive wine list, all available by the glass. The desserts are sensational.

Listings

Bike rental Numerous places around town rent bikes. For getting about town and the easy trails get hardtail machines from Good Sports, Dunmore St ($30 a day, $20 a half-day; ☎ 03/443 7966). For serious mountain biking try Mountain Bikes Unlimited, 99 Ardmore St (☎ 03/443 7882), who rent high-spec off-road machines for around $40 a day ($25 a half day).
Buses Atomic (☎ 03/442 9708) run to Christchurch, Dunedin, Queenstown, Invercargill, Te Anau and Greymouth; Catch-a-Bus (☎ 03/479 9960) runs to Dunedin; InterCity (☎ 03/474 9600) stop in Wanaka on the Queenstown to Franz Josef and Queenstown to Christchurch runs; Southern Link Shuttles (☎ 03/358 8355) run to Queenstown and Christchurch; and Wanaka Connexions (☎ 03/443 9122) run along SH8 to Dunedin.
Camping and outdoor equipment Good Sports, Dunmore St (☎ 03/443 7966), rents out fishing tackle ($10 a day), hiker tents (from $10 a day), sleeping bags ($7.50 a day) and just about everything else imaginable for use in the outdoors.
Car rental Aspiring Car Rentals (☎ 03/443 7883) have the cheapest cars in town starting at around $45 a day, with unlimited kilometres and insurance.
Internet Places all over town including fast machines at Wanaka Web, upstairs at 3 Helwick St ☎ 03/443 7429; daily 10am–10pm.
Medical treatment Wanaka Medical Centre, 21 Russell St ☎ 03/443 7811.
Pharmacy Wanaka Pharmacy, 33 Helwick St ☎ 03/443 8000.
Police Helwick St ☎ 03/443 7272.
Post office The post office at 39 Ardmore St (☎ 03/443 8211) has poste restante facilities.
Ski rental Harris Mountain Heliskiing, 99 Ardmore St (☎ 0800/684 468), and Racers Edge, 99 Ardmore St (☎ 03/443 7882), rent out skis and snowboards for $32–42 per day, and also run a ski tuning and repair service – as does Good Sports on Dunmore St (☎ 03/443 7966).
Taxis Wanaka Taxis (☎ 03/443 7999).

Around Wanaka

Wanaka is the only town of any size within a huge area of western Central Otago, and the only resort with easy access to tramps in the **Mount Aspiring National Park**. Consequently, it's a popular base for exploring the surrounding countryside, principally the open and mountainous areas to the north and west, the Haast Pass road over to the West Coast (see p.817), and the tortuous **Crown Range Road**, the most direct route to Queenstown, passing through the **Cardrona Valley** at perilous altitudes.

The Cardrona Valley

The most direct (though not necessarily the quickest) route from Wanaka to Queenstown is on the all-paved **Crown Range Road** (SH89), through the **Cardrona Valley**. Reaching an **altitude** of 1120m, it is one of New Zealand's highest public roads and is windy enough in places that anyone towing a caravan or trailer is discouraged from using the road. Nonetheless, on a fine day, it is a rewarding drive past the detritus of the valley's gold-mining heyday with views across the tussock high country.

Rumours of William Fox's unwitting discovery of gold in the Arrow River at Arrowtown in 1862 sparked a frenzy of activity. Prospectors spread far and wide, quickly moving north along the Crown Range and stumbling into the

Cardrona Valley, where **gold** was discovered later that year. Five years on, the Europeans legged it to the new fields on the West Coast, leaving the dregs to Chinese immigrants, who themselves had drifted away by 1870.

It is an easy drive from Wanaka 26km to the tiny community **CARDRONA**, with a few cottages, a long-forgotten cemetery and the *Cardrona Hotel* (see Accommodation, p.866) which stands in a state of arrested decay. Built in 1863, it survived the floods of 1878 that destroyed most of the old town, battling on until 1961. After years of neglect it was reopened in 1984, with its original facade and a completely renovated interior opening onto a great beer garden; it's now a popular watering hole for skiers in winter, and a good spot for bar and restaurant **meals** ($10–20) at any time.

Access roads to the Cardrona Alpine Resort and Waiorau Snow Farm (see "Winter in Wanaka" box on p.876) leave SH89 a couple of kilometres on the Wanaka side of Cardrona, right by the **bra fence**. A few years ago an ordinary section of farm fencing beside the road spontaneously sprouted a collection of bras which seems to grow each year.

Nearby, a cluster of activity operators have created a petrolhead's heaven. If you've ever wondered what it feels like hurtling towards a right angle corner at 100km/hr and spraying gravel everywhere, then find out **rally driving** with Extreme Rally (☎0800/872 559, ✉ride@mmrally.co.nz) who'll take you for a short but intense spin (2.5km for $135, 5km for $195) and even let you get behind the wheel (20min for $250, 1hr for $450). For something a little more leisurely go **quad biking** with Criffle Park Safaris (☎03/443 1711, ⓦwww.crifflepeaksafaris.com) who take you across farmland with some wonderful views. Go for a couple of hours ($95) or half a day ($200), and there are less powerful bikes for those aged thirteen to fifteen.

There's a more esoteric, testosterone-fuelled appeal to Monster Mountain Monster Trucks (☎03/443 6363, ⓦwww.monstertrucks.co.nz) where you can ride in a monster truck ($150), drive it yourself ($250), ride in a monsterized school bus ($25), or be driven for over 500m on the two wheels on one side of a car by the world's finest proponent of the art ($75). All three companies run year-round but call ahead outside the summer season.

South from here, the road twists and turns a further 26km through grassy flanks of bald, mica-studded hills to a great viewpoint overlooking Queenstown and Lake Wakatipu. It then steeply switchbacks down towards SH6 and Queenstown.

The Matukituki Valley and Mount Aspiring National Park

The **Matukituki Valley** is very much Wanaka's outdoor playground, a 60km tentacle reaching from the parched Otago landscapes around Lake Wanaka to the steep alpine skirts of Mount Aspiring, which at 3030m is New Zealand's highest mountain outside the Mount Cook National Park. Extensive high-country stations run sheep on the riverside meadows, briefly glimpsed by skiers bound for Treble Cone, rock climbers making for the roadside crags, Matukituki-bound kayakers, and trampers and mountaineers hot-footing it to the **Mount Aspiring National Park**.

The park, first mooted in 1935 but not created until 1964, is one of the country's largest, extending from the Haast Pass (where there are tramps around Makarora) in the north, to the head of Lake Wakatipu (where the Rees–Dart Track and parts of the Routeburn Track fall within its bounds) in the south. The pyramidal Mount Aspiring undoubtedly forms the centrepiece of the

Winter in Wanaka

May signifies the end of the summer season, and Wanaka immediately starts gearing up for **winter**. Mountain-bike rental shops switch to ski rental (see "Listings", p.874), watersports instructors don their baggy boarder pants, pot-bellied stoves replace parasols at restaurants, and frequent shuttle buses run up to the ski fields, calling at the hotels, hostels and sports shops along the way. Reports on snow conditions can be heard on the local radio at around 6.45am, and shops around town post up the morning's report in their windows – you can't miss them. If you plan to drive up to the ski fields, you'll need tyre chains, which can be rented at petrol stations in Wanaka.

Cardrona

Cardrona Alpine Resort (ⓣ03/443 7341, ⓦwww.cardrona.com) sprawls over three basins on the southeastern slopes of the 1934-metre Mount Cardrona, the 12km unsealed toll-free access road branching off 24km south of Wanaka and just short of the hamlet of Cardrona. Predominantly a family-oriented field – they run a junior ski school and a crèche – Cardrona is noted for dry snow and an abundance of gentle **runs** ideally suited to beginners and intermediates. Currently there are two quads, a double chair and learner tows, giving a maximum vertical descent of 390m and, though there is little extreme terrain, snowboarders have the run of four half-pipes. As you would expect, there's a full programme of lessons, ski packages and gear rental, plus full restaurant and bar facilities. An adult lift **pass costs** $65.

Through most of the long season (late June to early October), you'll need snow chains to negotiate the access road which drops you at the base facilities halfway up the field. Non-drivers can get **buses** from Wanaka, and from Queenstown, an hour and a half away.

Cardrona is unique in New Zealand in offering **accommodation** actually on the mountain – in luxury, fully self-contained studios for two (7x), or two- and three bedroom apartments ($270–450; ⓣ03/443 7411).

Treble Cone

More experienced skiers tend to frequent the excellent steep slopes of **Treble Cone** (ⓣ03/443 7443, ⓦwww.treblecone.co.nz), 22km west of Wanaka, where additional snow-making equipment has extended the season, which now lasts from mid-June to early October. Its appeal lies in open uncrowded slopes, spectacularly located high above Lake Wanaka, and a full 610 vertical metres of skiing, served by New Zealand's first detachable six-seater chair, a couple of T-bars and a learner tow. The **terrain** is very varied with moguls, powder runs, gully runs and plenty of natural and

park, rising with classical beauty over the ice-smoothed broad valleys and creaking glaciers. It was first climbed in 1909 using heavy hemp rope and none of the modern climbing hardware used by today's mountaineers, who still treat the mountain as one of the grails of Kiwi mountaineering ambition.

Travelling along Mount Aspiring Road beside the Matukituki River, you don't get to see much of Mount Aspiring, as Mount Avalanch and Avalanche Glacier get in the way. Still, craggy mountains remain tantalizingly present all the way to the **Raspberry Creek**, where a car park and public toilets mark the start of a number of magnificent tramps (see box on pp.878–879) into the heart of the park.

Buses operated by Mount Aspiring Express (ⓣ03/443 8422; $25 one-way, $45 return), and Alpine Coachlines (ⓣ03/443 7966, ⓔinfo@good-sports.co.nz; same prices) run 55km along Mount Aspiring Road to the national park's main trailhead at Raspberry Creek. Bikes cost $5 each way. Both

created half-pipes; the limited extent of wide, groomed slopes makes it hard work for beginners, but snowboarders will have a ball. Day **lift passes** go for $75 and there's a first-timer's package (skiers $86, boarders $96) including a lift pass, rental and two hours' instruction.

Lessons, gear rental and food are all on tap, and the field is easily reached along a 7km toll-free access road. Morning **buses** leave from Wanaka, and a shuttle bus takes skiers from the start of the access road on Mount Aspiring Road up to the tows.

Snow farm

With so many Kiwi skiers committed to downhill, it comes as a surprise to discover the **Snow Farm** (☏03/443 7542, ⓦwww.snowfarmnz.com), a Nordic ski area across the valley from Cardrona, some 24km south of Wanaka, then 13km up a winding dirt road. At $25 for access to the field and $20 for ski rental, it is a relatively inexpensive way to get on the snow; and Nordic or cross-country skiing is beginning to catch on. From July to September, exponents negotiate the 42km of marked and groomed Nordic trails designed to cater to beginners and experts in both the Nordic and telemark disciplines. The ski school caters to all levels with improvers' clinics and children's programmes running throughout the season, though more frequently at weekends.

Heli-skiing

No one is going to fool you into believing that **heli-skiing** is cheap, but there's no other way of getting to runs of up to 1200 vertical metres across virgin snow on any of six mountain ranges. From June to October Harris Mountains Heli-Ski (☏03/442 6722, ⓦwww.heli-ski.co.nz), New Zealand's biggest heli-skiing operator, offers almost 400 different runs on 150 peaks – mainly in the Harris Mountains between Queenstown's Crown Range and Wanaka's Mount Aspiring National Park.

Strong intermediate and **advanced skiers** generally get the most out of the experience, though those with more limited skills can still participate provided they meet the minimum standard determined by an ability questionnaire. **Conditions** are more critical than at the ski fields, but on average there's heli-skiing on seventy percent of days during winter, typically in four- to five-day weather windows separated by storms. Of the multitude of packages, the most popular have to be a three-run day ($645),"The Classic" ($695), with four runs in a day, and "Maximum Vertical" ($895), comprising seven runs for advanced skiers only; **bookings** should be made well in advance and accompanied by a substantial deposit (around 40 percent).

also run a charter service, which gives you greater flexibility and works out cheaper if you can get at least five people together.

Towards the West Coast: Lake Hawea and Hawea

Mountain-backed **Lake Hawea**, immediately east of Lake Wanaka, receives a fraction of the attention of its western neighbour. With its milky, azure waters this might seem surprising, but much of its appeal was shorn away in 1958 with the completion of a small dam, which raised the lake level by twenty metres, in the process drowning the lake's beaches and gently shelving shoreline. Nevertheless, the lake is still popular with anglers intent on bagging landlocked rainbow and brown trout, and salmon. Otherwise there is little reason to spend time here – except to recharge your batteries in the peace and quiet of

The DOC's *Matukituki Valley Tracks* and *Rees–Dart Tracks* leaflets ($1 each) are recommended for these walks, along with the all-new and very detailed *Mount Aspiring National Park* map ($15). These walks can be tackled by relatively fit and experienced trampers, but the climatic differences in the park are extreme, and the half-metre of rain that falls each year in the Matukituki Valley is no indication of the six metres that fall on the western side of the park; as ever, go prepared.

Several huts in this area are owned by the New Zealand Alpine Club (NZAC) but are open to all: pay at the DOC visitor centre in Wanaka.

Raspberry Creek to Aspiring Hut

The popular and mostly pastoral day walk from **Raspberry Creek to Aspiring Hut** (9km one way; 2hr 30min–3hr; 100m ascent) starts along a 4WD track which climbs gently from the Raspberry Creek car park beside the western branch of the Matukituki River, only heading away from the river to avoid bluffs en route to Downs Creek, from where you get fabulous views up to the Rob Roy Glacier and Mount Avalanche. Bridal Veil Falls is only a brief distraction before the historic Cascade Hut, followed twenty minutes later by the relatively luxurious stone-built **Aspiring Hut** (NZAC; 38 bunks; Nov–April $20 with gas; May–Oct $10 no gas), a common base camp for mountaineers off to the peaks around Mount Aspiring, which is wonderfully framed by the hut's picture windows. There's also **camping** ($5) near the hut.

Rob Roy Valley

The **Rob Roy Valley Walk** (6km one way; 2hr; 400m ascent) is shorter and steeper than the walk to *Aspiring Hut* and more spectacular, striking through beech forest to some magnificent alpine scenery, snowfields and glaciers. From the Raspberry Creek car park, follow the true right bank of the Matukituki for fifteen minutes to a swingbridge; cross to the true left bank of the Rob Roy stream, which cuts through a small gorge into the beech forest. Gradually the woods give way to alpine vegetation – and the Rob Roy glacier nosing down into the head of the valley.

Aspiring Hut to the head of the valley

An excellent day out from *Aspiring Hut* involves exploring the headwaters of the Matukituki River to the north. The **Aspiring Hut to Pearl Flat** (4km; 1hr 30min; 100m ascent) stretch follows the still-broad river as it weaves in and out of the bush to Pearl Flat. From **Pearl Flat to the head of the valley** (3.5km; 1hr 30min; 250m ascent) the path follows the right bank, crosses a huge avalanche chute off the side of Mount Barff and climbs high above the river through cottonwood and into open

HAWEA, a village that clings to the lake's southern shore 15km northeast of Wanaka. The Lake Hawea Store (daily 7.30am–7pm), right in the centre of the village, sells one-day fishing licences ($17) and can put you in touch with local angling experts; expect to pay $300–400 a day for fly-fishing guides.

If you stay, you'll find **camping** and basic **accommodation** in the cabins of the spacious, leafy *Lake Hawea Motor Camp*, SH6 (T & F 03/443 1767; camping $11, cabins & flats 2x–4x) right by the lakeshore. The *Lake Hawea Motor Inn*, 1 Capell Ave (T 03/443 1224 & 0800/429 324, E lakehawea@xtra.co.nz; dorms 1x, motel units 5x–6x), is optimally sited for uninterrupted lake and mountain views; the backpacker-style lodge has pleasant four-bunk dorms complete with bedding and self-catering facilities. The best of the **B&Bs** is *Sylvan Chalet*, 4 Bodkin St (T 03/443 1343, W www.inow.co.nz/sylvanchalet; 4x), where a couple of balconied rooms tucked atop a craft-filled A-frame boast fine mountain views.

WANAKA | Around Wanaka

⑬

country. Scott Rock Bivvy, marked on some maps, is little more than a sheltering rock 50m east of the river and reached by a bridge.

An alternative, initially following the same route, goes very steeply from **Aspiring Hut to French Ridge Hut** (9km; 4hr; 1000m ascent); the **French Ridge Hut** (NZAC; 20 bunks; $15) has great mountain views but is usually only below the snowline from December to March.

Cascade Saddle Route

The most challenging and most satisfying of the local tramps connects the Matukituki Valley to the Rees–Dart Circuit centred on Glenorchy (see p.862), via the arduous **Cascade Saddle Route** (4–5 days one way), a magnificent alpine crossing with fine panoramic views of the Dart Glacier and the Barrier Range. Long stretches of exposed high country and a finishing point 150km (by road) from the start mean that the route is not one to be undertaken lightly, though it is usually possible to send your excess gear ahead to Queenstown with Wanaka Connexions (☎03/443 9122), who charge around $10 per bag. Cascade Saddle can only be negotiated without specialized mountaineering equipment for around four months a year (typically Dec–March), and requires totally waterproof clothing, while a tent gives you the option of breaking the longest day by spending a night just beyond the alpine meadows at the saddle.

The first part of the route follows the track from **Raspberry Creek to Aspiring Hut** (9km; 2hr 30min–3hr; 100m ascent – see description on p.878). From **Aspiring Hut to Dart Hut** (13km; 8–11hr; 1350m ascent) views of Mount Aspiring improve as you rise above the tree line onto the steep tussock and snowgrass ridge above. The route is marked by orange snow poles which lead you to a steel pylon (1835m) that marks the top of the ridge, down to Cascade Creek and across it before climbing gently to the meadows around Cascade Saddle (1500m); four to six hours so far. Non-campers will have to press on another four or five hours to the *Dart Hut*, some 500m lower down, along the upper **Dart Valley**. The initial steep descent beside snow poles is treacherous when wet, but on a warm afternoon enjoys expansive views towards the mouth of the rubble-topped Dart Glacier, where chunks of ice periodically crash into the milky river that surges beneath it. In 1914, the terminus of the glacier had crept to within a kilometre of *Dart Hut*, but it is retreating an average of 50m a year and could all but disappear within eighty years. After following lateral moraine, rounding bluffs and fording streams, you eventually reach the new **Dart Hut** ($10; 32 bunks), from where it is two days to Glenorchy, following either the Dart or Rees river valleys.

The Lake Hawea Store has a café and a pizza and pasta **restaurant**, or head to the *Lake Hawea Hotel* for substantial bar meals and its beer garden.

The Central Otago goldfields

Though Queenstown's gold-rush heritage has largely been swamped by adventure tourism, the mining past remains one of the main attractions of the **Central Otago goldfields**, a historically rich region which has begun to adapt and evolve into a tourist destination of moody splendour covering much of the country east of the Queenstown–Wanaka axis to the coast at Dunedin. This barren, rugged and peculiarly beautiful high-country hinterland is where, from the 1860s to the end of the century, gold was panned from the streambeds, dredged from the deeper rivers, and eventually mined and blasted from the land. Small-time panners still extract a little "colour" from the streams and a few commercial mines still operate, but for the most part the gold has turned its back on the country it helped build. The landscape is now littered with abandoned mines, perilous shafts and scattered bits of mysterious-looking machinery, while shingle banks in the rivers occasionally reveal the remains of huge dredges, or the detritus of hare-brained schemes to divert the waters and reveal the gold-bearing riverbed.

Towns that boomed in the 1860s were mostly moribund by the early years of the twentieth century, but a few either struggled on as way-stations between the coast and the farmlands of the interior, or developed into prosperous serv-ice towns for the stone-fruit orchards which thrive in the region's crisp, dry winters and searingly hot summers. A shortage of water to irrigate these fertile lands was subsequently addressed by building a couple of controversial hydro dams on the Clutha River, drowning many of the orchards in the process. However, the microclimate and abundant water has allowed the development of a burgeoning **wine region** full of unique flavours and enormous potential (see p.884).

Many of the significant locales in the gold country fall under the auspices of the DOC's **Otago Goldfields Park**, which encompasses a score of diverse sites scattered throughout the region – all of which are listed in the free *Otago Goldfields Heritage Trail* leaflet, available from local visitor centres. When out exploring, take **precautions**: deep shafts and heavy machinery are potentially hazardous, so at recognized sites, keep to marked paths and heed safety barri-ers; elsewhere tread extremely carefully.

The reconstructed nineteenth-century boom town at **Cromwell** probably won't delay you long, but the town is a good jumping-off point for the former mining settlements of **Bannockburn** and **Bendigo**. Cromwell's Lake Dunstan is actually a reservoir backed up behind a dam, adjacent to the peaceful town of **Clyde**, now an attractive knot of restaurants and guest houses. **Alexandra** acts mainly as a service town at the fork of two roads penetrating deep into the less-visited part of the gold county: SH85 heads northeast onto the **Maniototo**, skirting the dilapidated former gold towns of **St Bathan's** and **Naseby** on the way to workaday **Ranfurly**, and the only accessible working mine at **Macraes Flat**; while SH8 dives southeast towards the coast through dull **Roxburgh** and **Lawrence**, where the gold rush initially started.

To really explore this region you need your own vehicle but there is some **public transport**. The Taieri Gorge Railway (see p.728) runs from Dunedin to Pukerangi where it is met by Track & Trail buses (℡03/477 5577, ⓦwww.transportplace.co.nz) to Queenstown; Catch-A-Bus (℡03/479 9960) run a once-daily service between Wanaka and Dunedin through the Maniototo; and fairly frequent buses run along SH8 between Queenstown and Dunedin.

Some history

New Zealand's greatest gold rush kicked off in 1861 when Gabriel Read, an Australian who had previously worked the Californian fields, unearthed flakes of the precious metal beside the Tuapeka River, south of Lawrence. Within weeks Dunedin had all but emptied and thousands were camping out on the **Tuapeka Goldfield** around Gabriels Gully. The excitement at Tuapeka soon fizzled out, although by the winter of 1862 Californian prospectors Horatio Hartley and Christopher Reilly teased their first flakes out of the Clutha River, bagging a 40kg haul in three months. This sparked off an even greater gold

Gold from dirt

The classic image of the felt-hatted old-timer **panning** merrily beside a stream is only part of the story of gold extraction, but it's a true enough depiction of the first couple of years of the Otago gold rush. Initially all a miner needed was a pick and shovel, a pan, and preferably a special wooden box known as a "rocker" for washing the alluvial gravel. Periodic droughts lowered the river levels to reveal unworked banks, but as the easily accessible gravel beds were worked out, all manner of ingenious schemes were devised to gain access to fresh raw material. The most common technique was to divert the river, and some far-fetched schemes were hatched, especially on the Shotover River: steel sheets were driven into the riverbeds with some success, landslides induced to temporarily dam the flow, and a tunnel was bored through a bluff.

When pickings got thinner miners turned their attentions to the more tightly packed banks of the gorges. Hillside dams were constructed and water was piped under pressure to **sluicing** guns that blasted the auriferous gravel free, ready for processing either by traditional hand-panning or its mechanical equivalent, where "riffle plates" caught the fine gravel and carpet-like matting trapped the fine flakes of gold. Eventually the scale of these operations put individual miners out of business and many pressed on to fresh fields.

To get at otherwise inaccessible gravel stock, larger companies began building **gold dredges**, great clanking behemoths anchored to the riverbanks but floating free on the river. Buckets scooped out the river bottom, then the dredge processed the gravel and spat the "tailings" out of the back to pile up along the riversides.

Otago's alluvial gold starts its life underground embedded in reefs of quartz, and when economic returns from the rivers waned, miners sought the mother lode. **Reef quartz mining** required a considerable investment in machinery and whole towns sprang up to tunnel, hack out the ore and haul it on sledges to the stamper batteries. Here, a series of water-driven (and later steam-powered) hammers would pulverize the rock, which was then passed over copper plates smeared with mercury, and onto gold-catching blankets, before the remains were washed into the berdan – a special kind of cast-iron bowl. Gold was then separated from the mercury, a process subsequently made more efficient with the use of cyanide.

rush, this time centred on Cromwell, which mushroomed as wagon trains made their way over the rough muddy trails from the coast into the interior. Tent cities sprang up, soon to be replaced by more permanent buildings as merchants moved in founding banks, hotels, shops, bars and brothels. Later in 1862, Thomas Arthur and Harry Redfern struck lucky at what is now Arthur's Point on the Shotover River, sparking a mass exodus for the fresh fields of what soon became known as "the richest river in the world". Miners flooded into Skipper's Canyon, but a few months later some of the heat was taken from its banks by discoveries on the Fox River near Arrowtown, the last of the major gold towns to be built and still the best preserved. Within a few years returns had dwindled and many headed off to investigate reports of richer finds on the West Coast. As fortunes waned and traders saw their profits diminishing, Chinese miners were co-opted to pick over the tailings (discarded bits of rock and gravel) left behind by Europeans, and were occasionally allowed to work unwanted claims.

Though the boom and bust cycle was as rapid here as in gold country elsewhere, some form of mining continued for the best part of forty years, and the profits fuelled a South Island economy, which, for a time at least, dominated New Zealand's exchequer. Dunedin's economy boomed, and the golden bounty funded the majority of the grand civic buildings there.

Many claims were eventually abandoned – not for lack of gold, but because of harsh winters, famine, war, a dip in the gold price, lack of sluicing water, or just disinterest. Although returns are far from spectacular, there are still people eking out a living from gold mining; stakes are still claimed and you'll find small- and medium-scale operations all over the province. There's very little appliance of science and despite a fair bit of sophisticated machinery, these are very much backyard operations where instinct counts for much and fancy mining theories not at all. Bigger capital-intensive companies occasionally gauge the area's potential, and as one mining engineer pithily put it, "there's still a shitload of gold out there".

Cromwell

East of Arrowtown, SH6 runs for 40km through the scenic Kawarau Gorge, past the Gibbston Valley wineries (see p.836) and the Goldfields Mining Centre (see p.883), to **CROMWELL**, a dull, flat little service town with its gold-mining roots waterlogged below the shimmering surface of the **Lake Dunstan** reservoir. Formed by the Clyde Dam 20km downstream (see p.885), Lake Dunstan swamped much of Cromwell's historic core. The present-day town centre is uninspiringly modern, but the surrounding region is beginning to find its place on the tourist map with its cluster of quality wineries, fruit orchards, gold diggings and a couple of water-borne leisure activities.

Soon after Hartley and Reilly's 1862 discovery of **gold** beside the Clutha River, a settlement sprouted at "The Junction" at the fork of the Kawarau and Clutha rivers. Local stories tell that it was later renamed when a government survey party dubbed it Cromwell to spite local Irish immigrant workers. Miners low on provisions planted the first fruit trees in the region, little expecting that Cromwell would become the centre of the Otago orchard belt. Its location, further from the sea than any other town in New Zealand, dictates an extreme temperature range – hot and arid in summer with still, cool, dry winters – making it perfect for growing dripping, toothsome **stone fruit**, and grape vines.

The town

Modern Cromwell is centred on a giant fibreglass fruity confection. Behind it, **The Mall** contains the combined visitor centre (see p.883) and **museum** (free, but donations welcome), packed full of gold-mining memorabilia, together with material on the construction of Clyde Dam. Free leaflets outline the self-guided **Cromwell Tour**, mind-numbingly dull but for the section around **Old Cromwell Town** (unrestricted entry), a kind of historic reserve on Melmore Terrace, where Lake Dunstan now laps the increasing number of restored old shopfronts. In the mid-1970s when the Clyde Dam was planned and the death knell sounded for the heart of old Cromwell, the preservation instinct kicked in and a dozen buildings due to be submerged were dismantled stone by stone and have now been rebuilt on the water's edge. You can spend a pleasant half-hour browsing the art, craft and gourmet food shops before retiring for an espresso and cake at the *Grain & Seed Café*.

Aquatic activities are still in their infancy here, though you can join Eco Experience (☏03/445 0788, ✉EcoExperience@xtra.co.nz) who provide binoculars on their three-hour **bird-watching trips**, which explore the eerie and ensnaring waterlogged-forest at the north-eastern tip of Lake Dunstan ($160 for the first two birdwatchers, then $60 each). For lake **fishing**, contact Dick Marquand (☏03/445 1745, ⊛www.troutfishingservices.co.nz) who is enthusiastic, experienced, knowledgeable and will guarantee a trout on his fly fishing trips for up to three people ($240 for 2hr, $300 3hr, $650 full day).

Practicalities

Queenstown- or Wanaka-bound **bus** travellers may well have to change in Cromwell, using the stop behind the Shell petrol station on Murray Terrace right by The Mall. In the heart of The Mall, Cromwell's **visitor centre** (Mon–Fri 9am–5pm Sat & Sun 10am–4pm; ☎03/445 0212, ⦿www.cromwell .org.nz) provides the free and comprehensive *Discover Cromwell* and *Walk Cromwell* leaflets.

The cheapest **place to stay** is at the *Cromwell Top 10 Holiday Park*, 1 Alpha St (☎03/445 0164 & 0800/107 275, ⦿www.cromwellholidaypark.co.nz), which has camping for $12–13 and a range of cabins, flats and motel units (2x–4x). Across the street there's a welcoming and comfortable homestay at *Cottage Gardens*, 3 Alpha St (☎ & ℻03/445 0628, ℮info@fiordland.gen.nz; 4x), with en-suite accommodation, a mature garden and dinner on request ($20). For a decent motel, head across town to *Anderson Park Motel*, 9 Gair Ave (☎03/445 0321 & 0800/220 550; 4x). Moving upscale you'll need to head 5km north along SH6 to *Villa Amo* (☎03/445 0788, ℮VillaAmo@xtra.co.nz; 6x), friendly and with two doubles in a large and airy house sitting right on the lake foreshore.

Cromwell does well for coffee, snacks and **lunch** with: modern café fare at *Fusée Rouge*, 75 The Mall; good pub food a couple of doors down at *The Pub*, 71 The Mall; a range of light meals at the *Grain & Seed Café* overlooking Lake Dunstan at Old Cromwell Town; and great fresh juices squeezed from their own orchards at *Juice Café*, SH8 close to the bridge over Lake Dunstan. For something more leisurely, visit the Bannockburn **wineries** (see p.884), just five minutes' drive away.

Dinner is more of a challenge. Apart from *The Pub* and Friday pizza evenings at *Juice Café*, consider heading to the *Bannockburn Hotel* in Bannockburn or one of the places in Clyde, 20km southeast (see p.885).

Around Cromwell

Tour buses disgorge their load at the half-dozen **fruit stalls** that encircle Cromwell. Pick of the bunch is Jones' Fruit Orchards, 5km west on SH6, which is stacked with fresh and dried fruit, the former blended to form wonderful fruit ice creams, best consumed in the adjacent rose garden.

Heading 2km further in the same direction the **Goldfields Mining Centre** gives a good sense of what it must have been like in these parts in the late nineteenth century, something further illustrated in the sluicings at Bannockburn.

If you're still craving for gold, venture 15km north of Cromwell towards the Lindis Pass to the quartz-mining district of **BENDIGO** and its acolytes Logantown and Welshtown. None comprises much more than a few scattered remains and deep **mine shafts**, but a (careful) amble among the ruins makes a fine way to pass a summer evening.

All this exploring is thirsty work and you'll welcome the chance to sample the Bannockburn **wineries**. A good starting point is **The Big Picture**, SH6, 4km west of Cromwell (daily 9am–8pm; $14; ☎03/445 4052, ⦿www.wineadventure.co.nz) where the idea is to sniff all manner of aromas used to describe wine – citrus, clove, leather, truffle, liquorice etc. You then venture into a small movie theatre where you find five wines waiting to be sampled. The film rolls and you are transported around Central Otago by helicopter as you are introduced to the landscape, the terroir, and lastly the winemakers themselves who discuss the making and qualities of their wine as you sit there tasting it.

If you'd prefer not to drive around the wineries, engage Clyde-based The Grape Escape (☎03/449 2696) who run **tours** in a 1971 Bedford school bus. They're very entertaining but only go when there are at least four people. Prices come down as numbers go up, but expect around $70 for half a day, $90 for a full day.

Lower Kawarau Gorge

The only real tourist attraction around Cromwell is the **Goldfields Mining Centre** (daily 9am–5pm; $14; ☎03/445 1038, ⓦwww.goldfieldsmining .co.nz), approached by footbridge over the brooding Kawarau 7km west of Cromwell on SH6. The extensive site occupies a longstanding though not especially lucrative alluvial mining site where ground-sluicing eventually gave way to Californian-style water jets used to loosen the shingle beds. Museum pieces are stationed on a thirty-minute self-guided tour, but while this was an authentic site, and is surrounded by engaging country, there is an overriding staginess about the mining displays themselves. The stamper battery has been brought in, a turbine was recovered from the river before Lake Dunstan filled and the Chinese Village was constructed as a film set in the early 1990s. Entry price includes a **guided tour** (departs on the hour), worth joining to handle some large gold nuggets, see the stamper battery cranked up using a water-powered Pelton wheel, and try your hand at extracting a flake or two. A good café and leafy garden make this an especially pleasant stop for families.

There's also a chance to sample the only Otago-based jetboat ride that actually negotiates rapids: **Goldfields Jet** (☎0800/111 038; $75) run forty-minute trips on the Kawarau just below the site.

A short distance upstream from the Goldfields site the small **Roaring Meg** power station marks both an important rapid run by sledgers and river surfers, and the "natural bridge", a point where the river narrows into a twisting gorge below cliffs which almost touch. Maori *moa* hunters and nineteenth-century gold men used the narrows as their main crossing point until ferries and bridges were constructed elsewhere.

Bannockburn and the wineries

Dedicated ruin hounds can head out to remote clusters of cottage foundations such as those in the Carrick Range or the Nevis Valley (both south of Cromwell), but for most goldfield aficionados the best bet is **BANNOCK-BURN**, a scattered hamlet 9km southwest of Cromwell. Armed with the *Walk Cromwell* leaflet from the Cromwell visitor centre, make for the **Bannockburn Sluicings** (unrestricted entry), a tortured landscape that was once home to two thousand people desperately washing away the land to reveal the gold-rich seams below. A two-hour **self-guided trail** dotted with information boards starts 1.5km along Felton Road and weaves around tail-races, sluicing and tunnelling operations up to Stewart Town with its handful of dilapidated mud-brick huts and ageing pear and apricot trees that still fruit.

Since the early 1990s, the warm, north-facing hillsides around the sluicings have been increasingly planted in grape vines, and the vintages from them – primarily Pinot Noir and Pinot Gris – have garnered considerable praise. Five **wineries** are open for tasting, all listed on the free *Central Otago Wine Map*. During winter it's worth calling in advance to check opening times.

Two wineries worth trying are: Olssens, 306 Felton Rd (summer daily 10am–5pm; ☎03/445 1716, ⓦwww.olssens.co.nz) which offers tasting ($4, refundable with purchase) and has a lovely sculpture garden that's perfect for whiling away the time as you tuck into one of their lunch platters ($16–20) or a picnic you've brought with you; and for something a little more formal, visit Carrick, Cairnmuir Road (summer daily 11am–5pm; ☎03/445 3840, ⓦwww.carrick.co.nz), housed in a lovely modern building with art on the walls and long views down to Lake Dunstan. There's tasting ($4, refundable with purchase) and an excellent daytime restaurant that's fine for a coffee or something more substantial like their panfried haloumi with Mediterranean vegetables ($16) or sesame crusted salmon ($22) and a glass of their wine.

There's no real town of Bannockburn but the *Cairnmuir Camping Ground*, 219 Cairnmuir Rd (☎ & ⓕ03/445 1956; camping $10, cabins 2x) offers basic **accommodation** close to Lake Dunstan, and there are good bar and restaurant **meals** at the *Bannockburn Hotel*, Bannockburn Road (☎03/445 0615).

Clyde

SH8 cuts southeast from Cromwell through 20km of the bleak and windswept **Cromwell Gorge**, hugging the banks of Lake Dunstan through what used to be New Zealand's most fertile apricot-growing country. The orchards are now all submerged below the waters of the lake, which are held back by the dam at **CLYDE**. The tiny associated town, peacefully situated off the main highway, languished for a number of years but is resurgent as a sybaritic retreat. Notwithstanding a few minor sights, there is nothing much to distract you from lounging around some excellent places to stay and dining in a small cluster of great cafés and restaurants.

Clyde's streets are lined with ornate stone buildings and simple cottages left over from the gold-mining days of the 1860s. Originally known as Dunstan, the town sprang up just downriver from the spot where Hartley and Reilly made their big find in 1862. As tens of thousands of fortune-seekers flooded in from Dunedin and Lawrence, it quickly became the centre of the Dunstan goldfields, but by 1864 waning fortunes and swift river currents forced out the miners in favour of river dredges.

The town and activities

Since the mid-1980s, the town has been dominated by the giant grey hydro-electric **Clyde Dam**, 1km north of town on SH8, which generates five percent of New Zealand's power and provides water for irrigation. Initially controversial, the dam is nevertheless considered something of an engineering marvel, with special "slip joints" providing the dam wall with flexibility in case of earthquakes.

Clyde's other attractions are limited to the panoramic views from the **Clyde Lookout** hill (500m from town; 30min walk) and three small but well-kept museums within easy walking distance of one another. The 1864 stone courthouse on Blyth Street now operates as the **Clyde Museum** (Tues–Sun 2–4pm; $2), worth a peek for its intriguing coverage of Clyde's Great Gold Robbery of 1870. One George Rennie made off with £13,000 in bullion and banknotes, but his horse was so weighed down with the gold that he left a trail of bags hidden behind rocks at intervals. Unfortunately the co-conspirator for whom this trail had been intended had already ratted on Rennie to the police, and the ill-fated villain was easily tracked down and arrested. The **Briar Herb Factory Complex**, corner of Fraser Street and Fache Street (Tues–Sun 2–4pm; $2), was established in the 1930s as New Zealand's first herb factory, and thrived for several decades, making use of the common thyme which still grows wild hereabouts, with entire hillsides flowering purple throughout November. The factory closed in the 1970s but lives on as an exhibition space, housing well-maintained displays of drying trays, presses and home-made machines used for processing the herbs. Other parts of the factory are given over to horse-drawn vehicles, a rabbiter's hut and an early hospital full of ghoulish medical instruments. The former Clyde Railway Station next door houses the **Station Museum** (Sat & Sun 2–4pm; $1), with its collection of stationary engines and railway ephemera. Also worth a look is the **Clyde Cemetery**, which has a number of ornate gravestones.

Clyde is the northern terminus for the Otago Central Rail Trail (see box, p.889) and the home of Trail Journeys, cnr SH8 and Springvale Road (℡0800/724 587, 🅦www.trailjourneys.co.nz) who **rent bikes** and panniers ($30 & $7 a day respectively) and organise pretty much everything to do with riding the trail including picking you and the bike up from the far end ($50) and booking accommodation along the way. They also do guided rides around Alexandra, **rent kayaks** (single $35 a day, double $70) and canoes ($40), and lead guided kayak trips on local rivers and lakes.

Practicalities

Buses stop in Clyde on demand, pulling up on Sunderland Street, which is where you'll find the majority of the good **places to stay** and eat. Those on a tight budget will want to **stay** at *Hartley Arms*, 25 Sunderland St (℡03/449 2700, 🅔hartleyarms@xtra.co.nz; dorms 1x, room 2x), a small and cosy backpackers partly built into Clyde's original gold assay office. Dorms have four bunks and there are doubles made up with sheets and towels. With a fuller wallet, *the* place to stay is at the relaxing and extremely atmospheric *Olivers Restaurant & Lodge*, 34 Sunderland St (℡03/449 2860, 🅦www.olivers.co.nz; 6x), which has a range of eclectically-styled luxury rooms in rustic buildings that were once part of a large general store catering for the gold-miners. The Smokehouse room ($300) comes with a huge bathroom fashioned like a Turkish bath, and all come with a delicious breakfast. Alternatively there's *Dunstan House*, 29 Sunderland St (℡03/449 2295, 🅦www.dunstanhouse .co.nz; room 5x, ensuite 6x), a boutique B&B in a fine house dating from 1865, which offers spacious comfortable rooms and a wraparound veranda on the first floor; and *Clyde Holiday and Sporting Complex*, Whitby Street (℡03/449 2713, 🅔crrc@ihug.co.nz; camping $9, vans and cabins 2x), a pleasant **campsite**, surrounding a sports ground with fully self-contained cabins and several on-site caravans, plus a swimming pool and book exchange.

Lunch on a fine day is best taken in the gardens at *Olivers*, which has an excellent and characterful **restaurant** serving breakfast and wholesome lunches (mostly around $15) and dinners (mains $28–30; book ahead especially at weekends), featuring the likes of lamb and kumara gateau in red wine and thyme jus. Once unchallenged, *Olivers* cuisine is now matched by that at *The Blues Bank*, 31 Sunderland St (closed Mon), which dishes up wonderful Louisiana Cajun and Creole plates – many named after the legendary blues players that also provide the decorative theme. Tuck into Creole chilli crabs ($22) or Muddy Waters mussels ($12) selected from menus encased in old record covers. This is also the best place to listen to jazz and blues from Friday through to Sunday. Cheaper pub-style snacks can be obtained 300m away at the attractive *Post Office Café*, on the corner of Blyth and Matau streets, built into the former 1865 post office and with a bar serving delicious Post Office Dark ale along with some excellent blackboard and BBQ specials, inside or in the garden bar out the back. They also have occasional live entertainment.

Alexandra and around

A large white clockface – visible from as far away as 5km – looms out of the cliff which backs **ALEXANDRA** (affectionately known as Alex), 10km southeast of Clyde. Alexandra sprang up during the 1862 gold rush, and flourished for four frenzied years before settling into decline, although the gold-dredging boom at the end of the century breathed some life back into the town. Now a prosperous service town for the fruit-growing heartland of Central Otago, it's the largest place for some distance, and its modest clutch of sights and stark mountain scenery may well persuade you to stop, particularly if your visit coincides with the longstanding **Alexandra Blossom Festival**, held on the fourth weekend in September.

Though currently in temporary lodgings, the **Alexandra Museum** is set to move into a new Museum, Arts & Visitor Information Complex, due to open in mid-2005 in Pioneer Park, near the centre of town on Centennial Avenue. It should contain displays on the golden years of the late nineteenth century, along with entertaining coverage of the sorry tale of rabbits, which were introduced into the area in 1909 and did what rabbits do – so well that they soon became a major menace throughout the South Island. To combat the problem, the town holds an **Easter Bunny Shoot** every year, and hunters from all over New Zealand congregate on Good Friday to slaughter as many as they can.

In the early years, the only way across the Manuherikia River was by unstable punt, but in 1879 the town built the **Shaky Bridge**, a suspension **footbridge** – originally wide enough for wagons but since narrowed – now crossed to reach the *Shaky Bridge Café* (see p.888), and a **lookout point** (2km one way; 40min) high above the town on Tucker Hill, which affords great views of the whole area.

With its long hours of hot sun, the region is now gaining a reputation for its wines, the **wineries** all highlighted on the free *Central Otago Wine Map*, available from visitor centres. The pick is Black Ridge, Conroys Road (☎ 03/449 2059; daily 10am–5pm), one of the world's most southerly wineries, in an unlikely setting amid black schist 6km southwest of Alex.

Activities

An abundance of treeless hills all around makes Alex a good base for **mountain biking**, with plenty of trails to tackle on your own with a *Mountain Biking* trail guide leaflet (50¢) from the visitor centre. Alternatively, get along to Altitude Adventures, 88 Centennial Ave (☎03/448 8917, ⓦwww.altitudeadventures.co.nz) who specialise in guided singletrack mountain biking tours from a half-day local trip ($69) to a four-day grand tour of the area ($525, including bike rental and accommodation). They're also well set up for getting you on the Otago Central Rail Trail (see p.889) and rent bikes from around $30 a day.

Several other operators run **tours** from Alex into the surrounding mountain ranges: you can go **horse trekking** in the thyme-scented hills of the Dunstan Trail (1hr; $25), with longer treks by arrangement (☎03/449 2445 evenings or 7.30–8am); or try a fantastic **4WD safari** up the Dunstan Mountains, the Old Man Range or other remote gold-mining areas, with Safari Excursions (☎03/448 7474, or through the visitor centre; $30–65 for half day, $55–125 full day), who have an extraordinary range of knowledge about the area and its plant- and bird-life and take you to places that are unusual and spectacular.

InterCity and Wanaka Connexions **buses** drop off at the monument at the intersection of Tarbert Street and Centennial Avenue; while Catch-a-Bus and Atomic stop outside the **visitor centre** (daily 9am–5pm; ☎03/448 9515, ⓦwww.centralotagonz.com). The centre is currently at 22 Centennial Ave, but with the opening of the new visitor complex (see p.887) will move across the road to Pioneer Park. The **post office**, 66 Tarbert St (☎03/448 7500), has poste restante facilities; and email@alx, 33 Tarbert St, has fast **Internet** access.

There's plenty of low-cost **accommodation** in Alexandra, including the new *Alexandra Backpackers*, 8–12 Skird St (☎03/448 7170; dorms 1x), right in the heart of town with six- and four-bed dorms. They're also adept at organising orchard work. For motels, go for either the budget *Alexandra Garden Court*, 51 Manuherikia Road/SH85 (☎03/448 8295 & 0800/736 116, ⓔalex.gardencourt@xtra.co.nz; 4x), a fifteen-minute walk from the centre, with six fully self-contained units and a swimming pool set in extensive landscaped gardens; or the more upscale and central *Alexandra Heights Motels*, 125 Centennial Ave (☎03/448 6366 & 0800/862 539, ⓔalexandraheightsmotel @xtra.co.nz; 5x). For something special, drive 2km southeast along SH8 to the French provincial-style *Rocky Range* (☎03/448 6150, ⓦwww.rockyrange .co.nz; 9x), perched high on a hill amid schist outcrops with stunning panoramic views; accommodation is around $300 and dinner can be arranged for an extra $70.

Campers need to walk fifteen minutes from the centre to *Alexandra Holiday Park* 44 Manuherikia Road/SH85 (☎03/448 8297, ⓕ448 8294; cabins 2x, flats 3x), a large well-kept and tree-sheltered site offering camping for $9.50 and mountain bikes for rent.

The best **places to eat** hereabouts are in Clyde, 8km to the north (see p.886); in town go for *Briar & Thyme*, 26 Centennial Ave (book for dinner ☎03/448 9189), which specializes in the likes of camembert and vegetable turnovers or oven-baked blue cod (around $17 each), as well as elegant dinners ($20–25), in a comfortable historic house with a wine bar. For some modern sophistication wander across the Shaky Bridge to the *Shaky Bridge Café*, Graveyard Gully Road (daytime and Friday evening; ☎03/448 5111), which does great coffee, has nicely prepared lunches ($15–22) and serves a range of mostly Central Otago wines by the glass.

Fans of quality burgers and seafood at low prices should eat at the nautically themed *Nuno's*, 73 Centennial Ave (☎03/448 5444), which does the best greasies in town to eat-in or take out and also has a passable bar.

North of Alex: the Maniototo

The most interesting route to the east coast from Alexandra is through the **Maniototo**, a generic name for the flat high country shared by three shallow valleys – the Manuherikia River, the Ida Burn and the Taieri River – and the low craggy ranges that separate them. Despite easy road access, the Maniototo seems a world apart, largely ignored by foreign visitors, though it is a common summertime destination for Dunedinites who appreciate the dry climate and the quality of the light some 500 metres up. This is beginning to change with the upsurge in popularity of the **Otago Central Rail Trail** (see box, p.889), but numbers remain low.

Predictably, Europeans first came to the area in search of gold. They found it near **Naseby**, but returns quickly declined and farming on the plains became more rewarding. This was especially true when **railway** developers looking for

13

THE GOLD COUNTRY | The Central Otago goldfields

One of the finest ways to explore the Maniototo is on the **Otago Central Rail Trail** (ⓦ www.otagocentralrailtrail.co.nz), a largely-flat 150km route – open to walkers, cyclists and horse-riders – from Clyde to Middlemarch and passing through all the main towns except for St Bathan's and Naseby. It follows the trackbed of the former Otago Central Branch railway line and includes modified rail bridges and viaducts (several spanning over 100m), beautiful valleys and long agricultural plains. At Middlemarch it meets the Taieri Gorge Railway (see p.728), though unless you arrive on Sunday (when there is a service to Middlemarch) you'll have to cycle along the road 18km to Pukerangi for the daily train.

Passenger trains ran through the Maniototo until 1990, but by the end of 1991 all the track had been pulled up. It wasn't until February 2000 that the trail opened, and since then its existence has galvanised a dying region. A few people walk or ride horses, but most cycle, and all sorts of accommodation has sprung up close to the trail to cater to bikers' needs. Pubs and cafés located where the trail crosses roads aren't shy to advertise the opportunity to take a break.

The route is fully outlined in the comprehensive and widely available *Otago Central Rail Trail* leaflet (free) with further context in Gerald Cunningham's *Guide to the Otago Central Rail Trail* (Reed Outdoors; $25).

The route is generally hard-packed earth and gravel making it possible to ride most bikes, though fat tyres make for a more comfortable ride. The whole trail takes most people three days, but if you're just out to pick the choicest bits (or are walking and don't fancy the whole thing) aim for a couple of 10km stretches, both with tunnels, viaducts and interesting rock formations: Lauder–Auripo in the northern section, and Daisybank–Hyde in the east. A torch is handy (though not essential) for the tunnels.

Bikes and customized packages with accommodation can be organised through various agencies. The best bets are: Cycle Surgery in Dunedin (see "Listings", p.727); Blind Billy's Holiday Camp in Middlemarch (see p.893; offering bikes at $30 a day and panniers $10 a day); Altitude Adventures in Alexandra (see p.887) and Kayak & Outdoor in Clyde (see p.886). If you don't fancy hauling a load, talk to Catch-a-Bus (☏03/479 9960) about having your bags transported to your next stop.

For more information peruse ⓦ www.otagorailtrail.co.nz and ⓦ www.railtrail.co.nz.

---

the easiest route from Dunedin to Alexandra chose a way up the Taieri Gorge and across the Maniototo. In 1898, the line arrived in **Ranfurly** which soon took over from Naseby as the area's main administrative centre, an honour held to this day even though the rails were pulled up in the early 1990s.

The main road through the region is SH85 from Alexandra to Palmerston, which is fast, largely straight and paved, and usually known as "**The Pigroot**"; it began life as the easiest route from the east coast to the Central Otago Goldfields. Scattered on the way are a handful of old gold-mining communities, among them **St Bathans**, **Naseby** and Ranfurly, each worth a brief visit for their laid-back atmosphere, calm seclusion and subtle reminders of how greed transforms the land. In between you'll see dozens of small cottages, many abandoned – a testament to the harsh life in these parts.

These days the highway also provides access to a rugged route further northeast to the Waitaki Valley (see p.707), via Dansey's Pass. The main public **transport** through these parts is the Catch-a-Bus service (☏03/479 9960; daily except Sat) between Dunedin and Wanaka which leaves Dunedin at 8am, arriving in Wanaka around noon and then setting back at 1pm. Visitors planning to use the Taieri gorge Railway (see p.728) may appreciate the Track & Trail buses (☏03/477 5577, ⓦ www.transportplace.co.nz) which meet the train and continue to Queenstown.

Omakau and Ophir

Heading northeast from Alexandra you are immediately in the high country plain, passing through inconsequential hamlets until you reach the twin settlements of Omakau and Ophir after 20km. **Omakau** is handily sited right beside the rail trail and is chiefly of interest for the *Commercial Hotel*, Main Road (ⓣ 03/447 3715, ⓔ omakaucommercial@xtra.co.nz; dorms 1x, rooms 3x), with campervan parking ($16 per site), en-suite rooms and a bar/restaurant serving decent and well-priced meals.

Omakau became the area's commercial hub with the arrival of the railway, but the original gold town hereabouts was **OPHIR**, 2km to the south. Make the brief detour to see the small but imposing 1886 **Post & Telegraph Office** which still handles the mail (Mon–Fri 9am–noon) and the nice little **suspension bridge** across the Manuherikia River, 1km further south. There's simple and welcoming **accommodation** here at the small but well-set-up *Ophir Lodge Backpackers*, 1 Macdonald St, Ophir (ⓣ 03/447 3339, ⓔ blgaler@xtra.co.nz; closed June–Aug; dorms 1x, rooms 2x), the local pub does weekend meals and you can get a coffee along the street at the *Old Bakery Café* on the main street.

St Bathans

The first place with genuine appeal is the minute former gold town of **ST BATHANS**, 80km north of Alexandra and accessed 17km along St Bathans Loop Road from Becks. St Bathans began life as a boom town called Dunstan Creek in 1863, following a gold strike at the foot of Mount St Bathans. Within six months two to three hundred miners were working the area, and the tent town comprised twenty stores and four pubs. The population peaked at 2000, but when the gold ran out in the 1930s everything went with it. These days it's virtually a ghost town with just seven permanent residents and an attractive straggle of ancient buildings strung in a crooked line along a single road. Some of the residents manage the atmospheric 1882 *Vulcan Hotel* (ⓣ & ⓕ 03/447 3629; singles $30, twins 3x, doubles 4x), where local farmers and visitors prop up the old wooden bar, which serves *St Bathans Gold*, a single malt bottled on the premises. With its garden bar across the road and cosy interior the pub makes a great place to stop for good lunches, espresso and full evening meals. There's also reasonable accommodation, though be warned that the place is haunted; doubters should book Room 1. The hotel also manages **accommodation** in cottages around town including the converted *Old Gaol* (5x) and the former *Constable's Cottage* ($220) which sleeps six.

Just up the street from the hotel, the former post office is once again performing that role as part of Despatches, as well as being a kind of mini-museum-cum-Victorian-**gift shop**.

The prettiest thing about the area is the striking **Blue Lake** right beside the town, where mineral-rich water has flooded a crater left by the merciless sluicing of Kildare Hill, which used to be 120m high until it was entirely washed away. A short track leads from the *Vulcan* to a vantage point over the intensely azure lake, now used for water-skiing, swimming and picnics.

Naseby

The small settlement of **NASEBY**, 25km east of St Bathans and 9km off SH85, clings to the Maniototo some 600m above sea level. At its 4000-strong peak in 1865, Naseby was the largest gold-mining town hereabouts, but today numbers have dropped to around 200 huddled in a collection of small houses (many of them originally built by miners from sun-dried mud brick), with a shop, a garage, a couple of pubs, a café, and a great campsite.

The town's story is told through two tiny museums, both at the junction of Earne Street and Leven Street. The **Maniototo Early Settlers Museum** (Nov–May Tues–Sun 1.30–3.30pm; $2) is packed with black-and-white photos of past residents' lives alongside a small collection of items left by Chinese miners, while the **Jubilee Museum** (daily 10am–5pm; $1 token available from the general store across the street) houses the remains of an old watchmaker's shop together with displays on the local gold rush of the 1860s and 1870s and the history of the town since then.

In summer, visitors are either cooling off at the shaded **swimming dam**, ten minutes' walk up Swimming Dam Road or exploring the surrounding **Naseby Forest**. Mostly larches, Douglas firs and pines, the forest harbours myriad trails that make it one of New Zealand's best destinations for single-track **mountain biking**. Entry is free and you can rent bikes from Naseby Mountain Bike Hire ($25 half day, $40 full day) who operate from the *Royal Hotel* (see below); they also do half-day guided bike trips around the forest ($100). They'll give you a map of the trails, which also highlights a number of pleasant forest **walks**. The best is the **One Tree Hill Track** (1.6km; 1hr return), which starts on Brooms Street in town and snakes uphill along the eastern side of Hogburn Gully, past dramatic honey-coloured cliffs entirely carved by water – a free sheet on the walk is available from the visitor centre.

The **Maniototo Ice Rink** (early June to mid-Aug; $12), a kilometre down Channel Road at the southern end of town, is New Zealand's home of the Scottish sport of **curling** (a sort of bowls on ice). Arm yourself with the *Spectators' Guide to Curling* leaflet, available free at the rink, or join in. Stone, broom and instruction will set you back $10 for two hours. By 2005 it is hoped that Naseby will be the proud owner of a new indoor, international-standard curling rink which may be opened up in summer.

Practicalities

Naseby's **visitor centre** (daily 11am–2pm; ☎03/444 9961) is in the former Post Office on Derwent Street. The town's range of **accommodation** is growing, the cheapest being the pretty and tranquil *Naseby Larchview Holiday Park* (☎03/444 9904, ⓦ www.nasebyholidaypark.co.nz; camping $10, cabins & vans 2x, tourist flats 3x), in the forest about five minutes' walk along Swimming Dam Road. In town, the *Ancient Briton* pub in Leven Street (☎03/444 9992; 3x–4x), has a number of neat, good-quality motel units, and rooms with access to a communal kitchen; and *The Royal Hotel*, 1 Earne St (☎03/444 9990; dorms 1x, rooms 2x) has bargain shared-bath doubles and twins. For comfortable if somewhat chintzy B&B visit *Monkey Puzzle House*, cnr Derwent & Oughter Sts (☎03/444 9985, ⓔmonkeypuzzle@xtra.co.nz; 5x); or head to

Dove Cote, 1 Channel Road (☎03/444 9260, ⓦwww.bedandbrekkie.co.nz; 4x) with continental breakfast served at the *Cottage Garden Café* (see below).

Eating means calling in for hearty meals at one of the two pubs or visiting *Cottage Garden Café*, on Derwent Street, for reasonable café meals, coffee and **Internet access**.

Dansey's Pass

The gravel Kyeburn Diggings Road, running east out of Naseby, continues as a narrow barren and beautiful route climbing northeast across the Kakanui Mountains via **Dansey's Pass** (about 40km from Naseby), to eventually emerge at Duntroon in the Waitaki Valley (see p.707). Though reasonably well maintained, the route is sometimes closed in summer and always marginal in winter, so check in Naseby before setting out. Old gold workings are visible from the roadside, where water-jets from sluices have distorted the schist and tussock landscape, leaving rock dramatically exposed.

At Kyeburn Diggings, 16km from Naseby, you'll come across the charming **Dansey's Pass Coach Inn** (☎03/444 9048, ⓦwww.danseyspass.co.nz; 6x), a comfortable lodge at the foot of the pass but in the middle of nowhere, built from local schist stone in 1862 and the only remnant of a 2000-strong gold-rush community. The stonemason was reputedly paid a pint of beer for each stone laid. The inn offers good beer, affordable lunches and fairly pricey dinners, as well as nicely modernized en-suite accommodation, which is booked up most weekends throughout the year. They also rent out mountain bikes ($10 per hour, $30 a half day), and in winter will take folk cross-country skiing up at the pass. There's **budget accommodation** at the far end of the route, about 15km north of the pass itself, at the excellent small and quiet *Dansey's Pass Holiday Park* (☎03/431 2564, ⓕ431 2560; camping $10, cabins 2x–3x), down by the riverside.

Ranfurly

Back on SH85 and 5km southeast of the Naseby turn-off lies the largest settlement on the Maniototo, **RANFURLY**. It is a compact place which is newly resurgent with the popularity of the rail trail and attempts to brand the place as New Zealand's **Rural Art Deco** centre. Apparently an arsonist torched many of the town's key buildings which were then replaced in the early 1930s in the prevailing Art Deco style. In truth, there's only a handful of noteworthy buildings, but Ranfurly has gone all out to make the best of what it has.

Almost everything happens on Charlemont Street East where the **former train station** contains the **visitor centre** (daily 10am–4pm; ☎03/444 9970, ⓦwww.maniototo.com), which has a free audio-visual show on the region and pictorial displays tracing the history of the town and the Otago Central Railway. Along the street at #1, the **Art Deco Exhibition** (daily: Nov–April 10.30am–4.30pm May–Oct 11am–4pm; $2 donation) contains all manner of Deco furnishings and houseware, but the star is the building itself, the 1948 Centennial Milk Bar. Opposite the visitor centre the *Ranfurly Lion Hotel* and the Ranfurly Auto Repairs shop both exhibit a few Deco features, but elsewhere much is achieved with imaginative paint jobs and period signage.

In summer, anyone with a 4WD or high-clearance vehicle can set out from Ranfurly to explore part of the magnificent **Old Dunstan Road** (often snow-bound May–Sept), the original route to the Central Otago goldfields across the Rock and Pillar and Lammerlaw ranges. The thought of gold prospectors guiding their horse-drawn drays and bullock wagons through this tough country for the sake of a dream fills you with admiration. From Ranfurly head 20km south to Patearoa and from there a further 25km to Paerau (aka Styx), where a 50km section of the Old Dunstan Road begins its gruelling journey to Clarks Junction and the easier SH87 heads towards Dunedin.

Practicalities

Ranfurly's range of **accommodation** is expanding and now includes several budget options. In town there's the *Ranfurly Motor Camp*, Reade Street (☏ & ☏03/444 9144; camping $10, cabins 2x), which has a covered swimming pool, and *Old Po Backpackers*, 11 Pery St (☏03/444 9588, ☺oldpobackpackers @hotmail.com; dorms 1x, rooms 2x), with bargain accommodation in made-up beds. The best of the local backpackers is *Peter's Farm Hostel* (☏03/444 9083 & 0800/472 458, ⓦwww.petersfarm.co.nz; camping $10, dorms 1x, rooms 2x), in a comfortable and very relaxing 1880 farmhouse 12km south of Ranfurly and 3km from the rail trail: call for pick-ups from both. With free use of bikes, kayaks, fishing rods and gold pans, several good walks, and breakfast ($5) and evening meals ($12–15) available it is a great place to take a break.

Back in town, the *Ranfurly Lion Hotel* (☏03/444 9140, ☺ranfurly.hotel@xtra.co.nz; dorms 1x, rooms 3x, ensuites 4x) has a range of rooms with free use of a spa pool; and there's the quiet *Ranfurly Motels*, 1 Davis Avenue, off Caulfield Street (☏ & ☏03/444 9383; 4x). For an extreme Deco experience, stay at *Moyola*, 38 Charlemont St E (☏03/444 9010, ☺edna@nzsouth.co.nz; 6x), a very comfortable B&B jam-packed with assorted Deco furniture and fittings.

The best **eating** in town is at the daytime BYO *E-Central Café*, 14 Charlemont St E, which does bikers' breakfasts, decent coffee and a range of light meals. Also try the *Highland Wine Bar*, 8 Charlemont St E, which dishes up some reasonably priced hearty staples and serves a much-needed drink.

Macraes Gold Mine, Middlemarch and SH85 to Dunedin

At Kyeburn, 15km east of Ranfurly, the slow **route to Dunedin** (SH87) branches south off SH85 and twists through the eastern Maniototo, a barren yet scenic landscape squeezed between the towering Rock and Pillar Range and the Taieri River. Fifty kilometres south of Kyeburn you'll reach the tiny community of **Middlemarch**, the Sunday-only terminus of the **Taieri Gorge Railway**, which makes a delightful two-hour run between here and Dunedin (see p.728 for details). Anyone planning to tackle the Otago Central Rail Trail from east to west should definitely consider starting by riding the railway either to Middlemarch or to **Pukerangi** (the weekday turn-around point), 18km to the south.

Either way you can **spend the night** in Middlemarch. Opposite the station, *Middlemarch Lodge & Backpackers*, 5 Snow Ave (☏03/464 3170, ☺middlemarchaccom@xtra.co.nz; bunks 1x, rooms 3x), a house converted into a combined hostel and lodge with polished wood floors, all beds made up, free continental breakfast and an attractive barbecue area. Most cyclists stay across the tracks at *Blind Billy's Holiday Camp*, Mold Street (☏03/464 3355, ⓦwww.railtrail.co.nz; camping $10, dorms 1x, vans 2x, cabins 3x, unit 4x), a campsite with cooking facilities in a converted railway carriage and a nice out-door seating area. There are also simple dorms, a couple of basic on-site vans, modern cabins, and a spacious two-bedroom motel unit. Alternatively, try the comfortable *Middlemarch B&B*, Swansea St/SH87 (☏03/464 3718, ⓦwww.middlemarch.co.nz; 3x) with its indoor spa area and optional breakfast ($5–8) and evening meal ($15).

Eating is limited to the daytime *Kissing Gate Café*, SH85 at the southern end of town, weekend meals at the *Strath Taieri Hotel*, opposite the station on Snow Ave, and takeaways.

The most renowned of Otago's operating gold mines, the huge opencast **Macraes Gold Mine**, lies on windswept hills between Ranfurly and Palmerston and can be visited on a two-hour tour (bookings essential on ☎0800/465 386; $15), which also takes in a historic reserve and a fully operational stamper battery. Should you want to **eat or stay** in the area, the ancient *Stanley's Hotel* (☎03/465 2400, ℱ465 2056; B&B 5x), a schist-stone construction, has a restaurant and bar, a few rooms with shared bathrooms, and a swimming pool.

Back on SH85 it's a further 14km from Dunback to Palmerston, where SH1 heads south to Dunedin and north towards Oamaru.

Southeast along SH8: Roxburgh and Lawrence

The fastest route from Alexandra to the coast is SH8, partly because there are few enticing stop-offs en route. The road follows the meandering course of the Clutha River, passing through rugged hill country between the Old Man and Lammerlaw ranges to the east, and the Knobby Blue Mountain range to the west. Along the way are a couple of mildly interesting gold towns, **Roxburgh** and **Lawrence**, both served by **buses** running between Queenstown or Alexandra and Dunedin InterCity, Atomic Shuttle, Catch-a-Bus and Wanaka Connexions.

Roxburgh

Thirteen kilometres south of Alexandra you pass through the **Fruitlands**, a tiny settlement where orchards were once planted in the hope that they'd flourish, only to fail and be replaced by livestock farming. The roadside *Fruitlands Gallery* (daily 10am–5pm), occupies a restored stone pub of 1866 and functions as a **café** exhibiting local arts and crafts. Close by, Symes Road runs 10km west into the hills to the 27-metre-tall **Old Man Rock**, an extraordinary stone obelisk from which the Old Man Range takes its name.

Some 15km further on, a **viewpoint** overlooks the large, concrete **Roxburgh Dam** and the shimmering turquoise of Lake Roxburgh, which backs up for over 30km. Eight kilometres south of the dam, the bland former gold town of **ROXBURGH** sits hemmed in by orchards, farmland and open-cast coal mines. Soon after the discovery of gold here in 1862, Roxburgh turned its attention to fruit growing. The vast orchards now yield bountiful crops of peaches, apricots, apples, raspberries and strawberries, all harvested by an annual influx of seasonal pickers; the season's surplus is sold from a phalanx of roadside stalls from early December through to May.

Should you need **to stay**, try the central *Villa Rose*, 79 Scotland St (☎03/446 8761, ℮remarkableorchards@xtra.co.nz; dorms 1x, rooms 2x), a backpackers equipped with dorms and several doubles, frequented by orchard workers; or *Lake Roxburgh Lodge*, SH8, 8km north (☎03/446 8220, ℗www.lakeroxburghlodge.co.nz; 5x), which offers wonderful en-suite motel-style rooms and a very good licensed **restaurant**.

Lawrence

From Roxburgh SH8 runs 32km south to **Raes Junction** (where SH90 spurs off southwest to Tapanui and Gore), and continues 26km to **LAWRENCE**, Otago's original gold town. It's hard to believe that this sleepy farming town,

THE GOLD COUNTRY | The Central Otago goldfields

with its population barely nudging 550, was once the scene of frenetic activity, as 12,000 gold-seekers scrambled to try their luck in the gold-rich Gabriel's Gully, discovered by Gabriel Read on May 23, 1861 (see below). This short-lived boom (it was over in barely a year) is recalled in a smattering of Victorian buildings, hastily constructed in a variety of materials and styles. A few have now been converted into chi-chi **galleries** that provide some reason to linger.

The combined **visitor centre** and **Goldfields Museum** on Ross Place/SH8 (Mon–Fri 9.30am–5pm, Sat & Sun 10am–4pm ☎03/485 9222) brings something of those heady days to life through imaginative displays and rents out gold pans ($5 per day). From here, a 3.5km drive along Gabriel's Gully Road passes the **Pick and Shovel Monument** commemorating the pioneer miners, en route to **Gabriel's Gully Goldfield Park**, where a series of plaques explaining the old workings should take you an hour or so to explore. A climb up the steep rise of **Jacob's Ladder** gives a good view of the gully, long since filled with tailings that reach nearly 20m in depth. It is possible to visit Gabriel's Gully as part of a loop walk from town (8.5km loop; 2.5hr) returning along a ridge.

After something to **eat** from one of the tearooms on Ross Place, or from the smart *Jazzed on Java* café, at #26, you'll probably want to press on. If you decide **to stay**, try the pleasant *Oban House Backpackers*, 1 Oban St (☎03/485 9259, ⓔobanhouse@xtra.co.nz; dorms 1x, rooms 2x), set in a big old house; or the fairly basic, creekside *Goldpark Motor Camp*, 1km south of the main road on Harrington Street (☎03/485 9850, ⓔsouthenrshearing@xtra.co.nz; camping $7, cabins 2x). *The Ark*, 8 Harrington Place (☎03/485 9328, ⓦwww .thearknz.homestead.com; 3x) offers B&B in a fine old home with beautiful gardens.

From Lawrence it's another 33km southeast to the junction with SH1 on the east coast, which strikes north towards Dunedin or south to Balclutha (see p.739).

Travel details

Queenstown is very much the region's hub with buses fanning out to Christchurch, Dunedin, Franz Josef Glacier, Milford Sound, Te Anau and Wanaka. Its airport is equally pivotal, though Air New Zealand has recently started flying into Wanaka.

Buses

The following lists the direct scheduled bus services in summer and doesn't include the scores of tour buses which ply the Queenstown to Milford Sound route daily – see p.916 for details of these. In winter services are cut back considerably.

From Alexandra to: Dunedin (4–5 daily; 3hr); Lawrence (4–5 daily; 1hr 15min); Ranfurly (daily except Sat; 1hr); Queenstown (4–5 daily; 1hr 30min).

From Arrowtown to: Queenstown (5–7 daily; 30min).

From Lawrence to: Alexandra (4–5 daily; 1hr 15min); Cromwell (4–5 daily; 2hr); Dunedin (4–5 daily; 1hr 30min).

From Cromwell to: Alexandra (4–5 daily; 30min); Dunedin (4–5 daily; 3hr 15min); Lawrence (4–5 daily; 2hr); Queenstown (7–9 daily; 1hr); Wanaka (4 daily; 45–60min).

From Glenorchy to: Queenstown (4 daily; 1hr).

From Queenstown to: Alexandra (4–5 daily; 1hr 30min); Aoraki Mount Cook (1 daily; 4hr); Arrowtown (5–7 daily; 30min); Christchurch (6–7 daily; 7hr–9hr); Cromwell (7–9 daily; 1hr); Dunedin (4–5 daily; 4–5hr); Franz Josef Glacier (2 daily; 8hr); Glenorchy (4 daily; 1hr); Greymouth (1 daily; 10hr 15min); Invercargill (2 daily; 3–4hr); Kingston (1 daily; 1hr); Milford Sound (2 daily; 5hr 15min); Te Anau (2 daily; 2hr 15min); Wanaka (4 daily; 1hr 45min).

From Wanaka to: Christchurch (2–5 daily; 6hr 20min–9hr); Cromwell (4 daily; 45min–1hr); Dunedin (2 daily; 4hr); Invercargill (1 daily; 4hr 15min); Queenstown (4 daily; 1hr 45min); Ranfurly (daily except Sat; 3hr).

Flights

Apart from scheduled services to the South Island's main centres, most flights are geared towards the lucrative Milford Sound market (see p.916), with half a dozen fiercely competitive companies flying out of Wanaka and Queenstown daily. Below we have only listed direct flights.

From Queenstown to: Auckland (3–5 daily; 1hr 45min); Christchurch (7–10 daily; 1hr); Milford Sound (5 daily; 35min); Te Anau (3 daily; 30min); Wanaka (3 daily; 20min).

From Wanaka to: Christchurch (1 daily; 1hr); Queenstown (3 daily; 20min).

Fiordland

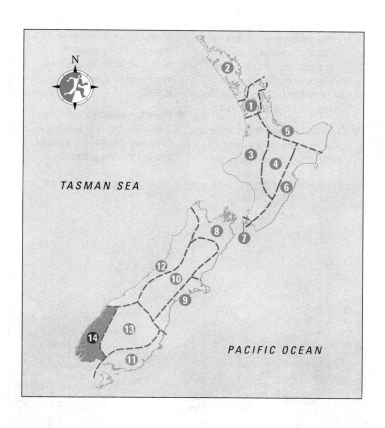

CHAPTER 14

Highlights

* **The Milford Track** Put up with the sandflies to find out why this beautiful tramp is New Zealanders' favourite. See p.920

* **Milford Sound** In a country full of scenic splendour, Milford Sound is hard to beat. A day-cruise is great, but for a little more solitude go overnight, or even dive into the dark water to see creatures normally living at much greater depths. See p.914

* **Doubtful Sound** Experience grandeur almost on a par with Milford Sound but with-out the bustle, all even better when seen from a kayak. See p.927

* **Hump Ridge and Waitutu Tracks** Explore this relatively little visited area on some fine tramping tracks in this historic logging area centred on the huge Percy Burn Viaduct. Combine it with excellent jetboating on the Wairaurahiri River. See p.932

* **Riverton** Learn to flax weave and carve bone in laid-back Riverton, the Paua capital of the world. See p.933

△ Kayaking, Milford Sound

14

Fiordland

For all New Zealand's scenic grandeur, no single region quite matches the concentration of stupendous landscapes found in its southwestern corner. Almost the entirety of **Fiordland** falls within the generous boundaries of the Fiordland National Park, a land of superlatives, boasting New Zealand's two deepest lakes, its highest rainfall and some of the world's rarest birds. This hasn't gone unnoticed at the United Nations, which has gathered pretty much the whole region – along with the Mount Aspiring National Park and parts of south Westland and the Aoraki Mount Cook area – into the **Te Wahipounamu World Heritage Area**.

The **Fiordland National Park**, New Zealand's largest, stretches from Martins Bay, once the site of New Zealand's remotest settlement, to the southern forests of Waitutu and Preservation Inlet where early gold prospectors set up a couple of short-lived towns. The 12,500 square kilometres of the park embraces a raw and heroic landscape with deep, icy and mountain-fringed lakes in the east and a western coastline of fifteen hairline fiords gouged out over the last two million years by glaciers creaking off the tail of the Southern Alps.

Maori legend tells how the **fiords** were formed at the hands of the great god Tu-to-Rakiwhanoa (see box on p.901), while scientific explanations point to a complex underlying geology, which evolved over the last 500 million years. When thick layers of seabed sediment were compressed and heated deep within the earth's crust, hard crystalline granite, gneiss and schist were formed. As the land and sea levels rose and fell, layers of softer sandstone and limestone were overlaid; during glacial periods, great ice sheets deepened the valleys and flattened their bases to create the classic U-shape, invaded by the sea lapping at their mouths.

After a few days in the inhospitable conditions created by Fiordland's copious rainfall and pestilent **sandflies** (*namu*), you'll appreciate why there is little evidence of permanent Maori settlement in these parts, though they certainly spent summers hunting here and passed through in search of greenstone (*pounamu*). **Cook** was equally suspicious of Fiordland when, in 1770, he sailed up the coast on his first voyage to New Zealand: anchorages were hard to come by; the glowering sky put him off entering Dusky Sound; slight, shifting winds hardly encouraged entry into what he dubbed Doubtful Harbour; and, uncharacteristically, he missed Milford Sound altogether.

Paradoxically, for a region that's now the preserve of hardy trampers and a few anglers, the southern fiords region was once the best-charted in the country. Cook returned in 1773, after four months battling the southern oceans, and spent five weeks in Dusky Sound. His midshipman, George Vancouver, returned in 1791, with the first bloodthirsty sealers and whalers hot on his heels. Over the mountains, **Europeans** seized, or paid a pittance for, land on

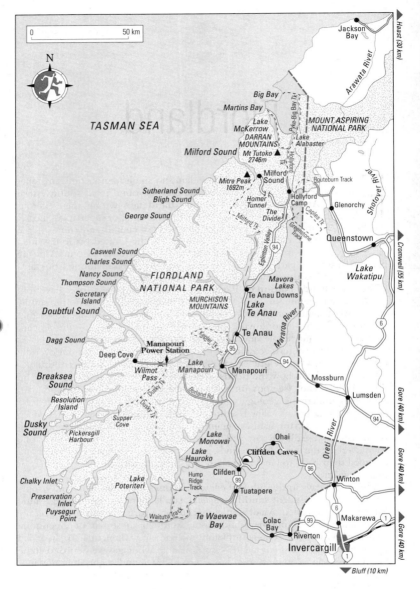

the eastern shores of Lake Te Anau and Manapouri for the meagre grazing it offered, while **explorers** headed for the interior. More egotistical than their seafaring kin, they conferred their own names on the passes, waterfalls and valleys they came across – Donald Sutherland lent his name to New Zealand's highest waterfall and Quentin McKinnon scaled the Mackinnon Pass (but failed to persuade cartographers to spell his name correctly).

One feature of Fiordland you can't miss is the **rain**: the region is sodden for much of the year. Milford Sound is particularly favoured, being deluged with up to seven metres of rainfall a year – the second-highest in the world (after the mountains of Tahiti). Fortunately the area's settlements are in a relative rain shadow and receive less than half the precipitation of the coast. Despite its frequent soakings, **Milford Sound** sees the greatest concentration of traveller activity, its skies alive with planes and choppers through most of the day. However, the Sound is still quite beautiful particularly when it's raining, with ribbons of water plunging from hanging valleys directly into the fiords – where colonies of red and black coral grow and dolphins, fur seals and Fiordland crested penguins gambol. Many visitors on a flying visit from Queenstown see little else of Fiordland, but a greater sense of remoteness is gained by driving along the dramatically scenic **Milford Road** between the sound and the lakeside town of **Te Anau**. Better still, trudge here along the **Milford Track**, widely promoted as the "finest walk in the world", though others in the region – the **Hollyford Track**, the **Kepler Track** and the **Dusky Track** – shouldn't be overlooked. A second lakeside town, **Manapouri**, is the springboard for trips to the West Arm hydroelectric power station, **Doubtful Sound** and the isolated fiords to the south. From Manapouri, the Southern Scenic Route winds through the western quarter of Southland through minor towns along the southwestern coast of the South Island.

Almost all **buses** in Fiordland ply the corridor from Queenstown through Te Anau to Milford Sound: most are tour buses (in various guises), stopping at scenic spots and regaling passengers with a jocular commentary, but others are scheduled services that disgorge trampers at the **trailheads**. Elsewhere, services are skeletal. Drivers are well disposed to giving **lifts**, though the Milford Road from Te Anau to Milford Sound is notoriously fallow ground for hitchers and, bearing in mind the number of diversions along the way, teaming up with like-minded souls and renting a car for the day, or joining a tour bus, is a much better bet. The only **flights** you are likely to take are the scenic jaunts from Milford Sound to Te Anau or Queenstown, although others do exist.

Tu-to-Rakiwhanoa and Te Namu

Fiordland came into being when the great god **Tu-to-Rakiwhanoa** worked with his axe to carve the rough gashes of the southern fiords around Preservation Inlet and Dusky Sound, leaving Resolution and Secretary islands where his feet stood. His technique improved further north, where he formed the more sharply defined lines of Nancy Sound, Caswell Sound and, the most famous of all, Milford Sound (Piopiotahi), the acme of Tu's skill.

After creating this spectacular landscape, Tu was visited by Te-Hine-nui-to-po, the goddess of death, who feared that the vision created by Tu was so wonderful that people may wish to live in Piopiotahi forever. To remind humans of their mortality, she liberated *namu*, or **sandflies**. The place of this liberation, Te Namu-a-Te-Hine-nui-te-po, at the end of the Milford Track, is now known as Sandfly Point. And the pesky critters have certainly had the desired effect. In 1773, when James Cook entered Dusky Sound, he was already familiar with the sandfly:

The most mischievous animal here is the small black sandfly which are exceedingly numerous and are so troublesome that they exceed everything of the kind I ever met with, wherever they light they cause swelling and such an intolerable itching that it is not possible to refrain from scratching and at last ends in ulcers like the small Pox. The almost continual rain may be reckoned another inconvenience attending this Bay.

Te Anau

The growing town of **TE ANAU** (pronounced Teh AHN-ow) straggles along the shores of its eponymous lake, one of New Zealand's deepest and most beautiful. To the west, the lake's watery fingers claw deep into bush-cloaked mountains so remote that their most celebrated inhabitant, the takahe (see box on p.905), was thought extinct for half a century. Civilization of sorts can be found on the lake's eastern side, where Te Anau has set itself up in recent years as a viable alternative to Queenstown, a major way station on the route to Milford Sound, and as a base and recuperation spot for the numerous tramps, including several of the most famous and worthwhile in the country. Top of most people's list is the **Milford Track**, which is reached across the lake from here, as is the newer **Kepler Track**, while the **Dusky Track**, accessible from Lake Hauroko, covers part of Lake Manapouri and ends at Supper Cove on the shores of Dusky Sound. To the north, the Milford Road passes The Divide, the western end of the Routeburn, Greenstone and Caples tracks (see pp.861–862), beyond that there's the Hollyford Valley and its tramp to the Tasman Sea, and at the southeastern end of the national park is the new, privately run Hump Ridge Track.

Arrival, information and transport

Buses either drop off around town or stop on the town's main shopping and restaurant street, known as Town Centre. The best sources of information are the **visitor centre**, at the junction of Town Centre and Lake Front Drive (daily 8.30am–5.30pm, later in summer; ☏03/249 8900, ⊛ www.fiordland.org.nz), and DOC's **Fiordland National Park visitor centre**, 500m south along Lake Front Drive (daily: late Dec–Jan 8am–8pm, Oct–late Dec Feb & March 8.30am–6pm, April–Sept 8.30am–4.30pm, ⊛ fiordlandvc@doc.govt.nz). The latter has a **Great Walks Booking Desk** (Nov–April daily 8.30am–5pm; May–Oct Mon–Fri 9am–noon & 1–4.30pm ☏03/249 8514, ⊛ greatwalksbooking@doc.govt.nz), as well as plenty of general information. From here, DOC run an excellent summer visitor programme of hour-long evening talks (throughout Jan; $3) plus full-day, unhurried conservation-themed trips in the forests ($70–82), all of which need to be booked in advance.

The **post office** and **banks** with 24hr ATMs are all found along Town Centre. While away on the tracks, trampers can usually **store gear** (free or for a small fee) at their accommodation, though it helps if you're staying with them on your return. Tramping **gear rental** is available from Bev's Tramping Gear Hire, 16 Homer St (☏03/249 7389, ⊛ www.ubd.co.nz/bevs.hire). Individual items are charged by the day, or you can save a few dollars with the Great Walks Package Special ($100) – containing all you need except boots and food for up to four days.

Local transport

Getting around Te Anau is no problem: everywhere in town is easily walkable, and there's a plethora of transport to the various trailheads. If you yearn for pedals, **bikes** can often be rented from most backpackers and from Fiordland Mini Golf & Bike Hire, 7 Mokonui St (☏03/249 7211; around $20 half day, $25 per day), whose tandems ($10 an hour) make exploring fun. For ranging slightly further afield, Scenic Shuttle (☏0800/277 483) run to Manapouri in the morning, and Tracknet (☏0800/483 628, ⊛ www.tracknet.net) run fairly frequent buses to Milford Sound, Queenstown and the Kepler and Routeburn

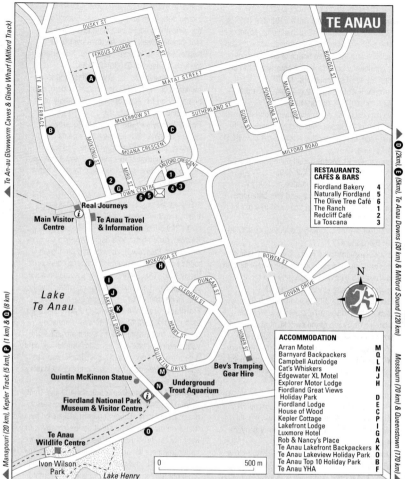

To An-au Glowworm Caves & Glade Wharf (Milford Track)

Manapouri (20 km), Kepler Track (5 km), P (1 km) & Q (8 km)

D (2km), **E** (5km), Te Anau Downs (30 km) & Milford Sound (120 km)

Mossburn (70 km) & Queenstown (170 km)

RESTAURANTS, CAFÉS & BARS

Fiordland Bakery	4
Naturally Fiordland	5
The Olive Tree Café	6
The Ranch	1
Redcliff Café	2
La Toscana	3

Lake
Te Anau

ACCOMMODATION

Arran Motel	M
Barnyard Backpackers	Q
Campbell Autolodge	L
Cat's Whiskers	N
Edgewater XL Motel	J
Explorer Motor Lodge	H
Fiordland Great Views	
Holiday Park	D
Fiordland Lodge	E
House of Wood	C
Kepler Cottage	P
Lakefront Lodge	I
Luxmore Hotel	G
Rob & Nancy's Place	A
Te Anau Lakefront Backpackers	K
Te Anau Lakeview Holiday Park	O
Te Anau Top 10 Holiday Park	B
Te Anau YHA	F

Real Journeys
Main Visitor Centre
Te Anau Travel & Information

Quintin McKinnon Statue
Bev's Tramping Gear Hire
Underground Trout Aquarium
Fiordland National Park Museum & Visitor Centre
Te Anau Wildlife Centre
Ivon Wilson Park
Lake Henry

0 ____ 500 m

N

14

FIORDLAND | Te Anau

---

trailheads. Taking an organized trip is generally cheaper, but you can rent a **car** for $90–100 a day from either First Choice (☎03/249 7140), or Hertz (☎03/249 7516) at Te Anau Travel and Information on Lake Front Drive, diagonally opposite the visitor centre.

Accommodation

Good motels string the length of Lake Front Drive and Quintin Drive a block back. There are also a number of reasonable budget options and plenty of good B&Bs. At motels, hotels and some B&Bs, **rates** tend to drop dramatically between June and August, and may be negotiable in the shoulder seasons (mid-April to May & Sept).

Hotels and motels

Arran Motel 64 Quintin Drive ☎03/249 8826 & 0800/666 911, ✉arran@teanau.co.nz. Motel cum B&B with attractive en-suite rooms, some cooking facilities and the added bonus of either a cooked or continental breakfast, plus courtesy car to and from the local transport options. ❺

Campbell Autolodge 42–44 Lake Front Drive ☎03/249 7546 & 0800/249 942, ⓦwww.cal.co.nz. Attractive place with lake views and flower-bedecked one-bedroom units, each with bath, shower and full kitchen, microwave, TV and phone. ❻

Edgewater XL Motel 52 Lake Front Drive ☎03/249 7258 & 0800/433 439, ✉edgewater.xl.motels@xtra.co.nz. Fairly basic waterfront motel with one- and two-bedroom units, full kitchen, TV, barbecue and free use of canoes. ❺

Explorer Motor Lodge 6 Cleddau St ☎03/249 7156 & 0800/477 877, ⓦwww.explorerlodge.co.nz. These spacious studios and one-bedroom units come complete with microwaves. The decor is slightly faded and quirky, with walls at weird angles. ❺

Fiordland Lodge 472 Te Anau-Milford Highway, 5km north ☎03/249 7832, ⓦwww.fiordlandlodge.co.nz. Some of the swankiest accommodation around set on a hill with great lake views. Lodge suites ($620–780) are spacious and very comfortable, and there are some self-contained cabins sleeping up to five. Great off-peak savings. Cabins ❽, suites ❾

Lakefront Lodge 58 Lake Front Drive ☎03/249 7728 & 0800/525 337, ⓦwww.lakefrontlodgeteanau.com. Modern, luxurious motel units, some with spa bath and all with every convenience. ❻

Luxmore Hotel Town Centre ☎03/249 7526 & 0800/589 667, ⓦwww.luxmorehotel.co.nz. Big, posh central hotel that deals with lots of the more expensive coach tours and offers standard and (newer) superior doubles and twins with ensuites and all the usual paraphernalia, as well as a variety of eating options. ❻–❼

B&Bs and homestays

Cat's Whiskers 2 Lake Front Drive ☎03/249 8112, ⓦwww.catswhiskers.co.nz. Excellent and very welcoming lakeside guesthouse with four pleasantly decorated en-suite rooms: one with a bath, and all with TV and full cooked breakfast. ❻

House of Wood 44 Moana Crescent ☎03/249 8404, ✉housefowood@xtra.co.nz. Four tastefully decorated, modern rooms, two with bathroom,

make up this fine homestay, which takes its design cues from an alpine chalet. Guests share the welcoming hosts' cosy lounge and it is only two minutes' walk from the town centre. ❺

Kepler Cottage William Steven Rd, 2km south towards Manapouri ☎03/249 7185, ✉kepler@teanau.co.nz, ⓦwww.fiordlandaccommodation.co.nz. A very comfortable modern, rural homestay on the edge of town, with plenty of space and friendly hosts. ❻

Rob & Nancy's Place 13 Fergus Square ☎03/249 8241, ✉rob.nancy@xtra.co.nz. Pleasant, peaceful homestay rooms and a self-contained apartment five minutes' walk from town. Cooked breakfast is accompanied by fresh home-made bread. ❻

Hostels and campsites

Barnyard Backpackers 80 Mount York Rd, ☎03/249 8006, ✉rainbowdowns@xtra.co.nz. Relaxed, rural hostel on a deer farm 9km south of Te Anau at Rainbow Reach, centred on a lovely lodge hand-built from natural timbers. There are lovely, long views, four-shares and some en-suite units, plus horse trekking along the Waiau River. Shares ❶, rooms ❷

Fiordland Great Views Holiday Park Milford Rd, 2km north ☎03/249 7059, ⓦwww.fiordlandgreatviewsholidaypark.co.nz. Small attractive site with a range of well-priced cabins and tourist flats. A courtesy bus does daily Kepler Track drop-offs and there's free gear storage. Camping $9, cabins ❷, flats ❸

Te Anau Lakefront Backpackers 48 Lake Front Drive ☎03/249 7713, ⓦwww.teanaubackpackers.co.nz. Slightly shabby former motel saved by a friendly atmosphere and small dorms, mostly with their own bathroom and kitchen. They're well set up for trampers, being five minutes' walk from the DOC office and offering free gear storage and with a big hot tub for when you get back. Bike rental for $25 a day. Dorms ❶, rooms ❸

Te Anau Lakeview Holiday Park 1 Manapouri Rd, 1km south ☎03/249 7457, ⓦwww.teanau.info. Te Anau's largest site, with spacious camping areas, dorms, a range of cabins and units and a sauna ($8 for 1hr). Camping $12, dorms ❶, cabins ❷–❸, tourist flats ❹, motel units ❺

Te Anau Top 10 Holiday Park 128 Te Anau Terrace ☎03/249 7462 & 0800/249 746, ⓦwww.teanautop10.co.nz. Central, cramped campsite that's mostly in demand for its fine on-site accommodation and abundant facilities. Camping $13.50, cabins ❸, units ❹, motels ❻

Te Anau YHA 29 Mokonui St ℡03/249 7847, @ yha.teanau@yha.org.nz. Modern, comfortable two-storey hostel close to the town centre with large dorms, double rooms (including en suites), free gear storage, helpful and informative staff, separate TV lounge, and barbecue area. Dorms **①**, rooms **③**

Sights and activities

There is little in Te Anau itself to distract you from simply admiring the scenery across the lake and taking gentle strolls along its shore. Ten minutes' walk south, a statue of Milford Track explorer Quintin McKinnon heralds the Fiordland National Park Visitors Centre (see p.902), where a short video (20min; $3) introduces the **Fiordland National Park Museum** inside the centre (same hours; free), with its fascinating displays on the construction of the Homer Tunnel and the undersea life of the national park, including an eighteenth-century cannon salvaged from Dusky Sound.

Across the road you can drop $1 in a turnstile to view the dismal tank of fish which masquerades as the **Underground Trout Aquarium**, or stroll on to

---

The takahe

For half a century the flightless blue-green **takahe** (*Notornis mantelli*) was thought to be extinct. These plump, turkey-like birds – close relatives of the ubiquitous pukeko – were once common throughout New Zealand. By the time Maori arrived, however, their territory had become restricted to the southern extremities of the South Island. When Europeans came, only a few were spotted by early settlers in Fiordland. No sightings were recorded after 1898; the few trampers and ornithologists who claimed to have seen its tracks or heard the takahe's call in remote Fiordland valleys were dismissed as cranks.

One keen birder, **Geoffrey Orbell**, pieced together the sketchy evidence and concentrated his search on the 500 square kilometres of the **Murchison Mountains**, a virtual island surrounded on three sides by the western arms of Lake Te Anau and on the fourth by the Main Divide. In 1948, he was rewarded with the first takahe sighting in fifty years. However, the few remaining birds seemed doomed: deer were merrily chomping their way through the grasses on which the takahe relied. Culling of the deer population averted the immediate crisis and, despite periodic setbacks from harsh winters, management programmes have brought takahe numbers to about 250.

Meanwhile, studies at the **Burwood Bush** rearing facility (closed to the public), in the Red Tussock Conservation Area east of Te Anau, have shown that takahe often lay three eggs but seldom manage to raise more than one chick. DOC officers now enter the Murchison Mountains each November to manipulate the **egg quota** so that each pair has only one viable egg to hatch. Any "surplus" eggs are removed to Burwood Bush, where rearing techniques pioneered here and at the **Te Anau Wildlife Centre** (see p.906) are employed to raise takahe for release back into the wild. Taped takahe noises encourage the chicks to hatch; then, to prevent them imprinting on their carers, the chicks are fed using **hand puppets** designed to look like adult takahe. And to help them hold their own against marauding stoats, young birds have their defensive instincts reawoken by watching DOC "Punch and Judy" shows, featuring stuffed stoats and juvenile takahe glove puppets.

Fear of having all their eggs in one basket has prompted DOC to establish several takahe populations on predator-free **sanctuary islands** – Maud Island in the Marlborough Sounds, Mana Island and Kapiti Island (both northwest of Wellington), and Tiritiri Matangi in Auckland's Hauraki Gulf – where the birds appear to be breeding well.

FIORDLAND | Te Anau

the **Lake Henry Walk** in the Ivon Wilson Park planted with native and exotic trees (about 20min circular walk). Once back at the visitor centre head a kilometre or so along the Te Anau lakeside path to the DOC's **Te Anau Wildlife Centre**, 178 Manapouri Rd (unrestricted entry; $1 donation box), where you can amble through the park-like setting and see parakeets, morepork and other bush birds, notably the takahe in specially constructed enclosures (see box on p.905 for more on the centre's ground-breaking work).

Te Anau's main paying attraction is Real Journeys' **Te Anau Glowworm Caves** (guided tours only: Oct to mid-May daily 8.15pm; mid-May to Sept 2pm, 5pm & 6.45pm; around 2hr 30min; $46), though its main appeal lies in its ability to occupy long evenings in Te Anau stopping you spending all your cash in the local bars. It has been spruced up a little but remains Victorian in spirit with a short underground boat ride, a glowworm grotto and a couple of nice waterfalls. Access is by a thirty-minute boat trip across to the western side of Lake Te Anau where you are herded into a visitor centre and taken through the caves in small groups on foot and by punt, spending thirty minutes in a 200-metre length of the Aurora cave system which tunnels under the Murchison Mountains.

Alternatives include a one-hour **jetboat ride** past *Lord of the Rings* locations on the placid Waiau River with Luxmore Jet (T0800/253 826, W www .luxmorejet.co.nz), and **quad-biking** with Highride Four Wheeler Adventures (T03/249 8591, W www.highride.co.nz) who offer a three-hour ride ($120, including the shuttle from Te Anau) that takes in the high backcountry and includes some stunning views of lakes Manapouri and Te Anau. No prior experience is necessary. They also have **horse riding** ($70), again taking around three hours.

Day walks from Te Anau

If you're kicking around Te Anau wondering what to do before your big tramp, consider some short walks as training. If you're not doing the Milford Track, it may even be worth joining one of the one-day guided walks at it southern end, though you can find better walks along the Milford Road (see box, p.913).

DOC visitor centre to Control Gates (4km one way; 50min; flat). Easy lakeside walk past the Te Anau Wildlife Centre to the point where the Waiau River leaves Lake Te Anau for Lake Manapouri. The control gates mark the start of the Kepler Track (see p.907).

Control Gates to Brod Bay (5km one way; 1hr 30min; gently undulating). The first section of the Kepler Track goes easily to Dock Bay (30min) where there's good swimming, and continues through mountain and silver beech forest past some limestone bluffs to the campsite at Brod Bay.

Control Gates to Rainbow Reach (9.5km one way; 2hr 30–3hr 30; mostly flat). Easy walking following the course of the Waiau River through red and mountain beech. By using the Tracknet buses to the control gates and back from Rainbow Reach (see "Kepler Track" account, p.909) you can spin this walk out over 5–7 hours, going perhaps 3km beyond Rainbow Reach to a wetland viewing platform.

Milford Track Real Journeys (T0800/656 501) and Trips 'n' Tramps (T03/249 7081) jointly run easy day-walks (Nov–March daily 9.15am; $125) beside the Clinton River at the start of the Milford Track. Trips involve a bus to Te Anau Downs, boat to Glade Wharf, 5–6 hours hiking and relaxing including lunch at Clinton Hut and return.

Lake cruises

Having exhausted the possibilities on shore, it pays to get **cruising** on the lake. If you're going tramping, this can best be accomplished en route to the start of the Kepler or Milford tracks (see p.907 & p.920). The operators who provide trailhead transport also provide a number of other trips.

Fiordland Wilderness Experiences ☎03/249 7700 & 0800/200 434, ⊛www.fiordlandseakayak.co.nz. These are the guys to see about paddling on Doubtful and Milford sounds, but they can get you kayaking on Te Anau or Manapouri either independently ($50 a day) or on one-day or overnight guided trips ($100 a day): stunning scenery at an easily attainable level.

Flights

Air Fiordland ☎03/249 7505, ⊛www.airfiordland.com. This company's wheeled planes are mostly used on flights to Milford Sound, the best deal involving a flight over the Milford Track to Milford Sound, a cruise and a bus back (6hr; $290).

Southern Lakes Helicopters Lake Front Drive ☎03/249 7167 & 0508/249 7167, ⊛www.southernlakeshelicopters.co.nz. Helicopter flights from a waterside helipad start at $120 for ten minutes and range up to a couple of hours including flights to Milford, Doubtful and Dusky sounds with landings in a narrow canyon known as Campbell's Kingdom or on snow high in the hills.

Sinbad Cruises ☎03/249 7106, ⊛www.sinbadcruises.co.nz. Murray – a chatty, knowledgeable lake-version of the typical Kiwi bushman – captains the hand-built gaff ketch *Manuska* doing the usual runs to the trailheads for the Milford ($68) and Kepler ($20) tracks, scenic cruises of the lake ($50), overnight specials ($60) and *Mount Luxmoore Hut* day walks on the Kepler ($35).

They also do various flight/walk/cruise combinations and do drop-offs for the tracks.
Wings & Water Lake Front Drive ☎03/249 7405, ©wingsandwater@teanau.co.nz. Float-plane flights that are ideal for an aerial view of southern Fiordland or a quick route to the track trailheads. They also do local loops (10min; $65), Kepler Track overflights (20min; $125), Doubtful Sound overflights (40min; $225), Milford Sound overflights (1hr; $320), and run into Supper Cove on Dusky Sound. One worthwhile combo involves jetboating down the Waiau River to Lake Manapouri and then flying back to Te Anau via the hidden lakes (1hr; $180).

Eating and drinking

Diners have little culinary genius to look forward to in Te Anau, though there are plenty of decent cafés and **no-frills places** selling modest food at reasonable prices. The **drinking** picture is much the same, and entertainment is mostly BYO.

Fiordland Bakery Town Centre, adjacent to *La Toscana*. Produces some excellent Trampers Bread for the tracks (lasting 3–4 days), particularly the four-grain. The daytime bakery café also offers a generous all-day breakfast (around $8). Closed Sun in winter.
Naturally Fiordland Town Centre. Relaxing bareboards café serving good coffee, delicious sandwiches and cakes at modest prices, and also has Internet access.
The Olive Tree Café Jailhouse Mall, 52 Town Centre. Licensed and open all day, this stylish café is one of the top spots to stop at. They produce some rich and delicious Mediterranean mains, a lovely green chicken curry, excellent pizza and pasta dishes and tasty brunches, as well as eye-opening coffee and sticky homemade cakes.
The Ranch Milford Rd. Rumbustious locals' haunt with bog-standard, but plentiful and cheap, Kiwi

grub and drinks deals, it also has its own local, music-only radio station, and offers lively DJ-run entertainment most nights and sometimes a band at weekends in summer.
Redcliff Café 12 Mokonui St ☎03/249 7431. Probably the best spot in town, good for an early evening sundowner or a late night tipple, but primarily a casual restaurant serving a range of modern Kiwi dishes in quantities to satisfy trampers' appetites. Expect the likes of rosemary chicken pasta ($20), mushroom crusted rack of lamb ($32), green Thai fish curry ($23) and white chocolate and passionfruit crème brûlée ($10). There's also a garden bar and occasional live bands.
La Toscana 108 Town Centre. Reasonable Italian restaurant that tries hard to please with a wide range of good pizza and pasta dishes. Licensed & BYO for wine only, plus takeaway.

The Kepler Track

The **Kepler Track** (60km; 3–4 days), finished in 1988, was intended to take some of the load off the Milford and Routeburn tracks and its success has now made it almost equally popular. Tracing a wide loop through the Kepler Mountains on the western side of Lake Te Anau, the track takes in one full day of exposed sub-alpine ridge walking and some lovely virgin beech forest, and has the added advantage of being easily accessible (on foot if you are keen) from Te Anau. The track is typically walked anti-clockwise. Throughout its length it is well graded and maintained but the long haul up to *Luxmoore Hut* makes this a strenuous tramp, and sections can be closed after snowfalls. DOC's *Kepler Track Independent Tramping* leaflet (free) is adequate, but for more detailed information, consult the 1:50,000 *Kepler Track Trackmap*.

Access and accommodation

The Kepler Track is one of New Zealand's Great Walks and through the summer season (Nov–April) its three main **huts** ($25, or $63 for 3 nights if pre-booked at the DOC centre, $50 per night if purchased on the track) – Luxmoore (50 bunks), Iris Burn (50 bunks) and Moturau (40 bunks) – all come with a warden, gas rings and flush toilets. You don't need to book specific nights in particular huts, but a Great Walks hut **pass** for the required number of nights must be bought in advance either online at ⓦ www.doc.govt.nz or through the Great Walks Booking Desks in Te Anau, Glenorchy or Queenstown. During the winter, these huts lose their warden and their gas rings and revert to serviced hut status ($10). Trampers are discouraged from using the simple and very small *Shallow Bay Hut* ($5), just off the track beside Lake Manapouri.

Camping ($12) is permitted at only two places, Brod Bay and Iris Burn, making for one very short and two very long days – assuming you walk the

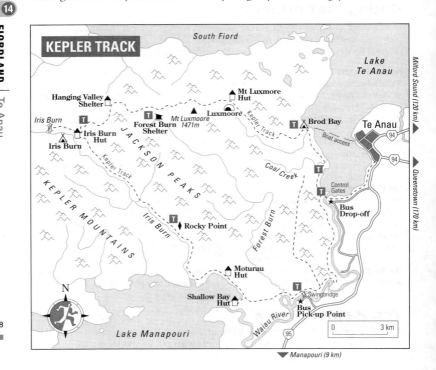

track anticlockwise – but getting the bulk of the climbing over with on the first long day.

Trailhead transport

The Kepler Track starts at the Control Gates, 5km southwest of Te Anau. It is a pleasant enough walk around the southern end of the lake, but most people engage the services of the Tracknet **bus** (☎0800/483 262; Oct to April only; $5), which picks up at accommodation around town from 8.30am and drops off at the Control Gates at 9.30am. On the return leg, most trampers stop 11km short of the Control Gates at the swingbridge over the Waiau's Rainbow Reach. Tracknet pick up at Rainbow Reach at 10am, 3pm and 5pm and charge $10 back to Te Anau.

You can skip another 5km of lakeside walking (and get ahead of the crowds) by **boating** across Lake Te Anau from Te Anau wharf to Brod Bay with Kepler Water Taxi ($18; ☎03/249 8364). Sinbad Cruises (☎03/249 7106) sail the *Manuska* across at 9am for $20.

The route

If you're setting out from Te Anau, head south along Lake Front Drive, then right, following the lakeshore and taking the first right to the Control Gates. From the **Control Gates to Brod Bay** (5.5km; 1hr–1hr 30min; flat) the track follows the lakeshore around Dock Bay and over Coal Creek, passing through predominantly beech and kamahi forests but with a fine stand of tree ferns. Brod Bay has good swimming off a sandy beach and makes a lovely place to camp. Non-campers must press on from **Brod Bay to Luxmoore Hut** (8.2km; 3–4hr; 880m ascent), following a signpost midway along the beach. The path climbs fairly steeply for a couple of hours to limestone bluffs, from where it is almost another hour to the bushline and fine views over Te Anau and Manapouri lakes and the surrounding mountains. The hut is almost an hour from the bushline.

With the hard ascent done, the section from **Luxmoore Hut to Iris Burn Hut** (14.6km; 5–6hr; 300m ascent, 900m descent) is testing but OK by comparison. This is an exposed, high-level section where any hint of bad weather should be treated seriously. The track climbs to just below the summit of Mount Luxmoore (from where you can scramble up to the 1471m peak), then descends to Forest Burn Shelter before following a ridge to Hanging Valley Shelter and turning sharply south to trace another open ridge towards Iris Burn. The Iris Burn is reached by zigzagging west into the forested Hanging Valley then following the stream to the hut and campsite in a large tussock clearing.

The track from **Iris Burn Hut to Moturau Hut** (16.2km; 4–6hr; 300m descent) starts behind the *Iris Burn Hut* and makes a steady descent through beech forest and riverside clearings beside Iris Burn. About halfway you pass toilets at Rocky Point, then enter a short gorge before hugging the river for several magical kilometres. Just before Iris Burn spills into Lake Manapouri, the track swings east and skirts Shallow Bay to the pleasant lakeside *Moturau Hut*. The hut is seldom full since some trampers prefer to continue on to the simpler and older **Shallow Bay Hut** ($5; 6 bunks) about forty minutes further on, while others continue from **Moturau Hut to Rainbow Reach** (6km; 1hr 30min; flat) through gentle beech forest to catch the last shuttle bus.

Walkers who persevere with the final stretch along the Waiau River from **Rainbow Reach to the Control Gates** (9.5km; 2–3hr; negligible ascent) are in for an easy forest walk with opportunities for fishing and swimming.

Milford Sound and around

Milford Sound is the most northerly and most celebrated of Fiordland's fifteen fiords, with vertical sides towering 1200m above the sea and waterfalls plunging from hanging valleys. While many of the other fiords approach Milford for their spectacular **beauty**, none come close for **accessibility**. Before the road was pushed through in 1952 visitors had to arrive by boat or walk the much-lauded **Milford Track** to reach the head of the fiord, but the opening of the Homer Tunnel paved the way for the phalanx of tourist buses that disgorge patrons onto fiord cruises. The tiny airport hardly seems to rest for a second as planes buzz angrily in and out, while all day in the summer and around the middle of the day during spring and winter, the crowds can certainly detract from the grandeur of the spot – but don't let that put you off. Even torrential rain adds to the atmosphere of this magical place, as an ethereal mist descends, periodically lifting to reveal the waterfalls at their thunderous best.

Like the other sounds, Milford is a drowned glacial valley rather than a river valley, making it technically a fiord. Maori know it as **Piopiotahi** ("the single thrush"), and attribute its creation to the god Tu-to-rakiwhanoa, who was called away before he could carve a route into the interior, leaving high rock walls. These precipitous routes are now known as the Homer and Mackinnon passes, but were probably first used by Maori who came here to collect *pounamu*. The first European known to have sailed into Piopiotahi was sealer John Grono who, in 1823, named the fiord Milford Haven after his home port in south Wales. The main river flowing into the Welsh Milford was the Cleddau, so naturally the river at the head of the fiord took that name too.

The earliest settler was Scot **Donald Sutherland**, who arrived with his dog, John O'Groat, in 1877; he promptly set a series of thatched huts beside the freshwater basin of what he called the "City of Milford", funding his explorations by guiding the small number of visitors who had heard tell of the scenic wonder hereabouts. By 1890 Sutherland had married a Dunedin widow, Elizabeth Samuel, and together they built a twelve-room hotel to serve the growing number of steamer passengers – "ashfelters" (city dwellers) and "shadow catchers" (photographers) – who flocked to admire the beauty of his remote home and to walk the newly opened Milford Track.

The predations of today's influx of visitors and the operation of a small fishing fleet have necessitated strategies to preserve the fiord's **fragile ecosystem**. Like all fiords, Milford Sound has an entrance sill at its mouth, in this case only 70m below the surface as compared to the deepest point of almost 450m. This effectively cuts off much of the natural recirculation of water and hinders mixing of sea water and the vast quantities of fresh water that pour into the fiord. The less-dense tannin-stained fresh, surface layer (up to 10m deep) builds up, further diminishing the penetration of light, which is already reduced by the all-day shadow cast by the fiord walls. The result is a relatively barren intertidal zone that protects a narrow – but wonderfully rich and extremely fragile – band of light-shy red and black **corals**; these normally grow only at much greater depths, but thrive here in the dark conditions. Unfortunately, Milford's fishing fleet use crayfish pots, which tend to shear off anything that grows on the fiord's walls. A marine reserve has been set up along the northeastern shore, where all such activity is prohibited, but really this is far too small and conservation groups are campaigning for its extension.

The road to Milford Sound

The 120-kilometre road from Te Anau to Milford Sound has to be one of the world's finest, though this hasn't stopped folk from hatching outlandish plans to circumvent it (see box below). This two-hour drive can easily take a day if you grab every photo opportunity, and longer still if you explore some of the excellent hiking trails outlined on the *Milford Road* leaflet ($1 from visitor centres). Anywhere else the initial drive beside Lake Te Anau would be considered obscenely scenic, but it is nothing compared to the Eglinton Valley, where the road penetrates into steeper, bush-clad mountains and winds through a sub-alpine wonderland to the bare rock walls of the seemingly impassable head of the Hollyford River. The Homer Tunnel then cuts through to the steep Cleddau Valley, the home straight down to Milford Sound.

Maori parties must have long used this route on their way to seek *pounamu* at Anita Bay on Milford Sound, but no road existed until two hundred unemployment-relief workers with shovels and wheelbarrows were put on the job in 1929. The greatest challenge was to puncture the headwall of the Hollyford Valley: work on the 1200-metre-long **Homer Tunnel** began in 1935, but was badly planned from the start. Working at a one-in-ten downhill gradient, the builders soon hit water and were forced to pump out continuously; a pilot tunnel allowing the water to drain westwards was finished in 1948 – when the

---

Cableways and soggy roads

A visit to **Milford Sound** is undoubtedly one of the highlights of most visitors' South Island experience. For most, the journey to this remote spot is half the enjoyment, but tour operators catering to short-stay-must-see tourists are constantly on the lookout for new ways to get punters in and out quickly. Milford Sound's topography largely prevents further development of the airport, so boosters have concentrated on two schemes: shortening the Queenstown to Milford journey by means of a monorail; and linking the Hollyford Valley with Jackson Bay and Haast to the north. Both schemes threaten the dynamics of the whole region, though neither look likely to happen in the near future, if ever.

The **monorail** plan was originally mooted by the Ngai Tahu *iwi*, which claims land rights over much of the Greenstone Valley, the shortest route from Queenstown to The Divide, just 40km east of Milford Sound. An alliance of greenies and outdoor enthusiasts raised enough public concern to force the shelving of plans in 1994. Of several subsequent proposals, the current favourite is a $100-million, 13km state-of-the-art aerial cableway system through the Greenstone Valley linking Lake Wakatipu with the Milford Road near The Divide. Detractors claim that the inconvenience of transferring between catamaran, cableway cabins and bus would offset any time gains, while investors still need to obtain consent from DOC and several local councils.

For every supporter of the venture in Queenstown, there is an opponent in Te Anau – a town that relies as heavily on Milford-bound traffic for its livelihood as Queenstown does on its jetboating, bungy-jumping reputation. More importantly, the plans are actively opposed by almost every wilderness walker, tramper and environmentalist in New Zealand (and abroad) because of the disastrous effect it would have on the infra-structure, ambience, plant- and animal-life of this unique environment.

The current **Hollyford Valley Road** was approved in 1936, but only 16km of it were built as a spur off the SH94 to Milford; between the Hollyford end of this spur and existing roads around Jackson Bay lie around 80km of valley floor, across which a new toll-road could be constructed. Fortunately, the plan was rejected by the Queenstown council, and the project is hopefully now on the backburner permanently.

whole project was relegated to the too-hard basket until 1952. After a concerted push, the road was finally completed in 1953, and officially inaugurated the following year, opening up Milford Sound to road traffic for the first time.

Despite recent improvements, such as passing bays for buses, the tunnel remains rough-hewn, forbiddingly dark and is often choked with diesel fumes (which make the headlights of oncoming vehicles appear to change from red to yellow to white). The sub-alpine section of the road is one of the world's most **avalanche**-prone. Since the last death on the road, in 1984, there has been a sophisticated avalanche-monitoring system in place and, if necessary, explosives are dropped from helicopters to loosen dangerous accumulations of snow while the road is closed. This mostly happens between May and November, when motorists are required to carry chains (available from service stations in Te Anau for around $30). Whatever the season, drivers should bear in mind that there is heavy bus traffic, which tends to be Milford-bound from around 11am to noon and Te Anau-bound between 3 and 5pm. Apart from the store in the Hollyford Valley, 8km off your route, there is nowhere to buy **food** until you reach Milford, so go prepared. **Petrol** in Milford is pricey so fill up in Te Anau.

Campers will definitely want to spend a night in one of the dozen simple DOC **campsites** ($5) along the way, almost all with giardia-free stream water, long-drop toilets and fireplaces. Two are between Te Anau and Te Anau Downs, and the remaining ten pack into the next 50km, either on the grassy flats of the Eglinton Valley or in the bush nearby. Mackay Creek, Totara Creek and East Branch Eglinton, all around 55km north of Te Anau, are particularly good.

Driving to Milford Sound

Heading north from Te Anau, there's little reason to stop in the first 30km to **Te Anau Downs Harbour**, where boats leave for the start of the Milford Track. The road then cuts east away from the lake, before veering north into the **Eglinton Valley** through occasional stands of silver, red and mountain beech interspersed with open flats of red tussock grass. Surprisingly in a national park, these plains are grazed, an anomaly resulting from longstanding leases which had to be honoured. The mountains that hem in the valley are, when the weather is calm, picturesquely reflected in the roadside **Mirror Lakes**, 56km north of Te Anau.

As you get nearer to the head of the valley the road steepens to **The Divide**, 84km north of Te Anau, at 532m the lowest east–west crossing of the Southern Alps. The car park has toilets and a walkers' shelter with a noticeboard advertising the times of passing buses (though it is far better for hikers to pre-arrange a pick-up).

Pressing on a couple of kilometres towards Milford, you descend into the valley of the Hollyford River, which is best seen from a popular viewpoint just before the Hollyford Road shoots off north. The Milford Road continues west towards the Hollyford's source, a huge glacial cirque in which an Alpine Club hut marks the start of the Gertrude Saddle walk (see box, p.913).

A kilometre further on, the **Homer Tunnel**, home of many curious kea, forges through the rock, emerging at the top of a long switchback down to the Cleddau River. Almost 10km on from the tunnel all buses stop at **The Chasm**, while their passengers stroll (15min return) to the near-vertical rapids where the Cleddau has scoured out a deep, narrow channel. Tantalizing glimpses through the foliage reveal sculpted rocks hollowed out by churning stones or tortured into free-standing ribs that resemble flying buttresses. From there it is another 8km to Milford Sound.

Hikes from the Milford Road

Curmudgeonly old-timers grumble about tourists wasting their time, effort and money on prize tramps like the Milford and the Routeburn when there are so many excellent walks easily accessible from the Milford Road. It is true there are many challenging hikes off this road, but we've restricted ourselves to commonly tackled day walks. For tougher stuff, obtain the local topographical maps and pick your own route: you can hardly go wrong.

Lake Gunn (3km loop; 45min; negligible ascent). Wheelchair-accessible nature walk with explanation of the area's forest and birdlife. Starts 74km north of Te Anau.

The Divide to Key Summit (5km return; 2–3hr; 400m ascent). Great panoramic views over three valley systems are the reward for this tramp along the western portion of the Routeburn Track. Starts 84km north of Te Anau.

Lake Marian (5km return; 2–3hr; 400m ascent). Excellent walk which ascends to a beautiful alpine lake, passing some wonderful cataracts (30–40min return) where boardwalks are cantilevered out from the rock wall. Starts 1km along Lower Hollyford Road, 88km north of Te Anau.

Homer Hut to Gertrude Saddle (10km return; 4–6hr; 600m ascent). Starting just by the Homer Hut this hike starts relatively gently up the dramatic Gertrude Valley, ringed by sheer rock walls. The track becomes a steep and poorly marked route up the final ascent to the saddle where there's a wonderful view of Milford Sound and the 2756m Mount Tutoko, Fiordland's highest point.

The Hollyford Valley

The Milford Road drops down from The Divide into the Hollyford Valley, which runs 80km from its headwaters in the Darran Mountains north to the Tasman Sea at Martins Bay. The 16km gravel Lower Hollyford Road (originally planned to reach Haast – see box on p.911) provides access to the Hollyford Track (see box on p.914 and the Lake Marian walk (see box above), a couple of other diversions. The first of these is a walk or more of a scramble to **Lake Marian** (5km return; 2–3hr; 400m ascent), which starts 1km along Lower Hollyford Road and climbs to a beautiful alpine lake, passing some wonderful cataracts (30–40min return) where boardwalks are cantilevered out from the rock wall.

The only habitation is 8km along the valley road at *Hollyford Camp* (no phone; bunks ❶, rooms ❷), a huddle of simple old 1930s cabins which served as married families' quarters for the long-suffering road-builders. Each cabin has a double room and a four-berth bunk room, linked by a kitchen/lounge area equipped with a coal-burning range and cold water supply. Trampers supplies (along with postcards, good books, maps, some rare greenstone and souvenirs) are sold in the **shop** (daily 8.30am–8pm), and there's a **museum** (shop hours; $1, free to guests) containing photos, pioneer artefacts and some interesting paraphernalia relating to the building of the Milford Road and the Homer Tunnel, the one-time community at Martins Bay, and the devastating floods that periodically afflict the region. All is overseen by the idiosyncratic, knowledgeable and entertaining Murray Gunn who'll spin you a headful of tales.

The road runs 8km beyond Hollyford Camp to the Road End – the beginning of the Hollyford Track and a shorter walk to **Humboldt Falls** (20–30min return), a three-step cascade leaping some two hundred metres and apparently the highest falls near a road in Australasia.

The **Hollyford Track** (56 km; 3–4 days one way) is long, but mostly flat, and open year round, though it can still be muddy after rain. DOC's *Hollyford Track* **leaflet** ($1) is fine for following it, though the 1:75,000 *Hollyford Track Trackmap* is more detailed. Running from the end of the Hollyford Valley road to Martins Bay, the track follows Fiordland's longest valley but suffers from being essentially a one-way tramp. It requires four days' backtracking – unless you're flash enough to fly out from the airstrip at Martins Bay or tough enough to continue around a long, difficult and remote loop known as the **Big Bay–Pyke route** (9–10 days total; consult DOC's *Big Bay–Pyke Route* leaflet for details). The joy of the Hollyford is not in the sense of achievement that comes from scaling alpine passes, but in the appreciation of the dramatic mountain scenery and the kahikatea, rimu and matai **bush** with an under-storey of wineberry, fuchsia and ferns. At Martins Bay, Long Reef has a resident **fur seal** colony, and from September to December you might spot rare Fiordland crested **penguins** (tawaki) nesting among the scrub and rocks.

Trampers who hate carrying a big pack, prefer more comfortable lodgings and having hearty meals cooked for them should consider a **guided walk** with Hollyford Track (PO Box 360, Queenstown ☎03/442 3760 & 0800/832 226, ⊛www.hollyford-track.com): small groups are led by knowledgeable guides, and nights are spent at the relatively luxurious *Martins Bay Lodge* and the similar standard *Pyke River Lodge* (3 days plus fly-out $1550).

Accommodation and access

The six DOC **huts** (all 12 bunks; $10) are each equipped with platform bunks, mattresses, water and toilets and do not need to be booked, though hut tickets or an annual hut pass should be bought in advance.

Buses on the Te Anau–Milford run will drop off at Marian Corner, where the Hollyford and Milford roads part company and 16km from the Road End, but it is best to go with Tracknet (Oct–April; ☎0800/483 262) who run from Te Anau right to the Road End for $38.

Milford Sound

After all the superlatives feted on Milford Sound, initial impressions can be a little deflating. The smattering of buildings that comprise the small settlement are hardly in keeping with such magnificent surroundings and the best of the fiord can only really be seen from the water. Nevertheless, it is a fine spot on the edge of a basin where the Cleddau and Arthur rivers surge into the fiord, and the whole scene is dominated by the triangular glaciated pinnacle of **Mitre Peak** (1694m), named for its resemblance to a bishop's mitre when viewed from this angle. So appealing is the place that most of Fiordland's tourism is focussed on Milford, and at the height of the summer, in good weather this area is buzzing with coaches, boats, planes and choppers.

Arrival and getting around

The most worthwhile way to get to Milford Sound, and the one which conveys the greatest sense of place, is to **walk** the Milford Track (see p.920), though **drivers** and **cyclists** do get the freedom to stop, sightsee and camp at the numerous basic campsites along the dramatic road from Te Anau (see p.911). Failing either of those, you can fly, hop on a bus, or do a combination of both, often with a cruise on the fiord thrown in (see box on p.916 for a rundown of the options).

There isn't much to the settlement at Milford Sound. The air strip, fishing harbour, cruise terminal, post office, pub and café, and expensive petrol station

Hollyford Track also work in with local air companies to offer **flights** (which must be pre-booked) between Milford Sound and Martins Bay. Since most people choose to fly out from Martins Bay (from $200), it often works out cheaper taking a "backload" trip from Milford Sound to Martins Bay (around $110) then walk the track in reverse.

Finally, you can avoid most of the long day's walk beside the attractive but samey Lake McKerrow with Hollyford Track's **jetboat service** (Nov–April only; $70) to the head of Lake McKerrow; if you're really pushed for time, a similarly priced run up the Hollyford River can further reduce the walk by a day.

The route

The track from **Road End to Hidden Falls Hut** (9km; 2hr 30min–3hr; negligible ascent) follows a disused section of road which soon crumbles into a track with some riverbank walking to the *Hidden Falls Hut*. Keen walkers will probably want to push on from **Hidden Falls Hut to Alabaster Hut** (10km; 3–4hr; 100m ascent) through ribbonwood and beech to Little Homer Saddle and past Little Homer Falls. From **Alabaster Hut to Demon Trail Hut** (15km; 3–4hr; negligible ascent), you soon pass a side track to the nicely sited *McKerrow Island Hut*, before continuing beside Lake Alabaster to *Demon Trail Hut*. The section from **Demon Trail Hut to Hokuri Hut** (10km; 5–6hr; 100m ascent) is probably the toughest on the walk, following the shore of Lake McKerrow on rough ground with some tricky stream crossings, to *Hokuri Hut*. The path continues from **Hokuri Hut to Martins Bay Hut** (13km; 4–5hr; negligible ascent), by way of the scant remains of Jamestown, a cattle-ranching settlement that prospered briefly in the 1870s. Passing the small airstrip served by Hollyford Track's flights, you'll stumble across some of the dozen dwellings that comprise Martins Bay; no one lives here permanently, but they are used by opportunistic whitebaiters and hunters. Continuing parallel to Martins Bay, and occasionally glimpsing the Hollyford River through wind-shorn trees, you reach the new *Martins Bay Hut*.

are scattered along the shore. Though they are not more than a few hundred metres apart, there is a sporadic free **shuttle bus** connecting them all. Boats all leave from the cruise terminal which bills itself as a **visitor centre** (daily: Oct–April 8am–5.30pm, May–Sept 9am–4pm) but is really just a place to buy boat tickets.

Accommodation and eating and drinking

For many years, what is not now known as *Mitre Peak Lodge* was the sole place to stay in Milford, but that is now completely devoted to customers on the Milford Track guided walk and is closed to the general public. Currently, the only **accommodation** is on boats on the sound (see "Overnight cruises" on p.919) or at *Milford Sound Lodge* (℡03/249 8071, ⓦwww.milfordlodge.com; camping $12, dorms ❶, rooms ❸), a well-run backpackers with spacious dorms, four-shares and doubles, a comfortable lounge with Internet access, a small pricey shop and a licensed restaurant-cum-pizzeria (open to all) serving evening meals for around $20. It is almost 2km back from the wharf and linked to it by a courtesy bus.

The only other **place to eat** is the *Mitre Peak Café* (daily: 8.30am–late) and associated **pub**, which jointly sell sandwiches, espresso, full meals (around $20), all served where you can watch the weather sweeping along the fiord.

As **Milford Sound** is on most visitors' itineraries, there's no shortage of operators willing to get you there from almost anywhere in the country. **From Queenstown**, a stream of luxury **buses** make the tiring four-to-five-hour drive via Te Anau to Milford, complete with frequent photo-opportunity stops and a relentless commentary, decanting their passengers for a cruise on the fiord then running them back again – a hurried twelve hours in all. This so-called coach-cruise-coach format is too much for many people who opt for a fly-cruise-coach trip (which may mean you don't go if the weather is bad) or the coach-cruise-fly variation (which guarantees you get there, though if the weather clags-in you may need to coach back).

Bus trips **from Te Anau** involve the middle (and most interesting) section of Queenstown-based trips and are appreciably shorter, generally taking a leisurely eight hours. Most tours also include a **cruise** on the sound once you get there – see p.919 for a run-down of the various vessels that ply its waters.

From Te Anau

The cheapest trips are those which don't include cruises – good value if you're going kayaking: try the track-transport specialists Tracknet (Oct–April; ☎0800/483 262), who will get you there and back for $66, but you'll have to put up with detours to the trailheads. The big boys such as Real Journeys (☎0800/656 501), InterCity (☎03/379 9020) and Great Sights (☎0800/744 487) all run luxury **bus and cruise** packages from around $110, though there are small reductions for backpackers and substantial standby **discounts** outside the peak season.

The **most interesting** possibilities include kayak trips with Fiordland Wilderness Experiences (see p.919), or joining Bike 'n' Cruise (☎03/249 7098, ⓦwww .bikefiordland.co.nz) who give you the opportunity to ride the downhill parts of the Milford Road, shuttling you along the tougher sections. It is all very gentle but fun and costs $99 just for the biking, $125 if you want to include a Milford Sound cruise. Another good company is Trips 'n' Tramps (☎03/249 7081, ⓦwww.milfordtourswalks.co.nz)

Around Milford

You are pretty much surrounded by water here, and you should waste little time before getting out on it. If tales of his pioneering days have inspired you, pay homage at **Donald Sutherland's grave**, hidden among the staff accommodation behind the pub. Otherwise, there's a five-minute stroll up to a **lookout** behind *Mitre Peak Lodge*, or a boardwalk and track beside the cruise terminal which leads to the 160-metre **Lady Bowen Falls** (15min return), named after the wife of George Bowen, New Zealand's governor in the 1860s. Though most impressive in spate when the upturned lip sends a spume out across the fiord, the falls are worth the walk at any time to observe the village's source of water and hydroelectricity. Three old graves at the foot of the falls guard the remains of nineteenth-century sealers and whalers.

The only other sight attached to terra firma is the **Milford Deep Underwater Observatory** (Oct–April 9.30am–5.30pm, reduced hours in winter; ☎03/249 9442, ⓦwww.milforddeep.co.nz), which is accessible by water taxi ($45 for taxi and entry) and on several of the major cruises ($20–25 more than the equivalent non-observatory cruise). The observatory consists of a floating platform moored to a sheer rock wall in Harrison Cove, part of the marine reserve about a third of the way along the fiord. A series of explanatory panels on the surface prepare you for the main attraction, a spiral staircase which takes you nine metres down through the relatively lifeless freshwater surface layer to a circular gallery where windows look out into the briny heart of the fiord. Sharks

who run year-round and concentrate on relaxed short bushwalks along the way before joining one of the sound cruises.

From Queenstown

If you don't have the time to stay in Te Anau and visit Milford from there, you'll have to opt for a **coach-cruise-coach** day trip from Queenstown, typically starting at 7am, returning just before 8pm. Prices kick off at $145 with Eco Fiord Tours (℡0800/107 505), rising to $149 with Kiwi Experience (℡03/442 9708) and $155 with the small-bus Kiwi Discovery (℡03/442 7340). Probably the best value is the backpacker-oriented BBQ Bus (℡03/442 1045, ⊛www.milford.net.nz; $169, $20 YHA discount) which runs full-day trips with stops for short bushwalks and a barbecue in the Hollyford Valley.

More upmarket tours using air-conditioned vehicles, complete with multilingual commentary or interpretation material, are offered by several companies, including Real Journeys (℡0800/656 503; $185), whose unusual wedge-profiled coaches give the best all-round views.

Many shy away from such a long day and opt instead for a more expensive package involving the forty-minute **flight** to Milford's small airfield, a **cruise** and a **return flight**: Air Fiordland (℡03/442 3404, 0800/103 404, ⊛www.airfiordland.com) charge around $305–325. A good compromise giving you a chance to see the scenery from the road in one direction, is to opt for a **fly-cruise-coach** combo. Most of the bigger bus and flight companies offer these including Air Fiordland/Great Sights who charge $305 for the fly-cruise-coach and $435 for coach-cruise-fly, reflecting the greater demand for flights back from Milford.

Travellers locked into the Kiwi Experience or Magic Bus circuit have to pay extra to do the Milford Sound leg; if you can get a group of four or five together, you can get here as cheaply, and with greater flexibility, by renting a car from Queenstown (see p.846).

and seals have been known to swim by, but most of the action happens immediately outside in window-box "gardens", which have been specially grown from locally gathered **coral** and plant species. Lights pick out colourful fish, tubeworms, sea fans, huge starfish and rare red and black coral. This might all sound a little naff, but unless you're an experienced diver this is the only chance you'll get to see these corals, which elsewhere in the world grow only at depths greater than forty metres. Cruises stop for around twenty minutes, which isn't quite long enough, so if you're really interested, a water taxi's your best bet.

Day cruises

Dramatic though it is, the view from the shore of Milford Sound pales beside the incomparable spectacle from the water, with waterfalls plunging hundreds of metres into the fiord. It is still difficult to grasp the heroic scale of the place, unless your visit coincides with that of one of the great cruise liners – even these formidable vessels are totally dwarfed by the cascades and cliff faces.

The majority of cruises explore the full 22km of Milford Sound, all calling at waterfalls, a seal colony and overhanging rock faces; at Fairy Falls, boats nose up to the base of the fall, while suitably attired passengers are encouraged to edge out onto the bowsprit and collect a cup of water. Longer trips sometimes anchor in Anita Bay (Te-Wahi-Takiwai, "the place of Takiwai"), a former greenstone-gathering place at the fiord's mouth, but still sheltered from the wrath of the Tasman Sea. In short, having come this far, it's essential to get out

△ Pebbles on Milford Sound

on the water by some means or other – even if it means putting up with corny cruise commentaries.

The simplest option is one of the twenty-odd two- to four-hour **day cruises** (best booked a few days in advance in summer) either on one of the large fast and comfortable boats or one of the more intimate small boats. Apart from the amount of company you wish to keep, there is little to choose between them.

Mitre Peak Cruises ☎03/249 8110, ⊛www.mitrepeak.com. For something a little more personal than the big boats, try Mitre Peak who take up to sixty people and regularly head out beyond the mouth of the fiord (4 daily; 1hr 40min–2hr 10min; $49–56).

Real Journeys ☎0800/656 501, ⊛www .realjourneys.co.nz. The biggest operator in the sound, running a range of big-boat trips starting with short scenic cruises (1hr 40min; $47–60)

which cost more in the middle of the day when demand is highest. More leisurely nature cruises (2hr 30min; $60–65) are better, and you can opt for a more intimate small-boat cruise (2hr 15min; $47) with only a few dozen on board.

Red Boat Cruises ☎03/441 1137 & 0800/657 444, ⊛www.redboats.co.nz. The major competition for Real journeys, offering a similar range of big-boat trips (1hr 45min–2hr 15min; $46–65).

Overnight cruises

Only Real Journeys (see above) run **overnight trips** on Milford Sound. Three of the vessels used for day cruises are equipped with beds, and each offers a slightly different experience, though all involve a leisurely cruise around, a chance to go kayaking, good meals and a night spent at anchor in some sheltered cove. The backpacker-orientated 61-berth *Milford Wanderer* (Oct–April daily 5pm–9am; $195) is a motor-driven replica of a sailing scow with cosmetic sails which makes an impressive sight as it ploughs along the fiord. On-board accommodation is somewhat institutional, with cramped four-bunk rooms equipped with sheets, sleeping bags and towels, but a hearty three-course evening meal is served (drinks extra). The more luxurious, 60-berth *Milford Mariner* (Sept–May daily 5pm–9am; $248) has very comfortable private cabins with en suites and serves a higher class of meal; while their much smaller 12-berth *Friendship* (Nov–March daily 5pm–9am; $195) is considerably more intimate with accommodation in six-bunked shared cabins: a very traditional nautical experience.

Kayaking and scuba diving

Fine though the cruises are, the elemental nature of Milford Sound can best be appreciated without the throb of an engine. The **kayaking** can be sublime, both companies organizing transport from Te Anau as well as picking up trampers coming off the Routeburn, Greenstone or Caples tracks at The Divide.

If you'd rather get under the water (and are PADI or SSI certified), join exciting and rewarding **scuba diving** trips. With the tannin-stained fresh water surface layer, the water gets dark quickly fooling the flora and fauna into thinking it is deeper than it really is. Consequently black coral (white but with a black skeleton), brachiopods (living dinosaurs), purple and white nudribranchs, scarlet wrasse and telescope fish are all visible at surprisingly modest depths.

Fiordland Wilderness Experiences ☎03/249 7700 & 0800/200 434, ⊛www.fiordlandseakayak .co.nz. The best kayaking on Milford Sound, on ecologically-oriented 4–5hr guided trips ($95 from Milford, $115 from Te Anau).

Rosco's Milford Sound Sea Kayaks ☎03/249 8500, ⊛www.kayakmilford.co.nz. An extensive

range of kayaking trips taking single and double sea kayaks to Harrison Cove and Sandfly Point (mid-Oct to mid-April; $90–250).

Tawaki Dive Company ☎03/249 9006, ⊛www .tawakidive.co.nz. Two guided dives cost $185 plus $55 for gear hire, and there's an additional fee of $40 if you want transport to and from Te Anau.

The Milford Track

More than any other Great Walk, the **Milford Track** has become a Kiwi icon and it sometimes seems that walking it is the dream of every New Zealander. Unlike other major tramps where foreigners, and particularly Europeans, predominate, Kiwis are in the majority here.

Its exalted reputation is partly accidental and partly historical. It seems likely that southern **Maori** paced the Arthur and Clinton valleys in search of *pounamu*, but there is little direct evidence. The first **Europeans** to explore this section of Fiordland were Scotsmen Donald Sutherland and John Mackay

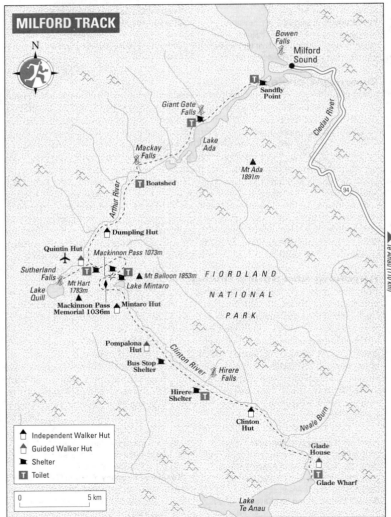

MILFORD TRACK

N

Bowen Falls
Milford Sound

Cledau River

T Sandfly Point

Giant Gate Falls
T

Lake Ada

Mackay Falls

▲ Mt Ada 1891m

94

Arthur River

T Boatshed

▲ Dumpling Hut

Te Anau (110 km) ▶

Quintin Hut
Mackinnon Pass 1073m

Sutherland Falls
▲ Mt Balloon 1853m   F I O R D L A N D
T
Lake Quill
▲ Mt Hart 1783m   *Lake Mintaro*   N A T I O N A L

Mackinnon Pass ▲ Mintaro Hut
Memorial 1036m   P A R K

Pompalona Hut

Bus Stop Shelter   *Clinton River*   ⚡ *Hirere Falls*

Hirere Shelter T

Clinton Hut   *Neale Burn*

Glade House

Legend:
- 🏠 Independent Walker Hut
- 🏠 Guided Walker Hut
- ◼ Shelter
- T Toilet

Glade Wharf

0   5 km

Lake Te Anau

Boat from Te Anau Downs & Te Anau ▼

who, in 1880, blazed a trail up the Arthur Valley from Milford Sound. The story goes that while working their way up the valley they came upon the magnificent Mackay Falls and tossed a coin to decide who would name it, on the understanding that the loser would name the next waterfall. Mackay won the toss but rued his good fortune when, days later, they stumbled across the much more famous and lofty Sutherland Falls. They may well have climbed the adjacent Mackinnon Pass, but the honour of naming it went to **Quintin McKinnon** who, with his companion Ernest Mitchell, reached it in 1888 after having been commissioned by the Otago Chief Surveyor, C. W. Adams, to cut a path up the Clinton Valley.

The route was finally pushed through in mid-October 1888 and the first **tourists** came through the next year, guided by McKinnon. The greatest fillip came in 1908 when a writer submitted her account of the Milford Track to the editor of London's *Spectator*. She had declared it "A Notable Walk" but, in a fit of editorial hyperbole, the editor retitled the piece "The Finest Walk in the World". From 1903 until 1966 the government, through its Tourist Hotel Corporation (THC), held a monopoly on the track, allowing only guided walkers; the huts were supplied by a team of packhorses, which weren't finally retired until 1969.

Wider **public access** was only achieved after the Otago Tramping Club challenged the government's policy by tramping the Milford in 1964. Huts were built in 1966 and the first independent parties came through later that year.

Practicalities

The Milford Track (54km; 4 days) has become a victim of its own hype. There is no doubt that it is a wonderful route through some of Fiordland's finest scenery, but many trampers disparage it as over-regimented, expensive, and not especially varied, while other complaints focus on the huts, which are badly spaced and lurk below the tree line among the sandflies. While these criticisms aren't unfounded – the tramp costs around $250 in hut and transport **fees** alone – the track is extremely well managed and maintained, the huts are clean and unobtrusive, and because everyone's going in the same direction you can go all day without seeing a soul. The Milford is also tougher than many people expect, packing the only hard climb and a dash for the boat at Milford Sound into the last two days. Nevertheless, almost anyone of any age can walk the track, though DOC recommends that unfit aspirants build up to it over 6–8 weeks. DOC's *Milford Track Independent Tramping* **leaflet** (free) is adequate for route-finding, though the 1:75,000 *Milford Track Trackmap* ($15) provides much more information. The 1:250,000 *Fiordland National Park* **map** is too small a scale to be of much use.

Booking and accommodation

Independent walkers tackling the Milford Track during the November to April tramping season are subject to a rigid system of advance-booking **accommodation passes** – use DOC's Great Walks Booking Desks in Queenstown, Glenorchy and Te Anau – for the three special category huts. Bookings are made for specific days and you can only walk the track from south to north, spending the first night at *Clinton Hut*, the second at *Mintaro Hut* and the third at *Dumpling Hut*. No backtracking or second nights are allowed and there is strictly **no camping**. Numbers are limited to forty per day, so you'll need to book as far ahead as possible; a couple of months if you are adaptable, six months if you need a specific departure date or are part of a large group. This does have the huge advantage that you are guaranteed a bed.

Huts all have wardens and are equipped with flush toilets, running (but not drinking) water, heaters and gas rings, but not pans and plates; the **cost** is $105 for the three nights, and family discounts of twenty percent apply throughout the season. Bookings are taken for the following season from July 1 and can be made online at Ⓦ www.doc.govt.nz, or through the Great Walks Booking Desk, DOC (PO Box 29, Te Anau ℡03/249 8514, Ⓔ greatwalksbooking @doc.govt.nz); pick up your accommodation passes from Te Anau before 11am on the day of departure. If the track is closed due to bad weather or track conditions, full refunds are made but new bookings can only be taken if there is space.

Outside the season the huts revert to serviced hut status ($10). They are unstaffed with no heating, clothes-drying or cooking facilities; bookings are not required and annual hut passes are valid.

Trailhead transport

Both ends of the Milford Track can only be realistically approached **by boat**. There are several possibilities, but all must be arranged and paid for before, or at the same time as, accommodation passes are issued. Independent walkers starting early should catch the 9.45am Tracknet bus (30min; $15) from Te Anau to Te Anau Downs, 30km north of Te Anau, where you board the 10.30am Real Journeys launch across Lake Te Anau to Glade Wharf (1hr 15min; $42). Since the first day's walk is very easy, it makes sense to make a late start using the 1.15pm Tracknet bus ($15) and the 2pm launch ($54).

At the Milford end of the track, the majority catch either the 2.15pm or the 3.15pm launch from Sandfly Point (Nov–April; $26) for the journey to Milford Sound (20min). **Buses** back to Te Anau can be picked up at 9.30am, 3pm and 5pm (3hr; $38).

Other operators offer different ways to approach and leave the track. They can all be booked individually, but most have combined to marginally under-cut the total price you'd pay for independent arrangements. Probably the best way to start from Te Anau is on the *Manuska*, a wooden ketch run by Sinbad Cruises (10.30am; 5–6hr; $68; ℡03/249 7106, Ⓦ www.sinbadcruises.co.nz), which sails under canvas whenever possible to Glade Wharf. A full package ($130) includes the *Manuska* cruise, being met at the other end with some kayaking on the sound and a bus back to Te Anau.

Guided walks

For many years, the only way to walk the Milford Track was on a **guided walk**. Some would argue that this is still the case, with just your personal effects to carry and comfortable beds to sleep in. Accommodation is in clean, plain huts which aren't exactly luxurious, but do boast hot showers, duvets on the bunks, three-course dinners with wine and cooked breakfasts. Staff prepare the huts, cook the meals, make up the lunches and tidy up after you. All you have to do is walk, but there's a price to pay for all this pampering. The **Milford Track Guided Walk** (Nov–March daily departures; ℡03/441 1138 & 0800/659 255, Ⓦ www.ultimatehikes.co.nz) is a four-night, five-day affair and costs $1750 ($1490 in Nov & April). For that you get a pre-track briefing in Queenstown, transport from there to the trailhead, accommodation and food on the track, a night at the *Mitre Peak Lodge*, a Milford Sound cruise and a return bus ride to Queenstown. Accommodation on the walk is in shared bunkrooms but for an extra $350 you can upgrade to a private en-suite room.

For keen hikers also wanting to walk the Routeburn the same company runs the eight-day **Ultimate Hike** (Dec–March $2840, Nov & April $2440) which follows the Milford Track schedule but only returns as far as Te Anau to begin the Routeburn Guided Walk (see p.860).

Anyone wanting a taste of the track without having to walk more than a couple of kilometres can join a Milford Track day-walk from Te Anau (see p.906).

The route

The track starts at the head of Lake Te Anau and follows the Clinton River into the heart of the mountains, climbing over the spectacular Mackinnon Pass before tracing the Arthur River to Milford Sound.

The first day is a doddle. **Glade Wharf to Clinton Hut** (8km; 1–2hr; 50m ascent) starts along a 2km 4WD track which serves *Glade House* (guided walkers only). The path then crosses a long swingbridge to the right bank of the gentle, meandering Clinton River; keen anglers can spend an hour or two fishing for trout in the deep pools. The track runs through dense beech forest, only occasionally giving glimpses of the mountains ahead beyond *Clinton Hut*.

From **Clinton Hut to Mintaro Hut** (16.5km; 4–6hr; 350m ascent), the track follows the true right bank of the Clinton River to its source, Lake Mintaro, right by the *Mintaro Hut*. Again this is easy going and, by the time you reach a short side track to Hidden Lake, Mackinnon Pass should be visible ahead. The track steepens a little to Bus Stop Shelter, then flattens out to *Pompolona Hut* (guided). From here it's a further hour to *Mintaro Hut* where, if it looks like it will be a good sunset, it pays to drop your pack and head up Mackinnon Pass.

The walk so far does little to prepare you for the day from **Mintaro Hut to Dumpling Hut** (14km; 5–6hr; 550m ascent, 1030m descent). Though the surface of the broad path is firm and well graded, bushwalking neophytes will find the haul up to Mackinnon Pass (1hr 30min–2hr) very strenuous. Long breath-catching pauses provide an opportunity to admire the wonderful alpine scenery, notably the headwall of the Clinton Valley, a sheer glacial cirque of grey granite. As the bush drops away behind you, the slope eases to the saddle at Mackinnon Pass, a great place to eat lunch, though you'll have the company of kea and the incessant buzzing of pleasure flights from Milford. A memorial to McKinnon and Mitchell marks the low-point of the saddle, from where the path turns east and climbs to a day shelter (with toilets and a gas ring) just below the dramatic form of Mount Balloon. From there it is all downhill, and steeply too, initially skirting the flank of Mount Balloon then following the path beside the picturesque Roaring Burn and down to the Arthur River. The confluence is marked by *Quintin Hut* (guided) which was originally built by the Union Steamship Company as an overnight shelter for sightseers from Milford visiting the Sutherland Falls. Though it remains a private hut, toilets and shelter are provided for independent walkers – who mostly dump their packs for the walk to the base of the 560m **Sutherland Falls** (4km; 1hr–1hr 30min return; 50m ascent), the highest in New Zealand. *Dumpling Hut* is another hour's walk from *Quintin Hut*.

After a tiring third day, you're in for an early start and a steady walk from **Dumpling Hut to Sandfly Point** (18km; 5–6hr; 125m descent) to meet your launch or kayak at 2pm or 3pm. After rain this can be a magnificent walk, as the valley walls stream with waterfalls and the Arthur River is in spate. The track follows the tumbling river for a couple of hours to the Boatshed (toilets), before crossing the Arthur River on a swingbridge and cutting inland to the magnificent MacKay Falls. More a steep cascade than a waterfall, they are much smaller than the Sutherland Falls but equally impressive, particularly after rain. Don't miss Bell Rock, a water-hollowed boulder that you can crawl inside. The track subsequently follows Lake Ada, created by a landslip 900 years ago, and named by Sutherland after his Scottish girlfriend. A small lunch shelter midway along its shore heralds Giant Gate Falls, which are best viewed from the swing-bridge that crosses the river at the foot of the falls. From here it is roughly an hour and a half to the shelter at Sandfly Point.

Manapouri, Doubtful Sound and the southern fiords

There is no shortage of contenders for the title of New Zealand's most beautiful lake, and sloshing 178m above sea level, **Lake Manapouri** is definitely among them, with its long and indented bush-clad shoreline contorted into three distinct arms. The lake has a vast catchment area, guzzling all the water that flows down the Upper Waiau River from Lake Te Anau and unwittingly creating a massive hydroelectric generating capacity – something which almost led to its downfall.

The one good thing to come from the hydroelectric project has been the opening up of **Doubtful Sound**, following the construction of the Wilmot Pass supply road. What was previously the preserve of the odd yacht and a few deer-stalkers and trampers is now accessible to anyone prepared to take a boat across Lake Manapouri and a drive over the Wilmot Pass. Costs are unavoidably high and you need to be self-sufficient (no burger joints or corner shops here), but any inconvenience is easily outweighed by glorious isolation and pristine beauty. Wildlife is a major attraction, not least the resident pod of sixty-odd bottlenose dolphins, who frequently come to play around ships' bows and gleefully cavort near kayakers. Fur seals slather the outer islands, Fiordland crested penguins come to breed here in October and November, and the bush, which comes right down to the water's edge, is alive with kaka, kiwi and other rare bird species.

Cook spotted Doubtful Sound in 1770 but didn't enter as he was "doubtful" of his ability to sail out again in the face of winds buffeted by the steep-walled fiord. The breeze was more favourable for the joint leaders of a Spanish expedition, Malaspina and Bauza, who in February 1793 sailed in and named Febrero Point, Malaspina Reach and Bauza Island.

In fact, Cook seemed more interested in **Dusky Sound**, 40km south, where he spent five weeks on his second voyage in 1773, while his crew recovered from an arduous crossing of the Southern Ocean. At Pickersgill Harbour, Cook endeavoured to ward off scurvy by using manuka leaves to brew a kind of "spruce beer" which, helped along with a touch of brandy, apparently tasted like champagne; obviously, the good captain hadn't supped champagne for some time. On Astronomer's Point nearby, it is still possible to see where Cook's astronomer had trees felled so he could get an accurate fix on the stars; not far from here is the site where 1790s castaways built the first European-style house and boat in New Zealand. Marooned by the fiord's waters, Pigeon Island shelters the ruins of a house built by Richard Henry, who battled from 1894 to 1908 to save endangered native birds from introduced stoats and rats.

Manapouri

The scattered community of **MANAPOURI**, 20km south of Te Anau, drapes itself prettily around the shores of the lake of the same name which, in the 1960s became a cause célèbre for conservationists opposed to the raising of the

Lake Manapouri's **hydroelectric** potential had long been recognized, but nothing was done to realize it until the 1950s. Consolidated Zinc Pty of Australia wanted to smelt their Queensland bauxite into **aluminium** – a tremendously power-hungry process – as cheaply as possible, and their beady eyes alighted upon **Lake Manapouri**. They approached the New Zealand government, who agreed to build a power station on the lake, at taxpayers' expense, while Rio Tinto's subsidiary Comalco built a smelter at Tiwai Point, near Bluff, 170km to the southeast.

The scheme entailed blocking the lake's natural outlet into the Lower Waiau River and chiselling out a vast powerhouse 200m underground beside Lake Manapouri's West Arm, where the flow would be diverted down a 10km tailrace tunnel to Deep Cove on Doubtful Sound. By the time the fledgling **environmental movement** had rallied its supporters, the scheme was well under way, but the government under-estimated the anger that would be unleashed by its secondary plan to boost water storage and power production by raising the water level in the lake by as much as 30m. The threat to the natural beauty of the lake sparked **national protests**, the "Save Manapouri Campaign" presenting to parliament a 265,000-signature petition, after which the plan was reluctantly dropped. The full saga is recounted in Neville Peat's book *Manapouri Saved* (see "Books" in Contexts, p.986).

The **West Arm Power Station** took eight years to build. Completed in 1971, it remains one of the most ambitious projects ever carried out in New Zealand. Eighty percent of its output goes straight to the **smelter** – which consumes something like fifteen percent of all the electricity used in the country, and yet Comalco are charged only a fraction of what domestic users pay. It is widely perceived to be an unnecessary drain on the country's resources and every time a new power station is proposed, the cry goes up for the plug to be pulled on the smelter. Because of the unexpectedly high friction in the original tailrace tunnel the power station had always run below 85 percent capacity and to boost power production a second parallel tailrace tunnel was built in the late 1990s. Power companies are much more sensitive now, and the project was completed without major protest.

⑭

lake level as part of the massive West Arm hydroelectric power scheme (see box above). With the power station complete, the lake left at its original level and the passage of three decades, there is little tangible evidence of the passions that once threatened the community's cohesion, but scratch below the surface and you'll find a lingering antipathy between economic rationalists and environmentalists.

Arrival and information

To get to Manapouri without your own transport, hop on the Te Anau–Invercargill Scenic Shuttle (☏03/249 8900), which leaves Te Anau at 8.15am and returns from Manapouri to Te Anau mid-afternoon. Real Journeys buses connecting with boats to West Arm and Doubtful Sound also take extras ($9 one way, $15 return) if their cruise passengers don't fill the bus.

The road from Te Anau reaches Manapouri as Cathedral Drive and then becomes Waiau Street, passing almost everything of interest on the way to Pearl Harbour and the office of Real Journeys (daily: Nov–Feb 7.30am–8pm; March–Oct 8am–5.30pm; ☏03/249 6602 & 0800/656 502, ⊛www .realjourneys.co.nz), the closest thing the village has to an information centre, and the jumping-off point for lake cruises. The sole shop and the post office both occupy the same building as the *Cathedral Café* on Cathedral Drive – find one and you've found the lot.

Accommodation and eating

Though most people prefer to base themselves in Te Anau, Manapouri does offer a reasonable selection of **places to stay**. **Eating** is more problematic, with the best bet being the *Cathedral Café*, Cathedral Drive (℡03/249 6619), which serves teas and snacks, but also stays open for $18–20 evening meals (in the summer only) until 8pm, later if you make a reservation. Failing that, the *Lakeview Motor Inn*, 68 Cathedral Drive, has the *Beehive Café* which dishes up generous portions of café fare and bar meals ($12–25).

Beechwood Lodge 40 Cathedral Drive ℡03/249 6993, ⓦ www.beechwoodlodge.com. Easily the nicest place in Manapouri, a purpose-built, wooden house in which the en-suite guest rooms ($400 each room or $600 for the whole house) both have lake views. The wonderful breakfasts include muffins and homemade bread, and the hosts are friendly and helpful. He's a fishing guide so there is always the chance he'll let slip where you can pick up some lake-fresh supper. ❾

The Cottage Waiau St ℡03/249 6838. Attractive en suites, both with decks, in a cutesy house with a cottage garden close to the wharf. Continental breakfast is included, cooked is $6 extra. ❺

Deep Cove Hostel Deep Cove, Doubtful Sound ℡03/216 1340, ⓦ www.deepcoveoutdooredu.org.nz. This two- and four-bed bunkroom accommodation overlooking Doubtful Sound is available only from mid-Dec to mid-Feb. There are mattresses, all eating and cooking utensils and good hot showers, but the nearest shop is Manapouri, so bring everything you'll need. The one-way fare with Real Journeys' Doubtful Sound service from Manapouri is around $60. Dorms ❶, rooms ❷

Freestone Backpackers, SH99, 3km east of Manapouri ℡03/249 6893. Attractive backpackers in a series of comfy wooden chalets with great mountain and lake views. Dorms ❶, rooms ❸

Manapouri Glade and Possum Lodge 13 Murrell Ave ℡03/249 6623, ⓔ possumlodge@xtra.co.nz. Appealingly old-fashioned, peaceful and well maintained campsite and hostel located right where the Waiau River meets the lake. Tent and powered sites go for $12, cabins ❸, motel units ❹

Manapouri Lakeview Motor Inn 50 Cathedral Drive, 1km from the wharf ℡03/249 6624, ⓔ fiordland@xtra.co.nz. Fully equipped motor park with sauna, kids play area and excellent vistas. Camping $10, cabins ❷, tourist flats ❸, motel units ❹

Around town

The several dozen houses that constitute Manapouri cluster at the outlet of the Waiau River, which the hydroelectric shenanigans have turned into a narrow arm of the lake now known as Pearl Harbour.

Apart from cruises and kayak trips (see below), the only thing to do in Manapouri is to saunter along some of the **walking trails** detailed in the DOC's *Manapouri Tracks* leaflet ($1, from DOC in Te Anau and some local accommodation). On the Manapouri side there's the **Pearl Harbour to Fraser's Beach** trail (45min), which follows an easy track through lakeshore beech forest with fantails and silvereye flitting about the thin understorey. For all the other tracks, you'll need to row across the Waiau River in a boat rented from Adventure Kayak & Cruise, 33 Waiau Street, next to the Mobil station (daily 8am–6pm; ℡03/249 6626). Boats cost $10 a day for up to two people, $15 a day for four, and you pay another $3 per boat to stay on the other side overnight, either camping or in one of the two DOC huts (both $5).

The most frequently walked is the **Circle Track** (3hr loop; 7km; 330m ascent) initially contouring west around the lake then turning southeast to climb the ridge up to a point with stupendous views over the lake then north back the to start.

The lake: cruises and kayaking

Most of the lake cruises are operated by Real Journeys (see p.925), who run three- to four-hour trips across Lake Manapouri to the impressive, if controversial, **West Arm Power Station** (Oct–April, 12.30pm daily; $55 from Manapouri, $70 from Te Anau). The ride across the lake terminates at a visitor centre, which highlights the European "discovery" of Fiordland, its flora and fauna and, plenty on the construction of the power station. A bus then takes you down a narrow, 2km-long tunnel to a viewing platform in the Machine Hall. All you can see are the exposed sections of seven turbines, but there's an interesting model of the whole system and some panels assaulting you with yet more statistics; read quickly before you're whisked back to the bus for the return to the surface.

For greater independence, you'll need **kayak rental**: Adventure Kayak & Cruise (see p.926) rent reasonable-quality single and double sea kayaks (1day $45, 3 days $115); and Te Anau-based Fiordland Wilderness Experiences (see p.907), rent out better boats for a fraction more.

Doubtful Sound and the southern fiords

To fully appreciate the beauty and sense the isolation of the **southern fiords**, you really need to spend a few days among them, travelling either by boat or kayak. If time is limited, plump for a full-day or overnight trip to **Doubtful Sound**; with more time to spare, spending a few days weaving between these mystical waterways is an unforgettable experience.

Real Journeys run two trips to Doubtful Sound, the cheapest being the full-day Wilderness Cruise (1–2 daily; $195 from Manapouri, $210 from Te Anau; lunch $20 extra) which includes a trip across Lake Manapouri and a visit to the power station. You're then transferred to a bus for the 20km ride over Wilmot Pass – the costliest stretch of road in the country and completely unconnected to any other road – to Deep Cove, where the tailrace tunnel spews out vast quantities of lake water. Here you board a three-hour cruise to the mouth of the fiord, where fur seals loll on the rocks, and into Hall Arm, where bottlenose dolphins often congregate.

Pleasant though this is, it is no substitute for the overnight cruise on the *Fiordland Navigator* (Oct–May daily at 12.30pm; quad-share $285, twin-share $445), a comfortable modern cruiser designed to look like a traditional sailing scow. The trip doesn't visit the power station but you're away from Manapouri for a full 24 hours, time enough to explore the fiords at a leisurely pace, join a nature walk, go kayaking and even swim. Food and accommodation are very good and there are savings of around 25 percent in October and May, and a ten percent YHA discount throughout the summer.

There's a more personal feel to Doubtful Sound one-day trips run by Pearl Harbour-based Fiordland Explorer Charters ($170; ☎03/249 6616 & 0800/434 673, ⓔexplorercharters@xtra.co.nz) with a maximum group size of twelve. Trips include a powerhouse visit and a three-hour cruise on Doubtful Sound in a glass-bottomed boat.

For a more in-depth encounter with the fiords, join one of the superb multi-day **trips** organized by Fiordland Ecology Holidays (☎03/249 6600, ⓦwww.fiordland.gen.nz; 3–10 days; $225 per day; book as far in advance as you can). The skipper of the motor-sailer *Breaksea Girl* spent twelve years running DOC's research vessel in these waters and holds passionate views on the non-extractive use of the fiords. Fishing is out and, though snorkelling and scuba diving are in, care is taken to minimize the impact on this fragile environment. Trips typically take in Doubtful, Dusky and Breaksea sounds, spending time with dolphins and seals and calling at places frequented by Cook and by turn-of-the-century bird conservationist Richard Henry. A worthy alternative to

FIORDLAND | Manapouri

At its most extensive, the **Dusky Track** is one of the **longest** and **most remote** tracks in New Zealand and is much tougher (and muddier) than any of the Great Walks. Even a cursory exploration of the area is likely to take 3–4 days. The high cost of transportation and the commitment involved make it one of the least-walked tracks, but anyone with sufficient experience and stamina shouldn't miss this opportunity to walk from one of New Zealand's largest lakes (Manapouri) to its longest fiord (Dusky Sound). DOC's *Dusky Track* **leaflet** ($1) is the best single resource for this walk, though tricky route-finding makes the 1:50,000 *Wilmot* (S148; $12.50) and *Heath* (S157) **maps** invaluable adjuncts.

There are three basic elements, each following a major river valley and connecting to form an inverted Y. Any two of these can be combined to make a tramp of four to six days, or all three can be attempted in eight to ten days. On a tramp of this length it is especially important to have plenty of spare food and stove fuel in case of bad weather or flooding. In **summer**, be prepared for a lot of stream crossings and precarious walkwires to negotiate. In **winter** you can also expect snow and ice, which often render the track impassable, though you will be advised of conditions when you notify either the Tuatapere or Te Anau DOC office of your intentions; remember to check in on your return from the track.

Accommodation and access

There is no need to book for the eight backcountry **huts** (almost all 10–14 bunks; $5) which operate on a first-come-first-served basis and have mattresses, tank water and long-drop toilets. There are four ways of tackling the track: walk in from Lake Hauroko, via Supper Cove and on to Lake Manapouri; doing it the other way round; flying in to Supper Cove and walking out to Lake Manapouri (ignoring Lake Hauroko); or doing this in reverse. Most trampers enter the region by boat across Lake Hauroko with Lake Hauroko Tours (Nov–April Mon & Thurs; $60; ☎03/226 6681, ⓦwww.duskytrack.co.nz), who'll pick you up at 9am in Tuatapere (see p.931). For walkers coming in the opposite direction, pick-ups from *Hauroko Burn Hut* are on the same days at noon, but must be confirmed in advance.

cruising is to take a research holiday (also run by Fiordland Ecology Holidays, and also booked way in advance), monitoring skinks and weevils, short- and long-tailed bats and native birds on the coastal islands (no experience required; around $1450 for 5 days).

A similar ethical vein flavours the energetic and excellent **kayaking trips** run by Fiordland Wilderness Experiences (☎03/249 7700 & 0800/200 434, ⓦwww.fiordlandseakayak.co.nz), who sometimes run joint trips with Fiordland Ecology Holidays which enable kayakers to reach unsullied waters by hitching a ride aboard the *Breaksea Girl* (6 days for $1800). Otherwise, their regular guided trips involve the usual bus ride from Te Anau, boat ride from Manapouri, 4WD trek over the Wilmot Pass and then idyllic kayaking on the almost silent Doubtful Sound and camping out in one of its spectacular remote arms where they have set up comfortable, ecologically-minded, camping sites. On day two you'll be paddling and sailing back with a satisfied glow (2 days departing daily in summer, otherwise Tues, Thurs & Sat; $300). For even remoter alternatives there are also three- to five-day guided trips ($130 a day), to Breaksea and Dusky Sounds, and freedom rentals for experienced paddlers. Adventure Kayak & Cruise (see above) offer a variation on the theme with cruise and kayak options on Doubtful Sound (1-day $170, 2 days $295).

During the **winter months** (May–Sept), the *Milford Wanderer* (☎03/249 6602

From Lake Hauroko, it's three days' walk to *Loch Maree Hut*, which is poised at the junction of the three "legs". Some trampers then turn west to **Supper Cove** and leave with Wings & Water scheduled **flights** (Nov–April daily 11am; $225; ☏03/249 7405), while others head north to **West Arm** (3 days) to pick up Real Journeys' daily 4.30pm **launch** across Lake Manapouri ($55), also worth confirming in advance.

The route
You won't want to hang around the *Hauroko Burn Hut*, and mid-morning boat drop-offs leave you plenty of time to walk from **Hauroko Burn Hut to Halfway Hut** (12km; 4–6hr), following Hauroko Burn as it runs through a short gorge and gradually steepens to *Halfway Hut*. The tramp from **Halfway Hut to Lake Roe Hut** (7km; 3–5hr) goes easily for a couple of hours then climbs above the bushline and follows snow poles to the magnificently sited *Lake Roe Hut*. Continuing from **Lake Roe Hut to Loch Maree Hut** (10km; 4–6hr), the track veers west along the tops of the Pleasant Range, with spectacular views to Dusky Sound, before descending very steeply to *Loch Maree Hut*.

Trampers wishing to walk from **Loch Maree Hut to Supper Cove Hut** (12km; 6hr) continue west from Loch Maree following the Seaforth River. At low tide, the last rough section of track can be avoided by cutting across the flats to *Supper Cove Hut* – where it is traditional to take out the dinghy and fish for your supper. Anyone not flying out has to retrace their steps to *Loch Maree Hut*.

From **Loch Maree Hut to Kintail Hut** (11km; 4–5hr), you follow the Seaforth River upstream on fairly difficult ground that can be boggy and becomes impassable when the river is high. The route from **Kintail Hut to Upper Spey Hut** (7km; 5–6hr) involves a steep ascent to the scenic sub-alpine Centre Pass, then an equally precipitous descent to *Upper Spey Hut*. The last day takes you fairly painlessly from **Upper Spey Hut to West Arm Hut** (11km; 4–5hr), down the Spey River to the Wilmot Pass road between West Arm and Doubtful Sound. Forty minutes' walk brings you to the wharf at West Arm – hopefully in time to catch the last launch. Otherwise you'll have to spend the night at *West Arm Hut* (only 6 bunks) 200m east of the power-station visitor centre.

& 0800/656 502, ☏www.realjourneys.co.nz) leaves its beat on Milford Sound and indulges in some leisurely cruises around the southern fiords: five days in Doubtful, Dusky and Breaksea sounds or six days around Stewart Island both cost $1600; seven days all the way down to Preservation Inlet goes for $2200.

The Southern Scenic Route

The vast majority of visitors to Te Anau and Manapouri retrace their steps to Queenstown and miss out on the fringe country, where the fertile sheep paddocks of Southland butt up against the remote country of the Fiordland National Park. The minor towns of the region are linked by the understated **Southern Scenic Route**, small roads where mobs of sheep are likely to be the biggest cause of traffic problems. From Te Anau it runs via Manapouri to SH99, following the valley of the Waiau River to the cave-pocked limestone country around **Clifden**. A minor road cuts west to Lake Hauroko, access point the Dusky Track, while the Southern Scenic Route continues south through the small service town of **Tuatapere** (base for hiking the Hump Ridge Track) to estuary-side little **Riverton** and on to Invercargill.

Scenic Shuttle **buses** (☎03/249 7654 & 0800/277 483, ⓔscenicshuttle @xtra.co.nz) do the trip from Te Anau through Manapouri, Tuatapere and Riverton to Invercargill and back daily (departing Te Anau 8.15am and Invercargill at 2pm in summer, 1pm in winter).

Borland Road and Lake Monowai

Some 35km south of Manapouri, **Borland/Lake Monowai Road** cuts west to Lake Manapouri's South Arm. Built in 1963, it provides hunting, fishing, mountain-biking and tramping access to a huge swathe of untouched country south of Lake Manapouri.

Passing the dam which controls the flow of water from Lake Manapouri down the Waiau River, the road runs 12km to the *Monowai River Lodge* (☎ & ⓕ03/225 5191; dorms ❶, rooms ❸), a lagoonside retreat geared to both the rod-and-gun set and backpackers. The fully self-contained lodge – complete with piano – sleeps twelve, and when not booked by groups, individual **rooms** are rented out; failing that, there are beds in rustic but comfortable bunkhouses. Immediately past the lodge, a spur runs 6km to **Lake Monowai**, the water level of which was artificially raised as part of an early, small-scale hydro scheme in 1925. The scars can still be seen on its shores, where there's a primitive **campsite** ($5) with long-drop toilets and barbecues. Monowai is a popular spot for fishing – mostly done from boats to avoid snagging lines in the submerged skeletons of drowned trees. Back on Borland Road it is another 4km west to *Borland Lodge* (☎03/225 5464; ❶), a youth **adventure centre** where you can stay in twin chalets (bring your own bedding). They also rent out reasonably priced tents and stoves to those wanting to explore the excellent **walking** country and huts hereabouts, all detailed in DOC's *Lake Monowai/Borland Road* leaflet ($1).

Beyond *Borland Lodge*, the increasingly narrow, steep and landslip-prone road can be driven another 40km to **Lake Manapouri's South Arm**, where there are toilets and a shelter (Oct–May; key from the DOC in Tuatapere or Te Anau). Close to the end of the road, a spur (open to trampers only) leads 15km over the Percy Saddle to **West Arm** and eventually to Doubtful Sound.

Clifden and Lake Hauroko

Back at the junction with the main highway, it is 32km further south to **CLIFDEN**, barely a town at all but of some interest for the historic **Clifden Suspension Bridge**, one of the longest in the South Island, built over the Waiau River in 1899 and in use until the 1970s. The north abutment overshadows a **free campsite** and barbecue area. Clifden most likely gets its name from low cliffs made of the same limestone that is riddled with the **Clifden Caves** (unrestricted access) where Maori once camped on summer foraging trips. They're signposted around 1km north of the bridge along SH 96 and 1km down Clifden Gorge Road. With no one to guide you there's a palpable sense of adventure as you head into this 300m-long labyrinth lined with flowstone and stalactite formations and dotted with glowworms. The passages are never tight but you'll need to do some crouching, scrambling and climbing ladders as you follow a series of reflective strips. Most can be explored without getting wet, but if you want to go the whole way you'll need to swim about five metres: wear clothes you don't mind getting wet and muddy.

Languishing at the end of a dirt road, 30km west of Clifden, **Lake Hauroko** is New Zealand's deepest lake (462m). Low bush-clad hills surround the lake, leaving it open to the "sounding winds" immortalized in its name. There are no facilities at First Bay, the road end, just a primitive campsite midway between Clifden and Lake Hauroko and, at the north end of the lake, the *Hauroko Burn Hut* (accessible by boat, or on foot via the Dusky Track – see p.928).

To explore, engage one of the companies running excellent wilderness **jetboating trips** on the lake and along the 27km of the Grade III **Wairaurahiri River** down to the coast. Some of the best trips are with Hump Ridge Jet (☎03/225 8174 & 0800/270 556, ⓦwww.humpridgejet.com), who run a one-day adventure ($140) jetboating downriver, allowing 4hr to relax or hike into the impressive Percy Burn viaduct then jetboating back. A two-day variation (also $140) has you walking the Waitutu Track (see box, p.932) from Bluefields Beach to Port Craig Hut, staying there then hiking across the Percy Burn Viaduct to the Wairaurahiri River where you're picked up by jetboat and taken upstream to Lake Hauroko. Good trips are also run by Wairaurahiri Jet (☎03/226 6845 & 0800/376 174, ⓦwww.wjet.co.nz), and both companies can arrange transport from Tuatapere (see below) or Clifden.

Tuatapere and around

Two sawmills and one feeble stand of beech and podocarp forest is the only evidence that **TUATAPERE**, on the banks of the Waiau River 14km south of Clifden, could once have justified its epithet of "The Hole in the Forest". As the largest town in southwestern Southland, Tuatapere makes a good geographical though otherwise poor base for exploring the very southern limits of Fiordland. To fight the apparent stagnation, the community banded together to create the **Hump Ridge Track** (see box, p.932), which, it is widely hoped, will draw travellers who will feel encouraged to stay in the area. The Waitutu Track is another attraction, and beyond that there's some great jetboating based nearby at Clifden (see p.930).

The Town

Maori legend records the great war canoe Takitimu being wrecked on the Waiau River bar at Te Waewae Bay some six hundred years ago. Maori set up summer foraging camps along the river and used these as way-stations on the route to the *pounamu* fields around Milford Sound, but it wasn't until European **pioneers** arrived around 1885 that Tuatapere came into being. By 1909 the **railway** had arrived from Invercargill, bringing with it increasingly sophisticated steam-powered haulers that made short work of clearing the surrounding bushland. More recently, foresters' attention shifted west to the fringes of the Fiordland National Park where, in the 1970s, the Maori owners proposed clear felling stands of rimu. Environmentalists prevailed upon the Conservation Minister who eventually, in 1996, agreed to pay compensation in return for a sustainable management policy. The bush's last stand – a riverside clump of beech, kahikatea and totara on the Domain – forms one station on the **Tuatapere Walkway**, a 5km stroll around town guided by a leaflet from DOC. For a rose-tinted version of pioneer history, visit **Bushman's Museum** accessed through the visitor centre (same hours; donation appreciated) where the displays are well presented if one-sided.

There is no reason to spend much time in Tuatapere itself, though you might use it as a base for jetboat trips.

Practicalities

For such a small town, Tuatapere is thinly spread on both sides of the Waiau River. On the eastern side, the **Hump Ridge Track visitor centre**, 31

Tuatapere makes an excellent base for two markedly different hiking experiences: the traditional, mostly coastal Waitutu Track and the Hump Ridge Track, which is gradually capturing the imagination of trampers for its hard-to-beat combination of coastal walking, historic remains, gorgeous sub-alpine country and relatively sophisticated huts.

Sections of both tracks are historically some of the country's most interesting as they follow a portion of the 1896 track cut 100km along the south coast to gold-mining settlements around the southernmost fiord of Preservation Inlet. This paved the way for wood cutters, who arrived en masse in the 1920s. Logs were transported to the mills on tramways, which crossed the burns and gullies on viaducts built of Australian hardwood – four of the finest have been faithfully restored including the 125m bridge over Percy Burn that stands 40m high in the middle and has become a star attraction.

The **trailhead** for both tracks is the Bluefields Beach car park, 28km west of Tuatapere, accessible by bus ($15 each way) organized through the Hump Ridge Track office. Here there's the *Rarakau Lodge* (see below). Hump Ridge walkers can also get access from Tuatapere to Track Burn ($60 return), 8km along the track.

To further complicate matters, various **jetboat** operators (see "Clifden and Lake Hauroko" account on p.930) allow you to walk sections of the tracks combined with a ride up or down the Wairaurahiri River.

The Waitutu Track

The historic, coastal **Waitutu Track** (DOC leaflet and map $1) slices through the largest area of lowland rainforest in New Zealand. Although it is easy-going and well-graded it takes the best part of four days to reach Big River and you'll just have to turn around and walk back unless you prearrange a jetboat out of Wairaurahiri Hut with Wairaurahiri Jet (T03/225 8318) or Wairaurahiri Wilderness Jet (T03/225 8174). A popular alternative is to make a three-day excursion staying at Port Craig Hut for two nights and exploring the environs on the second day. Three huts ($5) spaced four to seven hours' walk apart provide accommodation on the South Coast Track and camping is free.

The first day's walk is typically Bluecliffs Beach to Port Craig Hut (20km; 5–7hr; negligible ascent), following either the old logging road or, tide permitting, the beach – which should shave an hour off your walking time. On the section from Port Craig Hut to Wairaurahiri Hut (16km; 4–6hr; 200m ascent) the track follows the old tramway, crossing all four of the restored viaducts, before dropping down to the Wairaurahiri River. The path from Wairaurahiri Hut to Waitutu Hut (13km, 4–6hr,

Orawia (daily: Dec–Feb 8.30am–6pm; March–Nov 9am–5pm; T03/226 6399), is primarily for organizing hikers heading off for the Hump Ridge Track, but will also help with local accommodation, transport and the like.

Accommodation is limited but improving with the comfortable, new *Tuatapere Motel*, 73 Main St (T03/226 6250 & 0800/009 993; ❺), the traditional *Waiau Hotel*, 49 Main St (T03/226 6409, W www.waiauhotel.co.nz; rooms and ensuites ❸, B&B ❺), and the fairly basic *Five Mountain Holiday Park & Hump Track Backpackers* (6 Clifden Rd T & F03/226 6418; camping $10, dorms ❶, rooms ❷), a former forest workers' camp with grassy sites, a row of twin rooms and free vehicle storage for hikers. It is also worth considering staying at *Rarakau Lodge* (T03/225 8192; dorm ❶, rooms ❸), at Bluecliffs Beach at the beginning of the Hump Ridge and Waitutu tracks, which has bunkrooms, and private rooms and space for campervans and camping. Bring your own sleeping bag and pillow.

negligible ascent) largely follows the coastal flats across Maori land. Fit trampers with camping equipment might want to continue from Waitutu Hut to Big River (12km; 5–7hr; negligible ascent), the boundary of the Fiordland National Park and the end of the track; note that there are no facilities of any kind at Big River.

The Hump Ridge Track

The privately-managed **Hump Ridge Track** (book in advance ☎03/226 6739 & 0800/486 774, ⓦwww.humpridgetrack.co.nz or at the office in Tuatapere, see p.931) is done in three days with nights spent at two comfortable forty-bunk huts (each $40; May–late Oct $25), each with lights, gas cookers, tables, hot and cold running water, four-bunk rooms, and ablution blocks with flush toilets and wash basins. You still need to bring all the usual tramping gear including sleeping bags, cooking pots and utensils and all your food. It also requires a good level of fitness and isn't a hike for beginners or kids under ten.

If this all sounds too difficult you can arrange for helicopter **bag transfer** to the next hut with Southwest Helicopters (☎03/249 7402, ⓦwww.southwesthelicopters .co.nz). Either go for the full package ($135) or just have your stuff lifted up the steep climb to the first hut on the first day when the pack is heaviest ($45): everything, including empty bottles, must be carried out.

In addition there's a **Freedom Plus** package ($395) which includes two nights backpacker accommodation in Tuatapere, full heli-packing, return transport to Track Burn, hot showers, a sleeping bag supplied at the huts and a souvenir T-shirt. The trip can also be done as a **guided walk** with Kiwi Wilderness Walks (☎03/442 6017, ⓦwww.NZwalk.com) who run a four-day three-night trip ($1195) with everything Freedom Plus provides plus all meals, superior accommodation at the huts, hotel accommodation in Tuatapere and return transport from Te Anau or Invercargill.

Everyone walks **the track** in the same direction starting at Bluecliffs Beach Car Park. **Day One** (18km; 8–9hr; 900m ascent) starts along the coast but quickly becomes an uphill slog through podocarp/beech forest to the **Okaka Hut** on the Hump Ridge with its thoroughly rewarding views. On **Day Two** (18km; 7–9hr; 100m ascent, 900m descent) the track undulates past beautiful sandstone tors to a lunch spot with mountain and coastline views. After lunch you descend along Edwin Burn to the Edwin Burn Viaduct, then follow the coast past the more majestic **Percy Burn Viaduct**, to the hut at **Port Craig Village**. **Day Three** (17km; 6–7hr; undulating) wanders through towering coastal rimu and then down on to sandy beaches and back to the Bluecliffs Beach car park.

The best **eating** around is at the *Waiau Hotel*, 47 Main St, which is very much the social centre of town. Apart from that it is basically takeaways and self-catering.

Colac Bay and Riverton

South of Tuatapere, SH99 follows the wind-ravaged cliffs behind the wide and moody Te Waewae Bay, where fierce southerlies have sculpted some much-photographed macrocarpa trees into compact forms not unlike giant broccoli. Beyond the small town of Orepuki, the road cuts inland, regaining the sea 45km southeast of Tuatapere, at the quiet community of **Colac Bay** – a name eighteenth-century whalers derived from the name of the local Maori chief, Korako. Swimming aside, there's little reason to stop here, and you might as well press on a further 12km to **RIVERTON** (Aparima), one of the country's

The **eastern continuation** of the Southern Scenic Route through the Catlins to Dunedin is covered in Chapter Eleven, starting on p.738.

oldest settlements. Used by whalers from New South Wales as early as the last decade of the eighteenth century, the town was formally established in 1836 by another whaler, John Howell – who is also credited with kick-starting New Zealand's now formidable sheep-farming industry.

Strung along a spit between the sea and the Jacob's River Estuary (actually the mouth of the Aparima and Pourakino rivers), where fishing boats still harbour, Riverton has a relaxed almost comatose feel that might just lull you into staying for a day or so. The town is trying to pitch itself as some kind of paua capital, with a couple of giant paua shells in town, long-delayed plans to inlay the pavements with bits of shell, and several shops selling the **shells** by the score, best of which is the Riverton Paua Shoppe Factory, 134 Palmerston St. Alternatively, the Maori Craft Studio at 130 Palmerston St (☎03/234 9965, ⓦwww.solo1nz.faithweb.com), although it looks like a shop, is actually a great place to learn to **weave flax** in the traditional Maori-style or **carve bone** (both $90, including overnight accommodation). You should reserve an hour for the interesting local history and hoard of knick-knacks in the **Wallace Museum**, 172 Palmerston St (daily: Nov–April 10.30am–4pm May–Oct 1.30–4pm; $2 donation requested; ☎03/234 8698). Otherwise, consider one of the many boat charters to take you out trout or saltwater **fishing** (check at the visitor centre to see which ones are awake).

Practicalities

Local information, including a leaflet detailing leisurely beach and hilltop walks, is available in the **visitor centre,** 172 Palmerston St (Oct–April daily 10am–4pm; ☎03/234 9991), in the museum opposite the combined SuperValue market and post office. Easily the best **place to stay** is *Riverton's Guesthouse*, at 136 Palmerston St (☎03/234 8886, ⓔrivertonrockguesthouse @paradise.net.nz; ❶–❺), where beautifully decorated standard (❸ & ❹) and en-suite (❺) rooms occupy a tastefully renovated 1870s building along with a couple of four-shares (❶); everyone gets to use the well-equipped kitchen area and spacious, comfortable lounge overlooking the lagoon. If they're full, head next door to the *Globe Hotel Backpackers*, 144 Palmerston St (☎03/234 8527 & 0800/843 456, ⓦwww.theglobe.co.nz; dorms ❶, rooms ❷) where they have a good bar which serves gourmet pizzas. There's also the *Riverton Caravan Park and Holiday Homes* on Hamlet Street (☎ & ⓕ03/234 8526; camping $8, bunkhouse ❶, cottages & chalets ❷–❸). Of the limited range of **places to eat**, the most appealing is the *Nostalgia Country Café*, 108 Palmerston St (closed winter Mondays), which is good for coffee, light meals, their speciality homemade pies and predominantly seafood specials. Alternatively there's the stylish *Beach House Café and Bar*, on Rocks Highway, 2km west of Riverton town centre, with lovely views out over the sea, where you can pick up delicious lunches and dinners from a blackboard menu of predominantly tasty seafood, veggie and steak options or some gorgeous desserts.

Beyond Riverton, SH99 heads into the hinterland of Invercargill, 40km away.

Travel details

Fiordland is off the main transport routes. There are no trains or scheduled flights from the main airlines, and even buses are relatively few. One bus service worth pointing out is Tracknet's Backroad Bus which runs daily (Dec–April) between Queenstown and Te Anau using the *TSS Earnslaw* to get across Lake Wakatipu, then a bus along gravel roads past Mavora Lakes.

Buses

From Manapouri to: Clifden (1 daily; 1hr 30min); Te Anau (2 daily; 20min); Riverton (1 daily; 3hr); Tuatapere (1 daily; 2hr).

From Milford Sound to: Te Anau (2–5 daily; 2hr 15min); The Divide (2–5 daily; 1hr 30min); Queenstown (2 daily; 5hr 15min).

From Te Anau to: Dunedin (1 daily; 4hr 30min); Invercargill (1 daily; 4hr); Manapouri (2 daily; 20min); Milford Sound (2–5 daily; 2hr 15min); Queenstown (2 daily; 2hr 15min); Queenstown via backroads (1 daily; 4hr); Te Anau Downs (2 daily Nov–April; 30min); The Divide (2–5 daily; 1hr 20min).

From The Divide to: Milford Sound (2–5 daily; 1hr 30min); Te Anau (2–5 daily; 1hr 20min).

From Tuatapere to: Invercargill (1 daily; 2hr 30min); Riverton (1 weekly; 1hr 30min).

Flights

From Milford Sound to: Queenstown (at least 20 daily; 35min).

From Te Anau to: Queenstown (3–5 daily; 30min).

Contexts

Contexts

History

W hite New Zealanders have long thought of their country as a model of humanitarian colonization. Most Maori take a different view, however, informed by generations of their ancestors witnessing the theft of land and erosion of rights that were guaranteed by a treaty with the white man. Schoolroom histories have long been faithful to the European view, even to the point of influencing Maori mythology, but in the last couple of decades revisionist historians have largely discredited what many New Zealanders know as fact. Much that is presented as tradition, on deeper investigation turns out to be late nineteenth-century scholarship, often the product of historians who bent what they heard to fit their theories and, in the worst cases, even destroyed evidence. What follows is inextricably interwoven with Maori legend and can be understood more fully with reference to the section on Maoritanga (see p.957).

Pre-European history

Humans from southeast Asia first started exploring the South Pacific around five thousand years ago, gradually evolving a distinct culture as they filtered down through the islands of the Indonesian archipelago. A thousand years of progressive island hopping got them as far as Tonga and Samoa, where a distinctly Polynesian society continued to evolve, the people honing their seafaring and navigational skills to the point where lengthy sea journeys were possible. Around a thousand years ago, Polynesian culture reached its classical apotheosis in the Society Islands, a group west of Tahiti. This was almost certainly the hub for a series of migrations heading southwest across thousands of kilometres of open ocean, past the Cook Islands, eventually striking land in what is now known as New Zealand (Aotearoa).

It is thought that the first of these Polynesian people, the ancestors of modern **Maori**, arrived in double-hulled canoes between 1000 and 1100 AD, as a result of a migration that was planned to the extent that they took with them the *kuri* (dog) and food plants such as taro (a starchy tuber), yam and kumara (sweet potato). It seems likely that there were several migrations and there may have even been two-way traffic, although archeological evidence points to a cessation of contact well before 1500 AD. The widely believed story of a legendary "Great Fleet" of seven canoes arriving in 1350 AD seems most likely to be the product of a fanciful Victorian adaptation of Maori oral history, which has been readopted into contemporary Maori legend.

Arriving Polynesians found a land so much colder than their tropical home that many of the crops and plants they brought with them wouldn't grow. Fortunately there was an abundance of large quarry in the form of marine life and flightless birds, particularly in the South Island, where most settled. The people of this **Archaic Period** are often misleadingly known as "Moa Hunters" and while some undoubtedly lived off these birds, they didn't exist in other areas. By 1300, settlements had been established all around the coast, but it was only later that there is evidence of horticulture, possibly supporting the contention that there was a later migration bringing plants for cultivation. On the other hand, it may just signal the beginning of successful year-round food storage allowing a settled living pattern rather than the short-lived campsites used by earlier hunters. Whichever is the case, this marks the beginning of the **Classic Period** when *kainga* (villages) grew up close to the kumara grounds, often supported by *pa* (fortified villages) where the people could retreat when under attack. As tasks became more special-ized and hunting and horticulture began to take up less time, the arts – particularly carving and weaving (see pp.961–964) – began to flourish and warfare became endemic, digs revealing an armoury of *mere, patu* and *taiaha* (fighting clubs) not found earlier. The decline of easily caught birdlife and the relative ease of growing kumara in the warmer North Island marked the beginning of a northward population shift, to the extent that when the Europeans arrived, ninety-five percent of the population was located in the North Island, mostly in the northern reaches, with coastal settlements reach-ing down to Hawke's Bay and Wanganui.

European contact and the Maori response

Ever since Europeans had ventured across the oceans and "discovered" other continents, many were convinced of the existence of a *terra australia incognita*, an unknown southern land thought necessary to counterbalance the northern continents. In 1642, the Dutch East India Company, keen to dominate any trade with this new continent, sent Dutchman Abel Tasman to the southern oceans where he became the first European to catch sight of the South Island of Aotearoa. He anchored in Golden Bay, where a small boat being rowed between Tasman's two ships was intercepted by a Maori war canoe and four sailors were killed. Without setting foot on land Tasman turned tail and fled up the west coast of the North Island and went on to add Tonga and Fiji to Euro-pean maps. He named Aotearoa "Staten Landt", later renamed Nieuw Zeeland after the Dutch maritime province.

New Zealand was ignored for over a century until 1769 when Yorkshireman **James Cook** sailed his *Endeavour* into the Pacific to observe the passage of Venus across the sun. He continued west arriving at "the Eastern side of the Land discover'd by Tasman" where he observed the "Genius, Temper, Disposition and Number of the Natives" and meticulously charted the coast-line – the only significant errors were to show Banks Peninsula as an island and Stewart Island as a peninsula – and encouraged his botanists, Banks and Solander, to collect numerous samples.

Cook and his crew found Maori a sophisticated people with a highly formalized social structure and an impressive ability to turn stone and wood into fabulously carved canoes, weapons and meeting houses – and yet they were tied to Stone Age technology, with no wheels, roads, metalwork, pottery or animal husbandry. Cook found them aggressive, surly and little inclined to trade, but after an initial unfortunate encounter near Gisborne (see p.439) and another off Cape Kidnappers, near Napier (see p.463), he managed to strike up friendly and constructive relations with the "Indians". These "Indians" now found that their tribal allegiance was not enough to differentiate them from the Europeans and subsequently began calling themselves *maori* (meaning "normal" or "not distinctive") while referring to the newcomers as Pakeha ("foreign").

Offshore from the Coromandel Peninsula, Cook deviated from instructions and unfurled the British flag, claiming formal possession without the consent of Maori, but was still allowed to return twice in 1773 and 1777. The French were also interested in New Zealand, and on his 1769 voyage Cook had passed **Jean Francois Marie de Surville** in a storm without either knowing of the other's presence. Three years later, **Marion du Fresne** spent five amicable weeks around the Bay of Islands, before most of his crew were killed, probably after inadvertently transgressing some *tapu* (taboo).

The establishment of the Botany Bay penal colony in neighbouring Australia aroused the first commercial interest in New Zealand and from the 1790s to the 1830s New Zealand was very much part of the Australian frontier. By 1830 the coast was dotted with semi-permanent **sealing** communities which, within thirty years, had almost clubbed the seals into extinction. Meanwhile the British navy was rapidly felling giant kauri trees for its ships' masts, while others were busy supplying Sydney shipbuilders. By the 1820s **whalers** had moved in, basing themselves at Kororareka (now Russell, in the Bay of Islands), where they could recruit Maori crew and provision their ships. This combination of rough whalers, escaped convicts from Australia and all manner of miscreants and adventurers combined to turn Russell into "the Hellhole of the Pacific", a lawless place populated by what Darwin, on his visit in 1835, found to be "the very refuse of Society".

Before long, the Maori way of life had been entirely disrupted. Maori were quick to understand the importance of guns and **inter-tribal fighting** soon broke out on a scale never seen before. Hongi Hika from Ngapuhi *iwi* of the Bay of Islands was the first chief to acquire firearms in 1821, adding 300 muskets to his stock by trading the gifts showered on him by London society when he was presented to George IV as an "equal". Vowing to emulate the supreme power of the imperial king, he set about subduing much of the North Island, using the often badly maintained and inexpertly aimed guns to rattle the enemy, who were then slaughtered with the traditional *mere*. Warriors abandoned the old fighting season – the lulls between hunting and tending the crops – and set off to settle old scores, resulting in a massive loss of life. The quest for new territory fuelled the actions of Ngati Toa's **Te Rauparaha** (see p.939), who soon controlled the southern half of the North Island.

The huge demand for firearms drove Maori to sell the best of their food, relocating to unhealthy areas close to flax swamps, where flax production could be increased. Even highly valued tribal treasures – *pounamu* (greenstone) clubs and the preserved heads of chiefs taken in battle – were traded. Poor living conditions allowed European **diseases** to sweep through the Maori population time and again, while alcohol and tobacco abuse became widespread, Maori women were prostituted to Pakeha sailors, and the tribal structure began to crumble.

Into this scene stepped the **missionaries** in 1814, the brutal New South Wales magistrate, **Samuel Marsden**, arriving in the Bay of Islands a transformed man with a mission to bring Christianity and "civilization" to Maori, and to save the souls of the sealers and whalers. Subsequently Anglicans, Wesleyans and Catholics all set up missions throughout the North Island, playing a significant role in protecting Maori from the worst of the exploitation and campaigning in both London and Sydney for more policing of **Pakeha** actions. In return, they destroyed fine artworks considered too sexually explicit and demanded that Maori abandon cannibalism and slavery; in short Maori were expected to trade in their Maoritanga and become Brown Europeans. By the 1830s, self-confidence and the belief in Maori ways was in rapid decline:

the *tohunga* (priest) was powerless over new European diseases which could often be cured by the missionaries, and Maori had started to believe the Pakeha, who were convinced that the Maori race was dying out. They felt they needed help.

The push for colonization

Despite Cook's discovery claim in 1769, imperial cartographers had never marked New Zealand as a British possession and it was with some reluctance – informed by the perception of an over-extended empire only marginally under control – that New South Wales law was nominally extended to New Zealand in 1817. The effect was minimal; the New South Wales governor had no official representation on this side of the Tasman and was powerless to act. Unimpressed, by 1831 a small group of northern Maori chiefs decided to petition the British monarch to become a "friend and the guardian of these islands", a letter that was later used to justify Britain's intervention.

The Treaty of Waitangi: in English and Maori

The main points set out in the **English treaty** are as follows:
- The chiefs cede sovereignty of New Zealand to the Queen of England.
- The Queen guarantees the chiefs the "full exclusive and undisturbed possession of their Lands and Estates Forests Fisheries and other properties which they may collectively or individually possess".
- The Crown retains the right of pre-emption over Maori lands.
- The Queen extends the rights and privileges of British subjects to Maori.

However, the **Maori translation** presents numerous possibilities for misunderstanding, since Maori is a more idiomatic and metaphorical language, where words can take on several meanings. The main points of contention are as follows:

The preamble of the English version cites the main **objectives** of the treaty being to protect Maori interests, to provide for British settlement and to set up a government to maintain peace and order. On the other hand, the main thrust of the Maori version is that the all-important rank and status of the chiefs and tribes will be maintained.

In the Maori version, the concept of **sovereignty** is translated as *kawanatanga* (governorship), a word Maori linked to their experience of the toothless reign of British Resident James Busby. It seems unlikely that the chiefs realized just what they were giving away.

In the Maori text, the Crown guaranteed the *tangata whenua* (people of the land) the possession of their properties for as long as they wished to keep them. In English this was expressed in terms of **individual rights** over property. This is perhaps the most wilful mistranslation and, in practice, there were long periods when Maori were coerced into selling their **land**, and when they refused, lands were simply taken.

Pre-emption was translated as *hokonga* – a term simply meaning "buying and selling", with no explanation of the Crown's exclusive right to buy Maori land, which was clearly spelled out in the English version. This has resulted in considerable friction over Maori being unable to sell any land that the government didn't want, even if they had a buyer.

The implications of **British citizenship** may not have been well understood: it is not clear whether Maori realized they would be bound by British law.

Britain's response was to send the pompous and less-than-competent **James Busby** as British Resident in 1833, with a brief to encourage trade, stay on good terms with the missionaries and Maori, and apprehend escaped convicts for return to Sydney. Feeling that New Zealand was becoming a drain on the colony's economy, the New South Wales governor, Bourke, withheld guns and troops, and Busby was unable to enforce his will. Busby was also duped by the madness of Baron de Thierry, a Brit of French parents, who claimed he had bought most of the Hokianga district from Hongi Hika and styled himself the "sovereign chief of New Zealand", ostensibly to save Maori from the degradation he foresaw under British dominion. In a panic, Busby misguidedly persuaded 35 northern chiefs to proclaim themselves as the "**United Tribes of New Zealand**" in 1835. As far as the Foreign Office was concerned, this allowed Britain to disclaim responsibility for the actions of its subjects.

By the late 1830s there were around two thousand Pakeha in New Zealand, the largest concentration around Kororareka in the Bay of Islands, where there were often up to thirty ships at anchor. Most were British, but French Catholics were consolidating their tentative toehold, and in 1839 James Clendon was appointed American consul. Meanwhile, land speculators and colonists were taking an interest for the first time. The Australian emancipationist, William Charles Wentworth, had "bought" the South Island and Stewart Island for a few hundred pounds (the largest private land deal in history, subsequently quashed by government order) and British settlers were already setting sail. The British admiralty finally began to take notice when it became apparent that the Australian convict settlements, originally intended simply as an out-of-sight, out-of-mind solution to their bulging prisons, looked set to become a valuable possession.

It was a combination of these pressures and Busby's continual exaggeration of the Maori inability to control their own affairs that goaded the British government into action. The result was the 1840 **Treaty of Waitangi** (see box on p.942, and also p.942), a document that purported to guarantee continued Maori control of their lands, rights and possessions in return for their loss of sovereignty, a concept poorly understood by Maori. The annexed lands became a dependency of New South Wales until New Zealand was declared a separate colony a year later.

Settlement and the early pioneers

Even before the Treaty was signed, there were moves to found a settlement in Port Nicholson, the site of Wellington, on behalf of the New Zealand Company. This was the brainchild of Edward Gibbon Wakefield, who desperately wanted to stem American-style egalitarianism and hoped to use New Zealand as the proving ground for his theory of "scientific colonization". This involved preserving the English squire-and-yokel class structure by encouraging the settlement of a cross-section of English society, though without the "dregs" at the bottom. It was supposed to be a self-regulating system, whereby the company would buy large tracts of land cheaply from the government then charge a price low enough to encourage the relatively wealthy to invest, yet high enough to prevent labourers from becoming landowners. The revenue from land sales was then to fund the transportation of cheap labour to work the land, but the system ended up encouraging absentee landlordism as English "gentlemen", arriving to find somewhere altogether more rugged and less refined than they had been promised, hot-footed it to Australia or America.

Between 1839 and 1843 the New Zealand Company dispatched nearly 19,000 settlers and established them in "**planned settlements**" in Wellington, Wanganui, Nelson and New Plymouth. This was the core of Pakeha immigration, the only substantial non-Wakefield settlement being **Auckland**, a scruffy collection of waterside shacks which, to the horror of New Zealand Company officials, became the capital after the signing of the Treaty of Waitangi. Maori welfare and social justice had no place in all this, despite the precarious position of Pakeha settlements, which were nothing but tiny enclaves in a country still under Maori control. Transgressing the protocols of the local *iwi* was likely to have graver implications than offending the Pakeha government.

The company couldn't buy land direct from Maori, but the government bought up huge tracts and sold it on, often for ten or twenty times what they paid for it. Maori must have been well aware that they were being swindled and could have negotiated better prices themselves, but sold almost the whole of the South Island in a number of large blocks. Some was bought by two more organizations expounding the Wakefield principle: the dour Free Church of Scotland founded **Dunedin** in 1848, while the Canterbury Association established **Christchurch** in 1850, fashioning it English, Anglo-Catholic and conservative. In 1850 the New Zealand Company foundered, leaving well-established settlements which, subject to the hard realities of colonial life, had failed to conform to Wakefield's lofty theories and were filled with sturdy workers from labouring and lower middle-class backgrounds.

In 1852 New Zealand achieved self-government and set about dividing the country into six **provinces** – Auckland, New Plymouth, Wellington, Nelson, Canterbury and Otago – which took over land sales and encouraged migrants with free passage, land grants and guaranteed employment on road construction schemes. The same people drawn to the Wakefield settlements heeded the call, hoping for a better life away from the oppression and drudgery of working-class Britain. The new towns were alive with ambitious folk prepared to work hard to realize their high expectations, but many felt stymied by the low-quality land they were able to buy. At this point Maori still held the best land and were doing quite nicely growing potatoes and wheat for both local consumption and export to Australia, where the Victorian gold rush had created a huge demand. Pakeha were barely able to compete, and with the slump in export prices in the mid-1850s, many looked to pastoralism. The Crown helped out by halving the price of land, allowing poorer settlers to become landowners but simultaneously paving the way for the creation of huge pastoral runs and putting further pressure on Maori to sell land.

Maori discontent and the New Zealand Wars

The first five years after the signing of the Treaty were a disaster, first under governor Hobson then under the ineffectual FitzRoy. Relations between Maori and Pakeha began to deteriorate immediately, as the capital was moved from Kororareka to Auckland and duties were imposed in the Bay of Islands.

The consequent loss of trade from passing ships precipitated the first tangible expression of dissent, a famous series of incidents involving the Ngapuhi leader Hone Heke, who repeatedly felled the most fundamental symbol of British authority, the flagstaff at Russell (see p.194). The situation was normalized to some degree by the appointment of George Grey, the most able of New Zealand's governors and a man who did more than anyone else to shape the country's early years. He was economical with the truth and despotic, but possessed the intelligence to use his deceit in a most effective (and often benign) way. As Maori began to adapt their culture to accommodate Pakeha in a way that few other native peoples have – selling their crops, operating flour mills and running coastal shipping – Grey encouraged the process by establishing mission schools, erecting hospitals where Maori could get free treatment, and providing employment on public works. In short, he did what he could to uphold the spirit of the Treaty, thereby gaining enormous respect among Maori. Sadly, he failed to set up any mechanism to perpetuate his policies after he left for the governorship of Cape Town in 1853. Under New Zealand's constitution, enacted in 1852, Maori were excluded from political decision-making and prevented from setting up their own form of government; although British subjects in name, they had few of the practical benefits and yet were increasingly expected to comply with British law.

By now it was clear that Maori had been duped by the Treaty of Waitangi: one chief explained that they thought they were transferring the "shadow of the land" while "the substance of the land remains with us", and yet he now conceded "the substance of the land goes to the Europeans, the shadow only will be our portion". Growing **resistance** to land sales came at a time when settler communities were expanding and demanding to buy huge tracts of pastoral land. With improved communications Pakeha became more self-reliant and dismissive of Maori, who progressively began to lose faith in the government and fell back on traditional methods of handling their affairs. Self-government had given landowners the vote, but since Maori didn't hold individual titles to their land they were denied suffrage. Maori and Pakeha aspirations seemed completely at odds and there was a growing sense of betrayal, which helped to replace tribal animosities with a tenuous unity. In 1854, a month before New Zealand's first parliament, Maori held inter-tribal meetings to discuss a response to the degradation of their culture and the rapid loss of their land. The eventual upshot was the 1858 election of the ageing **Te Wherowhero**, head chief of the Waikatos, as the Maori "King", the leader of the **King Movement** (see box in Chapter Three, p.247) behind which Maori could rally to hold back the flood of Pakeha settlement. Initially just the Waikato and central North Island *iwi* supported the King, but soon Taranaki and some Hawke's Bay *iwi* joined in a loose federation united in vowing not to sell any more land. This brave attempt to challenge the changes forced upon them gave Maori a sense of purpose and brought with it a resurgence of ancient customs such as tattooing. While some radical Maori wanted to completely rid the country of the white menace, most were moderates and made peaceful overtures that Pakeha chose to regard as rebellious.

By now, most settlers felt that the Treaty of Waitangi had no validity whatsoever and sided with the land sellers to drive the government to repress the Maori landholders. There had been minor skirmishes over land throughout the country, but matters came to a head in 1860, when the government used troops to enforce a bogus purchase of land at Waitara, near New Plymouth. The fighting was temporarily confined to Taranaki but soon spread to consume the whole of the North Island in the **New Zealand Wars**, once known by Pakeha as the Maori Wars and by Maori as *te riri* Pakeha (white man's anger). Maori were divided: most of the supporters of the King movement, particularly the Waikatos, traced their *whakapapa* (genealogy) back to the Tainui canoe and some others chose this opportunity to settle old grievances by siding with the government against their traditional enemies. Through the early 1860s the number of Pakeha troops was tripled to around 3000, providing an effective force against Maori who failed to adopt a co-ordinated strategy. The warrior ethic meant there was no place for more effective guerrilla tactics, except in the east of the North Island, where **Te Kooti** (see box, p.449) kept the government troops on the run. Elsewhere Maori frequently faced off against ranked artillery and, though there were notable successes, the final result was inevitable. Fighting had abated by the end of the 1860s but peace wasn't finally declared until 1881, when the Maori fastness of the "King Country" (an area south of Hamilton which still goes by that title) was finally opened up to Pakeha once again.

British soldiers had been lured into service with offers of land and free passage and, as a further affront to defeated Maori, many of them were settled in the solidly Maori Waikato. Much of the most fertile land was **confiscated** – in the Waikato, the Bay of Plenty and Taranaki – with little regard to the owners' allegiances during the conflict. By 1862 the Crown had relinquished its right of pre-emption and individuals could buy land directly from Maori, who were forced to limit the stated ownership first to ten individuals and later to just one owner. With their collective power smashed, there was little resistance to voracious land agents luring Maori into debt then offering to buy their land to save them.

Between 1860 and 1881 the **non-Maori population** rose from 60,000 to 470,000, swamping and marginalizing Maori society. An Anglo-Saxon world view came to dominate all aspects of New Zealand life, and by 1871 the Maori language was no longer used for teaching in schools. A defeated people were widely thought to be close to extinction: Anthony Trollope in 1872 wrote "There is scope for poetry in their past history. There is room for philanthropy as to their present condition. But in regard to their future – there is hardly a place for hope."

Meanwhile, as the New Zealand Wars raged in the North Island, **gold fever** had struck the South. Flakes had been found near Queenstown in 1861 and the initial rushes soon spread to later finds along the West Coast. For the best part of a decade, gold was New Zealand's major export, but the gold provinces never had a major influence on the rest of the country, nor does the gold era retain the legendary status it does in California and Victoria. The major effect was on population distribution: by 1858 the shrinking Maori population had been outstripped by the rapidly swelling horde of Pakeha settlers, most settling in the South Island where relations with Maori played a much smaller part. The South Island prospered, with both Christchurch and Dunedin consolidating their roles, serving the surrounding farms and more distant sheep stations. Dunedin became the largest town in the country, the influx of the "New Iniquity" radically changing the city's staunch front of the "Old Identity".

Consolidation and social reform

The 1870s were dominated by the policies of Julius Vogel, an able Treasurer who started a programme of borrowing on a massive scale to fund public works.

Within a decade what had previously been a land of scattered towns in separately governed provinces was transformed into a single country unified by improved roads, an expanding rail system, 7000 kilometres of telegraph wires and numerous public institutions. Almost all the remaining farmable land was bought up or leased from Maori and acclimatization societies sprang up with the express aim of anglicizing the New Zealand countryside and improving farming. New Zealand quickly began to realize the agricultural expectation created by fertile soils, a temperate climate and relatively high rainfall. Arable farming was mostly abandoned and pastoralism was taking hold, particularly among those rich enough to afford to buy and ship the stock. With no extensive market close enough to make perishable produce profitable, wool became the main export, stimulated by the development of the Corriedale sheep, a Romney–Lincoln cross with a long fleece. Wool continued as the mainstay until 1882, when the first refrigerated meat shipment left for Britain, signalling a turning point in the New Zealand economy and the establishment of New Zealand as Britain's offshore larder, a role it maintained until the 1970s.

From 1879 until 1896 New Zealand went into the "long depression", mostly overseen by the conservative "Continuous Ministry" – the last government composed of colonial gentry. During this time **trade unionism** began to influence the political scene and bolstered the Liberal Pact (a Liberal and Labour alliance), which, in 1890, wrested power from those who had controlled the country for two decades and ushered in an era of unprecedented social change. Its first leader, **John Ballance**, firmly believed in state intervention and installed **William Pember Reeves**, probably New Zealand's most radically socialist MP, as his Minister of Labour. Reeves was instrumental in pushing through sweeping reforms to working hours and factory conditions that were so progressive that no further changes were made to labour laws until 1936. On his own initiative, with no apparent demand from workers, he introduced the world's first **compulsory arbitration system**, which went on to award numerous wage rises, so increasing the national prosperity. He had become too radical for most of his colleagues, however, and only remained in office until 1896. When Ballance died in 1892 he was replaced by **Richard "King Dick" Seddon**, a blunt Lancastrian who became, along with Grey, one of the country's greatest, if least democratic, leaders. Following Ballance's lead he introduced a graduated income tax and repealed property tax, hoping to break up some of the large estates (something eventually achieved much later, as technological changes made dairying and mixed farming more prosperous). New Zealand was already being tagged the "social laboratory of the world", but more was to come.

In 1893, New Zealand was the first nation in the world to enact full **female suffrage**, undoubtedly in line with the liberal thinking of the time, but apparently an accident nonetheless. The story goes that Seddon let an amendment to an electoral reform bill pass on the assumption that it would be rejected by the Legislative Council (an upper house which survived until 1950), thus diverting the ill will of suffragists. Others contend that female suffrage was approved not for any free-thinking liberal principle but in response to the powerful quasi-religious temperance movement, which hoped to "purify and improve the tone of our politics", effectively giving married couples double the vote of the single man who was often seen as a drunken layabout. In 1898 Seddon further astonished the world by weathering a ninety-hour continuous debate to squeeze through legislation guaranteeing an **old age pension**. Fabian Beatrice Webb, in New Zealand that same year, allowed that "it is delightful to see a country with no millionaires and hardly any slums".

By the early twentieth century, the radical impetus had faded along with the memory of the 1880s depression, and Pakeha could rest easy in the knowledge that their standard of living was one of the highest in the world. But things were not so rosy for Maori, whose numbers had dropped from an estimated 200,000 at Cook's first visit to a figure thought to be below 50,000 in 1896. However, as resistance to European diseases grew, numbers started rising, accompanied by a new confidence buoyed by the rise of Maori parliamentary leadership. **Apirana Ngata**, **Maui Pomare** and **Te Rangi Hiroa** (**Peter Buck**) were all products of Te Aute College, an Anglican school for Maori, and all were committed to working within the administrative and legislative framework of government, convinced that the survival of Maoritanga depended on shedding those aspects of the traditional lifestyle that impeded their acceptance of the modern world.

Seddon died in 1906 and the flame went out of the Liberal torch, though the party was to stay in power another six years. This era saw the rise of the "**Red Feds**", international socialists of the Red Federation who began to organize Kiwi labour. They rejected the arbitration system that had kept wage rises below the level of inflation and prevented strikes for a decade, and encouraged **strikes**. The longest was at Blackball (see p.773) on the West Coast, where prime movers in the formation of the Federation of Miners, and subsequently the Federation of Labour, led a three-month stoppage.

The 1912 election was won by William Massey's Reform Party, with the support of the farmers or "cow cockies". Allegiances were now substantially polarized and 1912 and 1913 saw bitter fighting at a series of strikes at the gold mines of Waihi, the docks at Timaru and the wharves of Auckland. As workers opposed to the arbitration system withdrew their labour, the owners organized scab labour, while the hostile Farmers' Union recruited mounted "specials" to add to the government force of "special constables". All were protected by naval and military forces as they decisively smashed the Red Feds. The Prime Minister even handed out medals to strike-breaking dairy farmers. Further domestic conflict was only averted by the outbreak of war.

Coming of age: 1916–1945

Though New Zealand had started off as an unwanted sibling of Mother England, it had soon transformed itself into a devoted daughter who could be relied upon in times of crisis. New Zealand had supported Britain in South Africa at the end of the nineteenth century and was now called upon to do the same in World War I. Locally born Pakeha now outnumbered immigrants and, in 1907, New Zealand had traded its self-governing colony status for that of a Dominion, giving it control over its foreign policy; but the rising sense of nationalism didn't dilute a patriotism for the motherland far in excess of its filial duty. Altogether ten percent of the population were involved in the war effort, 100,000 fighting in the trenches of Gallipoli and elsewhere. Seventeen thousand failed to return, more than were lost in Belgium, a battleground with six times the population.

At home, the **Temperance Movement** was back in action, attempting to curb vice in the army brought on by the demon drink. Plebiscites in 1911, 1914 and 1919 narrowly averted national prohibition but the "wowsers" succeeded to the point that from 1917 pubs would close at 6pm for the duration of the war. Six o'clock closing entered the statute books in 1918: not until

1967 did its repeal end half a century of the "**Six o'clock swill**", an hour or so of frenetic after-work consumption in which the ability to tank down as much beer as possible was raised to an art form. This probably did more to hinder New Zealand's social development than anything else: pubs began to look more like lavatories, which could be hosed down after closing, and the predilection for quantity over quality encouraged breweries to churn out dreadful watery brews.

The wartime boom economy continued until around 1920 as Britain's demand for food remained high. Things looked rosy, especially for Pakeha returned servicemen, who were rehabilitated on newly acquired farmland; in contrast, Maori returned servicemen got nothing. These highly mortgaged and inexperienced farmers began to suffer with the rapid drop in produce prices in the early 1920s, fostering a sense of insecurity which pervaded the country. Political leadership was weak and yet New Zealand continued to grow with ongoing improvements in infrastructure – hydroelectric dams and roads – and enormous improvements in farming techniques, such as the application of superphosphate fertilizers, sophisticated milking machines and tractors. New Zealand remained a prosperous nation but was ill-prepared for the **Great Depression**, when the Wall Street Crash sent shock waves through the country. The already high national debt skyrocketed as export income dropped and the Reform government cut pensions, health care and public works' expenditure. The budget was balanced at the cost of producing huge numbers of unemployed. Prime Minister Forbes dictated "no pay without work" and sent thousands of men to primitive rural relief camps for unnecessary tasks such as planting trees and draining swamps in return for a pittance. With the knowledge of the prosperous years to come it is hard to conjure the image of lines of ragged men awaiting their relief money, malnourished children in schools and former soldiers panhandling in the streets.

Throughout the 1920s the Labour Party had gradually watered down some of its socialist policies in an attempt to woo the middle-ground voter. In 1935 they were swept to power and ushered in New Zealand's second era of massive social change, picking up where Seddon left off. Labour's leader **Michael Joseph Savage** felt that "Social Justice must be the guiding principle and economic organization must adapt itself to social needs", a sentiment translated by a contemporary commentator as aiming "to turn capitalism quite painlessly into a nicer sort of capitalism which will eventually become indistinguishable from socialism". State socialism was out, but "Red Feds" still held half the cabinet posts. Salaries reduced during the depression were restored; public works programmes were rekindled, with workers on full pay rather than "relief"; income was redistributed through graduated taxation; and in two rapid bursts of legislation Labour built the model **Welfare State**, the first in the world and the most comprehensive and integrated. State houses were built and let at low rental, pensions were increased, a national health service provided free medicines and health care, and family benefits supplemented the income of those with children.

Maori welfare was also on the agenda and there were moves to raise their living standards to the Pakeha level, partly achieved by increasing pensions and unemployment payments. Much of the best land had by now been sold off but legal changes paved the way for Maori land to be farmed using Pakeha agricultural methods, while maintaining communal ownership. In return, the newly formed **Ratana Party**, who held all four of the Maori Parliamentary seats, supported Labour, keeping them in office until 1949.

New Zealand's perception of its world position changed dramatically in 1941 when the Japanese bombed Pearl Harbor. The country was forced to recognize its position half a globe away from Britain and in the military sphere of America. As in World War I, large numbers of troops were called up, amounting to a third of the male labour force, but casualties were fewer and on the home front the economy continued to boom. Foreign wars aside, by the 1940s New Zealand was the world's most prosperous country, with a fabulous quality of life and the comfortable bed of the Welfare State to fall back on.

More years of prosperity

The Reform Party and the remnants of the Liberals eventually combined to form the National Party which, in 1949, wrested power from Labour. With McCarthyite rhetoric, National branded the more militant unionists as Communists and succeeded in breaking much of the power of the unions during the violent and emotional 1951 Waterfront Lock-out. From the late 1940s until the mid-1980s, National became New Zealand's natural party of government, disturbed only by two three-year stints with Labour in power. The conservatism always bubbling under had now found its expression. Most were happy with the government's strong-arm tactics, which emasculated the militant unions and the country settled down to what novelist C.K. Stead viewed as the Kiwi ideal: "to live in a country with fresh air, an open landscape and plenty of sunshine; and to own a house, car, refrigerator, washing machine, bach, launch, fibre-glass rod, golf clubs, and so on." This ideal had a flipside, which the historian Tony Simpson expressed with "we used to run a smug little society in which all was forbidden unless it was specifically permitted, in which case it was compulsory". Nonetheless, such a life had huge appeal for Brits still suffering rationing after World War II, and between 1947 and 1975, 77,000 British men, women and children became "ten pound poms", making use of the New Zealand government's assisted passage to fill Kiwi job vacancies.

While the egalitarian myth still perpetuated by many Kiwis may never have existed, by most measures New Zealand's wealth was evenly spread, with few truly rich and relatively few poor. The exception at least in economic terms were Maori, many now migrating in huge numbers to the cities, especially Auckland, responding to the urban labour shortages and good wages after World War II. By the 1970s the deracination of urban Maori was creating social unrest which, left unchannelled, resulted in high Maori unemployment and a disproportionate representation in prisons. Increasing contact between Maori and Europeans exposed weaknesses in the Pakeha belief that the country's race relations were the best in the world. Pakeha took great pride in Maori bravery, skill, generosity, sporting prowess and good humour, but were unable to set aside the discrimination which kept Maori out of professional jobs.

On the economic front, major changes took place under **Walter Nash**'s 1957–60 Labour government, when New Zealand embarked on a programme designed to relieve the country's dependence on exports. A steel rolling mill, oil refinery, gin distillery and glass factory were all set up and an aluminium industry was encouraged by the prospect of cheap power from a hydroelectric project on Lake Manapouri (see box, p.924). When **Keith Holyoake** took over at the helm of the next National government, in 1960, Britain was still by far New Zealand's biggest export market but was making overtures to the economically isolationist European Common Market. New Zealand was becoming aware that Britain was no longer the guardian she once was. This was equally true in the **military** sphere, where New Zealand began to court its Pacific allies, signing the anti-Communist SEATO (South-East Asia Treaty Organization) document, and the ANZUS pact, which provided for mutual defence of Australia, New Zealand and the US.

Dithering in the face of adversity 1972–1984

In a landslide victory, the third Labour government took control in 1972. Again it was to last only a single three-year term, largely due to the difficulties of having to deal with international events beyond its control. Most fundamental was the long-expected entry of Britain into the Common Market. Some other export markets had been found but New Zealand still felt betrayed. Later the same year oil prices quadrupled in a few months and the treasury found itself with mounting fuel bills and decreasing export receipts. The government borrowed heavily but couldn't avoid electoral defeat in 1975 by National's obstreperous and pugnacious Robert "Piggy" Muldoon, who denounced Labour's borrowing and then outdid them. In short order New Zealand had dreadful domestic and foreign debt, unemployment was the highest for decades, and the unthinkable was happening – the standard of living was falling. People began to leave in their thousands and the "brain drain" almost reached crisis point. Muldoon's solution was to "Think Big", a catch-all term for a number of capital-intensive petrochemical projects designed to utilize New Zealand's abundant natural gas to produce ammonia, urea fertilizer, methanol and synthetic petrol. Though undoubtedly self-aggrandizing it made little economic sense. Rather than use local technology and labour to convert New Zealand vehicles to run on compressed natural gas (a system already up and running), Muldoon chose to pay international corporations to design and build huge prefabricated processing plants which were then shipped to New Zealand for assembly, mostly around New Plymouth.

Factory outfalls often jeopardized traditional Maori shellfish beds, and where once *iwi* would have accepted this as inevitable, a new spirit of protest saw them win significant concessions. Throughout the mid-1970s Maori began to question the philosophy of Pakeha life and looked to the Treaty of Waitangi (see box, p.942) to correct the grievances that were aired at occupations of traditional land at Bastion Point in Auckland (see p.105), and Raglan, and through a petition delivered to parliament after a march across the North Island.

Maori also found expression in the formation of **gangs** – Black Power, the Mongrel Mob and the bike-oriented Highway 61 – along the lines graphically depicted in Lee Tamahori's film *Once Were Warriors*, which was originally written about South Auckland life in the 1970s. Fortified suburban homes still exist and such gangs continue to be influential among Maori youth, a position occasionally positively exploited to bring wayward Maori youth back into the fold.

Race relations were never Muldoon's strong suit and when large numbers of illegal **Polynesian immigrants** from south Pacific islands – particularly Tonga, Samoa and the Cook Islands – started arriving in Auckland he responded by instructing the police to conduct random street checks for "overstayers", many of whom were deported. Muldoon opted for a completely hands-off approach when it came to sporting contacts with South Africa and in 1976 let the pig-headed rugby administrators send an All Black team over to play racially selected South African teams. African nations responded by boycotting the Montreal Olympics, putting New Zealand in the unusual position of being an international pariah. New Zealand signed the 1977 Gleneagles Agreement requiring it to "vigorously combat the evil of apartheid" and yet in 1981 the New Zealand Rugby Union courted a **Springbok Tour**, which sparked New Zealand's greatest civil disturbance since the labour riots of the 1920s.

Economic and electoral reform 1984–1996

Muldoon's big-spending economic policies were widely perceived to be unsuccessful, and when he called a snap election in 1984, Labour were returned to power under David Lange. Just as National had eschewed traditional right-wing economics in favour of a "managed economy", Labour now changed tactics, addressing the massive economic problems by shunning the traditional left-of-centre approach. Instead, they grasped the baton of Thatcherite economics and sprinted off with it. Under Finance Minister Roger Douglas's Rogernomics, the dollar was devalued by twenty percent, exchange controls were abolished, tariffs slashed, the maximum income tax rate was halved, a Goods and Services Tax was introduced, Air New Zealand and the Bank of New Zealand were privatized, and state benefits were cut. Unemployment doubled to twelve percent, a quarter of manufacturing jobs were lost, and the moderately well-off benefited at the expense of the poor; nevertheless, market forces and enterprise culture had come to stay. As one of the world's most regulated economies became one of the most deregulated, the longstanding belief that the state should provide for those least able to help themselves was cast aside.

In other spheres Labour's views weren't so right-wing. One of Lange's first acts was to refuse US ships entry to New Zealand ports unless they declared that they were nuclear-free. The Americans would do nothing of the sort and withdrew support for New Zealand's defence safety net, the **ANZUS** pact. Most of the country backed Lange on this but were less sure about his overtures towards Maori who, for the first time since the middle of the nineteenth century, got legal recognition for the Treaty of Waitangi. Now, Maori grievances dating back to 1840 could be addressed.

The rise in apparent income under Rogernomics created consumer confidence and the economy boomed until the **stock market crash** of 1987, which hit New Zealand especially hard. The country went into freefall and all confidence in the reforms was lost. In 1990 National's **Jim Bolger** took the helm, and throughout the deep recession National continued Labour's free-market reforms, cutting welfare programmes and extracting teeth from the unions by passing the Employment Contracts Act, which established the pattern of individual workplaces coming to their own agreements on wages and conditions. By the middle of the 1990s the economy had improved dramatically and what for a time had been considered a foolhardy experiment was seen by monetarists as a model for open economies the world over. Meanwhile, the gap between the rich and the poor continues to widen and New Zealand's classless society is increasingly exposed for the myth it always was.

Ever since New Zealand achieved self-government from Britain in 1852, it had maintained a first-past-the-post Westminster style of parliament, with the exception of the scrapping of the upper house in 1950 and the provision for four (now seven) **Maori seats**. Maori can choose to vote for their general or Maori candidate but not both. In the depths of the recession in 1993, New Zealand voted for **electoral reform**, specifically Mixed Member Proportional representation (MMP), which purports to give smaller parties an opportunity to have some say. In the three MMP elections since then, this has certainly proved to be the case with minor parties making significant showings each time. The inclusion of smaller parties after the 1996 election brought a new Maori spirit into parliament, with far more Maori MPs than ever before and maiden speeches received with a *waiata* (song) from their *whanau* (extended family group) in the public gallery. Unfortunately, most were political neo-phytes and few weathered that first term intact.

Modern New Zealand

Bolger's poor handling of the first MMP coalition government saw his support wane, and he was replaced in a palace coup, in which **Jenny Shipley** became New Zealand's first female prime minister. Her brand of right-wing economics and more liberal social policies succeeded in holding the coalition together but failed to bolster the polls on the lead up to the 1999 election. Suddenly, out of left-field came the **Green Party**, long-sidelined but newly resurgent under MMP. The vagaries of the MMP system meant that, on a nail-biting election night, the Greens were teetering between getting no seats at all and racking up six seats, a tally they eventually achieved with the counting of special votes. They formed a government with Labour and the Alliance under **Helen Clark**, and sent New Zealand's first Rastafarian MP to parliament, one **Nandor Tanczos**. Resplendent in waist-length dreads and a new hemp suit he quickly became both a bogeyman for the opposition and something of a hero to disenfranchised youth. As if the political landscape weren't topsy-turvy enough, the staunchly conservative Wairarapa district returned the world's first transgender MP, Carterton's former mayor, **Georgina Beyer**.

Nine years in opposition left Labour (the senior coalition partner) with a considerable agenda for change including stopping logging of beech forests on the West Coast and replacing the Employment Contracts Act with more worker-friendly legislation. They failed to deliver on education and health care, but Clark weathered every brickbat and minor scandal and swept to victory in the 2002 election with an increased majority.

The kind of **republican rabble-rousing** championed across the Tasman largely falls on deaf ears in Aotearoa, where, despite the maturing of the nation over the last twenty years, and a progressive realignment with the Pacific and Asia, most seem happy to maintain links with Britain. Nonetheless, Labour uni-laterally abolished knighthoods in 2000 and, in 2003, brooked no debate when it came to abolishing the right of final legal appeal to London's Privy Council.

Labour's popularity remained high until rise of the **foreshore and seabed debate** late in 2003. During her four years in power, Helen Clark has taken a benign approach to restitution for Maori, encouraging Treaty of Waitangi clauses to be built into all new legislation. Pakeha New Zealanders were gen-erally happy about this as it appeared to have no detrimental impact on their lifestyle. Meanwhile, Maori were beginning to feel under siege from the large numbers of immigrants from east Asia, whose taste for shellfish was threatening the viability of traditional Maori gathering grounds. One Maori group then decided to make a legal claim for Maori rights over the foreshore and seabed. It quickly escalated to a nationwide debate and all of a sudden Pakeha New Zealanders (who have always valued the freedom of the beaches) began to get worried.

As the foreshore and seabed debate raged, the new leader of the near-moribund National Party, former Reserve Bank Governor **Don Brash**, started to question the apparently preferential treatment given to Maori. Suggesting that all benefits should be needs-based rather than race-based, Brash obviously struck a chord and National's popularity rating rocketed past Labour's. Tensions have risen all round, and it remains to be seen how the foreshore and seabed issue will be resolved and how Clark will tough out Brash's more hard-line approach.

Chronology of New Zealand

c.1000AD	Arrival of first **Polynesians**.
c.1350	The traditional date of arrival of the "Great Fleet" from Hawaiki.
1642	Dutchman **Abel Tasman** sails past the West Coast but doesn't land.
1769	Englishman **James Cook** circumnavigates both main islands and makes first constructive contact.
1772	French sailor **Marion du Fresne** and 26 of his men killed in the Bay of Islands.
1809	Whangaroa Maori attack the *Boyd*; most of the crew killed.
1814	Arrival of **Samuel Marsden**, the first Christian missionary.
1830s	Sealing and whaling stations dotted around the coast.
1833	James Busby installed as British Resident at Waitangi.
1835	Independence of the United Tribes of NZ proclaimed.
1840	**Treaty of Waitangi** signed; capital moved from Kororareka to Auckland.
1840s	Cities of Auckland, Christchurch, Dunedin, Nelson, New Plymouth, Wanganui and Wellington all established.
1852	NZ becomes a self-governing colony divided into six provinces.
1858	Settlers outnumber Maori.
1860–65	**Land Wars** between Pakeha and Maori.
1860s	Major gold rushes in the South Island.
1865	Capital moved from Auckland to Wellington.
1867	Maori men given the vote.
1870s	**Wool** established as the mainstay of the NZ economy.
1876	Abolition of provincial governments. Power centralized in Wellington.
1882	First **refrigerated meat shipment** to Europe. Lamb becomes increasingly important.
1890	NZ become "social laboratory" with introduction of compulsory arbitration and graduated income tax.
1893	Full **women's suffrage**; a world first.
1898	Old age pension introduced.
1910s	Rise of organized labour under the socialist Red Federation. Strikes at Blackball, Waihi and Auckland.
1914–18	NZ takes part in WWI with terrible loss of life.
1917	**Temperance Movement** gets pubs closed after 6pm. Only repealed in 1967.
1920s	Initial prosperity evaporates as the Great Depression takes hold.
1935	M.J. Savage's Labour government ushers in the world's first **Welfare State** with free health service, family benefits, state housing and increased pensions.
1941	Bombing of Pearl Harbor and WWII begins NZ's military realignment with the Pacific region.
1947	New Zealand becomes fully independent from Britain.
1950	Parliament's upper house abolished.
1951	NZ joins **ANZUS** military pact with the US and Australia.
1950s	NZ comfortable as one of the world's most prosperous nations.
1957–60	Infrastructure improvements: steel mill, oil refinery, and numerous hydroelectric power stations built or planned.
1960s	Start of **immigration from Pacific Islands**. Major **urbanization of Maori** population.

1972–75	Third Labour government. NZ economy struggles to cope with huge oil price hikes and Britain's entry into the Common Market.
1975	**Waitangi Tribunal** established to consider Maori land claims.
1975–84	National's Robert "Piggy" Muldoon tries to borrow NZ out of trouble, investing heavily in ill-considered petrochemical projects.
1976	African nations boycott Montreal Olympics because of NZ's rugby contacts with South Africa.
1977	NZ signs Gleneagles Agreement banning sporting ties with South Africa.
1981	**Springbok Tour**. Massive protests as a racially selected South African rugby team tours NZ.
1983	NZ signs Closer Economic Relations (CER) Treaty with Australia.
1984	The "Hikoi" land march brings Maori grievances into political focus.
1984	Labour regains power under David Lange. Widespread privatization and deregulation of NZ's protectionist economy. Refusal to allow American nuclear warships into NZ ports severely strains US–NZ relations.
1985	French secret service agents bomb Greenpeace flagship the **Rainbow Warrior** in Auckland Harbour.
1987	New Zealand becomes a **Nuclear-Free Zone**.
1987	Stock market crash devastates NZ economy.
1990–96	Jim Bolger leads National government, pressing on with Labour's free-market reforms and further dismantling the welfare state.
1996	First **MMP election** returns an alliance of National and NZ First.
1997	Jenny Shipley ousts Bolger to become NZ's **first woman Prime Minister**.
1999	**Labour** regain power under Helen Clark in coalition with the Alliance and the Green Party. The Greens' Nandor Tanczos installed as NZ's first Rastafarian MP and Labour's Georgina Beyer becomes the world's first transgender MP.
2000	British knighthoods replaced by NZ's own honours system.
2001–03	NZ in the tourist spotlight as first *Lord of the Rings* movies released to general acclaim.
2003	Privy Council in London replaced by a Supreme Court as NZ's highest legal body.
2003	Debate over the rights to the foreshore and seabed brings Maori grievances to a head.
2003	NZ population reaches four million. Continued immigration from east Asia brings the Asian population up to ten percent of the nation.

Maoritanga

When the Pakeha first came to this Island, the first thing he taught the Maori
was Christianity. They made parsons and priests of several members of the
Maori race, and they taught these persons to look up and pray; and while they
were looking up the Pakehas took away our land.

Mahuta, the son of the Maori King Tawhiao, addressing the New Zealand Legislative Council in
1903.

The term **Maoritanga** embodies Maori lifestyle and culture – it is the
Maori way of doing things, embracing social structure, ethics, customs,
legends and art, as well as language (see p.993). In the Anglo-European
dominated society that New Zealand has always been, and to a large
extent still is, it has been easy to see Maori culture as harping back to some
fond-remembered idyll of the past, but Maoritanga has remained very much
alive, and in the last few decades has seen a dramatic resurgence. By most measures, Maori make up over ten percent of New Zealand's population, but
Maori–Pakeha marriage since the early nineteenth century has left a complex
inter-racial pool; many third- or fourth-generation Pakeha can claim a Maori
forebear or two, and some contend that there are no full-blooded Maori left.
Maori ancestry remains the foundation of Maoridom, but a sense of Maori
belonging has become a question of cultural identity as much as bloodlines.

Until very recently, white New Zealanders liked to promote the image of the
two races living in harmony as one people, citing scenes of Maori and Pakeha
elbow to elbow at the bar and Maori rugby players in the scrum alongside their
Pakeha brothers. Pakeha prided themselves on successful integration that
seemed a world away from the apartheid of South Africa or the virtual geno-
cide exacted on North American and Australian aboriginal peoples; after all,
Maori could claim all the benefits of Pakeha plus dedicated seats in parliament,
extra university grants and various other concessions. Yet this denied the undercurrent of Maori dissatisfaction over their treatment since the arrival of the first
Europeans; the policy of **assimilation** relied entirely on Maori conforming to
the Pakeha way of doing things and made no concession to Maoritanga. Maori
adapted incredibly quickly to Pakeha ways but were rewarded with the loss of
their **land**. It is impossible to overestimate the importance of this: Maori spirituality invests every tree, every hill and every bay with a kind of supernatural
life of its own, drawn from past events and the actions of the ancestors. It is by
no means fanciful to equate the loss of land with the diminution of Maori life-
force; little surprise, then, that much of the spirit went out of Maori people.

It is only really since the 1980s that the Pakeha paternal view has been
challenged, with the country reacting by adopting **biculturalism**. As Maori
rediscover their heritage and Pakeha open their eyes to what has been around
them for generations, knowledge of Maoritanga and some understanding of
the language is seen as desirable and even advantageous. The government has
increasingly channelled resources towards the "flax roots" of Maoridom,
fostering a rapid take-up in the learning of Maori language, a resurgence in
interest in Maori arts and crafts and a growing pride in Maoridom. At the same
time, Maori have won back customary rights to fisheries and resources, and
parcels of land have been returned to Maori ownership. Nonetheless, there is
a sense in some quarters that Maori are only getting as much as the Pakeha-
dominated government feels it is prepared to give back.

For many Pakeha, however, there is considerable unease over what is perceived as the government's soft stance on Treaty of Waitangi land claims (see box on p.942). Some envisage a future where Maori will own the land (including private land not currently up for redistribution under Treaty claims), will reclaim the rights granted them by the Treaty, and will have more influence than Pakeha. Quite frankly, they're afraid. So far, reaction to the strengthening Maori hand in this climate of conciliation has only been voiced quietly, and just how this scenario will pan out remains to be seen. True power-sharing and biculturalism seems a long way off, and Maori aspirations for "sovereignty" – a separate Maori government and judiciary – look far-fetched at present, but the Maori juggernaut is moving fast.

Maori legend

Maori culture remains highly oral, with chants, storytelling and oratory central to ceremonial and daily life. This was doubly so when Europeans arrived and first recorded the traditions and legends normally passed down verbally. Different tribal groups often had different sets of stories, or at least variations on common themes, but European historians with pet theories to promote often distorted the stories they heard and even destroyed conflicting evidence, creating their own Maori folklore. This generalizing trend served the purpose of creating a common Maori identity, and many of the stories have been accepted back into the Maori tradition, leaving a patchwork of authentic and bowdlerized legends. Nonetheless, there are fixed themes common to most.

Creation

From the primal nothingness of **Te Kore** sprang **Ranginui** the sky father and **Papatuanuku** the earth mother. They had numerous offspring, principally the major gods: **Haumia Tiketike**, the god of the fern root and food from the forest; **Rongo**, the god of the kumara and cultivation; **Tu Matauenga**, the god of war; **Tangaroa**, the god of the oceans and sealife; **Tawhirimatea**, the god of the winds; and **Tane Mahuta**, the god of the forests. Through long centuries of darkness the brothers argued over whether to separate their parents and create light. Tawhirimatea opposed the idea and fled to the skies where his anger is manifested in thunder and lightning, while Tane Mahuta succeeded in parting the two, breaking their primal embrace and allowing life to flourish. Ranginui's tears filled the oceans and even now it is their grief that brings the dew, mist and rain.

Having created the creatures of the sea, the air and the land, the gods turned their attentions to humans and, realizing that they were all male, had to create a female. They fashioned clay into a form resembling their mother and the responsibility again fell to **Tane**, who breathed life into the nostrils of the first woman, the Dawn Maiden, **Hinetitama**. It is from their union that the whole human race is descended.

Maui the trickster and Kupe the navigator

Maori mythology is littered with half-human demigods, and none is more celebrated than **Maui-Tikitiki-a-Taranga**, whose exploits are legend throughout Polynesia. With an armoury of spells, guile and boundless mischief,

Maui gained a reputation as a trickster, using his abilities to turn any situation to his advantage. Equipped with the powerful magic jawbone of his grandmother, he set about taming his world, believing himself invincible. He even took on **the sun**, which had taken to passing so swiftly through the heavens that the people had no time to tend their fields before it disappeared back into its fiery pit. Maui vowed to solve the problem and, with the aid of his older brothers, plaited super-strong ropes, which they tied across the sun's pit before dawn. As the sun rose into the net, Maui set upon the sun with his magic jawbone, beating him and imploring him not to go so fast. The sun was weakening rapidly and, in return for his release, agreed to do as Maui asked.

In the New Zealand context, Maui's master work was the creation of **Aotearoa**. With his reputation for mischief, Maui's brothers would often leave him behind when they went fishing, but one morning he stowed away under the seats. Far out at sea he revealed himself, promising to improve their recent poor catch. Maui egged them on until they were well beyond the normal fishing grounds before dropping anchor. In no time at all Maui's brothers filled their canoe with fish, but Maui still had some fishing to do. They scorned his hook (secretly armed with a chip of his grandmother's jawbone) and wouldn't lend him any bait, so Maui struck his own nose and smeared the hook with his own blood. Soon he had hooked a fabulous fish that, as it broke the surface, could be seen stretching into the distance all around them. Chanting an incantation, Maui got the fish to lie quietly on the surface where it became the North Island, known as Te ika a Maui, the fish of Maui. As Maui went off to make an offering to the gods, his brothers began to cut up the fish and eat it, hacking mountains and valleys into the surface. To fit in with the legend, the South Island is often called Te waka a Maui, the canoe of Maui, and Stewart Island is the anchor, Te punga o te waka a Maui.

With more historical veracity, Maori trace their ancestry back to **Hawaiki**, the semi-legendary source of the Polynesian diaspora, for which the Society Islands and the Cook Islands are the most likely candidates. According to legend, the first visitor to Aotearoa's shores was **Kupe**, the great Polynesian navigator. In one version of the tale he was determined to kill a great octopus that kept robbing his bait; drawn ever further out to sea in pursuit, he finally reached landfall on the uninhabited shores of Aotearoa, the "land of the long white cloud". He named numerous features of the land, then returned to Hawaiki with instructions on how to retrace his voyage.

Social structure and customs

Maori society remains **tribal** to a large extent, though the deracination resulting from the widespread move from the tribal homelands to the cities has eroded some of the closer ties. In urban situations the finer points of Maoritanga are having to be rediscovered, but the basic tenets remain strong and formal protocol still reigns for ceremonies as diverse as funeral wakes, meetings and Maori exhibition openings.

The most fundamental and tightest division in Maori society is the extended family or **whanau** (literally "birthing"), which extends from immediate relatives to cousins, uncles and nieces several times removed. A dozen or so *whanau* jointly form a localized sub-tribe or **hapu** (literally "gestation or pregnancy"), perhaps the most important tribal group, comprising dozens of extended families of common descent. *Hapu* were originally economically autonomous and today continue to conduct communal activities, typically through their *marae* (see below). Neighbouring *hapu* are likely to belong to the same tribe or **iwi** (literally "bones"), a looser association of several thousand Maori spread over a fairly large geographical area. The thirty-odd major *iwi* are even more tenuously linked by their common ancestry traced back to semi-legendary canoes, or *waka*. In troubled times, especially during the eighteenth-century New Zealand Wars, *iwi* from the same *waka* would band together for protection. Together these are the **tangata whenua** (literally "the people of the land"), a term that may refer to Maori people as a whole, or just to one *hapu* if local concerns are being aired.

The literal meanings of *whanau*, *hapu* and *iwi* can be viewed as a metaphor for the Maori view of their relationship with their ancestors or **tupuna**, who are considered to exist through their genetic inheritors; the past is very much a part of the present. Evidence of this is seen in the respect accorded the **whakapapa**, an individual's genealogy tracing descent from the gods via one of the migratory *waka* and through the *tupuna*. The *whakapapa* is often recited at length on formal occasions such as **hui** (meetings).

Maori traditional life is informed by the parallel notions of **tapu** (taboo) and **noa** (mundane, not *tapu*). These are not superstition but a belief system designed to impose a code of conduct: transgressing *tapu* brings ostracism and ill fortune and is thought to cause sickness. Objects, places, actions and even people can be *tapu*, demanding extra respect – for example, the body parts of a chief, especially the head, menstruating women, sacred items to do with ritual, earrings, pendants and hair combs, burial sites, and the knowledge contained in the *whakapapa* are all *tapu*. There is a practical aspect too, with the productivity of fishing grounds and forests traditionally maintained by imposing *tapu* at critical times. The direct opposite of *tapu* is *noa*, a term applied to ordinary items that, by implication, are considered safe; a new building is *tapu* until a special ceremony renders it *noa*.

People, animals and artefacts, whether *tapu* or *noa*, possess **mauri** (life force), **wairau** (spirit) and **mana**, a term loosely translated as prestige, but embodying wider concepts of power, influence and charisma. Birthright brings with it a degree of *mana* that can then be augmented through battle or brave deeds, and lost through inaction or defeat. Wartime cannibalism was partly ritual but by eating an enemy's heart a warrior absorbed his *mauri*; likewise personal effects gain *mana* from association with the *mana* of their owner, accruing more as they are passed down to descendants. Any slight on the *mana* of an individual was felt by the whole *hapu*, which must then exact **utu** (a need to balance any action with an equal reaction), a compunction that often led to bloody feuds, sometimes escalating to war and further enhancing the *mana* of the victors. Pakeha found this a hard concept to grasp and deeds that they considered deceitful or treacherous could be correct in Maori terms.

The responsibility for determining *tapu* fell to the **tohunga** (priest or expert), the most exalted of many specialists in Maoritanga, who is conversant with tribal history, sacred lore and the *whakapapa*, and considered to be the earthly presence of the power of the gods.

Marae

The rituals of *hapu* life – *hui*, **tangi** (funeral wakes) and **powhiri** (formal welcomes) – are conducted on the **marae**, a kind of combined community, cultural and drop-in centre (and much more), where the cultural values, protocols, customs and vitality of Maoritanga find their fullest expression. Strictly, a *marae* is simply a courtyard, but the term is often applied to the whole complex, comprising the **whare runanga** (meeting house, or *whare nui*), *whare manuhiri* (house for visitors), *whare kai* (eating house) and possibly even an old-fashioned **pataka** (raised storehouse). Marae belonging to one or more *hapu* are found all over the country, though they're concentrated in rural areas where a larger number of Maori live. In recent years, pan-tribal urban *marae* have started up, partly to help wayward Maori youth find their roots but also to cope with the growing awareness of Maoritanga on the part of urban Maori, many of whom have lost their *whakapapa*.

Visitors, whether Maori or Pakeha, may not enter *marae* uninvited, so unless you have Maori friends, you're most likely to visit on a commercially run **tour**. Invited guests are expected to provide some form of **koha** (donation) towards the upkeep of the *marae*, but this is included in tour fees. Remember that the *marae* is sacred and due reverence must be accorded the **kawa** (protocols) governing behaviour. There's no need to feel intimidated, though, as you aren't expected to know *kawa* and will be instructed as to what is required of you.

Following long tradition, **manuhiri** (visitors) approaching the *marae* are ritually challenged to determine friendly intent. This **wero** might involve a fearsome warrior (often the teenager you see driving away after the show) bearing down on you with twirling **taiaha** (long club), flickering tongue and bulging eyes. The women then make the **karanga** (welcoming call), which is followed by their **powhiri** (sung welcome), which breaks the *tapu* and acts as a prelude to ceremonial touching of noses or **hongi**, binding the *manuhiri* and the *tangata whenua* both physically and spiritually. On commercial trips, the welcoming ceremony is followed by a concert comprising songs, dances and chants, and a **hangi** (a feast cooked in an earth oven).

Arts and crafts

Although the origins of **Maori art** lie in the traditions of eastern Polynesia, over half a millennium of isolated development has resulted in a unique richness and diversity. Eastern Polynesia has no suitable clay, so Maori forebears had already lost the skills of pottery and focused their talents on wood, stone and weaving, occasionally using naturalistic designs but most often the highly **stylized forms** that make Maori art unmistakable.

As with other *taonga* (treasures), many superb examples were taken out of the country by Victorian and later collectors, but there is a determined move on the part of *iwi* and the Department of Maori Affairs to restore as many *taonga* as possible to New Zealand, including over a hundred severed heads that are scattered through museums all over the world.

Wood carving

Maori handiwork finds its greatest expression in **wood carving**, a discipline applied with as much care to a water bailer or ornamental comb as it is to the pinnacles of Maori creativity, *waka* (canoes) and *whare whakairo* (carved houses).

The earliest examples of wood carving feature the sparse, rectilinear styles of ancient eastern Polynesia, but by the fifteenth century these had been replaced by the cursive style still employed by more traditional carvers today. In the Northland forests, kauri wood was used, but in the rest of the country the durable yet easily worked totara was the material of choice. Carvers worked with shells and sharp stones in the earliest times, but the artist's scope increased dramatically with the invention of tools fashioned from **pounamu** (greenstone, a form of jade; see box on p.797), and again with the transition to steel tools. Some would say that the quality of the work declined with the coming of the Europeans: not just through the demand for quickly executed "tourist art", but as a consequence of pressure to remove the phallic imagery that the missionaries considered obscene. As early as 1844, carving had been abandoned altogether in areas with a strong missionary presence, and it continued to decline into the early years of the twentieth century, when Maori pride was at its lowest ebb. By the end of the 1920s the situation had become so lamentable that Maori parliamentarian Apirana Ngata established Rotorua's pan-tribal **Maori Arts and Crafts Institute**, viewed as the foundation on which Maoritanga could be rebuilt, and still the guardian of what is now a much more secure art.

The role of a carver has always been a highly respected one, with seasoned and skilled exponents having the status of *tohunga* and travelling the country both to carve and to teach. The work is a *tapu* activity and *noa* objects must be kept away – cooked food is not allowed near, and carvers have to brush away shavings rather than blow them – though women, previously banned, have now become carvers.

Maori carving exhibits a distinctive **style**, not just in its visual elements but in the approach to the material. Typically, relief forms are determinedly hewn from a single piece of wood with no concession to the natural forms, shapes and blemishes of the material. There is no attempt to represent perspective and while landscapes are represented, they are not actually depicted – figures stand alone. Unadorned wood is rare, carvers creating a stylistic rather than symbolic bed of swirling spirals, curving organic forms based on fern fronds or sea shells, and interlocking latticework. Superimposed on this are the key elements, often inlaid with paua shell. The most common is the ancestor figure, the **hei tiki**, a grotesquely distorted, writhing human form, either male, female or of indeterminate gender, often stylized to the point of unrecognizability except for the challenge of a protruding tongue and the threat of a hand-held *mere*. Almost as common is the mythical *manaia*, a beaked birdlike form, often with an almost human profile. Secondary motifs such as the *pakake* (whale) and *moko* (lizard) also occur.

While the same level of craftsmanship was applied to all manner of tools, weapons and ornaments, it reached its most exalted expression in *waka taua* (**war canoes**), sleek and formidable vessels that were the focus of community pride and endeavour. Gunwales, bailers and paddles would all be fabulously decorated, but the most detailed work was reserved for the prow and sternpost, usually a matrix of spirals interwoven with *manaia* figures. As guns and the European presence altered the balance of tribal warfare in the 1860s, the *waka taua* was superseded in importance by the *whare whakairo* (**carved meeting house**). Originally the chief's residence, the *whare* gradually adopted the symbolism of the *waka* – some even incorporated wood from *waka*. Each meeting house could be seen as the tangible manifestation of the *whakapapa*, usually representing a synthesis of the ancestors: the ridgepole is the backbone; the rafters form the ribs, enclosing the belly of the interior; the gable figure is the head; and the barge boards represent arms, often decorated with finger-like decoration. Inside, all wooden surfaces are carved and the spaces are filled with intricate woven-flax panels known as *tukutuku*.

Greenstone carving

When not using wood, Maori carvers work in **pounamu** (greenstone). In pre-European times complex trade routes developed to supply Maori throughout the land from the sources on the West Coast and in Fiordland; the South Island even became known as Te Wai Pounamu, the Water of Jade. The stone was fashioned into adzes, chisels and clubs for hand-to-hand combat; tools that soon took on a ritual significance and demanded decoration. Pounamu's hardness dictates a more restrained carving style and *mere* and *patu* in particular tend to be only partly worked, leaving large sweeping surfaces ending in a flourish of delicate swirls. Ornamental pieces range from simple drop pendants worn as earrings or neck decoration, to *hei tiki*, worn as a breast pendant and, for women, serving as a fertility charm and talisman for easy childbirth. Like other personal items, especially those worn close to the body, an heirloom *tiki* possesses the *mana* of the ancestors and absorbs the wearer's *mana*, becoming *tapu*.

Tattooing

A stylistic extension of the carver's craft is exhibited in *moko*, an ornamental and ceremonial form of **tattooing** that largely died out with European contact. Women would have *moko* just on the lips and chin, but high-ranking men often had their faces completely covered, along with their buttocks and thighs; the greater the extent and intricacy of the *moko*, the greater the status. A symmetrical pattern of the traditional elements – crescents, spirals, fern fronds and other organic forms – were painfully gouged into the flesh with an *uhi* (chisel) and mallet, then soot rubbed into the open wound. In the last decade or so the tradition of full-face *moko* has been revived both as an identification with Maoritanga and as an art form in its own right; since 1999, *moko* artists have been eligible for government funding through the Creative New Zealand organization.

Weaving and clothing

While men were busy carving, the women dedicated themselves to weaving and the production of clothing. When Polynesians first arrived in these cool, damp islands their paper mulberry plants didn't thrive and they were forced to look for alternatives. In time, they found *harakeke* (New Zealand **flax**), which became the foundation of all Maori fibre-work. The strong, pliable fibres were used as fishing lines and cordage for lashing axe-heads onto shafts and, most importantly, for protection from the elements and floor matting. With the arrival of the Pakeha, Maori quickly adopted European clothes, but they continued to wear cloaks on formal occasions and today these constitute the basis of contemporary design.

Flax will grow on marshy land all over the country and so the long, spindly leaves were almost always on hand. They were used in something close to their raw form for *raranga* (plaiting) into *kete*, handle-less baskets used for collecting shellfish and kumara, triangular canoe sails, sandals and *whariki*, patterned floor mats still used in meeting houses. For finer work, the flax must be treated by trimming, soaking and beating, a laborious process that produces a wonderfully strong and pliable fibre. Most fibre is used in its natural form, but Maori design requires some **colouring**: black is achieved by soaking in a dilute extract of the bark from a *hinau* tree then rubbing with a black swamp sediment known as *paru*; the red-brown range of colours requires boiling in a dye derived from the bark of the *tanekaha* tree then fixed by rolling in hot ashes; and the less popular yellow tint is produced from the bark of the Coprosma species. Economic necessity and consideration for the tree species concerned have seen the introduction of synthetic dyes, but traditional dyes are still used whenever possible.

Natural and coloured fibres are both used in *whatu kakahu* (**cloak-weaving**), the crowning achievement of Maori women's art, the finest cloaks ranking alongside the most prized *taonga*; the immense war canoe now in the Auckland Museum was once exchanged for a particularly fine cloak. The technique is sometimes referred to as finger-weaving as no loom is used, the women working downwards from a base warp strung between two sticks. Complex weaving techniques are employed to produce a huge array of different textures, often decorated with *taniko* (coloured borders), cord tags tacked onto the cloth at intervals and, most impressive of all, **feathers**. Feather cloaks (*kahu huruhu*) don't appear to have been common before European contact, though heroic tales often feature key players in iridescent garments undoubtedly made from bird feathers. The appeal of the bright yellow feathers of the *huia* probably saw to its demise, and most other brightly coloured birds are now too rare to use for cloaks, so new feather cloaks are very rarely made. Existing examples have become the most prestigious of garments, and you'll come across some fine examples in museums, the base cloth often completely covered by a dense layer of kiwi feathers bordered by zig-zag patterns of tui, native pigeon and even parakeet feathers. More robust *para* (rain capes) were made using the water-repellent leaves of the cabbage tree, and a form of coarse canvas that could reportedly resist spear thrusts was used for *pukupuku* (war cloaks). Some *pukupuku* were turned into *kahu kuri* (dog-skin cloaks) with the addition of strips of dog skin, arranged vertically so that the natural fur colours produced distinctive patterns.

As with other aspects of Maoritanga, weaving and plaiting have seen a resurgence. Cloaks are still an important element of formal occasions, whether on the *marae* for *hui* and *tangi*, or elsewhere for receiving academic or state honours. Old forms are reproduced directly, and also raided as inspiration for contemporary designs, which interpret traditional elements in the light of modern fashion, sometimes incorporating non-traditional colours and designs.

The haka and Maori dance

Opposing rugby teams quiver as the New Zealand All Blacks perform the ferocious, thigh-slapping, foot-stomping, tongue-poking, eye-bulging chant *Ka mate, Ka mate, Ka ora, Ka ora* ("It is death, it is death, It is life, it is life"), from the intimidating Te Rauparaha Haka. This is just the best known of many posture dances (often wrongly referred to as war dances) designed to demonstrate the fitness and prowess of warriors. It was composed by Te Rauparaha himself as he lay in a kumara pit trying to avoid detection by his enemies. Its use by what are often predominantly Pakeha sides might seem inappropriate, but it is so entrenched that there was considerable backlash when in 1996 the All Black coach suggested the *haka* might be changed to mollify southern Maori who were decimated by Te Rauparaha.

At commercial **Maori concerts** (predominantly in Rotorua but also in Christchurch, Queenstown and elsewhere) there will always be some form of *haka*, usually the Te Rauparaha version, which is almost always performed by men. Though women aren't excluded from the *haka*, they normally concentrate on **poi dances**, where balls of *raupo* (bulrush) attached to the end of strings are deftly swung around in rhythmic movements originally designed to improve co-ordination and dexterity.

The drums of eastern Polynesia don't appear to have made it to New Zealand, and both chants and the *haka* go unaccompanied. To the traditional bone flute, Pakeha added the guitar, which now accompanies **waiata** (songs), relatively modern creations whose impact comes as much from the tone and rhythm as from the lyrics (which you probably won't understand anyway). The impassioned delivery can seem at odds with music that's often based on Victorian hymns: perhaps the most well known are *Pokarekare ana* and *Haere Ra*, both post-European-contact creations. Outside the tourist concert party, Maori music has developed enormously in recent years to the point where there are tribal and Maori-language music stations almost exclusively playing music written and performed by Maori, often rap and hip-hop with a Pacific twist.

Landscapes and wildlife

Despite its diminutive size, New Zealand packs in an enormous diversity: unspoiled sub-tropical forest, rich volcanic basins (and volcanoes), mudpools and geysers, intricate and rugged coastline with golden sand beaches and spectacular alpine regions. This diverse landscape supports an extraordinary variety of animals and plant life, with almost ninety percent of the flora not found anywhere else in the world. Thanks to the efforts of a vociferous minority, since the late 1800s, examples of the many habitats, plants and wildlife are still easily accessible, protected within national parks and scenic reserves. For more on green issues, see p.976.

Mountain building

Land has existed in the vicinity of New Zealand for most of the last 500 million years: the earliest rocks found in the country are thought to have originated in the continental forelands of Australia and Antarctica, part of Gondwanaland, the massive continent to which New Zealand belonged. The oceanic islands were created by continental drift, the movement of the large plates that form the earth's crust, which created a distinct island arc and oceanic trench about 100 million years ago.

Roughly 26 million years ago, the land that makes up New Zealand rose further from the sea, and the landscape you see today was formed by **volcanic** activity and continuous movement along fault lines, particularly the Alpine Fault of the South Island. New Zealand lies on the boundary between the Australasian and Pacific tectonic plates. In the North Island the two plates crash into one another, the Pacific plate sliding underneath the Pacific resulting in prolific volcanic activity. Under much of the South Island the Pacific plate is riding over the Australian causing rapid **mountain building** and creating the Southern Alps. All this tectonic posturing gives New Zealand about four hundred **earthquakes** every year, though only a quarter are big enough to be noticed. The volcanoes on the North Island either lie dormant or periodically become impressively active. White Island (just off the coast of the Bay of Plenty) regularly blows off steam, while Mount Ruapehu erupted violently in 1995 and again in 1996.

Isolated evolution and human intervention

As far as we know, the first human didn't reach Aotearoa until around a thousand years ago, so New Zealand's flora and fauna evolved untouched for aeons. Little wonder that botanists and biologists have regarded these oceanic islands as a kind of evolutionary laboratory.

Before the arrival of early Maori, the only mammals around New Zealand were the seals, whales and dolphins on the coast and a couple of species of **bat** in the trees and caves. Land mammals were non-existent, a unique situation which allowed **birds** to fill the niches in the food chain usually held by mammals. With no predators, the birds became fearless, learning to walk amid the dense bush, gradually becoming flightless and growing in size. The largest sub-species of moa is thought to have been up to three metres high and would have been heavier than an ostrich. Who knows, if they had continued on this evolutionary path perhaps they would have become serious competitors to mammals, but their perfect adaptation to the environment brought about their downfall. With the arrival of man and other aggressive, fast-moving mammals they couldn't compete. Many died out, and most of those that remain – takahe, kokako, saddleback and even the kiwi – cling precariously, often surviving only with human help.

When Maori arrived around 1000 AD, they brought their dogs (*kuri*) and (presumably unintentionally) the Polynesian rat (*kiore*) in their canoes. While the dogs and rats were taking care of the smaller birds, Maori hunted the large, flightless **moa** into extinction. Periodically, cranks still claim to have seen live moa in remote parts, but it is thought the last died out before 1500. Some evidence suggest a few survived into the late 1700s.

Pre-Maori New Zealand was covered in thick **forest** composed of over a hundred species of tree, the floor carpeted by moss and lichen with a thick tangled undergrowth of **tree ferns**, some species over ten metres high. Amongst the trees and ferns were twining creepers, nikau palms and palm lilies, all intermingled and forming an impenetrable bush alive with native birds. Perhaps to make moa hunting easier, Maori burnt great swathes of **bush**, but left the remaining forest intact. Prime examples of forest still exist, though much reduced in size and often largely silent.

Maori impact pales in comparison with the devastation at the hands of Europeans. Even Cook's first exploratory visits left a legacy of pigs, sheep and potatoes: the wild pigs that are hunted in the bush are still referred to as Captain Cookers. In the early 1800s whalers and sealers bloodied the coastal waters, while logging campaigns cleared vast swathes of native trees, leaving land suitable for grazing cattle. Pioneers continued to tamper with the delicately balanced ecosystem in an attempt to turn New Zealand into a "New England". Encouraged by immigrant farmers and settlers, **acclimatization societies** sprung up everywhere in the late 1800s to introduce familiar animals and plants from their European homelands. Many of the introductions have worked out fine, and New Zealand would never have become the successful pastoral nation it is without introduced grasses, introduced birds, bees and butterflies to pollinate the grasses, and introduced sheep and cattle to eat the grasses. But many releases were much less successful: possums, stoats, ferrets, rabbits, rats, mice, hedgehogs, goats, thar, chamois, deer and many more have all become **pests** along with blackberry, gorse, broom and numerous other "weeds". While the weeds began to choke the land, the animals either outcompeted the native birds for food, killed their young or simply killed the adult birds. Even the national bird, the **kiwi**, is under threat (see box, p.971).

The lowlands

The archetypal image of New Zealand is of a pastoral land of steep grassy hills flecked with bouncy white lambs. In large part this is fair, and you won't have to go far from the airport to see flat paddocks full of **sheep** often backed by shelter belts of macrocarpa trees. The sheep population is currently around 40 million, roughly half of what it was a couple of decades back, and much of the grazing land has been turned over to other uses. High prices for milk products in the last few years have encouraged a rise in **dairying**, partly in the traditional dairy areas like the Waikato and Taranaki, but also in former sheep strongholds like Southland.

Deer farming is also big business (with much of the meat being exported to Germany) and you may even see farmed ostriches. Elsewhere land has been turned over to horticulture, one of the most visible crops being **grapes**. Vineyards seem to be cropping up everywhere with the biggest concentrations around Gisborne, Hastings, Martinborough, Blenheim, Nelson, Waipara and Cromwell. Growers are now toying with growing **olives** (with some success) and a few adventurous souls have planted oak and hazel trees in the hope of creating a truffle industry.

One almost constant companion throughout farmed New Zealand and in forests is the native **cabbage tree** (ti kouka) with its thin grey trunk up to 10m high topped by spear-shaped leaves and clusters of hundreds of white flowers. The leaf shoots were eaten by Captain Cook and his men who found them tolerably like cabbage – undoubtedly they were pretty desperate.

Lowland forests

This rural picture is a far cry from what greeted early settlers when most of lowland Aotearoa was swathed in thick forest. Much was logged, burnt and cleared to carve out farms, but pockets of **native bush** survive. The forests of Northland, the Coromandel Peninsula, the west coasts of both islands, around Wellington and on Stewart Island contain a great variety of native trees. There are also sixty endemic native flowering plant species in lowland areas, whose blooms are almost all white or yellow. With no pollinating bees to attract there was little need for vibrant petals. Much colour in gardens, parks and mixed forest comes from introduced species such as roses, azaleas and rhododendrons.

New Zealand's best-known tree, the **kauri**, is found in mixed lowland forest, particularly in Northland (see p.222). With a lifespan of two to four thousand years, this magnificent king of the forest rises to thirty metres, two-thirds of its height being straight, branchless trunk. It was greatly revered by Maori canoe-builders who have always enacted solemn ceremonies before hacking them down. European shipbuilders quickly caught on and coveted the trees for ships masts and timbers, though many of the kauri were also turned into frames, cladding and floorboards for New Zealand's typical wooden houses. The tree is also the source of the kauri gum, dug from ancient forests and exported in the late nineteenth and early twentieth century.

Open spaces along forest edges and river banks are often alive with tui (see p.970) sucking nectar from golden clusters of **kowhai**, the national flower. These hang from the kowhai tree whose wood was once fashioned into Maori canoe paddles and adze handles. Another useful tree, the **maire,** stands up to 20m tall and is covered with whitish bark, thick narrow leaves and tiny pink flowers that look like open umbrellas. Its wood is heavy and close-grained, ideal for war clubs, and when burned it gives off very little smoke. Now quite rare, the 30m **matai** was also once used by Maori as a source of timber for canoe prows and by settlers for buildings; it can be identified by a thick, dark grey bark that flakes off.

The North Island and the top third of the South Island is home to New Zealand's only native **palm**, the **nikau**, whose slender branchless stem bears shiny leaves of up to 30cm, long pink spiky flowers and red fruit. Early European settlers used to use the berries as pellets in the absence of ammunition.

The **pohutukawa** is an irregularly branched 20m tree found as far south as Otago, seen in forests around the coast and at lake edges. It typically bears bright crimson blossoms around Christmas time giving a suitably festive look to the beaches.

Another well-known red-blooming tree is the gnarled **rata**, found in quantity in South Island forests and in ones and twos around the North Island. It starts out life as a climber, its windblown seeds establishing it high in other trees, and then its aerial roots gradually take over the host, eventually draining it of life.

New Zealand is also known for its unusual family of pine species known as **podocarps**, which don't look much like traditional pines. One such is the majestic **rimu** (red pine) which grows to 60m with small green flowers, red cones and tiny green or black fruit. It was heavily milled for its timber (and its charcoal was mixed with oil and rubbed into tattoo incisions) and yet is still widespread throughout mixed forests. Other podocarps include **matai** (black pine), **miro** (brown pine), **kahikatea** (white pine), and **totara** which usually lives for a thousand years and was again used by Maori to make war canoes. The tree's thick brown bark was also used: it peels in long lengths, suitable for weaving baskets.

A common shade-loving tree found in stands in the forests is the **tawa**, with a long, thin blackish trunk and spear-shaped leaves. The tree produces black berries which, although initially unpleasant, develop a better flavour some time after picking. Below the canopy of these large trees you'll find an enormous variety of **tree ferns**, many of them hard to tell apart. The most famous, adopted as a national emblem, is the **ponga** (silver fern). Reaching about 10m in height, it has long fronds that are dull green on top and silvery white underneath.

Lowland wildlife

Most of the animals you'll commonly see as you travel around New Zealand have been introduced, but patient observers can see a reasonably range of **native birds**. You probably won't see New Zealand's national bird, the flightless, nocturnal **kiwi** (see box on p.971) in the wild. It has been on the endangered list for many years, and these days the only place that's possible is on Stewart Island; however, they can be seen all over the country in specially designed kiwi houses: those in Otorohanga, Napier, Wellington and Greymouth are all good.

Of the other flightless birds in New Zealand the most common is the **weka**, which is a little like the kiwi but slimmer, far less shy, and is generally dark brown with marked golden flecks, especially on the heavily streaked breast. Like the kiwi, the weka grubs around at dusk but can be seen regularly during the day: many are bold enough to approach trampers and take titbits from their hands. The bird's whistle is a loud and distinctive "kooo-li". There are four subspecies found in a variety of habitats throughout the country. The North Island bird flourishes in Poverty Bay and has been reintroduced around Auckland and in the forests. The South Island bird is found on the west coast of the South Island and Fiordland; and the bluff weka has thrived on the Chatham Islands and is being reintroduced in Canterbury. The last subspecies is ever present on Stewart Island.

The **kaka** is a member of the parrot family and closely related to the kea, though it does not venture from its favoured lowland forest environments in Northland, around Nelson, the Marlborough Sounds, the West Coast and Stewart Island. You can recognize the bird by its colour: bronze with a crimson belly and underside of the tail and wings.

When walking among the forests of New Zealand, it is not unusual to hear the cry of the **morepork**, an owl that's named after the distinctive sound of its call. A small brown bird, it sometimes appears in town and city gardens. Alongside the morepork is the distinct musical "mackmacko" of the **bellbird**, a shy green and blue, curve-billed bird. In contrast, the **fantail**, another common forest dweller, is more likely to be seen than heard, constantly opening and closing the tail that gives it its name. Often flying alongside walkers on trails, the bird is not keeping you company but feeding on the insects you disturb.

The **tui**, with its white throat and mostly green and purple velvet-like body, is renowned for mimicking the calls of other birds and the copious consumption of nectar and fruit. Its song has greater range than the bellbird and contains some rather unmusical squeaks, croaks and strangled utterances. Just as noisy is the **saddleback**, a rare but pretty bird, mostly black except for a tan-coloured saddle, whose chattering call welcomes you if you stumble into its patch of the forest. The thrush-sized saddleback belongs to the endemic family of wattle birds, of which the North Island kokako is also a member – see below.

Among the smaller birds regularly glimpsed as they flit around the forest the most distinctive are the **robin** family, which range from black with a cream or yellow breast to all black, depending how on far south you have travelled. They have a prolonged and distinctive song lasting for up to thirty minutes with only brief pauses for breath.

The **kereru** (the world's second largest pigeon) was a favourite Maori food but is now protected. It is a very ancient New Zealand species, which seems to have no relatives elsewhere. A handsome bird with metallic green, purple and bronze colouring and a pure white breast, you'll often see it flashing along in the low-lying forests. Another of New Zealand's oldest birds is the rare **kokako**, an abysmal flyer that lives around the Pureora Forest, Little Barrier Island (see p.158) and Rotorua (see p.307). If you're lucky you'll see it grouchily walking around the forest floor or climbing trees for another crack at flying, or catch a glimpse of its distinctive bright blue wattle.

The forest are also home to some impressive snails and the ancient **weta**, a grasshopper-like insect that has changed little in 190 million years. There are several species, the most impressive being the giant weta, which is the heaviest insect in the world, weighing up to 71g and about the size of a small thrush. Weta aren't dangerous, despite their vicious-looking mandibles (they're said to have been the model for Ridley Scott's *Alien*). Several species live in the bush and caves but they're hard to spot and you're most likely to see them in museums and zoos.

Another elusive animal is the lizard-like **tuatara** which eats insects, small mammals and birds' eggs, a diet which sees them grow to sixty centimetres in length and keeps them alive for well over a hundred years. The tuatara is one of the country's oldest inhabitants, dating back at least 260 million years, making it, to all intents and purposes, a mini dinosaur. It's nocturnal so you're unlikely to see one in the wild, although they have been reintroduced to many pest-free offshore islands – your best chance of spotting one is in a zoo or kiwi house.

Rivers, lakes and wetlands

High mountains and a good deal of rain mean that New Zealand is not short of rivers. Most run steeply to the sea, though a few meander along the east coast of the South Island. Canterbury and the Waitaki/Mackenzie Basin

The kiwi

Flightless, dull brown in colour and not exactly beautiful, **the kiwi** is nonetheless New Zealand's national symbol and is much loved by the general populace. It is also a unique bird. Stout, muscular, shy and nocturnal, it is a member of the ratite family – which includes the ostrich, emu, rhea, cassowary and the long-extinct moa – and is one of the few birds in the world with a well-developed sense of **smell**. At night you might hear them snuffling around in the dark, using the nostrils at the end of their bill to detect earthworms, beetles, cicada larvae, spiders and also koura (freshwater crayfish), berries and the occasional frog. Armed also with sensitive bristles at the base of its bill and a highly developed sense of hearing, the kiwi can detect other birds and animals on its territory and will readily attack them with its claws. The females are bigger than the males and lay huge eggs, weighing a fifth of their own body weight. After eighty days, the eggs hatch and the chicks live off the rich yolk; neither parent feeds them and they emerge from the nest totally independent. They sleep for up to twenty hours a day, which probably explains why it normally lives to the age of 20 or 25.

Sadly there are probably fewer than 15,000 birds left in the country and numbers are going down, rapidly. Attempts to halt the decline have been going on for decades but unless efforts are stepped up the kiwi may become **extinct in the wild**, possibly as early as 2020. The main problem is that stoats and feral cats kill 95 percent of kiwi in their first year before they can effectively defend themselves. But even then they have to contend with stray dogs. In six weeks during 1987, one stray dog killed 500 of the estimated 900 kiwi living in the Waitangi State Forest.

The will is there, but often the money is not. If you want to help save these iconic birds you can make a **donation** to the *Restoring the Dawn Chorus* programme run by the Royal Forest and Bird Protection Society, PO Box 631, Wellington (℡0800/200 064, ⊛www.forest-bird.org.nz), either online or by phone (using your credit card) or by cheque made out to "Forest and Bird".

There are six recognised sub-species.

The **Brown Kiwi** (*Apteryx australis*), the largest species, is famous for its big nose, bad temper and for being a tough fighter against intruders on its territory. They live in a wide range of vegetation, including exotic forests and rough farmland on the North Island. In 1993 the **Okarito Brown** (*rowi*) and the **southern Tokoeka**, which is almost identical, were identified as a separate species. Inhabiting the South Island and Stewart Island, these subspecies are the most communal of the kiwi family and can be seen poking about along the tideline within a few metres of one another. A further subspecies, the **Haast Tokoeka**, is found only in Fiordland.

The **Little Spotted Kiwi** or **Kiwi Pukupuku** (*Apteryx owenii*) is the smallest and rarest of the kiwi, for decades only found on offshore islands until a few were transferred to the Karori Sanctuary in Wellington in 2000. Predators and land clearance are largely responsible for the low numbers, although a programme to remove predators from the offshore islands has seen their fortunes revive. This species is mellow and docile by nature and pairs often share daytime shelter, going their separate ways to feed, grunting to one another as they pass. They rarely probe for food, instead finding prey on the ground or in the forest litter. In spring, during courtship, birds stand with bills crossed and pointing downwards while shuffling around each other, grunting, for up to twenty minutes. The best time to hear them is just after dark from high points around an island. Listen carefully for the male's shrill whistle and the female's gentle purr.

The **Great Spotted Kiwi** (*roa* or *Apteryx haastii*) inhabits regions of snow-covered peaks, herb fields, with rocky outcrops, valleys of red tussock and mountains clothed in beech forest and alpine scrub. The severe living conditions account for the many legends that surround them. Early European explorers told stories of remote kiwi the size of a turkey with powerful spurs on its legs, whose call was the loudest. Their harsh home has also helped preserve these big handsome birds, keeping them relatively safe from the pigs, dogs and stoats that have killed so many other kiwi.

specialize in distinctive **braided rivers**, their wide shingle beds and multiple channels providing a breeding ground for many birds, insects, fish and plants. Numerous lakes provide rich habitats for fish and birds; many of New Zealand's wetlands, on the other hand, have been drained for agriculture and property development, although some areas are preserved as national parks and scenic reserves. It's in low wetland areas that you're likely to come across the tallest of the native trees, the kahikatea (white pine), which reaches over 60m. There's a particularly fine stand in the central western North Island close to Te Awamutu.

One bird you're bound to see in the vicinity of a lake is the **pukeko** (swamp hen), a bird which is still in the process of losing the power of flight. The pukeko is mostly dark and mid-blue with large feet and an orange beak, and lets out a high-pitched screech if disturbed.

New Zealand is renowned for its great fresh-water fishing, with massive brown and rainbow **trout** and **salmon** swarming through the fast-flowing streams. All introduced species, these fish have adapted so well to their conditions that they grow much larger here than elsewhere in the world; as a result, many native species have been driven out. Another delicacy commonly found in New Zealand's waters are native **eels**, much loved by Maori who built complicated eel traps along many rivers. Curiously, despite spending most of their lives quietly in New Zealand rivers, they migrate to breed in the waters off Fiji.

Keeping the fishermen company along the river banks of the Mackenzie country and Canterbury are **black stilt** or **kaki**, one of the world's rarest wading birds. A thin black bird with round eyes and long red legs, the stilt is incredibly shy – if you do see one in the wild, keep well away. Usually found in swamps and beside riverbeds, the best place to see them is in the specially created reserve near Twizel (see p.702). A slightly more adaptable member of the family is the **common pied stilt**, a black and white bird that has been more successful in resisting the attentions of introduced mammals, particularly feral cats.

Another inhabitant of the Canterbury braided riverbank is the **wrybill**. This small white and grey bird uses its unique bent bill to turn over stones or pull out crustaceans from mud. In winter the species migrates to the north of North Island and the mudflats of Kaipara, Manukau and the Firth of Thames. The wrybill's close cousin, the **banded dotterel**, favours the sides of rivers, lakes, open land with sparse vegetation and coastal lagoons and beaches. It is a small brown and white bird with a dark or black band around its neck and breeds only in New Zealand, though it does briefly migrate to Australia.

The **blue duck** is one of four endemic species with no close relatives anywhere in the world. Its Maori name, **whio**, is a near perfect representation of the male bird's call. You can spot it by its blue-grey plumage, with chestnut on both breast and flanks; it also has an unusual bill with a black flexible membrane along each side, and beady yellow eyes. Mountainous areas are where it makes its home, preferring the swift mountain streams and approaching the coast only where the mountains are close to the sea. Unfortunately this is now an endangered species, preyed upon by mammals and forced to compete for food with the salmon and trout in the rivers.

The highlands

With most of the lowland forests cleared for farming, you really need to get into the hills to really appreciate the picture that greeted first the Maori and early European immigrants. Your best bet is in the many scenic reserves or national parks. The Tongariro, Whanganui, Taranaki, Nelson Lakes, Arthur's Pass and Aoraki Mount Cook national parks are all cloaked in highland forests, particularly New Zealand's native beech trees. Unlike most northern hemisphere beeches, the Kiwi variety are evergreen. The straight 20m high **mountain beech** (tawhairauriki) grows close to the top of the tree line and has sharp dark leaves and little red flowers. Also at high altitudes, often in mixed stands, are **silver beech** (tawhai), whose grey trunks grow up to 30m. Slightly lower altitudes are favoured by black and red beech. Often mixed in with them is the thin, straggly **manuka** (tea tree), which grows in both alpine regions and on seashores.

New Zealand has five hundred species of flowering alpine plant that grow nowhere else in the world. Most famous are the large white-flowered yellow-centred **Mount Cook lilies**, the world's largest buttercup. It flowers from November to January. Another interesting plant found on the high ground of the South Island is the **vegetable sheep**, a white hairy plant that grows low along the ground and, at a great distance, could just about be mistaken for grazing sheep.

Among alpine caves and rock crevices you might come across the black **alpine weta** (also known as the "Mount Cook flea").

The red-beaked, green and blue **takahe** is one of the most famous of the country's flightless birds. A close relative of the more common pukeko, the takahe was thought to have been extinct until rediscovered in 1948. Its survival is currently in the hands of the DOC, who have set up protection programmes in a few highland regions (see p.905). Another highland forest bird to watch out for is the **New Zealand falcon** or bush hawk, seen sometimes in the north of the North Island and more often in the high country of the Southern Alps, Fiordland and the forests of Westland. It has a heavily flecked breast, chestnut thighs and a pointed **head**.

New Zealand boasts the only flightless **parrot** in the world, the green and blue, nocturnal **kakapo**. Once widespread, there are now under a hundred birds left, all on two managed, predator-free islands in deep south of the South Island. You're much more likely to come across the **kea**, regarded as the only truly alpine parrot in the world (see p.680). Finally, of the smaller birds in the sub-alpine areas, the yellow and green **rock wren** and the **rifleman**, a tiny green and blue bird with spiralling flight, are commonly seen in the high forests of the South Island.

The coast, islands and sea

New Zealand's indented coastline, battered by the Tasman Sea and the Pacific Ocean, is a meeting place of warm and cold currents, which makes for an environment suited to an enormous variety of fish. Tropical fish species such as barracuda, marlin, sharks and tuna are attracted by the warm currents, locally populated by hoki, kahawai, snapper, orange roughy and trevally. The cold Antarctic currents bring blue and red cod, blue and red moki, and fish that can tolerate a considerable range of water temperatures, such as the tarakihi, grouper and bass, all avidly sought after by an army of weekend anglers.

Many people visit New Zealand with the express intention of seeing the marine mammals that grace the waters, and most leave satisfied. The rare **humpback whale** is an occasional visitor to the shores of Kaikoura and Cook

Strait, while **sperm whales** are common year round in the deep sea trench near Kaikoura. **Orca** are seen regularly wherever there are dolphins, seals and other whales, particularly around Banks Peninsula, Kaikoura, Dunedin, Stewart Island, the Marlborough Sounds, Cook Strait, the Bay of Plenty and the Bay of Islands. One frequent visitor is the **pilot whale**: up to 200 pass by Farewell Spit each year and some strand themselves there. Despite the efforts of the locals to refloat them, a few die nearly every year. Pilot whales are also seen in Cook Strait and the Bay of Plenty.

Common dolphins congregate all year round in the Bay of Plenty, Bay of Islands and around the Coromandel Peninsula. Of the three other species seen in New Zealand, **bottlenose dolphins** hang around Kaikoura and Whakatane most of the year, while **dusky dolphins**, the most playful, can be spotted near the shore of the Marlborough Sounds, Fiordland and Kaikoura, from October to May. At any time of year you might get small schools of tiny **Hector's dolphins** accompanying your boat around Banks Peninsula, the Catlins and as far down as Invercargill.

Until recently there were few opportunities to see the Hooker's (now called New Zealand) **sea lion** except on remote Antarctic islands; now these rare animals with their round noses and deep, wet eyes are appearing once more around the Catlins and Otago Peninsula. If you do see them, be careful: they bite and can move fast over short distances, so don't go any closer than ten metres and avoid getting between them and the sea. The larger New Zealand **fur seal** is in much greater abundance around the coast, easily spotted basking on rocks or sand and gracefully turning in the waters, their broader, pointy heads popping above the surface. You're most likely to come across them in the Sugar Loaf Marine Reserve off New Plymouth, around the Northland coast, in the Bay of Plenty, near Kaikoura, around the Otago Peninsula and in the Abel Tasman National Park. Both seals and sea lions can become aggressive during the breeding season (Dec–Feb), so remember to keep your distance (at least 30m) at these times. If you are lucky enough to visit the Nuggets in the Catlins, you may be rewarded by a sighting of one of the few **elephant seals** still breeding on the New Zealand coast; more extensive colonies exist on the offshore islands.

Also drawn by the fish-rich waters of the coast are a number of visiting and native seabirds, the most famous being the graceful and solitary **royal albatross**, found on the Otago Peninsula and, just offshore, the smaller **wandering albatross**. A far more common sight are **little blue penguins**, which you're almost guaranteed to see on any boat journey, all year round. The large **yellow-eyed penguin** is confined to parts of the east coast of the South Island, from Christchurch to the Catlins, while the **Fiordland crested penguin** with its thick yellow eyebrows is rarely seen outside Fiordland and Stewart Island. Other common sea birds include **gannets**, their yellow heads and white bodies unmistakable as they dive from great heights into shoals of fish; and **cormorants** and **shags** (mostly grey or black), usually congregating on cliffs and rocky shores. On and around islands you're also likely to see the **sooty shearwater**, **titi** (also known as "muttonbirds"), while the **black oystercatchers** and the black and white **variable oystercatchers**, both with orange cigar beaks and stooping gait, can be spotted searching in pairs for food on the foreshore almost everywhere.

975

△ Yellow-eyed penguin

Green issues

New Zealand comes with an enviable reputation for being "clean and green", a mantra chanted incessantly by the tourist machine. There is no doubt that it is a verdant land and much of it appears barely touched by human hand, but in large part this is more by accident than design. With a small population, generous winds and flushing rainfall, much of the pollution is dissipated and goes unseen. Dilution is New Zealand's typical solution to pollution. Although many New Zealanders are trying to preserve the country's environment, their efforts are often hampered by a vacillating government and the paramount interests of big business – wildlife has had to pay the price for some short-sighted and flagrant profiteering.

Traditionally meat, wool and dairy products have been New Zealand's main exports, but today a greater proportion is made up of forestry, machinery, aluminium and chemicals, all of which take their toll on land usage, pollution and energy demands. None of the animals or crops and few of the trees harvested are endemic to New Zealand: the countryside is a confusion of native, European and Australian birds, exotic and indigenous trees, and a profusion of plants and animals from each hemisphere. Since human habitation began, forty-three indigenous birds have become extinct, and New Zealand now accounts for eleven percent of the world's endangered bird species. Some of the worst culprits are introduced pests like possums (see box), stoats, wild deer, goats and rabbits which all either kill birds or damage their habitat.

Land usage

With a population of only 4 million and a relatively short recorded history, you might expect human impact on the land would be limited. But in just a thousand years (and mostly in the last 150) humans have managed to rid the country of 85 percent of its forest cover and convert a full three-quarters of the land area to the production of food and commercial forestry, the latter essential to the national economy. Most of the trees are quick-growing radiata pine, an American species (aka Monterrey Pine) introduced because it grows far quicker than any native variety; these days just ten percent of native forest remains.

Once European immigration got underway in the mid-1800s the immediate need was for food and settlers began hacking out their patch from the bush. With limited flat land, best pickings were quickly taken and settlers had to go for increasingly marginal land. This came to a head after World War I when returning veterans were promised a patch of land. Often they were assigned steep bush covered hills which they then spent years taming. Only really suitable for raising sheep, these farms were profitable when wool and lamb prices were high, but in recent years farming such land has become uneconomic and some areas are being allowed to slowly revert to their natural state.

Far more often, marginal lands are being planted with rows of **pines** – nice enough when they're standing though every 25 years areas they get logged, turning them into unsightly fields of stumps and discarded branches.

Meanwhile, the ever-growing need for housing, roads and associated infrastructure gobbles up productive farmland and threatens fragile wetland.

Possums

Visitors to New Zealand soon become familiar with the nocturnal possum, if only as road-kill. To see a live specimen you'll probably need to go tramping when you'll see them around the hut at night, their eyes reflecting your torchlight. They may look furry and cute, but you'll soon learn that even mild-mannered New Zealanders have an almost pathological hatred of this introduced Australian marsupial. Green MP Nandor Tanczos even has a possum-fur cover on his seat in parliament.

Even before the start of controlled European migration in 1840, enterprising individuals had started liberating **brushtail opossums** (*Trichosurus vulpecula*, more commonly known as **possums**) in New Zealand with the aim of establishing a fur industry. Acclimatization societies subsequently hastened their spread with both authorized and illegal releases. As early as the 1890s people recognised the damage possums were causing to orchards, gardens and native trees, and were advocating control. But in 1920 a Professor of Botany and Zoology at Wellington's Victoria University released a report supporting the possum, and stating that the harm to native forests was negligible. Releases only stopped around 1930.

There followed a series of ineffective regulations until 1947, when heavier penalties for harbouring and liberating opossums were brought into effect and all restrictions on the trapping or killing of possums were cancelled. Control measures were finally introduced in 1951 when a bounty was to be paid on all killed possums from which skins had not been taken – a scheme that continued until 1960.

Until the 1980s possums were still killed for their fur, but successful anti-fur lobbying saw pelt prices plummet and possum numbers skyrocket. Possums now number in excess of **seventy million**, and it is thought that they currently munch their way through 21,000 tonnes of vegetation every day. They are also carriers of bovine TB, an added menace to the dairy, beef and deer industries. Not only do they compete directly with native birds for food, they also eat birds' eggs and have been known to kill chicks.

Many believe rewarding possum hunters would solve the problem, but possums are now so widespread it seems only aerial poisoning will do the trick. Most studies indicate aerial drops of 1080 poison provide the most cost effective control, but the controversial nature of aerial poisoning means that DOC are still persisting with ground poisoning and trapping. Whatever the solution it is clear that if the possums are allowed to continue unchecked they will turn New Zealand into a barren wasteland.

Pollution

Influenced by commerce, past governments have favoured some decidedly unfriendly environmental policies, although the current Labour coalition is now trying to redress the balance. Despite a record of admirable moral stands, such as banning ships and submarines carrying nuclear warheads from its shores (see p.952), governments have usually managed to disregard environmental initiatives related to air pollution and industrial emissions – in fact, New Zealand has the fourth-worst record for CO emissions in the OECD. Although it's perceived abroad as a country with enviably clean air, its quality in many cities, if measured, is shocking (check out Christchurch in the winter), and there have been massive increases in asthma and other respiratory problems amongst the young. Auckland's 450,000 cars create levels of air pollution worse than most of the world's major cities and this seems unlikely to improve while current policies stay in place: New Zealand imports huge numbers of secondhand cars from Japan that would not be allowed off the boat in many other countries; there is no requirement for vehicles to be regularly emission tested; and fuel available from pumps could be a lot cleaner. This situation has even led to a ban on swimming in some of Auckland suburban bays after a couple of days rain, because the high levels of heavy metals deposited in the atmosphere by car pollution reappear in the run-off water that sloshes into storm drains that empty directly into the bays.

And it's not just cars. Greenpeace rates the **industrial pollution** from the Tasman pulp and paper mill in Kawerau as one of the country's worst problems. The mill is apparently responsible for the largest discharge of toxic organochlorine chemicals in the country and the nearby river has been contaminated by some of the most harmful chemicals known to man – it's known as the "black drain" by the locals. New Zealand also scores badly on **waste disposal** and the monitoring of chemical usage and contaminated sites – with 700 potentially contaminated sites, it is on a par with the USA. Every day more than a billion litres of sewage and industrial waste is discharged into rivers and the sea.

Another contentious issue is the use of **1080 poison** to kill possums. The chemical is banned in almost every other country in the world and farmers claim it kills their stock and the native birds it is designed to protect. On balance, DOC favour its use and the campaigning organization Forest & Bird are keen for DOC to use widespread aerial 1080 drops as a more effective attack on pests than the hand-place bait stations currently used.

Intensive farming also deserves to take some blame for pollution levels. Heavily depleted soils require massive amounts of phosphate fertilizer which then run off into streams and lakes often promoting weed growth and depriving the water of oxygen: some central North Island lakes are now virtually dead. There is no requirement for farmers to fence streams so cattle regularly defecate directly into waterways, compounding the problem. Once-clean waterways are now unsafe for swimming and drinking.

Thankfully, there is a strong groundswell of informed opinion leaning towards **organic smallholdings** in tandem with a rising consumer demand for natural, untreated food. The food industry has even introduced a carefully monitored "eco-label", where rigorous standards provide an independent endorsement of the quality of food production. However, more recently, under threat of trade sanctions from the US, the New Zealand government sanctioned trials of GM crops and produce, a real missed opportunity to stand alone as a GM-free nation and, in all probability, command higher prices for its all-natural produce.

Energy

New Zealand is about eighty percent energy self-sufficient with domestic coal, oil and gas providing the bulk of the energy, supplemented by renewables like geothermal, hydro and a little wind. But the known reserves of gas and oil are thought to be good for less than twenty more years and production is already in decline. Per capita demand is always increasing, and the country's population is also growing, putting ever greater demands on supply. In recent years, dry winters have seen South Island hydro lake levels drop and only pleas to reduce domestic power usage have avoided rolling blackouts. Although the nation is surrounded by sea water and buffeted by high winds, the efforts to exploit **alternative power sources** have been token at best with the Palmerston North wind-farm being a notable exception (see p.293). **Hydroelectricity** is, on the face of it, an environmentally friendly way to produce more power, but the reservoirs created behind grand dams have already destroyed numerous natural habitats, especially riverbanks, where threatened species of birds live, nest and feed. Public opposition to further dam-building was seen when the Government-owned Meridian Energy proposed Project Aqua, a hydro scheme along the Waitaki River inland from Oamaru. The project was eventually canned, and the energy industry is now casting around to find where the next petajoule is coming from. The obvious answer is **coal**. New Zealand still has huge reserves, but burning coal creates vast quantities of greenhouse gases which goes against the Government's commitment to the Kyoto Protocol.

Preserving the environment

As early as the 1880s, the more enlightened Pakeha were beginning to realise that their Europeanizing zeal was having a detrimental effect on the land and that measures needed to be taken to preserve the environment. Pressure was exerted by the eco warriors of the time to conserve the forest, wetlands and volcanic areas by creating **national parks**. In this way, native flora and fauna could be preserved, encouraging regeneration and restocking. In 1887 Te Heuheu Tukino IV (Horonuku) set the ball rolling by giving the nucleus of the Tongariro National Park to the nation, in order to preserve the integrity of a venerated tribal area. New Zealand's stock of national parks has been growing ever since and is now under the auspices of the Department of Conservation (DOC) which is charged with both preserving the environment and making it accessible to the people. It generally manages this apparently contradictory brief well and now administers fourteen such parks including two fairly recent additions: Kahurangi National Park set aside the northwestern tip of the South Island in 1996; and in 2002 the bulk of New Zealand's third largest island, Stewart Island, became Rakiura National Park.

DOC also manage hundreds of small **scenic reserves** dotted around the country, which alleviate pressure on the national parks and help preserve some aspect of the local environment. They are often patches of native bush requiring great vigilance as the stands grow slowly and are constantly under threat from development and introduced animals. It takes at least a hundred years for the bush to grow to maturity.

Despite valiant efforts in many quarters, conservationists' efforts to preserve populations of native birds have often failed and DOC has gone to great lengths to create **bird sanctuaries** on islands around the coast. In fact, New Zealand has become a world leader in eradication techniques and now has over a dozen predator-free islands to which some (sometimes all) of an endangered species have been moved. Once protected in this way, most species have recovered well and as the population swells the "excess" can be moved back to their original environments, or more likely so-called "mainland-islands" where intense trapping and poisoning of predators is used to give the birds a chance. Most wildlife sanctuaries are closed to the general public, but there are some **open sanctuaries** where you get a chance to experience the cacophony of birdsong once found all over the country and appreciate just how fearless these birds can be around humans. The main open sanctuaries are Tiritiri Matangi near Auckland (see p.156), Kapiti Island north of Wellington (see p.299), Motuara Island in Queen Charlotte Sound (see p.533) and Ulva Island just off Stewart Island (see p.760).

Books

K iwis are avid readers, and almost equally keen writers, producing more glossy picture books and wildlife guides than you would think possible. In a climate of growing confidence and with a more honest approach to issues that concern and reflect on New Zealanders' lives there have been an increasing number of excellent novels. Almost all of the following titles can be easily found in bookstores or online: where a book is out of print but still worth trying to track down, it is marked ◙ .

History, society and politics

James Belich *The New Zealand Wars* An extraordinary, well-researched, and in-depth work on the received version of the colonial wars, which re-examines the Victorian and Maori interpretation of the conflict. A book for committed historians and those fanatically interested in the subject, since it gives more detail than most people will ever need to know. *Paradise Reforged* is a history of New Zealanders from 1880 to the year 2000 that concentrates on the relationship they have with the outside world, written by one of the country's more original thinkers.

Alistair Campbell *Maori Legends* A brief retelling of selected stories in an accessible way with some evocative illustrations.

R.D. Crosby *The Musket Wars* An account of the massive upsurge in inter-*iwi* conflict before the start of European colonization, that was exacerbated by the introduction of the musket and led to the death of 23 percent of the Maori population, a proportion far greater than that of Russian casualties in World War II.

Alan Duff *Out of the Mist and Steam Duff* Author of *Once Were Warriors* (see p.983) has created a strangely vivid memoir of his life that falls short of autobiography but gives the reader a good idea where all the material for his novels came from.

A.K. Grant *Corridors of Paua* A light-hearted look at the turbulent and fraught political history of the country from 1984 to the introduction of MMP in 1996.

Tom Hewnham *By Batons and Barbed Wire* (o/p). A harrowing account of the 1981 Springbok Tour of New Zealand that stirred up more social hatred than any other event and proved conclusively that there is more to New Zealand society than just a bunch of good blokes.

★ **Michael King** *The Penguin History of New Zealand* Published in 2003 this is a highly readable and thoroughly up-to-date general history of New Zealand. Maori oral history gets good coverage and there's plenty on uneasy Maori–Pakeha relations, recent political changes and the Maori renaissance. *Death of the Rainbow Warrior* is a brilliant account of the farcical, though ultimately tragic, efforts of the French secret service to sabotage Green Peace's campaign against French nuclear testing. *Wrestling with an Angel* is a sensitive and comprehensive biography of Janet Frame. *Maori* is a newly updated and revised edition of a comprehensive pictorial history of all aspects of Maori life and an engrossing account of how it changed as a result of European influence.

Hineani Melbourne *Maori Sovereignty: The Maori Perspective*; and its companion volume *Maori Sovereignty: The Pakeha Perspective* by Carol Archie. Everyone from grass-roots activists to statesmen gets a voice in these two volumes, one airing the widely divergent Maori visions of sovereignty, the other covering the equally disparate Pakeha view on the subject. They assume a fairly good understanding of Maori structures and recent New Zealand history, but are highly instructive nonetheless.

★ **Claudia Orange** *The Story of the Treaty* A concise, illustrated exploration of the history and myths behind what many believe to be the most important document in New Zealand history, the Treaty of Waitangi. Well written but probably more than the casual traveller needs to know. Much the same criticism applies to the author's *The Treaty of Waitangi*, which covers the lead-up to the signing, and the treaty's first sixty years.

Margaret Orbell *A Concise Encyclopaedia of Maori Myth and Legend* A fairly comprehensive rundown on many tales and their backgrounds that rewards perseverance even though it's a little dry.

Jock Phillips *A Man's Country? The Image of the Pakeha Male* Classic treatise on mateship and the Kiwi bloke. This thorough exploration ranges through the formative pioneering years, rugby, wartime camaraderie, the development of the family-man ideal and Nineties man. It comes to life with the partial dismantling of the stereotype in the light of developments of the last thirty years.

D.C. Starzecka (ed) *Maori Art and Culture* A kind of Maori culture primer, with concise and interesting coverage of Maori history, culture, social structure, carving and weaving, spiced up by excellent colour photos of artefacts from the British Museum's collection.

K. Taylor and P. Moloney *On the Left: Essays on Socialism in New Zealand* A comprehensive survey of political essays spanning over a century that illustrates why New Zealand society has such a strong egalitarian spine.

P. Temple *A Sort of Conscience – The Wakefields* A tireless unravelling of the facts and fictions written about the Wakefields, once famed as New Zealand's founding fathers – now the villains of post-colonial dogma – who played an important part in the country's development and its progress toward self-government.

Dorothy Urlich *Cloher Hongi Hika* Compelling biography dealing with the foremost Maori leader at the time of the first contact between Maori and the Europeans, and his subsequent participation in the Musket Wars.

David Wilkie *Year of the Dove* The edited diaries of a Kiwi anaesthetist who, after his divorce, volunteered to become a health professional in Vietnam during the war. It is a fascinating view of what happened to the man, how he fell in love and what on earth possessed the NZ government to support this well-documented tragedy.

Ross Wiseman *The Spanish Discovery of New Zealand in 1576* Wiseman puts the case for pre-Abel Tasman European discovery based on wreckage from ships, Spanish-sounding Maori names and a clutch of other circumstantial but convincing evidence.

Travel and impressions

Mark Lawson *The Battle for Room Service: Journeys to all the Safe Places* On the basis that Timaru is rumoured to be the most activity-challenged city in New Zealand, itself the world's most differently interesting place, Lawson selects this modest South Island city as the first port of call, and first chapter, of his wonderfully entertaining world tour of such dull places.

Austin Mitchell *The Half-gallon, Quarter-acre, Pavlova Paradise* A humorous and insightful vision of 1960s New Zealand as seen through the eyes of a British Labour MP and self-declared Kiwi commentator. Though wildly out of date, in many ways the lifestyles and values he describes still have the ring of truth, and the book stands as a measure of how much New Zealand has progressed, and at the same time how little.

Fiction

Graeme Aitken *Fifty Ways of Saying Fabulous* An extremely funny book about burgeoning homosexuality in a young farm boy, who lives in a world where he is expected to clean up muck and play rugby. Brilliant and touching, but it loses its way in the final third and serves up an anticlimactic ending.

Eric Beardsley *Blackball 08* Entertaining and fairly accurate historical novel set in the West Coast coal-mining town of Blackball during New Zealand's longest ever labour dispute.

⭐ **Graham Billing** *Forbush and the Penguins* Described as the first serious novel to come out of Antarctica, it is the compelling description of one man's lonely vigil over a colony of penguins and the relationship he develops with them. Well worth the effort.

Samuel Butler *Erewhon Journey* to a utopian land, initially set in the Canterbury high country (where Butler ran a sheep station) but increasingly devoted to a satirical critique of mid-Victorian Britain.

⭐ **Ian Cross** *The God Boy* This first and only novel of note from Ian Cross is widely considered to be New Zealand's equivalent to *Catcher in The Rye*. It concerns a young boy trapped between two parents who hate each other and describes the violent consequences of this situation.

⭐ **Barry Crump** *A Good Keen Man; Hang on a Minute Mate; Bastards I Have Met; Forty Yarns, The Adventures of Sam Cash and a Song* Just a few of the many New Zealand bushman books by the Kiwi equivalent of Banjo Patterson, who writes with great humour, tenderness and style about the male-dominated world of hunting, shooting, fishing, drinking, and telling tall stories. Worth reading for a picture of a New Zealand and a lifestyle that have now largely disappeared.

Sigrid Crump *Bushwoman* Light, fresh and highly evocative account of a young German woman's solo travels on foot in New Zealand's backcountry during the 1960s and 70s. Infusing each page with her deep love of the Kiwi bush and fiercely independent spirit, Barry Crump's sister-in-law leaves you full of admiration.

Alan Duff *Once Were Warriors* A shocking and violent Social Realist book set in 1970s south Auckland and adapted in the 1990s for Lee Tamahori's film of the same name. At its heart are good intentions concerning the predicament of urban Maori, but at times this is a clumsy book with an oddly upbeat ending. Duff has also published a sequel, *What Becomes of the Broken Hearted*, which lacks the conviction, immediacy and passion of the first novel.

Janet Frame *An Angel at My Table* Though undoubtedly one of New Zealand's most accomplished novelists, Frame is perhaps best known for this three-volume autobiography, dramatized in Jane Campion's film which, with wit and a self-effacing honesty, gives a wonderful insight into both the author and her environment. Her superb novels and short stories use humour alongside highly disturbing combinations of events and characters to overthrow readers' preconceptions. For starters, try *Faces in the Water*, *Living in the Maniototo*, *Scented Gardens for the Blind*, *Daughter Buffalo* and *Owls Do Cry*.

Maurice Gee *Crime Story*; *Going West; Prowlers; The Plumb Trilogy* These from an underrated but highly talented writer. Despite the misleadingly light titles, Gee's focus is social realism, taking an unflinching, powerful look at motivation and unravelling relationships.

Patricia Grace *Potiki*. Poignant and poetic tale of a Maori community redefining itself through a blend of traditional and modern values, while its land is threatened by coastal development. Exquisite writing by an outstanding author who ranks among the finest in New

Zealand today. *Baby No Eyes* is a magical weaving of real events with stories of family history told from four points of view, where a deceased baby becomes a living character acting as the eyes of a stranger to further increase the reader's understanding of Maori ways and traditions. *Dogside Story*, short-listed for the 2001 Booker Prize, is a wonderful story concerning the power of the land and the power of *whanau* at the turn of the Millennium.

Peter Hawes *Leapfrog with Unicorns* and *Tasman's Lay* Two from the unsung hero, cult figure and probably only member of the absurdist movement in New Zealand, who writes with great energy, wit and surprising discipline about almost anything that takes his fancy. It's not much of a secret that Peter is also W.P. Hearst who has written the not-to-be-missed *Inca Girls Aren't Easy*, a series of joyous, sad and slippery tales. A brilliant late edition to Hawes' eccentric canon, *Royce, Royce the People Choice* is a sort of *Old Man and the Sea* plus *Moby Dick*, reinterpreted for New Zealand.

Keri Hulme *The Bone People* Celebrated winner of the 1985 Booker Prize, and a wonderful first novel set along the wild beaches of the South Island's West Coast. Mysticism, myth and earthy reality are transformed into a haunting tale peopled with richly drawn characters.

Witi Ihimaera *Bulibasha – King of the Gypsies* The best introduction to one of the country's finest Maori authors. A rollicking good read, energetically exploring the life of a rebellious teenager in 1950s rural New Zealand, where two mighty sheep-shearing families are locked in battle. It's an intense look at adolescence, cultural choices, family ties and the abuse of power, culminating in a masterful twist. Look out also for the excellent *The Matriarch* and *The Uncle Story*, the brilliant *Whale Rider* and *Star Dancer* by the same author.

Elizabeth Knox *The Vintner's Luck* A very curious book indeed that for no great reason became an international best seller, all about "a man, his vineyard, love, wine and angels."

Shonagh Koea *The Grandiflora Tree* A savagely witty yet deeply moving study of the conventions of widowhood, with a peculiar love story thrown in. First novel from a journalist and short-story writer renowned for her astringent humour.

Katherine Mansfield *The Collected Stories of Katherine Mansfield* All 73 short stories sit alongside 15 unfinished fragments in this 780-page tome. Concise yet penetrating examinations of human behaviour in apparently trivial situations, often transmitting a painfully pessimistic view of the world, and startlingly modern for their time.

Ngaio Marsh *Opening Night*; *Artists in Crime*; *Vintage Murder* Just a selection from the doyenne of New Zealand crime fiction. Since 1934 she has been airing her anglophile sensibilities and killing off innumerable individuals in the name of entertainment, before solving the crimes with Inspector Allen. Perfect mindless reading matter for planes, trains and buses.

Ronald Hugh Morrieson *Came a Hot Friday* Superb account of the idiosyncrasies of country folk and the two smart spielers who enter their lives, in a comedy thriller focusing on crime and sex in a small country town.

Vincent O'Sullivan *Let the River Stand* Deftly conjuring the minutiae of homestead and rural school life in a Waikato farming community of the 1930s, Sullivan weaves disparate tales around the life of his gawky anti-hero, Alex. Tragic, humorous and captivating. *Believers to the Bright Coast* is O'Sullivan's disappointing follow-up and little more than an impenetrable confusion repeating the themes and obsessions of the first.

Frank Sargeson *The Stories of Frank Sargeson* Though not well-known outside New Zealand, Sargeson is a giant of Kiwi literature. His writing, from the 1930s to the 1980s, is incisive and sharply observed, at its best in dialogue, which is always true to the metre of New Zealand speech. This work brings together some of his finest short stories. *Once is Enough, More than Enough* and *Never Enough!* make up the complete autobiography of a man sometimes even more colourful than his characters; Michael King has written a fine biography, *Frank Sargeson: A Life*.

Maurice Shadbolt *Strangers and Journeys* On publication in 1972 this became a defining novel in New Zealand's literary ascendancy and its sense of nationhood, putting Shadbolt in the same league as Australia's Patrick White. A tale of two families, of finely wrought characters, whose lives interweave through three generations. Very New Zealand, very human and not overly epic. Later works, which have consolidated Shadbolt's reputation, include *Mondays Warriors*, *Season of the Jew* and *The House of Strife*.

C.K. Stead *The Singing Whakapapa* Highly regarded author of many books and critical essays who is little known outside New Zealand and Australia. A combination of a powerful historical novel about an early missionary and a dissatisfied modern descendant who is searching for meaning in his own life. An excellent and engaging read. His 1998 collection of short stories, *The Blonde with Candles in her Hair*, was less critically acclaimed, but still entertaining and readable.

 Damien Wilkins *The Miserables* One of the best novels to come

out of New Zealand, shorn of much of the colonial baggage of many writers. It is surprisingly mature for a first novel, sharply evoking middle-class New Zealand life from the 1960s to the 1980s through finely wrought characters.

Anthologies

Fergus Barrowman (ed) *The Picador Book of Contemporary New Zealand Fiction* A good combination of extracts and short stories from most of the best living writers in the country.

Warwick Brown *100 New Zealand Artists* The companion to the above but also allowing room for sculptors, printmakers, photographers and graphic artists.

James Burns (ed) *Novels and Novelists 1861–1979, a Bibliography* A sweeping and comprehensive intro-duction to the history of the New Zealand novel and the characters who have made it such a powerful art form.

Bill Manhire (ed) *100 New Zealand Poems* A very manageable selection of Kiwi verse that provides an excellent introduction to the poetry of the nation.

 Owen Marshall (selected by) *Essential New Zealand short Stories* A truly representative collec-tion of fascinating short stories by

some of New Zealand's finest, including Frame, Ihimera, Mansfield, Shadbolt, Stead and Gee.

 C.K. Stead (ed) *Contemporary South Pacific Stories* A great collection from authors as diverse as European Kiwi, Maori, Fijian-Indian, Samoan, Tongan and Cook Islanders, with a brilliant introduction.

Hone Tinwhare (trans Frank Stewart) *Deep River Talk: Collected Poems* Tinwhare is a respected and established Maori poet with a bawdy sense of humour that is reflected in the collected old and new poems, showcased in this anthology.

 Ian Wedde and Harvey McQueen (eds) *The Penguin Book of New Zealand Verse* A compre-hensive collection of verse from the earliest European settlers to contem-porary poets, and an excellent intro-duction to Kiwi poetry; highlights are works by James K. Baxter, Janet Frame, C.K. Stead, Sam Hunt, Keri Hulme, Hirini Melbourne and Apirana Taylor.

Reference and specialist guides

Ian Brodie *The Lord of the Rings Location Guidebook* Popular but poorly written book that purports to give location-specific information but really doesn't tell you much more than this guide.

 Angie Errigo *Rough Guide to The Lord of the Rings* An essential companion for background on the whole JRR Tolkien phenomenon with exhaustive detail about the man, the books, the films, fan websites and even the books' influence on Seventies prog rock.

Rosemary George *The Wines of New Zealand* Entertaining and informative look at New Zealand's most important wine regions, the history, the people and the product.

John Kent *North Island Trout Fishing Guide* and *South Island Trout Fishing Guide* Laden with information on access, seasons and fishing style, and illustrated with maps of the more important rivers.

Terry Sturm (ed) *The Oxford History of New Zealand Literature* A massive and comprehensive guide to non-fiction, novels, plays and poems by a variety of academics, which is fascinating for anyone with an academic interest in the subject but otherwise as dry as an old stick.

Vic Williams *The Penguin New Zealand Wine Guide* A comprehensive breakdown of over 1200 wines from the land of the long white cloud that will keep you interested and turn you into a big fan, if you are not already.

Flora, fauna and the environment

D.H. Brathwaite *Native Birds of New Zealand* Brilliant colour photographs and lots of information pinpointing thirty rare birds that, with a little effort and some patience, you can observe while travelling around.

Andrew Crowe *Which Native Tree?* Great little book, ideal for identification of New Zealand's common native trees – though not tree ferns – with diagrams of tree shape, photos of leaves and fruit, and an idea of geographic extent.

John Dawson *New Zealand Coast and Mountain Plants* A luxuriant book filled with colourful and unusual illustrations.

Susanne & John Hill *Richard Henry of Resolution Island* Comprehensive and very readable account of a man widely regarded as New Zealand's first conservationist. The book serves as a potted history of this underpopulated area of Fiordland, peopled by many of the key explorers.

Geoff Moon *The Reed Field Guide to New Zealand Birds* Excellent colour reference book, with ample detail for species identification.

Geoff Moon *The Reed Field Guide to New Zealand Wildlife* Separate chapters, stuffed with colour photos, cover forest, open country, the coast and offshore islands, but facts are too thin on the ground for it to succeed as a reference work.

Rod Morris & Hal Smith *Wild South: Saving New Zealand's Endangered Birds* A fascinating companion volume to a 1980s TV series following a band of dedicated individuals trying to preserve a dozen of New Zealand's wonderfully exotic bird species, including the kiwi, kakapo, takahe and kea.

Neville Peat *Manapouri Saved* Full and heartening coverage of one of New Zealand's earliest environmental battles when, in the 1960s, a petition signed by ten percent of the country succeeded in persuading the government to cancel its hydroelectric plans for Lake Manapouri.

Murdoch Riley *New Zealand Trees and Ferns* An excellent, pocket-size guide with colour illustrations identifying the most-often-seen trees and ferns.

Tramping

Pearl Hewson *New Zealand's Great Walks* Pearl is a no-nonsense DOC officer working out of the Wellington Office and what she doesn't know about the Great Walks isn't worth knowing. This is a practical, concise guide that concentrates her experiences into a useful aid to trampers.

Moir's Guide (NZ Alpine Club, NZ). Probably the most comprehensive guide to tramping in the South Island. It is divided into two volumes: North, covering hikes between Lake Ohau and Lake Wakatipu; and South, which concentrates on walks around the southern lakes and fjords including the Kepler Track, plus the less popular Dusky and George Sound tracks.

Mark Pickering *Wild Walks* (Shoal Bay Press, NZ). Sixty short and easily accessible walks on the North Island, mixed in with historical anecdotes and precise descriptions of the local environment.

Cycling and adventure sports

Mike Bhana *New Zealand Surfing Guide* Pragmatic handbook to the numerous prime surf spots around the New Zealand coast, with details on access, transport, the best wind and tide conditions and expected swells.

Graham Charles *New Zealand Whitewater: 120 Great Kayaking Runs* (Craig Potton, NZ). An indispensable, comprehensive and entertaining guide to New Zealand's most important kayaking rivers. River maps and details on access are supplemented by quick reference panels with grades, timings, and handy tips like which rapids not to even think about running.

Bruce Ringer *New Zealand by Bike* (The Mountaineers, NZ). The definitive Kiwi cycle touring guide with 14 regional tours (with many side-trips), which can all be knitted together into a greater whole. Plenty of maps and altitude profile diagrams.

Nigel Rushton *Pedallers' Paradise* (Paradise, NZ; ⊛www.paradise-press.co.nz). Separate lightweight North Island and South Island volumes covering recommended routes, maps, gradient profiles, attractions along the way and lists of services and accommodation: the perfect complement to the Rough Guide.

Marty Sharp *A Guide to the Ski Areas on New Zealand* Exactly what you'd expect, with full descriptions of the fields complete with tow plans and information on access, local towns and ski rental.

Paul Simon and Jonathan Kennett *Classic New Zealand Mountain Bike Rides* (Kennett Bros, NZ). All you need to know about off-road biking in New Zealand with details of over four hundred rides. Paul Simon runs the www.mountainbike.co.nz site.

Film

I n the wake of *Lord of the Rings* films, all shot in New Zealand at the same time, the Kiwi film industry has enjoyed another of its intermittent revivals, previously most notable from 1988–1994 when *The Navigator, An Angel at my Table, The Piano, Once Were Warriors* and *Heavenly Creatures* all gained international recognition and success. Yet while each of the directors involved went on to greater successes, usually in Hollywood, along with one or two of the actors, the renaissance in New Zealand itself effectively faded away like a closing shot. In fact, New Zealand was primarily used as a relatively inexpensive back-drop for American TV series like *Hercules* and *Xena Warrior Princess* and for movies that needed the big outdoors. As a result the local film industry, with a few notable exceptions, is known mainly for technical back-up and providing a few extras.

An Angel at my Table Jane Campion, 1990. Winner of the Special Jury prize at the Venice Film Festival. One of the most inspiring events in New Zealand film, based on the brilliant autobiographies of Janet Frame (see "Books", p.983).

Bad Blood Mike Newell, 1981. A New Zealand/British collaboration set in New Zealand in World War II that relates the true story of Stan Graham, a Hokitika man who breaks the law by refusing to hand in his rifle. The ensuing events give rise to a discussion of the Kiwi spirit.

Bad Taste Peter Jackson, 1988. Winner of the special jury prize at the Paris Film Festival. Aliens visit earth to pick up flesh for an inter-galactic fast-food chain and have a wild old time. A witty and irreverent spoof that derides many of the portentous alien-to-earth films.

Broken English Gregor Nicholas 1996. A tough, uncompromising movie about Croatian immigrants and the relationship between a young Croatian girl and a Maori, with excellent performances and a powerful message about discrimination.

Came a Hot Friday Ian Mune, 1984. Rightly regarded as the best comedy ever to come out of New Zealand, concentrating on two incompetent confidence tricksters whose luck runs out in a sleepy country town.

Crush Alison Maclean, 1992. A competitor at Cannes. An offbeat, angst-ridden psychological drama set around Rotorua, where the boiling mud and gushing geysers underline the manipulative tensions and sexual chaos that arise when an American femme fatale enters the lives of a New Zealand family.

Desperate Remedies Peter Wells and Stewart Main, 1993. An acclaimed winner of the Certain Regard Award at Cannes that comments wryly on the intrigues and desires of a group of different people whose lives all somehow interconnect.

Flying Fox in a Freedom Tree Martyn Sandersson, 1989. Winner of the best screenplay award at Tokyo. A moving film about a young Samoan who rejects the old ways and his father who is obsessed with money and success.

Forgotten Silver Peter Jackson, 2000. Jackson at his tongue-in-cheek best in a fake documentary about a Kiwi movie pioneer, who invents film, sound, colour and the biblical epic, all in the bush on the West Coast.

Goodbye Pork Pie Geoff Murphy, 1980. A much loved and underrated comedy/road movie following the adventures of two young men in a yellow mini, the cops they infuriate, and the mixed bag of characters they encounter.

Heavenly Creatures Peter Jackson, 1994. Winner of the Silver Lion at Venice and an Oscar Academy-Award nominee for best original film script. An account of the horrific Parker/Hulme matricide in the 1950s that follows the increasingly self-obsessed passion, friendship and secrets of two adolescent girls. An evocative and explosive film that brings all Jackson's subversive humour to bear on the strait-laced real world and, best of all, the girls' fantastic imaginary one. Kate Winslet's film debut.

Kombi Nation Grant Lahood, 2003. Charming and clever low-budget road movie about the big OE (overseas experience), where young kiwis head off to explore Europe in a VW van (hence title).

The Locals Greg Page, 2003. One time pop promo' director, Page brings all his skills and professionalism to bear on a slight but engaging horror flick – one of the surprise hits of the year.

Lord of the Rings Peter Jackson, 2000–2003. The trilogy that harvested a crop of Oscars and single-handedly boosted New Zealand's tourist industry. Not much can be added to the small forest of reviews written on this spectacular evocation of Tolkein's teen-pleaser.

The Navigator Vincent Ward, 1988. A well-received competitor at Cannes, this atmospheric and stylistically inventive venture employs all Ward's favourite themes and characters, including the innocent visionary, in this case a boy who leads five men through time from a four-

teenth-century Cumbrian village to New Zealand in the twentieth century in a quest to save their homes.

Once were Warriors Lee Tamahori, 1994. A surging fly-on-the-wall style comment on the economically challenged Maori situation in modern south Auckland, bringing to mind kitchen-sink dramas of the 1950s and 1960s. More a study of class than a full-blown racial statement, it revels in the ordinary drudgery that creates despair, with a warts-and-all story about human weakness and strength of spirit against a background of urban decay. A true reflection of part of New Zealand life, giving expression to many of the conflicts and fears that rest beneath the surface of wider society. Based on the novel by Alan Duff (see "Books", p.980).

Patu Merata Mita, 1983. A powerful documentary recording the year of opposition to the 1981 Springbok rugby team tour of New Zealand, which goes some way to showing just what extraordinary passions were ignited by the event.

Perfect Strangers Gayllene Preston, 2003. Sam Neil gets another chance to trot out his "obsessed man" acting in a beautifully photographed thriller, with a rather unbelievable storyline about a man who takes a woman to a desert island.

The Piano Jane Campion, 1993. With Holly Hunter (Oscar winner), Harvey Keitel, Sam Neill and Anna Paquin (another Oscar winner) as the young girl. The film that made Campion bankable in Hollywood, a moody evocative winner of the Palme d'Or, Cannes. With a mixture of grand scenes and personal trauma it knowingly synthesizes paper-back romance, erotica and Victorian melo-drama – and includes Keitel's attempt at the worst Scottish accent of all time.

Rain Christine Jeffs, 2002. An evocative, dark portrayal of lazy summer beach holidays that grows more complicated when a young girl decides to compete for a man with her unhappily married mother.

Scarfies Robert Sarkies, 2000. Surprise hit of the year in NZ and art houses worldwide, a darkly funny story about students taking over a deserted house in Dunedin only to discover a massive dope crop in the basement. Things get progressively more unpleasant when the dope grower returns.

Sleeping Dogs Roger Donaldson, 1977. Perhaps the birth of the real New Zealand film industry based on C.K. Stead's book *Smith's Dream*. Sam Neill plays a paranoid anti-hero hunted by the repressive forces of the state for being a nonconformist. Although a slick thriller, the film struggles to get beyond its fast-paced rush to a violent conclusion.

Smash Palace Roger Donaldson, 1981. Like *Sleeping Dogs*, this is another Kiwi man-alone, in this case a dissection of a marriage break-up and custody chase that follows a racing driver attempting to get his child back at any price. A serious film with touches of humour, it suffers from being slick and a little too

like *Kramer Versus Kramer* on speed (or in *Speed*).

The Ugly Scott Reynold, 1996. Shown at the 1997 Cannes Film Festival, and winning rave reviews in the US, this movie revolves around a serial killer who has been locked away and wants to convince the world he is cured. An edgy comment on incarceration, reform and mistrust.

Utu Geoff Murphy, 1983. One of the official selections at Cannes, this portrays a Maori warrior in the late 1800s setting out to revenge himself on the conquerors of New Zealand, in the form of a Pakeha farmer. A tense, well-acted representation of many modern as well as historic issues.

Vigil Vincent Ward, 1984. A Cannes competitor, this dark, rain-soaked story portrays a young girl's coming of age and her negative reaction to a stranger who is trying to seduce her mother, adding to tension of her own sexual awakening.

Whakataratara Paneke Don C. Selwyn, 2001. The Maori *Merchant of Venice*, with English subtitles, an ambitious home-grown film that brings much local acting talent to the screen in an involved, if overly long, epic.

Language

Language

Language

English and te reo Maori, the Maori language, share joint status as New Zealand's official languages, but on a day-to-day basis all you'll need is English, or its colourful Kiwi variant. All Maori speak English fluently, often slipping in numerous Maori terms that in time become part of everyday Kiwi parlance. You may find television, radio and newspaper articles – especially those relating to Maori affairs – initially confusing without a basic grounding, but with the aid of our glossary (see p.996) you'll soon find yourself using Maori terms all the time.

A basic knowledge of Maori pronunciation will make you more comprehensible and some understanding of the roots of place names can be helpful. You'll need to become something of an expert, though, to appreciate much of the wonderful oral history, and stories told through waiata (songs), but learning a few key terms will enhance any Maori cultural events you may attend.

To many Brits and North Americans, **Kiwi English** is barely distinguishable from its trans-Tasman cousin, "Strine", sharing much of the same lexicon of slang terms, but with an accent marginally closer in tone to South African English. Australians have no trouble distinguishing the two accents, repeatedly highlighting the vowel shift which turns "bat" into "bet", makes "yes" sound like "yis" and causes "fish" come out as "fush". This vowel contortion is carried to new levels in remoter country areas, but there is really very little regional variation, only Otago and Southland – the southern quarter of the South Island – distinguishing themselves with a rolled "r", courtesy of their predominantly Scottish founders. Throughout the land, Kiwis add an upward inflection to statements, making them sound like questions; most are not, and to highlight those that are, some add the interrogative "eh?" to the end of the sentence, a trait most evident in the North Island, especially among Maori.

Maori

For the 50,000 native speakers and 100,000 who speak it as a second tongue, **Maori** is very much a living language, gaining strength all the time as both Maori and Pakeha increasingly appreciate the cultural value of te reo, a language central to Maoritanga and forming the basis of a huge body of magnificent songs, chants and legends, lent a poetic quality by its hypnotic and lilting rhythms.

Maori is a member of the Polynesian group of languages and shares both grammar and vocabulary with those spoken throughout most of the South Pacific. Similarities are so pronounced that Tupaia, a Tahitian crew member on Captain Cook's first Pacific voyage in 1769, was able to communicate freely with the Aotearoa Maori they encountered. The Treaty of Waitangi was written in both English and Maori, but te reo soon began to lose ground to the point where, by the late nineteenth century, its use was proscribed in schools. Maori parents keen for their offspring to do well in the *Pakeha* world frequently promoted the use of English, and Maori declined further, exacerbated by the mid-twentieth-century migration to the cities. Though never on the brink of extinction, the language reached its nadir in the 1970s when perhaps only ten percent of Maori could speak their language fluently. The tide began to turn towards the end of the decade with the inception of *reo* **pre-schools** (literally "language nests") where Maoritanga is taught and activities are conducted in Maori. Originally a Maori initiative, it has now crossed over and progressive *Pakeha* parents are increasingly introducing their kids to bicultural-ism at an early age. Fortunate kohanga *reo* graduates can progress to the small number of state-funded Maori-language primary schools known as kura kaupapa. For decades, Maori has been taught as an option in secondary schools, and there are now state-funded tertiary institutions operated by Maori, offer-ing graduate programmes in Maori studies.

The success of these programmes has bred a young generation of Maori speakers frequently far more fluent than their parents who, shamed by the loss of their heritage, are beginning to attend Maori evening classes. Legal parity means that Maori is now finding its way into officialdom too, with government departments all adopting Maori names in recent years and many government and council documents being printed in both languages. The increasing knowledge and awareness has spawned Maori TV and radio broadcasts. With the backing of the Labour government, a nationwide Maori TV channel started broadcasting in 2002.

In your day-to-day dealings you won't need **to speak Maori**, though both native speakers and *pakeha* may well greet you with *kia ora* ("hi, hello"), or less commonly *haere mai* ("welcome"). On ceremonial occasions, such as *marae* visits, you'll hear the more formal greeting *tena koe* (said to one person) or *tena koutou katoa* (to a group).

Maori words used in place names are listed below, while those in common use are listed in the general glossary (see p.996). If you are interested in learn-ing a little more, the best handy reference is Patricia Tauroa's *The Collins Maori Phrase Book*, which has helpful notes on pronunciation, handy phrases and a useful Maori–English and English–Maori vocabulary.

Maori place names

The following is a list of some of the most common words and elements you will see in **town and place names** throughout New Zealand. A. W. Reed's *A Dictionary of Maori Place Names* gives more detailed coverage of the same field.

Cloud **Ao**	End **Muri**
Road or path **Ara**	Big **Nui**
River or valley **Awa**	The place of **O**
Wind **Hau**	Sand, beach **One**
Fish **Ika**	Fortified settlement **Pa**
Small **Iti**	Ridge **Pae**
Food, or eat **Kai**	Flat, earth, floor **Papa**
Home, village **Kainga**	Chants **Patere**
Rippling **Kare**	Hill **Puke**
Bad **Kino**	Spring **Puna**
White, clear **Ma**	North **Raki**
Stream **Manga**	Sky **Rangi**
Bird **Manu**	Long, high **Roa**
Headland **Mata**	Lake **Roto**
Mountain **Maunga**	Hole, cave, pit, two **Rua**
Speeches **Mihi**	Top **Runga**
Sea, lake **Moana**	Light **Tahu**
Island or anything isolated **Motu**	Sea **Tai**

LANGUAGE | Maori

Man	Tane	Water	Wai
Sacred	Tapu	Canoe	Waka
Peak	Tara	Bay, body of water	Whanga
The	Te	Land or country	Whenua
Cave	Tomo		

Pronunciation

Laziness and arrogance have combined to give *Pakeha* – and consequently most visitors – a distorted impression of Maori pronunciation, which is usually mutated into an Anglicized form. Until the 1970s there was little attempt to get it right, but with the rise in Maori consciousness since the 1980s, coupled with a sense of political correctness, many *Pakeha* now make some attempt at Maori pronunciation. As a visitor you will probably get away with just about anything, but by sticking to a few simple rules and keeping your ears open, the apparently unfathomable place names will soon trip off your tongue. The key to **pronunciation** is in knowing where to split long compound words; scanning the place name elements above) should help a great deal, and it is worth remembering that all syllables end in a vowel. Each syllable is then stressed equally, so that, for example, Waikaremoana comes out as a flat Wai-ka-re-mo-ana. The other trick for the unwary is that Maori words don't take an "s" to form a plural, so you'll find many plural nouns in this book – kiwi, tui, kauri, Maori – in what appears to be a singular form; about the only exception is Kiwis (as people), a Maori word wholly adopted into English.

Maori was solely a spoken language before the arrival of British and French missionaries in the early nineteenth century, who transcribed it using only fifteen letters of the Roman alphabet. The five **vowels** come in long and short forms; the long form is sometimes signified in print by a macron – a flat bar above the letter – but usually it is simply a case of learning by experience which sound to use. When two vowels appear together they are both pronounced, though substantially run together. For example, "Maori" should be written with a macron on the "a" and be pronounced with the first two vowels separate, turning the commonly used but incorrect "Mow-ree" into something more like "Maao-ri".

The eight **consonants**, **h**, **k**, **m**, **n**, **p**, **r**, **t** and **w**, are pronounced much as they are in English. Finally, there are two digraphs: **ng**, pronounced much as in "sing", and **wh**, which sounds either like an aspirated "f" as in "off", or like the "wh" in "why", depending on who is saying what and in which part of the country.

Glossary

ACC Accident Compensation Commission.

All ribs and balls like a muster's dog thin.

ANZAC Australian and New Zealand Army Corps; every town in New Zealand has a memorial to ANZAC casualties from both World Wars.

Aotearoa Maori for New Zealand, the land of the long white cloud.

Ariki Supreme chief of an *iwi*.

Bach (pronounced "batch") Holiday home, originally a bachelor pad at work camps and now something of a Kiwi institution that can be anything from shack to palatial waterside residence.

Back-blocks Remote areas.

Biddy-bid A burr-bearing bush (from Maori piripiri).

Blat Travel at great speed.

Bludger Someone who doesn't pull their weight or pay their way, a sponger.

Boomer Excellent.

Bro Brother, term of endearment widely used by Maori.

Captain Cooker Wild pig, probably descended from pigs released in the Marlborough Sounds on Cook's first voyage.

Chilly bin Insulated cool box for carrying picnic supplies.

Choice Fantastic.

Chook Chicken.

Chuddy Chewing gum, also "chutty".

Chunder Vomit.

Coaster (Ex-) resident of the West Coast of the South Island.

Cocky Farmer, comes in "Cow" and "Sheep" variants.

Crib South Island name for a bach.

Cuz or **Cuzzy** Short for cousin, see "bro".

Dag Wag or entertaining character.

Dairy Corner shop selling just about everything, open seven days and sometimes 24 hours.

Dally Semi-derogatory name for descendants of Dalmatian immigrants from the Balkans.

Dob in Reporting one's friends and neighbours to the police; there is currently a dobber's charter encouraging drivers to report one another for dangerous driving.

DOC Department of Conservation. Operators of the national parks, conservation policy, track administration and much more.

Docket Receipt.

Domain Grassy reserve, open to the public.

Eftpos card-based debit system found in shops, bars and restaurants.

Fizz boat Small powerboat.

Flicks Cinema, movie theatre.

Flog Steal.

Footie Rugby, usually union rather than league, never soccer.

Freezing works Slaughter house.

Give it a burl Try it.

Godzone New Zealand, short for "God's own country".

Good as (gold) First rate, excellent.

Good on ya Expression of approbation or encouragement, frequently appended with "mate".

Gorse in your pocket To be slow to pay your share.

Greasies Takeaway food, especially fish and chips.

Greenstone A type of nephrite jade known in Maori as pounamu.

Haka Maori dance performed in threatening fashion before All Black rugby games.

Handle Large glass of beer.

Hangi Maori feast cooked in an earth oven (see p.45).

Hapu Maori sub-tribal unit. Several make up an *iwi*.

Hard case See "dag".

Hard yacker Hard work.

Hollywood A faked or exaggerated sporting injury used to gain advantage.

Hongi Maori greeting, performed by pressing noses together.

Hoon Lout, yob or delinquent.

Hori Offensive word for a Maori.

Hui Maori gathering or conference.

Iwi Largest of Maori tribal groupings.

Jandals Ubiquitous Kiwi footwear, thongs or flip-flops.

Jug Litre of beer.

Kai Maori word for food, used in general parlance.

Kaimoana Seafood.

Karanga Call for visitors to come forward on a *marae*.

Kaumatua Maori elders, old people.

Kawa-Marae Etiquette or protocol on a *marae*.

Kete Traditional basket made of plaited flax.

Kiore Polynesian rat.

kiwi the national bird and mascot of NZ, always set lower case.

Kiwi An alternative label for a New Zealander.

Koha Donation.

Kohanga Reo pre-school Maori language immersion (literally "language nest").

Kumara Sweet potato.

Kuri - Polynesian dog, now extinct.

Lay-by Practice of putting a deposit on goods until they can be fully paid for.

Log of wood Slang for the Ranfurly Shield, New Zealand rugby's greatest prize.

Mana Maori term indicating status, esteem, prestige or authority, and in wide use among all Kiwis.

Manaia Stylized bird or lizard forms used extensively in Maori carving.

Manchester Linen section of a department store and its contents.

Manuhiri Guest or visitor, particularly to a *marae*.

Maoritanga Maori culture and custom, the Maori way of doing things.

Marae Place for conducting ceremonies in front of a meeting house – literally "courtyard". Also a general term for a settlement centred on the meeting house.

Mauri Life force or life principle.

Mere War club, usually of greenstone.

Metalled Graded road surface of loose stones found all over rural New Zealand.

MMP Mixed member proportional representation – New Zealand's new electoral system.

Moko Old form of tattooing on body and face that has seen a resurgence among Maori gang members.

Ngati Tribal prefix meaning "the descendants (or people) of". Also Ngai and Ati.

No fear Expression indicating refusal or disagreement.

OE Overseas experience, usually a year spent abroad by Kiwis in their early twenties.

Pa Fortified village of yore, now usually an abandoned terraced hillside.

Paddock Field.

Pakeha A non-Maori, usually white and not usually expressed with derogatory intent. Literally "foreign" though it can also be translated as "flea" or "pest". It may also be a corruption of *pakepakeha*, which are mythical human-like beings with fair skins.

Pashing Kissing or snogging.

Patu Short fighting club

Paua Abalone, a type of shellfish with a wonderful iridescent shell.

Pavlova Meringue dessert with a fruit and cream topping.

Pike out To chicken out or give up.

Piss Beer.

Pissed Drunk.

Piss head Drunkard.

Plunkett rooms Childcare centre.

Podocarp Family of pine, native to New Zealand including rimu, kahikatea, matai, miro, totara etc.

Poms Folk from Britain; not necessarily offensive.

Pounamu New Zealand greenstone, a unique type of jade.

Powhiri Traditional welcome onto a *marae*.

Puckerooed Broken. Derived from the Maori for broken, pakaru.

Puku Maori for stomach, often used as a term of endearment for someone amply endowed.

Queen Street farmer City businessman owning rural property.

Ranch slider Sliding glass door giving onto the garden or decking.

Rangatira General term for a Maori chief.

Rapt Well-pleased.

Rattle your dags Hurry up.

Root Vulgar term for sex.

Rooted To be very tired or beyond repair, as in "she's rooted, mate" – your car is irreparable.

Rough as guts Uncouth, roughly made or operating badly, as in "she's running rough as guts, mate".

Scroggin Trail mix, essentially nuts and raisins.

Sealed road Bitumen-surfaced road.

Section Block of land usually surrounding a house.

She'll be right Everything will work out fine.

Shoot through To leave suddenly.

Shout To buy a round of drinks or generally to treat folk.

Skull To knock back beer quickly.

Slutted Greatly annoyed.

Smoko Tea break.

Snarler, snag Sausage.

Sparrow-fart Early, as in "up at the sparrow-fart."

Spinner A jerk.

Squiz A look, as in "Give us a squiz".

Station wagon Estate car.

Stoked Very pleased.

Taiaha Long-handled club.

Tall poppy Someone who excels. "Cutting down tall poppies" is to bring overachievers back to earth – every Kiwi's perceived duty.

Tane Man.

Tangata whenua The people of the land, local or original inhabitants.

Tangi Mourning or funeral.

Taniwha Fearsome water spirit of Maori legend.

Taonga Treasures, prized possessions.

Tapu Forbidden or taboo. Frequently refers to sacred land.

Te reo Maori Maori language.

Tiki Maori pendant depicting a distorted human figure.

Tiki tour Guided tour.

Togs Swimming costume.

Tohunga Maori priests, experts in Maoritanga.

True Left on the left facing down stream.

True Right on the right when facing down stream.

Tukutuku Knotted latticework panels decorating the inside of a meeting house.

Tupuna Ancestors; of great spiritual importance to Maori.

Ute Car-sized pick-up truck, short for "utility".

Varsity University.

Wahine Woman.

Waiata Maori action songs.

Wairau Spirit.

Waka Maori canoe.

Waratah Stake, a term used to describe snow poles on tramps.

Wero Challenge before entering a *marae*.

Whakapapa Family tree or genealogical relationship.

Whanau Extended family group.

Whare Maori for a house.

Whare runanga Meeting house.

Whare whakairo Carved house.

Within cooee Within reach.

Wop-wops Remote areas.

Yahoo To be or act like a lout.

Rough
Guides

advertiser

Rough Guides travel...

UK & Ireland
Britain
Devon & Cornwall
Dublin
Edinburgh
England
Ireland
Lake District
London
London DIRECTIONS
London Mini Guide
Scotland
Scottish Highlands &
 Islands
Wales

Europe
Algarve
Amsterdam
Amsterdam
 DIRECTIONS
Andalucía
Athens DIRECTIONS
Austria
Baltic States
Barcelona
Belgium & Luxembourg
Berlin
Brittany & Normandy
Bruges & Ghent
Brussels
Budapest
Bulgaria
Copenhagen
Corfu
Corsica
Costa Brava
Crete
Croatia
Cyprus
Czech & Slovak
 Republics
Dodecanese & East
 Aegean
Dordogne & The Lot
Europe
Florence
France

Germany
Greece
Greek Islands
Hungary
Ibiza & Formentera
Iceland
Ionian Islands
Italy
Languedoc & Roussillon
Lisbon
Lisbon DIRECTIONS
The Loire
Madeira
Madrid
Mallorca
Malta & Gozo
Menorca
Moscow
Netherlands
Norway
Paris
Paris DIRECTIONS
Paris Mini Guide
Poland
Portugal
Prague
Provence & the Côte
 d'Azur
Pyrenees
Romania
Rome
Sardinia
Scandinavia
Sicily
Slovenia
Spain
St Petersburg
Sweden
Switzerland
Tenerife & La Gomera
Tenerife DIRECTIONS
Turkey
Tuscany & Umbria
Venice & The Veneto
Venice DIRECTIONS
Vienna

Asia
Bali & Lombok
Bangkok
Beijing
Cambodia
China
Goa
Hong Kong & Macau
India
Indonesia
Japan
Laos
Malaysia, Singapore &
 Brunei
Nepal
Philippines
Singapore
South India
Southeast Asia
Sri Lanka
Thailand
Thailand's Beaches &
 Islands
Tokyo
Vietnam

Australasia
Australia
Melbourne
New Zealand
Sydney

North America
Alaska
Big Island of Hawaii
Boston
California
Canada
Chicago
Florida
Grand Canyon
Hawaii
Honolulu
Las Vegas
Los Angeles
Maui
Miami & the Florida

Keys
Montréal
New England
New Orleans
New York City
New York City
 DIRECTIONS
New York City Mini
 Guide
Pacific Northwest
Rocky Mountains
San Francisco
San Francisco
 DIRECTIONS
Seattle
Southwest USA
Toronto
USA
Vancouver
Washington DC
Yosemite

**Caribbean
& Latin America**
Antigua & Barbuda
Antigua DIRECTIONS
Argentina
Bahamas
Barbados
Barbados DIRECTIONS
Belize
Bolivia
Brazil
Caribbean
Central America
Chile
Costa Rica
Cuba
Dominican Republic
Ecuador
Guatemala
Jamaica
Maya World
Mexico
Peru
St Lucia
South America

1000

Rough Guides are available from good bookstores worldwide. New titles are published every month. Check www.roughguides.com for the latest news.

...music & reference

1002

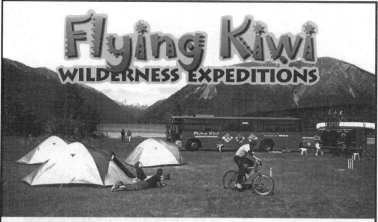

small print

and

Index

A Rough Guide to Rough Guides

In the summer of 1981, Mark Ellingham, a recent graduate from Bristol University, was travelling round Greece and couldn't find a guidebook that really met his needs. On the one hand there were the student guides, insistent on saving every last cent, and on the other the heavyweight cultural tomes whose authors seemed to have spent more time in a research library than lounging away the afternoon at a taverna or on the beach.

In a bid to avoid getting a job, Mark and a small group of writers set about creating their own guidebook. It was a guide to Greece that aimed to combine a journalistic approach to description with a thoroughly practical approach to travellers' needs – a guide that would incorporate culture, history and contemporary insights with a critical edge, together with up-to-date, value-for-money listings. Back in London, Mark and the team finished their Rough Guide, as they called it, and talked Routledge into publishing the book.

That first *Rough Guide to Greece*, published in 1982, was a student scheme that became a publishing phenomenon. The immediate success of the book – with numerous reprints and a Thomas Cook prize shortlisting – spawned a series that rapidly covered dozens of destinations. Rough Guides had a ready market among low-budget backpackers, but soon also acquired a much broader and older readership that relished Rough Guides' wit and inquisitiveness as much as their enthusiastic, critical approach. Everyone wants value for money, but not at any price.

Rough Guides soon began supplementing the "rougher" information about hostels and low-budget listings with the kind of detail on restaurants and quality hotels that independent-minded visitors on any budget might expect, whether on business in New York or trekking in Thailand.

These days the guides – distributed worldwide by the Penguin group – offer recommendations from shoestring to luxury and cover more than 200 destinations around the globe, including almost every country in the Americas and Europe, more than half of Africa and most of Asia and Australasia. Our ever-growing team of authors and photographers is spread all over the world, particularly in Europe, the USA and Australia.

In 1994, we published the *Rough Guide to World Music* and *Rough Guide to Classical Music*; and a year later the *Rough Guide to the Internet*. All three books have become benchmark titles in their fields – which encouraged us to expand into other areas of publishing, mainly around popular culture. Rough Guides now publishes:

SMALL PRINT

- Travel guides to more than 200 worldwide destinations
- Dictionary phrasebooks to 22 major languages
- History guides ranging from Ireland to Islam
- Maps printed on rip-proof and waterproof Polyart™ paper
- Music guides running the gamut from Opera to Elvis
- Restaurant guides to London, New York and San Francisco
- Reference books on topics as diverse as the Weather and Shakespeare
- Sports guides from Formula 1 to Man Utd
- Pop culture books from *Lord of the Rings* to Cult TV
- World Music CDs in association with World Music Network

Visit **www.roughguides.com** to see our latest publications.

Rough Guide credits

Editor: Lucy Ratcliffe
Layout: Ajay Verma, Umesh Aggarwal
Cartography: Miles Irving, Katie Lloyd-Jones & Ed Wright
Picture research: Sharon Thomas and Harriet Mills
Proofreader: Madhulita Mohapatra and Rima Zaheer
Editorial: London Martin Dunford, Kate Berens, Helena Smith, Claire Saunders, Geoff Howard, Ruth Blackmore, Gavin Thomas, Polly Thomas, Richard Lim, Clifton Wilkinson, Alison Murchie, Fran Sandham, Sally Schafer, Alexander Mark Rogers, Karoline Densley, Andy Turner, Ella O'Donnell, Keith Drew, Andrew Lockett, Joe Staines, Duncan Clark, Peter Buckley, Matthew Milton; **New York** Andrew Rosenberg, Richard Koss, Hunter Slaton, Chris Barsanti, Steven Horak
Design & Pictures: London Simon Bracken, Dan May, Diana Jarvis, Mark Thomas, Jj Luck, Harriet Mills; **Delhi** Madhulita Mohapatra, Umesh Aggarwal, Ajay Verma, Jessica Subramanian

Production: Julia Bovis, John McKay, Sophie Hewat
Cartography: London Maxine Repath, Ed Wright, Katie Lloyd-Jones, Miles Irving; **Delhi** Manish Chandra, Rajesh Chhibber, Jai Prakash Mishra, Ashutosh Bharti, Rajesh Mishra, Animesh Pathak, Jasbir Sandhu, Karobi Gogoi
Cover art direction: Louise Boulton
Online: New York Jennifer Gold, Cree Lawson, Suzanne Welles, Benjamin Ross; **Delhi** Manik Chauhan, Narender Kumar, Shekhar Jha, Rakesh Kumar
Marketing & Publicity: London Richard Trillo, Niki Smith, David Wearn, Chloë Roberts, Demelza Dallow, Kristina Pentland; **New York** Geoff Colquitt, Megan Kennedy
Finance: Gary Singh
Manager India: Punita Singh
Series editor: Mark Ellingham
PA to Managing Director: Julie Sanderson
Managing Director: Kevin Fitzgerald

Publishing Information

This 4th edition published September 2004 by **Rough Guides Ltd**,
80 Strand, London WC2R 0RL.
345 Hudson St, 4th Floor,
New York, NY 10014, USA.
Distributed by the Penguin Group
Penguin Books Ltd,
80 Strand, London WC2R 0RL
Penguin Putnam, Inc.
375 Hudson Street, NY 10014, USA
Penguin Books Australia Ltd,
487 Maroondah Highway, PO Box 257,
Ringwood, Victoria 3134, Australia
Penguin Books Canada Ltd,
10 Alcorn Avenue, Toronto, Ontario,
Canada M4V 1E4
Penguin Books (NZ) Ltd,
182–190 Wairau Road, Auckland 10,
New Zealand
Typeset in Bembo and Helvetica to an original design by Henry Iles.

Printed in Italy by LegoPrint S.p.A

1024pp includes index
A catalogue record for this book is available from the British Library.

ISBN 1-84353-325-1

The publishers and authors have done their best to ensure the accuracy and currency of all the information in **The Rough Guide to New Zealand**; however, they can accept no responsibility for any loss, injury, or inconvenience sustained by any traveller as a result of information or advice contained in the guide.

1 3 5 7 9 8 6 4 2

Help us update

We've gone to a lot of effort to ensure that the fourth edition of **The Rough Guide to New Zealand** is accurate and up to date. However, things change – places get "discovered", opening hours are notoriously fickle, restaurants and rooms raise prices or lower standards. If you feel we've got it wrong or left something out, we'd like to know, and if you can remember the address, the price, the time, the phone number, so much the better.

We'll credit all contributions, and send a copy of the next edition (or any other Rough Guide if you prefer) for the best letters. Everyone who writes to us and isn't already a subscriber will receive a copy of our full-colour thrice-yearly newsletter. Please mark letters: **"Rough Guide to New Zealand Update"** and send to: Rough Guides, 80 Strand, London WC2R 0RL, or Rough Guides, 4th Floor, 345 Hudson St, New York, NY 10014. Or send an email to **mail@roughguides.com**

Have your questions answered and tell others about your trip at **www.roughguides.atinfopop.com**

Acknowledgements

Laura would like to thank everyone who helped her during her research trip and during the writing-up period. Special thanks to my brother Damian for moral support throughout; Joe and Mel for giving me peace and quiet in their beachside hideaway at Onepoto Bay when I sorely needed it, and for their excellent company; to their friend Angela for her bold healing work; Tony Lyons at Ace Rentals in Auckland for a great car that carried me around for five months, and for his outstanding generosity (you're an angel); Clyde and Gloria for tremendous hospitality and laughs at Matangi Oaks; Cherrie for light-hearted companionship once the writing started and for supplying such inspiring reading material and several tasty meals at the bach; Rachel for her friendship, Thai massage and all the lessons she taught me; Els for being a sister to me and giving so much help in preparation for my return to the UK; the Mahamudra Centre at Colville for providing such a beautiful and harmonious place in which to write for two months, with plenty of good company and assistance; Lindy, Ian and family for one of the best Christmases I can remember; and all the friends in the UK who kept in regular contact and welcomed me home.

Tony Thanks to Peter Hawes and Elizabeth Barker; Topcat; Fuller's Ferries, Great Barrier Airlines, DOC, Tony at ACE Rentals (Auckland), the Saltmarsh Partnership in London, all the operators I visited, the people I stayed with, Active Earth, and Hiking New Zealand. Thanks too to the YHA in New Zealand, Chris McKellar for advice on the Kiwi gay scene and Roy Colbert for his help on Dunedin Sound. Mention must also be made of the wonderful hospitality of Gerry Hill at The Ponsonby Bed and Breakfast, Auckland; Hamish and all the other folk who helped, walked, talked or supped with me and generally made their feelings known on how to improve the book – particularly Izzy, Kate Mere, Caitriona McLean, Francesca

Elston, Sarah Clarke and the Tongariro Crossing crew. Finally, special thanks to Violet and Don for their unfailing support and Kate, John, Clare, James, Stan and Rachel for trying, against the odds, to keep me sane.

Paul would like to thank everyone who helped by providing information or just lightening the load during long research trips. As ever, respect is due to the helpful staff of visitor centres throughout the land who have been unstinting of their time and efforts in the face of long, detailed and tedious questioning. How do they remain so patient day in day out? In particular, thanks to Janet McDonald in Timaru, Tracey Lucas in Geraldine, Margaret Tait in Takaka, Beryl Anderson in Lyttelton, Lesley Gray in Oban and Brent Mathews in Havelock.

Mention must also be made of the assistance provided by Jo Roberts and Shelley Bourke at the Interislandline, Rob Naughton at Tranz Scenic, Lisa Wharton at Real Journeys, and both Hamish Allardice and Nicole Bain at the YHA. Research always has its fun side, especially with Even Bloomfield and Emelie at Kiwi Wilderness Walks, Greg McIntyre of Fat Tyre Adventures, Adrian Fogg at Rivers Wild, Amy & Dan at Dolphin Watch. Cheers, too, to all the friends and acquaintances around New Zealand who provided a bed for the night, suggested favourite restaurants, reported back from festivals, waxed lyrical about everything from hostels to luxurious retreats and generally helped make this fourth edition what it is. Mostly thanks to Phil and Wendy in Arrowtown, Richard and Raewyn in Wellington, and John Boon for two-wheeled explorations. Credit to all the readers who took the trouble to write in, especially multiple emailer Rebecca Smith; and big thanks to Irene for a sympathetic ear and support through long absences down country. And lastly a dedication to Roger, and his able successor, Pharaoh.

Readers' letters

Our continued thanks to everyone who has contributed letters, comments, accounts, and suggestions over the years, and especially to this 2004 edition. In particular: Sarah-Jane Anscomb, Amanda Armitage, Colin Armstrong, Jennifer Atkins, Jemma Baker, Trevor Barnes, Bob Beechey, Carol Lynn

Benoit, Gillian Birch, Trevor and Sue Boreham, Joanna Bradbury, Andy Brice, Rosemary Broadhurst, Geoff, Tara and Rory Brooks, Sophie Brookes, Richard Brown, Katy Buess, Thomas Bull, Sally Burgess, Anne Busby, Jean Cartwright, Pat Clough, Rocky Coles, Jenny Cook, Eddy le Couvreur,

Photo credits

Cover

Main front, Aoraki Mount Cook, Mackenzie © Rob Suisted, naturespic.com

Small front top picture, Kiwi crossing sign © Alamy

Small front lower picture, Maori motifs © Alamy

Back top picture, Lupins, Aoraki Mount Cook © Alamy

Back lower picture, Metal Palm, Wellington © Alamy

Colour introduction

Maori Carving © Munichslide/Alamy

Overview of Islands, Abel Tasman NP © Tourism New Zealand

Kiwi fruit © Steve Allen/Alamy

Sky City Tower, Auckland © Tourism New Zealand

Bungy over Queenstown © Doug Pearson/Jon Arnold/Alamy

Sheep, Glenorchy © Bob McCree/Alamy

Peter Jackson directing actors during the *Return of the King* © Capital Pictures

Rugby shirts hanging out to dry © Tourism New Zealand

Paua Shell House © Focus New Zealand

Things not to miss

01 Routeburn Track, Lake MacKenzie and Emily Peak © Focus New Zealand

02 Whale diving off Kaikoura © Jerry Dennis

03 Whanganui River © Jerry Dennis

04 Kauri Museum © Kauri Museum

05 Hot Water Beach © Paul Whitfield

06 Rugby © Tourism New Zealand

07 Bungy jumping on the Kawarau River © Robert Harding

08 Karori Sanctuary © Tourism New Zealand

09 Oparara Basin, Little Arch © Paul Whitfield

10 Hokianga Harbour © Paul Whitfield

11 Sunset on Moeraki Boulders © Paul Whitfield

12 Canoeing, Tawhai Falls, Tongariro National Park © Tourism New Zealand

13 White Island © Paul Whitfield

14 Tree Ferns © Paul Whitfield

15 Hangi © Paul Alamsy/Corbis

16 Ninety Mile Beach © Andrew Brice/Sylvia Cordaiy Photo Library Ltd/Alamy

17 Surfing © Craig Levers/Surfing NZ Magazine

18 East Coast: Anglican Church, Ruakokore © Paul Whitfield

19 Tongariro Crossing © Paul Whitfield

20 Wine, Marlborough/Blenheim © Focus New Zealand

21 Christchurch Art Gallery © Christchurch Art Gallery

22 Daily Telegraph Building, Napier, Hawke's Bay © Jerry Dennis

23 Wai-O-Tapu thermal area, Rotorua © Jerry Dennis

24 "Lost World" abseil, Waitomo Caves © Waitomo Adventures Ltd

25 Taieri Gorge Railway © Focus New Zealand

26 Yellow-eyed Penguins, Taiaora Heads, Otago Peninsula © Jerry Dennis

27 Nugget Point, The Catlins Coast © Paul Whitfield

28 Hikers on Fox Glacier © Mathieu Lamarre/Alamy

29 Jetboat on the Shotover River © Jerry Dennis

30 Farewell Spit © Focus New Zealand

31 Milford Sound © Richard Hamilton Smith/Corbis

32 Abel Tasman kayaking © Focus New Zealand

33 Kiwi spotting © Focus New Zealand

34 Maori Carver, Christchurch © Robert Harding

35 Te Papa - Exterior view at night © Focus New Zealand

Black-and-white photos

Auckland yachts and Sky City © Tourism New Zealand (p.78)

Aotea Square with macrocarpa wood waharoa by Maori sculptor Selwyn Muru © Macduff Everton/Corbis (p.97)

Zoanthid polyps, Poor Knights Island © Focus New Zealand (p.160)

Waikokopu Cafe, Waitangi Treaty House © Focus New Zealand (p.188)

Caving, Waitomo © Focus New Zealand (p.232)

Egmont National Park © Focus New Zealand (p.277)

Champagne Pool, Wai-O-Taipu © Paul Whitfield (p.304)

Maori cultural performance, Tamaki Village © Paul Whitfield (p.322)

Coromandel Peninsula © Neil Rabinowitz/Corbis (p.368)

Driving Creek Railway © Focus New Zealand (p.387)

Gannet colony, Cape Kidnappers © Tourism New Zealand (p.436)

Pania of the Reef, Napier © Focus New Zealand (p.459)

Beehive and Parliament House, Wellington © Chris Whitehead (p.482)

Te Papa © Te Papa (p.495)

Abel Tasman National Park © Tourism New Zealand (p.522)

Waterfall © Tourism New Zealand (p.568)

Oamaru © Focus New Zealand (p.600)

Moeraki Boulders © Kevin Schafer/Corbis (p.661)

Church of the Good Sheperd, Lake Tekapo © Jeremy Bright/Robert Harding (p.666)

Arthur's Pass © Tony Mudd (p.682)

Interior, Dunedin Public Art Gallery © Dunedin Public Art Gallery (p.710)

Lonekers Beach, Stewart Island © Focus New Zealand (p.719)

Franz Josef Glacier (Nevee) © Focus New Zealand (p.766)

Pancake Rocks, Paparoa NP © Paul Whitfield (p.790)

Makeshift sign advertising wine tasting, Wanaka © Charles O'Rear/Corbis (p.822)

Post Office, Arrowtown © Jerry Dennis (p.851)

Kayaking on Milford Sound © Paul A. Souders/Corbis (p.898)

Pebbles on Milford Sound © Richard Hamilton Smith/Corbis (p.918)

Yellow-eyed penguin, Dunedin © Tourism New Zealand (p.975)

SMALL PRINT

Index

Map entries are in colour.

INDEX

F

G

H

I

J

K

INDEX

INDEX

Map symbols

Maps are listed in the full index using coloured text.

━━	Railway	▲	Peak
═◇═	State highway	⭺	Viewpoint
═══	Road	⊔⊔	Cliffs/rocks
⅏	Pedestrianized street	♀	Lighthouse
▬▬	Steps	⫞	Waterfall
-----	Path	⤳	Marshland
- → -	Ferry route	⋀⋀	Spring
───	Waterway	) (	Bridge/tunnel
─ ─ ─	Chapter division boundary	∴	Ruins
♦	Place of interest	←	One-way street
▣	Restaurant	✈	Airport
◉	Hotel	P	Parking
⚊	Campsite	★	Bus stop
⌂	Hut	T	Toilet
▬	Shelter	⊞	Hospital
⚲	Church (regional maps)	ⓘ	Tourist office
♛	Castle	⊠	Post office
♀	Museum	☏	Telephone
⊙	Statue	@	Internet access
⟱	Public gardens	⚐	Fuel station
⚜	Winery	▬	Building
⬵	Swimming pool	→	Church
⤳	Surf beach	⊞	Cemetery
⚝	Ski area	▦	Park/National park
⚑	Golf course	▨	Forest
⬢	Cave	▦	Beach
⌇	Mountains	▨	Glacier